Wissenschaftliche Untersuchungen
zum Neuen Testament

Herausgeber / Editor
Jörg Frey (Zürich)

Mitherausgeber / Associate Editors
Markus Bockmuehl (Oxford) · James A. Kelhoffer (Uppsala)
Tobias Nicklas (Regensburg) · Janet Spittler (Charlottesville, VA)
J. Ross Wagner (Durham, NC)

516

Morna D. Hooker

Old and New

Essays on Continuity and Discontinuity
in the New Testament

edited by

Ahreum Kim

Mohr Siebeck

Morna D. Hooker, 1931; BA and MA Bristol University; PhD Manchester University; DD Cambridge University; 1961–70 Lecturer, King's College London; 1970–76 Lecturer, University of Oxford; 1976–98 Lady Margaret's Professor, University of Cambridge; Lady Margaret's Professor Emerita, University of Cambridge; Life Fellow, Robinson College Cambridge.

Ahreum Kim recently completed her PhD under the supervision of Professor George van Kooten at the University of Cambridge.

ISBN 978-3-16-162454-4 / eISBN 978-3-16-162455-1
DOI 10.1628/978-3-16-162455-1

The Deutsche Nationalbibliothek lists this publication in the Deutsche Nationalbibliographie; detailed bibliographic data are available at *https://dnb.dnb.de*.

© 2024 by Mohr Siebeck, Tübingen, Germany. www.mohrsiebeck.com

This book may not be reproduced, in whole or in part, in any form (beyond that permitted by copyright law) without the publisher's written permission. This applies particularly to reproductions, translations and storage and processing in electronic systems.

The book was typeset by Martin Fischer in Tübingen, printed by Gulde Druck in Tübingen on non-aging paper and bound by Buchbinderei Spinner in Ottersweier.

Printed in Germany.

Acknowledgements

I am grateful to Markus Bockmuehl for the invitation to gather these essays together in one volume. A suggestion that I prepare such a volume had indeed been made to me many years earlier by another publisher, but for various reasons the plan had never come to fruition. Even with this new stimulus of an invitation to publish them in the distinguished WUNT series, the process of collecting the essays together was delayed by my own inability to devote the necessary time and labour to the project. I am therefore indebted to friends for their encouragement to complete the task, and extremely grateful to colleagues in the University of Cambridge Divinity Faculty for forcing my hand by finding the necessary funding for the project. My thanks are due also to Jörg Frey and his committee for accepting the resulting volume for inclusion in the series. Finally, I am enormously grateful to Dr Ahreum Kim for preparing the typescript for publication: without her careful work, the book would never have appeared.

I must also express my thanks to the following publishers for permission to include previously published articles and essays in this volume: 1517 Media/Fortress Press, Bloomsbury Publishing Plc, Boydell and Brewer, Brill, Cambridge University Press, Eerdmans, Hymns Ancient and Modern, John Wiley & Sons, Manchester University Press, Oxford University Press, Peeters, *Proceedings of the Irish Biblical Association,* SAGE Publishing, The Society of Biblical Literature, *Svensk Exegetisk Årsbok,* and Wipf and Stock.

February 2023   Morna D. Hooker

Table of Contents

Acknowledgements V
Abbreviations XI

General Introduction 1

Section One
Introduction

1. New Wine in Old Bottles 11

Section Two
Methodology

2. Christology and Methodology 29
3. On Using the Wrong Tool 38
4. In His Own Image? 50

Section Three
The Development of Christology

5. T.W. Manson and the Twentieth-Century Search for Jesus 67
6. Is the Son of Man Problem Really Insoluble? 90
7. The Son of Man and the Synoptic Problem 103
8. Did the Use of Isaiah 53 to Interpret His Mission Begin with Jesus? 115
9. Good News about Jesus Christ, the Son of God 128
10. The Nature of New Testament Theology 143
11. Chalcedon and the New Testament 160

Section Four

Creative Conflict and the Gospel Tradition

12. 'What Doest Thou Here, Elijah?' 179
13. Mark's Use of Scripture 190
14. Isaiah in Mark's Gospel 200
15. Trial and Tribulation in Mark XIII 216
16. Traditions about the Temple in the Sayings of Jesus 235
17. Creative Conflict: The Torah and Christology 248
18. Uncomfortable Words: The Prohibition of Foreign Missions
    (Matt 10:5–6) 265

Section Five

Beginnings and Endings

19. The Beginning of the Gospel 275
20. Beginning from Moses and from All the Prophets 285
21. John's Baptism: A Prophetic Sign 298
22. John the Baptist and the Johannine Prologue 316
23. The Johannine Prologue and the Messianic Secret 321
24. 'There's Glory for You!': Death and Glory in John's Gospel 341

Section Six

Adam, Law, and Cult

25. Paul: Apostle to the Gentiles 359
26. Adam *Redivivus*: Philippians 2 Once More 371
27. Christ: The 'End' of the Law 384
28. On Becoming the Righteousness of God: Another Look
    at 2 Cor 5:21 401
29. Another Look at πίστις Χριστοῦ 416
30. 2 Corinthians 5:1–10 in Context 432
31. Artemis of Ephesus 460
32. The Authority of the Bible: A New Testament Perspective 468
33. Where is Wisdom to Be Found? Colossians 1:15–20 488
34. Christ, the 'End' of the Cult 497

Section Seven

Living in the New Age

35. 1 Thessalonians 1:9–10: A Nutshell – But What Kind of Nut? ... 521
36. Called to be God's Holy People 534
37. Christ Died for Our Sins, and Was Raised for Our Acquittal:
    Paul's Understanding of the Death of Christ 549
38. Raised for Our Acquittal (Rom 4:25) 562
39. A Partner in the Gospel: Paul's Understanding of His Ministry ... 579
40. Paul the Pastor: The Relevance of the Gospel 596
41. From God's Faithfulness to Ours: Another Look
    at 2 Corinthians 1:17–24 610
42. Philippians: Phantom Opponents and the Real Source of Conflict 616
43. 'Submit to One Another': The Transformation of Relationships
    in Christ (Eph 5:21–6:9) 632
44. 'The Sanctuary of His Body': Body and Sanctuary in Paul
    and John 654
45. 'Sola Fide': The Wrong Slogan? 668

Details of First Publication 683
List of Illustrations 687
Bibliography 689
Index of Ancient Sources 715
Index of Modern Authors 752
Index of Subjects 757

Abbreviations

AB	Anchor Bible
AnBib	Analecta Biblica
ANRW	*Aufstieg und Niedergang der römischen Welt*
AV	Authorized Version
BETL	*Bibliotheca Ephemeridum Theologicarum Lovaniensium*
BFBS	British and Foreign Bible Society
BGBE	Beiträge zur Geschichte der biblischen Exegese
BHT	Beiträge zur historischen Theologie
BJRL	*Bulletin of the John Rylands Library*
BNTC	Black's New Testament Commentaries
BZNW	Beihefte zur Zeitschrift für die neutestamentliche Wissenschaft
CBQ	*Catholic Biblical Quarterly*
CNT	Commentaire du Nouveau Testament
ConBNT	Coniectanea biblica: New Testament Series
EBib	Études bibliques
ETL	*Ephemerides Theologicae Lovanienses*
ExpTim	*Expository Times*
FRLANT	Forschungen zur Religion und Literatur des Alten und Neuen Testaments
HNT	Handbuch zum Neuen Testament
HTR	*Harvard Theological Review*
ICC	International Critical Commentary
ITQ	*Irish Theological Quarterly*
JB	Jerusalem Bible
JBL	*Journal of Biblical Literature*
JSNT	*Journal for the Study of the New Testament*
JSNTSup	Journal for the Study of the New Testament, Supplement Series
JSOT	*Journal for the Study of the Old Testament*
JSOTSup	Journal for the Study of the Old Testament, Supplement Series
JTC	*Journal for Theology and the Church*
JTI	*Journal of Theological Interpretation*
JTS	*Journal of Theological Studies*
KEK	Kritisch-exegetischer Kommentar über das Neue Testament
LSJ	Liddell-Scott-Jones Greek-English Lexicon
LW	*Luther's Works (American Edition)*. Edited by Jaroslav Pelikan, Helmut T. Lehmann and Christopher B. Brown. 83 vols. Philadelphia and St. Louis: Fortress and Concordia, 1955–.
NCB	New Century Bible Commentary
NEB	New English Bible
NIB	*New Interpreter's Bible*
NICNT	New International Commentary on the New Testament

NIGTC	New International Greek Testament Commentary
NJB	New Jerusalem Bible
NRSV	New Revised Standard Version
NS	New Series
NT	*Novum Testamentum*
NTSup	Novum Testamentum, Supplements
NTS	*New Testament Studies*
PL	Patrologia Latina
REB	Revised English Bible
RGG	Die Religion in Geschichte und Gegenwart
RHPR	*Revue d'Histoire et de Philosophie Religieuses*
RSR	*Recherches de Science Religieuse*
RSV	Revised Standard Version
RV	Revised Version
SBL	Society of Biblical Literature
SBT	Studies in Biblical Theology
SJT	*Scottish Journal of Theology*
SNTS	Society for New Testament Studies
SNTSMS	Society for New Testament Studies Monograph Series
TDNT	*Theological Dictionary of the New Testament*. Edited by Gerhard Kittel and Gerhard Friedrich. Translated by Geoffrey W. Bromiley. 10 vols. Grand Rapids: Eerdmans, 1964–76.
TWNT	*Theologisches Wörterbuch zum Neuen Testament*. Edited by Gerhard Kittel and Gerhard Friedrich. 11 vols. Stuttgart: Kohlhammer, 1932–1979.
TSK	*Theologische Studien und Kritiken*
UBS	United Bible Societies
UNT	Untersuchungen zum Neuen Testament
VTSup	Vetus Testamentum Supplements
WA	*D. Martin Luthers Werke: kritische Gesamtausgabe (Weimarer Ausgabe)*. 73 vols. Weimar: Böhlau, 1883–2009.
WBC	Word Biblical Commentary
WMANT	Wissenschaftliche Monographien zum Alten und Neuen Testament
WUNT	Wissenschaftliche Untersuchungen zum Neuen Testament
ZNW	*Zeitschrift für die neutestamentliche Wissenschaft*
ZTK	*Zeitschrift für Theologie und Kirche*

General Introduction

When I first began biblical research, seventy years ago, the issue that most fascinated me was the relationship between the Old Testament and the New – in other words, the continuity and discontinuity between the Judaism of the first-century CE and early Christianity. The question I focused on at that time was that of the possible influence of the so-called 'Servant concept' of Deutero-Isaiah in the New Testament.[1] The results of my investigations may, to be sure, have appeared very negative, since I concluded that there was no evidence to support the view that Jesus saw his own role in terms of Isaiah 53 – a conclusion that was contrary to the almost universal assumption of New Testament scholars at that time. It seemed, moreover, that Christians of the first generation had been slow to exploit the implications of that passage. My conclusions were not wholly negative, however, for I suggested that there were other passages in the scriptures that were influential, both for Jesus' own understanding of his role and for the interpretation given to it by the early church: among these were those psalms which speak of the suffering of those who are faithful and obedient to God, and the image of the one like a son of man in Daniel 7.

This research led me to ask further questions, however. One concerned the letters of Paul: if they, our earliest Christian documents, show scarcely a trace of Isaiah 53, then what *was* the source of his conviction that Jesus' sufferings and death were redemptive? I began to explore the idea of 'interchange' as a clue to Paul's interpretation of Christ's death.[2] This research soon pointed me towards the figure of Adam, and I found myself considering the significance of Adam for Paul, in particular in Romans 1.[3] Work on Paul was set aside in 1959, however, and it was not until many years later that I took it up again; invited to give the T.W. Manson memorial lecture in 1977, it seemed appropriate to speak on the theme of 'Interchange and Atonement', since it was Professor Manson who had been appointed to supervise my work 20 years earlier, and who had sadly died in 1958, six months after I first met him.[4]

---

[1] Old Testament scholars had for many years debated the identity of the individual or group referred to as my 'servant' in Isa 42:1–9; 49:1–6; 50:4–11; 52:13–53:12.

[2] The concept of 'interchange' is best summed up in the words of Irenaeus: 'Christ became what we are, in order that we might become what he is' (*Adv. Haer. 5 praef.*).

[3] This led to the publication of an essay, 'Adam in Romans I', *NTS* 6 (1960): 297–306, to be followed by a later postscript, 'A Further Note on Romans I', *NTS* 13 (1967): 181–183.

[4] Morna D. Hooker, 'Interchange and Atonement', *BJRL* 60 (1978): 462–481.

My change in direction in 1959 from the study of Paul was influenced by two factors. The first was the reaction to my work on the Servant, which was completed in 1956, and had finally been published, essentially unchanged, in 1959.[5] I was challenged by one reviewer, Professor C. F. D. Moule (who broadly agreed with my conclusions),[6] to explain why Isaiah 53, which 'is virtually the only Old Testament passage which recognizes undeserved suffering as redemptive for others', was apparently bypassed by both Jesus and the early church. Why is this so? 'Is it possible that the general use of Isa. 53 was precluded by some apologetic circumstance unknown to us?' My own explanation had been that the importance of Isaiah 53 had been exaggerated by scholars, as a result of their isolation of the 'Servant Songs' from the rest of Deutero-Isaiah and their assumption that the prophet had in mind a particular figure, known as 'my Servant', who thus needed to be identified. Moreover, when at a later time references to 'my Servant' *were* interpreted of a particular figure – namely 'the Messiah' (in the Targum) – the descriptions of suffering in Isaiah 53 were removed from the Messiah and applied to others, which meant that the notion of vicarious suffering was significantly absent. There was thus no precedent for the idea of a Messiah who suffered vicariously for others. But was this sufficient explanation for the non-use of what seemed to later interpreters to be the 'obvious' passages? I turned back from Paul to the Gospels, and began to look at the use of the term 'the Son of man', which was, according to all four evangelists, the term used by Jesus himself to refer to his suffering. Would this study perhaps help me to answer Professor Moule's questions? And would it perhaps also – since the idea of 'the Son of man' was clearly rooted in speculation about Adam – offer a foundation on which to return to my work on Paul? Perhaps the roots of 'interchange' lay in the Gospel tradition.

My research into the use of the idea of 'the Son of man', however, like that on Paul, was also broken off prematurely, since the topic proved a vast one, and I completed only my investigation of the term in Mark.[7] So although my work had led me to argue that Jesus understood his sufferings as a necessary outcome of his role as the Son of man, I was no nearer to a more satisfying explanation as to why Isaiah 53 had been ignored. It was many years later before I was able to look at this question once again.[8]

---

[5] Morna D. Hooker, *Jesus and the Servant: The Influence of the Servant Concept of Deutero-Isaiah in the New Testament* (London: SPCK, 1959).

[6] C. F. D. Moule, review of *Jesus and the Servant*, by Morna D. Hooker, *Theology* 62, no. 472 (1959): 429–430.

[7] Morna D. Hooker, *The Son of Man in Mark* (London: SPCK, 1967). I returned to the subject in later essays, reprinted here as essays 6 and 7.

[8] Morna D. Hooker, 'Did the Use of Isaiah 53 to Interpret His Mission Begin with Jesus?', in *Jesus and the Suffering Servant: Isaiah 53 and Christian Origins*, eds. William H. Bellinger Jr.

Looking back at my work over the past 70 years, I realize that the underlying theme of it all has been that of continuity and discontinuity, and I have therefore chosen to introduce this volume of essays with a lecture on that theme delivered in the University of London in 1984.[9] How was Jesus understood by those who met him, and by those who found themselves trying to comprehend his death and resurrection? How did he himself understand his role? How did his followers explain their conviction that he was of supreme importance for their lives? The answer to all these questions is, of course, that they did so in terms that made sense to them. If we are to understand Jesus and those who first believed in him, then we have to locate him in his Jewish background, in a culture where scripture and tradition were all-important. At the same time, however, the coming of Jesus heralded a radical change: he clearly acted and spoke with an authority that struck his contemporaries as revolutionary, and his disciples' conviction that he had been raised from the dead was interpreted as the beginning of a new era. Inevitably, the tension between old and new led to confrontations and conflicts between his followers and their fellow Jews. What we find in the New Testament are indications of the various ways in which Christians struggled to relate the givenness of the past – expressed, above all, in the words of scripture – with the exhilarating experience of the present. Inevitably, their attempts to do so frequently reflect the tensions and conflicts that arose between his followers and their fellow Jews.

Over time, the balance between these two forces – scripture and experience – shifted. Since the primary authority for first-century Jewish Christians was scripture, their problem was to interpret their experience of Christ in relation to scripture. 'Beginning from the scriptures' they 'searched the scriptures', and concluded that what had taken place in him was 'according to the scriptures': their experience had to be tested against scripture. In time, however, the process became reversed. Instead of interpreting Jesus in terms of scripture, believers' starting point was now Christ; their experience of him was so overwhelming that he became as it were the 'canon', by whose light scripture itself was now interpreted.[10]

---

and William R. Farmer (Harrisburg, PA: Trinity Press International, 1998), 88–103 = below, essay 8 (pp. 115–127).

[9] Morna D. Hooker, *New Wine in Old Bottles: A Discussion of Continuity and Discontinuity in Relation to Judaism and the Gospel*, the Ethel M. Wood Lecture delivered at the Senate House, University of London on 14 February 1984 (London: University of London, 1984) = below, essay 1 (pp. 11–26). A later series of lectures on this topic was delivered as the W.A. Sanderson Lectures in Melbourne and published as Morna D. Hooker, *Continuity and Discontinuity* (London: Epworth, 1986).

[10] See further, Morna D. Hooker, 'Where is Wisdom to Be Found? Colossians 1:15–20', *Reading Texts, Seeking Wisdom: Scripture and Theology*, eds. David F. Ford and Graham Stanton (London: SCM Press, 2003), 116–128 = below, essay 33 (pp. 488–496).

The essays in this volume, written over more than 50 years, explore various aspects of this tension between old and new. The public lecture delivered in 1984 serves as a general introduction to them all. Those in sections two to five deal chiefly with the Gospels, while those in sections six and seven are concerned with Paul and other letter writers.

I have made no attempt to update the essays, because so much has been written since most of them were first published, making it impossible to deal with all the scholarly developments that have taken place: the essays are themselves part of the story of the development of ideas. Occasional references to publications which were 'recent' when I was writing have been left unchanged, since these publications were part of the context in which I was writing, and these references are indications of how scholarship has moved on. Some of the essays, inevitably, engage with issues which were of particular relevance when they were written, but the problems underlying them are nevertheless still relevant. One change that has come about over the years that I have been writing is the awareness of so-called 'sexist' language, which was normal usage when the essays were first written, but which may jar with some readers today. I have left the original pronouns unchanged; they too are part of the ethos of a time when terms such as 'men' and 'mankind' were understood to refer to the entire population. As a woman, I certainly have no intention of excluding the feminine! Sadly, masculine terms referring to scholars were invariably correct, since when I began my research there were virtually no female biblical scholars at work.

The essays gathered here are a mixture of popular presentations and more scholarly discussions. Some of the former have been included because they form useful introductions or summaries of my work, others because I have received requests to do so, since they have been often cited, and have proved of particular usefulness to students. Inevitably, this has added to the overlap between essays which is in any case inevitable in a collection of this kind – notably between essays 2 and 3 – but I hope that readers will simply choose the version which is appropriate to them.

An earlier volume included fourteen essays on Paul published between 1960 and 1989.[11] Some of the topics dealt with in the present volume were taken up and explored more fully in books. Others – in particular those on Paul – have emerged from many years of lecturing on his theology to undergraduates.

There is much left unexplored which I would have liked to pursue, had I had time and stamina. In particular, I would have liked to look at the possibility that the theme of 'interchange' is not just a Pauline insight, but is rooted in the Old Testament and reflected in the Gospels. The Fourth

---

[11] Morna D. Hooker, *From Adam to Christ: Essays on Paul* (Cambridge: Cambridge University Press, 1990).

Evangelist, for example, whose theology is in many ways close to Paul's, speaks of 'the word made flesh' who 'dwelt among us' as one whom he terms 'only Son of God'; the result of his coming is that those who accept him are given the right to become 'children of God', and described as 'born of God' (John 1:12–14). Unlike Paul, John uses the term τέκνα rather than υἱοί, but though the language is different, the underlying thought is similar. The Word became flesh, and as a result, those who were originally born of flesh[12] can be born of God.

The Prologue is the key to understanding the rest of the Gospel,[13] which sometimes echoes its terminology, and sometimes uses other language. In a shocking image in chapter 6, we learn that those who 'eat his flesh' – an echo of the 'became flesh' of 1:14 – will have eternal life, because he is the living bread who comes down from heaven: in other words, by participating in what he is, they 'dwell in him and he in them', and so share his life. We already know from 3:13–15 that the one who came down from heaven was the Son of man, who was lifted up on the cross and has returned to heaven. The food that the Son of man now gives to his followers is his own flesh, which is given for the life of the world. This is close to Paul's concept of interchange (*pace* my comments below, essay 11!), and like him, John uses language that shocks us to express it. Like him, too, John's ideas embrace what later theologians described separately as 'incarnation' and 'atonement'. Like Paul, again, John speaks of God sending his only Son in order that those who trust in him might be saved (John 3:16). Later, the evangelist uses the image of the Vine to express the dependence of believers on Christ, and in the famous 'prayer' of chapter 17 speaks of a unity of believers 'in us' similar to the unity of Father and Son. These are just two of a number of passages that spell out the participation of believers in Christ.[14]

In an essay on Hebrews, I noted the parallel between Hebrews 2 and the Pauline notion of interchange.[15] The author describes how the one who is God's Son, and who now sits at God's right hand, was made for a short time lower than the angels; through his suffering, God brought many sons (υἱοί) to glory. As the pioneer of their salvation, it was necessary for him to share in the flesh and blood of the children – παιδία – and through his dying he liberated those who were in fear of death, since he experienced death 'for all

---

[12] John contrasts the new birth with that which was 'from bloods, from the will of flesh … from the will of men'.

[13] See below, essays 19 and 20.

[14] The theme has been explored by Andrew J. Byers, *Ecclesiology and Theosis in the Gospel of John*, SNTSMS 166 (Cambridge: Cambridge University Press, 2017). Like the 'Finnish school' of Pauline scholars, Byers uses the language of theosis to describe the transformation of believers.

[15] See below, essay 34.

mankind'. Like both Paul and John, the author to the Hebrews here expresses what I have termed 'incarnational soteriology'. And like John, where the one who has 'descended from heaven' is identified as 'the Son of man', he regards this language as the appropriate language to describe Christ's role. Quoting Psalm 8, he describes how man/the son of man was for a while made lower than the angels, but is now crowned with glory and honour (vv. 6–8). It is as 'son of man' that Jesus accomplishes his work 'for all mankind'.

This, of course, takes us back to the Synoptic Gospels, where Jesus is frequently referred to as 'the Son of man'. In earlier work, I have noted how the term is used especially in relation to his authority, as well as to his sufferings and vindication – precisely the ideas expressed in Psalm 8 and in Daniel 7. I have noted, also, how closely related the Son of man is in the Gospels to the vocation of his disciples; as those who want to belong to 'the Kingdom of God' (i.e. to obey God's rule), they are called to 'share' the sufferings of the one who is utterly obedient to his will – and so share also in his glory.[16] The Synoptic Gospels, of course, express their theology in narrative form, and it is worth noticing that both Mark and Matthew underline Jesus' experience of human suffering and alienation from God in the cry of dereliction, followed immediately by his identification as Son of God.[17] At the very beginning of the story, Matthew stresses Jesus' identification with the human condition in the story of his baptism, where he requests baptism along with those in need of repentance, even though it is he who will bring them forgiveness. The Baptist protests that it is inappropriate for him to come for baptism, and Jesus insists on 'fulfilling all righteousness' by being baptized with water – whereupon he is baptized with the Holy Spirit and identified as God's beloved Son.[18] In the story that follows, he baptizes others with the Holy Spirit.[19] There are hints here that the evangelists were familiar with ideas expressed by Paul and John in theological statements about one who was both truly 'Son of God' and fully human. As such, he is able to fulfil God's intention for Israel – and through Israel all humanity – to be God's son. We are brought back full circle to Paul's 'Adam' theology.

As for the answer to that question posed to me so long ago by Charlie Moule, my predecessor in the Lady Margaret's chair, the answer seems to me now, as it seemed then, that we need constantly to re-examine the assumptions with which we read the text. Are we approaching it with preconceptions which have been shaped by centuries of biblical study, by doctrinal

---

[16] See, e.g., Mark 8:31–38; it is clear from the narrative surrounding the other 'passion predictions' (Mark 9:31 and 10:33) that the disciples are expected to identify with Jesus' attitude and so share his sufferings as the path to glory.
[17] Mark 14:33–39 // Matt 27:45–54. Cf. 2 Cor 5:21.
[18] Matt 3:13–17.
[19] See below, essay 21.

formulations, and by liturgical practices? Are we indeed asking the right questions? Those who compose surveys know that the questions one poses can skew the answers that are given. It is all too easy to read our assumptions into the text, rather than allowing the text to speak for itself. If we are to understand texts written two thousand years ago and more, then we need to forget what we think we know and immerse ourselves, as far as is possible, in the world of those who wrote them – and beyond that, the world in which Jesus himself lived. The caveat 'as far as is possible' is of course all-important; we can never fully understand a culture that is so different from our own. But we must always beware of importing ideas which seem to be so obvious to us into the text, and of ignoring the clues which that text itself offers to us.

Section One

Introduction

1. New Wine in Old Bottles*

A Discussion of Continuity and Discontinuity in Relation to Judaism and the Gospel

'No one pours new wine into old wineskins; if he does, the wine will burst the skins, and the wine will be wasted, and the skins as well. New wine must be put into fresh wineskins' (Matt 9:17; Mark 2:22; Luke 5:37). This familiar parable is by no means as straightforward as it seems at first hearing. Clearly, it suggests the incompatibility of old and new, and the call for fresh wineskins to hold new wine implies that what is new is superior to what is old. Moreover, the setting of the parable, in a debate which contrasts the behaviour of Jesus' disciples with that of other religious groups among the Jews suggests that we are meant to understand that the new wine of the gospel cannot be contained within the confines of Judaism. Yet the loss of the wineskins is apparently as much of a disaster as the spillage of the wine. Matthew spells this out: 'new wine must be put into fresh wineskins – that way, both the wine and the skins are preserved'. As for Luke, his concern reaches not only to the old wineskins but to the old wine, for he adds a postscript to Jesus' words to the effect that no one who has tasted old wine wants to drink new, since the old is better. And though connoisseurs of wine might agree with Luke's assessment, it is a strangely conservative sentiment to find in Luke's Gospel – so strange, indeed, that commentators generally assume the statement to be ironic. How could Luke believe that the old wine of Judaism was preferable to the new wine of Christianity?

The ambivalent attitude towards what is old displayed in these different versions of the parable reflects an underlying tension which runs throughout much of the New Testament – the tension between old and new, between the beliefs and assumptions which the first Christians inherited from the past and the new insights of the gospel, between the framework of ideas which formed part of their heritage and the events which made them think again about their understanding of God and his world. To what extent was the faith of the church new? In what ways was it related to the past? These are crucial questions for our understanding of the New Testament and of early Christianity,

---

* The Ethel M. Wood Lecture delivered at the Senate House, University of London on 14 February 1984.

but the problem which they attempt to tackle is by no means confined to the pages of the New Testament. The particular focus of our investigation this afternoon is the emergence of Christianity from Judaism, and the questions confront us there in a particularly acute form – but they are relevant to any period of the church's history where past traditions prove inadequate to contain new insights. I do not mean to suggest, of course, that the situations are identical: for Christians, the events concerning Jesus remain unique, and cannot be explained simply by comparing them with other historical happenings. Yet Christians may well argue that continuing tensions between old and new are a sign of the ongoing activity of the Spirit. Certainly, in present-day debates about doctrine and hermeneutics, we find ourselves grappling with questions such as these: to what extent are the traditional ways of expressing the faith essential to it? How is the tradition that has been handed down from the past to be related to new ways of understanding the faith?

If such questions cause problems today, they must have been far more pressing in the early years of the church. And though of course we are well aware of the clashes between Paul on the one hand and the so-called 'Judaizers' on the other, I suspect that we do not always appreciate the subtlety of the problem they faced – partly because we tend to put the protagonists in opposing camps, and forget that most of them had a foot in *both* camps. The dangers which confronted them were, on the one hand, of clinging too closely to past beliefs and practices, and on the other, of cutting loose from the past altogether.

Now the tendency from a very early stage and throughout the history of Christianity has been to stress the newness of the Christian revelation and therefore the discontinuity between Judaism and Christianity. This is one of the inevitable consequences of the cleavage between the two religions: Judaism refused to accept Jesus as Messiah, Christians in turn denounced Judaism. The destruction of Jerusalem was seen as divine punishment; Jews became the scapegoats of Europe, and the blame for Jesus' death was laid at their feet. As a result, Christians forgot that most of the New Testament was written by men from within Judaism – who not only were themselves Jews, but saw Christian faith as orthodox Judaism, rather than as a separate religion. When we read Paul, and find him using the first-person plural, we automatically assume that he means 'we Christians'; most of the time, in fact, he means, 'we Jews'. The Gospels of Matthew and John show signs of being written for Jewish Christians who thought of themselves as true Jews – but who found themselves pushed out of Jewish synagogues, all the time protesting that they, not their opponents, were being true to the teaching of Moses. Their position was analogous to that of the early Methodist societies in this country in the eighteenth century, springing up within the Church of England, but finding it more and more impossible to stay there. Because our New Testament was written before the break between Jew and Christian, and because we look back at it from long after that break, we inevitably see Christianity as standing over against Judaism, instead of understanding it within the context of Judaism.

Another important factor which has led to a stress on *dis*continuity is the enormous influence exercised by Lutheran theology on biblical scholarship. For centuries, our understanding of Paul's theology has been dominated by the antithesis between Law and gospel; Bultmann, for example, sees Paul as the great opponent of Law. Even the recent book by Professor E. P. Sanders,[1] with its sympathetic portrait of first-century Judaism, has a very unsympathetic portrait of Paul, and leaves him as much opposed to the Law as ever. Talk about the old and new covenants has emphasized the contrast between the two religions rather than the continuity. There have, of course, been reactions to all this. The biblical theology movement stressed the *unity* of biblical revelation and for a time the pendulum swung the other way. But the general tendency over the years has been to oppose old and new, Judaism and Christianity, Law and gospel. As a result, the very word 'Law' has become for us a derogatory one; perhaps we should use the Jews' own term, 'Torah', to remind us that we are talking about a religious ideal, and not the caricature we have sometimes made of it.

This basic tendency to assume a cleavage between old and new affects our whole approach to the New Testament. An interesting example of this can be seen in critical work on the Gospels. Attempting to recover the authentic words of Jesus, scholars devised certain criteria, by which they might be tested. The most important of these was the criterion of dissimilarity.[2] This particular test pushed the notion of discontinuity to the limits, for it required a process of what we may perhaps term 'double declutching': it assumed that the words we can attribute with confidence to Jesus himself are those which do not overlap either with the beliefs of contemporary Judaism or with those of the early church. The absurdity of the method is self-evident (or so one would have thought): it can only produce a picture of a Jesus who has no roots in Judaism and no influence on the Christian community.[3] Because the notion of discontinuity is built into the method, its results inevitably give us a picture of discontinuity rather than continuity, and suggest not one gap but two between Judaism and the church. Once again, there have been reactions to this approach. Jewish scholars, for example, remind us that Jesus was a Jew, but the more they do this the more they blame the writers of the

---

[1] E. P. Sanders, *Paul and Palestinian Judaism* (London: SCM Press, 1977).

[2] For an example of this method see Norman Perrin, *Rediscovering the Teaching of Jesus* (London: SCM Press, 1967), 39–43.

[3] For criticism of this method, see Morna D. Hooker, 'Christology and Methodology', *NTS* 17 (1971): 480–487 = below, essay 2 (pp. 29–37).

New Testament for ignoring their past heritage and introducing what were essentially new notions: while they seek to narrow the gap between Judaism and Jesus, Judaism and Christianity remain as far apart as ever.

Our basic problem is, I believe, the difficulty of understanding what the authors of New Testament documents were trying to say in their own situation. We read the New Testament inevitably in our own context – we read it, first of all, as 'the New Testament' – that is, as the definitive statement of faith, the tradition from which Christians begin – whereas for those who wrote it, the beliefs they were setting out were the very opposite; they were new, daring, challenging, and rejected as heresy by those who began from what was then the accepted basis of faith, the Jewish scriptures. Our problem is to detach ourselves from a perspective in which Christian faith is the norm, and put ourselves back into a situation where Christians were seen as schismatics. But if we are to understand them, it is worth making the attempt, and asking the question – What were their problems? What were they trying to do? How did they relate their experience of Christ in the present with their beliefs about God's activity in the past? I want to look at some of the ways in which they wrestled with this problem, remembering that their two 'givens' were, on the one hand, their experience of Christ, and on the other, their roots in Judaism.

The difficulty of deciphering the evidence is summed up for us in one sentence by Paul; in Rom 10:4 he writes: 'Christ is the end of the Law'. But the Greek τέλος, like the English 'end', is ambiguous, and can mean either 'abolition' or 'fulfilment'. What does Paul mean? Does he regard the gospel as being in opposition to the Law, or as its completion? In what sense does the Law come to an 'end' with Christ?

The *earliest* answer to this question must surely have been that Jesus was seen as the fulfilment of both Law and Prophets. The idea that his life, teaching, death and resurrection were in accordance with scripture seems to have been the very earliest form of argument that was used to support the gospel, and the very first line of defence in any apologetic. We hardly need to look at examples. The method was either to appeal to particular proof-texts, or to scripture in general: what happened in Christ was interpreted as being 'according to the scriptures'. When appeal was made to particular proof-texts, then one could either quote chapter and verse, or weave the Old Testament passage into the narrative – sometimes so subtly that we, nineteen centuries later, do not always recognize the allusion. We need only compare the first two chapters of Matthew with the first two of Luke to find examples of these two approaches. Matthew quotes passages from the prophets, introducing them with the declaration that the gospel events took place in order to fulfil the prophets' words; Luke tells the story of Jesus' birth in language which is soaked in the vocabulary and style of the Septuagint. Whatever method was used, the purpose of the appeal to scripture was to demonstrate that God was at work in Christ, and that what he did – and even more mysteriously, what was done to him – were in accordance with God's purpose.

Such an approach begins, of course, from the assumption that the Old Testament scriptures were the authoritative witness to God's purpose, and the medium of God's self-revelation to mankind. It means, also, that Christ is seen as the fulfilment of God's purpose. The more these writers stressed the lines of continuity between their understanding of scripture and their experience of Christ, the more they came to see Christ as the *content* of God's plan – a plan which is traced back not simply to the time of David, Israel's ideal king, but to Moses, the nation's first redeemer, to Abraham, the father of the nation, and finally to Adam. Jesus is thus seen as part of God's plan from the very beginning.

When *we* talk about Jesus being seen as the fulfilment of scripture, we tend to think in terms of the fulfilment of prophecy. To judge from the evidence of the New Testament, however, it seems that the first Christians may have seen things somewhat differently. For a start, in understanding Jesus as the fulfilment of the prophets, they seem to have been thinking less in terms of straightforward 'predictions' than in terms of Jesus 'matching-up' to what was written in the prophets – as though, with an overhead projector, one were sliding one transparency over another until the two patterns merge. They began, that is, with their experience of Jesus, and looked for illumination in the prophets – and sometimes they found illumination in what appear to us to be strange places. Secondly, they seem to have thought of Jesus as 'fulfilling the Law' as well as the prophets. Indeed, from their point of view, this may well have been the more important. And though the evangelists show Jesus in constant conflict with scribes and Pharisees over his *interpretation* of the Law, the point of these skirmishes again and again is to prove that it is Jesus, not the Jewish religious authorities, who is faithful to the Law. Mark sets the scene at the beginning of his Gospel, when Jesus sends the leper to offer the sacrifice prescribed by Moses (Mark 1:44); and throughout Mark's story, Jesus turns the tables on his opponents (who are supposedly the upholders of the Law) by quoting the Law, and showing how his own teaching is in keeping with its demands. In Matthew, Jesus' teaching on the Law in the Sermon on the Mount begins with the words:

Think not that I have come to abolish the Law and the Prophets; I have come not to abolish them but to fulfil them. For truly, I say to you, till heaven and earth pass away, not an iota, not a dot, will pass from the Law until all is accomplished. (Matt 5:17–18)

Luke pushes the theme back to the very beginning of his story, and relates how Jesus' parents circumcised him and presented sacrifices in the temple, and so 'performed everything according to the Law of the Lord' (Luke 1:39).

Clearly the evangelists were concerned to stress the idea that Jesus fulfilled the Law. The fact that many of these passages occur in conflict situations suggests that there were those outside the Christian community who denied what is here affirmed. To 'scribes and Pharisees', Jesus was a lawbreaker – and worse, for he had apparently dared to attack Moses' teaching. To such accusations, the saying in Matthew 5:17 is clearly relevant: 'Think not that I have come to abolish the Law and the Prophets: I have come not to abolish them but to fulfil them'. Similarly, v. 19: 'Whoever relaxes one of the least of these commandments and teaches men so, shall be called least in the kingdom of heaven'. It is often suggested that these words reflect internal church disputes, and that it is the Hellenistic wing of the church, perhaps Paul himself, that is here under attack. But since the paragraph ends with the demand that Jesus' disciples must be more righteous than the scribes and Pharisees, it looks very much as though the accusations came from Jewish opponents. And the Christian response to these accusations was to say: 'we are in no way unfaithful to the Law; neither was Jesus unfaithful. We stand within the tradition of Judaism and at the end of the day, we shall be seen to be more faithful to Moses than you'. This is precisely the kind of argument one expects to be used by a minority group trying to establish its own position over against the parent body: 'it is we', they say, 'not you, who are being faithful to the traditions of the past; it is you, not we, who have gone astray'.

We see, then, that the belief that Jesus is the fulfilment of scripture can be conveyed in other ways than simply by quoting proof-texts. I have referred already to the way in which Luke weaves scriptural echoes into his account of the births of John and Jesus. His purpose seems to be to persuade us that he, too, like the writers of the Old Testament scriptures, is writing Salvation-history – writing about God's activity among his people. And he has another way of making the same point – namely, his frequent references to the Spirit of God; they establish that it is God himself who is at work in Jesus and his followers. Luke has an apologetic task; he has to persuade his readers that the story he tells – the story about Jesus, and the story about the activities of the apostles – are part of the same story which has its beginning in the Old Testament. What happened in the life, death and resurrection of Jesus, and what is continuing to happen in the life of the Christian community are, for Luke, all part of God's dealings with mankind: appeals to scripture and to the work of the Holy Spirit both showed that this was so. Yet commentators do not always appreciate Luke's own concern with continuity; indeed, the influential book by Conzelmann[4] suggests the very opposite, since he argues that Luke divides time into three distinct epochs – the period of the Old Testament, the

---

[4] Hans Conzelmann, *The Theology of St Luke,* trans. Geoffrey Buswell (London: Faber and Faber, 1960).

period of Jesus, and the period of the church. Whether or not that is a correct inference from Luke's two-volume work I am not sure; but if it is, it should not be stressed at the expense of Luke's emphasis on continuity, for he has gone out of his way, in the opening verses of both his volumes, to link first Jesus with all that happened before him, and then the events concerning the apostles with Jesus himself.

And if we want another example of the way in which the continuity with the past was important for the evangelists we can turn to the Fourth Gospel, where in the Prologue John underlines the theme in his own highly distinctive way, by showing that it was the same word of God spoken at the beginning of time which came again in the prophets, and finally in Jesus, the word made flesh.

In exploring this theme of continuity, I have begun with the Gospels rather than Paul, even though they were written later than Paul's letters, because of the difficulty in analysing Paul's view; but it is clear that he, too, understands Jesus to be the fulfilment of God's promises, and uses Old Testament proof-texts to support his argument. Indeed, Paul uses the Old Testament as a quarry from which to gather ammunition, and he does this especially when he is arguing with those who wish to impose circumcision and observance of the Law on his converts. Just as we find Jesus, in the Gospels, quoting the Law in arguing with those who claim to be upholding the Law, so, too, Paul appeals to the Law to show that it supports *his* case, and not that of his opponents. Whatever opposition there may be between Law and gospel, it has to be understood within this framework of the continuity of God's promises. But Paul, like Jesus, is accused of teaching what is contrary to the Law, and he indignantly rejects the charge. 'Is the Law contrary to God's promises?' he asks – 'μὴ γένοιτο – God forbid!' (Gal 3:21). 'Do we overthrow the Law by faith? μὴ γένοιτο – God forbid! We uphold the Law' (Rom 3:31).

To spell out all this is perhaps merely to state the obvious: of course these New Testament writers stressed, in their various ways, that Jesus was the fulfilment of the Old Testament promises – and if we were to look at later documents, at the Epistle to the Hebrews, for example, or 1 Peter, we should find a similar use of scripture as proof-texts, and the same conviction that they had been fulfilled in Christ. But it is as well to recognize what is happening. It was *not* that the first Christians inherited some kind of messianic 'checklist', and ticked off the items one by one: first-century Judaism did not have a ready-made list of messianic prophecies which had to be fulfilled by anyone who was a candidate for the title – there was no such list,[5] no such prophecies,

---

[5] A possible exception to this is the so-called 'Messianic Anthology' or 'Testimonia' found at Qumran (4Q175), consisting almost entirely of Old Testament texts. However, the three 'messianic' texts which are quoted seem to refer to three different figures – a prophet, a king,

and come to that, there probably wasn't a title of 'Messiah' either. Christians *began* from their experience of Jesus, and looked for ways of expressing what that meant. Old Testament passages which could be used as proof-texts were an obvious source; so were what we call the messianic titles, which probably weren't ready-made titles at all; so were various familiar symbols and images. They used these texts and terms, not simply because they were familiar parts of their thought-world, but because, in a variety of ways, they served to express the belief that Jesus was the fulfilment of Israel's hopes. The idea that there was a ready-made 'identikit' picture of the coming Messiah, waiting to be filled out, is the result of reading back our own ideas. At this point, the so called 'biblical theologians' were wrong, because they misunderstood the significance of the emphasis on continuity. Its thrust is from the experience of Jesus back to the past, rather than from the Old Testament to the New.

Now one of the interesting aspects of all this is that images, symbols, titles and proof-texts culled from the Old Testament are applied by these writers not only to Jesus himself, but to the community which believes in him. Indeed, some of them are used both of Jesus and of the church; and some bind the two together. The reason, of course, is that the early community was very much aware of itself as true Israel; we tend to speak of the new Israel – but that is because we have severed our cords with what we call 'old Israel'. But for the earliest Jewish Christians, Jesus was God's anointed, the fulfilment of God's promises to his people, Israel. If the nation's religious authorities had rejected him, they would be replaced; if Israel refused to respond, that did not mean that God's promises had failed: dead branches can be lopped off and new ones grafted in, but the tree remains; the tenants of the vineyard are driven out because of their villainy, but new ones will be appointed; the temple is destroyed, but it is rebuilt after three days; those who should have sat down to the messianic banquet are thrown out, but the feast goes on and vagabonds are brought in to feast instead; the sons of Abraham inherit the promises, but what a very odd lot these sons of Abraham are – Gentiles as well as Jews – and what links them to Abraham is not circumcision, but faith. If Jesus is the fulfilment of God's promises to his people, then those who believe in him must be the inheritors of those promises, and the true people of

---

and a priest; the various prophecies do not supply a 'job-description' for the 'Messiah', but evidence to back up the Community's expectations of several leaders. Moreover, the purpose of the collection seems to be primarily to stress the opposition which these leaders will meet, and the punishment which will overtake all those who withstand the Lord and his people. It is possible that the Teacher of Righteousness was thought to be the fulfilment of all three figures, but if so, then the Old Testament quotations are being used in a way similar to that in which such quotations are employed in the New Testament – as a way of spelling out the significance of the Teacher of Righteousness, not the messianic hopes for the future: in other words, the starting point is past experience of a particular individual, and not a job description which candidates for messiahship were required to match.

God; the new temple is built on him; the new sons of Abraham are sons only when they live in Christ. Arguments about Christology and about the identity of the Christian community inevitably belong together.

So the first answer that we find in the New Testament to the question – In what sense is Christ the 'end' of the Law? – is that he fulfils it.

In apparent contrast, however, we have passages in which Law and gospel appear to be opposed. The most obvious examples occur in the writings of Paul, since he argues the case for Christ as the replacement for the Law. 'What the Law could not do', he declares, 'God has done by sending his Son' (Rom 8:3). It is impossible to gain righteousness before God by the works of the Law; righteousness comes only through union with Christ, and by faith in him. God's people are no longer defined as those who accept the Law and receive the mark of circumcision; they are those who are in Christ, and who have been baptized into the community of men and women who believe in him. Reading Paul's words from a Gentile perspective, we are likely to see this argument in terms of stark alternatives – Law on the one hand opposed to the gospel on the other; and because Paul is always waging war with Judaizers of some kind when he speaks of the role of the Law, his words naturally come across in this way. In Galatians, in particular, the Law itself appears to be opposing God! But this is only because of the weakness of the flesh: the Law, which is in itself good, divine in origin, has as it were been hijacked by alien powers. Nevertheless, Paul never finally surrenders the Law. How can he? The Law was delivered by God to Moses on Mount Sinai; its commandments are holy, righteous, and good (Rom 7:12); the Law expressed God's will. But it cannot save; it cannot make men and women righteous in the sight of God. But since the Law comes from God, it must have a place in the divine plan, and Paul therefore looks for another function for the Law. In both Galatians and Romans, he explains this in terms of an interim measure; the Law was necessary, he argues, between the giving of the promises and their fulfilment. *Why* the Law was necessary, he does not really explain satisfactorily. The Law, he suggests, was our custodian – in charge, that is, of the Jews – until the time was ripe for Christ to come. Paul's problem, quite simply, is that the Law is there, and he cannot deny its divine origin without denying everything that has spoken to him of God in the past. He has to weld together this heritage with his new experience of God in Christ.

We have noted already the passage in Romans (3:31) where Paul indignantly denies that he is destroying the Law; he is not overthrowing the Law, but upholding it. Many commentators hold that Paul's attitude to the Law is inconsistent, and varies from one epistle to another.[6] Whether or not they are

---

[6] E.g. Heikki Räisänen, 'Paul's Theological Difficulties with the Law', in *Studia Biblica 1978*, ed. Elizabeth A. Livingstone, JSNTSup 3 (Sheffield: JSOT Press, 1980), 301–320.

right, it is unlikely that Paul would affirm in Rom 10:4 what he so vehemently denies a few chapters earlier, in Rom 3:31: 'Do we overthrow the Law by faith? μὴ γένοιτο – God forbid! We uphold the Law'. When he describes Christ as the end of the Law in 10:4, therefore, he cannot be thinking of a fundamental antithesis between Law and gospel – though we find no less an exegete than Käsemann insisting that he is.[7] Yet it seems clear from the context that Paul's meaning is that Christ achieves – finally and fully – what the Law was able to do only partially and temporarily. The passage in Romans 10 is an exposition of Deuteronomy 30, and it is a typical New Testament 'takeover bid' for an Old Testament text. What was originally said about God's Law is now interpreted as referring to Christ, not to the commands given on Sinai: the word which God sets in the mouths and hearts of his people is no longer interpreted as the word of command, but as the word of the gospel. In that sense, the Law is indeed ousted. Yet it is the Law itself – the book of Deuteronomy – which is being quoted! We see here how Paul understands the continuing function of the Law: it is the witness to Christ. In other words, even when Paul appears to be attacking the Law, he maintains that he is upholding its true meaning; Christ is still being seen as the fulfilment of the Law, even when he replaces it. God's revelation in the past was not inconsistent with his revelation in Christ, but was pointing towards what happened in him. Paul's argument is therefore based on the Law itself, for we are still arguing within the context of those who take the Jewish scriptures as authoritative; the crucial difference between Jew and Christian is the way in which those scriptures are understood and interpreted.

Commentators on Paul do not always appreciate that he remained a convinced Jew, and believed that he was being faithful to his Jewish heritage – and that meant, of course, to the Torah. It is true that his commission to evangelize the Gentiles led him to regard the Mosaic covenant as something binding on the Jewish people only, and something, moreover, which had been a temporary measure. But long before the Mosaic covenant, God had made certain promises to Abraham, and these have now been fulfilled in Christ. Of course there is continuity! God does not go back on his promises.

It seems, then, that even the apparent antithesis between Christ and the Law which serves to spell out the notion of Christ as the replacement of

---

[7] Ernst Käsemann, *Commentary on Romans,* trans. Geoffrey W. Bromiley (London: SCM Press, 1980). Käsemann is careful to distinguish between Paul's own antithesis of Law and gospel, and the dialectic of a later period. Nevertheless, he dismisses all attempts to interpret τέλος as 'goal' as unjustified. He points in particular to the idea that the Law is a 'custodian', whose role ends when Christ comes (Gal 3:24; cf. Rom 7:1–6). Even in Galatians, however, Paul dismisses any suggestion that the Law is 'against God's promises' (3:21), and introduces the image of the παιδαγωγός with the statement that scripture imprisoned everyone under sin *in order that* the promises might be fulfilled through faith in Jesus Christ. However negative the Law's role may be, it still has a positive purpose.

the Law should be seen in terms of continuity rather than of opposition. The suggestion that τέλος should be translated 'goal' in Rom 10:4 is an appropriate one (despite the strenuous opposition it has aroused) since it conveys admirably the tension between negative and positive in Paul's thought: if Christ is the goal of the Law, then the Law itself is designed with built-in obsolescence. When Christ arrives, the Law is at an end, not because Christ destroys what the Law stood for, but because he achieves the Law's aims.

Paul argued his case with vigour and passion, but he was by no means alone in his stance. What he did in his way, other writers did in theirs. The author of the Fourth Gospel, for example, vigorous in his condemnation of 'the Jews', claims for Jesus everything which had once been claimed for the Law. He does this by his use of imagery, since most of the symbols he applies to Jesus have their origins in Jewish beliefs about the Law. The word which was once spoken in the Law is now embodied in him: *he* is the light, the life, the way, the truth, the living manna, the source of water. Equally significant, the worship which had once been centred in Jerusalem is now focussed on Jesus: all the significance pertaining to the various religious festivals is now subsumed in Jesus. The Fourth Evangelist claims that truth and revelation and communion with God are to be found in Jesus, and not in the commands and ritual set out in the Torah. But this antithesis makes sense only within a context which accepts the validity of the Torah itself. John's argument is with Jews, who cling to the traditions of the past; but their trouble – according to John – is that they do not understand their own scriptures. 'You search the scriptures', says Jesus to the Jews, 'because you think that you have eternal life in them – but they bear witness to *me* … if you believed Moses, you would believe me, because he wrote of me' (John 5:37 ff.). The argument, therefore, is not between Moses and Christ: Moses is the witness to Christ, and not his opponent. In John, as in Paul, and as in the Synoptic Gospels, the argument is about how one interprets Moses; what John does is to hold together the traditions of the past and the new experience of God's grace in Christ.

And so we could go on. But already, we are being pushed, by *both* these lines of enquiry – both by the arguments which stress the continuity between old and new by seeing Jesus as the *fulfilment* of scripture, and by those which suggest a certain discontinuity between them by seeing Jesus as the *replacement* of the Law – to our third theme: this is the superiority of Christ to the Law.

In a sense, this is not really a separate theme at all. The superiority of Christ seems to have been implied in some of the passages we have considered already, and this not merely because what is newer is necessarily better – indeed, as we shall see in a moment, from the Jewish point of view, what was *earlier* was superior: as Luke puts it, the old wine is better than the new. The idea that Jesus fulfils various Old Testament promises does not necessarily in itself suggest that he is greater than they; but once we move into arguments that in some sense he replaces the Law, and that the Law witnesses to him, then his superiority is clearly implied – for why do we need a replacement unless it is in fact better than the old? Any manufacturer who improves his product has to substantiate his claim to have produced a superior version of it. New 'Tide' always washes even cleaner than old 'Tide' – a remarkable feat, since for years we will have been assured that the original product could not be bettered. What had once seemed to us – in our ignorance – perfect, now bears testimony to the superior quality of a product whose performance is even better. And so the Law, once seen as the embodiment of God's self-revelation and of his will for mankind, gives way to Christ, and plays a subsidiary role as witness to his superiority. It was a bold conclusion for those brought up within the Jewish faith.

One of the notable passages where this theme is worked out is 2 Corinthians 3. At first sight, Paul appears to be contrasting Moses and Christ. In fact he is comparing Moses with himself – to the former's detriment! – a bold, indeed a courageous, thing to do. Like Moses, Paul and his fellow apostles are ministers, but of a new, superior dispensation. Paul spells out the differences between them in a series of contrasting images: stone tablets are contrasted with living hearts; the carved letter with the Spirit; death with life; condemnation with righteousness; the face concealed under a veil with an open face. The passage suggests that Paul sees a clear antithesis between the two. But that would be to misunderstand his position, for to Paul the continuity is as important as the contrast, and what binds together Moses' ministry with that of Paul is the theme of glory. True, Paul regards Moses' glory as inferior, since it was only temporary: the glory which shone from Moses' face when he came down from Mount Sinai faded away, whereas Paul's glory grows brighter and brighter. Nevertheless, there is a link between the two, since the *ultimate* source of the glory reflected by both Paul and Moses is the same: the glory which Moses glimpsed on Sinai was the self-revelation of God – and that was the glory which was embodied in Jesus, and is now reflected by those who gaze at him. This whole passage is a good exposition of the ideas that we have been exploring: there is a continuity in God's self-revelation to his people, and it is *within* that context of continuity that we have to see the contrast between the dispensation of the Law, which led to death, and the dispensation of the Spirit, which leads to life. It is significant, too, that the contrast drawn here is not between Moses and Christ, but between Moses and Paul. The reason is Christ's superiority to Moses: he is, as it were, one higher up the scale, since he is not simply one who reflects God's glory – though he does that (2 Cor 4:6) – but is himself the *source* of glory; he is the true image of God (4:4), and the light which shines from his face is the creative light of God himself, which shone forth on the day of creation (4:6). So the glory which is seen in Jesus is regarded by Paul as primary, and this is why it is superior to the second-hand glory or revelation mediated through Moses. What Moses received was temporary, but what Jesus gives is permanent. But does Paul think of Christ himself as the source of the glory seen by Moses? Does his permanence stretch *backwards* through time as well as *forwards?* The link with creation suggests that this is indeed the way in which Paul's mind is moving. The logical implication of his argument is that Christ is not only *superior* to Moses but *prior* to Moses; but this he does not spell out.

There is, however, an interesting parallel with the imagery used by Paul in 2 Corinthians 3 in the language of the first chapter or the Fourth Gospel. Here, once again, we find the theme of glory: 'the word became flesh, and dwelt among us, and we saw his glory, the glory that belongs to one who is an only-begotten son of his father, full of grace and truth' (John 1:14). Once again, we have a contrast with Moses: the Law came through Moses, but grace and truth – qualities which are referred to in Exodus 34 in an account of God's self-revelation – have come through Jesus Christ.[8] But once again, this contrast must be seen within the context of continuity: the word which became flesh among us in the person of Jesus, whose glory we have seen, is the word which was in the beginning, the word which was with God, and which was the source of light and life. The glory which shone forth in Jesus, who makes the Father known to mankind, is the glory which no man has ever seen – not even Moses, who glimpsed only a rear view as God passed by on the mountain (Exod 33:22 ff.) – for Jesus embodies the grace and truth which belong to God himself. The parallels between 2 Corinthians 3 and John 1 are intriguing – especially since they both appeal to the same Old Testament texts, Genesis 1 and Exodus 33–34. But John spells out what was not made explicit in 2 Corinthians: he identifies this self-expression of God – his glory or word – with the word made flesh in Jesus; the light which shone at creation, the word which spoke at the beginning, is the light which shines in Jesus, and the word embodied in him. If Jesus is superior to the Law, he is also *prior* to the Law; it is the Law which reflects *his* glory, and not vice versa.

Similar claims that Jesus is not only continuous with God's past revelation but superior to everything that has been experienced previously appear elsewhere in the New Testament. In the opening verses of the Epistle to the Hebrews, for example, we are told: 'In many and various ways God spoke of old to our fathers by the prophets; but in these last days he has spoken to us by a Son, whom he appointed the heir of all things, through whom also he created the world: he reflects the glory of God and bears the very stamp of his nature, upholding the universe by his word of power'. Or again, in Col 1:15 ff., Christ is said to be 'the image of the invisible God, the firstborn of

---

[8] Exod 34:7. Cf. Morna D. Hooker, 'The Johannine Prologue and the Messianic Secret', *NTS* 21 (1974): 54 = below, essay 23 (pp. 321–340).

all creation; for in him all things were created, in heaven and on earth, visible and invisible ... all things were created through him and for him. He is before all things, and in him all things hold together'. It is no accident that these passages are examples of so-called 'Wisdom Christology', and that the ideas used here have been traced back to the descriptions of Wisdom in places such as Proverbs 8, Wisdom 7 and Sirach 24. But why did these passages come to be used of Christ? Was it perhaps because already in Judaism the identification had been made between the Law and the figure of Wisdom? The Law had already been interpreted as God's word, as the expression of God's glory, as the emanation of his splendour, and as present with God from the foundations of the world. If Christians were now claiming that in Jesus God reveals *more* of his character than he had done in either the prophets or the Mosaic covenant, then certainly everything that had hitherto been said about the Torah must be said about him – and more. If Jesus is understood to be God's supreme and final self-revelation, then what came previously must be seen as partial and incomplete. Law and Prophets both declared the word of God, yet they were derivative, secondary, and Christ is the authentic norm. He represents God's plan and purpose from the beginning – and inevitably, one begins to speak about his priority, and his pre-existence. Jesus is God's true image, the source of glory, and whatever other glimpses of God's glory have been caught hitherto are secondary to God's self-revelation in him. It is possible, even though he does not spell this out, that Paul believes that the glory Moses glimpsed on Mount Sinai was the glory of Christ himself. Certainly in 1 Corinthians 10 he says that the Rock from which the Israelites drank was Christ; this is an allusion to the rock which was struck by Moses in the wilderness in order to provide water for Israel, and which, according to Jewish legend, followed the people on their wanderings. Water is a familiar symbol for the Torah in rabbinic writings, so that the 'supernatural drink' from which the Israelites drank would normally be understood as a reference to the Torah; but Paul now identifies the *source* of this 'supernatural drink' – the Rock – with Christ.[9] Once again he seems to have taken over a familiar image in order to claim the superiority of Christ, but the logic of his argument suggests – whether intentionally or not – that Christ is prior, as well as superior. And if we turn back to the pages of the Fourth Gospel, we find not only the opening declaration that the Word was in the beginning, but later, in 12:41, an exposition of Isaiah's vision in the temple which explains that what Isaiah in fact saw was the glory of Jesus.

In this third approach to the question – how is Christ the end of the Law? – the theme of continuity has, as it were, been turned inside out. No longer is Christ seen simply as the fulfilment of scripture – as the one to whom Law

---

[9] Philo identifies the rock with Wisdom. See *Leg.* 2.86; *Det.* 115.

and Prophets point forward. He is seen now as the *source* of revelation, as the blueprint of creation. No longer does scripture validate Christ – rather, he validates scripture: he is the reality, and scripture is secondary to him, for the word of God is enshrined in Jesus, and not in the pages of the sacred text. Jesus is now seen, not so much as the goal of God's revelation, as its origin; not simply as the content of scripture but as the one who inspires its understanding. When we look at Christ, declares Paul, we understand the real significance of the scriptures, and the Spirit writes in our hearts the truth to which they bear witness.

If we attempt to put ourselves back in the shoes of these men, we can understand the logic of what they were saying. Of course they believed that there was continuity between the old and the new; the only alternative was to attribute what had been understood as God's self-revelation in the past to some other god: that was Marcion's solution – and his interpretation was equally logical, beginning from where he did. Seen from outside the context of Jewish Christianity, the claims which were made for Christ seem, inevitably, to denigrate the Law. Yet they were *not* a denigration, for the Law is God's Law, and its commandments, as Paul affirms (Rom 7:12), are 'holy, just and good'. Has the Law, then, been dethroned? There is a sense in which it has – but not if that image suggests to us, as it well might, a coup in which one ruler topples another. A better analogy might be that of a dowager duchess, who retains her title and her dignity when her son and daughter-in-law take over and become the new Duke and Duchess; although she is replaced, she is nevertheless still honoured, and in a paradoxical way finds fulfilment in those who succeed her. From the perspective of a later time, the antitheses of Matthew 5 sound like an attack on the Law: 'You have heard that it was said of old ... but I say to you ...'. Yet they are *not* an attack, as the introduction in verses 17–21 makes clear. From within the Jewish Christian community, those six antitheses made perfect sense: of course Matthew did not mean to suggest that Jesus had attacked the teaching of Moses! But the revelation which came through Moses was only partial, and now God's word is being spoken clearly and directly by one who is greater than Moses. Matthew certainly does not suggest that God has changed his mind, or has decided to replace an imperfect Law with a 'revised' version; nor does he suggest that Jesus is giving a *new* Law; rather, because he is superior to Moses, his words are more direct, more authoritative, and his presentation of God's demands makes no concession to human weakness.

Similar arguments go on elsewhere in the New Testament – though we do not always appreciate what is happening. In Acts 7, we find Stephen being accused by the Jews of teaching against the Law and the temple. Commentators frequently complain that Stephen's speech is irrelevant to the charges brought against him; in fact, it is highly relevant, for what he does, according to Luke's account, is to turn the tables on his accusers. It is they, he declares, who are disobedient to God's commands, delivered on Mount Sinai, and it is they who do not realize that the temple is only a symbol of something much greater, whereas the Christian community are obedient to God's commands and worship God as he should be worshipped. Taken out of its original context, Stephen's speech does sound like an attack on the Law and the temple, but in fact both are put in their place, and seen as symbols of something greater than themselves, which Christians claim to have experienced in the person of Jesus Christ.[10]

But the old bottles of Judaism could not contain the new wine of the gospel. The pity is, not that the wine was lost – for it was poured into fresh bottles – but that the old bottles were thrown away. When Christianity finally broke away from the parent body, then it lost part of its Jewish heritage. And when the Jewish context of the early debates was forgotten, then the claims being made for Jesus took on new interpretations; the attacks on Jewish opponents came to sound like total condemnation. What had been tension became antithesis, and the opposition between Christianity and Judaism was complete. The irony is that in time some of the fresh wineskins themselves became old and brittle, unable to contain the heady wine of the gospel. But that is another story, and a problem for another lecture altogether.

---

[10] Cf. Graham Stanton, 'Stephen in Lucan Perspective', in *Studia Biblica 1978,* ed. Elizabeth A. Livingstone, JSNTSup 3 (Sheffield: JSOT Press, 1980), 345–360.

Section Two

Methodology

2. Christology and Methodology*

New Testament scholarship of the 70's begins from the position which 50 years ago still needed to be hotly argued, but today seems axiomatic: the gospel material as it stands reflects the beliefs and interests of those through whose hands – or mouths – it has been handed down; to separate out the views of each evangelist from those of his predecessors – still more to isolate the original sayings of Jesus from the tradition as it is presented to us – is an intricate, perhaps an impossible task. How are we to proceed?

The so-called 'traditio-historical' method followed by many scholars suggests that the only safe way to proceed in recovering the teaching of Jesus is to adopt the principles of 'dissimilarity' and 'coherence'. The idea of dissimilarity as the standard by which we establish the distinctive teaching of Jesus is used by Bultmann,[1] and by Käsemann,[2] Conzelmann,[3] Perrin[4] and Fuller, among others, after him. Fuller[5] explains the principle in these terms:

> As regards the sayings of Jesus, traditio-historical criticism eliminates from the authentic sayings of Jesus those which are paralleled in the Jewish tradition on the one hand (apocalyptic and Rabbinic) and those which reflect the faith, practice and situations of the post-Easter church as we know them from outside the gospels.

To the small body of material extracted in this way there can then be added other sayings which are regarded as being consistent with it. As Perrin[6] expresses it: 'material from the earliest strata of the tradition may be accepted as authentic if it can be shown to cohere with material established as authentic by means of the criterion of dissimilarity'.

Some of us, however, feel uneasy about the way in which these two principles are applied, and doubt whether they are the means of recovering

---

* This paper was read at the Seminar on Christology, under the chairmanship of Professor Norman Perrin, during the General Meeting of the SNTS held at Newcastle in August 1970.

[1] Rudolf Bultmann, *The History of the Synoptic Tradition,* trans. John Marsh (Oxford: Blackwell, 1963), 205.

[2] Ernst Käsemann, *Essays on New Testament Themes,* trans. W.J. Montague (London: SCM Press, 1964), 34–37.

[3] Hans Conzelmann, 'Jesus Christus', in *Die Religion in Geschichte und Gegenwart,* vol. 3, eds. Hans von Campenhausen et. al. (Tübingen: Mohr, 1959), col. 623.

[4] Norman Perrin, *Rediscovering the Teaching of Jesus* (London: SCM Press, 1967), 39–43.

[5] Reginald H. Fuller, *The Foundations of New Testament Christology* (London: Collins, 1965), 18, 116.

[6] Perrin, *Rediscovering the Teaching,* 43.

the teaching of Jesus.[7] There are serious faults in the logic of using these particular criteria to establish his authentic message.

1. Use of the principle of dissimilarity, it is claimed, gives us what is distinctive in the teaching of Jesus. But the English word 'distinctive' can have two senses – it can mean 'unique' (what makes it distinct from other things, the German *verschieden*), or it can mean 'characteristic' (the German *bezeichnend*). In which sense is it being used here? Clearly the method is designed to give us the former – but what we really want is the latter; and the two are by no means necessarily the same. As an example, we might consider three typical speeches by three political leaders at election time; if we were to eliminate what was common to all three, how much would be left of any one speech? Probably very little! The result might give us what was distinctive of a party in the sense of what its members believe and members of other parties do not, but it would certainly not be representative of the policy of the party. This particular method of procedure has this inevitable drawback – that it will eliminate from the teaching of Jesus those areas in which he was in agreement with Judaism and those in which he was in agreement with the church. This is, of course, recognized by those who use the method, and accepted as a drawback.[8] It is, however, a very serious drawback indeed, for to take the remaining material as the basis of our reconstruction will inevitably lead to serious distortion. No one can seriously doubt that in some things Jesus' views must have overlapped those of the Jewish leaders and those of his followers, yet these must be set aside from our reconstruction. But to exclude details from our picture of Jesus may lead to distortion as serious as (or worse than) that which comes if we include too much. Moreover, since it inevitably detaches Jesus from his contemporaries, we are perhaps justified in suggesting that this distortion is serious. In this attempt to recover what is distinctive, it seems that the two senses of 'distinctive' are being confused – what makes Jesus distinct from others is being regarded as that which is characteristic of him.[9] We must be clear as to what this particular criterion can do: it may perhaps be able to give us a collection of sayings concerning whose authenticity we may be reasonably confident – but those sayings will not

---

[7] We must therefore disagree with the statement of Heinz Zahrnt, *The Historical Jesus*, trans. John Bowden (London: Collins, 1963): 'There is today general agreement on this basic principle of method'.

[8] Perrin, *Rediscovering the Teaching*, 43.

[9] Fuller, for example, refers to sayings which pass this test as 'the more characteristic parts of Jesus' teaching' (Fuller, *The Foundations of New Testament Christology*, 103). What he means is that they are 'distinctive' in the other sense. Cf. Perrin, *Rediscovering the Teaching*, 39: 'If we are to seek that which is most characteristic of Jesus, it will be found not in the things which he shares with his contemporaries but in the things wherein he differs from them'. This assertion of Jesus' uniqueness is a dogmatic assumption. Cf. the criticism of F. Gerald Downing, *The Church and Jesus: A Study in History, Philosophy and Theology* (London: SCM Press, 1968), 116.

necessarily represent the kernel of Jesus' teaching, or be his most characteristic thought.[10] Indeed, they would seem to offer us those sayings which the early church treated as peripheral.

2. 'It may' – but here we come to a second ground for misgiving. Since the method proceeds by eliminating ideas found in Judaism and early Christianity, it presupposes a fairly confident knowledge of both areas. To what extent is this justified? Use of this criterion seems to assume that we are dealing with two known factors (Judaism and early Christianity) and one unknown – Jesus; it would perhaps be a fairer statement of the situation to say that we are dealing with three unknowns, and that our knowledge of the other two is quite as tenuous and indirect as our knowledge of Jesus himself.[11] As far as Judaism is concerned, the discovery of the Qumran material should be sufficient warning against over-confidence in supposing that we know the whole truth about first-century Judaism. Any comparison between the beliefs of Judaism and the teaching of Jesus which claims to find ideas in the latter unparalleled in the former is inevitably an argument from silence, and should be treated as such. And if our knowledge of Judaism is only partial, so, too, is our knowledge of early Christian belief, and here, too, we must tread with caution. The traditio-historian is the first to recognize that the material as we have it today in the New Testament represents only part of the picture; there may have been other beliefs about Jesus and christological statements which are not now represented in our canonical material. It could be that if we knew the whole truth about Judaism and the early church, our small quantity of 'distinctive' teaching would wither away altogether.[12]

3. But even if we had perfect knowledge of Jesus' contemporaries, the method must be suspect because it begs the question. We begin our examination of the gospel material with a tool which denies the possibility of overlapping, and which insists on Jesus' uniqueness. Such a tool is bound to produce a picture in keeping with its assumption – and that is precisely what we get: a Jesus who stands out from his contemporaries as distinctive in his attitudes, who makes no messianic claims for himself, and who finds himself in opposition to the Jewish leaders. The method dictates its own conclusions.

4. The application of the method is bound to be subjective. How do we decide what is 'dissimilar'? – especially when we are reminded, also, that an 'authentic' saying of Jesus should be 'at home' in first-century Palestine. To be acceptable as genuine, a saying of Jesus must at one and the same time be

---

[10] Cf. Morna D. Hooker, *The Son of Man in Mark* (London: SPCK, 1967), 6 ff. D. E. Nineham 'Jesus in the Gospels' in *Christ for Us Today*, ed. Norman Pittenger (London: SCM Press, 1968), 58, n. 18.

[11] Perrin's statement that 'the Gospels offer us directly information about the early church' (Norman Perrin, *What is Redaction Criticism?* [London: SPCK, 1970], 69) is over-optimistic.

[12] Cf. Downing, *The Church and Jesus,* 114 ff.

'dissimilar' from contemporary Judaism, and yet use its categories and reflect the language and style of Aramaic.[13] In other words, authentic sayings must not be reflected in Judaism (as far as it is known to us) but must sound as if they could have been spoken at that time! It is difficult to know how to apply these apparently contradictory criteria simultaneously. When Perrin,[14] for example, argues that Jesus could not have used 'the Son of man' as a title because it did not exist in Judaism at the time, he is apparently using the second criterion; but if the title had (in his opinion) existed, he would presumably have eliminated it by applying the criterion of dissimilarity!

5. Subjectivity is even more of a danger when we turn to the second principle – that of coherence or consistency. We may be able to sort out what seems coherent (or incoherent) to us, but we are living in a completely different world, and what seems incoherent to us may have seemed coherent in first-century Palestine, and vice versa. Moreover, some of Jesus' sayings, if they are genuine, are paradoxical, and that alone should perhaps warn us against looking for what seems to us to be consistent.

6. When one adds the coherence principle to that of dissimilarity, then any errors in the results obtained by that method are liable to be magnified by the use of this second criterion. If the core of material upon which we build our reconstruction of the teaching of Jesus is inaccurate, then the addition of material which seems to be consistent with that core is likely to reflect those same inaccuracies.

7. Those who advocate the use of these criteria are strangely inconsistent in applying them. This may be illustrated by looking at the word 'Abba'. Here is a good example of something which is Aramaic in form but to which an exact parallel has not been found in Judaism; but it is used by the early church (see Rom 8:15 and Gal 4:6), and by the strict application of the principle of dissimilarity it should be eliminated. Yet it seems to be almost universally accepted that Jesus addressed God as 'Abba', and taught his disciples to do the same. Why? Perrin writes: '[these two verses] may not be regarded as representing early Christian tradition as such',[15] but this seems like special pleading. The real criterion being used here is not the principle of dissimilarity, but our own understanding of the situation.

As a contrasting example, let us take the term 'Son of man'. The 'orthodox' position today seems to be that Jesus spoke of a future, eschatological Son of man (not himself), and justification for this is found in 1 Enoch. Yet by the application of the principle of dissimilarity, the words of Enoch, if they did

---

[13] Cf. Fuller, *The Foundations of New Testament Christology*, 18; Perrin, *Rediscovering the Teaching*, 37 ff.; and the criticisms of Downing, *The Church and Jesus*, 113 ff.

[14] Perrin, *Rediscovering the Teaching*, 164–175, 197–198.

[15] Perrin, *Rediscovering the Teaching*, 41.

indeed exist at the time, as is assumed on this view, should eliminate all eschatological 'Son of man' sayings from the teaching of Jesus! Strict application of this rule would either reduce us to the position of Vielhauer,[16] Conzelmann[17] and others – that none of the 'Son of man' sayings are authentic – or leave us with the sayings about the earthly and suffering Son of man, which do not seem to have parallels in first-century Judaism.[18] As far as comparison with the church's beliefs is concerned, it is difficult to know how to apply the principle. We could argue that, since the evangelists identified Jesus with the Son of man, we must eliminate all the sayings. On the other hand, there is little sign outside the Gospels of a 'Son of man' theology, and no confessional formulae in the Synoptic Gospels that 'Jesus is the Son of man'. Yet there is a marked increase in the eschatological sayings as time goes on. By the principle of dissimilarity, we might argue that it seems probable that the original, authentic sayings are those which refer to the humiliation and suffering of the Son of man, and that the eschatological sayings are inauthentic – this would give us 'a good example of the things for which the criterion of dissimilarity seeks: radical difference from Judaism and later modification towards Judaism'.[19] Yet those who advocate this method come, surprisingly, to very different conclusions; they desert their principle at this point and use instead the principle of multiple attestation, arguing that the eschatological sayings are found in all the Gospel sources, but the others are chiefly Marcan. Once again, the real criterion being used is a particular view of the situation – in this case, the belief that Jesus made no messianic claims for himself, and so could not have spoken of himself as Son of man.

The 'Son of man' problem illustrates also the point made earlier, of our insufficient knowledge of Judaism, though in this particular case we may be *assuming* knowledge with undue foundation. It is strange how often it is accepted without question that 'the Son of man' was a well-known title for the eschatological redeemer in first-century Palestine. But was it? Was it well-known? Was it even a title? Was the book of the Similitudes of Enoch yet written? These questions are all open to debate, and many would feel that the evidence tends towards negative answers.[20] Yet the assumption that we do know the meaning of the phrase and understand how it would have been

---

[16] Philipp Vielhauer, 'Gottesreich und Menschensohn in der Verkündigung Jesu', in *Festschrift für Günther Dehn,* ed. Wilhelm Schneemelcher (Neukirchen: Kreis Moers, 1957), 51–79; Philipp Vielhauer, 'Jesus und der Menschensohn', *ZTK* 60 (1963): 133–177.

[17] Hans Conzelmann, 'Gegenwart und Zukunft in der synoptischen Tradition', *ZTK* 54 (1957): 277–296.

[18] So Eduard Schweizer; see 'Der Menschensohn', *ZNW* 50 (1959): 185–209; 'The Son of Man', *JBL* 79 (1960): 119–129; 'The Son of Man Again', *NTS* 9 (1963): 256–261.

[19] See Schweizer, 'Der Menschensohn'; 'The Son of Man'; 'The Son of Man Again'.

[20] See most recently, the article by Ragnar Leivestad, which challenges these assumptions: 'Der apokalyptische Menschensohn ein theologisches Phantom', *Annual of the Swedish*

interpreted at the time of Jesus lies at the basis of the kind of approach we have been examining.

How, then, can we proceed in our attempt to analyse early Christian beliefs about Jesus, and any christological statements and claims which he himself may have made? Much has been written recently about 'the burden of proof' regarding a saying's authenticity. From the old assumption that a Gospel saying was authentic unless proved otherwise, the pendulum has swung over to the opposite approach – the belief that sayings must be treated as non-authentic unless they can be proved dominical. This, it is suggested, is a more cautious method – the only 'safe' way of proceeding.[21] Yet perhaps a debate about 'the burden of proof' is not very profitable, and is appropriate only if one takes the extreme position that the Gospels represent historical reports of the words of Jesus, or the equally extreme view that Jesus himself said nothing sufficiently memorable to have come down to us. Similarly, perhaps, the question 'Who is the more creative, an individual or a community, Jesus or the church?' is not particularly helpful, for these are not the real alternatives. What we have is a body of material which has been handed on, shaped, moulded, used, and perhaps created, by the early Christian communities. It is perhaps more appropriate to suggest that the 'burden of proof' lies upon each scholar who offers a judgement upon any part of the material, to give a reasonable explanation for the existence of that saying, and to suggest a suitable *Sitz im Leben* for every saying or pericope. Too often, material is simply rejected as non-dominical, and attributed to 'the early church'; but this is only one step in the process, and though it is taken as a first step it ought, perhaps, more often to be the last, taken only when we have considered every possibility. For we are being no more 'cautious' or 'safe' in our procedure if we discard doubtful material than if we retain it – and if we unknowingly attribute dominical sayings to the church, our resulting pictures of Jesus and the development of Christology will be just as prone to error as if we wrongly attribute the church's formulations of their belief to Jesus.

Those of us who are less than optimistic about the possibility of reconstructing the process by which the tradition developed simply by using the tools of 'form criticism' and 'traditio-criticism' are sometimes described as 'opponents of form criticism'. Professor Perrin, for example, has recently written: 'Miss Hooker is convinced that form criticism has failed to make its point'.[22] This is a complete misunderstanding and misrepresentation of our position. I myself wrote in the study which Professor Perrin attacks: 'It

---

Theological Institute 6 (1968): 49–105. Cf. also Perrin's discussion, referred to above (Perrin, *Rediscovering the Teaching*, 164–175, 197–198).

[21] Perrin, *Rediscovering the Teaching*, 39.

[22] Perrin, *What is Redaction Criticism?*, 70. A similar misunderstanding is found in A.J.B. Higgins' essay 'Is the Son of Man Problem Insoluble?', in *Neotestamentica et Semitica: Studies in*

is certainly not our intention … to attack the form-critical method. Form criticism has established itself as an invaluable tool which can tell us a great deal about the history of the gospel material'.[23] But it cannot tell us everything; it is not a key which can unlock all mysteries. Too often it is treated as though it can.

My chief plea, then, is for less dogmatism in our conclusions, and the recognition that all our results are only tentative. We know too little to be dogmatic, and it is probable that any rigid division of material into 'authentic' and 'non-authentic' distorts the picture. All the material comes to us at the hands of the believing community, and probably it all bears its mark to a lesser or greater extent; to confine our picture of Jesus to material which passes all our tests for genuineness is too restricting. British readers are familiar with the tests on various commodities carried out by the magazine *Which?* to discover which brand is the best buy. The results are printed in the form of tables, with points being scored for reliability, efficiency, comfort, etc., and the greater the number of 'blobs' appearing in a column the better. Our approach to the gospel material must be something like this; few sayings will score the maximum number of points, but the greater the score the greater will be our confidence.

The criteria that we use will be various. They will include the principle of dissimilarity which we have been discussing, but we shall use this in a positive way, to increase our confidence about a saying, and not in a negative way, to blackball one. Equally, the principle of multiple attestation can be used positively, not negatively. The presence of Aramaisms, also, will be a point in a saying's favour, though it can no more prove a saying's genuineness than any other criterion. Parables are likely to go back to Jesus, though details may have been added, and the original point lost. The use of paradox and irony might also be thought to strengthen a saying's claim to be genuine.

But most important, perhaps, is the demand that a saying must be given a reasonable 'pedigree', whether it is attributed to Jesus or the church. Too often this is thought to be unnecessary. Let us take the 'confession' at Caesarea Philippi as an example. This is now commonly explained as a complete rewriting by Mark of an originally totally different story. The command to secrecy is eliminated as a typically Marcan theme, and the passion prediction is regarded as *ex eventu;* we are left with a narrative in which Jesus asks the disciples who they think he is, the reply of Peter, and the words of Jesus, 'Get behind me, Satan'.[24] Granted that this story is credible within the life

---

Honour of Matthew Black, eds. E. Earle Ellis and Max Wilcox (Edinburgh: T&T Clark, 1969), 73.

[23] Hooker, *The Son of Man in Mark,* 5.

[24] See Fuller, *The Foundations of New Testament Christology,* 109; John Knox, *The Death of Christ: The Cross in New Testament History and Faith* (London: Collins, 1959), 78–80.

of Jesus (which some of us may doubt), no satisfactory explanation is given as to how it came to be remembered and repeated (and it certainly fails to comply with the form critical requirement that it should answer a demand within the Christian community), or how it came to be so drastically altered as to take on a diametrically opposed meaning. It may be suggested that the very difficulty of the pericope led to the alteration – but the whole process has been based upon a completely hypothetical reconstruction, obtained by a rigid use of certain principles regarding what can and cannot be authentic.

Attempts to trace the history of the tradition must therefore take into consideration, at every step, the relation of any reconstruction to what we know (tentatively!) about Jesus and the church. We cannot solve problems simply by eliminating sayings from one stage and attributing them to another, for we may find ourselves confronted by even greater difficulties. Remembering always the danger of subjectivity mentioned above, we may here apply the principle of 'consistency' or 'coherence' in seeking to discover the most likely *Sitz im Leben* for a saying, and fitting it – tentatively – within the life of Jesus or of the Christian community. It is primarily for this reason that those of us who maintain the authenticity of the term 'Son of man' as a self-designation of Jesus do so. With all the difficulties involved, it is nevertheless easier to understand its use within the ministry of Jesus, the growing emphasis on the eschatological hope of the Son of man's return, and the final fossilization of the term within the tradition, than to suppose *either* that Jesus did not use the term at all, and that the community are responsible for all the sayings, *or* that he spoke of a coming Son of man, and that his followers completely misunderstood both his identity and his functions.[25]

Finally, we may perhaps put a question mark against the common assumption that Jesus made no direct messianic claims, and used no messianic titles of himself. This is part of an understandable reaction against the idea that we could recover Jesus' 'messianic self-consciousness' – but in its place we seem to be offered Jesus' 'unmessianic self-consciousness'! It is suggested that Jesus acted with extraordinary authority but offered no explanation in terms of his own person. It is perhaps worth quoting here some words of Reginald H. Fuller, writing about the relationship between Hebrew and Greek ways of expressing christological belief.[26] 'It is not just a quirk of the Greek mind,

---

[25] Cf. Hooker, *The Son of Man in Mark*, 182–193; Leivestad, 'Der apokalyptische Menschensohn', 80–91.

[26] Fuller, *The Foundations of New Testament Christology*, 248. Fuller himself recognizes this when he writes on page 130: 'Jesus understood his mission in terms of eschatological prophecy and was confident of its vindication by the Son of man at the End ... Take the implied self-understanding of his role in terms of the eschatological prophet away, and the whole ministry falls into a series of unrelated, if not meaningless fragments'. We may accept the underlying truth of this statement, without necessarily agreeing that the term 'eschatological prophet' is the correct one.

but a universal human apperception, that action implies prior being – even if, as is also true, being is only apprehended in action'. If Fuller is right, then his words should apply also to Jesus, who shared human apperceptions: we must at least pose the question whether his own understanding of the ground of his actions coincided with that of the church.

3. On Using the Wrong Tool*

My text is taken from the words of R. H. Lightfoot, according to a tradition recorded for us by D. E. Nineham, who tells us that R. H. Lightfoot 'was often to be heard lamenting: "If only they [NT scholars] would say 'we do not know'."'[1] My subject is that much used (and usually misused) term 'methodology'. My plea is that we should stop pretending to know the answer when we do not. My argument is that the tools which are used in an attempt to uncover the authentic teaching of Jesus cannot do what is required of them.

I was accused recently of believing 'that form criticism has failed to make its point'.[2] My immediate reaction to this terrible charge was to spring to my own defence by quoting what I had in fact written on the subject: 'It is certainly not our intention ... to attack the form-critical method. Form criticism has established itself as an invaluable tool which can tell us a great deal about the history of the gospel material'.[3] But recently I have begun to wonder whether I was right in describing form criticism as an invaluable tool. Was I simply paying lip service to the phrase which is now part of the NT scholars' creed: 'form criticism is a useful tool'? I sometimes set my pupils an essay with the title 'The uses and abuses of form criticism'; the results of their researches are illuminating, for the abuses are often found to outweigh the uses. Form criticism is a useful tool. But useful for what?

First, and most obviously, it is a literary tool. It tells us about the form of the material; it examines the shape of a piece of tradition and classifies it. This may be interesting to those who like doing that sort of thing, but I do not think it is particularly illuminating to be told that a miracle story is a miracle story, or that a paradigm is a paradigm – or an apophthegm – nor even that such stories take on certain shapes; one can learn that any evening by watching TV commercials. At this stage, form criticism is being used simply as a literary tool, to sort the material into piles according to its shape – and my reaction is a somewhat bored but polite 'How interesting'.

Much more interesting is the second stage of the discussion, when we begin to examine the *Sitz im Leben* of the material. The *Sitz im Leben* is defined by

---

* A lecture delivered to the Oxford Society for Historical Theology.

[1] D. E. Nineham, '... *et hoc genus omne*', in *Christian History and Interpretation: Studies Presented to John Knox*, eds. William R. Farmer, C. F. D. Moule, and R. R. Niebuhr (Cambridge: Cambridge University Press, 1967), 209.

[2] Norman Perrin, *What is Redaction Criticism?* (London: SPCK, 1970), 70.

[3] Morna D. Hooker, *The Son of Man in Mark* (London: SPCK, 1967), 5.

Bultmann[4] as the 'situation or occupation in the life of a community', and the form of the material is linked with its use by the community. It is at this stage that form criticism becomes exciting and that one may rightly speak of something which has proved invaluable – since it has revolutionized the way in which we look at the Gospels; though it is perhaps not so much form criticism itself which is invaluable in illuminating the material as the insight which goes with it – or rather underlies it – that the material comes to us *via* the community and was being used by the community. Form criticism itself, as a critical tool, attempts to discover the way in which the material was being used and applied to the life of the community at the time when it came into the written tradition. The difficulty is that it is not a very precise tool, since (as Bultmann stresses in the Preface to his *Die Geschichte der Synoptischen Tradition*), there is an inbuilt circularity in the method: as in all historical work 'it has to move in a circle. The forms of the literary tradition must be used to establish the influences operating in the life of the community, and the life of the community must be used to render the forms themselves intelligible'.[5] We have no independent knowledge of the groups which formed the pericopes which we are discussing, and we can only deduce the needs and interests of the community which shaped the material from that material itself. The *Sitz im Leben* to which a pericope is assigned – often with great confidence – is only a hypothesis, and sometimes one feels that the hypotheses demonstrate an excessive endowment of imaginative ability on the part of those who put them forward; as Humphrey Palmer has nicely put it: whether or not the early church was adept at thinking up stories about Jesus to fit church situations, the form critics are certainly adept at thinking up church situations to fit the stories about Jesus.[6]

Form criticism, then, tells us something about the shape of the material, and it attempts on the basis of that shape to tell us something about the way in which the material was being used – about its function within the community. It is at this stage, it seems to me, that the form critic gets carried away. For he next tries to deduce, from the material which he has before him, what the earlier forms *might* have been; it is at *this* stage that he begins to use form criticism as a historical tool. The aim of form criticism, wrote Dibelius, is 'to rediscover the origin and the history of the particular units and thereby to throw some light on the history of the tradition before it took literary form'.[7]

---

[4] Rudolf Bultmann, *The History of the Synoptic Tradition,* trans. John Marsh (Oxford: Blackwell, 1963), 4.

[5] Bultmann, *The History of the Synoptic Tradition,* 5.

[6] Humphrey Palmer, *The Logic of Gospel Criticism* (London; New York: St. Martin's Press, 1968), 185.

[7] Martin Dibelius, 'Zur Formgeschichte der Evangelien', *Theologische Rundschau* 1 (1929): 187.

In order to do this, one has to establish certain 'laws' about how oral tradition is changed: this is done by looking at certain tendencies in the Synoptic material, and reading them back into the oral period. Certain dangers in this method are immediately apparent. One is the assumption that the same developments apply at the oral stage as at the written; those who have conducted experiments maintain that they do not. The issue is complicated by the fact that, at the time when the Gospels were being written, the oral tradition was still a present reality, and it is possible that the processes of handing on tradition, on the one hand in an oral form, on the other in a written, were moving in opposite directions – that, for example, traditions could at the same period become shorter as they were repeated orally and lost details, and longer as they were written and attracted detail. The other obvious danger is that of generalization; however much one tries to establish 'laws' about the material, there are always some stories which refuse to fit the theory. One may discover a general tendency but that means only that the majority of cases behave in a certain way; any particular case may well belong to the minority, and behave in a quite contrary manner.[8]

In attempting to suggest earlier forms than those which at present exist, therefore, the form critic is once again postulating hypotheses; there can be no certainty that his suggestions are correct. Moreover, in attempting to reconstruct earlier forms behind those which we now have, we can never be sure that we have got back to the earliest form. For the form is shaped according to the purpose to which the early community put it – and the purpose is deduced from the form. We do not know what earlier forms there may have been, shaped in accordance with purposes no longer recoverable; the evidence for both forms and purposes has vanished. All we can do is to examine the existing material and, where the material is found in different forms, to discuss which of them is likely to be the earliest – though even that may be difficult (perhaps impossible) to determine. But we can never be certain that the form we have is the original – that there is no pre-history of the material.

The trap into which the form critic so often falls is that he equates the *Sitz im Leben* with the *origin* of the material; the *Sitz im Leben* is not simply the 'setting' of the material but, according to Fuller,[9] its 'creative milieu'. Now this is all right so long as by 'creative' is meant 'that which licked the material into its present shape'. But at this stage the form critic too often makes

---

[8] Cf. E. P. Sanders, *The Tendencies of the Synoptic Tradition* (Cambridge: Cambridge University Press, 1969), 272, who at the end of his investigation concludes: 'There are no hard and fast laws of the development of the Synoptic tradition. On all counts the tradition developed in opposite directions. It became both longer and shorter, both more and less detailed, and both more and less Semitic'.

[9] Reginald H. Fuller, *The New Testament in Current Study: Some Trends in the Years 1941–1962* (London: SCM Press, 1963), 40.

the mistake of confusing form with content. Because he has no knowledge of earlier forms, and because he can see the relevance of the material in its present form to the life of the early community, as he understands it, he thinks he has discovered the origin of the *material*. Of course he *may* be right: but he is making an assumption on the basis of insufficient evidence. Explorers have often been misled into thinking they have discovered the source of a river – and NT scholars have perhaps sometimes similarly been misled, though with less excuse.

The tool of form criticism can tell us about form; it also tries to tell us about the use which has shaped the material into that form. But it cannot tell us anything about the material itself and its reliability – except where, by a comparison of parallel traditions, it can be clearly seen that elements have been added to the material or changed. Nor can form criticism tell us about the history of the material before it took its present shape. To suppose that it can is to assume a knowledge about Jesus and the community which we lack.

But of course, in trying to dig behind the tradition as we now have it, the NT scholar has other criteria, other tools, to aid him. In this task of historical reconstruction, we have moved beyond the confines of form criticism into the wider field of 'traditio-historical criticism'. Are there other methods here which can help us in the perennial task of trying to rediscover the teaching of Jesus?

At this stage of the argument we meet two criteria which are, we are often assured, 'universally' recognized as the proper method of undertaking this task. They are the two principles of 'dissimilarity' and 'coherence'.

The idea of dissimilarity as the standard by which we establish the distinctive teaching of Jesus has been used by Bultmann, Käsemann, Conzelmann, Perrin, and Fuller, among others. Fuller explains the principle in these terms:

As regards the sayings of Jesus, traditiohistorical criticism eliminates from the authentic sayings of Jesus those which are paralleled in the Jewish tradition on the one hand (apocalyptic and Rabbinic) and those which reflect the faith, practice and situations of the post-Easter church as we know them from outside the gospels.[10]

To the small body of material extracted in this way there can then be added other sayings which are regarded as being consistent with it. As Perrin expresses it: 'material from the earliest strata of the tradition may be accepted as authentic if it can be shown to cohere with material established as authentic by means of the criterion of dissimilarity'.[11]

---

[10] Reginald H. Fuller, *The Foundations of New Testament Christology* (London: Collins, 1965), 18.
[11] Norman Perrin, *Rediscovering the Teaching of Jesus* (London: SCM Press, 1967), 43.

There are, however, serious faults in the logic of using these particular criteria to establish the authentic message of Jesus.

1. Use of the principle of dissimilarity, it is claimed, gives us what is distinctive in the teaching of Jesus. But the English word 'distinctive' can have two senses — as usual, the Germans use two words: 'distinctive' can mean 'unique' (what makes it distinct from other things, the German *verschieden*), or it can mean 'characteristic' (the German *bezeichnend*). In which sense is it being used here? Clearly the method is able only to give us the former — but what we really *want* is the latter; and the two are by no means necessarily the same. As an example, we might consider three typical speeches by three political leaders at election time; if we were to eliminate what was common to all three, how much would be left of any one speech? Probably very little! The result might give us what was distinctive of a party in the sense of what its members believe and members of other parties do not, but it would certainly not be representative of the policy of the party. This particular method of procedure has this inevitable drawback: that it will eliminate from the teaching of Jesus those areas in which he was in agreement with Judaism and those in which he was in agreement with the church. This is, of course, recognized by those who use the method, and accepted as a drawback. It is, however, a very serious drawback indeed, for to take the remaining material as the basis of our reconstruction will inevitably lead to serious distortion. No one can seriously doubt that in some things Jesus' views must have overlapped those of the Jewish leaders and those of his followers, yet these must be set aside from our reconstruction. But to exclude details from our picture of Jesus may lead to distortion as serious as (or worse than) that which comes if we include too much. Moreover, since it inevitably detaches Jesus from his contemporaries, I think we are justified in suggesting that this distortion is serious. In this attempt to recover what is distinctive, it seems that the two senses of 'distinctive' are being confused. What makes Jesus distinct from others is being regarded as that which is characteristic of him. We must be clear as to what this particular criterion can do: it *may* perhaps be able to give us a collection of sayings concerning whose authenticity we may be reasonably confident, but those sayings will not necessarily represent the kernel of Jesus' teaching, or be his most characteristic thought. Indeed, they would seem to offer us those sayings which the early church treated as peripheral.

2. 'It may'. But here we come to a second ground for misgiving. Since the method proceeds by eliminating ideas found in Judaism and early Christianity, it presupposes a fairly confident knowledge of both areas. To what extent is this justified? Use of this criterion seems to assume that we are dealing with two known factors (Judaism and early Christianity) and one unknown — Jesus; it would perhaps be a fairer statement of the situation to say that we are dealing with three unknowns, and that our knowledge of the other two is

quite as tenuous and indirect as our knowledge of Jesus himself. But one can solve x+y = z only if one knows the value of two of the three 'unknowns'. As far as Judaism is concerned, the discovery of the Qumran material should be sufficient warning against overconfidence in supposing that we know the whole truth about first-century Judaism. Any comparison between the beliefs of Judaism and the teaching of Jesus which claims to find ideas in the latter unparalleled in the former is inevitably an argument from silence, and should be treated as such. And if our knowledge of Judaism is only partial, so, too, is our knowledge of early Christian belief, and here, too, we must tread with caution. The traditio-historian is the first to recognize that the material as we have it today in the New Testament represents only part of the picture – but he apparently underestimates the importance of that fact. There may have been other beliefs about Jesus and christological statements which are not now represented in our canonical material: certainly there was no uniformity in expressing belief in Christ. It could be that if we knew the whole truth about Judaism and the early church, our small quantity of 'distinctive' teaching would wither away altogether.

3. But even if we had perfect knowledge of Jesus' contemporaries, the method must be suspect because it begs the question. We begin our examination of the Gospel material with a tool which denies the possibility of overlapping, and which insists on his uniqueness. Such a tool is bound to produce a picture in keeping with its assumption – and that is precisely what we get: a Jesus who stands out from his contemporaries as distinctive in his attitudes, but who makes no messianic claims for himself (he cannot, because the church will make messianic claims on his behalf), and who finds himself in opposition to the Jewish leaders. The method dictates its own conclusions.

4. The method presupposes that much of the Gospel material is due to the creative activity of the early Christian community; stories about Jesus came into being to deal with certain situations; inspired prophets spoke to the community in the name of the Risen Lord. But did not those same inspired prophets sometimes utter sayings which have no known parallel in contemporary Judaism and the early church? If individuals in the Christian community were as creative as is supposed, then presumably some of them at times spoke – as Jesus had done – in 'distinctive' ways. So perhaps in the small 'hard core' of sayings which this method attributes to Jesus, we may again have included too much!

5. The application of the method is bound to be subjective. How do we decide what is 'dissimilar'? Especially when we are reminded of another criterion which we should be using – namely, that an 'authentic' saying of Jesus should be 'at home' in first-century Palestine. To be acceptable as genuine, a saying of Jesus must at one and the same time be 'dissimilar' from contemporary Judaism, and yet use its categories and reflect the language and

style of Aramaic. In other words, authentic sayings must not be reflected in Judaism (so far as it is known to us) but must sound as if they could have been spoken at that time! It is difficult to know how to apply these apparently contradictory criteria simultaneously. When Norman Perrin, for example, argues that Jesus could not have used 'the Son of man' as a title because it did not exist in Judaism at the time, he is apparently using the second criterion; but if the title *had* (in his opinion) existed, he would presumably have eliminated it by applying the criterion of dissimilarity!

6. Subjectivity is seen also in the suggestion that authentic teaching can be guaranteed by the presence of 'the distinctive eschatological temper which characterized the preaching of Jesus'.[12] Here, clearly, we are in danger of going round in circles. For how do we know what was characteristic of Jesus' teaching, or what was his distinctive eschatological outlook, until we have established which sayings are authentic?! It is well-known that different people look at the evidence regarding eschatology and get very different answers. Bultmann, for example, sees the eschatological emphasis of Jesus as wholly future; others have looked at the same evidence and drawn a very different picture. At the moment, there is something of a truce – it is usually said that the kingdom is both present *and* future. But it may not be so simple. One of the worrying things about Jeremias' discussion of the parables[13] is the very Lucan character of his reconstruction of Jesus' message, with its emphasis on the present character of salvation: Jesus and Luke are found to be in remarkable agreement, and this seems very odd. May it be that Jeremias is reading Jesus through Lucan spectacles? The old danger of looking down a well and seeing one's own reflection still exists.

7. Subjectivity is still a danger when we turn to the principle of coherence or consistency, by which similar sayings are added to the core (or rump) of teaching which has been separated by the principle of dissimilarity. *We* may be able to sort out what seems coherent (or incoherent) to us – but we are living in a completely different world, and what seems incoherent to us may have seemed coherent in first-century Palestine – and *vice versa*. Moreover, some of Jesus' sayings – if they are genuine – are paradoxical, and that alone should perhaps warn us against looking for what seems to us to be consistent.

8. When one adds the coherence principle to that of dissimilarity, it is clear that any errors in the results obtained by that method are liable to be magnified by the use of this second criterion. If the core of material upon which we build our reconstruction of the teaching of Jesus is inaccurate, then the addition of material which seems to be consistent with that core is likely

---

[12] Bultmann, *The History of the Synoptic Tradition,* 205.
[13] Joachim Jeremias, *The Parables of Jesus,* rev. ed., trans. S. H. Hooke (London: SCM Press, 1963).

to reflect those same inaccuracies. If, for example, our core contains only 'future references to the Son of man', then any 'present' references will be automatically excluded.

9. Those who advocate the use of these criteria are strangely inconsistent in applying them. This may be illustrated by looking at the word 'Abba'. Here is a good example of something which is Aramaic in form but to which an exact parallel has not been found in Judaism; but it *is* used by the early church (see Rom 8:15 and Gal 4:6), and by the strict application of the principle of dissimilarity it should be eliminated. Yet it seems to be almost universally accepted that Jesus addressed God as 'Abba', and taught his disciples to do the same. Why? Perrin writes, 'These [two verses] may not be regarded as representing early Christian tradition as such'.[14] But why not? This seems like special pleading. The real criterion being used here is *not the principle of dissimilarity, but the scholar's own understanding of the situation.*

As another example, let us look at the very different treatment which is given, on the one hand to the term 'the kingdom of God', and on the other to the phrase 'the Son of man'. The two terms have much in common. The 'spread' of their occurrences throughout the Gospels and sources is remarkably similar.[15] Both are without real parallel in the Old Testament – though appeal can be made in each case to extra-biblical Jewish material. Both appear to have sometimes a present reference, sometimes a future one. Both refer to something possessing divine authority, which at present suffers reverse. The treatment which is handed out to these two phrases, however, is remarkably different. Although there is a certain overlap between Jesus and the early church regarding the kingdom of God – since the phrase *does* occur in the NT outside the Gospels – it is nevertheless regarded by all NT scholars as the core of Jesus' teaching. References to the Son of man, however, which with one famous exception is not used outside the Gospels, are reduced to a mere handful – if that. It is commonly assumed, either that Jesus did not refer to the Son of man at all, or that his only authentic utterances are to a future, glorious coming of the Son of man. On the principle of dissimilarity, it would be more logical to maintain that Jesus never used the expression 'the kingdom of God' than that he did not speak of 'the Son of man'.

Similarly, if one really applied this principle rigidly to the Son of man sayings, one would find that it was the eschatological group which was eliminated, and the present and suffering sayings which were left. But this must not be. Since the principle of dissimilarity has let the investigators down at this point, they fall back on another principle – the old one of multiple

---

[14] Perrin, *Rediscovering the Teaching of Jesus,* 41.
[15] Cf. the tables given by Joachim Jeremias in his *New Testament Theology, Part 1: The Proclamation of Jesus,* trans. John Bowden (London: SCM Press, 1971), 31, 260.

attestation; we have returned to dear old source criticism and dragged out Q, in support of the argument that since the suffering Son of man sayings are almost entirely Marcan, they are clearly inauthentic. Now it may be proper for the NT scholar to use whatever tools are available; but when he throws down one tool and picks up another like this, it certainly looks as though he is selecting his tool to fit his conclusion. In fact, the real criterion which is being applied in this case is a rule which is based on certain presuppositions: first, that the background of the phrase 'Son of man' is to be found in a messianic figure in 1 Enoch, who will ride on clouds of glory at the last day – which, as Dr Vermes reminded us, is a very dangerous assumption[16] – and secondly, that Jesus did not apply any messianic titles to himself and therefore could not possibly have referred to himself as Son of man.

Of course NT scholars recognize the inadequacy of their tools; when different people look at one passage, and all get different answers, the inadequacy is obvious, even to NT scholars! But they do not draw the logical deduction from this fact. They go on, hammering or chiselling away with their pet tools, and using the pieces which are left as the sure foundation on which they then erect their edifice. But if *these* tools fail us because they are too imprecise, can we not find others? The history of NT criticism is a continuous search for such criteria. There were, for example, Schmiedel's famous pillar sayings[17] – sayings which the early community clearly could not have invented; but if we are to apply this rule, then we must first be sure that we have understood the saying; and then, when it comes to asking whether there could have been a situation at some stage in the community's life to fit it, some commentators prove to have more lively imaginations than others; the force of the argument depends once again on our knowledge of the early community – and that is inadequate. Or perhaps you prefer Jeremias' appeal to Aramaisms; in his recent *New Testament Theology, Part 1*, he has an impressive list of Aramaic words which occur on the lips of Jesus;[18] my confidence in this as a method of approach was shaken badly when I discovered that a third of the words listed are found in a sentence attributed to Jesus in a polemical passage in the Babylonian Talmud! The remainder turned out to be words like abba, mammon, Gehenna, and the word from the cross. And of course, even if we succeed in showing that the form of the material,

---

[16] A previous paper to the Society, by Dr Vermes, had maintained that 'the Son of man' was not a messianic title in 1 Enoch. There is in any case very little evidence to support the commonly held belief that first-century Palestinian Judaism was expecting the coming of an 'apocalyptic' Son of man; see Hooker, *The Son of Man in Mark*, 33–48, 182–189; Ragnar Leivestad, 'Exit the Apocalyptic Son of Man', *NTS* 18 (1972): 243–267.

[17] Paul Wilhelm Schmiedel, in his article on 'Gospels' in *Encyclopaedia Biblica*, vol. 2, eds. Thomas Kelly Cheyne and John Sutherland Black (London: A&C Black, 1901), referred to certain sayings as 'the foundation-pillars for a truly scientific life of Jesus'.

[18] Jeremias, *New Testament Theology, Part 1*, 5 ff.

its sentence structure and so on were Aramaic, we could *with certainty* claim only to have dug back to a layer belonging to a Palestinian community – which would not necessarily even be early: we should not have proved that these were 'words of the Lord'. Jeremias uses another criterion in looking at the Son of man sayings; he suggests eliminating as dubious any which have parallels in an 'I form'.[19] The existence of such parallels may well be a matter of chance however – as is demonstrated when we have to turn to the Gospel of Thomas to find some of them; once again, our material is too limited to justify our using this kind of method. And the whole thing founders when we discover that the majority of the Son of man sayings which have no 'I parallel' are those which refer to the Son of man coming in glory; for by their very nature these are precisely those sayings which *cannot* be put into an 'I form'; once again we have been going round in a circle. Then there is the principle that any reference to the Old Testament *must* be credited to the early church, and represents the earliest Christian exegesis; why Jesus himself must be presumed never to have referred to scripture has never been clear to me. This principle is no more valid as a criterion than the older, opposite view that OT references are a sign of the *authentic* teaching. And finally, we have an old criterion in a new guise with the advent of redaction criticism. It is suggested that anything which is incompatible with an evangelist's plan and purpose could be regarded as authentic teaching of Jesus.[20] Such incompatibility would, however, prove nothing – except that the author has included material which he found already existing in the tradition. And, of course, to establish even that we should first need to discover the plan and purpose of the evangelist, with which the material is said to be incompatible. One glance at the innumerable and widely differing interpretations of the redaction critics will show how far we are from discovering that.

The fact that I have questioned the value of form criticism and certain other critical methods as tools in getting back to the Jesus of history does not mean that I am trying to offer comfort to those who have all along maintained a traditional 'conservative' approach. I venture to suggest that I am being more radical than those who are commonly labelled 'radical'. For it seems to me that conservative and radical alike have both succumbed to the temptation to seek for certainty – and to believe that it can be achieved. The 'radical', though he may eschew the old form of certainty, is seeking another. He looks for some kind of scientific verification – a litmus paper test which can be applied to the sayings of Jesus, which turns either pink or blue, according to

---

[19] Jeremias, *New Testament Theology, Part 1*, 262–264. Jeremias' argument is set out in full in 'Die älteste Schicht der Menschensohn-Logien', *ZNW* 58 (1967): 159–172.
[20] Suggested tentatively by D.G.A. Calvert in 'An Examination of the Criteria for Distinguishing the Authentic Words of Jesus', *NTS* 18 (1972): 219.

whether they are or are not authentic, so that he may sort his material into neat piles.

Nevertheless, because these tools have, in general, been applied in a very negative way, it is true that any reaction must make the pendulum swing back to what appears, in its assessment of the material, to be a more 'conservative' one. It is over-confidence in our tools that has led to the very minimal accounts of the Jesus of history. But if my own assessment tends to be a more traditional one, it is with the proviso that any attempt at reconstructing what lies behind our Gospels is highly speculative, and will in large measure reflect our own presuppositions about the material.

One important area of presupposition concerns the *likelihood* of the material being 'authentic'. From the old assumption that a Gospel saying was authentic unless proved otherwise, the pendulum has swung over to the opposite approach – the belief that sayings must be treated as non-authentic unless they can be proved dominical. This, it is suggested, is a more cautious method – the only 'safe' way of proceeding. It is, of course, nothing of the kind: if we attribute dominical sayings to the church, the resulting pictures both of Jesus and of the development of Christology will be just as prone to error as if we wrongly attribute the church's formulations of their belief to Jesus. The old assumption that we can recover Jesus' messianic self-consciousness was no more of a distortion than the present tendency to assume that he had no self-consciousness at all. The presuppositions come to the surface when one side declares, 'The burden of proof is on those who maintain that any of the material is authentic', or when the other asks 'Who is more likely to have been creative – Jesus or the church?' But these are not the real alternatives. All the material comes to us *via* the church, and is likely to have been coloured by the beliefs of those who have handed it on. But the burden of proof, to prove or disprove authenticity, lies neither on one side nor on the other. It is the duty of every scholar, in considering every saying, to give a reasonable account of all the evidence; for he is not entitled to assume, simply in the absence of contrary evidence, either that a saying is genuine or that it is not.

And what tools should he use in this task? He must, alas, use the tools we have been discussing, for there are no others, and there are unlikely to be any better ones discovered. But he must not use them arbitrarily, selecting only the one which seems to give the answer he wants. Neither must he use them negatively – to blackball a saying. The critic who tries with his knife to carve away the thick layers of the church's theology and give us the bare skeleton of the Jesus of history will no doubt shudder at my unscientific analogy, but it seems to me that all his criteria can only give us results like those which appear in the tables of the magazine *Which?*. The more blobs in the column, the more confidence one may have in that particular product, and the better buy it is. So with our Gospel sayings. The saying which is found in all the

Synoptic strata, which has no known parallel outside the Gospels, which is Aramaic in structure, will perhaps rate more blobs than one which has none of these features. But I am not suggesting that we should assume that those which score so many blobs are authentic, and those at the bottom of the table are not. We are moving here only from the more to the less probable.

For in the end, the answers which the New Testament scholar gives are not the result of applying objective tests and using precision tools; they are very largely the result of his own presuppositions and prejudices. If he approaches the material with the belief that it is largely the creation of the early Christian communities, then he will interpret it in that way. If he assumes that the words of the Lord were faithfully remembered and passed on, then he will be able to find criteria which support him. Each claims to be using the proper critical method. Each produces a picture of Jesus – and of the early church – in accordance with his presuppositions. And each claims to be right. The man who gets a different answer is accused of being a bad critic, because he has got the wrong answer. But who is right and who is wrong? They cannot all be right – though they may well all be wrong.

Every scholar likes to produce assured results. To say, as I am doing, that there are none, and can be none, may seem like a counsel of despair. But assured results are dangerous things. Too many hypotheses have been regarded as proved, and have become accepted dogmas. Of course one must have working hypotheses; but it should never be forgotten that these are only hypotheses, and that they must constantly be re-examined. Perhaps every NT scholar should have before him on his desk, as he writes, as a constant reminder of the dangers of dogmatism, the words of R.H. Lightfoot: 'We do not know'.

4. In His Own Image?

Spies at King's College London report that the Professor of New Testament Studies,[1] exasperated by excessive undergraduate reference to the 'wrong tool', exploded with a denunciation of the wretched woman with her wrong tools,[2] declaring that the real problem was that the right tools were used in the wrong way. He is, of course, correct – the real problem is the misuse of tools; though if someone applies a sledgehammer to a nut with disastrous consequences, it may fairly be said that the wrong tool has been used for the particular job in hand. Whichever way one describes it, New Testament scholars do often show a remarkable – dare one say 'naive'? – confidence in the particular scholarly method which happens to be in vogue at any time, and tend to use it to the near exclusion of other methods. As a result, successive generations of scholars are classified according to the method which they pioneered or used, so that source critics were followed by form critics, who in turn gave way to redaction critics; the categorisation implies that no one may examine the material in more than one way!

This picture is of course an oversimplification. It is obvious that every scholar builds on the foundation of those who have gone before, and accepts the results of previous work as the basis of his own. Both the historian of the tradition and the redaction critic rely on the conclusions of the source critic regarding the relationship of the documents, and their investigations follow on naturally from the insights of the form critic. To this extent, each scholar may claim to be 'using' various disciplines. Nevertheless, there is always a danger in assuming that the results in a certain area are 'assured'; conclusions which are not constantly re-examined become the presuppositions upon which new hypotheses are based. It is not enough to accept the conclusions reached yesterday and move on to new methods; for yesterday's problems may look rather different if viewed from today's position, and may yield different answers. The questions must therefore be continually reformulated and grappled with, however tiresome this may be: the New Testament scholar must not simply set certain questions aside as 'solved', but like a juggler, endeavour to keep all his balls in the air – sometimes, indeed, adding new ones to the number in play, but never allowing any of them to drop.

---

[1] Christopher F. Evans. This essay was written in his honour.
[2] Morna D. Hooker, 'On Using the Wrong Tool', *Theology* 75 (1972): 570–581 = above, essay 3 (pp. 38–49).

A study of the history of biblical interpretation demonstrates the way in which the answers which are given to questions in any particular period are largely determined by the outlook of those who ask the questions. If it is true to say that those who have hunted for the historical Jesus have often looked down a well and seen a reflection of their own faces, it is also true that students of the Gospels have tended to picture those who wrote them in their own image. When source criticism was in its heyday, and B.H. Streeter and his friends presented their solution of the Synoptic problem in terms of a four-document hypothesis, the evangelists appeared, through their eyes, in the guise of Oxford scholars, poring over their sources, meticulously piecing together the evidence of various documents, and taking care to record all available material and to lose no scrap of evidence. The scope of the hypothetical Q could therefore be determined with some confidence, and even the other sources used by Matthew and Luke – envisaged now as documents – could be reconstructed. Not only were the evangelists seen in the likeness of Oxford scholars in their method of working, but the underlying motives of scholars and evangelists were also understood to be remarkably similar: the evangelists, it was assumed, carefully preserved historical material about the Lord, since their concern was primarily to record what happened; they therefore provided valuable evidence which would lead the scholar back from the evangelist to the historical Jesus and his authentic words.

Form criticism, by contrast, threw the emphasis neither on the evangelists nor on the figure of Jesus, but on the interim period and the units of tradition. Its exponents saw the evangelists as collectors of pericopae, each of which confronts those who hear it with the word of the gospel. Once again, the philosophy of the scholar is reflected in the picture which is drawn – not, this time, in any portrait of the evangelists, now mere faceless stringers of pearls – but in the presentation of the 'community', that strange collective entity with the face and philosophy of a Lutheran preacher.

The implications of the form-critical approach for the search for the historical Jesus have been under continual discussion for the past fifty years; the hopes of the English source critics for recovering the real Jesus and his authentic words crumbled before the advance of the new method. Strangely, its relevance for source criticism itself is less often realized; the important role of the individual units of tradition – and possibly of small collections of units in the community – suggests that the idea of a monolithic Q is an unnecessary and indeed unlikely explanation of the phenomena it was devised to explain.[3] But if the existence and shape of a document Q is uncertain, it is, to say the least, remarkable to find a redaction critic writing a recent book on 'The Theology of Q' without really considering the question whether Q ever

---

[3] See C.K. Barrett, 'Q: A Re-examination', *ExpTim* 54 (1943): 320–323.

existed!⁴ The old questions must be constantly asked, and the old answers be continually questioned.

Redaction critics, too, may fairly be said to have recreated the evangelists in their own image. For many of them, it is axiomatic that the evangelists had no interest in history, but were creative theologians; their supposed creativity has surely met its match in the imaginative ability of many redaction critics! Redaction criticism, in its turn, ought to open up again some of the questions 'solved' when certain presuppositions held good. If the evangelists were as free with their material as is now being suggested, do the reasons once given for the priority of Mark, for example, still hold good?

As an illustration of the extent to which one's presuppositions and basic method influence one's conclusions, we may take the different interpretations given by different scholars to Mark 2:1–3:6. Henry B. Swete, in his commentary on Mark published in 1898, believed that 'the writer intended to follow the relative order of time' and that there is 'a progress in the history of the Galilean Ministry, as it is depicted by St Mark, which bears the stamp of truth'.⁵ He was therefore able to treat the links between the sections in 2:1–3:6 as historical. Most commentators in the past fifty years have accepted the conclusion of the form critics that the section is a pre-Marcan collection of conflict stories, grouped together because of their common theme. Recent emphasis on the evangelists as men with theological purposes, and not mere gatherers of tradition, however, would seem to suggest that this grouping may be due to Mark himself, and should be seen in the context of the structure of the whole Gospel; it may be in the plan of Mark's book that we shall discover the motive for bringing these particular narratives together. Hardly surprisingly, we find Eduard Schweizer, who writes his commentary from the viewpoint of a redaction critic, attributing most of the collection to Mark himself.⁶ These three very different explanations of the Marcan arrangement demonstrate the way in which assumptions about the material determine the interpretation which is given: responsibility for the ordering of events has shifted from the historical Jesus to the early community and finally to the evangelist. The final stage in this progression may indeed be to place the emphasis on the interpretation of the commentator (where, one suspects, it is in reality already hovering!) and to say with some literary critics that the original author's own purposes are immaterial, and that the meaning of what is written is found in the interpretation given to it by the reader.

---

⁴ Richard A. Edwards, *The Sign of Jonah in the Theology of the Evangelists and Q*, SBT 2/18 (London: SCM Press, 1971).

⁵ Henry B. Swete, *The Gospel According to St. Mark* (London: Macmillan, 1898), 53.

⁶ Eduard Schweizer, *The Good News According to Mark,* trans. Donald H. Madvig (London: SPCK 1971).

It is in fact reasonable to suggest that Jesus, the community, the evangelist, and the modern interpreter all play their part in the understanding of any Gospel passage, and that the relative importance of each factor varies from one passage to another. We shall hear the voice now of one, now of another. But how does one distinguish between these voices, and decide who is playing the major role? The difficulty of knowing whether the material mediated to us by 'the community' reflects only the beliefs of the community, or whether it speaks to us also about the historical Jesus, is matched by a similar difficulty when we turn to redaction criticism. Can we distinguish between the beliefs of the redactor and those who went before him? A recent guide to redaction criticism says:

> In order for redaction criticism proper to develop we had to learn to trace the various stages through which tradition has passed. Only then was it possible to recognize the nature and extent of the redaction. In other words redaction criticism proper is dependent upon the ability to write a history of the tradition.[7]

The author of this guide is confident that we have this ability: the tools to do this, he says, 'were developed through the ... discipline known as form criticism'.[8] Yet it is precisely in this attempt to trace the history of the tradition that we have seen the difficulties and dangers of coming to any certain conclusions; if the tools we use in tracing the tradition turn out to be inadequate, and if the method involves circular arguments and presuppositions, then we must recognize that we are in danger of building our redaction-critical house on foundations of shifting sand.

The redaction critic does, of course, have one great advantage over those whose primary concern was to trace the history of the tradition in the oral period. When he comes to Matthew and Luke, at least, he is able to point to actual verbal changes which an evangelist has made in his sources. Or is he? He may feel that present scholarly opinion makes it reasonable for him to assume the priority of Mark, and therefore to argue that any changes made by Matthew and Luke to the Marcan wording are significant. Already, however, difficulties arise: is it the text of Mark as we know it (insofar as we do know it! – perhaps here, too, we are overconfident) that was used by the later evangelists? Where they diverge from Mark, is it because their theological motives compel them to make changes? Are the alterations due to other reasons – perhaps stylistic or accidental? Most important of all, are such divergences perhaps not primarily alterations of Mark, but due to the fact that an evangelist has chosen to follow a tradition other than Mark's, even where the two Gospels are to some extent parallel? This particular difficulty occurs most frequently in Luke: suggestions that Luke prefers a non-Marcan source

---

[7] Norman Perrin, *What is Redaction Criticism?* (London: SPCK, 1970), 13.
[8] Perrin, *What is Redaction Criticism?*, 13.

to Mark tend to be treated with suspicion, since they are usually understood to be part of the unpopular proto-Luke hypothesis. Nevertheless, it is undeniable that Lucan parallels to Mark are frequently remarkably dissimilar. If we assume that Luke is deliberately altering his source, then we are likely to see these changes as evidence for his theology, and perhaps build important conclusions on them; if, however, Luke has not changed Mark, but in fact preferred to use another source, then – although his choice of source may be significant – we shall need to enquire carefully about the reasons for his choice.

An obvious example of this particular problem is Luke's 'omission' of Mark 10:45. On the basis of his failure to reproduce this saying, Luke has been accused of having no *theologia crucis,* and of deliberately altering Mark's interpretation of Christ's death.[9] Yet an examination of the Marcan section and its parallels in Matthew and Luke suggests that, while Matthew is clearly following Mark at this point, Luke is using a different version of the saying, for there is little verbal similarity.[10] Moreover, he has placed the pericope in a different setting, where it is in some ways more appropriate. These two factors seem to indicate that Luke was not consciously using Mark at all at this point – and therefore not altering or 'toning down' his interpretation of the significance of the cross. Now of course it may still be argued that the fact that Luke has preferred his non-Marcan source at this point can tell us something about his theology. But we must be very cautious how we use this kind of argument: for Luke may have had many reasons for doing what he did – among which must be included the fact that he often uses non-Marcan material in preference to Mark. The use of an alternative tradition, together with his placing of this particular pericope in a different setting (where possibly it was already embedded), suggest that it may simply not have occurred to Luke that he was 'altering' Mark or that he was rejecting a Marcan emphasis, and he might well have been astonished by the verdicts of his commentators and the motives attributed to him.[11] Too often, the discussion about this passage iso-

---

[9] For a recent example of this approach, cf. Edwards, *The Sign of Jonah*, 37: 'Luke has been careful to modify the very significant statement in Mark 10.45'.

[10] Bultmann regards Mark 10:45 as a dogmatic reformulation of a more primitive saying preserved in Luke 22:27. See Rudolf Bultmann, *The History of the Synoptic Tradition,* trans. John Marsh (Oxford: Blackwell, 1963), 93. Luke's version has parallels also with the tradition recorded in Mark 9:34 ff. and Luke 9:46–48.

[11] There is another factor which enters into our judgement on Luke's intention in this passage, and which demonstrates the importance of our own assumptions in handling the material; for the answer we give to the question of Luke's handling of the saying depends to a large extent on our interpretation of the Marcan version! Those who understand Mark 10:45 in the light of Isa 53 naturally regard the absence of the 'ransom' saying from Luke as significant; if the Marcan saying is understood in the tradition of Old Testament ideas about God's redemption of his people at the exodus and from the exile, and the hope of a future redemption, then the contrast between Mark 10:45 and Luke 22:27 is not so great. See

lates the Lucan verse from its context, and overlooks the fact that while Mark 10:45 is the climax of a pericope about glory, which points out the paradoxical path which the Christian disciple must follow, the Lucan version is set in the account of the Last Supper, and the theme of the significance of the death of Jesus for his followers is present in the context, immediately before and after the pericope: the death of Jesus is linked with the coming of the kingdom, in which Jesus has the right to apportion places,[12] and he gives these places to those who have continued with him in his 'trials' – though in the supreme trial immediately following, Jesus stands alone, his disciples having failed him. As in Mark, the themes of honour, lowliness, service, sharing the suffering of Jesus, and the central role of his lonely death – in Mark a 'ransom' for many, in Luke a 'covenanting' to the disciples – are all present.[13]

The question of the changes made to the Marcan material by the later evangelists is difficult enough. The problem becomes even more complex, however, when Mark is left behind, and the only source the redaction critic has for comparison is the unknown and unknowable Q. If Q ever existed in the solid form once envisaged, then the discussions as to whether Matthew or Luke has preserved its wording more exactly in various places might offer us some interesting evidence for the theological motivations of those two evangelists. But the more significant are the differences between the Matthean and Lucan forms of a saying, the more doubtful is it whether either evangelist

---

C.K. Barrett, 'The Background of Mark 10.45', in *New Testament Essays: Studies in Memory of Thomas Walter Manson, 1893–1958,* ed. A.J.B. Higgins (Manchester: Manchester University Press, 1959), 1–18; Morna D. Hooker, *Jesus and the Servant: The Influence of the Servant Concept of Deutero-Isaiah in the New Testament* (London: SPCK, 1959), 74–79. We may also note that Luke adds to the Marcan framework of the journey to Jerusalem the story of Zacchaeus (19:1–10) which leads up to another saying about the Son of man: 'The Son of man came to seek and to save that which was lost'. Here we have what seems to be a typical Lucan emphasis on salvation as already present in the ministry of Jesus, and had Luke inserted it before the story of Bartimaeus, it might have been argued that he was deliberately substituting this for the saying in Mark 10:45 linking the saving activity of the Son of man with his death: but Luke places the Zacchaeus incident in Jericho, and has Jesus heal Bartimaeus on the way *into* Jericho, instead of on the way out!

[12] In Mark 10:40, Jesus does not have the right to apportion the two chief places next to himself, though sharing his suffering is understood as a necessary qualification for sharing in his glory.

[13] A similar argument to that about Luke's treatment of Mark 10:45 is often used regarding his failure (according to the shorter text, which surely has the better claim to originality) to copy Mark's saying over the cup in 14:24. Once again, however, this ignores the setting in which Luke places the giving of the cup in vv. 17 ff., the cup from which Jesus will not drink, and which is firmly associated with the coming of the kingdom. The pericopae immediately following, as we have already seen, link the kingdom with the theme of the covenant. Luke's expression of the association between the cup and the covenant may not be as succinct as Mark's, but is his understanding so very different? Is the difficulty with Mark's version perhaps not the significance which is given to the death of Jesus, but rather the apparent identification of wine which is drunk with blood?

is making deliberate changes, and the more possible is it that the tradition has come to them in different forms. Once again, the choice of material which an evangelist makes may be important (especially if he is consciously rejecting an alternative version of the tradition) but it is less significant than changes which he may deliberately have made in the tradition he received, in order to fit his theological purpose. Those who argue that Luke used Matthew and not Q are in a much better position for showing the significant changes which have been made to the material by Luke; but if their basic assumption about Luke's sources is wrong – and the arguments for it are far from convincing – their interpretation collapses.[14]

The redaction critic therefore faces a formidable task: in order to understand his author, he needs to be able to trace the history of the tradition which has been used; yet at every step, both at the oral and at the written stage, the uncertainties are such that he must beware of any easy solutions. It is dangerously overconfident to assert:

> Our knowledge of the redactional activity of Matthew and Luke is ... both firm and extensive; we not only have one of their major sources, Mark, but we can also reconstruct another, the sayings source, Q.[15]

How then is the redaction critic to proceed? In many cases what he in fact does – or tries to do! – is to allow the evangelist to speak for himself; to study the structure and language of a Gospel, and to deduce from this evidence the purpose and position of the author. This approach has produced some illuminating insights in the hands of cautious scholars such as R.H. Lightfoot.[16] Yet this method, too, has its dangers. For it is all too easy to see patterns where none exist, and to impose our own interpretation on the material; when Mark is interpreted with the help of algebraic formulae,[17] or John with the aid of liturgical calendars which still fit even when shifted through six months,[18] then one is bound to ask whether the interpreter has not taken over

---

[14] The case for Luke's use of Matthew was argued by Austin M. Farrer, see 'On Dispensing with Q', in *Studies in the Gospels: Essays in Memory of R.H. Lightfoot,* ed. D.E. Nineham (Oxford: Blackwell, 1955), 55–88. Those who have used this thesis as the basis for redaction-critical work include M.D. Goulder, 'Characteristics of the Parables in the Several Gospels', *JTS* NS 19 (1968): 51–69, and John Drury, *Luke,* J.B. Philipps' Commentaries (London: Collins, 1973).

[15] Perrin, *What is Redaction Criticism?,* 57.

[16] See especially R.H. Lightfoot, *The Gospel Message of St. Mark* (Oxford: Clarendon Press, 1950).

[17] Cf. Austin M. Farrer, *A Study in St Mark* (London: Dacre Press, 1951). Farrer subsequently revised his own interpretation of Mark in *St Matthew and St Mark* (London: Dacre Press, 1954; 2nd ed., 1966).

[18] Cf. Aileen Guilding, *The Fourth Gospel and Jewish Worship* (Oxford: Clarendon Press, 1960). Some of the difficulties of this interpretation are discussed by Leon Morris in *The New Testament and the Jewish Lectionaries* (London: Tyndale Press, 1964).

from the evangelist. Sometimes the redaction critic ignores awkward pieces of evidence which do not fit his theory: Conzelmann, for example,[19] has often been justly criticized for making a generalization in speaking of the absence of Satan from the ministry; perhaps even more important is his failure to consider the significance of Luke 1–2, since, whatever their origin, these chapters now stand at the beginning of Luke's work, and may well provide vital information about his purpose.[20]

At other times, the redaction critic's analysis will lead him to speak of an evangelist's 'characteristics'. Undoubtedly each writer has his characteristics, but it is often extremely difficult to be certain what belongs to the evangelist and what to his source. Overconfidence in one's ability to distinguish the two can lead to false conclusions when the discovery of 'characteristics' is then used as a tool to separate sayings which have come to the evangelist as part of the tradition from sayings which he has created.[21] Even if we did conclude that a saying in Mark, for example, contains Marcan characteristics, this does not mean that it was a Marcan 'creation'; Mark may well have left his own fingerprints on the tradition which he has handled. Form critics have often fallen into the trap of supposing that when they have unearthed the earliest recoverable form of a saying and reconstructed its setting in the community, they have also discovered its origin. Redaction critics can easily fall into a similar trap, in supposing that a Marcan form means a Marcan origin. In the analysis of a book's structure, too, we find that very different interpretations are given

---

[19] Hans Conzelmann, *The Theology of St Luke,* trans. Geoffrey Buswell (London: Faber and Faber, 1960).

[20] Cf. Paul S. Minear, 'Luke's Use of the Birth Narratives, in *Studies in Luke-Acts,* eds. Leander E. Keck and J. Louis Martyn (London: SPCK, 1968), 121, and Morna D. Hooker, 'The Johannine Prologue and the Messianic Secret', *NTS* 21 (1974): 51 ff. = below, essay 23 (pp. 332 ff.).

[21] An example of this is to be found in Perrin's discussion of Mark 9:1 (Perrin, *What is Redaction Criticism?,* 48): he notes that 'Mark speaks of seeing the parousia here in 9.1, again in 13.26, and for a third time in 14.62'; moreover Mark uses the words 'power' and 'glory' in 'parousia contexts'; hence 'the reference to "seeing" the parousia and the use of the words "power" and "glory" in this kind of context' are Marcan characteristics. One confusion in this argument is immediately obvious: Mark 9:1, with its reference to 'seeing' and to 'power', is not a 'parousia' saying at all, but describes the coming of the kingdom of God: it is Matthew who transfers it to the Son of man. There are therefore *two* Marcan parousia sayings which promise that men will see the Son of man coming with clouds; these two sayings are similar, and they occur in similar contexts, promising future vindication in spite of present humiliation and suffering. There seem to be three possible explanations: (i) Mark has created both sayings, and the reference to 'seeing' is therefore a Marcan characteristic, as Perrin suggests. (ii) One saying came to Mark in the tradition, and he doubled it, in drawing the parallel between the situation of persecuted Christians and Jesus himself. (iii) Both sayings are traditional, and the reference to 'seeing' the Son of man is a natural one, for the words are in both places clearly referring to Daniel's vision; since the sayings have their setting in the context of suffering, it is not surprising that they are found, like the prediction of the passion, in Mark alone. It seems rash to conclude that the first of these suggestions is the only possible explanation, and that the saying in Mark 9:1 about the kingdom of God coming with power must be a Marcan creation!

according to the prior assumptions – or 'critical method'! – adopted by the investigator. Whereas source critics, for example, have tended to regard inconsistencies in a document as indications of a piecing-together of traditions by editors who were unconcerned by apparent contradictions, redaction critics assume that the redactors were rational men, and the same inconsistencies can therefore be explained as important indications of theological intent![22] But Mark and his successors were handling traditional material, and though each of them used it in his own way, it is unwise to assume that they carefully organized every detail of its arrangement. It is possible to concentrate on the evangelists to such an extent that one ignores the prior history of the tradition – and that means, inevitably, a distorted understanding of the evangelist and his aims.

Perhaps the greatest danger before the redaction critic, however, is that of imposing his own philosophy upon the material, and seeing the Gospel in the light of his own situation. The modern New Testament critic has weathered the storm which assailed his faith when he first discovered that the Gospels are not biographies, and do not present him with 'history as it happened'; for many Christians, the discovery that the Gospels are primarily theological documents, telling us as much about the faith of the community as about the things which Jesus did and said, has proved a liberating experience. Yet liberation from the shackles of historicity and its problems has led some to a position where they happily cut the ties with the historical Jesus and refuse all historical props to faith. This kind of criticism has often been brought against Bultmann, whose interest has been with the tradition – and with its history! The same tendency is now seen in redaction criticism: the evangelists, too, are understood as interested only in 'what it means' and not in 'what happened'.

The swing of the pendulum is seen in a comment by Perrin on Mark: 'After several generations of being read mistakenly, as a historian, he has earned the right to be read as a theologian'.[23] With this statement we must surely agree. But the pendulum is given a remarkable push in a revealing comment which Perrin makes on a study in Marcan theology written by Ernest Best, which he describes as 'a strange book in that the author combines redaction criticism with the assumption "that Mark believes that the incidents he uses actually happened"!'[24] Now this is really an extraordinary statement. Why should the fact that Mark is a 'theologian' preclude him from writing about events which he thought had happened? Can a 'theologian' write only about imaginary events? This is obviously sheer nonsense. Against Perrin, we must

---

[22] See, for example, Quentin Quesnell, *The Mind of Mark: Interpretation and Method through the Exegesis of Mark 6,52* (Rome: Pontifical Biblical Institute, 1969).

[23] Perrin, *What is Redaction Criticism?*, 53.

[24] Perrin, *What is Redaction Criticism?*, 83, quoting Ernest Best, *The Temptation and the Passion: The Markan Soteriology* (Cambridge: Cambridge University Press, 1965), xi.

quote Perrin himself: 'Mark has the right to be read on his own terms'.[25] And what is the most obvious thing about Mark's method of writing? It is that he presented his theology in a form which 'misled' generations of scholars into believing that he was writing an historical account! This, says Perrin, 'is mute testimony to the skill of Mark as an author'.[26] Mark may well be more skilful than has sometimes been allowed – but not if he succeeded only in concealing his purpose until the twentieth-century critic uncovered it! Was he perhaps using his skill to do precisely what he seems to be doing? He certainly gives the impression that he is writing *Heilsgeschichte*, and that theology and history are for him inextricably bound together. Is it not likely that he has chosen 'to introduce his particular theology of the cross' in narrative form because it is an exposition of what he understands to have actually happened? Perrin continues: 'That he chose to do this in the form of narrative rather than theological treatise is his business'.[27] It is perhaps sufficient comment on this to quote again his own remark made a few lines later: 'Mark has the right to be read on his own terms'!

When we turn to Luke, it is impossible to deny that his theology is presented as being grounded in history: he, certainly, believed in *Heilsgeschichte*. Is it, perhaps, the modern theologian's unease with the idea of God at work in history which has led to the accusation that Luke has 'historicised' the material? Yet even in Lucan studies, we find the assumption that theology and history do not mix appearing in a new guise in Perrin's summary of Conzelmann's views: 'Luke is in no way motivated by a desire to exercise historical accuracy, but entirely by his theological concept of the role of Jerusalem in the history of salvation'.[28] But does not Luke also have 'the right to be read on his own terms'? His own statement of intent in 1:1–4 scarcely seems to support this antithesis between historical accuracy and theology!

It may not be an accident that this kind of one-sided emphasis on theology over against history has grown up in connection with a stress on the Hellenistic influence on the Christian community; yet we would surely expect those soaked in the tradition of the Jewish scriptures to place more emphasis on history than is now often allowed. The dismissal of the past and its importance for the evangelists is in part also the result of stressing the *Sitz im Leben* of the evangelist himself; this concentration on the period of the redaction and denial of historical interest on his part continues a tendency already seen in form criticism. Undoubtedly the early Christian writer selected and used material which spoke to his condition – and, he presumably hoped, to that of

---

[25] Perrin, *What is Redaction Criticism?*, 53.
[26] Perrin, *What is Redaction Criticism?*, 52.
[27] Perrin, *What is Redaction Criticism?*, 53.
[28] Perrin, *What is Redaction Criticism?*, 29.

his readers — but did his interest stop there? Luke's answer, in 1:1–4, is clearly 'no'. And since Mark chose to write his 'gospel' in the form of an account of 'what happened then', he also does not appear to have thought 'now' and 'then' unrelated. The twentieth-century critic must not build the first-century evangelist in his own image, and assume that because he himself has despaired of discovering certainty regarding the historicity of his material, and has come to terms with this by placing more and more emphasis on its theological meaning, the evangelists did the same.

Such extreme expressions of the antithesis between 'theology' and 'history' are not necessarily part of the redaction-critical approach: indeed, they must be regarded as over-enthusiastic statements which distort the picture by exaggerating certain aspects neglected in previous study.[29] Our discussion has concentrated in particular on Perrin's *What is Redaction Criticism?* because this is offered as an introduction to the discipline for the 'ordinary student'. It is unfortunate that the account is so likely to mislead its readers.

The evangelist, we have already suggested, must be allowed to speak for himself; we must not impose our ideas upon him. But it is extraordinarily difficult to hear what he is trying to say. We have lost his *Sitz im Leben*; just as there is disagreement about the setting of the pericopae, so there is no certainty about the situation of the books, and the variety of interpretations presented by commentators demonstrates the difficulty. We try to put ourselves into the evangelist's shoes, and only succeed in forcing him into ours! Some have seen liturgical interests as paramount; the Gospels are linked with lectionaries, and the epistles with baptismal rites. But where is the evidence for this kind of liturgical organization at this early period? And where is the evidence in the material itself? It surely appears only when one wears liturgical spectacles. The most popular model in current exegesis, however, is a doctrinal one: the New Testament writers' main concern was to combat 'false christologies'. The Fourth Gospel and the Colossian 'hymn' have long been interpreted in this way,[30] and Paul is certainly frequently found in debate with opponents of one kind or another — now understood to be 'gnostics' as often as they are Judaizers, teaching a false Christology. Recently Mark has been understood as a defence against 'heresy'. This theory has been most fully expounded by T.J. Weeden, who argues that Mark presents us with two

---

[29] There are signs that Perrin himself does not always mean what he seems to say. In an article, 'The Literary *Gattung* "Gospel" — Some Observations', *ExpTim* 82 (1970): 7, for example, he speaks of a gospel (of which form Mark is in his estimation the only pure example) as 'a narrative of an event from the past in which interests and concerns of the past, present and future have flowed together'.

[30] But see Morna D. Hooker, 'Were There False Teachers in Colossae?', in *Christ and Spirit in the New Testament: Studies in Honour of Charles Francis Digby Moule,* eds. Barnabas Lindars and Stephen S. Smalley (Cambridge: Cambridge University Press, 1973), 315–331.

contrasting christologies – first, in chapters 1–8, a *theios-aner* Christology, and secondly, in the rest of the Gospel, his own suffering-Son-of-Man Christology; the Caesarea Philippi incident describes a conflict between these opposing christologies, and 'since there is no historical basis for a christological dispute of this nature having taken place between Jesus and the disciples, the only way to account for Mark's consuming interest in it is that it has some existential importance for the situation in his own community'.[31] If we ask Weeden what evidence there is for such a dispute in Mark's own situation, he will no doubt simply refer us to Mark himself: it has become axiomatic that the Gospel material is direct evidence for the evangelist. Yet even if we grant this initial assumption, there are grave difficulties with Weeden's thesis: that the disciples' understanding of Jesus is represented as *inadequate* is clear, but that it is *wrong* is by no means evident. If Mark is trying to attack a false Christology which he has put into the mouth of Peter, then he was remarkably unsuccessful, since innumerable readers of his Gospel, from Matthew onwards, have interpreted him completely otherwise! Certainly the disciples fall under Mark's disapproval; but this is not because they uphold a *theios-aner* Christology (whether the *theios-aner* theme is as significant for the New Testament as the current fashion for the title suggests is also questionable), but because they are blind to the significance of Jesus' words and actions. There is nothing in Mark's Gospel which supports the idea that he is presenting us with a wrong interpretation in chapters 1–8 which must be rejected: the story of the two-stage opening of the blind man's eyes in 8:22–26 suggests, on the contrary, that a proper understanding of Jesus as presented in these chapters is a necessary first stage before the mystery of the suffering Son of man can be understood.

The danger of reading later christological beliefs back into the Gospels has long been recognized by New Testament scholars; the documents must not be read through Chalcedonian spectacles. But we may wonder whether this current 'heresy hunt' is not also something of an anachronism. Were there already 'false christologies' to combat? No doubt those who wrote the documents now incorporated in the canon sought to emphasize certain aspects of the Gospel as they understood it. Mark perhaps felt it necessary to remind his readers that as disciples of Jesus they must expect to suffer – but did he feel this because they were *forgetting* this aspect (like the Corinthians), or because he wished to assure them that their present sufferings, of which they were possibly very much aware, were a necessary part of their discipleship, and that if they were faithful they would receive their reward? The emphasis of a particular theme does not mean that we have to look for a 'heresy' which is being opposed. Weeden's analysis brings out the two themes in Mark's

---

[31] Theodore J. Weeden, *Mark – Traditions in Conflict* (Philadelphia: Fortress Press, 1971), 69.

presentation of Jesus – his mighty acts, and the paradoxical path of suffering, which his disciples must also follow. Mark's writing is of course christological, since the whole New Testament is christological, attempting to express this new faith centred on Jesus: Mark does not need 'heresy' to make him write in this way.

False teaching certainly creeps into the Christian communities – though it is in the later New Testament epistles that we find the defences against it being set up. But does not this notion belong to a situation where Christian truth has established some kind of norm, and 'heresy' is a deviation? And can this be already the situation when Mark was written? In looking for the setting of the New Testament books it is apparently all too easy to overlook the obvious – that is, the fact that most of them were written before the final break with Judaism came: that the most pressing and urgent controversy which faced these men was the controversy with the orthodoxy of Jewish faith and practice. There was as yet no 'Christianity'; the movement was still a Jewish sect – claiming to be in the succession of Judaism, its members indeed the only true adherents to the Jewish religion. These early writers are concerned to establish that Jesus is the Messiah of God – and that if 'the Jews' do not accept him, then it must be because they are blind and deaf, and have cut themselves off from the promises of God; it is for these authors vitally important to demonstrate that their belief is entirely in accordance with the scriptures – which remain for them authoritative, since it is God's word through Moses and the prophets – and indeed that it is only they who really understand the scriptures, since 'Israel' has failed to grasp their meaning. This may well be the kind of controversy which lies behind Mark, where it is the Jewish people who demonstrate the false understanding of Jesus, the disciples who – in the end – have their eyes opened: if the disciples seem slow in understanding, then we may at this point agree with Weeden in supposing that this reflects in part the situation of Mark's own time; the process of showing how Jewish heritage and Christian experience could be reconciled was not completed in a day, and it was a process which was continued in many different ways, as the New Testament itself demonstrates.

The same kind of controversy is reflected elsewhere in the New Testament. That Paul had much to say on this particular topic is obvious. The other great theologian of the New Testament, John, is also concerned to show how Jesus fulfils all that Judaism promises, and completes the role of the Torah, which pointed forward to him. Matthew, too, with his enigmatic comments on the Law, is interpreted by commentators in many ways, but his words cease to seem contradictory when we stop trying to make him answer our questions, and allow him to put his own: What is the relation of the Christian community to the Law? And of Christ to Moses? Are Christians lawbreakers? Or are they in fact the true doers of the Law in contrast to Israel? The letter to the

Hebrews also, which is often said to be addressed to those in danger of lapsing into Judaism, was perhaps more probably written by someone who was grappling with the problem 'Why then the Old Testament?' and who solved it by seeing the cultic system as a foreshadowing of the work of Christ. We forget too easily the difficulty – and the excitement! – of discovering and demonstrating how Christ fulfilled the scriptures, which could be interpreted in a variety of ways – taken atomistically as simple proof-texts, used allegorically or typologically, or commented on by *midrash*. The Jewish scriptures are for these writers part of God's revelation, of which Christ is the fulfilment; since God is not fickle, the two cannot be contradictory, and the scriptures must point to Christ. With this dominating concern it is understandable why, for example, Luke might wish, as Christopher Evans suggested,[32] to present the central section of his Gospel as a Christian Deuteronomy.

This formulation of Christian belief against the givenness of the Old Testament is the particular setting which suggests itself to me as a likely background for much of the New Testament. In a book devoted to asking questions, it would be improper to indulge myself by exploring this theme any further. I must content myself with revealing my own particular presuppositions. Perhaps I, too, am reading my own concerns into the minds of the New Testament writers, and interpreting their work and their use of scripture in the light of present-day discussion about how Christians should use the Christian Bible! It is at least arguable, however, that in regard to this particular problem of relating the givenness of the past with the exhilarating experience of the present, we today have much in common with the writers of the New Testament.

---

[32] C. F. Evans, 'The Central Section of St Luke's Gospel', in *Studies in the Gospels* (see n. 14), 37–53.

Section Three

The Development of Christology

5. T.W. Manson and the Twentieth-Century Search for Jesus

It was my great privilege to meet T.W. Manson during the last six months of his life. I had taken up residence in Manchester in order to study for a second research degree under his guidance. Sadly, owing to his final illness, I met with him to discuss my research work on only a couple of occasions, but he made a lasting impression on me. I have remembered him with affection ever since, as a true exemplar of all that a humble scholar should be. In the event, the topic I had planned to study with him was put on the back burner, but twenty years later, when I had the honour of delivering the Manson Memorial Lecture, I was able to present to him, post-mortem, a short discussion of Paul's understanding of the atonement, the theme on which I had planned to work with him.[1]

Manson continued to lecture for as long as he was able, and his lectures were a delight, offering his audience theological substance leavened by shafts of wit.[2] He was anything but dogmatic: having set out different possibilities, he would look round the room with a sparkle in his eye and conclude with the words 'You pay your money and you take your choice'. As it happens, few scholars *have* chosen to follow many of Manson's suggestions, although many – whether consciously or unconsciously – have profited from his work and been influenced by it.

1. Pauline Studies

During his twenty-two years in the Rylands Chair at Manchester, Manson lectured regularly, once a year, in the John Rylands Library. Many of these lectures were subsequently published in the Library's *Bulletin*.[3] In these, he apparently succeeded in conveying the results of his scholarship (making full use of Greek and Hebrew sources) to a mixed audience. Here, too, we find the same happy expressions and wry comments that lightened his undergraduate

---

[1] Morna D. Hooker, 'Interchange and Atonement', *BJRL* 60, no. 2 (1978): 462–481.
[2] A selection of Manson's class lectures on New Testament theology was published after his death: T.W. Manson, *On Paul and John: Some Selected Theological Themes*, ed. Matthew Black (London: SCM Press, 1963).
[3] These were reprinted subsequently in T.W. Manson, *Studies in the Gospels and Epistles*, ed. Matthew Black (Manchester: Manchester University Press, 1962).

Fig. 1. Thomas Walter Manson (1893–1958)
Rylands Professor 1936–1958

lectures, such as his remark that 'Ecclesiastical gatherings have before now achieved remarkable results in the way of pompous platitude'.[4] Half a dozen of these lectures are on the Pauline letters, and they are mostly characterized by original suggestions that make one look at an epistle from a new angle. There is, for example, the lecture on Philippians (1939) which, under the innocuous title 'The date of the epistle to the Philippians', proceeds to challenge orthodoxy by suggesting that the letter was not written from prison, as is always assumed, but *after* Paul's release from a period of captivity. That would mean that Philippians 1 describes Paul's experiences in Corinth when brought before Gallio. The letter itself, Manson suggests, was written soon

---

[4] Manson, *Studies*, 183–184.

after, from Ephesus. This enabled him to explain the fact that Paul speaks of some of his fellow Christians having been *encouraged* by his imprisonment (Philippians 1:14): it was because Paul had been delivered from danger that the members of the Corinthian church were now proclaiming the gospel with boldness. Manson's suggestion was, to use his own expression, 'adventurous', but certainly worth exploring. As so often, he looked at what was regarded by other scholars as part of the 'given', and demonstrated that what seemed certain was frequently only another assumption.

This particular essay reveals something of Manson's own assumptions. For him, the fact that 'Acts knows nothing of an Ephesian imprisonment'[5] was important. Like most scholars of his generation, he spoke of 'the necessity of fitting Paul's account into the narrative of Acts'.[6] Yet this comment, in his essay on 'The problem of the epistle to the Galatians', which was primarily concerned with the difficulty of reconciling Galatians 2 with Acts 11 and 15, is immediately followed by the statement that 'Where Acts and Galatians conflict, the preference should generally be given to Galatians'. On this basis, he suggested a solution: that one should take 'Paul's narrative as the foundation'.[7] Subsequent work on the relationship between Paul and the Acts framework has endorsed this insight as to where the priority should lie.

Manson's Rylands lectures on Paul are rarely referred to today. The exception is his paper on Romans, in which, in light of the recent discovery of P^{46}, he developed a suggestion made much earlier that Romans 16 was originally addressed to the Ephesians.[8] Building on the puzzling textual evidence, which has one blessing at the end of chapter 15, another which appears as 16:20, 24 or 27, and a doxology which occurs not only at the very end but also after 14:23 or 15:33, and using the evidence of Origen that Romans had once concluded without chapters 15–16, it was clear that the original form of the epistle was uncertain. Manson's solution was that the first fifteen chapters of Romans were sent to the church in Rome, while at the same time a copy was sent to Ephesus with a covering note – i.e. Romans 16 – which commended Phoebe to the community and sent greetings to friends in Ephesus from Paul and from those Christians presently with him who would be known there. Although this theory is still mentioned in commentaries, it is generally rejected.[9]

---

[5] Manson, *Studies*, 150.
[6] Manson, *Studies*, 171.
[7] Manson, *Studies*, 186.
[8] The suggestion was first made by David Schulz: *Theologische Studien und Kritiken* 2 (1829), 609 ff.
[9] See, for example, C. K. Barrett, *A Commentary on the Epistle to the Romans*, 2nd ed., BNTC (London: A&C Black, 1991), 12 ff.; C. E. B. Cranfield, *A Critical and Exegetical Commentary on the Epistle to the Romans*, vol. 1: *Introduction and Commentary on Romans I–VIII*, ICC (Edinburgh:

Of the papers on Paul published by Manson elsewhere, two are of particular interest. An essay on 2 Corinthians 2:14–17 stresses that 'the followers of Christ, and in particular the Apostle himself, are participants in the spiritual activity which is focused in Christ'.[10] What is referred to in this passage as 'the fragrance of the knowledge of [God]' (v. 16) is Christ himself, for this knowledge is now found in Christ, as it had previously been found in Torah. Paul goes on to describe the apostles as the aroma of Christ, and Manson argues that this image of Paul's is illuminated by rabbinic writings in which the Torah is described as a drug that brought life to some, death to others, commenting that 'there is no reason why the pupil of Gamaliel should not have thought in a similar way of Christ'.[11] This essay is interesting because of its stress on the corporate bond between Christ and Christians (an idea found also in Manson's interpretation of the term 'the Son of man'), for its careful exegesis linking 2 Corinthians 2:14–17 with Paul's argument in chapter 3 and, above all, for its appeal to Paul's Jewish roots. Scholars today might hesitate to rely on Acts' reference to Paul as a pupil of Gamaliel (Acts 22:3), and be far more cautious about using rabbinic material which dates from a later century than Paul himself to explain his thought. Nevertheless, Manson's stress on the unity between Christ and believers and his emphasis on Paul's Jewish background were sound, and his suggestion about the roots of Paul's imagery may well be correct.

A similar recognition of the Jewish roots of Paul's theology is found in another of Manson's essays, this time on Romans 3:25.[12] In this, he argued that the origin of the word ἱλαστήριον is to be found (as in Hebrews 9:5) in its use in the LXX to translate the Hebrew *kappōreth*, the word used in the Pentateuch to refer to the covering of the ark, or 'mercy seat', and that Paul's language in this verse reflects the imagery of the Day of Atonement. Although others had championed the translation 'mercy seat',[13] Manson's article has been perhaps the most influential presentation of this interpretation. Once again, few scholars have concurred with his findings, but recently one of my own students has made a convincing case in support of his conclusions.[14]

T&T Clark, 1975), 9–11; James D. G. Dunn, *Romans 9–16*, WBC 38B (Dallas: Word Books, 1988), 884–885.

[10] T. W. Manson, '2 Cor. 2¹⁴⁻¹⁷: Suggestions Towards an Exegesis', in *Studia Paulina: In Honorem Johannis de Zwaan Septuagenarii*, eds. Jan N. Sevenster and W. C. van Unnik (Haarlem: Erven F. Bohn, 1953), 155.

[11] Manson, 'Suggestions', 160.

[12] T. W. Manson, 'ΙΛΑCΤΗΡΙΟΝ', *JTS* 46 (1945): 1–10.

[13] Tyndale translated the word ἱλαστήριον as 'seat of mercy', following Luther's translation, 'Gnadenstuhl'.

[14] Daniel P. Bailey, 'Jesus as the Mercy Seat: The Semantics and Theology of Paul's Use of *Hilasterion* in Romans 3:25' (PhD thesis, University of Cambridge, 1999). I had myself previously been persuaded that Manson's interpretation was probably correct: Morna D. Hooker,

2. Jesus

Manson's chief contribution to New Testament scholarship, however, was his work on the Gospels. Here we see the same features that characterized his work on Paul – original insights based on careful exegesis of the text and on the conviction that the material was rooted in Judaism. His first book, an investigation of the teaching of Jesus, has been described as his finest; remarkably, it was written while Manson was serving as minister of the Presbyterian church in Falstone, Northumberland, before he took up an academic post.

For Manson, study of Jesus' teaching was 'of vital importance both to New Testament Theology, of which it is the kernel, and to the study of the life of Jesus, a life in which, more than in any other, word and deed are united in indissoluble harmony'.[15] It was important for the study of Jesus because 'no attempt to write the life of Jesus ... could be considered complete without some account of his words', and it was important for New Testament theology because 'any work on New Testament Theology must necessarily take as its foundation the Theology of the Founder of Christianity'.[16] Manson's aim was 'to look as it were through the eyes of Jesus and to see God and man, heaven and earth, life and death, as he saw them'.[17] It is hardly surprising, then, that Manson was concerned to explore the roots of Jesus' teaching in Judaism, as evidenced in his understanding of the Old Testament, his use of Aramaic and his familiarity with the teaching of the rabbis.

Manson's study of the Gospels is based on acceptance of the priority of Mark and the four-document theory – regarded at the time as 'firmly established'[18] – and on the assumption that Mark provided 'a biographical sketch', which meant that 'one of the first steps toward the understanding of the teaching will be to fit it as far as possible into the framework of the life of Jesus',[19] since 'The mission of Jesus, like the careers of many of the great masters in music and literature, falls into periods'.[20] Accordingly, he emphasized the importance of Caesarea Philippi as a turning point in the ministry, and suggested that the fact that Jesus is described as delivering different kinds of teaching to different audiences is important for our understanding of Jesus himself. At the same time, he acknowledged the difficulty not only of

---

Not Ashamed of the Gospel: New Testament Interpretations of the Death of Christ (Carlisle: The Paternoster Press, 1994), 43–44.

[15] T.W. Manson, *The Teaching of Jesus: Studies of Its Form and Content* (Cambridge: Cambridge University Press, 1931), 5.

[16] Manson, *Teaching*, 3.

[17] Manson, *Teaching*, 5.

[18] Manson, *Teaching*, 7.

[19] Manson, *Teaching*, 12–13.

[20] Manson, *Teaching*, 13.

attempting to discover the *ipsissima verba* of Jesus but also, assuming this were possible, of comprehending them.

Underlying Manson's investigation of Jesus' teaching, then, is a consideration of the source in which a saying occurs (Mark, Q, M, or L), as a first step towards discovering its earliest form; of the audience to which it is addressed (disciples, opponents, general public), since this might affect its meaning; and of the position in the narrative in which it is found, above all in relation to Caesarea Philippi. He made no reference, at this stage in his work, to the investigations of form critics such as Karl Schmidt, Martin Dibelius and Rudolf Bultmann,[21] even though one British commentator, A. E. J. Rawlinson, had already argued, in his commentary on Mark, that the Marcan chronology was useless.[22] Rawlinson, however, was an exception, since by the time of the publication of Manson's book, in 1931, few scholars in the United Kingdom had yet taken real note of the work on form criticism coming out of Germany.

In *The Teaching of Jesus*, Manson was concerned to look at the central themes of Jesus' message, rather than to analyse the whole body of teaching attributed to him. That kind of detailed analysis was undertaken later in *The Sayings of Jesus*[23] (although he confined himself there to the material found in Q, M, and L). The bulk of his first book was taken up with an examination of 'The contents of the teaching': God as father, God as king (four chapters), and religion and morals. Significantly, his innovative exposition of Jesus as 'the Son of man' is one section in one of the chapters on 'God as king'. For Manson:

'Son of Man' in the Gospels is the final term in a series of conceptions ... the Remnant (Isaiah), the Servant of Jehovah (II Isaiah), the 'I' of the psalms, and the Son of Man (Daniel). ... it is the idea of the Remnant which is the essential feature about each ... Son of Man in the Gospels is another embodiment of the Remnant idea. In other words, the Son of Man is, like the Servant of Jehovah, an ideal figure and stands for the manifestation of the Kingdom of God on earth in a people wholly devoted to their heavenly King.[24]

Manson's understanding of the terms 'the kingdom of God' and 'the Son of man' is his most original contribution to New Testament research. His interpretation is based on a careful investigation of the biblical and rabbinic sources, and shows the influence of scholars such as Dalman and Billerbeck. At

---

[21] Karl L. Schmidt, *Der Rahmen der Geschichte Jesu* (Berlin: Trowitzsch, 1919); Martin Dibelius, *Die Formgeschichte des Evangeliums* (Tübingen: Mohr, 1919); Rudolf Bultmann, *Die Geschichte der synoptischen Tradition* (Göttingen: Vandenhoeck & Ruprecht, 1921).

[22] A. E. J. Rawlinson, *The Gospel According to St Mark*, Westminster Commentaries (London: Methuen, 1925).

[23] First published as Part II of H.D.A. Major, T.W. Manson, and C.J. Wright, *The Mission and Message of Jesus* (London: Nicholson and Watson, 1937); repr. as *The Sayings of Jesus as Recorded in the Gospels According to St Matthew and St Luke*, by T.W. Manson (London: SCM Press, 1949).

[24] Manson, *Teaching*, 227.

the same time, it is typical of much British scholarship, refusing to be forced into a choice between the diametrically opposed views emanating from the Continent at the time – on the one hand, the view 'represented by the religio-ethical humanitarian school of interpreters', on the other, 'thorough-going eschatology'. Commenting on these two very different ways of understanding the kingdom of God, he remarked, 'Both cannot be right, but both may be wrong', and goes on to argue that both are based on a 'fundamental misinterpretation' of the kingdom, before setting out his own interpretation.[25]

For Manson, the kingdom of God was essentially 'the reign of God'. Like the fatherhood of God, it was 'a personal relation between God as King and the individual as subject', although it quickly manifested itself as 'a society, something which might be called the People of God. This society consists of all those who are linked together by the fact of their common allegiance to one King'.[26] A greater manifestation, however, lies in the future. Thus:

… there is no point in asking whether it [the kingdom] is present or future, just as there is no point in asking whether the Fatherhood of God is present or future. It is something independent of temporal and spatial relations. It is a standing claim made by God on the loyalty and obedience of man.[27]

When the kingdom of God was seen in its Jewish setting, then, there was a cohesion in the various Gospel sayings about it. Although there seemed to be three different ways of referring to God's reign, these 'three interdependent conceptions of the Kingdom as an eternal fact, as a manifestation in the present life of men, and as a consummation still to come, can be paralleled in Jewish thought before and after the days of Jesus as well as in the early Christian literature'.[28] In the next three chapters he examines these three aspects of the kingdom: the eternal sovereignty, the kingdom in the world and the final consummation, considering each of them in the light of material from the Old Testament, pseudepigrapha and rabbinic writings.

In the same way, Manson saw no difficulty in holding that Jesus spoke of the Son of man in relation both to the passion and to the parousia. In twenty-two pages he set out his understanding of the meaning of the term, arguing that it was based on the imagery of Daniel 7:13. He pointed out that in apocalyptic literature the phrase was used 'not in its literal sense but as a symbol for something else',[29] a fact that was ignored by the large number of scholars on the Continent who assumed that it would have been understood, in Jesus' time, to refer to an eschatological saviour and judge. In Daniel

---

[25] Manson, *Teaching*, 117.
[26] Manson, *Teaching*, 134.
[27] Manson, *Teaching*, 135.
[28] Manson, *Teaching*, 136.
[29] Manson, *Teaching*, 212.

the one like a son of man is said to represent the saints of the Most High, and in the Gospels Manson noted the striking correspondence 'between the "Son of Man" predictions and the demands made by Jesus on his disciples',[30] and suggested that 'when Jesus speaks of the sufferings of the Son of Man he means something in which he and his followers should share'.[31] Although Jesus appeals to others to accept, with him, the role of the Son of man, the ideal is fulfilled in Jesus alone. Manson remarks that in Paul's thought there is a similar link between Christ's sufferings and those of believers,[32] and that Paul's use of the term ἄνθρωπος may be his equivalent to the phrase ὁ υἱὸς τοῦ ἀνθρώπου.

Manson's original contribution to the debate about the meaning of the phrase 'the Son of man' has been frequently quoted in subsequent discussion, but although it was influential in Great Britain, it gained little support elsewhere. This was largely owing to the widespread conviction (based chiefly on 1 Enoch 38–71) that Jews of the first century CE were expecting an eschatological 'Messianic' figure known as 'the Son of man'.[33] Later, when confidence in this view faded, the alternative suggestion was put forward that the phrase was nothing more than an idiomatic expression for 'man', and that most of 'the Son of man' sayings were based on a misunderstanding of his words, which were mistakenly read in the light of Daniel 7:13.[34]

Today, the method adopted by Manson in this book seems dated: confidence in Streeter's source hypothesis has dwindled; the assumption that the audience posited by an evangelist indicated its original setting in the life of Jesus now seems questionable; above all, Manson's belief that Mark presents us with a historical outline of Jesus' ministry, with Caesarea Philippi as its central pivot, has been shattered. Nevertheless, many of his concerns were justified: finding a saying in more than one possible source is still taken as an indication of its authenticity, and Manson's instinct that one should try to recover the earliest form of a saying was correct; his realization that the audience *posited* by an evangelist affected the meaning of a saying was sound; and although we can no longer rely, as he did, on the 'historical' framework apparently provided

---

[30] Manson, *Teaching*, 231. Note, in particular, Mark 8:34, 10:32–40, 14:26–31.

[31] Manson, *Teaching*, 232.

[32] See Colossians 1:24; 2 Corinthians 1:5; Philippians 1:29, 3:10; Romans 8:17; Galatians 6:17.

[33] Classic statements of this view are found in Rudolf Bultmann, *Theology of the New Testament*, vol. 1, trans. Kendrick Grobel (London: SCM Press, 1952), 26–32; Ferdinand Hahn, *The Titles of Jesus in Christology*, trans. Harold Knight and George Ogg (London: Lutterworth Press, 1969), 15–53; H.E. Tödt, *The Son of Man in the Synoptic Tradition*, trans. Dorothea M. Barton (London: SCM Press, 1965).

[34] Significant contributions were made by Geza Vermes, *Jesus the Jew: A Historian's Reading of the Gospels* (London: Collins, 1973), 160–191; Maurice Casey, *Son of Man: The Interpretation and Influence of Daniel 7* (London: SPCK, 1979); Barnabas Lindars, *Jesus Son of Man* (London: SPCK, 1983).

by Mark, Manson's insistence that if we are to understand Jesus we have to understand him in his own – Jewish – world, and try to see things through his eyes, is as true now as it was then.

3. Materials for a Life of Jesus

These same concerns are demonstrated in a series of lectures delivered at the John Rylands Library during the 1940s. In 1942 he had published a short article in *The Expository Times* entitled 'Is It Possible to Write a Life of Christ?'[35] Outlining the problem, he admits that 'the narrative matter' in the Gospels 'does not suffice to cover the ministry at all adequately'. Indeed, it leaves 'huge gaps', even if we assume the reliability not only of the material itself but also of the order in which it is arranged.[36] Moreover, the work of the form critics had raised questions regarding the form of the material and its use in the primitive church. Manson is by no means dismissive of form criticism itself. Nevertheless, the fact that a story or saying was useful to the church does not mean that it could not also have had a place in the ministry of Jesus. While acknowledging that it was necessary to consider how the church's needs might have shaped the material, he believed that:

> … far too much has been made of the Church and its need and its influence in shaping the materials now presented to us in the Gospels. … It is not higher criticism but the higher credulity that boggles at a verse of Mark and swallows without a qualm pages of pure conjecture about the primitive Christians' psychology and its workings on the pre-literary tradition.[37]

Manson then turns to the danger in trying to construct a 'life of Jesus' when there is so little material available. An obvious temptation is to 'indulge in padding'. In the early days of the church, attempts were made to fill the lacunae in the Gospels with apocryphal stories, and modern writers sometimes followed a similar path, filling the gaps with what they imagined might have happened. Recent books on Jesus, such as those by Bultmann and Dibelius, had tended to be short, and to concentrate on his teaching. Manson preferred the method adopted by Eduard Meyer, whose work set Jesus firmly in a Jewish context.[38] That meant that the ministry of Jesus had to be understood against the background of the centuries-long Jewish fight for freedom, his teaching had to be seen in a context stretching from Ezra the scribe to the redaction of the

---

[35] T.W. Manson, 'Is It Possible to Write a Life of Christ?', *ExpTim* 53 (1942): 248–251.
[36] Manson, 'Is it Possible?', 248b–249a.
[37] Manson, 'Is it Possible?', 249b.
[38] Eduard Meyer, *Ursprung und Anfänge des Christentums*, 3 vols. (Stuttgart: J.G. Cotta, 1921–1923).

Mishnah at the end of the second century CE, and the religion of Jesus had to be set against the background of the ritual of temple and synagogue:

> ... the characteristic features of the teaching of Jesus can be linked up with the Old Testament on one side and with the Church on the other. ... in order to see the full bearing of the fragments of evidence about the ministry, we must learn to see them in their Jewish and Christian context.[39]

Manson here affirms what the next generation of scholars was to deny: that if we want to understand Jesus we have to look at the links between him and Judaism on the one hand, and the church on the other. One wonders what his reaction would have been to the work of one of his own students, Norman Perrin, who claimed to have been greatly influenced by *The Teaching of Jesus*, and who paid lip-service to the fact that the 'teaching of Jesus was set in the context of ancient Judaism',[40] and yet applied the test of 'double dissimilarity' in the attempt to discover the authentic teaching of Jesus, and followed the principle of 'When in doubt, discard'![41] This is a very different approach from Manson's own conviction that the task of uncovering a reasonably clear portrait of Christ is not 'for those who impatiently brush aside most of the evidence as unreliable'.[42]

It is noteworthy that Manson says little about the Marcan chronology in this essay, beyond the fact that it had come under attack from Karl Schmidt. His approach in *The Teaching of Jesus* had been to see the teaching of Jesus in its Marcan framework; his approach now is more cautious, although ambitious, aiming to see the ministry of Jesus in its historical context, with Jesus as the decisive factor at the critical juncture between the history of post-exilic Judaism and the history of the early church. Since there is insufficient material to write a biography of Jesus, he is content to attempt a much more impressionistic portrait.

The first of the John Rylands lectures, published the following year in the *Bulletin*, takes the argument further.[43] This time he refers to the problem of the reliability of the Marcan framework; postponing discussion for another time, he notes that 'it is no longer possible to regard the Marcan framework, in all its details, as a rigid and unalterable scaffolding, into which everything must somehow be fitted'.[44] Just how far he was from regarding the Marcan frame-

---

[39] Manson, 'Is it Possible?', 250b.
[40] Norman Perrin, *Rediscovering the Teaching of Jesus* (London: SCM Press, 1967), 39.
[41] Perrin, *Rediscovering the Teaching of Jesus*, 11.
[42] Manson, 'Is it Possible?', 251b.
[43] T.W. Manson, 'The Life of Jesus: A Study of the Available Materials', *BJRL* 27, no. 2 (1943): 323–337. This essay, like his other Rylands lectures on Jesus, was subsequently reprinted in Manson, *Studies in the Gospels and Epistles*.
[44] Manson, *Studies*, 26.

work as 'rigid and unalterable' is demonstrated in his 1950 Rylands lecture on 'The cleansing of the temple',[45] in which he argues that the events described in Mark 11 took place at the Feast of Tabernacles, six months before Jesus' final visit to Jerusalem. Yet he did not retract his judgement that 'while many concessions may have to be made to the disruptive criticism of Mark, it is nevertheless the case that a good deal of structure remains. When the lath and plaster is removed, it appears that there is some solid masonry underneath'.[46]

In his next essay, 'The Foundation of the Synoptic Tradition: The Gospel of Mark',[47] Manson returned to the question of the reliability of Mark. Beginning from the Papias tradition, and considering other tradition about Mark, he argues that the evangelist would have been able to draw not only on the reminiscences of Peter but on other early Christian tradition. He quotes approvingly the conclusion of C.H. Turner, who had described Mark's Gospel as 'autobiographical', meaning that it recorded the account of Peter, who had been an eyewitness to the events described. If this view were correct, then there was reason to believe that the links between the pericopae also went back to Peter, so providing a reliable chronological framework.

In his lectures on Luke and Matthew, Manson is less concerned with the question of writing a 'life' of Jesus. He does, however, express confidence in Luke's faithfulness to his sources, and supports the theory of Proto-Luke; he also argues that Matthew, said by Papias to have compiled the λόγια, or Oracles, was responsible for composing Q. Turning to John, he comments that 'it is no longer possible to say "If the Fourth Gospel contradicts the Synoptics, so much the worse for the Fourth Gospel."'[48] Each case has to be settled on its own merits: the Synoptics are likely to be right in dating the cleansing of the temple at the end of the ministry, but John may be right on the nature of the Last Supper and the dating of the crucifixion.

In the final lecture in this series Manson returned to the theme of 'The Son of Man in Daniel, Enoch and the Gospels'. While he reiterates his earlier conclusions, he makes considerable amendments to the details. Once again, he begins from the conviction that the one like a son of man in Daniel 7 is a symbolic figure representing 'the people of the saints of the Most High'. He is 'not a divine, semi-divine, or angelic figure coming down from heaven, to bring deliverance, but a human figure going up to heaven to receive it'.[49] This

---

[45] T.W. Manson, 'The Cleansing of the Temple', *BJRL* 33, no. 2 (1951): 271–282.
[46] Manson, *Studies,* 26.
[47] T.W. Manson, 'The Foundation of the Synoptic Tradition: The Gospel of Mark', *BJRL* 28, no. 1 (1944): 119–136.
[48] Manson, *Studies,* 117.
[49] Manson, *Studies,* 126. Manson refers here to the work of T. Francis Glasson, *The Second Advent* (London: Epworth Press, 1945), 14 ff.

time, Manson examines the evidence of Enoch in more detail, and suggests that we have there an oscillation between the individual and the group. He believes that something similar is found in the use of the term 'the Son of man' in the sayings of Jesus, who took the term from Daniel 7.

The Son of man problem has become immensely complex, and seems to be even further from a solution today than it was in Manson's day. On the one hand, the 'thorough-going eschatological' interpretation, which understands Jesus to be speaking of someone else as the expected 'Son of man', lacks the necessary evidence in Jewish sources to make it likely. On the other, the 'idiomatic' interpretation fails to explain why Jesus would have used a phrase that apparently puzzled many of his own contemporaries, or how it came to be misunderstood and so give rise to so many other sayings. Neither theory can explain why Jesus spoke and acted with authority, and why his followers should have taken the step of identifying Jesus himself as *the* Son of man. Manson's interpretation of 'the Son of man' – like his understanding of 'the kingdom of God' – showed how apparently diverse statements in the Gospels were rooted in the biblical and Jewish material; aspects of the Son of man's vocation which seem at first sight to be contradictory are discovered to be integral parts of one pattern. Moreover, he took seriously the link between Jesus and his disciples implied in many of the sayings. His 'third way' may yet prove to be the best.

In the same year that he delivered this lecture on the Son of man (1949), Manson gave the Commemoration Day address at Westminster College, Cambridge, on 'The Quest of the Historical Jesus – Continued'.[50] He was now convinced that form criticism did not offer a way forward. The proper function of the discipline – the structure of the various units of narrative and teaching – was:

> ... interesting but not epoch-making. ... a paragraph of Mark is not a penny the better or the worse as historical evidence for being labelled, 'Apothegm' or 'Pronouncement Story' or 'Paradigm'. In fact if Form-criticism had stuck to its proper business, it would not have made any real stir.[51]

Form criticism had, however, been 'mixed-up' with other things: with the attack on the Marcan framework and with study of the *Sitz im Leben* of the tradition, which had led scholars to believe that the community that *used* sayings or stories had also *created* them. To Manson, both of these ideas were wrong-headed: he was 'increasingly convinced by prolonged acquaintance

---

[50] Manson, *Studies*, 3–12. Manson reworked the substance of this lecture for his contribution to the Festschrift for C.H. Dodd: T.W. Manson, 'The Life of Jesus: Some Tendencies in Present-day Research', in *The Background of the New Testament and Its Eschatology*, eds. W.D. Davies and D. Daube (Cambridge: Cambridge University Press, 1956), 211–221.

[51] Manson, *Studies*, 5.

with *Mark* that it is *not* a patchwork-quilt, but that in the main it presents an orderly and logical development',[52] and declared that 'a return to the study of the Gospels as *historical documents* concerning Jesus of Nazareth, rather than as psychological case-material concerning the early Christians'[53] was long overdue. Manson concludes:

> After many years of work at the problems, I confess that I am increasingly convinced that in the Gospels we have the materials – reliable materials – for an outline account of the ministry as a whole. I believe it is possible to produce such an outline and that, when produced, it will dovetail into the rest of the picture, that it will fit with what we otherwise know about contemporary Jewish faith and life in Palestine. It will also make sense in the context of Roman imperial policy in the Near East. And it will give an adequate explanation of the existence of the Church. We shall not be able to fit in all the details. … The gaps are enormous. But we have *some* details; and I think it is true to say that these short stories, parables, sayings, poems, and so on, which go to make up the Gospels themselves, epitomize the whole story.[54]

It was this task of producing 'an outline account of the ministry' that Manson attempted in his third book on Jesus, *The Servant-Messiah*, which is the printed version of lectures delivered several years earlier.[55] As we would expect, he is concerned to set out the context in which Jesus lived and worked: the book begins with a discussion of 'the Messianic hope', and ends with 'the Messianic succession'. On Jesus himself, he spells out the belief adumbrated in his 1949 lecture on the Son of man, that Jesus had 'defined the "Son of Man" in terms of the "Servant of the Lord"'.[56] It was Jesus who had brought together these two embodiments of the remnant, and in accepting the role of the Son of man, Jesus fulfilled the Israelite ideal, since the Son of man is the true Israel.

---

[52] Manson, *Studies*, 5–6.
[53] Manson, *Studies*, 8.
[54] Manson, *Studies*, 11.
[55] T.W. Manson, *The Servant-Messiah: A Study of the Public Ministry of Jesus* (Cambridge: Cambridge University Press, 1953).
[56] Manson, *Studies*, 144; Manson, *The Servant-Messiah*, 64, 73. In support, Manson merely refers to the work of William Manson, *Jesus the Messiah* (London: Hodder & Stoughton, 1943), 155–158. We should note an important difference between the two namesake scholars, however: for William Manson (*Jesus*, 98–103, 113–119), the figure of the son of man in Daniel was essentially a 'celestial figure', while T.W. Manson argued that it had originally been a symbol for the saints of the Most High, the 'remnant' of Israel. Nevertheless, T.W. Manson agreed that 'the apocalyptic tradition' saw 'the Son of man' as a glorious, triumphant figure, not a suffering one, and that the disciples would therefore have interpreted Jesus' words in these terms: T.W. Manson, 'Realized Eschatology and the Messianic Secret', in *Studies in the Gospels: Essays in Memory of R.H. Lightfoot*, ed. D.E. Nineham (Oxford: Blackwell, 1957), 209–222.

4. The Continuing Quest

In a sense, Manson's work on Jesus marks the end of an era. Like his predecessor in the Rylands Chair, C.H. Dodd, he was confident that Mark provided a historical outline of Jesus' ministry.[57] But times were changing, and from now on the challenge of form criticism had to be faced. Although Dodd himself was more influenced by the work of the form critics than was Manson, he argued that the 'historical outline' which formed the framework of Mark was itself part of the tradition: Mark's arrangement of the material was part historical, part topical. His theory proved popular in the English-speaking world, for it seemed to have proved a historical link with the historical Jesus. But in 1955 Dennis Nineham published a devastating critique of the theory, demonstrating that the outline was too brief to be useful, that there was no guarantee that the pericopae had been attached to it at the 'correct' chronological point, and that there was in any case no conceivable purpose for such a skeletal outline to have existed.[58] In sharp contrast to the standard commentary on Mark by Vincent Taylor,[59] which had laid stress on historical questions, Nineham's own commentary on Mark, published some eleven years after Taylor's,[60] demonstrated the results of approaching that Gospel from a form-critical stance.

At the end of the nineteenth century, Martin Kähler had pronounced the quest of the historical Jesus to be at a dead end: Jesus could be met only in the kerygma of the community. Shortly afterwards, the monumental survey of Jesus research by Albert Schweitzer, translated into English under the title *The Quest of the Historical Jesus*,[61] demonstrated just how futile the attempt to discover the Jesus of history had been. Yet the quest of the historical Jesus continued to dominate study of the Gospels throughout the twentieth century. To be sure, the work of form critics such as Dibelius and Bultmann seemed to confirm Kähler's conclusion. Barth and Bultmann had both insisted that knowledge of Jesus was a matter of faith, not history. For Barth that had meant the freedom to ignore historical questions and to concentrate on dogmatics, while for Bultmann it had led to the famous remark: 'I do indeed think that we can now know almost nothing concerning the life and

---

[57] Cf. C.H. Dodd, 'The Framework of the Gospel Narrative', *ExpTim* 43 (1932): 396–400. Dodd later wrote his own account of Jesus' life: *The Founder of Christianity* (London: Collins, 1971).

[58] D.E. Nineham, 'The Order of Events in St. Mark's Gospel – an examination of Dr. Dodd's Hypothesis', in *Studies in the Gospels*, ed. Nineham, 223–239.

[59] Vincent Taylor, *The Gospel According to St. Mark* (London: Macmillan, 1952).

[60] D.E. Nineham, *The Gospel of St Mark*, Pelican New Testament Commentaries (Harmondsworth: Penguin, 1963).

[61] Albert Schweitzer, *The Quest of the Historical Jesus*, trans. W. Montgomery (London: A&C Black, 1910).

personality of Jesus'.[62] For Bultmann, the historical Jesus was of no concern. Using form criticism as a tool, he demonstrated that most of the pericopae in the Gospels had been relevant to the life and worship of the early church, and argued that they had originated there.

The work of Bultmann in Germany and of T.W. Manson in England typifies two very different approaches to the Jesus question in the 1930s and 1940s. They were also, to a certain extent, typical of attitudes in their two countries. There were, however, some in England (such as R.H. Lightfoot) who were more appreciative of form criticism than Manson, and there were many in Germany who did *not* belong to the Bultmann school. Among the latter we may mention Ethelbert Stauffer, whose (somewhat eccentric) book on Jesus was based on the belief that it was still possible to separate the 'facts' about Jesus from the 'interpretation of the evangelists'.[63] For Bultmann, any concern to discover historical evidence about Jesus was a distraction from true faith, which must not rely on historical props. For Manson, on the other hand, God had revealed himself in history, and there was therefore no escape from historical enquiry. Yet these two scholars did have something in common, and it was what motivated their work, namely their Christian faith and their pastoral concern for their fellow Christians, struggling to believe the gospel.

It was in the 1950s that some of Bultmann's own students challenged his approach. In 1953 Ernst Käsemann delivered a lecture in which he declared that, in spite of the enormous difficulties in finding any reliable information about the historical Jesus, he was not prepared to accept that:

... defeatism and scepticism must have the last word and lead us on to a complete disengagement of interest from the earthly Jesus. If this were to happen we ... should also be overlooking the fact that there are still pieces of the Synoptic tradition which the historian has to acknowledge as authentic if he wishes to remain an historian at all.[64]

Even though it was impossible to write a 'life' of Jesus, then, one must be careful not to divorce Christian faith totally from its roots.

Käsemann still stood very clearly in the tradition of Bultmann, and was in no way advocating a return to the original quest. Nevertheless, a significant shift had been made, and similar statements were being issued by other German scholars. In 1956 Günther Bornkamm ventured to write a book entitled *Jesus von Nazareth*. While insisting that 'faith cannot and should not be dependent on the change and uncertainty of historical research', he

---

[62] Rudolf Bultmann, *Jesus and the Word*, trans. Louise Pettibone Smith and Erminie Huntress (New York: Scribner, 1934), 8.

[63] Ethelbert Stauffer, *Jesus and His Story*, trans. Dorothea M. Barton (London: SCM Press, 1960), 13.

[64] Ernst Käsemann, 'Das Problem des historischen Jesus': the English translation may be found in his *Essays on New Testament Themes*, trans. W.J. Montague, SBT 41 (London: SCM Press, 1964), 15–47 (here at 45–46).

nevertheless protested that faith could not 'be content with mere tradition, even though it be that contained in the Gospels', and that it must 'seek behind it to see the thing itself'.[65] That meant that 'it cannot be seriously maintained that the Gospels and their tradition do not allow enquiry after the historical Jesus. Not only do they allow, they demand this effort'.[66]

Yet even Bultmann had thought it possible to speak about the teaching of Jesus. In his book *Jesus and the Word*, he had written: 'Little as we know of his life and personality, we know enough of his *message* to make for ourselves a consistent picture' – even though he goes on to say that 'What the sources offer us is first of all the message of the early Christian community, which for the most part the Church freely attributed to Jesus'.[67] The difference between him and Käsemann centred on the dogmatic question concerning the relation between faith and evidence, rather than on any difference in method. The approach adopted by those who initiated what came to be called 'the new quest for the historical Jesus' was very much within the form-critical tradition.

In advocating his approach, Käsemann set out his basic criterion for establishing the authentic teaching of Jesus, which was later dubbed 'the criterion of double dissimilarity': 'In only one case do we have more or less safe ground under our feet; when there are no grounds either for deriving a tradition from Judaism or for ascribing it to primitive Christianity'.[68] He had in fact taken this over from Bultmann himself, who had written:

> We can only count on possessing a genuine similitude of Jesus where, on the one hand, expression is given to the contrast between Jewish morality and piety and the distinctive eschatological temper which characterized the preaching of Jesus; and where on the other hand we find no specifically Christian features.[69]

The focus of investigation was now the teaching of Jesus, and various criteria were applied in the attempt to isolate what was 'authentic'. In addition to the criterion of dissimilarity, there was the criterion of coherence or consistency, which meant that sayings which were thought to agree with other material regarded as authentic could also be treated as genuine. The objections to these criteria are now so well-known that it seems unnecessary to spell them out.[70]

---

[65] Günther Bornkamm, *Jesus of Nazareth*, trans. Irene and Fraser McLuskey with James M. Robinson (London: Hodder & Stoughton, 1960), 9.
[66] Bornkamm, *Jesus*, 22.
[67] Bultmann, *Jesus and the Word*, 12.
[68] Käsemann, *Essays*, 37.
[69] Rudolf Bultmann, *The History of the Synoptic Tradition*, trans. John Marsh (Oxford: Blackwell, 1963), 205.
[70] See Morna D. Hooker, 'Christology and Methodology', *NTS* 17 (1971): 480–487 = above, essay 2 (pp. 29–37); Morna D. Hooker, 'On Using the Wrong Tool', *Theology* 75 (1972): 570–581 = above, essay 3 (pp. 38–49); R.S. Barbour, *Traditio-Historical Criticism of the Gospels* (London: SPCK, 1972); Tom Holmén, 'Doubts about Double Dissimilarity: Restructuring the Main Criterion of Jesus-of-history Research', in *Authenticating the Words of Jesus*,

The criterion of multiple attestation, on the other hand, sometimes viewed with suspicion,[71] rested on firmer ground.

Assessments of the teaching of Jesus based on the criteria of dissimilarity and coherence inevitably tended to be negative. The 'burden of proof' was assumed to rest on those who wished to argue for a saying's authenticity. Only so, it was argued, could one be sure that one was not distorting the teaching of Jesus by attributing to him the words and thoughts of others. The 'distinctive' teaching of Jesus was assumed to be that which was unique to him. But the method distorted the teaching in another way, by excluding genuine sayings. If these criteria were to be rigorously applied, then the majority of sayings attributed to Jesus by the evangelists would be excluded; by removing anything which seems to echo Jewish beliefs or foreshadow the faith of the early church, one is left with a Jesus who said little of note and who had no links with past or future. Such a figure is a far cry indeed from the Jesus whom T.W. Manson had insisted must be seen in the context of Jewish beliefs and the faith of the church.

In practice, the criteria were rarely rigorously applied, but were tempered by the beliefs of those who applied them! But the negative approach which they engendered influenced much of New Testament study in the third quarter of the twentieth century, both in Germany and America. The criterion of dissimilarity was endorsed even by the more conservative Joachim Jeremias, although he was aware of its weaknesses, and in practice made little use of it, while fulfilling his promise to 'keep it in mind'.[72] Like Manson, Jeremias stressed Jesus' Jewish setting, and argued that many of his sayings reflected the language and style of Aramaic, and so could be regarded as reliable. Unfortunately, as others were to point out, Jesus was not the only one to speak in Aramaic in the first century CE! Jeremias also brought together the imminent eschatology of Schweitzer and the realized eschatology of Dodd, arguing that Jesus' proclamation of the kingdom of God reflects an 'eschatology in the process of being realized'. In this, too, he was close to Manson. In Scandinavia, meanwhile, scholars such as Birger Gerhardsson were arguing that the disciples would have learnt the teaching of Jesus by heart, as was customary when taught by a rabbi, and that it was therefore possible to hear the authentic voice of Jesus in the sayings recorded by the evangelists.[73]

---

eds. Bruce Chilton and Craig A. Evans, New Testament Tools and Studies 28/1 (Leiden: Brill, 1999), 47–80.

[71] Perrin, *Rediscovering*, 46.

[72] Joachim Jeremias, *New Testament Theology, Part 1: The Proclamation of Jesus*, trans. John Bowden (London: SCM Press, 1971).

[73] Birger Gerhardsson, *Memory and Manuscript: Oral Tradition and Written Transmission in Rabbinic Judaism and Early Christianity* (Lund: Gleerup, 1961).

The focus of attention had shifted, however, to the christological 'titles' of Jesus – above all to 'the Son of man', the title which Manson had argued was not a title at all, but rather the description of a role, and one which possibly had a collective dimension. Few, however, followed Manson's lead.[74] In Germany, H. E. Tödt[75] and Ferdinand Hahn[76] argued (as had Bultmann) that Jesus had spoken of the future eschatological judge as 'the Son of man', and that the church had identified him with this figure.

Meanwhile, Ernst Fuchs was suggesting that we need to look at Jesus' *conduct* as 'the real framework of his proclamation', arguing that 'This conduct is neither that of a prophet nor of a teacher of wisdom, but that of a man who dares to act in God's stead'.[77] In England, S. G. F. Brandon was arguing that Jesus had to be seen in terms of his political setting, and had been a Zealot sympathizer who was expecting the coming kingdom of God to overthrow Roman authority over Palestine.[78] He, too, was trying to see Jesus in his Jewish context, although his conclusions won few followers.

5. Changes in Method and Perspective

Critical work on the Gospels in the twentieth century had so far gone hand in hand with the search for the real Jesus. The theory of Marcan priority, which had won widespread acceptance in the nineteenth century, had led in turn to the formulation of the four-document hypothesis. The work of source critics such as Streeter had been largely motivated by the desire to establish which sources were closest to Jesus.[79] It was on this foundation that Manson had done his work. Form criticism might seem to have nothing to

---

[74] Among the exceptions are Morna D. Hooker, *The Son of Man in Mark* (London: SPCK, 1967); Morna D. Hooker, 'Is the Son of Man Problem Really Insoluble?', in *Text and Interpretation: Studies in the New Testament Presented to Matthew Black*, eds. Ernest Best and R.McL. Wilson (Cambridge: Cambridge University Press, 1979), 155–168 = below, essay 6 (pp. 90–102); C. F. D. Moule, *The Origin of Christology* (Cambridge: Cambridge University Press, 1977), 11–22.

[75] Tödt, *The Son of Man in the Synoptic Tradition*.

[76] Hahn, *The Titles of Jesus in Christology*.

[77] Ernst Fuchs, *Studies of the Historical Jesus*, trans. Andrew Scobie, SBT 42 (London: SCM Press, 1964), 22.

[78] S. G. F. Brandon, *Jesus and the Zealots: A Study of the Political Factor in Primitive Christianity* (Manchester: Manchester University Press, 1967).

[79] A fascinating recent example of such motivation is found in the work of William R. Farmer, who became a passionate supporter of the hypothesis that Matthew was the earliest Gospel, and that Mark had used Matthew and Luke. In his book *The Gospel of Jesus: The Pastoral Relevance of the Synoptic Problem* (Louisville: Westminster/John Knox, 1994), he revealed that his real concern was to establish as historical a Jesus who spoke of the atoning efficacy of his death in terms of Isaiah 53 – a Jesus who was, he believed, to be found most clearly in the Gospel of Matthew.

do with 'the historical Jesus' for, as Manson had rightly said, it was concerned with the literary form of the material, and not with its origin: in spite of the claims made for it, it could, in itself, tell one nothing about the reliability of the material or its 'pre-history'. But the form critics asked questions about the *Sitz im Leben*, and that inevitably led to the issue of authenticity. For some scholars, form criticism underlined the futility of the search for the historical Jesus, and its results were thus negative. Yet form criticism was used by those who wanted to recover the 'authentic' teaching of Jesus, as well as by those who were concerned to demonstrate that the tradition as it is preserved in the Gospels originated in the early church. For some, mostly in Germany and America, enquiry into the *Sitz im Leben* meant that one could ask only about how the material was used by the community: questions about Jesus himself were either off-bounds or led to largely negative results. For others, such as Jeremias, Dodd and Vincent Taylor, questions about the *Sitz im Leben* could be usefully employed in the attempt to establish the teaching of Jesus himself. For them all, however, enquiry into the *Sitz im Leben* was of lasting importance. For it was the realization that material *used* by the community would also have been *shaped* by it which subtly altered the way in which scholars came to view the evidence. There was now a recognition that 'fact' and 'interpretation' were fused together, and that it was impossible to prise them apart. The so-called 'Jesus of history' could not be detached from the 'Christ of faith'.

The next development in Gospel criticism, however – redaction criticism – shifted the spotlight away from the 'historical' Jesus and on to the evangelists and their *understanding* of Jesus. This brought a realization that the possibility of knowing anything about the historical Jesus was even less than had been hitherto recognized. The tradition had not only been used and shaped by the early community but had been selected and arranged by the evangelists to bring out their own particular theological understanding of him. Despairing of discovering Jesus, scholars sought to understand the evangelists instead – only to be brought back, full circle, to the importance of knowing which of the evangelists had written first, and which had built on his work. Source criticism was once again of vital importance if we were to understand the teaching of the evangelists, let alone of Jesus himself.

Remarkably, by the end of the twentieth century, research into the figure of Jesus surged. Books on Jesus poured from the presses – especially those of North America. The change has been so remarkable that some have dubbed it 'the third quest'. Such labels are not entirely helpful; here, too, there is more continuity between the various phases of investigation than one might suppose.

What was it that sparked this enormous interest in the figure of Jesus? It seems that it arose out of the conviction that there was more continuity between Judaism and Jesus, and between Jesus and the church, than had been supposed by some scholars. In other words, the two links that so many critics had been endeavouring to cut, in an attempt to discover the 'authentic' teaching of Jesus, were of utmost importance! To understand Jesus, one had to see him in the context of the Jewish world into which he was born; to understand the church, one had to comprehend how Jesus' words and actions could have led to the beliefs that first-century Christians came to hold about him. Unwittingly, scholars were now emphasizing precisely the points that had been made by T.W. Manson in his article on the life of Jesus in *The Expository Times* in 1942.

One of the contributory factors towards the rediscovery of first-century Judaism was undoubtedly the discovery of the Dead Sea Scrolls at Qumran, which provided new insights into the world in which Jesus lived. The work of scholars such as David Daube, W.D. Davies and Martin Hengel brought a new awareness of the importance of understanding Jesus in his Jewish setting, as did the new edition of Schürer.[80] As for Jesus himself, the work of Geza Vermes in England had done much to re-establish his Jewish identity.[81]

At the same time, scholars became aware that it was necessary to explain how the early Christian community came to worship Christ and to acknowledge him as Lord. There had been much debate about the relation between 'history' and 'faith'. Was Bultmann right to say that faith must not depend on historical evidence? Were his students right to insist that faith demanded historical enquiry? Certainly there was a historical issue to be settled, for there was a need to explain *why* and *how* the church had come to believe. Thus E.P. Sanders, who set Jesus firmly within the context of first-century Judaism, spoke also of searching for 'a thread which connects Jesus' own intention, his death and the rise of the movement', and claimed to have 'found a specific chain of conceptions and events which allows us to understand historically how things came about'.[82] Unlike many, Sanders begins not with the teaching of Jesus but – picking up Fuchs' suggestion – with his behaviour and actions: among the 'bedrock' of known facts about Jesus are his activity as a healer and the controversy regarding the temple.[83] In marked contrast to Bultmann's pessimistic comment that we can know almost nothing about Jesus, he writes: 'The dominant view today seems to be that we can know pretty well what Jesus was out to accomplish, that we can know a lot

---

[80] Emil Schürer, *The History of the Jewish People in the Age of Jesus Christ (175 BC–AD 135)*, eds. Geza Vermes and Fergus Millar, 3 vols. (Edinburgh: T&T Clark, 1973–1987).

[81] Geza Vermes, *Jesus the Jew* (London: Collins, 1973); *Jesus and the World of Judaism* (London: SCM Press, 1983); and *The Religion of Jesus the Jew* (London: SCM Press, 1993).

[82] E.P. Sanders, *Jesus and Judaism* (London: SCM Press, 1985), 334.

[83] For the importance of Jesus' actions see also Morna D. Hooker, *The Signs of a Prophet* (London: SCM Press, 1997).

about what he said, and that those two things make sense within the world of first-century Judaism'.[84]

It is significant that the majority of recent books on Jesus have taken seriously the question of the context in which Jesus lived. Anthony Harvey, for example,[85] asked questions about the political, religious, and social constraints which Jesus would have experienced, and the options that would have been open to him. Ben Meyer[86] attempted 'to understand the Jesus of ancient Palestine'.[87] John P. Meier revealed his hand in the title of his massive three-volume work, *A Marginal Jew*.[88] Dominic Crossan looked further afield to try to understand the world in which Jesus lived:[89] Jesus emerged as a Jewish Cynic, an interpretation close to one that had already been argued by Downing[90] and Mack.[91] For them, Jesus is very much on the borders of Judaism – as he is, too, for the members of the 'Jesus Seminar', still attempting to establish what Jesus said by using discredited criteria, and producing a very strange portrait of Jesus as a result.

For the great majority of scholars, however, Jesus is not a Cynic or a teacher of wisdom, but is to be understood as a Jew, who continues in either the prophetic or the apocalyptic tradition. In this (if not in everything!) Tom Wright is typical: 'If he belongs anywhere in history, it is within the history of first-century Judaism'.[92] The origins of the Christian movement – and so of Jesus himself – are now seen as being within Judaism.[93]

With Jesus firmly embedded within the context of Judaism, the question of continuity – or lack of it – between Jesus and the faith of the church also needs to be addressed. If *both* links are to be maintained, then it is necessary to show a line of development from Judaism, through Jesus, to the church.[94] This was also, as we have seen already, one of the points stressed by Sanders: Jesus

---

[84] Sanders, *Jesus*, 2.

[85] A.E. Harvey, *Jesus and the Constraints of History* (London: Duckworth, 1982).

[86] Ben F. Meyer, *The Aims of Jesus* (London: SCM Press, 1979).

[87] Meyer, *Aims*, 19.

[88] John P. Meier, *A Marginal Jew*, 3 vols. (New York: Doubleday, 1991, 1994, 2001).

[89] John Dominic Crossan, *The Historical Jesus: The Life of a Mediterranean Jewish Peasant* (Edinburgh: T&T Clark, 1991).

[90] F. Gerald Downing, *Jesus and the Threat of Freedom* (London: SCM Press, 1987); F. Gerald Downing, *Christ and the Cynics* (Sheffield: JSOT Press, 1988).

[91] Burton L. Mack, *A Myth of Innocence: Mark and Christian Origins* (Philadelphia: Fortress Press, 1988).

[92] N.T. Wright, *Jesus and the Victory of God* (London: SPCK, 1996), 91.

[93] See, for example, Christopher Rowland, *Christian Origins: An Account of the Setting and Character of the Most Important Messianic Sect of Judaism*, 2nd ed. (London: SPCK, 2002).

[94] For attempts to explain this development see William Horbury, *Jewish Messianism and the Cult of Christ* (London: SCM Press, 1998), and Larry W. Hurtado, *Lord Jesus Christ: Devotion to Jesus in Earliest Christianity* (Grand Rapids: Eerdmans, 2003). The line of continuity is an underlying assumption for Gerd Theissen's sociological study, *A Theory of Primitive Christian Religion* (London: SCM Press, 1999).

had to be understood in relation to the church's faith, as well as in relation to Judaism. The question of the relationship between Jesus himself and the faith of the church is once again a matter of historical investigation.

6. Summary

We have not attempted, in this article, to survey the whole course of the 'quest' (or 'quests')[95] of Jesus over the past century. Not only would it be impossible to do so adequately within the confines of this journal, but there are many other surveys available.[96] Rather, we have attempted to show how some of Manson's insights are relevant to the ongoing question, and how they have been in turn ignored, then vindicated, by the work of later scholars.

Manson was a man of his time. One would have no desire to adopt his methods and presuppositions today. But his work is of more than antiquarian interest, for some of his underlying assumptions are certainly relevant today. His conviction that 'the characteristic features of the teaching of Jesus can be linked up with the Old Testament on one side and with the Church on the other. ... in order to see the full bearing of the fragments of evidence about the ministry, we must learn to see them in their Jewish and Christian context'[97] could hardly be more topical. It was unfortunate that scholars of the generation after Manson lost sight of what today seems an obvious truth.

In some ways, Manson was ahead of his time. In *The Teaching of Jesus* he comments: 'We are so accustomed, and rightly, to make Jesus the object of religion that we become apt to forget that in our earliest records he is portrayed not as the object of religion but as a religious man'.[98] In his survey of the teaching of Jesus, he lists the 'contents' of that teaching as being 'God as father' and 'God as king', with a final chapter on 'Religion and morals'. The focus of this teaching is God – certainly not Jesus' own person. His understanding of the term 'the Son of man' also deflects attention away from Jesus himself. Manson was not concerned, as were so many scholars of his generation, with trying to recover the 'Messianic self-consciousness of Jesus', but rather with discovering his understanding of Israel's calling, and how it might be fulfilled. Many today, although not adopting Manson's theory

---

[95] Clive Marsh ('Quests of the Historical Jesus in New Historicist Perspective', *Biblical Interpretation* 5 [1997]: 403–437) identifies nine quests!

[96] See, for example, Bruce Chilton and Craig A. Evans, eds. *Studying the Historical Jesus: Evaluations of the State of Current Research*, New Testament Tools and Studies 19 (Leiden: Brill, 1994); Craig A. Evans, *Life of Jesus Research: An Annotated Bibliography*, rev. ed., New Testament Tools and Studies 24 (Leiden: Brill, 1996); Markus Bockmuehl, ed. *The Cambridge Companion to Jesus* (Cambridge: Cambridge University Press, 2001).

[97] Manson, 'Is it Possible?', 250b.

[98] Manson, *Teaching*, 101.

regarding the Son of man, would agree that this is a more appropriate way to evaluate the evidence.

A century after Martin Kähler pronounced the quest for the historical Jesus to be over, scholars continue to ask questions about him. But there is now a recognition that the real Jesus is to be found, not in any historical reconstruction, but in what we make of him. Manson the pastor would surely approve of that conclusion.

6. Is the Son of Man Problem Really Insoluble?

Many years ago, Principal Black, hearing that I was working on the problem of the meaning of the phrase 'the Son of man', sought to deter me by issuing the simple warning: 'Don't!' I hope it will not seem inappropriate if, in spite of his warning, I now offer to him yet another article on this hoary problem. For in an earlier volume of essays published in his honour there appeared an article by A.J.B. Higgins entitled 'Is the Son of Man Problem Insoluble?'[1] which took issue with my own 'solution' to the problem.[2] Perhaps I may be forgiven, then, for failing once again to heed Principal Black's advice, and returning to a question which he, too, has found irresistible.

'Who is this Son of man?' The most popular answer to this ancient question has been, in recent years, that he is an eschatological figure expected by Jesus as the vindicator of his message and mission, with whom he himself, after his death and resurrection, was identified by the early church.[3] This widely held belief is based upon three assumptions, all of which have recently come under attack.

Firstly, this interpretation of the evidence depends upon the conviction that there was already in existence, at the time of Jesus, a Jewish expectation of a heavenly Son of man. It has been widely assumed that this belief was a commonplace of first-century Judaism, but the evidence for it is flimsy in the extreme; it is drawn mainly from the Gospels themselves (which offer us primarily a Christian reinterpretation of the phrase), from a messianic interpretation of the passage in Daniel 7 which disagrees with the author's own interpretation of it, and above all from chapters 37–71 of 1 Enoch, whose early dating is becoming more and more unlikely.[4] Although it

---

[1] A.J.B. Higgins, 'Is the Son of Man Problem Insoluble?', in *Neotestamentica et Semitica: Studies in Honour of Matthew Black,* eds. E. Earle Ellis and Max Wilcox (Edinburgh: T&T Clark, 1969), 70–87.

[2] Morna D. Hooker, *The Son of Man in Mark* (London: SPCK, 1967).

[3] Among many presentations of this view, see e.g. John Knox, *The Death of Christ: The Cross in New Testament History and Faith* (London: Collins, 1959), 52–125; H.E. Tödt, *The Son of Man in the Synoptic Tradition,* trans. Dorothea M. Barton (London: SCM Press, 1965); Ferdinand Hahn, *The Titles of Jesus in Christology,* trans. Harold Knight and George Ogg (London: Lutterworth Press, 1969), 15–53.

[4] See most recently, *The Books of Enoch,* edited by J.T. Milik with the collaboration of Matthew Black (Oxford: Clarendon Press, 1976), 89–98; Milik places the Similitudes very late, at the end of the third century CE. Cf. also J.C. Hindley, 'Towards a Date for the Similitudes of Enoch. An Historical Approach', *NTS* 14 (1968): 551–565, who suggests the early second century CE. In a private communication, Dr Michael A. Knibb (editor of *The Ethiopic Book of*

seems probable that Daniel's vision was increasingly interpreted in terms of an individual 'messianic' figure, this is a long way from the suggestion that there was a widely-held expectation of a glorious, heavenly Son of man in first-century Judaism.[5]

Secondly, the idea that Jesus proclaimed a coming Son of man rests upon the assumption that he made no messianic claims for himself: sayings about the future role of the Son of man, therefore, if they are authentic, must refer to someone else. Some scholars have, of course, challenged the basic assumption that Jesus made no messianic claims. More significant for our present discussion, however, is the fact that the argument rests on the assumption that 'the Son of man' was a messianic title. If the phrase was not, after all, a messianic title, then its use by Jesus as a self-designation may well have been appropriate.

Thirdly, this theory is based upon what Dr Higgins described as 'the results of traditio-historical study, according to which the only authentic sayings are to be found among those referring to the eschatological functions of the Son of man'.[6] These 'results', however, are based upon the previous two premises, and if these prove to be uncertain, so is the conclusion that only 'eschatological' sayings can be authentic.

In spite of its popularity, therefore, this solution has little firm evidence to support it. Moreover, it raises many problems: what was Jesus' understanding of his own function if he expected another figure in the future, and what was the relation between them? What is the relation between the coming Son of man and the kingdom of God, which Jesus also (separately) announced? Why did the church invent 'Son of man' sayings which are totally different from those 'eschatological' sayings in their understanding of the function of the Son of man?

It is, perhaps, not surprising if the rival theory set out by Dr Vermes in an appendix to the third edition of Principal Black's book *An Aramaic Approach to the Gospels and Acts*[7] has recently been gathering support. Dr Vermes argued that the Aramaic phrase *bar nāsh(ā)* could be used in first-century Palestinian Aramaic not only to mean 'a human being' and 'someone' but also as a circumlocution for 'I'. Some scholars have taken issue with Dr Vermes

---

Enoch [Oxford: Clarendon Press, 1978]) tells me that he is inclined to date the Similitudes at the end of the first century CE.

[5] Ragnar Leivestad, 'Exit the Apocalyptic Son of Man', *NTS* 18 (1972): 243–267; Morna D. Hooker, *The Son of Man in Mark*, 11–74; Norman Perrin, *Rediscovering the Teaching of Jesus* (London: SCM Press, 1967), 164–173; Maurice Casey, 'The Use of the Term "Son of Man" in the Similitudes of Enoch', *Journal for the Study of Judaism in the Persian, Hellenistic and Roman Period* 7 (1976): 11–29.

[6] Higgins, 'Is the Son of Man Problem Insoluble?', 79.

[7] Matthew Black, *An Aramaic Approach to the Gospels and Acts* (Oxford: Clarendon Press, 1967), 310–328. See also Geza Vermes, *Jesus the Jew* (London: Collins, 1973).

over the question of the date of the relevant material.⁸ Even if we allow that his examples provide fair evidence for the time of Jesus, however, it is questionable whether, in the passages which he quotes, the phrase is really being used in place of the pronoun 'I', since in every case it would be more natural to substitute 'one' or 'a man'; the examples which he gives are in fact general statements which could refer to any man but which happen to refer to the speaker because he is known to be in the particular circumstances described.

Now this does not mean, of course, that the suggestion that Jesus used the phrase in accordance with this idiom must therefore be excluded: indeed, it has recently been argued that it is precisely this general application of the term which explains its use by Jesus.⁹ Dr Vermes' solution runs into several difficulties, however. Firstly, we must explain how the phrase came to be carefully preserved in the oral tradition, mistranslated into Greek, and then misunderstood to the extent that wholly inappropriate sayings (this time the eschatological ones) were created around it. If the phrase was a common expression for 'I' in Aramaic, then the use of the barbaric Greek phrase ὁ υἱὸς τοῦ ἀνθρώπου seems an inexplicable blunder; the fact that it was thought necessary to use this translationese suggests that there was already something a little unusual and special about the Aramaic phrase, even in an Aramaic-speaking community.

Secondly, if the phrase is simply a circumlocution for 'I', then the only sayings which can be accepted as original are presumably those which refer to his experiences of suffering and deprivation, such as Mark 8:31 and its parallels and Matt 8:20 (// Luke 9:58); taken in this sense, the phrase offers no explanation for claims to authority or hopes of future glory.¹⁰ Nor is there anything in the phrase to explain the note of necessity which characterizes the passion predictions, and this must be understood as part of the interpretation which has been introduced after the event. In other words, the original core of sayings is reduced to little more than 'the Son of man has nowhere to

---

⁸ E.g. Joseph A. Fitzmyer in a review of Matthew Black's book in *CBQ* 30 (1968): 426ff. Vermes cites material from the Palestinian Pentateuch Targum, the Palestinian Talmud and Genesis Rabba.

⁹ P. Maurice Casey, 'The Son of Man Problem', *ZNW* 67 (1976): 147–154, who suggests that the sayings have two levels of meaning – the general statement and the statement about the speaker in particular. He lists twelve authentic sayings: Mark 2:10, 28; Matt 8:20 (// Luke 9:58); Matt 11:19 (// Luke 7:34); Matt 12:32 (// Luke 12:10); Luke 22:48; Mark 10:45; 14:21a and b; Luke 12:8; Mark 8:38; Mark 8:31 (9:31; 10:33ff.).

¹⁰ Vermes comments on the contexts where he argues for the circumlocutional use of *bar nāsh(ā)* as follows: 'In most instances the sentence contains an allusion to humiliation, danger, or death, but there are also examples where reference to the self in the third person is dictated by humility or modesty' (in Black, *An Aramaic Approach to the Gospels and Acts,* 327). It might perhaps be argued that Jesus used the term for motives of modesty in speaking of power and glory, but this would not explain why he felt entitled to make such extraordinary claims to authority and honour.

lay his head' and 'the Son of man expects to suffer'. This seems an insufficient explanation of the way in which the phrase came to be regarded as Jesus' characteristic self-designation, and a slender basis on which so many other Son of man sayings came to be built.

If, on the other hand, these sayings about suffering and death are understood as general statements about mankind which apply to Jesus in particular, then either they are manifestly untrue ('a man has nowhere to lay his head') or they are so obvious as to be trite ('a man must die').

The understanding of the phrase as a simple periphrasis for 'I' fails, therefore, to explain why it should appear in the particular contexts where it is found, or be remembered as in any way distinctive of Jesus' speech. Nevertheless, Dr Vermes' evidence is important in demonstrating that the phrase was unlikely to have been understood by Jesus' hearers as a messianic title, and in suggesting that it would have been possible for him to use this phrase to refer to himself in contexts where this application was clear. His arguments therefore add strength to the view that there was no expectation of an eschatological Son of man in first-century Palestine, and that Christians were misled by the literal Greek translation into assuming that it had been used by Jesus as a title. What still needs to be explained is why Jesus should have chosen to use this particular phrase (which, *pace* Dr Vermes, seems to have been rare, if not unknown, as a self-designation at this period) and whether he attached to it any particular meaning which might explain why it occurs in such varied sayings in the tradition.

A final piece of evidence which demonstrates how unlikely it is that the term 'the Son of man' was in use as a messianic title in first-century Judaism is the way in which the early church failed to employ it as a title for Jesus. It is true that some at least of the Son of man sayings must have been created in the Christian community; but all of them are placed in the mouth of Jesus, and there is no evidence that 'the Son of man' was used (as were 'Lord' and 'Christ') as a title to refer to Jesus. However much significance may have been poured into the phrase, it continued to be understood as a self-designation of Jesus, and was not taken over as a living messianic title by the community.

These two rival interpretations of the phrase 'the Son of man' in the Gospels, one taking it as a messianic title, the other as a modest self-designation, appear to be incompatible. But since each of them succeeds in offering a satisfactory explanation of only half the evidence, it is arguable that their insights are complementary. The phrase cannot be a messianic title – yet the theory which interprets it as such at least offers a reason for its use; the view that it was an acceptable self-designation offers a possible explanation as to *how* Jesus could have used it of himself – but fails to explain *why* he should have employed a colourless phrase which has no particular function. Each theory is able to offer an interpretation of only part of the evidence: those who hold the messianic interpretation have to explain all but the eschatological sayings as the result of a misunderstanding in the Christian community, while Dr Vermes' interpretation reverses this procedure, and it is the eschatological sayings which are seen as the product of misunderstanding.

These two diametrically opposed approaches thus highlight the basic problem of the Son of man passages in the Gospels – namely, the apparent incompatibility of the various types of Son of man sayings found there. All explanations of the term have to solve the problem of the relationship between present and future sayings, and the tendency in recent scholarship has been to abandon attempts to reconcile them and to jettison one group as unauthentic. Yet the juxtaposition of ideas which seem to twentieth-century scholars incompatible may itself be the key to the problem: is it perhaps the phrase 'the Son of man' itself which links together these disparate ideas?

I have argued previously that the division of the sayings into different groups, though sometimes convenient, can be a misleading exercise.[11] It is worth noting also that the labels which are given to these groups of sayings can be equally misleading. A saying such as Mark 8:31, e.g. is commonly described as 'a prediction of the passion' or 'a suffering saying'. Yet this is to give the saying a particular slant by emphasizing only part of it: certainly the suffering is described in more detail than the resurrection, but it would be more accurate to label the saying as 'a prediction of death and resurrection' than as 'a passion prediction'. The details of the passion which have been included in these sayings are likely to have been added *ex eventu*; the idea that the sayings are primarily 'passion predictions' is perhaps due to the use which Mark has made of them, as pointers towards the death of Jesus. In themselves, however, they are predictions of resurrection as well as of death, of vindication as well as of suffering.

Similarly, it is worthy of note that all the 'eschatological' sayings in Mark occur in contexts which refer to suffering, and ought therefore to be described as promises of vindication rather than as prophecies of the parousia of the Son of man.[12] Just as the 'passion predictions' combine the ideas of death and resurrection, so these 'eschatological' sayings hold together the persecution which belongs to the present era and the glorious vindication of the future.

It could be argued, of course, that the context of these sayings is due to Mark, just as it has been argued that the passion predictions are creations of Mark. The other 'eschatological' sayings in Matthew and Luke are not found in this kind of context – indeed, as will be noted presently, their whole emphasis is somewhat different. However, the linking together of suffering

---

[11] Hooker, *The Son of Man in Mark*, 80.
[12] Hooker, *The Son of Man in Mark*, 180 ff.

and exaltation is found elsewhere in the New Testament tradition about the Son of man – to such an extent, indeed, that Matthew Black has suggested that the oldest stratum of the Son of man tradition may have referred to rejection and exaltation, rather than to death and resurrection.[13] In addition to the Johannine sayings (where the two ideas are combined by the play on the words 'glory' and 'lift up') and the one reference to the Son of man outside the Gospels at Acts 7:56, he lists the quotation from Ps 8 in Heb 2 (where the argument points the contrast between humiliation and glory) and Phil 2, which he considers to be dependent on tradition about the Son of man. If this is correct, it would be in accord not only with the vision of the one like a son of man in Dan 7, where a promise of future vindication is set in the context of the persecution presently being experienced by the author's readers, but with the wider background in Judaism of confident expectation that the suffering and righteous within Israel will be vindicated in the coming judgement.[14] It is therefore arguable that the central problem of the Son of man sayings – the incompatibility of the 'suffering' and 'eschatological' sayings – is an unreal one, and results from emphasizing one element in each saying at the expense of another, as well as one group of sayings over against the other. If this is so, however, it is a process which has already been begun by the evangelists. If they include different selections of sayings about the Son of man, this process is likely to reflect their different interests and purposes; the extent to which each has created sayings or merely chosen them remains, of course, debatable.

Because Mark's references to the death and resurrection of the Son of man have no real parallels in non-Marcan material, it has often been suggested that they are Marcan creations. The standard response to this argument, that such prophecies have a place only in a 'Gospel', and not in a collection of Jesus' sayings, may well receive support from redactional critical work on the Gospels. If Mark is responsible for the inclusion of these sayings it is because for him the death of Jesus is central; whether because he is concerned to answer the question 'Why did the Messiah die?' or because he is anxious to encourage Christians facing persecution or because he is trying to correct the beliefs of those for whom he writes, these sayings are relevant to his theme. Unless it can be shown that the remaining New Testament evidence for the Son of man's humiliation-exaltation is based solely upon Mark, it seems unlikely that the idea is a Marcan creation, though the emphasis on this particular theme may be due to his interests.

---

[13] Matthew Black, 'The Son of Man Problem in Recent Research and Debate', *BJRL* 45 (1963): 305–318.

[14] See the discussion in Eduard Schweizer, *Lordship and Discipleship* (London: SCM Press, 1960), 22–31.

Attention has less often been concentrated on the character of those sayings which are found in Matthew and Luke but not in Mark. Matthew takes over all the Marcan sayings, and Luke the great majority, but each of them uses in addition a considerable number of non-Marcan sayings. Those which speak of the suffering of the Son of man[15] are similar to the Marcan sayings and are usually held to be editorial.[16] The great increase is in sayings which refer to the future role of the Son of man. Examination of these sayings shows that, almost without exception, they refer explicitly to this role as one of judgement; even the exceptions occur in passages which are concerned with judgement.[17] This feature does not normally excite comment, since it is widely assumed that judgement is the obvious characteristic of the Son of man. Yet it is remarkable that the role of judge is never predicated of the Son of man in Mark. The closest that any of the Marcan sayings comes to ascribing this role to the Son of man is Mark 8:38, where it is said that he will be ashamed of those who have been ashamed of following Jesus; the scene depicted here is one in which the Son of man acknowledges Jesus' disciples and recognizes those who make up the elect community. It is possible that Mark understands the role of the Son of man to be that of judge, but the language is more appropriate if the Son of man is understood to be acknowledging his own before the judgement throne of God.[18] The role of witness is made explicit in the parallel saying in Q where the Son of man acknowledges or denies men before the angels of God;[19] the Q form of the saying is probably more original than the one found in Mark 8:38,[20] but in both Matt 10 and Luke 12 it has been set in a context of future judgement, which suggests a shift of emphasis in its interpretation.[21] A similar shift is seen in the Matthean version of Mark 8:38, which adds the words 'he will requite each according to what he has done'[22] to the Marcan saying, and so indicates

---

[15] Matt 26:2; Luke 17:25; 22:48; 24:7.

[16] E.g. by A.J.B. Higgins, *Jesus and the Son of Man* (London: Lutterworth, 1964), 78–82, 99 ff.

[17] The sayings occur in Matt 10:23; 13:41; 16:28; 19:28; 24:30, 39; 25:31; Luke 17:22, 30; 18:8; 21:36; Matt 10:32 (// Luke 12:8); Matt 12:40 (// Luke 11:30); Matt 24:27, 37, 44 (// Luke 17:24, 26; 12:40).

[18] It is possible that the 'coming' in 8:38 is understood by Mark as a coming to God, though the phrase 'in the glory of his Father' suggests that he is thinking of a coming to earth (to gather those who belong to him). See the discussion in John A.T. Robinson, *Jesus and His Coming: The Emergence of a Doctrine* (London: SCM Press, 1957), 53–56.

[19] Luke 12:8 ff. Luke's version of this saying, with its reference to the Son of man and the angels of God, is more likely to be original than that found in Matt 10:32 ff., which uses 'I' and 'my Father'.

[20] Cf. T. Francis Glasson, *The Second Advent*, 3rd ed. (London: Epworth Press, 1963), 68.

[21] Hahn assumes that Luke 12:8 ff. 'refers to the function of the Son of man as judge' (*The Titles of Jesus*, 33), but Tödt is surely correct when he says that in this passage 'the Son of Man does not appear as a judge, but as the guarantor' (*The Son of Man in the Synoptic Tradition*, 56).

[22] A quotation from Ps 62:12 (LXX 61:13).

that the Son of man himself is understood to be the judge; it is significant that Matthew also changes Mark's 'the kingdom of God coming in power' in the following verse to 'the Son of man coming in his kingdom' (Matt 16:28).

The Son of man also appears in the role of head of the elect community in Mark 13:26, where he is again said to come in power and glory: he sends angels throughout the world to gather the elect. It is natural for us to interpret this as a judgement scene – but nothing is in fact said about the Son of man as judge. Insofar as the theme of judgement is present in Mark 13 at all, it appears in the description of the disasters which are going to come upon the world before the appearance of the Son of man.[23] The coming of the Son of man is the climax of the chapter – but it is described as a promise, and not as a threat; those who endure suffering and persecution as followers of Jesus may be confident that finally, when the Son of man appears in power and glory, they will be acknowledged by him and receive a reward. The disciples are to watch – not for fear of impending disaster, but lest they fail to be ready to welcome their master. Once again, it is noticeable that Matthew has altered the significance of the saying about the Son of man; instead of the parable of the absent householder (Mark 13:34–37) he has followed the statement that no one knows the time of the end with a saying comparing the coming of the Son of man to the coming of the flood, a warning that when disaster comes 'one will be taken and one left', and another parable about a householder which is totally different in emphasis from that in Mark, since this time what is unknown is the time of the thief's arrival (Matt 24:37–44); an additional parable then describes the rewards and punishments meted out to his servants by a householder when he returns home unexpectedly (24:45–51). Matthew has extended the time of tribulation, which in Mark belongs to the period before the coming of the Son of man, and has interpreted that coming as itself a judgement on the wicked. Luke, too, has added a section warning his readers to be ready for a final day of judgement, on which they will be called upon to stand before the Son of man (Luke 21:34–36).

The third and final saying in Mark which refers to a future role for the Son of man is that in 14:62. This promises vindication for the Son of man, who will be seen 'at the right hand of power and coming with the clouds of heaven'; the ὄψεσθε suggests that the vindication is imminent – an impression confirmed by Matthew's ἀπ' ἄρτι, and Luke's ἀπὸ τοῦ νῦν. Commentators have tended to assume that the 'coming' of the Son of man means a coming to earth, and Luke's omission of the verb perhaps indicates that he also

---

[23] Once again, it may be asked whether the 'coming' of the Son of man was originally understood, even here, as a coming to earth. It is probable that Mark was thinking of a 'parousia', but the saying could be interpreted as a coming to God, and may have had that significance at an earlier stage, even if Mark has interpreted it in accordance with later understanding.

interpreted it in this way and left it out in order to solve the problem of an unfulfilled prophecy. Remarkably, Matthew has not only retained the phrase about coming with the clouds of heaven but has intensified the problem by adding the words ἀπ' ἄρτι: it seems that he has understood it as parallel to 'sitting at the right hand of power' – another way of speaking of a vindication which is to follow immediately, and which presumably takes place at the resurrection (cf. Matt 28:18). There is no reference in any of the gospels to the idea of judgement, though this may be implied in the sitting at the right hand of God.

To suggest that the theme of the suffering Son of man is a Marcan one is to isolate part of the evidence. It is of course true that the great majority of the sayings about the death and resurrection of the Son of man occur in Mark – though almost all of them are taken over by both the other evangelists, who also make editorial additions; it is also true, however, that almost all the so-called 'eschatological' sayings occur in Matthew and/or Luke, and that the content of these is significantly different from the three Marcan sayings. Whereas the sayings in Mark suggest vindication, the non-Marcan sayings all refer to judgement, and Matthew adapts two of the Marcan sayings to fit this theme.[24]

In asking whether Mark is responsible for the tradition about the suffering Son of man, therefore, we ought also to ask whether he is responsible for this particular emphasis in those 'future' sayings which he has included. The alternative is that the sayings in Matthew and Luke reflect a later development. Has Mark synthesized two different types of sayings about the Son of man (only one of which goes back to Jesus) into a pattern of suffering-exaltation, or have the other evangelists used tradition which stresses and develops the Son of man's future role, and so distorted an original pattern which linked this more closely with the theme of present suffering?

It is perhaps significant that whereas in Mark 14:62 an affirmation is made about the Son of man – namely that he will be seen in power and glory, and so be acknowledged as vindicated by God – many of the sayings used by Matthew and Luke take the status of the Son of man as a given factor: he is assumed to be the judge, and what is at issue is when he will come, and whether men and women will be prepared for his coming. In Mark 14:62 the saying about 'the Son of man' represents the claim about future vindication made by Jesus at the moment of challenge before the high priest; but in the eschatological sayings found in Matthew and Luke and not in Mark, the phrase is understood to be a well-known title (though one that is used only by Jesus of himself), and it is assumed that his authority as the Son of man will be accepted by those who hear his words. If a development has taken

---

[24] In Mark Jesus warns of coming judgement, but does not himself act as judge.

place it seems probable that it is from the understanding of the Son of man as one who expects to be vindicated to the belief that he is the one who will exercise authority in judgement.[25] This is precisely the kind of development which we see taking place between the picture of the one like a son of man in Dan 7 and the Son of man who acts with the authority of God in 1 Enoch.

The beginning of this development can in fact be traced already within the Gospel of Mark itself, as the Son of man is increasingly understood to be the one who vindicates others, and as the time of vindication shifts from an imminent to a more distant future. A comparison of the three so-called 'eschatological' sayings shows that in Mark 14:62 the Son of man himself is to be vindicated – presumably at the resurrection; in Mark 8:38 it is implied that he is to vindicate his followers, and though the original meaning may have been that Jesus expected his disciples to share his suffering and his vindication,[26] Mark's setting of the saying suggests that he has understood it of a subsequent event; just as Jesus suffered and was vindicated, so his followers may expect to suffer and to be vindicated. This timescale is made explicit in Mark 13, where the link between the sufferings of Jesus and of his disciples is seen in the way in which theirs 'conform' to his,[27] but where their sufferings are clearly subsequent to the death and resurrection of Jesus, and their vindication belongs to the distant future.

This kind of development is what we would expect if, as seems probable, sayings of Jesus expressing confidence in a future vindication by God were divided after his death and interpreted, on the one hand in terms of the resurrection, and on the other in terms of a future and final scene of vindication, in which the Son of man came to play a more and more central role.

It is time to return to our original question: if 'the Son of man' was, as Dr Vermes argues, an acceptable (though unusual) circumlocution for 'I' in Aramaic, and if Jesus would therefore have been understood to be referring to himself, why should he have chosen to use this particular phrase? Has the early Christian community totally misunderstood him in supposing that it was intended as a claim to future vindication and authority? Any satisfactory solution to the problem of the Son of man must demonstrate not only why Jesus was thought to be referring to himself but also how the term came to be interpreted as denoting a figure who exercised superhuman authority and who would play a central role in the future as judge.

---

[25] Cf. Eduard Schweizer, 'The Son of Man Again', NTS 9 (1963): 256–261: 'Only in the course of a "re-apocalyptization" of the eschatology of Jesus, in a Jewish-apocalyptic group of the early church, did the decisive witness in the last judgement become the judge himself' (259 ff.).
[26] Cf. C.K. Barrett, *Jesus and the Gospel Tradition* (London: SPCK, 1967), 49–51.
[27] Cf. R.H. Lightfoot, *The Gospel Message of St. Mark* (Oxford: Clarendon Press, 1950), 48–59.

In spite of comparative neglect in recent years, the traditional view that the term refers primarily to Dan 7 still offers a more complete answer to the problem than any other explanation. The following factors support this particular solution:

1. It is clear that Dan 7:13 has influenced many of the Gospel sayings. It is sometimes assumed that any allusion to the Old Testament must necessarily be secondary, but this is an illogical generalization which has transformed a trend in the tradition (to add Old Testament allusions) into a rule (that all such allusions are additions). The reference to Dan 7 certainly belongs to a very early stage of the tradition, and therefore deserves to be considered seriously as original.

2. In Dan 7 the phrase 'one like a son of man' is not a title but a claim to a role and status – a claim which is based on a relationship of obedience to God. There are indications, as we have seen, that in the earliest stratum of the Synoptic tradition also, the phrase signified a role rather than a title.

3. In later Jewish literature, one can see how 'the Son of man', clearly understood as a reference to the passage in Daniel, develops into or towards being understood as a title. The phrase lends itself to the kind of interpretation which we can see developing in the Synoptic tradition.

4. In spite of frequent denials by New Testament scholars that the figure of the 'one like a son of man' in Daniel has any knowledge of suffering, the problem which concerns the author of Dan 7 is that of the suffering of 'the saints of the Most High' who are clearly represented by the man-like figure in the vision. We find in this chapter precisely the theme of suffering-vindication which characterizes the Marcan understanding of the Son of man.

5. The 'one like a son of man' in Dan 7 represents a community and is to be understood as a corporate figure, even though an individual interpretation was given later to the passage when it was understood to refer to the Messiah. It has recently been argued that the corporate interpretation, as well as the messianic, was known in first-century Judaism.[28] The suggestion has often been made that 'the Son of man' in the Gospels is to some extent at least a corporate figure,[29] a view which has received support from Matthew Black.[30] Certainly the Synoptic Son of man – when he does not stand over against

---

[28] Maurice Casey, 'The Corporate Interpretation of "One like a Son of Man" (Dan. VII 13) at the Time of Jesus', *NT* 18 (1976): 167–180. His evidence is particularly interesting in view of the fact that he does not himself argue for a corporate interpretation of the phrase in the Gospels.

[29] Notably by T.W. Manson, in *The Teaching of Jesus*, 2nd ed. (Cambridge: Cambridge University Press, 1935), 211–234 and 'The Son of Man in Daniel, Enoch and the Gospels', *BJRL* 32 (1950): 171–193. Manson's view has never received much support, partly perhaps because he linked it with the idea that one could trace an historical development from corporate to individual in Jesus' use of the term.

[30] See Black, 'The Son of Man Problem'.

mankind as judge – is closely linked with other men, and seems to be understood as the head of a community.

The weakness of the view which links 'the Son of man' in the Gospels with Dan 7 is that it seems a very odd way for Jesus to have spoken of himself. This difficulty has led many to the belief that he must in fact have been referring to someone other than himself. Could Jesus have been referring to himself *and* to Dan 7 when he used this phrase, or do we have to choose between these two views?

In a recent article (one of three which he has contributed to the problem of this term) Maurice Casey[31] has argued that the Ethiopic phrases for 'Son of man' in 1 Enoch are used in exactly the same way as the Aramaic and Hebrew equivalents – i.e. to mean 'man'. The figure referred to, he argues, is not a heavenly one at all, but an exalted man (later identified with Enoch himself); although the phrase 'Son of man' is used in the sense of 'man', it is chosen because of the influence of Dan 7:13 upon the author's thought.

We suggest that in a similar way the phrase 'the Son of man' was chosen by Jesus as a self-designation because of the vital influence of Dan 7 on his thought. The phrase was used in contexts where it was clear that the 'man' referred to was none other than Jesus himself,[32] and the reason why he chose this somewhat unusual way of referring to himself was that the sayings in which it occurs make claims which could not be justified by a simple 'I', since they are based on Jesus' identification with the mission of the people of God, who are symbolized by the 'one like a son of man' in Dan 7. Jesus chose to use this particular Aramaic phrase, not only because it could be understood by his hearers in these particular contexts to refer to himself, but also because it would be understood to point to the Danielic idea of the suffering and vindicated righteous community. As in Daniel, the phrase is better understood as a reference to a role than as a title. At the same time, since it is only the context which can make plain whether *bar nāshā* is to be understood as 'I' rather than as 'man', the sayings are not necessarily to be understood as referring exclusively to Jesus. The Son of man sayings contain a challenge to others to be included and to make a corporate interpretation a reality instead of a possibility.

---

[31] Maurice Casey, 'The Use of the Term "Son of Man" in the Similitudes of Enoch', *Journal for the Study of Judaism in the Persian, Hellenistic and Roman Period* 7 (1976): 11–29. See also n. 9 and n. 28 above.

[32] English readers who remember the radio programme 'Itma' will be familiar with an example of the way in which a neutral phrase ('that man') can be given a special nuance. Every listener to the programme was aware that the statement 'It's that man again' in this particular context must refer to Tommy Handley: the phrase 'that man' was therefore transformed by its associations into something approximating to a title.

In 1 Enoch the Ethiopic phrases are preceded by the demonstrative 'that' – an indication, perhaps, that the author is pointing us to the vision of the Danielic son of man. In the Synoptic phrase, the pointer to Daniel may have left its mark in the use of the distinctive ὁ – described recently by C. F. D. Moule as one of the 'neglected features in the problem of the Son of man'.[33] Jesus is not, after all, speaking of himself as any man, but as man understood in terms of Daniel's vision. Jesus can speak of his mission and his future role as 'man' only because he sees himself in the light of 'the Son of man' whose obedience and authority, suffering and exaltation, are described in visionary terms in Dan 7.

Appropriate enough within the ministry of Jesus, as an expression of his obedience to God and his trust in him for future vindication, the term ceased to be appropriate in the same way after the resurrection. The Christian community understood it as a title, but did not adopt it for their own use, preferring to use 'Messiah' or 'Son of God' or 'Lord'. Nevertheless, it continued to be important within the tradition of Jesus' sayings, and to be understood as expressing the hope for vindication – now seen as a final vindication taking place at the parousia of the Son of man.

Is the Son of man problem really insoluble? It would perhaps be optimistic to hope that any 'solution' will be accepted in the near future as an 'assured result'. But assured results are always dangerous in New Testament scholarship. We shall perhaps move towards a solution, however, if we recognize that there is sometimes merit in very diverse views; like the Son of man sayings themselves, each may convey part of the truth, distorted when taken on its own, but playing its own part in the total pattern.

---

[33] C. F. D. Moule, 'Neglected Features in the Problem of "the Son of Man"', in *Neues Testament und Kirche, Festschrift für Rudolf Schnackenburg,* ed. Joachim Gnilka (Freiburg: Herder, 1974), 413–428. Geza Vermes' claim that the definite and indefinite forms of the phrase were indistinguishable in meaning has been disputed by Joseph A. Fitzmyer (see notes 7 and 8 above). The use of the definite article is certainly a striking feature in Greek, and as Moule comments, suggests 'something in the traditions of the sayings of Jesus which is more distinctive than simply an Aramaic phrase meaning "a man" or "somebody" or even ... "I"' (Moule, 'Neglected Features', 21). See also C. F. D. Moule, *The Origin of Christology* (Cambridge: Cambridge University Press, 1977), 14–17.

7. The Son of Man and the Synoptic Problem

In a short paper given at the Rome gathering of SNTS, William O. Walker suggested that one way of approaching the Synoptic problem would be to determine which of the proposed solutions was 'most compatible ... with what has been learned, quite independently of the Synoptic problem, regarding the development of particular themes or motifs in early Christianity'.[1] Though the examination of any one theme could not prove decisive in the debate between supporters of the Griesbach and the two-source hypotheses, the cumulative evidence of several such discussions might, he suggested, prove significant. He illustrated this approach by pointing to what he considered to be the likely development of the Son of man motif, and concluded that the theory most compatible with the evidence was neither the two-source nor the Griesbach hypothesis, but the proposal that Matthew and Luke used a common source and that Mark used both Matthew and Luke.

It is a bold man who attempts to solve one problem by appealing to another! Like the Synoptic problem itself, the enigma of the meaning of the term 'the Son of man' has been described as 'insoluble', and with perhaps even more justification; while this has not discouraged many of us from continuing our attempts to solve it, there is certainly no unanimity on the issue. Far from pointing a way forward, Walker has, by choosing this particular problem, demonstrated the danger of attempting to build conclusions on presuppositions. Moreover, he overlooks the fact that many of the assumptions behind the reconstruction of the 'development' of the Son of man motif which he uses as his norm were themselves based on the two-source hypothesis which he rejects.

Walker's argument is built on six propositions about the Son of man which he has no space to defend, but simply accepts as valid; he admits that they 'come from only one "wing" of recent Son of Man research', though he suggests that there is a 'growing consensus' in support of 'at least some' of them.[2] This 'consensus' is scarcely as impressive as he suggests, however, since some of the scholars referred to in the footnotes as presenting 'similar conclusions' to some

---

[1] William O. Walker, 'The Son of Man Question and the Synoptic Problem', *NTS* 28 (1982): 375.

[2] Walker, 'The Son of Man Question', 375 n. 11. It is somewhat surprising to find Walker appealing to a consensus, in view of the fact that in an earlier article he rejected an approach which had emerged out of 'a significant consensus among NT scholars'; see William O. Walker, 'The Origin of the Son of Man Concept as Applied to Jesus', *JBL* 91 (1972): 482.

of the six points would be surprised by the implication that they are therefore supporting the overall position.[3] In fact, if the propositions are taken together, they amount to a theory with which perhaps the majority of scholars would be in profound disagreement. Nevertheless, since there is considerable support for some of them, these proposals present us with a useful test case in considering the possibilities and pitfalls in pursuing this particular approach to the Synoptic problem.

The six propositions are as follows:[4]

1. 'There was no Son of Man title or concept as such in first-century Judaism; therefore, the titular use of the term and the concept associated with it must have originated either with Jesus himself or within the early Christian community'. We have no quarrel with the first statement, since it represents a view for which many of us have argued in opposition to the once dominant belief that a heavenly Son of man was part of first-century Judaism's eschatological hope. The second, however, seems to exclude the possibility that there were no developments in first-century Judaism which might help to explain the titular use of the phrase by the early Christian community: it is certainly arguable that 1 Enoch provides evidence that the phrase had come to be interpreted as a title by at least some Jews by the end of the first century CE, and it is unlikely that the two developments were entirely independent.

2. 'No Son of Man title or concept as such can be detected in the authentic sayings of Jesus; therefore, the titular use of the term and the concept associated with it must have originated within the early Christian community'. Again, while many of us would agree that Jesus did not use the phrase as a title, the evidence nevertheless points overwhelmingly to the belief that he used the phrase in some sense or other, and if we rule out the notion that there was in first-century Judaism any expectation of an eschatological Son of man, then it seems that he must have used the phrase as a way of referring to himself; it is arguable, too, that it was intended in some way to denote his own role. But if the phrase 'the Son of man' was used by Jesus himself, then however much later developments may have transformed its meaning, it is misleading to say that the concept and titular use of the phrase had their origin in early Christian circles: the growth of the title and 'concept' from Jesus' self-reference is an important part of the evidence in tracing the development from one strand of tradition to another.

3. 'The origin of the Son of Man title and concept can be found within the early Christian community as the product of a *pesher*-type exegetical process similar to that which has been discovered among the sectaries of Qumran'.

---

[3] Ragnar Leivestad is quoted in n. 12, Geza Vermes in n. 13, and Vermes and M. Casey in n. 15.

[4] Walker, 'The Son of Man Question', 375 ff.

This had been argued by Walker in an earlier article published in 1972;[5] building on the work of Norman Perrin, who had seen a crucial development in the Son of man tradition taking place with the combination of Psalm 110:1 and Daniel 7:13, Walker suggested that Psalm 8 had played an important role in linking these two texts. His argument at that time, however, was based on the hypothesis of Marcan priority, for Perrin had ascribed 'to the author of Mark the major role in the creative use of Son of Man traditions in the NT period',[6] and Walker himself argued that the crucial stage in this development is to be found in Mark 12:36b.[7] He can hardly argue now against Marcan priority by appealing to a theory which was based on that hypothesis! At the very least, the earlier arguments of Perrin and Walker need to be re-examined, since the case which Walker is now arguing must mean that the major role in the development of the titular use of the phrase was played by someone earlier than Mark.

4. 'Of the various types of Son of Man sayings preserved in the gospels, those that reflect the influence of Daniel 7.13 and thus are eschatological in nature most nearly represent the earliest stage in the development of the Son of Man title and concept; all other types are secondary and derivative'. This, of course, is the view of one 'wing' of scholarly opinion, and a very different approach is represented in the work of Geza Vermes, Maurice Casey, and Barnabas Lindars;[8] Walker refers to Vermes and Casey in a footnote, but treats them as supporting his conclusion because they do not regard Jesus' use of the phrase as titular.[9] Once again, however, we must insist that Jesus' use of the phrase is an important part of the evidence in tracing the development of the titular usage. The recognition that Daniel 7:13 played an important part in 'the development of the Son of man title and concept' does not necessarily mean that all non-eschatological sayings are 'secondary and derivative'.

5. 'Relatively speaking, the Son of Man christology originated and developed rather late within the exegetical tradition of the early church, and it apparently originated among Greek-speaking, not Aramaic-speaking, Christians'. This argument is based on the preceding propositions, in particular on the belief that the origin of the titular usage is to be traced to a link between Psalm 110:1 and Daniel 7:13 via Psalm 8. In defending this fifth proposition, Walker refers in a footnote to the probability that there were several stages

---

[5] Walker, 'The Origin of the Son of Man', 482–490.

[6] Walker, 'The Origin of the Son of Man', 484.

[7] Walker, 'The Origin of the Son of Man', 487.

[8] Geza Vermes, 'The Use of בר נש / בר נשא in Jewish Aramaic', in *An Aramaic Approach to the Gospels and Acts,* by Matthew Black, 3rd ed. (Oxford: Clarendon, 1967), 310–330 (Appendix E); Vermes, *Jesus the Jew* (London: Collins, 1973), 160–191; Vermes, *Jesus and the World of Judaism* (London: SCM Press, 1983), 89–99. Maurice Casey, *Son of Man: The Interpretation and Influence of Daniel 7* (London: SPCK, 1979). Barnabas Lindars, *Jesus Son of Man* (London: SPCK, 1983).

[9] Walker, 'The Son of Man Question', 383 n. 16.

in the exegetical process before 'the final stage of the process – the stage that actually produced the Son of Man christology'.[10] But the later he places what he terms 'the final stage', the more likely it is that Son of man traditions had already developed independently of the fusion with Psalm 110:1.

6. 'Outside the canonical gospels, early Christian literature contains almost no traces of the Son of Man christology found in these gospels; therefore, it must be concluded that this christology never became widely established in the early church'. This statement assumes a particular version of 'Son of Man christology'; the question is not, in our opinion, so easily settled,[11] but must be left on one side in our present discussion. It will, however, be useful to consider whether the Fourth Gospel may have important light to shed on this problem.

It is on the basis of these six propositions that Walker now explores 'the possible relationship between the Son of Man question and the Synoptic Problem'. He assumes, that is to say, 1. that the Son of Man title and concept originated, developed, and flourished within the limited circle of a particular Christian exegetical tradition; 2. that they originated relatively late within this tradition; 3. that their earliest form was eschatological in nature; and 4. that they never became widely known or accepted in the early church as a whole. As a probable corollary, he suggests that within the limited circle where the Son of Man christology originated, developed, and flourished, there would have been a tendency to create new Son of Man sayings and to add the title to already existing sayings lacking it but that, outside this circle, the tendency would have been to eliminate or change the Son of Man title where it was found.[12]

It is obvious that when the Synoptic problem is approached on the basis of these assumptions, the two-source hypothesis is immediately found to be incompatible with it, for Mark has only three eschatological sayings, but has included nine sayings about betrayal, suffering, death, and resurrection and two about the Son of man's present authority, whereas Matthew and Luke contain far more sayings, many of them eschatological. If Walker's assumptions are right, the eschatological sayings represent the earliest stage in the Son of man Christology, which flourished and developed in one Christian circle; within that circle Son of man sayings would have been created, whereas outside it, the tendency was 'increasingly to eliminate rather than to add Son of Man references to the tradition'.[13] On this basis, it seems clear

---

[10] Walker, 'The Son of Man Question', 383 ff. n. 16.

[11] In particular, the question as to whether Son of man imagery lies behind Paul's Adam Christology is still an open one.

[12] Walker, 'The Son of Man Question', 376.

[13] Walker, 'The Son of Man Question', 378.

that Matthew and Luke must be earlier than Mark, since they include a large number of Son of man sayings of all types, whereas Mark represents a later stage where Son of man sayings are being deleted from the tradition, and the understanding of the phrase is moving away from the eschatological, towards interpreting it in terms of suffering. The Griesbach theory seems to be more compatible with this particular theory about the origin of the Son of man sayings, except that such sayings are found both in Matthew (where approximately half of them are eschatological, the remainder being either about his present activity or his suffering) and in the special material used by Luke (where they are primarily eschatological), suggesting that they are more widespread than Walker's theory allows. He therefore proposes yet another solution to the Synoptic problem – namely, that Matthew and Luke used a common source (which we may conveniently refer to as 'Q'), in which were to be found sayings of all three kinds, though the majority were eschatological in nature. The 'Q' community may, he suggests, be the one which is responsible for the crucial first stage in the creation of the Son of man sayings, but that suggestion is not essential to his thesis. Mark wrote last, using Matthew and Luke as his principal sources.

By contrast, the two-source hypothesis suggests 1. that Son of man sayings were widespread in the early church, being found in at least two sources (Mark and Q), and possibly in Matthew and Luke also; 2. that Son of man sayings in Mark were primarily about suffering, death, and resurrection, whereas in the other sources they were primarily eschatological; 3. that Matthew and Luke added Son of man sayings to their Marcan source; 4. that the development was away from 'suffering' sayings towards eschatological sayings.[14] Indeed it does! And many of us would argue that this summary of Walker's is a good account of the way in which the Son of man tradition actually developed. If our two hypotheses are incompatible, we must certainly abandon one or other of them. But which? Walker assumes that his hypothesis about the Son of man is right, and that the two-source hypothesis is therefore wrong, but if we reverse the argument, and start from the assumption that the two-source hypothesis is correct, then it is his Son of man hypothesis that is demonstrated to be in error!

One of the points which has emerged in our criticism of Walker's assumptions is the fact that he assumes that the 'titular' use of the phrase 'the Son of man', though the last stage of an exegetical process, marks the beginning of 'the Son of man' tradition in the Gospels; the possibility that Jesus might have used the phrase to refer to himself or to his own role is totally ignored. But if there is any possibility that Jesus in fact used the phrase in any sense whatever, then 'the Son of man' tradition clearly had its origins before the point at

---

[14] Walker, 'The Son of Man Question', 377 ff.

which exegetical developments created what Walker terms the 'concept' of an eschatological Son of man. In other words, there must have been 'Son of man' sayings in existence in the period before the titular use developed, something which occurred 'rather late' in the exegetical tradition of a particular Greek-speaking Christian community. But if such 'Son of man' sayings were already in existence, then the assumption that all non-eschatological sayings can be understood as developments within that community falls to the ground, and we need to trace the development of the phrase before the titular use emerges.

The method Walker proposes is clearly circular. If we begin with his theory about the Son of man sayings, we will end with one 'solution' to the Synoptic problem, but if we begin with an alternative theory, we will reach a very different conclusion. There is as yet no agreement on the Son of man problem, for on the one hand we have those who argue that the earliest sayings (whether they originated with Jesus himself or within an early Christian community) are eschatological, in which case the development in the tradition will be away from the eschatological sayings and towards those that are ordinary and non-eschatological; and on the other, we have those who believe that the phrase was used by Jesus as some kind of self-reference,[15] in which case the development will be in the opposite direction. The theory of Marcan priority fits one theory about the development of the Son of man tradition, and the Griesbach hypothesis (or rather Walker's variant of it) fits another. We need firmer ground beneath our feet if this method is to throw any light on the issue.

It is worth asking, however, whether there is any other kind of development within the Son of man tradition which has so far been ignored in this argument. When 'Son of man' sayings are divided into the customary three 'types', we find that examples of each kind are to be found in each of the Gospels. An examination of those concerned with suffering shows that the very few sayings in this category which occur either in Matthew or in Luke alone are very similar to those found in all three Gospels, so there is no indication of development here. When we look at the sayings which refer to the activity of the Son of man in the present, we discover that the very opposite is true: the sayings are so very diverse that it is impossible to speak of development between one Gospel and another. When we turn to the eschatological sayings, however, the evidence is much more interesting, since here we find indications of development between one Gospel and another.

Mark has only three sayings about the future glory of the Son of man. The first is found in Mark 8:38, which speaks of the Son of man coming in the

---

[15] See Vermes, Casey, Lindars (n. 8 above). Also, Morna D. Hooker, 'Is the Son of Man Problem Really Insoluble?', in *Text and Interpretation: Studies in the New Testament Presented to Matthew Black*, eds. Ernest Best and R.McL. Wilson (Cambridge: Cambridge University Press, 1979), 155–168 = above, essay 6 (pp. 90–102).

glory of his Father with the holy angels, and being ashamed of those who have been ashamed of Jesus. Mark (who clearly identifies Jesus with the Son of man) envisions a scene in which those men and women who have not been prepared to share in Jesus' shame and suffering are not acknowledged by the Son of man. A similar saying in Matthew 10:32 ff. and Luke 12:8 ff. puts the idea positively as well as negatively, though in Matthew's version, Jesus speaks of himself in the first person throughout. In this 'Q' form of the saying, however, the acknowledgement of those who have previously acknowledged Jesus is made 'before my Father' (Matthew) or 'before the angels of God' (Luke): the language here suggests a court of law, in which Jesus appears as a witness – or perhaps as a counsel – either for the prosecution or for the defence. It seems, therefore, that in Mark 8:38, the Son of man occupies a more exalted role than in Luke 12:8 ff., since he himself apparently receives or rejects men and women into his company. Another interesting shift is seen when we compare Mark 8:38 with the parallel sayings which occur at the equivalent point in the narrative in Matthew 16:27 and Luke 9:26. Luke's version here is almost identical with Mark's, but Matthew's contains an extra line at the end: 'and then he will give everyone his due reward'. The italicized words are generally understood to be a quotation from Psalm 62:12 (LXX 61:13) = Proverbs 24:12, which suggests that they are an addition, and that the version in Mark 8 and Luke 9 is therefore earlier than that in Matthew 16. It is interesting to note, too, that these final words make a significant change to the meaning of the saying, since Matthew clearly depicts the Son of man as a judge, meting out punishment and reward.

Mark's second saying is found in 13:26. This time the Son of man is to come 'in clouds, with great power and glory, and then he will send out the angels to gather his chosen ones'. The scene complements that in 8:38, and presents the positive side of the Son of man's coming, for instead of being ashamed of those who are not worthy of him, he now sends out angels to gather the elect into his company. As in Mark 8:38, the Son of man is not described as exercising a judicial role; nevertheless it is clearly crucial to be included among his elect, to be one of those whom he recognizes as his. This time, comparison with the parallels in Matthew 24:30b and Luke 21:27 reveals few differences in the saying itself, the major one being that Luke omits the reference to the angels gathering the elect and substitutes a declaration that the coming of the Son of man is the sign that the liberation of those whom Jesus addresses is at hand. Matthew is closer to Mark, but has an extra phrase, 'with the blast of a trumpet', which echoes Isaiah 27:13. The significant differences are in the context, which we will examine shortly.

The final saying in Mark comes at 14:62, where Jesus replies to the high priest's question as to whether he is the Christ, the Son of the blessed, with the words 'I am, and you will see the Son of man sitting at the right hand of power and coming with the clouds of heaven'. This time there are very significant differences indeed, since in neither Matthew nor Luke does Jesus reply with the words 'I am';[16] both Gospels, moreover, contain a temporal reference: in Matthew 26:64, they will see the Son of man sitting ἀπ' ἄρτι, and in Luke 22:69, the Son of man will be sitting ἀπὸ τοῦ νῦν. Luke omits the reference to the Son of man coming with the clouds; for him, Jesus' words refer to the authority he will be given at his ascension, not to the parousia. Matthew's much more awkward construction combines the idea of Jesus' imminent enthronement with that of his return. The three evangelists are agreed in seeing the saying as a claim by Jesus that he will be vindicated and (as the Son of man) will be given the seat at God's right hand: what his duties or functions will be is not specified, but both Matthew and Luke stress the belief that this authority will be exercised by Jesus immediately after his resurrection.

In Mark, then, we find that the so-called 'eschatological' sayings are used consistently to express claims and promises about the future vindication of Jesus himself (14:62) and of his followers (13:26, and, by implication, 8:38). All three sayings are found in contexts which have to do with shame and suffering: in 14:62, Jesus is on trial for his life; in 8:38, it is those who are ashamed of Jesus, and who are unwilling to share his suffering, of whom the Son of man will be ashamed; and in 13:26, the gathering of the elect is their reward for faithfulness in the face of suffering and persecution. A comparison with the parallel sayings in Matthew and Luke has revealed that Matthew 16:27 understands Jesus to exercise a judicial role, while Matthew 26:64 and Luke 22:69 emphasize his kingly role in the period before the end.

We need now to consider the use made of the eschatological sayings by Matthew. First, we have Matthew 10:23, from which we learn that the coming of the Son of man marks the dramatic conclusion to the present age; nothing is said about what he will do, but the reference to the day of judgement in v. 15 suggests that his coming marks the arrival of that day, even though he is not specifically described as acting as judge. In 13:41, however, judgement (or at least, punishment) is certainly in mind, for a saying very similar to that in Mark 13:26/Matthew 24:30b describes the Son of man once again sending out his angels, this time to remove from his kingdom all who tempt others to sin and all who do evil; they are thrown into the fire, and there will be wailing and gnashing of teeth. The righteous, on the other hand, will shine like the sun in the kingdom of their father. Matthew has included here not only the reference to punishment, but an idea that we have not met explicitly stated before – namely, that the Son of man himself has a kingdom. The parable itself

---

[16] In Luke's account, however, these words are used in an oblique way, in answer to the second part of the question.

(in Matt 13:24–30) is about the kingdom of heaven; the explanation has the righteous enjoying the kingdom of their father. But the owner of the field who sows good seed and who sends out reapers at harvest time is the Son of man, and the angels gather the weeds out of his kingdom.

The same idea is found in the next of these sayings in Matthew which occurs at 16:28: 'Truly I tell you, there are some of those standing here who will not taste death until they see the Son of man coming in his kingdom'. This is a particularly significant passage, since it is almost identical to the parallel sayings in Mark 9:1 and Luke 9:27; there is, however, one crucial difference, since both Mark and Luke refer to the coming of the kingdom of God. Once again, we have a difference which suggests that Matthew's version of the saying is later than that used by Mark and Luke, since we know that the kingdom of God was central to Jesus' own message, and the emphasis on the kingdom of the Son of man begins to look like a late development in the tradition. This idea continues in the next saying, in Matthew 19:28, where we learn that 'when the Son of man sits on his glorious throne, [the disciples] will sit on twelve thrones judging the twelve tribes of Israel'. Here the Son of man sits on his own throne (rather than simply at God's right hand, as in Mark 14:62) and the glory is also his own (rather than being the glory of his father, as in Mark 8:38, or the glory which simply accompanies him in Mark 13:26). Moreover, he is clearly understood to exercise judgement, since his followers also sit on thrones and judge the people. Leaving aside for a moment the sayings in Matthew 24, we find both these ideas once again in 25:31, which describes what will happen 'when the Son of man comes in his glory, and all the angels with him'. In this account of the future judgement of the nations, we are told that the Son of man 'will sit on his glorious throne, and before him will be gathered all nations, and he will divide them from one another, as a shepherd divides sheep from goats'. This is the clearest and most detailed description of the judgement which will be exercised by the Son of man, and once again we find that the glory and the throne belong to him, and that after the initial reference to him as the Son of man, he is described as 'the king'. We note, too, that although the story is far more elaborate and specific than the prediction in Mark 14:62, it follows a similar pattern (i.e. coming and sitting enthroned).

Returning to Matthew 24, we note that there are six Son of man sayings, one of which we have already considered (24:30b, parallel to Mark 13:26). The first, in v. 27, compares the coming of the Son of man to a flash of lightning; the implication seems to be that his arrival is both sudden and unmistakeable. The word for 'coming', παρουσία, though it became a technical term for the second coming of Christ, is used by Matthew alone among the evangelists, and found only in this chapter; it occurs in the disciples' opening question in v. 3, as well as in three of our sayings, in vv. 27, 37 and 39. The use of the word indicates that for Matthew the arrival of the Son of man is now an expected event about which teaching can be given, whereas in the three eschatological sayings found in Mark, the idea that he would come was being introduced. Similarly, v. 30a refers to the sign of the Son of man in heaven, a sign which either precedes the coming of the Son of man in the second part of the verse or else is to be identified with that coming. Whichever interpretation we choose, his coming is expected, and this verse provides the answer to the disciples' introductory query, 'What is the sign of your coming and of the end of the age?' The sayings in vv. 37 and 39 compare the coming of the Son of man to the days of Noah, and to the coming of the flood, which reminds us that the theme of this whole passage is that of eschatological judgement. The final saying, in v. 44, demands readiness, because the time of the Son of man's arrival is unknown. A comparison with Mark at this point shows that v. 42 is parallel to Mark 13:35, but that instead of Mark's parable about a returning householder (13:35–37), Matthew has a straightforward command to the disciples to be ready for their Lord, followed by another parable in vv. 43 ff. (// Luke 12:39 ff.) comparing the coming of the Son of man to the arrival of a thief in the night. In their Matthean context, these six sayings present a much more detailed picture than that offered by Mark 13:26. The coming of the Son of man is part of the eschatological expectation, and his coming means not simply vindication for the elect, but judgement for everyone.

A similar picture is found in Luke. An enigmatic saying in 11:30 refers to the Son of man as a sign to this generation, but both the context and the comparison with Jonah suggest that Luke has understood the sign to be the presence of Jesus, rather than his future coming.[17] In Luke 12:8, 40, we have two 'Q' sayings to which we have already referred. Moving on to chapter 17, we find a cluster of sayings similar to those in Matthew 24: in v. 22, the disciples long to see one of the days of the Son of man; vv. 24 and 26 give us the sayings about his coming being like a lightning flash and like the days of Noah, and v. 30 compares 'the day when the Son of man is revealed' to the day when fire and brimstone rained down on Sodom. Once again, the coming of the Son of man is an event which is expected, and which involves judgement. It is interesting to note, however, that this teaching is given in response to queries from the Pharisees about the time of the coming of the kingdom of God: as in Matthew 13, the shift from the kingdom of God to sayings about the Son of man suggests later development. In 18:8, in a saying unique to Luke, Jesus asks whether, when the Son of man comes, he will find faithfulness on earth; once again, the saying fits awkwardly at this point, since it is used to conclude a parable which is about God, not the Son of man, vindicating his elect.

---

[17] Matthew, on the other hand, understands the saying of Jesus' death and resurrection (Matt 12:39ff).

Finally, in Luke 21, we find the saying parallel to Mark 13:26 in v. 27, followed by exhortations to be ready and by a warning to the disciples to watch, praying that they will be able to stand before the Son of man, an indication that he is understood to be coming in judgement (v. 36).

Our examination of the way in which the eschatological sayings are employed by the three Synoptic evangelists suggests that Matthew and Luke reflect a later stage in the development of the concept of the Son of man than does Mark. Whereas in Mark the three eschatological sayings serve to affirm the future vindication of Jesus and his disciples, many of those in Luke and Matthew refer to the day of the Son of man as an event which is expected. In both Matthew and Luke, the Son of man exercises a far more active role than in Mark: in Matthew he is referred to as a king and has a kingdom, and his role in judgement is emphasized; in Luke, too, we meet the idea of judgement. What we see here is a growing emphasis on the future authority and role of Jesus, a shift from the idea that he will be vindicated and will be given authority by God to various descriptions of the ways in which he will exercise the authority and power entrusted to him. Such developments no doubt reflect the interests and situation of the early Christian communities, as well as being a natural elaboration of the earlier sayings. It is illuminating to compare this difference in emphasis with the change we find between Daniel 7 and 1 Enoch 37–71. In this case, since the description of the Son of man in 1 Enoch is based on Daniel 7, we know that the account in 1 Enoch of the figure who exercises judgement is a development from the description of one like a son of man who comes with clouds and is given dominion and glory and kingdom. In 1 Enoch, the Son of man himself deposes kings from their thrones and punishes sinners (46:4–8); he is enthroned in glory and exercises judgement (62:5–14; 69:26–29). The author has spelt out what the kingly power given to the one like a son of man in Daniel 7 involves.

Finally, it is perhaps worth considering whether the evidence of the Fourth Gospel can throw any light on the development of the concept of the Son of man. The fact that John is usually dated late might seem to rule out this possibility, yet there is good reason to believe that the evangelist has made use of early traditions.[18] It is obvious that the Son of man sayings in the Fourth Gospel are very different from those in the Synoptics: John has nothing about the sufferings of the Son of man, nor about the parousia. Yet closer examination reveals interesting similarities with the Synoptic tradition. A number of the Johannine sayings speak of the Son of man being lifted up (3:14ff.; 8:28; 12:34) or glorified (12:23; 13:31ff.), thus coalescing the themes of his death and subsequent vindication. These sayings hold together

---

[18] Barnabas Lindars, *The Gospel of John,* NCB (London: Marshall, Morgan and Scott, 1972), 25–28; John A.T. Robinson, *The Priority of John* (London: SCM Press, 1985).

ideas which seem in the Synoptics to be divided between the so-called passion predictions and the declarations of future vindication. Yet further reflection reminds us that in Mark the 'passion predictions' are predictions of resurrection as well as of death, and that the sayings about vindication occur in contexts which are concerned with suffering. The two ideas necessarily belong together. It is arguable that these sayings simply represent the evangelist's own meditations on the term 'the Son of man', and cannot help us in tracing the development of its use in the early Christian communities. Nevertheless, the fact that this particular 'title' is used in making the fusion of suffering with vindication is suggestive, for if John is using independent traditions, and not basing his Gospel on the Synoptics, then we have supporting evidence for the belief that the sayings about the suffering and vindication of the Son of man belong to an early stratum, and that it is the sayings about judgement and kingship which represent a later development.[19]

Other Johannine sayings are about ascent and descent, either of the Son of man himself (3:13; 6:62) or of the angels on him (1:51), and about the bread which he gives, which is then identified with his own flesh, pointing to his death (6:27, 53). Only one (5:27) refers to the Son of man's role as judge.

John's evidence must remain problematic. But we suggest that in the Synoptic Gospels themselves there is sufficient evidence of a development from those eschatological sayings about the Son of man which speak of his vindication to those which describe his kingdom and judgement to suggest that Mark, who uses only the former, must be earlier than Matthew and Luke. Perhaps Walker's suggestion that the Son of Man sayings may throw light on the Synoptic problem can be used after all – but with very different results from those which he proposed.

---

[19] Matthew Black, 'The Son of Man Problem in Recent Research and Debate', *BJRL* 45 (1963): 305–318, suggested that the saying in John 3:14 represented 'the most primitive version' of the tradition regarding the rejection and resurrection of the Son of man; see p. 317.

8. Did the Use of Isaiah 53 to Interpret His Mission Begin with Jesus?*

It was 1956 when I finished typing the final copy of my M.A. dissertation, which appeared in book form a long three years later as *Jesus and the Servant*.[1] Forty years on is an appropriate time to look back, and so I am particularly grateful for this opportunity to take stock and to think again about a topic which has lost none of its fascination and importance. I have to warn you, however, that having done so, I am, by and large, unrepentant. I have no intention of recanting! To the question posed in the title of this lecture, I have to reply that I can find no convincing evidence to suggest that Isaiah 53 played any significant role in Jesus' own understanding of his ministry.

But let us begin with what no one will deny: that for centuries Christians have read Isaiah 53 in the light of their knowledge of Christ's ministry and death and of their experience of the forgiveness which has come through him. Isaiah 53 is by no means the only text that has been read through what we may term christological spectacles. Looking back, all sorts of passages – Isaiah 7:14, for example, or 35:5–6 – seem to Christian eyes and ears to be clear 'messianic' prophecies; Old Testament scholars usually see things differently. But Isaiah 53 has, above all other passages, seemed to be the most relevant and divinely inspired: here, apparently, we have a vision of one man suffering vicariously for the sins of others. What Christian can read that moving passage in Isaiah 53 and fail to say 'Amen'?

But therein lies our problem. Isaiah 53 seems *so* appropriate, *so* apposite, that we find it difficult to rid ourselves of the assumption that its relevance was seen from the very beginning – even, perhaps, that it was read as a prophecy of a suffering Messiah by the Jews themselves. Isaiah 53 has become part of our Christian culture, and its relevance is reinforced every year when we hear its words sung to the music of Handel's *Messiah*. We have, in a sense, been brainwashed into thinking that, because Christians have found that their reading of Isaiah 53 expressed the deepest truth about Jesus, he too must have seen in it a description of his own calling. The very suggestion that it could have been otherwise has seemed to some an undermining of Christian faith itself. How, asked one commentator, could the church continue to believe about Jesus what he did not know to be true about himself?

---

* Paper read at Seminar convened by Professor William R. Farmer (a well-known supporter of Matthean priority) at Baylor University in February 1996 to discuss this question.
[1] Morna D. Hooker, *Jesus and the Servant* (London: SPCK, 1959).

Well, the answer to that question is 'very easily'. The judgements of history are not to be despised because those who were involved in the original events did not know everything that would result from them. When, at the end of the so-called Battle of Britain, Winston Churchill said of those who had flown the Spitfires and defended British shores against enemy attack, that 'never in the course of human history have so many owed so much to so few', he was summing up what a grateful nation felt they had achieved. It is unlikely, however, that any of those pilots had thought of what they were doing in those terms: they had simply seen a job to be done and done it. Perhaps you will think that with Jesus it was different. But was it? When the Fourth Evangelist spoke of him as the eternal word made flesh, he was surely not suggesting that this was how the earthly Jesus had thought of himself; and when the fathers of the church drew up the creeds, they were certainly articulating their own beliefs, not his. It is true that the Christian church must look for continuity between Jesus and their own beliefs about him: if the church uses Isaiah 53 of Jesus, then it can only be because it believes that Jesus behaved in such a way, and that God worked through his ministry and death and resurrection in such a way, that Isaiah 53 is an *appropriate* text to use of him. But if we take the incarnation seriously, then it is not necessary to trace the use of this passage back to Jesus himself. Unfortunately, however, Christians do not always take the incarnation seriously! They frequently attribute to him complete knowledge, and in doing so, strip him of his trust in God, and his obedience to God's will, a trust and obedience which he maintained even when he did not know where they would lead him.

So let us be clear that if I question Jesus' use of Isaiah 53, it is not because I wish to question the church's affirmation that the passage can be read in the light of Jesus' death and be found meaningful. I would suggest, however, that to do so is an example of what we these days call 'reader response' – the response of *Christian* readers to a text. The question with which I am concerned is a historical one: did Jesus himself see the passage as particularly significant for his own role? But there are two related questions that we shall also need to consider: one concerns the way in which Isaiah 53 was read by Jews in the time of Jesus; the other is the question as to when it was that Christians first saw the relevance of that passage. It is with this latter question that I begin. For convenience sake, I shall continue to refer to the passage as Isaiah 53, even though, of course, the crucial text begins in 52:12.

1. Clear Quotations

Let us begin by glancing at those passages in the New Testament where we have clear quotations of Isaiah 53. By these I mean passages where there is no

8. Did the Use of Isaiah 53 to Interpret His Mission Begin with Jesus?

possible doubt that Isaiah 53 is being quoted. In seven out of the eight passages, as though to dispel all doubt, the quotation is introduced by an introductory formula, such as 'it is written'. The first, 'he took our infirmities and bore our diseases', in Matthew 8:17, is particularly interesting, because it is applied in what seems to us a surprising way – not to Jesus' sufferings and death, but to his miracles of healing. But why not? Matthew's quotation is not taken from the LXX of Isaiah 53:4, which speaks of the Servant as 'bearing our sins', but it is in fact a fair translation of the original Hebrew, which speaks of afflictions and pain. Taken out of its original context, and used as a proof-text, the quotation is an entirely appropriate one for Jesus' miracles of healing. It is only because we have grown accustomed to Isaiah 53 being used of Jesus' death that we are surprised by this passage; it is, in fact, a far more appropriate passage to have used of the miracles than the quotation of Isaiah 42:1–4 found in a similar context in Matthew 12:17–21.

The quotation of Isaiah 53:12 in Mark 15:28, where it is used of Jesus' crucifixion between two thieves, is surely a later addition to Mark's text. Note, however, that it is not used to explain the *meaning* of Jesus' sufferings, but simply as a proof-text: scripture was fulfilled in the fact that Jesus was put to death *in the company of* wrongdoers. The same verse is used, in a similar way, in Luke 22:37, but this time, the wrongdoers are Jesus' own disciples. The implication, in both contexts, is that Jesus himself is innocent.

The Fourth Evangelist also has one clear quotation; it comes in John 12:38, and is from Isaiah 53:1: 'Lord, who has believed our report?' The same quotation is used by Paul, in Romans 10:16. Both authors use it in the same way, as a reference to Israel's failure to respond to the gospel. Also in Romans, we have a quotation of Isaiah 52:15 in 15:21, again with reference to Paul's ministry, but this time the quotation and application are both positive, for the Gentiles *have* responded to his gospel.

The longest quotation is found in Acts 8:32 ff., and consists of the second half of Isaiah 53:7 and the first three lines of v. 8. That reference to the first three lines is significant, since the quotation consists of a description of the Servant's sufferings, and breaks off at precisely that point where the passage begins to speak of their interpretation:

> As a sheep is led to the slaughter,
> And as a lamb before its shearers is dumb
> so he opens not his mouth.
> In his humiliation, justice was denied him.
> Who can describe his generation?
> For his life is taken up from the earth.

There is nothing here about the sin and iniquities which are mentioned immediately before and immediately after these words in Isaiah 53. *Why?* 'There was no need,' suggest some commentators, 'because these verses would represent the whole chapter: Luke expected his readers to think of it all'. Really? Did they *know* the rest of the chapter? And if they did, and Luke meant them to think of it all, why is it that he chose these particular verses? If he had been trying deliberately to avoid the theme of atonement, he could not have done better! Is it not odd that the ideas which seem so important to us are not quoted? At the very least, that suggests that these ideas were not so important to Luke. The passage is quoted without any reference to the meaning of Jesus' death; like the verse quoted in Luke 22:37, it serves as a simple proof-text.

The final quotation is found in 1 Peter 2:22–25, where we have scattered phrases from vv. 9, 4, 12, 5, and 6 of Isaiah 53. This is, of course, a rather different use of Old Testament material, and perhaps we ought not to include it among the quotations at all. It is not introduced with a formula, and the phrases quoted are certainly not consecutive: rather, they are woven into the argument – or perhaps we should say into the hymn, since this passage is clearly hymnic in form. But their source is clear, and there are several phrases which are closely parallel to the LXX, so we may perhaps include it among the clear quotations. The fascinating thing about this passage in 1 Peter is its purpose: the author is appealing to slaves to be submissive to their masters and to put up with undeserved punishment. For this, he says, they have been called, because Christ himself suffered for them, leaving them an example, in order that they might follow in his steps. How he did this is then spelt out in terms of Isaiah 53. But having begun with the appeal to Christ's sufferings as an *example* to be followed, he progresses to the idea that they have atoning value – an idea which, strictly speaking, is not relevant to his argument. Here, in this final passage, then, we at last find an example of Isaiah 53 being used in the way in which, as Christians, we *expect* it to be used. Is this perhaps *the* significant moment in the exegesis of that passage, when it was first interpreted of the *meaning* of Christ's death?[2]

We find this remarkable fact, therefore: that in none of the seven passages where a quotation from Isaiah 52–53 is introduced by a formula indicating that a citation from scripture follows is that quotation interpreted *of the meaning* of Jesus' death. In other words, it is not used here in the way we expect – the way which seems so self-evident to the later church. It is used once of his miracles, and two or three times as a proof-text concerning the fact of his death; it is used several times of reaction to the gospel. It is only by cheating a little, and including 1 Peter 2, where the allusion to Isaiah 53 is so clear as to be beyond reasonable doubt, that we find a passage where the prophet's words are understood in terms of what Jesus' death achieved. The

---

[2] In fact, as we shall see later, there appears to be an earlier allusion to Isaiah 53 in another passage dealing with Jesus' death, at Romans 4:25.

importance we attach to that last passage will, of course, depend very largely on the answers we give to questions regarding the date and authorship of that epistle. But I am more intrigued by another question, and that is this: is it significant that it is precisely here, where Isaiah 53 is not being used as a 'proof-text', that we find it being used *creatively* for the first time? We have moved here beyond simple appeal to 'what is written' to the exploration of its *significance*.

Now of course, it may be that we shall find evidence for the use of Isaiah 53 elsewhere, in phrases that echo that passage, and we must return to consider that possibility before we conclude. But I want to turn now to consider the central question which has been put to me: did *Jesus* interpret his own mission in terms of Isaiah 53?

2. Jesus

Asking any historical question about Jesus is, I need hardly say, fraught with difficulties. We need, then, to consider first of all two questions regarding our assumptions in handling the material. One way of proceeding is to begin by considering the question of the authenticity of the teaching attributed to Jesus by our evangelists. If one takes a somewhat negative approach to that question, then one is almost bound to come to a negative conclusion regarding his use of Isaiah 53; most of the possible allusions will have been eliminated, not on the grounds that they do not echo that great passage, but because they are not considered to be authentic words of Jesus. Not surprisingly we find Bultmann following that path, and coming to a negative conclusion as a result. The method I adopted forty years ago was to give the material the benefit of the doubt and to treat it as authentic, in order that all the evidence should be considered, and that still seems to me the best way to proceed, even if it is not fashionable. Had I come to a positive conclusion I would then, of course, have had to consider the nature of the tradition. In fact, I came to a negative conclusion, in spite of including everything: but my negative results were not based on negative assumptions regarding authenticity.

The other methodological question concerns the relationship between the Synoptics. Forty years ago, there was no need for me to justify the assumption of Marcan priority. Today, and certainly in present company, I must at least explain that I still believe Marcan priority to be the most likely hypothesis, and that I am unpersuaded by the arguments of those who support other views. But again, fortunately, it seems to me that assumptions for or against any theory are largely irrelevant to this particular inquiry. I mention this, *not* because I think it would be helpful for us to discuss the matter, but simply to justify the fact that I am ignoring it.

So what is the evidence for the use of Isaiah 53 in the so-called passion predictions attributed to Jesus himself? Many commentators assume that Jesus' conviction that he must suffer *must* have been based on Isaiah 53, because there is no other passage to explain it. No other passage? The Old Testament scriptures are full of the sufferings of the righteous! Could he not have read the psalms? Did he not know Daniel? Is it not significant that he spoke, not of the sufferings of the Servant, but of the Son of man? There is no justification for assuming, as has so often been done, that Jesus believed himself to be the Messiah, preferred the title Son of man, but understood his role to be that of the Servant. That kind of piecing together of Jewish hopes and predictions belongs to the period of the church, when he was seen as the fulfilment of all the scriptures, and when Christian writers built up a kind of identikit picture[3] of Old Testament promises, juxtaposing images, and ideas from various sources. So I say again, where is the evidence *in these sayings* for the use of Isaiah 53 by Jesus? The only word reminiscent of the LXX of Isaiah 53 is παραδίδωμι, used in Mark 9:31 and 10:33 and parallels in a sense very different from the sense in which it is used in Isaiah 53:12. Nor do these passion predictions take up the idea of vicarious suffering. If we are looking for an Old Testament background against which to understand these sayings, we should take the hint we are offered in the reference to the Son of man, and look to Daniel 7, rather than Isaiah 53.

The other saying attributed to Jesus which is often said to show the influence of Isaiah 53 is Mark 10:45 (// Matt 20:28). But the similarities are superficial. The verb διακονέω is never used in the LXX to translate עָבַד, and λύτρον, which is often traced to אָשָׁם in Isaiah 53:10, is never used for that word, and has a quite different meaning. The LXX text of Isaiah 53:10 is in fact very different from both Mark 10:45 and from the Hebrew, for it reads 'if you [presumably the listeners] offer a sin-offering' – i. e., περὶ ἁμαρτίας. Of the three words traced to Isaiah 53, only πολλῶν (used there three times) is relevant, and that is a term which is used frequently elsewhere. I do not find this evidence persuasive.

3. Isaiah 53

My work on Jesus and the Servant has come under attack, as is well-known, by those who remain convinced that Jesus must have seen himself in terms of the Servant of Isaiah. What seems so obvious to us, it is said, must surely have been obvious also to him. But I have also come under what can be described

---

[3] An identikit picture is built up by the police by piecing together smaller pictures – a nose, a chin, etc. – answering to witnesses' descriptions.

as 'friendly fire' from those who believe that though I was right in arguing that Isaiah 53 was not a particularly important text for him, I had not gone far enough! I should, I was told, have examined the assumptions that Old Testament scholars make about that text, as well as the assumptions that New Testament scholars make about *their* material.

Two scholars, Norman Whybray[4] and Harry Orlinsky,[5] have suggested that Christian scholars have misunderstood Isaiah 53. They have both argued that the passage is not, in fact, a description of vicarious suffering at all; Whybray, indeed, has argued that the Servant was not even understood to have died, and that the references to his apparent 'death' should be understood rather as meaning that he came close to death. He points to some interesting parallels in other prophetic passages and in the psalms, but it has to be said that on neither point does he seem to have persuaded many others that his interpretation of the passage is correct.

Obviously if Orlinsky and Whybray were correct, we should have an explanation as to why what appears to us to be the unique theme of Isaiah 53 was for so long ignored. The idea was not taken up and used because it was not there in the first place! So it is worth asking what their evidence is. At this point, we have to raise the question as to what we mean by the word 'vicarious'. In English, the term is unfortunately ambiguous; my *Oxford English Dictionary* understands it, firstly, to refer to that which 'takes or supplies the place of another thing or person', and so to mean someone who acts as a substitute; in theological contexts, this is generally interpreted in terms of Christ suffering in the place of sinners. This is the concept that our German colleagues refer to as 'exclusive place-taking' (*exkludierende Stellvertretung*), and this is how Isaiah 53 has traditionally been understood. But there is a second definition in my dictionary, which takes the word to refer to an action 'performed or achieved by ... one person on behalf of another', and so to mean someone who acts as a representative, and this, I think, is what is referred to in German as 'inclusive place-taking' (*inkludierende Stellvertretung*).[6] The point made by Orlinsky and Whybray is not that the Servant does not suffer, but that he does not suffer *instead of* others (as their substitute); rather, he suffers *alongside* them (as their representative). They point to the fact that in Isaiah 40:2, Israel is said to have suffered 'double for all her sins'; if that passage is relevant to Isaiah 53, and if the speakers in that chapter are understood to be

---

[4] R. Norman Whybray, *Thanksgiving for a Liberated Prophet: An Interpretation of Isaiah Chapter 53,* JSOTSup 4 (Sheffield: JSOT Press, 1978).

[5] Harry M. Orlinsky and Norman H. Snaith, *Studies on the Second Part of the Book of Isaiah*, VTSup 14 (Leiden: Brill, 1967).

[6] See Daniel P. Bailey, 'Concepts of *Stellvertretung* in the Interpretation of Isaiah 53', in *Jesus and the Suffering Servant: Isaiah 53 and Christian Origins,* eds. William H. Bellinger Jr. and William R. Farmer (Harrisburg, PA: Trinity Press International, 1998), 237–241.

Israel, as seems most probable, then the Servant cannot be said to have suffered *instead of* Israel. There is no question of the guilty onlookers getting away scot-free. This cannot, then, be 'substitutionary' suffering.

What, then, is meant by the kind of statement we find in v. 5?

> He was wounded for our transgressions,
> crushed for our iniquities.

Orlinsky and Whybray point to the fact that in Hebrew the preposition is מִן, not בְּ, while in Greek we have διά. The most natural meaning, in both languages, is that the transgressions and sins are understood to be causal:

> He was wounded *because of* our transgressions,
> crushed *because of* our iniquities. ...

In other words, the Servant suffered *as a result of* the sins of others. This is certainly not vicarious in the substitutionary sense; after all, it could be said of the Jews who perished in the Holocaust, that they were wounded because of Hitler's transgressions, crushed as a result of his iniquities. In other words, it was his wickedness which led to their suffering. The Servant's sufferings were also the result of the misdemeanors of others. In his case, however, we do not have someone who suffers *instead of* his guilty compatriots, but rather someone who *shares* in their sufferings, even though he himself, unlike them, is innocent.

But what of a statement such as we find in v. 4, that the Servant bore our infirmities and carried our diseases, or in v. 12, that he bore the sin of many? Once again, if we remember that the Servant was not the only person to be suffering, these statements read rather differently from the way in which they are normally interpreted. The so-called Servant did not escape suffering, even though he was innocent; on the contrary, he seems to have borne the brunt of the suffering. The suffering which he endured belonged by right to his people. What we have is not 'vicarious suffering', *if* by that we mean substitutionary suffering – the anomalous 'exclusive place-taking' which is without parallel in Old Testament thought; rather we have an example of '*inclusive* place-taking' or of what we in English normally term 'representation'.

If this is a correct interpretation, then what is being said in this chapter is, first of all, that the Servant suffers *as a result of the sins of others*. The onlookers thought him guilty, but now that he has been vindicated by God, they realize that he was innocent. He suffered, not because of his own sins, but because of theirs. If we forget our Christian presuppositions, and read the text in that light, it comes across in a new and interesting way, and perhaps explains some of the readings of both the LXX and the Targum.

So far so good. But at this point I find myself parting company with Orlinsky and Whybray, because it seems to me that they have played down too much what the Servant's sufferings *achieved*. We still have to explain v. 5b:

upon him was the punishment that made us whole,
and by his bruises we are healed,

as well as the enigmatic statement in v. 10 about the אָשָׁם, and the statement in v. 10 that the righteous one will make many righteous. There is no doubt that the sufferings of the Servant are understood here, both in the Hebrew and in the LXX texts, to have had atoning power, even though the text of v. 10 is uncertain and obscure. It is no longer simply that the sins of others have caused the Servant to suffer: now his sufferings lead in turn to their restoration and forgiveness. Once again, however, there is no need to interpret this in terms of 'substitution': there are many ways in which the sufferings of one person can save a whole community.

Nevertheless, the work of these two scholars reminds us that the meaning of Isaiah 53 is by no means as obvious as Christians have often assumed. In addition, the Hebrew is, to say the least, difficult: much of it is obscure or unintelligible, and the Septuagint, like the Targum, often seems to say something rather different. Taken together, these facts may explain to some extent why there is so little reference to the idea of 'vicarious suffering' in Judaism, and why the Christian community was so slow to exploit this passage.

What I find of particular interest in all this, however, is that the idea which Otfried Hofius[7] *denies* to Isaiah 53 and finds in the New Testament application of the passage is, in my view, present in the original also. What we have in Isaiah 53 is much better described as *representative suffering* rather than *vicarious suffering*: as *inclusive* place-taking rather than *exclusive* place-taking. But before we explore the implications of that idea, let us return to Jesus.

4. Explanation

Isaiah 53 was, it is often said, the obvious text for Jesus to use. Why then, is there so little evidence that it was in fact important for him? Perhaps because what seems to us, after the event, to be the obvious text was not necessarily the obvious text at the time. The important question for us to ask, therefore, is not necessarily about the original meaning of the Hebrew, but rather: 'How was this passage read in the first century CE?' Now one of the remarkable things about Isaiah 53 is that Jewish exegesis of this chapter in the period between its composition and the first century CE seems virtually to ignore

---

[7] Otfried Hofius, 'Das vierte Gottesknechtslied in den Briefen des Neuen Testamentes', *NTS* 39 (1993): 414–437. The article was one of those referred to by Daniel Bailey in his contribution to the colloquium. Hofius argues that in Isaiah 53 itself the Servant's sufferings are interpreted as substitutionary ('exclusive place-taking'), and that it was our New Testament writers who transformed the meaning by understanding it as 'inclusive place-taking'. I suggest, on the contrary, that the 'representative' interpretation has its roots in the original text.

the idea that one person's suffering can have atoning power for others.[8] It is, of course, possible that the idea was used, and that the literature in which this happened has not come down to us, but certainly we have no evidence to suggest that this was so. Later Jewish literature shows the influence of some of the themes found in Deutero-Isaiah, but not of this particular idea. It has frequently been said that the Qumran literature picks it up, but once again it is echoes of the Servant passages in general, rather than of this particular idea, that are to be found there. So how was the chapter understood? One problem in answering this question is the problem of the Targum: does its very strange interpretation of the chapter indicate the way that the passage was understood in the first century CE, or does it reflect a process of anti-Christian rewriting? If the former, it suggests that the sufferings described in that chapter were not being interpreted in a positive way; if the latter, it offers us no help at all in understanding first-century Jewish interpretation, since we cannot recover the original text. If the early Christian community ignored for so long what appears to *us* to be the key theme of Isaiah 53, was this perhaps because in the Jewish milieu of the first century this was *not* the key theme? If we are to understand the thoughts of first-century men and women, we need to put ourselves into their shoes, and not try to make them wear ours.

But there is another way in which we muddy the waters, and that is by our constant reference to the Servant 'Songs' or to the 'suffering Servant' or even to the 'Servant' – each of these words being, of course, spelt with a capital S. It is necessary to remind ourselves that in the first century CE no one talked about 'Servant Songs', or even about 'Deutero-Isaiah'. The question 'Did Jesus think about himself as "the Servant"?' (with a capital S) is a meaningless one. To the author of Isaiah 53, 'my servant' (without a capital) had seemed an appropriate way of describing one who had been utterly obedient to God; to others, it had seemed an appropriate way of describing men such as Moses and David. In time, it seemed an appropriate way for the church to describe Jesus. But there was no notice in the 'Jobs Vacant' column of the papers reading 'Wanted: The Servant of the Lord'; no expectation that there would be a Servant who would suffer; there was simply a description of one who had been faithful to God and who had therefore been termed God's 'servant'.

I suggest, then, that the reason that Jesus did not model himself on the so-called suffering Servant of Isaiah 53 was because it was by no means the obvious passage of scripture to which he would turn. During his ministry, he proclaimed the forgiving love of God, which welcomed repentant sinners back without condition: particular acts of 'atonement' were apparently

---

[8] Evidence for the idea of vicarious atoning suffering itself (quite apart from possible influence by Isaiah 53) is equally scant. See Sam K. Williams, *Jesus' Death as Saving Event: The Background and Origin of a Concept* (Missoula, MT: Scholars Press, 1975), 121–135.

unnecessary. As he faced death, he appears to have seen his role in terms of the one like a son of man in Daniel 7, who stood for the righteous saints, persecuted because of their faithfulness to God. The psalms, too, provided a description of what happened to those who were faithful to God; Isaiah 53 *may* have been part of this pattern, but apparently added nothing to it. And beyond death, Jesus trusted in God for vindication, in accordance with the promise contained in all these Old Testament texts. If Mark 10:45 and 14:24 are authentic sayings, then it seems that Jesus may have seen his death as an event comparable to the exodus, bringing into existence a new people of God: certainly this seems to have been the way in which all the evangelists interpreted it.[9] There was, in a sense, no need for him to link his death specifically with the notion of atonement for sin. It was his followers who took that step, because it corresponded with their experience of forgiveness.

Let us return, then, to those clear quotations of Isaiah 53 with which we began, since now, I suggest, the apparently perverse way in which they are used should no longer surprise us. I have already suggested that the quotation from v. 4, used of the miracles in Matthew 12, is entirely appropriate, provided that we forget the LXX rendering. The use of proof-texts, without reference to the notion of vicarious suffering, in Mark 15, Luke 22, and Acts 8 no longer surprises us: the verses quoted are sufficient explanation of Jesus' suffering. The use of Isaiah 53:1 in John 12 and Romans 10 of the Jews' refusal to respond to the gospel is an obvious one, as is the more positive use of Isaiah 52:15 in Romans 15. And what we have in 1 Peter 2 is perhaps an indication of the way in which the use of Isaiah 53 developed: first it is used to show that Jesus' suffering was innocent; then a second theme appears, as the same passage is used to show how the Servant's suffering brings healing and forgiveness to others.

Is this passage in 1 Peter the beginning of the second stage of Christian exegesis of Isaiah 53? Or was that stage already begun by Paul? Are there echoes of Isaiah 53 in his writings? Who first used Isaiah 53 to interpret Jesus' death as an atonement for sin?

5. Paul

Now it seems to me that there is one clear echo of Isaiah 53 in Paul, and that is in Romans 4:25: an interesting passage which is often said to be pre-Pauline, though I can see no good reason for denying it to Paul himself. Forty years ago, I did not appreciate the importance of this verse: I followed C.H. Dodd

---

[9] See Matt 20:28; 26:28 ff.; Luke 9:31; 22:24–30; John 18:28; 19:33.

in assuming that Paul's language here was rhetorical,[10] and many other commentators have interpreted the passage in the same way. Thus, Grayston writes: 'The formula was constructed to be verbally memorable rather than theologically precise'.[11] I would argue now that Paul has in fact chosen his language with care, and with an eye to theology rather than rhetoric: Christ, he says, was delivered up on account of our trespasses; he was raised for our justification or 'rightwising'.[12] This antithesis corresponds with what he says elsewhere in his letters about Christ's identification with the situation of sinners and our identification with his – an identification which he spells out in different passages in various ways: he speaks, for example, of Christ being made sin, becoming a curse, being born under the Law, coming in the likeness of sinful flesh for our sake, in order that we might share his righteousness, receive blessing, be set free from the Law, and receive adoption as the children of God.[13] Christ shares our condemnation in order that we might share his vindication by God, a vindication which was made known when he was proclaimed as Son by the resurrection of the dead.[14] In other words, what Paul says in Romans 4:25, where he links Christ's death with our sins, and his resurrection with our justification, is understandable in the light of the idea that some of us refer to as 'interchange in Christ',[15] an idea which is widespread in his writings: Christ shares our situation – the situation of those who are born of Adam – but transforms it by his obedience, so that those who, through baptism into his death and resurrection are now *in* Christ, share *his* vindication and *his* righteousness. The one who is innocent shares the suffering and death which are deserved by Adam's descendants, and his vindication is shared by those who acknowledge him as Lord. These ideas are summed up admirably in the words of Romans 4:25, 'he was delivered up because of our trespasses; he was raised for our justification' (δικαίωσις). But the explanation as to *why* his death and resurrection are effective 'for us' is found only in the context: the meaning of 4:25 is spelt out in chapters 5, 6, and 8. The language of 4:25 is echoed in the argument about Adam and Christ in 5:12–21, where Paul emphasizes that it was the *trespass* of Adam which led

---

[10] C.H. Dodd, *The Epistle of Paul to the Romans* (London: Hodder & Stoughton, 1932), 70. Hooker, *Jesus and the Servant*, 195.

[11] Kenneth Grayston, *Dying, We Live: A New Enquiry into the Death of Christ in the New Testament* (London: Darton, Longman, and Todd, 1990), 92.

[12] The two uses of διά are formally parallel, but the first is causal, the second final.

[13] 2 Cor 5:21; Gal 3:13 ff.; 4:4 ff.; Rom 8:3 ff., 14–20.

[14] Romans 1:3 ff.

[15] I have explored various facets of this idea in essays collected in Morna D. Hooker, *From Adam to Christ* (Cambridge: Cambridge University Press, 1990). See also Morna D. Hooker, 'A Partner in the Gospel: Paul's Understanding of His Ministry,' in *Theology and Ethics in Paul and His Interpreters*, eds. Eugene H. Lovering, Jr. and Jerry L. Sumney (Nashville: Abingdon, 1996) = below, essay 39 (pp. 579–595).

the many to sin and to die, and the grace of God in Christ which made them *righteous*.[16] In chapter 6, Paul spells out *how* this happens: believers are baptized into Christ and share his death (vv. 3, 5–11); they also share his risen life and his righteousness (vv. 4, 6–7, 12–14). This is why there is now no condemnation for those who are in Christ (8:1). It is clear, as we read on, that 4:25 is based on a belief that Christ shares the death of those who are 'in Adam', and that those who are 'in him' share his righteousness before God.

The language of Romans 4:25 – παραδίδωμι and δικαίωσις – echoes Isaiah 53:11 ff. But what is said in Romans 4:25 is very close also to the interpretation I have been offering of the *meaning* of Isaiah 53, which should be understood, I have suggested, in terms of representation rather than substitution, of 'inclusive' rather than 'exclusive place-taking'. Thus Isaiah 53:5: 'He was wounded because of our transgressions; and with his bruises we are healed'. Paul: 'Christ was delivered up because of our trespasses; and through his resurrection we are brought into a right relationship with God'. In Romans 4:25, then, we have not only distinct echoes of the *language* of Isaiah 53:11 ff., but similarities in thought; this passage clearly meets the criteria I suggested should be applied to possible echoes of Old Testament texts.

So is this one reference to Isaiah 53 accidental? Or is it an indication that it was Paul who first exploited the idea of atoning suffering in that passage? Was that chapter the raw material out of which his understanding of atonement in terms of an interchange between Christ and the believer was built?[17] If so, why is it only in Romans that the link becomes clear? And why has the passage left so few traces elsewhere? Or did Paul develop the idea and *then* see the relevance of Isaiah 53? These are the questions which intrigue me, and I am particularly glad that this colloquium is concentrating on the writings of Paul. To the question that has been put to me, 'Did the use of Isaiah 53 to interpret his mission begin with Jesus?' I remain convinced that the answer is 'No'. To the question, 'Where, then, *did* it begin?' I am far more ready than I was forty years ago to suggest that it may well have been with Paul.

---

[16] Note the frequent occurrence of παράπτωμα (vv. 15 [*bis*], 16, 17, 18, and 20) and the root δικαιό- (vv. 16, 17, 18 [*bis*], 19, 21).

[17] There are interesting echoes of this idea of interchange outside Paul, and one of them is in 1 Peter 2:24, in the exposition of Isaiah 53: 'He himself carried our sins in his body up to the tree, so that, freed from sins, we might live for righteousness'. Significantly, however, this passage does not express the theme that is essential to the idea of 'interchange' – namely, that of *sharing*. The author does not say or imply that Christ shared our human death, or that we share his righteousness – simply that Christ dealt with our sins by his death so that we might live for righteousness. The passage reads like an echo of Paul's ideas, minus the idea that everything takes place through our union with Christ; cf. 1 Thess 5:10: 'Christ dies for us, so that … we might live *with him*'.

9. Good News about Jesus Christ, the Son of God*

It is difficult today to think ourselves back to the time when Mark was *not* regarded as 'story'. Yet for almost two thousand years, it was neither thought of, nor listened to, as such. According to the earliest tradition, recorded by Papias around 140 CE, the Evangelist had done no more than record what he remembered from the teaching of Peter: the content was reliable, but the order was not.[1] Then, for centuries, Mark was supposed to have abbreviated Matthew – though why he should have done so was not clear! Since almost all the material contained in Mark was reproduced in either Matthew or Luke or both, there was a natural tendency to regard Mark as less important than the other Gospels.

With the emergence of the theory of Marcan priority in the nineteenth century, Mark came to be seen as an historian and biographer, and his ordering of events was now regarded – *pace* Papias – as reliable. In the ensuing quest for the historical Jesus, therefore, Mark – now regarded as the first Gospel – was seen as the primary source, and his narrative was regarded as an outline of the life of Jesus. In the early twentieth century, however, the rise of form criticism concentrated attention on the individual pericopes, which were likened to 'pearls on a string', arranged in haphazard order, just as Papias had said – though the material itself was no longer regarded as reliable. Redaction criticism, the next major development, looked at the ways in which the Evangelists had *changed* the tradition, so was unhelpful in looking at the earliest Gospel, though attempts were made to distinguish Mark's style.[2] It was, however, the growing emphasis on literary-critical approaches that led scholars to consider the Gospel as *narrative*, an insight set out definitively in the original edition of *Mark as Story*.[3]

One significant obstacle to thinking of the Gospel as 'story' was the fact that it was normally heard as part of the liturgy, and so in snippets, rather than as a whole: the hearers' attention was thus concentrated on the individual pericopes. But while Mark's Gospel was certainly intended to be *heard* rather

---

* Originally written as a contribution to *Mark as Story*, 2nd ed. (see note 3 below).

[1] Papias, as recorded by Eusebius, *Hist. eccl.* 3.39.15. Similarly the *Anti-Marcionite Prologue* and Irenaeus, *Adv. Haer.* 3.1.2.

[2] E.g., Ernest Best, *The Temptation and the Passion*, SNTSMS 2 (Cambridge: Cambridge University Press, 1990).

[3] David Rhoads and Donald Michie, *Mark as Story: An Introduction to the Narrative of a Gospel* (Philadelphia: Fortress, 1982). See also David Rhoads, Joanna Dewey, and Donald Michie, *Mark as Story: An Introduction to the Narrative of a Gospel*, 2nd ed. (Minneapolis: Fortress, 1999).

than read privately, the drama of the story is inevitably lost when it is divided up into short sections.[4] The fact that his Gospel was designed to be heard has affected Mark's manner of writing: repetitions and summaries remind listeners of what has already taken place and help them to understand where the story is going, while the breathless style – so often criticized by literary scholars – carries us along in its enthusiasm. As we listen, the tension rises: the short scenes in the early part of the story give way to a more connected narrative, and the Gospel comes to a climax with Jesus' crucifixion.

Whether by accident or design, the shape of the Gospel seems to fit Aristotle's description of a tragedy, though the final epilogue (16:1–8) means that the story is not, in fact, a tragedy, but – as the opening words declare – 'good news'.[5] A Greek tragedy would open with a 'prologue' that provided essential information enabling the audience to understand the significance of the events they were about to see on the stage. Mark's opening verses (1:1–13) fulfil this function.[6] He begins by assuring us that what he is telling us is 'good news'. This phrase translates the Greek word *euangelion* (εὐαγγέλιον), which is normally translated 'gospel'. In the ancient world, the word was often used of the announcement of a special event, such as the birth or accession of a new emperor. Here the good news concerns Jesus the Messiah, 'as it is written in the prophet Isaiah'. If we turn to the later chapters of Isaiah, from which the quotation in Mark 1:3 comes, we find that the verb *euangelizomai* (εὐαγγελίζομαι, 'to announce good news') occurs frequently. The good news announced there, and in Mark, is about God's salvation of his people.

The subject of the good news he is about to relate is Jesus, the Messiah. To be sure, Mark's wording – 'the good news of Jesus Christ' – is ambiguous and could mean simply that he is relating the good news *proclaimed by* Jesus, but though the story that follows will tell how Jesus announced good news, the way in which that story is told concentrates attention on the figure of Jesus himself. Jesus proclaims the kingdom of God, but Mark's concern is to proclaim Jesus. When Mark begins his book with the words 'The beginning of the good news', therefore, we realize that there is a double entendre. The phrase could perhaps be a way of getting started and mean no more than the old introduction to lessons read in church worship, 'Here beginneth …'. But perhaps Mark means that the *whole* of his book, which recounts the ministry,

---

[4] See Bridget Gilfillian Upton, *Hearing Mark's Endings: Listening to Ancient Popular Texts Through Speech Act Theory* (Leiden: Brill, 2006).

[5] Aristotle, *Poet.* 10–12, 18; *Rhet.* 3.14.

[6] Some commentators regard vv. 1–15 as the prologue, e.g., Leander E. Keck, 'The Introduction to Mark's Gospel', *NTS* 12 (1966): 352–370. For arguments supporting vv. 1–13, see Morna D. Hooker, 'The Beginning of the Gospel', in *The Future of Christology: Essays in Honor of Leander E. Keck,* eds. Abraham J. Malherbe and Wayne A. Meeks (Minneapolis: Fortress, 1993), 18–28 = below, essay 19 (pp. 275–284). On the function of the opening verses, see Morna D. Hooker, *Beginnings: Keys That Open the Gospels* (London: SCM Press, 1997).

death, and resurrection of Jesus, is the beginning of the good news. What he recounts is simply 'the beginning of the good news' that is now being proclaimed by Jesus' followers. The abrupt ending of the Gospel in 16:8 suggests that the story continues in the lives and witness of Jesus' disciples.

1. Jesus, Messiah

Mark's opening words assure us that this Jesus is the Messiah – a fact that remains hidden from the characters in the story until Peter acknowledges him to be such at Caesarea Philippi (8:29). Peter's recognition of Jesus as Messiah has long been regarded as an important turning point in the narrative, and it corresponds to the crucial scene in a Greek tragedy identified by Aristotle as the moment when the course of the play changes. This scene is often a moment of recognition when the characters grasp something of the significance of what is taking place (e.g., the true identity of the central figures).[7] At this point in Mark's narrative, Jesus' true identity begins to dawn on those closest to him. Strangely, however, Jesus neither accepts nor rejects the title, and his response has led some to suggest that in fact he rejected it, but at his 'trial' before Caiaphas he is said to have responded to the high priest's question, 'Are you the Messiah, the Son of the blessed?' with a clear 'I am' (14:62).[8] His claim is echoed by the chief priests, who taunt him at Golgotha with the words, 'Let the Messiah, the king of Israel, come down from the cross' (15:32). These clear declarations of Jesus' identity at the beginning, at the turning point of the narrative, and at its climax, make it clear that Mark wants us to believe in Jesus as God's anointed one, the Messiah.

It is the story of Jesus' crucifixion, however, that spells out what it *means* to be 'the Messiah, the king of Israel', since Jesus is crucified, not in spite of his messiahship, but precisely *because* he is the Messiah. Pilate begins his investigation by asking Jesus, 'Are you the king of the Jews?' (15:2), and although Jesus' reply is ambiguous, it appears to mean that Pilate is stating the truth, even though he does not understand it. When Pilate realizes that the accusations brought against Jesus are false, he offers to release 'the king of the Jews' (15:9). Throughout these proceedings, he persists in referring to Jesus as 'king of the Jews' (15:12). The soldiers mock Jesus as king, clothing him in purple and crowning him with thorns; they salute him – 'Hail, king of the Jews' – kneel to him, and pay mock homage (15:16–20). The charge against

---

[7] See above, n. 5. Aristotle describes the scenes between the prologue and this recognition scene as the 'complication' and those that follow as the 'dénouement'.

[8] On Jesus' supposed rejection of the title, see Theodore J. Weeden, *Mark – Traditions in Conflict* (Philadelphia: Fortress, 1971), 64 ff.

him is that he is 'the king of the Jews' (15:26), and the passers-by mock him as 'the Messiah, the king of Israel' (15:32).

Jesus is revealed to us, the hearers of the Gospel, as Messiah (*Christos*) at the beginning of the story, he is acknowledged to be Messiah by the disciples at its turning point, and he is proclaimed Messiah – a *suffering* Messiah – at its end. The word *Christos* (Χριστός) is also used three times between Caesarea Philippi and the trial, but not to *identify* Jesus. In 9:41 and 13:21, the reference is clearly to the future, after Jesus' messiahship has been openly proclaimed. In 12:35, Jesus is depicted as referring to himself obliquely as Messiah.[9] To the great majority of those taking part in the story, these references are unintelligible. To those in the know, however – those who have heard Mark's opening words – they are significant.

We may set out the way in which Mark uses the term *Christos* (Χριστός) in tabular form. The terms *prologue, complication, discovery*, and *dénouement* are those used by Aristotle. In Mark, however, the final scenes are more than the inevitable conclusion to the dénouement: they form a series of ironic recognition scenes. Here, in the climax to the story, Jesus' identity is openly revealed on the cross, even though no one fully comprehends.

2. Christ: A Marcan Summary

Prologue	1:1–13	1:1, title
Complication	1:14–8:21	(1:34, text dubious)
Discovery	8:22–9:13	8:29, Caesarea Philippi
Dénouement	9:14–13:37	9:41; 12:35; 13:21
Climax	14:1–15:47	14:61, high priest's question
		15:32, mockery
		15 *passim*, Jesus crucified as king

3. As It Is Written

According to the opening line of Mark's Gospel as we have it today, Jesus is not only 'Messiah' but 'Son of God'. There is, to be sure, some doubt about the authenticity of the words here, and so we shall for the moment postpone looking at their significance.[10] Before he begins the narrative, Mark sets out the information we need in order to understand why the story he is about to relate is 'good news', and first of all he assures us that this good news is in

---

[9] In 1:34, where we are told that the demons recognized Jesus, some manuscripts read 'they knew that he was the Messiah'.

[10] They are missing from the original version of ℵ and Θ.

accordance with what was written in the prophet Isaiah. After 1:1, we might expect a passage about the Messiah or the Son of God, but what we are given speaks rather about the coming of the Lord. In Mark, this 'anchoring' of the story in scripture is unique. To be sure, there are many allusions to scripture and even quotations in what follows, but these are all found in the mouths of the characters in the story. It is only here that the author himself spells out the important fact that what is about to take place is the fulfilment of scripture. Mark's method contrasts with that of Matthew, who in his early chapters points out several times that what occurred in the birth and infancy of Jesus took place 'in order to fulfil what had been spoken by the prophet'.[11] For Mark, one such comment is sufficient: we are meant to hear his whole story in the light of what was said by the prophet.[12] The good news he is about to tell us is the fulfilment of God's promises, since it is 'as it is written'.

Mark begins, then, by assuring us that the story he is about to tell fulfils the promises written by the great prophet Isaiah. In fact, part of what follows comes from elsewhere, being an amalgam of Exod 23:20 and Mal 3:1; only verse 3 is from the book of Isaiah (Isa 40:3). How are we to explain this mistake? If Mark were a modern author, we might blame him for failing to check his source. But in his day, this was not so easy! The only way that Mark could have checked the passages would have been by working laboriously through scrolls, and one wonders whether he had access to them. He would almost certainly have been quoting from memory and not consulting any text. It may well be that he is quoting a 'proof-text' that was already being used by other Christians, and wrongly assumed that the whole passage was from Isaiah. Or he may himself have been responsible for joining two such 'proof-texts', only one of which was from Isaiah, together.[13] But had Mark been challenged and told that his reference was wrong, he might well have been unrepentant. For first-century Jews, Isaiah was the great prophet whose book contained the promises of God's coming salvation, and it was his words that were now being fulfilled! If Mark singled out Isaiah, this may well have been deliberate. Perhaps, therefore, we should classify this as a 'deliberate mistake'.

Interestingly, the passages quoted concentrate, not on the figure of Jesus, but on the messenger who is sent to prepare his way. The messenger's task is to announce the coming of the Lord in salvation and judgement. His only function is to prepare his way by urging men and women to be ready: he is simply 'a voice, crying in the wilderness'. So it is that the first figure to appear

---

[11] Matt 1:22–23; 2:5–6, 15, 17–18, 23; cf. 4:14–16.
[12] Cf. Rikki E. Watts, *Isaiah's New Exodus in Mark,* WUNT 88 (Tübingen: Mohr Siebeck, 1997).
[13] While both Matthew and Luke quote Isa 40:3 when introducing John the Baptist's ministry (Matt 3:3; Luke 3:4–6), each of them uses the first half of the quotation (from Exodus and Malachi) elsewhere (Matt 11:10; Luke 7:27).

on the stage will be that of John, crying in the wilderness and proclaiming a baptism of repentance.

Although Mark's appeal to scripture in 1:2–3 is unique, there are interesting echoes of it throughout the narrative. First of all, we are reminded on various occasions of the importance of Isaiah's prophecies: Jesus is said to quote Isaiah (Isa 29:13) in 7:6–7 (where Isaiah is specifically mentioned), when he complains about the insincerity of the Pharisees' worship, and in 11:17 (quoting Isa 56:7), when he again protests about the failure of the religious authorities to worship God and the fact that they are preventing others from doing so. In a similar vein, though without specifically referring to scripture, he declares that the crowd's reaction to his teaching is a fulfilment of words taken from Isa 6:9–10 (Mark 4:12) and describes the Jewish leaders' failure to respond to his preaching in a parable that is clearly based on Isa 5:1–2 (Mark 12:1). There are further echoes of Isaiah in other passages, such as Mark 3:27 (Isa 49:24); 5:3 (Isa 65:4); 7:37 (Isa 35:5–6); 9:48 (Isa 66:24); 12:32 (Isa 45:21); 13:24–25 (Isa 13:10; 34:4); 13:31 (Isa 51:6).

It seems clear, then, that Mark does indeed see the story of Jesus as the fulfilment of the promises and warnings made through Isaiah. The messenger of God was sent to prepare the way of the Lord, who has now come to his people, bringing salvation to those who receive him and condemnation to those who do not.

Throughout the story, too, there are quotations from other passages of scripture. In disputes between Jesus and the Jewish religious authorities, for example, appeal is made to Moses in 10:4 and 6–7 (regarding divorce), in 10:19–20 (regarding the greatest commandment), and in 12:19 and 26 (regarding resurrection). Jesus is hailed by the crowd on his entry into Jerusalem with words taken from Pss 118 and 148 (Mark 11:9–10), while he himself is said to have quoted Ps 118 in Mark 12:10–11 regarding his forthcoming rejection and vindication and Ps 110 in 12:36 regarding his messianic status. His only words on the cross are taken from Ps 22 (Mark 15:34).

These various quotations and allusions demonstrate the truth of Mark's opening assertion that the good news about Jesus is the fulfilment of scripture. There is another, more ominous way, however, in which the story demonstrates that this is true. In two other passages, Jesus is said to have appealed to scripture without any indication as to *what* scriptures might be in mind: in both cases, he is referring to his own destiny. The first of these occurs once again at the turning point of the Gospel, immediately after the transfiguration, where Jesus' true identity is revealed to three of the disciples. As they come down from the mountain, Jesus warns Peter, James, and John that they must say nothing about what they have seen and heard until the Son of man has been raised from the dead (9:9), a saying that baffles the disciples, who ask about the promised coming of Elijah. Jesus then explains that Elijah has already come and that 'they have done to him whatever they wished, as it is the scriptures say of him' (9:13). It is clear that the returning Elijah is here identified with John the Baptist, but the reference to the scriptures is puzzling, since, although Mal 4:5 promises that Elijah will be sent before the day of the Lord, apparently identifying him with the 'messenger' of 3:1, it says nothing about suffering. Possibly the reference is to what 'they *wished*' to do to the first Elijah (1 Kgs 19:1–3). In the case of John, 'they' have already carried out what they wished to do.

Linked with these words is Jesus' declaration that the scriptures say of the Son of man that he must 'endure great suffering and be treated with contempt' (9:12). By now, readers of the Gospel (and even the disciples) will have grasped that, when he speaks of the Son of man, Jesus is referring to his own mission (see 2:10, 28; 8:31, 38). At the turning point in the narrative, therefore, we learn that this mission includes suffering and death (8:31; 9:12) and that this is foretold in scripture. Once again, there is no indication as to what scriptures are in mind.

The link with Elijah, who comes first and 'puts everything in order' points us back to 1:2–3. The coming of the messenger sent to prepare the way was announced in scripture. In these opening verses of the Gospel there is no indication that John's mission will not be successful: the first hint of this comes in 1:14, which speaks of his 'handing over' or arrest. Many refused to respond to Jesus himself, however, as the quotations from Isaiah in Mark 4:12 and 7:6–7 indicate. 'The way of the Lord' that John was summoned to prepare proves to be the 'way' that leads to Jerusalem and to death (9:33–34; 10:32, 52).[14] The 'good news' about Jesus, Messiah, Son of God, will prove to be about his suffering, death, and resurrection, but all this nevertheless takes place according to scripture.

This insistence that what happens to the Son of man takes place 'as it is written' reappears in the passion narrative. In 14:21, 'the Son of man goes as it is written of him', while in 14:27 Jesus is said to have quoted Zech 13:7, which speaks of the shepherd being struck and the sheep scattered. When he is arrested in Gethsemane, Jesus declares, 'let the scriptures be fulfilled' (14:49).

Although there are many references to scripture throughout Mark's Gospel – in particular to Isaiah – we see that this emphasis on the fulfilment of scripture in relation to Jesus' mission is especially marked in the prologue, at the turning point of the Gospel, and at its climax.

---

[14] The repetition of the phrase 'in the way' in 9:33–34, which seems unnecessary, is perhaps meant to remind us that the road that Jesus is following leads to Jerusalem. If so, then Mark is subtly underlining the disciples' total misunderstanding of the situation. While accompanying Jesus on the way that leads to the cross, they argue about which of them is the greatest!

4. As It Is Written: A Marcan Summary

Prologue	1:1–13	1:2–3, as it is written
Complication	1:14–8:21	4:12, quote from Isaiah
		7:6–7, quote from Isaiah
		allusions to Isaiah in 3:27; 5:3; 7:37
Discovery	8:22–9:13	9:12–13, as it is written of the Son of man/Elijah
Dénouement	9:14–13:37	11:17, quote from Isaiah
		12:1, parable (from Isaiah)
		allusions to Isaiah in 9:48; 12:32; 13:24–25, 31
		quotes from Law in 10:4, 6–7, 19–20; 12:20, 26
		quotes from Psalms in 11:9–10; 12:10–11, 36
Climax	14:1–15:47	14:21, as it is written of the Son of man
		14:27, for it is written (Zech 13:7)
		14:49, let scripture be fulfilled
		15:34–35, quote from Ps 22

5. John the Baptist

After being told that Mark is going to give us good news about Jesus, the Messiah, it is something of a surprise when the first person to appear on the stage is not Jesus himself but John. But of course the quotation in 1:2–3 has spoken of the one who is going to prepare the way for the Lord, and in John the Baptist we recognize Elijah, who is sent to announce the day of the Lord (Mal 4:5–6). The arrival of John is a reminder of just how important his role is. John's mission is described in Mark 1:2–8. His baptism signifies the people's repentance, in preparation for forgiveness. He prepares the way for one who is far greater than he, whose baptism will be with Spirit rather than water. In 1:7–8, Mark sets out John's message. It contains three statements, each of which makes the same point: the one who follows him, and whose coming John announces, is far greater than he. Jesus' story will begin only after John has been 'handed over' (1:14). John's role is that of the forerunner who heralds the coming of his successor.

As we have seen, John is referred to again, immediately after the transfiguration, now clearly identified with the returning Elijah, sent to prepare the way (9:11). Jesus tells his disciples that Elijah has already come and that 'they' have done to him what they wished. To hearers of the Gospel, the meaning of Jesus' words is immediately clear, since in the section between the prologue and the recognition scene, Mark told at length the story of John's death (6:14–29). Arrested because his preaching was unpalatable to the authorities, he was put to death when Herodias found an opportunity to outwit her husband Herod. King Herod, knowing John to be a righteous and holy man, and therefore reluctant to execute him, nevertheless succumbed to pressure. The account ends with John's disciples taking his body and laying it in a tomb, and though there are rumours of John's resurrection (6:14–16), they are untrue. Elijah has indeed come: he has prepared the way of the Lord, 'and they have done to him whatever they wished' (9:13).

To those of us who have heard the story of Jesus before, the significance of this account of John's death has ominous overtones. No wonder that we are reminded, in 9:12, that 'Elijah's' fate is linked to that of the Son of man. Just as John's baptism in water pointed forward to Jesus' baptism in Spirit,[15] so his death points forward to that of Jesus himself. Like John, Jesus – the Son of man – will be 'handed over' and put to death. Jesus' own story will in a sense mirror that of John, for when we come to the passion narrative we hear how the religious authorities, finding Jesus' teaching unpalatable, seized the opportunity to bring about his death (14:1–2, 10–11). They, too, managed to outwit the political leader, Pilate, even though he believed Jesus to be innocent (15:1–15). Jesus' death is inevitable, and the story seems to end when Joseph of Arimathea lays Jesus' body in a tomb (15:42–47). This time, however, rumours of a resurrection are replaced by the scene at the empty tomb, where someone who appears to be a heavenly messenger assures us that Jesus has indeed been raised from the dead (16:6).

But what of John, alias Elijah? We look for him in the passion narrative in vain, but then realize that this is because his enemies have disposed of him. Yet his failure to appear is noted, when the crowd misunderstands Jesus' words from the cross and think that he is calling for Elijah to assist him (15:35–36). But how *could* Elijah come, when he, too, has been put to death? Jesus' forerunner has been silenced. Since 'they' have done to him what they wanted, Jesus' own fate is sealed.

Mark clearly thinks of John as Jesus' forerunner, and we are reminded of this fact once again in the section between the recognition scene and the climax, when Jesus challenges his enemies to say whether John's authority was human or divine (11:27–33). The answer they give – or fail to give – will determine the answer to the question they have posed him regarding his *own* authority. If John's authority came from God, so too does that of the one whose coming John foretold. But if the religious authorities failed to recognize the source of John's authority, they will inevitably fail to recognize that of Jesus.

---

[15] Influenced by Luke, we are accustomed to thinking of this Spirit baptism as something that took place at Pentecost. Mark, however, does not relate this story, and it is likely that he regarded the ministry of Jesus, who received the Spirit at his own baptism, as a 'baptism with Spirit'. See Morna D. Hooker, 'John's Baptism: A Prophetic Sign', in *The Holy Spirit and Christian Origins: Essays in Honor of James D. G. Dunn*, eds. Graham N. Stanton, Bruce W. Longenecker, and Stephen C. Barton (Grand Rapids: Eerdmans, 2004), 22–40 = below, essay 21 (pp. 298–315).

6. John the Baptist: A Marcan Summary

Prologue	1:1–13	1:4–8, John: forerunner
Complication	1:14–8:21	1:14, handed over
		6:14–29, John's death
Discovery	8:22–9:13	9:11–12, John (= Elijah): forerunner in suffering
Dénouement	9:14–13:37	11:27–33, authority
Climax	14:1–15:47	15:35–36, Elijah unable to help

7. Jesus, Son of God

As we have noted, the words 'Son of God' may be an addition in 1:1, but if so they clearly represent fairly Mark's own understanding, for as we shall see, the true meaning of the term 'Christ' is found only when it is explained by that of 'Son of God'. The words occur again in 1:11, and this time there is no doubt at all about their authenticity. Here Jesus is addressed as 'my beloved Son' by the heavenly voice at his baptism. According to 1:11, the heavenly voice speaks to Jesus alone, but the affirmation that he is Son of God is repeated at the transfiguration (9:7), which follows closely after Caesarea Philippi,[16] forming part of the 'turning point' of the Gospel, and this time it is heard not only by Jesus but by three of his disciples. When we turn to the 'trial' scene, at the end of the Gospel, the high priest's question seems to equate 'Messiah' with 'the Son of the Blessed' (14:61), and as with 'Messiah', Jesus' clear acknowledgement of his identity as 'Son' is echoed at the crucifixion, for when he dies, the Roman centurion declares, 'Surely this man was [the] son of God' (15:39). Although a Roman centurion could hardly have used these words with the significance that Mark gave to them, they echo the words of the heavenly voice in 1:11 and 9:7, and as though to ensure that we see the connection, Mark links the centurion's confession with the statement that the temple curtain was torn in two, using the same verb that he used in 1:10 of the tearing apart of the heavens.[17] When the barrier between God and humankind is removed, the truth about Jesus is revealed.

Jesus' identity as Son of God is thus made plain at the beginning (in Mark's 'prologue'), at the turning point (where Jesus' identity is first revealed to humans), and at the climax of his story (in the passion narrative). It seems as though, while it is natural for humans to consider the possibility that Jesus may be the Christ, God's anointed one (1:1; 8:27; 14:62; 15 *passim*), Mark is pushing us to recognize that the most profound understanding of what this

---

[16] Unusually, Mark links the two narratives with the phrase 'six days later', ensuring that we see the link between the two narratives.

[17] See Rhoads, Dewey, and Michie, *Mark as Story*, 48.

means is conveyed by the words of the heavenly voice (1:11; 9:7), picked up in mockery in 14:61 and in astonishment in 15:39.

As with the term *Christos* (Χριστός), 'Son of God' occurs in between these three significant passages, either in addressing or referring to Jesus. In 3:11 and 5:7, Jesus is addressed as 'Son of God' by unclean spirits, and in 12:6 and 13:32 Jesus appears to be speaking of himself as 'Son', though in neither case openly. Once again, however, these identifications are unheard or uncomprehended by the characters in the story, although they ring bells for those of us who are 'in the know', since we have been privileged to witness the baptism and the transfiguration and to overhear the words spoken from heaven.

8. Son of God: A Marcan Summary

Prologue	1:1–13	(1:1, text dubious)
		1:11, voice from heaven
Complication	1:14–8:21	3:11, 5:7, recognized by unclean spirits
Discovery	8:22–9:13	9:7, voice from heaven
Dénouement	9:14–13:37	12:6; 13:32, Jesus' self-reference
Climax	14:1–15:47	14:61, high priest's question
		15:39, centurion's 'confession'

9. The Shape of Mark's Story

If we look at the shape of Mark's story, we find that there are certain themes that occur in the opening prologue, at the fulcrum of the narrative – the moment when some of his followers begin to understand who he is – and at its conclusion. These themes are Jesus' identity as Messiah; the fact that what takes place is 'in accordance with scripture'; the witness of John, both in his proclamation of Jesus' coming and in his death; and Jesus' identity as Son of God. At these three points in the narrative, these facts about Jesus are revealed to a few of the characters in the story or to us, its hearers. There are also allusions to all these facts in the intervening narrative, though their significance here is hidden from the characters.

The good news is, as we are told in Mark's prologue, essentially about Jesus, the Messiah and Son of God, and is witnessed to by scripture and John the Baptist, who is himself fulfilling the role set out for him in scripture. What we might never have guessed from these opening verses is that the story would end with Jesus' rejection, suffering, death, and resurrection. True, when we hear the story for a second or third time, we notice possible hints of what is to come: Jesus, here baptized by John in Jordan, will later speak of a far more terrible 'baptism' that he will have to undergo (10:38). Further, the fact that we are not told the outcome of Jesus' testing by Satan may hint that the battle is not finally over, even though the strong man has been bound and his property is being plundered (3:27). Certainly at Caesarea Philippi Peter is addressed as 'Satan' and rebuked for tempting him, and in Gethsemane Jesus is said to be 'troubled and distressed' (14:33) as he prays to be spared from drinking the cup prepared for him; he is surely being 'tested' here, and he urges Peter to pray that *he* might be spared from being tested. But these hints in 1:1–13 are 'echoes' of what is to come rather than clear indications of what lies ahead. In any case, we do not need to be told the *plot* of the story in the prologue; we simply need to be told who Jesus is so that we can understand the narrative that follows.

If we begin to read Mark's narrative at 1:14, we may well conclude that the story is about the kingdom of God. This, after all, is what Jesus proclaims, not himself. But the question of his identity continually intrudes. The unclean spirits recognize him as God's 'Holy One' or 'Son' (1:24, 34; 3:11; 5:7). In various ways, he is said to do what God alone can do: he forgives sins – and is accused of blasphemy (2:5–7); he stills a storm, and the disciples, astonished at his control over wind and waves, ask 'Who is this?' (4:41) – unsurprisingly, since only God can exercise such power (Ps 89:8–9)! He claims to be working in the power of the Holy Spirit (3:29). He raises a dead child (5:35–43). In his hometown, his neighbours acknowledge his wisdom and power but reject him (6:1–6). Elsewhere, however, he is acknowledged to be a prophet (6:14–16).

In a miracle reminiscent of one attributed to Elisha (2 Kgs 4:42–44), Jesus feeds a large crowd (6:30–44), though the emphasis placed on the numbers involved – a crowd of five thousand fed with five loaves and two fish – indicates a far greater miracle than that performed by Elisha, who is said to have fed one hundred men with twenty loaves. Mark's story suggests, too, that Jesus is seen as a second Moses; yet he is surely greater than Moses, since the exodus story tells us that it was *the Lord* who provided the manna, not Moses (Exod 16; cf. John 6:32). Moreover, there is food left over and to spare (6:43), whereas the manna could not be kept. Finally, although Moses walked *through* the sea, he certainly did not walk *on* it, which is what Jesus then does (6:47–52).[18] Again, this is something that God alone could do (Job 9:8). Jesus greets his disciples with words we normally translate as 'It is I' but that also mean 'I am'. Does Mark understand Jesus to be using the divine name? A second feeding narrative (8:1–10) is followed by another boat trip, in which the disciples fail to understand Jesus' teaching and comment on the fact that they have no bread with them (8:14–21). But why should they be concerned

---

[18] It was God, of course, who parted the waters of the Red Sea to enable the Israelites to pass through: Exod 14:21; Ps 77:19–20; Isa 43:16; 51:10.

about that when one who is greater than Moses and the prophets, and has twice supplied the crowds with food, is with them? They are blind and deaf to the truth, as were the crowds in 4:10–12, still unaware of who Jesus really is.

The recognition scene of 8:27–30 contrasts the idea we have already met in 6:14–16 that Jesus is John the Baptist, Elijah, or one of the prophets, with the truth: he is the Messiah. But like the blind man whose eyes are at first only partly restored (8:22–26), Peter can grasp only half the truth. He rejects the notion that Jesus must suffer, but Jesus continues by telling would-be disciples that they, too, must be prepared to share his sufferings (8:34–38). The truth half-grasped at Caesarea Philippi is confirmed by the story of the transfiguration, which Mark has firmly linked to it by the unusual use of the phrase 'six days later' (9:2). Now Jesus is seen by Peter, James, and John conversing with Moses and Elijah, but is revealed as greater than they, since 'This is my beloved Son'. Again, however, they are told that Jesus' destiny is to suffer. Jesus sees messiahship and sonship as involving suffering, and this is because he sees his role as that of the Son of man, given authority by God but rejected by others.[19] From now on, the narrative will show Jesus traveling to Jerusalem, followed by disciples who continually show that they do not understand why he is going there (9:30–37; 10:32–45).

As Jesus approaches Jerusalem, he heals another blind man, who hails him as 'Son of David': even though he is blind, he already recognizes something of the truth. This time, the man's sight is immediately fully restored, and he follows Jesus 'on the way' to Jerusalem; he is prepared to become a disciple of one who is heading for suffering and death. His healing signals the time of disclosure. Jesus then deliberately stages his entry into Jerusalem, riding into Jerusalem on the back of a donkey, an extraordinary action in view of the fact that all pilgrims *walked* into the city. This provocative action has to be seen as a claim to messiahship (cf. 1 Kgs 1:28–40). The cursing of the fig tree (11:12–14, 20) is best understood as a sign of Israel's imminent fate, since she, too, has failed to produce fruit when the Lord looked for it (see Jer 8:13; Hos 9:10, 16; Mic 7:1). The cleansing of the temple (11:11, 15–19) suggests the coming of the Lord to his temple foretold in Mal 3:1–4. Jesus condemns the commerce taking place in the temple, which is preventing people from worshipping God, and in the ensuing conversation with the religious authorities implicitly claims that his authority comes from God (11:27–33).

In his teaching, Jesus hints that he is God's Son (12:6) and greater than David (12:35–37), while privately to four disciples he again hints that he is

---

[19] There is enormous debate about the significance of the term 'the Son of man'. Whatever Jesus himself may have meant by the term, however, Mark appears to have understood it in terms of Dan 7:13 (see Mark 8:38; 13:26; 14:62). The Son of man represents the faithful in Israel, presently suffering but promised vindication because of their obedience to God.

Messiah (13:21) and Son (13:32), and he affirms that the Son of man will come with great power and glory (13:26). Then, immediately before the passion story unfolds, a woman pours costly ointment over his head, a preparation, says Jesus, for his coming burial (14:3–9). But – anomalous as it may seem, since the action is performed by a woman – the fact that she pours the ointment *on his head* suggests that he is being anointed king.

And so we move into the passion narrative itself, where the truth about Jesus is found in the mouth of the high priest – a fact of great significance, even though he refuses to recognize the truth of his own words, since it was the high priest's task to anoint and proclaim Israel's king. The irony of a woman who anoints Jesus and a high priest who dismisses his own proclamation as blasphemy is then continued in the account of Jesus' condemnation and crucifixion as 'the king of the Jews'.

The story reaches its climax with the centurion's declaration that Jesus was 'son of God'. These are the last words spoken by a human in the Gospel, and they provide the moment of full revelation. With the death of Jesus, the temple curtain has been torn in two (15:38), and a Gentile has access to the presence of God. Jesus' executioner (no matter that he does not understand it) sees the truth.

Mark's story has an epilogue (16:1–8). We are told how the women who witnessed Jesus' death and burial come to the tomb and find it empty. They are told by a young man dressed in white that he has been raised, and they are commissioned to tell Jesus' disciples to follow him to Galilee. Terrified, they flee from the tomb and fail to tell anyone what they have seen and heard.[20]

The story ends, then, with total human failure. The religious authorities have failed to accept Jesus, Pontius Pilate has caved in to pressure, the crowds have melted away, the disciples have run away, Judas has betrayed him, Peter has denied him, and at the end even the women – hitherto faithful – have failed him. In spite of the centurion's confession, the story appears to be a tragedy. Yet Mark introduced it as 'the beginning of good news', and now we realize that it is, indeed, only the beginning. The very fact that the story is now being told means that the women must have overcome their fear and that the disciples did indeed obey the command to go to Galilee. There they had to learn all over again what discipleship meant: taking up the cross and following Jesus. The message entrusted to the women is a message of forgiveness. The disciples – even Peter! – are being given a second chance.

---

[20] Neither of the endings that follow Mark 16:8 was written by Mark himself: the style and vocabulary of both are quite different from Mark's own. They seem to have been composed by early scribes who were dissatisfied with Mark's abrupt ending and who felt the need to add information about appearances of the risen Jesus.

But Mark's abrupt ending means that the final scene concerns not just the disciples but becomes an invitation to those who hear his story. 'If you want to see the risen Christ', he seems to be saying, 'You, too, must set out on a journey — set out on the way of discipleship, believing that he has indeed been raised. Go in spirit to Galilee, the place where men and women were challenged by the mighty acts and words of Jesus, and learn what discipleship means'. The story Mark tells is only the beginning of a story that he invites his readers to continue for themselves, as they come to acknowledge Jesus as Messiah and Son of God and to preach the good news to the world (cf. Mark 13:10).

10. The Nature of New Testament Theology*

1. Introduction

What *is* New Testament theology? The answers to this question are so many and so various that they would appear to be largely dependent on the understanding of those who attempt to define it. To the New Testament scholar, however, New Testament theology is primarily an historical discipline. Our difficulties lie chiefly in knowing how to approach it and analyse it.

The editors have helped us here by allocating a particular topic to each contributor. Yet to be asked to focus on Christology can hardly be said to narrow down the field of research, for in a sense *all* New Testament theology is Christology. Our New Testament books focus on the figure of Jesus precisely because he is the new element in the situation. New Testament authors were not concerned to write a systematic 'theology', but were reacting to the life, death, and resurrection of Jesus, whom they believed to be God's Messiah or Christ. The evangelists were concerned to write 'the good news about Jesus Christ' (Mark 1:1). The letter writers – above all, Paul – wrote pastoral letters to those who responded to this good news and were endeavouring to live by it. Christological statements often seem to occur in these letters only incidentally, but the fact that they are introduced at all demonstrates how relevant Christology was to Christian life. As we read the New Testament, it would seem that Christ is in the foreground, while God is in the background.

Yet it is precisely because God *is* 'in the background' that we have a New Testament at all. We must beware of being misled by the fact that its books focus so dearly on the figure of Jesus, for the basic assumption that undergirds them all is this: that in Christ, *God* has been at work, revealing his salvation. For Paul, this meant that what took place in and through Jesus was due to 'the grace of God' (Rom 5:15–16) who, 'in Christ, was reconciling the world to himself' (2 Cor 5:19).[1] John expressed the same belief, in statements attributed to Jesus himself: Jesus was sent by God (John 5:30), and the words Jesus speaks and the works he does are the words and works of God, so that once again, God can be said to be 'in him' (John 8:46–47; 10:37–38). Although

---

* Originally written as a contribution to a book with this title.

[1] The translation of this verse is notoriously difficult: does Paul mean that 'God was in Christ, reconciling the world to himself', or that 'in Christ, God was reconciling the world to himself'? Whichever way we translate these words, it is clear that the reconciliation that took place through Christ's death and resurrection was understood by Paul to be the work of God.

Mark heads his story 'the good news about Jesus Christ', the origin of this 'good news' is God himself, and was promised by him long before, in holy scripture (Mark 1:2; cf. Rom 1:1–4). The Epistle to the Hebrews opens with the declaration that '*God*, who spoke in time past to our fathers in many different ways through the prophets, has now spoken to us by a son', while the message preached by Peter in the early chapters of Acts speaks of *God* raising Jesus from the dead and making him Lord and Messiah (Acts 2:32, 36), and of the way in which *God* has fulfilled his promises through him (Acts 3:13, 15, 18–21, 26). Above all, it was this conviction that God had raised Jesus from the dead that was crucial for Christian faith.

We see, then, that though Jesus is in the foreground throughout the New Testament, with the result that the vital question for believers came to be the one he is said to have put to his disciples, 'Who do you say that I am?' – a question that dominated the early church's doctrinal controversies – the more fundamental question was: 'What has *God* done – in Christ?' It was the answers they gave to this question that not only enabled them to answer the question about Jesus' identity, but led to a new understanding of God as the 'Father of our Lord Jesus Christ' (2 Cor 11:31).

In the New Testament, as in the old, the nature of God is revealed by what he does. In Christ, God showed his love for humankind (Rom 5:8); in Christ's death, God revealed his glory, that is his nature (John 12:28); through Christ, men and women came to recognize that God's salvation was meant for all people (Luke 2:30–32), and that the Gentiles were included in God's covenant with Israel. New Testament theology is focused on Christ, not merely because he was at the forefront of their experience, but because it was in pondering the meaning of his life, death, and resurrection that Christian believers found themselves reshaping their entire theology. Their experience of Christ affected their understanding of God and his purpose for the world, their grasp of the work of the Holy Spirit and the nature of God's people, together with their hope for the future, and forced them to rethink the way in which God's demand that his people be holy as he himself is holy might be fulfilled.

2. Dynamic, Not Static

Summing up the implications of the opening paragraphs of his *New Testament Theology*, George Caird wrote: 'it follows that there is no such thing as New Testament theology'.[2] It might seem an unpropitious beginning! Yet Caird was right, for as we have noted already, our New Testament authors were not

---

[2] G.B. Caird, *New Testament Theology*, ed. L.D. Hurst (Oxford: Clarendon, 1994), 4.

attempting to write a 'theology', but were engaged in apologetic and dialogue. The real problem with talking about 'New Testament theology', however, is that it suggests something static and complete, whereas what we have in the New Testament is a number of different people all 'doing theology' in different situations. We do not have an inanimate corpse, labelled 'New Testament theology', laid out on a mortuary slab and waiting for dissection; rather we have a series of photographs of people vigorously engaged in the process of 'theologizing', trying to work out the significance of their faith. To use a biblical metaphor, we have something that was in the process of being written by the living Spirit on hearts of flesh, not a closed system that had been carved on tablets of stone, and was no longer capable of development and change (2 Cor 3:1–6).

In reading the New Testament, we find ourselves conversing with first-century Christians who were attempting to think out the meaning of the life, death, and resurrection of Jesus. In the early years that meant primarily trying to understand the 'Christ event' in relation to the holy scriptures and to what, as Jews, they already knew about God. We find that their ideas developed as they did so, and as they realized the implications of what they were claiming for Jesus. And as new situations and problems arose, they expressed their faith in new ways. The content of their belief was inextricably bound up with the context in which they lived and worked, so that the form in which they expressed their belief necessarily changed as their circumstances changed, in order to be meaningful. But that context itself changed and shaped their belief.

We see an example of this at the simplest level in the basic response to the question 'Who is Jesus?' The earliest confession of faith seems to have been 'Jesus is the Messiah' (Mark 8:29), a message that would have been understandable in the Jewish context in which it was first proclaimed (Acts 2:36; 5:42). The evangelists all make plain that the 'good news' they are announcing concerns Jesus the Messiah (Matt 1:1, 18; Mark 1:1, 34; Luke 2:11, 26; John 1:18, 41; 20:31). Paul, preaching the gospel in the Gentile world, could hardly expect his converts to find such a confession meaningful. Although he continually referred to Jesus as *Christos*, the Greek form of *Messiah*, the confession which made most sense in this new context was 'Jesus is Lord' (Rom 10:9; 1 Cor 12:3; Phil 2:11). Questions regarding the origin and background of this term are endlessly asked, and are given widely divergent answers: some argue that it derives from the Old Testament understanding of God as 'Lord' (cf. Rom 10:13); others that it reflects pagan belief in 'gods many and lords many' (1 Cor 8:5); others that it is a direct denial of the claims of Caesar (Phil 2:11; 3:20). We need, however, to distinguish *origin* from *context*. If we are asking who first used the title 'Lord' for Jesus, the answer seems to be 'Jewish Christians', since the phrase *marana tha* (1 Cor 16:22), meaning

'Our Lord, come!' (or 'Our Lord has come'), which Paul apparently expected his readers to understand, is Aramaic. It is clear that Paul's own use of the term was shaped by the Old Testament; he appears, for example, to have been influenced by Ps 110:1 (Rom 8:34; 1 Cor 15:25). Gentiles listening to his message, however, would have heard it against the background of their previous belief in many gods and many lords: now they were assured that there was only *one* Lord (1 Cor 8:6), who had been enthroned by the one true God (Phil 2:9–11). But at some stage it came to have a more particular resonance, because they were living in the Roman Empire, where exclusive claims came to be made in time for Caesar. Whether the cult of the emperor was already a political force in the time of Paul is not clear; what is certain is that the confession 'Jesus is Lord' took on a new significance when it was seen as fundamentally opposed to the confession of Caesar as Lord (*Martyrdom of Polycarp* 8.2).

New terms are needed to express belief as the gospel moves into different contexts, and as new circumstances arise. The old terms, when they are used in new settings, are interpreted differently. Inevitably, then, the belief itself changes: something is gained, and something is lost. Once again, the term 'Messiah' provides a good example. It is unlikely that the Greek form of the word, 'Christos', had already replaced 'Jesus' as a name by the time that Paul took the gospel to Gentiles, and he could easily have referred to Jesus by his name, which would have been more comprehensible to his converts. The fact that Paul continued to use the term 'Christ' in an alien context suggests that it was important to his understanding of the gospel. And indeed, the word 'Messiah' reflects his understanding of God's purpose for the world and the role of Israel in the divine plans, for it was through his 'Messiah' ('anointed one') that God had fulfilled his promises to Israel (Rom 9:5, cf. 1:3): it was because Jesus was the Messiah that, like the kings before him, he could be the representative of his nation, and that God could recreate his people 'in Christ'. In the Gentile world, however, the full significance of the term was easily forgotten, if it was ever understood. It therefore rapidly came to be used merely as another name for Jesus. Yet this change signalled far more than a forgetting of the term's full meaning; when Christians forgot the real significance of the name 'Christ', it became easier for them to cut adrift from Judaism.

If 'Messiah' lost its significance in the Gentile world, another appellation, 'the Son of God', gained new layers of meaning. In Old Testament usage, the phrase was used of Israel herself (Exod 4:22; Hos 11:1) or of Israel's king (2 Sam 7:14; Ps 2:7). The dual use is unsurprising since, as we have noted already, the king was regarded as the representative of his people. As 'son of God', however, the king was also the representative of God. It is hardly surprising, then, if we find both Paul and John speaking of God 'sending' his son (Rom 8:3; Gal 4:4; John 3:17; 1 John 4:9–10, 14; the verbs vary, but the meaning appears to be the same). Because children often resemble their parents, a son of God was naturally understood to have been obedient to his father. In the book of Wisdom, written shortly before the Christian era, the righteous man is described as 'God's son'. Whatever Jesus did as God's son must, then, have been the will of God. This understanding is reflected in the Gospels, and in particular in the passion narratives. In an extraordinary twist to the story in Mark and Matthew, Jesus' executioner watches him die and proclaims him to be 'Son of God'. Both evangelists had earlier linked the disciples' realization that Jesus is 'Son of God' with Jesus' attempts to explain that this meant suffering and death (Matt 16:16, 21; Mark 9:7, 12). For Jesus, sonship meant obedience to the will of God, whom he addresses as 'Abba', meaning 'Father' (Matt 26:39, 42; Mark 14:36). All three Synoptic evangelists describe how Jesus is challenged by the high priest to say whether or not he is 'the Son of God', and how it is his response (however enigmatic) to this final question that leads to his crucifixion (Matt 26:63–65; Mark 14:61–63; Luke 22:70–71). In the Fourth Gospel, the 'hour' of Jesus' death is seen as the purpose of his ministry, and by his death he glorifies God (John 12:27). In dying, Jesus both discloses (17:1–5) and achieves (19:30) God's plan for the world, which is to give eternal life to all who trust in him (3:16).

For Paul, too, the term 'Son of God' expresses Jesus' closeness to his Father. The gospel of God which Paul proclaims is the gospel 'about God's Son' (Rom 1:1–3, 9). That gospel concerns the death and resurrection of his Son (Rom 5:10). Paul speaks not only of God giving up his Son to death (Rom 8:32), but of the Son giving himself up (Gal 2:20): Father and Son are united in purpose, and the Son is obedient to the Father's will. So God 'sent his Son' (Rom 8:3; Gal 4:4); but, as in the Johannine literature, this 'sending' has redemptive purpose: the Son of God shares human weakness, and by identifying himself with men and women, enables them to share his death and resurrection, and so to be 'conformed to his image' (Rom 8:29) and to become 'sons of God'[3] addressing God as 'Abba' (Rom 8:14–15; Gal 4:4–6). In Christ, their future is secure, for the Son of God will come again from heaven (1 Thess 1:10) but though everything will finally be subject to him, the Son himself is subject to God (1 Cor 15:24–28).

Paul's insistence that those who trust in God and in what God has done in Christ share the likeness of God's Son points us back to the Jewish origins of his thought. God had called *Israel* to be his Son; now, 'in Christ' – that is, in the Messiah – Christian believers had inherited the promises made to Abraham, and had been made 'sons of God' (Gal 3:26).[4] This 'sonship' brought

---

[3] Many modern translations obscure Paul's logic, by choosing to use politically correct language and substituting 'children' for 'sons'; Paul's point, however, is that men and women all become like him; for him, the term 'sons' was inclusive, not exclusive.

[4] Once again, Paul's term is meant to include women as well as men, a point he specifically spells out in v. 28, where he makes it clear that race, gender and status are all irrelevant 'in

them immense privileges, for they were now heirs of God's promises, but it also brought the requirement to obey God: for Paul, however, 'obedience' no longer meant obedience to the Law, but the obedience that sprang from faith, which he termed the 'obedience of faith' (Rom 1:5; 16:26). As an apostle, Paul believed himself to have been called by God to be a role model of the Christian life, since God had been pleased 'to reveal his Son in me' (Gal 2:16);[5] his task was like that of a mother giving birth to children who would be like Christ, their elder brother (Gal 4:19). Those who were truly 'like Christ' were truly human, for they were what God had intended men and women to be – like God himself.

In a pagan world, however, Paul's words would once again have been understood somewhat differently. The term 'Son of God' would have suggested a divine being of some kind, and according to the myths of the ancient world, the sons of the gods were not characterized by obedience to their parents. The notion that the Son of God had been sent would have been interpreted as indicating not so much the purpose of the sender as the descent of a 'heavenly' being into the world. Inevitably, then, new questions began to be asked – e.g. about the Son's pre-existence. As time went by, Paul's language about Jesus as Son of God was understood as spelling out his 'divinity', and the term no longer reminded Christians of their calling, but separated Christ from them. According to the later exegesis of the church, 'the Son of God' expressed Christ's divinity, while the term 'the Son of man' referred to his humanity. Were those who read New Testament language in this way distorting its meaning, or were they drawing out the implications of its teaching in ways that were appropriate to their own culture? Unfortunately, what tended to happen was that the later interpretation came to be seen as the authoritative and only way of understanding the text, with the result that 'New Testament theology' was not only identified with the theology of a later community, but was itself regarded as though it were set in stone.

3. The Gospel of/about Jesus

The most fundamental shift of perspective had, of course, taken place even earlier when the Christian faith was first born. With the death and resurrection of Jesus (to quote Bultmann's famous words), 'the proclaimer

---

Christ'. His insistence that women had equal standing with men in the new people of God is remarkable, in view of the cultural assumptions of his day.

[5] The phrase is usually translated 'to me', but the normal meaning of the Greek preposition used by Paul here is 'in'. For Paul, the revelation on the Damascus Road was far more than an apparition; it was a call to reveal God to the Gentiles; cf. Acts 9:15; 22:15; 26:16–18.

became the proclaimed'.[6] New Testament scholars agree on very little, but on one thing there is unanimity: what Jesus proclaimed was the kingdom of God. Yet the message of his followers was clearly centred on Jesus himself. The shift is nicely reflected in the enigmatic opening words of Mark's Gospel: 'The gospel (good news) of Jesus Christ'. Mark might perhaps mean the good news proclaimed *by* Jesus, but what he goes on to write is the good news *about* him.

This shift is even clearer, of course, when we turn to the Fourth Gospel. While it is true that the Synoptic tradition reflects the beliefs of the community, the focus of Jesus' teaching in the Synoptic Gospels is the kingdom of God, not Jesus himself. Jesus speaks only rarely about himself, and when he does, he demands secrecy (Mark 8:27–30 and //s), or refers enigmatically to his approaching suffering and vindication (Mark 8:31–33 and //s). It is only during the 'trial' before the high priest that Jesus is said to have agreed that the terms 'Messiah' and 'Son of God' were appropriate ways of referring to him (Mark 14:61–62 and //s). The evangelists preferred to show their readers how they should interpret the figure of Jesus by their editorial comments and through their arrangement of the material rather than by putting claims into the mouth of Jesus. In John, however, we are dealing with tradition that has been radically modified by Christian belief. There are, to be sure, echoes of sayings and stories found in the Synoptics, but the picture of Jesus presented by John is very different. Instead of implicit Christology, we have explicit claims. Jesus speaks of himself openly as 'the Son' (John 5:20–23 etc.), and acknowledges that he is the Messiah (John 4:25–26; 11:24–25). He makes extraordinary claims for himself in the 'I am' sayings. No longer is Jesus' message about the kingdom of God: rather, it is about Jesus himself. This is a different kind of apologetic, which spells out clearly the claims of the Christian community about Jesus by placing them in the mouth of Jesus himself. John's concern was to persuade his readers to 'believe that Jesus is the Christ the Son of God, and through believing, might have life in his name' (20:31). But though his method was very different from that of the other evangelists, their purpose was similar, for they, too, were concerned to write 'the good news about Jesus'.

The difference between the message of Jesus and the message about Jesus is not, however, as great as might at first appear, since the message of Jesus himself contained implicit claims. Although Jesus proclaimed the kingdom of God – or rather the rule of God – that rule was very closely bound up with his own person, so that in a very real sense it was embodied in him. His message – directed to his own people, the Jews – was a message of good news

---

[6] Rudolf Bultmann, *Theology of the New Testament*, vol. 1, trans. Kendrick Grobel (London: SCM Press, 1952), 33.

(Matt 4:23; Mark 1:14; Luke 4:18), for while he demanded repentance (Matt 4:17; Mark 1:15; Luke 5:32), he offered 'release to the captives and recovery of sight to the blind' (Luke 4:18). According to all the Gospels, the salvation he spoke of was experienced by those whom he healed. While there are obvious historical problems surrounding some of the miracle stories, there seems to be a firm tradition that Jesus did possess extraordinary powers of healing, and that what he did made as much impact as what he said. Although it is only in the Fourth Gospel that the miracles are described as 'signs' and that their significance is spelt out, it is clear that the other evangelists, too, see the healing miracles as integral to Jesus' message. All three Synoptic writers spell this out at the beginning of their accounts of Jesus' ministry: Matthew tells us that Jesus travelled through Galilee, 'proclaiming the good news of the kingdom, and curing every disease and every sickness' (Matt 4:23); Mark describes how Jesus taught in the synagogue at Capernaum, amazing everyone with the authority with which he taught and expelled unclean spirits (Mark 1:22, 27); and Luke tells how Jesus read the opening verses of Isaiah 61 in the synagogue at Nazareth, and then declared, 'Today this scripture has been fulfilled in your hearing' (Luke 4:16–21).

The evangelists interpreted the miracles, not as mere 'signs and wonders', but as embodying Jesus' message. It is not surprising if the authority with which he spoke and acted raised questions about the source of his authority (Mark 3:22 and //s; 11:28 and //s). The evangelists provide their answer to this question in their opening paragraphs, and though their methods are very different, their answer is the same: the story of Jesus is the story of how God fulfilled his promises to his people, the story of what God did in and through him. They expect us to read their narratives in the light of this knowledge, while providing reminders from time to time, in words attributed to Jesus, of why he is acting as he does: thus we are told that his exorcisms are the work of the Holy Spirit (Matt 12:28; Mark 3:23–30); that he is sent by God (Matt 15:24; Mark 9:37 and //s; 15:24; Luke 4:18; John *passim*); that he came for a purpose (Mark 10:45; Luke 19:10; John 10:10); and that what happens to him – even his suffering and death – is in accord with God's will (Mark 14:35–36 and //s; Matt 26:56: Mark 14:49; John 12:27–28).

Many of these statements are honed by opposition, and those who raise questions about Jesus' authority in the Gospels are his opponents. The reaction of those who took exception to his teaching was, in effect, to say, 'Who does he think he is?' So we see that the question about Jesus' authority moves easily into the question 'Who, then, is this?' (Mark 4:41). For his followers, it was not enough to say 'he was sent by God'; faith required labels, definitions, confessions, all of which would summarize and express what they believed about him.

4. The Use of Titles

Much of the discussion of New Testament Christology in the twentieth century centred on the investigation of titles. This was hardly surprising, since terms such as 'Messiah', 'Lord', and 'Son of God' tend to be used in confessions of faith. Yet it is important to remember that these 'titles' are succinct ways of expressing beliefs, shorthand summaries which, as we have seen, convey a range of ideas that differ according to the situation of those who hear them. Indeed, 'Son of God' is primarily an expression of a relationship rather than a title (Ps 2:7; Rom 1:3; John 3:16). There is little in the Synoptic tradition to suggest that Jesus referred to himself as 'Son of God' (Matt 11:25–27 // Luke 10:21–22 is the remarkable exception), but there are clear indications that he thought of God as his Father (Mark 14:36 and //s), and could therefore be described by God himself as his Son (Mark 1:11 and //s; 9:7 and //s). 'Messiah' is used in the Old Testament only as an adjective (1 Sam 2:10), not as a title, and once again expresses a relationship to God. Was Jesus perhaps thought of as 'anointed' by God, or by the Spirit of God (Luke 4:18, quoting Isa 61:1), before he was confessed as 'the Messiah'?

The Gospels preserve answers to the question of Jesus' identity that were later considered inadequate: he was addressed as 'teacher' by both friends and enemies (Matt 8:19; Mark 4:38; 12:14, 19; Luke 12:13; John 11:28); he was considered by many to be a prophet (Mark 6:15 // Luke 9:8; Mark 8:28 and //s; Luke 24:19; John 4:19), perhaps even *the* prophet spoken of by Moses (Deut 18:15; John 6:14; 7:40). Jesus is said to have spoken of himself in terms of a prophet (Matt 13:57 // Mark 6:4; Luke 4:24; 13:33). But is that how he thought of himself? Or did he believe himself to be 'the Messiah'?

The question of the 'messianic self-consciousness of Jesus' dominated a great deal of christological investigation in the twentieth century. The answer was regarded by many scholars as being of great significance for Christian faith. Typical of their approach is this comment, dating from 1945: *'The Church cannot indefinitely continue to believe about Jesus what he did not know to be true about himself!'* (italics original).[7] The conviction expressed so forcefully here was diametrically opposed to the position of those such as Rudolf Bultmann, who denied that Jesus thought of himself as Messiah, as Servant, or as Son of man, and considered this unimportant for Christian belief.[8] Such titles, it was argued, can tell us only about the beliefs of the early Christians, not those of Jesus himself. Moreover, it would seem that Jesus himself was not as obsessed with his own person as he was later assumed to be. The important question which emerged from this scholarly battle proved to be a rather different one;

---

[7] John W. Bowman, *The Intention of Jesus* (London: SCM Press, 1945), 108.
[8] Bultmann, *Theology of the New Testament*, 26–32.

not 'Did Jesus or did he not think of himself as "the Messiah"?' but rather 'Is there continuity, as well as discontinuity, between the beliefs, words, and actions of Jesus and those of the early church? Did he behave in such a way that his followers felt themselves compelled to speak of him as "Messiah"?'

Undoubtedly the most enigmatic of all the so-called 'messianic titles' applied to Jesus is the one which he himself is said to have used: 'the Son of man'. The Greek phrase ὁ υἱὸς τοῦ ἀνθρώπου – 'the son of the man' – is a literal translation from Aramaic, and must have puzzled Greek-speaking audiences. Unlike all other titles, it was not used by others (with the exception of Acts 7:56), but by Jesus alone. This means that there can be little doubt that Jesus used the phrase. But was he thinking of himself, as the Gospels suggest, or of a future eschatological figure, as has been argued by some twentieth-century scholars (typical of this view is Hahn[9])? Or was the phrase an Aramaic idiom, a modest way of referring to oneself, which was misunderstood by the Greek speaking church (as argued by Vermes[10])? A more traditional view understands Jesus to have been referring to himself, but questions whether the phrase should properly be described as a 'title'.[11] Rather, as in Dan 7:13, to which many of the Son of man sayings allude, 'the Son of man' is the description of a role. The phrase hints at the role of the man 'Adam', who was created by God to rule under him over the earth (Ps 8:4–8).[12] In particular, it points to the role of Israel, God's people (Dan 7:13; Ps 80:17;[13] 2 Esdras 6:53–59). Although Jesus used the term as a self-designation, it is notable how frequently what is said about 'the Son of man' clearly involves others: the Son of man must suffer, die and be vindicated, but his disciples must be prepared to follow his example (Mark 8:31–38 and //s); the Son of man came to serve, and his disciples must also serve one another (Mark 10:43–45 and //s); when the Son of man comes in glory, his elect will share his triumph (Matt 24:30–31 // Mark 13:26–27).

The answers we give to these questions about the origin and use of the phrase 'the Son of man' are important, not only because of the light they throw on Jesus' own understanding of his ministry, but also because of their relevance to the question of the relationship of Jesus' own beliefs to the development of 'New Testament theology'. Is Jesus' *own* theology part of the picture, and how much continuity do we expect between the way Jesus saw

---

[9] Ferdinand Hahn, *The Titles of Jesus in Christology,* trans. Harold Knight and George Ogg (London: Lutterworth Press, 1969), 15–67.

[10] Geza Vermes, *Jesus the Jew: A Historian's Reading of the Gospels* (London: Collins, 1973), 160–191.

[11] Morna D. Hooker, 'Is the Son of Man Problem Really Insoluble?', in *Text and Interpretation: Studies in the New Testament presented to Matthew Black,* eds. Ernest Best and R.McL. Wilson (Cambridge: Cambridge University Press, 1979), 155–168 = above, essay 6 (pp. 90–102).

[12] Once again, modern translations which opt for political correctness disguise the significance of the Hebrew, which speaks in v. 4 of 'man' and of 'son of man'.

[13] As in Ps 8:4, 'man' and 'son of man' are used in parallel.

his own mission and the way the church interpreted him? If Jesus used the phrase 'the Son of man' to refer to his own mission, why did the early church not consider it to be an appropriate way to express their beliefs about him? If he spoke of someone else as 'the Son of man', did the church radically distort his teaching in identifying him with this figure? If he used the phrase merely as an idiomatic way of saying 'I', is there anything in his teaching to explain why the church created so many sayings about 'the Son of man'? These last two explanations of the phrase both require that we assume that the early church misunderstood Jesus' own words and gave them a very different meaning. And neither of them provides us with any insight regarding Jesus' understanding of his own mission. How did he perceive his own role?

Yet the fact that the Gospels all testify to Jesus' use of the term as a way of referring to his mission suggests that there is an important element of continuity here. Jesus clearly used the phrase, and it was sufficiently distinctive and characteristic of him to be remembered. Why was it important to him? Can we find other signs of continuity, not necessarily in the 'title' itself, but in what Jesus is recorded as saying *about* 'the Son of man'? In other words, are these sayings echoed elsewhere in the New Testament? Those who regard the sayings as creations of the church will, of course, argue that any parallels between the Son of man sayings and the theology of Paul and John merely confirm that the sayings reflect the church's beliefs. But might those beliefs in fact be founded on what Jesus himself said about 'the Son of man'?

One of the remarkable features of New Testament Christology is the close association between Jesus and the believing community which is assumed to exist by the majority of its authors. The clearest expression of this idea is perhaps to be found in Paul, in his use of the phrase 'in Christ' to describe the believer's relationship to Christ. He spells out that relationship in different ways, describing Christians as joined to Christ – and to each other – by being members of Christ's body (1 Cor 12:12–27; Rom 12:4–5) or by being built into the temple whose foundation is Christ (1 Cor 3:11–17). Such is the close relationship of believers with Christ that they can be said to have been baptized into Christ, and so into his death (Gal 3:27; Rom 6:3), but those who share his death will also share his resurrection (Rom 6:5) – indeed, Christ already lives within them (Gal 2:20).

It would seem that, for Paul, this close relationship is founded on the fact that as *Christos,* that is *Messiah,* Jesus is a representative figure. It is by union with him that Gentiles are made 'the seed of Abraham' (Gal 3:16, 26–9), and it is through him that they share in the promises made to Israel (Rom 9:1–5). What happens to Christians takes place because they are *in* Christ – or it takes place *with* Christ or *through* Christ. It is surely for this reason that Paul rarely uses the name 'Jesus' on its own, preferring to speak of 'Christ', of 'Jesus Christ', or of 'Christ Jesus'.

In the opening paragraph of Romans, Paul tells us that Christ was born 'of the seed of David' (1:3): by birth, then, he was qualified to be 'Messiah'. Elsewhere, Paul speaks of Jesus being born of a Jew (Gal 4:4). Christ's identity with his people is important – as is his identity with the human condition in general (Rom 8:3; 2 Cor 5:21; 8:9). It is necessary for him to be Jewish, in order to represent Israel, just as it is necessary for him to be human, in order to represent humanity. But his Davidic descent is 'according to the flesh'. God, on the other hand, is Spirit, and acts in power: the reason why Christ is able to save his people is that by the resurrection of the dead, God proclaimed him Son of God in power (Rom 1:4). Remarkably, Paul speaks here of the resurrection of the dead in the plural: is he perhaps already hinting at Christ's representative role? In Romans 5, we realize that this representative role is not confined to his relationship with Israel, since now he is compared and contrasted with Adam. Paul's argument here is based on the Jewish understanding of Adam (the name means 'man') as a representative figure, whose sin brings death to all his descendants. In contrast to Adam's disobedience, which brings condemnation to all, we have Christ's obedience, which brings life to all (Rom 5:12–21). Yet Paul insists throughout that though this is effected by Christ's obedience, it is God who is at work, and it is because of his grace that the results of Adam's fall are reversed (5:15–17, 20–21).

In Christ, therefore, we have what is in effect a new creation (2 Cor 5:17; Rom 8:19–25). Christ's resurrection will be shared by believers (6:5), who will be openly revealed to be what *he* is, God's 'sons' (8:19, 29). So, in him, men and women attain to the glory which comes from those who see God face to face (8:30; 2 Cor 3:18), a glory which they lost when Adam sinned (Rom 1:23; 3:23). In terms of what Paul terms the flesh, men and women are like Adam, made from dust and returning to dust; but at the resurrection of the dead they will share the likeness of Christ, who is 'the last Adam' (1 Cor 15:20–27a, 42–49). Christ is thus the model of what men and women should be, the true 'image of God' (2 Cor 6:6), after whom Adam was fashioned (Gen 1:26). Not surprisingly, he fulfils the words of Ps 8:7 about the role of humanity in the world (1 Cor 15:27). We find, then, that when Paul attempts to spell out *how* men and women are affected by Christ's obedient death and resurrection he uses 'Adam' language, and that the ideas, as well as the language, are reminiscent of the Son of man sayings in the Gospels.

The Fourth Evangelist, too, emphasizes the union between Christ and his followers: they are dependent on him, as are branches on a tree (John 15:1–11). The fact that John speaks of a vine tree is significant, since the vine was a symbol for Israel (Ps 80:8, 14, where it is linked with the 'son of man' in v. 17). John does not refer to the Son of man here, but at the beginning of this section he has described how Jesus washed his disciples' feet – a dramatic representation of the saying found in Mark 10:45. Since 'servants are not greater than their master' (13:16), the disciples must do the same, but *because* they 'are not greater than their master' (15:20) they, like him, will be persecuted. 'Son of man' Christology underlies passages such as these, even where the term is not used.

In Heb 2:6–7 we have the one clear citation of Ps 8:4 ff. in the New Testament. The passage refers to humans, and the author comments that, contrary to the promise in the Psalm, all things are *not* yet subject to them; but, he adds, it *has* been fulfilled in the case of Jesus, who has 'tasted death for everyone'. He is 'the pioneer of their salvation', who sanctifies those who, with him, share the same heavenly Father. Thus Heb 2:5–18 elaborates the idea of Jesus as the Man who fulfils the divine plan and enables others to do so too.

Even though 'the Son of man' is not used as a title, therefore, the ideas linked with it are important. Narrowing Christological investigation down to a consideration of titles is clearly bound to distort our understanding of the way in which our New Testament authors understood Jesus. And if we ask *why* this term was not used as a title for Jesus, then the answer may be partly because Jesus himself had not used it as a title, but rather employed it as a way of describing his mission, and partly because it seemed inadequate for expressing all that the early church now wanted to express about the status and authority of the one who had, by the resurrection, been made Lord and Christ (Acts 2:36).

5. The Use of Narrative

Towards the end of the twentieth century, New Testament scholars placed increasing importance on what they termed 'narrative theology', and though Paul's letters do not set out to tell a story, we can see that underlying his theology there is a story about God's purpose for the world he had made. This is most clearly seen in Romans, which speaks of human sin, which has corrupted the world (1:18–32), of God's promises to his people Israel (4; 9:1–5; 11) and the gift of the Law (7), or his redemption of Jew and Gentile alike in Christ (3:21–31), which reversed what had happened through Adam (5:12–21), and of the final, hoped for restoration of all creation (8:18–39; 11:25–36; cf. 1 Cor 15:20–28).

The use of narrative as a way of 'doing theology' is, of course, much clearer in the Gospels. The evangelists' aim is to write 'gospel' – 'good news' – not biography, and in their presentation of Jesus, the so-called 'historical Jesus' is already fused with the 'Christ of faith'. The developing concern of the Christian community with Christological definitions inevitably affected the way in which the evangelists wrote their stories. John, as we have seen, makes his meaning clear by placing Christological claims into the mouth of Jesus. But *all* the evangelists tell their stories in such a way as to spell out the significance of the one whom they believe to be 'Jesus Christ the Son of God' (Mark 1:1).[14] All of them have 'prologues', which spell out the significance of who Jesus is, using Christological terms such as 'Messiah', 'Son of God', and 'Lord' (Matt 1–2; Mark 1:1–13; Luke 1–2; John 1:1–18), and they clearly expect this revelatory material to inform the way in which the stories that follow are read. Although, in the Synoptics, Jesus so rarely speaks about himself, all four evangelists arrange their material in such a way that the reader's attention is focused on him. They use narrative to spell out their understanding of who Jesus is.

We have a good example of this in Mark's Gospel, in the passage where he describes how Jesus taught the people in parables, beginning with the parable of the Sower, which is introduced and concluded with the injunction to listen (Mark 4:3, 9). The response of the hearers to Jesus' teaching is clearly of vital importance, and the interpretation that follows explains that what they are being asked to respond to is 'the word' (4:14). The word spoken by Jesus concerns the rule of God, which is at present invisible, but which will be given to those who respond to Jesus' message and enjoy the harvest (4:11, 26, 30). Yet it is clear that for Mark, those who respond to Jesus' message respond to Jesus himself, and that 'the word' is, in effect, the word – the Gospel – about *him*. It is his followers – 'those who were around him, with the Twelve' – who are given the secret of the kingdom (4:10–11). Moreover, Mark has positioned this group of parables immediately after the story of how opinion concerning Jesus divided the community: on the one hand, the scribes who accused him of working under the control of Satan, together with the members of his own family who believed that he was out of his mind, had clearly *rejected* the word; on the other, those who were around him and who did God's will had *received* it. Immediately *after* the parable collection, we have the story of Jesus stilling the storm, which leads the disciples to ask, 'Who then is this?' This is the question with which Mark, by his arrangement of the material, continually confronts his readers, leaving them to supply the answer. At the same time, he reminds them that the truth is hidden from those who have no eyes to see it (4:12).

It is the failure of Jesus' own people to perceive the truth that is stressed by Matthew in *his* arrangement of the tradition, since he not only introduces the parables with the story of the refusal of Jesus' own family to acknowledge his authority, but concludes them with an account of how he came to his hometown and was rejected there. Though Jesus speaks of a prophet being rejected in his own country, the implication of this story is that he is far

---

[14] The words 'the Son of God' may or may not belong to the original text of 1:1, but certainly represent Mark's views; cf. 1:9; 9:11; 15:39.

greater than any prophet. For Matthew, too, the parables confront the reader with a choice about how they respond to Jesus himself.

All our evangelists have chosen to shape their narratives in ways that help to demonstrate the truth of the good news about Jesus the Messiah. Matthew, for example, includes far more teaching than Mark, and we might assume at first sight that his aim is simply to preserve the teaching of Jesus. But when we look at the way in which he introduces the first block of teaching material in chapters 5–7, we realize that he is deliberately presenting Jesus as greater than Moses (Matt 5:1, 17, 21–22 etc.). The 'Sermon' ends by pointing to the choice which faces all who hear Jesus' words: will they act on them or ignore them? The decision they take is crucial (7:24–27).

Luke, also, arranges material in such a way as to point to the truth of Jesus' identity. In 4:16–21, Jesus announces that in him, the words in Isaiah 61 have been fulfilled: he is bringing good news to the poor, the recovery of sight to the blind (4:18). He then records various stories of healings and his version of the Sermon (6:17–49): Jesus is seen proclaiming good news to the poor (6:20) and healing the sick. When John's disciples come to enquire whether he is 'the one who is to come' (7:19), Jesus makes no direct reply, but tells them to report to John what they have seen and heard: 'the blind receive their sight, the lame walk, the lepers are cleansed, the deaf hear, the dead are raised, the poor have good news brought to them' (7:22). Luke leaves us, his readers, in no doubt as to the correct answer to the question.

John's method is to arrange his material around the great Jewish feasts (John 2:13; 5:1; 6:4; 10:22; 11:55); each of his 'signs' is linked with a discourse which brings out its meaning, and the themes of the discourse are appropriate to the festival with which it is associated (2:1–11 and 13–22 with 3:1–21 and 4:1–26; 4:46–54 and 5:2–9 with 5:19–47; 6:1–14 and 16–21 with 6:25–59; 9:1–12 with 8:12–59 and 9:13–41; 11:1–53 with 10:1–39. Jesus teaches openly about his relationship with the Father (10:22–38), and about his coming death and glorification (12:23–33).

It is clear that all our evangelists consider the truth about Jesus to be plain to those with eyes to see and ears to hear. Although Jesus may not make explicit claims for himself, his words and actions are evidence enough for those who believe. Others, moreover, whether intentionally or not, declare the truth. This often leads to irony, as in the Marcan passion narrative. It is the high priest who speaks of Jesus as 'the Messiah, the Son of the Blessed One' (14:61), Pilate – together with the Roman soldiers – who declares him to be 'the King of the Jews' (15:9, 18, 26), and his executioner who declares him to be 'Son of God' (15:39). The evangelist thus uses the story of Jesus' death to reveal the truth about him, and also stresses the fact that obedience, suffering and death are all integral to Jesus' Messiahship. It is only because he refuses to save himself that he is able to save others (15:30–31). It is only because he does not come down from the cross that he is the true Messiah and King of Israel (15:32).

6. The Origins of New Testament Christology

In using narrative, our New Testament writers were following in the tradition of the Old Testament, where God consistently reveals himself by what he does – in creation, in history, and in what is said and done by his prophets. When Moses catches a glimpse of God's glory on Sinai, this proves to be a revelation of God's steadfast love for his people (Exod 33:18–23; 34:4–7). And when the Son reveals the glory of God, he reveals, by his death, God's love for the world (John 3:16; 12:23–28; 13:31–32). If biblical theology is about how God reveals himself to men and women, then Christology must be about how he is revealed in Christ. It is essentially about the way in which God acts.

In spite of the fact that the New Testament consists of documents written by different authors in very different circumstances, so that they describe who and what Jesus is and does in such different ways, there is an underlying consistency in their Christology: they present Jesus as the one who is sent by God, and who acts with the authority of God – the one through whom God is working. They give him the name of God himself – 'Lord' (Rom 10:9; Phil 2:11; John 20:28). At the same time, they insist that Jesus is obedient to his Father (Rom 5:19; Phil 2:8; John 5:30), and that he is our representative, the model of what men and women should be. Behind their very different presentations of Jesus there lies the conviction that God created men and women in his likeness, intending them to be 'sons of God'; that Israel was called to fulfil this purpose; and that now, in Christ, it is possible for men and women of all races to become God's children by trusting in Christ, who is the pattern of what men and women should be, since he is 'the image of God' himself.

One of the formative elements in the development of New Testament Christology appears to have been the discussion of Christ's relation to the Law. On Sinai, God had revealed his will in the Law; it was impossible that God could have made a mistake, or changed his mind. But Jewish Christians found themselves increasingly isolated from their fellow Jews, while the influx of Gentile Christians into the church raised questions as to whether or not the Law was binding upon them. Different answers were given, according to the situation, but underlying them all is the conviction that Jesus is the fulfilment of the Law: that is, that through him, the *intention* of the Law is fulfilled. For Matthew, in conflict with fellow Jews, this seems to mean continuing to obey the Law, but going beyond its literal demands (Matt 5). For the Fourth Evangelist, it seems to imply that now that God has spoken fully in Christ, the Law is no longer necessary (1:17–18). The author of Hebrews makes a similar point (Heb 1:1–4); for him, there is no need for the sacrifices set out in the Law, since Christ, our high priest has offered a sacrifice that requires no repetition (Heb 9–10). For Paul, too, Christ seems to have replaced the Law: the Law points forward to him (Rom 10:8), but what the Law promised has now been achieved by God through Christ (Rom 8:3). Instead of living by the Law, Christians now live by 'the law of Christ' (Gal 6:2).

It is hardly surprising, then, that we find signs of the influence of the so-called 'Wisdom Christology' in at least three of our New Testament books: John 1:1–18, Col 1:15–20, and Heb 1:1–4 (cf. also Matt 11:19, 25–30). All seem to be drawing on the interpretation of the Law found in the Wisdom literature. The Law is identified with God's word, and since God created the world by his word (Gen 1:1–3), this word is personified as Wisdom, God's master-workman (Prov 8:22–35; Wis 7:22–26; 9:1–2).

It is surely significant that it is these passages, which attempt to spell out how God reveals himself through Christ, that we find some of the most exalted language about Christ himself. Although the concerns that shaped the theology of our New Testament authors were very different from those that led the fathers of the church to produce the creeds, we can understand how, building on what the New Testament says about him, they would wish to define him in terms both of 'God' and of 'Man'.

11. Chalcedon and the New Testament

When more than 500 bishops gathered together in the Church of St Euphemia at Chalcedon in October 451 CE, a copy of the scriptures was placed in the centre of the Council as a symbol of the fact that their deliberations began from scripture, and that they believed themselves to be expounding scripture. The definition they eventually produced was an interpretation of the Nicene Creed, and that in turn was understood to be an exposition of scripture.

It is, then, a little disconcerting to a New Testament scholar to find the careful definition of Chalcedon couched in language which is utterly foreign, not simply to the ideas and language with which we are familiar today, but also to those we identify as belonging to the writers of the New Testament: how very different is this description of Christ's person from what the New Testament writers have to say about him! We might perhaps have expected the fathers of the church, being closer in time, to have been closer in understanding. Yet the gap between the approaches of the first and the fifth centuries appears to be as great as that between those of the fifth and the twentieth. Nothing could be a clearer demonstration of the way in which scripture is always interpreted in the language and thought-forms of the age – in this particular case an age whose ideas are as far removed from those of our own time as they are from those of our New Testament writers.

The problem in this particular instance, of course, lies in the fact that the interpretation of the Christian story which was laid down at Chalcedon became normative for later understanding of the scriptures. Because of its crucial role in the formation of Christian doctrine, this particular interpretation (albeit in less complex terms) became the yardstick for future understanding of the person of Christ. Whereas the interpretations which emerged in other periods can be laid aside and abandoned, as belonging to the *Zeitgeist* which helped to create them, the Chalcedonian definition became part of the given, with the result that generations of Christians have read the New Testament through Chalcedonian spectacles, unaware of the fact that they were imposing not simply the interpretations of their own age on to a first-century text, but those of the fifth century also.

Now whether the Chalcedonian definition was a proper interpretation of the New Testament for the fifth century is an interesting hermeneutical question which I must leave to others better qualified to answer; so, too, with the question as to whether or not it is a necessary starting point for Christian understanding of the person of Christ today – a question which has been much debated recently, not least by Maurice Wiles, to whom this essay is offered in grateful acknowledgement of his work, support, and friendship over many years. The question which concerns me here is the extent to which the influence of Chalcedon is still a positive hindrance to our understanding of what the New Testament authors were trying to say about Jesus in their own very different time and circumstances. The fathers of the church held that the Son, being 'of one substance with the Father ... became incarnate'. This may have been a natural way for them to interpret the Fourth Gospel in their own time, but it was not, as we shall see, what the Fourth Evangelist himself said.

Students of the New Testament interpret its evidence in very different ways, as became evident during the debate which followed *The Myth of God Incarnate*. But while there is disagreement as to whether or not 'incarnation' is an appropriate word to use at any point in describing New Testament Christology, there is widespread agreement that none of its authors speaks explicitly about Jesus as *God* incarnate. Indeed, many would go so far as to say that nowhere in the New Testament is Jesus actually referred to as 'God': the few passages which might be interpreted in this way are in fact all ambiguous. The idea of 'incarnation' is used explicitly only in John 1:14, and even that refers to the Logos, rather than to God. Moreover, that passage has to be balanced by statements in some of our other New Testament books which sound suspiciously like what we today would term 'adoptionism'. As for the notion of pre-existence, one well-known New Testament scholar has attempted to explain away almost all the passages where this is generally assumed to be implied.[1] Clearly we need to look at the evidence a little more closely.

Let us begin with our earliest writer, Paul. One of the obvious starting points here is what may loosely be described as 'incarnational formulae': Galatians 4:4, 'When the time had fully come, God sent forth his Son, born of woman, born under the law', and 2 Corinthians 8:9, 'You know the grace of our Lord Jesus Christ, that though he was rich, yet for your sake he became poor'. The first passage explicitly refers to Jesus' birth (*contra* Dunn[2]), and the second is also most reasonably understood in the same way. Attempts to explain it away by referring it to Jesus' decision to leave his home in Nazareth are frankly absurd: Jesus was no Francis of Assisi, giving up a life of luxury for an itinerant life, but a humble Galilean carpenter. It is true, of course, that the prophets were also thought of as having been 'sent' by God – but these two passages suggest that we are dealing here with the kind of idea which the creeds expressed in the phrase 'and became man'. But what is the point that Paul is wishing to emphasize? It is Christ's oneness with humanity, and

---

[1] James D. G. Dunn, *Christology in the Making: A New Testament Inquiry into the Origins of the Doctrine of the Incarnation* (London: SCM Press, 1980).

[2] Dunn, *Christology*, 40–42.

in particular with the fact that he shared in the limitations and deprivations to which humanity itself has been subjected: he was born under the law; he became poor. We can find similar ideas elsewhere. Thus Romans 8:3 tells us that God sent 'his own Son in the likeness of sinful flesh'; Philippians 2:7–8 describes the way in which one who was in the form of God took 'the form of a slave, being born in the likeness of men; and being found in human form he humbled himself and became obedient unto death, even death on a cross' – the cross being the manner of death appropriate for a slave.

The fact that Christ became identified with humanity at his birth suggests first that he himself stands apart from fallen humanity, and secondly that he is also pre-existent. But we must not assume that the former statement necessarily implies that Paul is thinking of him as 'God'. As for the second, though Christ is clearly pre-existent, that does not, at this stage, lead to speculation or discussion by Paul about what the pre-existent Christ was or did; rather, it is a way of stressing that what the earthly Jesus did was part of God's eternal plan and purpose.

In order to understand more clearly what Paul is saying in these two passages in Galatians and 2 Corinthians, we need to remember that so far we have quoted only half of them. Thus Galatians 4:4 continues, 'in order to redeem those under the law, in order that we might receive adoption as sons', while 2 Corinthians 8:9 concludes, 'in order that by his poverty you might become rich'. For want of a better term, I have sometimes termed these passages 'formulae of interchange',[3] since what they say is reminiscent of Irenaeus' terse saying: 'he became what we are, in order that we might become what he is' (Irenaeus, *Adv. Haer.* 5 *praef.*). We become rich – as he was rich; we become children of God – as he was Son of God; we are redeemed from the Law – as he was free from the Law. If we examine the context of Romans 8:3 we discover that there, too, the result of God sending his Son in the likeness of sinful flesh is that we become children of God; and following on from Philippians 2 we discover in Philippians 3:20–21 that we are to be conformed to the glorious body of the exalted Lord – the one who was, we have been told, in the form of God. If we now broaden the enquiry a little, we discover other texts – Galatians 3:13 and 2 Corinthians 5:21 – which speak of Christ sharing in our human condition (becoming a curse, and being made sin) in order that we might share in his, though of course these two passages are generally held to refer to what we would label 'the atonement' rather than 'the incarnation'.

It is clear that what we become through Christ is what, in the purpose of God, we are meant to be – truly human; men and women are recreated in

---

[3] Morna D. Hooker, 'Interchange in Christ', *JTS* 22 (1971): 349–361; reprinted with other essays on the same theme in Morna D. Hooker, *From Adam to Christ: Essays on Paul* (Cambridge: Cambridge University Press, 1990).

God's image, they are children of God, enjoying the liberty and privileges of God's children, and reflecting his glory. It is no accident that the language Paul uses when describing the redemptive activity of Christ refers to him in language which is appropriate to one who is truly what Man is meant to be: he is the Son of God – and as Son, obedient to God; he is the Man from heaven – standing in contrast to Adam, the man from earth; he is the image of God, and is in the form of God – as Adam was before the fall; and like Adam in the Garden of Eden, he reflects the glory of God; even the authority Christ exercises reminds us of Adam, for the first man was commanded to have dominion over the earth and its creatures. To use the language of Colossians, Christ is the firstborn of creation, as well as the firstborn from the dead, and therefore pre-eminent both in the universe and in the church.

Now I suspect that Paul took it for granted that Christ was pre-existent, though until we get to Colossians (which may or may not have been written by Paul himself) there is little sign of any interest in what he did in his pre-existence. Christ represents God's purpose for mankind, and he is certainly no afterthought or addition to the plan: he must therefore have been from the beginning. But pre-existence does not necessarily imply divinity. I believe that it was in fact in thinking out Christ's relationship with the Law that the idea of pre-existence became important.[4] It is suggestive that the first indication of Christ's pre-existence (1 Cor 8:6) speaks of him as the one through whom creation exists – a role attributed in Jewish thought to the Law (Midr. Rab. Gen. 1.1). It would take us too far afield to explore Paul's teaching on the Law in any detail: suffice it to say that in Paul's understanding of the relationship between God and his people there is a sense in which Christ replaces the Law; or rather, since Paul insists that his teaching *establishes* the Law, the Law is discovered to be a temporary dispensation which points forward to the finality which is revealed in Christ. Compared with Christ, the Law is a kind of rough first draft – an inadequate metaphor, since it suggests that God found it necessary to have several attempts before producing the perfect version. And this, of course, is precisely where the idea of pre-existence comes in, for in Jewish thinking the Law was pre-existent – inevitably, because it expressed God's will for his people. If Christ has taken over from the Law, and is found to represent God's will for his people even more profoundly than the Law, then of course he must be pre-existent also; the Law is not so much a first draft as a somewhat blurred xerox copy, whereas Christ is the perfect image. Christ is thus greater than the Law: he embodies God's will for his people more completely than the Law; moreover, what the Law could not do

---

[4] Cf. G.B. Caird, 'The Development of the Doctrine of Christ in the New Testament', in *Christ for Us Today*, ed. Norman Pittenger (London: SCM Press, 1968), 66–80.

God has now done, working through Christ – namely, recreated mankind in the image and likeness of God.

In the various passages we have considered so far, Paul speaks sometimes of God sending his Son, and sometimes of Christ taking or becoming subject to human limitation. In the same way, when he writes of Christ's death, he refers sometimes to God giving up his Son for our sake, sometimes to Christ giving himself up. The essence of Sonship is that the Son is obedient to his Father's will, so that in speaking of God's purpose it makes little difference whether one refers to God sending or giving up his Son, or whether one attributes the action to Christ himself. Close examination of Paul's references to Christ as 'Son' suggests to me that he used this particular term (whether consciously or unconsciously) in speaking about God's saving activity in Christ in order to underline the fact that God's purpose of salvation is brought about through one who (being Son) acts in accordance with and in obedience to that purpose.[5] The term 'Son' thus reminds us that, in all he does, Christ acts in obedience to God.

But this means, of course, that everything that happens through Christ is the activity of God himself. To use Paul's classic phrase: 'God was in Christ, reconciling the world to himself'. Thus when the disobedience of the one man Adam is weighed against the obedience of the one man Christ in Romans 5, the scales come down heavily on the side of Christ, who is a better man than Adam, precisely because the grace of God is at work through him. Because Christ is Son of God, truly obedient to God's will, the power of God is channelled through him. He stands over against the rest of humanity, even though he is one with them. Moreover, the same set of terms serves at one and the same time to identify him both as one with God and as one with mankind. We have already listed the language which Paul uses in speaking of Christ as the true Adam: he is Son of God; in the form of God; the image of God; Lord. This is language which *we* consider more appropriate for expressing what we would term Christ's 'divinity'. For Paul, these terms express the fact that Christ is one with God, precisely because they express his obedience as man. But because he speaks in terms of activity, rather than in terms of being, he thinks of Christ as one with God in purpose and will, rather than in nature.

The language which Paul used in speaking about Christ is thus language which is appropriate primarily to the proper relationship of men and women to God. Christ is the epitome of what humanity was meant to be: he is in the image of God (as was Adam), the Son of God who is obedient to God, and who, under God, by right enjoys the world's resources and exercises lordship over creation. This is what Christ was, before what we call his incarnation,

---

[5] Morna D. Hooker, *Pauline Pieces* (London: Epworth Press, 1979), 55–68.

and it is what he continues to be. But, equally important, it is what he enables men and women to become: for they, too, become 'sons of God' (Gal 4:5).[6] Christians share Christ's status before God – his righteousness (2 Cor 5:21), blessing (Gal 3:14), riches (2 Cor 8:9), and glory (Phil 2:9–10, 3:21). They do not, of course, become his equals: the relationship is a dependent one, for what they receive is always due to the fact that they are in him. Christ continues to stand apart from men and women, even while enabling them to share in what he is. Nevertheless, the terms and statements which later theologians regarded as pointers to Christ's 'divinity' are for Paul the very terms and statements which describe the true humanity which becomes a possibility for those who are redeemed by Christ.

Thus it would seem that statements which appear at first sight to be 'incarnational formulae' are not, strictly speaking, 'incarnational' at all. Rather, for Paul, they refer to the conviction that by sharing our fallen humanity (i.e. life in Adam) Christ enabled men and women to become what he is: but Paul does not, as did Athanasius, understand that as meaning that they become divine *(De Inc.* 54). Paul's use of the pattern of 'interchange' suggests that he understands Christ's willing identification with our fallen humanity to be balanced by our resultant identification with his true humanity. If we use the term 'incarnation' of the statement that 'he became what we are', then what word are we to use of the balancing statement that we in turn become what he is? It is better to speak of 'Second Adam' Christology: a new creation has taken place, and humanity has been redeemed through one who is (in Luther's phrase) 'proper Man'.

The closest any of our New Testament writers come to speaking of Jesus as the incarnate God is of course the famous statement in John 1:14. In fact this passage speaks of the *Word* of God becoming flesh, not of God himself becoming flesh; it could of course be argued that since in 1:1 we are told that the Word was God, there is little difference between the idea of 'God incarnate' and 'the Word of God incarnate', but that, I think, would be to misunderstand what John is attempting to say.

The Johannine Prologue is, I believe, wrongly interpreted if it is taken in isolation from the rest of the Gospel. It is a true 'prologue' – it serves to introduce the theme of the Gospel and to explain it; without it, we will make little sense of the rest of the Gospel, for it provides the clues which help us to make sense of everything which follows.[7] Much of the Gospel is made up

---

[6] The 'sexist' language jars on us, but it is necessary to retain it in order to stress the fact that Christians share Christ's relationship to God. For Paul, of course, the term 'sons' was not intended to be exclusive; indeed, he stresses the fact that it is inclusive – women are included on equal terms with men as heirs of the inheritance offered in Christ; see especially Gal 3:28.

[7] Morna D. Hooker, 'The Johannine Prologue and the Messianic Secret', *NTS* 21 (1974): 40–58 = below, essay 23 (pp. 321–340).

of a series of signs, the meaning of which is spelt out in discourses: signs and discourses together demonstrate the extraordinary authority of Jesus in both actions and words, which amount, in effect, to a claim to be the fulfilment of Judaism. Everything said in the past about the Law is now claimed by Jesus to be true of himself; everything achieved in the past in Jewish worship is now achieved by him. He is the total fulfilment of God's self-revelation in the past; and since the partial is no longer needed, he is also its replacement.

Interlaced with these signs and discourses we have a number of disputes between Jesus and the Jews, who are resisting the truth of the revelation. In these disputes we in fact overhear debates which were going on between Jews and Christians in the synagogues at the time when John was writing (5:16–47; 6:41–65; 7:14–52; 8:12–59; 9:35–41; 10:19–39). The Christian claims about Jesus are rejected by the Jews, who cling to the revelation of God in the past in the Law; the Christian retort is that if only the Jews understood Moses, they would realize that he pointed forward to Christ (5:39–47; 9:28–29). The issue in dispute is thus whether Jesus was an imposter or whether he came from God; again and again it is put in terms of Jesus' origin: where does he come from? The Christian claim is that he comes from above – i.e. from God.

The Prologue provides the justification for these claims about Jesus. The Word of God, active in the past in creation, in history, in the prophets, was believed by Jews to have been embodied in the Law given to Moses on Mount Sinai. Christians are now claiming that a fuller, more complete embodiment of God's word, or Logos, has taken place in Jesus Christ. But it is the same God who speaks at creation, on Sinai, and through the prophets who now speaks in his Son: his Word is constant; his self-revelation is of a piece; he has not changed his mind. In speaking of this Word, the Fourth Evangelist naturally uses language which reminds us that in Hebrew thought a word once spoken had a dynamic life of its own. The Logos is referred to as though a separate being, over against God; but in a similar way, Jewish writers had already spoken of Wisdom as God's master-workman, helping in the work of creation, dwelling among God's people, speaking through the prophets (Prov 8:22–31; Wis 7:22–10:21; Sir 24); Wisdom had been identified with the Law (Sir 24:23), which was described also as God's word (Ps 119; *Migr.* 130). If Christ is to be slotted into this understanding of God's dealings with his people, it is hardly surprising if the evangelist speaks of him in these terms: God has spoken again; he has revealed himself once more. The Word which was with God at the beginning, through which all things came into being, by which light and life were created, has now come among us in the flesh. The glory of God, glimpsed on Sinai, but never seen by any human being, has now been fully disclosed in the person of God's Son, who is the full embodiment of all God's grace and truth.

Reading the rest of John's story, after reading the Prologue, we are able to appreciate the claims which the evangelist makes on Jesus' behalf. Since God speaks in him, his words are the words of God; his deeds, also, are the deeds of God (10:37–38). He comes from above (8:23). He is 'from God' (9:33). He is one with the Father (10:30).

Ought we, then, to speak of John's understanding of Jesus in terms of a doctrine of 'God incarnate'? After all, he declares in 1:1 that 'the Word was God'; in 1:18 he speaks of Jesus, according to what may well be the correct reading, as *monogenēs theos*. Moreover, at the end of the Gospel he has Thomas confess Jesus as 'my Lord and my God'. Is this not what we understand as 'incarnation'?

I think not. I suspect that it is misleading to use that term because it disguises the very different frames of reference within which our evangelist, on the one hand, and the fathers of the church, on the other, were working. It is worth noting how, in each of these three instances, John also makes it quite clear that the Word, or Jesus, stands over against God. Thus in 1:1 the declaration that the Word was God is sandwiched in between two statements that 'The Word was *with* God'. Whether or not 1:18 does in fact describe Jesus as 'only God' (rather than as 'only Son'), this comment follows a declaration that 'No one has ever seen God'. And though in 20:28 the risen Jesus is acknowledged by Thomas as 'my Lord and my God', Jesus himself, a few verses earlier, declares that he is ascending 'to my Father and your Father, to my God and your God'. Similarly, in the rest of the Gospel, though we find Jesus proclaiming 'Before Abraham was, I am' (8:58), he also declares 'My Father is greater than I' (14:28). The relationship between Father and Son is one of dependence on the Son's part: 'the Son can do nothing of his own accord, but only what he sees the Father doing' (5:19); 'My teaching is not mine, but his who sent me' (7:16). Though the term 'Son' is much more common in the Fourth Gospel than in Paul, its function is similar. This understanding of Jesus is greatly illuminated by study of the Jewish understanding of the agent who has been commissioned to work on behalf of someone else and as his representative: the claims made on behalf of Jesus can be explained, at least in part, when we see that he is presented as God's agent in the world, who acts in total accord with his will.[8]

The context in which a passage is read determines its meaning. To Christians of a later generation, it is natural to interpret John 20:28 as a declaration of Jesus' 'divinity'. Yet commentators often point out that this passage is a

---

[8] Peder Borgen, 'God's Agent in the Fourth Gospel', in *Religions in Antiquity*, ed. Jacob Neusner (Leiden: Brill, 1968), 137–148, and Peder Borgen, *Logos Was the True Light* (Trondheim: Tapir, 1983), 121–132; Jan-Adolf Bühner, *Der Gesandte und sein Weg im vierten Evangelium*, WUNT 2/2 (Tübingen: Mohr, 1977), 181–267; John Ashton, *Understanding the Fourth Gospel* (Oxford: Clarendon Press, 1991), 308–329.

confessional statement, not a dogmatic formula, and thus has to be treated with caution. It is also illuminating to consider alongside it a passage in John 10, where Jesus' claim in verse 30, 'I and the Father are one' (a claim to unity in will and activity, not in essence), is followed by Jewish protest at his 'blasphemy', which leads Jesus to respond by quoting and expounding Psalm 82:6: 'I said, you are gods'. The argument here seems to depend on a tradition that the words were addressed to the Jewish people after the giving of the Law on Sinai.[9] If so, the reasoning is clear: if those to whom the word of God comes are addressed as 'gods', how much more appropriate is it to think of the one who embodies the Word (and who thus does the works of his Father) in these terms. It is hardly surprising, then, if Thomas' acknowledgement of Jesus as his Lord and God forms the climax to the Gospel in 20:28. But the evangelist's line of reasoning in chapter 10 reminds us that the debate underlying Thomas' confession was very different indeed from that about the divine and human natures of Christ which occupied the fathers of the church.

What John is trying to express is the notion of revelation. God has revealed himself in the past in various ways; now, supremely, he has revealed himself in the Son. No one has ever seen God, but the Son has 'exegeted him' (1:18). He has revealed his glory: a statement which is equally true, however you explain the 'he' and the 'his'; above all, God has been glorified through the cross – in other words, his true nature has been revealed there. The Revealer God is encountered in his revelation, and when one encounters the revelation, one encounters God. But it is surely more accurate to speak (as John himself does) of the incarnate Word, rather than of the incarnate God.

In many ways, the issues with which the Fourth Evangelist is concerned are those which occupy Paul: both are concerned to show how the self-revelation of God in Christ relates to his self-revelation in the past. Both are concerned to show how Jesus brings life and salvation to men and women. But Paul's notion of 'interchange' finds no echo in John: to be sure, through the coming of Christ, men and women are enabled to become 'children' of God (1:12); but

---

[9] B. *'Abod. Zar.* 5a; Midr. Rab. Exod. 32:1, 7; Lev. 4.1; 11.3; Num. 7.4; 16.24; Deut. 7.12; Song 1.2.5; Eccl. 3.16.1. See James S. Ackerman, 'The Rabbinic Interpretation of Psalm 82 and the Gospel of John: John 10:34', *HTR* 59 (1966): 186–188. Another rabbinic tradition understood the words to have been addressed to the judges of Israel appointed by Moses (Deut 1:15–18). J.A. Emerton, 'The Interpretation of Psalm 82 in John 10', *JTS* NS 11 (1960): 329–332 argues that the 'gods' in John 10:34 are to be understood as evil angels, as in the Peshitta, an interpretation since reinforced by the discovery of 11Q Melch., where the first *'elohîm* in Ps 82 is interpreted of Melchizedek (Marinus de Jonge and A.S. van der Woude, '11Q Melchizedek and the New Testament', *NTS* 12 [1966]: 301–326), and the second of evil angels. Though he is probably right in arguing that this interpretation is closer to the *original* meaning of the psalm, it seems less appropriate to the Johannine context. The reference to 'the Law' and the description of those who are addressed as those 'to whom the Word of God came' point us to Sinai.

is the choice of the word *tekna* here perhaps a deliberate differentiation from the *huios* who is *monogenēs*? Certainly the giving and sending formulae in John 3 are expressed very differently from those in Paul: God gave his Son in order that believers might have eternal life, and sent him into the world in order to save the world. The end result is the same – salvation and life – but the way in which it is expressed is quite different. The Word may have 'become flesh', but the emphasis is on the Son's oneness with God rather than with men and women; as for those to whom he came, the Johannine vocabulary and imagery stress their dependence *on* him, rather than their unity *with* him: they see, believe, and live.[10]

John's portrait of Jesus is of course in many ways very different from those we find in the other Gospels. Though we can certainly find interesting parallels in the Synoptics to some of the Johannine sayings, their significance for understanding the person of Jesus has not been explored by the other three evangelists. There is nothing in the Synoptics remotely parallel to the explicit Johannine presentation of 'the Word made flesh'. Whereas, in John, Jesus proclaims himself, in the other Gospels, he proclaims the kingdom of God. In spite of recent attempts to rehabilitate John, on this point at least the Synoptics are more historically reliable. What is interesting about this, however, is that though in the Synoptics Jesus teaches about God and his kingdom, and has very little to say about himself (and even that is in the form of enigmatic statements about the Son of man!), the way in which the evangelists tell their stories means that our attention is focused on Jesus throughout. The all-important question which arises is: who is this? We find Jesus forgiving sins, walking on water, stilling storms, providing bread, raising the dead. But only God is able to do these things! No wonder the common reaction of the crowds is one of fear. Men and women are confronted with the power of God in the person of Jesus; the Synoptic evangelists explain this, not in terms of 'incarnation', but by speaking of the Spirit of God at work in Jesus. But all of them make it clear that this is a unique experience. For though he calls men and women to follow him in the way of discipleship, he himself stands over against them: in the saying which is closer than any other to the Johannine teaching, we are reminded that 'Everything is entrusted to me by my Father; and no one knows the Son except the Father, and no one knows the Father except the Son and those to whom the Son chooses to reveal him' (Matt 11:27 // Luke 10:22). Jesus is acknowledged by God himself as his only Son, and acts with an authority far greater than that of Moses. Once again,

---

[10] E.g. the Johannine images of bread and water. Cf. John's use of the 'vine' whose branches are totally dependent on the tree in ch. 15 with Paul's image of the body, in which the limbs cooperate in the body's functioning. It is worth noting, too, that in the Synoptics Jesus and his disciples walk together 'on the way', but in John Jesus *is* the way.

all-important questions about how Jesus fits into the divine purpose for Israel lie in the background: he is God's last word to his people.

And what of Hebrews — frequently said to set out Christ's 'divinity' in the first two chapters, followed by his 'humanity'? Hebrews begins with a remarkable passage which has interesting parallels with the Johannine Prologue: God has spoken in past ages to our fathers through the prophets (including Moses), but now he has spoken through a Son. This Son reflects the glory of God and bears the very stamp of his nature; through him he created the world. The language once again echoes that which is used in the wisdom literature both of Wisdom and of the Law; Jesus has replaced the Law as the figure who embodies the plan of God. It may well reflect also Jewish speculation about an angelic figure who, though not God, is enthroned in heaven and shares God's glory and even his name; interestingly, this speculation seems to tie up with the kind of thing which is said about the figure like a son of man in Daniel 7 and the Son of man in 1 Enoch — a figure who represents mankind. We are somewhat surprised to find this kind of speculation in Judaism, so passionately monotheistic, but however exalted these various angelic figures may be, the power and authority which they exercise are derived from God himself. Perhaps, then, such speculation may help us to understand how Jewish monotheists came to make this kind of exalted statement about Christ.[11]

Hebrews continues by showing the superiority of Christ, first to angels, then to Moses. We are inclined to be more impressed by the former than the latter. Christ is superior to angels — an assertion which is backed up by a catena of passages from the psalms: no angel was ever addressed by God as Son; on the contrary, the angels were commanded to worship him; the Son shares in the rule of God and in the work of God in creation; he is eternal, and sits at God's right hand. The final proof-text is introduced with the statement that the world was not subjected to angels; to whom, then, was it subjected? Psalm 8 says that it was to man, and to the son of man. So the climax of the author's argument is that Jesus is crowned with glory as man and as son of man! We are then told that through Jesus and his sufferings God has brought many sons to glory; Jesus is the pioneer of their salvation; he and they have one origin, and he therefore acknowledges them as brethren. This is why he shared their nature of flesh and blood and shared their death. Here is something remarkably close to Paul's notion of interchange. As in Paul, we have the idea of Christ as one who deliberately shares human nature and human suffering and who thereby is able to bring many sons to glory — that

---

[11] Alan F. Segal, *Two Powers in Heaven: Early Rabbinic Reports about Christianity and Gnosticism* (Leiden: Brill, 1977), 182–219; Christopher Rowland, *The Open Heaven: A Study of Apocalyptic in Judaism and Early Christianity* (London: SPCK, 1982), 94–113.

is, enables them to share in his glory and sonship. And as in Paul, we find that the exalted terms which suggest to us what we would call 'divinity' are linked by the author with Christ's humanity and with the conviction that God's eternal purpose is achieved through him: the one who reflects God's glory and bears the stamp of his nature is in fact the Son who is obedient to his Father's will, and the glory and sonship which he bestows on others are his by right because he is 'son of man'.

Next comes the comparison with Moses: both Moses and Jesus were faithful, but Moses was a servant, whereas Jesus is a son. This comparison is in fact just as important for our author as that with the angels, since Moses represents the Law, and we thus see how the revelation of the past stands in comparison with the revelation in Christ. Moreover, Moses set out the various sacrifices which were to be offered up in Israel – sacrifices which have now been rendered obsolete by the once-for-all self-offering of the heavenly high priest. Like Paul and John (and to a lesser extent the Synoptic evangelists), the author of Hebrews is concerned to relate Christ to God's self-revelation in the past, both in creation and in his dealings with Israel.

Paul, the Fourth Evangelist, and the author to the Hebrews all declare that God's self-revelation in Christ is final and complete: there is nothing to be known of God which is not known in him. In the language of Colossians, 'in him all the fullness of God was pleased to dwell'. All our writers are concerned to relate this self-revelation to what had gone before. All of them are faithful to their Jewish heritage: God has been active in creation, in the salvation of his people, in the giving of the Law, in prophecy, and now in Christ. Each of them uses the language of pre-existence, because it is inevitable in talking about Christ as the one who fully expresses God's will, and who represents God's purpose for mankind. And each of them sees Christ as the prototype of a new humanity: Jesus is the Son of God, but he brings many sons to glory; through him, men and women become children of God.

This brief survey of some of the more significant christological statements in the New Testament will perhaps explain why I feel that there is a great gulf between the thought-world in which they were fashioned and that which gave rise to the Chalcedonian definition. Though it is easy to see how the sayings of the Fourth Gospel came to be interpreted in terms of 'incarnation', none of our writers was in fact describing 'how God became man'. Moreover, those passages in the Pauline epistles and in Hebrews which seem to us like references to 'incarnation' are in fact concerned primarily to express the purpose of God for humanity, now fulfilled in Christ. Let me sum up by suggesting three reasons why the language of Chalcedon is so different from that of the New Testament.

First of all, Chalcedon was primarily intended as a bastion against heresy. Definition was necessary in order to make quite clear which heretical views were being excluded. In the days of the New Testament, on the other hand, Christianity was itself the heresy. This is something which is frequently forgotten by exegetes, who tend to read back later situations into the New Testament and suppose that our writers were defending the true Christian gospel against this or that heresy. But for most of the time they were not; they were propagating a message which was itself seen as heretical, and were still in the process of working out its significance. The orthodoxy was Judaism; the Christian sect was trying to work out its position *vis-à-vis* the parent body and to reconcile faith in Jesus as God's Messiah with the conviction that God was indeed the God who had revealed himself to his people in the past. What our writers say about Christ has to be seen in this context.[12] By the time of the Chalcedonian Council, the statements which had once been heresy had become orthodoxy, and were therefore handled in a completely different way.

Secondly, our New Testament writers were primarily concerned to describe the activity of God: he had acted, he had redeemed his people. They used a great variety of imagery – anything and everything available to them – in order to describe this activity; it was natural to them to employ narrative and metaphor. Their concern was not to offer definitions of the being of God or the being of Christ. The nature of God is known by what he does: many of the most important New Testament christological passages are hymns extolling God for what he has done through Christ. This is what is meant by describing New Testament Christology as 'functional' rather than as 'ontological'; it seems to me to be a valid distinction. Nor is this simply an aberration on the part of our New Testament writers: it is part of the biblical tradition. Nowhere in the Old Testament does one find God being spoken of in terms of pure being: even in Deutero-Isaiah, where the description of God is at its most majestic, God is still celebrated as the one who acts. He is the God who reveals himself to his people and acts on their behalf, 'the God of Abraham, Isaac and Jacob', the 'Lord your God, who brought you out of the land of Egypt' (Exod 3:6; 20:2). But by the time of Chalcedon things had changed radically; after four centuries in which Christians had grown accustomed to the idea of a divine Father and a divine Son and were used to speaking of them as peers, the fathers of the church approached the questions of Christology in a very different way.[13] What had been for our New Tes-

---

[12] In his recent book (*Understanding the Fourth Gospel*), John Ashton argues that it is possible in the Fourth Gospel to trace the way in which beliefs about the person of Christ were developed by one particular community as it thought out its faith in the context of Jewish opposition.

[13] See Maurice F. Wiles, *The Spiritual Gospel: The Interpretation of the Fourth Gospel in the Early Church* (Cambridge: Cambridge University Press, 1960), 112–147; Maurice F. Wiles, *The Divine Apostle: The Interpretation of St. Paul's Epistles in the Early Church* (Cambridge: Cambridge University Press, 1967), 73–93.

tament authors helpful images used to describe their experience of God have now become doctrines which themselves need to be defined and analysed.

Thirdly, leading on from there, our New Testament authors write from within a Jewish context and not a Greek philosophical one. One hesitates these days to make contrasts between Greek and Hebrew language, but in spite of the pitfalls involved in easy contrasts it is still true to say that there are differences in outlook. Paul, for example, could never have spoken of Christ as 'consisting of a reasonable soul and a body'. He speaks of man as *sōma psuchikon,* and the contrasts he uses are not between God and man, but between spirit and flesh. The debate at Chalcedon makes no sense to those accustomed to think in Jewish terms. Most important of all, the issues were quite different: our New Testament authors were wrestling with the question: 'How do our new beliefs about Christ relate to what we have always believed about God – about the creation of the universe, his election of Israel, and his promises to his people?' Their concern was to show that it was the same God who had been at work in the past who was now at work in Christ, and that his new work in Christ was the fulfilment of everything that had gone before: hence the importance of showing his superiority to Moses.

The idea of an incarnate God is, we suggest, foreign to Jewish thinking. Remember the prayer of Solomon: 'Will God indeed dwell on the earth? Behold, heaven and the highest heaven cannot contain thee' (1 Kgs 8:27). To be sure, the Shekinah dwelt on earth, but the Shekinah was a particular manifestation of God's universal presence, and like other manifestations (angels, wisdom, the Spirit, the Word) was a way of speaking of God's self-revelation.[14] Again, individuals were accorded divine honours: Moses, in particular, was said by Philo, elaborating Exodus 7:1, to have been given the name of god and king (e.g. *Mos.* 1.158; *Somn.* 2.189). Ezekiel the Tragedian relates a dream of Moses, in which he is enthroned by God on his own throne and given the emblems of rule – symbols of his future authority over men (68–89); the passage is reminiscent of that in 1 Enoch 45, where it is said that the Elect One (i.e. the Son of man) will sit on God's throne of glory. In these passages and others,[15] men share in divine honour because they are given divine authority, but this does not mean that they are themselves 'divine' beings: rather their authority and honour are manifestations of the fact that God is revealing his power and purpose through them.[16]

In his essay 'Does Christology Rest on a Mistake?' Maurice Wiles argued that the doctrine of incarnation arose within the Jewish framework of belief

---

[14] Rowland, *The Open Heaven,* 80.

[15] There is an interesting example at Isa 9:6, where the future king is addressed as *'el.*

[16] It is sometimes suggested that these figures were in fact regarded as 'divine', but this goes far beyond the evidence; these figures were thought to exercise divine authority and to share divine honour because they had been appointed by God as his representatives.

in creation-fall-redemption, and that it 'has been from its earliest origins ... closely interwoven with the doctrines of creation and of the fall'.[17] The mistake, he suggests, was to tie each of these doctrines to a particular event, and since many Christians have long since recognized that there is no need to link creation to a specific creative action of God, or to take the story of the fall literally, they should be ready to accept that the redemptive act of Christ must be understood in a similar way: if creation and fall are no longer seen in temporal terms, what of redemption and restoration? Whether or not Professor Wiles is right in suggesting that if we demythologize what is said about Adam we must also demythologize what our New Testament writers say about Christ is an interesting question. We should perhaps remember that the mythological ideas used by our writers were the appropriate ones for them to use, but that they were simply that — appropriate: while it was inevitable that the first Christians hammered out their new faith in these terms, this mythological language was not necessarily capable of conveying everything that had to be expressed, and it may be that at this point the Jewish eschatological framework is inadequate — as inadequate as the metaphysical language of Chalcedon! Perhaps it is significant also that Paul, at least, appears at times to 'demythologize' Adam[18] and insofar as restoration remains an eschatological expectation rather than an accomplished fact, there is a sense in which the work of Christ is not in fact tied to a specific point in history, but remains a possibility.

Be that as it may, it is significant that in discussing the early stages of Christian belief Professor Wiles finds it necessary to speak in terms of 'redemption' rather than of 'incarnation', for our brief survey of the evidence has indicated that 'redemption' is the more appropriate term within the Jewish complex of ideas. In keeping with traditional Jewish expectation, our New Testament writers thought in terms of the restoration not simply of humanity, but of the entire universe, and it was this that they claimed had been initiated in Christ. Equally significant was the fact that it was assumed that God's purpose for the universe would be achieved through his people Israel, and that redemption therefore centred on her: the first significant affirmation about Jesus was that he was the Messiah, and Moses is almost as important a figure in the schema as Adam. Though the belief that God acted in and through Christ belongs within this framework, and Professor Wiles is right to say that 'the doctrine of the incarnation arose in the closest conjunction with' the doctrines of the creation and the fall,[19] this doctrine was not yet, in New Testament times, what we would now recognize as one of 'incarnation', for the simple

---

[17] Maurice F. Wiles, 'Does Christology Rest on a Mistake?', *Religious Studies* 6 (1970): 70.
[18] Morna D. Hooker, 'Adam in Romans I', *NTS* 6 (1960): 297–306.
[19] Wiles, 'Does Christology Rest on a Mistake?', 72.

reason that our writers were not thinking in metaphysical terms. As he himself argues elsewhere, the idea of incarnation is anachronistic in the New Testament setting, and developed when New Testament writings were interpreted in a non-Jewish environment.[20] In other words, the earliest Christians used language which led others to speak of 'incarnation', rather than thinking in terms of incarnation themselves. The really significant development took place when the mythical was translated into the metaphysical, and what our New Testament writers spoke of in terms of 'redemption' was interpreted in terms of 'incarnation'. To impose precise metaphysical definitions on to a mythical framework may well be regarded as a mistake, for the focus is now on the pre-existence, incarnation, exaltation, and *parousia* of Christ, rather than on creation-fall-redemption, and concern is now with the salvation of individual souls, rather than with the redemption of the universe. But from the point of view of a student of the New Testament, the most serious mistake of all is the way in which this later resolution of the gospel story has been read back into our New Testament texts.

One of the false assumptions that has often confused the debate is the belief that the kind of interpretation of the New Testament evidence which we have been giving is of a 'low' Christology, in contrast to the 'high' Christology which focuses on incarnation. But it would be quite wrong to suppose that what we have discovered in the New Testament is a 'low' Christology. Our New Testament writers are convinced that God acts through Christ, that he speaks through him, and that he reveals himself in him. They use terms which are dynamic rather than metaphysical, but in their own way they express the conviction that in Christ they have 'seen' God. To insist that the New Testament should be read in its own terms is in no sense to advocate a 'reductionist' Christology. It is not a question of 'high' and 'low', but rather of *different* Christologies, worked out in totally different thought-worlds in answer to different problems: to judge one in terms of the other and to find it wanting is to misunderstand what is taking place.

Whether or not Chalcedon was a proper development from what is said about Christ in the New Testament is, as I said earlier, another question. I suspect that – given the philosophical climate – it was an inevitable development. In that sense, the claim symbolized by placing the scriptures in the centre

---

[20] Maurice F. Wiles, *The Remaking of Christian Doctrine* (London: SCM Press, 1974), ch. 3; see also Frances Young, 'A Cloud of Witnesses', in *The Myth of God Incarnate,* ed. John Hick (London: SCM Press, 1977). G.N. Stanton speaks of 'incipiently incarnational christology' ('Incarnational Christology in the New Testament', in *Incarnation and Myth: The Debate Continued,* ed. Michael Goulder [London: SCM Press, 1979], 163), but admits that 'there may be more appropriate ways of expressing the convictions of the New Testament writers' than the statement 'Jesus is God incarnate' ('Mr Cupitt on Incarnational Christology in the New Testament', in *Incarnation and Myth,* 171).

of the Council was justified: though there was disagreement at Chalcedon, the debate reflected the only kind of way in which the texts could be approached at that time. But the Chalcedonian definition is not a direct 'translation' of what is being said in the New Testament into another set of terms, for the questions its authors addressed were totally different from those which exercised the authors of the New Testament. When it comes to interpreting what the latter were trying to say, we must always remember to take off spectacles which have in any way been tinted with Chalcedonian beliefs. If we want to do justice to the ways in which the first Christians were trying to express their faith we must not suppose that when they speak of Jesus as 'Son of God' they meant the second person of the Trinity, or thought of him as being 'of one substance with the Father'; they were aware only that in Jesus of Nazareth God had spoken to them in a way which led them ever more confidently to identify the revealer with the revealed.

Section Four

Creative Conflict and the Gospel Tradition

12. 'What Doest Thou Here, Elijah?'

A Look at St Mark's Account of the Transfiguration

'The Transfiguration is at once the commentator's paradise and his despair'. It was with these words that George Caird introduced a study of the narratives of the transfiguration[1] in which he explored some of the ideas he had already hinted at in his unpublished Oxford DPhil thesis on 'The New Testament Concept of Doxa'. Finding myself – as often – in fundamental agreement with his approach, though questioning some of his conclusions, it seems a fitting theme on which to offer this essay in his memory, in gratitude for the many happy and often stimulating hours we spent together, trying to hammer out the meaning of New Testament texts.

Mark's account of the transfiguration begins with an intriguing and unusual reference to time: it took place 'after six days'. The only parallel in Mark to this precise dating is found at 14:1, while Luke, whom one might have expected to be precise, has the vague 'after about eight days'. But six days after what? After Peter's declaration that Jesus is the Messiah (8:29)? After Jesus' own prediction of his death and resurrection (8:31)? Or after the affirmations about the coming of the Son of man and the kingdom of God (8:38 and 9:1)? There are obvious links between the story of the transfiguration and all three of these themes. The declaration in 9:7 appears to be a divine confirmation of Peter's 'confession' in 8:29 – for though the heavenly voice addresses Jesus as 'Son', while Peter called him 'Messiah', the two terms stand together, rather than over against each other (compare 14:61). The theme of suffering (8:31) is taken up again immediately after the story of the transfiguration, when Jesus warns his disciples to tell no one what they have seen, until the Son of man has risen from the dead (9:9). This particular demand for secrecy suggests that the vision which the disciples have shared is of the glory which belongs to Jesus after the resurrection; this would mean that Mark intends us to see the transfiguration as a confirmation not only of Jesus' messianic status, but of the necessity of the way of suffering, death, and resurrection which lie before him.[2] The story itself is often interpreted as a fulfilment (or a foretaste) of the promise in 9:1 about the coming kingdom of God; but it seems more

---

[1] G.B. Caird, 'Expository Problems: The Transfiguration', *ExpTim* 67 (1956): 291–294.
[2] Caird, 'Expository Problems', 291.

likely that Mark sees it as a prefigurement of 8:38, which speaks of the future glory of the Son of man.[3]

The opening words of the story thus bind it closely to its context, and it is doubtful whether we need to choose between these three themes, for they belong together. But the words may well be intended to link the story with an incident quite outside the Marcan narrative altogether. In Exod 24:16, we read how Moses went up Mount Sinai, and how 'the glory of the Lord rested upon Mount Sinai, and the cloud covered the mountain for six days; on the seventh day he called to Moses out of the cloud'. The parallels, of course, are not exact, but if we find further echoes of the Exodus story in Mark's narrative, we shall be justified in assuming that Mark intends these opening words as a pointer to that story.[4]

Moses was accompanied by Joshua, who later succeeded him; Jesus takes three of his disciples with him – those who, in Mark's account, are closest to him – and goes up a 'high mountain'. The traditional site of the transfiguration is Mount Tabor, which is hardly a high mountain, but the exact location is unimportant, for the mountain is the place of worship, the place of revelation, perhaps also the new Sinai of the messianic era. The statement that Jesus 'was transfigured before them' reminds us of the gulf between him and his disciples: he is revealed as sharing in God's glory, while they are the witnesses to his glory. Unlike Matthew, who refers to Jesus' face shining like the sun (Matt 17:2),[5] Mark does not explain in what way Jesus himself was transfigured: he refers only to the transformation of his clothes, which became whiter than any earthly whiteness. The whiteness of garments often features in apocalyptic writings which attempt to describe heavenly scenes,[6] and Mark himself describes the young man in the tomb on Easter Day as wearing white – a hint, perhaps, that he is a heavenly being. Jesus' garments are described also as 'glistening' (στίλβοντα) – a word used only here in the New Testament – presumably with the reflection of heavenly radiance. The verb μεταμορφοῦν itself is an interesting one, used in the New Testament only in this story (by Mark and Matthew), in Rom 12:2 and in 2 Cor 3:18; this last passage is of particular interest to us, since it refers to Christians who with unveiled faces see (or reflect) the glory of the Lord, and are transformed into the same image, from glory to glory. This statement forms the climax of a section in which Paul has demonstrated the superiority of Christ over Moses

---

[3] G.H. Boobyer, *St Mark and the Transfiguration Story* (Edinburgh: T&T Clark, 1942), 58–61. Cf. Matt 16:28, which interprets the saying found in Mark 9:1 as a reference to the coming of the Son of man.

[4] The link is made by many commentators; see, e.g. Hugh Anderson, *The Gospel of Mark* (London: Oliphants, 1976).

[5] Exod 34:29 ff. refers to the skin of Moses' face shining.

[6] E.g. Dan 7:9.

by expounding the story related in Exod 34 of Moses' descent from Sinai, his face aglow with the reflection of divine glory: Paul contrasts the glory which faded from Moses' face with the lasting glory of Christ. There is no necessary direct link between 2 Corinthians and Mark 9, but Mark's narrative may well have been influenced by the tradition about Moses.

The disciples see two figures talking with Jesus, and these are identified as 'Elijah with Moses'. Why should these two individuals have been present with Jesus? The traditional answer has been that they represent the Law and the Prophets: the choice of Moses to represent the Law is obvious, and Elijah is the first major prophet in the books known as 'the Former prophets' in the Hebrew scriptures. Now Matthew and Luke may well have interpreted the scene along these lines, for they have 'corrected' Mark's account and refer, as is natural, to 'Moses and Elijah', but Mark's enigmatic phrase, 'Elijah with Moses', which suggests that Moses is playing a secondary role, hardly supports this interpretation. Is there an alternative explanation of the presence of these two figures? Perhaps they were seen as suitable companions for Jesus because they both suffered on account of their faithfulness (a theme taken up in vv. 12–13): like those disciples who are prepared to follow Jesus' path of suffering, they share in his glory (8:34–38).[7] Another link between Elijah and Moses, and one that is clearly relevant to the transfiguration, is the fact that both of them experienced theophanies on mountains. Or again, Elijah was said to have been carried up into heaven, and was therefore one of the few people who did not 'taste death' (9:1), and according to Jewish tradition Moses had shared a similar experience.[8] But none of these explanations of the presence of these two figures solves the riddle of Mark's phrase: why is Elijah mentioned first, when Moses was the earlier, and always remained the more significant figure in Judaism?

The explanation may well lie in the context of Mark's own narrative. The returning Elijah certainly played a part in Jewish eschatological expectation, and this tradition was already known in the first century CE, since it goes back to Malachi 3 and 4. Mark himself makes clear use of this tradition: immediately following the transfiguration, we have the conversation between Jesus and the three disciples, in which they ask him about the coming of Elijah, and Jesus affirms that Elijah has already come. The returning Elijah is here identified with John the Baptist, who is presented once again in the role which he regularly occupies in Mark's Gospel, as the messenger who points forward to the one who follows him, who is greater than he. But Elijah appears also in

---

[7] Morna D. Hooker, *The Son of Man in Mark* (London: SPCK, 1967), 127 ff.

[8] So Margaret E. Thrall, 'Elijah and Moses in Mark's Account of the Transfiguration', *NTS* 16 (1970): 305–317; this explanation leaves us wondering why Enoch was not also present on the mountain.

the complex of material immediately preceding the transfiguration. Here, it is Jesus who puts the questions: asked to say what men think of him, the disciples reply that they assume him to be John the Baptist, or Elijah, or one of the prophets (8:28): the same three suggestions have already appeared earlier in the Gospel, in the account of John's death, at 6:14 ff. It is clear that Mark intends his readers to reject these answers as wrong: John the Baptist has not been raised from the dead; Jesus is not the returning Elijah who prepares the way of the Lord – we know already from the opening verses of the Gospel what will be affirmed in 9:13, that this is John's role; nor is Jesus 'one of the prophets' – a phrase to which we must return. Mark has thus tied the story of the transfiguration into the popular hope for Elijah's return – a hope which he sees fulfilled in John the Baptist, who is the herald of Christ's coming. It is, then, not so strange after all that Elijah is present on the mountain, and that he is mentioned first.

But if Elijah is present as Jesus' forerunner – as the one who prepares his way and witnesses to his superiority – why is Moses there? Moses was not expected to return before the day of the Lord.[9] In explaining why Elijah is mentioned first, we seem to have reduced Moses to the status of a mere hanger-on. At this point we need to return to the story of Caesarea Philippi, and to the third of the answers given to the question 'Who is Jesus?' He is, it is suggested, 'one of the prophets'. Like the previous two suggestions, this seems to indicate a figure returning from the past – an idea which is spelt out in Luke's version of the story, where this third suggestion is that 'one of the prophets of old has arisen'. In contrast to these assumptions, we have Peter's declaration that Jesus is the Christ, a new and unique figure, not one returning from the past. But the reply given in the earlier section of Mark, at 6:15, varies slightly: here the third suggestion is that Jesus is a prophet in the succession of prophets, rather than one of the prophets returning from the dead. Mark's phrase may well be a deliberate echo of Deut 18:15, where Moses promises Israel that God will raise up another prophet like himself, in which case the speculation is that Jesus is this 'new Moses', the prophet whom God has promised to send to lead his people. But this suggestion is attributed, like the others, to popular rumour, and if Mark is indeed referring to 'the prophet' rather than to 'a prophet' in 6:15, he presumably considers this judgement to be as inadequate as those given in 8:28. The belief that Jesus is a prophet – whether old or new, whether the returning Elijah or the prophet like Moses – even though it springs from a desire to honour Jesus, is mistaken.

In two earlier scenes, then, Mark has already contrasted a false understanding of Jesus – that he is John, Elijah, or one of the prophets – with the truth,

---

[9] It is sometimes suggested that some such expectation had already arisen, but the evidence is all very late.

as yet only partially grasped. Elijah and Moses belong to the group of God's messengers who are most worthy of honour – yet Jesus is greater than they. It seems as though the traditional interpretation may have been mistaken in suggesting that Moses represents the Law and Elijah the prophet. Moses is as much a representative of the prophets as is Elijah: indeed, in Jewish thought Moses is the prophet *par excellence*, and none of his successors has lived up to him.[10] We must return to the question of the exact function of Elijah and Moses in Mark's story when we have looked at the rest of the narrative; for the moment, we note that their presence on the mountain could have something to do with Mark's belief that Jesus is *not* to be identified either with Elijah or with one of the prophets, and that they thus play a negative role.

Elijah and Moses converse with Jesus. It is only Luke who tells us the topic of their conversation – 'his exodus, which he was to fulfil in Jerusalem' (Luke 9:31). By using the unusual word ἔξοδος, Luke not only links the transfiguration with Jesus' death, but points to a very positive and significant interpretation of that death. It is notable, too, that Luke twice (vv. 31, 32) uses the word δόξα, which is picked up in the words of the risen Christ on the way to Emmaus in 24:26: 'Was it not necessary that the Christ should suffer these things and enter into his glory?' It looks very much as if Luke has understood the glory of Jesus at the transfiguration as a 'preview' of the glory he obtains through suffering. Luke, however, has no reference to the conversation between Jesus and his disciples on the way down from the mountain, in which Jesus links what they have seen with his Resurrection, and then underlines the necessity for suffering. In this scene, Mark and Matthew make a link between the transfiguration and Jesus' future exaltation similar to that made by Luke, even though the conversation they depict is different from Luke's, as is their terminology. For all three evangelists, the link with future suffering and vindication is part of their understanding of the event.

Peter's contribution is recorded by all the evangelists, and Luke agrees with Mark that he spoke without understanding. In Mark, he addresses Jesus as 'Rabbi' – a term used for Jesus elsewhere in this Gospel, but reading strangely so soon after Caesarea Philippi. Has Mark used it deliberately, to indicate the inadequacy of Peter's understanding of Jesus? In spite of his 'confession' of Jesus as the Christ, he is thinking of him still on the level of a mere teacher; however honourable the title 'rabbi' may be, it is clearly not a sufficiently exalted form of address.[11] Peter suggests building three σκηναί – tents or booths. His error is often said to be that he is premature; ignoring

---

[10] Cf. Hos 12:14 (13); Deut 34:10.
[11] Luke, similarly, uses the word ἐπιστάτα, a vocative form which occurs regularly in his Gospel; the term indicates one who has authority of some kind. Matthew prefers the term κύριε, which is capable of bearing much more meaning than the simple polite 'sir'.

the predictions of suffering and death, he assumes that the End has already come – the eschatological period which will be symbolized by the people living once again in booths, like those used in the wilderness.¹² But the σκηναί Peter offers to build are for Jesus, Moses, and Elijah, not for the people in general, or even for the disciples themselves: why do they alone need booths? An alternative explanation for Peter's mistake is that he ranks Jesus with Moses and Elijah: he thinks that he is honouring Jesus in treating him on a par with the great figures of old, and has failed to grasp that he is greater than they.¹³ This solution fits the context, but fails to explain why Peter should suppose that building booths was an appropriate way of showing honour. At this point we need to consider the possible significance of these booths.

The term σκηνή is used in the LXX in a variety of ways. Its most common use is as a translation of the Hebrew אֹהֶל meaning 'tent' – usually referring to an ordinary dwelling, but occasionally to the 'tent of meeting'. This latter structure is also termed מִשְׁכָּן in Hebrew – literally 'dwelling-place' – once again translated by σκηνή in the LXX, and usually referred to in English as the 'tabernacle'. Thirdly, σκηνή is used to translate the Hebrew סֻכָּה which means some kind of matted construction. The plural was regularly used of the structures erected at the Feast of Tabernacles or Booths. Although these were made of plaited branches, and were used in the fields at harvest time, the explanation given to them in Leviticus linked them with the dwellings of the nomad period, which were no doubt tents (Lev 23:42 ff., where סֻכּוֹת = σκηναί is used in both verses): a custom belonging to the agrarian society is explained and justified by appeal to the wilderness experience, even though tents and booths were very different structures. This means that though Peter must be understood to be referring to 'booths' of branches, since the disciples will hardly have come equipped with camping gear, the term σκηναί can be assumed to evoke a whole range of ideas. Just as a Renaissance painter saw nothing incongruous in painting the Annunciation against a fifteenth-century Italian landscape, so first-century Jews apparently saw no problem in portraying the tents of the wilderness period as 'booths'.

Was it then the Feast of Tabernacles, and was this why Peter wished to construct appropriate shelters for Elijah, Moses, and Jesus?¹⁴ If so, the festival has left no other mark on the narrative – and we are again left wondering why the disciples do not plan to build booths for themselves. Similar objections apply, as we have already seen, to the suggestion that the disciples might be thought to be assuming that the eschatological Feast of Tabernacles had arrived.¹⁵

---

¹² So Boobyer, *St Mark and the Transfiguration Story*, 76–79.
¹³ R.H. Lightfoot, *The Gospel Message of St. Mark* (Oxford: Clarendon Press, 1950), 43 ff.
¹⁴ Harald Riesenfeld, *Jésus Transfiguré* (Copenhagen: E. Munksgaard, 1947).
¹⁵ This suggestion seems to have been first made by Ernst Lohmeyer, in 'Die Verklärung Jesu nach dem Markus-Evangelium', *ZNW* 21 (1922): 185–215.

Moreover, the idea that the End was visualized as a perpetual celebration of Tabernacles has not been substantiated.[16] Professor Caird found the explanation of the term σκηναί in another of its Old Testament uses: 'The idea of the tabernacles was drawn from the story of Israel's sojourn in the wilderness where the tabernacle had been the shrine of the Divine glory, and Peter was proposing to build the tabernacles for three such manifestations of God's presence'.[17] But though both the Hebrew אֹהֶל and מִשְׁכָּן and the Greek σκηνή are used of God's tabernacle, and though Moses at least was understood to be a mediator of God's glory, Peter does not suggest building three tabernacles for the 'manifestations of God's presence': he suggests building them for Moses, Elijah, and Jesus themselves. It is true that Peter's intervention is ignored, presumably because it was considered inappropriate: but to identify the dwellings of God's glory as in any sense belonging to mere humans would surely have been unthinkable rather than merely inappropriate; such a tabernacle could only have been for God himself.[18]

Why then should Peter wish to erect booths? Perhaps the explanation is basically more simple. After all, if unexpected visitors drop in, one feels obliged to entertain them in some way, to invite them in and offer them hospitality. Without house or even tent to throw open, how could the disciples show proper respect, except by building some kind of temporary shelter? And indeed, what more appropriate dwelling for these men of the desert than σκηναί?[19] If Jesus is included, perhaps that is because the disciples have seen him transfigured, and now realize that he belongs in the company of Moses and Elijah, as worthy of honour as they. If they require three tents rather than one, that is because the idea of 'each man in his tent' is the norm.

Peter's suggestion is foolish for three reasons. Firstly, because Moses and Elijah are not here to stay: in a few moments the disciples will see 'no one, except Jesus'. Secondly, the reason why they are not here to stay is that, in different ways, they are Jesus' predecessors. The role of Elijah has been played out by the Baptist, whose task in all the Gospels is to act as a witness to Jesus, a signpost who points the way to the one who follows him. Moses, also – astonishingly – is a witness to Jesus, since Jesus is the fulfilment of what was written by 'Moses and all the prophets'; the phrase is Luke's, but the belief is again common to all the evangelists. But this means, thirdly, that Moses and

---

[16] The 'promise' in Hos 12:9 (LXX 12:10) that Israel will again live in booths refers to her future punishment; Zech 14:16–19 is concerned with the yearly celebration of the festival.

[17] Caird, 'Expository Problems', 292. Cf. Ulrich Mauser, *Christ in the Wilderness* (London: SCM Press, 1963), 113 ff.

[18] Cf. Exod 40:35, where Moses is not allowed to enter the tabernacle, because the glory of the Lord fills it.

[19] Cf. J.A. Ziesler, 'The Transfiguration Story and the Markan Soteriology', *ExpTim* 81 (1970): 263–268.

Elijah are in no way Jesus' equals – the truth half-grasped by the disciples at Caesarea Philippi. Moses, the greatest figure in Judaism, and Elijah, the prophet of the last days, fade from the picture as the heavenly voice draws the disciples' attention to Jesus alone: 'This is my beloved Son; hear him'. Jesus is not simply 'John the Baptist or Elijah or one of the prophets', but greater than all who came before him.

Mark attributes Peter's response to the disciples' fear – the common reaction of men and women to manifestations of God's power at work in Jesus.[20] The next verse contains further echoes of the story of Moses, to whom God spoke from the cloud which covered the mountain (Exod 24:15 ff.; 34:5). The words attributed to the voice also echo Deut 18:15, another incident concerning Moses, where he commands the people to hear the prophet whom God will raise in his place. Is Jesus here being identified with that prophet? We have already argued that Mark found that an inadequate understanding of Jesus. Moreover, what we have in the transfiguration story is far more than one prophet commanding obedience to his successor:[21] it is the voice of God himself, commanding obedience, not to a prophet but to his Son. The combination of reflected radiance, cloud, and voice indicate that the story is to be understood as a theophany, and in this context the frequent demands in the Old Testament to hear and obey the words of God himself are more significant than the injunction to hear one particular prophet. If prophets could declare 'the word of the Lord' to his people, how much more the one who is now identified as God's beloved Son?

There is of course another important parallel with the words spoken from heaven, in the similar declaration addressed to Jesus himself earlier in the story at the Baptism. If Mark repeats the words in almost the same form, that is hardly surprising: a heavenly revelation may be relied on to remain constant. But presumably he expected his readers to remember that earlier occasion;[22] we must therefore ask what light this first story may be able to throw onto the second.

The words spoken from heaven in Mark 1:11 form the climax of Mark's opening paragraphs. He begins by telling us that the coming of John fulfilled the prophecies that God would send a messenger to 'prepare the way of the Lord'. The description of John as a man of the wilderness, wearing camel's hair and leather girdle, and eating locusts and wild honey, suggests that he is seen as the returning Elijah. John's only function in Mark is to point the way to the one who follows him: he appears in the wilderness, to prepare the way

---

[20] Cf. Mark 4:41; 5:15, 33; 6:50; 16:8.
[21] Contra. J. Ziesler, 'The Transfiguration Story', 267.
[22] Matthew apparently added the phrase ἐν ᾧ εὐδόκησα to Mark's second story, so bringing it into closer conformity with the earlier account.

of the Lord by preaching a baptism of repentance for the forgiveness of sins; his only message is about the one who follows him. Three times he stresses the superiority of this coming one, who is mightier than John, whose sandals John is unworthy to untie, who will baptize with Holy Spirit instead of water. John's words are followed by the arrival of Jesus on the scene, and the heavenly declaration that he is God's Son. John's function here is precisely, but far more explicitly, that of Elijah in 9:2–13: he is Jesus' forerunner, whose task is to bear witness to him, and who must fade from the scene when his task is done; in 1:14 he is put into prison – and 'they did to him whatever they pleased, as it is written of him' (9:13). If the disciples, on the Mount of Transfiguration, are privileged to glimpse the glory of Jesus, and hear the proclamation of his identity, it is hardly surprising if they also glimpse Elijah, and have John's true identity explained to them.

The parallel story of the baptism thus spells out the role of John, and provides us with good reasons for the presence of Elijah on the Mount of Transfiguration, but does nothing to explain Moses' presence. We have already discovered a negative role for Elijah and Moses – their presence confirms that Jesus is not to be identified with Elijah (nor, as the ensuing conversation makes plain, with John, since he is Elijah), nor even with Moses, the greatest of the prophets (and clearly for Mark it is inconceivable that he should be a lesser prophet than Moses). But does Moses have a positive role, like that of John alias Elijah, who is the forerunner and witness to Jesus?

The conversation between Jesus and his disciples on the way down from the mountain has already supplied us with a clue about Elijah; does it offer us any guidance about Moses? Mark and Matthew are in close agreement in their accounts of this conversation, but there is one feature of the Marcan narrative which Matthew does not take up: in Mark, Jesus asks specifically what it is that is written concerning the Son of man, and links this with the fact that what has happened to the returning Elijah was also written concerning him. One of the puzzles which commentators have never solved is that of knowing where in the Old Testament such things could be supposed to be written, and since Mark does not single out any particular text, he may well be appealing to scripture in general, rather than individual passages. If we were to press Mark to name his sources, then as far as the Son of man is concerned, he might appeal to the prophets, to the psalms, and to Daniel; Elijah remains a conundrum, unless the reference is to Jezebel's attempts on the first Elijah's life in 1 Kings. We thus seem to have possible leads in every area of the Hebrew scriptures except for the Law, and may well wonder whether this is of any relevance at all to our original question about Moses. Surprisingly, the answer may well be 'yes', since elsewhere – both in the New Testament and in rabbinic writings – we find 'the Law' being used as a blanket term for

Old Testament citations, even when the Pentateuch itself is not quoted;[23] on other occasions, appeal is made to 'Moses and all the prophets', where Moses is differentiated from the prophets, though they are joint witnesses.[24] In Mark 9:12 ff., where no particular reference is given, it would be natural to a first-century Jewish Christian to regard this as an appeal to 'Moses and all the prophets'. All this reminds us that Moses is the obvious figure to represent not just the Law, but everything that 'is written'. We must ask, therefore, whether Moses' role on the mountain top may not be parallel to Elijah's. Elijah – in the person of John the Baptist – is the forerunner of Jesus, and witness to the authenticity of Christian claims about him. Moses, too, the first and greatest of God's prophets, is also a witness to those claims: the things which happen to Jesus – death and resurrection – are the things which are 'written concerning the Son of man'. Moses, like Elijah, appears in the role of Jesus' sponsor.

But Jesus is greater than his sponsors – greater than Elijah, his forerunner, and greater even than Moses. We have no room here to explore the role of Moses in Mark's Gospel, and must be content with the observation that in various passages Jesus is depicted as appealing to the teaching of Moses (1:44; 7:10 ff.; 10:3, 19; 12:26, 29 ff.) At the same time, however, the Mosaic commands are set in the context of superior commands, which show Jesus acting with an authority greater than that of Moses: Jesus both fulfils the Law and points beyond it.[25] Like Elijah, Moses functions as a predecessor of Jesus, whose role is to witness to the one who is greater than he. It is appropriate, then, that these two witnesses to Jesus should be present on the mountain top – Elijah, whose coming has restored all things, and Moses, whose writings bear witness to Christ.

Finally, we must ask whether this interpretation of the story helps us to understand the form of Mark's narrative. We have already seen that there are very clear echoes of the story of Moses on Mt. Sinai, but we have rejected as inadequate the suggestion that Jesus is being presented as 'the prophet like Moses'. Jesus is not simply in the tradition of the prophets, but the unique Son of God. Now there are several other passages in the New Testament where a comparison is made between Moses and Jesus, and on every occasion there are echoes of this same story about Sinai. The most obvious is perhaps 2 Corinthians 3, where the temporary glory of the old διακονία is contrasted with the permanent glory of the new, reflected from the face of Christians; the whole passage can fairly be described as a midrash of Exod 34:29–35, and the essential point is the superiority of Christ's ministers to Moses. How

---

[23] See John 10:34; 12:34; 15:25; Rom 3:19; 1 Cor 14:21. In *b. Sanh.* 91b, Ps 84:5 (4) and Isa 52:8 are quoted as 'Torah'; similarly Zech 12:12 in *b. Sukkah* 51b.

[24] See Luke 16:29, 31; 24:27; John 1:45; Acts 28:23.

[25] Cf. the apparent paradox in Matt 5, where vv. 17–20 introduce the antitheses of vv. 21–48.

much greater, then, the glory of Christ himself, who is the image of God and the source of our glory (4:1–6). Much more succinct – though nevertheless clear – is the allusion to Sinai in John 1:14–18. Again, the passage is concerned with glory – the glory we have seen in Christ, the glory (as in Mark 9:7) appropriate to one who is God's only Son.[26] Again, there is a contrast between Moses (through whom the Law was given) and Christ, who embodies grace and truth,[27] and who is (as in 2 Cor) the source of blessing for Christians. Finally, there is Hebrews 3, where Jesus is said to be worthy of greater glory than Moses, since the one is a Son, the other a servant (3:1–6); this contrast picks up the opening words of the book, in which we are told that God has spoken to his people in the past through the prophets, but has now spoken through a Son – 'the effulgence of his glory'. It is worth noting, too, that in 2:9, the glory and honour with which Jesus is crowned is said to be διὰ τὸ πάθημα τοῦ θανάτου. This same paradox of glory through death is the theme of 2 Cor 4:6 ff., where Paul spells out what it means for Christians to reflect Christ's glory. In John, this truth is so self-evident that the moment of Christ's death is spoken of as his glorification. And if we return to Mark 9, we find that there the glory seen on the mountain cannot be spoken of until the Son of man has been raised from the dead, and the prophecies of his suffering and rejection been fulfilled. Nor is this a 'fluke' in Mark, since on the rare occasions when he uses the word δόξα, he links it every time with the suffering and death of Jesus and his followers.[28]

Mark's account of the transfiguration, then, presents in narrative form ideas found in at least three other New Testament writers – quite apart from the use made by Matthew and Luke of the story. The echoes of the story of Moses on Sinai remind us that the glory of Jesus is even greater than the glory of Moses. The story of the transfiguration spells out the truths of the preceding paragraphs, 8:27–9:1. Jesus is not John, nor Elijah, nor one of the prophets, but a much greater figure – the Christ (or Son of God, cf. Mark 14:61); his destiny is suffering and death, and those who wish to follow him must expect to share his fate; but his final destiny is glory – a glory which he will share with those who are loyal to him. It looks very much as though the enigma of the story may be largely due to the fact that we fail to realize that Mark is here presenting in dramatic form ideas which were part of the common beliefs of the early Christian communities.

---

[26] Here, too, the witness of John the Baptist is referred to (v. 15); but in this Gospel the identification of John with Elijah is denied (1:21).

[27] Cf. Morna D. Hooker, 'The Johannine Prologue and the Messianic Secret', *NTS* 21 (1974): 52–58 = below, essay 23 (pp. 321–340).

[28] See Mark 8:38; 10:37; 13:26.

13. Mark's Use of Scripture

It is perhaps understandable that the original version of this essay, commissioned for a book on the use of Hebrew scriptures in the New Testament,[1] was assigned a mere 4,000 words by the book's editors, for at first sight Mark seems to make little appeal to the Old Testament. In contrast to Matthew and Luke, who in their different ways emphasize the fulfilment of scripture, Mark includes only one explicit editorial quotation, in 1:2 ff., and gives that a wrong attribution.

But appearances are deceptive. Mark handles the material in his own distinctive way, and the opening quotation is significant: his story is good news precisely because it is the fulfilment of scripture.[2] Thereafter, Jesus' words and activities constantly echo OT scenes and language, until what is 'written' of the Son of man (9:12; 14:21) is finally fulfilled. There is no dearth of references: one recent article[3] listed 57 quotations and approximately 160 allusions (not counting passages which had possibly 'influenced' Mark) in chapters 11–16 alone! But they do not all fit into the pattern of 'fulfilment', for in some cases Jesus appears to take issue with scripture, notably in discussions about the Law.

To deal adequately with the use of the OT in Mark's Gospel in one chapter is clearly an impossible task. In order to reduce the problem to manageable proportions, we shall confine our attention to those quotations and allusions which can be traced to the Pentateuch.[4] Inevitably, this will raise the crucial question of Mark's attitude to the Law, even though that particular term is never used by Mark: does he believe that the Law has been abrogated by the gospel?[5]

---

[1] D.A. Carson and H.G.M. Williamson, eds., *It is Written: Scripture Citing Scripture: Essays in Honour of Barnabas Lindars, SSF* (Cambridge: Cambridge University Press, 1988).

[2] Contra Alfred Suhl, *Die Funktion der alttestamentlichen Zitate und Anspielungen im Markusevangelium* (Gütersloh: Mohn, 1965), who denies that the theme of fulfilment is important for Mark.

[3] H.C. Kee, 'The Function of Scriptural Quotations and Allusions in Mark 11–16', in *Jesus und Paulus,* eds. E. Earle Ellis and Erich Grässer (Göttingen: Vandenhoeck & Ruprecht, 1975), 165–188.

[4] Problems of space also compel us to leave on one side the question of the particular form of text which Mark has used. We shall concentrate here on the theological significance of Mark's handling of the Pentateuchal texts.

[5] See the discussion by Siegfried Schulz, 'Markus und das Alte Testament', *ZTK* 58 (1961): 184–197, and Hans Hübner, *Das Gesetz in der synoptischen Tradition* (Witten: Luther-Verlag, 1973), 213–226. The question is more often posed in terms of Jesus' own attitude to the Law.

1. Quotations

Turning first to those passages from the Pentateuch which are introduced specifically as quotations, we leave aside the possible use of Exod 23:20 in 1:2 – since Mark himself attributes the quotation to Isaiah and is apparently unaware of the source of these particular words[6] – and move on to 7:10, where Jesus appeals to what 'Moses said' in Exod 20:12 and 21:17. The context of this appeal to scripture is an argument between Jesus and a group of Pharisees and scribes arising from the lax behaviour of his disciples, who eat with 'unclean' hands. Throughout this section, Mark emphasizes that the issue in dispute is not one of the provisions of the Mosaic law, but part of 'the tradition of the elders'. At the beginning of the pericope he explains that the Pharisees do not eat without washing their hands, so observing the tradition of the elders – and he goes on to list some of the other traditions that they observe.[7] The challenge of the Pharisees and the scribes in v. 5 concerns the fact that his disciples do not observe these traditions; in reply, Jesus complains that his opponents abandon the commandment of God, while maintaining the tradition of men (v. 8). As an example of their 'hypocrisy', he contrasts what 'Moses said' – the commandment of God – with what 'you say' (v. 11). The clear commandment to honour father and mother is thus annulled by the tradition which allows a man to declare his goods 'corban'.

In this first example, therefore, we find that though the story begins with Pharisees and scribes challenging the behaviour of Jesus' disciples, it is Jesus who appeals to the Torah and who in turn, on the basis of Torah, challenges the practice of the Pharisees and scribes; the accusation of failure to keep the Law is brought, not against Jesus, as we might have expected, but against the Pharisees and scribes. Thus far Mark has presented Jesus as a loyal son of Moses. This is the more remarkable, since the argument in vv. 9–13 might well have been conducted in terms of the relative weight to be given to different parts of the Law, for the inviolability of an oath is affirmed in the Law itself (Num 30:2; Deut 23:21–23), and Jesus' opponents would presumably have argued that in this particular instance of 'corban' they were maintaining the divine command. Nevertheless, this example is both introduced and concluded with an accusation by Jesus that they maintain their own traditions and make void the word of God. Again and again throughout vv. 1–13 Mark insists that this is the real issue.

---

[6] If not Exod 23:20, then Mal 3:1.
[7] It is clear that the story in its present form is being told for the benefit of the Gentiles; the fact that the quotations from Isa 29 follows the LXX, not the Hebrew text, suggests that the conversation reflects a debate between Jews and Christians, rather than between Jesus and his contemporaries, *pace* Kenneth J. Thomas, 'Torah Citations in the Synoptics', *NTS* 24 (1977): 85–96.

The situation becomes more complex when we move on to the 'parable' in vv. 14–16 and its explanation in vv. 17–23. On its own, the saying in v. 15 might seem compatible with the story so far: in declaring that it is what comes out of a man (i.e. evil thoughts and desires, vv. 21 ff.) rather than what enters him that defiles him, Jesus could well be summing up his position in the previous dispute: it is not the failure to observe traditions about the washing of hands or utensils which defile a man, but the failure to honour father or mother. But the issue in vv. 2 ff. concerns the ritual preparation of hands and utensils, not the food itself, whereas v. 15 is most naturally interpreted as referring to the food which is eaten; certainly this is the way it is understood in the private explanation to the disciples which follows. To be relevant to the dispute in vv. 1–5, we must assume that the Pharisees believed that cultic impurity could be passed from unwashed hands to food to eater.[8] Moreover the radical nature of the saying – 'not this but that' – fits uneasily into a context where the issue has so clearly been a conflict between human tradition and divine command, for the prohibition of certain foods as unclean certainly belongs to the Law. We might perhaps interpret v. 15 as a declaration of priorities, and understand it to mean: 'You must not be so busy with ritual cleanliness that you ignore moral cleanliness'. But this interpretation becomes impossible when we come to v. 19, where Mark spells out what he understands to be the significance of the saying with the comment: 'making all foods clean'.

This second section thus introduces a new idea into the question of Jesus' relationship with the Law: whereas in vv. 1–13 we found Jesus appealing to the Law, he now appears to be dismissing it! Having attacked the Pharisees for setting the tradition of men over the commandments of God, we now find him apparently abandoning another of the commandments altogether: the comparison is no longer between the tradition of men and the commandments of God, but between the teaching of Moses and that of Jesus. We can, of course, explain this inconsistency in terms of the different traditions used by Mark, but this hardly explains his own position. On the one hand, he sees Jesus as obedient to the commandments of God given through Moses and attacking the tradition of men; on the other, as setting his own authority above that of Moses. We must return to this problem later.

The next quotations from the Pentateuch occur in ch. 10, once again in a debate with the Pharisees, this time on the question of divorce. Here too, the argument is initiated by the Pharisees, and once again Jesus responds by appealing to the teaching of Moses. But here he invites his opponents to quote the Law, and on this occasion 'what Moses said' proves to be inadequate,

---

[8] Roger P. Booth, *Jesus and the Laws of Purity* (Sheffield: JSOT, 1986) argues for this belief: see chs. 4 and 5.

not because it was 'the tradition of men', but because it was adapted to human weakness. So in contrast to Moses' concession in Deuteronomy 24, Jesus appeals to Gen 1:27 and 2:24, where the ideal for marriage is set out. This time we are clearly comparing one part of the Law with what is understood to be a superior command. The logical outcome of this argument is set out in v. 9, which in effect annuls the provision of Deuteronomy 24. We have therefore reached a conclusion very similar to that in 7:19: the authoritative pronouncement of Jesus takes priority over that of Moses. But once again, the argument which leads up to this pronouncement affirms the inviolability of God's decree in scripture.

On this occasion also, Mark adds a private scene between Jesus and his disciples in which the implications of his teaching are brought out. And once again this private teaching takes matters a further step, since Jesus' pronouncement in vv. 11–12 declares that those who take advantage of the Mosaic provision are guilty of adultery. As in 7:19, the authoritative teaching of Jesus is now challenging the Law itself. Later in this chapter, in vv. 17–22, Mark records the incident of a man who comes to Jesus asking what he must do to inherit eternal life. Once again, Jesus appeals to the Torah; this time he quotes the last six commandments (Exod 20:12–16/Deut 5:16–20) – those concerned with human relationships. When the man protests that he has kept all these from his youth, he is told to sell all his possessions, give them away, and follow Jesus.

In the first part of this incident, Jesus is portrayed as loyally upholding the Law, but in the second part, loyalty to the Law proves to be insufficient: the one thing that the man lacks can be found only by abandoning all his possessions and becoming Jesus' disciple. As in the previous incidents, therefore, we find that the Law is first upheld, but that the authority exercised by Jesus is then shown to be even greater than that of the Law.

In ch. 12, Mark presents a series of incidents in which Jesus engages in dialogue with various groups. In vv. 18 ff. he is challenged by Sadducees, who mock the notion of resurrection by appealing to Moses' provision for levirate marriage in Deuteronomy 25. Since the Sadducees regarded the Pentateuch alone as authoritative, the argument here is quite different from the dispute with the Pharisees in ch. 7. Jesus protests that in fact they do not understand the scriptures to which they appeal: nor do they understand the power of God, which can raise the dead. Scripture itself bears witness to this power, as is seen 'in the book of Moses' – namely, in the words of God at the burning bush.

In this incident, one passage of scripture is played off against another: the quotation from Exodus 3:6 overthrows the conclusion which had been drawn from Deuteronomy 25. Yet how does Mark establish that Jesus' interpretation is correct, and the Sadducees' is wrong? As before, the matter is decided by the authoritative pronouncement of Jesus himself, who in effect gives the verdict in favour of his own position. In order to underline this authority, Mark has Jesus introduce and conclude his response with the declaration that the Sadducees are in error: this 'enclosure' is parallel to the one used in 7:9, 13, where Jesus sets out the error of the Pharisees. There is, however, another hint as to why Jesus' position should be accepted as correct: Mark sets the incident in the temple, where Jesus has just told the parable of the vineyard, ending with a proof text which points forward to his own resurrection; following the teaching in and concerning the temple, the story moves on to tell of Jesus' passion, death and resurrection. If the Sadducees do not know the power of God, therefore, is it because they do not recognize that power at work in the resurrection of Jesus himself? Jesus appeals to Moses as a witness to the power of God to raise the dead to life, but for Mark and his readers, that power has been seen in the risen Jesus, and this is why his words have authority.

The final pericope in which the Torah is appealed to is 12:28–34, where a scribe questions Jesus about the commandments, and he replies by quoting Deut 6:4 ff. and Lev 19:18. This is an unusual story, since encounters between Jesus and the representatives of official Judaism normally take the form of conflict stories, whereas in Mark's account (in contrast to those of Matthew and Luke) the questioner is friendly. Nevertheless, the story represents a struggle: the scribe presents a challenge, and Jesus responds. The scribe – the official teacher of the Mosaic law – then approves and endorses that response. Mark tells us that Jesus, in turn, approved the scribe's wise reply – a somewhat surprising comment, since this reply consisted of little more than a repetition of Jesus' own words.[9] It is possible that Mark has adapted a story in which the scribe himself was challenged to make the reply – as in Luke 10:25–28 – and that he has clumsily retained Jesus' commendation of the scribe's words, but the story as it stands makes good sense. The scribe naturally assumes that he has the authority to vet Jesus' teaching, and he gives it his approval: he acknowledges Jesus as a true son of Moses. But Jesus turns the tables, by giving his *imprimatur* to the scribe: 'You are not far from the kingdom of God'. It is Jesus who has the authority to judge, not the representative of Moses. 'After that,' comments Mark, 'no one dared to ask him any question'.

It should be noted that both the original question as to which is the first commandment, and the scribe's comment on Jesus' reply, assume that it is proper and necessary to compare one part of the Law with another, and to decide which should have precedence over the other.

In these five passages Mark presents us with a picture of Jesus as one whose teaching is in accordance with that of Moses, but who does not merely repeat the Mosaic teaching, since his authority goes beyond that of Moses. As Mark

---

[9] There is perhaps an echo of Deut 4:35 in the first part of his summary.

expressed it in 1:22: 'he taught them as one with authority, and not as the scribes'. It is notable that in three of these five passages Jesus makes specific appeal to Moses, while the other two refer to the Decalogue; four of the five use the word ἐντολή.[10]

2. Allusions

It is notoriously difficult to decide what is and what is not an allusion to another text: some echoes of the Pentateuch may be accidental, and not the result of influence at all; others may be unconscious, and not due to any deliberate association with the OT on Mark's part, but they could nevertheless be important in betraying what was going on in his subconscious mind; others may well indicate that a link with the OT has been seen, either by Mark or by someone else before him, and that this link is important for the interpretation of the particular passage. The first reference noted in the margin of NA[26] is a good example. If the statement in 1:6 that John ate locusts is simply part of the tradition, then the link with Lev 11:21 ff. may be accidental; but Lev 11:21 ff. reminds us that locusts – unlike other insects – are 'clean' and may be eaten. Did it occur to Mark that John's diet was in accordance with the Law? And if so, is this significant? Was it important enough to lead to the inclusion of this detail in the narrative? It seems more probable that the reference to locusts was included because it indicated that John's diet was desert food.

Another problem in this opening section occurs in v. 11. The voice from heaven uses words which are reminiscent of Ps 2:7, and possibly also of Isa 42:1, but the phrase υἱὸς ἀγαπητός is used by the LXX in Gen 22:2, 12, 16 of Abraham's only son Isaac. It is used again by Mark in 9:7, and in the parable of the vineyard in 12:6. Whether or not the parallel with Isaac occurred to Mark, it was not long before other Christian writers saw its relevance.

It is hardly surprising that many of the allusions to the Pentateuch in Mark concern what is lawful. Several of these occur in the two stories about the Sabbath in 2:23–3:6, where the accusation of doing what is not lawful is brought first against the disciples, then against Jesus himself.[11] It is important to realize that the behaviour of the disciples does not necessarily contravene the Law: plucking ears of corn is clearly distinguished from reaping in Deut 23:25, so that it is questionable whether their action could properly be described as 'work'. The dispute thus concerns the interpretation of the Mosaic

---

[10] The word is used only six times by Mark – all of them in these four passages: 7:8, 9; 10:5, 19; 12:28, 31. The word νόμος does not occur at all.

[11] The accusation in 2:24 refers to the command set out in Exod 20:8–11 and other passages; cf. 34:21. The prohibition in v. 26 refers to Lev 24:5–9. The reaction of the Pharisees in 3:6 could presumably be justified by appealing to Exod 31:14.

command to 'remember' the Sabbath. So, too, in the second incident, where Jesus declares that it is proper to do good on the Sabbath, not evil, and to save life, not kill. Since at the end of the story the Pharisees 'immediately' (i.e., on the Sabbath), plot to destroy him, the implication seems to be that they are doing precisely what Jesus declares to be contrary to Sabbath observance: as in ch. 7, it is not Jesus but his opponents who are shown to be guilty of breaking the Law.

In the first incident, Jesus responds to his opponents in a way which is by now familiar to us, by quoting scripture – though not, on this occasion, the Pentateuch: he justifies the behaviour of his disciples by appealing to the precedent set by David. But the analogy will hardly work unless Jesus is in some way comparable to the figure of David, so that already the argument depends on the authority of Jesus, as well as on the appeal to scripture, and it is the declaration of this authority – that of the Son of man – which clinches the argument in 2:28. In the second incident, his authority to pronounce is demonstrated in the healing of the man with a withered hand. Jesus does not merely interpret the Law, but fulfils it in a uniquely authoritative way, by doing good and saving life. Once again we are reminded of the earlier scene in the synagogue in ch. 1, where Mark links together Jesus' authoritative teaching and healing in the comment of the congregation in v. 27.

Jesus' loyalty to the Torah has already been demonstrated in an earlier allusion to the Pentateuch in 1:44. On this occasion, he sends the leper whom he has just healed to the priest, instructing him to make the offering for his cleansing which Moses commanded, 'as a proof to them'.[12] Are we to understand this as a proof of the man's healing? If so, why has Mark used the plural αὐτοῖς when only one priest has been mentioned? Or is he thinking of this command as a demonstration of the way in which Jesus himself kept the Law? In this case, we must presumably understand the αὐτοῖς as referring to all those who might question his loyalty to Moses – those who later in the Gospel emerge as Jesus' opponents. Whatever the explanation, we find here the same combination of ideas which we have already met in several other passages: Jesus is shown at one and the same time as upholding the Law, and yet exercising a far greater authority than Moses. In this particular instance he does this by healing the man of his leprosy, where the Law could make provision only for what should be done once the disease has been cured: when the Law is fulfilled, it is seen to bear witness to the authority and power of Jesus.

It is perhaps worth noting that a similar theme will be spelt out in Mark's next story, where Jesus forgives sins – something which no man can do – though there is, of course, provision in the Law for dealing with sins which have already been forgiven, just as there is provision for dealing with a leper.

---

[12] The regulations for this offering are set out in Lev 14:2ff.

It is possible that Mark himself made this connection between the two stories, and understood them both as examples of the superiority of Jesus to the Law.

The next three passages containing allusions to the Pentateuch are of a somewhat different kind: each recalls an incident in the story of Moses. The first is the story of the feeding of the five thousand, in which we are told that the crowds were 'like sheep without a shepherd'; these words in 6:34 are reminiscent of a phrase used in Num 27:17, where Moses requests Yahweh to appoint someone to lead the people after his death, and is instructed to commission Joshua.

The second passage is the story of the transfiguration, and in this instance there are several reminiscences of the story of Moses: the introductory 'after six days', together with the setting on the mountain, point us to Exod 24:15 ff., and this association is confirmed by the presence of the cloud and the voice which speaks from it; the story alluded to on this occasion is the giving of the two tables of the Law. The words of command addressed to the disciples from the cloud echo another passage, Deut 18:15, in which Moses is again looking ahead to the time following his death, and promises that God will raise up for the people another prophet like himself. But the most remarkable feature of Mark's story as far as our present theme is concerned is the appearance of Moses himself on the mountain, conferring with Jesus and Elijah. It is impossible to consider Mark 9:2–13 here in the detail it deserves,[13] but already we have seen that the chief parallel to the story is the account of the giving of the Law to Moses, and that when Moses vanishes from the scene, the divine voice commands the disciples to heed Jesus in words that demonstrate that he is Moses' successor. On the other hand, we must note that Jesus is singled out as God's beloved Son – a clear indication of his superiority to both Moses and Elijah. The summit conference signifies agreement between the parties, but not equality.

The third passage occurs later in this chapter (9:38–40), when one of the disciples reports that they have attempted to stop someone casting out demons in Jesus' name, 'because he does not follow us'. The parallel here is found in Num 11:26–29, where Moses is told that two men who had not been included among the seventy elders whom he has just appointed as his helpers are nevertheless prophesying; Joshua asks him to stop them, but Moses recognizes that Yahweh has put his spirit on these men, as well as on the chosen seventy. Though Mark does not refer here to the spirit, we know from 3:22–30 that he understands exorcism to be the work of the spirit. Unlike

---

[13] I have discussed the role of Moses and Elijah in the transfiguration narrative in Morna D. Hooker, "'What Doest Thou Here, Elijah?'": A Look at St. Mark's Account of the Transfiguration', in *The Glory of Christ in the New Testament: Studies in Christology in Memory of George Bradford Caird,* eds. L.D. Hurst and N.T. Wright (Oxford: Clarendon Press, 1987), 59–70 = above, essay 12 (pp. 179–189).

the other stories we have considered, this particular incident is not concerned with the position of Jesus himself, but with that of men and women who claim to act in his name. But in their case, too, the 'mighty works' they do is of vital significance in demonstrating who they are.

With the arrival of Jesus in Jerusalem in 11:1, the story becomes dominated by the approaching death of Jesus, and references to all parts of the OT multiply. Some possible allusions are tenuous: the colt which is tied in 11:2 (but not specifically to a tree!) may echo Gen 49:11; the plot in 12:7 to kill the favourite son is similar to that against Joseph in Gen 37:20. But the echo of Exod 22:22 in 12:40, following closely after the conversation with the scribe in vv. 28–34, appears deliberate: in condemning those scribes who oppress widows, Jesus once again accuses those who claim to be the guardians of the Law of doing, themselves, what the Law forbids.

Mark 13 is full of OT allusions, and several of these come from the Pentateuch. The promise of v. 11 echoes Num 22:35, and the language of v. 19 is reminiscent of Deut 4:32. The warning against false prophets working signs and wonders in v. 22 may well be based on Deut 13:1–3, and the promise that the elect will be gathered from the corners of the earth reminds us of the promise to gather the scattered people of God in Deut 30:4. In the passion narrative, the majority of allusions can be traced to the psalms and prophets, but there are several echoes of the Pentateuch. The saying about the poor in 14:7 is reminiscent of Deut 15:11; the reference to the blood of the covenant in v. 24 recalls Exod 24:8. The problem in 14:55–59 arises from the need for two witnesses set out in Deut 17:6 and 19:15, and the speed of burial in 15:42 is based on Deut 21:22 ff.

3. Summary

Many of the passages we have referred to in section 2 support the picture derived from those in section 1. Mark's attitude is surprisingly consistent, and if we find his material confusing, this results from the inherent tension in the position that he maintains. For he presents us with a picture of Jesus who both upholds the Mosaic law, and yet exercises an authority which is greater than that of Moses. In spite of all attempts by his opponents to fault him, Jesus cannot be faulted in his loyalty to the Law; on every occasion it is they who are shown to be the lawbreakers, not he. The many references to Moses, both direct and allusive, serve to show that Jesus is Moses' successor, but again and again the successor is shown to be superior.

Obvious tensions arise if the actions and teachings of Jesus appear to challenge those laid down in the Law. Sometimes, as in 3:1–6, this is resolved by showing that the vital issue is the way in which the Law is interpreted.

Elsewhere, as in 10:2 ff., one part of the Law is shown to be more fundamental than another; but in this particular instance the tension cannot be resolved, for Jesus' authoritative interpretation of one command leads to the annulment of another in the follow-up to the incident in vv. 10–12. So, too, in the scene in ch. 7, where Mark attempts to solve the problem by insisting that the debate is really about the conflict between God's commands and human tradition; but once again, the tension cannot be resolved in this way, and this emerges in the evangelist's comment in v. 19 that Jesus made all food clean, a statement which certainly cannot be reconciled with Mosaic regulations![14] It is perhaps significant that both these developments are said by Mark to have been private revelations to the disciples: the challenge of Jesus to the Law itself is something that emerged as the Christian community thought out the implications of his teaching.

If there are anomalies in Mark's picture, this was inevitable. They reflect the tensions of a Christian community which attempted to reconcile the traditions of the past with their new experiences in Christ. His evidence supports the belief that neither Jesus himself nor the earliest generation of Christians regarded the teaching of Moses as abrogated: his commands were indeed those of God himself. But interpretation and adaptation led inevitably to the point of rupture – a point which had not yet been reached when Mark wrote, but which must eventually come. The problem reflected in Mark is one which in one form or another has continued to exercise the church ever since. The way in which he addressed the problem in his own day may perhaps offer some guidance to those who seek to meet it in our own.

---

[14] Matthew avoids this tension in his version of these two stories. He omits the comment in Mark 7:19 from the first story (Matt 15:1–20), so that the issue remains that of eating with unwashed hands, not that of eating unclean food. In the second (Matt 19:3–12), Matthew's arrangement of the material is such that he avoids the impression that Jesus is attacking the Law; moreover, Jesus himself allows divorce 'for unchastity' (v. 9) and concedes that the ideal cannot be kept by all (v. 11). In neither story, therefore, is there any suggestion that the Law itself is under attack. Luke has no parallel to either story.

14. Isaiah in Mark's Gospel

That the book of Isaiah was of particular importance for Mark seems clear, for he begins his 'Gospel about Jesus Christ' with a quotation which he attributes to Isaiah. It is, moreover, the only 'editorial' quotation in the whole Gospel, since the quotations he uses elsewhere are always attributed to one of the characters in the story, normally Jesus himself. Like Rom 1:2 – but more specifically – it establishes straight away that the gospel proclaimed here was 'announced beforehand in sacred scriptures through his prophets'. This one quotation, in Mark 1:2–3, is thus the equivalent of all the 'fulfilment-quotations' in Matthew put together.[1] It would seem, then, that this opening quotation is understood by Mark to be programmatic: the key to understanding what this 'gospel' – or 'good news' – might be is to be found in the book of Isaiah.[2]

It is all the more remarkable, then, that what Mark introduces as 'written in the prophet Isaiah' begins with words written elsewhere! The opening sentence – 'Behold, I send my messenger before you, who will prepare your way' – appears to be an amalgam of promises taken from Exod 23:20 and Mal 3:1. This is even more surprising when we compare the Synoptic parallels to Mark 1:3, since though both Matthew and Luke use this Exodus–Malachi quotation elsewhere (Matt 11:10; Luke 7:27), the quotation from Isa 40:3 is found here on its own (Matt 3:3 and Luke 3:4, in both cases attributed to Isaiah). If Matthew and Luke were independently using Mark 1, then they must both have decided to drop the first quotation at this point because each of them was planning to use it in another context. This would suggest that they had already thought out exactly what they would be including later in their narratives. Critics who argue that Mark used Matthew, rather than the other way round, see this passage as evidence that Mark, having decided to omit the story about John the Baptist sending messengers to Jesus from prison, took the Exodus–Malachi quotation from that story and joined it to the words from Isaiah.

---

[1] It is, of course, true that Mark, unlike Matthew, is using scripture broadly, not to show how particular details were fulfilled. Cf. Hugh Anderson, 'The Old Testament in Mark's Gospel', in *The Use of the Old Testament in the New and Other Essays: Studies in Honor of William Franklin Stinespring*, ed. James M. Efird (Durham, NC: Duke University Press, 1972), 280–306.

[2] Alfred Suhl, *Die Funktion der alttestamentlichen Zitate und Anspielungen im Markusevangelium* (Gütersloh: Mohn, 1965), denies the importance of 'fulfilment' for Mark, but ignores the importance of this opening quotation.

Both these explanations appear to envisage the evangelists poring over documents and piecing them together with scissors and paste. It seems more probable that both quotations were already being used in the pre-Marcan tradition to refer to John, and came to the evangelists independently.[3] All made use of a tradition quoting Isa 40:3, while Matthew and Luke knew of a different story in which Jesus referred to Exodus–Malachi. Further evidence that Isa 40:3 was an important one in the early Christian community[4] is to be found in the fact that it is used also in the Fourth Gospel, where it is once again employed of John the Baptist (John 1:23).[5] It may well have been Mark, then, who was responsible for bringing the two quotations together.[6]

Why did Mark attribute this 'mixed' quotation to Isaiah? Was it a mistake? Did he, that is, *assume* that both halves of the quotation must be from Isaiah? Or was it a 'deliberate' mistake? In other words, was Isaiah so important for him that it seemed necessary to establish straight away that the good news about Jesus Christ was the fulfilment of what had been promised through Isaiah?[7] This question can be answered only by examining the way in which he uses Isaiah, not only in this passage but elsewhere in his Gospel.[8] Before doing that, however, we must gauge its importance here.

First, we need to remember that the later chapters of Isaiah (generally known as 'Deutero-Isaiah' and 'Trito-Isaiah') make his book the obvious source for proclamations about God's eschatological salvation. Moreover, what Mark sets out to write is the 'good news' or 'gospel', and the noun he uses (εὐαγγέλιον) is related to a verb that is used several times in the later chapters of Isaiah, where it is used of proclaiming the good news of God's rule.[9] It has, to be sure, been pointed out that the noun itself is not used with this eschatological sense in the LXX, and attempts have therefore been made to derive Christian use of the term from the imperial cult, where the plural

---

[3] Comparison of Mark 1:1–13 with its parallels in the other Gospels suggests that Matthew and Luke were not following Mark closely at this point, but using another, parallel, tradition.

[4] The use of the opening verses of Isaiah 40 in the New Testament is discussed by Klyne R. Snodgrass, 'Streams of Tradition Emerging from Isaiah 40:1–5 and Their Adaptation in the New Testament', *JSNT* 8 (1980): 24–45.

[5] It is possible, of course, that the author of the Fourth Gospel was here drawing on one of the Synoptics, rather than using an independent tradition.

[6] An alternative explanation suggests that the first quotation was an early gloss, copied into the text of Mark from Q 7:27. This solution is favoured by some commentators, e.g. Vincent Taylor, *The Gospel According to St. Mark* (London: Macmillan, 1952), 153. There is, however, no textual evidence to support this suggestion.

[7] See in particular Rikki E. Watts, *Isaiah's New Exodus and Mark,* WUNT 2/88 (Tübingen: Mohr Siebeck, 1997), 88–90.

[8] Recent discussions of this are to be found in Watts, *Isaiah's New Exodus*; and Joel Marcus, *The Way of the Lord: Christological Exegesis of the Old Testament in the Gospel of Mark* (Louisville: Westminster/John Knox, 1992).

[9] See 40:9; 52:7; 60:6; 61:1.

form is used of 'good news' about the emperor. No doubt those living in the Roman Empire would have made that link, but the frequent use of the verb, which certainly has an Isaianic background, suggests that we should look for the origin of both terms in the LXX.[10] The fact that Mark claimed that the beginning of the gospel was 'as it is written in the prophet Isaiah' suggests that he was well aware that the prophet had proclaimed 'good news'.

Secondly, it is worth noting *why* Mark needed to use the Exodus–Malachi quotation to introduce the lines from Isaiah. Matthew and Luke both begin their accounts of John's mission with a reference to him in the wilderness, and to the fact that he was preaching (Matt 3:1; Luke 3:2–3): they then use the quotation from Isaiah to back this up. Mark, however, *begins* with scripture, and since he has not yet mentioned John, the first quotation, from Exodus–Malachi, serves to introduce him, and to explain who the 'voice crying in the wilderness' is. The quotation from Exodus–Malachi underlines the specific role of John: his whole purpose is to prepare the way of the one who follows him. By beginning in this way, rather than by introducing John by name, Mark ensures that his readers will immediately understand that John's only purpose is to point forward to the one who follows him. Not surprisingly, then, in contrast to Matthew and Luke (Matt 3:7–10; Luke 3:7–14), John's message in Mark consists of three pithy statements which concentrate our attention on the one who is so much greater than he. The quotation from Isa 40:3 is sandwiched between the words from Exodus–Malachi and the description of John vv. 4–6 which identifies him as a prophet – and in particular the prophet Elijah (2 Kgs 1:8), who was expected to return before the coming of the Lord (Mal 4:5) – and so underlines the fact that the one for whom John has prepared the way is none other than 'the Lord':

> a voice crying in the wilderness –
> 'Prepare the way of the Lord;
> make his paths straight'.

In Isa 40:3, 'the Lord' was, of course, God himself: the LXX (which Mark follows exactly, apart from substituting 'his' for 'our God' at the end) used the word κύριος here in place of the divine name. Mark, it would seem, has identified 'the Lord' of Isaiah 40 with Christ, for by the end of Mark 1:8 all eyes are focused expectantly on the one who comes after John, and in vv. 9–11 Jesus not only appears on the scene, but is addressed by the heavenly voice as God's beloved Son, and is revealed to Mark's readers as the one in whom God's holy Spirit is at work.

Although Isa 40:3 is interpreted by Mark as being fulfilled in John the Baptist, therefore, its real significance – like that of John himself – is to point

---

[10] For further discussion of this issue, see Watts, *Isaiah's New Exodus*, 96–99.

to the one who follows him, and to inform us that in Jesus the salvation promised in Isaiah has arrived. It is in the light of this text, therefore, that Mark wishes us to read his narrative.

Before we turn to the rest of Mark's Gospel, however, we must consider what these introductory quotations tell us about the message of John. When he appears, in v. 4, he prepares the way of the Lord by proclaiming a baptism of repentance for the forgiveness of sins. It is noticeable that Mark, unlike Matthew and Luke, does not present John as a prophet of judgement: the Baptist's message is entirely positive, and indeed is echoed by Jesus himself in 1:15. God offers the forgiveness of sins to those who repent, and nothing is said in these introductory verses about the fate of those who refuse to do so. Nevertheless, the promised forgiveness requires repentance. The fact that Mark's account of the ministry of Jesus begins, in 1:14, with the words 'After John had been handed over', indicates straight away that not everyone has welcomed his proclamation, and that the coming of the Lord will inevitably mean judgement, as well as salvation.

1. Other Clear Quotations of Isaiah

The theme of repentance and forgiveness is echoed in the next clear quotation of scripture, in 4:12. This quotation, too, is from Isaiah, although this time Mark gives no hint of its source. It occurs in 4:12, in the brief comment about the purpose of parables which links the parable of the Sower (4:1–9) with its interpretation (4:13–20). Mark tells us here that before explaining the parable itself, Jesus told his disciples why he taught the people in parables. It was

in order that they may look and look, yet perceive nothing; that they may listen and listen, yet understand nothing. Otherwise they might turn and be forgiven.

The saying itself, together with the setting (a private explanation to Jesus' disciples), bears the hallmark of teaching emanating from the early Christian community. The quotation is from Isa 6:9–10, though it is by no means exact, since the order of 'seeing' and 'hearing' has been reversed, and the first part of v. 10 has been omitted. Mark's version shows no clear dependence on either the Masoretic text or the LXX or the Targum. The introductory ἵνα suggests, however, that Mark intended his readers to understand these words as a quotation.[11]

---

[11] Although Matthew has a saying similar to Mark 4:12a (Matt 13:13; cf. Luke 8:10), he follows it with a clear citation of Isa 6:9–10. It seems that he recognized the allusion, but did not regard Jesus' words as a quotation.

Although the quotation raises considerable theological difficulties, its meaning for Mark seems clear. Jesus taught in parables in order that his hearers should *not* understand and respond to his teaching. This harsh statement appears to clash with what Mark tells us elsewhere about Jesus' proclamation of God's kingdom. Indeed, in 4:33–34, he explains that Jesus taught the people 'the word, as they were able to hear it', and that he invariably used parables to do so. These parables were a challenge – one could respond to their message or ignore it – and the so-called 'parable of the Sower' is in fact a parable about parables. Sandwiched between the parable itself and its explanation, this quotation from Isaiah 6 offers an explanation as to why so much of the crop had failed – in other words, why so many of Jesus' fellow Jews had failed to respond to his message. Since God was omnipotent, the fact that men and women were apparently unable to see and hear the offer of salvation must be part of his purpose. Just as the call of Isaiah was interpreted, after the event, as a call to *prevent* men and women responding to his message, so Jesus is depicted as preaching in parables in order to conceal his message. Mark 4:11–12 reflects the early Christian community's attempt to deal with a problem that left its mark elsewhere in the New Testament – above all in Romans 9–11. The same verses from Isaiah 6 are quoted in John 12:40 and Acts 28:26–27, which are concerned with the same problem.

Set as it is in a pivotal position in this collection of parables – which is Mark's first major section of Jesus' teaching – this quotation reminds us that seeing and hearing the good news which Jesus is proclaiming and enacting is not enough: it needs to be perceived and understood. The salvation which the Lord brings must be grasped: those who have not turned again and repented do not receive the forgiveness promised by John, and so are not ready for the coming of the Lord announced in Isa 40:3. Although the quotation's function is negative, however, the reference to 'turning' and to 'forgiveness' points to the fact that the *primary* purpose of the Lord's coming is to bring salvation.

The third clear quotation in Mark is once again from Isaiah, and this time it is introduced as a prophecy of Isaiah concerning the 'hypocrites' whom Jesus is here addressing (7:6–7). These are 'the Pharisees and some of the scribes, who have come from Jerusalem' (7:1) and who are criticizing him because of his disciples' failure to observe the traditions of the elders. The form of the text is closer to the LXX of Isa 29:13 than to the Hebrew, which would be less appropriate here, since it is concerned solely with the contrast between worship with the heart and with the lips. Jesus' comment in vv. 9–13, which contrasts divine and human commandments, picks up the accusation in the final line of the LXX:[12]

---

[12] It is undoubtedly true, as Watts, *Isaiah's New Exodus*, 216–218, has argued, that the religious authorities' concern with petty regulations was also interfering with their worship

> This people honours me with their lips,
> but their heart is far from me.
> In vain they worship me,
> teaching human precepts as doctrines.

The quotation is not only introduced with the words 'as it is written', but is ascribed specifically to Isaiah, as in 1:2. This offers some support to the suggestion noted earlier that Isaiah was of particular importance to Mark. In contrast to that introductory quotation, however, what we have here (as in 4:12) is a saying which condemns God's people for their failure to respond to him: those who worship with their lips but not their hearts are not ready for the coming of the Lord. The words of Isaiah pronounce judgement on the religious leaders of Israel, who oppose the teaching and practice of Jesus. Isaiah announced the coming of the Lord (Mark 1:2–3), but he also announced that his people would fail to respond to him (4:12) or worship him wholeheartedly, because they were more concerned with their own teaching than with God's commandments (7:6–7). One of the inevitable results of the Lord's coming is judgement.

Mark 7:1–23 appears to be a collection of different sayings which have been brought together at some stage. The first few verses (1–5) describe the incident which provokes the Pharisees' criticism of the disciples, and vv. 6–8 provide Jesus' first response to that criticism, based on Isa 29:13. The quotation is then echoed, rather clumsily, in v. 9, which introduces an example of the way in which the Pharisees 'abandon the commandment of God and hold to human tradition' (v. 8), using two more biblical quotations (vv. 9–13). The particular example seems to have no obvious relevance to the matter of handwashing, and may well have originally been part of a different dispute. The relevance of Isa 29:13 to the argument is brought out better by Matthew, who tells us that Jesus threw back the accusation brought by his opponents; he places Jesus' discussion of what 'Moses' said and what 'you' say before the Isaiah quotation, which he uses to effect as the punchline of the incident.

The specific example given of the way in which Jesus' critics abandon the commandment of God in favour of human tradition is the commandment to honour one's father and mother, given through Moses (Exod 20:12 and 21:17). Jesus accuses them of allowing the commandment to be set aside by declaring goods to be 'corban', or dedicated to God by an oath. The human tradition can hardly be the refusal to break a vow, since the irrevocable nature of oaths is also a divine commandment (Num 30:2; Deut 23:21–23). It must therefore be the ruling that the vow takes precedence over one's duty to father and mother.

---

of God, which is the main theme of the Hebrew text of Isaiah. Nevertheless, the specific application of the passage in the Marcan context – to the priority being given by the religious leaders to human tradition – requires the LXX version rather than the Hebrew.

Jesus' attitude is similar to the judgement expressed in the third century CE in the Mishnah *(Ned.* 9:1), where the honour due to father and mother is said to overrule all vows. The fact that this is spelt out in the Mishnah suggests that someone had at some stage argued the opposite, and that the dispute with the Jewish religious authorities described in Mark 7:1–13 – whether this involved Jesus himself or his later followers – was therefore a possible one.

Following this argument about the divine commandment and human tradition, Jesus is said to have summoned the crowd (Mark 7:14) in order to give a second, quite different, answer to the question regarding handwashing. He now declares that what enters the mouth does not defile, only what leaves it (v. 15), a saying that is then explained, privately, to the disciples (vv. 17–23). The saying in v. 15 seems a far more apposite response to the criticism levelled at the disciples than the sayings in vv. 6–8 and 9–13,[13] and may well represent an earlier tradition.[14] It is possible that vv. 6–13 have been inserted into the story at some stage. If Mark himself was responsible for the somewhat clumsy introduction of these verses here, it may have been because he thought the Isaiah quotation of particular importance, as showing, once again, that Israel's failure had been foreseen by the prophet. We have no way, however, of knowing whether or not Mark was responsible for introducing it here.

A brief quotation from Isaiah occurs in the description of Gehenna in Mark 9:48: it is the place where 'their worm never dies, and the fire never goes out'.[15] The words are taken from the final verse of Isaiah, and are close to, but not identical with, the LXX. This time, the words are used as a warning to the disciples themselves, not as a comment about 'those outside' (4:11–12) or about Jesus' critics (7:6–7). Even Jesus' followers need to be on their guard lest they stumble and fall. Like the original words in Isaiah, this warning of possible destruction stands in stark contrast to the promise of reward, which is described in Mark in terms of entering into life (9:43, 45) or entering the kingdom of God.

The next plain quotation of Isaiah occurs in 11:17, in the story of the so-called 'cleansing of the temple'. Whatever the nature of the original incident, it is clear that for Mark the event is part of Jesus' judgement on Israel for her failure to worship God aright. The words of Isa 29:13 might well have been used appropriately here, but instead Mark quotes a positive text from Isa 56:7 – 'my house shall be called a house of prayer for all the nations'. These words were originally part of God's promise regarding his temple, but in Jesus' mouth here they become a condemnation, because the temple is *not* a house

---

[13] Cf. also Luke 11:37–41, which links criticism of Jesus' failure to wash before eating with a saying about the 'outside' and the 'inside'.

[14] See, e.g. Joel Marcus, *Mark 1–8,* AB (New York: Doubleday, 1999), 447–448.

[15] The description is found three times in some MSS (as vv. 44, 46 and 48), but the shorter version is almost certainly original.

of prayer for all the nations but – in the words of Jeremiah – has been made 'a robbers' den' (Jer 7:11). The Greek, both of the quotation from Isaiah and of the phrase from Jeremiah, agrees exactly with the LXX, but since this provides an accurate translation of the Hebrew, we cannot be certain that Mark was using it.[16]

Debate about the meaning of this incident continues unabated: is it a 'cleansing' or a 'sign of future destruction'? The answer may well be that Jesus himself intended it to be the former, but that Mark, writing after the event, saw it as the latter.[17] Certainly the setting he gives it suggests that he sees it as signifying judgement and destruction. He interweaves the story (11:11, 15–19) with that of the barren fig tree (11:12–14, 20–24). The temple is first inspected, then condemned, because those to whom it was entrusted are robbers; the tree is inspected for fruit, then cursed, and is later discovered to have withered. Following this, we have a confrontation between Jesus and the religious authorities, who question him about his authority. In reply, Jesus questions them about the authority by which John baptized. It is obvious from this that readers are intended to understand that Jesus' ministry is closely related to that of John. Mark apparently expects us to think back to the first eight verses of his Gospel, in which the baptism of John was shown to be the preparation for the one who followed him, and John himself was identified as the messenger of Exod 23:20 and Mal 3:1, who was also the voice crying out in the wilderness: 'Prepare the way of the Lord, make his paths straight' (Isa 40:3).

In view of this reference to the baptism of John, it is a source of surprise to all commentators that Mark failed to make any reference in chapter 11 to Mal 3:1, since that verse announces that 'the Lord', whose way the messenger was sent to prepare, 'will suddenly come to his temple'. Jesus, the Lord (11:3), has now ridden into Jerusalem, has entered the temple, and has condemned, in God's name, what is happening in 'my house'. Perhaps Mark failed to recognize the importance of Mal 3:1, having referred specifically only to Isaiah in 1:2; perhaps, in any case, that passage would have seemed irrelevant, since he appears to have assumed that Jesus came to the temple in judgement, and not to refine and purify (Mal 3:2–4).

The theme of judgement is continued in the next two chapters of Mark's Gospel. Chapter 12 represents the second block of teaching in Mark, and like chapter 4, its first and most memorable element is a parable about the produce of a crop. The parable of the Sower (4:1–9) pointed to the urgency of responding to the good news proclaimed by Jesus; the comment from

---

[16] A.E. Harvey's comment that the quotation cannot have been taken from the Hebrew, *Jesus and the Constraints of History* (London: Duckworth, 1982), 132, is mistaken; he appears to have been looking at the wrong half of the Hebrew verse.

[17] Cf. Morna D. Hooker, 'Traditions about the Temple in the Sayings of Jesus', *BJRL* 70 (1988): 7–19 = below, essay 16 (pp. 235–247).

Isaiah 6 in 4:12 offered some explanation of Israel's failure to understand. The parable of the vineyard in 12:1–12 contains clear echoes of the imagery of the vineyard in Isa 5:1–2. Isaiah describes Israel as the Lord's vineyard, which, being planted on fertile ground, should have produced a splendid crop, but which produced only wild grapes. Some of Mark's vocabulary is close to that of the LXX: 'built a wall round it' (not in the Hebrew of Isa 5:2, though v. 5 refers to both a wall and a hedge). The major difference between the two stories is that in Isaiah the vineyard itself fails to produce a good crop, and so is destroyed by its owner: the moral is spelt out in Isa 5:3–7, where the Lord brings destruction on his people. In Jesus' story, however, the vineyard produces a crop, but the tenants refuse to hand any of it over to the landlord, and ill-treat his messengers. Finally, when they kill his only son, he comes in person, kills the tenants and lets the vineyard out to others. Mark's final comment, in v. 12, indicates that he understands the parable to be directed against 'them' – i.e. the religious leaders who have been questioning Jesus at the end of chapter 11. It is the religious leaders, rather than the crowd, who here fall under divine judgement.

Once again, a scriptural quotation has been added to the story, either by Mark or by someone before him. This time it is taken from Psalm 118 (LXX 117):22–23, and – remarkably – this injects a message of hope into the parable. The stone rejected by the builders will become a cornerstone. The quotation seems totally inappropriate here: the cornerstone of a building has nothing to do with a vineyard. It is *so* inappropriate, however, that its use must be deliberate. In fact, it is more relevant than we might suppose.

First, as we have already noted, the vineyard in Jesus' parable is not destroyed but handed over to new tenants. Although judgement descends on the previous tenants, the vineyard remains in the owner's possession. Israel's leaders will be punished, but Israel herself will be saved. However 'mixed' the metaphor may be, the rejected stone that is raised as a cornerstone illustrates the continuity in God's plan for his people.

Secondly, the reference to the cornerstone, like the reference to the beloved son who features in the parable, means that our attention is inevitably focused on the figure of Jesus. Christology is central to this parable, but it also dominates this entire section, from the moment that Jesus rides into Jerusalem like a king. The question regarding his authority to challenge what was happening in the temple (11:27–33), his teaching about the Messiah (12:35–37), and his warning about the coming of the Messiah/Son of man in 13:21–31, all focus our attention on Jesus himself.

Thirdly, Mark has placed this block of teaching in the setting of the temple (11:27; 12:41; 13:1). Reference to the 'cornerstone' thus links the parable to Jesus' provocative action there. Even though Mark has interpreted that event as a sign of coming destruction – a theme which will be elaborated in chapter 13 – the hint here of a new building suggests that there is to be a 'new' temple which will fulfil the intention expressed in Isa 56:7 of being 'a house of prayer for all the nations'. Further hints of this hope for the future are expressed in 12:28–34, in the story of the scribe who is 'not far from the kingdom of God', in the account of the poor widow who throws everything she has into the temple treasury (12:41–43), and in Jesus' words about the fig tree, apparently dead, which is in fact merely dormant, and bursts into leaf when summer approaches (13:28). Although the accusation that Jesus said that he would destroy the temple and raise another, not made with hands (14:58; 15:29), is said to be false, the fact that Mark uses it in his story of Jesus' trial and crucifixion, together with the account of the tearing of the temple veil in 15:38, suggests that he saw it as a distortion of Jesus' teaching about a judgement that would bring both destruction and restoration. Through him, therefore, Isa 56:7 will, finally, be fulfilled.

This coming judgement is the theme of Mark's final quotation from Isaiah, in 13:24–25. Here we have another composite citation, which begins with lines drawn from Isa 13:10, a passage which announces the coming of the day of the Lord. These lines are similar to the LXX translation, though they may be an independent translation of the Hebrew. The second part of the citation echoes phrases from the LXX version of Isa 34:4, though there are similar passages elsewhere, e.g. Joel 2:10. Although these lines in Mark 13:24–25 are not introduced as a citation, they would clearly evoke memories of the prophetic threat of judgement among Mark's Jewish readers, together with those Gentiles familiar with the Jewish scriptures.

These verses occur at the climax of the so-called 'Apocalyptic Discourse' in Mark 13, which is itself the conclusion to the section dealing with Jesus' arrival and activity in Jerusalem (chapters 11–12). Jesus here finally announces the coming judgement on Jerusalem: the temple will be destroyed, and its inhabitants will endure suffering and death. Before that happens, however, the good news will be proclaimed among the nations, and his own followers will be persecuted: in other words, the pattern of Jesus' own ministry will be repeated, but on a worldwide scale. When the end finally comes, it will be heralded by the traditional signs accompanying the arrival of the day of the Lord. Then the Son of man will be seen, coming in clouds – a clear allusion to Dan 7:13 – and will gather his elect (13:26–27).[18]

In 1:1–3, Mark used the quotation from Isa 40:3 to introduce 'the good news about Jesus Christ'. We might have expected him to employ other 'positive' texts from Isaiah, such as 9:1–2 (used by Matthew in 4:15–16), 42:1–4 (used by Matthew in 12:18–21) or 61:1–2 (used by Luke in 4:18–19). In fact,

---

[18] For a discussion of the Old Testament texts which may lie behind Mark 13 see Lars Hartman, *Prophecy Interpreted: The Formation of Some Jewish Apocalyptic Texts and of the Eschatological Discourse Mark 13 Par.*, ConBNT (Lund: Gleerup, 1966).

'the way of the Lord', which John prepared and which Jesus has walked, has proved to be the way of suffering and death for them both, even though it has brought forgiveness and health and salvation to others. Many of Jesus' fellow Jews have been blind and deaf to his message, and the religious authorities have been implacably opposed to him. The quotations from Isaiah in chapters 4 and 7 were used by Mark to show that Israel's failure to respond to the Gospel was decreed in scripture; even in 11:17, the fact that God's purpose for the temple set out in Isa 29:13 had been thwarted was apparently foreseen by Jeremiah. In 9:48, words from Isaiah were used in warning the disciples of the punishment that awaited those who failed to follow Jesus and to gain life thereby. Now, in chapter 13, this final quotation announces the coming judgement, which will inevitably mean destruction for all who are not acknowledged to be his own by the Son of man. This consistently 'negative' use of Isaiah may seem surprising, but the coming of the Lord inevitably means judgement, and that can lead to punishment as well as to salvation.

2. Possible Allusions to Isaiah

Appendix 4 to the 27th edition of the Nestle-Aland edition of the *Novum Testamentum Graece* (1993), 'Loci citati vel allegati', lists a further eighteen places in Mark's Gospel where there are possible allusions to Isaiah.[19] This list is by no means complete, however, since we find that some possible allusions which are noted as occurring in Matthean passages are ignored in their Marcan parallels. Thus Isa 28:16 and 8:14 are listed as influencing Matt 21:42, but there is no reference to Isaiah for the identical Mark 12:10, while for the equivalent verse in Luke (20:17), Isa 28:16 is mentioned, but not Isa 8:14! In fact, any reference to Isaiah here is superfluous, since all three Gospels give an identical word-for-word quotation of Psalm 118 (LXX 117):22.[20] Of greater significance is the fact that a more likely reference to Isa 43:16 is ignored at Mark 6:48, though noted for Matt 14:25.

It also has to be remembered that Nestle-Aland sometimes uses an exclamation mark to refer to parallel passages where important information is given in the margin. If we work through the text of Mark, we find that the editors have failed at 1:10 to warn us to turn to Matt 3:16, which refers us to Isa 11:2. In the following verse, however, an exclamation mark alerts us to turn from Mark 1:11 to Matt 3:17, which refers us to Isa 42:1 and 62:4. When we

---

[19] These are: Mark 2:7; 3:21, 27; 4:30; 5:3; 7:37; 9:12; 10:34, 45; 12:1, 32, 40; 13:8, 31; 14:24, 49, 61; 15:27.

[20] The same is probably true of Mark 12:32, where Nestle-Aland suggests a quotation from Isa 45:21. It is more likely, however, that it derives only from Deut 6:4 and 4:35. Deut 6:5 is quoted in the next verse.

come to Mark 9:7, we are referred back to 1:11 and its parallels (and hence to Matt 3:17 and the references to Isaiah). Similarly, Mark 14:36 indicates that we should turn back to 10:38 and its parallels, a verse which alerts us to Matt 26:39 and its parallels (Mark 14:36!), and this in turn points us to Isa 51:17, 22. The same kind of detective work takes us from Mark 14:65 to 10:34, which refers us back to Isa 50:6.

Other possible references are missed altogether by Nestle-Aland: it fails, for example, to give any reference to Isa 64:1 (63:19 in Hebrew and LXX) for Mark 1:10 or its parallels in Matthew and Luke, though commentators frequently suggest that there is an echo of that verse in this passage.[21]

A number of the suggested allusions seem fanciful.[22] Others seem to have more substance. Mark's description of a demoniac who lives among tombs near pigs (5:3, 11) is reminiscent of Isa 65:4; the comment in 7:37 that Jesus 'makes the deaf hear and the dumb speak' may put us in mind of Isa 35:5; Jesus' denunciation of those who oppress widows (12:40) echoes the charge of Isa 10:2, and his prediction of coming disaster in 13:8 reminds us of similar predictions in passages such as Isa 19:2, 13:13 and 8:21; the comment that heaven and earth will pass away but Jesus' words endure (13:31) may well have been based on Isa 51:6. The most convincing suggestion in the early chapters is the possible allusion to Isa 49:24 ff. in Mark 3:27, for though there are no clear verbal allusions to the LXX, both passages describe taking prey from the strong.[23] The suggestion that Mark had that passage in mind is strengthened by the fact that Jesus' words here echo those of John the Baptist in 1:7, where he spoke of his successor as 'stronger' than himself; moreover, they appear to point back to Jesus' confrontation with Satan in the wilderness in 1:12–13. What is happening in Jesus' ministry, then, demonstrates the truth of what we were told in Mark 1:1–13 – that what is now taking place in him was written in the prophet Isaiah.

Another possible echo of Isaiah is found in the words of the heavenly voice in 1:11 – 'You are my beloved Son; with you I am well pleased' – and in the similar words used in the account of the transfiguration (9:11). These words have frequently been traced to Isa 42:1, where God declares:

> Here is my servant, whom I uphold,
> my chosen, in whom my soul delights.

---

[21] The verb used by Mark for 'breaking open' (σχίζω) is not the one used in the LXX. Matthew and Luke both use the verb used in the LXX (ἀνοίγω). Does Mark's version reflect the Hebrew? Were Matthew and Luke aware of the link? Or are the coincidences accidental?

[22] Mark 2:7 (Isa 43:25); 3:21 (Isa 28:7); there is little, if any, verbal similarity in either case. Isa 40:18 and Mark 4:30 are linked only by a question about whether or not one can make a comparison: in the former case the answer is 'No', while in the latter, this is then done.

[23] The reference to the demoniac's strength in 5:4 may also be suggestive, indicating Jesus' superior strength.

Although there are obvious similarities with that passage, however, there is no overlap whatever between Mark's Greek and the LXX. Not surprisingly, therefore, other passages (in particular, Gen 22:2 and Ps 2:7) have been suggested as possible backgrounds. Perhaps the strongest claim of Isa 42:1 for consideration lies in the fact that the next line reads, 'I have put my spirit upon him'. The relevance to Mark 1:10 is plain.

The significance of this possible allusion to Isa 42:1 was much distorted in the era when, having isolated the so-called 'Servant Songs' in Isaiah (42:1–4; 49:1–6; 50:4–9; 52:13–53:12), scholars assumed that there was a particular figure (present or future) known as 'the Servant of Yahweh', with whom Jesus was here being identified. In fact, God is said to have addressed various individuals as 'my Servant' in the Old Testament (e.g. Gen 26:24; Exod 14:31; 2 Sam 3:18; Isa 20:3). Moreover, Jesus is not addressed as 'Servant' in chapters 1 and 9, but as 'Son'; if any 'title' is being used, this is it. In the absence of linguistic links, there is little to indicate that Mark had Isa 42:1 in mind. What we can say is that, since Mark understood the gospel to be the fulfilment of what was written in the book of Isaiah, he may well have been familiar with Isaiah 42. Whether or not he (or anyone before him) thought this particular verse relevant is not clear, and certainly he was not *quoting* from it.

In all these cases, it is difficult to be certain as to whether possible allusions are deliberate. Those who shaped the tradition before Mark may or may not have been aware of the biblical echoes it contained; Mark himself may or may not have been consciously using Isaiah's words; Mark's first readers may or may not have picked up allusions. What is certain is that subsequent readers, alerted by Mark's opening reference to Isaiah, would have read his Gospel in the light of their knowledge of that book.

This may be the case with many of the references to Isaiah given in the margins of Nestle-Aland concerning passages which relate to Jesus' death. In 9:12 ff., Mark alerts us to the fact that what is about to happen 'is written about the Son of man' without indicating *where* it is written. The passage is notoriously difficult, because it refers also to the things written about the sufferings of the returning Elijah. Commentators have been unable to find an appropriate biblical reference for Elijah, but for the Son of man confidently refer to Isa 53:3 (presumably through the idea of treating with contempt), even though there is no linguistic link with that verse.[24] Similarly, when Jesus is arrested in the garden, and is reported as saying 'Let the scriptures be fulfilled' (14:49), the margin refers us to Isa 53:7 – though why this particular verse should have been singled out is not clear. In both cases, however, the editors seem to have assumed that if the scriptures are being invoked in

---

[24] A more appropriate biblical passage is Ps 22:7 (LXX 21:8), which is also listed by Nestle-Aland; this uses the same verb as Mark.

connection with Jesus' death, then Isaiah 53 must have been in mind. A third reference to what is written, in 14:21, appears to have escaped the notice of the editors of Nestle-Aland. Many commentators, however, attribute this also to the influence of Isaiah 53, because of the use of the verb παραδίδωμι, usually translated here as 'betray', in vv. 18 and 21. The verb is used in the sense of 'to hand over' or 'to deliver up' in Isa 53:6, 12.

We can be certain, from these general references, that Mark intended his readers to understand the sufferings of Jesus to be seen as the fulfilment of scripture. Yet he does not refer to Isaiah by name, and he uses no clear quotations from that book in either the passion narrative or the predictions of Jesus' coming death and resurrection. The only quotations he uses in connection with the passion are from Zech 13:7 (Mark 14:27), Dan 7:13 (Mark 14:62), and Ps 22:1 (LXX 21:2) (Mark 15:34).

Once alerted to the idea that Jesus' suffering, death, and vindication were the fulfilment of scripture, one becomes aware of words used by Mark which 'echo' words in Isaiah. The verb παραδίδωμι, just mentioned, is a good example. It is, nevertheless, the obvious verb for Mark to have used, especially as it can convey a *double entendre:* Jesus is 'handed over' to the authorities by Judas, but also by God himself. Mark 10:34 and 14:65 both refer to spitting, as does Isa 50:6, but did Mark have that passage in mind?[25] Mark 10:38 and 14:36 speak of a cup that Jesus is reluctant to drink, and Isa 51:17 refers to a cup of wrath; the image of drinking from a cup, however, is used elsewhere (e.g. Ps 75:8). Mark 10:45 and 14:24 both refer to the benefits of Jesus' death 'for many', a word used in Isa 53:11, where many are made righteous because of the sufferings of God's righteous one,[26] but the word is a common one. In Mark 14:61 Jesus is at first silent, reminding us of the image of a sheep silent before its shearers in Isa 53:7,[27] but again, we cannot know whether Mark was thinking of that passage. The fact that Jesus was crucified between two robbers (Mark 15:27) was linked at an early date with the statement that 'he was numbered with the transgressors' in Isa 53:12, as is demonstrated by the gloss in v. 28, but this does not mean that Mark himself necessarily realized how appropriate these words were for his narrative.[28]

The passage, above all others, where the influence of Isaiah has been detected is Mark 10:45. Here, the reference to service, to a ransom, to the

---

[25] See also 15:19. 14:65 is the closest to Isaiah, having three words in common with the LXX: ἐμπτύειν, πρόσωπον, ῥαπίσμασιν.
[26] Mark uses the same Greek word, πολλῶν, as the LXX of Isa 53:11. The verb ἐκχυννόμενον, 'poured out', has also sometimes been traced to the Hebrew verb used in Isa 53:12.
[27] See also Mark 15:5.
[28] Others have found still more allusions to Isaiah 53 in the passion narrative. See, e.g., Douglas J. Moo, *The Old Testament in the Gospel Passion Narratives* (Sheffield: The Almond Press, 1983).

voluntary giving-up of one's life, and the use of the word 'many', have all been said to derive from Isa 53:10–11. The word 'many', as we have already noted, is indeed used in Isa 53:11, but there is no other linguistic echo of that passage. True, the LXX speaks of God's righteous one 'serving many', but the verb it uses is a different one from that used by Mark.[29] If we turn back to the Hebrew, that speaks, not of 'serving many', but of 'my Servant' – i.e. God's Servant – a title of great honour. The idea of a 'ransom' (λύτρον) may well come from these later chapters of Isaiah, for the cognate verb (λυτρόω) is used of God's expected redemption of Israel (Isa 43:1; 44:22–23; 52:3; 63:9), while Israel is to be set free without a ransom (λύτρον) being paid (Isa 45:13). God himself is described as 'Israel's Redeemer' (Isa 41:14; 43:14; 44:24), and his people as 'the redeemed' (Isa 35:9; 62:12). These passages reflect the belief that there would be a new exodus, which would deliver Israel from exile, just as she had been delivered in the past from Egypt. The image of redemption is particularly appropriate for rescuing a people in bondage, since it reflects the practice of paying a ransom in exchange for someone or something, especially a slave.[30] This redemption of his people is now to be fulfilled, according to Mark 10:45, by the Son of man surrendering his own life as a 'ransom'. Isa 53:10–11, however, contains a different idea. This passage speaks of God's Servant being made a 'guilt offering', which involved making restitution to the injured party and offering a sacrifice as a means of expiation. This is a very different image, and it is taken over in the LXX version, which translates that term by the phrase 'for sin'. Once again, readers of Mark's Gospel in a modern translation who know Isaiah 53 may well think the relevance of the passage is clear; there is little evidence, however, to show that Mark himself saw the connection with that particular passage.[31]

3. Conclusion

If we look at the overall pattern of citations in Mark's Gospel, it would seem significant that more of these are drawn from Isaiah than from any other book.[32] This is in keeping with Mark's opening claim that the good news is the fulfilment of what was written in the prophet Isaiah. Apart from these,

---

[29] Mark uses διακονέω; the LXX, δουλεύω.

[30] E.g. Exod 30:12; Lev 25:24–26, 51; Isa 45:13.

[31] On Mark 10:45, see Morna D. Hooker, *Jesus and the Servant* (London: SPCK, 1959), 74–79; C.K. Barrett, 'The Background of Mark 10.45', in *New Testament Essays: Studies in Memory of Thomas Walter Manson*, ed. A.J.B. Higgins (Manchester: Manchester University Press, 1959), 1–18. Werner Grimm, *Weil ich dich liebe: Die Verkündigung Jesu und Deuterojesaja* (Bern: Herbert Lang, 1976), 231–265, has argued that Mark 10:45 owes more to Isa 43:3 ff. than to Isa 53.

[32] There are, to be sure, a similar number of appeals to 'Moses'. In the passion narrative, echoes and quotations from the psalms predominate.

there may also be allusions to images and expectations found in Isaiah at various points in Mark's narrative,[33] though there can be no certainty that these were indeed drawn from that book, either by Mark or by his sources, and there is little sign that he was quoting from the LXX.

It is important to remember, however, that Mark was a man of his own age. We should not imagine him doing what we might do – thumbing through the pages of Isaiah, checking references, or even finding relevant passages with the aid of a computer! 'Looking things up' in a scroll was not simple. Certain passages of Isaiah may well have been familiar to him (perhaps because they had already been incorporated into the tradition), but he would not have known Isaiah by heart. Some phrases may already have become part of Christian vocabulary, without Mark being aware of their source. Which of *us* knows that 'the apple of his eye' is used in Deut 32:10, or that Shakespeare's statement that 'We are such stuff as dreams are made on' is found in *The Tempest* Act IV Scene 1 (or, indeed, can quote it accurately!)? Scholars often echo ideas they have picked up from others, often totally unaware that they are 'recycling' something that they have heard or read. In the same way, some of Mark's debt to Isaiah may well be unconscious. We should not exclude the possibility that he owes more to the prophet than appears on the surface – but neither should we assume that he was aware of many of the links with Isaiah which have been suggested subsequently. Readers of Mark may well discover that the story he tells is one that is 'as written in Isaiah the prophet' in more ways than Mark himself ever imagined.

---

[33] It has been possible here to mention only those that have been most frequently suggested.

15. Trial and Tribulation in Mark XIII*

1. An Enigma

There are few things that can be said about Mark 13 without fear of contradiction; but if I begin with the statement that it presents us with an enigma – or even a series of enigmas – I shall perhaps be on safe ground. Few other chapters in the Bible can have been the subject of so many special studies, and it is not without reason that so much attention has been devoted to it. The chapter is full of exegetical problems, but its greatest oddity is that it exists at all. For it is totally unlike anything else in Mark. This is the only occasion on which we find a long, connected discourse in the mouth of Jesus. The passage which comes closest to being similar in format, Mark 4, is not only considerably shorter – approximately 50 lines of Greek text, over against 70 – but is broken up into shorter sections. Moreover, whereas Mark 4 is a collection of parables – albeit on similar themes – Mark 13 is the exposition of a particular topic. And, of course, that topic in itself marks out Mark 13 from the rest of the gospel, for only here do we have teaching about the end of all things.

The ways in which the problems of Mark 13 have been formulated and approached have varied considerably over the years. As we might expect, they reflect in large measure the concerns and methods of the times. The theory of the Little Apocalypse, a document which Mark is supposed to have taken over and expanded, was first put forward by Colani in 1864.[1] The reasoning that led him to propound this particular theory seems to have been very largely the result of his attempt to answer the problem of the authenticity of some of the sayings in the discourse. Did Jesus prophesy the end of the world and his own return on the clouds of heaven within the lifetime of his own generation? If he did, then he was mistaken. But if we begin with the assumption that Jesus could not have been mistaken, then we must conclude that the prophecies could not have been his. Colani's theory is based both on his conviction that Jesus could not have been mistaken, and also on his dislike of eschatology, for he regarded the eschatological beliefs of Jewish Christians

---

* A lecture delivered in the John Rylands University Library on Wednesday, 10 March 1982.
[1] Timothée Colani, *Jésus-Christ Et Les Croyances Messianiques De Son Temps,* 2nd ed. (Strasbourg: Truettel et Wurtz, 1864).

as unworthy of Jesus.[2] It is a fascinating exercise to trace the extent to which subsequent exegesis of the chapter has reflected the rejection by certain exegetes of the possibility that Jesus might have been mistaken, and their refusal to reckon with the idea that he might have accepted the eschatological and apocalyptic ideas of his day. At any rate, Colani's theory offered a solution to this dilemma – and did so in terms which made sense to New Testament scholarship of the late nineteenth and early twentieth centuries. For this was the period of source criticism, and Colani suggested a source, behind Mark, to explain the problems of this chapter.

Now whether or not Colani's theory is correct I do not know. Certainly there are tensions and apparent contradictions within the chapter which lend support to the view that a variety of material has been pieced together. The somewhat artificial setting and the structure of the discourse are explained if Mark has taken over a document and edited it, and it is hardly surprising that the Little Apocalypse theory has enjoyed great popularity, even if there is considerable disagreement as to which verses to assign to it. But the fact that we can extract certain verses from the chapter and find a pattern in them does not mean that Mark has necessarily taken over an existing structure; it may be that we are imagining the pattern, or that Mark himself has created it. Certainly it seems safer to start with the problem of the way in which Mark has handled the tradition.

When the term 'apocalypse' was first used of Mark 13 itself I have not discovered. Certainly it was used by Bultmann and gained popularity in the form-critical period when everything was given a label – even though the discourse did not fall into any form-critical category, being a collection rather than a unit. But in recent years the terms 'Marcan apocalypse' or 'apocalyptic discourse' have been challenged. Is this, in fact, true apocalyptic at all? Granted that it bears some of the characteristics of apocalyptic writing, and that certain verses are closely parallel to passages in Jewish apocalyptic books, there are nevertheless important dissimilarities. If one draws up a checklist of characteristics which one might expect to find in apocalyptic literature, many are absent. There is no heavenly vision, no bizarre imagery; there is a cosmic catastrophe, but the time of its arrival is unknown; nothing is said about judgement, or about the fate of the righteous and unrighteous. There is at least as much material that can be described as paraenesis as there is material that unfolds the future.

Now I am inclined to side with those who argue that, strictly speaking, Mark 13 is not an apocalypse at all. If one confines the term 'apocalyptic' to a particular form of literature, instead of using it loosely as a synonym for

---

[2] See the discussion by George R. Beasley-Murray in *Jesus and the Future* (London: Macmillan, 1956), 14–21.

'eschatology', as so often happens, then Mark 13 is certainly an unusual kind of apocalyptic. However, we cannot say that the term is inappropriate in this case simply because some of the features of apocalyptic are missing; for few pieces of apocalyptic literature bear them all, and it is well-known that similar arguments have been held as to whether there is any true apocalyptic in the Old Testament. The dispute as to how we should classify the chapter raises in my mind a more fundamental uneasiness about the desirability of attaching this particular label: is it helpful, or is it misleading, in that it predisposes us to interpret the material in a particular light? At the very least, it seems to me that attaching the label 'apocalypse' may not be particularly helpful. Sorting out material into various pigeonholes is a favourite pastime with scholars, but it is questionable whether one is doing much more than clarify things in one's own mind. Even among our scientific colleagues, the taxonomist sometimes has to reclassify his specimens; his choices are to some extent subjective. If we wish to discover the purposes and meaning of Mark 13 for Mark, then attaching a particular label may be far from helpful. For I doubt very much whether Mark said to himself: 'I am going to write an apocalypse'. It is salutary to remember that the one clear example of apocalyptic writing in the New Testament, the book of Revelation, is described by its author as prophecy! That there is a link between prophecy and apocalyptic most scholars would agree; but where does prophecy end and apocalyptic begin? There is no clear divide – rather there is a spectrum of writings, and Mark 13 falls somewhere in the middle. If the discourse fits uneasily into the category of apocalyptic, that of prophecy is no more appropriate. This suggests that if we want to understand what Mark was doing, we should certainly be prepared to look at contemporary apocalyptic literature for help in understanding the way in which his mind was working; but we should beware of ready-made stick-on labels.

I have already betrayed that the question which primarily concerns me is that of Mark's own handling and understanding of the material. In concentrating on that problem, I am, of course, reflecting the mood of New Testament scholarship at the moment as much as Colani and Bultmann reflected the interest of *their* periods. It is the redaction-critical questions that interest us now, and I make no excuse for concentrating on them – not least because I find them particularly fascinating. No longer do we assume that Mark simply put down all the material he knew; what, then, was he aiming to do?

2. Context

First, then, let us look at the context of the chapter. A recent study of Mark 13, published in the Rylands *Bulletin,* began with the remark: 'The existence of Mark xiii between chapters xii and xiv requires explanation'.[3] If Mark is indeed a passion narrative with a long introduction, then chapter 13 is the end of the introduction, for 14:1 begins the passion narrative proper. What can we say about its placement at this juncture? I would like to offer just three comments. First, if we want a literary precedent for a speech about future events being placed on a great man's lips at the very end of his life, then there are plenty of examples in the biblical material. In Gen 49, for example, Jacob predicts what will happen to his descendants; in Deut 32, Moses addresses the people shortly before his death, and in 1 Chron 28, David hands over his kingdom to Solomon. In the intertestamental period whole books were written in the form of farewell discourses – namely The Testaments of the Twelve Patriarchs and The Assumption of Moses – and in the New Testament we find Paul making a speech when he takes leave of his mission field in Acts 20. Most interesting of all, the Farewell Discourse attributed to Jesus in the Fourth Gospel comes at precisely the same point in the narrative as in Mark – between the final scene of Jesus teaching in the temple and the beginning of the passion narrative.[4]

Secondly, the discourse comes at the climax of Mark's account of Jesus' teaching in the temple. The whole of chapters 11 and 12, following Jesus' triumphal entry into Jerusalem, are set in the temple. The one exception to this is the story of the withered fig tree, which is set on the route to and from the temple, and which is itself an indictment of the temple worship. Like the so-called cleansing of the temple, around which Mark has set it, this story seems to have been interpreted by Mark as a symbolic action pointing forward to the destruction of the temple. Now it is arguable that for Jesus himself, the incident of the cleansing of the temple was just that – a demand for sincere worship and for reform. Mark, however, has interpreted it as a prophecy of judgement; its insertion into the story of the fig tree shows that he understood

---

[3] Kenneth Grayston, 'The Study of Mark XIII', *BJRL* 56 (1974): 371–387. Cf. also the discussion by Rudolf Pesch, who argued from the structure of Mark's Gospel that ch. 13 was a later addition, though written by the same author, *Naherwartungen: Tradition und Redaktion in Mark 13* (Düsseldorf: Patmos-Verlag, 1968), 48–73. Such an analysis, if it is accepted, makes the problem all the more acute: why did Mark destroy his own symmetrical arrangement? For an analysis of the role of Mark 13 in the overall structure of the gospel, see Jan Lambrecht, *Die Redaktion der Markus-Apokalypse: literarische Analyse und Struktururuntersuchung* (Rome: Päpstliches Bibelinstitut, 1967), 15–63.

[4] In John, of course, the discourse is placed after Jesus' last meal with his disciples, not before. However, there is no account of the supper itself, and the only introduction to the discourse is the incident of the footwashing, which is followed in John 13 by material parallel to the synoptic tradition of Jesus' conversation with his disciples at the Last Supper. Although the theme of the Johannine discourse is very different from that in the Synoptics (though still concerned with the future), it is worth nothing that here, too, the disciples are warned about the persecution they must expect as followers of Jesus.

Jesus' actions as a prophecy of destruction.[5] It is hardly surprising if the end of this section leads into the discourse in chapter 13.

Thirdly, the discourse is followed by the passion narrative. It was, I think, R.H. Lightfoot,[6] who first pointed out the remarkable echoes of this chapter in the passion narrative – or perhaps we should put it the other way round: for it is Jesus who suffers first, and the disciples are warned that they must expect similar experiences, so that what is said about them 'echoes' what will be said about Jesus in the passion narrative. Now this link between the sufferings of Jesus and of his disciples is a very common theme in Mark. Each of the passion predictions is followed by a passage which brings out the implications for the disciples of pledging loyalty to Jesus. Mark 13 plays the same kind of role *vis-à-vis* the passion narrative; although the theme and structure of the chapter are concerned with the last things, it contains also warnings about what the disciples must expect to endure because of their discipleship before the end arrives.

If the position of Mark 13 requires explanation, then, it is surely to be found in the fact that the most appropriate setting for such a discourse is either here or 'after supper' (where John has placed it), and that in view of the subject matter of the Marcan version, it is more appropriate here. Moreover, the chapter forms a link between the theme of chapters 11 and 12 (the condemnation of Israel, because of her failure to receive her Messiah)[7] and that of chapters 14 and 15 (the spelling-out of the story of the Messiah's rejection). The two themes are, of course, woven together throughout; e.g. in 12:8 we have a reference to the death of Jesus, while in 14:58, 15:29 and 38, there are references to the fate of the temple.

It is often said that the introduction to the discourse is artificial, and serves simply as a peg on which to hang Jesus' words. That the disciples should have been overawed by the sight of the temple is, of course, understandable enough; Josephus tells us that visitors were amazed at its size and magnificence.[8] The basis for describing the setting as artificial is partly that the chapter contains two introductions, partly that the destruction of the temple itself is not mentioned in the whole of the discourse. Yet it is not entirely fair to complain, as Victor of Antioch did long ago, that the disciples asked one question and Jesus answered another. For the abomination that makes desolate in verse 14 is certainly to be set up in the temple, and the disaster

---

[5] This theme has recently been explored in detail by William R. Telford in *The Barren Temple and the Withered Tree*, JSNTSup 1 (Sheffield: JSOT Press, 1980).

[6] R.H. Lightfoot, *The Gospel Message of St. Mark* (Oxford: Clarendon Press, 1950), 48–69.

[7] Matthew underlines this theme by adding ch. 23 immediately before his parallel to Mark 13. The chapters consists of a series of 'Woes' pronounced against the scribes and Pharisees, followed by the lament over Jerusalem in verses 37–39.

[8] Josephus, *Ant.* 15.11.5; *J.W.* 5.5.4–6.

which follows will bring desolation in Judaea. However, the fact that Mark has chosen to introduce the discourse with the prediction of the temple's destruction in verses 1–2 is certainly a clue to his understanding of the material. If Jerusalem and her temple are to be destroyed, this is due to Israel's wickedness; her punishment will herald the end of all things, and the judgement of all mankind. The setting of the chapter, on the Mount of Olives, was the natural site from which to admire the temple's magnificence, but in view of Zech 14:4, it was an equally appropriate setting for an eschatological discourse. The disciples' double question – 'When will these things be, and what is the sign that all these things are going to take place?' links together the fate of Jerusalem and the final judgement.[9]

3. Section 1

The discourse itself consists of five sections, followed by two parables and associated sayings. Let us look at these seven paragraphs in turn.

The first section, in 13:5–8, opens with the warning which is characteristic of the discourse: βλέπετε. The disciples have asked for a sign of the imminence of the catastrophe. Jesus warns them not to be misled by *false* signs. Various disasters are going to occur – disasters that play a familiar role in prophetic announcements of doom and apocalyptic warnings. But these disasters are *not* the sign of the End, nor even of Jerusalem's fall; the end is *not yet* (v. 7), for these things are only the beginning of sufferings (v. 8). The phrase ἀρχὴ ὠδίνων, with its suggestions of birthpangs, may be a technical term of apocalyptic. Some have described this section as *anti*-apocalyptic, but that seems hardly fair. Phrases such as δεῖ γενέσθαι in v. 7 echo the language of apocalyptic predictions. It would be more accurate to describe it as anti-apocalyptic-fervour; as intended to dampen down wild enthusiasm which saw any disaster as the prelude to the last days. To describe such disaster as the 'birthpangs of the End' is to admit that they are indeed the prelude, but also to emphasize how many other things must take place before the end of all things arrives. There is an interesting parallel between this section and 2 Thess 2, where we find a similar injunction not to be alarmed or agitated – μὴ θροεῖσθε – by reports that the day of the Lord has arrived. This suggests that the origin of the warning in Mark 13 will have been a similar kind of situation.

But the *crux interpretum* in this particular section is found in the warning in verse 6. Who are the 'many' who come 'in my name' saying 'I am'? The obvious explanation is that they are pseudo-messiahs, messianic pretenders;

---

[9] The final words of verse 4 echo the LXX version of Dan 12:7: συντελεσθήσεται πάντα ταῦτα.

this makes sense in a Jewish setting – but why should such men claim to speak in Jesus' name – i.e. with his authority – while making messianic claims for themselves? And how could they mislead the Christian community, for whom Jesus was already the only Messiah? William Manson's solution was to suggest that what they announced was 'I am is here' – just as the false prophets in 2 Thess 2 announced that the day of the Lord had arrived.[10] But that hardly seems to be how Mark understood the situation, for it is difficult to see how ἐγώ εἰμι can mean *he* is here; whoever these men were, they seem to have been making false claims about *themselves*. An alternative solution is to take the phrase ἐπὶ τῷ ὀνόματί μου to mean 'claiming to be me' or 'usurping my name'.[11] But were there really 'many' in the Christian community who believed themselves to be the returning Jesus, and who misled the faithful? Perhaps this suggestion is possible, in a time of prophetic fervour and enthusiasm, but it must be admitted that there is no evidence elsewhere for such claims. This impasse leads me to return to the obvious interpretation, and suggest that these men were indeed messianic pretenders, but to understand them as *Jewish* claimants to messiahship. We must then take the phrase ἐπὶ τῷ ὀνόματί μου in its second possible meaning, 'usurping my name' – i.e. the name Christ, not the name Jesus. Matthew seems to have understood the claim this way, since he interprets Mark's ἐγώ εἰμι as 'I am the Christ'. But how, one may well ask, could such men mislead the faithful? Now the interesting point to notice here is that Mark does not in fact suggest that they do. They are to mislead 'many'; and the disciples are not to be misled by the appearance of these Jewish messianic pretenders, any more than by the wars and rumours of wars, by the earthquakes and famines. This is not an internal church problem – an early Christian aberration – but part of the familiar pattern of troubles which are part of the unwinding of history.

Now if verses 6–8 are, as is often suggested, part of a pre-Marcan apocalypse – or even if they are simply an independent piece of tradition – it may well be that they are Jewish in origin, rather than Jewish-Christian. It may be that Mark used them here because of the verb πλανήσουσιν, which formed a link with his introductory warning where the same verb is found. At any rate, it seems to me that *we* should not be misled by the double occurrence of the verb into thinking that because the initial command not to be misled is directed to disciples, it is disciples also who are in danger of being misled into following false messiahs; the danger that awaits them is of assuming that the appearance of these upstarts is the sign of the End.

---

[10] William Manson, 'The ΕΓΩ ΕΙΜΙ of the Messianic Presence in the New Testament', *JTS* 48 (1947): 137–145.

[11] Cf. George R. Beasley-Murray, *A Commentary on Mark Thirteen* (London: Macmillan, 1957), *in loc.*

4. Section 2

The second section, verses 9–13, is totally different, though it begins with a repetition of the warning to the disciples in verse 5 to take heed. This time, however, they need to take heed for themselves – βλέπετε δὲ ὑμεῖς ἑαυτούς. Unlike the sufferings in 5–8, those in 9–13 are experienced specifically by Christians. The warning is, of course, to *expect* these things – *not* to try to escape them. It would not be true to suggest that these sufferings are totally foreign to the theme of apocalyptic, since apocalyptic writings were often addressed to those who were being persecuted because of their faith. Nevertheless, the sufferings are different in kind from the cosmic disasters associated with the end of the world. The theme is the familiar Marcan one – that disciples must expect to suffer the same kind of vilification and ill-treatment as their master. Matthew and Luke include similar sections in their versions, but it is noteworthy that Matthew omits verses 9, 11, and 12, having used them already in the instruction to the Twelve in Matt 10:17–21. And since Mark 13:9–13 are concerned with the cost of discipleship, it looks as if the Matthean setting, in chapter 10, is an indication of the kind of context in which this material was first used. Its function was *not* originally to convey information about the timing of the End, but to warn Jesus' disciples about what following him would mean. They must expect to be handed over to the Jewish courts – much as Jesus himself is about to be handed over to the Sanhedrin; here we have not only the term συνέδρια but the verb παραδίδωμι, which sounds like a knell through Mark's story. They can expect to be beaten, put on trial before governors and kings, betrayed by members of their own families, and hated by all for the sake of Jesus' name. Those who endure εἰς τέλος, to the end, will be saved – this final sentence in the paragraph echoes Theodotion's rendering of Dan 12:12. Taken without reference to the Marcan setting, the meaning seems to be: those who are faithful to the uttermost, i.e. until death, will be saved – a paradoxical saying of the kind we find in Mark 8:35. But what are we to make of the word τέλος in the *Marcan* context? It seems to suggest that Christians who endure (and who survive!) until the End will be saved – a promise at variance with the warning in the previous verse that they must expect to be handed over to death! Once again, one wonders whether we have in τέλος a link word, which led Mark, or someone before him, to place this section here.

But the real problem in this section is the saying in v. 10: the gospel must first be preached to all nations. Let me say straight away I am not persuaded by the arguments of Professor Kilpatrick that the traditional punctuation is wrong.[12] It is true that there are difficulties in believing that Jesus himself gave

---

[12] G.D. Kilpatrick, 'The Gentile Mission in Mark and Mark 13:9–11' in *Studies in the Gospels,* ed. D.E. Nineham (Oxford: Blackwell, 1957), 145 ff.

such clear directions regarding a mission to the Gentiles; but the saying in any case looks like an intrusion into the context and therefore a Marcan editorial comment. And there are no problems in believing that Mark pointed forwards to such a mission. But how did Mark understand the word 'first'? Πρῶτον here could have the sense 'before you are arrested': before you are arrested, you must preach the gospel to the Gentiles. In the context of Mark 13, however, it is more likely to refer to the events which signify the arrival of the End. Matthew has clearly understood the saying in this way, since in his version he adds the words 'and then the End will come' (Matt 24:14). Moreover, we find that a similar idea occurs in Matthew 10, following Jesus' warning to the disciples about persecution. After the passage that is almost identical with Mark 13:9, 11–13, Matthew adds the enigmatic saying in 10:23: 'if they persecute you in this city, flee to the next; indeed I tell you, you will not have completed the cities of Israel before the Son of man comes'. Now there are obvious differences between the two sayings. Matt 10:23 concerns an unfinished mission to Israel, Mark 13:10 and Matt 24:14 a mission to the Gentiles which must be completed – it is to *all* the Gentiles – before the End comes. Matt 10 suggests a sense of urgency, Mark 13 and Matt 24 emphasize that the End is not yet here. But all three passages stress the need to preach before the parousia, and link this idea with warnings about the persecution which those who follow Jesus must expect. The fact that Matthew makes this link in two different places (using non-Marcan material as well as Marcan) suggests that the ideas of preaching, persecution, and the parousia were related ones, and that Mark 13:10 may not be such an arbitrary insertion as at first appears.

A comparison between Matt 10 and Mark 13 demonstrates very well the way in which tradition can be differently used in different contexts. In Matt 10, the sayings about persecution form part of the warnings to the disciples about the treatment they can expect in the course of their mission; the reference to the parousia in v. 23 stresses the urgency of this mission. In Mark 13, on the other hand, the same sayings are a warning about what the disciples must expect to endure before the End, while the reference to preaching in v. 10 serves the same function as the comment in v. 7 that the End is not yet: the emphasis is on endurance instead of urgency. For Mark, the sufferings of the disciples are not signs that the End is at hand, but signs that the proclamation of the gospel is taking place; the End *cannot* come until the Gentile mission is completed. Now if Johannes Munck was right about the interpretation of the restrainer in 2 Thess 2, we should once again have a remarkably similar idea in that chapter.[13] Unfortunately, it seems unlikely to

---

[13] Johannes Munck, *Paul and the Salvation of Mankind,* trans. Frank Clarke (London: SCM Press, 1959), 36 ff. Munck was, of course, picking up an idea that goes back to patristic times, as well as building on the earlier work of Oscar Cullmann, 'Le caractère eschatologique du

me that he *was* right! Nevertheless, we do find in Rom 11:25 ff. the idea that the preaching of the gospel to the Gentiles was only a first stage in the eschatological countdown. This suggests that Mark may have been writing in a similar situation.

If I am right about the function of the saying, then perhaps this explains its position. Mark could not have begun the section with it, since it does not belong with his warning to take heed. He might have ended with it, as Matthew does in chapter 24; this is neater, but in Matthew the comment has no real relevance to the warnings about persecution, and is simply treated as a reference to one more thing that must take place before the End. In Mark, however awkward the order may be, and however intrusive verse 10 may seem, the saying nevertheless belongs within Mark's overall structure. The disciples must expect to suffer as followers of Christ: but those sufferings are not to be misunderstood as signs that the End is at hand. Rather *they result from the preaching of the gospel*. But that preaching is itself one of the events that must take place before the End: only when the proclamation of the gospel is completed – that is, when it has been preached to *all* the Gentiles – can the disciples expect the End of all things.

5. Section 3

With the third section, verses 14–20, we have another abrupt change in mood. Instead of general predictions about wars and catastrophes or prophecies of persecution for Jesus' followers, we have a reference to a particular, local disaster. The pace of the discourse alters, and we are given an answer to the disciples' initial question, 'When?' Until this point the message has been 'Wait! Endure! The End is not yet'. But now the time for action has arrived. The sign will be the abomination of desolation, standing where he ought not. The phrase is of course a quotation from Daniel – one of many echoes of Daniel in this chapter, 'Let the reader understand!' Those who have attributed the whole discourse to Jesus have been obliged to understand these words as meaning 'Let the reader of Daniel understand'. Others have supposed that Mark has simply copied them from his written source, not noticing the absurdity of attributing them to Jesus. But there is no need for these explanations; it is better to treat the words as a parenthesis of Mark's own, alerting his readers to the fact that his somewhat enigmatic language needs to be decoded. But why the enigma? Why does Mark use such obscure language? One suggestion is that he avoids speaking plainly because of

---

devoir missionaire et de la conscience apostolique de S. Paul: Étude sur le κατέχον (-ων) de 2. Thess. 2:6–7', *RHPR* 16 (1936): 210–245.

the dangerous political situation. Another is that he himself has no precise idea of what his words mean. Up to this point, the 'prophecy' has described events already experienced by the Christian community; if this is the point at which Mark himself moves into the unknown, this may explain his mysterious language. This would mean, of course, that Mark wrote *before* 70 CE. The most likely explanation, however, seems to me to be that Mark intends us to take note of the full significance of his words. What is going to take place in the temple will be the fulfilment of Daniel's prophecy, and it will be the sign of the arrival of the last things, for in Dan 12:11 the setting up of the abomination of desolation marks the beginning of the countdown to the End. Mark's use of a masculine participle, ἑστηκότα, suggests that he is thinking of a person, but this person is the embodiment of evil – the antichrist of later apocalyptic literature. Behind the historical event in the temple, then, Mark intends us to see its real significance, and to understand *why* this should be the sign that unparalleled disasters are to be let loose in the world. The role of this evil figure in Mark is remarkably similar to that played by the man of lawlessness in 2 Thess 2. There we read that the day of the Lord will not come until he has been revealed – the son of perdition who takes his seat in the temple of God, proclaiming himself to be God.

The urgency of the instructions to flee when this event occurs suggest a sudden invasion or uprising. Whatever it is, it brings terrible suffering – the kind of suffering which has accompanied many other disasters in the course of history. Only, says Mark, this is *not* that kind of suffering. For this tribulation, θλῖψις, is far greater than anything that has been known in the course of history. The words are a clear reference to Dan 12:1, and indicate that Mark is interpreting this as the eschatological tribulation. It is only because God in his mercy has set a limit to its duration that anyone will be able to survive it.

The problematic verse in this section is, of course, 14, and the unsolved problem is whether for Mark this is a future or a past occurrence. For the moment, I do not see the solution to this one. Let us for the moment simply take note of the fact that, future or past, it is here that the programme, as Mark presents it, changes gear. After the 'not yet' of the previous two sections, we have at last a 'Now!'

6. Section 4

We move on to the fourth section, and experience a sense of déjà vu, for the appearance of false Christs reminds us of the warning in verse 6. Verses 21–23 look very much like a variant of that saying. There are further interesting parallels in Luke 17: first in verse 21, where, however, the 'not here ... not there' refer to the kingdom of God, and then in verse 23, where what is being looked for is the coming of the Son of man; Matthew seems to have incorporated a version of this last saying into his account of the discourse (Matt 24:26–28). The idea that the Messiah will be discovered 'here' or 'there' suggests a human figure rather than a heavenly one descending to earth, and once again the saying may have referred originally to Jewish expectation of a Messiah. This time, however, Mark understands the warning as specifically addressed to the disciples; the danger is such that even the elect may be led astray – if such a thing is possible! The situation depicted now is quite different from that in verse 6. A sign has been given; the days to the End are numbered on the heavenly calendar; the time to expect the Son of man is near. In this context, the saying certainly reminds us of the false rumours mentioned in 2 Thess 2 to the effect that the day of the Lord has come. The faithful must beware false rumours and false prophets who announce the End, beware even false Christs. Who can these false Christs be? We have already said that the elect were unlikely to have been misled into following Jewish messianic pretenders, and that we have no evidence of Christians claiming to be the returning Jesus. Should we perhaps understand the warning, in this context, as linked with the prediction of the arrival of the Antichrist in 14? It is worth noting that the arrival of the lawless one in 2 Thess 2 is also to be accompanied by 'signs and wonders'. Equally suggestive is the reference to Antichrist in 1 John 2:18: 'You have heard that Antichrist has come, and now there are many antichrists'. For the writer of 1 John, the false teachers are manifestations of the power of Antichrist. Mark's warning against ψευδόχριστοι may well refer to something similar. Because the term is for us so specific, we are of course inclined to assume that anyone termed a ψευδόχριστος must have been setting himself up as a unique leader, probably of a political kind, but the fact that Mark links the ψευδόχριστοι with ψευδοπροφῆται suggests that his warning is directed against charismatic figures of some kind.[14] If so, then these are teachers who emerge during the troubled period following the downfall of Jerusalem, misleading the Christian community with false teaching about the time of the End; but their predictions are further false alarms. By contrast, Jesus' own prophetic words will be seen to be true (v. 23).

7. Section 5

But finally the last stage of the drama is reached, in verses 24–27: cosmic disasters herald the arrival of the Son of man. The description of what will take place is lifted from a couple of chapters in Isaiah, typical of Old Testament

---

[14] So Beasley-Murray, *Commentary, in loc.* The words ψευδόχριστοι καὶ are omitted by D 124 1573 d i k, but are probably original.

passages which use the imagery of cosmic breakup and darkness to describe the wrath which will overtake the world on the day of the Lord.[15] It is often said that apocalyptic writers took over this poetic imagery and understood it literally, though the evidence that they did so is in fact somewhat scant; references to the sun and moon ceasing to function are surprisingly rare in apocalyptic.[16] Certainly they seem to have expected strange phenomena in the heavens, portents of the approaching End.[17] How does Mark understand these words? It seems unlikely that he is using them simply as poetic imagery, forceful ways of describing the terrors of war, earthquake, and famine, since these disasters have been described already, in 6–9, and again in 15–20. We seem to have moved on beyond the course of historical events to the winding-up of history. Are the failure of sun and moon and stars to be understood literally, as signs of the approaching End? If so, then, unlike earlier false alarms, there can be no mistaking these particular portents! It is not simply that the heavens have gone awry, but that they are breaking up. We must, of course, be careful not to read back into Mark's words our own understanding of the universe. To us, his picture suggests total cosmic disintegration. Luke is perhaps closer to understanding Mark when he speaks about 'signs in sun and moon and stars'. But it is doubtful whether Mark had worked out the logic of the picture which he presents. The language he used was the traditional language used by the prophets for the day of the Lord, and it is used because it evokes all the ideas associated with that day of judgement. It is more than metaphorical, less than literal; the closest parallels are in the passages he uses – Isa 13 and 34 – which are equally ambiguous. In this context, sensible questions about what will actually happen are out of place, for the language is the language of myth. When these things happen, *then* 'they'[18] will see the Son of man coming with great power and glory, and *then* he will send out his angels and gather the elect from all corners. Once again, the *then* provides an answer to the disciples' initial question, 'When?' – or rather, to their second question, about the time when all things were to be fulfilled. The first sign was set in the temple, and heralded its destruction; the second sign is set in the heavens, and heralds the advent of the Son of man and the vindication of the elect.

---

[15] Isa 13:10; 34:4.

[16] The failure of the sun, moon, and stars is apparently seen as part of God's judgement on the world in As. Mos. 10:5, and as part of the disorder of nature that man brings upon himself through his wickedness in 1 En. 80:4 ff.

[17] In 4 Ezra 5:4 ff. the reversal of day and night is a sign of the coming of the End; the quenching of the sun in T. Levi 4:1 is a sign of coming judgement that unbelieving men ignore; Sib. Or. 3:798 ff. sees the sun's failure as a sign of the end of all things. Cf. Joel 2:30 ff. (3:3 ff.), where the darkening of sun and moon are 'portents' of the day of the Lord.

[18] The subject of the verb is not specified. The fact that this verse is not addressed to the disciples suggests that we have here an independent saying.

8. Parables and Sayings

The first of the two parables that follow is about the fig tree, the harbinger of summer; its green shoots are the sign that summer is about to follow. Placed at this point in the discourse, the parable seems to confirm the idea that in the previous paragraph, 24–27, Jesus had at last provided the answer to the disciples' question – that *second* question, about the sign of the fulfilment of everything. When they see these things – presumably the cosmic phenomena in verses 24 ff. – then they will know that something or somebody is at the door; the context demands that we understand the subject of ἐστιν as 'he': when these things take place, the Son of man will be on the threshold. The intriguing thing about this parable is that it refers to a fig tree. The fig tree is, of course, the obvious tree to have chosen, since it is not an evergreen, unlike most trees in the area. But a fig tree has already been used, at the beginning of the section on the temple, in Mark 11, to symbolize the destruction of the temple. Here, by contrast, the bursting into new life of an apparently dead tree is to be the sign of the Son of man's arrival, and it is a fitting sign of what is, for the elect, a joyous event. Nor is it an arbitrary sign, for, as Dr Telford, in his recent study *The Barren Fig-tree*,[19] has demonstrated, the fig tree was commonly used to symbolize the joys of the messianic age.

The sayings which follow are often said to be contradictory, but I see no problem in supposing that Mark could maintain both that what has been predicted is certain, and will take place within a certain time (vv. 30 ff.), and that the precise time is unknown (v. 32). The real problem comes in the final verses of the chapter, the second of the two parables. It is introduced with the familiar warning to take heed, which occurs repeatedly in the discourse. But this time the reason for the warning is that the time of the End is unknown. The situation of the disciples is like that of servants waiting for their master to return from a journey in the middle of the night; they do not know at what hour he will return, and therefore they must watch through the whole night. In Mark's version, the parable bears obvious marks of artificiality. Nobody would have returned from a long journey in first-century Palestine in the middle of the night; Luke's version of the parable is about a man who had gone out to a banquet, and this makes much better sense.[20] Mark seems to have combined a story about a man expected home at night with the parable recorded elsewhere in Matthew and Luke about a man away from home who entrusts his servants with various responsibilities.[21] The point of his version is not that the master's arrival is unexpected, but that his servants are given

---

[19] Cf. n. 5.
[20] Luke 12:36–40.
[21] Matt 25:14–30 // Luke 19:12–27.

no warning about the precise time that he will come, and must therefore be constantly vigilant. The detail about giving his servants work to do, which seems to have come from the parable of the talents, will have reminded Mark's readers that keeping watch for the master's return does not excuse the servants from faithfully carrying out their duties. Mark's allegorical interpretation of the parable is plain, and the moral is spelt out with only a thin disguise in v. 35: the disciples must keep watch, since they do not know when their master will come. This suggests that he is already at hand, and the urgency of this command is at odds with the earlier part of the discourse, which emphasized that the End could not be expected yet. It may be, however, that Mark has added the detail about the work that is entrusted to the household servants in order to emphasize that the command to keep watch for the master's return does not in his view conflict with the belief that a certain period of time must elapse first.

9. Mark's Purpose

How, then, are we to understand Mark's overall purpose in this discourse? In contrast to Marxsen, who suggested that it was designed to urge Mark's readers to flee from Jerusalem to Galilee,[22] it seems to me that it urges inaction rather than action. It is true that three of its sections refer to signs that some great event is about to occur; but interwoven with these are three other sections describing events that *might* be taken as signs but which in fact are not to be misunderstood as such. These three sections are introduced by the warning to take heed in verses 5, 9, and 23 – and this warning is against misunderstanding what is happening and not, as we might perhaps expect, against being caught off guard by the parousia. But taken together, these first six sections can be understood to present a coherent message which runs: 'Do not be alarmed by these events ... the End is not yet; but when this event occurs – then watch out!' This message is repeated twice, the first climax coming in verse 14, and the second in 24 ff., and is rounded off by 28–31. The final section, however, although it too contains the command to take heed in verse 33, apparently contradicts *all* the previous six paragraphs by urging the need to watch constantly, since the time of the parousia is unknown to anyone. It offers no signs, either true or false, but demands constant vigilance; the Lord's coming cannot be pinned down to any particular period of the night.

Paradoxically, it may well be this last section, which seems out of place in the discourse, which comes closest to representing Jesus' own teaching.

---

[22] Willi Marxsen, *Der Evangelist Markus: Studien zur Redaktionsgeschichte des Evangeliums* (Göttingen: Vandenhoeck & Ruprecht, 1959), 101–140.

It is understandable if a message which originally ran 'Be prepared; watch; the kingdom of God may come at any time' encouraged the early Christian community to expect an imminent end to the world. Expectation of the coming kingdom tended to be overlaid by expectation of the coming Son of man.[23] In time, a new warning was necessary in a situation of over-enthusiasm: 'Do not get *too* excited: the End is near – but not as near as all that'. This, in fact, is precisely the development which – if the epistles addressed to the Thessalonian church are both genuinely Pauline – took place in the Christian community at Thessalonica. At the same time, events that had been interpreted as signs that God was working his purpose out, and therefore as warnings to Christians to be on the alert, became distorted into signs by which one could plot the time of the Lord's return, and were welcomed as indications that the period of the church's suffering was over. Mark's chapter seems to reflect this second situation, and it looks very much as though he has adapted the material to fit it. Events which were being interpreted by some of his contemporaries as signs that salvation was near were indeed part of the eschatological programme, but they could not pinpoint the time. Mark's overall message is a warning that there may be more suffering yet in store – a familiar enough theme in a Gospel which has emphasized that following Jesus means taking up the cross. Nevertheless, Mark encourages his readers by his confidence in the final parousia of the Son of man in glory, which brings victory not only for the Son of man but also for the elect. As for what I have suggested is the earliest eschatological message, in verses 33 ff., Mark has adapted the original warning about the End coming 'at any time' to suggest that it may be later rather than sooner: in the meantime the Lord's servants must faithfully perform the tasks he has given them and be prepared to face temptation and trial, however long they may have to wait.

10. The Situation

However great the tension between the material in the earlier sections and this last paragraph, therefore, an attempt has been made to hold them together. But there are tensions, also, between these earlier sections. Let us investigate first the pattern that emerges if we concentrate on the four sections in the discourse that begin with the warning: βλέπετε. These are the three sections which warn about things that must not be misunderstood as signs (numbers 1, 2, and 4), and the final paragraph which warns that there is to be no sign at all. Taken together, the message of these four sections is as follows:

---

[23] An obvious example is seen in Matt 16:28, compared with Mark 9:1. Cf. also Luke 17:20–30; Matt 10:5–7, 23; 13:24–30, 36–43.

Take heed. There will be all kinds of turmoil and disaster, but these are not the sign; the End is not yet. You will be persecuted – but this is not the sign: persecution shows rather that the gospel is being preached. There will be false teachers, and even Christians will be led astray – but this is not the sign. There is no sign of his coming, and you must therefore be continually alert.

Might these four paragraphs perhaps come from one source? If so, its message seems to have been a warning against *all* attempts to calculate the time of the End. But the warning of the final paragraph, with its emphasis on the need to watch, is at variance with the insistence of the earlier paragraphs that the End is not yet, even though it has been adapted to suggest a period of waiting. Do these other three paragraphs, then (sections 1, 2 and 4), perhaps have a common origin? Or does the repeated βλέπετε indicate Marcan editing, since the same warning is found on three other occasions in the gospel?[24] And whatever their previous history, how do these four paragraphs fit with the three sections in which a sign *is* mentioned? Now the interesting thing to note in these three sections is the speed, in every case, with which the sign is followed by the event that it heralds. When you see the abomination of desolation standing in the temple, then get out! There is no time to do anything except flee. When you see the heavens disintegrate, then there certainly cannot be any mistaking the sign, nor any time to make further preparations. When you see the fig tree burst into leaf, then summer is at hand. There is nothing arbitrary about any of these images. When the temple is invaded by Antichrist, then it will be destroyed; when the heavens break up, the End is here; when the leaves unfold, summer has come. There is no time for anything. The signs are not detached phenomena, but rather the beginning of the disaster itself. The message of the final paragraph is certainly appropriate to this situation, for if things happen so suddenly, then clearly the disciples need to be continually on the alert.

When Mark pieces all this material together (and it looks very much as though the various traditions may have been used in very different situations at an earlier period), the whole thing looks like this:

> The disciples ask for a sign of the temple's destruction, and a sign that all things are going to be fulfilled. Jesus replies as follows: world disasters are not the sign; persecution of Christians is not the sign. There *is* a sign of Jerusalem's fall – but it will be instantaneous and demand immediate action. As for the End, false teachers will announce that it is here – but even that is not the sign. When it comes, there will be no mistaking the sign of its arrival. To all of this, the theme of the final parable is surprisingly relevant: since the crisis comes suddenly, there is need to keep alert, but since its coming may not be immediate, there is need to work.

---

[24] Mark 4:24; 8:15; 12:38. Rudolf Pesch, *op. cit.*, argues that the phrase is part of Marcan redaction.

What kind of situation lies behind Mark's discourse? We have already noticed the interesting parallels with 2 Thess 2, and it looks very much as though a similar situation exists in both communities. In other words, Mark's teaching is aimed at Christians who are unduly excited and agitated by eschatological expectation; he reminds them that Christian discipleship involves mission and persecution before the final time of vindication. However, there is a significant difference between the two passages. The readers of 2 Thessalonians are urged not to believe rumours that the End has arrived, because the man of lawlessness must first be revealed. He will seat himself in the temple, proclaim himself to be God, and his activity will be marked by false signs and wonders. In Mark, the desecration of the temple is interpreted as a sign of the temple's destruction, and though this is of course firmly linked with the End, the two apparently take place at different times. There are two crises, one local, one global. Why? One possibility is that the emphasis on Jerusalem reflects the interests of a Palestinian community. Another is that it reflects Mark's own interests, and his insistence on Israel's failure and coming punishment. But it may well be that Mark is writing between the two crises – i.e. after 70 CE; in other words, that he separates the two because Jerusalem has fallen, the temple been destroyed, Israel been judged, and the End is still not here. If the prophecy of verse 14 does not accord directly with historical events, this suggests that Mark is not writing in Palestine, and that he is using traditional material, rather than recording what happened.

Finally, we should note another difference between 2 Thessalonians and Mark. What is said in 2 Thess 2 about the man of lawlessness who is revealed before the End is in Mark divided between three groups of figures. First, there are those who usurp Jesus' name and say 'I am' (Mark 13:6); in 2 Thessalonians the man of lawlessness proclaims himself God (2 Thess 2:4). Secondly, there is the abomination of desolation, standing where he ought not (Mark 13:14) – the man of lawlessness sits in the temple (2 Thess 2:4); and thirdly, there are false Christs and false prophets who perform signs and wonders (Mark 13:22) – activities associated with the man of lawlessness (2 Thess 2:9). It looks very much as though the three groups in Mark represent different parts of the tradition about the opposition which will mark the last days.[25] Interestingly enough, Mark insists that two of these groups are *not* to be interpreted as signs of the impending crisis, whereas one of them *is*.

If that provides us with a puzzle with which to end this study of Mark 13, it may perhaps provide us also with a clue to understanding the problem with which this discourse was intended to deal. For the tradition preserved in 2 Thess 2 might well have led to the kind of misinterpretation – the hunting

---

[25] Cf. Lars Hartman, *Prophecy Interpreted: The Formation of Some Jewish Apocalyptic Texts and of the Eschatological Discourse Mark 13 Par.*, ConBNT (Lund: Gleerup, 1966), 178–205, 235–238.

for signs – to which Mark seems to be opposed. If the unleashing of evil was said to be the sign of the End, then we can understand how all sorts of different manifestations of evil were being interpreted as *the* sign, and how many false rumours could arise. Mark's message is a warning against looking for false signs. Neither international disturbances nor persecution are signs that the End is imminent. Even when tribulation is at its most intense and false prophets announce that the End is here – still these are false signs. When Antichrist comes, then destruction will follow, instantly. As for the coming of the Son of man, that will be sudden, and judgement will follow immediately. Mark's readers must not be misled by talk about the signs of the End. This is why he adapts the final parable. They need to wait patiently and to work faithfully, as well as to watch. For Mark, the antichrist figure has become the symbol of Israel's judgement and the temple's destruction. Beyond that, the disciple can only wait and watch for the coming of the Son of man.

16. Traditions about the Temple in the Sayings of Jesus*

This essay owes its origins to a paper given some years ago by Professor E. P. Sanders, at my Cambridge Seminar, in which he explored the problem of trying to recover the *ipsissima verba Jesu*, and of reconstructing the events which led to his death. That paper has subsequently been published, as part of his book on *Jesus and Judaism*.[1] One of the positive conclusions to emerge from a somewhat bleak picture was that one could at least conclude that there was some kind of controversy between Jesus and the Jewish religious authorities regarding the temple, and that it was this controversy which ultimately led to Jesus' death. This set me thinking about the temple sayings in the tradition, and the result was this essay.

There is a surprising amount of material on this topic, and it is not confined to the Gospels. I suggest that we begin with the story of the incident in the temple (Mark 11 and parallels). I call it 'incident' in order not to beg any questions, for the usual appellation, 'cleansing', certainly does that. It may be that, in an hour's time, we shall feel justified in referring to it by that term – but, for the moment, let us reserve judgement and look, first, at the way in which the evangelists present this story.

There can be no doubt that Mark has understood Jesus' actions in the temple as a demonstration of condemnation and an indication of judgement which is to follow. This is quite clear from the way in which he has sandwiched this story and that of the withered fig tree together. In 11:11, Jesus enters the temple, inspects it and withdraws. On the following morning, he inspects a fig tree, finds no fruit on it and curses it. On entering the temple, he protests about what is going on – and about what is not going on, i.e. true worship of God – in a dramatic way. On the third day, the fig tree is discovered to be dead, v. 20. But, in the meantime, the religious authorities – priests and scribes – have already determined to destroy Jesus, v. 18. *His* fate is bound up with that of the temple. There can be no doubt, I think, that Mark intends us to see a parallel between Jesus' two dramatic actions: he pronounces judgement on the temple, as on the tree, and for the same reason – because of the failure to produce the harvest that was intended. And there is one final hinge that links the two stories together – the saying in v. 23 about

---

*A lecture delivered in the John Rylands University Library of Manchester on Wednesday, 6 May 1987.
[1] E. P. Sanders, *Jesus and Judaism* (London, SCM Press, 1985).

the mountain being cast into the sea. As a saying about the power of faith, this seems strangely out of context; but if Mark understood 'this mountain' as the temple mountain, it begins to make sense. Instead of being exalted, Zion is going to be destroyed and cast into the abyss (Micah 4:1).

But it is perhaps worth looking also at the wider context in which Mark has set this complex of tradition. In the opening verses of chapter 11, he describes the entry of Jesus into Jerusalem – a story which has clear messianic significance for the readers of the Gospel, even though this is hidden from those taking part in the procession: it is as Messiah that Jesus enters Jerusalem. William Telford, in his fascinating study *The Barren Temple and the Withered Tree*,[2] has recently shown how appropriate the story of the fig tree is to the theme of Jesus' messiahship. In the messianic age, the fig tree should yield fruit; instead, when Jesus arrives in Jerusalem, it proves to be barren. And when Mark has finished with the fig tree and takes Jesus back into the temple again in v. 27, we have a dispute between Jesus and the religious authorities about the nature of his authority. In reply, Jesus asks about the authority of John the Baptist. This is not, of course, just a trick question, which puts the opposition on the spot. The role of Jesus himself is linked with that of John the Baptist. If John was the forerunner, and if his mission was from God, then who does that make Jesus, and what is the nature of *his* authority? Mark has already given his readers the answer to these questions, back in the opening verses of chapter 1. So in this debate in the temple, at the end of chapter 11, we are reminded of the nature of Jesus' messianic authority. (I am using the term 'messianic' here in a broad sense, for want of any better term, without wanting to narrow it down to any particular understanding of messiahship.) In other words, Mark has put his temple-tree sandwich inside another sandwich to form a double-decker, with vv. 1–10 and 27–33 reminding us just who it is who has arrived in the Jerusalem temple.

Chapter 12 is equally illuminating. Jesus teaches in the temple (cf. 14:49). First, we have a parable. It tells of a vineyard owner who expects, at harvest time, to receive fruit from his vineyard; but the tenants to whom he has entrusted it rob him of his due. Worse still, they kill the owner's only son; and they, in turn, are destroyed. The theme of the parable is a retelling of the temple-tree sandwich – but it goes a little further: we have the same legitimate demand for fruit; the failure to do what is required, which amounts to robbery (cf. 11:17, quotation of Jeremiah 7:11); the carrying out, this time, of the threat to kill the son and heir (cf. 11:18); the destruction of the tenants themselves. And then, at the end of the story, two interesting developments. First of all, the vineyard is given to others, v. 9. How does Mark understand

---

[2] William R. Telford, *The Barren Temple and the Withered Tree*, JSNTSup 1 (Sheffield: JSOT Press, 1980).

this? Who are the *original* tenants? Are we to think of Israel as the old tenants – which is what Isaiah 5 might lead us to expect – and the Gentiles as the new? If so, then perhaps Isaiah 56:7, quoted in 11:17 (a house of prayer for the nations), is now being fulfilled – and maybe that is why that verse is quoted in chapter 11. What was intended for the original temple is now being worked out – in the vineyard! And, if that seems to be a mixed metaphor, do not blame me, for Mark himself is going to introduce it in v. 10. But before we look at that verse, let us consider the alternative interpretation of the new tenants. In v. 12, Mark tells us that 'they' knew that Jesus had told the parable against them. Unfortunately, he omits to tell us who 'they' are, but since 'they' are contrasted with the crowd one may assume that he means the religious authorities again; and if 'they' are represented in the story as the original tenants, that suggests that the 'others' might be, for Mark, either the '*am ha-aretz* or the leaders of the new Christian community. But the second development is the more intriguing. This is the addition, in verses 10–11, of a proof text, taken from Psalm 118:22 (the stone rejected by the builders). It is not, of course, a Marcan addition; it is found in the same place in the Gospel of Thomas. In one sense it is totally inappropriate here: it is the tenants who have been destroyed, not the vineyard – and, anyway, you do not plant a vineyard on a corner-stone (not if you want any grapes!). This is temple-imagery – or, at least, it is building imagery. The text is used twice more in the New Testament: in Acts 4:11 of the resurrection and in 1 Peter 2:7 of the offence that the Jews found in Jesus – but the context there is about the Christian community as a spiritual house of living stones and holy priesthood. What is the text doing in Mark 12? Matthew Black[3] argued that it is original, and that the parable is in fact a *pesher* on it based on the pun between 'stone' and 'son', but I do not find this persuasive, though the pun may well have led to the *addition* of the proof-text. I imagine that the text was added at some early stage in the tradition because the parable was felt to be incomplete. The only son has been killed and his body thrown out of the vineyard, v. 8; but, for the church, that was not the end of the story, and a reference to the resurrection was needed. By adding this particular proof-text, someone has not only introduced the idea of Jesus' resurrection, but has also, deliberately or not, linked the new community which takes over the vineyard of Israel with the idea of a new temple, built on the resurrected Lord.

The rest of chapter 12 consists of more teaching in the temple. Notice the theme: Jesus has condemned the religious leaders of Israel; in the next two incidents they condemn themselves. First, the Pharisees and Herodians try to catch him out with a trick question; the punchline of Jesus' reply, in v. 17, is

---

[3] Matthew Black, 'The Christological Use of the Old Testament in the New Testament', *NTS* 18 (1971): 1–14.

'Give to Caesar what belongs to Caesar, and to God what belongs to God'. Once again we have the suggestion that they are failing to give God his due (cf. 11:17; 12:3). Then the Sadducees try similar tactics with a question about the resurrection (a natural tack for the Sadducees, but certainly relevant to Mark's theme). In contrast, a scribe asks Jesus about the greatest commandment and declares that to love God and one's neighbour is more important than all the sacrifices offered *in the temple* (v. 33). Next, a question from Jesus himself – challenging the teaching of the scribes – reminds us that Jesus is greater than any mere Davidic Messiah. Finally, we have in verses 38–44 Jesus' denunciation of the scribes for their hypocrisy and false piety and, by contrast, the incident of the widow who puts her entire wealth into the temple offertory and thus gives more than all the other worshippers.

And with that incident we are brought up to chapter 13 and the prophecy of the temple's destruction in 13:2. After the last two chapters, it is hardly surprising to meet this, but it is in fact the first clear reference to the temple's destruction that we have met. And it is, of course, the *only* clear prophecy of the temple's destruction in chapter 13. Although it is clear from the arrangement of the material that the destruction of the temple is bound up with the events of vv. 14 ff., when the abomination of desolation stands where it ought not – i.e. desecrating the sanctuary – the temple itself is not mentioned again specifically. But disaster and desolation and judgement for those in Judaea are. It is worth asking what other themes are found in this chapter. On the one hand, we find warnings addressed to the disciples, the company of God's people, about the persecution and sufferings which they may expect to endure for the sake of the Gospel, vv. 9–13; on the other, we have the promise that the Son of man will gather his elect. As R. H. Lightfoot pointed out, the sufferings of the disciples 'echo' those of Jesus in the passion narrative; the promise in v. 26 of vindication by the Son of man 'echoes' Jesus' own vindication in 14:62. In Mark 13, also, we have a surprise reappearance of the fig tree. When the fig tree starts to shoot, then you know that the summer, the time of harvest, is here. And when all these things happen, then you will know that the Son of man is at the doors. So the prophecy of the temple's destruction is linked in this last discourse of Jesus with the theme of eschatological judgement for Israel, with the warning of suffering for the Christian community (who are to share Jesus' own suffering) and with the promise of the gathering of a new community, brought together from all corners of the earth (v. 27) and ready for the final coming of their Messiah.

Moving on to the account of the 'trial' before the high priest in 14, we find a saying about the temple being attributed to Jesus by his accusers: 'we heard him say, I will destroy this temple, made with hands, and in three days I will build another, made without hands' (v. 58). Did Jesus ever utter such a saying? Mark says that the accusation was made by *false* witnesses, and that

16. Traditions about the Temple in the Sayings of Jesus 239

their witness did not agree, so clearly he does not believe that Jesus spoke these words. Rather, they are a distortion of what Jesus has said. Certainly he has prophesied the destruction of the temple and hinted at something which might replace it, but that is not a threat to destroy it himself. Indeed, in Mark's account it is the religious authorities, more than anyone, who are responsible for the coming disaster. But the accusation is certainly evidence that there was a well-established tradition that Jesus was believed to have uttered threats of some kind against the temple. And it is repeated in 15, in the story of the crucifixion, where it is used by those who mock Jesus (v. 29). Finally, in Mark, we have the comment in 15:38: at the moment when Jesus died, the curtain of the temple was torn in two, and his executioner confessed him to be Son of God. It is worthy of note that these last three references, the false accusation, the mockery and the rending of the curtain, all use the term ναός rather than ἱερόν. Is the torn curtain seen by Mark as a symbol of the temple's destruction? Or as 'opening up a new and living way' into God's presence for the Gentiles? In view of his arrangement of the material over the last few chapters, there can be no doubt that the death of Jesus – the Messiah, rejected by his people – and the destruction of the temple belong together. By engineering the death of Jesus, the religious authorities themselves have sealed the fate of the temple. But I doubt if we need to choose between the torn curtain as a symbol of destruction or of the opening up of something new. For when the centurion confesses faith – even though he may not have comprehended what he was saying – then the new community is born.

What about the other evangelists? Going back to the incident in the temple (Matthew 21), we find that Matthew has unscrambled Mark's temple-tree sandwich; in Matthew the tree withers instantly, so there is no need for a second visit. But the two incidents stand side by side, and the parallel between them is still clear. Moreover, Matthew has added another incident in the temple, verses 14–16: Jesus heals the blind and the lame and the children cry out 'Hosanna to the son of David', echoing the greetings on the road in v. 9. If we look back at 2 Samuel 5, we find that the first story told of David, after he is made king, is about his capture of Jerusalem. He takes the city, in spite of the taunts that the blind and the lame would be able to keep him out, as a result of which incident, so it is said, the blind and lame are not permitted in the temple (2 Samuel 5:8). But now the blind and lame come to Jesus in the temple and are healed, and the children hail him as David's son. So Matthew emphasizes what is already implied in Mark: that it is as Messiah that Jesus comes to the temple. Perhaps because he concentrates on the blind and lame, the reference to the Gentiles is omitted from the quotation from Isaiah 56. Like Mark, Matthew then describes the challenge to Jesus concerning his authority, but follows this, not with one parable but with three: the two sons; the vineyard tenants; the marriage feast. All three make the same point – and one that is spelt out: tax-gatherers and sinners will enter the kingdom of God before the religious leaders of the nation, v. 31; the kingdom will be taken away from you and given to a nation that produces fruit, v. 43; those invited to the marriage feast are destroyed, and others invited, 22:7–10. So Matthew emphasizes the point already made in Mark – that the vineyard will be given to new tenants – but seems to interpret it in terms of Jewish sinners rather than Gentiles. He then returns to the Marcan account of Jesus' teaching – except that the scribe now becomes an opponent of Jesus rather than an admirer – until we come to the denunciation of the scribes, where Matthew goes to town with a whole chapter of woes pronounced on scribes and Pharisees. Mark's warnings have been sharpened into wholesale condemnation. This ends with a pronouncement of judgement, 23:35–36, and a lament over Jerusalem, verses 37–39, which refers specifically – echoing Jeremiah – to Jeremiah's 'house' being abandoned; this leads into the prophecy of the temple's destruction, 24:2. Once again, Matthew expands Mark's discourse with extra sayings about judgement and then, in chapter 25, emphasizes this theme with the parable of the wise and foolish virgins, the parable of the talents and the judgement of the nations by the Son of man. The feature of much of this material in Matthew is, of course, that, while judgement is already pronounced on Israel, the *warnings* are now addressed to the members of the church lest they share the same fate (cf., for example, the two-moral version of the parable of the marriage feast, Matthew 22, compared with Luke's version, Luke 14). The material thus has a double function.

Turning to the account of the trial before the high priest in chapter 26, we find an interesting development from Mark; Matthew does not describe the two witnesses who report Jesus' saying about the temple as false (indeed, he seems to distinguish them from the false witnesses of v. 60) and apparently they agree in their testimony. Jesus is reported as saying: 'I am able to destroy the temple of God, and to build it in three days'. Presumably Matthew believes that Jesus did claim something of the kind; but the form of the saying is neither a straightforward claim that he *will* destroy and rebuild the temple nor a prophecy of the temple's destruction, but a claim to have the power to destroy it – very much like the saying in v. 53 about Jesus' divine resources. Asked by the high priest to respond to this charge, Jesus is silent. Since the high priest's next question is to ask if Jesus is the Messiah, the Son of God, Matthew may well have regarded these two questions as parallel. Since Jesus is Messiah and Son of God, of course he is able to destroy the temple and build it again if he wishes to do so. Moving on to the crucifixion, we have the scene where Jesus is mocked by the passers-by; as in Mark, so in Matthew, Jesus is mocked first of all as having claimed that he would destroy the temple and build it in three days, then as King of the Jews, 27:39–42. But Matthew expands Mark's account by adding v. 43: he said 'I am the Son of God'.

Interestingly, the two claims – that Jesus is the destroyer of the temple and Son of God – again occur in parallel. And finally, in v. 51, we have the rending of the temple curtain, which in Matthew is accompanied by an earthquake and the resurrection of the saints – a foretaste of the new people of God.

Luke gives us a somewhat different picture. He omits the story of the cursing of the fig tree and gives a brief, straightforward account of Jesus' actions in the temple. Nevertheless, he links this story with the theme of destruction in a different way. In between the Triumphal Entry (or rather Approach) and Jesus' arrival in the temple, we have Jesus' lament over Jerusalem in 19:41–44. Immediately after this clear prediction of the city's coming destruction, Jesus enters the temple and casts out the merchants; the interpretation of Jesus' actions as a symbol of future events is thus even clearer in Luke than in Mark.

But what has happened to the fig tree? In Luke, of course, we have a *parable* about a fig tree, in 13:6–9, which is interpreted as a warning: if the tree continues in failing to bear fruit, then it will be cut down. Immediately before the parable, in 13:1–5, we have Jesus' comment on the Galileans slain by Pilate and the victims of the tower in Siloam; their fate is a warning to his hearers – 'Unless you repent, you will all perish in the same way'. At the end of chapter 13, we have sayings about Jerusalem: Jesus must go to Jerusalem, since it is only in Jerusalem that prophets perish, verses 31–33; the last two verses, 34–35, are a lament over Jerusalem, parallel to Matthew 23:37–39: Jerusalem, which kills the prophets, and whose house will be abandoned. It is worth noting that the parable which immediately precedes this, in verses 22–30, about the householder who locks his door, contrasts those who find themselves excluded from the kingdom of God (to their own surprise) and those who come from the far corners of the earth to sit down at the feast: for the last will be first, and the first will be last.

Has Luke's parable developed into Mark's miracle? Whatever the relationship between these two units of tradition, it is interesting that they are interpreted by the evangelists in similar ways. But for Luke the parable is a *warning*, and for Mark the blighting of the tree is a sentence of *judgement*; the tree is already dead, and there is no hope. It seems reasonable to suggest that Mark's interpretation represents a later stage of development, when Israel had finally failed to respond to her Messiah and had therefore brought judgement upon her own head. In Luke 13:1–9, we are still at the stage of warnings and appeals. And yet we know – and *Luke* knows – that the warnings and appeals are themselves fruitless: Jerusalem's fate is already sealed, and the temple will be no more.

Before we abandon the fig tree, it is worth noting an interesting echo of the theme, in Luke 23:31. The setting is the *via dolorosa*. Immediately before his own execution, Jesus warns the inhabitants of Jerusalem of the disaster which will come on *them*; once again, the two themes are closely linked together. For if they do these things now, when the wood is green, what will happen when the wood is dead? The tree has now been chopped down – it can only die and become dry and brittle.

There is another interesting omission from Luke – the accusation at the trial before the Sanhedrin that he has threatened to destroy the temple. In Luke, the two questions put to Jesus take up the two titles used in the second question in Mark and Matthew: 'Are you the Christ? ... Are you the Son of God?' So the mockery at the cross (repeated three times) is all about his claim to be the Christ. But Luke does include the tearing of the temple curtain, though it comes before, not after, Jesus' death (v. 45).

But, as with the fig tree, so with the accusation about threats to destroy the temple: the tradition appears elsewhere – this time, of course, in Acts 6:13 ff. It is Stephen who is accused of speaking against 'this holy place and the Law'; more specifically, of saying that 'Jesus of Nazareth will destroy this place'. Now Luke describes the witnesses as false, which suggests that he believes Stephen to be innocent of the charge brought against him, and, though commentators often complain that Stephen's speech in Acts 7 is no defence against the charge and serves only to demonstrate that Stephen *has* spoken against the temple, I doubt whether this can be Luke's intention. Certainly Luke himself is not anti-temple. Stephen is accused of speaking against the temple and against the Law, and the point of his reply is to demonstrate that it is in fact his accusers (i.e. the Jewish nation) who have proved, by their repeated disobedience and idolatry, their failure to accept the Law and to honour the God who cannot be contained in any temple. Stephen defends himself, not by saying 'I have not attacked either the Law or the temple', but by saying 'It is *you* who have done these things – you who have failed to keep the Law you claim to uphold and to honour the God whose temple you claim to revere'. If Stephen has spoken of future destruction, it is as judgement on Israel's sin. What is intriguing about this is that the underlying theme is exactly parallel to that which has emerged in the other Gospels in the accounts of Jesus' actions in the temple and the accusations brought against him at his trial. The destruction of the temple is the result of the disobedience of Israel; it is they, ultimately, who are guilty of blasphemy against the temple, because they are guilty of blasphemy against God. And there is another fascinating link with the Synoptic tradition. The end of the story in Acts 7 is the martyrdom of Stephen and his vision of the Son of man; similarly, in Mark 13, the prophecy of the temple's destruction leads up to the coming of the Son of man, who gathers together the elect after their sufferings; and in Mark 14, the accusation against Jesus as threatening to destroy the temple leads into his confident declaration of his own vindication as Son of man. In contrast to those whose condemnation and exclusion from God's presence is symbolized by the destruction of the temple, we have the emergence of a new community, who are acknowledged by the Son of man.

Finally, we come to John. In Chapter 2, John describes the first of Jesus' signs: Jesus changes water into wine. The water was meant for Jewish rites of purification; the wine is superior to any made by man. Immediately after, Jesus goes to Jerusalem and creates havoc in the temple; one interesting addition to the story, in John's account, is that Jesus drives the sacrificial animals out of the temple. Another addition is the quotation from Psalm 69:10: the zeal of your house shall consume me, v. 17. As in the Synoptics, Jesus is challenged – typically, in John, by 'the Jews' – and asked (once again, this is typical of John) for a sign. The sign will be given – it is the sign of Jesus' resurrection: 'Destroy this temple, and in three days I will raise it'. Here, the saying is actually put into Jesus' mouth, not attributed to him in garbled form by opponents, and we note that it is *they* (not he) who will destroy this temple. Lest we miss the point, as we well might, John tells us that Jesus was speaking of the temple of his body. John has here brought together the tradition of the incident in the temple (Mark 11 and parallels) and the saying attributed to Jesus about the destruction and rebuilding of the temple (Mark 14 and parallels) and shows that he too understands the 'sign' in the temple to be a symbol of its future destruction. But, remarkably, John switches at this point from speaking about the temple as ἱερόν to the term ναός, so that we have an exact parallel, linguistically, with what happens in Mark and Matthew. Moreover, he has shown, by his commentary on these events, as well as by his arrangement of the material, that he believes the risen Jesus to be the replacement of the old temple, the focus of Christian worship. It is a theme which John spells out in the rest of the Gospel, since John demonstrates how Jesus is the fulfilment of Jewish worship, as well as of the Law, but we should perhaps note especially chapter 4, with its discussion of the place of worship, and 7:38, where Jesus is the source of living water, the eschatological temple of Ezekiel's vision (Ezekiel 47).

What emerges from this rapid examination of the Gospel material? First, it seems that *all* the evangelists interpret the incident in the temple as a sign of its coming destruction: the Fourth Gospel simply makes explicit what is implicit in the other three. Secondly, they all link the temple's destruction with the death of Jesus, and this in two ways:

(a) Jesus' words about and actions in the temple are seen as triggering off the events which led up to his death. This is brought out even by John, who places the story at the beginning of the Gospel, yet makes the link with the words 'zeal for thy house will consume me'.

(b) Jesus' death made the destruction of the temple and of Jerusalem inevitable.

Now the *second* of these two themes looks very much like the theologizing of the church. Because Israel has rejected her Messiah and killed him, therefore

God will punish her; she is doomed. What has happened is the result of Israel's own actions. A similar line of reasoning can be seen in 1 Thessalonians 2:15 ff. It is because the Jews killed the Lord Jesus that the wrath of God has come upon them.

But what of the first? Did Jesus act and speak against the temple in such a way as to lead the authorities to take action against him? And, if he *did*, was it in quite the way that the evangelists suggest? The evidence that Jesus predicted the temple's downfall (as in Mark 13:2), and that of Jerusalem, seems overwhelming; it seems safe to assume that he uttered warnings, possibly even laments. But did he *threaten* the temple? Are the evangelists right in seeing the incident in the temple as a sign of its destruction? And did he ever say anything like the saying attributed to him in Mark 14:58: 'I will destroy this temple, and in three days build another'? Now that particular saying worries me because it is absent from Luke, who has transferred the whole scene to the trial of Stephen. But *has* he transferred it? Or is Luke perhaps right? Is this in fact a dispute between church and synagogue which the other evangelists have transferred to the lifetime of Jesus? Does Mark perhaps give this away by his use of the terms χειροποίητος and ἀχειροποίητος?

I hoped in this essay to look at the evidence outside the Gospels, but there is no time to do more than mention the most obvious passages. In Paul we have 2 Corinthians 6:14–7:1, where the Christian community are said to be the temple of God; the point of Paul's imagery here is to stress the presence of God among his people and therefore the need for purity. The same imagery is used in 1 Corinthians where, in 3:16–17, Paul stresses that the Christian community is God's temple, and therefore holy, and in 6:19 he speaks of individual Christians as being severally the temple of the Holy Spirit which makes purity essential. There is a fascinating link in these passages between the terms σῶμα and ναός which we cannot explore now, but it is worth noting that Paul sees the temple as the community of Christians and stresses the need for purity.

In Ephesians 2:18–22 we have the image once more. The new community grows out of the cross and becomes the temple of God. Gentiles are brought into the household of God, and Jesus is the chief cornerstone. Similar ideas are used in 1 Peter 2:4–8. Christ is the living stone, rejected by men, but chosen by God; we are living stones, built into a spiritual house, in order to be a spiritual priesthood. Again, in these two passages, we have the theme of the Christian community as God's temple.

So we have clear evidence that the theme of the Christian community as the temple of God was being discussed by Paul and others: the contrast between the spiritual sanctuary and the sanctuary made with hands has an obvious setting in this period. It seems less likely that the contrast goes back to Jesus himself, for though parallels can also be found at Qumran, they emerged from a community which was cut off from the temple.

As for the incident in the temple, is there anything in the story itself which makes it a prophecy of destruction, or is it simply the evangelists' arrangement of the material which makes it that? Could it be that what the evangelists see as clear pronouncements by Jesus were in fact much less clear? That warnings about future judgement have been sharpened into final condemnations in the light of subsequent events? That a parable about what will happen to a fruitless fig tree has been developed into an action which demonstrates both the sentence and its execution?

Sanders asks us to believe that Jesus proclaimed the forthcoming destruction of the temple, not because he wished to purify it, but simply 'to indicate that the end was at hand and that the temple would be destroyed, so that the new and perfect temple might arise'.[4] But *why* was the old temple doomed to destruction? And why was a new one promised? The act of destruction implies judgement and condemnation. So for what was the old one condemned? We accept Sanders' point that there is nothing to indicate that Jesus condemned temple sacrifices in themselves or the way in which they were being carried out. But he *did* condemn those who failed to produce fruit (12:1–12), those who liked honour, who oppressed widows and made long, sham prayers (12:38–40); he singled out for praise the scribe who set love of God and neighbour above all else and the woman who gave everything she had to the temple treasury. In other words, we have a *reason* for Jesus' judgement on the temple: if it was to be destroyed, it was because the behaviour of those worshipping there belied their worship.

But was that destruction inevitable? Or was Jesus' action to be seen as a warning of what might happen? Was it an expression of final judgement? Or was it a cleansing – a demand that worship should be genuine and not a sham?

Now Mark has given us two clues, which so far we have not considered, in the shape of Old Testament quotations. One is from Isaiah 56:7 – 'My house shall be called a house of prayer for all nations', and the other from Jeremiah 7:11 – 'Has this house become a den of robbers?' The former verse is from an oracle of restoration, the latter from a passage of judgement and condemnation. Sanders dismisses both texts from consideration, as far as questions about Jesus' own understanding of the passage are concerned, referring us to Anthony Harvey's discussion of this story, and suggesting that he has shown conclusively that these Old Testament texts could not have been used by Jesus himself, and that the incident could therefore not have been originally a 'cleansing' of the temple, as the quotations imply.[5] Now it may be that Harvey is right in his conclusion that the Old Testament quotations are additions to the story at some stage, but he is certainly wrong in the method

---

[4] Sanders, *Jesus and Judaism*, 75.
[5] A. E. Harvey, *Jesus and the Constraints of History* (London: Duckworth, 1982), 132 ff.

by which he reaches that conclusion. For his chief argument is that the quotation from Isaiah 56:7, as it is given by Mark, represents the LXX version and 'could hardly be extracted from the Hebrew version which Jesus would have used'. But what Hebrew version is *Harvey* using? For the words in question are there in *my* Hebrew text, as well as those which Harvey quotes; he seems to have looked at only half the text. So I do not think we can dismiss the Old Testament quotations, and with them the notion of cleansing/purifying the temple, quite so quickly.

As for the reference to the den of robbers, this has been dismissed as an inappropriate way of referring to the money changers. But this is to miss the significance of the quotation, which comes from the famous chapter in which the people are told not to trust 'in these deceptive words: this is the temple of the Lord, the temple of the Lord, the temple of the Lord'. The accusation that they have turned God's house into a den of robbers arises from their behaviour – 'you steal, murder, commit adultery, swear falsely, burn incense to Baal – then come and stand before me in my house'. Yet side by side with these accusations is the promise: 'If you truly amend your ways ... if you truly execute justice one with another, if you do not oppress the alien, the fatherless or the widow ... then I will let you dwell in this place'. But if not – 'I will do to the house which is called by my name and in which you trust, and to the place which I gave to you and to your fathers, as I did to Shiloh' (Jer 7:5–15).

So what was Jesus doing when he entered the temple and overthrew the money changers' tables? Was he, perhaps, after all, *cleansing* the temple rather than destroying it? Was he, in other words, protesting against those who worshipped there while failing to love God with all their heart and soul and mind and strength? Was he protesting in the only way possible, by interrupting the sacrifices? Are not his actions more appropriate against such false worship than as a symbol of coming destruction? Certainly the quotations from Isaiah and Jeremiah make sense in that context. And if the Triumphant Entry took place at the Feast of Dedication, as has sometimes been suggested,[6] how appropriate that Jesus should cleanse the temple on his arrival. Was it, then, this action and his demand for radical reform that led to his arrest and death?

One final suggestion, for which I have no evidence at all! All the Synoptics link the incident in the temple with the challenge to Jesus' authority. Jesus replies by linking his own activity with that of John. But those who have rejected the preparation of John will reject the activity of Jesus. Now, according to Mark 1, John is the messenger of Malachi 3:1, who prepares the way of the Lord – the Lord, who (so Malachi tells us) will suddenly come to his temple, who will be like a refiner's fire and fuller's soap, and who will

---

[6] F.C. Burkitt, 'W and Θ: Studies in the Western Text of St Mark (continued)', *JTS* 17 (1916): 139–149.

purify the sons of Levi and purge them like gold and silver. Now none of the evangelists makes use of that part of the quotation. Perhaps it is not surprising, since in Malachi the cleansing is successful, and the refined sons of Levi once more offer acceptable offerings to the Lord. For the evangelists, the cleansing of the temple by Jesus is *un*successful; instead of the reform he asked for, he met opposition, arrest and death. But is the link between Jesus and John the Baptist in that pericope in Mark 11 perhaps a leftover from an earlier tradition, in which the action of Jesus *was* seen as a cleansing, and as the coming to the temple of the Lord whom John had announced? Is Paul's emphasis on the purity of the new temple an echo of this theme?

Maybe not! But what I do suggest is that sayings and actions which are basically hopeful and call for reform, repentance, and renewal can easily be adapted to express judgement and execution. All the images we have explored – the tree, the temple, the vineyard – are essentially images which suggest response, life, fruit; it is only a short step from a call to produce fruit and to offer worship which is worthy of the Lord, to a picture of a barren tree, an unproductive vineyard and a temple in ruins.

17. Creative Conflict: The Torah and Christology

The great majority of the books of the New Testament reflect, to a greater or lesser extent, the controversies between Jews and Christians that marked the emergence of the Christian faith and its separation from Judaism. But to what extent was it Christian claims about Jesus which led to disputes between Christians and Jews regarding the Torah or Law, and to what extent was it disputes regarding the Torah, and Jesus' relation to it, which led to the development and formulation of christological claims? This may well prove to be something of a chicken-and-egg question! Certainly the Gospels suggest that controversy over the Torah was inextricably linked with the question of Jesus' authority from the beginning. The purpose of this essay is to explore that link. Pressures of space mean that our exploration will be confined to the Synoptics. It is a pleasure to offer the essay as a modest tribute to David Catchpole, whose own work on the Synoptic Gospels has contributed so much to our understanding of them.

There are four distinct ways in which Jesus and the Torah are related in the Gospels. First, the Torah – together with the Prophets and the Writings – is understood to be *fulfilled* in Jesus. Each of the evangelists emphasizes, in his own way, that the scriptures point forward to him. Secondly, Jesus is portrayed as himself *faithful* to the commands of the Torah: he fulfils the Torah in the sense that he keeps it. In both these approaches, the authority of the Torah is assumed; their purpose, however, is not to stress the authority of the Torah, but to emphasize the significance of Jesus. Thirdly, the teaching of the Torah is from time to time *challenged* by Jesus, whose authority is demonstrated to be greater than that of the Torah. Fourthly, the era of the Torah is seen as *giving way* to the era of Christ. Although these last two approaches might suggest a break between Torah and Gospel we find, remarkably, that the links are firmly maintained. Seeming challenges to the Torah regularly occur in contexts that affirm the validity of the Torah; the belief that the old has been replaced by the new arises from the assumption that there is continuity between the two: even when the Torah is superseded, it continues to have a role.

1. Mark

In order to trace what is taking place we turn first to Mark which, with the great majority of scholars, we believe to be the earliest Gospel. Although Mark never uses the word νόμος (law), he depicts many controversies regarding its regulations and interpretation, and he shows how scripture in general is fulfilled in the Gospel.

In his opening lines, Mark declares that his story is the fulfilment of prophecy which he attributes to Isaiah (Mark 1:2–3). This theme is echoed in the rest of the Gospel in quotations – the majority of which are also taken from Isaiah – found in the mouth of Jesus. Mark does not always specify that these are quotations, but unless we suppose that he was using tradition without being aware of its significance, and that this therefore represents an early *pre-Marcan* method of handling scripture, he must have considered it unnecessary to spell out its origin. Interestingly, these subsequent quotations are invariably negative: scripture is 'fulfilled' by Israel's hard-heartedness and rejection of God's plan (4:12; 7:6; 11:17); judgement is inevitable (13:24–25). Even the disciples succumb (8:18). Israel's failure leads to Jesus' death (12:10–11; 14:27), and this is said to correspond to what is 'written', even when specific quotations are not given (9:12 ff.; 14:21, 49). The passion narrative itself contains clear allusions to scripture (15:24, 34). The nature of these quotations suggests that the purpose underlying their use was to deal with the major theological problem created by Israel's rejection of 'the gospel about Jesus Christ' and by what Mark believed to be Israel's own rejection by God.

The one quotation that stands apart from this pattern is Ps 110:1, interpreted in 12:35–37 as a 'messianic' prophecy. Yet this is not cited as straightforward 'fulfilment', but raised as a question which hints that 'Davidic' messianism is an inadequate category for Jesus. The passage almost certainly reflects christological debates within the Christian community, as it endeavoured to explain Jesus' status by appealing to Old Testament texts.

Mark portrays Jesus as faithful to the Torah: Jesus 'keeps' the Sabbath by attending synagogue (1:21; 3:1), orders the healed leper to carry out the procedure laid down by Moses (1:44); he celebrates Passover in Jerusalem (14:12–16). In his teaching, Jesus appeals to the Torah – to the commandment to honour father and mother (7:10); to the creation story (10:6–8); to the commandments (10:19); to God's self-revelation to Moses (12:26); to the Shema (12:29–30) and to the demand in Leviticus to love one's neighbour (12:31).

This picture of Jesus as faithful to the Torah helps to demonstrate the falsity of the accusations constantly brought against him by his enemies. Accused by the Pharisees of allowing his disciples to break the Sabbath law (2:23–28), Jesus appeals to the divine purpose behind the Sabbath law – a purpose which is being realized in what he and his disciples are doing. The accusation brought by the Pharisees is false, because what is at issue is the way in which the Sabbath law is interpreted. In the incident that follows this, Jesus counters the unspoken accusation that, by healing, he himself is breaking the Sabbath, with the question 'Is it lawful to do good on the Sabbath, or to do evil? To save life or to kill?' Once again, Jesus points to the purpose underlying the Torah; the story demonstrates that it is he who in fact observes the Law – by giving life – while the Pharisees break it – by plotting how to destroy him.

The first of these stories, however, is less straightforward than the second. The Pharisees' objections are based on their interpretation of the disciples' actions as 'reaping' and 'threshing', and the obvious response would have been that such an interpretation was 'human tradition' (cf. 7:1–23) not 'divine law'. Instead, Jesus is said to have appealed to the action of David and his companions in eating the shewbread, which only priests were allowed to eat (1 Sam 21:1–6). But what is the connection? The only link seems to be the action of eating, but while David's men are described as having been hungry (Mark 2:25), no explanation is given for the disciples' action. Is the meaning, then, that scripture itself does not apply the regulations with the rigidity exercised by the Pharisees? That they are losing sight of the purpose of the Law by concentrating on its details? Yet the fact that Jesus is said to appeal to David is significant, for it suggests that Mark sees it as a statement about Jesus' own authority.[1] It was David and his companions who ate the shewbread, Jesus' companions who eat the grains of wheat. If David and his companions could break the command of the Torah, how much more can Jesus and his companions dispense with the regulations *surrounding* the Law. The comparison is christological – between David and Jesus (who, we learn at 12:35–37 is greater than David) – but the question of authority touches the Torah. The Son of man is not subject to the Sabbath, but is Lord of the Sabbath (2:28).

Leaving aside the question of what light this material might shed on Jesus' own attitude, we can see that these stories reflect disputes between early Christians and Jews. To the former, it seemed clear that Jesus was faithful to the Torah, and that what he rejected was the particular interpretation of its commandments espoused by scribes and Pharisees. Nevertheless, his words and actions presented a radical challenge to traditional assumptions about what the Torah required, and thus raised questions about his authority and identity. To non-Christian Jews, his teaching and behaviour appeared to undermine the Torah, enabling his followers to sit loose to all its commandments.

This clash is demonstrated in chapter 7, where scribes and Pharisees again attack Jesus because of the behaviour of the disciples. This time their criticism concerns the disciples' failure to observe 'the tradition of the elders' which demanded the ceremonial washing of hands before eating, and once again Jesus turns the tables, quoting Isa 29:13 to accuse his opponents of deserting

---

[1] This incident occurs in a section – Mark 1:14–3:6 – which underlines very clearly the authority of Jesus.

the Torah in order to keep the tradition – an accusation that is then backed up with the example of 'corban', which could be used to make void 'the word of God', the commandment to honour father and mother to which Jesus has himself appealed.

So far Jesus is clearly in the right in the eyes of the Torah and his opponents at fault, because they allow concern for the tradition to obscure the demands of the Torah. At this point, however, Jesus seems to challenge the Torah itself, declaring that one cannot be defiled by what one eats (v. 15), an apparent flat contradiction of Leviticus 11. Since the saying is couched in the form 'Not this, but that', however, it may well be an emphatic way of affirming that ritual cleanliness is less important than moral cleanliness (cf. Hos 6:6). Nevertheless, what is 'less important' is part of the Torah, and Jesus is clearly understood to be challenging the attitude which devotes so much attention to those aspects of the Torah that can be easily regulated that the less-easily definable commands are ignored. This is radical teaching, but it is not unique: the saying in v. 15 stands firmly in the prophetic tradition (cf. Hos 6:6; Jer 7:22 ff.). Mark, however, understands it as far more radical still. The 'parable' of v. 15 is explained in subsequent teaching given to the disciples alone (7:17–23), and Mark adds the comment that Jesus thereby 'declared all foods clean': in a Gentile Christian environment, Jesus' words were understood as annulling the Mosaic command. This interpretation clearly cannot be reconciled with Mark's overall presentation of Jesus as *faithful* to the Torah. The fact that it is nevertheless found in the context of a passage where Jesus is presented as more faithful to Moses than the Pharisees demonstrates the way in which the argument developed. The original conviction that Jesus was loyal to the Torah was breaking down, and Jesus' own teaching was being seen as more authoritative than that of Moses.

A similar shift occurs in Mark 10, where Jesus is questioned by the Pharisees as to whether or not divorce is permissible.[2] Jesus replies by asking what Moses commanded, but they respond by referring to what Moses *permitted*. Jesus then appeals to the divine intention for male and female expressed in the creation story (Mark 10:6–8; Gen 1:27; 2:24).[3] This time it is not Mosaic command and human tradition that are in conflict, but the 'command' implicit in the Genesis texts and the permission implicit in Deut 24:1–4. The Mosaic

---

[2] For a detailed discussion of the way in which this story is handled see David R. Catchpole, 'The Synoptic Divorce Material as a Traditio-Historical Problem', *BJRL* 57 (1974): 92–127.

[3] There is an interesting parallel in CD 4.20–5.5, where Gen 1:27 is also quoted, together with Deut 17:17. This passage is sometimes understood to prohibit divorce as well as polygamy; so, e.g., Joseph A. Fitzmyer, 'The Matthean Divorce Texts and Some New Palestinian Evidence', *Theological Studies* 37 (1976): 197–226. The issue there, however (as in 11QTemple 57:17–19), seems to be not marriage after divorce, but marriage to more than one wife, since David is exonerated from blame on the grounds that in his time the book of the Law had not yet been opened.

regulation in Deuteronomy 24, which allows for divorce, is interpreted as a concession, of lesser significance than the divine plan in Genesis.[4] Once again, however, in the subsequent scene, what Jesus teaches his disciples in private appears to challenge the Torah itself, since those who remarry after divorce are said to 'commit adultery' (10:10–12). The antithesis seems to have sharpened and the rule set out in Genesis now precludes altogether the possibility of remarriage implicit in Deuteronomy 24. As with 7:17–23, the setting of this scene 'in the house', where Jesus addresses only his disciples, suggests that we have here Christian reinterpretation of Jesus' teaching. Jesus' authority is again seen as greater than that of Moses.

These are the only two scenes in Mark in which Jesus appears to challenge the teaching of Moses, and the fact that both are presented as explanations of Jesus' teaching, given to the disciples in private, is significant. This was how, in time, the teaching of Jesus was understood by at least some first-century Christians. For the most part, Mark portrays Jesus as challenging the authority of the *teachers* of Torah, the scribes, and Pharisees. The comment at the beginning of the story, in 1:22, that he taught with authority, not as the scribes, is echoed at the end of the Gospel, where it is presented in dramatic form when a scribe questions Jesus, endorses his teaching – and is then himself commended by Jesus (12:28–34): the scribes, who considered themselves the guardians of the Torah, thought it their task to judge Jesus' faithfulness to Torah, but Mark's story suggests that *he* was judging *them*, since his authority was greater. A few verses later, we find Jesus condemning the scribes in general, because they oppress widows while making a public show of piety (Mark 12:38–40; Exod 22:22; cf. Deut 24:17–22; Mal 3:5). In this chapter, too, we find Jesus berating the Sadducees for failing to understand the Torah (12:18–27): they, too, have concentrated on the Mosaic regulations (Deut 25:5–10) and ignored the implications of the divine self-revelation in Exodus 3.

But there are hints in Mark's narrative that support the idea that he thought of Jesus as superior to the Torah itself, and not just to its teachers. He makes a leper clean – something the Law cannot do, though it can authenticate the cure (1:40–45); although Jesus himself commands that the Mosaic regulations should be obeyed, the healed leper does not bother to carry them out: in the new community, the Torah's commands seem irrelevant, since Jesus' power is demonstrably greater than that of the Torah. In the next scene, Jesus declares a man's sins to be forgiven – in marked contrast with the Torah, where sacrifice and ritual cleansing are required. Here too, Jesus is depicted as claiming an authority greater than that of Moses.

---

[4] 'Jesus' restrictive pronouncement, while radical, does not have the same force as would permitting what Moses prohibited', W.D. Davies and E.P. Sanders, 'Jesus: From the Jewish Point of View', in *Cambridge History of Judaism,* vol. 3, eds. William Horbury, W.D. Davies, and John Sturdy (Cambridge: Cambridge University Press, 1999), 656–657.

Moses typology may well lie behind the feeding narratives (6:30–44; 8:1–10), and possibly the miracles on the sea (4:35–41; 6:45–52). If so, however, Mark leaves us to work this out for ourselves. But the story of the transfiguration (9:2–8) reminds us forcefully of the continuity between Moses and Jesus, and the superiority of the latter. Elijah, Moses and Jesus are not equals, as Peter supposes, for it is Jesus alone who is singled out by the divine voice as 'my beloved Son': once they had listened to Moses, but now they are to listen to Jesus.[5]

The new situation is presented in dramatic form in Mark 10:17–22, where a man asks Jesus how to inherit eternal life. Jesus, faithful to the Torah, reminds him of the Mosaic commandments, whereupon he declares that he has kept them all. He lacks only one thing, responds Jesus: he must sell everything he has, give the proceeds to the poor, and follow him. Jesus here plainly endorses the old, but offers something better, the way of Christian discipleship.

These passages suggest, not that Jesus is seen as challenging Moses by overturning his teaching, but rather that Moses is seen as pointing forward to Jesus:[6] the old era is being replaced by the new. The time for fasting has given way to the time for feasting because the bridegroom is here (2:18–20). The appointment of twelve disciples indicates that Israel is being re-formed (3:13–19); Jesus' death is seen as a covenant which brings this community into being (14:24). But the new must not be allowed to destroy the old: the old cloak must not be torn, nor the wineskins be destroyed, even though there is new wine to be enjoyed (2:21–22). Mark seems anxious that the old should be preserved: to change the image, he is determined, not simply to eat his cake, but to have it.[7]

2. Matthew

Matthew presents a similar picture to Mark, but the various elements in it are all intensified. The theme of fulfilment is clearly of prime importance to Matthew, and is seen above all in the ten quotations introduced by a formula explaining that events took place 'in order that what was said through the

---

[5] Cf. Morna D. Hooker, '"What Doest Thou Here, Elijah?" A Look at St Mark's Account of the Transfiguration', in *The Glory of Christ in the New Testament: Studies in Christology in Memory of George Bradford Caird,* eds. L.D. Hurst and N.T. Wright (Oxford: Clarendon, 1987), 59–70 = above, essay 12 (pp. 179–189).

[6] I have argued earlier (see n. 5) that Elijah and Moses are both seen as Jesus' 'forerunners' in Mark.

[7] I have discussed Mark's use of the Pentateuch at greater length in 'Mark's Use of Scripture', originally entitled 'Mark', in *It is Written: Scripture Citing Scripture: Essays in Honour of Barnabas Lindars,* eds. D.A. Carson and H.G.M. Williamson (Cambridge: Cambridge University Press, 1988), 220–230 = above, essay 13 (pp. 190–199).

prophet might be fulfilled'. These various quotations all function as broadly 'messianic' proof-texts: they explain who Jesus is (1:22–23; 2:15; 2:23; 21:4–5 [cf. 21:9]) and the effect of his coming (2:18; 4:14–16); describe the nature of his ministry (8:17; 12:17–21; 13:35) and the price of his betrayal (27:9). A slightly different formula introduces a similar 'messianic' prophecy in 2:5–6, and another the quotation from Isa 40:3 which identifies John as the forerunner in 3:3 (cf. Mark 1:3). Other quotations showing how scripture is being fulfilled are found in the mouth of Jesus at 11:10 (// Mark 1:2); 13:14–15 (cf. Mark 4:12); 15:7–9; 21:13 (// Mark 11:17); 21:16; 21:42 (// Mark 12:10–11); 22:44 (// Mark 12:36); 24:29 (// Mark 13:24–25); 26:31 (// Mark 14:27). Elsewhere, there are clear allusions to scripture being fulfilled (11:2–6; 24:15; 26:54, 56).

Jesus is depicted as living by the Torah: tempted by the devil, he repeatedly quotes from Deuteronomy (4:4, 7, 10; Deut 8:3; 6:13, 16); twice, in disputes with the Pharisees, he complains that they do not understand the saying 'I desire mercy, not sacrifice' (9:13; 12:7; Hos 6:6). Clearest of all is 5:17–20, where he declares that he has come to fulfil the Law and the Prophets, not to abolish them. As with the Qumran community, it is Law and Prophets together that must be obeyed.[8] None of the commandments can be annulled. It is hardly surprising then, that Matthew modifies the implications of Mark 7 and 10. In the story of the dispute about handwashing, Matthew records, in different words from Mark's, the saying that 'it is not what enters the mouth that defiles a person, but what comes out of the mouth', but it is quite clear from the subsequent conversation that 'what enters the mouth' is understood to refer back to the original question about eating with unwashed hands, not to 'clean' and 'unclean' food (Matt 15:1–20). Jesus is not challenging the Law but, as in 9:13 and 12:7, insisting that 'mercy' is more important than 'sacrifice'.[9] The account of the question about divorce has also been modified, and the order in which the Old Testament passages are quoted has been reversed, so that the rule is mentioned before the concession (Matt 19:3–9). In his response Jesus appeals immediately to Gen 1:27 and 2:24, which he interprets as a prohibition of divorce. Asked about Moses' provision for divorce he replies, as in Mark, that this was because of their hardness of heart; nevertheless, anyone who divorced his wife *except for unchastity* and married someone else committed adultery. In first-century Judaism this position would not have been seen as challenging the Law, but as supporting the interpretation of Shammai, who held that Deut 24:1–4 permitted divorce only on the grounds of unchastity.

---

[8] 1QS 1:2–3: the members of the community are to 'do what is good and right before [God] as He commanded by the hand of Moses and all his servants the Prophets' (Vermes' translation).
[9] Cf. also 23:23.

In both these scenes, Matthew has retained Mark's picture of general teaching followed by teaching addressed specifically to the disciples, even though this special teaching is no longer given in private. This continues the pattern he has already set in the Sermon on the Mount, where Jesus teaches his disciples (5:1), although the crowds are present and listening (7:28). The implication is that all are invited to respond, though few will be able to accept this more difficult teaching. In 15:12–20, Jesus merely spells out the meaning of the saying in v. 11 which his disciples ought to have understood (v. 16), but in 19:10–12 the disciples' question leads to teaching on a somewhat different subject – those who adopt celibacy for the sake of the kingdom. This certainly goes beyond anything that the Law required, but suggests that Matthew saw the kingdom as presenting demands far greater than the Torah.

The teaching on divorce in Matt 19:3–9 is similar to that which forms the third of the six antitheses in Matthew 5. These antitheses present a contrast between what was said in the past (i.e. by Moses) and what Jesus now says. Is Jesus, like a Jewish rabbi, simply contrasting previous interpretation of the Torah with his own?[10] The emphatic ἐγὼ δὲ λέγω ὑμῖν suggests that what Jesus is presenting is more than mere 'interpretation' of the Torah. Is he then challenging the teaching of Moses? Matthew cannot have believed this, since the antitheses follow immediately after 5:17–20.[11] In fact, none of the antitheses contradicts the teaching of Moses; on the contrary, they all intensify it. What is true of the teaching on divorce is true of the antitheses in general: *Jesus forbids what is permitted in Torah, but he does not permit what is forbidden.* Not only are murder and adultery forbidden, but anger and lust as well; divorce – except for adultery – is ruled out; not only is false swearing prohibited but oaths of any kind; the Law that limited revenge is insufficient – there should be no revenge at all; love for one's neighbour must be extended to embrace one's enemy as well.

Although Matthew's Jesus does not challenge the teaching of Moses, he does far more here than simply interpret its meaning, since his words stand in contrast to those of Moses. What he is demanding of his followers is a righteousness greater than that of scribes and Pharisees (5:20), a righteousness greater than anything that Moses demands. But on what authority? Matthew has already given us the clues. In his opening chapters, the story of Herod's attempt on the life of Jesus, the Massacre of the Innocents and Jesus' escape to Egypt all echo the story of Moses. Now, however, Jesus emerges as greater

---

[10] Cf. David Daube's discussion of the rabbinic formula in *The New Testament and Rabbinic Judaism* (London: Athlone Press, 1956), 55–62.

[11] For a recent discussion of these issues, see W.D. Davies and Dale C. Allison, *A Critical and Exegetical Commentary on the Gospel According to Saint Matthew*, vol. 1, ICC (Edinburgh: T&T Clark, 1988), 505–509.

than Moses. Like Moses, he ascends a mountain,[12] but whereas Moses stayed on the mountain for forty days and then descended to pass on the teaching he had received to the people, Jesus sits down *on* the mountain, and his disciples come to him there. If the setting suggests that Jesus is for Matthew a 'new Moses', it also suggests that he is *superior* to Moses, and that the teaching he gives is closer to the source of divine revelation, being delivered from the mountain itself. The teaching of Jesus is delivered to the disciples, the people who have left everything to follow him (4:18–22) – much as the Israelites abandoned everything to follow Moses – and they form the nucleus of a new community (cf. 19:28). The Sermon begins with the Beatitudes – the blessings God gives his people; like the story in Exodus, grace precedes demand, for Moses also, when he came *down* the mountain, began by reminding the people of what God had done for them and told them of the blessings he was now promising them (Exod 19:3–7). Two short sayings then describe the role of God's people: their task is to be the salt of the earth and the light of the world. Both sayings contain a reference to possible failure to carry out the task – is this a criticism of Israel? Both sayings indicate that the task is now seen as a universal one.

The teaching Jesus gives is new, because it is the fulfilment of both Law and Prophets (v. 17), but precisely *as* their fulfilment, it does not destroy them. What Jesus demands does not contradict Torah but surpasses it, because what he demands from his followers is nothing less than perfection (v. 48). The commands are *his* commands, as we are reminded by the repeated use of the phrase '... but *I* say to you ...'. To be sure, we are reminded at the end that allegiance to Jesus is insufficient, and that what is required from men and women is obedience to God's will (7:21–23); but it is *Jesus* who will sit in judgement, and who will vindicate or reject! This idea is spelt out at length at the end of the Gospel, when Jesus describes the judgement carried out by the Son of man when he comes in glory as king (25:31–46). And the sermon closes with the parable of the wise and foolish builders; the man who builds on rock is not the man who obeys Torah, but the man who hears *these words of mine* and does them. The choice reminds us of the one placed before Israel after the giving of the Law (Lev 26; Deut 30:15–20). No wonder Matthew ends with the comment that Jesus taught with authority, not like the scribes!

The Jesus who delivers the Sermon on the Mount does not challenge the Mosaic law: on the contrary, he confirms the Law, for not an iota or a tittle will be abolished until heaven and earth pass away. Nevertheless, those who are Jesus' disciples and who belong to the new community obey *his* words – words which, like the word of God himself (Isa 40:8; Ps 119:89), will endure even *after* heaven and earth pass away (24:35). The era of the Torah is giving

---

[12] The phrase is used repeatedly of Moses in the LXX: e.g. Exod 19:3; 24:15; 34:4.

way to the era of Christ, for 'the prophets and the Law prophesied' until the coming of John, whose arrival announced the coming of Jesus himself (11:7–15). This strange statement in 11:13, with the prophets preceding the Law, and the use of the verb 'prophesied', betrays Matthew's concerns.[13] Prophets and Law are not abolished in the new era but fulfilled. When the era of Christ *finally* takes over, the Torah given through Moses will no longer be necessary. But that time has not yet come, for the rule of heaven is at present subject to violent attack (11:12). In the meantime, the regulations of the Law should be observed (e.g. 5:23; 17:27; 24:20).[14]

Confirmation of our understanding of the Sermon on the Mount is found in Matt 11:25–30. The thanksgiving in v. 25 reminds us of the Beatitudes: it is the νηπίοι, the simple, to whom 'these things' have been revealed. In the LXX psalms, the νηπίοι are God's faithful ones, who receive wisdom in the shape of the Law (Ps 18:8 [19:7]; 118 [119]:130). Now the wisdom comes from Jesus, who is the source of revelation, for 'all things have been handed over' to the Son by the Father (v. 27). The mutual knowledge of Father and Son is strongly reminiscent, it has been suggested, of the reciprocal knowledge requested by Moses in Exod 33:12–13 (cf. Deut 34:10), the promise of rest (v. 28) of the promise in Exod 33:14.[15] But now the mutual knowledge is between the Father and the Son. Does this passage, then, contrast the revelation to God's servant Moses and the revelation through the Son? If so, it points us in the direction of John 1:17 and Heb 1:1–2; 3:1–6: in Matthew's setting at least, this passage well deserves its description as a 'Johannine thunderbolt'! The Son reveals the Father (cf. John 1:18) to those whom he chooses. The rest is now given *by Jesus*, and he summons men and women to take up *his* yoke. Jer 5:5 speaks of the Torah as a yoke, and Sirach 51:26 of the yoke of wisdom, which is identified with the Torah. Now Jesus offers his yoke, for he is himself wisdom (Matt 11:19); Jesus is authentic Torah, 'the full revelation of God and of his will for man'.[16]

---

[13] See David R. Catchpole, 'The Law and the Prophets in Q', in *Tradition and Interpretation in the New Testament: Essays in Honor of E. Earle Ellis for His 60th Birthday*, eds. Gerald F. Hawthorne with Otto Betz (Grand Rapids: Eerdmans, 1987), 95–109.

[14] Each of these passages raises problems. How are we to understand the reference to sacrifice in 5:23, since Matthew was writing after 70 CE? Can 17:27 be construed as an attack on the regulation in Exod 30:13, or does it reflect the view that the tax should be given only once in a lifetime, not annually (cf. 4Q159)? Does 24:20 assume that flight on the Sabbath is impossible, or merely that it would offend Jewish neighbours? On this last point, see Graham N. Stanton, *A Gospel for a New People: Studies in Matthew* (Edinburgh: T&T Clark, 1992), 192–206.

[15] See W.D. Davies and Dale C. Allison, *A Critical and Exegetical Commentary on the Gospel According to Saint Matthew*, vol. 2, ICC (Edinburgh: T&T Clark, 1991), 271–297, and literature cited there.

[16] Davies and Allison, *Matthew*, vol. 2, 290.

Matthew uses much of the Marcan material we have looked at with very little alteration, but there are one or two significant changes. In 9:17 he underlines the meaning of the parable about the wine and wineskins with the words 'and both are preserved'. To the teaching on parables he adds the saying in 13:52 about the scribe who rightly treasures 'what is new and what is old'. In Matt 12:1–8 Matthew has retained the strange reference to David eating the shewbread, but has made the conversation more relevant to the matter under debate, first by noting that the disciples, too, were hungry, and secondly and more significantly by adding another example – that of the priests, who 'break the Sabbath' (12:5, presumably by offering the Sabbath sacrifice, and so working on the Sabbath, Num 28:9–10). The argument now runs smoothly: the Pharisees have failed to understand the principles set out in Hos 6:6: 'I desire mercy, and not sacrifice'. The priests 'break the Sabbath' in order to serve the temple, but 'something greater than the temple is here', and that 'something greater' appears to be Jesus himself, 'for the Son of man is Lord of the Sabbath' (cf. 12:38–42). Another interesting change is found in Matt 19:16–22 (// Mark 10:17–22), where a man asks Jesus how to possess eternal life. Instead of addressing Jesus as 'Good Teacher' as in Mark, he asks Jesus 'what good deed' is necessary. Matthew thus avoids the danger of interpreting Jesus' reply as a denial that he is good. There is one who is good, and his commandments are plain, and must be obeyed: nevertheless, if the man wishes to be perfect, he must sell everything and follow Jesus. The story neatly encapsulates the message of the Sermon on the Mount. Finally, we note that in 22:41–46 the question about the significance of Ps 110:1 is addressed to the Pharisees and given a new introduction: 'What is your opinion about the Messiah? Whose son is he?' The implication, of course, is that he is not son of David, but Son of God (cf. 11:27; 28:19).

As in Mark, it is those who *teach* the Law who are condemned, notably in Matthew 23, where Jesus pronounces woe on scribes and Pharisees. But this passage is introduced with the command to do whatever the scribes and Pharisees teach, since they sit on Moses' seat (23:2). One must do what they say, but not what they do, since their actions show them to be hypocrites.

There is just one passage in Matthew which could be interpreted as a challenge to the Law itself. This is 8:21–22, where a disciple is forbidden permission to bury his father before following Jesus. Does this contradict the teaching in Matt 15:1–20 (cf. Mark 7:1–23), where Jesus himself condemns the Pharisees and scribes for not observing the commandment to honour one's parents? It seems unlikely that Matthew would have understood it in that way. Are we perhaps to suppose that the man's father was not yet dead, and that he is simply offering an excuse for postponing his commitment to Jesus? Or does Jesus' reply reflect rather the importance of the enterprise on which he is engaged? When God's call demands, then certain obligations under the Law no longer apply (cf. Lev 21:11; Num 6:6; Jer 16:1–9; Ezek 24:15–18; Matt 10:37). If this is how we should understand the saying, then it is similar to others in which one demand in the Law is weighed over against another.

Matthew has emphasized three of the four themes found in Mark: the fourth is firmly refuted. He has shown how Jesus fulfils the Torah and is faithful to Torah; he has shown also that Jesus' authority is greater than the authority of Moses; at the same time, he has stressed that Jesus in no way challenges Moses' teaching. Nevertheless, though the Torah will last while heaven and earth endure, it will finally be subsumed in the era of Christ.

Yet for Jesus' followers, members of the new community, his teaching has already taken over, and nowhere is that clearer than in the closing verses of the Gospel. Allusions to the Moses tradition have often been found in this story,[17] but there is one aspect of this that seems to have escaped attention. The scene is reminiscent not only of those in which Moses commissioned Joshua (Deut 31:14–15, 23; Josh 1:1–9) but, even more importantly, of Moses' own commissioning in Exodus 3, and his return in Exodus 19–20 to receive the Law. In Exodus 3, Moses meets with God and is commanded to bring his people out of Egypt: when he protests that he is unfit for the task, God replies 'I am with you' (Exod 3:12) and tells Moses to return with the people to the same mountain and worship him there. God then reveals his name as 'I am who I am'. If the parallel between that story and Matthew's has largely gone unnoticed, that is because in the latter Jesus is the one who commissions, not the one who is commissioned: it is *Jesus* who meets the disciples on the mountain that he has appointed (though Matthew has made no previous reference to this!) and who is worshipped by them there – even though some doubted, much as Moses and the Israelites doubted. Jesus has been given all authority, not only on earth but in heaven, and it is with that authority – the authority of God himself – that he acts here. It is *he* therefore, who sends the disciples out to make disciples of the nations, so creating a new community. Moses received the Law and passed it on to the people, but the disciples have been instructed by Jesus, and now it is *they* who are commanded to pass on *his* teaching. The God who revealed himself to Moses was the God of the Jewish patriarchs, the God of Abraham, Isaac and Jacob, and his name was 'I am'; now this God is revealed as 'Father, Son and Holy Spirit', and it is into this name that all nations are to be baptized. But he is still 'I am'! Moses was sent to Pharaoh with the promise 'I am with you' (Exod 3:12), even before he understood the significance of the divine name (3:14), and now Jesus' promise to the disciples – 'I am with you always' – echoes that promise and that name. The echo can hardly be accidental, for in Matt 1:23 we were told

---

[17] For details, see W.D. Davies and Dale C. Allison, *A Critical and Exegetical Commentary on the Gospel According to Saint Matthew*, vol. 3, ICC (Edinburgh: T&T Clark, 1997), 676–687.

that Jesus' birth fulfilled the words of Isa 7:14, including the promise that 'they shall call his name Emmanuel'. The reference to this promise followed somewhat strangely after the angel's instruction to call the child 'Jesus', but Matthew certainly intended to include the whole quotation from Isaiah, for he spells out the word's meaning – 'God with us'. He has, in fact, made one slight alteration to the LXX version, changing the singular καλέσεις to the plural καλέσουσιν: this part of the promise will be fulfilled, not at Jesus' birth, but when Christian believers come to acknowledge him as 'God with us'.[18] Now, at the close of Matthew's Gospel, the words are fulfilled in Jesus' own promise 'I am with you'.[19]

3. Luke

In Luke, the emphasis is very much on the fulfilment of scripture, and though there is opposition from Jesus' fellow Jews, there is no hint of conflict with the Law itself. The emphasis on fulfilment is seen in the opening chapters – not, indeed, in 'fulfilment' quotations, as in Matthew, but in the allusions that pervade the whole account, and which clearly show Jesus to be the fulfilment of God's promises. There are just three references to 'the Law', all in 2:22–24, and all referring, not to the way in which prophecies were fulfilled in Jesus, but to the way in which Jesus – through his parents – fulfilled the regulations of the Law. Mary and Joseph did what the Law required, bringing Jesus to Jerusalem to present him to the Lord, and making the appropriate sacrifice. They are shown to have been a pious, law-abiding family, observing the Passover (2:41), as indeed was Jesus himself, attending synagogue on the Sabbath 'as was his custom' (4:16). As in Matthew, Jesus quotes scripture in his conflict with Satan (4:4, 8, 12), for he lives in accordance with the Law. At his death, the centurion declares him to be righteous (23:47), innocent of the charges brought against him.

Luke has just one 'fulfilment' prophecy, but that dominates the first few chapters of Jesus' ministry. The long quotation from Isaiah 61 in 4:16–19 is placed in the mouth of Jesus himself, and forms the agenda for the material from 4:31–7:23. On hearing Jesus' words, 'all in the synagogue' are enraged and attempt to kill him: their objection is not to anything that Jesus has yet done, but to the claim that he is the promised anointed prophet of Isaiah 61. The theme of fulfilment is implicit in Jesus' message to John the Baptist in 7:18–23 and in 9:31, where he discusses his coming 'exodus' with Moses and Elijah.

---

[18] See Graham Stanton, 'Matthew', in *It is Written* (see n. 7), 215.

[19] I hope to explore the ideas set out in this paragraph in a forthcoming book on the theme of 'endings'.

Luke's presentation of Jesus in the role of a prophet serves to emphasize the continuity of what is taking place with God's self-revelation in the past. In 4:24, and again in 13:33, Jesus himself accepts that prophetic role: both passages refer to rejection and death. He is acknowledged by the people as a prophet (7:16; 9:8, 19; 24:19; cf. 7:39). Specifically, he is linked with Elijah (and Elisha) in 4:25–27; the story in 7:11–17 echoes stories about Elijah and Elisha (1 Kings 17:17–24; 2 Kings 4:32–37) and 9:59–62 the call of Elisha by Elijah (1 Kings 19:19–21); the people think that he may be Elijah (9:8, 19). Like Elijah (2 Kings 2:1–12), Jesus will be 'taken up' (9:51). There are hints, too, that he is seen as the prophet like Moses (cf. 9:35; Deut 18:15), for in the long journey to Jerusalem which begins in 9:51 there are possible echoes of the story of Moses.[20]

Towards the end of the story, Luke emphasizes that what happens to Jesus was 'written by the prophets' (18:31; 22:37), and in the closing scenes the risen Christ explains the things written about himself in all the scriptures, 'beginning from Moses and all the prophets' (24:27, 44–45).

In Luke, all suggestion that Jesus might be challenging Moses has vanished. The squabble about unwashed hands (Mark 7:1–23 // Matt 15:1–20) is absent, and the argument about divorce is reduced to a single saying (16:18). Without the setting of controversy provided by Mark and Matthew, it would not have occurred to Luke's readers that the prohibition of divorce and remarriage might be held to contradict Moses. Luke provides his own setting:[21] first, we have the saying in v. 16 that contrasts the era of the Law and Prophets, which lasted 'until John', with the new era, in which the rule of God is proclaimed, and everyone is eager to accept it. The urgent necessity of proclaiming and entering the kingdom is demonstrated in Jesus' sayings to would-be disciples in 9:57–62. The saying in v. 17 makes clear that this does not mean that the Law is therefore obsolete: on the contrary, what the Law demands accords with the demands of the kingdom, and v. 18 is presumably meant to illustrate this! Luke is clearly not interested in the niceties of rabbinic debate, and sees the ethical issues as paramount. The parable that follows hints at the continuity between the demands of the Torah and the demands of the kingdom. The rich man ignored the needs of the poor: he, like his brothers, has ignored 'Moses and the prophets', but those who ignore Moses and the prophets will fail to listen, 'even if someone rises from the dead' (16:29–31).

In Luke, the so-called 'Johannine thunderbolt' is found in a passage which stresses the theme of fulfilment (10:17–24). It follows the account of the

---

[20] Cf. C.F. Evans, 'The Central Section of St. Luke's Gospel', in *Studies in the Gospels: Essays in Memory of R.H. Lightfoot,* ed. D.E. Nineham (Oxford: Blackwell, 1957), 37–53.

[21] The three sayings in 16:16–18 are all found in totally different settings in Matthew. Either Luke has brought the sayings together himself, or he has taken the combination over from 'Q' (so David R. Catchpole, *The Quest for Q* [Edinburgh: T&T Clark, 1993], 235).

return of the Seventy and Jesus' vision of the fall of Satan from heaven, and it is followed, not by sayings about finding rest and accepting Jesus' yoke, but by Jesus' declaration that the disciples are blessed, because they see and hear what many prophets and kings longed in vain to see and hear.

Luke sees no conflict between the Torah and the gospel. The teaching in the Sermon on the Plain (6:17–49), though similar to that in the Sermon on the Mount, is not contrasted with previous teaching. There are, to be sure, many incidents in which the Pharisees are depicted as rejecting Jesus' teaching, a theme which is continued in Acts, where 'the Jews' continually reject the gospel. The Pharisees, in turn, come under attack from Jesus. But the problem of reconciling Jesus' teaching with that of Moses is no longer a real one.[22]

The change is demonstrated by Luke's remarkable version of the saying about patching a garment (5:36). No one, we are told, takes a patch out of a new garment in order to mend an old one! The absurd image reveals Luke's concern lest the gospel be treated as a 'repair job' on Judaism: he is worried, not about losing the old, but about destroying the new. The new must be recognized for what it is. The saying, absurd as it is, reminds us (like that in 16:16) that something essentially *new* has happened: its meaning now corresponds with that of the parable about new wine which cannot be contained in old wineskins (5:37–38). In view of this, v. 39 must be seen as an ironic comment, not a commendation of the old wine! Whatever the origin of this saying, it is an appropriate description of the reaction of Jesus' contemporaries to his message.

4. Synthesis

Can we draw any conclusions from this brief survey?

Underlying all the Gospels we have tradition which indicates that Jesus spoke and acted with an authority that led to conflict during his lifetime. This authority and this conflict inevitably raised questions regarding his identity in the minds of his contemporaries. Whether or not these questions were formulated in christological terms, they would certainly have included the suggestion that he was a prophet.[23]

Mark suggests that the conflict continued in arguments between Christians and Jews, and that Jesus' authority was now being linked with particular

---

[22] There are, however, echoes of this controversy in Acts, where the charge of prophesying that Jesus will destroy the temple and overturn the Mosaic teaching is brought against Stephen in Acts 6:14; his subsequent speech ignores the charge and demonstrates that it is his *accusers* who are guilty of rejecting the demands and promises of God.

[23] For some of the evidence, see Morna D. Hooker, *The Signs of a Prophet* (London: SCM Press, 1997).

christological claims. Jesus acted as the Son of man, as someone like David, as one with greater authority than Moses. The transfiguration shows Jesus to be not only the successor of Elijah and Moses but greater than they, since he is the Son of God – for Mark the most significant of all the christological titles. Mark maintains that Jesus himself was in agreement with Moses, and that his only disagreement was with the interpreters of Moses. Nevertheless, he recognizes that, in the context of the Gentile mission, Jesus' teaching in effect overruled that of Moses (7:19).

Matthew has faced up to the problem that Mark failed to solve. Writing in a Jewish milieu, the situation of conflict is more obvious, the response more consistent. Matthew emphasizes the theme of fulfilment, but insists that the old has not been overthrown. His solution to the tension between old and new is to trace the continuity between Moses and Jesus in terms of partial and complete revelation. Moses instructed the Jews in what he was given, but he did not see the whole picture, which is now revealed to Christians by Jesus, who is not simply a teacher or a prophet but the source of the Torah. As the controversy intensifies, so the christological claims are sharpened. Matthew develops Mark's link between the idea that Jesus is greater than Moses and the revelation that he is Son of God: Jesus is the Son who reveals the Father, he is 'God with us'. Of course Jesus is greater than Moses! Nevertheless, Moses' teaching is endorsed, even while it is superseded.

Luke presents a very different story. His emphasis is on the theme of fulfilment, on the way in which the story of Jesus continues the story of Israel, and on how the Law and Prophets and writings point forward to Jesus. Although he uses some of the 'controversy stories' showing Jesus in conflict with scribes and Pharisees, there is little indication that he was involved in Jewish-Christian wrangling about possible conflicts between Moses and Jesus. His Christology is the Christology of fulfilment: Jesus is the expected prophet, the expected Messiah, he is Son of God, Lord, and Servant. But the era of Jesus succeeds the era of the Law and the Prophets, and the demands of the Torah are not relevant to Luke's Gentile community. Although in Acts Luke shows that Christians were still endeavouring to persuade the Jews that Jesus was the fulfilment of Israel's hope (Acts 28:20), the break between the Jewish and Christian communities is clear.

And what of the Fourth Gospel? To complete this survey, we would need to look at this also. Were we able to do so, we would find there the theme of fulfilment, not simply in the many references to scripture,[24] but in the introductory prologue in 1:1–18, and in the very Johannine presentation of Jesus 'fulfilling' the Law by offering to men and women everything that was offered

---

[24] See 1:23, 51; 2:17; 6:45; 7:38; 10:34; 12:13, 15, 38, 40; 13:18; 15:25; 17:12; 19:24, 28, 36, 37; 20:9.

not only in the Law (e.g. in the images of manna, water, light, and life[25]), but in the feasts (in particular the offering of Jesus as the true Passover lamb[26]) and in the worship of the temple (4:23). Jesus is clearly greater than Moses and the Torah – indeed, this theme dominates the Gospel (1:17–18) – but there is no contradiction between old and new, since the same divine λόγος, which spoke in creation and through Moses, was 'made flesh' in Christ (1:14). Moses pointed forward to Christ (5:39–47; 7:19–24), who is far greater than himself – and than Abraham too – since he is 'I am' (8:58).

Many studies have shown that John's Gospel reflects conflict between Christians and Jews, and some have attempted to trace the way in which his theology evolved from that situation.[27] It is surely no accident that Matthew, also facing opposition from fellow Jews,[28] and attempting to hold together old and new, developed a profound Christology which, though it is not spelt out in the Johannine manner, is remarkably similar.[29] Christology like this would certainly have led to further controversy, but controversy itself was undoubtedly one of the creative forces which helped to shape this Christology.

---

[25] 6:5–59; 4:1–15; 7:38–39; 19:34; 1:1–18; 3:19–21; 11:25, etc.

[26] 1:29, 36; 18:28; 19:36.

[27] See, in particular, John Ashton, *Understanding the Fourth Gospel* (Oxford: Clarendon, 1991).

[28] The situations are not, of course, identical. In John's time, the split between the two communities has taken place, and the opponents are 'the Jews', not 'the Pharisees'.

[29] Similar also, it should be added, to many Pauline passages, written after similar arguments with his fellow Jews.

18. Uncomfortable Words: The Prohibition of Foreign Missions (Matt 10:5–6)

'Go nowhere among the Gentiles ...'

The command of Jesus to his disciples to concentrate their mission upon the Jewish nation and *not* to evangelize the Gentile world is certainly a saying which Christians are likely to find 'uncomfortable'. Apart from queries which it may raise about the whole course of Christian history and the continuing missionary work of the church, the words offend our belief in the unlimited compassion of Jesus: they are, to say the least, surprising on the lips of one who has been proclaimed for nineteen centuries as *Salvator Mundi*. Their offence is, of course, no new problem; the early fathers found them perplexing, and resorted to allegory, but this attempt to remove the difficulty was unable to provide a lasting solution.

The saying has no parallel in the other Gospels, and is found in Matthew in the mission-charge to the Twelve, which forms the second of the major discourses of Jesus in this Gospel. This discourse includes a variety of material, some of which is paralleled in the other Synoptics. Matthew 10:5–16 gives Jesus' instructions regarding the mission, much of which is similar to the parallel passages in Mark 6:7 ff. and Luke 9:1 ff. and 10:1 ff. Verses 17–22 refer to persecution, and much of this section seems more appropriate to a later period than to a mission set in the course of Jesus' own lifetime – and indeed the parallel sections in Mark 13 and Luke 21 are found in a context where Jesus is pointing forward to a time of future conflict, when his disciples are likely to follow the pattern of his own suffering. The sayings which makeup the rest of the chapter also seem more appropriate if they refer to this later period.

The relationship between the various Synoptic accounts at this point is complex; but if one is correct in assuming Marcan priority, then Matthew appears to have gathered together a variety of material, combining Mark's account of the mission of the Twelve with another account (which Luke prefers to keep separate), and adding to this a number of other sayings on the theme of discipleship and persecution.[1]

---

[1] Already in vv. 2–4 he has inserted into Mark's account the names of the disciples, which Mark gives in a separate section at 3:13–19.

There are perhaps three possible explanations of the presence of Matt 10:5b–6 here. One is that it is an isolated saying – possibly a variant of Matt 15:24 – which Matthew has placed in this appropriate setting, having prepared for its use in Matt 9:36; its appropriateness is, however, somewhat marred by its proximity to the saying in v. 16, where the disciples are themselves likened to sheep sent among wolves! Its insertion by Matthew as the opening words of the discourse might however perhaps be partly explained by the fact that Mark's account of the sending out of the Twelve contains at this point the phrase which opens our saying – εἰς ὁδόν, Mark 6:8, meaning here 'for the journey' – though of course this link might have been made at a pre-Matthean stage rather than by Matthew himself.

A second possibility is that the saying was part of the non-Marcan version of the commissioning of disciples which seems to lie behind Luke 9:2 and 10:3–16, and that Luke omitted the saying for obvious reasons. If so, then this version apparently included both the reference to Israel as sheep, and that to the disciples as sheep among wolves (10:3),[2] but since Matthew was happy with this inconsistency, we cannot rule out the possibility that it was found also in the tradition which he and Luke used. It is noteworthy that whereas Matthew has the saying about sheep among wolves at the end of his section, Luke places it at the beginning of the discourse in 10:3, where it forms a striking introduction, but is not really relevant to the commands in verses 4 ff. It seems probably that Luke has changed the position, rather than Matthew; if so, then this lends some support to the possibility that the 'Q' version began with the saying now found in Matt 10:5–6, and that Luke replaced it by this other saying about sheep. In this case Matthew saw the saying preserved in 10:16 as a suitable introduction to the material about persecution which he has placed in verses 17 ff. – though one could indeed argue that it was for this very reason that *Matthew* altered the position of the saying from the beginning and that Luke's positioning is therefore the unedited one!

A third possibility is that the saying is due to the Matthean editing, and is intended to show that the disciples of Jesus were bound by the same limits as those which applied to Jesus; this might seem more likely if the commissioning of the disciples *followed* the similar saying in 15:24 rather than preceded it. The possibility of a Matthean origin is of course dependent upon the meaning of the saying and whether it reflects a Matthean viewpoint, and we must return to this question.

In the setting supplied by Matthew, the command effectively limits the sphere of the disciples' operations to Galilee, which was surrounded by Gentile territory on all sides except the south, where lay Samaria. The phrase

---

[2] Unless – as seems less likely – the latter was a separate saying, which has been independently added to the section by both Matthew and Luke.

εἰς ὁδόν reflects an Aramaic idiom meaning 'towards', 'to', which the AV and RV have translated too literally; the anarthrous εἰς πόλιν Σαμαριτῶν (into a city of [the] Samaritans) is probably also to be explained from the Aramaic, where one word can mean both city and province, and has apparently been incorrectly translated into Greek. We may therefore translate, with Jeremias:[3]

> Go not to the Gentiles,
> and enter not the province of Samaria;
> but go rather to the lost sheep of the house of Israel.

The reference to sheep not only echoes Jesus' words in Matt 9:36, but reflects the language of Jeremiah 50:6 and Ezekiel 34:6, 11 ff.; the genitive can be either partitive or explanatory, but in view of the contrast with non-Jews it is more probably the latter, the whole of Israel being regarded as 'lost'. The commissioning of the twelve disciples also implies, of course, a mission to the whole of Israel, and this is the more remarkable when it is remembered that the nine and a half tribes of the Northern Kingdom were 'lost' or scattered in a more literal sense: the sending of twelve apostles to the lost sheep of Israel suggests, symbolically, the gathering together of the twelve tribes at the eschaton. This idea has already been introduced in the image of the harvest in 9:37 ff., which represents the eschaton. If the disciples are sent out as harvest workers (i.e. reapers) as Matthew's ordering of his material clearly indicates, then they are not 'missionaries' in the usual sense of those who sow the seed. Rather, by offering a final opportunity to Israel, they act (like the angels in Jewish apocalyptic literature) as those who bring God's judgement, sifting the elect from those who are rejected.[4]

This eschatological note is dominant in the other difficult saying which is found in this chapter, at 10:23, a verse which also seems to be an isolated *logion,* since it is embedded in material which has parallels in the other Gospels. Verses 17–22 are closely parallel to Mark 13:9–13, part of which is found also in Matt 24, and it seems that Matthew has either chosen to incorporate the Marcan material at an earlier point, or followed a very similar tradition; since Matt 10:23a is reminiscent of Mark 13:14b // Matt 24:16, it is tempting to suggest that the whole of vv. 17–23a formed one unit of tradition, and that v. 23b has been attached to it because it contains words echoing the vocabulary of the previous section;[5] the separate saying, in vv. 24 ff. (// Luke 6:40), follows naturally after the references to persecution and to the Son

---

[3] Joachim Jeremias, *Jesus' Promise to the Nations,* trans. S. H. Hooke (London: SCM Press, 1958), 19 ff.

[4] Cf. Ferdinand Hahn, *Mission in the New Testament,* trans. Frank Clarke (London: SCM Press, 1965), 40 ff.

[5] Matt 10:22 ... εἰς τέλος ... (v. 23a) ἐν τῇ πόλει ταύτῃ ... (v. 23b) οὐ μὴ τελέσητε τὰς πόλεις τοῦ Ἰσραὴλ ...

of man. One may perhaps make the further, tentative suggestion that v. 23b originally belonged to our saying in vv. 5b–6, for it seems to explain and complete the injunction of Jesus to his disciples.[6]

But these proposals can only be speculative, and we must consider what Matthew himself has done with the material, and how he understood it. We have already referred to the saying very similar to Matt 10:6 in 15:24, where Jesus protests that his own mission is to the lost sheep of Israel alone and does not include the Gentiles; nevertheless, the point of the narrative is that in spite of this limitation, the Gentile woman is permitted a share in the benefits of the kingdom, because of her faith. Her case is exceptional however: the woman herself according to Matthew's account acknowledges from the outset the sphere of Jesus' mission when she addresses him as 'Son of David'; and in his own ministry, Jesus is depicted as adhering to the limits which he imposes on the Twelve. He withdraws into Gentile territory,[7] but does not preach there, and he does not enter Samaria.

There are, however, more positive references to the share of the Gentiles in the messianic blessings. In Matt 8:11 ff. Jesus declares that 'many will come from east and west and sit at table with Abraham, Isaac, and Jacob in the kingdom of heaven, while the sons of the kingdom will be thrown into the outer darkness'; both the antithesis within the saying, and the context given to it by Matthew, make it clear that the 'many' here refers to Gentiles. A similar antithesis between the rejected sons of the kingdom and those who take their place is found in 21:43 which underlines the meaning of the parable of the vineyard servants. Hope for the Gentiles is also offered in 25:31–46, in the so-called 'parable' of the sheep and goats, where it is 'all the nations' who are judged, and the righteous are given the kingdom prepared for them 'from the foundation of the world'. Constant application of this passage to Christian communities has obscured the fact that as it stands in Matthew the narrative refers to the Gentiles,[8] those who are outside the promises of Israel, to whom the gospel has not been preached and who have not known or heard of Jesus. If the process sounds like salvation by works, nevertheless for Gentiles to share

---

[6] Wilfred L. Knox, *The Sources of the Synoptic Gospels,* vol. 2, ed. Henry Chadwick (Cambridge: Cambridge University Press, 1957), 51, links together vv. 5 ff., 16b and 23 as an authentic saying of Jesus, which has been amplified by Matthew with other material. W. G. Kümmel, *Promise and Fulfilment: The Eschatological Message of Jesus,* trans. Dorothea M. Barton (London: SCM Press, 1957), 61–63, argues that v. 23b is an isolated saying, since v. 24 has a parallel in another context, and the two parts of v. 23 do not belong together: τελέσητε refers to the completion of a task – namely missionary work. Verse 23b thus fits the missionary charge of Jesus to his disciples.

[7] Matt 8:18–34; 15:21–28; 16:4 ff.

[8] The phrase πάντα τὰ ἔθνη should probably be understood as meaning the Gentiles; certainly it includes them. Cf. T. W. Manson, *The Sayings of Jesus* (London: SCM Press, 1949), 249 ff.; Joachim Jeremias, *The Parables of Jesus,* rev. ed. trans. S. H. Hooke (London: SCM Press, 1963), 209.

in the kingdom at all is an act of sheer grace on God's part, and one which might astonish the Jews, as well as the 'righteous' themselves.

Other passages in Matthew do speak of the gospel being preached to the Gentiles, however: 24:14 refers to worldwide evangelization in terms of 'a testimony to all nations', and the reference to testimony in 10:18 ff., should perhaps also be included. Finally, we have the words of the risen Jesus in 28:18–20, where he commands the Eleven to 'go … and make disciples of all nations'.

It is clear from this final passage alone that any particularist notions are foreign to Matthew. He himself, therefore, must have understood the limitation laid on the Twelve in 10:5 ff. as temporary, even though much of the material in the rest of that chapter seems to reflect the conditions appropriate to a period after that of Jesus' own ministry. The clue to his understanding of the matter is given us in the concluding words of his Gospel, where the command of Jesus is made dependent by the word οὖν (therefore) on what precedes: 'All authority in heaven and on earth has been given to me. Go *therefore* and make disciples …' The ministry of Jesus was limited to Israel, and the work of his disciples was similarly circumscribed; but now the authority of the risen and ascended Lord is without bounds – and the mission of his followers is equally extensive. This close correspondence between the mission of master and disciples is seen if we compare the message proclaimed by Jesus in Matt 4:17 with that which he entrusts to his disciples in Matt 10:7, or the account of Jesus' activity in 8 and 9 with the summary instructions of 10:8; possibly it is for this reason that Matthew has chosen to include in chapter 10 the warnings of persecution in vv. 17 ff., so closely reminiscent of Jesus' own sufferings, ending in vv. 24 ff. with the sayings which directly link the fate of the disciples with that of their master.

Matthew, then, we suggest, sees the limitation of 10:5b–6 as a temporary one, no longer applicable in the post-resurrection situation. If we were correct in our suggestion that these verses originally formed one saying with v. 23b, Matthew's rearrangement becomes understandable. For on their own, vv. 5b–6 no longer refer to a limitation that must continue until the parousia, while v. 23b, in its present context, underlines the predicament of Israel, and her guilt in persecuting the Messiah's messengers, and so rejecting her last opportunity to repent. Whether or not Matthew has made this alteration, however, it remains true that he understands the mission of Jesus as limited to Israel, and underlines the guilt of Israel in failing to respond – and this to a large extent comprises the so-called 'Jewishness' of this Gospel. The mission of the Jewish Messiah is naturally directed solely towards the Jews – they are offered the good news of the kingdom, but remain almost universally unrepentant or hard of heart; in rejecting their Messiah their guilt is established, and they bring judgement on their own heads in the terrible words of 27:25; therefore the kingdom is taken from them and given to others.

It seems unlikely, however, that Matthew himself created the saying in 10:5 ff.[9] Most commentators attribute it to a pre-Matthean source, suggesting that it reflects the views of a Jewish Christian community which was opposed to evangelization of the Gentiles on the ground that there was enough to do within Judaism without going beyond its confines;[10] certainly the form of the saying as a prohibition suggests that a contrary view was being espoused. If this is the saying's origin however, Matthew's use of it, as we have seen, reflects a very different viewpoint.

Some, however, have argued that the saying is an authentic *logion* of Jesus.[11] In support of this, it can be urged that the limitation appears to be in keeping with Jesus' own practice;[12] he himself announced the kingdom in Galilee, and though the population of Galilee was mixed, it was nevertheless Jewish territory; he spoke in terms of the fulfilment of Israel's hopes, and though non-Jews occasionally benefited from his ability to heal, these occasions were sufficiently rare and surprising to be noted and to attract comment. Nevertheless, one wonders whether there would have been occasion for such a saying within the ministry; a prohibition normally occurs where the opposing course of action has been suggested, and it seems very unlikely that it would have occurred to the disciples to announce the coming of the kingdom to the Gentiles; indeed, the evidence of Acts suggests that for some years after the crucifixion and resurrection there was no thought of such a mission.

---

[9] Francis Wright Beare, 'The Mission of the Disciples and the Mission Charge: Matthew 10 and Parallels', *JBL* 89 (1970): 1–13, believes that the saying *was* framed by Matthew in order to bring out the idea of Jesus' primary concern for Israel. In an earlier article, however, 'Sayings of the Risen Jesus in the Synoptic Tradition' in *Christian History and Interpretation: Studies Presented to John Knox*, eds. William R. Farmer, C.F.D. Moule and R.R. Niebuhr (Cambridge: Cambridge University Press, 1967), 176 ff., Professor Beare attributed the saying to 'an ancient and highly respected source'.

[10] E.g. Julius Wellhausen, *Das Evangelium Matthaei*, 2nd ed. (Berlin: Georg Reimer, 1914), *in loc.*; Willoughby C. Allen, *A Critical and Exegetical Commentary on the Gospel According to St. Matthew*, 3rd ed., ICC (Edinburgh: T&T Clark, 1912), *in loc.*; Benjamin W. Bacon, *Studies in Matthew* (London: Constable, 1930), 199; Rudolf Bultmann, *The History of the Synoptic Tradition*, trans. John Marsh (Oxford: Blackwell, 1963), 145; G.D. Kilpatrick, *The Origins of the Gospel According to St. Matthew* (Oxford: Clarendon Press, 1946), 26 ff. and 118 ff. Ferdinand Hahn, *Mission in the New Testament*, 55 ff. n. 5.

[11] So Marie-Joseph Lagrange, *Évangile selon Saint Matthieu*, 3rd ed. (Paris: J. Gabalda, 1927) *in loc.*; Alfred Plummer, *An Exegetical Commentary on the Gospel According to St. Matthew* (London: Elliot Stock, 1909), *in loc.*; Knox, *The Sources of the Synoptic Gospels*, 50 ff.; Joachim Jeremias, *op cit*, 19 ff., 26–28; A.M. Harman, 'Missions in the Thought of Jesus', *The Evangelical Quarterly* 41 (1969): 137–139.

[12] We may note here, not only the evidence of the evangelists, but Paul's description of Jesus at Romans 15:8 as διάκονος περιτομῆς.

But what of Jesus himself? Was a 'Gentile mission' a course of action that he was likely to consider? There have been attempts to argue that Jesus' attitude changed, and that at the end of his ministry, because of the obduracy of the Jews, he turned to the Gentiles.[13] But not only do we lack the kind of evidence which would enable us to trace such a development, there is a dearth of any evidence that Jesus himself turned to the Gentiles; in cases where non-Jews were healed, it was they who took the initiative, by coming to Jesus for help. Even Luke, who is obviously interested in the Gentile mission, does not picture Jesus himself as undertaking it; such references as there are in his Gospel and in Matthew's which might support this idea are not accounts of Jesus' activity, but Old Testament quotations.[14]

Another possibility is that Jesus saw his death as opening up the way for Gentiles. Certainly this belief is expressed in the New Testament: Mark seems to have understood the death of Jesus as sealing the rejection of Israel and also as the means by which Gentiles found salvation.[15] Paul's understanding of the way in which the hardening of Israel's heart (regarded by him as temporary) led to the salvation of the Gentiles is developed in Romans 9–11; and Matthew, similarly, emphasizes that it is the Jews' failure to respond to their Messiah which establishes their guilt and the handing over of their privileges to others.[16] But it is by no means certain that Jesus himself thought in these terms.[17]

Such a conclusion should not surprise us. Jesus was a Jew, and his understanding of his mission was naturally in terms of his own people; Christians have acknowledged him as the Messiah – but the Messiah, by definition, was concerned with the fate and fortunes of his people. What offends the Christian in the suggestion that Matt 10:5–6 is a true report of Jesus' attitude, even if the words are not actually his, is the idea that he might have shared the notion that privilege was confined to the chosen people. 'To them belong the sonship ... the covenants ... the Law ... the promises ... the Christ', wrote Paul in Romans 9:4–5; must we add, also, in Jesus' mind, 'the gospel'?

---

[13] Cf. Maurice Goguel, 'Jésus et les origines de l'universalisme chrétien', *RHPR* 12 (1932): 193–211.

[14] Luke 2:29–32, Matt 12:18–21.

[15] This idea has been developed by M. Kiddle, 'The Death of Jesus and the Admission of the Gentiles in St. Mark', *JTS* 35 (1934): 45–50.

[16] Cf. Wolfgang Trilling, *Das Wahre Israel*, 3rd ed. (München: Kösel, 1964), 103–105, 138–40.

[17] Mark 10:45 (perhaps authentic) has been thought to refer to the Gentiles, e.g. by M. Kiddle, 'The Death of Jesus'. But in the context it seems more likely that the πολλοί represent the many of Israel, over against Jesus. Mark 12:9 is perhaps an addition to the parable of the vineyard tenants, see C.H. Dodd, *The Parables of the Kingdom*, 3rd ed. (London: Nisbet, 1936), 126 ff.; Jeremias, *The Parables of Jesus*, 74; Vincent Taylor, *The Gospel According to St. Mark* (London: Macmillan, 1957), *in loc.* Even if original, however, we still have to face the problem regarding the extent of allegorization in this parable, and determine whether Jesus is referring directly to his own death.

But the concentration of Jesus' mission upon Jews is not to be interpreted as a 'particularist' attitude over against the idea of 'universalism'.[18] For what was at issue was not so much a question of privilege as of responsibility: true, the Jews had been given privileges – but they were in danger of throwing them away. The hour of judgement has arrived, and this is their last chance; of course Jesus is sent to the lost sheep of Israel – and time is running out. There can be no question of preaching to the Gentiles – indeed, the notion is irrelevant, for Jesus has not come to found a new religion; his message speaks of the fulfilment of Judaism, of the arrival of the kingdom of God which brings both salvation and judgement to the members of God's people. As for the Gentiles, their salvation belongs in Jewish thought to the time when the kingdom is established, and they are to be brought to God through Israel's witness. It is probable that Jesus shared the belief that God's purpose was to bring salvation to the Gentiles through the Jewish nation;[19] as we have noted, there are references in his words in Matthew to the final inclusion of the Gentiles, and these may reflect his attitude, though they stand in the Gospel as a warning to the Jews rather than as a promise to the Gentiles. Jesus' mission to his own people was natural and inevitable, and insofar as it was 'exclusive', that was because his message was to the existing people of God. The scandal of his words proved to be not in his particularity, but in his prophecy of the exclusion of his own people from the kingdom: salvation did indeed come to the Gentiles through Israel – but it was not through her witness, but through her rejection of the Messiah.

---

[18] Cf. Bengt Sundkler, 'Jésus et les païens', *RHPR* 16 (1936): 462–499.
[19] T.W. Manson, *Jesus and the Non-Jews* (London: Athlone Press, 1955).

Section Five

Beginnings and Endings

19. The Beginning of the Gospel

In an influential essay entitled 'The Introduction to Mark's Gospel', published in 1966, Lee Keck complained that 'almost never does the introduction figure in discussions of Mark's purpose', and he went on to argue that 'much more attention must be paid to the relation between the structure of Mark's thought and the structure of his text'.[1] In the past twenty-five years, Marcan scholars have taken his advice and have paid increasing attention to the way in which the evangelist ordered his material; at the same time, similar concerns have influenced study of the other Gospels. No longer can one complain that Mark's introduction is ignored.

In the course of his essay, Lee Keck argued (against R. H. Lightfoot) that the Marcan 'prologue' consisted of Mark 1:1–15 (not vv. 1–13) and that its function should not be compared with that of the Johannine prologue. If I take issue with him on these particular points, I hope that my basic agreement with him on the importance of Mark's structure will nevertheless make this a suitable birthday tribute to one whose contributions to New Testament scholarship constantly challenge us all to look at the evidence afresh. But whereas his concern was to ask whether the prologue helped us to understand Mark's purpose, mine is to inquire into the purpose of the prologue itself.

In recent years there has been growing support for the idea that Mark's Gospel was influenced by contemporary Greek tragedy. As long ago as 1931, Ernest W. Burch described the book as a 'closet drama, that is, drama whose power is felt by the reader without stage presentation'.[2] Burch was uncertain whether or not Mark was familiar with the work of Aristotle but concluded that his writing was 'clearly in correspondence with principles on which the drama of his day was constructed'.[3] Since then, an increasing number of scholars have used dramatic imagery to describe Mark's Gospel. More recently, two substantial studies of Mark, by Standaert and Bilezikian, have independently explored the parallels between Mark and contemporary Greek drama. According to Aristotle, the basic pattern of a tragedy moves from the complication (δέσις) to the dénouement (λύσις).[4] The change between the two is most effectively made when it takes the form of a discovery that brings

---

[1] Leander E. Keck, 'The Introduction to Mark's Gospel', *NTS* 12 (1966): 352, 369.
[2] Ernest W. Burch, 'Tragic Action in the Second Gospel: A Study in the Narrative of Mark', *The Journal of Religion* 11 (1931): 346.
[3] Burch, 'Tragic Action', 358.
[4] Aristotle, *Poet.* 18.

about a reversal.⁵ The opening scene of the drama is termed by Aristotle the 'prologue' (πρόλογος).⁶ In practice we find that this prologue serves to provide whatever information is essential to the comprehension of the play: it can be either dramatic or expository, and it may reveal to the audience events that took place before the action; it can also reveal what is about to take place in the play and can explain its real significance, a significance which will be concealed from the characters in the story.⁷ Whereas Bilezikian confines himself to the influence of Greek drama on Mark, Standaert explores parallels not only with the structure of tragedy but also with the five divisions into which an oration was divided by the rhetoricians, and he argues that Mark was influenced by the rules of rhetoric as well as by the conventions of drama.⁸

There is good reason to believe that, consciously or unconsciously, Mark was influenced in the presentation of his material by contemporary drama, not least because the turning point of his story at Caesarea Philippi conforms to Aristotle's description of a complex plot in which discovery or recognition (ἀναγνώρισις) and reversal (περιπέτεια) are accompanied by suffering (πάθος).⁹ The discovery involves a surprise that comes not to the audience (who know the general outline of the plot) but to the characters in the story.¹⁰ This situation leads to irony, since the events unfolding on the stage are comprehended by the audience, but not the participants. This is, of course, precisely the experience we have in reading Mark's Gospel, where we observe almost all the characters in the story bewildered by events and failing to understand what seems to us, who know their true significance, to be so obvious. According to Aristotle, the play produces fear and pity in the audience:¹¹ what effect listening to Mark's Gospel had on the original hearers we do not know, but it is noteworthy that one characteristic of the book is the emphasis on the fear of the characters in the story.

Mark's prologue, too, does precisely what a dramatic prologue is meant to do: it provides the information that is essential to our understanding of the story, before the main action of the drama begins. It enables us to follow the succeeding narrative and to comprehend all that takes place, in contrast to the participants in the story. The prologue is the key to the Gospel. And it may

---

⁵ Aristotle, *Poet.* 10–11.
⁶ Aristotle, *Poet.* 12.
⁷ Gilbert G. Bilezikian, *The Liberated Gospel: A Comparison of the Gospel of Mark and Greek Tragedy* (Grand Rapids: Baker, 1977), 53–54, 121–122. See also Friedrich Gustav Lang, 'Kompositionsanalyse des Markusevangeliums', *ZTK* 74 (1977): 1–24; Mary Ann Beavis, *Mark's Audience: The Literary and Social Setting of Mark 4:11–12* (Sheffield: JSOT, 1989), 31–35.
⁸ Benoît H.M.G.M. Standaert, *L'Evangile selon Marc: Composition et genre littéraire* (Brugge and Zevenkerken: Sint Andriesabdij, 1978).
⁹ Aristotle, *Poet.* 11.
¹⁰ Aristotle, *Poet.* 10, 16.
¹¹ Aristotle, *Poet.* 14.

well be that Mark has provided us with the key to the prologue itself by beginning with the word ἀρχή, a term Aristotle uses of the beginning of a well-constructed plot.[12] But these opening verses can be interpreted in this way only up to and including v. 13; up to this point, we are provided with information about Jesus that is not known to the characters in the story but will help us to make sense of it. In v. 14, Jesus comes into Galilee, and preaches the kingdom of God. From this moment on, the story unfolds from the viewpoint of those who are 'on stage' (though with occasional asides, as if from a Greek chorus, providing additional information to the audience through the words of unclean spirits and the heavenly voice). There is nothing secret in vv. 14–15, which means that it must belong to the story proper, and it is for this reason that I find myself in disagreement with Lee Keck about the ending of the prologue.

The notion that Mark should have modelled his Gospel on the form of a drama is not entirely odd. In the second century BCE, Ezekiel the Tragedian wrote at least one dramatic poem, *The Exagoge,* which retells the story of Moses and the exodus. The poem, of which only fragments survive, is based on Exodus 1–15. It is not clear whether the poem was intended to be presented on the stage, but its dramatic form is clear. Of particular interest is the opening scene, a monologue by Moses in which he recounts the story of Jacob's journey down into Egypt, Pharaoh's oppression of the people, and Moses' birth and rescue from death. In other words, before the story proper begins, this introductory monologue provides the background information that is necessary for our comprehension of subsequent events.

But plays were not the only form of ancient literature that began with a prologue. After discussing tragedy, Aristotle turns to epic poetry and suggests that its structure is similar.[13] In an oration, the first of the divisions was the προοίμιον, or exordium.[14] Others besides Standaert have commented on the similarities between the Gospels and oratorical compositions. George Kennedy remarks that 'the arrangement of each Gospel tends towards an oratorical structure. Each has some kind of proem …'[15] The function of the proem, however, was 'to obtain the attention of the audience and goodwill or sympathy toward the speaker',[16] and this hardly matches with the purpose of Mark 1:1–13 (or, indeed, of 1:1–15!).

---

[12] Aristotle, *Poet.* 7: 'Now a whole is that which has beginning, middle, and end. A beginning is that which is not necessarily after anything else, and which has naturally something else after it'. Cf. the more formal analysis in *Poet.* 12, which refers to prologue, episode, and exode.

[13] Aristotle, *Poet.* 23–24.

[14] Aristotle, *The Art of Rhetoric* 3.14.

[15] George A. Kennedy, *New Testament Interpretation through Rhetorical Criticism* (Chapel Hill; London: University of North Carolina Press, 1984), 97.

[16] Kennedy, *New Testament Interpretation,* 23–24.

Nevertheless, the growing recognition that these verses play an important function in the structure of the Gospel is significant. For it seems that in all kinds of writing, beginnings were important. We can find an obvious example of this in the New Testament itself. More than fifty years ago, Paul Schubert examined Paul's introductory thanksgivings and pointed out that they followed the pattern of thanksgivings in the epistolary papyri, where the thanksgiving is 'a conventional and familiar epistolary formula ... which serves to introduce the subject matter of the letter'.[17] At the very beginning of his letters, therefore, Paul provides us with an indication of the concerns which have led him to write and alerts us to the theme of what follows.

It is hardly surprising, then, when we turn to writings intended to be less ephemeral than epistles, that we find other kinds of formal prologues. Beginnings are, for example, of great importance in historiography. Both Greek and Latin historians frequently begin with a formal prologue, in which the subject of the work is set out in the very first sentence. Donald Earl, in a study of this prologue-form,[18] has suggested that the model for it is to be found in the introductory verses of *The Iliad* and *The Odyssey,* in which the themes of the two books are briefly set out. Early prologues, in Herodotus and Thucydides, provide this introduction in a single sentence; those of later writers are more elaborate. They inform the reader about the importance of the subject, the reasons for writing, the scheme of the work, and the name of the author. Josephus provides an admirable example in his prologue to *The Jewish War,* where he begins with an account of why previous attempts to relate the events he is going to describe were inadequate. He then provides a summary of the topics he intends to include, which probably deliberately selects those subjects which might attract potential readers. Earl sums up the evidence thus: 'If in Classical Antiquity you set yourself to write history, then your very first sentence must make it quite clear to the reader'.[19]

But this was in no way unusual, since writers of diverse kinds 'all make genre and subject absolutely plain at the beginning of their works'.[20] Thus 'the function of the first sentence is to establish, if not the specific topic to be treated, at least the literary genre to which the work belongs, history, dialogue, oratory and so on'.[21] Earl concludes his study by pointing out:

> There were good practical reasons why rigid rules were observed as to the form of opening sentences in written works. The technique of ancient book production, the physical nature of the volumen did not allow the reader easily to scan the body of the work to ascertain its

---

[17] Paul Schubert, *Form and Function of the Pauline Thanksgivings*, BZNW 20 (Berlin: A. Töpelmann, 1939): 161–163.

[18] Donald Earl, 'Prologue-Form in Ancient Historiography', *ANRW* 1/2 (1972): 842–856.

[19] Earl, 'Prologue-Form', 844.

[20] Earl, 'Prologue-Form', 846.

[21] Earl, 'Prologue-Form', 849.

subject. The first sentence and first paragraph performed much of the function of the title page and list of contents in a modern codex. Hence the obligation to make quite clear in your first sentence at least what type of literature you were writing.[22]

But this, of course, is precisely what Mark has failed to do — at least in the eyes of modern scholars, who continue to argue about the genre of his book. Yet in his introductory words, ἀρχὴ τοῦ εὐαγγελίου Ἰησοῦ Χριστοῦ, he provides us with an indication of what he intends to write: the gospel of Jesus Christ. Perhaps he was in fact offering what he considered to be an adequate description of his book. No matter that there was no such genre as 'gospel'! It is an appropriate title for what Mark has written, and the church acknowledged it when it labelled these books 'gospels'. But the phrase not only gives us a title for the book, it tells us that what immediately follows is to be understood as ἀρχή, the beginning of the story and the prologue to what follows. And clearly the dramatic analogy is more appropriate in this case than the historical: for Mark gives us, not a summary of future events, but the christological information that will provide us with the insight necessary to understand those events.

One of the great debates among gospel critics in recent years is whether, if we grant that Mark created a new genre in writing a 'gospel,' the other evangelists followed suit or did something different. What is certainly remarkable is that all four of them wrote prologues which, although different in content, functioned in very similar ways. If Earl is correct, then we should not be surprised to find each of them writing an introductory section that provides an indication of what is to come. In fact, all four of these introductory sections provide this information in a similar way, by setting out from a believer's point of view the significance of the story which is about to come. This is all the more remarkable because each evangelist does so by using his own material. In each of the Gospel prologues, the truth about Jesus is clearly stated, but this truth remains almost entirely hidden from the characters in the rest of the story, who fail to grasp the significance of what is happening: in this respect at least, all four introductions are close to the model of the dramatic prologue.

It is perhaps significant that in two of the Gospels, this change in gear between the prologue and subsequent chapters is so marked that there has been debate about whether or not the introductory sections 'belonged' to the Gospels. There has been endless discussion about the origins of both John 1:1–18 and Luke 1–2. Whatever we conclude about these issues, however, each of these sections forms part of the final redaction of the Gospel to which it is attached. And although in all four cases there is a clear difference in mood between the introductory section (where truth is spelt out without

---

[22] Earl, 'Prologue-Form', 856.

any concealment) and the rest of the Gospel (where ordinary mortals fail to comprehend what is taking place), there is also in every case a sense that each prologue belongs to its particular Gospel. The themes in Mark's prologue are those that are important for Mark's understanding of the gospel; so, too, with Matthew, Luke, and John.

But where does each prologue end? Here, too, there has been endless debate, this time in relation to all four Gospels. I have already argued that in Mark the divide comes after v. 13, because that is the point at which the theological information which is hidden from the characters in the story ceases. A similar break occurs after John 1:18, which makes the suggestion that the prologue consists of the whole chapter[23] improbable, even though vv. 19–51 do contain a remarkable amount of testimony to the person of Jesus: there is a marked difference between the theological exposition in vv. 1–18 and the narrative that begins in v. 19. In the case of Matthew, there have been similar debates about the extent of the prologue: does it end at 2:23,[24] at 4:11,[25] or at 4:17?[26] And in Luke we seem to have not only a 'theological prologue' (ending either at 2:52 or 4:13) but a literary preface in 1:1–4 of exactly the kind we expect in a book written by a historian.

What has led many scholars to argue for the inclusion of Matt 3:1–4:17 and Luke 3:1–4:13 in the Matthean and Lucan prologues is the fact that the material found here is parallel to Mark 1:2–13. To a certain extent, the same argument can be applied to John 1:19–51. Nevertheless, as Oscar Seitz pointed out, Matthew and Luke (and, we may add, to some extent John) shifted this material away from its 'prologue position', and provided 'a new and different kind of prologue'.[27] The Marcan tradition has been further modified in both Matthew and Luke by the addition of information about the teaching of John the Baptist, which means that the spotlight is no longer focused on Jesus as rigorously as it is in Mark. The baptism of Jesus, too, is no longer so clearly an other-worldly event: in Matthew because John recognizes Jesus, in Luke because it is mentioned almost in passing. In both Matthew and Luke, the temptation of Jesus becomes a conversation with Satan. The events which in Mark were 'the beginning of the Gospel' and stood over against the story proper have now become almost part of it. There is, in fact, a marked difference between the unusual events in the opening chapters of Matthew and Luke (angelic messages and dreams, Jesus' conception by the Holy Spirit, the

---

[23] Oscar J. F. Seitz, 'Gospel Prologues: A Common Pattern?', *JBL* 83 (1964): 262–268.

[24] David Hill, *The Gospel of Matthew*, NCB (London: Oliphants, 1972).

[25] Frans Neirynck, 'ΑΠΟ ΤΟΤΕ ΗΡΞΑΤΟ and the Structure of Matthew', *ETL* 64 (1988): 21–59.

[26] Jack Dean Kingsbury, *Matthew: Structure, Christology, Kingdom* (Philadelphia: Fortress, 1975).

[27] Seitz, 'Gospel Prologues', 262–263.

heavenly star, Spirit-inspired utterances by devout men and women) and the more down-to-earth narrative about John's ministry in Matthew 3 and Luke 3. It therefore seems appropriate for us to concentrate in our discussion on what is uniquely Matthean and uniquely Lucan, for it is in these introductory chapters that they provide us with what *they* consider it important for us to know.[28]

Now, in fact, the information that is provided in all four prologues is remarkably parallel, in spite of the fact that the actual material is so different. All tell us that the gospel about Jesus Christ is the fulfilment of scripture – Mark by his unusual quotation of scripture in 1:2, Matthew by his careful formula quotations, Luke by his pastiche of septuagintal expressions, and John by his use of ideas from Genesis 1 and Exodus 34. All four inform us that Jesus is 'Son of God'. In Mark, this is revealed by the voice from heaven (1:11); in Matthew (typically), it is confirmed by scripture (2:15); in Luke (again, typically), it is announced by the angel Gabriel (1:35); and in John, it is stated in 1:14 (and possibly in 1:18). All four describe Jesus as 'Christos': Mark in his introductory title, Matthew repeatedly (1:1, 16, 17, 18; 2:4), Luke twice (2:11, 26), and John when he first names Jesus (1:17). All three synoptists speak of the activity of the Holy Spirit: Mark describes the descent of the Spirit on Jesus at 1:10, while both Matthew and Luke attribute the conception of Jesus to the Holy Spirit (Matt 1:18, 20; Luke 1:35). Mark, Luke, and John all stress the superiority of Jesus over John the Baptist (Mark 1:7–8; Luke 1; John 1:6–8, 15), while both Matthew and Luke tell us that Jesus is descended from David (Matt 1:1, 20; 2:5–6; Luke 1:32, 69; 2:4, 11) – something which Mark and John do not mention, presumably because it is of no interest to them (cf. Mark 12:35; John 7:41–42). Not surprisingly, some of these themes are found also in Matthew 3–4 and in Luke 3–4, as well as in John 1:19–51, in the material that is parallel to Mark, so that if we include this in our analysis, all four Gospels include the first five of these six points.

While a comparison between the themes of the four introductory sections is illuminating, so, too, is a comparison between each introduction and its Gospel: each introduction fits its Gospel like a glove. Mark tells us that Jesus' coming is the fulfilment of scripture and that he is the Lord to whom both the prophets and John the Baptist point forward (cf. 9:1–13;[29] 11:27–33). Al-

---

[28] It may be a coincidence, but it is nevertheless interesting that when the prologues are defined as Matthew 1–2, Mark 1:1–13, Luke 1–2, and John 1:1–18, the 'story proper' in all four Gospels begins with the witness of John the Baptist to Jesus, although in Mark, who has already told the story of John, this consists of a brief reference to John being 'handed over'.

[29] Morna D. Hooker, "'What Doest Thou Here, Elijah?' A Look at St. Mark's Account of the Transfiguration', in *The Glory of Christ in the New Testament: Studies in Christology in Memory of George Bradford Caird,* eds. L.D. Hurst and N.T. Wright (Oxford: Clarendon Press, 1987), 59–70 = above, essay 12 (pp. 179–189).

though 1:2–3 is the only editorial quotation of scripture in the book, the belief that Jesus fulfils scripture is important for Mark – especially in relation to his death. The belief that Jesus is the Son of God reappears at crucial points in the story (9:7; 15:39; cf. 12:6), and the conviction that the Holy Spirit is at work in him and that he has defeated Satan is clearly of importance for understanding his exorcisms (3:20–30). Once we have read the rest of the story, we may recognize in his baptism a hint of the suffering to come (10:38).

Turning to Matthew, we find that the evangelist spells out what he considers to be the vital information about Jesus in the so-called birth narratives. The genealogy, with its careful scheme of 3 x 14 generations, traces his descent from both David and Abraham.[30] The fact that the Holy Spirit is at work in his conception is revealed in a dream. In chapter 2, we learn that Jesus was born in Bethlehem and was identified as 'king of the Jews' by a heavenly sign and by wise men from the East. Herod's plot to kill Jesus and his slaughter of the innocents point forward to the rejection of Jesus by his people and the suffering that follows rejection, while the homage of Gentiles reminds us that they are to be brought into the kingdom (cf. 8:11; 28:19). The parallels with the story of Moses and the exodus from Egypt remind us of the significance of what Jesus is to do in saving his people from their sins (1:21).

Luke spends much of chapter 1 drawing out the parallelism between the stories of John and Jesus, in a way that firmly establishes Jesus' superiority over his forerunner. At the same time, everything he tells us about John gives us additional information about Jesus. This information is found in the mouths of angels and inspired persons, who emphasize the role of the Holy Spirit (an important theme for Luke; see 4:1, 14, 18). Throughout the first two chapters we are assured that the Old Testament promises have been fulfilled and that the coming of Jesus means salvation – a salvation that involves the reversal of fortunes which is so typical of Luke and which extends even to Gentiles (2:32, a theme that becomes important in Acts). But salvation comes first to Israel, and in chapter 2 Luke explains how it came about that Jesus was born in the city of David; the rest of the chapter centres on the temple in Jerusalem (another theme taken up in Acts) and emphasizes that in the case of Jesus every requirement of the law of Moses was scrupulously performed (2:22, 23, 24, 27, 39). A passing reference in 2:35 points us forward to the passion.

John's prologue has at times been regarded as foreign to his Gospel, but in fact its themes are closely related to those in the rest of the book; I have explored the significance of the prologue for understanding the Gospel

---

[30] On the significance of the genealogy, see Krister Stendahl, 'Quis et Unde?', in *Judentum, Urchristentum Kirche: Festschrift für Joachim Jeremias*, ed. Walther Eltester, BZNW 26 (Berlin: Töpelmann, 1960), 94–105; Marshall D. Johnson, *The Purpose of the Biblical Genealogies*, 2nd ed. (Cambridge: Cambridge University Press, 1988); Raymond E. Brown, *The Birth of the Messiah* (London: Chapman, 1977).

elsewhere.[31] Once we have grasped the fact that Jesus is the Logos of God and the source of life and light, the one through whom God has acted in the past in creation and prophecy, we comprehend how he is able to perform the signs and to make the claims the evangelist attributes to him.

Thus it is not only Mark's Gospel whose opening paragraphs offer us a clue to its evangelist's purpose. Each Gospel provides us with an introduction that will guide us through the pages that follow.[32] This can hardly be accidental.[33]

There is one more intriguing similarity between the Gospels' opening paragraphs. I have mentioned already the literary preface in Luke 1:1–4, which has often been compared with classical historical prefaces[34] and is exactly the kind of introductory paragraph Earl had in mind when describing the prologue-form used by ancient historians. There is, of course, nothing strictly comparable in the other three Gospels. Nevertheless, each begins in a striking way, with a sentence that provides a kind of title for what follows.

There has been much discussion as to whether Mark's opening phrase, ἀρχὴ τοῦ εὐαγγελίου Ἰησοῦ Χριστοῦ, should be understood as a title, either of the prologue or of the whole book. Ernst Lohmeyer long ago pointed to the fact that many Jewish prophetic, didactic, and apocalyptic books begin with a title or brief heading.[35] If Mark means the word ἀρχή to refer to the prologue, then perhaps he intends the whole book to be seen as 'the gospel of Jesus Christ'. John uses the same word, ἀρχή, and at the same time echoes Gen 1:1: for him, 'the beginning of the gospel' is to be traced back to God's word at the creation. His opening sentence is hardly a title, but it serves as such, since it informs us straightaway in sonorous language that this book is about God's word at work in the world.[36] When we turn to Matthew, we find him using, in his first line, not the word ἀρχή, but γένεσις. Once again, there has been a great deal of discussion about the meaning of this opening. Is the

---

[31] Morna D. Hooker, 'The Johannine Prologue and the Messianic Secret', *NTS* 21 (1974): 40–58 = below, essay 23 (pp. 321–340).

[32] What has been said often of Mark and John has been admirably said of Matthew and Luke by Joseph A. Fitzmyer: 'The infancy narratives function as a sort of overture to the Gospels proper, striking the chords that will be heard again and again in the coming narratives' (*The Gospel According to Luke I–IX* [New York: Doubleday, 1981], 306).

[33] J.M. Gibbs argued that each prologue provided a guide to its Gospel's structure, a frame of reference in which each Gospel was to be understood, and a table of contents of major themes, but his analysis of the prologues was somewhat different from ours. See his 'Mark 1,1–15, Matthew 1,1–4,16, Luke 1,1–4,30, John 1,1–51: The Gospel Prologues and Their Function', in *Studia Evangélica*, vol. 6, ed. E.A. Livingstone (Berlin: Akademie Verlag, 1973), 154–188.

[34] For a recent discussion, see Joseph A. Fitzmyer, *The Gospel According to Luke I–IX*, 287–290.

[35] Ernst Lohmeyer, *Das Evangelium des Markus*, 17th ed. (Göttingen: Vandenhoeck & Ruprecht, 1967), 10. See Proverbs, Ecclesiastes, Canticles, the twelve Minor Prophets, Tobit, Baruch, Testaments of the Twelve Patriarchs, 1 Enoch, Testament of Job, Apocalypse of Abraham, 1QS, 1QM.

[36] Cf. the openings of Hosea, Joel, Micah, Zephaniah.

phrase βίβλος γενέσεως here a deliberate echo of Gen 5:1 and 2:4? Should we translate γένεσις as 'genealogy' and see these first few words as a heading to vv. 2–17? But why is the same word repeated (instead of the more obvious γέννησις) in 1:18? Does γένεσις in 1:1 mean 'origin', and does this first line stand as a heading to chapters 1–2 (or perhaps to 1:1–4:16)? Or should we perhaps, with W.D. Davies and others, think of the gospel events as a new Genesis and understand the word to be a reference to the new creation which is brought by Christ and, hence, a title for the whole book?[37] If so, then Matthew has deliberately drawn our attention to the fact by using the title of the first book of the Torah – just as John has done by echoing its opening words. Whatever we decide, Matthew has provided us here with some sort of title, and it takes us back to beginnings, with the reference to Christ's γένεσις. And when, finally, we turn back to Luke, we find the final, intriguing link in that he, too, uses the word ἀρχή, although in his case it is to refer to the tradition which has been handed down to him by those who were involved in these events ἀπ' ἀρχῆς.

I have not attempted here to solve the problem of the genre of the Gospels. What I have tried to do is to underline some of the remarkable features all four Gospels share in their opening pages. It would seem that each of the evangelists has consciously and deliberately spelt out at the beginning of his book both his purpose in writing and his interpretation of the story. If we attempt to read the Gospels without taking due note of the clues set out in the introductions, we shall certainly misunderstand them. Lee Keck's insistence that we need to pay attention to Mark's introduction in order to understand his purpose is true of all the evangelists: the vital importance of these introductory sections for our understanding of the Gospels as wholes cannot be overestimated.

---

[37] Most recently in W.D. Davies and Dale C. Allison, *A Critical and Exegetical Commentary on the Gospel According to Saint Matthew*, vol. 1, ICC (Edinburgh: T&T Clark, 1988), 149–154.

20. Beginning from Moses and from All the Prophets

1. Old Testament Roots

In his account of the encounter between the risen Christ and two disciples on the Emmaus road, Luke tells us how, 'beginning from Moses and from all the prophets, [Jesus] explained to them in the whole of scripture the things concerning himself' (Luke 24:27). There is no doubt that scripture plays a significant role in Luke's understanding of Jesus, though its importance is not always immediately apparent, because there are far more scriptural allusions than quotations in his writings. In this essay I shall confine myself to the Gospel, and concentrate on those passages which are specifically Lucan.

The first two chapters of Luke's Gospel highlight the problem of tracing Old Testament influence: the whole section is clearly saturated in Old Testament ideas and phraseology, yet there is no specific quotation. These two chapters, often referred to as 'the birth narratives', are perhaps better described as the prologue to the Gospel – like the equivalent chapters in Matthew and the opening verses of Mark and John, they provide us with key information as to who Jesus is, information which will enable us, the readers, to comprehend the rest of the Gospel, but which is hidden from almost all the participants in the story.[1] Not surprisingly, there is a difference between all these introductory sections and what follows – a difference so marked in the case of Luke and John that there has been considerable debate as to whether they are in fact later additions to the story. In all four Gospels, the truth about Jesus is unfolded in these chapters, and we learn that he is the Christ, the Son of God. Each of the evangelists emphasizes that the coming of Christ is the fulfilment of past hopes and promises, though each of them does so in a different way: Mark introduces the Gospel with a quotation which he attributes to Isaiah; John opens with a clear allusion to Gen 1:1, and writes what we may perhaps term a 'midrash' on Gen 1:1–5 and Exod 33:12–34:8;[2] Matthew quotes five

---

[1] See Morna D. Hooker, 'The Beginning of the Gospel', in *The Future of Christology: Essays in Honor of Leander E. Keck,* eds. Abraham J. Malherbe and Wayne A. Meeks (Minneapolis: Fortress Press, 1993), 18–28 = above, essay 19 (pp. 275–284).

[2] Peder Borgen, 'Observations on the Targumic Character of the Prologue of John', *NTS* 16 (1970): 288–295; Morna D. Hooker, 'The Johannine Prologue and the Messianic Secret', *NTS* 21 (1974): 40–58 = below, essay 23 (pp. 321–340).

passages in full, introducing each with a 'fulfilment' formula;[3] and what Matthew does in a somewhat heavy-handed way, Luke does in a much more agile fashion, using Old Testament imagery and vocabulary. Although there is no specific reference to the scriptures in the first two chapters of Luke, there is no mistaking the fact that the language – in particular, the language used by Gabriel and by men and women filled with the Holy Spirit – is reminiscent of that used in the Septuagint. Some of the events echo Old Testament stories (notably, the story of Hannah and Elkanah in 1 Samuel 1–2) or spell out the fulfilment of Old Testament hopes.

In emphasizing the importance of chs. 1–2 for understanding Luke's Gospel, I am clearly disagreeing with Conzelmann, who ignores these two chapters in his interpretation of Luke's theology.[4] But it is precisely because he leaves these two chapters on one side in his analysis that he is led to the conclusion that Luke is making sharp divisions between the three epochs of history – those of Israel, the ministry of Jesus and the church. In fact, Luke seems to go out of his way to stress the links between the epochs, first, by emphasizing that the scriptures were fulfilled in the birth, life, death, and resurrection of Jesus, and secondly, by indicating that the mission of the apostles mirrored that of Jesus himself.

These first two chapters fulfil another function, however, for they look forward as well as back. Luke's use of scriptural allusions serves to assure us that what happens in Jesus is the continuation of God's work in the past and the fulfilment of his promises, but these same allusions act as prophecies of what is to come, for the words of Gabriel and of the men and women who are inspired by the Holy Spirit describe what the ministry of Jesus will achieve.[5]

Even though the only words in Luke 1–2 italicized in Nestle-Aland's 26th edition of the Greek New Testament as an Old Testament quotation are those taken from Num 6:3 and applied to John the Baptist in 1:15, therefore, these two chapters are of great importance for understanding Luke's approach to the Old Testament. What we learn here is that the time of Israel's salvation has arrived; that John the Baptist will prepare the way of the Lord, as did Elijah of old; that Jesus will be called the Son of the Most High; that he will inherit the throne of David, and that his kingdom will have no end; that he

---

[3] Matt 1:22–23; 2:5–6, 15, 17–18, 23. A similar formula is used six times in the rest of the Gospel, at 4:14; 8:17; 12:17; 13:14, 35; 21:4; 27:9.

[4] Hans Conzelmann, *The Theology of St Luke,* trans. Geoffrey Buswell (London: Faber, 1960). Contrast Paul S. Minear, 'Luke's Use of the Birth Narratives', in *Studies in Luke-Acts: Essays Presented in Honor of Paul Schubert,* eds. Leander E. Keck and J. Louis Martyn (London: SPCK, 1968), 111–130; Stephen Farris, *The Hymns of Luke's Infancy Narratives,* JSNTSup 9 (Sheffield: JSOT Press, 1985), 151–160.

[5] Cf. Paul Schubert, 'The Structure and Significance of Luke 24', in *Neutestamentliche Studien für Rudolf Bultmann,* ed. Walther Eltester, BZNW 21 (Berlin: Töpelmann, 1954), 165–186.

is born through the power of the Holy Spirit; that his coming involves the putting of things to rights, which will mean the reversal of fortunes for high and low; that through him the promises made to Abraham will be fulfilled. The focus throughout is on Jesus, and the echoes of the Old Testament are thus christological.

This brief summary of the themes of Luke 1–2 reminds us of how very Jewish these chapters are: Jesus is the fulfilment of Jewish hopes. Moreover, it is only in 2:32, where Simeon speaks of a light which brings revelation to Gentiles, that we find a hint that the coming of Jesus will mean their salvation. This Jewishness is something of a surprise in what is often described as a 'Gentile' Gospel, and may seem to provide support for those who believe that the introductory chapters are a later addition. In fact, however, when we examine the rest of the book carefully, we find that it contains very little about salvation for the Gentiles. It is true that there are hints of that theme, but they are only hints, and almost all of them are promises for the future.[6] It is not until the very end of the Gospel, at 24:47, that the theme is brought out into the open with the command of the risen Christ to his disciples to preach to all nations. Significantly, Luke omits the whole of Mark 7, which contains Jesus' teaching about clean and unclean food and the healing of the Syro-Phoenician woman's daughter. It would seem as though Luke has deliberately saved references to Gentiles for his second volume, where their response to the gospel becomes the dominant theme. Because he has two books, he is able to spell out how the gospel was preached to the Jew first, and subsequently to the Gentiles.[7]

In view of this emphasis on the fulfilment of Jewish promises, it is no surprise to find that Jesus is said to have been born in Bethlehem: even though Luke's account of how this came about seems most unlikely, it is clear that all is done in order that Jesus should be a true son of David. Following his circumcision, Jesus is taken to Jerusalem to be presented to the Lord. Describing what took place in the temple, Luke points out no fewer than five times that what was done there was in accordance with the prescriptions of

---

[6] Exceptions are the stories of the healing of the Roman centurion's servant in 7:1–10, and of the Samaritan leper in 17:11–19; the demoniac in 8:26–39 may also have been understood to be a Gentile. Other hints are found at 3:6, where 'all flesh' is to see the salvation of God, in 4:16–30, where Jesus refers to Elijah and Elisha assisting Gentiles, and in the story Jesus tells in 10:30–37 about a good Samaritan. Those who flock into the kingdom of God in 13:28–30 could be Gentiles, as could those who receive a late invitation to the dinner party in 14:15–24 and the 'others' to whom the vineyard is given in 20:16, though Luke may have understood any of these to refer to Jewish outsiders. Although the 'seventy' or 'seventy-two' in 10:1 are often interpreted as missionaries to the Gentiles, Luke appears to have thought of them as having been sent through Jewish territory!

[7] Acts 13:46; cf. Rom 1:16.

the Law.⁸ Thus he presents Jesus as a quintessential Jew, born of David's line, in the city of David, and from his birth obedient to the Mosaic law.

It has sometimes been argued that this picture is in conflict with the rest of the Gospel. S.G. Wilson, for example, came to the conclusion that Luke is confused on the issue of the Law, and 'presents Jesus as sometimes opposed to and sometimes in league with the law'.⁹ It seems to us, however, that Luke himself sees no conflict between Jesus and the Law. In 4:1–13 he includes the story of the temptation, in which Jesus rebuts Satan's attack by appealing three times to Deuteronomy. Although in subsequent chapters Jesus (and his disciples) are accused by the Jewish authorities of breaking the Law, the real cause of these disputes is the interpretation of the Law. Thus in 6:9, and again in 14:3, Jesus poses the question 'Is it lawful to heal on the sabbath?', and it is clear that the implied answer is 'yes'.¹⁰ On two occasions, prominent Jews come to Jesus asking how they might inherit eternal life. On the first occasion (10:25–28), Jesus throws the question back, asking 'What is written in the Law? How do you understand it?' When his questioner replies with a summary of the Law, to the effect that one must love God and love one's neighbour as oneself, Jesus gives his approval. When the question is put a second time (18:18–27), Jesus himself replies by reciting the last five commandments. Clearly there is no contradiction between the Law and Jesus in either passage. Yet the teaching of Jesus makes new demands which go beyond those of the Law. In the first story, we find him making the requirements of the Law more stringent in the parable of the Good Samaritan, told in response to the question 'Who is my neighbour?' (10:29 ff.). In the second, when his questioner claims to have kept the commandments from his youth, he is told to give all his possessions to the poor and follow Jesus: if he wishes to enter the kingdom of heaven, obedience to the Law is insufficient.

A very similar picture emerges in Mark, where Jesus is presented as faithful to the Law, but in disagreement with the religious authorities over its interpretation.¹¹ In Mark, however, there are two passages where Jesus apparently challenges the teaching of the Law itself. The first occurs in Mark 7, where Jesus responds to the Pharisees' criticism of his disciples for eating with unwashed hands by accusing his opponents of concentrating on human

---

⁸ The phrase κατὰ τὸν νόμον (or a variant) is used in 2:22, 27 and 39, ἐν (τῷ) νόμῳ Κυρίου in vv. 23 and 24.

⁹ S.G. Wilson, *Luke and the Law* (Cambridge: Cambridge University Press, 1983), 57.

¹⁰ Cf. 13:10–17.

¹¹ Cf. Morna D. Hooker, 'Mark's Use of Scripture', originally entitled 'Mark', in *It is Written: Scripture Citing Scripture: Essays in Honour of Barnabas Lindars,* eds. D.A. Carson and H.G.M. Williamson (Cambridge: Cambridge University Press, 1988), 220–230 = above, essay 13 (pp. 190–199).

traditions and neglecting the commandments of God; afterwards, when the disciples question Jesus in private, he spells out the significance of his teaching, and Mark adds the comment 'By saying this he declared all foods clean' (v. 19), showing that he understood Jesus to be challenging the Law itself (not simply human tradition), by doing away with kosher food.[12] The second is in Mark 10, where Jesus responds to the Pharisees' question about divorce by setting the divine command in Gen 2:24 above the Mosaic provision in Deut 24:1; the final saying, in v. 9, prohibits what Moses allowed. In vv. 11–12, Mark again describes private teaching given to the disciples, in which Jesus declares that a man (or a woman!) who takes advantage of the Mosaic provision that a man may divorce his wife is guilty of adultery if he marries someone else. When we turn back to Luke, however, we find that he has omitted the first of these passages altogether – a surprising omission, if Luke was using Mark as a source, since teaching about clean and unclean clearly backs up the church's decisions about table-fellowship with Gentiles in Acts. We have noted already, however, that Luke prefers to save this development in understanding for his second volume. The question about divorce and Jesus' response are also missing from Luke; only the saying in Mark 10:11–12 survives, in Luke 16:18. But the very different context given to it by Luke indicates that he does not regard it as in any sense challenging the Law, for it follows immediately after the statement that 'it is easier for heaven and earth to pass away, than for one letter of the Law to lose its force'. Since heaven and earth have not passed away, this saying must be understood (*pace* the contortions of various commentators!) as an affirmation that Jesus maintains the authority of the Law, in spite of the arrival of the kingdom of God (v. 16). In this particular instance, the coming of the kingdom tightens the demands of the Law by forbidding remarriage after divorce.

It would seem, then, that Luke's portrayal of Jesus in his Gospel corresponds with his insistence in ch. 2 that everything following his birth was done in accordance with the Law.

2. The Prophets Fulfilled

Many of the Old Testament quotations used by Luke are found also in Matthew and Mark: a full investigation would need to consider whether there are significant variations.[13] The two most interesting concern quotations from

---

[12] The fact that the teaching was delivered in private to the disciples suggests that whatever we may decide about the rest of the passage, the interpretation in vv. 17–23 belongs to the period of the church.

[13] Cf. C.K. Barrett, 'Luke', in *It is Written: Scripture Citing Scripture*, 231–244.

Isaiah, the first in 3:4–6, where Luke extends the passage from Isaiah 40 cited by Matthew and Mark; the extra lines stress the significance of what is taking place and point forward to the salvation which will be seen by the whole of humanity. The second occurs in Luke 8:10, where instead of the quotation of Isa 6:9–10 found in Mark 4:12 we have only an echo of Isaiah: ἵνα βλέποντες μὴ βλέπωσιν καὶ ἀκούοντες μὴ συνιῶσιν. In Matthew, by contrast, where the quotation is attributed to Isaiah, it is considerably extended (13:14–15). But Luke makes use of the full quotation elsewhere, for it occurs at the climax of the story he tells in his second volume – in Acts 28:26–27 it forms Paul's final comment on his own preaching and on the failure of the Jewish people to respond to the gospel. Those who see without perceiving and who hear without comprehending are no longer Jesus' contemporaries, but the Jews of the next generation who reject Paul's message, and that which is hidden from them is now given, not to the disciples, but to the Gentiles (v. 28). As elsewhere, the fact that Luke wrote two volumes appears to have enabled him to avoid using something in the context of the ministry of Jesus which is more appropriate within the life of the early church.

Two other quotations from Isaiah used in Luke's Gospel do not occur in either Matthew or Mark. The first is found in the story of Jesus' sermon in the synagogue at Nazareth in 4:16–30, where he reads from Isa 61:1–2, a passage which seems to have been of considerable importance for the early church.[14] It is often pointed out that the reading stops immediately before the reference to God's day of vengeance in Isa 61:2. The quotation follows the LXX of Isaiah 61, but omits one phrase ('to heal the broken-hearted') and includes another ('to set at liberty those who are oppressed') taken from Isa 58:6; this minor variation is probably of no great significance. Jesus' exposition of the text consists in the claim that Isaiah's words have been fulfilled today, in the hearing of those in the synagogue. How are we to understand this fulfilment? Jesus has said nothing and done nothing in the synagogue except read the passage – how, then, is scripture fulfilled? The answer must be that it is fulfilled because Jesus here and now accepts it as the programme for his ministry, identifying his mission with that of the prophetic figure described in Isaiah 61. He is able to accept it because the Spirit of the Lord is indeed on him – something we know, because Luke has continually emphasized it, and backed up his statements with evidence: he has told us of the descent of the Spirit – in bodily form – at Jesus' baptism (3:22); in 4:1 he emphasized that Jesus was full of the Spirit and was led by the Spirit, as a result of which he was able to withstand the temptations of Satan; and in 4:14 he told us that Jesus returned in the power of the Spirit into Galilee, where he taught in their synagogues and everyone sang his praises (vv. 14–15). The Spirit of the Lord is indeed 'on'

---

[14] Cf. Matt 11:5–6 // Luke 7:22, and echoes in Matt 5:3–4 and Luke 6:20–21.

Jesus;[15] the rest of the quotation tells us what he is anointed to do, by providing a manifesto for Jesus' ministry.

The story has a partial parallel in Mark 6:1–6 and Matt 13:54–58, but Luke has placed his much fuller version considerably earlier in his narrative, at the very beginning of his account of Jesus' ministry, and we can see why. In the succeeding chapters we find references to exorcisms and healings, together with the cures of a leper, of a paralytic, and of a man with a paralysed hand; we read of Jesus calling Levi to follow him, and then joining a party of 'sinners' in Levi's house; we are given an account of the teaching Jesus addressed to his disciples, who are described as 'poor' and 'hungry'; we hear how he healed a centurion's servant and raised a widow's son to life. By the time John the Baptist sends messengers to him in 7:18 ff. asking whether he is the expected one or not, Jesus has preached the good news and set the prisoners of Satan[16] free: he has thus completed the task set out for him in Isa 61:1–2, except that Luke has not recorded any instances of the one form of healing which is specifically mentioned, which is the restoration of sight to the blind. It can hardly be accidental that when John's disciples pose their question, Luke tells us that Jesus promptly healed many people from their diseases and plagues and evil spirits, and bestowed sight on the blind, so establishing beyond all doubt that he is indeed the one who was to come (7:21).[17] Jesus' next words sum up his activity in language which echoes not only Isa 29:18–19 and 35:5–6, but 61:1–2 as well. Is this echo of the quotation of Isaiah 61 part of a deliberate *inclusio*? Certainly it seems that the programme spelt out in Luke 4 has been carried out, and that 7:18–23 is intended to underline this fact.

Jesus' exposition of Isaiah 61 in Luke 4 raises various interesting questions. Why, for example, does he quote the wrong proverb? The saying 'physician heal yourself' is surely irrelevant here, for Jesus has no need of healing. The appropriate proverb is found in Gospel of Thomas 31: 'No prophet is acceptable in his village; no physician heals those who know him'; this would have led neatly into Jesus' description of the way in which both Elijah and Elisha ministered to Gentiles rather than to Jews. But here is another puzzle, for though Jesus appeals to the examples of Elijah and Elisha in helping Gentiles, Luke depicts Jesus himself as apparently confining his own ministry to Jews. The references to Elijah and Elisha thus point forward to the mission to the Gentiles which lies beyond Jesus' rejection, death and resurrection,[18] but these

---

[15] The Greek ἐπ' echoes the phrase used at the baptism.

[16] Cf. 13:16.

[17] It is significant that Matthew, whose account is very closely parallel to Luke's at this point, does not include a parallel to vv. 20–21.

[18] B.J. Koet, *Five Studies on Interpretation of Scripture in Luke-Acts* (Leuven: Leuven University Press/Uitgeverij Peeters, 1989), 24–55, denies that the references to Elijah and Elisha are intended as prefigurations of the Gentile mission or of judgement on Israel, and argues that

latter events are themselves 'foretold' in the saying in v. 24, in the fury of his countrymen and their attempt to lynch him, and in his escape from their hands. This perhaps explains the form of the saying in v. 23, for at the end of the Gospel it will be Jesus himself who needs healing.[19] The story is thus a mini-presentation of the whole Gospel, with one interesting reversal – instead of Jesus' death and resurrection leading to the mission to the Gentiles, it is the promise of salvation for the Gentiles which stirs up his countrymen's hostility, and so leads to their attempt to kill him.

An interesting parallel to this story of biblical interpretation is found in Acts 8, where the Ethiopian eunuch reads from Isa 53:7–8, and asks Philip to explain to him whom the passage is about. As in Luke 4, the quotation stops abruptly; if in that passage the exclusion of Isaiah's reference to 'the day of God's vengeance' is seen as deliberate, the same logic demands that in Acts 8 the choice of these particular lines of Isaiah 53 and these only must also be understood as deliberate. The passage is used simply as a proof-text about Jesus, not as a key to the meaning of his death: 'and beginning from this passage Philip preached to him the good news of Jesus'.

The second important quotation from Isaiah found in Luke alone[20] among the Gospels occurs in 22:37. In the upper room, Jesus warns his disciples that they can no longer expect to be received and welcomed as messengers of the kingdom; they must equip themselves with swords, because the words of scripture, 'He was reckoned with the transgressors', must be fulfilled in him. The most obvious meaning of this highly enigmatic passage appears to be that Jesus is saying to his disciples, 'Buy swords, so that I can be arrested in the company of apparent gangsters'.[21] Most commentators shy away from this interpretation, probably because they dislike the highly mechanistic manner of fulfilling scripture which it apparently attributes to Jesus.[22] They suggest instead that the passage refers to Jesus' crucifixion with two thieves,[23] or that it is a reference to the passion narrative in general.[24] Neither of these solutions

---

they are intended to encourage Jesus' hearers at Nazareth to respond to his message. But they certainly do not function this way in the Gospel, where indeed they lead Jesus' audience to fury: the passage suggests rather that some Gentiles will respond to the gospel and some Jews reject it, and so exclude themselves from salvation.

[19] Cf. the similar jibe in 23:35.

[20] We assume that Mark 15:28 is a later addition to the text.

[21] So Paul S. Minear, 'A Note on Luke XXII 36', *NT* 7 (1964): 128–134.

[22] Minear's own suggestion is not that the command is an artificial literary device, but rather that it is intended to disclose the fact that the disciples have disobeyed Jesus' earlier instructions; 'Luke XXII 36', 132–133.

[23] As in the addition to Mark at 15:28. So Joseph A. Fitzmyer, *The Gospel According to Luke X–XXIV,* AB (New York: Doubleday, 1985), *in loc.* Cf. Martin Rese, *Alttestamentliche Motive in der Christologie des Lukas* (Gütersloh: Mohn, 1969), 155–158.

[24] See I. Howard Marshall, *The Gospel of Luke,* NIGTC (Exeter: Paternoster Press, 1978)

offers an explanation of the present context of the words, where they follow Jesus' instruction to his disciples to buy swords.

Whatever explanation we adopt, the interesting factor about this passage is the way in which it is used. We have here the one clear reference to Isaiah 53 in the whole of Luke – indeed, in all four Gospels – and it is used simply as a proof-text. There is no reference to the so-called Servant's vicarious suffering or to any atonement brought about through his death. As with the longer passage quoted in Acts, Luke does not exploit the theological significance of the passage, but simply refers to it being 'fulfilled'.

3. All Things Fulfilled

If the beginning of the Gospel is an important clue to Luke's theology, so too is the end; in the resurrection appearances in the final chapter of Luke the fulfilment of scripture is again an important theme, but now it is linked with a new theme – that of the fulfilment of Jesus' own words. There are three scenes. The first, in vv. 1–12, is set at the empty tomb. A comparison with Matthew and Mark reveals notable differences, one of which is significant for our purposes. Instead of the command to go into Galilee, we have a reminder of what happened there: 'Remember how he told you, while he was still in Galilee, that the Son of man must be delivered into the hands of sinners and be crucified, and rise on the third day'. These words point us back to the first passion prediction in 9:22 (echoed in v. 44), where Jesus announced that 'the Son of man must suffer many things and be put to death ... and the third day be raised'.[25] No explanation for the suffering is offered: it is simply stated that it is necessary, and the term used, δεῖ, is repeated in 24:7. The same word occurs in 13:33 ('I must go on my way today and tomorrow and the third day' – that is to Jerusalem and to death), in the passion prediction in 17:25, and in 22:37, where Jesus says that Isaiah 53 must be fulfilled. This necessity is clearly based in scripture, even though there is no clear reference in any of the passion predictions to any particular passage – but it is not scripture alone that has now been fulfilled but the words of Jesus himself, for it was he who said what would happen and what was 'necessary'. In other words, Jesus is presented as a prophet whose prophecies have been vindicated – an idea not unfamiliar in Luke, where Jesus actually refers to himself as a prophet on two occasions, each time as a prophet who is rejected by his people (4:24, in the passage we have already considered, and 13:33).[26] We have here an idea similar

---

in loc. Cf. Douglas J. Moo, *The Old Testament in the Gospel Passion Narratives* (Sheffield: The Almond Press, 1983), 132–138.

[25] The predictions in 17:25 and 18:31 ff. occur on the journey from Galilee to Jerusalem.

[26] The belief that Jesus is a prophet is raised elsewhere in Luke; see 7:16, 39; 9:8, 19; 24:19.

to one we met in the birth narratives, where men and women filled with the Spirit prophesied about the significance of John the Baptist and Jesus. But now it is Jesus who has prophesied his own death and resurrection, and his words that have been fulfilled.

The second scene takes place on the road to Emmaus in vv. 13–27. Jesus upbraids his companions for their slowness to believe all that the prophets have spoken (v. 25). Was it not necessary, he asks, that the Messiah should suffer all these things and so enter into his glory? Once again, the necessity is founded in scripture: 'and beginning from Moses and from all the prophets, he interpreted to them in all the scriptures the things concerning himself'. This time the words of the risen Christ link back to the final passion prediction in 18:31 ff., where Jesus refers to his coming sufferings, not as something which 'must' happen, but as the fulfilment of 'everything which is written of the Son of man through the prophets'. The interesting feature in 24:27 is that Jesus refers first to Moses; to what passages can this refer? Luke fails to tell us.[27] The reference is vague but inclusive, and becomes more so, as we progress from the prophets in v. 25 via Moses and all the prophets to all the scriptures in v. 27.

In the third scene, in vv. 36–49, the two ideas of Jesus' own prophecies and those of scripture are drawn together and coalesce. Jesus appears to the Eleven in Jerusalem and reminds them of what he has taught them earlier: 'These were my words to you when I was still with you; I told you that everything written about me in the law of Moses and the prophets and the psalms must be fulfilled' (v. 44). The events in Jerusalem have thus fulfilled not simply what was written in all three parts of scripture, but the words of Jesus himself. Jesus is thus proved to be the prophet like Moses (Deut 18:21–22). 'Then he explained to them that it is written that the Messiah should suffer and rise from the dead on the third day, and that repentance for the forgiveness of sin should be proclaimed in his name to all the Gentiles, beginning from Jerusalem' (v. 47). Once again, Luke fails to tell us where it is written. Nor do the predictions attributed to Jesus to which this passage refers assist us, since the only saying which Luke has quoted in connection with the sufferings of Jesus is the enigmatic quotation of Isa 53:12 in 22:37. This dearth of explicit quotations is remarkable, since Luke refers to a number of scriptural passages in other connections in the course of his story. It means that in this final chapter, as in chs. 1–2, we have no precise quotation, even though the conviction that everything is happening according to scripture is clearly underlined in both passages.

---

[27] This is hardly surprising, since the only passage he has quoted so far is Isa 53:12 in 22:37, but it corresponds with Traugott Holtz's contention that Luke did not have direct access to a text of the Pentateuch; see *Untersuchungen über die alttestamentlichen Zitate bei Lukas* (Berlin: Akademie Verlag, 1968), 60–130, 168–169.

Luke uses these conversations with the risen Christ to draw out the significance of events. In this sense, ch. 24 forms the epilogue to his Gospel, rather as chs. 1–2 form the prologue. One interesting fact is that whereas we are inclined to think that the scriptures being appealed to must be in the prophets and psalms, we twice find here reference to Moses. Where does Moses fit in?

4. Moses and All the Prophets

That Moses is an important figure for Luke is indicated already by the way in which the evangelist handles the Law. Significant, too, is the way in which he treats the transfiguration story in 9:28–36. Only Luke tells us the subject of the conversation between Jesus, Moses, and Elijah, namely Jesus' ἔξοδος, which he was to fulfil in Jerusalem – the unusual term establishes a link between the salvation achieved through Moses and the coming death of Jesus. The voice from heaven, identifying Jesus as God's Son, commands the disciples (as in Matthew and Mark) to 'hear him', words which suggest that Jesus is also understood to be the prophet like Moses who is spoken of in Deut 18:15. Almost immediately following, in 9:51, we are told that the time for Jesus' ἀνάλημψις approached: the term is reminiscent of the assumptions of both Moses and Elijah, and implies that Jesus, also, will be taken up to glory – the glory in which Moses and Elijah appear in 9:31 – though in his case by a painful death. But though we are told that the time has approached, and though Jesus is said to have set his face resolutely towards Jerusalem, Luke now begins a long section in which Jesus meanders around Palestine, often heading in the wrong direction. C.F. Evans made the fascinating suggestion that the stories between 10:1 and 18:14 have been carefully chosen and placed in an order which corresponds with the account of Moses leading Israel through the wilderness in Deuteronomy 1–26.[28] Some of his parallels seem far-fetched, and the notion of Luke carefully collating his material with the text of Deuteronomy is too reminiscent of the methods of a modern scholar to be wholly persuasive. There is more evidence to support his less ambitious suggestion that the first two stories in this section both echo stories of Elijah: in the first, we read how, in contrast to Elijah, Jesus refuses to call down fire on those who reject him (cf. 2 Kgs 1:9–12); then (again unlike Elijah) he refuses to allow a would-be disciple to bury his father (cf. 1 Kgs 19:19–21). When we

---

[28] See 'The Central Section of St. Luke's Gospel', in *Studies in the Gospels: Essays in Memory of R.H. Lightfoot,* ed. D.E. Nineham (Oxford: Blackwell, 1957), 37–53. Evans' suggestion is, of course, incompatible with Holtz's argument that Luke did not have access to a copy of the Pentateuch.

turn to the story of Christ's ascension in Acts 1, we find Luke emphasizing the way in which, after Jesus had promised his disciples that they would receive the Holy Spirit, they saw him lifted up into heaven (vv. 9–10), an interesting echo of Elijah's insistence that if Elisha were to inherit his spirit in its full power, he must see him depart into heaven (2 Kgs 2:9–15). These echoes confirm the belief that in 9:51 Luke is deliberately linking the assumption of Jesus with that of Elijah.[29]

In view of the hints at 9:31 and 35, we expect the figure of Moses to be of equal significance with that of Elijah, and certainly there are echoes of the Moses tradition in 10:1–18:30. The appointment of the Seventy is reminiscent of Moses' choice of seventy elders (Exod 24:1; Num 11:16); the commandments are quoted and endorsed (10:25–28; 18:18–21); the teaching of Moses is invoked (16:29–31); above all, these chapters contain the bulk of Jesus' teaching, which is delivered with great authority. The command to hear Jesus in 9:35 is repeatedly echoed – if men and women hear him, they hear the words of one sent by God (10:16); psalmists and kings longed to hear what the disciples now hear (10:24); in listening to the word of Jesus, Mary chooses the best part (10:39, 42); those who hear and obey God's word are blessed (11:28); Jesus is greater than Solomon, whose wisdom was listened to by the Queen of the South, and greater than Jonah, whose preaching converted the people of Nineveh (11:29–32); those with ears to hear are commanded to hear (14:35); and finally we are told that those who did not hear Moses and the prophets will not repent, even if one should rise from the dead (16:29–31), words whose true significance depends on knowing the end of the story. When we turn to Acts, we find confirmation that Luke thought of Jesus as 'the prophet like Moses' in 3:22, where Deut 18:15–19 is quoted and applied to Jesus. The reminiscences of Moses go beyond echoes of his teaching, however: we have already noted the reference to Jesus' death as an 'exodus' in 9:31, and in 22:19–20, 28–30, in the context of the Last Supper, we find Jesus linking his death with a covenant; this theme, associating Jesus' death with the covenant on Sinai, appears first in the disputed words over the second cup, but it is used again in the saying about the kingdom which God has covenanted to him, and which he now covenants to his disciples, appointing them as judges who will sit on thrones judging the twelve tribes of Israel.[30]

Whether or not we accept the suggestion that the travel narrative is meant to parallel the journey of Moses from Horeb to the promised land, therefore, it would seem that Luke intends to present Jesus as both the prophet like Moses

---

[29] There are, of course, other hints in Luke that he sees Jesus as the new Elijah, e.g. 7:11–17. Cf. P. Dabeck, '"Siehe, es erschienen Moses und Elias" (Mt 17,3)' *Biblica* 23 (1942): 175–189; John Drury, *Tradition and Design in Luke's Gospel* (London: Darton, Longman & Todd, 1976), 147–148.

[30] Cf. Deut 16:18.

and as the returning Elijah.[31] In doing so, he demonstrates another way in which 'Moses and all the prophets' are fulfilled in Jesus. Just as he spells out in 4:16–7:23 his conviction that the passage from the prophets which Jesus read in Nazareth was fulfilled in his actions, so he indicates in 9:51–62 that Jesus is a new Elijah, and spells out in 9:51–18:30 his belief that he is also the prophet like Moses and that the law of Moses is 'completed' in him. This typology perhaps appears to us to be subtle, but it is no more subtle than the use of septuagintal phraseology in chs. 1–2: Luke's manner of handling the scriptures and seeing their fulfilment in Jesus is not quite what we, from our twentieth-century perspective, expect. But if the relevance of Moses and the prophets is not immediately obvious, that is hardly surprising, for only in ch. 24 does the risen Christ open the eyes of the disciples 'to understand the scriptures'. It may be that modern scholars need similar illumination if they are to understand the subtleties of Luke's manner of expressing his conviction that 'the whole of scripture' referred to Jesus.

---

[31] Mal 4:4–5 links the figure of Moses and Elijah. It is possible that Luke saw significance in the fact that the end of the travel narrative brings Jesus and his disciples to Jericho (18:35) since Jericho features in both the story of the death of Moses, Deut 32:49, 34:1, 3, and the account of Elijah's assumption, 2 Kgs 2:4.

21. John's Baptism: A Prophetic Sign

It is self-evident that the unique feature that marked out John the Baptist from other prophets was the fact that he baptized: so unusual and distinctive was this that it gave him his name, 'the Baptist',[1] or 'the Baptizer'.[2] John's clothes marked him out as a prophet,[3] but his message was essentially contained in what he performed, which was primarily 'a baptism of repentance leading to the forgiveness of sins'.[4] Nowhere is it more plain than here that prophetic word and prophetic action belong closely together.[5] Although the baptism of Jews was without precedent, it was an appropriate symbol of cleansing. Not surprisingly, John's baptism has been described as an 'effective sign' or as a 'prophetic symbol'.[6] Our purpose in this chapter is to explore this idea of John's baptism as a prophetic sign more fully.

How would John's baptism have been understood? Attempts to trace the origin of his baptism to either proselyte baptism or the lustrations at Qumran have proved unconvincing to most scholars. The evidence for proselyte baptism, it is suggested, is too late; the rites at Qumran, unlike John's baptism, were repeated regularly.[7] The relevance of both to our argument is more basic: both employ the symbolism of water. The proselyte entering Judaism needs to be cleansed of the sins and impurity of his or her past life; the initiate at Qumran seeks to maintain his purity. In each case, *water is an obvious symbol for interior cleansing.*

The image of washing as a metaphor for removing impurity or sin is common in the Old Testament.[8] The outward action symbolizes an inner reality. It is, then, no surprise that Mark and Luke describe John as proclaiming βάπτισμα μετανοίας εἰς ἄφεσιν ἁμαρτιῶν. But how should we understand that εἰς?

---

[1] Matt 3:1; 11:11–12; 14:2, 8; 16:14; 17:13; Mark 6:28; 8:25; Luke 7:20, 33; 9:19.
[2] Mark 6:14, 24; also 1:4, according to B and some minuscules, including 33.
[3] Cf. Mark 1:6 and parallels with Zech 13:4 and 2 Kings 1:8.
[4] Mark 1:4 // Luke 3:3.
[5] For a discussion of the connection between word and action, see W. David Stacey, *Prophetic Drama in the Old Testament* (London: Epworth, 1990).
[6] For example, James D.G. Dunn, *Baptism in the Holy Spirit*, SBT 2/15 (London: SCM Press, 1970), 17.
[7] For brief accounts of the problem, see Morna D. Hooker, *A Commentary on the Gospel According to St. Mark*, BNTC (London: A&C Black, 1991), 39–43; John P. Meier, *A Marginal Jew*, vol. 2, AB (New York: Doubleday, 1994), 49–52.
[8] For example, Lev 17:16; 2 Kings 5:10–14; Ps 51:2, 7; Isa 1:16; Jer 4:14; Zech 13:1–2. Cf. Josephus' interpretation of John's baptism in *Ant.* 18.5.2.

Is forgiveness of sins something that takes place at the baptism in the Jordan? Or is it something that is *proclaimed* in this action but has not yet taken place? A comparison with Matthew is illuminating since he states only that John was preaching in the wilderness, calling on his hearers to repent – a theme echoed in John's declaration in Matt 3:11: ἐγὼ μὲν ὑμᾶς βαπτίζω ἐν ὕδατι εἰς μετανοίαν. John summons men and women to repent (3:2), and those who are baptized confess their sins (3:6), but for Matthew forgiveness lies in the future, since it is brought by Jesus (9:6) and is made available to many through his death (26:28). Since Mark and Luke interpret John's proclamation of baptism as preparation for what was to come, they would surely have agreed with Matthew that John's baptism pointed forward to the forgiveness brought by Jesus.[9]

1. Prophetic Signs

Whatever the background to John's baptism, it would certainly have been *understood* as a 'prophetic sign' – a dramatic action which, like prophetic words, proclaimed the divine will.[10] Once performed, the prophetic sign – like the prophetic word – could not be undone. John's message and baptism both point forward to the one who follows him. His baptism is 'the beginning of the gospel'.[11] What, then, does it signify?

In the Old Testament, the prophetic action mimics what God is doing or is about to do. Isaiah goes 'naked and barefoot' as a symbol of Israel's coming shame (Isaiah 20); Jeremiah smashes a pot to symbolize the destruction of Jerusalem (Jer 19:1–13); Ezekiel eats inferior bread, cooked with dung, and drinks a small measure of water each day to portray the terrible conditions that the people are going to endure (Ezek 4:9–17). John announces the coming of the Lord – a coming that brings rejoicing but also demands repentance. His baptism could well symbolize the inner cleansing effected by forgiveness. Being submerged in water might also symbolize the death and destruction that will overwhelm the wicked,[12] just as emerging again could suggest salvation and new life.[13]

The link made in all the Gospels between John's baptism with water and the baptism with the Holy Spirit supports all these interpretations. Old Testament prophets warned of a coming day of the Lord which would bring

---

[9] Cf. Meier, *Marginal Jew*, 53–55; Joel Marcus, *Mark 1–8*, AB (New York: Doubleday, 2000), 155–156.
[10] Stacey, *Prophetic Drama*, 260–282.
[11] Cf. Ernst Lohmeyer, *Das Evangelium des Markus*, 17th ed. (Göttingen: Vandenhoeck & Ruprecht, 1967), 19.
[12] Cf. Gen 6:17, Jer 47:2–4, and Ps 106:11.
[13] Cf. Jonah 2:5–6 and Ps 18:16.

judgement and salvation: on the one hand, there would be purification and purging, on the other, renewal and recreation. Both ideas are linked with the expectation of God's! as well as with the image of water. Like the Greek πνεῦμα, the Hebrew word רוּחַ can be translated into English by the word 'breath' as well as by 'wind' and 'spirit'. The wind that purifies and punishes comes from God himself. It is the Lord who will wash and cleanse Israel by means of 'a spirit of judgement' and 'a spirit of burning' in Isa 4:4. It is the breath of the Lord which, like an overflowing stream, will 'sift the nations with the sieve of destruction' in Isa 30:28.[14] The 'hot wind' that overwhelms Israel in judgement in Jer 4:11 comes from the Lord; the prophet goes on to appeal to the people to 'wash [their] hearts clean of wickedness, so that [they] may be saved' (4:14). All these passages link future cleansing with purging or judgement; all of them combine the imagery of water or washing with the Spirit/wind/breath of God.[15]

Especially interesting for our investigation is Ezek 36:25–28, where God promises on the one hand that he will remove his people's sins – a process that is symbolized by sprinkling them with water, an image taken from the cultic rite – and on the other that he will recreate them and put his own spirit within them, so that they obey his commands:

> I will sprinkle clean water upon you, and you shall be clean from all your uncleannesses, and from all your idols I will cleanse you. A new heart I will give you, and a new spirit I will put within you; and I will remove from your body the heart of stone and give you a heart of flesh. I will put my spirit within you, and make you follow my statutes and be careful to observe my ordinances. Then you shall live in the land that I gave to your ancestors: and you shall be my people, and I will be your God.

In Zech 13:1, we are told that 'on that day, a fountain shall be opened for the house of David and the inhabitants of Jerusalem, to cleanse them from sin and impurity': idols, false prophets, and the unclean spirit will be removed. A few verses earlier, in Zech 12:10, God had promised to 'pour out a spirit of compassion and supplication on the house of David and the inhabitants of Jerusalem'.

The Spirit of God is here a spirit of renewal. Water itself is, of course, greatly valued as the source of life,[16] and water in the wilderness, in particular, is seen as a symbol of regeneration.[17] The image of God 'pouring out' his Spirit, just as water is poured out, is used in Isa 44:3–4, where we read: 'I will pour water on the thirsty land and streams on the dry ground. I will

---

[14] Cf. 2 Esdras 13:11.
[15] For a similar link between the Spirit's cleansing from sin and the cleansing of flesh by water, see 1QS 3:6–9; 4:20–21. Cf. also Jub 1:23, which associates a 'holy spirit' with cleansing.
[16] Cf. Ezek 17:5–6; 47:1–12.
[17] Cf. Isa 35:6–7; 41:18.

pour my spirit upon your descendants and my blessing on your offspring'.[18] Here renewal, the other side of what is expected, is emphasized. The Spirit of God, active at the creation (Gen 1:2), will bring new life to the earth and to God's people.[19]

Although the 'spirit of judgement' and 'spirit of burning' expected by Isaiah (4:4) sound totally negative, closer examination shows that the *purpose* of this judgement was to purge: 'Whoever is left in Zion and remains in Jerusalem will be called holy' (v. 3). Moreover, this comes about 'once the Lord has washed away the filth of the daughters of Zion and cleansed the bloodstains of Jerusalem from its midst by a spirit of judgement and by a spirit of burning'. The image of God *purging* his people is common.[20] Washing and purging are likened to what takes place in the moral and spiritual sphere. Reward and punishment go together, as in Isa 61:1–4, where the prophet, claiming that the Spirit of God rests upon him, declares that his task is to proclaim not only 'the year of the Lord's favour' but also 'the day of vengeance for our God'. The Baptist is portrayed in 'Q' as having threatened wrath and destruction by fire; he is also said to have expected the wheat to be gathered into the granary.

We suggest, then, that John's baptism with water was intended, not simply as a symbol of cleansing, but as *a dramatic prophetic sign pointing to what God was about to do in a baptism with the Holy Spirit* – a pouring out of God's Spirit that would not only bring inner cleansing and punishment but would also renew his people. But how much of this is reflected in our Gospels?

2. Mark's Interpretation

Everything that the Evangelists tell us about John's baptism mark it out as preparatory. But each tells the story in a different way. Mark's brief account of John's activity begins with a quotation from scripture which identifies him with Isaiah's voice, summoning men and women to 'prepare the way of the Lord'. His message, like his baptism, prepares those who respond for one who follows him. It consists of three points, all of which bear witness to his successor:

1. Someone much stronger than John is coming after him.
2. John is unworthy even to unfasten the thongs of this coming one's sandals.

---

[18] The targum of Isa 44:3 specifically compares God's Spirit with water: 'As waters are poured upon a thirsty land, and flow down over the dry ground, so will I pour my holy spirit upon thy sons, and my blessing upon thy son's sons'.
[19] Isa 32:15; Ezek 39:29; and Joel 2:28–29 also speak of God pouring out his Spirit on Israel.
[20] For example, Job 23:10; Ps 66:10; Isa 1:25; 48:10; Jer 6:29–30; 9:7; Zech 13:9; Mal 3:2–4.

3. Whereas John has baptized with water, the coming one will baptize with the Holy Spirit.

Mark's next scene shows the baptism of Jesus, who is acknowledged by the heavenly voice as the beloved Son of God and as well pleasing to him. Jesus is clearly the one whose coming John has proclaimed. We understand now why John spoke of his unworthiness to serve him. As Mark's story unfolds, we see men and women recognizing this quality in Jesus, though rarely succeeding in expressing their awareness in words; indeed, it is only the centurion in charge of Jesus' execution who, echoing the words spoken in 1:11, confesses him to be 'Son of God' (15:39). Yet the belief that Jesus is the Son of God provides the explanation for the whole story. Unclean spirits acknowledge him to be 'the Holy One of God' (1:24), 'the Son of God' (3:11), and 'Son of the Most High God' (5:7). Men and women who see Jesus' mighty actions are overcome by fear (4:41; 5:15, 33) and terror (5:42), and ask wonderingly who he is (4:41). His opponents question him as to the source of his authority (1:27; 3:22; 11:28).

John's first promise was of someone 'stronger' than himself. Ἰσχυρότερος is hardly the word we would have expected, but it is clearly appropriate to Mark's story.[21] Following Jesus' baptism, we are told how he was tested by Satan in the wilderness, and though Mark does not tell us the outcome, the presence of wild beasts and angels suggests that he sees the confrontation as a cosmic battle. In 3:27, we realize from Jesus' parable that, since his exorcism of unclean spirits demonstrates that he has defeated Satan, he is clearly 'stronger' than Satan himself. Further proof of Jesus' strength is seen when he rebukes the wind and waves and subdues the storm (4:35–41). He then destroys a whole legion of unclean spirits and calms a man possessing supernatural strength, whom no one had previously been able to subdue (5:1–13).[22]

The promise concerning future baptism with the Holy Spirit appears at first sight to be the one that is most clearly picked up in Mark 1:9–13, for it is while Jesus is himself being baptized by John – with water – that the Spirit descends on him from heaven. This scene is linked by Mark to the next one with his favourite phrase – καὶ εὐθύς – suggesting that they belong together. The Spirit drives Jesus out into the wilderness to confront Satan. In the rest of his story, Mark leaves us in no doubt that what Jesus does is in the power of the Holy Spirit, for though the Spirit is rarely mentioned, the parable in which he compares Satan to a 'strong man' who has been bound concludes

---

[21] God himself is characterized by strength in the Old Testament; see, e.g., Deut 10:17; Ps 24:8.

[22] Cf. Mark 9:18, where it is said that the disciples did not have the strength to cast out an unclean spirit.

with the claim that what he is doing is in the power of the Holy Spirit (3:29–30).

But John's promise was that the coming one would baptize *you* – that is, those whom he himself has baptized with water – with the Holy Spirit. Mark's terse account of Jesus' baptism by John provides the explanation as to *how* the coming one is going to carry out this baptism, but there is no reference in the rest of Mark's Gospel to Jesus baptizing anyone, either with water or with the Spirit. Is this third element of John's message, then, unlike the other two, a promise whose fulfilment Mark fails to describe? This seems unlikely, since the three statements in Mark 1:7–8 clearly belong together: the first two refer to what Jesus is and does *during his ministry*, while the third saying points back to what we have been told about John's baptism: since his baptism prepared the way for the one who followed him, this suggests that it, too, pointed forward to something that Jesus would do *during his ministry*.

Is it possible that he thinks of Jesus as baptizing with the Holy Spirit *during his ministry*? This thesis was argued forty years ago by John Edmund Yates,[23] though it has been generally ignored or rejected by other scholars. Yet there is much to be said for it, as we shall see.

In Mark, the recipients of John's baptism are described as 'the whole district of Judaea, together with everyone from Jerusalem'. Although this is clearly an exaggeration, the statement that all Jews throughout the nearby area have responded to John's call is intended to indicate that the whole nation has been prepared for what is to come. In this prophetic action, the few represent the many. Those who, according to John, are to be baptized with the Holy Spirit are those whom he himself has baptized with water. If, then, it is *the whole nation* whom John has baptized and whom he addresses as ὑμᾶς, then it is *the whole nation* which is to be baptized with Holy Spirit,[24] and not Jesus' disciples alone.

We have seen that such a baptism with the Holy Spirit might well bring purification and destruction, as well as renewal and restoration. The day of the Lord would bring both judgement and salvation, and God's people must expect the Lord to refine them as well as to bless them.[25] Mark has depicted Jesus as empowered during his ministry with the Holy Spirit (1:9–11). Everything he does will be in the power of the Holy Spirit – a fact confirmed in 3:20–30. Specifically, Mark shows how Jesus' authority over 'unclean spirits' – a phrase he uses eleven times – and over Satan himself is the work of the Holy

---

[23] John Edmund Yates, *The Spirit and the Kingdom* (London: SPCK, 1963).
[24] Jesus, of course, begins his ministry in Galilee and does not reach Judaea until 10:1, but the crowds who come to hear him are said to come not only from Galilee, but 'from Judaea and from Jerusalem, from Idumea, from beyond Jordan, and from the region round Tyre and Sidon' (3:7).
[25] Mal 3:1–12

Spirit (1:12–13; 3:29–30). Jesus is said to 'destroy' these unclean spirits (1:24), but those whom they possess are released, cleansed, and restored to health and to society (5:1–15). Jesus also forgives sins (2:1–12) and makes a leper clean (1:40–45). His healing miracles purge the sick not only from unclean spirits but also from impurity and sin (1:40–2:12; 5:21–34).

Jesus' message, too, is a call to purification. Because the rule or kingdom of God has drawn near, he calls on men and women to '*Repent* and believe the good news' (1:15). He calls sinners to follow him, and symbolizes God's forgiveness by eating with them (2:13–17). He demands *inner* purity and true love of God, not outward purification (7:1–30). At the end of his ministry he comes into the temple and purges it of those who have substituted concern with the 'purity' of sacrifices for true worship (11:12–19; cf. Mal 3:1–4). Jesus' prophetic action is a protest against the sham piety of the temple and a demand for it to become a house of prayer, though Mark, writing after 70 CE, inevitably saw it as pointing forward to its destruction.[26] Throughout his ministry, then, Jesus purifies Israel from sinfulness and uncleanness.

Side by side with Jesus' work of purification goes restoration. Some of his miracles appear to symbolize renewal and plenty – for example, the feedings (6:30–44; 8:1–10) or the restoration of nature (4:35–41). In his healing miracles, he brings restoration of health, of limbs (2:1–12; 3:1–6), of sight (8:22–26; 10:46–52) and hearing (7:31–37), even of life itself (5:35–43). The verb σῴζω points us to the symbolic significance of these miracles, for salvation is what all long for (10:26; cf. 13:13, 20). Jesus' mission is to save life (3:4), and those who respond in faith are saved (5:34; 10:52). The sick are saved (5:23, 28; 6:56), since it is they who need a physician – but this physician has come to save sinners (2:17). He has come, too, to give his life as a ransom for many (10:45), and it is through his death that the many are saved: paradoxically, it is the one who refuses to save himself who is able to save others (15:30–31; cf. 8:35).

Apart from 1:1–13 and 3:29, Mark does not make the link between the Spirit and Jesus' ministry. Does this mean that it is unimportant? The emphasis on the Spirit in 1:1–13, which provides us with key information for understanding the Gospel, suggests the opposite. What we are told in the Prologue (Jesus as Messiah, Son of God, the fulfilment of scripture, endowed with the Holy Spirit, confronting Satan) is worked out in the following narrative.

From time to time, however, there are reminders that the baptism of John points forward to that of Jesus. One significant example of this is in 11:27–33, where Jesus is questioned about his authority. To justify his actions, Jesus appeals to *the baptism* of John: the implication is clear – the baptism of John pointed forward to what Jesus has been doing in the temple. As in 3:22–30,

---

[26] See Morna D. Hooker, *The Signs of a Prophet* (London: SCM Press, 1997), 44–48.

there are two possibilities regarding the source of John's authority and his own, but this time the choice is between God and men rather than between the Holy Spirit and Satan: to opt for 'men', however, is to deny Jesus' divine authority, and so in effect to opt for Satan.[27] Jesus invites his opponents to understand that what he is doing is the fulfilment of what John initiated in his baptism: just as John proclaimed the will of God, so now Jesus enacts it.

Other references to John suggest that Mark saw him as the forerunner of Jesus in his death. In 1:14, he is 'handed over' (παραδίδωμι); in 6:17–29, his death and burial foreshadow Jesus' own; in 9:12–13, the rejection of John, now identified as 'Elijah', seals Jesus' own fate. It is perhaps no accident that in 10:38–39, Jesus refers to his coming death as a 'baptism'. It will bring to others both condemnation (11:12–14, 20–21; 12:9) and salvation (10:45; 14:24).

In the light of Acts 2, commentators have tended to assume that the baptism with the Holy Spirit promised in Mark 1:8 must mean a pouring out of God's Spirit on believers, enabling them to prophesy, as foretold in Joel.[28] But if the Holy Spirit is understood as the *agent* of the baptism that Jesus brings (as water is the agent of John's baptism), then we see that what Jesus does in his ministry is to baptize men and women with the Holy Spirit – to plunge them into God's purifying and creative power – bringing them cleansing and forgiveness, renewal and life. Those who respond to Jesus' message find salvation. For those who refuse to repent, however, this baptism inevitably brings judgement and punishment, since for those who resist the Holy Spirit there can be no forgiveness (3:29). It would seem, then, that Mark understands his Gospel to be the story of how Jesus 'baptized' men and women with the Holy Spirit.

We should not forget, moreover, that the enabling of the disciples depicted by Luke in Acts 2 is also one of Mark's themes. Jesus begins his ministry by calling disciples to share his work (1:16–20), and he appoints twelve to proclaim the gospel and to have authority over demons (3:14–15). When he sends them out, he gives them authority over unclean spirits (6:7). The disciples, then, are called to carry on his work of baptizing with the Holy Spirit. But they are also called to share the cup and baptism of suffering – to be baptized *with* him in death and resurrection (10:38–39).[29] They, however, are only partially successful: they cast out many demons (6:13) but then fail with the epileptic boy (9:14–29). The command to feed a crowd leaves them baffled (6:37), while they flee from danger and suffering (14:50, 66–72). But after the resurrection, the Holy Spirit will be working through them (13:11).

---

[27] Cf. Mark 8:33, where Satan and 'men' are both opposed to what comes from God.
[28] For example, C.K. Barrett (*The Holy Spirit and the Gospel Tradition* [London: SPCK, 1958], 125) writes that Mark's form of this saying 'must doubtless have been understood by the Evangelist and his readers as a reference to the gift of the Spirit to the church'.
[29] Cf. 8:34–38. See also Romans 6.

How, then, did Mark interpret the relationship between baptism with water and baptism with the Holy Spirit? If we have understood Mark correctly, it would seem that he presents John's baptism with water as a dramatic action by John, symbolizing *another* baptism. Like all such prophetic actions, it was *a way of proclaiming what God was doing or was about to do,* a prophetic sign of the baptism with the Holy Spirit carried out by Jesus.

3. Luke and Matthew

A comparison of Mark with Matthew and Luke raises problems regarding sources. For our purposes, the important question is whether their version of John's preaching might be earlier than Mark's.

In both Matthew and Luke, the saying comparing the two baptisms is split, and the other two sayings are sandwiched in between:

1a: I have baptized you with water;
2:   The one who follows me is stronger than I;
3:   I am not worthy to undo his sandals;
1b: He will baptize you with Holy Spirit and fire.

The other notable difference from the Marcan version is the addition of the phrase 'and fire'. But *is* it an addition? Or is the 'Q' version[30] of the saying the more original?

The division and separation of the saying about baptism must surely be secondary. Instead of a comparison between the two baptisms we have a chiastic structure, with two short sayings about baptism surrounding the two other parallel sayings emphasizing Jesus' superiority. The effect is to relegate John to the past and focus our attention on Jesus.

What, however, are we to say about the reference to fire? Many commentators argue that this is original. Some of them argue that the earliest version of John's preaching contained no reference to the Spirit, referring only to a future baptism with fire: it should thus be understood as a threat of coming judgement.[31] This is supported by the context in Matthew and Luke, where John goes on to describe the way in which the coming one will winnow his wheat and burn the chaff with unquenchable fire.[32] Others suggest

---

[30] The term 'Q' is used here simply to denote the material used in common by Matthew and Luke, and not to imply the use of a particular source or sources.

[31] This suggestion has a venerable history. See, e.g., T.W. Manson, *The Sayings of Jesus* (London: SCM Press, 1949), 40–41; Rudolf Bultmann, *The History of the Synoptic Tradition,* trans. John Marsh (Oxford: Blackwell, 1963), 111. Similarly, Vincent Taylor, *The Gospel According to St. Mark* (London: Macmillan, 1952), 157: 'Probably, then, the reference to the Holy Spirit has been introduced under the influence of the Christian practice of baptism'.

[32] Matt 3:12 // Luke 3:17. Cf. also the threat of destruction by fire in Matt 3:10 // Luke 3:9.

that πνεῦμα originally referred not to Spirit but to *wind,* and that the word ἁγίῳ was added later:[33] the wind is necessary to separate the chaff from the grain,[34] so that the simple πνεύματι καὶ πυρί would make excellent sense in the Matthean and Lucan context. Both wind and fire would then be symbols of judgement and of destruction.[35]

Luke's inclusion of these 'harvest' sayings (3:17) is significant, since they are in apparent tension with his own understanding of John's promise that Jesus will baptize *with the Holy Spirit.* John's saying is echoed in Acts 1:5, where the risen Christ says, 'For John indeed baptized with water, but you shall be baptized in Holy Spirit, in a few days' time'.[36] This prophecy is fulfilled at Pentecost (2:1–4), and the phenomenon is associated with a noise 'like that of a rushing, violent wind' and the sight of 'divided tongues, as if of fire'.

Although Luke preserved the 'Q' sayings about judgement, therefore, he clearly understood John's words about the Holy Spirit as pointing forward to the gift of the Spirit to the disciples at Pentecost. Since he associated this experience with the image of fire, he apparently saw it as a purifying as well as an empowering experience.[37] The fire that destroys (Luke 3:9, 17) can also purge.[38] On the day of Pentecost, Peter urges the crowds to 'Repent, and be baptized … in the name of Jesus Christ, for the forgiveness of sins, and you will receive the gift of the Holy Spirit' (Acts 2:38). As in Luke 3:3, baptism points forward (εἰς) to the forgiveness of sins.[39] That this forgiveness is effected by the Holy Spirit is confirmed in Acts 10:43–44, where the Spirit is given *before* baptism and interpreted as proof that Cornelius and his household have already received forgiveness of sins. If we are puzzled by the fact that they are baptized *after* receiving the Spirit, that is because we do not appreciate the nature of the prophetic action, which does not necessarily precede what it signifies.[40]

---

[33] For example, Barrett, *Holy Spirit,* 126. He points to the slight ms. evidence for the omission of the word in Luke 3:16. It is arguable, however, that the omission from Luke is not due to a recollection of a 'Q' version, but to the fact that 'wind' makes excellent sense in the immediate Lucan context. It will certainly not be what Luke himself wrote, however, since he understood the saying to point forward to the gift of the Holy Spirit at Pentecost. Among others who support 'wind and fire' as the original form, see Ernest Best, 'Spirit-Baptism', *NT* 4 (1960): 236–243.

[34] The image is used of destruction in Isa 40:24 and 41:15–16.

[35] Cf. Isa 30:27–28; 66:15. The symbols are sometimes combined in images such as 'a hot wind' (Jer 4:11–12), and 'breath of fire' (2 Esd 13:10).

[36] Cf. also Acts 11:16 and Luke 24:49.

[37] The wind in Acts 2:2 is referred to as πνοή and so can hardly be an echo of πνεῦμα in Luke 3:16.

[38] God's Spirit is connected with the removal of sin in Jewish thought; cf. Isa 4:4; 1QS 3:6; 4:20–21.

[39] Cf. Acts 11:13–18; 15:8–9.

[40] Stacey, *Prophetic Drama,* 277.

In Luke 3:16, it seems likely that Luke understood the saying as primarily pointing forward to Pentecost and the experience of Christian believers. Yet this future baptism means also that they will be purged from sin. The Q context, which Luke has retained, stresses this negative aspect of what is expected, since it emphasizes the punishment and destruction of those who do *not* repent and respond. Luke has, however, tempered the negative element in John's teaching with positive advice to the repentant (3:10–14). Perhaps, then, Luke thought of two separate future baptisms – with the Spirit for some, and with the fire of judgement for others.[41] Yet 'Spirit' and 'fire' are linked together with καί, not presented as alternatives. Moreover, while the Spirit is poured out at Pentecost, condemnation and punishment still lie in the future, and will not occur until the coming of the Son of man and the restoration of Israel's kingdom (Luke 17:22–37; Acts 1:6).

Luke's references to the Spirit, like Mark's, are clustered at the beginning of the Gospel. In 4:14, Jesus comes into Galilee 'in the power of the Spirit'. Immediately following, he enters the synagogue in Nazareth, reads the passage from Isaiah 61 beginning 'The Spirit of God is upon me' (though the reference to 'the day of vengeance' is omitted), and declares, 'Today this scripture has been fulfilled in your hearing' (4:21). Like Mark, Luke thinks of Jesus as empowered by the Holy Spirit.

In the pages that follow, Luke shows Jesus fulfilling Isaiah 61's prophecy. He proclaims good news to the poor (4:43–44; 6:20–49), releases the captives and frees the oppressed – from unclean spirits (4:33–37), from sickness (4:38–41; 6:6–11), from leprosy (5:12–16), from sin (5:17–26), from death (7:11–17) – and announces the year of jubilee which changes everything (5:1–11, 27–28; 6:5). When John's disciples come to him in 7:18–20 to ask if he is 'the one who is to come', only the recovery of sight remains unfulfilled. In that very hour, says Luke, 'Jesus healed many from diseases, plagues, and evil spirits, and gave sight to many who were blind'. His message to John echoes Isa 26:19 and 35:5–6, as well as Isa 61:1. All that Jesus does he does because the Spirit of the Lord is on him; he is indeed the one proclaimed by John – 'the one who is to come' – the one who is to baptize with the Holy Spirit.

Jesus then asks the crowd about how they see John, and tells them that there is no one born of women who is greater than John; yet 'the least in the kingdom of God is greater than he' (7:28). Luke comments that the people, having been baptized by John, acknowledged God to be righteous, but the Pharisees and scribes, who had refused baptism, rejected his will. For Luke, who recognizes that the entire population was *not* baptized by John,[42] the baptism which Jesus exercises is seen as positive, bringing forgiveness and

---

[41] Cf. Origen, *Homiliae in Lucam* 24.
[42] Contrast Luke 3:3 with Mark 1:5 // Matt 3:5.

renewal,[43] while those who rejected John – and so Jesus – will be punished. The final paragraph about John – the 'parable' about children at play (7:31–35) – reminds us that those who rejected John will also reject Jesus.

Luke ends this section with the story of the penitent woman who anoints Jesus' feet (7:36–50), a story which includes the parable of the two debtors (7:41–43). The theme is forgiveness and salvation, and it provides a fitting end to a section which began with the reading of Isaiah 61. The Pharisee's comment (v. 39) that if Jesus were a prophet he would have known that the woman was a sinner points us to the significance of the situation. Jesus does indeed know that she is a sinner, and precisely because he is more than 'a prophet'[44] he brings her forgiveness and sets her free. In spite of Luke's Pentecost material, therefore, he presents Jesus throughout these chapters as the fulfilment of John's promise that his successor would baptize with the Holy Spirit. The 'power' that comes upon the disciples in Jerusalem (Acts 1:8) is *the power with which Jesus himself has worked*. They, too, now perform 'signs and wonders' (Acts 2:22, 43).

Matthew offers no parallel to the Pentecost story. Although his Gospel concludes with the dominical command to baptize 'into the name of the Father and of the Son and of the Holy Spirit' (Matt 28:19), there is no hint that this baptism is to be ἐν πνεύματι ἁγίῳ. Like Mark, Matthew envisages the disciples as empowered with the Holy Spirit in the future when, following in Jesus' footsteps, they are 'handed over' and face false accusations.[45] Yet already during his ministry, Jesus gives his disciples authority over unclean spirits, a story found in all three Synoptics,[46] and in Matthew this authority over unclean spirits is clearly identified with the Holy Spirit (Matt 12:28).[47] They are therefore clearly acting in the power and with the authority of the Holy Spirit.[48]

How, then, does Matthew understand John's promise that the coming one will baptize with the Holy Spirit and fire? Using the 'Q' tradition of John's teaching, he has emphasized the negative aspect of the Spirit's work. He points to a future judgement, when the wicked are destroyed in unquenchable fire (3:10, 12). Unlike Luke, he does not include teaching addressed to the repentant (Luke 3:10–14), so John's core teaching is immediately preceded by

---

[43] Is this why he omits the reference to 'the day of vengeance' from Isaiah 61 in 4:19?

[44] B* and Ξ read ὁ προφήτης, which is another way of making the same point.

[45] Matt 24:9 // Mark 13:11. Cf. Matt 10:19–20. These sayings all point to a specific occasion after the end of Jesus' ministry. Luke 11:13 suggests that his followers can ask for the Spirit at any time.

[46] Matt 10:1 // Mark 6:7 // Luke 9:1.

[47] This saying is part of Jesus' response to those who accuse him of casting out demons in the power of the prince of demons (Matt 12:24–37). Cf. Mark 3:22–30 and Luke 11:15–23. Luke has 'finger' in v. 20 instead of 'spirit'.

[48] See also Matt 10:20 (cf. Luke 12:11–20).

the denunciation of the Pharisees and Sadducees (Matt 3:7–10), and followed by the reference to the winnowing fork, the threshing floor, and the burning of chaff. Moreover, in Matthew coming judgement is an important theme,[49] and fire is frequently referred to as the means of future punishment.[50] This corresponds to the stress throughout his Gospel on the future judgement by the Son of man. For him, 'baptism with fire' appears to lie in the future.[51]

Nevertheless, Matthew has retained Mark's account of the confrontation between Jesus and the Pharisees (Matt 12:22–32 // Mark 3:20–30). Indeed, he has strengthened it, since he has added to it the saying, 'But if it is by the Spirit of God that I cast out demons, then the kingdom of God has come upon you' (12:28). Moreover, the incident is introduced with a quotation of Isaiah 42 which includes the words 'I will put my Spirit upon him' (12:18). Intriguingly, it is followed by sayings about the fruit of good and bad trees and the words 'You brood of vipers!' (12:33–34), echoing John's words in 3:7–10 and suggesting that what Jesus is doing 'by the Spirit of God' is seen as the fulfilment of John's promise that he would baptize 'with the Holy Spirit and fire', bringing both salvation and judgement. The continuity between John and Jesus is seen in the fact that both proclaim the same message (3:2; 4:17).

4. The Fourth Gospel

Finally, we turn to the Fourth Gospel, where John's ministry of baptism is mentioned only incidentally. The Evangelist's emphasis is on the Baptist's testimony to the one who follows him. Twice in the Prologue, John testifies: first to 'the light' (1:6–9), then to the one who comes after him, but who ranks before him (1:15). When the narrative begins, in 1:19, it is with 'the testimony of John' to 'priests and Levites from Jerusalem'. His three negative answers to their questions emphasize the fact that he is merely the witness to the one who follows him. In the Fourth Gospel it is the Baptist, not the Evangelist, who applies the words of Isa 40:3 to himself: he is simply 'a voice crying out in the wilderness', preparing the way of the Lord (John 1:23). Questioned by those who had been sent to interrogate him[52] as to why he is baptizing, he says merely that he baptizes with water, but immediately goes on to speak of

---

[49] The theme is especially prominent in passages which Matthew does *not* share with Mark, e.g., 5:27–30; 7:1–5, 13–27; 10:15; 11:20–24; 13:24–30, 36–43, 47–50; 18:23–35; 22:1–14; 23:1–39; 25:1–46.

[50] Matt 3:10, 12; 5:22; 7:19; 13:40, 42, 50; 18:8, 9; 25:41.

[51] Ulrich Luz, *Matthew 1–7: A Commentary,* trans. Wilhelm C. Linss (Edinburgh: T&T Clark, 1990), 171–172, maintains that Matthew distinguished between 'baptism by the Spirit' and 'baptism by fire'.

[52] These people are described as having been sent 'from the Pharisees' (1:24). Either the Evangelist was confused about the beliefs of the Pharisees and has used 'Jews' (1:19) and

the coming one who is already present, though unrecognized, whose sandal thong he is unworthy to untie (John 1:24–27). John's words seem a strange answer to the question, but they once again serve to emphasize his witness to Jesus.

On the following day, Jesus was identified by John as 'the Lamb of God' and as the one who ranks ahead of him because he was before him (1:29–30). This is the Johannine equivalent of the Synoptic saying about the coming one who is *stronger* than John. Its relevance to the rest of the Gospel is clear. It has been used already, in 1:15, to remind us that John's witness was to the pre-existent and incarnate Word, and it will be echoed later in the story.[53] Once again John speaks of his baptism: he 'came baptizing *with water in order that* [the one who ranks before him] might be revealed to Israel' (1:31). The sole purpose of John's baptism in the Fourth Gospel appears to be to provide the backdrop for John's testimony: 'I saw the Spirit descend like a dove from heaven and rest on him. I myself did not know him, but he who sent me to baptize with water said to me, "The one on whom you see the Spirit descend and rest, he it is who baptizes with Holy Spirit". I myself have seen and bear witness that he is the Son of God' (vv. 32–34). On the third day John sees Jesus again and repeats his testimony that he is the Lamb of God. The disciples who are with John then follow Jesus (1:35–37).

The way in which the Fourth Evangelist has used the tradition suggests a very different understanding of John's baptism from the one we find in the Synoptics. He has emphasized the role of John as witness to Jesus to the extent that his baptism no longer has any purpose in itself except to provide the setting for the revelation of Jesus' identity.[54] The Baptist himself denies that he is to be seen in the role of Elijah or 'the prophet', since he is only a voice bearing witness to his successor. Mark's comparison between the two baptisms, already separated in Matthew and Luke, is now pulled even further apart, so that John's statement that he baptizes with water occurs on the *first* day (1:26), his declaration that Jesus baptizes with the Holy Spirit on the *second* (1:33). The other two sayings comparing John with Jesus, which are closely linked in the Synoptics, are also divided between these two days.[55]

How did the Fourth Evangelist understand this baptism with the Holy Spirit? Like Luke, he seems to look forward to the future gift of the Spirit

---

'Pharisees' interchangeably, or he was thinking of *another* group of interrogators and *not* the 'priests and Levites' referred to in 1:19.

[53] John 8:58; 17:5.

[54] The two baptisms are thus neither compared (as in Mark) nor contrasted (as in Matthew and Luke) but simply referred to. It is perhaps for this reason that John refers later to Jesus himself baptizing (3:22, 26) – although in 4:1–2 he indicated that it was his disciples who did so, not Jesus himself.

[55] Cf. Matt 3:11 // Mark 1:17 // Luke 3:16 with John 1:30, 27.

to Jesus' disciples. In 7:39, the enigmatic remark that 'there was as yet no Spirit' is explained by the context, which shows that he is thinking of the gift of the Spirit to believers, something that could not take place until Jesus was glorified. It may well be significant, then, that when Jesus dies – or, in Johannine terms, is glorified – he 'gives up his spirit' (19:30). Certainly he is said, after the resurrection, to have breathed on his disciples and to have said, 'Receive the Holy Spirit' (20:22). Interestingly, the Fourth Evangelist apparently links *this* 'baptism' with the authority to forgive sins (20:23).

We find an echo of the Baptist's testimony in 3:5, where it is said that no one can enter the kingdom of God unless they are born of water and spirit.[56] Although John's water baptism is important for those who wish to be born from above, water is not mentioned again in this passage, and its significance is apparently subsumed in Spirit baptism. It is *the Spirit* who gives life (6:63).

In the Fourth Gospel, water is an image of the 'living water' that gives life to the believer (John 4:1–30); it is used in this sense as an analogy for the future gift of the Spirit in 7:37–39. The spring of water provided by Jesus (4:14; 7:38) brings renewal and life.

The work of the Spirit is described in chs. 14–16. The Spirit – or παράκλητος – is a Spirit of truth (14:16–17; 15:26; 16:13) who will teach (14:26) and guide (16:13–15) the disciples. The Spirit will also convict *the world* of sin, of righteousness, and of judgement (16:7–11). In this last passage we see the *negative* aspect of the Spirit's coming. How will this work be done? It will be done *through the disciples,* to whom the Spirit will be sent (16:7). This promise is fulfilled in John 20:21–23, when Jesus tells the disciples that he is sending them, *as the Father sent him,* breathes on them, and says, 'Receive the Holy Spirit: whoever's sins you forgive will be forgiven; whoever's you retain will be retained'. Although John, like Luke, sees 'baptism with the Holy Spirit' as something experienced by the disciples after Jesus' resurrection, for him (as for Luke) that baptism means that the disciples are *to continue the work that Jesus himself has done,* leading men and women into the truth and bringing forgiveness to some, condemnation to others (3:16–19). In other words, *receiving* the Spirit will enable them to *baptize* with the Spirit.

5. Conclusion

All our sources refer to John's baptism as a 'baptism with water', and to the expected baptism as a 'baptism with the Holy Spirit'. If any reliance can be placed on the criterion of multiple attestation, it would seem that the earliest

---

[56] This is the natural interpretation of 'water' here, especially in view of the references to the Baptist in 3:22–24. The suggestion that it refers to physical birth seems inappropriate, since the Evangelist goes on to contrast flesh and Spirit.

form of the saying referred to πνεῦμα ἅγιον, not to πνεῦμα. Although 'wind and fire' are associated in Jewish thought as purifying agents, there is evidence that the Spirit of God could also be expected to purge and punish. 'Wind' and 'fire', then, are metaphors that spell out part of what the 'Holy Spirit' might be expected to do. The fact that the 'Q' tradition links the Spirit with fire demonstrates that this interpretation of what 'baptism with the Holy Spirit' signified is an early one, whether or not it was part of the original saying.

All our sources see *some* link between John's baptism and the baptism which Jesus himself is expected to carry out. For all the Evangelists, John's primary function was to be the witness to Jesus, but by the time we come to the Fourth Gospel, this is his only function, and the only purpose of his baptism is to identify Jesus.

The striking differences in these accounts leave us with difficulties, however. Firstly, there is the obvious tension in Luke-Acts between the context of the saying – prophecies of judgement and of punishment – and its interpretation as a promise of the gift of the Spirit to Jesus' disciples at Pentecost. For Matthew this is not a problem because he has concentrated on the theme of judgement, while the Fourth Evangelist has taken the alternative route and omitted any reference to judgement, interpreting John's words as a promise that Jesus would give his followers the Spirit. Mark's enigmatic version has neither the 'Q' context suggesting judgement nor a Pentecost experience at the end of the Gospel to explain how he interpreted it.

Secondly, there is an anomaly in Matthew and Luke in the fact that the recipients of John's baptism on the one hand and of Jesus' on the other are all addressed as ὑμᾶς.[57] In Matthew, it is apparently those who are baptized with water 'for repentance' (Matt 3:11), 'confessing their sins' (3:6), who can expect to be baptized 'with the Holy Spirit and fire', and who will therefore experience judgement and punishment! The 'Q' context of the saying suggests that the logion *ought* to read, 'I have baptized you with water *lest* you are baptized with holy Spirit and fire' – that is, 'Repent, while you have time, lest you receive condemnation'. Luke, in spite of his use of the Q material, nevertheless suggests that many who came for baptism were repentant (Luke 3:10–15), and describes John's message as 'good news' (3:18). There is still an anomaly, however, since those who are baptized with water in Luke 3:16 are not the people who receive the gift of the Spirit in Acts 2. Why, then, is ὑμᾶς used in both halves of the saying? In other words, the form of the saying does not fit the Evangelist's interpretation, either in Matthew or in Luke. For the Fourth Evangelist there is no problem, since ὑμᾶς is missing: there is no indication as to *who* is baptized, whether with water or with the Holy Spirit.

---

[57] This point is stressed by James D.G. Dunn, 'Spirit-and-Fire Baptism', *NT* 14 (1972): 81–92.

In Mark, too, the word ὑμᾶς is used twice, addressed to the crowds who come to John for baptism. Is the baptism with the Holy Spirit that John announces expected to bring judgement, or is it an eschatological gift? In the absence of the context provided by Q, emphasizing judgement, and of any 'Pentecost' scene, we have only Mark's own narrative to guide us. Are the two interpretations offered by Matthew and Luke perhaps *partial* understandings of the significance of John's baptism? And is it possible that in Mark the ὑμᾶς who are baptized with water are identical with the ὑμᾶς to be baptized with the Holy Spirit?

As we have seen, there is good evidence that first-century Judaism would have understood the pouring out of God's Spirit as an eschatological gift which would renew creation: Joel 2:28–29, the passage quoted by Luke in Acts 2:16–21, is an obvious example. We have seen, too, that there was an expectation that God would purge his people from their sins by a spirit of judgement and a spirit of burning (Isa 4:4).

The fact that all our Evangelists preserve the link between the two baptisms suggests that John himself saw his baptism as a prophetic drama signifying baptism with the Holy Spirit. What he was expecting was an outpouring of God's Spirit, bringing judgement and destruction to the unrepentant,[58] forgiveness and renewal to those who responded.[59] In the words of Professor Dunn:

> What John held out before his hearers was a baptism which was neither solely destructive nor solely gracious, but which contained both elements in itself. … the repentant would experience a purgative, refining, but ultimately merciful judgement; the impenitent, the stiff-necked and hard of heart, would be broken and destroyed.[60]

'Q' emphasized the latter, and this influenced the way Matthew understood the tradition, while Luke balanced it with the more positive interpretation in Luke 4–11. The author of the Fourth Gospel stressed the *future* work of the Spirit. *All* our Evangelists portray Jesus as bringing both salvation and judgement to Israel in the course of his ministry, and *all* suggest that Jesus handed on the task of baptizing with the Holy Spirit to his disciples, who will extend his mission to the world.[61] Although Luke correctly understood 'baptism with water' to point forward to 'baptism with the Holy Spirit', he

---

[58] Cf. 1 Cor 10:1–5, where Paul refers to baptism into Moses and links it with drinking from the spiritual rock (i.e., Christ), which makes one liable to judgement. He uses a similar idea of the Eucharist in 1 Cor 11:29.

[59] Cf. 1 Cor 6:11.

[60] Dunn, 'Spirit-and-Fire Baptism', 86. All our Gospels portray Jesus as offering the choice to his hearers at the very beginning of his ministry – in Mark, in the parable of the Sower (Mark 4:1–20); in Matthew, in the Sermon on the Mount (Matthew 5–7; see esp. 7:13–27); in Luke, in the Sermon on the Plain (Luke 6:20–49). In John the choice is set out in 3:16–21.

[61] Matt 28:19; Mark 13:10; Luke 24:46, 49; John 20:21–23; Acts 1:8.

has misled us by *identifying* the enabling of a small company of disciples at Pentecost with the baptism itself. For John, and for Jesus, it was far more than this. Just as John's whole mission was to point forward to Jesus, so his baptism was intended to point forward to the baptism which Jesus would carry out. Behind *all* our traditions we can discern the powerful symbolism of a baptism with water that was intended to be a dramatic representation of a baptism with the Holy Spirit, bringing forgiveness of sins, renewal, and judgement. If we want to see how this baptism with the Holy Spirit was effected, we need look no further than to the ministry of Jesus himself.

22. John the Baptist and the Johannine Prologue

The Johannine Prologue is not only one of the most important passages in the New Testament, but also one of the most controversial. There is disagreement regarding its character, its relationship to the rest of the Gospel, and its integrity, as well as regarding detailed points of exegesis.

The great majority of modern commentators regard the Prologue as a hymn or poem which has been taken over by the author of the Fourth Gospel and adapted to his purpose by various additions. These additions can be detected, it is suggested, by changes not only in theme but also in the poetic structure. However, the changes are not so obvious as to lead to any unanimity regarding the precise limits of these additions. Although they are generally considered to include the references to John the Baptist in verses 6–8 and 15, there is a considerable variety of opinion as to how much more may be regarded as additional material.[1]

An exception to this approach is that of C.K. Barrett,[2] who points to the lack of agreement among those who seek to remove the 'insertions' as an indication that the original poetic structure which they are attempting to recover never in fact existed. Moreover, 'the whole passage shows, on careful exegesis, a marked internal unity, and also a distinct unity of theme and subject-matter with the remainder of the gospel'.[3]

Nevertheless, on either approach, the references to John the Baptist remain an enigma. If we agree with Professor Barrett that the Prologue is one with the rest of the Gospel, we are nevertheless left wondering why the author has introduced the references to John in such an abrupt manner. If we agree with those who think that the Prologue (in a shorter form) once had a separate existence, then the references to John are even more puzzling. It is not enough to dismiss these verses as the author's additions; we must explain why he made these additions at these particular points – and it must be admitted that they are very odd additions. They have aptly been described by John A.T. Robinson as 'rude interruptions'.[4]

---

[1] The variety of opinion is summarized by Raymond E. Brown, *The Gospel According to John, I–XII* (New York: Doubleday, 1966), 21–23.

[2] C.K. Barrett, *The Gospel According to St John* (London: SPCK, 1958), 125 ff.

[3] Barrett, *The Gospel According to St John*, 126.

[4] John A.T. Robinson, 'The Relation of the Prologue to the Gospel of St John', *NTS* 9, no. 2 (1963): 120–129.

To omit passages as 'additions' because their subject matter seems foreign to their context can never be an adequate explanation unless one can suggest also why they should have been placed precisely where they are. In the case of the references to John the Baptist, it has been suggested that they were 'perhaps originally the opening verses of the Gospel, displaced when the Prologue was prefaced to the Gospel by the final redactor'.[5] But why did this 'final redactor' insert them into the Prologue? Was he insensible to the poetic structure which the commentators have uncovered? Why not leave the 'original' introduction to follow after the Prologue, and lead into vv. 19 ff.? One possible explanation which has been offered is that vv. 6–8 deliberately contradict the claims of a sectarian group who thought of John the Baptist as the light.[6] This would explain the insertion at this point, though unfortunately direct evidence that any such claim was ever made is lacking.[7] The insertion of v. 15 is even more difficult to explain. Raymond E. Brown's suggestion 'that the final redactor, seeing that it might be useful here to emphasize the theme of pre-existence, copied into the Prologue the sentence from v. 30'[8] is no real answer. John A. T. Robinson is correct when he writes: 'It is hard to see it being added as an explanation, because (unlike other verses to be considered) it explains nothing in the context: it merely interrupts'.[9]

It will perhaps assist our investigation if we look a little more closely at these two references to John the Baptist, and consider their relationship to the evangelist's account of John the Baptist's witness to Jesus which is found in 1:19 ff.

The first statement, in vv. 6–8, introduces John as one who was sent from God to bear witness to the light. This section emphasizes the function of John as witness: we are told first that he came εἰς μαρτυρίαν, and this statement is twice amplified in the explanatory clause ἵνα μαρτυρήσῃ περὶ τοῦ φωτός. On the first occasion this clause is linked with a further, positive explanation of John's function as witness – ἵνα πάντες πιστεύσωσιν δι' αὐτοῦ – and on the second a negative statement makes clear that John's witness was not to himself – οὐκ

---

[5] Brown, *The Gospel According to John, I–XII,* 22. Cf. also Robinson, 'The Relation of the Prologue to the Gospel of St John', and Wilbert F. Howard, rev. C.K. Barrett, *The Fourth Gospel in Recent Criticism and Interpretation* (London: Epworth Press, 1955), 118 ff.

[6] Rudolf Bultmann, *Das Evangelium des Johannes,* 17th ed. (Göttingen: Vandenhoeck & Ruprecht, 1962), 4 ff.

[7] There is, of course, evidence (here and in the Clementine literature) that messianic claims were being made on John's behalf, and this would explain the Johannine denial – but not why it is placed *at this specific point* and in these terms. See the discussion of the Baptist sect in Walter Wink, *John the Baptist in the Gospel Tradition* (London: Cambridge University Press, 1968), 98–105, and Charlie Scobie, *John the Baptist* (London: SCM Press, 1964), 187–202.

[8] Brown, *The Gospel According to John, I–XII,* 35.

[9] Robinson, 'The Relation of the Prologue to the Gospel of St John', 125.

ἦν ἐκεῖνος τὸ φῶς ἀλλ' ἵνα μαρτυρήσῃ περὶ τοῦ φωτός. This brief statement is similar in substance to 1:19–28, the first section in the evangelist's material about John the Baptist. These verses are introduced with the words καὶ αὕτη ἐστὶν ἡ μαρτυρία τοῦ Ἰωάννου, and the theme of John as witness is continued in the words καὶ ὡμολόγησεν καὶ οὐκ ἠρνήσατο, καὶ ὡμολόγησεν … in v. 20. The substance of this section is a conversation between John and the priests and Levites from Jerusalem: the main point is John's denial of any role for himself save that of a voice preparing the way of the Lord, and his emphasis on his own unworthiness in comparison with the one who follows him. Questioned concerning his baptism, he links his water baptism with the one to whom he bears witness. In other words, John 'came for testimony, to bear witness to the light, that all might believe through him. He was not the light, but came to bear witness to the light' (1:7–8).

The second statement in the Prologue concerning the Baptist is found in v. 15. Again we find John introduced as one who bears witness – and presumably we are to conclude from the present tense, μαρτυρεῖ, that this witness continues. This time John himself is made to speak (κέκραγεν), and his words point the contrast between himself and the one to whom he bears witness. His successor is greater than he, and indeed comes before him, and this priority is based on his pre-existence. Again there is a parallel with the material regarding the Baptist which occurs later in the chapter, this time with the second section, vv. 29–34, which describe the events of 'the next day'. Unlike vv. 19–28 the emphasis here is entirely positive: John is said to have pointed out Jesus as the Lamb of God and to have witnessed to him (ἐμαρτύρησεν) as the one on whom he has seen the Spirit descend. John himself emphasizes his role as witness – μεμαρτύρηκα ὅτι οὗτός ἐστιν ὁ Υἱὸς τοῦ Θεοῦ. The closest link with v. 15, however, is found in the fact that John's words in v. 15 are repeated in v. 30, both passages referring to a previous statement which has not itself been recorded.

Isolated from their context in the Prologue, therefore, these two statements about John in vv. 6–8 and 15 seem to point forward to the two sections which are to follow, to his own denial of any position for himself and his emphasis upon the role of Christ who, though he follows John, has priority in every other way. But what is the function of these passages in their present setting? At this point we must examine the remaining material in the Prologue.

Once again we immediately meet difficulties because of the variety of opinions which are held. But there is at least some measure of agreement that a major division occurs at v. 14. This is supported both by the repetition of the term λόγος and by the introduction of a new stage in the argument at this point. It is, of course, by no means certain that this is the first reference to the incarnation; most commentators believe that it is first referred to in v. 9

or v. 10, or even earlier.[10] Nevertheless, the reference to the Logos 'becoming flesh' is certainly a new and significant statement.

If we omit for the moment the 'interruptions' in vv. 6–8 and 15, we find that the remaining material falls into the following pattern: A (i) vv. 1–5. The Logos in relation to God; active in creation; as life – which is light. (ii) vv. 9–13. The light lightens men; but the world (created by him) did not accept him; those who did were made children of God through him. B (i) v. 14. The incarnate Logos – his glory, full of grace and truth. (ii) vv. 16–18. Men have received of his fullness, and grace and truth have come through him; God, whom no one has seen, has been made known through him.

It will be noted that each main section is built to some degree in chiastic form. The first moves from the theme of the Logos' relation to God and to creation to the idea that he is life and so light. After the 'insertion' we move on from the theme of light to the reaction of the world (created by him, cf. v. 3) and to the new life as children of God given to those who receive him; the second part of this first main section, therefore, picks up from the first the ideas of life and light, of the relationship of the λόγος to creation and of a relationship with God. In the second main section, we are told that we have seen the glory of the incarnate Logos, as of the μονογενής, full of grace and truth. Again, these themes are taken up after the 'insertion' in v. 15; the language emphasizes the links – πλήρωμα, ἡ χάρις καὶ ἡ ἀλήθεια, ἑώρακεν, μονογενής Θεός, Πατρός. The references to John the Baptist occur at what may be described as the turning-points of the two sections – at that point in each where the themes already stated are taken up and developed; each of the 'development' sections works out more fully what has been stated in the preceding verses. In each case this is done in terms of the meaning for mankind of what has been already stated. The Logos, eternally with God and the agent of creation, is the bearer of life and light, which shines in the darkness: the world (made through him) did not know him and his own people rejected him, but to those who accepted him he gave power to become children of God. (Already we meet the division caused by Christ's presence among men, which is the theme of John's Gospel.) The Logos became flesh and we saw his glory: grace and truth have come to us through him, and he has made known to us God himself, whom no one has ever seen.[11]

---

[10] Cf. Barrett, *The Gospel According to St John*, in loc.; Brown, *The Gospel According to John, I–XII*, 29, points out how the phrases in this section link with the activity of Jesus in the rest of the Gospel. William H. Cadman, *The Open Heaven: The Revelation of God in the Johannine Sayings of Jesus*, ed. G.B. Caird (Oxford: Blackwell, 1969), 20–22, interprets v. 5 as a reference to the incarnation. Similarly Rudolf Schnackenburg, *The Gospel According to St. John*, vol. 1 (London: Burns & Oates, 1968) *in loc*.

[11] John here contrasts Jesus with Moses, through whom the Law was given to us, and who, according to Exod 33:17–23, was unable to see God.

The positioning of the references to John the Baptist suggests that they serve a particular function at these points, and that they are not mere parentheses. Their function becomes clearer when we remember that the passages are not primarily 'about John the Baptist'; rather, like John himself, they point to the one to whom John witnessed. They refer to the historical 'event' of Jesus Christ, that is, to the appearance of the Logos among men. Their importance lies in the fact that each refers to John as the witness who confirms the truth of what has just been said, that light is shining in the darkness, and that we have seen the glory of the incarnate Logos.[12] It is to these basic statements of truth that the Baptist, in his own way, witnesses. He bears witness that the one who follows him is 'the light' when he describes himself as a voice and as one who prepares the way; he bears witness to the incomparable superiority and pre-existence of his successor when he declares that he has seen the Spirit descend upon Jesus, and therefore knows and bears witness that he is the Son of God.

The function of John the Baptist in these two short passages is therefore the same as that which he has in the rest of the Fourth Gospel: his purpose is only to serve as a witness to Jesus. This interpretation of his mission is reflected in 1:31, where the Baptist states what might otherwise surprise us, that the purpose of his baptism is to reveal Jesus to Israel: having identified him as the Lamb of God, he declares ἵνα φανερωθῇ τῷ Ἰσραήλ διὰ τοῦτο ἦλθον ἐγὼ ἐν ὕδατι βαπτίζων. The same emphasis is seen in two later references which look back to John's witness, as those in the Prologue look forward. In 3:26 John's disciples speak to him of Jesus as the one ᾧ σὺ μεμαρτύρηκας, and John then repeats his witness. Again, in v. 33, Jesus himself refers to John's witness to the truth.[13]

Within the Prologue, the references to John the Baptist serve to link the subsequent historical statements with the metaphysical truths there outlined: they make clear that it is Jesus who is the true light which gives light to men, and who is the full revelation of God. Whether or not they are additions to an original 'hymn', they are by no means 'interruptions', as at first appeared. Rather the author has used them to link firmly the introductory philosophical passage (which may well be his own composition) to the events which he is going to portray in the rest of his Gospel. The Logos who was eternally with God is the one to whom the Baptist pointed: the Logos who became flesh is the one who follows John although he is before him. The references to John thus play as important a role within the Prologue as John himself plays in the Gospel.[14]

---

[12] The parallelism between these two statements, together with their similar positioning, supports the interpretation of v. 5 as referring to the incarnation; see above, n. 10.

[13] Note the use of ἐθεασάμεθα and ἑώρακεν in vv. 14–18, echoed by τεθέαμαι and ἑώρακα in vv. 32 and 34.

[14] I am grateful to Professor C. F. Evans for helpful criticism of the first draft of this article.

23. The Johannine Prologue and the Messianic Secret*

In 1892 Adolf Harnack, writing on the relation of the Prologue to the Fourth Gospel, posed the question in these words: 'What is the aim of the Gospel, what is the aim of the Prologue? Are these aims identical or is the Prologue really an introduction to the Gospel? ... Is it the key to understanding the Gospel?'[1] My aim in this paper is to consider once again this question of the function of these opening verses. What did the author – or redactor – of the Gospel aim to achieve by beginning his book in this way?

From the time of the earliest exegetes, the first eighteen verses of John's Gospel have been regarded as of special significance, and they have for many years been spoken of as the Prologue. The difference between these verses and the rest of the Gospel is obvious – so obvious, indeed, that they are often assigned to a separate source. Many assume that they could not have been written by the evangelist; some argue that they are a later addition to the Gospel. This last drastic solution raises as many problems as it attempts to solve: for not only does the Gospel begin strangely without these verses, but their later addition to the Gospel seems inexplicable; the more commentators emphasize (rightly or wrongly) the difference between these verses and the rest of the Gospel, the harder it becomes to understand how any redactor came to consider them a suitable introduction. Whatever the truth in this matter, however, as the Gospel stands at present, these verses are intended to offer an introduction to the events which follow.

Commentators on Mark's Gospel have in recent years drawn a parallel between the opening verses of that Gospel and the Johannine Prologue. The existence of a Marcan prologue is far less obvious, and seems to have been first suggested by R.H. Lightfoot.[2] The parallel was used by Lightfoot to elucidate Mark's purpose. The present paper attempts to reverse this process, and investigates the possibility that Mark's literary method may help us to understand John's.

Unlike John 1:1–18, the style of Mark 1:1–13 in no way distinguishes it from the rest of the Gospel. Nevertheless, there are certain noteworthy features in these introductory verses. The opening words of Mark 1:1 – probably to be

---

* A paper read at the meeting of SNTS at Southampton, 31 August 1973.
[1] Adolf Harnack, 'Über das Verhältnis des Prologs des vierten Evangeliums zum ganzen Werk', *ZTK* 2 (1892): 191.
[2] R.H. Lightfoot, *The Gospel Message of St Mark* (Oxford: Clarendon Press, 1950) 15 ff.

understood as a title – are, of course, in a class of their own. The next two verses are also unusual: for though there are explicit quotations of scripture elsewhere in the Gospel, as well as many scriptural echoes, it is only here that the evangelist himself explicitly states that the events which he is recording were happening καθὼς γέγραπται. Also noteworthy in these introductory verses are the threefold reference to the Holy Spirit (mentioned again only in 3:29, 12:36 and 13:11), the account of the voice from heaven (which has a parallel in 9:7) and the conflict with Satan (which is referred to again in 3:20–30). It is clear to us that these verses stand apart in a sense, from the account of the ministry which is to follow. Yet they are in narrative form, as is the rest of the Gospel, and the vocabulary, though unusual, finds echoes in later chapters; certainly the differences are not enough to suggest that these verses are by anyone other than the evangelist.

Mark, then, gives us a prologue in narrative form; John offers us something which, though it relates events, is much closer to being a theological discourse. Yet the difference should not be exaggerated. For if narrative is typical of Mark, discourse is typical of John. The bulk of the rest of John's Gospel – until we come to a passion narrative – is theological discourse, held together by a slight narrative framework: his material is essentially a brief account of certain activities of Jesus, together with lengthy theological comment on the significance of those activities, usually in the mouth of Jesus himself. In the Prologue, the order is reversed: we have theological statements, with a couple of references to John the Baptist to 'anchor' what is being said in history.[3] Yet the juxtaposition of historical narrative and theological interpretation is in many ways similar to the rest of the Gospel. Controversy regarding the Johannine Prologue has so concentrated on the question of the 'poetic' style that it has perhaps been overlooked that as far as form and content is concerned, we might well expect John to write a prologue in this way. The vocabulary of these verses, also with one or two exceptions which we must examine later, links it with the chapters which follow.[4]

R.H. Lightfoot, drawing attention to the special character of Mark 1:1–13, spelt out the parallelism between these verses and the opening verses of John:[5]

Both prologues dwell upon the relation of Jesus Christ to John the Baptist … and in each book it is shown that, however great and God-sent the forerunner, his work pales into insignificance when set against the arrival of Him whose way had been prepared by John. And just as St John's prologue reaches its highest point at verse 14, 'The Word became flesh'

---

[3] Morna D. Hooker, 'John the Baptist and the Johannine Prologue', *NTS* 16 (1970): 354–358 = above, essay 22 (pp. 316–320).

[4] There are echoes, for example, in 2:11; 3:19; 5:26, 37; 7:22 ff.; 8:12, 32, 38; 9:5; 11:4, 25; 12:35 ff., 46; 14:7 ff.; 16:3; 17:1–4, 14, 17. The references to John's witness are taken up in 1:19–36 and 3:25–30.

[5] Lightfoot, *The Gospel Message of St Mark*, 18 ff.

... so St Mark's prologue reaches its highest point in the words of verse 11, 'Thou art my beloved Son, in thee I am well pleased' ... And finally, just as in John the narrative proper only begins at verse 19, so also in Mark the narrative proper only begins with the account of the Lord's activity in verses 14 and 15, when He comes into Galilee with the announcement that the time is ripe, and God's promises are now in process of accomplishment.

To these parallels we can add the fact that Mark (by means of his reference to the Old Testament scriptures which have now been fulfilled) clearly demonstrates that Jesus is the culmination of God's purposes, the one to whom God's promises point; and that John sees in Jesus the λόγος made flesh – that λόγος which has been the expression of God's activity from the beginning. Mark records that Jesus is acknowledged from heaven as ὁ υἱός μου ὁ ἀγαπητός – a phrase almost identical in meaning with John's μονογενὴς υἱός.[6] According to Mark, the Holy Spirit is at work in what Jesus does: John, in his Prologue, refers to this same activity of God at work in Jesus in terms of the World made flesh. Mark, in his brief account of the temptation, depicts a conflict between Jesus and Satan: John speaks of light coming into darkness and the darkness being unable to master it.

The 'gain' of Lightfoot's interpretation of Mark, as he himself saw it, was that 'we find placed in our hands at the outset the key which the evangelist wishes us to have, in order that we may understand the person and office of the central Figure of the book'.[7] How successfully Mark has done this becomes apparent if we omit the first thirteen verses and begin to read the Gospel at verse 14, at the same time imagining that we know nothing about this 'central Figure of the book'. To do so is to find ourselves very much in the situation of those whose reaction is described in Mark's narrative. We meet a strange itinerant preacher, who announces with authority that God's kingdom is about to burst upon us, who performs certain remarkable miracles, and who continually challenges the authority of the religious leaders. If we read the book in this way, our reaction is to exclaim with some of the characters in the story: 'What is this new teaching? He commands even unclean spirits with authority and they obey him' (1:27);[8] 'Who then is this, that the wind and sea obey him?' (4:41); 'By what authority do you do these things? Who gave you authority to do them?' (11:28). The common people, the disciples, the religious leaders, are all shown by their reaction to be uncomprehending, and we can sympathize with their obtuseness.

Mark, however, does not allow us to read the Gospel in this way. He does what every writer of detective fiction studiously avoids doing – he spells out the solution for us on the first page. After that the clues are blatantly obvious.

---

[6] C.H. Turner, 'ὁ υἱός μου ὁ ἀγαπητός', *JTS* 27 (1926): 113–129.
[7] Lightfoot, *The Gospel Message of St Mark,* 17.
[8] Adopting the reading of ADW f 13, f 28, etc.

Those who know that Jesus is the fulfilment of God's promises, that he is God's beloved Son, that the Spirit of God is at work in him, and that he has fought with Satan, know the answers to the questions which are continually being asked by the participants in the story. Unlike the modern writer of detective fiction, Mark did not wish his readers to be puzzled. He wished them to see and recognize the truth which he was setting out before them: that Jesus was the Christ, the Son of God, and that the Spirit of God himself was at work in what he did. To read Mark's Gospel after reading the Prologue is to read with the spectacles of faith: the messianic secret is an open secret for those who have been allowed to overhear the words from heaven, for to them the significance of what is happening is obvious, and the obtuseness of crowds, disciples, and religious leaders who failed to comprehend seems culpable. Mark demonstrates the truth that the 'facts' alone are insufficient: those with eyes of faith interpret what is happening correctly – others deny Jesus' authority or attribute it to the wrong source. Men and women are divided in Mark's narrative into those who acknowledge Jesus and those who reject him – and to acknowledge him is to confess that he is the Christ, the Son of God, and to recognize the Spirit of God at work in him. The faith to which the disciples are called – together with the readers of the Gospel – is precisely that which is revealed to us in the opening verses: and it is precisely this estimate of Jesus which divides disciple from unbeliever, for those who do not see and understand the divine revelation are those who remain outside, and who are offended by what Jesus does.

The messianic secret in Mark was once interpreted as something which divided believer from unbeliever during the ministry of Jesus. Later, it was seen as representing the tension between the non-messianic ministry of Jesus and the messianic interpretation of the church – between 'then' and 'now'. Whether or not there is some truth in either or both of these positions, it is certainly true that the messianic secret in Mark indicates a tension in the *present* experience of the evangelist and his readers: their generation is divided into those who have eyes to see and those who have not. The problem is not simply that men and women failed to recognize *then* the one whom they *now* acknowledge to be Messiah; but that the question 'Who is he?' can still be given totally opposing answers.

When we turn to John we have, of course, no 'messianic secret'. Jesus is twice pointed out by John the Baptist as the Lamb of God.[9] The Baptist explains that his knowledge of this is not human, but has come to him by

---

[9] The title is puzzling, and no satisfactory solution has ever been given. Perhaps it is best understood in relation to the Evangelist's arrangement of signs and discourses, by which he shows Jesus to be the one who is the fulfilment of all the Jewish festivals: in him are brought together all the functions of the old rituals – but now they are effective for the world.

revelation; he has seen the Spirit descend and rest on Jesus – this is how he knows him to be the one who baptizes with the Spirit, and the Son of God. These words remind us again of the Marcan prologue – but what in Mark was spoken for the ear of the reader alone is in John shouted aloud by the Baptist. The disciples acknowledge Jesus as Messiah from the very beginning;[10] Jesus himself sets out his claims openly throughout the Gospel in no uncertain manner.[11] Yet just as in Mark we meet a division between those who accept the claims of Jesus (however imperfectly understood) and those who do not, so too in John there is a division between those who are 'his own' and 'the Jews'. The cause of the division, too, is very much the same as in Mark. Those who reject Jesus do so because the truth is hidden from them: they may converse with Jesus but they are unable to understand what he is saying, and the authority which he claims is in their view not God-given but an authority he has taken upon himself.

But if messiahship is spoken of openly, what is it that is hidden? An examination of those passages where Jesus meets opposition and where his hearers reject his teaching shows that for John the point at issue is the question of Jesus' origin: those who reject him fail to recognize that he is 'from above'. This question is raised in every debate between Jesus and the Jews, and the fundamental cause of the dispute is set out in the opening discourse between Jesus and Nicodemus: the latter is unable to understand Jesus because he has not been born ἄνωθεν, and therefore can understand only at a fleshly, not a spiritual level. Nicodemus cannot grasp heavenly things, while Jesus is the Son of man who descended from heaven (3:1–13). The monologue which follows (3:14–21) introduces the theme of Jesus as the light which has come into the world, and it is natural to find this reference to light followed by the final appearance of John the Baptist in this Gospel, once again bearing witness to Jesus as in chapter 1 by declaring that he himself is not the Christ, but is sent to bear witness to the greater one who follows him.[12] Here, too, we have a short monologue (whether in the mouth of the evangelist or the Baptist is not clear) whose themes echo those of the conversation between Jesus and Nicodemus. The Baptist, as the one who bears witness to Jesus and his divine origin, stands in contrast to Nicodemus, who fails to recognize the truth.[13]

The failure of 'the Jews' to recognize Jesus' divine origin is demonstrated throughout the Gospel. Their enmity arises from the fact that Jesus makes himself equal with God (5:17 ff.); they attempt to stone him because he claims

---

[10] 1:41, 49.

[11] For example in 4:26; 5:17; 8:28; 9:37; 10:24 ff.; 18:20 ff.

[12] As in 1:6–8, 15, and 1:19–28, 29–36, the Baptist's witness to Jesus here consists of a negative statement about himself, and a positive statement about Jesus. Cf. Hooker, *op cit*.

[13] Since the Baptist witnesses to the truth about Jesus, it can hardly be he, as some commentators suppose, who is referred to as ἐκ τῆς γῆς.

to be one with God (10:30–39); in both instances the Jews fail to recognize that the activity of Jesus is the activity of God. The crowds do not believe in him because they think they know where he comes from – though of course they do not, since he is sent from God (6:41 ff.; 7:25–30).[14] The great debate in chapter 8 is centred on the question to which Jesus knows the answer but the Jews do not (since they judge according to the flesh) – namely whence he comes and whither he is going (8:14 ff.; cf. 7:41 ff.); they are from below, and belong to this world, but he is from above, and does not belong to it, for he comes from God (8:23–30); he comes from God, but they do not understand him, because they are not children of God (8:42–47). When Jesus declares: 'Before Abraham was, I am', they again attempt to stone him (8:58 ff.). The same question of Jesus' origin appears in 9:29: 'We know that God has spoken to Moses, but as for this man, we do not know where he comes from'. Finally, the theme of Jesus' divine origin is prominent in the trial scene, where Jesus first tells Pilate that his kingdom is not ἐκ τοῦ κόσμου τούτου (18:36), and is later asked by Pilate: Πόθεν εἶ σύ; (19:9). In these scenes Pilate is cast in the role of a middleman who puts the questions, for the real dispute is between Jesus and the Jews.[15]

Underlying many of these disputes are themes central to the prologue – light (3:19–21; 8:12 ff.; 9:5, 39) and life (3:15, 36; 5:24–26; 6:51 ff.) and truth (3:33; 8:44–46; 18:37–38). As in Mark those who have read the introductory verses understand what is obscure to many of the main actors in the drama, so here those who have read the Johannine Prologue comprehend words of Jesus which otherwise seem irrelevant. The most puzzling Johannine discourse is immediately illuminated by a re-reading of the Prologue.

The theme of the λόγος, too, is recognizable in the disputes about the activity of Jesus interpreted as that of God himself (5:17 ff.; 10:30–39). Although λόγος is not used again in John in precisely the way that it is used in the Prologue, the word does occur significantly elsewhere. In 5:37–47, for example, the Jews fail to recognize the works of Jesus as the activity of the Father: 'His voice you have never heard, his form you have never seen; and you do not have his word abiding in you, for you do not believe him whom he has sent' (5:37 ff.). To fail to recognize Jesus is to fail to accept God's word.

In chapter 8, the difference between the disciples of Jesus and his opponents is that the former continue in his word (v. 31), whereas those who oppose him demonstrate that his word finds no place in them (v. 37). Those who accept him are children of God, and those who reject him are children of the devil (vv. 39 ff.); 'He who is of God hears the words (τὰ ῥήματα) of God;

---

[14] How far they are from comprehending is demonstrated by the fact that they argue about Galilee versus Bethlehem! See 7:41 ff.

[15] 18:34 ff.; 19:6 ff.

the reason why you do not hear them is that you are not of God' (v. 47). It is clear that Jesus' words are those of God himself, since he goes on to claim: 'before Abraham was, I am' (v. 58). The Jews should keep his word, as he has kept his Father's word (vv. 51–55). The words of Jesus are not spoken on his own authority, but have been given to him by the Father (12:44–50). The identification is explicitly made in 14:23 ff.: 'If a man loves me, he will keep my word ... He who does not love me does not keep my words; and the word which you hear is not mine but the Father's who sent me'. In 17:6, 8, 14, 17, Jesus says that he has passed on to the disciples the word or words given to him by the Father: they have received them, and know that Jesus has come from the Father and been sent by him.

The 'word of God' is crucial in 10:34–36, where Jesus quotes Ps 82:6 to demonstrate that those to whom the word of God came were properly called 'gods'. How much more, then, is it right to call him whom the Father consecrated and sent into the world 'the Son of God': the activity of Jesus is that of God himself, and demonstrates that God's word has indeed come in him. In all these disputes between Jesus and the Jews, the theme of God's word is central.

In Mark's Gospel it is the 'messianic secret' which divides men into those who, being blind, remain blind and incapable of recognizing the truth, and the disciples, who for all their incomprehension come to grasp the truth that Jesus is the Son of God. Even the disciples, however, because they find the secret hard to comprehend, share to a large extent in the general hardness of heart and blindness to the truth: their eyes are like those of the blind man at Bethsaida, only partly opened. They are liable to slip back into a position where they see things from men's viewpoint, instead of from God's (Mark 8:33).[16] In the Fourth Gospel there is a similar bewildering pattern of belief and disbelief: the twelve follow Jesus, though not fully comprehending him, but there are also disciples who cease to believe and 'Jews' who sometimes believe. It is worth asking what clues are given us regarding the causes of this belief and disbelief. In 6:60, many of Jesus' disciples take offence, declaring 'This is a hard saying: who can listen to it?' Even if we do not regard vv. 51–58 as a later addition to the discourse, the 'hard saying' seems to refer to the identification of Jesus with the bread which came down from heaven, rather than to the particular eucharistic interpretation. This is made clear by the reply of Jesus in verse 62: what will their reaction be if they see the Son of man ascend to where he was before? It is Jesus' claim to be the bread which comes down from heaven which causes many to turn back. Here we have

---

[16] According to their response, they are sometimes 'inside', sometimes 'outside'. See C. F. D. Moule, 'Mark 4:1–20 Yet Once More', in *Neotestamentica et Semitica,* eds. E. Earle Ellis and Max Wilcox (Edinburgh: T&T Clark, 1969), 98 ff.

the theme of heavenly origin. But we have also the very significant contrast with Moses: it was not Moses who gave bread to your fathers, but God who gives bread to you. This bread is already identified in Jewish thought with the Torah, the word of God. It is the claim of Jesus to be this bread (which readers of the Prologue will of course understand) which causes unbelief.[17] What Moses gave was not the true bread, but points forward to what is to come. By contrast with the failure of many disciples to believe this we have the confession of Peter in v. 68: 'You have the words of eternal life'.

In chapter 8 we have a more confused situation. In verse 31 we read of Jews who believed in Jesus. Immediately, however, they take on the normal character of Johannine Jews, hostile to Jesus and to his words. Why? One can of course explain such inconsistencies by referring to sources – though this does not explain why the evangelist was content with inconsistency. Once again, it is worth noting what it is which causes belief to change to disbelief. It is those who abide in the word of Jesus, who are truly his disciples; the truth sets them free. It is this suggestion that the Jews need to be set free which sparks off their indignation: 'We are descendants of Abraham, and have never been in bondage to anyone'. In the ensuing conversation, Jesus demonstrates that the proud descendants of Abraham are slaves to sin and therefore no true children of Abraham. Those in whom the word of Jesus finds no place seek to kill him, v. 37. They are not children of God, but children of the devil, because they do not love the one who comes from God, and cannot bear to hear his words, vv. 42 ff. Once again we have the claim of Jesus to come from God; we are told, moreover, that for the Jews to be true children of God it is not enough for them to be descendants of Abraham – indeed, to be merely that is to be in bondage! They must accept Jesus and his word. Those who have read John 1:11–13 understand why this step is necessary.

Moses pointed forward to the coming of Christ, the true bread; Abraham rejoiced to see his day. In 5:37–47 the evangelist has already spelt out the fact that Moses wrote of Jesus, and that, in refusing to hear Jesus, they are failing to accept the witness of Moses. 'If you believed Moses, you would believe me, for he wrote of me. But if you do not believe Moses' writings, how will you believe my words?' (vv. 46 ff.). The question at issue is how they read Moses: 'You search the scriptures', Jesus says to the Jews, 'because you think that in them you have eternal life; and it is they that bear witness to me; yet you refuse to come to me that you may have life'. Life has come into the world, but they will not accept it; they will not seek the glory which comes

---

[17] The contrast with Moses is even more pointed if John is contradicting an interpretation which identified Moses with the manna. This identification is perhaps found in Targum Neofiti Exodus 16:15; see Geza Vermes, 'He is the Bread', in *Neotestamentica et Semitica*, 256–263.

from God. They do not hear the testimony of God himself to Jesus. 'His voice you have never heard, his form you have never seen; and you do not have his word abiding in you, for you do not believe him whom he has sent' (vv. 37 ff.). To those who know that the word of God, active throughout history, and speaking in the Torah, has now been made flesh, and that the God whom no man has seen has been made known by his Son, the claims of Jesus here are comprehensible, since it is obvious that the scriptures point to Jesus: those who have not understood what is set out in the Prologue are, in every sense, in the dark.

In chapter 9 we have an acted parable on the theme of belief and unbelief. Jesus, the true light, opens the eyes of the man born blind. In the course of the chapter, his inner eyes of faith are gradually opened, while the Pharisees become confirmed in unbelief. The climax of their confrontation comes in their second meeting, and the irony of the situation is brought out in vv. 28 and 29, in the words of the Jewish authorities: 'You are his disciple, but we are disciples of Moses. We know that God has spoken to Moses, but as for this man, we do not know where he comes from'. The Pharisees fail to recognize that God not only spoke to Moses, but is speaking through 'this man'. The healed man is astonished: 'You do not know where he comes from', he exclaims. 'If this man were not from God, he could do nothing'. Once again it is the question of Jesus' origin which causes division, and which separates the believer from the non-believer. The man who confesses that Jesus comes from God is cast out of the synagogue. But in the final comment of Jesus we see that it is the Jews who have become blind. His coming has brought not only light but judgement, because men are blind to the truth.

These final words remind us of the words of Jesus in Mark about the blindness of those who do not accept him. Another close parallel is found in John 12. Here, as often, Jesus speaks of his presence in the world in terms of light, a reference which readers of the Prologue will understand: his hearers must walk in the light, lest they are overtaken by darkness. The failure of the crowd to believe is summed up by the evangelist in quotations from Isa 53:1 (used in similar circumstances by Paul, Rom 10:16) and 6:10: 'He has blinded their eyes and hardened their heart, lest they should see with their eyes and perceive with their heart, and turn for me to heal them'. This is said by the evangelist to refer to Christ's glory, which Isaiah saw; Isaiah therefore wrote of Christ. The 'secret' which is hidden from the crowd in John is not the mystery of the kingdom, nor the messianic identity of Jesus, but the glory spoken of in the Prologue. In the final verses of this chapter, Jesus spells out the meaning of belief: to believe in him is to believe in him who sent him. He has come as light into the world – but those who do not believe in him remain in darkness. Once again, the key to understanding this discourse of Jesus is put into the hands of those who have read the Prologue.

Fifty years ago, Ernest Findlay Scott suggested that 'in the fourth Gospel the Messianic idea is replaced by that of the Logos'.[18] Some have objected that, apart from the Prologue, the Logos idea is conspicuous by its absence. But Scott was surely right. The idea of the Logos is as central – and as hidden – in John as the idea of Jesus of Nazareth as Messiah is central in Mark. Just as the messianic identity of Jesus is a secret in Mark, so the identity of Jesus with the Logos is a secret in John – not deliberately hidden, but certainly not known to those who oppose Jesus, and never spelt out specifically in his debates with them; but as in Mark there are innumerable clues which can be understood by those who know the secret because they have become disciples of Jesus, so in John there are many mysterious passages, incomprehensible to those who think only in terms of the flesh, which make sense to those who have believed in Jesus and been made children of God,[19] and recognize in him the Logos of God.[20] And just as, in Mark, the secret is on occasion shouted aloud, but falls on deaf ears, so in John, Jesus speaks of himself in terms which to us seem obvious – but which the Jews fail to comprehend. The Johannine 'secret' explains the claims of Jesus to come from above: for Jesus is the divine λόγος. Those to whom this secret is not revealed are blind and uncomprehending – and yet culpable, since, having the scriptures, they should have recognized Jesus; the disciples, as in Mark, do not fully comprehend, and yet are prepared to follow, having glimpsed something of the truth, and to them, in chapters 14–17, the themes of 1:1–18 are set out most clearly. To those of us who read the Gospel, however, all is plain – provided that we first read the Prologue; for as in the case of Mark, if we leave these verses aside and begin at 1:19, we find ourselves sharing the bewilderment of Jesus' contemporaries: 'Isn't this Jesus, the son of Joseph, whose father and mother we know? How does he now say "I have come down from heaven"?' (6:42); 'Are you greater than our father Abraham who died? ... Who do you claim to be?' (8:53). It is only because we know that Jesus is the Word made flesh that we are able to understand his words in this Gospel; only because we have been given this clue to the significance of what he does that we are not offended by his claims.

A contrast is often drawn between Mark's use of miracle stories and the Johannine understanding of miracles as 'signs'. Yet the similarities are also worth noting. In both Gospels there are different levels in understanding the

---

[18] Ernest Findlay Scott, *The Fourth Gospel: Its Purpose and Theology* (Edinburgh: T&T Clark, 1920), 6.

[19] 1:12 ff.

[20] Cf. T.W. Manson, *On Paul and John* (London: SCM Press, 1963), 158 ff.: 'One is tempted to think that the peculiarity of the discourse in the Fourth Gospel arises just from this; that it is the Logos that speaks in the person of Jesus. The Jewish interlocutors get at cross-purposes with the Johannine Christ because they think they are holding a debate with Jesus the son of Joseph from Nazareth, whereas they are really listening to the incarnate word of God'.

miracles. In Mark, the common reaction is one of astonishment – the crowds marvel at the miracles; but for those with some understanding, they have greater significance, for they are pointers to the true identity of Jesus. 'Who then is this?' (4:41). In John, also, there are two levels of understanding. But here the messianic question is brought out into the open: 'Can this be the Christ?' (4:29). 'When the Christ appears, will he do more signs than this man has done?' (7:31). The deeper meaning of the miracles, which is hidden from the crowds who waver between belief and unbelief, is that they are manifestations of his glory. As in Mark, the miracles set out the secret of Jesus' person to those with eyes to see.

The Johannine discourses also, though they are so different from the Marcan parables, nevertheless serve the same function and produce the same effect. In Mark the parables are used christologically, presenting a challenge to discipleship, and setting out the supreme importance of the choice. The Johannine discourses have a similar role. In both Gospels, parable and discourse inevitably lead to division and rejection and dispute, as well as to discipleship and understanding. The parable becomes paradoxically a way of concealing the truth; the discourse leaves men bewildered instead of enlightened. The secret of Jesus' identity is in both cases the key to understanding.

Since the 'secret' to which men are blind is different in the two Gospels, we naturally find a difference in the way in which messianic terms are used. In Mark, the belief that Jesus is perhaps John the Baptist or Elijah or one of the prophets is contrasted with the confession that he is the Christ. The crowd – and Herod too, in chapter 6 – do not even begin to guess that Jesus is the Messiah. Throughout his ministry, the secrecy of his messiahship is concealed from them. Compare with this John's Gospel, where 'Messiah' is included with the other terms, in both 1:20 ff. and 25 and in 7:41. The messianic possibility is no longer, as in Mark, one that is not even mentioned: the secret in John is the truth that Jesus has come from above. There is already a hint of this in Mark 12:35–37; in John it has moved into the central place.

Similarly, the term 'Son of God' belongs in Mark to the 'secret' and is deliberately hidden: Jesus himself does not use the phrase – though for Mark himself it is a far more significant term than 'Messiah'. It is the sonship of Jesus which is acknowledged from heaven in 1:11 and 9:7, and by the centurion in 15:39, and in the early chapters it is as 'Son of God' that the unclean spirits acknowledge Jesus (3:11 and 5:7). In John, on the other hand, Jesus speaks of himself openly as 'Son of God' – but the true significance of the title is not grasped by his hearers. The real difference between Mark and John at this point is that in the former the sonship of Jesus is deliberately hidden, whereas in the latter it is simply not understood: the glory has been revealed, but men have been blind. To some extent this reflects the different ways in which the evangelists approach the problem of responsibility: although both emphasize the divine purpose on the one hand and human failure on the other, the emphasis in Mark is on the former, and in John on the latter: to use a Pauline metaphor, the 'veil' in John is on the human side. It is perhaps worth noting another link between the evangelists in their use of this title: in both Mark (1:10 ff.) and John (1:32–34), as also in Rom 1:3 ff., the designation of Jesus as Son of God is linked with the Spirit of God.

A final parallel between Mark and John may be seen in their treatment of Jesus' death. In Mark, the understanding of Jesus as Messiah and Son of God is linked closely with his death: no real explanation of this is ever given – but the acknowledgement of Jesus as Son of God comes about through his death. Readers of the Gospel are privileged to overhear the truth, spoken by the voice from heaven, in the Prologue – it would indeed be more accurate to describe it as a 'Son of God' secret rather than a messianic secret: in spite of manifest clues in the course of the Gospel, it is only by Jesus' death that the truth about him becomes generally known – see 9:7–9 and 15:39. In John, the Prologue sets out for us the truth about Jesus' glory; and though in the course of the Gospel signs of his glory are seen, it is only in the hour of his death that Jesus is fully glorified, and the truth made plain.

The Johannine Prologue, then, serves the same function as its Marcan equivalent; without it the chapters which follow are incomprehensible to us, as to the Jewish opponents in the story. Notwithstanding the arguments of those who have considered it an addition to the Gospel, it seems that these verses give us, as R.H. Lightfoot remarked, 'the key to the understanding of this gospel'.[21] They are not only closely related in theme to the rest of the Gospel, but are (to quote Lightfoot again) 'designed to enable the reader to understand the doctrines of the book'.[22] We are led to the conclusion that these verses have always formed the essential opening paragraphs of the Gospel.

It would be interesting to discover a parallel to this literary device of Mark and John. Did other authors set out to give an explanation to the ensuing drama in their opening pages? In some Greek plays, of course, we find prologues which set out the purpose of the dramatist, and summarize the plot: but the parallel is not close. Clayton R. Bowen, writing on 'The Fourth Gospel as Dramatic Material',[23] commented that the very term 'prologue' suggested a drama – but promptly mixed his metaphors by speaking of the verses as 'a striking of the great major chords whose harmony is to vibrate

---

[21] Lightfoot, *The Gospel Message of St Mark*, 78.

[22] Lightfoot, *The Gospel Message of St Mark*, 11. Cf. C.K. Barrett's comment on John 1:1: 'John intends that the whole of his gospel shall be read in the light of this verse. The deeds and words of Jesus are the deeds and words of God; if this be not true the book is blasphemous'. *The Gospel According to St John* (London: SPCK, 1955), *in loc.*

[23] Clayton R. Bowen, 'The Fourth Gospel as Dramatic Material', *JBL* 49 (1930): 292–305.

until the last curtain falls'.²⁴ Looking at Jewish literature, we find that the book of Sirach opens with a prologue – but it is closer to the literary model of Luke 1:1–4 than to John 1. Nor does Philo provide a parallel – the closest approach to one is found in the introductory section of *De Legatione ad Gaium*.²⁵

A better parallel is perhaps to be seen much closer to hand, in the other Gospels. The opening chapters of Luke, like the Johannine Prologue, are most often discussed in terms of authorship, style, and sources. If instead we think about the function of these chapters, it is noticeable that they provide us with the same kind of information as the Marcan and Johannine Prologues, and that they do so by spelling out the truth about Jesus with the help of titles and descriptions which are rarely used in subsequent chapters. In the 'infancy narratives' Luke gives his readers the key to understanding the events which follow: the angels announce the identity of Jesus, and the various psalms explain the significance of what is happening, and its relationship to God's activity in the past. As in Mark and John, we have emphasis in these chapters on a new significant activity of God (in terms of his Spirit, here associated especially with the birth of Jesus) and on the relationship between Jesus and John the Baptist. When Luke reaches the point which is for Mark the beginning of the Gospel, we find that we have embarked on the story proper, and these events no longer, as in Mark, form a key, but are part of the narrative. Those who have read chapters 1 and 2 know why John should now appear as forerunner; the descent of the Spirit and the voice from heaven confirm what we already know.²⁶

Matthew's infancy narrative offers us a less rewarding parallel, though once again we are given significant information about Jesus: his descent from Abraham and David; his conception through the Holy Spirit; the promise that he will save his people from their sins. The stories in chapter 2 symbolize the later events of the Gospel: the coming of the magi with their gifts, and the slaughter of the innocents, point to the kingship of Jesus – and to the rejection and suffering associated with it; the death of the children and the flight to Egypt mark him out as a Mosaic figure, who will shortly challenge the current interpretation of the Torah. Here, too, we find titles such as 'Christ' and 'the king of the Jews' being used of Jesus.²⁷

---

²⁴ Bowen, 'The Fourth Gospel as Dramatic Material', 298.
²⁵ Philo also begins *De Vita Mosis* with a declaration of his purpose in writing.
²⁶ The title 'Son of God' has already been used, together with 'Son of the Most High', 'Saviour', 'Christ', and 'Lord'; the fact that Jesus is the expected King of David's line has also been stressed. Throughout Luke 1–2 angels and Spirit-inspired men and women act in the role of a Greek chorus, pointing out the significance of events, and showing how Old Testament expectation is being fulfilled. Cf. Paul S. Minear, 'Luke's Use of the Birth Stories', in *Studies in Luke-Acts,* eds. Leander E. Keck and J. Louis Martyn (Nashville: Abingdon Press, 1966), 111–130.
²⁷ A similar suggestion that the birth narratives in Luke and Matthew are parallel to the

A parallel of a different kind with the Johannine Prologue can, of course, be found in the Wisdom Christology of Heb 1:1–4 and Col 1:15–20. There is perhaps a parallel in function, as well as content, since both these christological statements form a foundation on which the argument of the subsequent pages is based. In Hebrews, the first four verses set out the relation of Christ to God, to the universe, to God's previous activity in the world, to humanity, and to angels; the rest of the epistle spells out the consequences. In Colossians, the statements about Christ's relation to God, to the universe, and to mankind, set out in 1:15–20, form the basis of Paul's arguments in the rest of the epistle. In Hebrews, as in John, this Wisdom Christology demonstrates Christ's superiority to the revelation of the Old Testament, and this may well be the case, also in Colossians.[28]

Professor Käsemann, writing on the purpose of the Johannine Prologue,[29] has suggested that the key to understanding it is to be found in vv. 14–18. In the last part of this paper I turn to an examination of these verses.

It has been argued recently by Professor Borgen[30] that the opening verses of the Prologue are an exposition of Gen 1:1–5. It has also been suggested by several writers that the background of vv. 14–18 is found in the revelation on Sinai described in Exod 33.[31] The links with the latter passage are, I believe, even closer than has hitherto been recognized.

In 33:12–23, Moses makes two requests of Yahweh. First, in v. 13, he asks: 'If I have found favour in thy sight, show me now thy ways, that I may know thee and find favour in thy sight'. This request is apparently granted in the promise: 'My presence will go with you'; through God's presence with them, God's people will be distinct from all other people. The second request comes in v. 18, where Moses says: 'I pray thee, show me thy glory'. This request is only partly granted: the Lord will make his goodness pass before Moses, and will proclaim his name, Yahweh, but Moses may not see his face.

Marcan and Johannine Prologues (identified as Mark 1:1–15 and John 1:1–34) has been made by Oscar J. F. Seitz in 'Gospel Prologues: A Common Pattern?', *JBL* 83 (1964): 262–268. Contrast Henri van den Bussche, *Jean: Commentaire de l'Evangile Spirituel* (Paris: Desclée de Brouwer, 1967), 65, who compares with the Johannine Prologue the formal introductions in the other Gospels – Mark 1:1, Luke 1:1–4, and Matt 1:1–17.

[28] See W. D. Davies, *Paul and Rabbinic Judaism,* 2nd ed. (London: SPCK, 1955), 147–152, 172–175; Morna D. Hooker, 'Were There False Teachers in Colossae?', in *Christ and Spirit in the New Testament,* eds. Barnabas Lindars and Stephen S. Smalley (Cambridge: Cambridge University Press, 1973), 315–331.

[29] Ernst Käsemann, *New Testament Questions of Today,* trans. W. J. Montague and Wilfred F. Bunge (London: SCM Press, 1969), 152.

[30] Peder Borgen, 'Observations on the Targumic Character of the Prologue of John', *NTS* 16 (1970): 288–295.

[31] E.g. M. E. Boismard, *St John's Prologue,* trans. Carisbrooke Dominicans (London: Blackfriars, 1957), 136–140.

The subject of vv. 14–18 in John 1 is glory, and this, together with the contrast between Christ and Moses in v. 17, and the phrase πλήρης χάριτος καὶ ἀληθείας in v. 14, which has been interpreted by many commentators as equivalent to the phrase רַב־חֶסֶד וֶאֱמֶת found in Exod 34:6,[32] all point us at once to Exod 33–34. When we examine that passage more carefully, we discover other ideas which are echoed in John 1. We have already noted the promise that God will be present with his people, and that his presence will distinguish Israel from other nations. The term שכינה is used in 33:16 by the Targums, and already God's presence has been symbolised by the tent in vv. 7–11 (LXX σκηνή). With this we may compare the reference to 'his own' in John 1:11 and the phrase ἐσκήνωσεν ἐν ἡμῖν in v. 14. The form of Moses' request in Exod 33:13 is interesting: 'If I have found favour, show me thy ways, that I may ... find favour in thy sight'. The noun חֵן used twice here is, of course, the term which is normally translated by χάρις.[33] Is it this idea of favour given to one who has already received favour, which lies behind the notoriously difficult phrase in John 1:16, χάριν ἀντὶ χάριτος? Those who have received the grace of being God's own people receive also the grace of his presence among them (v. 14).

In Exod 33:17–23 the Lord promises that he will make his glory pass by Moses, who will see only a rear view, for 'you cannot see my face; for man shall not see me and live' (v. 20). As John puts it in 1:18, 'no one has ever seen God'; but John continues: he 'who is in the bosom of the Father, he has made him known'. Is John here deliberately contrasting Moses, who was placed at God's side, but allowed to see only God's rear view, and Christ, who is in the bosom of the Father?[34]

In Exod 33:19 we read that God is to make all his goodness pass before Moses, and that he will proclaim his name, Yahweh. In vv. 5–7 of the next chapter we read how God fulfils his promise: he descends in the cloud and stands with Moses there; passing before him, he proclaims 'Yahweh, Yahweh, a

---

[32] E.g. C.H. Dodd, *The Interpretation of the Fourth Gospel* (Cambridge: Cambridge University Press, 1953), 175; C.K. Barrett, *The Gospel According to St John* (London: SPCK, 1955), *in loc*. Note the equivalence between רַב and πλήρης.

[33] Although, as we have already noted, many commentators associate the phrase χάρις καὶ ἀλήθεια in v. 14 (see also v. 17) with the Hebrew חֶסֶד וֶאֱמֶת, the usual LXX rendering of that phrase is ἔλεος καὶ ἀλήθεια, and almost every occurrence of the word χάρις represents the Hebrew חֵן. It is used for חֶסֶד only in Esther 2:9 (and in 2:17, where it renders both terms). C.H. Dodd, *loc cit*, argues that occurrences in Sirach and in Symmachus and Theodotion indicate that χάρις later replaced ἔλεος as a translation for חֶסֶד. This may explain its use in John 1:14 and 17. As far as χάρις is concerned, however, the weight of Old Testament evidence suggests that the background is to be found in the term חֵן.

[34] Cf. John 5:37 and 6:46. The background of the former passage is perhaps also the theophany on Sinai; cf. Wayne A. Meeks, *The Prophet-King: Moses Traditions and the Johannine Christology*, NTSup 14 (Leiden: Brill, 1967), 299 ff. There may also be an intentional contrast with Sirach 45:1–5.

God merciful and gracious, slow to anger, and abounding in steadfast love and faithfulness' – וְרַב־חֶסֶד וֶאֱמֶת. Later Jewish exegesis understood these verses as an exposition of the thirteen divine attributes,[35] and we have already seen that two of these are echoed in the Johannine phrase πλήρης χάριτος καὶ ἀληθείας. They are all summed up, apparently, in the phrase used in Exod 33:19 – כָּל־טוּבִי:[36] are they perhaps also summed up by John in the word πλήρωμα? In Exod 34 the divine name, Yahweh, heads the list of divine attributes, all of which are concerned with God's dealings with his people; in the rest of John's Gospel the divine name, 'I am', will be used repeatedly by Jesus in making various claims – many of them associated in Jewish thought with the role of the Torah. In every case, the evangelist stresses the importance of what Jesus is for the believer;[37] as he puts it in 1:16, 'of this πλήρωμα we have all received'.

In Exodus, Yahweh himself proclaims the name Yahweh. In John 1:18 it is μονογενὴς Θεός (or Υἱός) who 'declares':[38] the verb used by John is ἐξηγεῖσθαι, and though this is not used by the Septuagint in Exod 33–34, it conveys well the sense of the divine proclamation – expressed in 33:19 and 34:5 in the rather odd Hebrew construction קָרָא בְשֵׁם – which reveals the character of God. John's language here seems to have been influenced also by Sirach 43:31: τίς ἑόρακεν αὐτὸν καὶ ἐκδιηγήσεται;[39] In John 17 Jesus says that he has manifested the Father's name to those who have kept God's word: the context links this with the mutual glorifying of Father and Son.

It may possibly be objected that the suggested use of Exodus lacks consistency, since John is at one and the same time seeing Christ's glory as continuous with that revealed on Mount Sinai, and contrasting Christ with the figure of Moses. This, however, is precisely John's point – and one repeated throughout his Gospel;[40] Christ is not only the one who has seen the face of God, but is himself the *source* of divine δόξα, full of grace and truth. The difference is brought out in the use of different verbs in 1:17; the Law was given through Moses (in the theophany on Mount Sinai) – but grace and truth themselves

---

[35] Cf. T. Bab Rosh Hashanah 17b; Rashi on Exod 33:19 and 34:6. Already within the biblical tradition, we see the beginning of this development, with the reiteration of the themes of these verses; cf. Num 14:18; Neh 9:17; Pss 86:15, 103:8, 145:8; Joel 2:13; Jonah 4:2.

[36] The LXX reads here: Ἐγὼ παρελεύσομαι πρότερός σου τῇ δόξῃ μου. This may reflect a variant Hebrew reading, בִּכְבוֹדִי, but more probably shows influence by v. 22. The reading underlines the fact that the disclosure of God's glory is his self-revelation.

[37] Note the verbs used with the 'I am' sayings; 'come' in 6:35, 'follow' in 8:12, 'enter' in 10:7, 9, 'know' in 10:11, 14, 'believe' in 11:25, 'come' (to the Father) in 14:6 and 'abide in' 15:1, 5.

[38] It is appropriate that it is the one who is the λόγος made flesh who performs this function. At this point in the Prologue, we are reminded again of the unity between God and the λόγος, now expressed in terms of unity between Jesus Christ and the Father. Cf. van den Bussche, *Jean*, 105 ff., who suggests that v. 18b corresponds to v. 1.

[39] Cf. also Ps 22:23 (21:24).

[40] Cf. T. Francis Glasson, *Moses in the Fourth Gospel* (London: SCM Press, 1963), 24 n.; Meeks, *The Prophet-King*, 288 ff.

have come through Jesus Christ. There is therefore not only a partial antithesis between Christ and Moses,[41] there is also an antithesis between Christians and Moses, who are both recipients of the revelation. So it is we (v. 16) who have received χάριν ἀντὶ χάριτος. This double theme – Christ as the revelation of God's glory, and as the fulfilment of the Torah, to which Moses only pointed forward – is the theme of the rest of the Gospel.

If this interpretation is correct, we can understand the strange insertion of the reference to the Baptist in v. 15; his witness is necessary at this point so that we may understand that the one who follows him in the story – Jesus – is in fact the one who was before him, whose glory is spoken of in the pages of the Old Testament.[42] We understand also why certain terms – χάρις, πλήρωμα – should be appropriate here, when they are not used elsewhere.

The term πλήρωμα gives us an interesting verbal link with another important passage where Wisdom Christology is employed, namely Col 1:15–20. The link is not merely a verbal one, however, for there is a close parallel between the two passages. In John 1 we are told first of the relation of the λόγος to God, of his work in creation, and of this continuing role in the world; then, in v. 14, we learn of the λόγος made flesh and the revelation of God's glory, and the fact that men receive of the πλήρωμα embodied in him. In Col 1:15–20 we are told first of the relation of the Son to God (ὅς ἐστιν εἰκὼν τοῦ Θεοῦ), of his work in creation, and his continuing sustaining role (vv. 15–17); then we are told of his role in relation to the church, and his work in redemption, which is dependent upon the fact that ἐν αὐτῷ εὐδόκησεν πᾶν τὸ πλήρωμα κατοικῆσαι.[43] In John, the glory of God is revealed in the λόγος made flesh, and those who see him receive of this πλήρωμα. In Colossians, the πλήρωμα dwells in Christ, and the church is filled in him (1:19; 2:9ff. Cf. Eph 1:23). In Heb 1:1–4, also, we find linked together the ideas of Christ's unique relationship with God, his role as agent of creation, his continuing work in upholding all things, his character as reflection of God's glory and expression of his being, and his work in redemption. These themes are expanded throughout chapters 1 and 2, and here too we find that men are given a share in what has been revealed in Christ – sonship and glory (2:10).

But why should John, in his exposition of these ideas, bring together the term λόγος and the imagery of Exod 33–34? There is, of course, an immediate and obvious link between the λόγος and the idea of the Torah, God's word, which was itself symbolized by light and life, terms which have been used

---

[41] Boismard, loc cit, understands the parallel with Exodus to mark Christ out as the new Moses of a new covenant. But in John, Christ is the one whose glory we see.

[42] See John 17:5. Cf. Anthony Tyrrell Hanson, *Jesus Christ in the Old Testament* (London: SPCK, 1965), 108–113.

[43] The two terms used to introduce the two sections in Col 1, εἰκών and ἀρχή, are used by Philo in association with the λόγος in *Conf.* 146.

already in the opening verses of the Prologue – just as there is an obvious link between the ideas of light and a glory which can be seen. Is there perhaps also another link with the word λόγος to be found in the Exodus passage in Yahweh's words to Moses in 33:17: 'even this word which you have spoken I will do'? Certainly John might have described his Gospel as the account of God performing the word spoken by Moses.

John spells out this truth for us in 5:37 ff., a passage which appears to be another echo of Sinai. In rejecting Jesus, the Jews are showing that they have never heard God's voice or seen his form or received his word. They search the scriptures – which bear witness to Jesus – and fail to recognize that they speak of him. God himself is glorified – i.e. revealed[44] – in what Jesus does: throughout the Gospel, discourses and signs and the arrangement of the material round the pattern of Jewish festivals spell out the truth that this revelation is the fulfilment of everything that went before, and that Moses is the witness who speaks of Jesus.

We have seen that it is Christians, as much as Christ, who stand in contrast to Moses in John 1. A similar idea is to be found in 2 Cor 3:1–4:6, where the contrast between Moses and Christ slides into a contrast between Moses and the Christian: for it is we whose faces are unveiled and unashamed. The theme of this passage, too, is glory – though now it is the glory which Moses reflected after speaking to God on Sinai; Moses' irradiation was, however, according to Paul, only temporary and imperfect, whereas the glory Christians now see and reflect is the glory of Christ. What kind of glory is this? Its source, we learn in 2 Cor 4:6, is God, who said, at creation, 'Let light shine out of darkness'; Paul, in a pattern the reverse of John's, leads us back from the light of the glory glimpsed on Sinai and seen in Jesus Christ to the light of creation. For both Paul and John, Christ is the fulfilment of God's eternal purpose, which was only partly revealed on Sinai. The full unveiling of God's glory is now seen by Christians.[45]

In the course of his argument in 2 Cor 3, Paul speaks of faith in Christ in terms of the removal of the veil; the veil is removed not only from Moses' face, but from the scriptures and from the hearts of those Jews who turn to Christ. So we return to the theme of the messianic secret. For the veil, here, serves the same purpose as the blind eyes and hard hearts spoken of by the evangelists. And the truth which is obscured is the same as in John – it is the glory of Christ; it is the fact that the old covenant points forward to the new, and that the glory as revealed by Moses is brought to completion in Christ. As

---

[44] Cf. G.B. Caird, 'The Glory of God in the Fourth Gospel: An Exercise in Biblical Semantics', *NTS* 15 (1969): 265–277.

[45] Paul brings out clearly the idea that Christians in turn reflect this glory by becoming what Christ himself is. See especially 2 Cor 3:18 and 4:4. Cf. similar ideas in John 1:12 ff., Col 2:9 ff., 3:10, and Heb 2:10.

Paul sums it up in Rom 10:3 ff., where he is grappling again with the problem of Israel's failure to see the truth, Christ is the τέλος of the Law. The Jews seek to establish their own righteousness, and are ignorant of the righteousness of God; they do not realize that though the Law speaks of a righteousness based on works, it also points forward to a righteousness based on faith.[46]

It seems likely that Paul's argument in 2 Corinthians has developed out of the kind of understanding of the Law which we find in Jewish writings, and which forms the background of the opening verses of John 1. In passages such as Proverbs 8 and Sirach 24, wisdom is associated with God's work of creation, and identified with the Law: the divine plan was with God from the beginning, and was revealed to Israel at Sinai.[47] We find the rabbis speaking of the Torah as part of the eternal purpose of God – created before the world: a passage in the Babylonian Talmud, for example, describes the angels as asking what Moses is doing on Mount Sinai. 'He has come to receive the Torah', replies the Lord, at which they exclaim, 'That secret treasure, which has been hidden by Thee for 974 generations before the world was created, Thou desirest to give to flesh and blood'.[48] To Paul it is clear that it is Christ himself who is the secret treasure or wisdom, hidden by God from all eternity.[49] John expresses this same belief in his own way: 'In the beginning was the word ... the word became flesh ... and we saw his glory ... full of grace and truth'. Over against the Jewish claim that God's eternal purpose was finally revealed at Sinai, we have the Christian claim that the Torah only pointed forward to the revelation made in Christ.[50]

---

[46] A similar argument is used by Paul in 1 Cor 2, where he speaks of a hidden wisdom, concealed from the rulers of this age, but revealed to Christians. Paul uses language appropriate to the Corinthian situation, speaking of wisdom instead of righteousness, but the argument that man must rely on God's wisdom, not his own, is parallel to his argument in Romans and Galatians that man must rely on God, and not his own works. The two ideas are brought together in 1 Cor 1:30, in the statement that Christ is both our wisdom and our righteousness. If Paul is thinking of Christ as the fulfilment of God's age-long purpose, the one to whom the scriptures pointed, though their meaning was until his coming veiled, it was perhaps a simple step for him to express this in terms of wisdom – not simply because the Corinthians had a special interest in that term, but because Judaism had already identified the Torah with wisdom. For other expressions of this idea of the secret now revealed in Christ, see Rom 16:25 ff.; Col 1:25 ff., 2:2 ff.; Eph 3:3 ff.

[47] Cf also the identification of Torah and wisdom in rabbinic writings, e.g. Rab. Gen. 1.1.4; Rab. Lev. 11.3.

[48] T Bab Šabb. 88b.

[49] 1 Cor 2:7; cf. Col 1:26. The 'end' in both cases, as in 2 Cor 3–4, is our glorification.

[50] The question which so often puzzles commentators, as to the precise point in the Prologue where the author first speaks of the incarnation, would perhaps be for him a meaningless question. The λόγος now made flesh was with God at the beginning, and has made God known throughout history; the light has always shone in darkness, and the coming of the light has continually been rejected by men, both in the past and in the events described by John in his Gospel. It is therefore entirely appropriate that the Baptist, whose function is to witness to Jesus, should appear in both sections of the Prologue, binding the two parts together and

In both 2 Corinthians and Romans we see Paul wrestling with the problem of reconciling faith in Jesus as Christ not only with his conviction that God had spoken through the Old Testament, but also with the failure of the Jews to recognize the truth. In thinking about possible situations in the early church, reconstructing various so-called false Christologies, heresies and problems, it is easy to overlook the obvious and most pressing problem which confronted these early Christians – the relation of Christian faith to their Jewish heritage. It is difficult for us, nineteen centuries or so after the division between Jew and Christian has been made, to appreciate the trauma of those who found the new wine of Christian faith bursting the skins of Judaism – yet knew that God had spoken both through Moses and the prophets, and most decisively in Jesus of Nazareth. It is not surprising to find the Fourth Evangelist, like Paul, still grappling with this basic problem – and this, I suggest, is the reason why he wrote his Gospel, and his Prologue, as he did. The secret which he and the readers share, but which is hidden from the Jewish nation, is the truth spelt out for us in the first eighteen verses of his Gospel – that in Jesus Christ the God who has spoken in time past is fully revealed. There is no contradiction between old and new, only glorious fulfilment, because the scriptures themselves speak of Christ. Those who are blind to this are indeed in darkness – but those who possess this key see the glory of God.

---

assuring us that the historical figure to whom he points is the λόγος made flesh – that the one who reveals the glory of God is himself the light which has shone since creation, and that the one who comes after the Baptist in time is the one who has existed since before time began.

24. 'There's Glory for You!': Death and Glory in John's Gospel*

'There's glory for you!' said Humpty Dumpty.

'I don't know what you mean by "glory"', Alice said.

Humpty Dumpty smiled contemptuously. 'Of course you don't – till I tell you. I meant "there's a nice knock-down argument for you!"'

'But "glory" doesn't mean "a nice knock-down argument"', Alice objected.

'When *I* use a word,' Humpty Dumpty said, in rather a scornful tone, 'it means just what I choose it to mean – neither more nor less.'

Lewis Carroll's words in this passage from *Through the Looking Glass* conceal, as his apparent nonsense so often does, profound truth. Words do not always mean what they at first sight appear to mean, and may, indeed, mean something very different from what we expect. Those of you old enough to remember the philosopher and broadcaster C. E. M. Joad know that he always began the answer to any question with the words 'It all depends on what you mean by …'. Words change their meaning over time and in different contexts. It can even be, as Humpty Dumpty rightly saw, that the meaning of a word can be changed by the way in which we ourselves use it.

'Glory' is one such word. The Greek word δόξα, which we translate by 'glory', is related to the verb 'to think', and so originally meant 'what one thinks', or 'opinion'. The opinion you have of *me* will therefore be my reputation – and since the word is almost always used in a positive way, that hopefully means that your opinion of me is good. By the time we get to the New Testament, however, the meaning 'opinion' has vanished, and though the word still occasionally means 'reputation', or 'honour', it is used far more often to convey the sense of 'glory'. To understand how the change came about, we have to look at what the Greek translators of the Old Testament did when they came to the Hebrew noun כָּבוֹד, a word that is related to the verb 'to be heavy'. Presumably because what you were worth in material terms could be weighed in gold, and those with wealth were highly regarded, the cognate noun was used of 'honour', 'splendour', and 'glory'. It was this Hebrew word which our Greek translators quite naturally translated by the word δόξα. In a figurative sense, too, those with less wealth but with gravitas are important, and impressive, to others.

---

* The Eileen Stamper Memorial Lecture, delivered at the Vacation Term for Biblical Study on 4 August 2019.

A search through the many occurrences of כָּבֹד in the Hebrew Bible and δόξα in the Septuagint quickly reveals that the majority of them are used in relation to God. He, above all, is glorious, and worthy of veneration. But here we have a paradox, for God himself is invisible, and men and women cannot see his face. How, then, can they see his glory? The glory of the Lord, we discover, is revealed indirectly – through his actions (which are, of course, clear only to those who look behind the scene), his words (which are spoken through prophets), and through various cosmic phenomena, such as thunder and lightning, earthquakes and floods. At one and the same time, the glory of the Lord is revealed and seen by all[1] – and yet remains invisible.

Stories of those who experienced visions of God demonstrate this paradox. Moses encountered the Lord in the phenomenon of the burning bush, the fire which burned but did not consume.[2] The incident is usually termed a 'theophany' – and yet God does not, in fact, *appear*. God cannot be seen – it is an angel, we are told, who appears in the fire; even so, Moses hides his face, because he is afraid to look at God. The Lord then reveals himself to be the God of his ancestors, the great 'I am', but in the long conversation that follows, Moses does not set eyes on God. Rather, God instructs Moses about what he, the Lord, will do through Moses.

The same anomaly occurs when Moses meets the Lord on Sinai after the exodus. In Exodus 33 we are told that whenever Moses entered the Tent of Meeting, the pillar of fire – the symbol of God's presence – used to descend and stand guard at the entrance, while the Lord spoke to Moses 'face to face'.[3] Yet this story has been juxtaposed with another, in which Moses asks to see God's glory, and is told that he *cannot* see his face. The story recounts how Moses is instructed to take up his position in a cave, and told that when the Lord's glory passes by, the Lord will cover him with his hand – because he must not see God's face. Moses will, however, be permitted to see God's back, as he disappears round the mountain. So Moses goes up Mount Sinai with two blank tablets of stone, in order to receive the Law, and there the Lord reveals his identity. Once again, God announces that he is 'I am', and spells out what this means. He is 'I am', the Lord, a God who is compassionate and gracious, long-suffering, faithful and true, forgiving yet just. Even though Moses' view of God's glory is partial, this glimpse of glory – like the name 'I am' – reveals to him the essential character of God. So too does the Law, which is now delivered to Moses, and which sums up God's will. And so in glimpsing God's glory, Moses understands something of who this God is – the great 'I am'.

---

[1] Isa 40:5.
[2] Exod 3:1–6.
[3] Exod 33:7–11.

Seeing — and yet not seeing. Biblical commentators explain such contradictions by suggesting that different traditions have been brought together. Yet we ourselves use equally contradictory imagery in trying to speak of God. A familiar hymn addresses God as 'immortal, invisible, ... in light inaccessible hid from our eyes', yet goes on to laud him as wise, blessed, glorious, almighty, victorious, the source of justice, goodness, love, and life. God is at once hidden, yet revealed.

Our biblical writers use anthropomorphic imagery to describe what is both hidden and revealed, speaking of God's face and his back. Moses cannot see God himself — he can only see something of God's glory — his rear view, as Exodus expresses it. Yet even this encounter with God makes Moses' own face shine with reflected glory — a glory of such magnitude that when, forty days later, Moses comes down from the mountain, his fellow Israelites are unable to look at him. His face shines, because he has been speaking with the Lord — and now his fellow Israelites are afraid to approach him. He has, as it were, become radioactive, and dangerous, reflecting the judgement of the Lord on those who fail to do his will.

Humpty-Dumpty's definition of 'glory' as 'a nice knock-down argument' is beginning to look a little less silly. Clearly the glory of God is enough to knock anyone down. His glory is overwhelmingly powerful.

Of course, Moses is not the only person in the Old Testament to glimpse the glory of God. There is, for example, the famous account of the commissioning of Isaiah in Isaiah 6. Although the prophet tells us that in his vision even the seraphim attending on God cover their faces with their wings, he reports that he himself 'saw the Lord', and describes God in terms of a great human monarch. Having seen God, he assumes, until reassured otherwise, that he will die. Ezekiel records a similar experience, describing how he saw 'as it were, a sapphire in the shape of a throne', with 'a form in human likeness' sitting on it, and surrounded by a radiance which was 'like the appearance of the glory of the Lord'.[4] The prophet is clearly attempting to describe the indescribable. How *does* one describe a personal God without using imagery normally associated with persons? It is hardly surprising if both Jewish and Islamic law forbade the portrayal of God's image, for it is difficult for the human mind to depict God except in our own image; he is — as Daniel 7 describes him — the Ancient of Days, clothed in a white robe and with hair like wool, and seated on a throne, presiding over a court of judgement.[5] The picture conveys meaning in a way that the equivalent words — eternal, pure, glorious, just — do not.

---

[4] Ezek 1:26–28.
[5] Dan 7:9–10.

The use of human imagery to describe God reminds us that the biblical tradition is the very opposite: men and women are created in the image of God. Genesis 1:26 ff. records God's decision to create men and women – male and female – in his image and likeness. In the Garden of Eden, Adam spoke to God face to face, and the result, according to Jewish apocalypses and rabbinic tradition,[6] was that his own face shone with astonishing glory. This glory was not, of course, his own, but derivative, a reflection of the great glory of God, the result of Adam acknowledging the worth of God; in giving God glory, he reflected the glory that was God's. After the fall, however, Adam was afraid to enter God's presence, and hid in the trees.[7] Not only had he disobeyed God, but he had submitted to the serpent, over whom he had been given dominion, and so reversed God's plan for creation. He and his descendants were no longer able to see God, and they no longer honoured him as they should. As a result, they no longer reflected his glory – either literally or metaphorically.

It would seem that the story of Moses on Mount Sinai was understood as a semi-reversal of the story of the fall. Moses has a glimpse of God's glory, and so partially reflects it. He honours God, to the extent that he is able. He is also given the Law, which spells out what obedience to God means, and with the Law, Israel is offered a chance to begin again, and reverse the failure of Adam. But Israel fails to accept that chance, and her story in the centuries that follow is seen by the prophets as a story of disobedience and failure. The prophets nevertheless continue to hope that one day the people will repent and return to God, and they express their hope in terms of a restored creation, when the whole of nature will live once more in harmony. This hope depends on the repentance and return of Israel to her God, to worship him as he deserved. Then 'he will build up Zion; he will appear in his glory', declares the psalmist. 'And so the name of the Lord will be declared in Zion, and his praise told in Jerusalem, when the nations gather together, and kingdoms, to worship the Lord'.[8] It is hardly surprising, then, to find the Qumran community expressing the belief that in the last days the elect would inherit 'all the glory of Adam'.[9]

1. New Testament

Our New Testament writers express similar hopes, although for them, glory is not just a future hope but a present reality, experienced by believers through Christ. In the Synoptic accounts of the teaching of Jesus, glory still belongs to

---

[6] Apoc. Mos. 20–21; Rab. Gen. 11:2; 12:6; Sanh. 38b.
[7] Gen 3:8.
[8] Ps 102:16, 21–22.
[9] 1QH 17:15; cf. CD 3:20.

the final days: the Son of man will come in glory to judge men and women. But who *is* this 'Son of man'? The storyline indicates that it is none other than Jesus himself, and his identity – as the Son of man who judges – will be revealed in his glory. Yet for some, Jesus is *already* recognized for who he is. For those with eyes to see, the ministry of Jesus is itself a manifestation of God's glory: in Luke's Gospel, the angels who proclaim his birth and announce his identity are surrounded by glory and offer glory to God;[10] at the transfiguration, Jesus is clothed with glory, together with his companions, Moses and Elijah.[11] It is no accident that in all three Synoptic Gospels, this story follows that of Peter's partial recognition of Jesus' identity at Caesarea Philippi. But full recognition comes after his death, and at the end of his Gospel, Luke describes how the Risen Lord explains to the travellers to Emmaus that it was necessary for the Christ to suffer, before he entered into his glory.[12] Future glory is seen as a reward for present suffering, not only for Jesus, but for his followers, as well. For Jesus, this means that his identity is finally acknowledged.

Throughout *his* Gospel, the Fourth Evangelist makes explicit what is implicit in the other three. For John, the story of Jesus' ministry is the revelation of glory – the glory of God, and that of his Son, though the two cannot be separated. Whereas the synoptic evangelists believed that glimpses of glory – of God and of Jesus himself – were to be seen in his ministry, John announces what is clear to all who believe in Jesus. He sets out his theme in the Prologue, in 1:14: 'And the Word became flesh and made his home among us, and we saw his glory, such glory as befits the Father's only Son, full of grace and truth.' The words 'grace and truth' echo words found in the account we looked at from Exodus of God's self-revelation to Moses on Sinai, and it is significant that the Prologue goes on to compare Moses with Jesus. Whereas the Law was given through Moses, grace and truth have come in the person of Jesus. Nobody – not even Moses! – has ever seen God, but his only Son, who is close to his heart, has made him known. John does not deny that the Law was a divine gift – but that gift pointed forward to something even greater. The contrast between Moses and Jesus is not simply between one who could not see God and one who *has* seen him, but between one who could not see God and one who makes him known – or, to use the biblical imagery, who radiates his glory. As Jesus explains in 14:9, anyone who has seen him has seen the Father.

So where is this glory to be seen? We naturally expect the answer to be 'in his miracles', and so we are not surprised when, in 2:11, the evangelist tells us

---

[10] Luke 2:9, 13
[11] Luke 9:31 ff.
[12] Luke 24:26.

that the miracle at Cana, where water was changed into wine, was 'the first of the signs that revealed his glory'. What *is* surprising, however, is the fact that nobody at the wedding-feast (apart from Mary and the servants who had filled the jars with water) was aware of what had happened. How, then, was Jesus' glory *revealed*? The disciples, we're told, 'believed in him'; or should we perhaps, with the REB, translate the aorist ἐπίστευσαν by 'came to believe' – i.e. afterwards? Once again, we have the theme of glory that is both hidden and revealed.

The introduction to this miracle tells us that it took place 'on the third day' – but what does *this* mean? Does it simply refer back to the previous incident, at the end of chapter 1, or does it have a symbolic meaning? Commentators have noticed that the same phrase is used in Exodus 19:16, introducing the story of Moses' first ascent of Sinai, where he was given the Ten Commandments. Does John have that story in mind? This seems to me very probable, since the 'sign' at Cana, like all the others, conveys the message that Jesus is the fulfilment of Judaism, and that the Law and the Jewish festivals point forward to him: indeed, Moses himself, we are told later, bore witness to Jesus.[13] Nevertheless, the new is definitely superior to the old, which in that sense becomes redundant. Like successive models of a car, the two are not opposed, since the old is clearly a forerunner of the new. The pots filled with water for the Jewish rites of sanctification as stipulated in the Law are replaced by the heady wine of the gospel. It is hardly surprising, then, that this event is seen by the evangelist as a manifestation of glory. If glory accompanied the giving of the Law to Moses, how much greater must be what is happening in Jesus.

But there is another theme that unites the signs in John's Gospel. Not only do they indicate that the gospel is the fulfilment of Judaism, but they all point clearly to the nature of that gospel, which concerns the death and resurrection of Jesus himself. Jesus rebuffs his mother with the words 'my hour has not yet come' – and so uses for the first time the word 'hour', which in this Gospel refers to the hour of Jesus' death, which is also the hour of his glorification. It is in the cross that Jesus' glory is revealed. It is no wonder, then, that the glory revealed in the signs remains hidden from Jesus' contemporaries.

The story of the wedding at Cana is linked with the so-called 'cleansing of the temple', which takes place a few days later in Jerusalem, where Jesus has gone to celebrate Passover with his disciples. He drives the money changers and sellers of sacrificial animals out of the temple, because they have turned his Father's house into a market. Challenged to produce a sign of his authority, Jesus speaks enigmatically of the destruction and restoration of the

---

[13] John 5:46.

temple – referring, as the evangelist explains, to his own coming death and resurrection. In other words, the sign the Jews demand in v. 18 has already been given, since Jesus' actions in the temple at Jerusalem point forwards to what is going to take place to the temple of his body. And once again, what he does indicates that he is the fulfilment of Judaism, since worship in his risen body – i.e. the church – will replace the worship in the Jerusalem temple. This time, there is no reference to glory, and apparently nobody understands what is happening; but, the evangelist adds, '*After* his resurrection his disciples recalled what he had said, and they believed the scripture and the words that Jesus had spoken'.[14] As for the theme of a new temple, is it coincidence, I wonder, that in 4:21, 23, in Jesus' conversation with the Samaritan woman, he looks forward to *the hour* when believers will worship God, not in Jerusalem nor in Samaria, but in spirit and in truth.

It is well-known that much of John's Gospel recounts a series of signs, which indicate who and what Jesus is. Encouraged by the reference in 4:54 to a 'second sign' in Galilee, commentators like to count them, and argue that there are seven – though they do not all agree as to which the seven are, which suggests that the total number may not be important. But certainly we have another 'pair' of signs, one in Galilee and one in Jerusalem, in 4:46–5:47, the second again being linked to Jesus attending a festival. First a young boy, then an elderly man,[15] are healed, but the common theme is the restoration of life. In the first healing, the boy's father learns that the hour when Jesus assured him that his child would live was the hour when the fever left him, and as a result his whole household became believers. Is John's threefold use of the word 'hour' accidental, or is it meant to suggest that what belongs to the future is already taking place? Unlike the jam in *Through the Looking Glass*, which is served every other day, meaning yesterday and tomorrow but never today, the glory of God is being seen here and now. The second healing leads the Jews to seek Jesus' death, and in the conversation between Jesus and the Jews that follows, Jesus claims that the Son does whatever he sees the Father doing; just as the Father raises the dead and gives them life, so does the Son.[16] He goes on to speak of 'the hour' that is coming *and now is* when the dead will hear the voice of the Son of God and will live (v. 25).

In both these stories, we see that the hour is already here, since Jesus is giving life. But the hour when *all* who are dead will hear his voice and rise from their graves is still to come.[17] What happens in the miracle is a sign of what *will* happen. The Father bears witness to the Son, but the Jews do not

---

[14] John 2:22.
[15] Life expectancy in first-century Palestine is said to have been approximately 35. This man had been crippled for 38 years, and was presumably older than that.
[16] John 5:19 ff.
[17] John 5:28 ff.

hear his voice; although they read the scriptures diligently, they do not understand that *they* witness to the Son; they accept glory from men, but ignore the glory of God – the glory that is displayed in Jesus; Moses himself wrote about him, but they have failed to believe him.[18] It is perhaps worth noting here that in chapter 7, in a passage which seems to refer back to this miracle,[19] Jesus is again said to contrast those who seek their own glory with the one who seeks the glory of him who sent him.[20] The healing of the paralytic is a revelation of the nature of God.

We have now learned a little more about Jesus' coming hour. It is in a sense already here, since these signs already reveal the glory of God, indicating the superiority of Jesus to Moses, and pointing forward to the coming death and resurrection of Jesus, and yet it still lies ahead.

It is tempting to explore all the signs, but I must stick to my theme and bypass the next pair – the feeding of the five thousand and the walking on the water[21] – simply noting that they both contrast Jesus with Moses and point to Jesus' coming death and resurrection, and move on to the final miracle in the Gospel in chapter 11. The raising of Lazarus is specifically described by Jesus as taking place 'to the glory of God',[22] and like previous signs, it leads the disciples to believe in Jesus.[23] Jesus is the resurrection and the life, and those who believe in him will live, even if they die.[24] The miracle clearly points forward to the death and resurrection of Jesus. Indeed, since it leads the chief priest and Pharisees to plot his death, it seals his fate. It is a 'prophetic action' which signifies what will inevitably happen to Jesus himself.[25]

In John 12:37–43, John summarizes the purpose and effect of the 'signs'. In spite of the fact that Jesus has performed so many, the Jews have failed to believe in him. This, he tells us, fulfilled the words of Isaiah in chapters 53 and 6, about the nation's failure to believe; the second passage – 'he has blinded their eyes and hardened their heart, so that they might not look with their eyes and understand with their heart and turn to me – and I would heal them' is quoted in various formats by all the Synoptics, though *they* link

---

[18] John 5:36–47.
[19] John 7:21–24.
[20] John 7:18.
[21] John 6. The two stories are woven together rather like one of Mark's famous 'sandwiches'. Moses divided the waters of the Red Sea, but Jesus walks *on* them; Moses fed the people with manna, which lasted only a day, but Jesus feeds them with the bread of life, and those who eat will never be hungry. This bread is of course Jesus himself, and he will give it to them through his death. Those who ate manna died, but those who eat this bread will have eternal life.
[22] John 11:4, 40.
[23] John 11:15; cf. v. 48.
[24] John 11:25 ff.
[25] Cf. W. David Stacey, *Prophetic Drama in the Old Testament* (London: Epworth 1990); Morna D. Hooker, *The Signs of a Prophet* (London: SCM Press, 1997), especially pp. 68–76.

it with Jesus' parables.[26] In John's Gospel, significantly, John concludes this second quotation with the comment: 'Isaiah said this *because he saw his glory* and spoke about him.' What the Jews have failed to comprehend is that in his 'signs' Jesus has revealed the glory of the Lord himself. Once again, glory is both hidden and revealed.

The reference here to blind eyes echoes the conversation between Jesus and the Jews following one of the signs we haven't looked at – the healing of a man born blind in chapter 9. In the conversation that follows, the Pharisees condemn Jesus for healing on the sabbath, and declare that they themselves are faithful disciples of Moses; while they know that God spoke to Moses, they know nothing about Jesus or his origins. Meanwhile the healed man puts his trust in Jesus, as the Son of man, thus showing that he has indeed been given sight. In contrast, the Pharisees, who fail to believe, are condemned for their blindness.

We think of 'signs' as acts of power, but we should note that not all the Johannine signs are miracles, and that John never uses the word δύναμις, an act of power, which is used often in the Synoptics to refer to a miracle. He is concerned to point to the *significance* of Jesus' actions, all of which indicate that God is at work. Since they reveal his glory, we are not surprised to find that they point to the resurrection. Paradoxically, however, John takes the extraordinary step of conflating Christ's *suffering* with his glory. Rather than telling us, as Luke does, that the Christ must suffer and so enter his glory, Jesus speaks of his coming death as itself the moment when he will glorify God and himself be glorified.

It is in those passages where Jesus speaks of '*being* glorified' that John's emphasis on Jesus' *death* as the hour when his glory is revealed is most clearly seen. In 12:23 ff. Jesus declares that the time has come for the Son of man to be glorified, and explains that a grain of wheat must fall into the earth and die, in order to bear a harvest. He prays to God to glorify his name, and a voice from heaven replies: 'I have glorified it, and I will glorify it again'. But this hour is also the hour of judgement, when Satan is defeated. When Jesus is lifted up from the earth, he will draw everyone to himself.

The verb ὑψόω, to lift up, found here, has both a literal meaning – 'to lift up' – and a metaphorical one, 'to exalt'. Commentators are in agreement that John is deliberately using the word ambiguously. Jesus has already used it of his death. Back in chapter 3:14 ff., he declared that just as Moses lifted up the serpent, so the Son of man must be lifted up. The serpent impaled on a stake in the Old Testament story brought healing to the sick and dying, and is now interpreted as a sign pointing forward to the crucifixion of Jesus, which will bring eternal life to all who believe. Jesus refers to his lifting up/exaltation

---

[26] Mark 4:12; Matt 13:14 ff.; Luke 8:10. Matthew has the fullest version.

again in 8:28. The dual meaning of the verb parallels the idea that the crucifixion is Jesus' glorification.

The saying in 12:23 about being glorified is affirmed by Jesus in 13:31 ff., and picked up once more in the so-called 'high-priestly prayer' in chapter 17. 'Father, the hour has come', says Jesus, and prays that God will glorify the Son, in order that the Son may glorify God. He continues: 'I have glorified you on earth by finishing the work which you gave me to do'; Jesus has spoken twice before of his intention to complete the work given to him by God,[27] and now he declares that he has done so. The Greek verb used here is closely related to the one used in 19:30, where Jesus' final words from the cross are 'It is finished'. And if we have any lingering doubts about whether John does indeed think of Jesus' death as the hour of his glorification, whoever wrote chapter 21 certainly had none, since in v. 19, writing about Peter, he speaks of the death by which *he* would glorify God.

The idea that Christ's death is the hour of glorification upsets all human expectations. Of course, the idea is well-known to us all. Indeed, we are so used to Johannine teaching that the absurdity of it no longer strikes us, and we cheerfully sing 'Lift high the cross' without thinking of the paradox. But imagine the shock this teaching must have given to the first hearers of this Gospel. Crucifixion was the most cruel, shameful, excruciatingly painful death that the ancient world could devise. Pinned naked to a cross, Jesus had been utterly humiliated, branded as a criminal, totally defeated, his plans apparently at an end. How could this be a revelation of God's *glory*?

To find the answer we need to go back once more to Exodus, for when God allowed Moses to glimpse his glory, he revealed himself as compassionate and gracious, long-suffering, faithful and true, forgiving yet just. It is no accident that when Jesus claims in 17:4 that he has glorified God on earth, he goes on to say that he had made known God's name – that is, he has made known who God is. If Jesus' crucifixion is the hour of glorification, it is the hour when, more clearly than anywhere else, the nature of God is revealed. When the Son of man is lifted up, like the serpent, on a cross, we know that God's love for the world led him to give his Son up to death.

Where did John get this extraordinary idea that turns our expectation of glory on its head? Is it simply his way of dealing with the scandal of the cross? Was he alone in his interpretation? The surprising answer is that he was not, for years before John wrote, Paul did something very similar. Did they develop their ideas independently, or had John read some of Paul's letters and put into story form what Paul had expressed in theological statements? We do not know, but I always think it is more interesting and exciting if different

---

[27] John 4:34; 5:36.

authors develop similar ideas independently rather than one building on the thought of another.

Now at first sight you may well dispute my statement that Paul's teaching is similar to John's. Indeed, commentators sometimes *contrast* their views. They point to Philippians 2, where Paul first describes Jesus' humiliation in death, and then his 'hyper-exaltation', using a compound of the verb ὑψόω, 'to lift up'. It was this exaltation which led to the glory of God the Father. In Romans 6:4, Paul writes about Christ being raised 'through the glory of God the Father'. C.K. Barrett translated the phrase as 'in a manifestation of the glory of God', and comments that glory has 'a predominately eschatological meaning', which means that Christ's resurrection was an eschatological event.[28] It is no surprise that in 1 Cor 15:43, the fate of believers is described as 'sown in humiliation … raised in glory'.

Elsewhere, however, Paul uses an idea that is remarkably similar to John's though the language is different. In 1 Cor 1:18–25, he describes the message of the cross as 'sheer folly' to outsiders. Jews demand signs – the word is the one used by John – and Greeks wisdom, 'but we proclaim Christ nailed to the cross, a scandal to Jews and foolishness to Greeks. Yet to those who are called, both Jews and Greeks, he is the power of God and the wisdom of God. The folly of God is wiser than human wisdom, and the weakness of God stronger than human strength'. The power of God, elsewhere linked to Christ's resurrection,[29] is here demonstrated in his death.

One of the remarkable things about this passage is the fact that Paul makes no reference to the resurrection – even though, later in the epistle, in chapter 15, he will say that without the resurrection, the Corinthians' faith is useless. Here, his only message is 'Christ nailed to the cross', and he delivered it in weakness and fear (1 Cor 2:2–5) – and with good reason, for it is 'a scandal to Jews'. But his word and gospel conveyed the power of God and brought them to believe. As for the Greeks, they regarded his message as foolishness – but in fact, says Paul in vv. 6–8, what he proclaimed was 'God's hidden wisdom – his secret purpose to bring *us* to our destined glory'. It was because this wisdom was hidden that 'the powers that rule the world … crucified the Lord of glory'.

Apparent weakness that is divine strength is very close to the Johannine understanding of glory, as is the wisdom hidden from human understanding – wisdom that concerns the Lord of glory who is crucified, and so brings *us* to glory. Are there other parallels? Let us look again at the well-known passage in Philippians 2, where our interpretation depends on our translation of

---

[28] C.K. Barrett, *A Commentary on The Epistle to the Romans*, BNTC (London: A&C Black, 1991), *in loc.*
[29] Rom 1:4; Phil 3:10.

v. 6. The standard translations render this 'who, *though* he was in the form of God, did not regard equality with God as something to be exploited' (NRSV) or 'He was in the form of God; *yet* he laid no claim to equality with God' (REB).[30] In other words, the translators assume that it would have been natural for one who was in the form of God to insist on exercising his rights as one who was equal to God.

But when we look at the Greek, we discover that there is no 'though' or 'yet' present. Interestingly, the King James' version got this right: 'Who, *being* in the form of God, thought it not robbery to be equal with God'. What does this mean for our understanding of the passage? The literature written on this passage is enormous, so rather than attempting to do it justice, let me simply suggest that if we *omit* the 'though', Paul seems to be saying that it was precisely *because* Christ was in the form of God that he did not consider his equality to God to justify exploitation or self-aggrandizement or power-grabbing.[31] Rather, he understood it to mean the very opposite: it meant emptying himself, taking the form of a servant, humiliating himself and becoming obedient to death – even death on a cross. Paradoxically, the nature of God is revealed in service and crucifixion. Paul is not *contrasting* being in the form of God with being in the form of a servant. No, to be in the form of God *meant* taking the form of a servant.

Some of us believe that this so-called 'hymn' was written with Adam in mind – Adam, who, created in the image of God, nevertheless grasped for equality and was disobedient.[32] Whether or not we are right, it is significant that the Philippians here are urged to share in the attitude of Christ – or rather, as Paul explains in the following chapter, to be conformed to him; and when he appears from heaven, he will transform the body of our humiliation and conform it to his body of glory. Humanity becomes what it was meant to be – recreated in the image of God, and reflecting his glory. His 'hidden purpose' is fulfilled.

One interesting feature of this passage is the way in which Paul uses himself as an example of what he is urging the Philippians to do. He gave up

---

[30] It was this contrast that led to the nineteenth-century kenotic theory.

[31] See C. F. D. Moule, 'The Manhood of Jesus in the New Testament', in *Christ, Faith and History: Cambridge Studies in Christology*, eds. S. W. Sykes and J. P. Clayton (Cambridge: Cambridge University Press, 1972), 95–110; cf. Michael J. Gorman, '"Although/Because He Was in the Form of God": The Theological Significance of Paul's Master Story (Phil 2:6–11)', *JTI* 1, no. 2 (2007): 147–169; Gorman writes (p. 163): 'Christ Jesus did what he did because this is what it means to be in the form of God. Cruciform kenosis is the counterintuitive "truth about God".'

[32] See Morna D. Hooker, 'Philippians 2:6–11', in *Jesus und Paulus: Festschrift für W. G. Kümmel*, eds. E. Earle Ellis and E. Grasser (Göttingen: Vandenhoeck & Ruprecht, 1975), 151–164; also Morna D. Hooker, 'Adam *Redivivus*: Philippians 2 Once More', in *The Old Testament in the New Testament: Essays in Honour of J. L. North*, ed. Steve Moyise (Sheffield: Sheffield Academic Press, 2000), 220–234 = below, essay 26 (pp. 371–383).

everything he valued in his Jewish heritage in order to gain Christ, and he longs to know Christ and the power of his resurrection and the fellowship of his sufferings, being conformed to his death. The order here puzzles commentators: why does he refer to the power of Christ's resurrection before his sufferings and death? Is it because – as we shall see in other passages – Paul himself already experiences that power in his own sufferings? Power, like glory, keeps invading the present, even in the middle of suffering and shame.

And that brings us to 2 Corinthians, where Paul spells out more fully than anywhere else his understanding of his ministry. We begin in chapter 3,[33] where he makes a remarkable comparison between his own ministry and that of Moses.[34] The ministry of Moses is symbolized by the glory which shone from his face after meeting with the Lord on Sinai – glory so great that the Israelites were unable to look at it. Moses therefore had to veil his face, and the veil was only removed when he turned to the Lord; once again, we have the idea that the glory of God is hidden. But now, in Christ, the veil has been removed. The glory on Moses' face is as nothing compared with the glory reflected in Paul's own ministry, for the veil has been removed. As a result, *all* believers see, as in a mirror, the glory of God, and the result is that we are all being transformed into the same image with ever-increasing glory. The gospel of which Paul is a minister is the gospel of the glory of Christ, and he is the image of God. The God who at the beginning of time commanded light to shine out of darkness has shone in our hearts, and that light is the knowledge of the glory of God in the face of Jesus Christ.[35]

Like the Johannine Prologue, this passage combines exegesis of Genesis 1 with the story of Moses in Exodus 33–34, and asserts the superiority of Christ to Moses, but whereas John 1 introduces John's Gospel, 2 Corinthians is concerned with what that gospel means for Christian living. Already in chapter 1, Paul has claimed that his suffering, like that of Christ, has brought consolation and salvation to others.[36] Now, in chapter 4, he describes how 'this treasure' – i.e. the light of the knowledge of the glory of God – is contained in 'earthenware jars'. Paul carries round in his body the death of Jesus – so that the life Jesus lives may be revealed in him. The hope remains a future one: he trusts in the God who raised the Lord Jesus to life and will raise him with Jesus; he expects 'an eternal glory'. But though (v. 11) he is continually being 'handed over' to death, it is in order that the life of Jesus may be revealed in his mortal body; death is at work in him, so that life may be at work in others.

---

[33] 2 Cor 3:7–18.
[34] For further discussion of 2 Cor 3, see Morna D Hooker, 'Beyond the Things That Are Written?: St Paul's Use of Scripture'. *NTS* 27 (1981): 295–309.
[35] 2 Cor 4:4–6.
[36] 2 Cor 1:3–7.

Future life is being enjoyed – like jam – today. God's glory is no longer concealed, but revealed – paradoxically – in suffering.[37]

Glory belongs to the future, when God's purposes are finally fulfilled. But of course in the biblical story it belonged also to the very beginning, as we noted when we were thinking about Adam. God created Adam in his own image, we are told, and we have noted that Jewish legends believed him to have reflected his glory. This tradition appears to be reflected in passages such as Rom 1:23 and 3:23. Now that Christ has reversed the consequences of Adam's sin (Romans 5) we hope for future glory (8:18, 21). Creation longs for this final redemption, when God's purpose is finally fulfilled.

When that happens, then those whom God has called will be conformed to the image of his Son – and that means not only that they are 'justified', or brought into a right relationship with God, but glorified.[38] No wonder, then, that glory is seen as God's hidden purpose for humanity. This is what God intended at creation, and what is now brought to fulfilment, in Christ. But it has come about because God's 'free gift of grace' was demonstrated in the actions of one who, unlike Adam, was righteous and obedient. 'God proved his love for us in the fact that Christ died for us'.[39] What is this but a demonstration of God's glory? And we are being conformed to his image, and so glorified.

It is obvious to us all that the Christian proclamation of a crucified Messiah was contrary to Jewish expectation of what God's anointed representative would be. It is hardly surprising if the ancient world dismissed the gospel as a scandal and as folly. What we do not always recognize is that this message is contrary to our expectations of *God*. The paradox that is grasped in their different ways by both Paul and John means that we need to revise our whole understanding of the nature of God, and in spite of centuries of Christian tradition – or perhaps because of much of that tradition! – we find this difficult to do. Our images of God assume that his power is expressed in victory and triumph, not in weakness and defeat. We associate glory with resurrection, not with the cross. As a result, countless Christians expect God to *save* them from suffering, and are puzzled when he does not. They forget that many others, like Paul, have found God present with them *in* their suffering.

There is, then, a paradox at the very heart of the Christian gospel: God reveals himself in suffering and death, in humility and shame, in weakness and defeat. While John states this boldly, Paul clearly understood that in human terms, it is sheer nonsense. It is hardly surprising if his so-called 'conversion'

---

[37] For further discussion of 2 Cor 4 see Morna D. Hooker, '2 Corinthians 5:1–10 in Context', in *2 Thessalonians and Pauline Eschatology: For Petr Pokorný on His 80th Birthday*, ed. Christopher Tuckett (Leuven: Peeters, 2013), 165–195 = below, essay 30 (pp. 432–459).

[38] Rom 8:29 ff.

[39] Rom 5:8.

meant that he had to rethink his beliefs about God. But this is the principle underlying the gospel. This is why the Son of man came to serve, and why his followers must do the same; this is why the first will be last and the last first; this is why true wisdom appears like foolishness, and strength like weakness.

The gospel as understood by these two early theologians appears to belong to a world that is back to front. But they, of course, would maintain, that it is *we* who are in 'Looking-glass land', and are out of touch with the divine plan. And that brings us back to Humpty-Dumpty and his definition of glory. Is it *we*, perhaps, who have made glory mean what we would *like* it to mean? And who has the knock-out argument? Is it the philosophers of Corinth, with their clever rhetoric, and their theology of success, or Paul and John, grappling with a truth so amazing that it blinds us all, until, as Paul expresses it, we turn to the Lord.[40]

---

[40] For discussion relevant to the topic of this lecture, see George J. Brooke, ed., *The Significance of Sinai Traditions About Sinai and Divine Revelation in Judaism and Christianity* (Leiden: Brill, 2008), and Jarl E. Fossum, *The Image of the Invisible God* (Göttingen: Vandenhoeck & Ruprecht, 1995).

Section Six

Adam, Law, and Cult

25. Paul: Apostle to the Gentiles

The 28th St Paul's Lecture, under the auspices of the London Diocesan Council for Christian-Jewish Understanding, given at St Botolph's Church, Aldgate on November 16th, 1989.

When I was invited to deliver this St Paul's Lecture, it seemed to me to be an open invitation to lecture on St Paul himself. Who, or what, I wondered, could possibly provide a more appropriate topic? Yet when I looked back over the titles of previous St Paul's Lectures, I could not find his name anywhere in the list. Unless he is hiding somewhere, in one of the more enigmatic titles, none of the previous lectures in a series which bears his name has ever been devoted to him. Now this omission is a very curious fact. Why, I wondered, have your previous lecturers studiously avoided him? Could it be because the popular image of Paul is of someone who was always attacking Judaism, who rejected the Jewish Torah, or Law, and who turned his back on the faith of his forefathers? Could it be because he is not normally regarded as having done anything to foster Christian-Jewish understanding? If so, then it is clearly high time to look at his teaching afresh, to demonstrate that this popular understanding is wrong, and that he is in fact a highly appropriate choice as the patron saint of this series.

But, you may well ask, did not Paul describe the Torah in highly derogatory terms? Did he not say that it had led him into sin, that it had brought judgement, even death? Did he not contrast the Law with faith, and contrast freedom in Christ with slavery under the Law? He did indeed. But he also described the Law as holy, and declared that its commands are holy, just, and good (Rom 7:12). He assumed that the Torah was divine in origin, and when he was accused of undermining the Law through his insistence on faith, declared indignantly that, on the contrary, he was upholding the Law (3:31). Now it is possible, as some have argued, that Paul did not know his own mind, and that he wrote contradictory statements about the Law; alternatively, it may be that he changed his mind over a period of time. It is possible, for example, that he modified the early, hostile stance towards the Law which he expressed in writing his somewhat bitter letter to the Galatians, and that by the time he wrote to the Romans he had mellowed in his approach and realized that there were good things to be said about it after all. If so, then we should at least give him the credit for having realized his mistake in his old age. In fact, however, this explanation will not work, since we can find apparently contradictory attitudes to the Law side by side in the same epistle. Thus in Romans we find him describing the Law one moment as good and holy, the next declaring that it was ineffectual; and whenever he attacks Torah as a system, he backs up his argument by quoting from the Torah itself. Could there be a clearer case of someone who liked to eat his cake and have it?

I am in fact persuaded that Paul was not as perverse as he appears, and that the reason why he appears to us to be, to say the least, a little confused, is that we misunderstand his purpose in writing to his churches, and therefore misinterpret his teaching. One of our problems is that we read him through the spectacles of a later age, and ask the wrong questions in trying to fathom his thought. We ask our own questions, and expect him to answer them, and so fail to recognize that he was dealing with a totally different set of questions. We ask about the salvation of individuals; about guilt, and how one can be set free from it; about how we may make peace with God; about what we term 'Paul's attitude to the Law'. I do not say that Paul would not have comprehended these questions, but I do not believe that they were his primary concern. I suggest that the questions which most interested him would have included these: how may *Gentiles* be included in the people of God? What is expected of those whom God has recognized as his people, and who live in the messianic age? What is going to happen to those whom God first called to be his people – that is, the Jewish nation? And what is God's plan for mankind, which he is now working out in history?

A second reason for our difficulty in understanding Paul's letters is that we expect to find in them what isn't there. In writing them, he was dealing with very particular problems, which were burning issues at the time; the letters are not statements of the Christian gospel, but applications of the gospel to those problems. That does not mean that you will not find the gospel in them, but you will have to search it out. It is rather as though we wished to improve on our school French, but could find no French grammar book to assist us, and the only useful book we could discover was a French novel. Reading the novel should certainly improve our understanding of the language, but it will be by being plunged into the use of the language, not by learning its first principles. Paul's letters *use* the gospel – they apply it to the problems of the day; and his problems were very different from ours.

So what exactly were his problems? And what was his situation? Let us begin at the beginning, with his call. I say 'call' deliberately, rather than 'conversion', because although we frequently talk about the conversion of St. Paul, I do not believe that that is the way he would have seen the event which we, taking our cue from Acts, refer to as the Damascus Road experience; indeed, it is perhaps in talking about his conversion that we begin to go wrong in our understanding of Paul. 'Conversion' implies either that one forsakes one religion for another, or that one abandons an irreligious life for a life centred on God. But Paul certainly did not abandon an irreligious life when he became a Christian; he tells us that he had lived a very strict life, scrupulously obeying all the commandments of the Jewish law in his zeal to serve God. Nor did he abandon one religion for another: he insists that his new faith is the culmination of the old, and cites text after text to demonstrate that what has happened through the life, death, and resurrection of Christ has been done by the God of Abraham, Isaac, and Jacob.

How, then, did Paul himself see that initial event? There is only one place in his letters where he describes what happened, though he several times refers to it by describing himself as 'called to be an apostle'. But in Gal 1:13 ff. he tells us about that initial call:

> You have heard of my former manner of life within Judaism: how savagely I persecuted the church of God and tried to destroy it; and how in the practice of Judaism I outstripped most of my contemporaries by my boundless devotion to the traditions of my ancestors. But then in his good pleasure God, who from my birth had set me apart, and who had called me through his grace, chose to reveal his Son in and through me, in order that I might proclaim him among the Gentiles.

The climax of this account comes in those last few words: the revelation of God's Son took place in order that Paul might proclaim him among the Gentiles. This is his own understanding of the most significant event in his life – it was a call to be the apostle to the Gentiles. It is a remarkable paradox that the man called for this task had been, as he puts it elsewhere, 'a Hebrew born and bred, of the tribe of Benjamin, in his practice of the Law a Pharisee, in zeal for religion a persecutor of the church, by the Law's standard of righteousness without fault' (Phil 3:5 ff.). It was this man, who prized his Jewish heritage above everything, who loved the Law and was eager to obey it, who was called to be the apostle to the Gentiles. There is no doubt that this is the way in which Paul saw his task, for he underlines it in the next chapter of Galatians, when he tells us that the church authorities in Jerusalem recognized that he 'had been entrusted to take the gospel to the Gentiles as surely as Peter had been entrusted to take it to the Jews' (Gal 2:7). Our problem is that when we think about what happened on the Damascus Road we naturally turn to Luke's account in Acts 9, since Luke tells it as a rattling good story, in marked contrast to Paul's somewhat cryptic reference in Galatians 1; and because Luke's story is so good, we tend to remember its details: the light from heaven and the voice, and the fact that Paul was temporarily blinded; but even in Luke's account, we find that the point of it all is because Paul is 'a chosen instrument, to bring the name of Jesus before the Gentiles' (Acts 9:15). Nor is this accidental, for in the other two, less well-known accounts of the event, found later in Acts (22:15; 26:17 ff.) precisely the same point is made, though this is not always made clear in our

English translations. So our sources are unanimous: the experience which led Paul to acknowledge Jesus as God's Son was interpreted by him as a call to be the apostle to the Gentiles.

Since this is so, and since in Galatians Paul clearly understands his mission to be distinct from that of Peter, who is charged with the mission to the Jews, we have to remember that Paul's letters were written to congregations which were predominantly Gentile in their make-up. I do not say that there were no Jews at all in the Christian churches of Corinth or Galatia or Thessalonika; certainly some Jews in these places must have responded to the gospel, and Paul may well have used the local synagogue in each town as the launching-pad for his preaching, just as Acts tells us. But many of those who heard him preach in the synagogues and who responded to the gospel were 'godfearers', that is, Gentiles who worshipped there without taking the decisive step of becoming Jews. Paul believed himself to be called by God to be the apostle to the Gentiles, and it was to them that he took the gospel, and it seems that this was his understanding from the very beginning. New Testament scholars are unsure whether Galatians or 1 Thessalonians is Paul's earliest letter: no matter. We have already seen that in Galatians Paul declares that he was called to be the apostle to the Gentiles from the word 'Go'. As for 1 Thessalonians, note how in 1:9 he reminds the congregation that they 'turned to God from idols, to serve a living and true God'. The Thessalonians really *were* 'converted'; they were Gentiles by birth, and had worshipped pagan gods, until Paul had brought them the gospel. Interestingly it is the epistle to the Romans, written to a church which Paul had not founded, which seems to be mostly clearly directed to Gentiles *and* Jews.

I stress the obvious because we do not always realize its implications. We are used to the idea that the Christian church is predominantly Gentile because it has been that way for the past 1900 years or so. But that was not how things began; and if Paul had not been commissioned to be the apostle to the Gentiles, Christianity might have remained what it was in its earliest days – a sect within Judaism. It is clear from the Gospels that Jesus himself confined his ministry to the Jews: he described himself as sent to the lost sheep of the house of Israel. His disciples were all Jews, and so were the earliest Christians, who believed him to be God's Messiah, or anointed one, who had brought the fulfilment of all Israel's hopes. I call them 'Christians' because it is a convenient term, but of course the word is anachronistic: these men and women were Jews who believed that Jesus had been raised from the dead, that he had been vindicated by God himself and acknowledged by the community of believers as Lord and Christ. Their conviction that God had fulfilled all his promises to Israel, and their joyous new way of life attracted others to join them; they, too, were Jews, who saw Jesus as the fulfilment of Old Testament hopes. They described themselves, not as 'Christians', but as followers of 'the way'. How would we expect such people to express their new faith? We know that they met together, for fellowship and 'the breaking of bread'; but in their everyday lives we would expect them to remain good Jews; to show their devotion to God and their thankfulness for what he had done by continuing to read scripture, by obeying its commands, and by worshipping God in the temple and in synagogue. If God had fulfilled his promises to his people, that was no reason to abandon his commands. Jesus himself had taught them that they must love God with heart and mind and soul and strength, and that the scriptures set out what that means; it is true that he sometimes disagreed with the religious authorities about the interpretation of the scriptures, but he did not question their authority as God's word to his people.

But it was not very long before a new development took place which was to change everything: Gentiles heard the gospel and responded to its message. One gathers from the account which Luke gives in Acts 10 of the conversion of Cornelius that this development was totally unexpected. It was open to Gentiles to become Jews by accepting circumcision, if they were male, and by accepting the obligation to keep the Law; but here was a Gentile who had accepted the gospel preached to him by Peter, and who had received the promises which God had made to Israel without ever *being* a member of God's people! But had he? Could the promises be fulfilled for someone who was outside the covenant which God had made with his people? To Peter, the answer to that question was clear: Cornelius and his household had received the Spirit of God. God's Spirit had, as it were, bypassed the old definition of God's people, and had included him in the blessings which were being poured out on Israel in the last days; the fact that he had received the Spirit was surely clear proof that he was now a member of God's people, even though he had never been circumcised. When Peter is called to explain to his fellow believers in Jerusalem why, as a pious Jew, he had stayed with Gentiles and had eaten with them he silences opposition by repeating the story: 'The Holy Spirit fell on them, just as on us at the beginning ... if then God gave Gentiles the same gift that he gave us when we believed in the Lord Jesus Christ, who was I, to withstand God?' (Acts 11:15–17).

And when we turn back to Paul, it is interesting to find that when he is writing to his Gentile converts in Galatia, he uses exactly the same argument. Their experience had been similar to that of Cornelius; they, too, had responded to the gospel and received the Spirit of God. 'You fools!' he writes to them. 'You have already received the Spirit! Do you really want to go back to the flesh?' In order to understand Paul's position, we have to remember that the gift of the Spirit was seen as the sign of the new age. Paul had preached the gospel to the Galatians; they had heard and believed, and they had received the gift of the Spirit: in other words, they had been recognized by God as his children, and they had already addressed him as 'Father'. The blessings of the new age were theirs, without their becoming Jews. And now they wish to become Jews, to accept circumcision and with it all the obligations of the Torah. It is because Paul believes that Christians are already living in the new age that he sees circumcision and all that it involves as a retrograde step which undermines the gospel and denies the reality of what has already taken place. He uses a similar argument elsewhere (2 Cor 3). Clearly, he saw the arrival of the Spirit as a crucial fact which altered everything.

So why, we may well ask, were the Galatians wanting to take another path? Why did they not see their new faith in the same way as Paul? Was it not patently obvious that circumcision was unnecessary, and that obedience to the Law was no longer required of those who claimed to be members of God's people? The answer is 'No'. What is so surprising is not that the Galatians assumed that their faith in Christ required obedience to the Jewish Torah, but that Paul declared that for them to accept it would be, not simply unnecessary, but equivalent to an annulment of the gospel.

The Galatians' position is in fact simple to understand. Paul had preached to them the good news: he had told them what all Christians believed, namely, that God's promises in the Jewish scriptures had been fulfilled; that he had sent Jesus, his Son, into the world, and had raised him from the dead, and that those who believed in him would share in the joys of the new age. Indeed, he claimed that this new age had already begun, with the sending of God's Spirit on men and women; all they had to do was to live their lives under his guidance. And then Paul had left them, hurrying off on his mission to evangelize yet more Gentiles. So what was the small group of very young Christians to do? We can imagine them meeting together, talking with astonishment about the experience which had come to them. They would surely want to worship God: how were they to do this? One or two of them were probably Jews; others would have been 'godfearers'; the only pattern of worship which they would have known, therefore, apart from the worship of the pagan gods they had abandoned, would be the worship of the synagogue. They would begin, then, with worship which must have seemed very much like that of the synagogue; the only sacred books they had were the Jewish scriptures, the only hymns they had, at least at the beginning, were the Jewish psalms. The new converts would also want to live out their new faith in their everyday lives: how were they to do that? Their previous behaviour as pagans would not provide a good example; but those among them who were Jewish knew what it meant to serve a righteous and holy God. Paul had talked vaguely about 'life in the Spirit'; he had told them to cultivate love, joy, peace, patience, kindness, goodness, faithfulness, gentleness, and self-control. But what did that mean in practical terms? What were they to do, day by day?

Where could they find guidance? Once again, the obvious place to look was in the Jewish scriptures, where very precise rules about how God's people should live were to be found. And where could they find out more about their new faith? Why in the Jewish scriptures, of course, the scriptures which their apostle, Paul, was always quoting, and which he said pointed forward to Christ and were fulfilled in him. So to the scriptures they turned, and when they did so, they discovered that at the very beginning God had made a covenant with the great ancestor of the Jewish people, Abraham, and promised that one day, through him, he would bless all the nations of the earth. And what was the sign of the covenant? Why, circumcision! And when they read a little further, they came to the story of Moses on Mount Sinai, and discovered that there God made another covenant with his people, and that they promised to obey all God's commandments. So what were the Galatians likely to conclude, when they read such stories? – especially when a group of so-called 'Judaizers' visited them. Who these Judaizers were we do not know: perhaps they were Jewish Christians; perhaps they were Gentile converts to Judaism, who naturally assumed that others should follow their example in becoming Jews: whichever they were, they were very willing to explain the meaning of the Jewish scriptures to the Galatian Christians. And their explanation would have gone like this: like Abraham, you have believed in God. Fine! How does the story go on? Abraham was circumcised, as a sign of the covenant which God made with him. If you want to enjoy the blessing which God promised to Abraham, you too must be circumcised. Like Moses and the children of Israel, you have been saved by God, and rescued from slavery. Fine! But what happened next? God gave his people the Law, and they promised to obey the Law. If you want to be members of God's people, then you too must accept the Law and obey all its commands.

The reasoning was obvious, the logic impeccable: if you wished to be what we would term a Christian, and enjoy the privileges of God's people, it was necessary first to become a member of that people, and that meant becoming a Jew. Surprisingly, it was Paul who did not accept the obvious view: it was Paul, Jewish to the roots, who insisted that Gentile Christians must *not* accept circumcision, must *not* take on the obligations of the Law. Why? It was because he believed that decisive events had taken place with the death and resurrection of Jesus: the new age had dawned, and that meant that the definition of those who belong to the people of God had been changed. It was no longer those who were Jewish by birth or by conversion who belonged to the people of God, but those who were 'in Christ' – that is, those who believed that God had raised Jesus from the dead and who acknowledged him as Lord (Rom 10:9) – and this new community included both Jews and Gentiles. But surely, people must have said to Paul, if Jesus is the Christ, the anointed one, that means he is the Jewish Messiah; he is the fulfilment of Jewish hopes. It is at this point that Paul reminds the Galatians of their conversion experience: they had heard the gospel, had believed in it, and been baptized with the Holy Spirit: in other words, God had already acknowledged them as his children (Gal 3). If Paul uses this as the basis of his argument in trying to persuade the Galatians that they were already members of God's people, was it perhaps because this was what had convinced *him* that God had saved these Gentile men and women quite apart from the Law (Rom 3:21)? When the Gentiles began to flock into the church, there was no denying that they had already received God's Spirit: and since they *were* Gentiles, not Jews, this must mean that God must have saved them on the basis of sheer grace. There was nothing unJewish about such a conclusion. The prophets had looked forward to the day when Gentiles would worship Israel's God; they had not suggested that it would be necessary for them to become Jews in order to do so (cf. Isa 2:2–4 = Mic 4:1–3; Isa 25:6; Zech 8:23). In the future age, such steps are unnecessary.

Paul's argument with the Galatians is simply this: you have arrived. You are already living in the new era – the era of the Spirit. Whatever happened in the past, good though it may have been, belongs to the past era – the era of the flesh. Even God's gifts to Israel, gracious as they were, belonged to the era of the flesh, because they were the provisions of a past age. The Jews were descendants from Abraham, according to the flesh; they had received the sign of the covenant, circumcision, in their flesh; all the privileges they enjoyed – the worship of God, their position as his children, the covenants, the Law, the promises which God had made to them – all belonged to them because they were descendants of Abraham. But now the new age has dawned; the promises have been fulfilled, and God has poured out his blessings upon all nations: not simply on the Jews, but on Gentiles as well – both are now included in the new community of God's people. And because we are living in this new era, the old definitions, which depended on fleshly matters, like birth, and physical descent and circumcision are no longer relevant. This is why he is adamant that his Gentile converts must not try to become Jews, and must not put themselves under the rule of the Law. If they do, then they are denying that God has already acted on their behalf, and that his action did not depend on faithfulness to the Law. As he puts it in writing to the Romans: 'Now, quite independently of Law, the righteousness of God has been made known, though with the Law and the Prophets bearing witness to it' (Rom 3:21).

We can perhaps begin to understand, then, why in writing to the Galatians Paul said some very harsh things about the Law: it is because he was writing to Gentiles who did not appreciate that they were already members of God's people, and because he believed that in attempting to 'improve' their situation they were in fact undermining the gospel. The Law, he argued, had been given to the Jews as an interim arrangement; it had promised something better – and that something had arrived through Christ. Paul's hope was that when Jews saw Gentiles enjoying the salvation which had been promised to *them*, they would be led to respond to the gospel (Rom 11:11); but if the Gentiles interpret their faith in Christ as the first step towards becoming Jews, what encouragement will they provide to Jews to take the momentous step of believing in Jesus?

But what, then, was the position of those Jews who believed in Jesus as Messiah? Were they still bound by the Law? We have already seen that it was entirely natural for the very first groups of Christians to show their love and devotion towards God by obeying the Law's precepts. Once again, Paul saw things differently! It is not difficult to follow his logic. God made certain promises to Abraham; these promises have now been fulfilled in Christ. Again, the Law, together with the prophets, contains certain promises: these, too, have been fulfilled in Christ. But once you enjoy the fulfilment, your perspective changes: you look back at the promises, instead of forwards to what you hope for. Once you arrive at your holiday destination, you enjoy the reality of the mountains and the lakes, and you no longer need the glossy brochures which enticed you there, except as a guide to the pleasures that are yours to enjoy. And once you have climbed the mountains and swum in the lakes, then the brochures seem a poor substitute: only a fool would spend his holiday hunting for the brochures in the tourist offices, rather than enjoying the scenery about him. Paul's argument is founded on his conviction that Christians have in a sense arrived: the last days are here. God has acted, he has saved his people, and he has saved, *not* those who had been most diligent in obeying the Law, but those who believed in Jesus.

One of the remarkable features stressed throughout the Gospels, as well as in the Acts of the Apostles and in Paul's letters, is the fact that the people who responded to Jesus and to the good news were outsiders – 'publicans and sinners' to use the old-fashioned phrase. It was not the righteous who were flocking into the kingdom of God, but sinners. This was not just Paul's understanding of things, but part of the common belief of the early Christian community. In Galatians 2, when he is reporting a somewhat acrimonious conversation he had had with Peter, Paul says that he reminded Peter of a belief which they held in common, namely, that no one, whether Jew or Gentile, is brought into a right relationship with God by fulfilling the works of the Law, but only through faith (Gal 2:16). So what is the Jew who becomes a Christian to do? Is he now free to break all the commandments? To murder, to steal, to commit adultery, to covet? Of course not! Paul certainly does not encourage his converts to break the commandments; indeed, it is interesting to discover that when he is giving them moral advice, he tends to quote from them (see Rom 13:9; 1 Cor 5:13; Gal 5:14; cf. Phil 2:15)! The Law, he insists, is holy, and the commandment is holy, just, and good (Rom

7:11). There is nothing wrong with the Law, *but* it is not God's final word. In Paul's eyes, those Jews who have not responded to the gospel have failed to respond to God's final word – the word to which the Law itself pointed forward: they have rejected the salvation which God has now offered through the death and resurrection of Christ, and have preferred to seek righteousness through the Law.

As Paul looked back on his previous existence, before he had come to faith in Christ, he saw it as a period of bondage and weakness. He certainly had not seen it like that at the time. On the contrary, he tells us that he had gloried in the Law (Phil 3:4–6). But now that he has experienced the new relationship with God which faith in Christ brings, he sees the past in a new light. He has arrived at his holiday destination, and the brochures have given way to the reality. And this is why he believes that for Jews who accept the Christian gospel, keeping the detailed regulations of the Jewish law is a matter of indifference; they are no longer bound by them. They have entered the promised land. But at the same time, he plunders the Jewish scriptures, in order to demonstrate that what Christians, both Jews and Gentiles, are now experiencing is the fulfilment of the promises made by God to his people long ago. Paul's audacious claim is that the righteousness which God demanded in the Law is in fact possessed, not by those who keep the Law, but by those who live 'in Christ'.

Now whatever else we may say about it, we have to agree that Paul's teaching was highly dangerous. To Jews who accepted the gospel, he said: your new life in Christ sets you free from the condemnation which the Law pronounces on all disobedience. To Gentiles, he said: you *must not* put yourself under the yoke of the Law, because that would be a denial of your new life in Christ. Like Augustine, centuries later, he appeared to be saying: love God, and do what you like! The rule works well as a guiding principle, provided that one understands fully the meaning of the two words 'love' and 'God'. And the trouble was that Paul's converts were not always clear about the meaning of either word. On the other hand, they had a pretty good idea of what they understood by the injunction to do what they liked! Paul's teaching was wide open to misunderstanding and abuse: the more he emphasized that the gifts of the last age were already here, the greater the temptation to enjoy life and ignore the concerns of their neighbours; the more he insisted that Gentiles must not put themselves under the Jewish law, the more likely they were to abandon all moral constraints. It is no good telling newly converted pagans to love God and do what they like; they need some kind of guidance.

To be fair to Paul, he didn't quite put it that way. Instead, he talked about a new way of life which he described as 'life in Christ', or as 'life in the Spirit'. What he meant was that Christians should be conformed to the character of

God himself, revealed in Christ, and in the life of the Spirit of God among them. Life under the Law has been replaced by life in Christ. Once again, it seems to me that even here, where Paul's teaching appears to be directly contrary to Judaism, he is in fact being true to his Jewish roots. For in Judaism, the Law is God's gift to his people, Israel, given to them when he made a covenant with them on Sinai. Their promise to keep the Law was based on the fact that God had saved them from Egypt. In other words, God had chosen them to be his people and had delivered them: now he established a covenant with them, and they promised to *be* his people by keeping the Law. The command of God to Israel was: 'Be holy as I am holy'. God and people were bound together in a covenant which required them to be what he was. And now, Paul believes, God has again delivered his people, only this time he has included Gentiles as well as Jews, and the deliverance has come about through the death and resurrection of Jesus. He has called a new community to belong to him, and has made a new covenant with them: and once again, he demands of his people that they should be holy as he is holy. The difference is that the parameters of their obedience are now spelt out, not by the Jewish law, which was God's gift to the Jewish people, but by life in Christ, who is God's gift to the whole of mankind. But when Paul gave his converts practical guidance about how to behave, a lot of his advice came straight out of the Jewish scriptures! The glossy brochures had not been confined to the wastepaper basket, and were still useful as guides to the beauties which one might expect to find in the mountains. But that is hardly surprising. For it was in the Torah that Paul himself had learned the nature of God – the God whom he believed to be the Father of Jesus Christ.

I have spent all my time in this lecture dealing with two of the questions which I suggested at the beginning were of crucial importance for Paul: namely, how may *Gentiles* be included in the people of God? And what is expected of those whom God has recognized as his people, and who live in the messianic age? I have no time to deal with the other two: what is going to happen to those whom God first called to be his people – that is, the Jewish nation? And what is God's plan for mankind, which he is now working out in history? Suffice it to say that Paul believed that ultimately the whole Jewish people would come to recognize the truth of the Christian claim for Jesus. In Romans 9–11 he expresses the passionate longing that Jew and Gentile together may worship God and enjoy the depth of the riches of the wisdom and knowledge of God: only when that happened would the last days be fully here, and the whole universe be restored to what God intended for it. I hope that I have done something to justify my claim that the popular picture of Paul as anti-Jewish is false. He was born a Jew, was nurtured in Judaism, and remained thoroughly Jewish in his thinking. He did not question the belief that the Law and Prophets were God's words to his people; but he *was* convinced that the promises of God set out in the Law and the Prophets had been fulfilled. This alone was what divided him from the majority of his fellow Jews, who did not accept the Christian gospel. And this remains the one honourable cause of division between Jew and Christian believer today. All the rest — anti-Semitism, hatred, fear, suspicion, enmity, persecution — is built on misunderstanding and prejudice, and is a travesty of the gospel which Paul proclaimed.

26. Adam *Redivivus*: Philippians 2 Once More

This paper is an attempt to respond to the article by Markus Bockmuehl published in the *Journal of Theological Studies* a few years ago on the meaning of the phrase ἐν μορφῇ θεοῦ.[1] That article had two main conclusions, the first of which was that there was 'insufficient evidence to establish an *explicit* link, or even a deliberate allusion, to Adam'.[2] The Adamic interpretation was accordingly described as being an 'interpretative cul-de-sac'.[3] The other, more positive, conclusion, was that the meaning of the word μορφή was 'visible form', and that the background of Paul's usage here was to be found in Jewish mystical tradition. With the second of these conclusions I have no quarrel. The evidence, though somewhat scanty, does indeed suggest that μορφή had this visual meaning, though whether or not this came to Paul via the mystical tradition I am not so sure. What I want to challenge is Bockmuehl's first conclusion, that the belief that the passage should be read in the light of the story of Adam is an 'interpretative cul-de-sac'.

Those of us who have argued for Adamic influence have found links with Adam not only in the phrase 'in the form of God' in v. 6, which *may* be reminiscent of Gen 1:26, but in the implicit contrast between Adam, who grasped at equality with God, and Christ, who did not grasp at/cling to/exploit that equality.[4] Whereas Adam was stripped of his privileges, Christ deliberately emptied himself, becoming what Adam had become – a slave, subject to death. In favour of this interpretation we may point to Paul's use of Adam elsewhere (most clearly in Rom 5:12–21 and 1 Cor 15:21–22, 42–50), and to the language Paul uses at the end of Philippians 3 (where the implications of the 'hymn' for Christians are set out), language which echoes that which he uses elsewhere to describe the restoration of men and women to the glory which Adam lost (Rom 8:18–30, 39; 1 Cor 15:35–57; cf. 2 Cor 3:12–4:6).

Bockmuehl begins by dismissing the traditional assumption that the phrase ἐν μορφῇ θεοῦ is the equivalent of κατ' εἰκόνα θεοῦ, the LXX translation of בצלם אלהים in Gen 1:26–27. He refers to an article by Dave Steenburg, who

---

[1] Markus Bockmuehl, '"The Form of God" (Phil. 2:6): Variations on a Theme of Jewish Mysticism', *JTS* NS 48 (1997): 1–23.
[2] Bockmuehl, '"The Form of God"', 11.
[3] Bockmuehl, '"The Form of God"', 6.
[4] My own interpretation ('Philippians 2:6–11') was published in *Jesus und Paulus: Festschrift für W. G. Kümmel,* eds. E. Earle Ellis and E. Grasser (Göttingen: Vandenhoeck & Ruprecht, 1975), 151–164.

argued that εἰκών and μορφή were not synonyms.[5] Although it is at least worthy of note that some of the Fathers believed εἰκών and μορφή to be synonyms,[6] I have to agree that Steenburg's case is a persuasive one: we cannot simply pretend that ἐν μορφῇ θεοῦ and κατ' εἰκόνα θεοῦ are the same thing. However, I find myself uneasy with the analogy that Bockmuehl then employs to illustrate this conclusion. With εἰκών, μορφή and δόξα he compares 'corn flakes, toast, and orange juice', which may all, he says, 'be discrete aspects of the same breakfast'.[7] So they may, but I do not think they are related in quite the same way as are εἰκών, μορφή and δόξα. Corn flakes, toast and orange juice are separate items on the menu, very different in origin, character, and taste; their only connection is that they may follow one another at the same meal. The fact that εἰκών, μορφή and δόξα are not synonyms does not mean that they do not belong together; it is possible that they overlap in a way that corn flakes, toast, and orange juice do not. Bockmuehl's own discussion shows that this is in fact so.

1. The Problem

The question of whether the figure of Adam is in view in Philippians 2 is linked with the debate as to whether or not in describing Christ as 'in the form of God' Paul is thinking of him as pre-existent, though the two issues should not be confused. Some of those who have supported the Adamic interpretation have tried to exclude the idea of pre-existence from Philippians 2, and have argued that it is the actions of the *human* Jesus that are contrasted with those of Adam. Since the man Adam was created in the image of God, the phrase 'in the form of God' must, they suggest, refer to the earthly Jesus. One of the strongest advocates of this interpretation has been James Dunn,[8] though he seems to have modified his views in his recent book on Paul's theology.[9] It is, however, difficult to make sense of what Paul says in v. 7 without acknowledging that it was the *pre-existent* Christ who became man: so difficult, I suggest, as to be impossible.

The attraction of the theory that Paul is thinking of the human Jesus is, of course, that it allows for a real comparison and contrast between Adam and Christ. If, however, we maintain that it was the pre-existent Christ who was

---

[5] Dave Steenburg, 'The Case Against the Synonymity of *Morphē* and *Eikōn*', *JSNT* 34 (1988): 77–86.
[6] E.g. Ambrosiaster, in his Commentary on Phil 2:6; see *PL* 17, col. 407 254C.
[7] Bockmuehl, '"The Form of God"', 8.
[8] James D.G. Dunn, *Christology in the Making* (London: SCM Press, 1980), 113–121.
[9] James D.G. Dunn, *The Theology of Paul the Apostle* (Edinburgh: T&T Clark, 1998), 281–288, 292–293.

'in the form of God', then Adam and Christ are no longer in alignment. The problem that now confronts us is this: How can we have a figure who is described in Adamic terms who then *becomes* man, and takes on Adam's likeness? Bockmuehl dismisses the notion of what he terms 'an eternally pre-existent *human* Jesus'.[10] But is this in fact the necessary alternative to the view that eliminates pre-existence in favour of an earthly Jesus? Is it possible, in other words, to combine the ideas of pre-existence and the comparison with Adam *without* thinking of the *human* Jesus as 'eternally pre-existent'?

2. Incarnation

Now the idea that Christ became man is found elsewhere in Paul, and it is perhaps wise to begin looking for an answer to this conundrum there. Particularly interesting is Rom 8:3, since what we have there is in many ways similar to Phil 2:6–7: ὁ θεὸς τὸν ἑαυτοῦ υἱὸν πέμψας ἐν ὁμοιώματι σαρκὸς ἁμαρτίας ... Instead of Philippians' ἐν ὁμοιώματι ἀνθρώπων we have ἐν ὁμοιώματι σαρκὸς ἁμαρτίας. The verse comes towards the climax of Paul's extended argument about the redemption of mankind in Christ, who has by his obedience reversed what Adam did when he brought sin and death into the world. In the rest of the chapter we read of the renewal of creation and the restoration of the glory lost by Adam. God, we are told, sent his Son in the likeness of sinful flesh; the result is that men and women are delivered from slavery, and themselves become children (lit. 'sons') of God (Rom 8:14–17), having been destined to be conformed (συμμόρφους) to the image (εἰκών) of his Son (8:29). Paul's expectation reflects the hope of future restoration found in later Judaism, which looks forward to a time when men and women will again be like God. Thus Rab. Gen. 21.7 interprets Gen 3:22 of the world to come, when God will say 'Behold the man *has become* as one of us'.

The same idea is expressed in Galatians 4: ἐξαπέστειλεν ὁ θεὸς τὸν υἱὸν αὐτοῦ, γενόμενον ἐκ γυναικός, γενόμενον ὑπὸ νόμον. This time we find verbal echoes in the word γενόμενον (although it is used in a slightly different sense) in a context which implies that, in being born of a woman under the Law, Christ became a slave in order that those who were slaves might become sons. In both Romans 8 and Galatians 4, unlike Philippians 2, the initiative is taken by God, who sends the one described as his Son. A parallel to Christ's *self*-emptying in Phil 2:7 is found in 2 Cor 8:9, where he is said to have become poor for the Corinthians' sake, with the result that they have been made rich. All three of these passages describe what we may term 'incarnation'.

---

[10] Bockmuehl, "'The Form of God'", 10.

Now Gal 4:4–5. and 2 Cor 8:9 are two of the so-called 'interchange' formulae, where the result of Christ becoming man is that men and women are made what he eternally is.[11] Romans 8:3 and Phil 2:6–11, on the other hand, though also about what we would call 'incarnation', appear to tell us only about Christ becoming man – until, that is, we read a little further; when we do, we discover that here, too, believers are transformed and take on Christ's likeness. In Romans 8, as we have just seen, this is spelt out later in the chapter; in Philippians, it occurs at the end of ch. 3. I find it intriguing that the idea of Christ's incarnation is always linked with the destiny of believers. Whether 2 Cor 5:21 and Gal 3:13 should also be classified as incarnational formulae is open to debate, though my own belief is that it is a mistake to regard them as concerned solely with the death of Jesus; the notion of Christ becoming 'sin' in 2 Corinthians 5 is remarkably similar to Rom 8:3, while that of Christ being made a curse in Galatians 3 is linked with the statement that he came under the Law in Gal 4:4. What Christ was in his death is the logical outcome of what he became by his birth, as Phil 2:6–11 reminds us. Certainly there is a link in both 2 Corinthians 5 and Galatians 3 with what believers become in Christ: the righteousness of 2 Cor 5:21 and the blessing of Gal 3:13 belong to those who are also 'in Christ', and therefore the children of God, sharing the glory and riches of Christ (cf. Rom 8:14–21; Gal 3:26–4:7; Phil 3:8–9, 20–21).

3. Image

In Romans 8, this idea of becoming like Christ is expressed in terms of being conformed to the image of God: συμμόρφους τῆς εἰκόνος τοῦ υἱοῦ αὐτοῦ (v. 29). It is worth noting the close proximity of εἰκών with σύμμορφος and with δοξάζω in v. 30; even though εἰκών, μορφή and δόξα are not synonyms, they have *something* to do with each other, and their relationship is apparently closer than that of orange juice, cereal, and toast. We find the same idea, expressed in the same language, in two other passages. In 2 Cor 3:18, Christians see the glory of the Lord reflected in the face of Christ, and are transformed into the same image; this time we have εἰκών, μεταμορφόομαι and δόξα linked together. In 2 Cor 4:4 we learn that Christ is himself 'the image of God'. Similar ideas are developed in Colossians, where Christ is described as 'the image of the invisible God' (Col 1:15), while Christians are said to have taken off 'the old man' and to have put on the new, which is being renewed after the image of his creator (Col 3:10; the 'sexist' language here is necessary if

---

[11] See, in particular, Morna D. Hooker, 'Interchange in Christ', *JTS* NS 22 (1971): 349–361, reprinted with other essays on the same theme in Morna D. Hooker, *From Adam to Christ: Essays on Paul* (Cambridge: Cambridge University Press, 1990).

we are to grasp the point). The figure of Adam is surely lurking in the background in all these passages; first of all the language is 'Adamic', since Adam was created after the image of God, and was understood to have reflected the glory of God before the fall; secondly, the context in each case points to Adam. Romans 8, as we have already noted, is the climax of an argument about Adam's fall and humanity's restoration in Christ, and the chapter ends with creation itself being set to rights. 2 Corinthians 4:6 is a quotation from Gen 1:3, but already in ch. 3 the midrash on the story of Moses on Mount Sinai in Exodus 33 has reminded us of the glory lost by Adam which, according to rabbinic legend, was almost restored to Israel through Moses. Colossians 1:15–20 is about Christ's primacy in the universe, and 3:10 sets the idea of our renewal according to the image of the creator side by side with the metaphor of taking off the old man and putting on the new. Similar ideas are certainly present in 1 Corinthians 15, and may well lie behind the passage at the end of Philippians 3, for though the word εἰκών is not used there, we are told that the Lord Jesus Christ will transform our bodies of humiliation and conform them (σύμμορφος) to his own body of glory.

There is one other εἰκών passage which we ought to include, though it is something of a conundrum, and that is 1 Cor 11:7. Here we are told that man (but not woman!) is the image and glory of God. The statement is backed up by references to Gen 2:18 and 22, and is clearly based on Gen 1:27, even though the phrase used there is κατ' εἰκόνα θεοῦ. The real problem with this passage is, of course, that Paul is attempting to use the biblical material to support a sexist hierarchy that conflicts with the view he expresses in Gal 3:28 that male and female are equal in Christ. It seems that his social conditioning when dealing with a practical situation is in conflict with his theological insight in Galatians. I suggest that he has tied himself up in a muddle here because he has tried to combine what is said in Genesis 1 (where both male and female are created in the image of God) with a justification for social convention based on Genesis 2 (where the woman is subordinate to the man). By interpreting Genesis 1 in the light of Genesis 2, he is able to argue for an important *difference* between male and female, for although he does not in fact deny that woman is 'the image of God', his argument clearly depends on the denial that she is the *glory* of God.

What is intriguing about this statement in 1 Cor 11:7, however, is the fact that Paul uses a phrase that we might expect him to use of Christ (εἰκὼν καὶ δόξα θεοῦ) of 'a man'. The assumptions that led him to do this are set out earlier in the chapter: if man is the glory of God, and woman is the glory of man, this is because the head of a woman is her husband, the head of a man is Christ, and the head of Christ is God. Yet we see at once that a stage in the 'hierarchy' is missing in v. 7: instead of God – Christ – man – woman (v. 3), we now have God – man – woman. What Paul *ought* to be saying in v. 7 is that it is the *head* of man (= Christ) who is the image and glory of God. Moreover, having said that *man* is the image and glory of God, he immediately has a problem in trying to draw a parallel with the relationship between man and woman, since now he is unable to say that woman is the image of man. Paul has approached the question with presuppositions of male superiority derived from Genesis 2, but these presuppositions do not fit with the idea expressed in Genesis 1, that both male and female were created in the image of God.

1 Corinthians 11 appears to be an aberration in Paul's usage, since elsewhere the phrase εἰκών θεοῦ refers to Christ. Moreover, like the passages which refer to Christ's incarnation, these other εἰκών passages are all linked with the destiny of believers (both men and women), who become *like* Christ.[12]

4. Adam

Let us turn now to two passages where the comparison between Adam and Christ, implicit in so many of these εἰκών passages, is made explicit. In Rom 5:12–21, this comparison is the climax of the argument in the preceding chapters, and we are told that what happened in Christ was in many ways *not* the equivalent of what happened in Adam (vv. 15–17), both because the grace of God was at work in Christ, and because Christ's actions were the very reverse of Adam's – a point which is then underlined in the comparisons of vv. 18–19, which are in effect contrasts. The nature of God's overwhelming grace was spelt out in the opening verses of the chapter, where we were told that Christ died 'for us' (v. 8), that is 'for the ungodly' (v. 6), and that we have been reconciled to God through the death of his Son (v. 10), being 'justified' or 'rightwised' (δικαιωθέντες) by his blood (v. 9).

In 1 Cor 15:21–22, Christ stands over against Adam as the one who brings life instead of death, and who is then identified as the Son who reigns until he hands everything over to his Father (vv. 24–28). Later in the chapter, Adam is described as the first man, who became a living soul (v. 45, quoting Gen 2:7), whereas Christ is the last Adam, who is a life-giving Spirit. Verse 46 underlines the fact that the σῶμα ψυχικόν ('the physical body') comes before the σῶμα πνευματικόν ('the spiritual body'). We are then told that the first man is from the dust, the second man from heaven, and just as men and women have borne the image of the first, so they will bear the image of the second (vv. 47–49). If 1 Cor 15:47 describes Christ as 'the second man', that is surely because, *as man,* Adam preceded Christ; in terms of our own experience, also, we share in the physical body of Adam *before* we are transformed

---

[12] Even in 1 Cor 11, Paul is appealing to what men and women were created to be – and perhaps also to what they *should* be in the Christian community; the angels referred to in v. 10 may be present to see that creation's purpose is fulfilled.

into the spiritual body of Christ. The fact that Paul found it necessary to emphasize this point is unlikely to be because he knew the teaching of Philo and wished to contradict it; it is more likely that he stressed it because he knew that it would have been natural for the Corinthians to think of the heavenly man as *preceding* the earthly since, of course, his heavenly origin meant that he was pre-existent. Paul is concerned here with the way in which humanity bears the image first of the earthly, then of the heavenly (v. 49) and not the question as to whether Adam or Christ existed first.

Once again, then, we find the idea that we bear Christ's image, which is here directly contrasted with the image of Adam. The point of Paul's argument is the nature of the future resurrection, when Christians will share the glorious body of Christ. In both 1 Corinthians 15 and Romans 5, Paul is again concerned with the destiny of men and women, and as elsewhere, this is to be like Christ. Christ is understood to have reversed the effects of Adam's fall, and the reason that he is able to do so is that he is both Man and Son of God. The relationship between Adam and Christ is not that of two competitors in a task, the first of whom fails while the second succeeds. Rather, Christ has to *undo* the failure of Adam, *reverse* his disobedience, and bring life where Adam brought death. He is thus *greater* than Adam. Christ and Adam are never regarded by Paul as equals. Rather he sees Christ as the pattern of what Adam was meant to be, and the eschatological goal of what men and women are to become.

5. Son of God

We are not surprised, therefore, to find that both these passages about Adam are associated with language about the Son of God. In Romans 5, Paul uses this title immediately before the 'Adam' passage. The summary in vv. 8–9 of what God has done in 'rightwising' sinners through Christ's death, and what he may therefore be relied upon to do – namely save us from wrath – is repeated in vv. 10–11, this time in terms of our reconciliation to God through the death of his Son and the fact that we may therefore rely upon him to save us by his love. If the 'he's in that summary are ambiguous, that is because the agent of the passive verb σωθησόμεθα is ambiguous; this is hardly surprising, since the parallel reminds us that God and Christ are at one. I suspect that the title 'Son of God' is used here because it expresses both Christ's unity of purpose with his Father and his obedience to God's will. These, as we have already seen, are important themes in vv. 12–18.[13]

---

[13] Cf. Morna D. Hooker, *Pauline Pieces* (London: Epworth Press, 1979), 53–68.

These, too, are ideas which belong to 1 Cor 15:28, the verse which concludes the paragraph that begins, in vv. 21–22, with the comparison of Adam and Christ. The resurrection that comes through Christ will take place at his coming (v. 23), and this is followed by his reign, in fulfilment of Ps 8:6, a passage which, significantly, refers to all things being put under *Man's* feet. What happens in Christ is the realization of God's purpose for humanity. But at the end Christ will hand over the kingdom to the Father, and the Son will himself be subject to God, as Ps 8:5 suggests (vv. 24, 28).

'Son of God' language is also prominent in Romans 8, another passage we have already looked at; in fact, all the themes I have so far considered – incarnation, image, and Adam – are to be found there. It is God's Son who is sent in the likeness of sinful flesh in v. 3 – a way of reminding us that what Christ achieved was the work of God. It is to the image of God's Son that believers are conformed (v. 29) – a way of reminding us that in being conformed to Christ, we too become children of God and so like him (vv. 14, 19). Verse 32 repeats the theme of 5:8–11: if God did not spare his own Son, but gave him up for us, we may expect him to give us all things.

Romans 8 may well be a later development of ideas already spelt out in Gal 4:1–7, where Paul again tells us that God sent his Son; the Greek verb is different,[14] but the brief clause combines once again the ideas of God's purpose and Christ's obedience. God also sent the Spirit of his Son, with the result that we, too, become 'sons'. Sayings about the Son of God, like those about Christ's incarnation, about εἰκών, and about Adam, seem to tell us as much about human destiny as about Christ himself.

Most of the remaining references to Jesus as 'Son of God' occur in brief references to the gospel, but there is one of these in particular which we should examine, and that is Rom 1:3–4. This passage is often said to be a pre-Pauline summary of the gospel, a view which I do not share, but if it is indeed such a summary, Paul has certainly made it his own; as usual with these introductory summaries, it is entirely appropriate to the theme of the letter. The gospel is said to be about God's Son, who was born of the seed of David; the word γενομένου puts us in mind immediately of the γενόμενος in Gal 4:3 and Phil 2:7. We, of course, tend to think of the phrase 'of the seed of David' as a messianic claim, and therefore interpret it as though it were some kind of exalted title; but Paul puts it in the context of σάρξ, using his familiar phrase κατὰ σάρκα. We see, then, that for him the statement that the Son of God was 'born of the seed of David according to the flesh' is the equivalent of 'being born in human likeness', or 'being born of a woman, under the law'. The Son of God shares in our humanity, and even his Davidic lineage is a part of being human. The second part of the summary speaks of his being 'declared to be

---

[14] Rom 8:3 uses πέμπω, Gal 4:4 ἐξαποστέλλω.

Son of God in power by the resurrection of the dead, Jesus Christ our Lord'. Here we have the equivalent of the second half of the Philippian 'hymn', where Christ is highly exalted and given the name that is above every name, so that all creation acknowledges him as Lord. In Philippians it is God who exalts Christ; Romans uses the divine passive and the phrase ἐν δυνάμει, 'in power', but also the phrase κατὰ πνεῦμα ἁγιωσύνης, balancing the κατὰ σάρκα in the first clause.

There are two interesting points for my purposes in this summary. The first is the fact that it speaks of the Son of God becoming man and then, at the resurrection, being declared Son of God. Is that first reference to 'Son of God' an indication of pre-existence? If so, what is the difference in status between what he was then and what he becomes at the resurrection? Is the resurrection simply an open acknowledgment of what he always was? Or should we understand the verb ὁρίζω to mean 'appoint' rather than declare. These are familiar problems, which have been met before in Philippians 2, suggesting that what we have here is a parallel summary. This passage even ends in a similar way to Phil 2:6–11, with the reference to Jesus Christ being proclaimed as Lord. The second point of interest is Paul's use of those phrases κατὰ σάρκα and κατὰ πνεῦμα, which are taken up in Romans 8, where we are told that Christ came ἐν ὁμοιώματι σαρκὸς ἁμαρτίας, ('in the likeness of sinful flesh'), so that those who have lived κατὰ σάρκα might live κατὰ πνεῦμα (vv. 3–4). What it means to live κατὰ σάρκα, and the way in which men and women come to a new life κατὰ πνεῦμα is in fact the theme of the first eight chapters of Romans, and is summed up in the key passage in 5:12–21, where the same idea is expressed in terms of the contrast between life in Adam and life in Christ. It is only by concentrating on Rom 1:3–4 in isolation and ignoring the argument of Romans 1–8 as a whole that one can deny the relevance of Adam to this passage.

6. Philippians

I suggest, therefore, that the links between these various passages indicate that they are united by an underlying coherent theme. The relationship between them is not that of separate items on a breakfast menu, but rather that of differently coloured threads which have been woven together into a tapestry. The fact that Adam seems to be present in so many of the passages I have mentioned, and not simply those where he is named, encourages me to suppose that Adamic imagery underlies Philippians 2–3, where we have similar ideas of Christ becoming man with the result that men and women become what he is. 'Adamic' language is used, moreover, in Phil 3:21, where we have several interesting echoes of 1 Corinthians 15. In Phil 3:21 we expect a Saviour from heaven (cf. the man from heaven in 1 Cor 15:47), we have an echo of Ps 8:6 (cf. 1 Cor 15:27–28), and we wait for our bodies to be changed and to be conformed to Christ's (cf. 1 Cor 15:35–49). How, then, are we to deal with the objection that Phil 2:6 cannot be intended as a contrast between Adam and Christ, since the *result* of Christ's action is that he became man, and took on human likeness? *I suggest that it is precisely in this anomaly that we find the solution to the problem.* As we have already seen, Paul does not regard Adam and Christ as exactly parallel, since for him Christ is always greater than Adam. In Romans 5, Adam and Christ are, as it were, placed in the two pans of a pair of scales, but the finger of God rests on one of the pans, with the result that what happens in Christ is *far greater* than what happens in Adam. In 1 Corinthians, the first man was created out of the dust, a living being, but the second man is from heaven, and is a life-*giving* spirit. As man, Adam precedes Christ; but as the pattern according to which Adam was created, Christ precedes Adam. Christ is the *true* 'image of God', after whom Christians are now being recreated, while Adam is the distorted copy, whose disobedience meant that humanity became enslaved to sin and death. If for a moment we assume that the background of Philippians 2 is to be found in this Adamic imagery, and attempt to set out the two actions of Adam and Christ diagrammatically, the pattern would be:

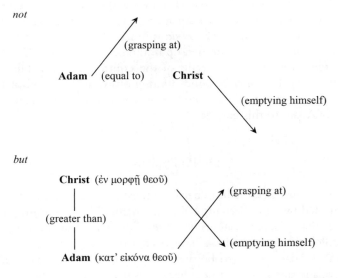

The chief problem with the idea that Adam is in mind in Phil 2:6 is due to the assumption that Adam and Christ are being viewed as equals; they are not. To make sense of any parallel with Adam in Philippians, we have to understand Christ to be the 'blueprint' of what Man was *meant* to be, the perfect image of God and the reflection of his glory. If Paul has chosen to use the phrase ἐν μορφῇ θεοῦ rather than the one used of Adam in Genesis, that is with good reason, for it would make no sense at all to say that one who was 'in the image of God' (i.e. man) *became* man! The pre-existent one was *not* κατ' εἰκόνα θεοῦ, but ἐν μορφῇ θεοῦ.

Why is it, then, that Paul here uses this particular term μορφή, whereas similar statements in Romans 1 and 8 and Galatians 4 refer to God's Son? It has, indeed, often been assumed that what we have in Philippians 2 is an example of Son-of-God Christology, and this idea has been explored by C.A. Wanamaker,[15] who examined Phil 2:6–11 alongside Gal 4:4, Rom 1:3–4, 8:3–4 and 1 Cor 15:24–28. If the basic meaning of the word μορφή is 'visible form', as Bockmuehl argues, then the suggestion that the phrase ἐν μορφῇ θεοῦ is in fact comparable to the title 'Son of God' is a viable one, since children are often like their parents. This visible form is perhaps to be identified with God's glory, which features in Old Testament theophanies (cf. Exod 32). Or perhaps, since Bockmuehl objects to the assumption that these terms are synonyms, we should understand it rather as the expression of the inner reality that is at one and the same time concealed by and revealed by the glory. The idea that God has a 'form' which normally cannot be seen by humans is found in various Jewish writings.[16] Particularly interesting is the well-known passage in the Talmud quoted by Bockmuehl which interprets Gen 1:27 as meaning that God created Man 'in the image (צלם) of the likeness (דמות) of his form (תבנית)' *(b. Ketub.* 8a). We do not know how early this particular interpretation is, but the fact that it distinguishes image (צלם is frequently translated in the LXX by εἰκών), likeness (דמות, commonly translated by ὁμοίωμα) and form (תבנית is mostly translated by ὁμοίωμα or παράδειγμα, but once, in Isa 44:13, by μορφή), may be significant. A parallel idea is found in Philo who, however, uses the term εἰκών to describe what is *closest* to God. So God is the pattern of the image (who is also God's word) and this image is in turn the pattern for humanity, since 'God made the Man after the image of God' (κατ' εἰκόνα θεοῦ, *Leg.* 3.96). Does a similar idea lie behind Paul's hierarchy in 1 Cor 11:3 (though there expressed in terms of κεφαλή), where we have God-Christ-Man? Is this why Christ is presented as *the* εἰκὼν τοῦ θεοῦ, to whom men and women must be conformed? And if μορφή is the 'visible form' of God, do we have a similar idea, expressed this time in terms of δόξα, in 2 Corinthians 3, where Christ is the image of God and the embodiment of his glory, and

---

[15] C.A. Wanamaker, 'Philippians 2.6–11: Son of God or Adamic Christology?', *NTS* 33 (1987): 179–193. Cf. Hans Conzelmann, who includes it, without apology, in his summary about Christ as 'Son of God', in *An Outline of the Theology of the New Testament,* trans. John Bowden (London: SCM Press, 1969), 79–80.

[16] See Bockmuehl, '"The Form of God"', 11–23.

therefore superior to the *reflected* glory of the Law? What Israel glimpsed at Sinai is embodied in Christ.

This parallel between Phil 2:6–11 and 2 Cor 3–4:6 is an interesting one, since the setting of the so-called 'hymn' in Philippians 2 is reminiscent of the Sinai traditions of Exodus and Deuteronomy. Just as God's revelation of himself to Moses on Sinai was followed by the demand for obedience from the people, so now the idea that the nature of God – the visible form of his glory – is revealed in the actions of Christ is followed by the demand that the Philippians are obedient to the gospel. In contrast to the Israelites, who grumbled and argued (Exod 16:1–12; 17:1–7), and proved to be 'a crooked and perverse generation' (Deut 32:5), they are to be 'blameless and innocent children of God'. Following the implicit contrast of Christ's obedience with Adam's disobedience, the obedience expected from those who belong to Christ is now contrasted with the disobedience of Israel, who repeated the sin of Adam when they turned their back on God's revelation in the Exodus and on Sinai and worshipped other gods.[17] Philippians 2 sets the theme of 'Adam' in the context of the Law. So, too, in 2 Corinthians 3, where the 'midrash' on God's revelation on Sinai reaches its climax in the description of the way in which Christians are being transformed into the image of Christ, and reflect his glory.[18] For Paul, Christ is the wisdom of God (1 Cor 1:24, 30), through which God created the world (Col 1:15–17), a wisdom that was partially revealed in the Law at Sinai (2 Cor 3:7–18). But this same wisdom can be described also as the image of God and the reflection of his glory (2 Cor 4:4; Col 1:15).[19]

Ideas about the creation of Adam such as those expressed in the Talmud and in Philo may well lie behind Paul's use of Adamic language. For him, Christ is the *true* 'image of God' (2 Cor 4:4; Col 1:15), the one who is 'in his form' and therefore Son of God, whereas Adam, who was created 'after' God's image, became subject to sin and death because of his disobedience (Rom 5:12–21), and is now only a distorted copy of what he was meant to be, a slave to the στοιχεῖα τοῦ κοσμοῦ. Those who have borne the image of the first Adam may, in turn, bear the image of the last Adam (1 Cor 15:42–49) – last, not in the sense that he came into existence last, but because he represents the eschatological goal of humanity, God's original purpose for creation. He is the one through whom all things exist (1 Cor 8:6; Col 1:15–16), the embodiment of God's glory, according to whose image men and women are being restored (Rom 8:28–30; Col 3:9). I have no difficulty with Wanamaker's suggestion that Phil 2:6 should be read alongside those passages which speak of *the*

---

[17] For the way in which Paul links the sin of Adam and of Israel in Romans, see Dunn, *The Theology of Paul the Apostle*, 93, 97, 99–100. Jewish tradition also linked the two.

[18] This 'Adamic' language is continued in ch. 4, with the reference to Christ as the image of God (v. 4), and the reference to the creation narrative (v. 6).

[19] These ideas are, of course, already associated in the Wisdom tradition and in Philo.

Son of God becoming man, but we do well to ask why Paul chose to use the phrase ἐν μορφῇ θεοῦ here rather than 'the Son of God'. I suspect that part of the answer at least to this question is to be found in the contrast between ἐν μορφῇ θεοῦ and μορφὴν δούλου), for the logic of the passage demands a contrast – between 'the form of a slave', which expresses the condition into which Adam fell, and 'the form of God', which expresses the condition of the one who is *greater* than Adam. *If Paul wished to emphasize the contrast between Adam and Christ,* then 'the Son of God' was not the most appropriate term to use. As we have already seen, κατ' εἰκόνα θεοῦ was also inappropriate. He might, of course, have written ὃς εἰκὼν θεοῦ ὑπάρχων, the 'Adamic' phrase he uses elsewhere. Why does he not use it here? Is it possible that part of the explanation is to be found in 1 Corinthians 11, where Paul surprises us by using εἰκών of man – and even more astonishingly, of the male of the species? Was εἰκὼν τοῦ θεοῦ perhaps insufficiently clear to be used in the context of Phil 2:6, where Paul wished to make a *contrast* between Christ and Adam? Might the phrase εἰκὼν τοῦ θεοῦ have suggested, in this context, that Adam and Christ were equal figures on a level playing-field? Or was it, after all, simply the parallel with μορφὴν δούλου λαβών that made him prefer ἐν μορφῇ θεοῦ ὑπάρχων?[20]

I am not sure of the answers to these questions, but the fact that Paul does not use the word 'image' here is certainly no reason to reject the reference to Adam. Contrary to the views of both Wanamaker and Bockmuehl, therefore, I want to suggest that Paul may well have used the phrase ἐν μορφῇ θεοῦ precisely because the theme of the contrast with Adam is fundamental to the argument of the passage, and because it was in fact the best and clearest way to express both that contrast and the superiority of the one who was and who remained, even during his humiliation, 'in the form of God'. If we take due note of all the evidence, we shall I think discover that the so-called Adamic cul-de-sac leads us to the key ideas underlying the Philippian hymn, and to fresh insights into Pauline Christology.

---

[20] Those who regard Phil 2:6–11 as a pre-Pauline 'hymn' have no need to wrestle with these problems!

27. Christ: The 'End' of the Law

Paul's description of Christ as τέλος νόμου in Rom 10:4 is a key text in Pauline interpretation. Whole monographs have been written about this one verse alone.[1] Does Paul mean that Christ is 'the end of the Law' in the sense that he is its termination, or in the sense that he is its fulfilment or goal?

In fact, of course, English words do not necessarily correspond to Greek words – though in this case there is an ambiguity in the word 'end' to match that in the Greek. The word τέλος here may well cover *both* our English senses: after all, if the goal – the purpose – of the Law has been achieved, it is no longer 'necessary'. Many commentators are thus happy to suggest that the phrase τέλος νόμου here conveys *both* meanings:[2] Christ is 'the end of the Law', both because he fulfils its purpose *and* because he brings it to an end as a system by which to live. If we stress the alternative meaning, however – that Christ is the termination of the Law – this does not necessarily imply that its *purpose* has been achieved.

So where is Paul's emphasis? Does he think of Christ primarily as *completing* the Law or as *competing* with it? For many centuries, the Lutheran influence dominating much exegesis meant that the Law and Christ were seen as antithetical: Recent scholarship has tipped the balance in the opposite direction, and stressed Paul's Jewish roots and his insistence that he was being faithful to the Law (Rom 3:31) – and, even more important, that *God* was faithful to his promises (Rom 3:2–3; 9:6). But what was it that led Paul to affirm that *Christ* was the goal of the Law? And if Paul does indeed see Christ as the goal of the Law, what are the implications of that belief?

Let us begin by looking at the context in which this statement occurs. In Romans 9–11 Paul is endeavouring to explain God's dealings with Israel. He insists that God's λόγος has not failed, and that the promises made to Abraham have been fulfilled. God's purposes have been worked out in extraordinary ways, but the result has been that he has made known 'the riches of his glory' for those whom he has called – not from the Jews only, but also from the Gentiles (9:23). It is, of course, this inclusion of the Gentiles that has led Paul

---

[1] E.g., Robert Badenas, *Christ the End of the Law: Romans 10.4 in Pauline Perspective*, JSNTSup 10 (Sheffield: JSOT Press, 1985).

[2] This is not to say (as Heikki Räisänen suggested, *Paul and the Law,* WUNT 29 [Tübingen: Mohr, 1983], 53) that they are assuming that Paul could not make up his mind between the two meanings: the word τέλος embraces both. Räisänen acknowledged that this was in fact possible in the second edition of his book (1987).

to rethink his attitude towards the Law. He concludes (9:30–32): 'What, then, are we to say? Gentiles, who did not strive after righteousness have obtained righteousness – that is, *righteousness* on the basis of faith, whereas Israel, who strove after the law of righteousness, did not attain that Law. Why not? Because she strove after it as though it could be fulfilled on the basis of works, not faith'.

Paul does not say here quite what we expect him to say! In particular, what he says about Israel surprises us – and we should note that he is talking here about *Israel,* and not about individual Jews. Contrary to the translators, he does *not* say that Israel 'did not succeed in *fulfilling* [the] Law';[3] nor does he say that Israel was striving 'for the righteousness that is based on the Law'[4] or that she 'did not attain *righteousness*'.[5] He says that she did not attain *the Law.* Why? The answer becomes clear when we turn back to the previous sentence. We might well have expected Paul to make a clear contrast with what he said in v. 30, and to write:

> Gentiles, who do not strive after righteousness ...
> Israel, who does strive after righteousness ...

In fact, however, he spoke of Israel striving after a *law* of righteousness: it is this 'law of righteousness' that Israel has failed to attain. But is this νόμος δικαιοσύνης simply the equivalent of the δικαιοσύνη ἐκ νόμου of 10:4? I suggest not. For here, already, in Romans 9, we have the idea of two contrasted goals. The goal for which Gentiles were *not* striving but which they nevertheless reached – was *righteousness.* The goal for which *Israel* was striving was *the Law itself* – the Law whose own goal was, indeed, righteousness. In striving to fulfil it, however, Israel lost sight of the Law's purpose: she treated it as an end in itself instead of pursuing its goal – righteousness. Since she did not attain the Law, there is no need to explain that she did not attain righteousness either. Her mistake was to pursue the Law as though it could be achieved on the principle of works, and not through faith (v. 32). Paul's accusation, then, is not simply that Israel did not attain righteousness, but that she pursued the wrong goal, which meant that inevitably she misunderstood the role of the Law.

What Paul says here is consistent with what he said in Romans 7, where he described the Law as ἅγιος and πνευματικός (7:12, 14), and the commandment as δικαία καὶ ἀγαθή. The Law is God's Law (7:22, 25) but is unable to do what it promised because of the weakness of the flesh (8:3), which has come under the power of the Law of sin and death (7:23; 8:2). But for the

---

[3] NRSV; cf. NJB.
[4] RSV; cf. JB
[5] Matthew Black, *Romans,* 2nd ed., NCB (London: Marshall, Morgan and Scott, 1989), 138. Paul Wilhelm Schmiedel's suggested emendation of the text is noted in the margin of the Nestle-Aland text.

contrast between the principles of 'works' and 'faith' we have to go back to 3:19–4:6. The Law itself, we are told there, supports Paul's assertion that 'no one will be "rightwised" in God's sight *by the works of the Law*', while both Law and Prophets witness to the fact that 'God's righteousness has been revealed to all who believe' (3:19–22). The νόμος which is τῶν ἔργων leads to boasting, but the νόμος which is πίστεως excludes boasting (v. 27). Paul appears to be opposing two interpretations of the Torah, one of which sees it as focused on 'works', the other as witnessing to faith. When the Torah is understood in terms of 'works' it leads to boasting, not to righteousness, which comes only by faith (v. 28). We have here the same contrast that we find in 9:31a. The contrast is not between *Law* and faith, but between two principles set out *in* the Law – 'works' (v. 20) and 'faith' (vv. 21–22). Turning to Abraham in chapter 4, Paul maintains that he embodies this principle that δικαιοσύνη comes through πίστις and not through ἔργων, and the evidence is found in scripture in Genesis 15, backed up by Psalm 31 (32), a psalm attributed to David.

In Romans 9, also, Paul backs up his argument with a quotation from scripture – here a mixed quotation from Isa 28:16 and 8:14 about a stone that leads to stumbling. In Isaiah 8, the stone is God himself, who nevertheless becomes a rock that causes Israel to stumble. In Isaiah 28, the rock is laid by God in Zion as a cornerstone and sure foundation: its significance is unclear, although here, too, it may symbolize the presence of Yahweh himself, on whom the new spiritual temple – the new society of God's people – depends. Or perhaps the foundation of this new community is the trust that Israel has in God. The LXX translation makes this trust more specific – it is ἐπ' αὐτῷ[6] – while the targum of Isaiah 28 understands the stone as referring to the Messiah. In Romans the stone, which is laid by God, is assumed by almost all commentators to refer to Christ – an interpretation that is supported by the christological interpretation of the two Isaiah texts in 1 Peter 2:4–8.[7] The final line of the quotation is repeated in Rom 10:11, where αὐτῷ appears to refer to Christ; the alternative possibility that it might refer to God himself in 10:11 seems to be excluded by the confession in 10:9 that 'Jesus is Lord' – the title that is central to the argument in 10:11–17 – and it is presumably 'the Lord' who is referred to in the term αὐτῷ (see vv. 12–13). The question therefore arises as to whether the clear christological meaning of the phrase ἐπ' αὐτῷ in Rom 10:11 determines the interpretation of the αὐτῷ in 9:33. Does the αὐτῷ in 9:33 also refer to Christ, or to something or someone else?

Furthermore, if this first αὐτῷ does refer to Christ, does this settle the meaning of the stone as well? Are we to conclude that the 'rock' over which

---

[6] These words are missing in B.
[7] 1 Peter interprets both Isa 8:14 and 28:16 (together with Ps 117 [118]:22) christologically.

Israel has stumbled is also Christ? Is Paul affirming here that Israel's problem is that she has failed to believe in him? The majority of commentators accept this interpretation, but the possibility that the stumbling-block is the Law, supported by some scholars,[8] should not be too easily dismissed. It should be noted, after all, that Christ has not been mentioned since 9:1–5, and that the two subjects under discussion in Rom 9:30–31 are the Law and righteousness. Moreover, what Paul has just stated is that Israel has misunderstood the function of the Law. Perhaps, then, the stumbling-block over which Israel has fallen is the Law. This interpretation of the 'rock' as symbolizing the Law finds some support in the structure of the mixed quotation from Isaiah, which inserts a phrase from Isa 8:14 into a framework drawn from Isa 28:16. The former is much closer to the Hebrew than to the LXX, which expands the text, emphasizing that to those who are faithful to him, God is a sanctuary rather than a stumbling-block. The words from Isa 28:16, on the other hand, appear to be drawn from the LXX text, though omitting the positive description of the stone as a cornerstone that has been tested and is sure.[9] The positive descriptions of the stone present in both LXX passages are thus ignored, and the emphasis is on the stone as a cause of stumbling. In contrast to this negative picture, the final line from Isaiah 28 speaks of 'believing in it/him'.

But the reason that a stone causes one to stumble is normally that it is hidden from view – hardly true of the Law. The metaphor suggests rather something obscure, which appears here to be the fact that the Law could not be attained by works, and that the righteousness promised in the Law came only through faith. It was this, says Paul, that Israel had failed to grasp, even though it is set out in the Law itself (3:19–22). In other words, she has tripped up because she has misunderstood the Law and been unaware of its true significance. The Law promises that those who have faith will not be ashamed. But in whom or what should they believe? And who or what is the true significance of the Law? The ambiguity in the quotation in v. 33 reminds us that the answer is still hidden from Israel. It will be spelt out in the next paragraph, where Christ is revealed as the 'purpose' or 'goal' of the Law, and where the promise that those who believe ἐπ' αὐτῷ clearly refers to him.

The chiastic structure of vv. 30–33 supports the suggestion that what has caused Israel to stumble is their understanding of the Law:

---

[8] So C.K. Barrett, 'Romans 9.30–10.21: Fall and Responsibility of Israel', in *Die Israelfrage nach Röm 9–11*, ed. Lorenzo De Lorenzi (Rome: Abbey of St Paul Outside the Walls, 1977), 99–130; also Barrett, *A Commentary on the Epistle to the Romans*, 2nd ed. (London: A&C Black, 1991) *in loc.* Cf. Paul W. Meyer, 'Romans 10:4 and the End of the Law', in *The Divine Helmsman*, eds. James L. Crenshaw and Samuel Sandmel (New York: Ktav, 1980), 59–78.

[9] Contrast the way in which this text is used in 1 Pet 2:6, where the stone is Christ.

A   Gentiles, who did not pursue *righteousness,* nevertheless attained it on the basis of faith (v. 30).
B   Israel, who pursued the *law* of righteousness, did not attain the Law – because she did so 'as though' its basis was works, not faith (vv. 30–31).
   [So what misled her? Her misunderstanding of the Law and its goal – i.e. righteousness.]
B' She tripped over the stone of stumbling, as scripture testifies.
A' Scripture also affirms that those who have faith will not be ashamed.

Seen in this context, the most natural explanation of the 'stone of stumbling' is that it represents the Law itself – or rather, *the true significance of the Law,* which was hidden from Israel. Her misunderstanding of the Law led her to pursue it as though the righteousness it demanded were based on works. In fact, this righteousness was based on faith. As we have seen, there are echoes here of what Paul wrote in 3:27 about a 'law of works' and a 'law of faith'. The Law's true purpose was to witness to the righteousness freely offered to those who believe, and Israel stumbled because she did not realize that the Law offered righteousness on the basis of faith. As we read on, we discover that the proper understanding of the Law – its true goal – is Christ, and that righteousness is based on faith in him. It would seem, then, that the ambiguous αὐτῷ in v. 33 must be understood as Christ – the one in whom the *Gentiles* (v. 30) have believed.

So far, however, Christ has not been specifically mentioned in the argument that began at 9:6. Nevertheless, no one who has read Paul's argument in Romans 1–8 can doubt that the references to πίστις and δικαιοσύνη are pointing towards him. The theme of Paul's epistle is the gospel, in which 'the righteousness of God is revealed through faith for faith' as Hab 2:4 testifies (Rom 1:17) – and this gospel 'concerns God's Son ... Jesus Christ our Lord' (Rom 1:3–4).

In 10:1, Paul speaks of the zeal that his fellow countrymen have for God – a zeal which, according to Phil 3:6, he himself shared. This zeal is misinformed, however, since it is not κατ' ἐπίγνωσις (v. 2): 'Being ignorant of God's righteousness, and seeking to establish their own righteousness, they have not submitted to the righteousness of God' (v. 3). The same contrast reappears in Phil 3:9, where Paul's own righteousness is said to be ἐκ νόμου, and God's is based ἐπὶ τῇ πίστει: Rom 10:3 thus restates the contrast already set out in 9:30–31. δικαιοσύνη θεοῦ is a key term in Romans, where it occurs eight times.[10] But what is this 'righteousness of God'? We know from earlier statements in the epistle that it is revealed in the gospel (1:17), that it is attested to by the Law and Prophets (3:21), and that it comes to all who believe διὰ πίστεως Ἰησοῦ Χριστοῦ (3:22) – though the meaning of this last phrase is, of course, disputed. In 3:25–26, Paul insists that God has demonstrated his

---

[10] 1:17; 3:5, 21, 22, 25, 26; 10:3 (*bis*).

righteousness in Christ. Paul might well have gone on to tell us that this righteousness was the goal of the Law. Instead, he tells us that Christ himself is the goal of the Law – but goes on to explain *why* in the phrase εἰς δικαιοσύνην παντὶ τῷ πιστεύοντι. He is the goal of the Law because he *is* righteousness (cf. 1 Cor 1:30), and because he realizes righteousness for every believer. This is the righteousness which has been granted to Gentiles (9:30). What Paul's fellow Jews failed to recognize, in seeking their own righteousness, was that the goal of the Law was the righteousness of God, a righteousness that is available to all who believe. Like climbers toiling up a mountain, they had set their sights on a ridge, mistaking it for the top, and had not noticed their real goal – the peak hidden behind it.

Once again, Paul appeals to scripture to back his argument – this time to Moses himself – and draws a contrast between the righteousness which is ἐκ νόμου and that which is ἐκ πίστεως. Even without the parallel in Phil 3:9, it is clear that the righteousness ἐκ νόμου is the righteousness that the Jews have sought to establish – their own righteousness – while the righteousness ἐκ πίστεως is the righteousness belonging to God. Since Paul clearly assumes that both of the passages he quotes[11] were written by Moses, he is appealing to the Law itself as the witness to these two kinds of righteousness. The Law, then, speaks of a righteousness based on works (v. 5) – a righteousness which, however, has already been described in 9:32 and in 10:3 in disparaging terms. There Paul has described how Israel had pursued the law of righteousness as though it could be attained by works, and how her people had *ignorantly* sought to establish their own righteousness. But, the Law *also* speaks of a righteousness that is based on faith (vv. 6–10), and witnesses to the fact that all that is necessary for salvation is the confession that Christ is Lord and faith that he has been raised from the dead. In a remarkable piece of hijacking, Deut 30:12 ff. is discovered to refer, not to the Law and to obedience to it, but to the gospel and to faith in Christ. The Law itself thus points beyond itself, to its 'goal', namely Christ.

The implication of Paul's argument is clear. If God's promises have been fulfilled, and his purpose – set out in the Law – is achieved in Christ, that purpose must be *prior* to the Law. Although he comes *after* the Law, Christ is certainly no 'afterthought', but represents God's purpose from the beginning of time. This is well summed up in Rom 16:25 (whether or not this passage was written by Paul himself): the proclamation of the gospel means the revelation of the μυστηρίον, which has been hidden for long ages but which is now made manifest, and has been made known through the prophetic writings – or rather (though this is not spelt out), through Christian exegesis of the prophets. If Christ is the τέλος νόμου, *the goal* of the Law rather than simply its

---

[11] Lev 18:5 and Deut 30:12–14.

ending, then he must also have been there at its beginning. What Paul does, therefore, is not to interpret Christ in relation to the Law, but to interpret the Law in relation to Christ.

Paul's understanding of the relationship between Christ and the Law in this passage is in keeping with his argument in the rest of Romans. Relying on the Law does *not* make one righteous before God (2:17–3:20); but God has now revealed his righteousness apart from the Law, yet witnessed to by the Law and Prophets, and this righteousness comes, through Christ, to all who believe (3:21 ff.). The Law, good though it was, had been unable to save, and had resulted in death (7), but God has now done what the Law, weakened by flesh, was unable to do (8:2). Yet when asked whether his teaching abrogated the Law, Paul responds with an indignant μὴ γένοιτο! Throughout his argument, Paul emphasizes that the gospel was the fulfilment of God's promises, set out in scripture, that his people would experience his righteousness – promises which are now revealed to include Gentiles as well as Israel. By sending his own Son, God has enabled the διαίωμα of the Law to be fulfilled (8:34), and the goal of the Law – righteousness – has been reached (10:4). Since Christ is the fulfilment of the Law, the obedience required by the covenant is achieved in him: so it is that the proclamation of the gospel leads to the obedience of faith (1:5; cf. 15:18; 16:26). The Law is not abrogated, but *fulfilled*.

But what of Paul's *other* writings? Galatians, so similar in theme, nevertheless seems far more negative in what it says about the Law. It was delivered through angels, by the hand of a mediator (3:19), and though its divine origin is not denied, it is clearly being regarded as inferior to Christ; the 'works of the Law' are linked with the curse of Deut 27:26 (3:10).[12] Can Christ be said to be the goal of the Law here? Indeed he can! For in 3:24, Paul specifically describes it as our παιδαγωγός, whose role was to bring us to Christ. The παιδαγωγός was not a teacher but a custodian, whose function was to protect the child from harm and ensure that he learned good manners. The role of the Law was thus to act as 'our' custodian until the coming of Christ, when righteousness on the basis of Christ became possible. But Paul expresses the idea more positively than this: it was *'in order that* (ἵνα) we might be "rightwised" on the basis of faith' that the Law held 'us' in custody: the *purpose* of the Law was to point to Christ, and thus to bring us to the righteousness that is based on faith. In the course of his argument Paul lists various opposing powers: the works of the Law are opposed to faith (3:2, cf. Rom 9:31), the

---

[12] Paul's argument is obscure, since the curse of Deuteronomy is pronounced on those who fail to do what the Law commands. It is possible, as Christopher Stanley has argued ("'Under a Curse": a Fresh Reading of Galatians 3.10–14', *NTS* 36 [1990]: 481–511), that we should understand the curse here to be potential rather than actual, but even if he is right, the tone is far more negative than in Romans – presumably because of the urgency of the situation which Paul was addressing in Galatians.

flesh to the Spirit (3:3), and the curse of the Law to the blessing of Abraham (3:10–14). In Gal 4, we find slavery opposed to sonship. One contrast that we might have expected is 'Law' and 'promise', since the argument of 3:15–20 is that the promises precede the Law and are not annulled by it. But in 3:21, Paul insists that the Law is *not* opposed to the promises. The role of the Law was *not* to bring righteousness or to make alive, but to 'imprison all things under the power of sin' (3:22) until the appointed time (4:1). Righteousness comes from faith, and the Law is not based on faith, but on works (3:11–12).

Paul's argument here differs in many ways from the one he uses in Romans 9–10. The Law itself, as well as its works, is contrasted with πίστις, and specifically described as *not* being ἐκ πίστεως (3:12). Nevertheless, it witnesses to the blessing promised to Abraham, and is a παιδαγωγός εἰς Χριστόν. There are differences, too, between Paul's use of Abraham here and in Romans 4: significantly, Paul identifies the 'seed of Abraham' with Christ himself, and stresses the priority of the promise of future blessing made to Abraham and to his seed to the Law. If the Law is a παιδαγωγός until the coming of Christ, that is because God's promises concerning Christ were already made *before* the Law was given. The Law is a temporary measure, but Christ came at 'the fullness of time', in order to bring God's eternal purpose to completion.

Paul's argument in Romans 9–10 is in many ways similar to the one he presents in Phil 3:4–10. Here, Paul lists his privileges as a Jew (cf. Rom 9:4–5), and contrasts what he has abandoned – his own righteousness, that which is ἐκ νόμου – with the righteousness that comes διὰ πίστεως Ἰησοῦ Χριστοῦ, and which is ἐκ θεοῦ. The contrast between a righteousness that is ἐκ νόμου and that which is ἐκ θεοῦ suggests that once again, as in Romans, Paul thinks of the Jews as having lost sight of the Law's true goal. One difference between the two passages is, of course, that Paul implies that he did 'attain the Law', since he was 'perfect' in respect of the righteousness contained in the Law (Phil 3:6). Yet the righteousness of God, available through faith, is incomparably greater. Another difference – probably arising from the different circumstances in which the letters were written – is that in Philippians the righteousness of the Law is simply *compared* – or rather contrasted! – with the righteousness of God, and the Law is not said to point forward to Christ. Nevertheless, the claim in v. 3 that '*we* are the circumcision' shows that the link with the past has not been broken: the *true* circumcision consists of those who have faith, *not* of those who bind themselves to fulfil the works of the Law.[13] There is a sense in which the great privileges enjoyed by Israel foreshadow the even greater privileges of those who are in Christ.

In 2 Corinthians 3 we find another passage where the old and new are compared and contrasted, even though the word νόμος is not used in this

---

[13] The phrase τοὺς κακοὺς ἐργάτας in v. 2 is presumably a parody of reliance on 'works'.

epistle. The comparison here is between the ministry of Moses, described as 'the ministry of condemnation' and 'of death' (vv. 7, 9), and 'the ministry of the Spirit' and 'of righteousness' (vv. 8–9), which is the ministry exercised by Paul himself (4:1). Paul begins by describing the Corinthians as a letter written on human hearts – a metaphor that echoes the hope expressed in Jer 31:31–33 of 'a new covenant', written on the people's hearts – and so leads Paul into a series of contrasts: ink is contrasted with the Spirit; hearts with stones; the letter which kills with the Spirit that gives life (v. 6), condemnation with righteousness; what was temporary with what is permanent (v. 11); concealment with revelation (vv. 12–18). One thing, however, has no opposite, and that is glory, which accompanies both the old and the new. True, the glory that attended the ministry of death fades in comparison with the glory of the ministry of righteousness (v. 10), but it was, nevertheless, genuine glory – such glory, indeed, that the Israelites could not bear to look at it (v. 7). The ministry of condemnation and death is the ministry of the Law, and the story to which Paul is alluding is that of Moses receiving the Law on Sinai. According to that story, when Moses, after speaking with God, came down from the mountain carrying the tablets of the Law in his hands, his face shone with reflected glory. This glory was so dazzling, that after he had delivered the Law to Israel, he was obliged to wear a veil over his face when he was in the people's presence: the glory was too great for them to bear.

Yet this glory, argues Paul, is as nothing compared with the far greater glory that has now been revealed in the ministry of righteousness. Paul now gives a different explanation for the veil: it was not intended solely to cover the glory on Moses' face, but to conceal 'the end of what was being done away with' (v. 13). Once again we have the word τέλος, and once again its meaning is disputed. There are other uncertainties. What is it that is being abrogated? It seems most likely that the participle καταργούμενον picks up the previous use of that word in v. 11. What is temporary, and is being abrogated, is the ministry of condemnation and death given to Moses in the Law. What Moses conceals is the τέλος of this system. As in Rom 10:4, τέλος here may mean either termination or goal. Here, however, there is less problem than there is there in taking it to mean 'termination', since we are not talking about the Law itself, but about Moses' ministry – a ministry of condemnation and death, which we have been told has been abrogated (v. 11).

Writing about this passage some 20 years ago, I understood τέλος to mean 'full stop'.[14] If this is right, Paul is now saying that what Moses was concealing was not the glory that was too bright to gaze on, but the fact that the glory was no longer there. Today, I am persuaded that τέλος means primarily

---

[14] Morna D. Hooker, 'Beyond the Things That Are Written?: St Paul's Use of Scripture', *NTS* 27 (1981): 295–309.

'goal', or 'purpose', as in Rom 10:4[15] – though here, as there, that sense will necessarily imply also 'termination'. Some commentators, objecting to this interpretation, ask why Paul might have thought that 'Moses wanted to hide the aim of the old covenant – that is, Christ – from Israel'.[16] But the question can be turned round: why should Paul have thought that Moses would wish to hide the fact that the glory was fading, and that the system based on the Law was only temporary? For certainly he is arguing that Moses concealed *something* from Israel, and in that sense can be accused of deception – the very charge that has been brought against Paul, and against which he is attempting to defend himself (4:2 ff.)!

The logic of 2 Cor 3:12–18 seems to me to demand that τέλος here means 'goal', since Paul goes on to describe what takes place when the veil is removed – in Christ. *Until* that happens, whenever Moses is read, the veil is still present – though it is now said to be on their (i.e. Jewish) hearts. 'But when someone turns to the Lord, the veil is removed' (v. 16). This quotation from Exod 34:34 is here understood to refer, not to Moses, but to the believer. But who is the Lord? Is it God or Christ? In v. 17 Paul explains: the Lord is in fact the Spirit, who brings freedom. Freedom from what? Presumably from γράμμα, and so from condemnation and death. If Moses veiled his face in order to conceal the fact that the old system had come to an end, then the removal of the veil should lead to the discovery that the glory had faded. Instead, however, its removal means that we see 'the glory of the Lord' – and, like Moses, reflect it. What we see is the fulfilment of the old system – which, though it brought condemnation and death, had nevertheless *promised* life. But the glory we now see does not need to be veiled – instead, 'reflecting that glory, we are transformed into the same image from glory to glory' (v. 18).

Are the ministry that led to condemnation and death and the ministry that leads to life unconnected? Is it simply that we once relied for illumination on a box of candles, but now have been connected to mains electricity? I once used that illustration to compare the glory revealed on the face of Moses with that revealed on the face of Christ. But it now seems to me to be inadequate, since it ignores the fact that Paul is convinced that the *source* of illumination is the same: it is more a case of replacing old, low-wattage bulbs with the newest and brightest bulbs on the market, and plugging them

---

[15] So e.g., Jean Héring, *The Second Epistle of Saint Paul to the Corinthians* (London: Epworth, 1967) *in loc.* R.P.C. Hanson, *II Corinthians* (London: SCM Press, 1954), *in loc.*; Anthony Tyrrell Hanson, *Jesus Christ in the Old Testament* (London: SPCK, 1965), 28–29. Cf. Margaret E. Thrall, *A Critical and Exegetical Commentary on the Second Epistle to the Corinthians,* vol. 1, ICC (Edinburgh: T&T Clark, 1994), 257–258.

[16] Victor Paul Furnish, *II Corinthians,* AB 32A (Garden City, NY: Doubleday, 1984), 207. Cf. C.K. Barrett, *A Commentary on the Second Epistle to the Corinthians,* BNTC (London: A&C Black, 1973), 120.

into the same sockets. In other words, there is an essential link between the two revelations of δόξα – even though, as in Gal 3:19, that which came by the hand of Moses was now seen by Paul to be inferior. Yet even my new image fails to convey Paul's full meaning: for the 'new' bulbs prove to be the original, the 'old' ones an inferior substitute. Christ is not just one who passes on God's glory, but the clearest expression of that glory. Moses' face shone because he had glimpsed the glory of God himself on Sinai. The glory that is *now* revealed is also the glory of the Lord, a glory which *we* reflect (κατοπτριζόμενοι, 3:18). Where do we see this glory? In the face of Jesus Christ (4:6), who is himself the embodiment of glory because he is the image of God (4:4). The τέλος of the old system was, in fact, not simply its goal but its original expression, the revelation glimpsed by Moses on Sinai. In place of the reflected glory of the Law, we have the undiminished glory of *the Lord*. And this glory is nothing less than the light which shone out of darkness when God created the world (4:6; cf. Gen 1:3).

We now discover, therefore, that the glory Paul has been talking about is the glory of *Christ,* who is the image of God (v. 4). The gospel Paul proclaims is that *Jesus Christ* is Lord (v. 5), so if we reflect 'the glory of the Lord' and are being changed into 'the same image' (3:18), Paul is clearly meaning that Christian believers become like Christ – a familiar enough Pauline theme. The veil, which has moved in Paul's exegesis from Moses' face to Jewish hearts, is now said to rest on the gospel – but it hides it only from those whose minds have been blinded, preventing them from seeing the light of the gospel – the gospel which proclaims Christ as Lord. Paul might well have said 'the glory glimpsed by Moses on Sinai was the glory now revealed in Christ'. In fact, however, he takes the continuity in revelation back to creation. The God who, at creation, said 'Let light shine out of darkness' (and who revealed his glory on Sinai) is the God who reveals himself to us in the light we now see on the face of Jesus Christ.

Although Paul's argument necessarily implies that the revelation granted to Moses was inferior, it is important to remember that he does not deny that it *was* a genuine revelation, and that it was 'glorious'.

Similar ideas are reflected in an earlier passage – 1 Cor 10:4 – another verse which attracts many divergent views! Using another of the Exodus stories – this time that of Israel's travels in the wilderness – Paul refers to the rock from which water poured when Moses struck it (Exod 17:6; cf. Num 20:7–13). The fact that Paul refers to the rock as having 'followed' the Israelites shows that he was familiar with an interpretation of the story that is found also in later rabbinical writings. Paul's contemporary, Philo, refers to the story of the rock which provided water, as does Wis 11:1–4. Whereas the latter simply remarks that Wisdom was at work in these events, however, Philo identifies the rock itself with Wisdom. The rock is the source of water, with which

Philo links manna, and both water and manna are symbols of the word of God – the Torah.[17] For Paul, the rock was Christ, and he was thus the source of nourishment. Most commentators point to the identification of Christ with Wisdom earlier in the epistle (1:24, 30), and suggest that this is the basis of the claim that he is the rock here. Recently, however, some scholars have questioned whether 'Wisdom Christology' is as important for Paul as has been claimed, and it has been pointed out that since, in chapter 1, Paul's concern is to persuade the Corinthians that their own wisdom is worthless and that they must rely on the power and wisdom of God, the language he uses there is likely to echo that being used by the Corinthians themselves.[18] We should note, moreover, that the term 'wisdom' is not used in 1 Cor 10:1–5, and there is no necessary link with the argument of chapter 1. We need to look carefully, therefore, at 10:1–5 itself.

Discussion of this passage has tended to centre on the question as to whether or not Paul is thinking about the pre-existent Christ as being present in the Old Testament. Such arguments, I suggest, miss the point. Paul is talking not so much about Christ being present *in* the story, as about him being the reality which lies *behind* the Old Testament story. Just as the source of Moses' glory was the glory of the Lord – the glory we now see fully revealed in the Lord Jesus Christ – so the source of the water (and the manna), symbols of the Torah, is said to have been Christ.

It is because Christ is the *source* of what was revealed in the Torah – the rock from which the water flowed – that Paul can go on to ascribe to him the role which was played, in Jewish thought, by God's Word or Wisdom in creation. If by his Word God brought the world into being (Gen 1:1), and if Wisdom was with him at the beginning (Prov 8:22; Sirach 24:1–12) and is the fashioner of all things (Wis 7:22), then this is the role which must now be attributed to Christ. It is he – not the Torah – who is God's Word or Wisdom. He is the divine agent *through* whom all things come into being. Paul sums it up in one tight formula in 1 Cor 8:6: 'There is one God, the Father, from [ἐξ] whom are all things and for [εἰς] whom we exist, and one Lord, Jesus Christ, *through* [διά] whom are all things and *through* [διά] whom we exist'. This formula is echoed by what Paul says of God himself in Rom 11:36, but unlike that passage, this summary attributes the agency of creation and redemption to Christ. We do not need to argue from 1 Cor 1:24 and 30 that 1 Cor 8:6 expresses so-called 'Wisdom Christology', for the basis of Paul's understanding of Christ's role in

---

[17] Philo, *Leg.* 2.86.
[18] On this point see Gordon D. Fee, 'Wisdom Christology in Paul: A Dissenting View', in *The Way of Wisdom: Essays in Honor of Bruce K. Waltke,* eds. J.I. Packer and Sven Soderlund (Grand Rapids: Zondervan, 2000), 251–279. *Contra,* Anthony C. Thiselton, *The First Epistle to the Corinthians,* NIGTC (Grand Rapids: Eerdmans, 2000), 728: 'We cannot readily underplay the role for Paul of Christ the Word of God (1:30)'.

creation is evident in 1 Cor 10:4 itself: if Christ was the source of spiritual food and drink for the Israelites, then he is the Word spoken by God at creation and on Sinai, the Wisdom that guided Israel in the wilderness. Paul begins, not from an identification of Christ with Wisdom, but with the recognition of his priority to the Law.

But though we do not need the identification with Wisdom in 1 Cor 1:24, 30 in order to support this interpretation of 1 Cor 10, they may well reflect similar ideas to those expressed in this passage. It is true that the argument in 1 Cor 1 begins from human wisdom, but the divine Wisdom that is opposed to it is the gospel itself (v. 23), and though the message of Christ crucified is described as 'folly' (the obvious contrast to wisdom) to Gentiles, it is said to be a σκάνδαλον to Jews, reminding us of Rom 9:33. And in his final summary (1:30), Paul describes Christ as σοφία ..., δικαιοσύνη τε καὶ ἁγιασμός. What is found in Christ is precisely what the Law promised.

Whether we think the epistle to the Colossians is Pauline or not, the Christology of Col 1:15–20 is not so very far from 1 Cor 8:6. I am still attracted by the theory of C. F. Burney, proposed 75 years ago, that this passage is based on an exposition of Gen 1:1 and Prov 8:22.[19] Here Paul spells out the relationship of Christ, the divine Wisdom, to his creation, in a series of images and prepositions: ἐν, διά and – significantly! – εἰς. In 1 Cor 8, εἰς – together with ἐξ – was used of God. These three prepositions are then repeated in the second section of this christological exposition, where Christ's relationship with the *new* creation is brought out. Christ, then, is not simply the one through whom and by whom all things came into being, and through whom and by whom all things are now reconciled; in Colossians he is seen as the one for whom all this took place. In other words, he is the goal of creation (τὰ πάντα ... εἰς αὐτὸν ἔκτισται) – the goal that is reached when all things are finally reconciled to him (v. 20). This passage, too, of course, bristles with problems – not least in that last phrase. Are all things reconciled to *Christ,* as the syntax suggests? Translators instinctively understand 'him' to refer to 'God' here, even though God has not been mentioned. I suggest that the symmetry of the passage demands that we understand this second εἰς αὐτὸν to mean that all things are reconciled 'to him' – i.e. to Christ – just as they are said to have been created εἰς αὐτὸν. This means that everything in the universe has been restored to the order intended by God.[20] This is possible because it pleased πᾶν τὸ πλήρωμα to dwell in Christ. This phrase suggests that he embodies all the attributes of God – another echo of the so-called 'Wisdom Christology'.[21] A similar idea

---

[19] C. F. Burney, 'Christ as the APXH of Creation', *JTS* 27 (1926): 160 ff.

[20] So Eduard Lohse, *Die Briefe an die Kolosser und an Philemon,* KEK (Göttingen: Vandenhoeck & Ruprecht, 1968), *in loc.*

[21] Philo speaks of God completely filling the Logos with incorporeal powers, *Somn.* 1.62, cf. 1.75.

is expressed in John 1:16 of the Logos, and seems there to reflect the language of Exod 33:19, which is part of the story of God's self-revelation to Moses on Sinai.[22]

A few verses later, Paul states his own aim: it is 'to present every man mature in Christ' – i.e. τέλειος. If creation reaches its goal in Christ, then of course man will do so also. Needless to say, modern translations shy away from using the word 'man' in this verse. Nevertheless, it is important! For of course, the opening phrase in Col 1:15 – ὅς ἐστιν εἰκὼν τοῦ θεοῦ τοῦ ἀοράτου – links the theme of creation and Adam. εἰκὼν is a term used of Wisdom and the Word, both in intertestamental literature and by Philo.[23] But we also find there the tradition, going back to Gen 1:26, that Adam was created κατ' εἰκόνα θεοῦ. To claim that Christ is εἰκὼν τοῦ θεοῦ, therefore, is to claim that he holds a special position, both in relation to creation *and* in relation to mankind. What can be said of Christ in relation to the cosmos (that he is πρωτότοκος and pre-eminent) can be said in relation to the new man, who is being renewed according to the image of the creator (Col 3:10). The parallels are not exact, but are nevertheless significant.

We have argued that what Paul says about Christ in relation to creation (his so-called 'Wisdom Christology') is dependent upon his belief that Christ is prior to the Law: his claim is, simply, that what Judaism said about the Word and Wisdom applied to Christ, *not* to the Law. It might, then, be better to speak about 'Torah Christology', rather than 'Wisdom Christology'. We now see that Col 1 brings the consequences of that belief into striking conjunction with a parallel belief about Christ's 'priority' to Adam.

One fascinating aspect of all this is that the argument that Paul appears to be using in relation to the Law is parallel to the argument that he uses in relation to Adam. For although, as he reminds us in 1 Cor 15:46, the physical man – the first Adam – came *before* the spiritual in temporal terms, nevertheless the *last* Adam is the *true* Adam. The first Adam was a *type of the one to come* (Rom 5:14), and it is the latter – Christ – who is *the* image of God (2 Cor 4:4),[24] after whose image we are being recreated (Rom 8:29; 1 Cor 15:49; 2 Cor 3:18). Interestingly, the ideas of glory surrounding the figure of Adam are similar to those associated with the Law, for in Jewish tradition both Adam and the Law reflected the glory of God. In Col 1 we find once again that in Christ we have moved to the *source* of the glory. He is *the* εἰκὼν τοῦ θεοῦ, the embodiment of God's Wisdom, glimpsed by Moses on Mount Sinai; he is *the* εἰκὼν τοῦ θεοῦ,

---

[22] Cf. Morna D. Hooker, 'The Johannine Prologue and the Messianic Secret', *NTS* 21 (1974): 40–58, esp. 54–56 = above, essay 23 (pp. 321–340).

[23] Wis 7:26 (cf. 9:1–2); *Leg.* 1.43; *Conf.* 147; *Fug.* 101; *Somn.* 2.45.

[24] See Morna D. Hooker, 'Adam *Redivivus*: Philippians 2 Once More', in *The Old Testament in the New Testament: Essays in Honour of J. L. North*, ed. Steve Moyise, JSNTSup 189 (Sheffield: Sheffield Academic Press, 2000), 220–234 = above, essay 26 (pp. 371–383).

in contrast to Adam, who was created κατ' εἰκόνα θεοῦ.²⁵ The conviction that the τέλος νόμου is Christ corresponds with the belief that Adam is the τύπος of the one to come.

Before I go back to the questions with which I began, it is worth reminding ourselves that what Paul is doing has parallels, not only in Jewish literature, but within the New Testament itself.

The link in 2 Cor 4, for example, between the glory revealed on Sinai and the light of creation, has an obvious parallel in John 1:1–18. where the author begins from the light in Genesis 1 and moves on to the glory of Exod 34.²⁶ For John, God's revelation to Moses in the Law is affirmed – but what we have in Christ is the embodiment of grace and truth, the glory belonging to an only son. No one (not even Moses!) has ever seen God, but Christ has made him known and revealed his glory. Significantly, the term John uses to sum up Christ's continuity with, superiority to, and priority to the Law is 'Word'. This introductory passage is of particular importance, since it explains the assumptions in the rest of the Gospel, where we see how Moses bears witness to Jesus as Son of God (5:39–47). Though the Son follows Moses, he in fact precedes him – he must do, since he precedes Abraham, and is greater than Abraham (8:39–59). The one who is near to God's heart is also nearest to the source of revelation – indeed, he *is* that revelation, since his mission is to reveal the glory which he shared with God before the world came into existence.

John's Gospel is written in a context of controversy, and the author's purpose is clearly to show that Christ is the true fulfilment of Judaism. What is said about Jesus echoes what was once said about Torah: he is, e.g., light, life, the way, the truth, bread, water. As Peder Borgen has expressed it: 'John transfers the Torah's function to Jesus'.²⁷ Paul's arguments were developed in a somewhat different setting, since his mission was to be the apostle to the Gentiles; nevertheless, his debates about Christ – the Messiah – and about the Law are shaped by his arguments with his fellow Jews. It is not surprising if there are interesting parallels between Paul and John.

And there are obvious parallels with other New Testament writers – most notably with Matthew,²⁸ but also with the author to the Hebrews.

---

²⁵ Gen 1:26; Sir. 17:3; *Leg.* 3.96.
²⁶ I have explored these parallels in 'The Johannine Prologue and the Messianic Secret'. See also Peder Borgen, 'Logos was the True Light', *NT* 14 (1972): 115–130.
²⁷ Borgen, 'Logos', 124.
²⁸ I have discussed these briefly in Morna D. Hooker, 'Creative Conflict: The Torah and Christology', in *Christology, Controversy and Community, New Testament Essays in Honour of David R. Catchpole,* eds. David G. Horrell and Christopher M. Tuckett (Leiden: Brill, 2000), 117–136 = above, essay 17 (pp. 248–264).

Concluding Questions

How, then, did Paul come to affirm that Christ was the τέλος νόμου? It is clear that he – and some of our other New Testament writers – have moved a long way from the simple notion that his life, death, and resurrection 'fulfilled' particular passages in the Law and the Prophets. What all these writers have in common is a background of controversy with their fellow Jews. The other authors I have mentioned – Matthew, John, and the writer to the Hebrews – all seem to be on the fringes of Judaism, showing a passionate devotion to their Jewish heritage and faith, yet all being 'sidelined' by orthodox Judaism. Paul, in a sense, had deliberately 'sidelined' himself by accepting the commission to be the apostle to the Gentiles – but he, too, continued to believe that God's self-revelation to Israel was true. What all of them had to do was to reconcile their conviction that something new and decisive had happened in Christ with their belief that God had spoken to Moses and the prophets. For Paul, four elements were crucial:

1. His experience of Christ, which had exploded his previous conviction that those who did what the Law commanded would live (Lev 18:5, quoted in Gal 3:12 and Rom 10:5).
2. His realization that the scope of the gospel included the Gentiles, and that he was commissioned to be their apostle, which meant that he had to think again about what God's purposes might have been; if God's Spirit had been poured out on Gentiles, then the Law was *not* the basis of righteousness (Gal 3:1–5).
3. His controversies with fellow Jews, which made him refine his arguments.
4. His Jewish education, which provided him with the necessary knowledge of the scriptures and the traditions based on them.

It was because Paul had discovered that the δικαιοσύνη ἐκ θεοῦ was *not* identical with the δικαιοσύνη ἐκ νόμου, but came διὰ πίστεως Χριστοῦ, that he had been forced to acknowledge that τέλος νόμου Χριστός. With that realization came the conviction that what he had once believed about the Torah was in fact true of Christ. The experience of his Gentile converts confirmed this. They had received the Holy Spirit through the proclamation of Christ crucified. Peder Borgen has pointed out that the same link is found in the story of Cornelius in Acts 10:34–48. Peter describes how Christ was hung on a tree (Acts 10:39, quoting Deut 21:22) and raised to life, and while he is still speaking, the Holy Spirit is poured out on those he is addressing (10:44).[29] For Luke, as for Paul, the pouring out of the Spirit on the Gentiles is proof that nothing more is necessary (cf. also Acts 11:1–18). The fact that Christ suffered the penalty prescribed in the Law, and that its verdict was reversed by God, meant that the curse of the Law was annulled and the promised blessing was achieved. For

---

[29] Peder Borgen, 'Jesus Christ, the Reception of the Spirit and a Cross-National Community', in *Jesus of Nazareth: Lord and Christ,* eds. Joel B. Green and Max Turner (Grand Rapids: Eerdmans, 1994), 220–236.

Paul, it was the gospel itself that demonstrated, on the one hand, that the Law's temporary rule was at an end, on the other, that what it promised had arrived, in Christ.

What, then, are the implications of the belief that Christ is the τέλος νόμου?

It is clear that they are enormous. 1. By speaking of Christ as the 'End', we have seen that Paul was necessarily brought to think of him also as the 'Beginning' – an idea that becomes explicit in Col 1. Hence we find statements that apparently imply pre-existence.

2. What had been said about the Law in relation to creation was now understood to be more appropriately said about Christ. It was he who was God's agent in both creation and in redemption – a sphere in which the Law was shown to have been ineffectual, because of the weakness of the flesh.

3. If Christ 'replaces' the Law, and occupies the position previously occupied by the Torah in Jewish thought, then God's people are redefined: they consist no longer of those obedient to the Law – those 'under the Law' – but of those who are 'in Christ', and who believe in him. God's purpose is discovered to be far greater than was hitherto imagined.

4. The way of life to be followed is no longer to walk in the ways of the Law, but to walk in the way of the Lord; it is to fulfil, not the Law given on Sinai, but 'the law of Christ' (Gal 6:2). Paul has adapted the pattern that E.P. Sanders has famously called 'covenantal nomism'. This covenant, however, is established in Christ, not at Sinai. But though Paul refers to it as a 'new covenant' (2 Cor 3:6, cf. 1 Cor 11:25), I suspect that he would have said that it is in reality the covenant of promise, once made to Abraham, and now ratified in Christ (Gal 3:15–29), and so the *original* covenant. Just as Christ, the 'Second Adam,' was in fact the *true* image of God, after whom Adam was created, and just as the glory revealed in Christ is the *source* of the glory reflected by Moses, so the covenant ratified in him is the *original* covenant, and the covenant with Moses the temporary, earthly counterpart of what is eternal and heavenly (Gal 4:21–31).[30] This covenant has been ratified through Christ's death and resurrection, and the 'law' that is linked with it is simply the requirement that one lives 'in Christ'. Pressed to spell out what that means, Paul usually gives a list of abstract terms, rather than specific rules. Above all, it means love – and those who love have fulfilled the whole Law (Gal 5:14).

Christology, cosmology, ecclesiology, ethics – four major topics, these! We take these developments for granted. Did they just evolve? Or are they, in fact, all derived from an idea that is often denied or simply overlooked – that Christ is the *End* of the Law, and therefore its *Beginning*?

---

[30] See Morna D. Hooker, '"Heirs of Abraham": The Gentiles' Role in Israel's Story', in *Narrative Dynamics in Paul: A Critical Assessment,* ed. Bruce W. Longenecker (Louisville: Westminster John Knox Press, 2002), 85–96.

28. On Becoming the Righteousness of God: Another Look at 2 Cor 5:21*

1. Introduction

2 Cor 5:21 is often – discouragingly! – described as 'one of the most difficult verses in the New Testament'. Its problems are obvious. Perhaps the most striking feature of the verse is Paul's extraordinary use of the terms ἁμαρτία and δικαιοσύνη. Why does he use nouns, and what does he mean by them? The statement that Christ was made sin startles us, but the parallel clause, informing us that we have become the righteousness of God, is equally puzzling, for the addition of the word Θεοῦ destroys the symmetry of the parallel and is certainly unexpected. Even the simple words in the verse cause problems: what does Paul mean by ἡμεῖς? Does Paul meander in his use of 'us' in this section between the apostolic (meaning Paul and his co-workers) to the general (meaning 'all Christians') and is he thinking in v. 21 of *all* Christians or of the role of the apostles? Finally, what is the relationship of this verse to the argument as a whole? Why, in the course of a lengthy exposition of his understanding of his ministry, does Paul throw in no less than three summary statements of the gospel, in vv. 14–15, 18–19, and 21? What is their precise relevance to his argument?

2. Gal 3:13

'Christ was made sin for us'. Attempting to understand the enigmatic statement in 2 Corinthians 5 by turning to another of equal complexity may seem foolish, but 2 Cor 5:21 and Gal 3:13 are so similar that they cry out to be examined together, and one passage may well illuminate the other. As with 2 Cor 5:21, Gal 3:13 is part of a longer argument. This begins back in 2:15, and concerns the way in which both Jews and Gentiles have been brought into a new relationship with God – a relationship which is defined by the verb δικαιόω. The difficulties of translating this verb into English are such that for the purposes of this paper I shall use the Old English 'rightwise', rather

---

* This paper was originally delivered at a special seminar held in Durham on 4 May 2007 on the occasion of Professor C.K. Barrett's 90th birthday. It is offered here as a tribute to someone whose scholarship and friendship meant so much to me over almost 50 years, and whose ministry was – like Paul's – modelled on the gospel.

than the usual 'justify'. Our new relationship with God has come about, Paul argues, not on the basis of the works of the Law, but on the basis of πίστις, 'faith' or 'trust'. We have trusted in Christ in order to be 'rightwised' with God through faith, and *not* through the works of the Law. A summary of the gospel in v. 20 explains that Christ's death means that 'I' have died (with Christ) to the Law, and that Christ now lives within 'me'.

To back up his argument, Paul now appeals to experience. The outpouring of God's Spirit which the Galatians have experienced is proof of their new relationship with God (3:1–5), and this Spirit was received, he reminds them, on the basis of πίστις, not on the basis of the works of the Law, which belong to the realm of the flesh. Next come scriptural proofs (3:6–9). First, Paul quotes the case of Abraham, who believed – that is, trusted in – God, and so was counted righteous (Gen 15:6). Abraham's descendants are those who – like him – trust in God. The promise made to Abraham was that all nations would be blessed in him: in other words, they would be his children, members of God's people, and would inherit the land.

The reference to blessing leads into a second scriptural proof. In contrast to those whom Paul describes as being ἐκ πίστεως stand those who are ἐξ ἔργων; just as the blessing belongs to the former, so a curse rests on those who rely on the works of the Law, since scripture says 'Cursed is everyone who does not persevere in doing everything that is written in the book of the Law' (3:10). Absurdly, as it seems to us, Paul uses Deut 27:26 here to support an argument which directly opposes what the verse in its original context clearly states. How can the curse pronounced in Deuteronomy on those who *fail* to persevere in the things written in the Law be said to have fallen on those who *observe* the works of the Law? The quotation appears to prove what Paul is attempting to deny!

Space precludes an attempt to answer this question, so we must simply note that Paul apparently believes that the quotation makes his case. He then comments that it is evident that no one is in fact 'rightwised' before God ἐν νόμῳ, since (Hab 2:4) 'the righteous one lives ἐκ πίστεως'. The Law, on the other hand, is *not* based on faith, but on the principle of works, since 'the one who does these things lives by them' (Lev 18:5). The assertion that 'it is evident' is apparently based on the fact that nothing is said in this text from Leviticus about being righteous, whereas Hab 2:4 links righteousness with faith. Why, then, we may reasonably ask, does the Law command Israel to 'do' and 'live by' the commands of the Law? The reason will be spelt out later in the chapter, when we discover that the Law was an interim measure, a παιδαγωγός 'until faith came' (v. 23). For Paul, that means that Hab 2:4 is understood to be a *promise* of what would happen once faith came. Until that time, all are under the curse of the Law, since the Law could not bring righteousness, or make alive (v. 21).

From this curse Christ has redeemed us, by himself *becoming* a curse – a fact demonstrated by the quotation of Deut 21:23, which pronounces a curse on everyone whose body is hung on a tree. The purpose, declares Paul, was that, in Christ, the blessing of Abraham might come to the Gentiles, and that we might receive the Spirit through faith. How can Christ's scandalous death bring blessing to others? Paul fails to explain, though in the rest of the chapter he tells us that the blessing comes to those who are 'in Christ', and that it comes through πίστις. Christ is the seed of Abraham, and so the one to whom the blessing belongs; those who by faith are baptized into him – Greeks as well as Jews, slaves as well as freemen, both male and female – share his status, and so become Abraham's heirs. The blessing promised to Abraham regarding his seed thus comes to those Gentiles who are united with Christ (v. 29), and who share Abraham's faith (v. 7).

A second ἵνα clause tells us that the reason why Christ became a curse was that we might receive the promised Spirit of God. Paul has already argued that the Galatians received the Spirit through faith, not by obedience to the works of the Law, and he has linked that argument to the example of Abraham by the word of καθώς, which introduces his quotation of Gen 15:6 in 3:6. It would seem that the blessing promised to Abraham is understood by Paul to be the gift of the Spirit to those who are 'rightwised' by faith. This Spirit is sent to those who are 'in Christ Jesus', and is a sign that they, like him, are 'sons of God' (3:26; 4:4–6).

Paul spells out clearly how Christ is the source of blessing, but fails to explain how the curse has been neutralised and transformed. Although he does not specifically refer to the resurrection in 3:13, it clearly underlies his argument, just as it does in 2:19–20, where again it is presumed. It is perhaps not accidental that Galatians begins – unusually – with the declaration that God raised Jesus Christ from the dead (1:1). The resurrection is fundamental to the argument.

Gal 3:13 and 2 Cor 5:21 are both statements of what some of us have described – for lack of a more adequate term – as an 'interchange' between Christ and the believer.[1] Christ is identified with our condition, in order that we may be identified with him, and so share in what he is. What Paul understood by this was expressed brilliantly by Irenaeus, in the classic summary: 'Christ became what we are, in order that we might become what he is'.[2] Interestingly, however, neither Gal 3:13 nor 2 Cor 5:21 offers us a statement that is as symmetrical as the one coined by Irenaeus.

In Galatians, the statement that 'Christ became … in order that we' is part of a much more complex sentence. First, we are told that 'Christ redeemed

---

[1] Cf. Morna D. Hooker, 'Interchange in Christ', *JTS* NS 22 (1971): 349–361.
[2] Irenaeus, *Adv. Haer.* 5 *praef.*

us from the curse of the Law' by becoming 'a curse' for our sake. Since it is those who base their lives on 'works' who are under the curse of the Law (v. 10), the 'us' here presumably refers to Jewish Christians,[3] even though the blessing – as Paul immediately makes clear – extends to Gentiles. Why, however, does Paul describe Christ as 'a curse' rather than as 'cursed'? This is the more intriguing, since his citation of Deut 21:23 follows the LXX in using an adjective, meaning 'cursed'.[4] Perhaps it is because Paul has been using the nouns 'curse' and 'blessing' in his argument, and wants to pick them up.[5] Perhaps, also, it is because the *Hebrew* of Deut 21:23 states that the malefactor's body is exposed as a sign that he is 'the curse of God'. That, of course, is an ambiguous phrase. Does it mean, as the LXX understands it to mean, 'cursed *by* God', or does it mean 'a curse – i.e. an insult – *to* God'? In an excursus to his commentary, Lightfoot cites Jewish and Christian evidence that the latter view was 'the popular Jewish interpretation (shared therefore by Jewish Christians) at all events from the second century of the Christian era'.[6] Does *Paul* have this sense in mind? Is this why he uses the noun, κατάρα, rather than the adjective? And is this why he omits the words ὑπὸ τοῦ θεοῦ from his quotation of the LXX? Pseudo-Jonathan explains that exposure on a tree is 'a disgrace before the Lord', because the executed man is made in the image of God. Most commentators assume that by using the LXX to explain the word 'curse', Paul is indicating that he means 'cursed *by God*', but his introductory words, 'Christ has redeemed us from *the curse of the Law*' suggest that he understands Christ to have fallen under the curse pronounced *by the Law*.

The third possible explanation of Paul's use of the noun κατάρα is found in the Jewish understanding that those who were under a curse became a source of contamination to others. Thus Pseudo-Jonathan goes on to explain that the malefactor's body must be removed from the tree by nightfall lest it should pollute the land. The well-known story of Achan[7] demonstrates how the wrongdoer brought a curse on others, and therefore had to be destroyed, together with everything belonging to him. To say that Christ became 'a curse' is to say more than that he was 'cursed': it suggests that he became a source of contamination to others. Logically, therefore, one might expect Paul to continue by saying that Christ brought a curse on others. In fact, however, the opposite is true: he became a source of blessing. Nevertheless, although

---

[3] So Hans Dieter Betz, *Galatians*, Hermeneia (Philadelphia: Fortress, 1979), *in loc. Contra*, James D.G. Dunn, *A Commentary on the Epistle to the Galatians*, BNTC (London: A&C Black, 1993), *in loc.*

[4] To be sure, Paul uses ἐπικατάρατος, rather than κεκατηραμένος – possibly because he wants to pick up the opening word of the quotation from Deut 27:26 (see Gal 3:10).

[5] So E.P. Sanders, *Paul* (Oxford; New York: Oxford University Press, 1991), 58.

[6] J.B. Lightfoot, *Saint Paul's Epistle to the Galatians*, 10th ed. (London; New York: Macmillan, 1890), 152.

[7] Joshua 7.

the divine purpose was to bring blessing to the Gentiles and to all who believe, yet to those who refuse to trust in him he remains a σκάνδαλον,[8] and so, for a time at least, the cause of Israel's failure and exclusion.[9]

What, then, of the blessing? The second part of our 'interchange' statement corresponds to the first in using a noun, but there the similarity ceases. If the two clauses were strictly parallel, we might expect Paul to write *either* that 'Christ became a curse in order that the Gentiles might *become* a blessing', or that 'Christ became cursed, in order that the Gentiles might be blessed' – which is, in effect, what most commentators understand him to mean. There is a further complication, however, since the symmetry is disturbed by the fact that Paul continues with a ἵνα clause – 'in order that we might receive the promised Spirit' – which apparently provides a definition of what it means to receive the blessing.

Now it may well be argued that if a pattern does not fit, we should not impose on it what Paul says – and I would have to agree. But I do not think that we should abandon the notion of 'interchange' quite so readily. For it is clear that in speaking of Christ being made a curse, Paul is thinking of his identification with humanity's condition. The curse, he has insisted, rests on all who do not have πίστις – and since this πίστις comes only with Christ (3:23, 25), this curse rests on all humanity until his coming. How, then, we may wonder, was *Abraham* able to trust God and to be counted δίκαιος? The answer seems to be that what Abraham trusted was the *promise* of God, a promise that was fulfilled in Christ. Abraham's faith was in a sense proleptic. 'Scripture, foreseeing that God would "rightwise" the Gentiles through faith, declared the gospel to Abraham beforehand' (v. 8). Between the promise and its fulfilment we have the Law, under which we were 'imprisoned' until the coming of faith (v. 23). This Law was unable to bestow either life or righteousness (v. 21). The blessing promised to Abraham is given to those who believe, on the basis of πίστις Χριστοῦ (v. 22). The fact that faith comes only with the coming of Christ (v. 23) offers support to the suggestion that Paul may be thinking here of Christ's own πίστις as the basis of ours – but that is by the way.[10]

By being born of a woman, and under the Law, therefore (4:4), Christ came under the curse of the Law,[11] and his scandalous death demonstrates

---

[8] Gal 5:11; 1 Cor 1:23; Rom 9:33; 11:9.

[9] Rom 11:7–10.

[10] See George F. Howard, 'On the "Faith of Christ"', *HTR* 60 (1967): 459–465; Richard B. Hays, *The Faith of Jesus Christ: An Investigation of the Narrative Substructure of Galatians 3.1–4.11*, 2nd ed. (Grand Rapids; Cambridge: Eerdmans, 2001); Sam K. Williams, 'Again Pistis Christou', *CBQ* 49 (1987): 431–447; Morna D. Hooker, 'ΠΙΣΤΙΣ ΧΡΙΣΤΟΥ', *NTS* 35 (1989): 321–342.

[11] Cf. Christopher D. Stanley, '"Under a Curse": A Fresh Reading of Gal 3.10–14', *NTS* 36 (1990): 481–511.

this. On the other side of the ledger, the gift of the Spirit demonstrates that the promise made to Abraham has been fulfilled: blessing has been poured out on the Gentiles. Since this blessing has come to the believing Gentiles as a result of their baptism into Christ, it is plain that the crucified Christ is not, after all, a 'curse', but a source of blessing. The resurrection has annulled the curse of the Law.

3. 2 Cor 5:21

We turn back, at last, to 2 Corinthians 5, and straight away we notice that here, too, we have a lack of symmetry. It is true that this time we have two nouns, so that we can reduce the central contrast to the statement that

> He made him to be a sin for us
> in order that we might become righteousness in him

– but that is to ignore the word Θεοῦ! Moreover, the introductory 'he who knew no sin' creates a further imbalance by forming an additional contrast to 'he made him to be sin'.

This introductory phrase is perhaps easy to understand. The description of Christ as ἁμαρτία is shocking – so shocking that Paul apparently considered it necessary to ensure that he was not misunderstood. This time there can be no question of the noun being used for an adjective: Christ was *not* made 'sinful'. Yet almost all commentators interpret the *second* noun as equivalent to an adjective. This can hardly be simply δίκαιος, however, since Paul qualifies δικαιοσύνη with Θεοῦ. Again, many commentators would endorse the comment of C.K. Barrett, who suggests that if the statement that 'Christ became *sin*' means that 'he came to stand in that relation with God which normally is the result of sin, estranged from God and the object of his wrath', then 'we became righteousness' means that we 'have come to stand in that relationship with God which is described by the term *righteousness*, that is, we are acquitted in his court, justified, reconciled'.[12] According to this forensic understanding of the term, δικαιοσύνη is treated as the equivalent of the participle δικαιωθέντες,[13] and Θεοῦ is regarded as a genitive of origin: it is *God* who has 'rightwised' us, and *God* in whose court we are acquitted. An alternative explanation suggests that δικαιοσύνη, like ἁμαρτία – and like κατάρα and εὐλογία in Gal 3:13 ff. – should be seen as an active power.

---

[12] C.K. Barrett, *A Commentary on the Second Epistle to the Corinthians* (London: A&C Black, 1973), 180.

[13] Barrett, *2 Corinthians*, 180.

28. On Becoming the Righteousness of God: Another Look at 2 Cor 5:21

Let us begin, once again, by looking at the passage in context. The theme of 2 Corinthians is Paul's ministry – and though the epistle opens with thanksgiving that he and the Corinthian congregation have been reconciled, the letter is in effect a defence of his ministry. Paul's understanding of his apostleship is nothing less than conformity to the gospel: his ministry is a revelation of glory (chapter 3) – but the glory is that of Christ, which means that Paul carries the death of Jesus in his body, in order that the life of Jesus may be displayed there. This means that he is given up to death for Jesus' sake, in order that others might live (4:11–12). Yet the revelation of the glory of Christ is not confined to apostles. 'We are *all* being transformed into [Christ's] image', writes Paul (3:18).[14] It is true that Paul seems to see his role as an apostle to be a channel of the 'interchange' of experience that has come to him in Christ. Sharing in the sufferings of Christ, he has been able to pass on the consolation he has received to the Corinthians (1:3–7); experiencing the dying of Jesus, he has been enabled to bring life to them (4:8–12); his weakness has been the means of conveying Christ's power (13:3–4). But the process does not stop there! The Corinthians themselves are a 'letter of Christ' (3:3), and the grace they experience extends to others (4:15).[15] Those who have been made rich through Christ's poverty (8:9) are urged to share their wealth with others in ministering to the saints in Jerusalem (9:10–15). In an earlier letter, 1 Corinthians, Paul had already defended his understanding of his apostolic role and urged the Corinthians to imitate him (1 Cor 4:15; 11:1). The apostle's life is modelled on the pattern of the gospel, but it is intended as a model for others.

The use of the first-person plural throughout these chapters clearly applies to Paul in particular; he is describing his own experience. Yet what he says is true – or *ought* to be true! – of Christians in general. The pattern of the gospel should be stamped on *all* their lives.

At the beginning of 2 Corinthians 5, Paul describes how 'our earthly tent' is being destroyed, and how 'we groan', longing for a better dwelling; he is undoubtedly drawing here on his own experience, and precisely because it *is* his experience, it is linked with his apostolic calling. Nevertheless, the experience of mortality is common to others, and the confidence he expresses should also be shared by others. Similarly, 'we must *all* appear before the judgement seat of Christ' (5:10). Immediately following this, however, the 'we' of v. 11 refers to Paul in particular: 'we try to persuade others', he says, and then describes what that means. Whatever he does is 'for God' and 'for you' (v. 13). Verse 14 spells out the reason, and introduces the first brief summary of the

---

[14] The πάντες is missing from P[46], but it seems more likely that it was accidentally omitted than that it was deliberately added.

[15] Margaret E. Thrall, *A Critical and Exegetical Commentary on the Second Epistle to the Corinthians*, vol. 1, ICC (Edinburgh: T&T Clark, 1994), 346.

gospel: 'The love of Christ controls us, since we hold that one died for all, therefore all have died. And one died for all, in order that the living might no longer live to themselves but to the one who died and rose for them'. At its heart, this summary in vv. 14–15 contains yet another statement implying an 'interchange':

> he died for all
> in order that [they] might live to [him].

Once again, however, the brief summary has been overlaid with various explanations. The fact that Christ died for all means, first, that 'all have died': in other words, his death was not a substitute for theirs, but in some sense brought it about. Secondly, his death for all means that 'those who live' should no longer live 'to themselves', but 'to him who died and was raised for them'. Whether οἱ ζῶντες means 'all who live' (i.e. all humanity) or 'those who share Christ's risen life' (i.e. all Christians) is not clear, but since the clause expresses purpose, perhaps we should understand him to mean the former. Moreover, the fact that Paul's argument is based on the statement that 'Christ died for all' suggests that he is thinking of life for all.

We have, then, a statement of the gospel that is both familiar – 'he died and was raised' – and yet distinctive in the way that it indicates the *purpose* of his death and resurrection. But *why* does Paul quote this summary of the gospel here? He does so *in order to apply it to his own ministry*: the gospel means 'living for Christ', and for him, that means being constrained by Christ to persuade others – by word and example – of the truth of the gospel. At the same time, he is anxious that the Corinthians should see the relevance of this gospel to their own lives.

A further consequence of what has happened is that judgements 'according to the flesh' are no longer appropriate (v. 16). This is because there is, in Christ, a new creation: the old has gone and the new has come (v. 17). Here, too, what Paul says applies to *all* who are in Christ: hence he uses τις in v. 17. But the reason *why* he says it is probably related to his own commission. Before he was 'in Christ' he *had* judged him 'according to the flesh', but he does so no longer. And it is precisely because his understanding of who Christ is is *not* 'according to the flesh' that he has what the Corinthians – who still have tendency to see things from that perspective (1 Cor 3:1–4) – regard as a strange understanding of what it means to be an apostle.

Everything that has happened, we are now told, is from God, 'who reconciled us to himself, and gave us the ministry of reconciliation' (v. 18). The *first* 'us' here cannot be limited to Paul and his colleagues: possibly Paul means 'us Christians', but the parallel statement in v. 19, which tells us that 'in Christ God reconciled the world to himself', suggests that he may be thinking of the whole human race. But to whom is the message of reconciliation entrusted (vv. 18b, 19b)? Is it to all who accept reconciliation? Or is Paul thinking of his own call to proclaim the gospel?

Since in v. 18 Paul speaks of God reconciling 'us' meaning 'us Christians', and since he immediately says that the ministry – or message – of reconciliation is entrusted to 'us', we expect the 'us' in v. 18b and v. 19b to have the same meaning as in v. 18a. Is this ministry, then, entrusted to Christians in general? Now there is certainly a sense in which we may say that all who accept reconciliation from God become themselves the agents of reconciliation. Paul rarely uses the verb καταλλάσσω; apart from the three occasions in vv. 18–20, we find it only in Rom 5:10 (where it is used twice, in both cases of our reconciliation to God) and 1 Cor 7:11, where the Christian woman is urged to be reconciled to her estranged husband. The noun καταλλαγή is found elsewhere only in Rom 5:11 and 11:15, where Paul describes Israel's failure as bringing about the reconciliation of the world. But though the term 'ministry of reconciliation' is unusual, the idea that Paul's ministry reflects the gospel is certainly not, and neither is his conviction that his converts should share his task. The Corinthians share his sufferings and consolation (1:7), and they are urged to help him by their prayers (1:11) and to imitate him (1 Cor 4:16; 11:1). This idea is stressed in Philippians, where Paul urges members of the Christian community to prove themselves to be 'innocent and above reproach', to 'shine like stars in a dark world, and to proffer the word of life' (2:15–16). Paul describes the Philippians as having shared in the work of ministry (1:5), and his purpose in writing seems to be to ensure that they continue his understanding of ministry as conformity to the gospel, appealing to them to imitate him (3:17; 4:9).[16]

Nevertheless, what he has in mind in 2 Cor 5:18–20 is clearly his own calling as an 'ambassador of Christ':[17] he is still trying to explain his understanding of his ministry to the Corinthians. In other words, the context suggests that we should understand the pronouns in vv. 18b, 19b and 20a to refer specifically to Paul and his fellow evangelists.[18] The fact that there is an obvious awkwardness in moving from 'us' meaning 'us men and women' in v. 18a to 'us' meaning 'us apostles' in v. 18b[19] is perhaps due to the fact that Paul is de-

---

[16] Morna D. Hooker, 'Philippians: Phantom Opponents and the Real Source of Conflict', in *Fair Play: Diversity and Conflicts in Early Christianity: Essays in Honour of Heikki Räisänen*, eds. Ismo Dunderberg, Christopher Tuckett, and Kari Syreeni (Leiden: Brill, 2002), 377–395 = below, essay 42 (pp. 616–631).

[17] For the significance of the term 'ambassador' here see Anthony Bash, *Ambassadors for Christ*, WUNT 2/92 (Tübingen: Mohr, 1997).

[18] Furnish, on the other hand, follows other commentators in taking vv. 18 and 19 to refer to believers, even though in v. 20 'the first-person-plural pronouns must refer to the Pauline apostolate'. See Victor Paul Furnish, *II Corinthians*, AB 32A (Garden City, NY: Doubleday, 1984), 320, 339.

[19] C.K. Barrett describes it as 'abrupt and difficult' (*2 Corinthians*, 176).

liberately narrowing down the meaning here because he wants to demonstrate how he has endeavoured to live out the gospel. It is perhaps for this reason that Paul has again summarized the gospel, using language which he then applies to his own mission. As a result of the gospel, God is described as

> giving to us the ministry of reconciliation ...
> entrusting to us the word of reconciliation ...
> entreating through us.

We suggest, then, that the language Paul uses here to summarize the gospel – that in it God reconciles the world to himself – has once again been chosen because it is appropriate to what he wishes to say about his ministry. In other words, he understands his role in terms of bringing about reconciliation between God and the gentiles.

So what, specifically, *is* the message of reconciliation? Verse 21 offers us yet a third summary. Once again, it speaks of the significance of Christ's death:

> The one who knew no sin
> God made sin on our behalf
> in order that we might become the righteousness of God in him.

The previous summaries spoke of Christ dying 'for all', and of his death being a means of reconciliation for 'the world', whereby transgressions are not 'counted'. The third, which is the 'appeal' made by Christ's ambassadors to the world, is more personal: 'Christ was made sin *for us*'.

Why ἁμαρτία? The noun cannot here be a substitute for an adjective, but is it perhaps shorthand for a phrase? Does it mean 'sin-offering'?[20] Attractive as this interpretation has been to some commentators, it must be rejected: Paul can hardly have used ἁμαρτία with two different meanings almost side by side. But how could Christ have been 'made sin'? In Galatians 3, the context offered some sort of explanation as to why Paul might have employed the nouns, 'curse' and 'blessing', but there is no help of this kind here. The horror of the word serves to underline the need of the world for 'reconciliation'; this is what we are without Christ – 'sin' – alienated from God. Sin is for Paul an alien power that corrupts the world and leads to death, because of the weakness of the flesh (Romans 6–7). The Old Testament provides an analogy of what it means to be identified with sin in the scapegoat, and Jesus' own experience of 'being made sin', cut off from God, is graphically portrayed in the cry of dereliction (Mark 15:34 // Matt 27:46).

The purpose, we are told, was 'that we might become the righteousness of God in him'. Once again we must ask 'who are the "we"?' The assumption that δικαιοσύνη is equivalent to δικαιωθέντες means that the majority of commentators conclude that the 'we' here must refer to all Christians: we are

---

[20] The LXX uses both ἁμαρτία and περὶ ἁμαρτίας for 'that which is for sin'.

all 'rightwised', 'accepted in God's court', and the 'righteousness' is understood to be a divine gift bestowed on believers. Θεοῦ then emphasizes the fact that we are talking about a righteousness whose origin is God, not man. But though the phrase 'the righteousness of God' is used elsewhere in contrast to 'my own righteousness' (Rom 10:3; Phil 3:9), this particular contrast hardly seems relevant here. Why, then, should Θεοῦ be used here? It may well be, of course, that Paul instinctively emphasized the fact that any 'righteousness' that Christians possessed came from God. But the phrase δικαιοσύνη Θεοῦ presents us with a *double* puzzle. If Paul has in mind here our 'rightwising', then why does he use the noun, δικαιοσύνη, rather than δικαιωθέντες? Is the noun used merely to provide a contrast to ἁμαρτία? Turning back to Gal 3:13, we remember that there was in fact no symmetry there, because Paul did *not* say that the Gentiles had *become* a blessing, but rather that the blessing came *to* them. On the analogy of that passage, we might expect him to say here that 'Christ became sin in order that righteousness might come to us' – or 'in order that we might *receive* righteousness' – the expression he uses in Rom 9:30. Instead, he declares that we *become* the righteousness of God.

Essential to understanding Paul's way of thinking is the phrase ἐν αὐτῷ, which features in so many of these 'interchange' passages. It is only when we are united with Christ that we become righteousness. Just as he was identified with our sin, so we – because we are in him – are now identified with God's righteousness. *We become what he is.* A similar idea is expressed in 1 Cor 1:30, where Paul declares that Christ 'became for us wisdom from God, righteousness and sanctification and redemption'.[21] He is seen here as the *source* of our righteousness, as well as of wisdom, sanctification, and redemption. These terms are all dynamic. If Christ is 'for us wisdom from God', that is because he is himself both 'the power of God and the wisdom of God' (1 Cor 1:24).

What, then, can it mean to 'become God's righteousness'? It was Ernst Käsemann who suggested that many exegetes of this passage had been misled because their understanding of the phrase 'the righteousness of God' in Paul had been largely shaped by the Reformation tradition. Käsemann argued that in some passages, at least, the phrase should be understood as a subjective genitive characterizing God's own nature and activity, rather than as a righteousness bestowed on men and women. In Jewish thought, God's righteousness is his integrity, his faithfulness to the covenant, his justice; it is demonstrated in putting things right, and is therefore revealed in both salvation

---

[21] One wonders whether, in saying that 'Christ became for us righteousness', Paul had in mind the words of Deut 6:25, where the *Hebrew* reads: 'It shall be to us righteousness if we diligently obey this whole commandment'. In contrast to 'our' righteousness, Christians now have Christ: no wonder, then, that boasting is excluded (1 Cor 1:29, 31). There is an interesting parallel to 1 Cor 1:30 in 1QS 10:11: 'To God I shall say "my righteousness"'. God is here seen as the judge who deals justly and mercifully with his servants, and is praised for his salvation.

and judgement. We should remember that 'δικαιοσύνη θεοῦ is for Paul, as it is for the Old Testament and Judaism in general, a phrase expressing divine activity'.[22] This meaning is clear in Rom 1:17; 3:5, 21–26, in all of which God's righteousness is revealed in salvation or (Rom 3:5) judgement, while in 1 Cor 1:30, 'it appears as the direct manifestation of the Christ'.[23] Käsemann concluded that in 2 Cor 5:21, God's righteousness becomes manifested on earth in 'those who live under the eschatological justice of God'.[24] Bultmann disputed Käsemann's interpretation, saying that it was unnecessary to hold that a phrase had the same meaning in every case.[25] This is certainly true – but the meaning elsewhere may nevertheless be a helpful guide![26] Not surprisingly, Bultmann understood the phrase here to mean that we are 'justified' by God. I wonder, however, whether Käsemann's suggestion has not pointed us to the key to understanding why Paul used this particular phrase here. Elsewhere, it seems clear from the context that for Paul, δικαιοσύνη Θεοῦ does indeed refer primarily to God's activity in setting things to rights. Even in Rom 10:3 and Phil 3:9, where God's righteousness stands in contrast to 'human righteousness', it is plain that his righteousness is manifested in the gospel (Rom 10:4; Phil 3:8–10). Is there anything in the context of 2 Cor 5:21, therefore, to suggest that when Paul uses the phrase there, he perhaps means that 'we' are in some sense partakers in this divine activity?

In looking at the previous two summaries of the gospel (2 Cor 5:14–15, 18–19) we suggested that Paul's purpose in quoting them was to apply them, in particular, to his own ministry. Is he perhaps doing something similar here? Has he once again chosen language that is particularly apposite to his understanding of his ministry? The context suggests that this is so. Already, in the first few chapters of 2 Corinthians, he has spelt out the way in which his own suffering has brought consolation to the Corinthians: 'Death is at work in us, but life in you' (4:12). Following 2 Cor 5:21 he continues 'Working together

---

[22] Ernst Käsemann, '"The Righteousness of God" in Paul', in *New Testament Questions of Today*, trans. W.J. Montague and Wilfred F. Bunge (London: SCM Press, 1969), 168–182. S. Lyonnet also argued that 'it is not so much a question of a divine attribute as of the divine activity which works the restoration of Israel'; see 'Pauline Soteriology', in *Introduction to the New Testament,* eds. A. Robert and André Feuillet (New York: Desclée, 1965), 834. See also Peter Stuhlmacher, *Gerechtigkeit Gottes bei Paulus,* FRLANT 87 (Göttingen: Vandenhoeck & Ruprecht, 1965), 74–78; Karl Kertelge, '*Rechtfertigung*' *bei Paulus* (Münster: Aschendorff, 1967), 99–107.

[23] Käsemann, '"The Righteousness of God" in Paul', 173.

[24] Käsemann, '"The Righteousness of God" in Paul', 181.

[25] Rudolf Bultmann, 'ΔΙΚΑΙΟΣΥΝΗ ΘΕΟΥ', *JBL* 83 (1964): 12–16. For further discussion of the phrase, see R. Bieringer, 'Sünde und Gerechtigkeit Gottes in 2 Korinther 5,21', in *Studies on 2 Corinthians,* eds. R. Bieringer and J. Lambrecht (Leuven: Peeters, 1994), 461–513.

[26] In an additional note to the 1969 reprint of his essay, Käsemann denies that he was assuming that the concept 'must have the same meaning throughout the Pauline corpus'. Käsemann, '"The Righteousness of God" in Paul', 168 (footnote).

with [Christ], we entreat you not to receive the grace of God in vain' (6:1). He has moved here from the general to the particular: picking up the verb παρακαλέω, used in v. 20, where the audience was not specified, he now addresses the Corinthians. 'Now is the day of salvation', he declares (v. 2) – they must not lose what they have been given! It is fear that they might do so that explains why he is so anxious lest they reject his ministry (6:3). Spelling out what this ministry has cost him, and the gifts that he has needed to exercise it, he declares that he has ministered 'in the power of God, with the weapons of righteousness in his right and left hands' (6:7).

In the exercise of his ministry, then, Paul demonstrates the power of God, even though he is enduring weakness and affliction. This experience reflects the paradox seen in Christ, who suffered weakness and shame, but who is the source of power and righteousness (1 Cor 1:23–25, 30). This is an idea that he will expound in 2 Cor 13:3–4:

> Christ was crucified because of weakness
> But he lives because of God's power
> So we are weak in him
> But live with him – towards you – because of God's power.[27]

The weapons of righteousness wielded by Paul are of course also supplied by God. The true minister of God, working in the power of God, embodies the gospel – the dying and rising of Christ – and so is himself an instrument of righteousness. So it is, in 6:10, that Paul claims that by sharing in the extraordinary paradox of Christ's incarnation, death and resurrection – which means that though he is dying, yet he is alive (v. 9) – he is able, though poor, to make others rich (6:10), thus sharing in the mission of Christ himself (8:9).

Although both Bultmann and Barrett rejected Käsemann's understanding of the phrase δικαιοσύνη Θεοῦ in 2 Cor 5:21, it was Bultmann himself – quoted approvingly by Barrett[28] – who summed up most clearly what I am suggesting is conveyed by understanding δικαιοσύνη Θεοῦ in an active, rather than a passive, sense. I use Barrett's translation: 'With the cross, God instituted the office of reconciliation, the word of reconciliation (2 Cor v. 18 ff.); in other words, the preaching itself also belongs to the event of salvation. ... in it Christ is encountered, God's own word ... is encountered: "So we act for Christ, while God at the same time preaches through our mouth"'.[29] And as Paul reminds us in Rom 1:16–17, it is in the gospel, which is the power of God, working towards salvation, that the righteousness of God is revealed. Should we be

---

[27] The repetition of 'God's power' suggests that Paul is anxious to emphasize here the fact that any power he exerts is not his own.

[28] Barrett, *2 Corinthians,* 178–179.

[29] Rudolf Bultmann, 'Jesus und Paulus', in *Exegetica,* ed. Erich Dinkler (Tübingen: Mohr Siebeck, 1967), 228.

surprised, then, if the apostle whose manner of life – as well as his preaching – is conformed to the gospel, and *in* whom the power of God is at work, has become 'the righteousness of God'? This is what it means for Paul 'to live for Christ', not himself, and to be an 'ambassador for Christ', entrusted with 'the message of reconciliation'. Could this explain why, in this third summary of the gospel, he uses the language he does?

Nevertheless, it is 'we' who become the righteousness of God, and that righteousness should therefore be revealed in the lives of *all* believers, not just those of the apostles. If Christ is the source of 'righteousness and sanctification' (1 Cor 1:30), then those who, in him, become what he is, should also embody righteousness and sanctification. Perhaps this explains why Paul goes on, in 6:14–7:1, to urge Christians to live holy lives: righteousness and lawlessness cannot be partners,[30] any more than can Christ and Beliar. Although this passage is often regarded as an intrusion into 2 Corinthians (in spite of the lack of textual evidence to support this view), it is certainly appropriate for Paul to remind his readers that righteousness is incompatible with idolatry and immorality.[31] Being the righteousness of God must mean being like him, since he is their God and they are his people (6:16). *Being* righteousness implies living righteously.

The passage's relevance to the theme of the letter becomes clearer when we recall that Paul has described the Corinthians as his letter of recommendation (3:2): what they are validates both his ministry and his gospel.[32] If the righteousness of God is revealed in the gospel and in the life of the apostle, it must be revealed also in the faith and lives of those who respond to the gospel – and that means that what they are and do will be the means of witnessing to the gospel. Paul is not demanding that Christians withdraw from the world – how could he, when he did not do so himself? What he does insist is that those who are called to be channels of righteousness and light must not compromise with the dubious morality of their neighbours, but cleanse themselves and 'make holiness perfect' (2 Cor 7:1; cf. 1 Cor 1:30). God himself will then live among them, and they will be his temple and his holy people. God's righteousness will be seen in them.

Paul's appeal to the Corinthians in chapters 8–9 can also be seen as a logical continuation from the conviction that Christians are agents of righteousness. This section begins with a reminder that the Macedonians have longed to share in Paul's ministry to the saints (8:4) and have done so by contributing

---

[30] Cf. Rom 8:19, where 'slaves of lawlessness' are contrasted with 'slaves of righteousness', owing allegiance to different masters.

[31] So Heinz-Dietrich Wendland, *Die Briefe an der Korinther*, 7th ed. (Göttingen: Vandenhoeck & Ruprecht, 1954), 187: 'Wer zur Gerechtigkeit geworden ist (5,21), kann nichts mehr mit der Ungerechtigkeit zu tun haben'.

[32] Thrall, *2 Corinthians*, 472.

to his collection. Paul then urges the Corinthians, also, to share in every kind of good work. Since God's righteousness abides forever, he will increase the yield of *their* righteousness (9:8–10): once again, we see the link between God's righteousness and that of Christians – and this righteousness is demonstrated in bringing assistance to those in need. It is certainly no accident that the key appeal in this section is made on the basis of another of Paul's 'interchange' statements: 'you know the grace of our Lord Jesus Christ, that – being rich – he became poor for your sake, in order that you, by his poverty, might become rich' (8:9). The Corinthians, too, must in their turn bring riches to others. By doing so, they will be sharing in Paul's ministry, and God's saving power will work through them.

In 2 Cor 5:14–21, Paul has given us three summaries of the gospel. I have suggested that the language he uses is chosen in order to draw out the particular relevance of the gospel for his own ministry. Nevertheless, the summaries speak of a universal salvation, and the experience Paul describes is shared by others – or should be! Christ died for *all*, so that *all* might live for him,[33] and living for him means offering the message of reconciliation to others and serving as instruments of God's righteousness. Christ became sin for *us*, in order that *we* might become the righteousness of God, and that 'we' can hardly be exclusive! The new creation embraces *all* who are in Christ. Becoming God's righteousness is not just a matter of being acquitted in God's court or of sharing Christ's status before God. If God's righteousness is a restorative power, bringing life and reconciliation, then those who 'become righteousness' will be the means of manifesting that power in the world. The 'we' in v. 21b, which has particular significance for Paul's own understanding of discipleship and ministry, becomes an invitation to others to share in the divine activity. What Christ is to us – righteousness, wisdom, sanctification, redemption – Christians must now be to the world.

---

[33] Cf. Rom 6:13, where Paul urges his readers to offer themselves no longer to sin, as instruments of wickedness, but to God, as instruments of righteousness.

29. Another Look at πίστις Χριστοῦ*

For Jan Lambrecht, on his 85th birthday

On the last occasion that I tackled the problem of the meaning of the phrase πίστις Χριστοῦ, I argued that the question of its translation 'cannot be settled on the basis of appeals to grammatical construction alone. This issue can be settled only by exegesis'.[1] In support of this view I might well have appealed, though I did not, to James Hope Moulton, who, writing in his famous *Prolegomena* on the application of the labels 'subjective' and 'objective' to any genitive, commented that 'It is as well to remember that in Greek this question is entirely one of exegesis, not of grammar'.[2]

Since my original lecture was delivered, a great deal more has been written about the grammatical complexities surrounding the phrase, but – not surprisingly – we seem to be no nearer to any definite conclusion. The appeal to grammar has, in effect, run into the sand. Meanwhile, it is clear that the very different interpretations given to Paul's use of the phrase continue to be influenced by exegetes' very different presuppositions. In the words of one recent contributor to the discussion: 'It is theology, not grammar, that continues to drive the debate'.[3]

One thing is certain: this debate cannot be ignored. As recently as 1975, Charles Cranfield dismissed in a brief footnote the suggestion that πίστις Χριστοῦ should be understood as a subjective genitive,[4] but by 1998 he felt obliged to spell out the reasons as to *why* he believed that the proposal was 'unconvincing'.[5] One of the reasons that the debate has sparked interest and continues to excite some Pauline scholars – though most of them, it has to

---

* Originally delivered at a seminar in honour of Jan Lambrecht's birthday held in Leuven, 14th October 2011.

[1] Morna D. Hooker, 'Πίστις Χριστοῦ', *NTS* 35 (1989), 321.

[2] James Hope Moulton, *Prolegomena,* vol. 1 of *A Grammar of New Testament Greek* (Edinburgh: T&T Clark, 1908), 72.

[3] Debbie Hunn, 'Debating the Faithfulness of Jesus Christ in Twentieth-Century Scholarship', in *The Faith of Jesus Christ: Exegetical, Biblical, and Theological Studies,* eds. Michael F. Bird and Preston M. Sprinkle (Milton Keynes: Paternoster, 2009), 26.

[4] C. E. B. Cranfield, *A Critical and Exegetical Commentary on the Epistle to the Romans,* vol. 1, ICC (Edinburgh: T&T Clark, 1975), 203.

[5] C. E. B. Cranfield, 'On the Πίστις Χριστοῦ Question', in *On Romans and Other New Testament Essays* (Edinburgh: T&T Clark, 1998), 81–97.

be said, are located on the other side of the Atlantic – is, indeed, its relevance to theology. 'The πίστις Χριστοῦ debate', it has been said, 'involves a conflict over the fundamental shape of Paul's theology'.[6] It is no accident that Richard Hays, whose book *The Faith of Jesus Christ* was largely responsible for bringing the whole question to scholars' attention at the end of the twentieth century,[7] titled a paper in which he defended his views, delivered to a meeting of the SBL in America in 1991, 'Πίστις and Pauline Christology: What is at Stake?'[8] In answer to his own question, he listed five issues: these concerned the relation between Christology and soteriology in Pauline theology; the humanity of Jesus; the tension between individual religious experience and the corporate nature of salvation; ethics; and the significance of the phrase 'the righteousness of God'.

It is clear that the meaning we give to the phrase πίστις Χριστοῦ influences the way we interpret the Pauline epistles. At the same time, however, our understanding of the epistles determines the way we interpret the phrase πίστις Χριστοῦ, since the stance we take on the issues that Hays lists as crucial influences our exegesis of the texts. We are locked firmly into the so-called hermeneutical circle.

1. Presuppositions

It is relatively easy to expose the presuppositions of others, not always so easy to analyse our own. The Greek phrase πίστις Χριστοῦ is ambiguous and can be translated either as 'Christ's faith'; or as 'faith in him' – though to English ears, at least, if we leave other considerations aside, the former seems more natural. The word πίστις itself is ambiguous, since it can mean not only 'faith', but 'faithfulness' – a meaning which seems to be common in the LXX. But 'faith' can also signify '*what* one believes', and thus mean something closer to the English word 'belief', which normally conveys the notion of 'belief that', rather than 'belief in'. And since English tends to have many synonyms, we can also translate πίστις by 'trust' or 'trustworthiness' – and the word 'trust' conveys well the notion of utter reliance on God – a reliance that is, of course, founded on the belief that he is trustworthy, and that he can be relied on to save his people. This problem of translation is not, of course, confined to English.

---

[6] Benjamin Myers, 'From Faithfulness to Faith in the Theology of Karl Barth', in *Faith of Jesus Christ*, eds. Bird and Sprinkle, 291.

[7] Richard B. Hays, *The Faith of Jesus Christ: An Investigation of the Narrative Substructure of Galatians 3:1–4:11*, SBL Dissertation Series 56 (Chico, CA: Scholars Press, 1983).

[8] Published as an appendix to *The Faith of Jesus Christ: An Investigation of the Narrative Substructure of Galatians 3:1–4:11*, 2nd ed. (Grand Rapids; Cambridge: William B. Eerdmans, 2002), 272–297.

The ambiguity of the Greek was carried over into the Latin and other early versions of the New Testament. Was it perhaps because there appeared to the translators to be no problem in comprehending Paul's meaning? But if there was in fact no problem, was that because the phrase was obviously objective, or because it was clearly subjective? Or was it perhaps because the distinction was meaningless, since the phrase could convey both meanings simultaneously? For all their definitions, the grammarians warn us against being over precise. 'It is ... important', writes Nigel Turner, 'not to sacrifice fullness of interpretation to an over precise analysis of syntax. There is no reason why a gen[itive] in the author's mind may not have been both subjective and objective'.[9]

We might expect the comments of the fathers to help us here, but – alas! – their comments seem to be as ambiguous as Paul's own writings, so it is hardly surprising if modern scholars interpret their evidence in diametrically opposite ways.[10] In fact, there is remarkably little evidence as to how they understood the phrase: were they, too, unaware of any problem? Did the phrase appear to them to be transparently clear? Where they do offer clear comments, these tend to favour the view that they understood Paul to be thinking of the objective genitive.[11] Thus Athanasius, commenting on Hebrews 3:2, rejects the Arian interpretation of that verse by insisting that the word πιστόν here means that Christ was one who should be believed, and that it does *not* mean that he himself had faith. Since this concerns the interpretation of Hebrews, it does not, of course, preclude the notion that *Paul* might have referred to Christ's own trust or trustworthiness. Nevertheless, for Athanasius the real debate concerned the humanity and divinity of Christ, and the suggestion that Christ had faith in God implied that he was merely human. The author of Hebrews, then, must be speaking of Christ's trustworthiness, and not of his trust in God.[12]

Athanasius' doctrinal assumptions are clear, and dictate his exegesis of the text. Later, we find Augustine, commenting on Romans 3:22, insisting

---

[9] Nigel Turner, *Syntax*, vol. 3 of James Hope Moulton, *A Grammar of New Testament Greek* (Edinburgh: T&T Clark, 1963), 210. Cf. also F. Blass and A. Debrunner, *A Greek Grammar of the New Testament and Other Early Christian Literature*, trans. Robert W. Funk (Cambridge: Cambridge University Press, 1961), § 163.

[10] Ian G. Wallis, *The Faith of Jesus Christ in Early Christian Traditions*, SNTSMS 84 (Cambridge: Cambridge University Press, 1995), finds evidence that several of the fathers interpreted Paul as teaching that believers share the faith of Christ. Roy A. Harrisville, III, 'ΠΙΣΤΙΣ ΧΡΙΣΤΟΥ: Witness of the Fathers', *NT* 36 (1994): 233–241, and Mark W. Elliott, 'Πίστις Χριστοῦ in the Church Fathers and Beyond', in *Faith of Jesus Christ*, eds. Bird and Sprinkle, 277–289, both argue the opposite.

[11] R. Barry Matlock, 'Saving Faith: The Rhetoric and Semantics of πίστις in Paul', in *Faith of Jesus Christ*, eds. Bird and Sprinkle, 87.

[12] Athanasius, *Orationes contra Arianos* 2.6.9.

that Paul cannot mean 'the faith with which he himself believes', since faith is a quality of man,[13] and later still we find Thomas Aquinas arguing, on the basis of Hebrews 11:1, that 'where divine reality is not hidden there is no point in faith. But from the moment of conception Christ had the full vision of the very being of God. ... Therefore he could not have had faith'.[14] For Athanasius, Augustine, and Aquinas, then, their exegesis of the text is driven by their presuppositions regarding Christ's divinity and humanity. Undoubtedly their beliefs were based on their reading of the text, but it is clear that those same beliefs influenced the way in which they read the text. Their assumptions clash totally with the convictions of those modern scholars for whom 'Christ's faith' is seen not simply as a necessary part of his humanity, but as the distinctive mark of the one human being who was truly what man was intended by God to be.

The ambiguity in the Greek phrase is reflected in Erasmus' literal Latin translation and reappears in the first English translations of the New Testament. The King James Bible, following Tyndale, translated it literally as 'the faith of Christ'. In English, this would most naturally mean 'Christ's faith'. Was that how the translators understood it? It seems more likely that this is simply an example of their tendency to be overliteral in their translation. Certainly later English commentators, such as John Wesley in his *Notes on the New Testament*, understood the phrase to refer to our faith in Christ. But Wesley was, of course, like other English exegetes, strongly influenced by Martin Luther, and Luther was the first to make the 'objective' meaning abundantly clear by translating the phrase 'der Glaube an Jesum Christum'. Luther's doctrinal assumptions are here plain to see. Rightly observing that in all the contexts where the phrase is used, Paul is talking about Christians' belief in/faith in/trust in Christ, he read this same meaning into the phrase πίστις Χριστοῦ. But was he right to do so?

Luther's understanding of the phrase dominated Protestant exegesis for the next four centuries: Paul's gospel was understood to be 'justification by faith', and πίστις Χριστοῦ was interpreted as meaning 'faith in Christ'. God had offered a means of reconciliation in the death of his Son, and all that was required of men and women was faith. When Paul uses the phrase ἐκ/διὰ πίστεως Χριστοῦ, therefore, it is to emphasize the contrast between the righteousness imputed to men and women on the basis of faith and the pseudo-righteousness which relies on the works of the Law. Catholic commentators, too, seem to have interpreted the phrase in a similar way, though

---

[13] Augustine, *De spiritu et littera* 9 (CSEL 60, 167); *St Augustine: On the Spirit and the Letter*, trans. W.J. Sparrow Simpson (London: SPCK, 1925), §15.

[14] Aquinas, *Summa Theologiae* 3a, q.7, a.3.

their motives are less obvious; probably they were following tradition, or thought, like Aquinas, that it was inappropriate to attribute faith to Christ.

2. Challenges to the Tradition

An interesting exception to the common view was expressed by the English poet Samuel Taylor Coleridge at the beginning of the nineteenth century. In a recent article J. Gerald Janzen has drawn attention to Coleridge's annotation on Christian writers, in which he refers to Christ's faith.[15] Janzen describes him as a 'solid British antecedent' to his own views,[16] since in commenting on saving faith Coleridge writes that 'even this Faith (see Gal. 2:20) is not ours but the Faith of the Son of God in us'.[17] Perhaps because Coleridge was commenting on later Christian texts rather than the Pauline epistles themselves, however, I have not seen his interpretation referred to elsewhere.

It seems to have been Johannes Haussleiter who set in motion the modern movement that has challenged the traditional view. In 1891, he argued that when Paul wrote about πίστις Ἰησοῦ, he was referring to the faith which Jesus himself maintained in God, even in the face of crucifixion.[18] Haussleiter was followed, among others, by Gerhard Kittel,[19] but an alternative solution was suggested by Adolf Deissmann, who proposed that the phrase represented 'a special type of genitive, which might be called the "genitive of fellowship", or the "mystical genitive", because it indicates mystical fellowship with Christ'.[20] We may perhaps be concerned by Deissmann's appeal here to 'a special type of genitive' – although grammarians do suggest far more options than the simple 'objective' and 'subjective' genitives. What is worthy of note, however, is first that Deissmann is thinking in terms of fellowship with the spiritual Christ, and not of the faith of the earthly Jesus;[21] secondly, that he approaches the problem with the conviction that, for Paul, faith is 'faith "in" Christ, that is to say, faith is something which is accomplished in union of life with the spiritual Christ'.[22] It is this conviction that determines his exegesis, and it is an idea that will be taken up by later commentators.

---

[15] J. Gerald Janzen, 'Coleridge and *Pistis Christou*', *ExpTim* 107 (1996): 265–268.
[16] Janzen, 'Coleridge and *Pistis Christou*', 268.
[17] Janzen, 'Coleridge and *Pistis Christou*', 266.
[18] Johannes Haussleiter, *Der Glaube Jesu Christi und der christliche Glaube: Ein Beitrag zur Erklärung des Römerbriefes* (Erlangen: Deichert, 1891).
[19] Gerhard Kittel, 'Πίστις Ἰησοῦ Χριστοῦ bei Paulus', *TSK* 79 (1906): 419–436.
[20] Adolf Deissmann, *St. Paul: A Study in Social and Religious History*, trans. William E. Wilson (London: Hodder & Stoughton, 1926), 162–163.
[21] Contrast Kittel, 'Πίστις Ἰησοῦ Χριστοῦ', 426.
[22] Deissmann, *St. Paul*, 262.

The notion that πίστις Χριστοῦ should be understood as a subjective genitive re-emerged in the English-speaking world in the 1950s. A.G. Hebert[23] and Thomas Torrance[24] both appealed to the equivalence between the Hebrew אמונה and the Greek πίστις, and so interpreted πίστις Χριστοῦ as 'the faithfulness of God manifested in Christ's human faithfulness'. Torrance's interpretation was built on that of Karl Barth, who had understood διὰ πίστεως Ἰησοῦ Χριστοῦ to mean 'through God's faithfulness in Jesus Christ'.[25] But Hebert's and Torrance's arguments were demolished by James Barr, who attacked their assumption that πίστις would convey a fundamentally Hebrew meaning.[26] Others rejected their interpretation for different reasons. Professor Charlie Moule, my predecessor at Cambridge, for example, protested that it reduced Paul's emphasis on human response to God's action in Christ.[27] But one might with more justification protest that to understand πίστις Χριστοῦ as 'our faith in Christ' reduces emphasis on the action of God itself! If, for example, we translate Galatians 2:16 as 'we know that a person is justified, not by the works of the Law but by faith in Jesus Christ; and we have come to believe in Christ Jesus, so that we might be justified by faith in Christ', we have no fewer than three references to our faith in Christ, and none at all to what God has done! Is Moule's objection not a case of the tail wagging the dog – the doctrine of justification by faith determining the exegesis of the text?

One scholar who did advocate the meaning 'the faith of Christ' at length was Pierre Vallotton, whose book *Le Foi de Christ* seems to have made little impact on the scholarly world.[28] I was interested to discover that the copy of his book that I consulted in the Cambridge University Library had clearly once belonged to Charlie Moule, since the margins are full of indignant comments and protests in Charlie's own unmistakable hand.

At the end of the twentieth century, the centre of discussion moved to the United States, with scholars such as George Howard[29] and Luke Timothy Johnson[30] arguing for the subjective genitive, but it was Richard Hays who argued the case most forcibly in his doctoral dissertation,[31] and who has been

---

[23] A.G. Herbert, '"Faithfulness" and "Faith"', *Theology* 58 (1955): 373–379.
[24] Thomas F. Torrance, 'One Aspect of the Biblical Conception of Faith', *ExpTim* 68 (1957): 111–114.
[25] Karl Barth, *The Epistle to the Romans*, trans. E.C. Hoskyns (Oxford: Oxford University Press, 1933), *in loc*.
[26] James Barr, *The Semantics of Biblical Language* (Oxford: Oxford University Press, 1961), 161–205.
[27] C.F.D. Moule, 'The Biblical Conception of "Faith"', *ExpTim* 68 (1957): 157.
[28] Pierre Valloton, *Le Christ et la foi: Etude de théologie biblique* (Geneva: Labor & Fides, 1960).
[29] George F. Howard, 'The "Faith of Christ"', *ExpTim* 85 (1974): 212–215; George F. Howard, 'Faith of Christ', in *The Anchor Bible Dictionary*, vol. 2, ed. D.N. Freedman (New Haven: Yale University Press, 2008), 758–760.
[30] Luke Timothy Johnson, 'Romans 3:21–26 and the Faith of Jesus', *CBQ* 44 (1982): 77–90.
[31] Hays, *The Faith of Jesus Christ*.

its champion ever since. His thesis as a whole dealt with 'The narrative substructure of Galatians 3:1–4:11' and demonstrated the importance of interpreting the phrase in the context of Paul's argument, not in isolation. Hays' book led to a flurry of articles, and to the debate at the 1991 SBL meeting, at which Hays confronted James Dunn, a staunch supporter of the traditional 'Lutheran' view. But that debate by no means settled the matter, and proponents of both views continue to argue their cases with vigour. The publication of a collection of seventeen new essays entitled *The Faith of Jesus Christ: Exegetical, Biblical, and Theological Studies* two years ago demonstrates the continuing interest in the topic.[32]

3. A Way Forward?

Is there a way forward? If by that we mean 'Will everyone come to a common mind on this matter?' the answer must clearly be 'No'! Nevertheless, fashions in New Testament interpretation, as in everything else, do change, and it is certainly true that there is more sympathy with the so-called 'subjective' explanation than there was fifty years ago, when Charlie Moule was making his indignant annotations to Vallotton's book. Why? Is it simply due to the brilliance of arguments brought forward in its support – arguments that have persuaded many of its truth? But equally brilliant arguments have been made on the opposite side. Or is it perhaps because other changes have taken place? It seems to me that it is more likely to be due to the latter, and in particular to four changing emphases: 1. the stress on righteousness as belonging to God; 2. the realization that much of Paul's argument concerns God's dealings with Israel and the Gentiles rather than the salvation of individuals; 3. the growing recognition of the importance for Paul of the idea of participation in Christ; and 4. the recognition that for Paul the humanity of Christ is essential both to his christology and to his soteriology.

In searching for a way forward, we should perhaps begin by analysing what we mean – or rather what *Paul* meant – by the word πίστις. According to Liddell and Scott, the primary meaning of the noun is 'trust in others' or 'faith', and so 'trustworthiness'; the second is 'that which gives confidence', hence 'assurance' or 'proof'. Arndt-Gingrich, on the other hand, list first 'that which *causes* trust and faith' – i.e. 'faithfulness', or 'proof' – and *then* the active sense of 'trust, confidence, faith in', the reason being, no doubt, that it is God's faithfulness that is seen as being of primary importance. When Paul uses the word πίστις of God, then it clearly indicates God's trustworthiness or faithfulness. If we ask 'to what is he faithful?' then the answer must be 'to

---

[32] Hunn, 'Debating the Faithfulness of Jesus Christ'.

himself' – i.e. to his own nature. But when the word is used of *Christians*, then the primary meaning of the word is 'faith' or 'trust'. In this sense, the word indicates a relationship: Christians have faith in God or in Christ. The lexica's different definitions reflect what is in fact a hen-and-egg situation. Our trust/faith is founded in the trustworthiness/faithfulness of God, but those who trust in him become *like* him, trustworthy in their turn. Paul makes use of this idea in 2 Corinthians 1:15–22, where he appeals to the faithfulness of God in order to defend himself from accusations that he himself is *un*trustworthy.[33] Both as a member of God's holy people – no longer because he is a Jew, but because, like the Corinthians, he is 'in Christ' – and as an apostle (2 Cor 1:1–2), Paul is called to be holy as God is holy (Lev 11:45). It is no wonder, then, that he reflects the faithfulness of God himself.

The phrase πίστις Χριστοῦ is thus doubly ambiguous. Not only are we confronted by a choice between the subjective and the objective genitive – or whatever other kind of label we decide to use – but, if we choose the subjective genitive, we again have two possible translations. Might Paul be speaking of the faith of Christ or of his faithfulness? The former emphasizes his humanity – since as man, he trusted in God – while the latter can be understood as a sharing in the nature of God. But once again, this may be a false dichotomy, since the choice which confronts us may have been forced on us because of the problem of translating from one language to another. Could Paul perhaps be referring both to Christ's faith/trust in God *and* to his faithfulness/trustworthiness? If Christ was – as Paul claims – the one who was all that Adam was *not*, then we would expect him not only to trust completely in God, but also to reflect God's trustworthiness. For if, as Paul claims, Christ was 'the true Adam', then this was because he was 'the image of God', as he expresses it in 2 Corinthians 4:4, and thus reflected the glory – the nature – of God.

4. Paul's Argument in Romans

The precise meaning of a phrase can be understood, however, only when we look at the context in which it is found. Richard Hays subtitled his book 'The narrative substructure of Galatians 3:1–4:11'. Romans, too, has a narrative substructure, but the epistle is primarily an argument, and we need to trace it if we are to understand our phrase. The book's theme is 'the gospel (or good news) of God', good news which was announced beforehand in the scriptures, and which concerns God's Son, who was the physical descendant of David, but who was proclaimed Son of God in power by the resurrection

---

[33] Hooker, Πίστις Χριστοῦ, 334–335.

of the dead (1:1–4). In what follows Paul sets out his understanding of this gospel, and how it is that it is intended for Gentiles as well as Jews, and in the rest of this paper I will look at how that argument may throw light on our problem.

Paul first sets out his own mission: it is to bring about the obedience of faith among all the Gentiles. Once again, we have a phrase that can be translated in many ways, and it has been suggested that the words 'faith' and 'obedience' are synonymous.[34] Certainly it seems that there is for Paul a close link between the two, and this corresponds with the Jewish conviction that God had called Israel to trust/have faith in him as their only God, and to obey his Law – in other words, what E.P. Sanders famously described as 'covenantal nomism'. Paul's expression 'obedience of faith' neatly sums up this idea, but hints also at a contrast between an obedience that is grounded in faith, and one that is defined by the Law. At the end of the letter, Paul again speaks of his work in winning obedience from the Gentiles,[35] thus framing the epistle with statements regarding his mission. Paul's mission includes the Christians in Rome, since they, too, are apparently Gentiles (1:6) – Gentiles who have been called to belong to Jesus Christ, and therefore called also to be saints (v. 7). This means that, like Israel of old, they have been called to be holy as God is holy, members of God's people – all this by virtue of the fact that they belong to Jesus Christ.

In 1:9 Paul refers once again to the fact that the gospel he preaches is about God's Son. This is the third time that Paul has spoken of Christ as God's Son, suggesting that it is a key term in his argument.

Romans 1:16–17 bring us another definition of the gospel. It is, we now learn, the power of God to bring salvation for all who believe – for the Jews first, and then Greeks – since in it, the righteousness of God is revealed. Others have pointed out that Paul's language here echoes that of Psalm 98, which speaks of God making known his salvation in the sight of the nations and revealing his righteousness to the house of Israel[36] – though according to Paul's gospel, salvation is no longer confined to the house of Israel. There seem to be clear echoes of the LXX in the words σωτηρία, δικαιοσύνη and ἀποκαλύπτεται. What has not been pointed out, however, is that the Psalmist goes on to say that God has remembered his steadfast love and his faithfulness to Israel; the LXX translates these terms with ἔλεος and ἀλήθεια, mercy

---

[34] See e.g. Cranfield, *Romans, I*, 66–67.
[35] Rom 15:18. See also 16:26, which uses the phrase 'the obedience of faith', though the final three verses may be a later addition to the letter.
[36] Most recently Douglas A. Campbell, 'An Echo of Scripture in Paul and its Implications', in *The Word Leaps the Gap: Essays on Scripture and Theology in Honor of Richard B. Hays*, eds. J. Ross Wagner, C. Kavin Rowe and A. Katherine Grieb (Grand Rapids; Cambridge: William B. Eerdmans, 2008), 367–391. The echo is noted already by NA[26].

and truth, but the Hebrew uses חסד and אמונה. Is Paul remembering the Hebrew here? If so, this could perhaps explain why he goes on to say that God's righteousness is revealed ἐκ πίστεως, so giving him a link to Habakkuk 2:4. God has remembered his faithfulness, and the revelation of his δικαιοσύνη springs from his πίστις. As we read on through Romans, we find that God's faithfulness is one of Paul's themes: the gospel is the demonstration of God's faithfulness to his promises (1:2).

It would seem, then, that the phrase ἐκ πίστεως in Romans 1:17a refers to God's faithfulness. But who is it who makes the answering response of faith referred to in the phrase εἰς πίστιν? Is it Christ, or Christian believers? Or is it perhaps both? Paul helpfully explains his meaning by quoting Habakkuk 2:4, but succeeds only in leaving the commentators more confused. Because God reveals his δικαιοσύνη, springing from his own faithfulness, to those who have faith, 'the one who is righteous, on the basis of faith, will live'. But who is this righteous one? Once again, it could be either Christ or the Christian. And to whose faith (or faithfulness) does *this* use of the phrase ἐκ πίστεως refer? Since the Habakkuk quotation picks up the phrase that Paul has just used, we would expect him to be interpreting it – as the LXX certainly does – to mean *God's* faithfulness. If so, then the righteous one lives because of God's faithfulness. Or does Paul understand it to refer to the faith/trust which the righteous one has in God? If so, then Paul could be thinking either of Christ or the Christian. But we have not yet finished with the possible permutations, since the phrase ἐκ πίστεως can be taken *either* with ὁ δίκαιος *or* with ζήσεται. Is Paul interpreting Habakkuk to mean that the one who is righteous by faith will live? Or that the one who is righteous will live by faith?

Once again, one wonders whether the variety of meanings is not a clue to the answer to our problem. Do we have to choose between them? First, does ἐκ πίστεως belong to ὁ δίκαιος *or* to ζήσεται? Later on, Paul spells out the fact that righteousness leads to life (Rom 5:17, 21). Indeed, so close is the relationship between them that in v. 18 he uses the expression δικαίωσις ζωῆς. The unusual word δικαίωσις occurs elsewhere only in 4:25, where Christ's resurrection means that we are made righteous. Faith in the one who raised Jesus to life leads to our being-made-righteous (4:25), and now (5:18), our being made righteous leads to life – a life which, as Paul explains in Galatians 2:20, is lived by faith in Christ, i.e. by union with him. If the relationship between righteousness, faith and life is so close, is it possible that Paul is here deliberately leaving both possibilities open, and that the phrase ἐκ πίστεως can refer *either* to ὁ δίκαιος *or* to ζήσεται?[37]

---

[37] Francis Watson insists that we must choose between these two interpretations, and argues forcefully that the former is correct, on the basis that πίστις and δικαιο- words occur together

Secondly, if righteousness is revealed 'from faith to faith', as Paul claims in v. 17a, then the righteous one will certainly live because of *God's* faithfulness. But Paul is going to go on to show how, *true* to his promises, God 'rightwises' those who have faith. So their faith, too, is important! If we were to ask Paul, then, to whose faithfulness/faith does the ἐκ πίστεως of Habakkuk 2:4 refer – that of God or of the believer – he might have well replied 'both'! And what of Christ? Do we not expect, in this summary of the gospel, some reference to *him*? As we shall find when we turn to 3:21–26, God's righteousness was made plain *through Christ*. In 1:17b, then, is Paul perhaps thinking of *Christ's* faith/faithfulness? And if so, is he then interpreting Habakkuk 2:4 as a messianic text, as some have claimed?[38] It is not modern exegetes alone who read texts in the light of their beliefs! Paul certainly did so, and he may well have interpreted 'the Righteous One' as a messianic title.[39] Christ is referred to as 'the Righteous One' by Luke,[40] and Paul himself would certainly have thought of Christ as 'righteous', since he is the source of righteousness for others – an idea expressed vividly in 1 Corinthians 1:30, where he is described as 'righteousness', and in 2 Corinthians 5:21, where Paul tells the Corinthians that in Christ we become the righteousness of God. In Romans 3:10, Paul concludes his lengthy indictment of Jews and Gentiles with the statement that 'there is none righteous, no, not one', and in the subsequent contrast between Adam and Christ, it is through Adam's disobedience that many are condemned, through Christ's obedience that the 'many' are made righteous (5:19) and so find life (v. 21). Christ is the source of righteousness for the many.

How is this achieved? The answer lies in Paul's important opening salvo to his argument in chapter 6: 'Do you not know that you have been baptized into Christ's death?' His question is prompted by the ludicrous notion that Christians should sin in order to allow God to show them even more grace. For Paul, the idea is absurd, because Christians have died to one way of life and been raised to another – *in Christ*. Because *he* died to sin and lives to God, they too should be dead to sin and alive to God (vv. 10–14), since by dying and rising with Christ they are no longer 'in Adam' but 'in Christ'. They must therefore now present themselves to God as instruments of righteousness. What this means is explained in v. 16: 'Don't you know that if you present yourselves to someone as slaves to obey him, you are slaves of the one

---

frequently elsewhere. See 'By Faith (of Christ): An Exegetical Dilemma and its Scriptural Solution', in *The Faith of Jesus Christ*, eds. Bird and Sprinkle, 147–163.

[38] See e.g. Anthony Tyrrell Hanson, *Studies in Paul's Technique and Theology* (London: SPCK, 1974), 40–45; Douglas A. Campbell, 'Romans 1:17 – A *Crux Interpretum* for the ΠΙΣΤΙΣ ΧΡΙΣΤΟΥ Debate', *JBL* 113 (1994): 265–285.

[39] 1 Enoch 38:2; 53:6. The date of this section of 1 Enoch is notoriously difficult to establish.

[40] Acts 3:14; 7:52; 22:14. See also Jas 5:16.

whom you obey?' The question seems tautologous, but it is clearly designed to emphasize the point. Paul now explains that one can either be a slave of sin – which leads to death – or of obedience – which leads to righteousness. This third use of obey/obedience is extraordinary. The choice we *expect* Paul to offer the Romans is between being slaves of sin or of righteousness – leading to *life*. Instead, the opposite of 'sin' is not righteousness, but obedience! Why? Once again, Paul's purpose may be to emphasize his point, which is hammered home in the next verse: 'You, who were once slaves of sin, have become obedient from the heart to the form of teaching delivered to you; having been freed from sin, you have become slaves of righteousness'. The following verses then draw the contrast we expect. Sin leads to death, but righteousness to life.

Four references to obedience in two verses can hardly be accidental. They appear to be picking up what Paul said in 5:19 about *Christ's* obedience – the obedience that made many righteous. Now we realize that Christians share not only Christ's righteousness but also his obedience – or should do! Those who die and rise with him must present themselves to God as slaves of righteousness instead of sin – and that means being 'obedient to obedience'. To be in Christ means being obedient as he was obedient. We notice that the same link occurs in Philippians 2, where the famous Christ-passage in vv. 6–11, in which Paul reminds his readers how Christ was 'obedient to death', is followed in v. 12 by the words: 'Therefore, my beloved, as you have always obeyed me … work out your own salvation with fear and trembling, for it is God who is at work in you'. In obeying Paul, they are of course obeying Christ, since in Paul they have an example of what it means to live in conformity to the cross of Christ (3:17–18).

Paul's argument in Romans 5–6 uses the idea of obedience rather than faith, but it is clear that the language of 'obedience' and 'faith' overlap: both words express our relationship to God, and both lead to righteousness. Paul's emphasis on obedience here also picks up what he said in the opening verses of the epistle, where he defined his mission as being 'to bring about the obedience of faith among all the nations'. This 'obedience of faith' was precisely what God had required of Israel, whom he had originally called to be his holy people, and what that entailed had been set out in the Law. Now, however, it is those who are 'in Christ' who are obedient as Christ was obedient, and who present themselves to righteousness for sanctification as God's holy people. God's righteousness has been made manifest 'apart from Law', to those who have been baptized into Christ and who belong to him. It is time to turn to 3:21–26, where the crucial phrase πίστις Χριστοῦ occurs.

5. Romans 3:21–26

The first thing to note is that 3:21 picks up the statement in 1:17 that the gospel concerns the revelation of God's δικαιοσύνη. The intervening verses have spelt out the failure of all, Jew and Greek alike, to worship and obey God. Israel has proved unfaithful, but God himself has remained faithful (3:2), and man's unrighteousness has served to demonstrate God's righteousness. No one is righteous (3:10), and the Law has served only to make this plain. But now God's δικαιοσύνη has been made known *apart from Law*, though both Law and Prophets bear witness to it – as Paul indeed affirmed in the letter's opening sentence. It has been made known, Paul now explains, διὰ πίστεως Ἰησοῦ Χριστοῦ εἰς πάντας τοὺς πιστεύοντας. The last few words clearly refer to Christians: it is they who trust/believe; but what does Paul mean by the phrase διὰ πίστεως Ἰησοῦ Χριστοῦ? We expect Paul to tell us here *how* God's righteousness is revealed, and this phrase seems to provide the explanation. From the summary of the gospel in 1:2–4, and those still to come in 4:24–25, and 5:6–11, the answer is plain: he has acted *in Christ*. This suggests that Paul is referring here to Christ's own πίστις, rather than that of believers. God's righteousness is revealed *through Christ himself*, not in our response *to* him. '*Pistis Christou*', suggests Lou Martyn, 'arises in Paul's vocabulary as his way of reflecting the tradition's reference to Christ's deed of rectification'.[41] And if we ask why he should use the phrase in this particular context, the answer must be because here, as in Galatians 2–3 and Philippians 3, his concern is to show how God's righteousness is revealed *apart from the Law, in Christ*. The contrast between a righteousness based on the works of the Law and one based on faith requires a reference to what *God* has done. And what the Law was unable to do has been achieved through God sending his Son (8:3). We are saved, not by faith, but by grace *through* faith. That faith belongs primarily to Christ, but *it can be shared by those who are 'in him'*. That is why the righteousness given to those who are 'in Christ' (8:1) depends, as Habakkuk 2:4 and Genesis 15:6 (quoted in 4:3) make clear, on faith.

So if Paul is referring in 3:21–26 to *Christ's* πίστις, is it to his faith in God or to his faithfulness? Let us turn back once more to Romans 5:12–21. Here Paul does not simply compare Adam and Christ, but contrasts them, since the contest between Adam and Christ is not an equal one. In v. 15 he affirms that what took place in Christ was not like what happened in Adam, because in Christ we see the grace of God and the gift in grace of the one man Jesus Christ. In v. 16 he repeats this: the gift cannot be compared with what happened through Adam, because the act of grace led to acquittal. And in v. 17 he says virtually the same thing! Paul's syntax is confused, but his meaning

---

[41] J. Louis Martyn, *Galatians,* AB (New York: Doubleday, 1997), 270–271.

is plain: the result of one man's trespass was that death ruled because of that one man; how much more momentous, then, are the grace and the gift of righteousness which lead to life for those who receive them through the one man Jesus Christ. Three times over, Paul emphasizes that what has happened concerns *the action of God, in and through Christ.*

In Romans 5:15–17, then, the one man Christ is pitched against the one man Adam, and it is essential for Paul's argument that Christ is fully human. But at the same time, he makes it abundantly clear that, to use the language of 2 Corinthians 5:19, *God* was at work in Christ, reconciling the world to himself. In being obedient, Christ was all that man *should* be, but at the same time God himself was clearly at work. It is no accident that immediately before the Adam/Christ passage in Romans 5:12–21, Paul reminds his readers that *God's* love to us is seen in the fact that Christ died for us. Having been 'justified' by his death, we can be confident that we will be saved through Christ from wrath; having been reconciled to God through the death of his Son, we can be confident that we will be saved by his life. The language points forward, of course, to that of chapter 6. It is not simply 'by' his death and resurrection that we are reconciled and saved but 'in' them, by sharing *in* his death and resurrection.

So is Christ's πίστις in 3:22 his faith in God or a sharing in the faithfulness of God? Romans 5 suggests that the answer may be 'both'. The logic of 3:22 requires us to suppose that here, too, Paul is thinking of God's action in Christ, and in v. 24 he spells out what this action is. 'God set forth Christ Jesus as a ἱλαστήριον – a mercy seat – through faith/faithfulness, by his death'. The phrase 'by his death' – ἐν τῷ αὐτοῦ αἵματι – will be picked up in 5:9. But what does the phrase διὰ πίστεως here mean? This time there is no reference to either Christ or to the believer, but I am inclined to agree with those who have argued that the strange order of words suggests that Paul must be thinking once again of the πίστις of Christ.[42] Our redemption was achieved both through the action of God *and* through Christ's trust in him. The paragraph is rounded off with yet another use of the phrase, but this time it refers to 'the faith of Jesus' rather than that of Christ,[43] which suggests that Paul is referring here to *his* faith rather than ours.[44]

Another echo of previous chapters is the reference in Romans 5:10 to Jesus as 'God's Son'. Paul does not use this term often, but when he does, it seems to be important. We have noted already that it occurs three times in the first nine verses of the epistle. It will recur again five times in chapter 8. And here, in 5:10, we find it in what is essentially a summary of the gospel – a summary

---

[42] E.g. Johnson, 'Romans 3:21–26', 79–80.
[43] A few MSS and versions read Ἰησοῦ Χριστοῦ, but the evidence for this reading is very weak.
[44] Cf. Johnson, 'Romans 3:21–26', 80.

that reminds us of why Christ was uniquely qualified to be the one who dealt with the aftermath of Adam's sin. To describe someone as 'the son of so-and-so' was to argue that he had the characteristics of so-and-so. To be a true son meant not only to be obedient to one's father, but to be fully in accord with one's father's will and purposes. Such a son would trust his father and prove trustworthy.

For Paul, the gospel or 'good news' concerns God's Son, who was son of David according to the flesh, and was declared to be Son of God according to the Spirit of holiness by the resurrection from the dead (1:3–4). In 5:10 he spells out what this good news means for us: if we were reconciled to God through the death of his Son when we were enemies, how much more, having been reconciled, shall we be saved by his life. And in 8:3–4 he explains its significance in relation to the Law: what the Law could not do, because of the weakness of the flesh, God has done; sending his own Son in the likeness of sinful flesh, and to deal with sin, he has condemned sin in the flesh, in order that the requirement of the Law might be fulfilled in us, who live according to the spirit, and not according to the flesh. As Jan Lambrecht has argued, Paul's declaration that the requirement of the Law is fulfilled in us picks up his indignant denial in 3:31 of the suggestion that in maintaining that God's righteousness has been revealed apart from Law, διὰ πίστεως Χριστοῦ, he was overthrowing the Law. Professor Lambrecht has suggested further that in 8:4 'Paul delicately balanced two aspects of obedience, i.e., human behavior and divine grace'.[45] This delicate balance between human behaviour and divine grace is precisely what, we have argued, is present in what Paul says about *Christ*, both in Romans 5:12–21, and in the phrase πίστις Χριστοῦ, which conveys divine faithfulness as well as faith. But in 8:4, instead of being seen in Christ, this balance is reflected in those who are 'in Christ'. God sent his Son in our likeness, sharing our flesh; but he defeated sin, and enabled us to live according to the Spirit – the Spirit that raised him from the dead. And so, as Paul goes on to explain, we become children of God, using the very name for God used by Jesus himself (vv. 14–17). We are predestined to be conformed to the image of God's Son, sharing his glory (vv. 29, 21), because God gave up his own Son for us (v. 32). Those who are conformed to his image will certainly share his obedience and his faith. It is no accident that every occurrence of the phrase πίστις Χριστοῦ is found in a context which speaks of the faith of Christians, for through death and resurrection his faith becomes theirs.

God has revealed his righteousness in Christ, who became what we are – yet without sin – and so enabled us to become what he is. This theme permeates Paul's letters, and illumines the passages where the phrase πίστις

---

[45] Jan Lambrecht and Richard W. Thompson, *Justification by Faith: The Implications of Romans 3:27–31* (Wilmington, DE: Michael Glazier, 1989), 70.

Χριστοῦ is used. In Galatians 4:4–5, he tells us that God sent his Son, born of a woman, under the Law, in order that we might be set free from the Law and become God's sons. For Paul, this means that he himself has died to the Law, and that Christ now lives in him, since he lives because of the πίστις Χριστοῦ (2:20); it is not through the Law, but through the faith of Christ, in whom we have put our trust, that we are set right with God (2:16). The promise given on the basis of faith is fulfilled for those who are 'in Christ' and so Abraham's seed (3:6–18).

In Philippians 2:8, Paul tells us that Christ took our human form and was obedient even to death – and his subsequent vindication and exaltation mean that those who live in him live in hope of sharing his resurrection and being conformed to his glory (Phil 3:11, 21). Why? Because those who are 'in Christ' share the righteousness that comes through his πίστις (Phil 3:9). The close links between Philippians 2:6–11 and chapter 3 suggest that Paul is thinking here of Jesus' obedient trust in God.[46] In Romans, the obedience of God's Son leads him to share our death, and his subsequent vindication means that those who are 'in him' share his resurrection and life (Rom 4:25; 5:12–21). In him, they are called to obedience, and their destiny is to be conformed to the likeness of God's Son, and so to become God's children (8:29), for they have been 'called to belong to Jesus Christ ... called to be saints', called to offer 'the obedience of faith' (Rom 1:5–7). And all this happens because God has revealed his righteousness through Christ's πίστις (3:21–26).

In this paper I have had time only to begin the exploration of the relevance of the notion of Christ's πίστις to Paul's argument in Romans. Nevertheless I have, I hope, succeeded in showing why interpreting the phrase to refer primarily to Christ's trust in God fits so well into Paul's conviction that *in the one man Jesus Christ*, men and women are enabled to become what he is. But, of course, this inevitably demonstrates how a particular interpretation of Paul's thought governs our exegesis of the text.

So were Luther and his followers wrong? They were certainly not wrong to emphasize the role of faith. And as with the answers to our questions about the other phrases we have briefly considered, it may well be that the answer to the question 'Does this phrase refer to Christ's faith or ours'? may be 'Both'. Nevertheless, that faith/faithfulness is primarily that of Christ, and we share in it only because we are in him. Although all the passages where the phrase πίστις Χριστοῦ is used refer to our faith in Christ, it would seem that this faith is possible only because it is a sharing in his. In Christ, and through him, we are able to share his trust and obedience, and so become what God called his people to be.

---

[46] I explored these links in 'Philippians 2:6–11', in *Jesus und Paulus: Festschrift für W. G. Kümmel*, eds. E. Earle Ellis and E. Grasser (Göttingen: Vandenhoeck & Ruprecht, 1975), 151–164.

30. 2 Corinthians 5:1–10 in Context*

It is disheartening, to say the least, to discover that the passage assigned to one for interpretation is described by commentators as 'notoriously difficult',[1] or even as 'arguably the most difficult passage in the whole Pauline corpus'.[2] In view of the difficulties encountered elsewhere in the Pauline literature, comments such as these mean that one inevitably approaches these verses with considerable trepidation. Nor can any consideration of their meaning be confined to these verses alone, for they form one part of a much longer argument, itself a notoriously difficult section, and looking at them in isolation, as is sometimes done, is bound to distort them.

Since monographs continue to be written on these verses,[3] and the authors of multi-volume commentaries find it impossible to deal with all the issues,[4] it would obviously be foolish to attempt to analyse the passage in detail, or to seek a new interpretation of Paul's words. My purpose in this paper will therefore be to explore the extent to which the hope expressed in this passage corresponds with what Paul writes elsewhere.

The main issue that has been endlessly debated by commentators can be summed up in the question, 'Has Paul changed his mind?' In 1 Corinthians 15 his future hope is centred on the parousia, and it seems clear that he himself expects to be alive at the Lord's return. Although some Christians will have died before then, all alike will be 'changed in a flash' at his coming. Paul uses two images to describe this transformation: the first is that of resurrection – 'the dead will be raised imperishable' (v. 52), and the second that of being clothed – 'for this perishable body must be clothed with the imperishable, and the mortal with the immortal' (vv. 53 ff.). Both metaphors depend on what is the crucial central truth for Paul – that *the believer shares the experience of Christ*. Christians will be raised to life because Christ was raised; they will be 'made

---

* Paper delivered to the Pauline Ecumenical Colloquium in Rome, 2012.

[1] C.K. Barrett, *A Commentary on the Second Epistle to the Corinthians*, BNTC (London: A&C Black, 1973), 150. So also Fredrik Lindgård, *Paul's Line of Thought in 2 Corinthians 4:16–5:10*, WUNT 2/189 (Tübingen: Mohr Siebeck, 2005), 1.

[2] Nigel Watson, *The Second Epistle to the Corinthians* (London: Epworth, 1993), 49.

[3] E.g. Lindgård, *Line of Thought*. A survey of the interpretation of the passage from Calvin to 1973 was made by Friedrich Gustav Lang, *2. Korinther 5,1–10 in der neueren Forschung*, BGBE 16 (Tübingen: Mohr, 1973). The literature was already immense.

[4] See the comment by Margaret E. Thrall (in a two-volume commentary!), *A Critical and Exegetical Commentary on the Second Epistle to the Corinthians*, vol. 1, ICC (Edinburgh: T&T Clark, 1994), 397, regarding the difficulty of doing this.

alive in him' (vv. 20–23); they will be clothed with imperishability because they are to 'wear the likeness of the heavenly man' (v. 49).

Resurrection is said to take place 'at his coming' (v. 23), when 'we shall all be changed' (v. 51), dead and living alike. Since the focus in this discussion is on this future resurrection, nothing is said about the condition of the dead *between* their death and resurrection, but since 'all' are changed 'in a moment, in the twinkling of an eye' (v. 52), it is clear that Paul regards the dead – like the living – as 'perishable' and 'mortal', and so in need of drastic change; their situation appears to be no more favourable than that of the living – but this is not an issue with which Paul is here concerned.

In 2 Corinthians 5:1–10, however, the focus has shifted from the parousia to what will take place to Paul himself after death. Facing up to the possibility that he is likely to die before the Lord's return, Paul apparently expects his mortal body to be swallowed up by life at his death (5:1–5). Moreover, he now regards it as a positive personal advantage to be one of those whom the world would classify as 'dead'. He would rather, he declares, be 'away from the body and at home with the Lord' than 'at home in the body and away from the Lord' (vv. 6–9). This is strange language from one who expressed so strongly his joy in living with Christ and in Christ, but is perhaps explained by the image he uses in Phil 3:20, where he describes Christians as those who have their citizenship in heaven. However joyful his present experience of living in Christ, it is only a foretaste of a future reality, and to be 'at home' with Christ – 'in heaven' – will be even better.

In 1 Corinthians 15, then, Paul describes a sudden change that takes place at the parousia, whereas in 2 Cor 5:1–10 he depicts the culmination of a process which begins in this life, and is seemingly completed at death. There is an obvious tension between these two pictures. Is the lapse of time between the two letters sufficient to account for the change in outlook? Have recent events – such as his near-experience of death in Asia (2 Cor 1:8 ff.) changed Paul's perspective? That may well be true, though it is clear from 1 Cor 15:30–32, as well as from the long list of dangers in 2 Cor 11:23–29, that Paul had long been aware that his mission might end in premature death. Could it be, then, that 2 Corinthians 5 reflects a significant change in belief? The change in eschatological perspective was described by C.H. Dodd as a 'definite change of outlook', and as of far more significance than a mere 'readjustment … of the eschatological time-table'.[5] Others explain the different approach

---

[5] C.H. Dodd, 'The Mind of Paul: II', in *New Testament Studies* (Manchester: Manchester University Press, 1953), 112. Dodd argues that differences between the epistles 'represent real development, and are not merely the result of the circumstances of the particular aim of the several epistles' (84). This essay was originally published in 1933. Contrast the view of John Lowe, who took issue with Dodd (among others) in a paper delivered to the Oxford Society of Historical Theology in May 1940 (subsequently published as 'An Examination of Attempts

in 2 Corinthians as due, neither to a change in belief nor a simple change in perspective, but rather to the fact that in this letter he is concerned with a different issue.

Turning back to 1 Corinthians 15, we note that the number of Christians who have died has already grown since Paul wrote 1 Thessalonians, as we would expect with the passing of time. Whereas in 1 Thessalonians the death of Christians was apparently exceptional, Paul now says that 'we shall not *all* die' (v. 51) – but since many have, he needs to explain what future resurrection means for them: it takes place at the parousia, and involves 'putting on' a new kind of body. By the time that 2 Corinthians 5 is written, Paul is facing the probability of his own death before the parousia, but though that letter may reflect an increased expectancy of death on Paul's part, the real issue with which he is concerned there, and which is in fact the dominant theme of the whole letter, is the defence of his ministry. Confronted by accusations concerning his understanding of ministry, Paul defends himself by insisting that his words and actions are a proclamation of the crucified and glorified Christ. If he always carries the death of Jesus in his body, it is so that the life of Jesus may be seen in his body. The life-through-death that he experiences already in this life cannot be broken by his own death.

Paul's hope of future resurrection, which is based on Christ's resurrection, is, of course found in all his letters. In Romans, he is concerned with the question which he had discussed earlier, in Galatians, of the role of Israel, and God's purpose concerning Jews and Gentiles. As in Galatians, discussion in Romans is centred very much on Christian experience in the present. There is no mention in either letter of the parousia as such, though there are references in Romans to the day of judgement (2:1–16) and the day of salvation, which is drawing near (13:11 ff.). The great eschatological passage in Romans 8 looks for a future resurrection (v. 11) and for the revelation of glory (v. 18), which surprisingly involves, not the revelation of God's Son, but that of God's sons (*sic*) and the restoration of creation (vv. 19–21). The climax of the passage comes with the declaration that neither death nor life nor anything else will be able to separate us from the love of God in Christ. Although the emphasis throughout Romans is on present experience, we see now that this is to become more intense hereafter, for what we enjoy at the moment is merely 'the firstfruits' of the Spirit. Present suffering cannot be compared with future glory (v. 18); we have already been saved, but it is in hope of something greater (vv. 24 ff.). And once again that hope is nothing less than a becoming like Christ – being conformed to the image of God's Son.

---

to Detect Developments in St Paul's Theology', *JTS* 42 [1941]: 129–142). He wrote, 'with one minor exception, the evidence available does not enable us to trace any development whatever in St Paul's thinking from beginning to end' (129).

In the well-known 'hymn' of Philippians 2, Paul speaks of the exaltation of Christ rather than his resurrection (2:9), and so not surprisingly goes on to refer to Christians' future transformation into the likeness of Christ's glorious body, rather than of their resurrection (3:20 ff.).[6] Written towards the end of Paul's life,[7] this letter undermines the notion that Paul changed his mind in any significant way between writing 1 Corinthians 15 and 2 Corinthians 5, for although in Philippians 3 we find Paul affirming his hope in the parousia (3:20 ff.),[8] when (as in 1 Corinthians 15) his body will be changed into the likeness of Christ's, this process has apparently already begun, since he speaks also of knowing already the power of Christ's resurrection as he shares the sufferings of Christ, and of being conformed to his death, in hope of attaining the resurrection from the dead (3:10 ff.). Moreover, a couple of chapters earlier, when considering the likely outcome of his impending trial, he declares that he would prefer to die and 'be with Christ', than remain alive (1:20–26). If his trial ends with execution, then that will be for him a gain, since he will be 'with Christ' in an even closer sense than at present.

Side by side, then, we find Paul expressing the hope of being with Christ immediately after death, the idea of a growing conformity to Christ through present suffering, and the expectation of Christ's arrival from heaven, when our bodies will be transformed into his likeness. If these ideas coexist in the same letter, it is clearly inappropriate to speak (as Dodd did) of Paul 'changing his mind'.[9] Nevertheless, his thinking on the future life may well have developed, as he thought through the implications of his faith in the light of events. The hopes he expresses in both 2 Corinthians 5 and Philippians 1 are clearly linked to his experiences – in the first case, his constant exposure to danger and to 'wear and tear', in the second, the possibility of imminent execution. The change from thinking of himself as among the living at the parousia (as in 1 Thessalonians 4) to realizing that he is unlikely to survive would naturally lead him to think out what might await him. Instead of thinking of death as a 'sleep' (as in 1 Thess 5:10; 1 Cor 15:20), he describes it in his later letters as being 'at home with the Lord' (2 Cor 5:9), or as being 'with Christ' (Phil 1:23). It has sometimes been suggested that in 2 Corinthians Paul has abandoned

---

[6] But see 3:10 ff., below.

[7] It seems far more likely that the letter was sent from Rome than from Ephesus or Caesarea, and thus was written when Paul faced a capital charge there. See the summary of the various arguments in Markus Bockmuehl, *The Epistle to the Philippians*, BNTC (London: A&C Black, 1997), 25–32.

[8] Cf. also the references to 'the day of Christ' in 1:10 and 2:16.

[9] It is sometimes argued that chapters 1–2 and 3–4 belong to different letters, but the language and argument of chapter 3 pick up those of 2, demonstrating the unity of the letter. Moreover, there are parallels to both 1 Cor 15 and 2 Cor 5 in Phil 3.

Jewish 'apocalyptic' and adopted Hellenistic ideas.[10] But is there perhaps a link that holds his various pictures of the afterlife together? To answer this question we need to look in greater detail at 2 Cor 5:1–10.

1. Sharing the Experience of Christ

Before we examine that passage, however, we must look at what Paul says in one or two earlier passages. We begin with 1 Thessalonians, where in 1:10 Paul introduces one of the main themes of the letter[11] when he reminds his readers that their response to the gospel had been 'to turn to the true and living God from idols, and to wait eagerly for his Son – whom he had raised from the dead – to appear from heaven'. Paul's chief concern in this letter is to reassure the Thessalonians that Christians who have died have not been lost (4:13),[12] and in v. 14 he assures them that 'God will bring *with Jesus* those who have fallen asleep'. Paul's conviction depends on the fact that 'Jesus died and rose' – a summary which may well be an early creed, since it refers to 'Jesus' rather than 'Christ' (as is more normal in Paul) and uses the verbs in the active, not passive. The link between belief in Christ's death and resurrection and the hope that God will bring with Christ those Christians who have died is expressed in the words οὕτως καὶ. Logically, we expect Paul to say, 'Christ died and rose; even so those who have died (with Christ) will be raised', but instead he speaks of God *bringing* 'with Jesus those who have fallen asleep'.

There is considerable debate as to whether the phrase διὰ τοῦ Ἰησοῦ in v. 14 should be taken with 'fallen asleep' or with 'bring'; the latter suggestion makes the phrase seem awkward and redundant, since σὺν αὐτῷ is already attached to that verb, but if it is correct, it stresses the role of Christ. Taking it with

---

[10] This idea was famously explored by Wilfred L. Knox, *St Paul and the Church of the Gentiles* (Cambridge: Cambridge University Press, 1961), 125–145.

[11] Cf. Morna D. Hooker, '1 Thessalonians 1:9–10: A Nutshell – but What Kind of Nut?', in *Geschichte – Tradition – Reflexion: Festschrift für Martin Hengel zum 70. Geburtstag*, vol. 3: *Frühes Christentum*, ed. H. Lichtenberger (Tübingen: Mohr Siebeck, 1996), 435–448 = below, essay 35 (pp. 521–533).

[12] The grief of the Thessalonians is most probably due to a fear that Christians who have died have missed out on salvation, not simply that they will in some way be disadvantaged at the parousia, as is argued among others by A. F. J. Klijn, 'I Thessalonians 4,13–18 and its Background', in *Paul and Paulinism: Essays in Honour of C. K. Barrett*, eds. Morna D. Hooker and S. G. Wilson (London: SPCK, 1982), 67–73, and by J. Delobel, 'The Fate of the Dead According to 1 Thes 4 and 1 Cor 15', in *The Thessalonian Correspondence*, ed. Raymond F. Collins (Leuven: Leuven University Press, 1990), 340–347. Whichever interpretation is adopted, however, Paul is reassuring the Thessalonians about the fate of Christians who have died. See, on this verse, a paper contributed to an earlier meeting of the Pauline Colloquium: John M. G. Barclay, 'Death and Early Christian Identity', in *Not in the Word Alone: The First Epistle to the Thessalonians*, ed. Morna D. Hooker, Monographic Series of *Benedictina*, vol. 15 (Rome: Abbey of St Paul Outside the Walls, 2003), 131–153.

'fallen asleep' is often regarded as difficult,[13] but perhaps Paul uses it to stress the fact that those who have fallen asleep were *already united with Christ*: those who fall asleep through Jesus – or 'in Jesus'[14] – will be *brought with him*. Although Best argues that 'it seems rather late in the passage to identify the dead as the Christian dead',[15] it would surely have seemed important to make this identification, since Paul is distinguishing between pagans (v. 13), who had no hope for the dead, and the Thessalonians, who *did* have (or *should* have had!) hope for those fellow Christians who had died. Whichever way we take the phrase, however, Paul affirms that Christians who have 'fallen asleep' will be brought with Christ, and that *this depends on the fact that Christ died and rose*.

There has been considerably less debate as to what is meant by the statement that God will bring the Christian dead with Christ. It is generally assumed that this is a reference to the parousia, and that Paul is thinking of Christ's return to earth. If Christ brings them to earth with him, does this mean that he is already thinking of the dead as in some sense enjoying being 'with him' immediately after death, as in 2 Cor 5:8 ff. and Phil 1:23? But in fact Paul has not yet mentioned the parousia, and we should beware of assuming that he is already thinking of Christ's return to earth. If that is what he meant, he would most naturally have written: '*Christ* will bring with him those who have died'. In fact he stresses the action of *God*, and it therefore seems more probable that he is thinking of Christ's final exaltation into heaven, taking believers with him, rather than of the parousia.[16] Otherwise, we have the strange notion that the dead-in-Christ are brought back to earth at the parousia, simply in order to be raised! Paul is *not*, after all, describing a 3-stage programme for the events surrounding the parousia, running:

1. God brings the dead-in-Christ to earth with him (vv. 13 ff.).
2. When Christ returns, the dead-in-Christ are then raised (v. 16).
3. Living Christians are then caught up into the clouds to meet the Lord, together with the dead-in-Christ (v. 17).

Rather, he is expressing his conviction about Christians who have died *in two different ways*. First, in vv. 13 ff., he contrasts the grief of pagans with the hope

---

[13] See, e.g., the discussion by E. Best, *A Commentary on The First and Second Epistles to the Thessalonians*, BNTC (London: A&C Black, 1972), 188 ff.

[14] Charles Masson, *Les deux épîtres de Saint Paul aux Thessaloniciens*, CNT 11a (Neuchâtel; Paris: Delachaux & Niestlé, 1957), 55 ff., insisted that διὰ τοῦ Ἰησοῦ should not be equated with ἐν Χριστῷ, but the meaning of the phrases is often similar: see 1 Thess 4:2, where we might have expected Paul to write ἐν Χριστῷ, and 1 Cor 1:10.

[15] Best, *1–2 Thessalonians*, 189.

[16] So, e.g., Ernst von Dobschütz, *Die Thessalonicher-Briefe*, KEK 10 (Göttingen: Vandenhoeck & Ruprecht, 1909), 191 ff.; James Everett Frame, *A Critical and Exegetical Commentary on the Epistles of St. Paul to the Thessalonians*, ICC (Edinburgh: T&T Clark, 1912), 170 ff.; Béda Rigaux, *Saint Paul: Les épîtres aux Thessaloniciens*, EBib (Paris: Gabalda, 1956), 537.

of Christians, and what this hope means, assuring the Thessalonians that God will 'bring' these 'sleeping' Christians with Christ (into God's presence?). Having affirmed this, Paul then quotes a 'word of the Lord' to the effect that the living will have no precedence over the dead, and goes on to describe, with apocalyptic imagery, how this is so (vv. 15–17): 'The Lord will descend from heaven, and the dead-in-Christ will be raised, following which we who are alive will be caught up *with them* to meet the Lord. And so we shall be with the Lord for ever'.

It seems more probable, then, that when Paul says, in v. 14, that 'God will bring with him those who have died', *he is thinking of Christ's final return to heaven, not of the parousia*. The dead-in-Christ will be brought with Christ into God's presence by God himself, following the resurrection. This, incidentally, makes more sense, not only of the fact that Paul uses both διὰ τοῦ Ἰησοῦ and σὺν αὐτῷ, but also of the οὕτως καί: just as Christ died and rose, *even so* will God exalt the dead-in-Christ (διὰ τοῦ Ἰησοῦ) *with* Christ (σὺν αὐτῷ) into his presence. Resurrection and exaltation belong together. The resurrection of Christ is truly a guarantee of what is still to come.

That this is the true meaning of ἄξει seems confirmed by a comparison with 2 Cor 4:14,[17] 'for we know that he who raised the Lord Jesus will raise us also with Jesus, and bring us, with you, into his presence'. As in 1 Thess 4:14, all is dependent on the death and resurrection of Jesus, and as there, God 'brings' us – this time, specifically, into his presence (παραστήσει). The main difference is the fact that the two groups here are referred to, not as 'the dead' and 'the living', but as 'us' and 'you' – presumably because Paul has just been describing how he is being given up to death, 'so that death is at work in us, but life in you'; he now realizes that he is likely to be among the dead, rather than the living. In 2 Cor 4:14, Paul compresses his earlier double explanation into one sentence:

> 1 Thess 4:14, we believe that Jesus died and rose again
> 2 Cor 4:14, the one who raised the Lord Jesus
> 1 Thess 4:16, the dead in Christ will rise.
> 2 Cor 4:14, will raise us also with Jesus,
> 1 Thess 4:14, God will bring with him those who have fallen asleep;
> 2 Cor 4:14, and will bring us with you
> 1 Thess 4:17, we shall be with the Lord for ever
> 2 Cor 4:14, into his presence.

1 Thess 4:14, then, is not a reference to the parousia, but an assurance that the dead-in-Christ will be brought into God's presence, an assurance that is then repeated, though expressed differently, in 'the word of the Lord' which

---

[17] The parallel is noted by Joseph Plevnik, *Paul and the Parousia: An Exegetical and Theological Investigation* (Peabody, MA: Hendrickson, 1997), 74.

follows. It is noticeable that, in his attempt to explain how it is that the dead will not be disadvantaged, Paul uses language in these verses which is picked up later in both 1 and 2 Corinthians.

In the following chapter, Paul warns the Thessalonians about the coming 'day of the Lord'. Christians can expect it to be a day of salvation, not wrath, because 'our Lord Jesus Christ died for us, so that whether we are awake or asleep we may live with him'. Once again, he insists that there is no distinction between those who are alive and those who are dead, and once again he speaks of being 'with Christ'. The credal summary is expressed in the familiar format of the so-called 'interchange' passages: 'Christ died for us, *in order that* we might live with him'.[18] But as in similar passages, this is *not an exchange*: Paul writes, *not* 'Christ died, in order that we might live', but 'Christ died, in order that we might live *with him*'. In other words, Christians share his resurrection: by sharing our human death, Christ enabled us to share his life. The credal statement has been curtailed, since what Paul clearly means (as in 4:14) is 'Christ died and rose'. In 4:14, the conclusion drawn from the credal summary was that since Jesus died and rose, God will bring the Christian dead *with him* (i.e. as sharers in his resurrection); here, it is that we may live *with him*. Does this refer to a life here and now – the dead 'in heaven', the living on earth? It is more probable, in view of the context, that Paul is thinking of the life that follows the day of the Lord. He is once again assuring the Thessalonians that the dead in Christ share 'the hope of salvation' (5:8).

In 1 Thessalonians 4–5, then, Paul expresses the eschatological hope in three different ways: the dead-in-Christ will be brought into God's presence 'with Christ'; they will be raised at his coming, and be caught up – with the living – in the clouds to meet the Lord; and they will live 'with him'.

2 Thessalonians, though largely concerned with eschatology, has nothing to say that is relevant to our purpose apart from 2:1, where the author (who may or may not have been Paul) discusses 'the parousia of our Lord Jesus Christ and our being gathered to him'. This image is closest to 1 Thess 4:17, where believers are to be 'caught up in the clouds … to meet the Lord', but adds nothing to the picture found there.

We turn next to 1 Corinthians 15, where we have Paul's fullest statement of what he understands by future resurrection. The problem Paul addresses appears to be very similar to that which caused the problem in Thessalonika – a failure to grasp Paul's teaching about future resurrection. In 1 Thess 4:13, he spoke of non-believers as those who had no hope. Here, he describes those whose hope in Christ is confined to this world as pitiable, since their faith is

---

[18] See Morna D. Hooker, *From Adam to Christ: Essays on Paul* (Cambridge: Cambridge University Press, 1990). Cf. Irenaeus, *Adv. Haer.* 5 *praef.*

vain. His argument stresses the link between Christ's death and resurrection and our own – a link which we have already seen in 1 Thess 4:14 and 5:10:

> If there is no resurrection of the dead, then Christ has not been raised.
> That means that our gospel and your faith are empty.
> If the dead are not raised, Christ has not been raised.
> That means that your faith is futile,
> and those who have fallen asleep in Christ have perished (vv. 12–19).

He goes on to insist that Christ *has* been raised, and that – as in 1 Thess 4:16 – those who belong to him will be raised at his coming (vv. 20–23). Paul's own hope of resurrection is demonstrated in his willingness to face constant danger (vv. 30–33).

But what does Paul mean by future resurrection? Paul spells out his answer to this question in vv. 35–58. At the heart of this description is his conviction that Christians will bear the image of Christ himself. Since their resurrection depends on his (vv. 12–19), it is hardly surprising that their resurrection body will be like his. The link is established in the use of Adam/Christ imagery: as all die in Adam, so all will be made alive in Christ (v. 22); as we have borne the image of the man of dust (Adam) so we will bear the image of the man of heaven (Christ, vv. 45–49).

Paul's imagery stresses both the continuity between what dies and what is raised, and the differences between them, expressed in a series of opposites. In spelling out what he believes will happen, Paul uses two metaphors; the first is taken from horticulture, and speaks of sowing a bare grain, which then comes to life (v. 37). The metaphor is appropriate in speaking of the dead, who are 'sown' and then 'raised', and is spelt out in a series of contrasts between what is sown and what is raised. The naked seed is exchanged for a living plant, dishonour and weakness give way to glory and power, the physical body to a spiritual body. All this is necessary because flesh and blood cannot inherit the kingdom of God, and neither can the perishable inherit what is imperishable (v. 50). But this principle applies to the living, as well as to those who have 'fallen asleep', which means that, although 'we shall not all die, we will all be changed' (v. 51). Paul next describes what this means for those who are alive at the parousia. We too (for Paul includes himself among their number) will be changed (v. 52); Paul now uses the metaphor of dressing – the perishable body will put on (ἐνδύω) imperishability, and the mortal body immortality (vv. 53–54). So death will be swallowed up in victory. It should be noted that whereas the metaphor of sowing entailed a dramatic exchange, that of clothing means a 'putting' on of something over what presently exists. The former is appropriate when talking about the resurrection of the dead (the main question under discussion), the latter when describing what happens to those who are alive at the parousia. Nevertheless, both groups are going to be changed, and take on the image of Christ.

In this section (1 Cor 15:42–54), then, we have a series of contrasts:

Perishable/imperishable
Dishonour/glory
Weakness/power
Physical/spiritual
First Adam/last Adam
Living physical being/life-giving spirit
From earth/from heaven
Mortal/immortal

If we are to bear the image of the man from heaven (glory, power, etc.), it is because he himself first bore the image of the man from earth (dishonour, weakness, etc.). In the familiar words of Irenaeus,[19] Christ became what we are, in order that we might become what he is. Paul will pick up much of the language used in this chapter in 2 Corinthians.

We have noted already that *Galatians* makes no reference to the parousia. The emphasis throughout the letter is very much on believers' present experience. The Galatians have already been set free from the present evil age (1:4), have already been set free from slavery and been adopted as God's children (4:1–7). Paul's language in the second passage stresses the link between Christ and ourselves: God has sent his Son, in order that we might become his sons (*sic*, 4:4 ff.); it is in Christ Jesus that we are God's sons (*sic*, 3:26), for those who have been baptized into Christ have clothed themselves with Christ (3:27). The verb (ἐνδύω) reappears in 1 Cor 15:53 ff., but there, as we have seen, it is used of what takes place at the parousia, whereas here it refers to what happened at baptism. *Already, then, we have in some sense taken on Christ's image.* In the case of the Galatians, however, this is far from complete, since Paul declares that he is once again 'in labour' with them until Christ is formed in them. Of his own experience, he says that he has been crucified with Christ, and so lives no longer: rather, Christ lives in him.[20] Yet this is only one way of expressing it, since either side of this statement he declares that having died to the Law he now lives to God, and that the life he now lives he lives by trust in the Son of God (2:19 ff.). Whether it is Paul who lives to God, or Christ who lives in him, we have here words that will be echoed in 2 Cor 5:15, 'He died for all, in order that the living might no longer live for themselves, but for him who died and was raised for their sake'.

---

[19] Irenaeus, *Adv. Haer.* 5 *praef.*
[20] A similar idea is expressed in 1:16 if we give ἐν its most natural meaning, and understand Paul to be saying that it pleased God to reveal his Son *in* him or through him – i.e. in his life and mission.

Life in Christ is therefore a present experience for Paul, as is life in the Spirit (3:1–5), under whose guidance the Galatians are urged to live (5:16–26). At the same time, however, the Spirit is a guarantee of what lies in the future. Through the Spirit, we are assured that we are God's sons (*sic*), and so heirs of God's promises (4:6). Those born of the Spirit are children of the inheritance (4:28–30). Through the Spirit we await the *hope* of righteousness (5:5), and that hope is to inherit the kingdom of God (5:21); in other words, if we live by the Spirit rather than the flesh, our reward will be eternal life (6:8).

Paul's concern in Galatians is not with the parousia, but with the issue of circumcision and obedience to the Law. It is not surprising, then, that the emphasis is on the present. At the same time, however, we see the tension which characterizes all his letters, between present Christian experience on the one hand and hope for the future on the other.

In *Romans*, this tension pervades the whole argument, especially in chapters 5–8. Although Paul refers to the coming day of wrath (2:5), the day of judgement (2:16), and the day of salvation (13:11 ff.), he makes no attempt to describe what takes place when the Lord returns. At the end of chapters 1–4, which discuss God's dealings with Jews and Gentiles, he concludes with a credal summary which declares that 'God raised Jesus our Lord from the dead' (4:25). This leads on to the conclusion, introduced in 5:1 with a triumphant 'Therefore': Therefore, since we have already obtained access to grace, we boast *in hope of sharing the glory of God*. The tension between what we already have and what we still hope for is set out in vv. 9–10:

> We *have been* 'rightwised' by his blood,
> we *will be* saved through him from the wrath of God.
> We *were* reconciled to God through the death of his Son,
> we *will be* saved by his life.

How this happens is then spelt out in terms of a contrast between Adam and Christ. Adam's sin led to death for all, but the grace of God, effective though Christ, means that the situation has been reversed. On the one hand, we have Adam's disobedience, on the other, Christ's obedience. Whereas Adam's sin led to condemnation and death for all, Christ's righteous act has led to acquittal and life for all. Sin is replaced by grace, which leads to eternal life. In this passage Paul picks up the contrast between Adam and Christ which he used in 1 Cor 15:20–22 and 42–49, and spells out the difference between them, not in terms of 'physical' and 'spiritual', but in terms of 'obedience' and 'disobedience', 'sin' and 'righteousness' – a contrast which was only hinted at in 1 Corinthians (15:17, 56), since Paul's concern there was to reassure his readers about the coming resurrection.

What Christ's reversal of Adam's fall means for the Christian is explained in chapter 6. In being baptized into Christ, we have been baptized into his death – buried with him into death, so that, as Christ was raised, 'we too might walk in newness of life. For if we have been united with the form of his death, we shall also be united with his resurrection' (vv. 3–5). These verses encapsulate the tension of the Christian life: already dead to sin, already buried with Christ, already sharing in his risen life, and yet not *fully* sharing his resurrected life, since conformity to his resurrection lies in the future.[21] But this future life is important for Paul's argument. 'Eternal life' was the goal of 5:21, and in 6:8 we are reminded again of the eschatological goal: 'if we have died with Christ, we believe that we shall also live with him'. That is why, in this present life, 'you must consider yourselves dead to sin and alive to God in Christ Jesus' (v. 11).

In chapter 8, Paul spells out at length his future hope. Once again, this is firmly rooted in what God has already done, and so we are aware of the eschatological tension between what characterizes Christians' lives here and now, and what awaits them in the future. God sent his Son in the likeness of our sinful flesh to deal with sin, and the result is that we, who live according to the Spirit, and not according to the flesh, are set free from the power of sin (vv. 3 ff.). Moreover, this Spirit is the guarantee that the one who raised Jesus from the dead will give life to our mortal bodies (v. 11). As in 6:5, it is possible to take this as referring to 'the vivifying energy of the Spirit'[22] in the present life, but most commentators take it to refer to the future resurrection.[23] The Spirit is the spirit of adoption (υἱοθεσία), so that we, too, are sons (*sic*) of God (vv. 15 ff.). And yet we still *await* adoption (v. 23)! This time the word υἱοθεσία refers to 'the redemption of our bodies'. Although we already know ourselves to be God's children, the whole of creation awaits 'the revelation of the sons of God' (v. 19). This dual use of υἱοθεσία, together with the ambiguity of verses such as 6:5 and 8:11, demonstrates again the eschatological tension that pervades the whole section. Paul's admonitions are not merely 'Be what you are', as Bultmann so famously expressed it, but 'Be what you *will* be' – or rather, since the Christian life is a process, 'Be what you are becoming'. Paul himself neatly sums this tension up in v. 24, 'you were saved in hope', and the hope is that Christians will be conformed to the image of his Son (v. 29). Yet clearly this hope, although

---

[21] It is possible (so Franz J. Leenhardt, *The Epistle to the Romans: A Commentary*, trans. H. Knight [London: Lutterworth, 1961], *in loc.*) to take the future indicative ἐσόμεθα in v. 5 as logical – 'we must be' – and so as a reference to the present, but most commentators agree that this does not fit the context. C. E. B. Cranfield, *A Critical and Exegetical Commentary on the Epistle to the Romans*, vol. 1, ICC (Edinburgh: T&T Clark, 1975), *in loc.*, understands it to refer to the moral life (as v. 4 suggests), but v. 8 clearly has a future reference.

[22] Leenhardt, *Romans*, 210.

[23] E.g. Ernst Käsemann, *An die Römer*, Handbuch zum NT 8a (Tübingen: Mohr Siebeck, 1980), *Commentary on Romans*, trans. G.W. Bromiley (London: SCM Press, 1980), *in loc.*; Cranfield, *Romans*, *in loc.*

defined in v. 24 as future, is in some sense already being realized, for the verbs he uses in v. 30 are all aorists. It is unsurprising to find Christians described as having been predestined, called, and 'rightwised', but in what sense have they *already* been glorified? As recently as v. 17 glorification was set out as a future promise. Is this aorist used merely in order to express certainty? Or is it rather that there is a sense in which glory is not simply a future hope, but something already in the process of realization – as in 2 Cor 3:18? Christians are already 'sons' of God, and so conformed (if not fully) to the image of his Son. But this glory remains hidden until the day when the sons of God are revealed (v. 19). This section of Romans ends with the confident declaration that nothing in all creation – including death itself – can separate us from the love of God in Christ Jesus our Lord. What this means in terms of post-mortem existence he is not here concerned to explain.

In another of Paul's late letters, *Philippians*, we find that he several times refers to 'the day of Christ', which is a day of judgement (1:6, 10; 2:16). This day is apparently imminent, since in Phil 4:5 Paul writes that 'the Lord is near'. In 3:20 ff., he again expresses his hope for Christ's parousia, declaring that we are expecting our Saviour, the Lord Jesus Christ, from heaven, and that he will transform our bodies of humiliation, conforming them to his own body of glory (v. 21).[24] As in 1 Corinthians 15, then, it is at the parousia that believers are to be transformed into Christ's likeness. Christ will effect a change in our 'body', but instead of speaking of perishable/imperishable and mortal/immortal, Paul uses the language of humiliation and glory – language picked up from the so-called 'hymn' of 2:6–11. Paul's description of what he hopes for in 3:20 ff. needs to be read alongside this earlier passage, in which Christ is said to have taken the form of a slave and the likeness of men, and to have humbled himself to a shameful death on a cross. It is *because* (διό) he did this that God exalted him (vv. 9–11) – and it is because he has been exalted above all things that he is able to conform us to his likeness, through the power given to him at his exaltation. Here we have a powerful expression of what some of us have termed 'interchange' – *not* an exchange, but an *inter*change of experience – whereby the fact that Christ identifies himself with humanity – becoming what we are – enables us to share in what he is.[25] This too, in different language, is the understanding of redemption expressed in terms of the First and Last Adams in 1 Corinthians.

When Paul writes in Phil 3:20 ff. that 'we are expecting a Saviour', who 'will transform the body of our humiliation', he appears once again to number himself among those who will be alive at the parousia, as he did in 1 Thess

---

[24] The language of v. 21 picks up that of 2:6–11: μετασχηματίσει, ταπεινώσεως, σύμμορφον, δόξης, πάντα.

[25] Cf. Irenaeus, *Adv. Haer.* 5 *praef.*

4:15 and 1 Cor 15:52 ff.[26] Yet his survival is far from certain, as Phil 1:12–26 makes plain. The subject here is Paul's forthcoming trial. Philippians may well be Paul's last letter, in which case it was probably written from prison in Rome.[27] Certainly it is in Philippians 1, more clearly than anywhere else, that he confronts the possibility of his imminent death. He looks forward to his coming trial, in the confident expectation that he will be enabled to speak with boldness, and will not be put to shame (1:20). He is apparently facing a capital charge and wondering what the outcome will be – and what he should hope for. 'To me,' he writes, 'to live is Christ and to die is gain (κέρδη)'. The statement that 'to live is Christ' recalls what he wrote in Gal 2:20, while his conviction that 'to die is gain' is similar to the hope expressed in 2 Cor 5:8. His words are also reminiscent of his argument in 1 Thessalonians, where he assured his readers that Christians who had fallen asleep would not be at a disadvantage: now, however, he considers it a positive advantage to die! 'My own desire', he writes, 'is to depart and be with Christ'. Yet he thinks that the churches need him, and that he should therefore 'choose' to remain; it would seem that his actions are governed, not by what he himself wants, but by what will serve others. Is Paul here deliberately modelling himself on Christ's example, which he describes in 2:1–11? Certainly he portrays his own Christian life in Philippians 3 in terms that suggest he saw it as a conscious 'imitation' of Christ[28] – and there, too, he rejects what might have seemed 'gain' (κέρδη) for something better (v. 7).

In Philippians 1, then, the idea that he will be 'with' Christ in a closer sense after death is dominant, as in 2 Cor 5:6–10, and it is in no sense dependent on the parousia. But in chapter 3, Paul confidently awaits the parousia! Yet the transformation that awaits believers when the Lord appears is not totally new, but the completion of a process described in 3:7–17. Paul's purpose is 'to be found in Christ' (3:9), and 'to know the power of his resurrection, by sharing his sufferings and becoming like him in death' (v. 10). 'Our citizenship is in heaven', writes Paul in 3:20, using a noun (πολίτευμα) which picks

---

[26] Even if, as some suggest, vv. 20 ff. are a non-Pauline fragment (so John Reumann, 'Philippians 3.20–21 – a Hymnic Fragment?', *NTS* 30 [1984]: 593–609), Paul presumably includes himself when reciting an article of faith.

[27] Philippians appears to be Paul's 'final testimony'. See Morna D. Hooker, 'Philippians: Phantom Opponents and the Real Source of Conflict', in *Fair Play: Diversity and Conflicts in Early Christianity: Essays in Honour of Heikki Räisänen,* eds. Ismo Dunderberg, Christopher Tuckett, and Kari Syreeni (Leiden: Brill, 2002), 377–395 = below, essay 42 (pp. 616–631).

[28] Paul picks up the verb ἡγέομαι from 2:6, and uses it to refer to what, as a Christian, he considered to be worthless; whereas the result of Christ's decision was that he was found in the fashion of a man (εὑρεθῶ, 2:7), Paul is found in Christ (3:9). His aim is to be conformed to Christ's death (συμμορφιζόμενος τῷ θανάτῳ αὐτοῦ, 3:10), picking up language used in 2:6–8. The final goal is expressed in 3:21, in language which echoes the vocabulary of the whole hymn: see n. 24 above.

up the verb used in 1:27 (πολιτεύεσθε). Those who live as citizens of heaven are *already* being conformed to the likeness of Christ, as Paul's argument in chapters 2 and 3 makes clear.

Philippians, we have suggested, may well be Paul's last letter. Although some may argue for an earlier date, that would not help the hypothesis that Paul abandoned expectation of an imminent parousia after writing 1 Thessalonians and 1 Corinthians, and came to believe instead in a transformation which took place immediately after death, unless one assumed also that Philippians consists of more than one letter, and that chapters 1 and 2 were written considerably later than chapters 3–4.[29] As we have noted, however, chapters 1 and 2 themselves contain references to the 'day of the Lord'! Philippians alone, therefore, should persuade us that it is incorrect to suggest that Paul 'changed his mind' in-between writing 1 Corinthians and 2 Corinthians.

This brief survey of Paul's letters (apart from 2 Corinthians) has demonstrated that it is impossible to trace a change in Paul's outlook, and that what appear to modern scholars to be incompatible images are used side by side. These are always relevant to the particular point that Paul is making, and are influenced both by his readers' circumstances and his own. Moreover, whether Paul is describing changes that occur at the parousia or at death, his hopes are expressed in language that he uses elsewhere of his present experience as someone who now lives 'in Christ'.

2. 2 Corinthians 5

We come, finally, to 2 Cor 5:1–10 – but these verses are only a short section in a much longer passage in which Paul is defending his ministry, and cannot be rightly understood without seeing them in that context. It is misleading to treat them as a 'digression', as do some commentators.[30] Although Paul is clearly already on the defensive in chapters 1 and 2, his argument really begins in 3:1 with the comparison between the ministry of the old covenant, entrusted to Moses, and the ministry of the new, entrusted to himself. With extraordinary boldness, he compares his own behaviour in openly proclaiming 'the gospel of the glory of Christ' (4:4) with that of Moses, who concealed God's glory from the Israelites with a veil (3:13). The glory of the earlier ministry of condemnation, which led to death, is nothing in comparison with

---

[29] The suggested division of the letter at 3:2 is unconvincing, however, since there are close links between chapters 2 and 3.

[30] The term is, for example, used of these verses by Barrett, *2 Corinthians, in loc.* The vast majority of commentators treat them as a separate paragraph, but Furnish is surely right in refusing to regard 5:1 as marking a break in the argument; see Victor Paul Furnish, *II Corinthians*, AB (Garden City, NY: Doubleday, 1984), *in loc.*

the glory of the ministry which leads to righteousness, and so to life (3:4–11). This glory is fully revealed in Christ, and those who turn to him not only see his glory but reflect it, while they are 'transformed into the same image, from one degree of glory to another' (3:12–18). The glory glimpsed by Moses and now fully revealed is of course the glory of God himself, and if it is revealed in Christ, that is because he is the image of God (4:4). The light first seen at creation now shines in Christ, and has shone in the hearts of believers (4:1–6). Christians are therefore being recreated after God's own image – restored to what God intended them to be. Paul explains here how transformation into the likeness of Christ and glorification are a *present* experience for Christians.[31] The creative light of Christ has *already* shone into them. He picks this up in 5:17, when he sums up his argument: 'if anyone is in Christ, there is a new creation. Everything old has passed away; see! new things have come into being'. In the verses in-between, however he spells out the paradoxical nature of that experience in his own life, which means that (in conformity to the pattern of Christ) he is handed over to death in order to bring life to others (4:10–12). Whatever happens to him is a means of spreading the gospel, and so glorifies God (4:13–15).

Paul's claim, then, is that he proclaims the glory of Christ, not only in his message, but in his life, since he himself reflects the message of the gospel.[32] To the Corinthians, however, Paul's claims do not seem to correspond with reality. No one looking at him would regard him as glorious! This 'treasure' is, he confesses, contained in 'clay jars' (4:7). He admits that he is afflicted, perplexed, persecuted, struck down (4:8 ff.). How, then, can he claim to reflect Christ's glory? The answer is that he interprets all these experiences as 'always carrying in his body the dying of Jesus – in order that, in his body, the life of Jesus may be revealed' – an idea so important that he spells it out again (4:10 ff.). By sharing in Christ's death – not only in baptism but in his ministry – Paul is enabled to share in his life, and so weakness and shame are turned into strength and glory. But this is not all, since this life overflows to others: 'death is at work in us but life in you' (v. 12).

Some commentators suggest that this could mean that Paul expects to die before the parousia, while the Corinthians will survive,[33] but there appears to be a direct causative link between Paul's sufferings and the 'life' that is at work in them. It is an idea that has already been expressed in the opening lines of the epistle, where Paul speaks of the consolation given to him in his affliction – consolation which allows him to console others who are themselves being afflicted:

---

[31] Cf. Rom 8:30.
[32] Cf. the probable meaning of Gal 1:16, 'It pleased God to reveal his Son *in* me'.
[33] Dodd, 'The Mind of Paul', 110 ff.

For as the sufferings of Christ overflow to us, so, through Christ, our consolation overflows to you. For if we are afflicted, it is for your comfort and salvation; if we are comforted, it is for your comfort.

In much the same way, the author of Colossians (who may or may not be Paul himself) speaks of *suffering for the sake of Christ's body, the Church*, and describes this as 'completing,' in his flesh, 'the sufferings of Christ' (Col 1:24).[34]

Paul's defence of his ministry is clearly rooted in his understanding of the gospel, which was, quite simply, 'Jesus Christ, and him crucified' (1 Cor 2:1). Yet this apparently foolish message was the power and wisdom of God (1 Cor 1:18–25), since he had raised Christ from the dead. Now Paul claims that his own life has taken on the pattern of the gospel, since he experiences life in the midst of death. Even more than this, *because he is in Christ, and shares his risen life, he becomes a mediator of Christ's risen life to the Corinthians*.[35]

But now Paul turns to the future. He shares the faith of the Psalmist, who believed, and therefore spoke. Paul, too, proclaims what he believes – and what he believes is expressed in another credal formula: 'he who raised the Lord Jesus will raise us also with Jesus, and make us stand, with you, before himself' (4:13 ff.). The reasoning corresponds with that in 1 Thessalonians 4 and 5 and 1 Corinthians 15, and Paul is surely referring to the final, future, resurrection. His words echo 1 Thess 4:16 ff., and suggest a distinction between what will happen to 'us' and to 'you', but this time Paul includes himself among those who will be raised. The Corinthians may well still be alive at the parousia, even if he is not – but as in 1 Thess 4:17, they will *all* be in God's presence. He then reminds the Corinthians that his motive for all his actions is not simply his own vindication, but their salvation, and the glorification of God (4:15).

The 'therefore' (διό) in v. 16 indicates that *the reason that Paul does not lose heart lies in his belief in the future resurrection*. Already, in the present, his 'outer man' is wasting away, but his 'inner man' is being renewed day by day. The word ἄνθρωπος picks up the word which Paul used in 1 Cor 15:21 and 42–49, in the contrast between Adam and Christ.[36] In other words, what he spoke of there as a future event is seen here as a process that has already begun.

---

[34] Cf. the essay by W. F. Flemington, 'On the Interpretation of Colossians 1:24', in *Suffering and Martyrdom in the New Testament: Studies presented to G. M. Styler by the Cambridge New Testament Seminar,* eds. William Horbury and Brian McNeil (Cambridge: Cambridge University Press, 1981), 84–90.

[35] For further discussion of this theme see Morna D. Hooker, 'A Partner in the Gospel: Paul's Understanding of His Ministry', in *Theology and Ethics in Paul and His Interpreters: Essays in Honor of Victor Paul Furnish,* eds. Eugene H. Lovering, Jr. and Jerry L. Sumney (Nashville: Abingdon, 1996), 83–100 = below, essay 39 (pp. 579–595).

[36] He uses it again in Rom 5:12–19, again with reference to the contrast between Adam and Christ. The phrase κατὰ τὸν ἔσω ἄνθρωπος is also used in Rom 7:22, but in a very different context and contrast.

Already he is taking on 'the image of the heavenly' (1 Cor 15:49), for he has seen the glory of the Lord in Christ, and 'is being transformed into the same image' (2 Cor 3:18). Yet Paul's present experience is only a foretaste of the future reality. The eternal weight of glory that is prepared for Christians is overwhelmingly greater than their present affliction. What can be seen is temporary, while the unseen is eternal (vv. 17 ff.).

The link to 5:1 is made with the word γάρ, since what follows is a continuation of the argument, though the image of 'earthenware pots', used in 4:7, has given way to that of a temporary dwelling. 'What is seen' is now described as an 'earthly house – a tent', while 'what is unseen' is 'a building from God, a dwelling not made with hands, eternal, in the heavens'. It is impossible within the constraints of this paper to debate the extent to which Paul might have adopted 'Greek' ideas.[37] The suggestion that he is thinking in Hellenistic terms of the body as the dwelling-place of the soul, which is released from it on death, seems unlikely, however, since the hope he expresses here is not for the release of the soul, but rather for the exchange of his present dwelling for a better one[38] – the hope, that is, which is expressed in different language, in 1 Corinthians 15.

The use of the term σκῆνος and the idea of a house not made with hands reminds us of the saying about the temple attributed to Jesus in Mark 14:58 (cf. John 2:19–22), and there are possible echoes also of Paul's image of believers as 'God's temple' in 1 Cor 3:16 ff. and 6:19. Whatever the origin of his terms, he here affirms his belief that, even if he dies, he will 'have' (ἔχομεν) an eternal building from God in heaven.[39] What is not yet clear is whether he now expects to inhabit this building immediately after death, or whether he will have to wait for the parousia. The significance of the verb ἔχομεν has been the subject of intense debate: does Paul's use of the present tense mean that he is now thinking of an immediate transformation, taking place at the moment of death,[40] or is it to be understood as an indication of his certainty about what *will* take place at the parousia – as described in 1 Corinthians 15?[41] Or is this perhaps the wrong question? Many commentators have pointed out that the idea that the Age to Come exists already in heaven is a common feature

---

[37] For discussion of this point, see the commentaries.

[38] Jan Lambrecht, *Understanding What One Reads II: Essays on the Gospels and Paul* (Leuven; Paris; Walpole, MA: Peeters, 2011), 248, suggests that though Paul's use here of language from Wis 9:15 indicates Hellenistic influence, one should not assume 'a radically Hellenized content'. Paul's thought is not strictly dualistic, since he does not envisage 'existence without a body'.

[39] Cf. John 14:2.

[40] So Thrall, *2 Corinthians, in loc.*

[41] Cf. Hans Lietzmann, *An Die Korinther I–II* (Tübingen: Mohr Siebeck, 1969), *in loc.*; Barrett, *2 Corinthians, in loc.*; Andrew T. Lincoln, *Paradise Now and Not Yet* (Cambridge: Cambridge University Press, 1981), 63–65.

in Jewish apocalyptic:[42] what exists already in heaven represents what *will* be on earth,[43] and so depicts what the righteous will finally enjoy. In 1 Enoch 39:4, for example, we find Enoch describing how he saw 'the dwelling-places of the holy, and the resting places of the righteous'.[44] It is in this tradition, perhaps, that Paul declares in Phil 3:20 that 'our citizenship is in heaven'. Does his use of the present tense and the phrase 'eternal in the heavens' in 2 Cor 5:1 indicate that Paul is thinking of the future as a present reality in heaven, as in some apocalyptic writings? If so, his image is not intended to answer the question 'When?' but to affirm the certainty that his hope will be fulfilled.

Other commentators have suggested that the echo of Mark 14:58 is significant.[45] Whether or not Paul is familiar with a tradition going back to Jesus, the idea of a heavenly temple – the pattern for what will be set up when the Age to Come is finally realized – is widespread in biblical and pseudepigraphal writings.[46] Paul's use of temple imagery in 1 Cor 3:16 (an image he picks up in 2 Cor 6:16) suggests that he is perhaps thinking in 2 Cor 5:1, not of individual resurrection 'bodies', but of corporate existence in the body of Christ.[47] This may well be true, but since this verse comes at the end of his discussion in 4:7–18, we may expect it to affirm his belief that he himself will not be 'crushed … forsaken … [or] destroyed'. As long as he continues 'in this tent' he groans, but is nevertheless sure of the final outcome, of which God's Spirit is the guarantee (5:2–5).

In v. 2, he picks up the idiom of dressing which he used in 1 Cor 15:53 ff., where he described the change that is to take place to the living at the parousia as a putting on of imperishability and of immortality. In a typically Pauline mixed metaphor, he speaks of his hope, not to be 'unclothed', but to be 'further clothed' with his heavenly dwelling, so that mortality may be swallowed up by life (vv. 2, 4). Like the image of the heavenly dwelling-place, the idea

---

[42] See e.g. W.D. Davies, *Paul and Rabbinic Judaism* (London: SPCK, 1955), 314–319; Furnish, *II Corinthians*, in loc.

[43] This is rooted in the idea that God's purposes go back to creation, and so are 'preexistent'.

[44] See also 4 Ezra 10:25–57; 2 Bar 4. Paul is perhaps influenced by this idea in Gal 4:21–31.

[45] André Feuillet, 'La Demeure Céleste et la Destinée des Chrétiens', *RSR* 44 (1956): 161–192, 360–402; for Feuillet, the heavenly dwelling is the resurrection body of Christ (377 ff.). Similarly Jean-François Collange, *Énigmes de la deuxième épître aux Corinthiens: Étude exégétique de 2 Cor. 2:14–7:4*, SNTSMS 18 (Cambridge: Cambridge University Press, 1972), 179–198. On the significance of the temple saying, see also R.F. Hettlinger, '2 Corinthians 5.1–10', *SJT* 10 (1957): 174–194; E. Earle Ellis, 'II Corinthians V. 1–10 in Pauline Eschatology', *NTS* 6 (1960): 211–224.

[46] In Exod 25:9, 40; 26:30; 27:8, we find the idea that the earthly sanctuary is a copy of the heavenly pattern. See also Wis 9:8, T. Levi 3:4–6, and Heb 8:2.

[47] John A.T. Robinson, *The Body: A Study in Pauline Theology* (London: SCM Press, 1952), 73–80; Ellis, *II Corinthians V. 1–10*.

of heavenly garments for the righteous can be found in Jewish tradition,[48] and this suggests again that Paul is more concerned with the certainty of his hope, than with the question 'When?' Some commentators, however, believe that – notwithstanding 2 Cor 4:14 – Paul is still hoping, as in 1 Corinthians 15, that he will be alive at the parousia. If so, then what he expresses in vv. 2–4 is a deep desire to be 'clothed upon' with the heavenly body *before he dies*. He groans (vv. 2, 4), longing for the time when he will be clothed, because he does not wish to have the old body stripped off, and longs rather to be covered by the new body, superimposed upon it (as in 1 Cor 15:53 ff.) – in other words, he longs for the mortal to be swallowed up (v. 4, καταποθῇ; another echo of 1 Cor 15:54) by life.

The problem with this interpretation is that it seems to be out of step, not only with 2 Cor 4:14, but with what follows, in 5:6–8, where Paul is apparently eager for death because this means that he will be 'at home with the Lord'. This does not in itself rule it out, since it is of course possible for Paul to put what appear to be contradictory ideas side by side: the frequent examples of 'eschatological tension' between present experience and future hope are a good example! But it is possible that his thought here is more consistent than this. Is he perhaps now hoping that he will 'put on' the resurrection body *immediately upon death*? Realizing now, in 5:1–5, that he is likely to die before the Lord's return, is he perhaps expecting his mortal body to be swallowed up by life at his death? If so, this would not mean that he has radically changed his views since writing 1 Corinthians, but rather that increasing sufferings have changed his perspective. Death may be 'the last enemy to be destroyed' (1 Cor 15:26), but by the time he writes Romans he is confident that not even death can separate him from the love of God in Christ Jesus (Rom 8:38 ff.), and perhaps that confidence lies behind his words here. Realistically, he knows that he is unlikely to be alive at the parousia, but he still longs to experience the transformation which he described in 1 Cor 15:51–57. So is he now perhaps hoping that this will take place *when he dies*? The mixed metaphor of a building with which one is clothed may, indeed, be due to a conscious desire to use the imagery he employed earlier. The compound verb, ἐπενδύομαι, corresponds to what he wrote in 1 Corinthians 15:53 ff. about the mortal putting on immortality, and the imperishable putting on immortality. There it described what happened to those who were alive at the parousia, and Paul apparently still hopes that this 'putting on' will be his lot, even if his death precedes the Lord's return.

But how confident is Paul that he will be *immediately* 'clothed upon' at death? What is the significance of his aside in v. 3? – and what is the correct reading of that verse? The Nestle-Aland text follows the Western text in

---

[48] Cf. 1 Enoch 62:15 ff.; 1QS 4:7 ff. Cf. 4 Ezra 2:45; Rev 6:11; 9:9.

reading ἐκδυσάμενοι, suggesting that Paul is here raising the possibility – and rejecting it – that he may have to 'put off' the earthly habitation before being clothed with the heavenly, and so be found 'naked' (presumably at the parousia). Many commentators prefer the reading ἐνδυσάμενοι, however,[49] and this has better manuscript support.[50] If we accept this reading, the meaning is very similar, though expressed with more confidence – especially if, with P[46] B D et al., we read εἴπερ for εἴ γε. Paul hopes that he will be able to 'put on' immortality and imperishability, as he described in 1 Cor 15:53–54.[51] In other words, he hopes that he will be clothed with the heavenly habitation over his present body, and so not be found 'naked' on that day (v. 3). The adjective 'naked', which picks up the term γυμνός used of the seed sown in the earth in 1 Cor 15:37, might be seen to support the view that Paul means that he hopes not to be among the dead.[52] The word γυμνός, however, refers not simply to the state of being dead, but rather to being without a habitation – disembodied – a suggestion that Paul immediately rejects, since he is confident that God has a heavenly habitation in store.[53] But *why* might one be found naked? Since we have assumed that the background here is not Hellenistic dualism, there is no reason to think that Paul is thinking of a 'soul' that has been stripped of its body, though he could, of course, be briefly dismissing the views of those who did think in those terms.[54]

An alternative interpretation is suggested by the fact that γυμνός is sometimes used in the LXX of those who are guilty and ashamed when judgement takes place.[55] Some commentators therefore suggest that Paul uses the word here in this sense, and that he has the last judgement in mind (as at v. 10).[56] He immediately dismisses the idea that he might be found naked as impossible,

---

[49] E.g. Barrett, *2 Corinthians*, in loc; Thrall, *2 Corinthians*, in loc.

[50] P[46] ℵ B C D[2] Ψ 0243 maj lat sy co; Cl.

[51] See C.F.D. Moule, 'St Paul and Dualism: The Pauline Conception of Resurrection', *NTS* 12 (1966): 122: 'death, even in [2 Corinthians 5], marks, not so much the escape of the soul from the prison of the body as the completion of the transformation of the σῶμα ψυχικόν into the σῶμα πνευματικόν'.

[52] Cf. Jan N. Sevenster, 'Some Remarks on the ΓΥΜΝΟΣ in II Cor. V. 3', in *Studia Paulina: In Honorem Johannis de Zwaan Septuagenarii*, eds. Jan N. Sevenster and W.C. van Unnik (Haarlem: Erven F. Bohn, 1953), 202–214.

[53] Cf. Thrall, *2 Corinthians*, in loc.

[54] It is possible, of course, that Paul is using the language of Corinthian 'Gnostics', only to dismiss it, but why should he do so here?

[55] Isa 47:3; Ezek 16:37; 23:29; Hos 2:3; Amos 2:16. Cf. also the parable of the wedding garments, Matt 22:11–14. According to Gen 3:7, 10ff., Adam and Eve *became aware* that they were naked as soon as they sinned; but in 2:25 they were *already* naked. Nakedness, then, can hardly be interpreted here as an indication of guilt. Later Jewish texts, however, understand Adam to have been naked because he had been stripped of his glory: 3 Bar (Gk) 4:16; Apoc Mos 20:1ff.

[56] See Ellis, 'II Corinthians V. 1–10', 219–221; Lang, *2.Korinther 5,1–10*, 188; Furnish, *II Corinthians*, in loc.; A. Oepke, γυμνός, *TDNT* 1/773–775.

since he has *already* been clothed, ἐνδυσάμενοι, and what he now longs for is to be *further* clothed, ἐπενδύομαι. If this is his meaning, then the most likely explanation of his language is that Paul is referring to the fact that he has already been clothed with Christ, at baptism (as in Gal 3:27), and that what he is now longing for is a further stage in this process.

Verse 4, however, seems to tell against this interpretation, since there Paul uses the image of 'taking off' clothes, which must refer back to the idea of the 'earthly tent' of v. 1 being destroyed. He picks up the verb στενάζω, 'to groan', from v. 2. He longs to be 'further clothed', rather than 'unclothed', and that means that mortality will be 'swallowed up' by life. The verb καταπίνω was used, as we have noted, in the same sense in 1 Cor 15:54, together with the image of 'putting on'. Here, certainly, the imagery refers to mortality, and not to the fact that he has 'put on' Christ.

We have to remember, however, that when Paul speaks of his 'earthly tent' in 5:1 this is an alternative way of describing the 'outer man' of 4:16, and that he has claimed that though this is being destroyed, the 'inner man' is being renewed. The basis of this claim is that he carries in his body the death of Jesus, in order that the life of Jesus may also be seen in his body (4:10). When he changes metaphors in chapter 5 to that of a tent versus a heavenly house, we might have expected him to declare that he will not be left homeless. Instead, he switches metaphors once again, and speaks about a change of garments. This, however, makes perfect (if somewhat confusing!) sense if we remember that he believes that *the process of taking on the image of Christ* (to revert to his original metaphor of 3:18!) *has already begun*. As long as he remains in his 'tent', he groans, longing for something better – namely to be 'clothed upon' (v. 2). The introduction of this new image leads Paul to make an aside:[57] since his 'inner man' is being renewed daily, he is of course presupposing[58] that he will not be left naked when he dies, since he has already 'put on' (ἐνδυσάμενοι[59]) Christ.[60] In v. 4 he repeats what he told us in v. 2: as long as he remains in the tent, he groans. He does not wish to be 'unclothed' (i.e. to

---

[57] Jerome Murphy-O'Connor, *The Theology of the Second Letter to the Corinthians* (Cambridge: Cambridge University Press, 1991), 52, regards v. 3 as a parenthesis, in which Paul 'uses the symbol of "clothed" in a new sense'.

[58] Commentators agree that both εἴ γε and εἴπερ, found in P⁴⁶ B D, convey assurance.

[59] This paraphrase assumes that the correct reading here is ἐνδυσάμενοι. As we have noted, however (n. 49), some mss read ἐκδυσάμενοι. If the reading ἐνδυσάμενοι is correct, we should note that Paul does *not* use here the verb ἐπενδύομαι of vv. 2, 4, a verb which implies putting on an additional garment. Barrett, *2 Corinthians*, says that the word is simply 'repeating the sense of the compound verb of the preceding verse', but we suggest that the change is deliberate. If we read ἐκδυσάμενοι, then Paul is affirming that even if his 'outer man' is completely destroyed, he will not be left naked, but the reason is the same – he has already 'put on' Christ.

[60] R. F. Hettlinger, '2 Corinthians 5.1–10', believes that the idea that 'the Christian is already clothed with Christ' is significant, and that Paul could not 'have regarded death as an interruption of ... incorporation [into Christ] – as nakedness' (188 ff.). He nevertheless translates v. 3

die), but to be 'clothed upon'. He is confident that – to put it another way – the mortal will be 'swallowed up' by immortality, since this is God's plan (v. 5).

Whatever happens, then (and however we interpret these four verses!), Paul is confident that a heavenly building awaits Christians, and that this hope is guaranteed by the presence of the Spirit, who is the ἀρραβών of what awaits us (vv. 5 ff.). But this reference to the Spirit as an ἀρραβών of what is to come reminds us that *already* we see the glory of the Lord, and are being transformed into the likeness of Christ, through the power of the Lord, who is the Spirit (3:18).

In v. 6, however, Paul introduces a new idea. We have already seen that what he says in 4:14 is reminiscent of the picture painted in 1 Thess 4:15, where dead believers are raised to life and are joined by 'those of us who are still alive', caught up in clouds to 'meet the Lord'. We have noted that one crucial difference is that Paul no longer expects to be among the survivors at the Lord's return. More radically, however, he now regards it as *a positive personal advantage* to be one of those whom the world would classify as 'dead'. Whereas, in writing to the Thessalonians, he had assured them that the living would 'have no advantage' at the parousia over those who had died (1 Thess 4:15), he now suggests that it may be better to be dead (in the Lord) than alive, since he believes that those who have died are 'at home with the Lord', while the living are in a sense in exile 5:6–8. This is strange language from one who expressed so strongly his joy in living with Christ and in Christ, but it corresponds to the belief he expresses in Phil 1:23, that 'to depart' is to 'be with Christ'. It is perhaps explained by the image he uses in Phil 3:20, where he describes Christians as those who have their citizenship in heaven. However joyful his present experience of living in Christ, it is only a foretaste of future joy, and to be 'at home' with Christ – 'in heaven' – will be even better. But 'whether at home or away', he declares in 2 Cor 5:9, 'our aim is to please the Lord'. This serves to introduce the theme of judgement (v. 10) – and so reminds us of Paul's original concern, which was a defence of his ministry; not, of course, that he was answerable to the Corinthians, for he – like them – must appear before the judgement seat of Christ.

In 2 Cor 5:11, then, Paul points out the relevance of his arguments for his main theme – the defence of his ministry – with the linking 'therefore'. What he has written is not intended to be a way of commending himself (v. 12) – for, as he wrote in 4:5, he proclaims not himself, but 'Jesus Christ as Lord'. In everything he is constrained by the love of Christ. The gospel he proclaims is that he 'died for all, and the consequence of this (ἄρα) is that all have died' (v. 14). Moreover, 'he died for all, in order that (ἵνα) those who live might live no longer for themselves, but for him who died and was raised for them'

---

as 'on the assumption *of course* that when we shall have put on this clothing *at death* we shall not be found naked *before God*' (190).

(v. 15). The repetition of the first clause emphasizes the importance of what is being said:

> One died for *all*, and the consequence of this (ἄρα) is that *all* have died.
> He *died* for all, in order that (ἵνα) those who live might *live*
> – no longer for themselves, but for him who died and was raised for them.

The reciprocal nature of the gospel – he died for all, *in order that* they might live for him – spells out a little more fully what Paul expressed in earlier letters. It is, for example, very similar to the early summary of belief in 1 Thess 5:10: 'Our Lord Jesus Christ died for us, so that whether we are awake or asleep we may live with him', while Gal 2:19 expressed Paul's own experience: 'I died to the Law, in order that I might live to God'.

Since all have died, and those who live no longer live for themselves, but for Christ, there is now 'a new creation' (v. 17). Paul's claim is equivalent to saying that the Age to Come is already here: 'the old has passed away, and the new has arrived'. The promises of Old Testament prophets such as Isaiah are fulfilled. Paul's claims emphasize the present reality of what had hitherto been only a future hope. This dramatic change is the result of God's action in reconciling us to himself through Christ. Now he has entrusted this ministry to Paul and others, who are ambassadors for Christ. Their message is that all should be reconciled to God, and if one wonders how this reconciliation is possible, it is because God made Christ, 'who knew no sin, to be sin, in order that in him we might become the righteousness of God' (5:21).[61]

Paul continues his appeal to the Corinthians in the following chapter, where he once again insists that his ministry has meant enduring both suffering (6:4ff.) and demonstrating Christian spiritual gifts (6:6ff.).[62] In the eyes of the world he has been as good as dead, and yet he is alive; he has been poor, yet has made many rich (and so shared the ministry of Christ, 8:9); has had nothing, yet possessed all things (6:8–10). So the Corinthians in turn, believers in Christ, must live as the people of God, called to holiness (6:14–7:1).

3. Conclusion

The different hopes expressed in Paul's letters appear to reflect changes in Paul's circumstances rather than a radical change of view, but far more importantly *they reflect the different subjects under discussion and the different problems addressed.*

---

[61] On the possible significance of this verse, see Morna D. Hooker, 'On Becoming the Righteousness of God: Another Look at 2 Cor 5:21', *NT* 50 (2008): 358–375 = above, essay 28 (pp. 401–415).

[62] Cf. Furnish, *II Corinthians, in loc.*

It is in 1 Thessalonians and 1 Corinthians that we find Paul spelling out what he believes will happen at the parousia, and in both cases, this is *because a particular problem about the future resurrection has arisen in the church that he is addressing*. His hopes about what might happen to him personally after death are found in 2 Corinthians and Philippians – in each case, *because of the particular situation in which he finds himself.* In Galatians and Romans there is no extended discussion of either question, since his main concern is to spell out what God has done and is doing for those who trust in Christ; nevertheless, the ultimate goal is always in sight, and in Romans especially we are aware of the eschatological tension between what has already been done and what lies in the future.

How, then, are we to make sense of 2 Cor 5:1–10? In 4:14, Paul has stated his faith that the one who raised the Lord Jesus will bring him into his presence. He is confident that the pattern of death/life already at work in him will continue after death: affliction is the preparation for glory (4:16–18). That means that if his 'earthly tent' is finally destroyed, there is an eternal house awaiting him in heaven. As long as he is alive, he groans, waiting for what is better, hoping for the day when he will be clothed with his heavenly dwelling, trusting that he will not be found naked. Although Paul does not refer directly to the parousia, he is using the language associated with the parousia in 1 Cor 15:51–55, and appears to be referring to that event. What he is describing is his present situation – confident of the future, and wishing that what is promised were already here, but meanwhile enduring the afflictions of the present. This is the burden he must bear, as long as his ministry continues. That is what it means to be 'at home in the body but away from the Lord' (5:6). That is what it means to walk by faith – the faith expressed in 4:14. In other words, what he is describing in 5:1–5 is a continuation of what he writes in 4:7–18, i.e. *a description of his present situation, as he awaits the Lord's return, rather than what he expects to happen to him if he dies before that occurs*. It sums up his confident hope that his present affliction is preparing 'an eternal weight of glory' (4:17). As long as he continues in this life, he groans, longing for the glory that awaits him. Of course he would *prefer* to be 'away from the body and at home with the Lord' (v. 8)! Whether that will take place immediately after his death or only after the parousia he does not specify. His concern is only to express his confidence in the final outcome (vv. 6 and 8).

If this interpretation is correct, then 2 Cor 5:1–10 is in no way opposed to the picture which Paul draws in 1 Corinthians – rather, it draws on it. As there, so here (4:14), what he says is founded on his belief in future resurrection. Those who live in Christ are eager for the parousia, when – as in 1 Cor 15:53 ff. – 'the mortal will be swallowed up by life' (5:4). Certainly Paul introduces a new idea – the thought that he himself may die before the parousia – but if that happens the heavenly habitation will still be his. Whichever happens, he is confident that what God has planned will be fulfilled (v. 5).[63]

In 5:8 Paul expresses the hope that it will be better to be 'away from the body, and at home with the Lord', a hope that reappears later in a bolder form in Phil 1:21, where he says that for him, 'to live is Christ, to die is gain', and goes on to declare that 'to be with Christ is far better' (v. 23). Bolder, too, is his declaration there that he is sure that Christ will be magnified in his body, whether by life or death (Phil 1:20). In 2 Corinthians, Paul already expressed that same idea, though somewhat more tentatively: his aim, he says, is to please the Lord, whether he is 'at home or away' (2 Cor 5:9), since (whether we live until the parousia or not), 'we must all appear before the judgement seat of Christ'. As we have noted, the nucleus of this idea is found already in the early summary of belief in 1 Thess 5:10: 'Our Lord Jesus Christ died for us, so that whether we are awake or asleep we may live with him', and in Gal 2:19, where Paul says that he died to the Law, in order that he 'might live to God'.

The fact that in two letters – 2 Corinthians and Philippians – Paul uses language about the future which seems to us to juxtapose incompatible ideas suggests that we are asking the wrong questions if we wonder whether his views changed radically with time.[64] The language of resurrection (found in 1 Corinthians, 2 Corinthians and Philippians) is a way of affirming confidence in the future, a confidence based on what God has done in Christ, and carrying with it all the ideas associated with new creation and new life. The hope of the parousia (referred to in 1 Corinthians and Philippians) expresses the conviction that all things will finally be put under the rule of Christ. When that takes place, death itself will be defeated (1 Cor 15:54). The conviction that those who die will be 'with Christ' (2 Corinthians and Philippians) arises from the belief that, in view of this final victory, death itself cannot separate those who have died and been raised with Christ from God's love in Christ (Rom 8:38 ff.). Paul does not bother to explain how this hope relates to the hope of the parousia – and had he been asked, he might well have dismissed the question as foolish, as in 1 Cor 15:36! The tension between the two is part of the eschatological tension that pervades *all* of Paul's writing – the tension between the now and not yet.[65] It is perhaps significant that in 1 Thessalonians,

---

[63] In view of Paul's changed circumstances, the development between 1 Corinthians 15 and 2 Corinthians 5 is a natural one. Cf. Moule, 'Dualism', 123: 'the essential distinction between his positions in I Cor. xv and II Cor. v is only that, in the former, he too lightly looked for addition, whereas, by II Cor. v, he was more realistically reckoning with exchange'.

[64] Cf. C. F. D. Moule, 'The Influence of Circumstances on the Use of Eschatological Terms', *JTS* NS 15 (1964): 1–15.

[65] Cf. Lowe, 'Developments', 136, commenting on the sudden transformation in 1 Corinthians and the gradual change in 2 Corinthians, writes: 'this is precisely that alternation

Paul already spoke both of the parousia *and* of future resurrection. Moreover, he spoke of living 'with Christ' as something experienced both by the living and by those who have died 'in Christ' (1 Thess 4:16; 5:10).

Finally we should note that we find this same tension between the now and the not yet in other New Testament writings, most notably in the Gospel of John. Although John does not refer to the parousia,[66] there is a tension between present and future experience. Jesus is said to have described himself as 'the resurrection and the life' (John 11:25). But what does this mean? It means that 'those who believe in me, even though they die, will live'; it also means that 'everyone who believes in me will never die'. These two statements are placed side by side. Elsewhere, he is said to claim that anyone who believes through hearing his word 'has eternal life and does not come under judgement, but has passed already from death to life' (John 5:24). Immediately after this, however, he speaks of a future resurrection to judgement (v. 28). Is he perhaps referring to a different group – i.e. non-believers? Not in 6:40, where we read that God's purpose is 'that all who see the Son and believe in him may have eternal life; and I will raise them up on the last day'. Although eternal life is continually spoken of as a present experience, resurrection remains in the future. The Fourth Evangelist apparently sees no problem in combining a belief in future resurrection with that of eternal life enjoyed here and now. The tension is well summed up in his phrase 'The time is coming and now is'.

It seems that Paul and John shared the problem of expressing the idea of the life given to believers except by using images which – logically – seem to us to be contradictory. The reason is perhaps that they are both attempting to describe a relationship with God, who is outside time, and for whom past, present, and future are all one.

4. Summary

1. The passage must be read in context, *not* taken as a digression. It is part of Paul's defence of his ministry. Following his description of what it means for him to experience sharing the sufferings and resurrection of Christ in his everyday life, he insists that this pattern of 'life through death' will continue even when his mortal body is destroyed. He is confident of the outcome of the final judgement (in contrast to the spurious judgements of the Corinthians).

---

between present process and final result which is characteristic of Paul's thinking from start to finish'.

[66] The references to Jesus coming again in John 17 are explained in terms of the coming of the Paraclete, and so applied to a *present* experience of the Gospel's readers.

2. There is no reason to suppose that Paul has changed his mind in any significant way since writing 1 Corinthians. There are many overlaps with what he says about his present experience of Christ and his future hope to suppose that this is so. Although Paul may be less confident than he was then that he will survive until the parousia, differences are mainly accounted for by the fact that the issue he is addressing in 2 Corinthians is his own situation, not the doubts of the Corinthians about the future resurrection.

3. In all these passages, Paul describes the Christian's future life in terms of life *with* Christ, *in* Christ, and *for* Christ. He understands this future life as the fulfilment of present experience, which he sees in terms of a growing conformity to Christ. This theme unites 1 Corinthians 15 and 2 Corinthians 5, and is far more important than any differences in imagery and perspective.

31. Artemis of Ephesus

1 Corinthians 15:32 has long been a *crux interpretum*. How could Paul, a Roman citizen, have been condemned to fight with wild beasts in the arena, and how, supposing such an unlikely event took place, could he have survived? Since Paul himself makes no reference to his citizenship, it is of course possible that the author of Acts was mistaken in describing him as a Roman citizen (Acts 16:37; 22:25–29), in which case our first difficulty disappears. Yet Paul's failure to refer to it may simply be due to the fact that he did not consider his citizenship to be relevant to the argument of any of the extant letters. For Luke, on the other hand, it was of fundamental importance, since it is the basis of Paul's appeal, and the reason why the book ends in Rome. If Paul were indeed a Roman citizen, it seems extremely unlikely that he would have been condemned to fight with beasts, but had he done so, then, as various commentators have observed, he would most certainly have lost his Roman citizenship[1] – and this, according to Acts 22, was clearly not the case. By fighting in the arena, however, he would have lost not only his citizenship but his life as well, for he could hardly have survived such an encounter. We may safely conclude, then, that a literal interpretation of Paul's words is impossible.

It would seem that Paul is using here one of the vivid metaphors of which he is so fond. But to what particular incident – or series of incidents – is he referring? All we know from 1 Corinthians itself is that it took place in Ephesus (from where Paul now writes his letter, 16:8), and that it was life-threatening (15:30), for Paul's train of thought suggests that it was an extreme example of the dangers which faced him every day (v. 31). This rules out Malherbe's suggestion that Paul is referring here to Paul's vigorous opposition to those who advocated self-indulgence, and even perhaps to his own battle for self-control in face of temptation,[2] for though it is true that Paul goes on to contrast his own faith in the resurrection with the attitude of those who advocated hedonism (such as is described in Isa 22:13), a battle of this kind would hardly have been life-threatening. Nor was such philosophy confined to Ephesus. Indeed, self-indulgence seems to have infected the Corinthian church, where some were apparently advocating sexual licence and excessive

---

[1] See e.g. C.K. Barrett, *A Commentary on the First Epistle to the Corinthians*, BNTC (London: A&C Black, 1968), 366.

[2] Abraham J. Malherbe, 'The Beasts at Ephesus', *JBL* 87 (1968): 71–80. The image of an inner struggle with a many-headed beast was used by Plato in *The Republic*, 589A, and was echoed by later philosophers.

eating: why, then, in writing to the Corinthians, should Paul refer to his struggle against such attitudes in *Ephesus* rather than in Corinth itself? Paul was, of course, writing the letter from Ephesus (1 Cor 16:8), but the fact that he used the aorist ἐθηριομάχησα in 15:32 indicates that he was thinking of a particular event located in Ephesus.

A more likely suggestion is that Paul is referring to violent opposition from human adversaries. In the Old Testament, powerful enemies are frequently referred to as wild beasts (LXX θηρία).[3] Paul himself describes opponents of 'his' gospel as 'dogs' (Phil 3:2), and – according to Luke – as wolves savaging the flock (Acts 20:29). Ignatius famously continued this tradition by describing his guard of Roman soldiers as leopards.[4] If this is the explanation of the metaphor in 1 Cor 15:32, it would have to refer to a confrontation with enemies that had proved so serious as to be life-threatening, but from which he had emerged victorious. Robert E. Osborne refers to a frieze found in the theatre at Corinth on which are seen men fighting with wild beasts, and notes the suggestion that it depicts *bestiarii,* i.e. gladiators trained to fight with animals, not prisoners condemned to die.[5] Paul is perhaps thinking of himself as one who, like a trained *bestiarius*, is able to defeat his opponents in the arena.[6] Osborne further notes that in 1QpHab 12 the θηρία of Hab 2:17 are interpreted as 'the simple of Judah who keep the Law', and asks whether it is 'eisegesis rather than exegesis' to suggest that Paul may be referring to 'Judaizers' in using the term here.[7] His question suggests that he was aware of the absurdity of his own proposal: not only do we have to imagine some link between the Qumran interpretation and Paul, but we are offered a remarkable progress in exegesis. Habakkuk uses the metaphor of wild beasts to refer to the *enemies* of Israel, due for punishment; for the Qumran community to reverse the imagery and the sense of the original by understanding the beasts to represent the *faithful* within Israel who keep the Law and are to be vindicated is strange enough, but for Paul then to reinterpret them as 'Judaizers' is a step too far.[8] This is indeed eisegesis gone mad.

Paul's reference to extreme danger is in no way surprising. By the time he wrote 2 Cor 11:23–27, he had experienced many such desperate situations. He 'boasts' there that he has frequently faced death, and describes how he has received 39 strokes from the Jews on five occasions, been beaten with

---

[3] E.g. Isa 56:9; Ezek 34:5, 8, 25, 28; Hos 2:12 (14 LXX); Ps 74:19; Daniel 7. Cf. also Ezek 29:3 ff. The same imagery is used in the book of Revelation; see especially ch. 13.

[4] Ignatius, *Rom.* 5:1.

[5] Robert E. Osborne, 'Paul and the Wild Beasts', *JBL* 85 (1966): 225–230.

[6] Cf. Paul's description of himself as a trained athlete in 1 Cor 9:25–27.

[7] Osborne, 'Paul and the Wild Beasts', 229.

[8] If Acts is to be believed, although some Jews refused to believe Paul's gospel, the only opposition he met in Ephesus came from worshippers of Artemis, not from 'Judaizers'.

rods (a Roman punishment) on three, and once been stoned. Among the many dangers he then lists he includes dangers from both his own people and from Gentiles. It would be understandable if he described a 'trial' before those in authority or a public confrontation with his opponents as 'fighting with beasts'.

Do we know of any such event that took place in Ephesus? The obvious answer is Yes – the gathering in the theatre described in Acts 19:28–41. There are, however, two problems with this. The first is that, according to Luke, Paul himself was not present. The crowd, he tells us, dragged Gaius and Aristarchus, Paul's travelling companions, to the theatre, and though Paul attempted to join them, he was prevented from doing so by his fellow Christians and by some local officials who were well disposed towards him, and who urged caution. Paul was therefore spared the confrontation with 'beasts' in the theatre. Even if Luke's account is correct, however, it is nevertheless true, as Barrett commented, that 'to have a theatre full of people thirsting for one's blood might well have seemed life-threatening'.[9]

Yet Paul's metaphor suggests that he had confronted his enemies face to face, and one must inevitably wonder whether he would have used it if he had not actually been present in the arena. And, if his description in 2 Cor 1:8–10 of the affliction that overtook him in Asia refers to this event, which is possible, this suggests that Paul's situation was even more dangerous than Luke depicts. Was Luke perhaps mistaken in saying that Paul himself was not present in the theatre? His desire to depict Roman officials as favourable to the Christian faith may have influenced his narrative, since the Asiarchs in Ephesus are said to have urged Paul not to enter the theatre. Nor would Luke have wished to portray Paul himself appearing before the mob in the theatre if he had then been unsuccessful in quelling the crowd: his hasty departure from Ephesus would look too much like a defeat. According to Luke (Acts 20:1), Paul left Ephesus when the uproar was over, and the implication seems to be that he lost no time in doing so. Any link between this and the riot is softened, however, by the fact that Paul's departure accords with his avowed intention, made earlier (19:21), of leaving Ephesus for Macedonia. This announcement and Paul's actual departure in fact frame the account of the riot, as though Luke is suggesting that this incident made no difference to Paul's plans.

The second difficulty with identifying the danger of 1 Cor 15:32 with the riot of Acts 19 is that Paul's hasty departure leaves no time for the composition

---

[9] C.K. Barrett, *A Critical and Exegetical Commentary on the Acts of the Apostles*, vol. 2, ICC (Edinburgh: T&T Clark, 1998), 918. The remark was made apropos the possible relation of the riot to 2 Cor 1:8–10, not 1 Cor 15:32. Barrett himself rejected the suggestion – which goes back at least to Tertullian (*On the Resurrection of the Flesh*, 48) – that 1 Cor 15:32 and 2 Cor 1:8 refer to the same event.

of 1 Corinthians, which we must therefore place *before* the riot took place. In this case Paul must be referring in 1 Cor 15:32 to something else.

There are in fact other problems with Luke's account of the riot,[10] but these are not so great as to make us deny that it took place. Moreover, it was serious — serious enough, Luke tells us, for Paul's friends, together with the Asiarchs, to persuade him not to appear. His absence from the theatre is not what we expect, since neither Luke nor Paul himself depict him as avoiding danger elsewhere, and this alone suggests that the danger was particularly great. But the more life-threatening the event, the more likely it is that Luke is correct in saying that Paul left Ephesus immediately afterwards, thus leaving no opportunity to write to Corinth. There are possible indications of this danger in Acts 20:16, where Paul, en route to Jerusalem, decides to bypass Ephesus. Was this, as Luke says, because he wished to save time, or was it because Ephesus had become too dangerous a place for him to visit? Was it merely to save time that he summoned the leaders of the Ephesian church to Miletus, rather than going to Ephesus himself?

It is possible, however, that Luke's link between the riot and Paul's departure from Ephesus was only an assumption — though a natural one. His introduction to the account of the riot in Acts 19:21 is far more vague than his conclusion: it took place κατὰ τὸν καιρὸν ἐκεῖνον i.e. at some time during the two or more years that Paul spent in Ephesus.[11] Since Luke also tells us that Paul's ministry had been extremely effective during that period (19:8–12),[12] we may assume that he had already come into conflict with the worshippers of Artemis, the great goddess of Ephesus, and with those who profited from her worship. The greater his success, the greater the challenge to Artemis. Was the riot caused by the silversmith Demetrius, then, perhaps only one of a series of confrontations between the Christians and those who opposed them? Paul's own comment in 1 Cor 16:9 that he is staying a little longer in Ephesus because 'a great opportunity for effective work has opened up, and there are many opponents' suggests that opposition was ongoing. The worship of Artemis was so long-standing and so well established in Ephesus that the conflict between her worshippers and the Christians was inevitable, and must also have been a protracted one.[13]

A further complication arises from the fact that, according to Acts, Paul had made an earlier visit to Ephesus. The first (Acts 18:8–21) is described as having been extremely hurried. Luke tells us only that Paul, having set sail for Syria,

---

[10] See Ernst Haenchen, *The Acts of the Apostles,* trans. Bernard Noble et al. (Oxford: Blackwell, 1971), 576–579.
[11] Acts 19:8, 10.
[12] See also vv. 17 and 26.
[13] See Richard Oster, 'The Ephesian Artemis as an Opponent of Early Christianity', *Jahrbuch für Antike und Christentum* 19 (1976): 24–44.

put into Ephesus, where he went to the synagogue, had a discussion with the Jews, was invited to stay longer, but declined. The reason for his haste to continue his voyage is not clear, and the whole episode is odd in the extreme.

In v. 18 Paul is described as having had his hair cut in fulfilment of a vow – an act which seems extremely unlikely, and is perhaps an attempt by Luke to depict Paul as a law-abiding Jew. Having arrived in Caesarea (which is in Judaea, not Syria) he went up and greeted the church, and then went down to Antioch (v. 22). After spending some time there, he set off back to Galatia and Phrygia. Why he undertook this journey is unexplained, and it is not surprising that in v. 21 the Western Text thought it necessary to add the information that Paul felt obliged to celebrate the coming feast in Jerusalem.[14] But did he in fact go to Jerusalem? Apart from this added note, Jerusalem is not even mentioned! The statement that Paul 'went up' may mean 'to Jerusalem', but leaves us wondering why, in this case, Luke did not spell this out. This whole paragraph suggests that Luke lacked information about Paul's movements at this point. Was it possible, then, that this earlier visit to Ephesus was more extensive than Luke suggests?

There are obviously far too many problems for us to be able to identify the event referred to in 1 Cor 15:32 with the riot of Acts 19:23–41. Nevertheless, we know that something happened in Ephesus that put his life in danger, and that he likened it to fighting with wild animals. It is significant that on the two occasions that Paul mentions the particular places where the dangers he encountered occurred, he refers to Ephesus and to Asia. What particular danger did he encounter in Ephesus? If he is not referring in 1 Cor 15:32 to the riot itself, then what was this great danger? Is there any special reason for him using the metaphor of fighting with wild animals in describing what happened in Ephesus? And, is it possible that Luke's account of the underlying causes of the Ephesian riot may provide a clue to help us understand Paul's metaphor?

The city of Ephesus was dominated by the great temple of Artemis, one of the seven wonders of the world. Her worship was identified with the city to such an extent that she was known throughout the region as 'Artemis of Ephesus'.[15] Inscriptions refer to Ephesus as the νεωκόρος of Artemis, implying that the city was regarded as responsible for guarding the goddess' honour.[16] Luke records that the town clerk of the city opened his appeal to the crowd with a reference to this fact (Acts 19:35). To such an extent was she identified with the city that on coins struck to commemorate treaties

---

[14] D (*) Ψ 𝔐 gig w sy.

[15] For the close links between Artemis and Ephesus, see Paul Trebilco, *The Early Christians in Ephesus from Paul to Ignatius,* WUNT 166 (Tübingen: Mohr Siebeck, 2004), 19–30.

[16] Steven J. Friesen, *Twice Neokoros,* Religions in the Graeco-Roman World 116 (Leiden: Brill, 1993), 55 ff.

with other cities, Ephesus was represented by an image of the goddess.[17] She was honoured by regular processions through the city. All this meant that her cult was the source of the city's wealth. Paul's gospel was inevitably regarded as an attack on the goddess, but since it was her worship that attracted the crowds to the city, it would have been seen also as a threat to the livelihood of the inhabitants. The silversmiths, in particular, enjoyed a lively trade manufacturing small statues of the goddess. Their real problem with Paul was that his success was undermining their trade, since those whom he converted to 'the Way' would no longer wish to buy shrines devoted to the goddess Artemis. They were able to present the danger, however, as an attack on Artemis herself, and it was this rather than the threat to their livelihood that gained them public support. In defending the goddess' welfare, the city entrusted with the task of acting as her νεωκόρος would, at the same time, be defending the welfare of its own citizens.

Artemis was worshipped elsewhere throughout the Roman Empire, as Demetrius reminds his fellow silversmiths in Acts 19:27, and like her Roman counterpart Diana, she is sometimes depicted with bow and arrows, since she was known as the goddess of hunting. Her connection with animals has a far more sinister side, however, for she was seen as being in command of all wild animals – in the water and the air, as well as on land.[18] In the Iliad she is described as 'Mistress of Beasts' (πότνια θηρῶν),[19] 'Lady of the Wilds', and 'Mistress of the Bow'. She is seen as fiercely aggressive, and is even said to have mocked her twin brother Apollo for his cowardice; Hera describes her as a lioness to women, whom Zeus allows her to destroy at her pleasure. Her worship was especially prevalent in Asia Minor,[20] where her cult had taken over elements associated with the local goddess Kybele, and so developed distinctive features. In art, for example, she was depicted with various beasts around her, or flanked by two lions, just as Kybele had been before her.

In the National Archaeological Museum in Naples, a remarkable second-century alabaster statue of Artemis of Ephesus which depicts her as Queen of Nature and Mistress of the Beasts brought home to the author how closely she was identified with wild beasts, so making Paul's metaphor particularly appropriate (see *Fig. 2*). The statue's head is a modern replacement, though it reproduces similar iconography found elsewhere: from it hangs a veil which bears

---

[17] Richard Oster, 'Numismatic Windows into the Social World of Early Christianity: A Methodological Inquiry', *JBL* 101 (1982): 215 ff.; Richard Oster, 'Ephesus as a Religious Center under the Principate, I: Paganism before Constantine', in *Aufsteig und Niedergang der römischen Welt* II/18/3, ed. H. Temporini and W. Haasa (New York: DeGruyter, 1990), 1661–1728.

[18] Walter Burkert, *Greek Religion: Archaic and Classical,* trans. John Raffan (Oxford: Blackwell, 1985), 149.

[19] Homer, *Iliad* 21.470.

[20] Note once again the words attributed to Demetrius, who is said to have described 'Asia and the world' as worshipping her (Acts 19:27).

Fig. 2. Second-century statue of Artemis of Ephesus, National Archaeological Museum in Naples. Photo: author.

the heads of lions and griffins. Round her neck are the signs of the Zodiac, while on her bust there are four rows of rounded protuberances. There has been considerable discussion about what these represent, but the long-held theory that they were breasts has been discredited, and it is now suggested that they depict the scrota of bulls which have been sacrificed to the goddess:[21] thus Artemis, identified with the Great Mother, is seen as the source of life.

---

[21] See Gérard Seiterle, 'Artemis – Die Grosse Göttin von Ephesos', *Antike Welt* 10 (1979): 3–16. See also Robert Fleischer, 'Neues zu Kleinasiastischen Kultstatuen', *Archaeologischer Anzeiger* 98 (1983): 86, and L. Portefaix, 'The Image of Artemis Ephesia – a Symbolic Configuration Related to Her Mysteries?', in *100 Jahre österreichische Forschungen in Ephesos,* eds.

The bottom half of the goddess' body is covered with rows of animal heads – lions, griffins, horses, bulls, and bees. This depiction is said to be typical of statues dating from the second-century BCE onwards.[22]

The goddess was clearly believed, then, to have strength superior to wild animals, and to have them at her command. The sight of her might bring comfort to those who thought of her as their protector, but would strike fear into her enemies. It would hardly be surprising if Paul were to describe a confrontation between himself and the enraged devotees of Artemis as 'fighting with wild beasts'. The Jewish metaphor depicting Israel's enemies as wild beasts would take on heightened significance in this context. For the reasons already discussed, the riot described by Luke in Acts 19 may not be the occasion Paul had in mind, but since we know that Luke failed to record many occasions when Paul (if he is to be believed) was in great danger,[23] then it is highly probable that considerably earlier in his two-year stay in Ephesus Paul would have been seen as a threat to the worship of Artemis, and would have been involved in dangerous confrontations with those who were devoted to her and whose livelihood he was thought to be undermining. The opportunities for preaching were enormous, but the dangers were real. As he wrote to the Corinthians, 'a wide door for effective work has opened to me, and there are many opponents'.[24] In proclaiming Jesus, rather than Artemis, he was, as *we* would say, putting his head into the lion's mouth. The riot described by Luke may have taken place *after* Paul wrote 1 Corinthians, but it could well have been the culmination of a series of incidents. By the time it took place the situation had very probably become so dangerous that his friends would think it prudent to keep Paul himself out of sight.

Whatever the precise occasion that Paul had in mind when he spoke of fighting with wild beasts, his metaphor seems a highly appropriate one for him to use in describing his resistance to the opposition aroused by his temerity in proclaiming the gospel of Jesus Christ in a city devoted to Artemis, Mistress of the beasts.

H. Friesinger and F. Krinzinger (Vienna: Verlag der Österreichischen Akademie der Wissenschaften, 1999), 611–617.
[22] Trebilco, *The Early Christians*, 23.
[23] 2 Cor 11:23–27.
[24] 1 Cor 16:9.

32. The Authority of the Bible: A New Testament Perspective*

A snippet of conversation on the radio, overheard by chance one day recently, focused my mind on the problem of the authority of the Bible. A man who firmly believed that the sun moved round the earth was being interviewed. Why did he hold this view, he was asked? The answer was that he based his whole life and philosophy on the Bible. So for an explanation of the universe, he turned first of all to Genesis 1. Blithely ignoring the statement that God's first action had been to create light, and that light had been separated from darkness, night from day, on the very first day of creation, he observed that the earth had been created on the second day, and that it was not until the fourth day that (somewhat belatedly!) God had created sun, moon, and stars, and had placed the sun in the dome of heaven to provide light to the earth. In this scheme, the sun clearly goes round the earth.

As far as this man was concerned, that was the end of the discussion. For him, everything was based on the Bible, so that it dictated even his understanding of science. Reminded that the Roman Catholic Church had recently, centuries after the event, apologized to Galileo for condemning his views, he remarked that the church had been right at the time, and that the apology had been a mistake.

Written centuries before modern scientific discoveries, the Bible reflects the views of a different age. In order to take its teaching seriously, this man clearly feels it necessary to deny the discoveries and views of the modern world. For him, the Bible is locked into a time capsule, and he is in effect imprisoned in it. Ironically, his very devotion to the teaching of the Bible makes it irrelevant to the world of today.

How does the Bible itself assist us with the problem of 'the authority of scripture'? If the biblical books have any kind of authority for Christians today, then the attitude of our New Testament writers to their scriptures is relevant to our quest. Since they rarely referred directly to the question of authority, however,[1] we need to look at the way in which they handled scripture. If we are to understand their approach, we need to remember that their worldview, too, was shaped by biblical teaching – which in their case meant, of course, the Jewish scriptures. Their starting point was the faith in

---

* A lecture given at North Park Theological Seminary, Chicago, in 2003.
[1] 2 Tim 3:14–17 is exceptional.

God and in his promises set out in what we call the Old Testament. For the early Christians, it was axiomatic that God was the creator of the universe, that he had entered into a covenant relationship with his people Israel, and that one day the world would be restored to peace and harmony and God's rule would be obeyed by everyone. The authority of scripture was self-evident. What they needed to understand and explain was how their new experience of what God had done in the life, death, and resurrection of Jesus Christ fitted into these beliefs.

Some might have argued – and indeed they did! – that the new experience and the old beliefs were irreconcilable. In that case, they must either reject the Christian gospel, as did many of the Jews, or abandon the writings of the Old Testament, as did Marcion and his followers in the second century. But our New Testament writers all insist that there is no conflict between old and new. In their various ways, the four evangelists all show how the 'good news' about Jesus is the continuation of God's purposes for Israel and for the world. For our purposes, however, it is perhaps best to concentrate on the teaching of Paul, who approaches the problem by using theological argument. Even in Paul, however, the question of 'the authority of scripture' is approached obliquely, rather than head-on, since for him, as for all Jews, the authority of scripture is axiomatic, and does not need to be discussed. Like all Jews, his faith and understanding of the world were shaped by the scriptures. Writing primarily to *Gentile* Christians in Rome, he reminds them that 'The scriptures written long ago were all written for our instruction' (Rom 15:4). The gospel that he proclaims was 'announced beforehand in sacred scriptures through the prophets' (Rom 1:2), and it is to those scriptures and the words of the prophets that he turns in order to expound it. If we want to understand how Paul understands the authority of scripture, then, we must see how he *uses* it; in particular, we must look at how he relates the teaching of what we call 'the Law' with the new life that has come to him through Christ. I shall concentrate on three passages where the issue of old and new demonstrates the kind of 'authority' that Paul gave to scripture.

Before we examine these passages, however, it may be helpful to make some introductory comments. First, in what follows, I shall normally render the Greek word *nomos*, as 'law'. Although *nomos* is used in the LXX to translate the Hebrew term *Torah*, meaning 'teaching', and so has a wider range of meaning than our word 'law', that teaching certainly included the commandments set out in the Pentateuch. It is with those commandments that Paul is concerned in the passages that we are to examine. The term should not be understood to imply that Judaism was of necessity a legalistic religion.[2]

---

[2] Paul sometimes uses *nomos* to refer to the Pentateuch, and even to all the Jewish scriptures (see e.g. Rom 3:19).

Second, Paul's methods of exegesis are those of his own day. They may well make preachers in the twenty-first century uneasy, for he tears passages out of context, uses allegory or typology to give new meanings to old stories, abandons the 'original' meanings of texts and turns them on their heads. We may well shy away from his methods, but the important issue for us is the authority that he ascribes to scripture, rather than his ways of interpreting it. The different ways in which he finds meaning in 'what is written' underlines its importance.

Third, Paul's explicit quotations of scripture occur in Romans, 1–2 Corinthians and Galatians. In Romans and Galatians, he is involved in arguing specifically about the relation between God's self-revelation in the past (as recorded in scripture) and his self-revelation in Christ. In these two epistles, Paul appeals to scripture in order to argue against what he regards as a false understanding of scripture. In 1–2 Corinthians, he is concerned to uphold the truth of the gospel and the genuineness of his own ministry over against the arrogant views of the Corinthians, who, influenced by the values prevalent in their city, boasted in their own wisdom, knowledge, and status. In both contexts – the 'Jewish' one in Romans and Galatians, and the 'pagan' one of 1–2 Corinthians – he appeals to Jewish scripture, in order to justify his gospel and its implications for his manner of life (and the manner of life appropriate for Christians).

We turn, then, to the three passages I have chosen as the focus for our thinking.

1. Second Corinthians 3–4

Second Corinthians 3:1–4:6 is a complex passage, about which many monographs have been written.[3] This is not the place to discuss the many exegetical difficulties found there. We are concerned only to consider the light the passage throws on Paul's use of scripture. Its relevance to our concern is, however, inevitably oblique, since here, as elsewhere, Paul is not concerned to discuss the authority of scripture, which for him is axiomatic. Nevertheless, the way in which he handles it is illuminating.

Paul's purpose in this passage is to defend his own ministry against those who have been attempting to undermine it. Hints of the accusations that have been brought against him are seen in the final verse of the previous chapter. He begins his defence by contrasting himself with those who come

---

[3] See, e.g., Linda L. Belleville, *Reflections of Glory: Paul's Polemical Use of the Moses-Doxa Tradition in 2 Corinthians 3.1–18,* JSNTSup 52 (Sheffield: JSOT Press, 1991). I have discussed the passage myself in 'Beyond the Things That are Written?: St. Paul's Use of Scripture', *NTS* 27 (1981): 295–309.

bearing letters of introduction, setting out their credentials. He has no need to commend himself, or to provide any kind of letter, since the Corinthians themselves are all the evidence he needs of his apostolic calling; the existence of the Christian community in Corinth is itself a 'letter', written on Paul's[4] heart, and this letter speaks for itself (3:1–2). The letter is from Christ himself, but it has been *delivered* by Paul. The verb Paul uses here (*diakoneō*) is, of course, related to the noun *diakonia*, meaning 'service' or 'ministry', a theme that Paul takes up a few verses later. This letter is written, not with ink, but with the Spirit of the living God. With a sudden change of metaphor, Paul now contrasts a letter written on tablets of stone with one written on tablets consisting of human hearts (v. 3). Letters written with ink and tablets of stone both stand over against what God himself effects.

Linda Belleville has rightly argued that the shift of metaphor from letters written with ink to tablets of stone is not accidental; the rest of the chapter, which focuses on the story in Exod 34, is not a mere diversion.[5] Paul's ministry is of a piece with his gospel, and both are about the work of the living God, whose Spirit is at work in human hearts. It is the Spirit who authenticates the truth of the gospel, over against reliance on carrying out the commandments of the Law (Gal 3:1–5). Fearing that what he claims may sound like boasting, Paul insists that his confidence is based, through Christ, on God, and that any competence he has comes from God (vv. 4–5), who has empowered the apostles 'as ministers of a new covenant'. Now Paul is using the language of Jeremiah 31:33. Jeremiah's vision was of a time when the covenant would be written on human hearts and so observed, in contrast to the covenant made by God with his people on Mt. Sinai – a covenant which they then broke. But Jeremiah was not alone in his hope for the future. Compare, e.g., this passage from Ezek 36:26–28:

> A new heart I will give you, and a new spirit I will put within you; and I will remove from your body the heart of stone and give you a heart of flesh. I will put my Spirit within you, and make you follow my statutes and be careful to observe my ordinances. Then you shall live in the land that I gave to your ancestors: and you shall be my people, and I will be your God.

The condemnation of Israel for failing to observe God's commandments, and the belief that God would not only punish her for her sins, but renew her through his Spirit, are constant themes in the prophets. The new covenant, Paul tells us, is characterized by Spirit (*pneuma*), not letter (*gramma*), for the letter kills, but the Spirit gives life (v. 6).

---

[4] There is a textual problem here: both *hēmōn* ('our') and *humōn* ('your') are well attested, and each makes sense in the context. If we read the former, the word presumably embraces Paul's fellow workers, who would share his lifestyle and so be criticized together with him.

[5] Belleville, *Reflections of Glory*, 146–149.

The ministry of Paul and his co-workers is now contrasted with the ministry of death – a ministry that was engraved in letters on stone. Yet that ministry was inaugurated with overwhelming glory, such that the Israelites could not bear to look at the face of Moses (v. 7). How much greater then, is the glory that accompanies the ministry of the Spirit (v. 8). Paul now repeats this same idea in several different ways. If glory accompanied the ministry that brought condemnation, how much more will the ministry that brings righteousness abound in glory (v. 9). Indeed, what had once been glorified has not been glorified at all in comparison with what is a far greater glory (v. 10). For if what was being abolished (i.e. Moses' ministry, which was concerned with an 'old' covenant[6]) was accompanied by glory, how much more is what endures accompanied by glory (v. 11).

The background of Paul's imagery is clear. He is thinking of the giving of the Law to Moses on Mt. Sinai; such was the glory that accompanied this event, that Moses' face reflected it when he descended from the mountain, and the Israelites were afraid to look at him.[7] It is extraordinary that in a passage where Paul is defending himself against accusations of being arrogant and commending himself, he should not only compare his own ministry with that of Moses, but claim that it is superior! He is surely asking for trouble. The only explanation is that his whole ministry depends on what he here describes as the 'new covenant', in contrast to the old. This new covenant is written in Spirit, not letter, and the implication is that the reverse was true of the 'old covenant'. The superior glory of the new ministry depends on the glory that is seen and reflected, and since 'glory' is nothing less than the self-revelation of God, what is being claimed is that God is more clearly revealed in the new dispensation, of which Paul is a minister, than in the old. The reason that he is called to be an apostle, and so proclaims the gospel with such boldness, is that what was 'promised beforehand in the holy scriptures and through the prophets' has been fulfilled (Rom 1:2).

The climax of Paul's argument comes in vv. 12–18. With extraordinary boldness, he now makes a direct contrast between his own ministry and that of Moses himself! No wonder he begins by explaining that it is on the basis of this hope (of enduring glory) that he is acting so boldly (v. 12). He now picks up another detail from the story in Exodus 34: having passed on the words of the Lord to the Israelites, Moses covered his face with a veil, removing it only when he spoke to the Lord and passed on God's commandments to the people; when he was not communicating with the Lord or with the people, he kept his face covered (Exod 34:33–35). In the Exodus narrative,

---

[6] Paul describes himself and his co-workers as ministers of a 'new covenant' in v. 6. In v. 14 he uses the contrasting phrase, 'old covenant'.

[7] Exod 34:29–30.

the explanation is that the people were afraid to look at Moses' face, which continued to reflect the glory of God: they needed to be protected from this ethereal light. Paul has already referred to this explanation in v. 7. Now, however, he gives another explanation for the veil: it was intended to prevent the Israelites from gazing at the end of what was in the process of fading away (v. 13). But, he adds in v. 14, their hearts were hardened.

What does Paul mean? That they did not realize that Moses was concealing anything from them? What does he mean by 'end' in v. 13? And what was it that was fading away? The word *katargoumenon* has been repeated from v. 11, and presumably refers to the ministry of Moses, for Paul is still contrasting his own ministry with that of Moses: it is Moses' ministry – that of the old covenant – that has what we would today describe as 'built-in obsolescence'. The word *telos* can mean 'end' both in the sense of 'termination' and 'goal'. Does Paul mean that the Jews failed to recognize that Moses' ministry was only temporary?[8] Or does he mean that they failed to recognize its true goal?[9] This, as we shall see, may well be the meaning of the word in Rom 10:4, where Christ is said to be the *telos* of the Law. If this is what he intends here, then he is suggesting that what was hidden from the Jews was the fact that Christ was the fulfilment of Moses' ministry. Whatever meaning we give to the word, however, it would seem that Paul is maintaining that the ministry of Moses, in passing on the Law to Israel, was temporary, and that the Jews had failed to recognize this.

At this point in Paul's argument the veil shifts from Moses' face to the 'old covenant' itself, from which it is taken away only by Christ (v. 14). Indeed, whenever Moses is read (for the old covenant is, of course, 'of letter, not of Spirit', v. 6), the veil lies over the hearts of those who hear his words (v. 15). It would seem that they failed to see that the 'old covenant' pointed to a 'new covenant', and that the true significance of the old covenant is revealed only in Christ. But (and here Paul quotes loosely from Exod 34:34) 'whenever he turns to the Lord, the veil is removed' (v. 16). The original passage refers to Moses going in to speak to the Lord. But who is now doing the turning? Is it still Moses? If so, then 'Moses' must stand for any Jew of Paul's own time. More difficult, perhaps, is the question 'Who is the Lord?' After the reference to Christ in v. 14 we might perhaps think that Paul is thinking of Jews turning to Christ, but the passage in Exodus was clearly referring to God himself: Moses was understood to be going into the tabernacle to speak to God. But

---

[8] So, e.g., Victor Paul Furnish, *II Corinthians*, AB 32A (Garden City, NY: Doubleday, 1984), 207; Margaret Thrall, *A Critical and Exegetical Commentary on the Second Epistle to the Corinthians*, vol. 1, ICC (Edinburgh: T&T Clark, 1994), 256–258. She argues that Moses concealed what was negative, not what was positive.

[9] So, e.g., Jean Héring, *The Second Epistle of Saint Paul to the Corinthians*, trans. A. W. Heathcote and P. J. Allcock (London: Epworth, 1967), 25.

there is more to be said on the matter: Paul's next words are probably a comment on the Exodus story. 'Now the Lord is the Spirit', he explains, 'and where the Spirit of the Lord is, there is freedom'. When one 'turns to the Lord', and speaks with him directly, one is confronted by the Spirit of God. Paul has neatly taken his argument back to the beginning, and to his claim that the letter that certifies his ministry is written by the Spirit of the living God. That is why he wears no veil over his face, but reflects openly the glory of the Lord. The claim to direct communication with God over against the 'hidden' revelation of the Law reminds us of what Paul says in Gal 3:19 about the Law having been administered through angels at the hand of an intermediary. The result is that the Lord who is Spirit is changing 'us' into his own likeness, so that the glory we reflect is increasing, not diminishing (v. 18). Men and women are being restored to what God created them to be.

Since God in his mercy has entrusted this ministry to Paul, he does not lose heart (4:1); there is nothing shameful or deceitful in what he does, neither does he distort the word of God. By declaring the truth of God openly, he commends himself to others in the sight of God (v. 2). His gospel (in contrast to the Law, 3:14) is not veiled – except, that is, to those who are on the way to destruction (4:3), whose unbelieving minds have been blinded by the god of this world. They are unable to see the light of the gospel of the glory of Christ, who is the image of God (v. 4). In what is probably a refutation of an accusation brought by his critics, Paul declares: 'We do not preach ourselves; we preach Christ Jesus as Lord, and ourselves as your servants for Jesus' sake, because the God who said "Let light shine out of darkness" has shone in our hearts to give the light of the knowledge of the glory of God in the face of Jesus Christ' (4:5–6). The glory seen in the face of Christ is reflected from the face of his ministers (3:18), and since Christ is the image of God, this glory is the glory of God himself, a glory that was revealed when God created the world (Gen 1:3).

It is important to recognize what Paul is doing in this passage. His purpose is to defend his own ministry: he has perhaps been accused of lacking the necessary credentials, but his authority is not from any human source, but from God (3:1–3; cf. Gal 1:1). For Paul, the commission to proclaim God's Son among the Gentiles went hand-in-hand with his acceptance of the gospel (Gal 1:15–16), and the gospel, too, is a direct revelation from God of his glory, seen in the face of Christ (4:6; cf. Gal 1:12). The revelation of God's Son was made both to him and through him.[10] The real source of Paul's confidence regarding his ministry is found in the nature of the gospel itself. For proof of

---

[10] Gal 1:15–16. The Greek phrase *en emoi*, though normally translated 'to me', should perhaps be rendered literally as 'in me'. See Morna D. Hooker, *Paul: A Short Introduction* (Oxford: One World, 2003), 107.

the superiority of 'the Spirit' to 'the letter', Paul turns, paradoxically, to what is written – not, of course, to letters of commendation, but to scripture. Just as in Rom 3:21, he maintains that the Law and Prophets witness to the fact that God's righteousness has been revealed 'apart from the Law', so here in 2 Corinthians he uses scripture to argue that it points to something greater than itself.

'Paradoxically', and yet inevitably, Paul turns to scripture since 'what is written' is also God-given. Paul nowhere denies that Moses saw God's glory: indeed, he stresses the fact that Moses' face reflected the glory that he had seen. But Moses' ministry was temporary, and the glory was therefore fading. Moses is said to have concealed this fact from the Jews, and this is matched by their inability to understand the 'old covenant' when it is read. The problem was that this ministry, engraved in letters on tablets of stone, brought death. The result was that the full glory of God was hidden. That glory is now revealed on the face of Jesus Christ (4:6). It was of course the same God who had called light out of darkness and who had spoken to Moses on Sinai who had now revealed his righteousness in his Son. Of course the scriptures were 'holy', and of course the ministry of Moses reflected the glory of God; but God had spoken more clearly and more directly in the person of his Son, and had revealed his lasting glory in him.

What Paul expresses in 2 Corinthians 3–4 in his exposition of Exodus 34 has parallels elsewhere. We see similar ideas in the opening verses of Hebrews, where we are told that whereas in the past God spoke to our forefathers in many ways through the prophets, he has now spoken to us in this final age in the person of his Son. The author goes on to contrast the Son not only with angels but with Moses, who was not a son but God's faithful servant, and whose glory is therefore less than that of the Son (Heb 3:1–6). Once again, the authority for all these statements is scripture itself.

A similar assumption appears to be reflected in the so-called 'antitheses' in Matthew 5:21–48. Six times over, we have a quotation from a commandment of Moses. The passage is introduced by the statement in 5:17–18:

Do not suppose that I have come to abolish the Law or the prophets; I have not come to abolish but to fulfil. Truly I tell you, that until heaven and earth pass away, not the smallest letter or stroke of a letter shall pass away from the Law, until everything is fulfilled.

It is clear that unless Matthew is totally unaware of the significance of what he is writing, the antitheses cannot be understood as contradicting the meaning of the original commandments. What they do is to point behind the purpose of the command and widen its scope. One should not simply avoid murder, one should not hate; one should not simply refrain from adultery, but from lust also; one should not simply spare a woman from disgrace by giving her a legal document of divorce, but refrain from divorcing her; one should not simply be true to oaths sworn before God, but be true to one's word in every circumstance; one should not merely limit revenge to the equivalent punishment – 'an eye for an eye' – but refrain from revenge altogether; one should not merely love one's neighbour, but one's enemy as well. Matthew, who appeals constantly to what is written, shows himself aware of the limitations of 'the letter of the Law'. Law points *beyond* itself to the will of God.

Perhaps the most interesting parallel to 2 Corinthians 3–4, however, is found in the Fourth Gospel. The Prologue of John's Gospel, which provides the key to understanding what follows, is, like 2 Cor 3:1–4:6, an exposition of Genesis 1 and Exodus 34. Through his Word, God created the world, and revealed himself to men and women, but they failed to comprehend his self-revelation. He gave his people the Law through Moses, but an even greater gift – 'grace and truth' – came in the person of his only Son: in other words, 'the Word made flesh' is the full revelation of God's nature, the embodiment of what he is. Not even Moses was able to see God, but God's only Son, who is closest to God's heart, has made him fully known. Because we have seen the glory of the only son, we have seen the glory of God himself. This passage does not deny the validity of the revelation to Moses; the Law was 'given' (John 1:17), and in the following narrative Jesus appeals to what was written by Moses. But the reason that he does so is because the scriptures bear witness to him (John 5:37–40, 45–46).[11]

Even more illuminating is the discourse on the theme of bread in John 6. This is linked to the miracle of the feeding of the five thousand in 6:1–14, which is interpreted as a 'sign' (v. 14). The story is expounded in terms of the gift of manna to the Israelites in the wilderness. Comparisons are drawn between Moses and Jesus, who is seen as 'the prophet who is to come into the world' (v. 14), since the prophet was expected to repeat what Moses had done. But the manna eaten in the wilderness, like the bread shared in the miracle of the loaves and fishes, is in fact a symbol pointing to something greater. The manna was not itself the bread that comes down from heaven, since the bread from heaven, which is given by God – the bread of life – is Jesus himself (vv. 32–35, 48–51). Those who ate the manna in the wilderness died, but those who eat the 'living' bread will live (vv. 48–51, 58).

Although the miracle of the feeding is ostensibly set against the story of the giving of the manna, there is clearly another Old Testament scene in John's mind, and that is the giving of the Law on Mt. Sinai. In Jewish exegesis, manna was seen as a symbol of the Torah, the word of God that feeds and nourishes his people.[12] What is being claimed here, then, is that the true

---

[11] For a more detailed exposition of this passage, see Morna D. Hooker, 'The Johannine Prologue and the Messianic Secret', *NTS* 21 (1974): 40–58 = above, essay 23 (pp. 321–340).

[12] For examples, see Peder Borgen, *Bread from Heaven,* NTSup 10 (Leiden: Brill, 1965), 147–192.

source of nourishment is not the Law, but Jesus himself; it is his words, not the words of Torah, that give life, because they are also spirit (v. 63). He has come down from heaven to do God's will (vv. 37–40), and those who come to him and who believe in him will have eternal life (vv. 44–47). What is written in the Prophets (Isa 54:13) has been fulfilled, for the people are now 'all taught by God', for they are taught by his Son, who has seen him face to face (vv. 45–46). The Law was said to offer life, but those who ate the manna all died, whereas those who eat the living bread will live (vv. 48–51). The Jews strive to 'do the works of God' (v. 28), but the true 'work of God' is to believe in the one whom God has sent (v. 29). The chapter ends with a scene in which the disciples are faced with a choice: others reject Jesus' teaching, but they confess that he is the Holy One of God, and has the words of eternal life (vv. 68–69).

Many of the ideas used in 2 Corinthians 3–4 reappear here: we find the same contrast between Moses and Jesus, between faith and works, between death and life, between something that was clearly transient and something that is eternal, because it is 'spirit and life'. The links are so close as to suggest that early Christians had to rethink their understanding of the story of the law-giving on Sinai. The question of the authority of the Law and the Prophets was clearly an important issue.

In Paul, John, Matthew, and the author to the Hebrews, then, we have four very different writers, all of whom appeal constantly to scripture as their authority, nevertheless all maintaining that scripture points beyond itself to a superior revelation in Christ.

2. Romans 2:12–16, 25–29

My second passage, like my first, is not specifically about scripture. Its purpose is very different from 2 Corinthians 3–4, since in Romans 2 Paul is arguing that Jews have dishonoured God because of their transgression of the Law; like the Gentiles, they do not give God the glory that is due to him, and so fail to reflect his glory (Rom 1:23; 3:23). Once again, however (v. 29), Paul uses the contrast between *pneuma* (spirit) and *gramma* (letter). No one, he says, will be accounted righteous before God simply by hearing the Law; it is necessary to *do* it (2:13). Gentiles who have what the Law requires written on their hearts will put to shame Jews who fail to observe it (vv. 14–15). So, too, with circumcision: neither 'written code'[13] nor physical circumcision is of value if one transgresses against the Law (vv. 25–27); the mark of the true Jew is 'circumcision of the heart', and is a matter of spirit not letter (v. 29).

---

[13] REB. Paul's word is *gramma*, lit. 'letter'.

The images of Law written on human hearts and circumcision of the heart both suggest once again Jeremiah's vision of the new covenant, which Paul has already used in 2 Corinthians 3. Remarkably, Paul is talking here about Gentiles, who are described as 'not having the Law' (v. 14) and as 'uncircumcised' (v. 27). There is considerable disagreement as to whether Paul is thinking of pagan Gentiles who instinctively do what the Law requires or of Christians who do not by birth have the Law but nevertheless fulfil it. Is Paul underlining his argument regarding the Jews' failure by suggesting that Gentiles are capable of natural goodness? Or is he already pointing forward to the fact that those who did not belong to Israel are, through Christ, included in the new dispensation (Rom 9:30)?[14] Whichever he means, he is pointing to a righteousness before God which does not depend on the Law, even though it is witnessed to by the Law and Prophets (Rom 3:21), a righteousness which will be disclosed when God judges human hearts through Christ Jesus (2:16).

In-between these two paragraphs in Romans 2, in vv. 17–24, Paul makes a most extraordinary attack on his fellow Jews, and specifically on those who rely on their observance of the Law. 'You, who teach others,' he asks, 'why do you not teach yourself?' Four accusations follow, though it is not clear whether we should understand these as statements of what certainly is the case, or questions about what may be true:

> While preaching 'do not steal', do you steal?
> While preaching 'do not commit adultery', do you commit adultery?
> While abhorring idols, do you commit sacrilege?[15]
> You boast in the Law, but through transgression of the Law you dishonour God.[16]

The proof that these charges are justified is to be seen in the words of scripture: 'The name of God is blamed because of you among the Gentiles' (Isa 52:5).

Many Old Testament passages have been suggested as parallels to Paul's extraordinary accusations. They are indeed in the tradition of the prophets. The most interesting is found in Jer 7:9–10: 'Will you steal, murder, commit adultery, swear falsely, burn incense to Baal, and go after other gods and then

---

[14] The matter largely depends on whether the word *phusei* ('by nature') is taken with the words that precede it, or with those that follow. In favour of the former interpretation is the order of words; in favour of the latter is the use of the term in v. 27, where it clearly means 'by descent'. Those who support the former view include C. K. Barrett, *A Commentary on the Epistle to the Romans,* BNTC (London: A&C Black, 1991), *in loc.*, and James D. G. Dunn, *Romans 1–8,* WBC 38A, (Dallas: Word Books, 1988), *in loc.* Among those who support the latter is C. E. B. Cranfield, *A Critical and Exegetical Commentary on the Epistle to the Romans,* vol. 1, ICC (Edinburgh: T&T Clark, 1975), *in loc.*

[15] Lit. 'rob temples'.

[16] The slight change in construction (to a relative pronoun with the indicative) suggests that this last accusation is a statement rather than a question.

come and stand before me in this house which is called by my name, and say "We are delivered" – only to go on doing all these abominations?'

Jeremiah's accusations include those listed by Paul when he writes 'do you steal, commit adultery, and commit sacrilege?' But instead of his summary statement that those who boast in the *Law* dishonour God, Jeremiah's accusations are addressed to those who trusted in the *temple*, saying: 'this is the temple of the Lord, the temple of the Lord, the temple of the Lord' (Jer 7:4). Both Jeremiah and Paul, however, have the same concern. Those they condemned were boasting in God, but failing to obey his will: their worship was external only, not a matter of the heart.

Those whom Paul attacks here regarded themselves as devout Jews, and believed that they were following exactly what the Law – scripture – decreed. While scrupulously following the letter of the Law, however, they were, he maintains, failing to do what in reality it demanded.

The contrast in 2:29 between 'letter' and 'Spirit' is picked up later in Romans 7, where Paul deals specifically with the inadequacy of the Law. Although the Law is holy, and its commandments are holy, righteous, and good (7:12), it is unable to prevent sin because of human weakness. Although it is 'spiritual', the Law operates in the sphere of 'flesh', not 'Spirit' (7:14). Christians, however, have been released from its demands, and so are able to serve God in the new life of the Spirit, instead of under the old written code (*gramma*, 7:6). This has come about because God himself has done what the Law could not do, by sending his Son to share our human condition, and in doing so has not only condemned sin but, paradoxically, enabled the demands of the Law to be fulfilled in those who live according to the Spirit instead of the flesh (Rom 8:3–4).

The idea that the Law is fulfilled in those who are 'in Christ' (Rom 8:1) is reflected in various other passages in Paul. In Rom 13:8, Paul declares that those who love others have fulfilled the Law; he then quotes four of the Ten Commandments, and says that all the commandments are summed up in the command to love one's neighbour, since love is the fulfilment of the Law. Out of context, we might suppose that Paul is simply insisting on obedience to the Law's commands, but of course he is appealing to the principle *behind* the Law, which is the law of love. He understands the commandments to be spelling out some of the implications of what it means to love one's neighbour. Paul is not, of course, alone. Jesus himself appeals to the same principle,[17] as do contemporary Jewish rabbis.[18] Once again, Paul is loyal to Jewish tradition, and to the demand to see the implication of the commands.

---

[17] See Matt 22:34–40 // Mark 12:28–31 // Luke 10:25–28.
[18] Similar sayings are attributed to R. Hillel (first century; see T Bab Šabb. 31a) and to R. Akiba (second century; see Sipra 89b, and are also found in Testament of Issachar 5:2; 7:6; and Testament of Dan 5:3.

We have to remember, however, that for Paul this 'new' commandment depends on the 'Therefore' of Rom 12:1. What Christians now do they do because they are enabled, in Christ, to offer themselves to God 'as a living holy sacrifice', and it is in him that their attitudes have been transformed (12:2). Moreover, Paul's argument in Rom 13:8–10 shows that he thinks there is a danger that in concentrating on each and every commandment, Christians may miss their point: what is important is not avoiding this or that action, but loving others. One must not limit the principle of loving others to particular examples.

The same idea is expressed in Gal 5:14. The whole Law, says Paul, is summed up in the commandment to love one's neighbour as oneself. Once again, we need to read this in context, for in this chapter Paul is insisting that Gentile Christians must not accept circumcision, and so put themselves under the Law (5:2–6). Christians have been set free (v. 13), and must be guided by the Spirit (v. 16). Those who are guided by the Spirit must express their love for others by bearing one another's burdens; in doing so they will fulfil 'the law of Christ' (6:1–2). What the Law commands is good and true, but men and women are unable to 'do' what the Law commands until they are in Christ, and the Holy Spirit takes over their lives. 'The Law' finds its 'fulfilment', its true significance, in the law of Christ: what is written points beyond itself, to the purpose of God.

3. Romans 9:30–10:10

In Rom 9–11 Paul is endeavouring to explain God's dealings with Israel. He insists that Israel's failure to respond to the gospel does not mean that God's word has failed; on the contrary, the promises made to Abraham have been fulfilled. God's purposes have been worked out in extraordinary ways, but the result has been that he has made known 'the riches of his glory' for those whom he has called, including Gentiles as well as Jews (9:23). He concludes (9:30–32):

> What, then, are we to say? Gentiles, who did not strive after righteousness have obtained righteousness – that is, righteousness on the basis of faith (that is, trust in God) – whereas Israel, who strove after the law of righteousness, did not attain that Law. Why not? Because she strove after it as though it could be fulfilled on the basis of works, not faith.

Paul does not say here quite what we expect him to say! In particular, what he says about Israel surprises us. Contrary to the translators, he does *not* say that Israel 'did not succeed in *fulfilling* [the] Law',[19] nor does he say that Is-

---

[19] NRSV; cf. NJB.

rael was striving 'for the righteousness that is based on the Law'[20] or that she 'did not attain *righteousness*'.[21] He says that she did not attain *the Law*. Why? The answer becomes clear when we turn back to the previous sentence. We might well have expected Paul to make a clear contrast with what he said in v. 30, and to write: 'Gentiles, who do not strive after righteousness.... Israel, who *does* strive after righteousness....' In fact, however, he spoke of Israel striving after a *law* of righteousness: it is this 'law of righteousness' that Israel has failed to attain. But is this law of righteousness simply the equivalent of the righteousness of the Law he refers to in 10:4? I suggest not. For what we have here is the idea of two contrasted goals. The goal for which Gentiles were *not* striving, but which they nevertheless reached, was *righteousness*. The goal for which *Israel* was striving was *the Law itself* – the Law whose own goal was, indeed, righteousness. In striving to fulfil it, however, Israel lost sight of the Law's purpose: she treated it as an end in itself instead of pursuing its goal – righteousness. Since she did not attain the Law, there is no need to explain that she did not attain righteousness either. Her mistake was to pursue the Law as though it could be achieved on the principle of works, and not through faith (v. 32). Paul's accusation, then, is not simply that Israel did not attain righteousness, but that she pursued the wrong goal, because she had misunderstood the role of the Law.

Paul backs up his argument with a quotation from scripture – here a mixed quotation from Isa 28:16 and 8:14 about a stone that leads to stumbling. In Isaiah 8, the stone is God himself, who nevertheless becomes a rock that causes Israel to stumble. In Isaiah 28, the rock is laid by God in Zion as a cornerstone and sure foundation. Its significance is unclear, although here, too, it may symbolize the presence of Yahweh himself, on whom the new spiritual temple – the new society of God's people – depends; the targum of Isaiah 28, however, understands the stone as referring to the Messiah. In Romans, the stone which is laid by God, and over which Israel has stumbled, is assumed by almost all commentators to refer to Christ.[22]

Is Paul affirming here that Israel's problem is simply that she has failed to believe in Christ? The majority of commentators accept this interpretation, but the possibility supported by some scholars that the stumbling-block is the Law[23] should not be too easily dismissed. It should be noted, after all, that

---

[20] RSV; cf. JB.

[21] F.F. Bruce, *Romans*, 2nd ed., NCB (Grand Rapids: Eerdmans, 1989), 138. Paul Wilhelm Schmiedel's suggested emendation of the text is noted in the margin of Nestle-Aland's text.

[22] This interpretation is supported by the christological interpretation of the two Isaiah texts in 1 Pet 2:4–8. The words that follow, referring to 'trusting in him/it' are normally understood to refer to Christ also. Certainly the phrase has this meaning when the words are repeated in Rom 10:11: 'the Lord' of vv. 12–13 must be 'the Lord' of v. 9.

[23] So C.K. Barrett, 'Romans 9.30–10.21: Fall and Responsibility of Israel', in *Die Israelfrage nach Röm 9–11*, ed. Lorenzo De Lorenzi (Rome: Abbey of St Paul Outside the Walls, 1977),

Christ has not been mentioned since 9:1–5, and that the two subjects under discussion in Rom 9:30–31 are the Law and righteousness. Moreover, what Paul has just stated is that Israel has misunderstood the function of the Law. Perhaps, then, the stumbling-block over which Israel has fallen is the Law.[24]

But the reason that a stone causes one to stumble is normally that it is hidden from view – hardly true of the Law. The metaphor suggests something obscure, which appears here to be the 'hidden' meaning of scripture. What was hidden from Israel seems to be the fact that the Law could not be attained by works, and that the righteousness promised in the Law came only through faith – i.e. trust in God. It was this, says Paul, that Israel had failed to grasp, even though it is set out in the Law itself (3:19–22). In other words, Israel has tripped up because she has misunderstood the Law and been unaware of its true significance. Scripture promises that those who have faith will not be ashamed (9:33). But in whom or what should they believe? The ambiguity in the quotation in v. 33 reminds us that the answer is still hidden from Israel. It will be spelt out in the next paragraph, where Christ is revealed as the 'purpose' or 'goal' of the Law, and where the promise that those who believe in him clearly refers to him. The 'hidden' meaning of scripture is, then, Christ himself and the righteousness that is found in him. Those who maintain that the 'stumbling-block' is Christ are also right!

The chiastic structure of vv. 30–33 supports the suggestion that what has caused Israel to stumble is their understanding – or rather, their misunderstanding – of the role of the Law. This misunderstanding led her to regard the Law as though the righteousness it demanded were based on works. In fact, this righteousness was based on God's faithfulness, and on faith in him.

a) Gentiles, who did not pursue *righteousness*, nevertheless attained it – on the basis of faith (v. 30).
b) Israel, who pursued the *law* of righteousness, did not attain the Law – because she did so 'as though' its basis was works, not faith (vv. 30–31).
b) She tripped over the stone of stumbling, as scripture itself testifies.
a) Scripture also affirms that those who have faith in it/him will not be ashamed.

99–130; also Barrett, *Romans, in loc.* Cf. Paul W. Meyer, 'Romans 10:4 and the End of the Law', in *The Divine Helmsman: Studies on God's Control of Human Events*, eds. James L. Crenshaw and Samuel Sandmel (New York: Ktav, 1980), 59–78.

[24] This interpretation of the 'rock' as symbolizing the Law finds some support in the structure of the mixed quotation from Isaiah, which inserts a phrase from Isa 8:14 into a framework drawn from Isa 28:16. Paul's quotation ignores the positive descriptions of the stone found in both LXX passages, and so places the emphasis on the stone as a cause of stumbling. His quotation of Isa 8:14 is much closer to the Hebrew than to the LXX, which expands the text, emphasizing that to those who are faithful to him, God is a sanctuary rather than a stumbling-block. The words from Isa 28:16, on the other hand, appear to be drawn from the LXX text, but omit the positive description of the stone as a cornerstone that has been tested and is sure.

So far, Christ has not been specifically mentioned in the argument that began at 9:6. Nevertheless, no one who has read Paul's argument in Romans 1–8 can doubt that the references to 'faith' and 'righteousness' are pointing towards him. What Paul says here is consistent with what he said in Romans 7, where he described the Law as holy and spiritual (7:12, 14), and the commandment as holy, righteous, and good. The Law is God's Law (7:22, 25) but is unable to do what it promised because of the weakness of the flesh (8:3), which has come under the power of sin and death (7:23; 8:2). But for the contrast between the principles of 'works' and 'faith' we have to go back to 3:19–4:6. The Law itself, we are told there, supports Paul's assertion that 'no one will be accounted righteous in God's sight *by the works of the Law*', while both the Law and Prophets witness to the fact that in the gospel 'God's righteousness has been revealed to all who believe' (3:19–22). The Law which is 'of works' leads to boasting, but the Law which is 'of faith' excludes it (v. 27). Paul appears to be opposing two interpretations of the written Law, one of which sees it as demanding 'works', the other as witnessing to faith. When the Law is understood in terms of 'works' it leads to boasting, not to righteousness, which comes only by 'faith', or trust, in God (v. 28). We have here the same contrast that we find in 9:30–33; that contrast is between seeing the Law as a means to achieving righteousness, and understanding it as witnessing to what is offered to those who have faith.

In 10:1, Paul speaks of the zeal that his fellow countrymen have for God – a zeal which, according to Phil 3:6, he himself shared. This zeal is misinformed, however, because they are 'ignorant of God's righteousness'. 'Seeking to establish their own righteousness, they have not submitted to the righteousness of God' (v. 3). The same contrast reappears in Phil 3:9.[25] We know from earlier statements in the epistle that the 'righteousness of God' is revealed in the gospel (1:17), that it is attested to by the Law and Prophets (3:21), and that it is effective for all who believe 'through the faith of Jesus Christ' (3:22), though the meaning of this last phrase is, of course, disputed. Now Paul tells us that because Christ himself is the goal of the Law he brings righteousness to all who believe (v. 4). Christ is the goal of the Law because he *is* righteousness (cf. 1 Cor 1:30), and because he realizes righteousness for every believer. This is the righteousness which has been granted to Gentiles (9:30). What Paul's fellow Jews lost sight of, in seeking their own righteousness, was the righteousness of God. Like climbers toiling up a mountain, they had set their sights on a ridge, mistaking it for the top, and had not noticed their *real* goal – the peak hidden behind it.

---

[25] Paul's own righteousness is there said to be based on the Law, while God's is based on trust.

The context of Paul's statement in Rom 10:4 demands that we understand *telos* to mean 'goal' rather than 'termination'.[26] The role of the Law is affirmed, but it is temporary. When we set out on a journey, we do so in order to reach our destination; when we take a college course and sit an examination, it is in order to obtain a certain qualification. The fact that we arrive at our destination is not a denial of the interest of our journey, neither is the degree certificate we receive a denial of the value of the work we have undertaken, but it is no longer necessary for us to sit on a train or to attend lectures. Similarly, the role of the Law, in terms of discipline, belongs to what is past.

Once again, Paul appeals to scripture to back his argument – this time to Moses himself – and draws a contrast between the righteousness which is based on Law and that which is based on faith. Even without the parallel in Phil 3:9, it is clear that the former is the righteousness that the Jews have sought to establish – their own righteousness – while the latter comes to those who trust in God. Since Paul clearly assumes that both of the passages he quotes[27] were written by Moses, he is appealing to the Law itself as the witness to these two kinds of righteousness. The Law, then, speaks of a righteousness based on works (v. 5) – a righteousness which, however, has already been described in 9:32 and in 10:3 in disparaging terms.[28] But the Law *also* speaks of a righteousness that is based on faith (vv. 6–10), and witnesses to the fact that all that is necessary for salvation is the confession that Christ is Lord and faith that he has been raised from the dead. In a remarkable piece of hijacking, Deut 30:12 ff. is discovered to refer, not to the Law and to obedience to it, but to the gospel and to faith in Christ. The Law itself thus points beyond itself, to its 'goal', namely Christ.

The implication of Paul's argument is clear. If God's promises have been fulfilled, and his purpose – set out in the Law – is achieved in Christ, that purpose must be *prior* to the Law. Although he comes *after* the Law, Christ is certainly no 'afterthought', but represents God's purpose from the beginning of time. This is well summed up in Rom 16:25 (whether or not this passage was written by Paul himself): the proclamation of the gospel means the revelation of the secret which has been hidden for long ages but which is now made manifest, and has been made known through the prophetic writings – or rather (though this is not spelled out), through Christian exegesis of the

---

[26] For a discussion of this passage, and a defence of understanding *telos* as 'purpose' rather than 'abrogation', see Robert Badenas, *Christ the End of the Law*, JSNTSup 10 (Sheffield: JSOT Press, 1985). Cf. also Morna D. Hooker, 'Christ: the "End" of the Law', in *Neotestamentica et Philonica: Studies in Honor of Peder Borgen*, eds. David E. Aune, Torrey Seland, and Jarl Henning Ulrichsen, NTSup 106 (Leiden: Brill, 2003), 126–146 = above, essay 27 (pp. 384–400).

[27] Lev 18:5 and Deut 30:12–14.

[28] Paul described there how Israel had pursued the law of righteousness *as though* it could be attained by works, and how her people had *ignorantly* sought to establish their own righteousness.

prophets. If Christ is the 'end of the Law', the *goal* of the Law rather than simply its ending, then he must also have been there at its beginning. The Law is seen as witnessing to Christ and finding its fulfilment in him.

Paul's understanding of the relationship between Christ and the Law in this passage is in keeping with his argument in the rest of Romans. Throughout, Paul emphasizes that the gospel was the fulfilment of God's promises, set out in scripture,[29] that his people would experience his righteousness – promises which are now revealed to include Gentiles as well as Israel. By sending his own Son, God has enabled the requirements of the Law to be fulfilled (8:3–4), and the goal of the Law – righteousness – has been reached (10:4). Since Christ is the fulfilment of the Law, the obedience required by the covenant is achieved in him: so it is that the proclamation of the gospel leads to the obedience of faith (1:5; cf. 15:18; 16:26). The Law is not abrogated, but *fulfilled*.

4. The Role of Scripture

Arguments about Paul's ministry, about the place of Jew and Gentile in God's design, and about the contrast between 'works' and 'faith', may seem to have little to do with the authority of scripture. Yet all these passages throw interesting light on the question, not only because Paul appeals in all of them to scripture itself, but because behind his discussion of all these issues lies the question of his understanding of the *role* of scripture. For in talking about 'the Law', Paul is talking about the five books of Moses; indeed, as we have already noted, the term is sometimes used in a way that includes other books of the Hebrew scriptures as well. The Law is what is written, it is *gramma*, 'letter', and what is written has authority. How, then, can Paul oppose what the Law says?

The answer, of course, is that he does not. Rather, he points *beyond* the Law to the purpose of God. The giving of the Law to Moses was accompanied by great glory, but Moses was unable to look on the face of God, and the glory that he glimpsed was hidden, since he was able to see only Yahweh's back (Exod 33:18–23). Although what is written is itself holy, it is only a witness to the far greater holiness of God. When Paul contrasts *gramma* and *pneuma*, he is not comparing different ways of interpreting scripture – what we might call 'literal' and 'spiritual' – since he uses various methods in his own interpretation – sometimes what we might term literal, sometimes allegorical. *Gramma* refers rather to the *function* of scripture: scripture is what is written, and its purpose is to witness to what God is and does. But what God himself does is the work of *pneuma*. What is written cannot in itself give life; it can only witness to the life that God desires to give us.

---

[29] This idea is set out in his opening sentence: the gospel of God was promised beforehand through his prophets in the holy scriptures (1:2).

In pointing to the meaning behind scripture, Paul stands within the tradition of Old Testament prophets, who had condemned their people for worshipping God with their lips but not their hearts, and for keeping the letter of the Law while ignoring its fundamental demands. He stands, too, in the tradition of Jesus himself, who is reported to have come into conflict with those who were scrupulous in their observance of the sabbath, while failing to see that to save life was to do God's will, and to take life was to deny it.[30] Other New Testament writers, as we have seen, continued that tradition.

Does any of this help us in considering the authority of scripture for us today? It is perhaps because so much of the discussion is couched in terms of the role of 'the Law' that we fail to see its relevance. But 'the Law' is 'that which is written'; 'the Law and the Prophets', together with the writings, made up the Jewish scriptures. The contrast Paul was making was between what had become static (that which was written) and that which was alive and which gave life (the Spirit).

Because 'Law' has been understood so often as standing over against Christ, Christian tradition has tended to oppose 'Old Testament' and 'New Testament'. But for Paul, the contrast between the 'old covenant' and the 'new' was between *gramma* and *pneuma*, between what was written 'with ink' and what is written by the Spirit. 'Gospel' for our New Testament writers did not mean a written account, but good news that is proclaimed by word of mouth. When John declared that 'the Word had become flesh', he was referring to the living Word of God, who revealed the nature of God in a way that the Pentateuch, given through Moses, was unable to do. The church, however, has frequently *identified* the words of scripture with the Word of God. As a child, I remember singing the hymn 'O Word of God incarnate', and assuming that I was singing a hymn addressed to the Bible; the hymn was, after all, in the section of hymns concerned with 'the Holy Scriptures'! Only later did I discover that it was Christ who was the incarnate Word. How many others, I wonder, have made the same mistake? And how many in effect make that mistake by thinking of the Bible as 'the Word of God'? If our exegesis of various passages teaches us anything, it is that the Bible is the *witness* to God's self-revelation — to his Word — and not that Word itself. We need to distinguish between the Word of God and the words of scripture.

Because the self-revelation of God witnessed to in the Bible is found above all else in Christ, the incarnation is in fact the best model for understanding the Bible's authority. In the incarnation, God chose to accept the limitations of time and space and culture, and to become vulnerable to misunderstanding and rejection. The image of the helpless child reminds us of the risk which is involved in the incarnation: of the vulnerability of God's self-revelation. In

---

[30] Matt 12:9–14 // Mark 3:1–6 // Luke 6:6–11 and 14:1–6.

Christ, God makes himself known to men and women, but his Word is always heard in a particular time and space and culture, and is always open to misunderstanding and rejection. When God spoke to prophets and evangelists and apostles, he ran the risk of being misunderstood, for to speak is to risk the danger of being misunderstood, rejected, or simply ignored. When the record of what men and women thought they heard God say to them became part of the canon, the danger was multiplied. When God speaks to us today through the pages of the Bible, he makes himself vulnerable again.

Scripture, then, is meant to be a witness to the truth; it is not a substitute for the truth. 'What the Law could not do,' writes Paul, God has done (Rom 8:3). God acts apart from Law, but the Law and Prophets witness to what he does (Rom 3:21). The danger is to treat what is written as a binding code rather than a witness to the reality beyond. The choice is well-expressed in the lines of George Herbert's hymn:

> A man that looks on glass
>   On it may stay his eye,
> Or if he pleaseth, through it pass,
>   And then the heaven espy.

Although the formation of the Christian canon in the early centuries CE was a necessary and inevitable step for the church to take, there were obvious dangers inherent in adopting a closed canon. It was now all too easy for Christians to treat all scripture as *gramma*, and to behave as though God's Spirit were no longer at work in the world. It was all too easy to assume that our biblical writers had encapsulated the whole truth, and so to confine Christ himself to the pages of scripture, forgetting that those who claim to follow the Risen Christ must be prepared to recognize that he continues to lead his people into a fuller understanding of the truth. If we today are to hear the Word of God, then we must remember that the written word is only a witness to that Word. The church must seek to interpret the Word of God – the will of God – *behind* the written word, by listening to the Spirit, who gives life. If we persevere, we shall find that God speaks to us *through* the Bible, and that behind its words we can begin to discern the Word, the self-revelation of God.

33. Where is Wisdom to Be Found?
Colossians 1:15–20*

Trained in the methods of tradition-historical scholarship, the questions I ask when approaching a text are instinctively 'Who?' 'When?' 'Why?' 'What?' In the case of Col 1:15–20, these are notoriously difficult to answer.

Who? Well – possibly Paul, possibly not – for even if we suppose that the epistle itself was written by Paul – as I tend to do – this section could well have been written by someone else, and so be an early credal composition, used here because it is appropriate for Paul's purpose. If, on the other hand, the epistle is pseudepigraphal, it is possible that the author is here quoting something composed by Paul himself.

Since the question of authorship is so problematical, the questions concerning date and place of composition must also remain unresolved, for they are inextricably linked with that of authorship. Only the question 'To whom?' permits us to give a reasonably confident answer. The letter claims to have been written to Christians in Colossae, and there seems no reason to doubt that it was intended for use by the church there.[1]

But *why* was the letter written – whether by Paul or by a disciple – and *why* was it addressed to Colossae? 'Were there false teachers in Colossae?' I used that question as the title of a paper I wrote some 30 years ago in honour of my predecessor in the Lady Margaret's chair,[2] and it seems appropriate that I should have been asked to look again at Colossians as my contribution to the celebration of the 500th anniversary of that chair's founding. Since my own answer to that particular question was 'No', and since the great majority of scholars appear to disagree with me[3] – though they are unable to agree among themselves as to what these hypothetical false teachers taught – we are left with yet more unresolved question marks.

Yet if the epistle *is* by Paul – or is written in the Pauline tradition – we can at least be sure that Col 1:15–20 has been included in the epistle because it is

---

* Lecture delivered in 2002 at the celebration of the 500th anniversary of the founding of the Lady Margaret's Professorship of Divinity at Cambridge.

[1] The only textual variant concerns the spelling of the name.

[2] Morna D. Hooker, 'Were There False Teachers in Colossae?', in *Christ and Spirit in the New Testament: Studies in Honour of Charles Francis Digby Moule,* eds. Barnabas Lindars and Stephen S. Smalley (Cambridge: Cambridge University Press, 1973), 315–331.

[3] Exceptions are N.T. Wright, *The Epistles of Paul to the Colossians and to Philemon* (Leicester: Inter-Varsity, 1986); and Roy Yates, '"The Worship of Angels": (Col 2:18)', *ExpTim* 97 (1985): 12–15; idem, *The Epistle to the Colossians* (London: Epworth, 1993).

relevant to the situation in Colossae as the author understands it, and to his insights into the bearing of the gospel *on* that situation. Is its purpose here perhaps to assure the community in Colossae that they need have no fear of astral forces, since Christ is greater than them all (2:8–10, 15)? In a world where pagan deities and superstitions abounded, such assurance would be very necessary.[4] Is it perhaps to remind them that, in Christ, they have already been reconciled to God, and so have no need to adopt the customs of their Jewish neighbours, who believe in the same God, but not in Christ (2:16–23)? Jewish customs and regulations must have seemed to offer an appropriate guide to appropriate behaviour to converted Gentiles wondering what their new faith required of them, and how they might best 'lead lives worthy of the Lord' (1:10). For our author, the answers to these questions are not to be found in abstaining from food or in observing festivals, but in living a life in conformity to Christ's.

Even if we could find the answer to the question concerning the purpose of this passage in its present context, however, this would not necessarily tell us why it was written in the first place. For if Col 1:15–20 is a quotation of traditional material, then what we have here may perhaps be a passage that was composed in one context being adapted and expounded for use in another. If that is so, then even though it is not a passage of *scripture* that is being interpreted here, the process of interpretation is nevertheless similar to that used when expounding scripture. Certainly the verses that follow build on what is said here and draw out its significance for the Christian community.

The passage itself is relevant to *our* purpose for an even more fundamental reason, however, for there is good reason to believe that Col 1:15–20 is itself an exegesis of scripture, drawing out what its author believed to be the true meaning of the text. It was C. F. Burney who suggested that the passage was an exposition of the Hebrew word *bereshith* – 'in the beginning' – the opening word of Gen 1:1, in the light of Prov 8:22?[5] Since his time, countless commentators have drawn our attention to the fact that the language of Col 1:15–20 is reminiscent of passages in the Wisdom literature which describe the wisdom of God.[6] Hence the use of the term 'Wisdom Christology' in relation to this passage.

'Where is wisdom to be found? And where is the place of understanding?' asked Job (28:12) – and the answer he gave was that God alone knows, since it was he who allocated wisdom a place at the creation (28:23–27). But though

---

[4] For an account of these pressures, see Clinton E. Arnold, *The Colossian Syncretism*, WUNT 2/77 (Tübingen: Mohr Siebeck, 1995).

[5] C. F. Burney, 'Christ as the ΑΡΧΗ of Creation', *JTS* 27 (1926): 160 ff.

[6] See, e.g., Job 28, Proverbs 8, Wisdom 6–10, Sirach 24. Among those who recognized the relevance of the Wisdom literature for this passage, see Jean-Noël Aletti, *Colossiens 1,15–20*, AnBib 91 (Rome: Biblical Institute Press, 1981).

mortals cannot find it or buy it (vv. 12–19), it is given to those who honour and obey God, for 'the fear of the Lord is wisdom, and to depart from evil is understanding' (v. 28). Many commentators explain this verse as an addition to vv. 1–27, reflecting a traditional approach equating wisdom with 'the fear of the Lord' that is found elsewhere,[7] but the same link is found in Proverbs 8, where wisdom is said to have been created 'the beginning of his way' – that is, 'the beginning of his works' (v. 22), and to have been at God's side – like a master craftsman when he created the world (vv. 23–31). Wisdom offers instruction to her children on how to fear God and do what is right. Whoever finds wisdom finds life (v. 35). Psalm 33 (LXX 32), also, links what God did at creation with instructions to fear him, though here it is 'by the word of the Lord' that the world is created (v. 6), and because his word is upright that he should be feared and obeyed.

In the book of Wisdom, wisdom is seen as operating in the world since the beginning, guarding and guiding God's people. She is described as 'the fashioner of all things' (7:22), God's agent at creation (9:1–2), and is understood to be the expression of God's very being, for she is

> a breath of the power of God
> and a pure emanation of the glory of the Almighty ...
> a reflection of eternal light,
> a spotless mirror of the working of God,
> and an image of his goodness. (7:25–26)

Wisdom demands righteousness, and those who love her keep her laws (6:18), but she condemns those who are unjust and fail to keep the Law (6:4).

Similar ideas are expressed in Sirach 24, where wisdom declares that 'before the ages, in the beginning, he created me' (v. 9), and describes how she was commanded to make her dwelling in Israel (v. 8). We are not surprised, therefore, when the gifts she offers are identified with 'the book of the covenant of the Most High God, the Law that Moses commanded us' (v. 23).[8]

In these various passages, the word, wisdom or Law of God are linked, sometimes identified. All these terms are used in statements that express the conviction that the will or purpose of God that was instrumental in the creation was revealed on Sinai. Once Israel's God had been identified as the creator, that link was inevitable. He had created the world by his word – and had spoken that word again on Sinai, where he revealed his wisdom in the Torah. A similar approach is found in the writings of Paul's contemporary, Philo, who says of this universe that 'its cause is God, by whom it has come into being ... its instrument the word of God, through whom it was framed'

---

[7] E.g. Prov 1:7; 9:10.
[8] Cf. also Sir 15:1.

(*Cher.* 127). For Philo, the word – or wisdom – of God is also the source of water and manna, symbols of the Torah (*Leg.* 2.86).

Belief in God as creator, however, had important implications for Israel's future salvation. Yahweh had laid the foundations of the earth and stretched out the heavens (Isa 51:13–16). It was the God of Israel who is the only God, the creator of the world and the only saviour. The link between creation and redemption is specifically made in Isaiah 40–55. At the Exodus, the power by which God created the world had been demonstrated when he bared his arm and blew with his breath: chaos had overwhelmed Israel's enemies, but she herself had been saved (Exod 15:1–19). It was because God was the creator of the world that Israel could rely on him to save them again – a theme that is reiterated again and again in these chapters (e.g. Isa 40:12–31). In these chapters, too, the new 'Exodus' is described in language deliberately reminiscent of the first (Isa 40:3–5; 43:2). Since Yahweh has already redeemed his people at the Exodus, he will do so again (Isa 43:11–21).

God's creative word is clearly relevant to this theme. God's salvation is sure because the word of Israel's God will stand forever (Isa 40:8). His word has gone out from his mouth and will not return – and that word proclaims him as the only God, to whom every knee will bow (Isa 45:21–23). His word will go out from his mouth and will accomplish his purpose, which is to restore his people and recreate paradise (Isa 55:10–13). Wisdom is specifically linked with redemption in the description of the Exodus in Wis 10:15–21. Creation and redemption belong together, and both depend on the word of God.[9]

Col 1:15–20 holds together these two themes of creation and redemption, which are set out in parallel verses (vv. 15–16 and 18b–20), linked by a parallel couplet summing up the same theme (vv. 17–18a). The passage is a eulogy of the one *through whom* God has worked, in creation and redemption. If the language used in Colossians 1 echoes the language of the LXX version of the various passages about wisdom which we have mentioned and also the language used by Philo, that is because what had been claimed by Judaism for the Torah – and more – was now being claimed for Christ. *He* was God's word of wisdom, by whom the world had been created and was now being restored.[10]

But Colossians 1 is not the only place in the New Testament where this language and these ideas occur. John 1 and Hebrews 1 are obvious examples. Like Col 1:15–20, John 1:1–18 appears to be based on an exegesis of Genesis 1.

---

[9] Cf. N.T. Wright, who specifically links both creation and redemption themes in the Old Testament with the wisdom tradition behind Colossians 1 in 'Poetry and Theology in Colossians 1.15–20', *NTS* 36 (1990): 444–468.

[10] For a recent detailed defence of the view that Col 1:15–20 is built on Jewish wisdom traditions, see Christian Stettler, *Der Kolosserhymnus*, WUNT 2/131 (Tübingen: Mohr Siebeck, 2000).

The exposition appears to be entirely Jewish, until we are told that the word through whom all things were created became flesh and dwelt among us, and that what has come to us through him is greater than the Law given through Moses. Christ's is the true glory, and he is the one who alone is able to reveal God fully, since – unlike Moses – he has seen God.[11] The familiar link between creation and Law is found here, and so, too, is the theme of restoration, for those who receive the word (who is the true light) are enabled to become children of God (v. 12). The same links reappear in 2 Corinthians 3–4 which – like John 1 – expounds both Exodus 33–34 and Genesis 1.[12] Here the glory reflected by Moses on Sinai is compared with the far greater glory of Christ – greater because Christ is the image of God, and the glory revealed in him is nothing less than the glory which shone at creation, when God said 'Let light shine out of darkness'. Those who see this glory in the face of Christ are being conformed to the image of the one who is himself the image of God (2 Cor 3:18; 4:4, 6): the glory lost by Adam is being restored.

Elsewhere in Paul, in 1 Corinthians, we find the idea of Christ as the agent of creation, 'through whom are all things and through whom we exist' (8:6).[13] In the same epistle he expounds the story of the rock which supplied the Israelites in the wilderness with water. According to the book of Wisdom, wisdom was at work in these events (11:1–4), while Philo identifies the rock with wisdom (*Leg.* 2.86). For Paul, however, the rock was Christ, and *he* was the source of the water (a symbol of the Torah) supplied to Israel (1 Cor 10:1–5). Similar ideas are of course expressed in John's Gospel in the miracles and discourses which reveal Jesus to be the source of living water, the true manna, light, life, way, truth – obvious corollaries to the opening declaration that he is the word.

The same understanding appears to have been held by the author of Matthew, in his portrayal of Jesus teaching from the Mount. What Jesus delivers is not a *new* Law, but the true understanding of what had been revealed to Moses on Sinai and only partly understood: he does not destroy the old but fulfils it (5:17–20), as he alone is able to do. Only he is able to reveal the Father – because he is the Son of the Father (11:25–27).

For the author of Hebrews, also, the sonship of Christ is important. Christ is the Son, Moses a servant (3:1–6), who delivered a Law which 'has only a shadow of the good things to come' (10:1). Christ is superior not only to him but also to all the angels, for he is the one through whom God has spoken and through whom he created the worlds; he is the reflection of God's glory and

---

[11] Cf. Morna D. Hooker, 'The Johannine Prologue and the Messianic Secret', *NTS* 21 (1974): 40–58 = above, essay 23 (pp. 321–340).

[12] Cf. Morna D. Hooker, 'Beyond the Things that are Written? St Paul's Use of Scripture', *NTS* 27 (1981): 295–309.

[13] Like Philo in *De Cherubim* 127, Paul here seems to distinguish between the cause (God the Father) and the agent (Christ).

the expression of his being (1:1–14), and through him many sons are brought to glory (2:10).

These passages were all written by men who were very much concerned with the problem of relating their growing understanding of the implications of their faith in Jesus with their Jewish roots, and reflect something of the conflict between their previous convictions regarding the Torah and the claims they were now making for Christ. They established their case by identifying Jesus with God's wisdom or word, through which the world had been created, and by which it would be restored.

Col 1:15–20 sums up these claims: Christ is the image of the invisible God, with him before all things began, the agent of creation, by whom, through whom and for whom all things have been created. In him the fullness of God was pleased to dwell, and was pleased, through him, to reconcile all things to him through his death.[14] Christ, not the Torah, is now understood to be the supreme revelation of God's will or purpose, the fullest expression of his word or wisdom. The parallelism between 1:15–16 and 1:18b–20, and between v. 17 and v. 18a, stresses the link between his work in creation and in redemption.

Colossians 1 is said to express 'Wisdom Christology' rather than 'Logos Christology' – perhaps because Christ is identified with wisdom elsewhere in Paul (1 Cor 1:24, 30). Interestingly, however, neither the word σοφία nor the word λόγος is used in this passage! They are not needed, since what was once said about them has been transferred to Christ. But notice the references to σοφία in the context, which draws out the significance of the passage for the life of the Christian community.[15]

1. Col 1:9: Paul says that he prays unceasingly for the Colossians, that they may be filled with knowledge of God's will, in all spiritual wisdom and understanding.

The language of the whole paragraph (vv. 9–12) is thoroughly Jewish. Knowledge of God's will would, for a Jew, come through the Torah. For Paul, it was now understood to come through Christ, in whom God's purpose for his world is revealed. Observing the Law brought wisdom and understanding (σοφία καὶ σύνεσις: Deut 4:6; Sir 24:23–26). These gifts are now offered to those who are in Christ, who will thus be enabled to 'lead lives worthy of the Lord' (1:10). The proper response to the revelation of God's will in Christ (as to his revelation on Sinai) is a life that conforms to the divine commands.

2. Col 1:28: Paul proclaims Christ, warning everyone and teaching everyone in all wisdom, in order to present everyone mature in Christ.

---

[14] The phrase εἰς αὐτόν is often translated as though it were εἰς ἑαυτόν, meaning 'to himself', because commentators feel that things should be reconciled to God, rather than to Christ. But the symmetry of the passage (2 x ἐν ... διά ... εἰς) demands that we should understand the phrase to refer to Christ. As we shall see, this interpretation makes good sense of the passage.

[15] Cf. also 1 Cor 3:16 and 4:5.

The phrase ἐν πάσῃ σοφίᾳ echoes what was said in 1:9: Paul works to make his prayer a reality. He claims to teach with wisdom, since his aim is to 'present everyone mature in Christ', who is the source of wisdom. The threefold use of 'everyone' in this verse might suggest hyperbole, except that 1:15–20 referred to the reconciliation of *all* things to Christ.[16] The one whom Paul proclaims is 'Christ in you, the hope of glory' (1:27). The glory which had been lost by Adam,[17] which accompanied the giving of the Torah, and which would, so it was said, be restored at the End to those who had kept the Law,[18] was in fact to be found in Christ, who is 'the image of the invisible God' (1:15). Maturity in Christ will mean sharing in this glory.

3. Col 2:3: God's mystery – a mystery hidden throughout the ages and generations but now revealed to the saints (1:26) – is Christ himself, in whom are hidden all treasures of wisdom and knowledge.

Once again, Paul affirms that his task is to ensure that even those Gentiles who have not seen him face to face (v. 1) should come to the knowledge of God's 'mystery' – that is, Christ himself (v. 2; cf. 1:26, 27). This time Christ is identified as the *source* of wisdom and knowledge – the one 'in whom are hidden all the treasures of wisdom and knowledge'. The verse sums up the implications of 1:15–20. Paul goes on to argue that all other claims to possible wisdom and knowledge are simply 'philosophy and empty deceit', whose origins are mere human tradition or the elemental forces of the universe, all of which are inferior to Christ (vv. 8–15).

4. Col 2:23: Jewish regulations have a reputation for wisdom, but are of no value.

What had once appeared to be the embodiment of wisdom – God's revelation on Sinai, and the regulations set out in Torah – are now discovered to belong to a partial and temporal revelation. They have the reputation for embodying wisdom, but do not possess the reality. Since the Colossian Christians no longer belong to the world ruled by the elemental spirits of the universe, they do not need regulations that belong to that world: they have been raised with Christ, and should therefore seek the things that belong to the new age, where Christ reigns at God's right hand (3:1).

The mystery hidden throughout the ages and generations – the wisdom sought by men and women in the past and glimpsed by Moses on Sinai – is now revealed to be Christ – or rather, Christ *in you,* the hope of glory (1:27). Why is it expressed in this way? Because he is the εἰκὼν Θεοῦ, not simply the agent of creation but also the *pattern* according to which Adam was created

---

[16] So James D. G. Dunn, *The Epistles to the Colossians and to Philemon: A Commentary on the Greek Text* (Grand Rapids: Eerdmans, 1996), 125.

[17] For this idea in later Jewish tradition, see Rab. Gen. 11.2; 12.6; Sanh. 38b. Cf. Rom 1:23.

[18] 2 Esdras 7:95, 97; 1 Enoch 38:4; 50:1.

and *to* which men and women (even Gentiles!) are now being restored. '*Christ in you*' because Christians have shed 'the old Adam' and have put on the new, which is being renewed *according to the image* of its creator, until it reaches full knowledge (3:10). As εἰκὼν Θεοῦ, Christ is both the agent of creation and the pattern for humanity – the one *by* whom all things were made, and *to* whom all things are reconciled (Col 1:16, 20).

As we read through Colossians, we see how the implications of this passage for the Christian community are brought out. If Christ is the agent of all creation, then those in him need have no fear of or concern for 'the elemental spirits of the universe' (2:8, 20). If God's 'fullness' dwells in him, then it is he who reveals God's purpose for humanity, and Christian ethics are a matter of living in Christ (2:6; 3:12–17). A passage which is itself an exegesis of scripture is in turn expounded and applied.

What, then, can we learn from the way in which the author of this passage handles scripture? Paradoxically, beginning from what he regards as authoritative, he *subverts* the text by pointing to a greater authority *behind* the text. Col 1:15–20 is not simply an example of exegesis; rather it points us to what its author regards as the fundamental *principle* of exegesis. The word spoken by God at creation and revealed on Sinai was not, after all, encapsulated in the written Torah, but dwells in Christ. In Johannine terminology, that means that the incarnate word reveals God in a way that Moses could not do; the role of the words of scripture is to witness to the word. In Pauline imagery, it means that the glory displayed in Christ is far greater than the glory glimpsed by Moses on Sinai, and the role of the Law and the Prophets is to witness *to* him. For Paul, something static – words inscribed on stone tablets – has been replaced by something alive – the Spirit at work in human hearts (2 Cor 3:1–3). Paul begins from scripture and appeals to it as authoritative, yet insists that the interpretation of scripture must not be fossilized. He has no interest in the question which I was trained to ask: 'What did this mean for the original author?' Rather, with the rabbis, he insists '*You* read it this way, but *I* interpret it in this. The text does not mean what you think it means, because it witnesses to the one who is *behind* the text, namely Christ'. For Paul, the 'canon' is not scripture itself, but Christ, which means that scripture must be read in the light of Christ. Where is wisdom to be found? Not in the written Torah – not even in the epistles of Paul! – but in the living Christ.

Is Paul's view sustainable? The way in which Christians down the ages have treated the words of scripture as authoritative and regarded the Bible itself as the word of God – offering clear guidance and hard-and-fast rules – suggests that they have found it difficult to follow him. Tablets of stone are easier to take hold of than the Spirit of Christ. How do we read the mind of Christ? For an answer, we turn back, inevitably, to the written word, though endeavouring to read it with the guidance of the Spirit.

We find ourselves confronted once again, therefore, with the question that has been raised again and again in other essays in this volume: *how* do we interpret scripture? How do we distinguish between an ethical or unethical reading? Between a reading that is legitimate and one that is illegitimate? Between one that is right and one that is wrong? Between one that is wise and one that is unwise? All those terms have been used by other contributors to this symposium. For Paul, the answer is: look at Christ, and at what *he* reveals to us of the love of God; interpret scripture in the light of Christ.

In giving that answer, Paul inevitably makes himself vulnerable, for he is in danger both of misunderstanding the text and of being himself misunderstood. But if God revealed himself by what he said to Moses on Sinai, he himself was in danger of being misunderstood; if he revealed himself in Christ and speaks to us through a man born of woman, then it is *God* who has made himself vulnerable. Men and women can so easily reject what is shown them, or simply misunderstand what they hear. If incarnation is at the centre of Christian faith, then we must surely expect the text that bears witness to the incarnate word to be open to the same vulnerability. Vulnerability is built into God's revelation.

Where is wisdom to be found? The answer we are given in Colossians in 'in Christ himself' (2:2–3). Christ, who is the image of the invisible God; Christ, through whose death all things have been reconciled (1:20). It is surely no accident that when, in 1 Cor 1:24, 30, Paul *identifies* Christ with the wisdom of God, it is in a passage where he is spelling out the significance of the message of *Christ crucified* – to Jews, a stumbling-block, and to Gentiles, folly. There could be no clearer demonstration of the vulnerability of God's revelation than the crucifixion: men and women had refused to listen to his incarnate word and attempted its destruction. Yet it is *here* that God's wisdom is to be found! The gospel message is that God's power is effective even here, and that he has triumphed over death itself in the resurrection.

Because scripture is the witness to God's revelation, it will be open to the same possibilities of misunderstanding and rejection, for it inevitably reflects the vulnerability of that revelation. But just as God has revealed himself in the crucified and risen Christ, so he has been able to reveal himself through the pages of scripture. Since scripture is the witness to God's revelation, it must be understood in the light of the birth, death, and resurrection of Christ, in whom all the treasure of wisdom are to be found.

34. Christ, the 'End' of the Cult*

Preachers, it has often been said, should begin where their congregations are. Since Hebrews appears – in spite of its epistolary conclusion – to have been written as a homily of some kind, we should perhaps assume that its author would have heeded this advice. Yet it is notoriously difficult to deduce from the epistle not simply where its first readers may have lived, but what their situation and problems might have been. Like the mysterious figure of Melchizedek, Hebrews appears on the scene without explanation, and we are told nothing about either its author or its intended readers. The latter, to be sure, were soon identified as Jews – hence the epistle's name, given some time in the second century – though they were clearly Greek-speaking Christian Jews, like the author himself. But what was their situation? The traditional explanation was that they were a group of Jewish converts to Christianity who were in danger of lapsing into Judaism. These young Christians, it was suggested, were feeling isolated from the worship which had formerly meant so much to them. Excluded from the synagogue, and cut off from the ceremonies centred on the temple in Jerusalem, they had lost their original fervour for their new faith, and were tempted to return to their former beliefs and practices.[1]

This interpretation of Hebrews assumes that the epistle was written before 70 CE, but fails to explain why the author refers to the 'tent' rather than the 'temple,' and why it describes the cult in language taken from the books of Exodus and Leviticus, rather than as something ongoing. Moreover, if the epistle was written to diaspora Jews, one wonders how much of a 'temptation' the pilgrimages to Jerusalem might have been.[2] However important the sacrificial system may have been for Judaism at this time, worship for these men

---

* Lecture delivered at the second St. Andrews Conference on Scripture and Theology in 2006.

[1] So, e.g., F. F. Bruce: 'We may think of them as converts from Diaspora Judaism ... who were strongly tempted to discontinue their Christian fellowship with its forward-looking challenge and slip back into the Judaism they had left' ('Hebrews', in *Peake's Commentary on the Bible,* ed. Matthew Black [London: Thomas Nelson, 1962], 1008). Although Bruce says that he was influenced by William Manson, the latter had, in fact, already challenged this view; see n. 17.

[2] It is, of course, possible that the congregation addressed by the writer was based in Palestine, perhaps even in Jerusalem, as Brooke Foss Westcott argued; *The Epistle to the Hebrews,* 2nd ed. (London: Macmillan, 1892), xxxv–xliii. The fact that the letter was written in Greek makes this unlikely, however.

and women in their pre-Christian past would in practice have been centred primarily on the synagogue.

The main drawback with this interpretation, however, is surely that it is anachronistic. It assumes that Christianity was already understood as 'another' religion, separate from Judaism. It treats faith in Jesus as incompatible with Jewish beliefs. But had the crucial parting of the ways yet taken place? Surely not! If we read Galatians, to be sure, we might suppose that 'Christianity' had already cut its Jewish links, since Paul there berates his Gentile converts for trying to adopt the practices of Judaism, a backward step which would put them once again under the power of τὰ στοιχεῖα τοῦ κοσμοῦ from which they have been delivered. Such a conclusion would, however, be false. Paul's stance in Galatians is related to a situation that arose within his Gentile mission, and his words are addressed to Gentiles. For them, it would certainly be a retrograde step to adopt Jewish practices, since that would be to deny that 'the fullness of the ages' (Gal 4:4) has arrived, and would mean that they were relying on the 'works of the Law', rather than trusting in what God has done through Christ. Similarly, Jewish Christians who insisted that Gentile converts must be circumcised and obey Jewish practices were in effect denying the significance of Christ's death and resurrection. Nevertheless, Paul's insistence on the importance of Christ's death and resurrection in no way cuts Christian faith from its Jewish roots, since his argument here rests on his assertion that Christ is the 'seed' of Abraham, and that *in him* Jew and Gentile alike are Abraham's heirs, members of God's people.

But what of those *outside* the Pauline mission – Jewish converts to Christianity? What practical difference did their acceptance of Jesus as Messiah make to their manner of life? If Acts is to be believed, the early Christians based in Jerusalem continued to worship in synagogues and in the temple. According to Acts 20:16 Paul himself travelled to Jerusalem to celebrate Pentecost, and Paul's own remark in 1 Cor 16:8, indicating that he still marked the festivals, may support this. Why should loyal Jews who were now convinced that Jesus was God's Messiah cease to worship God in the traditional ways, or abandon their observance of the Torah? The picture in Acts is entirely believable. The idea that old practices were at best irrelevant, at worst incompatible with Christian belief, has not yet developed.

The refusal of Jews to accept the claims made on behalf of Jesus by Jewish Christians inevitably increased tension between the two communities. In Matthew, criticism of the Jewish religious authorities is mounting; the Fourth Gospel reflects a time at the end of the first century when Christians were being expelled from the synagogues, and Heb 13:13 may reflect a similar situation. It was not the Christians who had concluded that confession in Jesus as Son of God was incompatible with Jewish beliefs, however, but the Jewish authorities. If the readers of Hebrews were being expelled from the synagogues or persecuted for their faith in Jesus as Messiah, they might well be tempted to abandon their new faith; but this was hardly a 'return' to something they had *left*.

An alternative explanation of the situation addressed in Hebrews is that it was written *after* 70 CE, and that the author's 'word of *paraclesis*' (13:22) was intended, not as a word of admonition, directed to those who were in danger of 'lapsing' into Judaism, but rather as a word of encouragement, addressed to those who were distressed by the news of the temple's recent destruction.[3] On this interpretation, our author's message to his readers is that there is no need for them to be distressed by the loss of the temple, since they have no need of the temple sacrifices. Christ has made the final, perfect offering of himself, so fulfilling the purpose of the Old Testament sacrificial system, and bringing it to an end. If the temple had been destroyed, this might explain our author's references to the 'tent', and his reliance on the biblical rubrics. It is nevertheless surprising that there is no reference to a cataclysmic event that had caused the community such trauma, and so triggered the writing of the epistle: the fact that the temple had been destroyed, and worship there had ceased, would surely support the author's claim that the prescribed sacrifices were no longer necessary, and it is strange indeed that it is not mentioned.

Unanswered questions about the date, authorship and purpose of Hebrews clearly abound. Who *was* our anonymous author? And who were the 'Hebrews' to whom he wrote? Was the epistle written before 70 CE or after? Was it intended primarily to admonish a congregation who were in danger of abandoning their faith, or to encourage those whose faith had been shaken? When obvious questions produce such different answers and raise so many problems, it is necessary to approach them in a different way.

1. Crisis in the Community?

Commentators frequently emphasize the danger which confronted the congregation.[4] Lindars writes of 'the urgency and anxiety which characterise the letter from end to end,'[5] and believes that 'the situation is extremely serious, and the leaders are at their wits' end to know how to cope with it'.[6] The letter is written to deal with a 'crisis',[7] since the author regarded the 'return

---

[3] Cf. Marie E. Isaacs, *Reading Hebrews & James: A Literary and Theological Commentary* (Macon, GA: Smyth & Helwys, 2002), 12–13.

[4] Cf. the comment by William L. Lane: 'The targeted audience was an assembly in crisis' (*Hebrews 1–8*, WBC [Dallas: Word Books, 1991], lxi).

[5] Barnabas Lindars, *The Theology of the Letter to the Hebrews*, New Testament Theology (Cambridge: Cambridge University Press, 1991), 5.

[6] Lindars, *Theology*, 8.

[7] Lindars, *Theology*, 8

to Judaism as virtual apostasy'.[8] No wonder, then, that Lindars believes that the author 'is extremely anxious to dissuade the readers from taking what he regards as a disastrous course of action'.[9]

But what is the basis for this assessment? Lindars points to the concluding verses of ch. 13, where the author appeals to his readers to bear with his λόγος τῆς παρακλήσεως, and suggests that the fact that he writes these final words in his own hand is an indication of 'the anxiety which he feels about the reception of the letter'.[10] He goes on to suggest that the author's request for the readers' prayers in vv. 18–19 demonstrates 'the same anxiety', and that his charge to 'obey your leaders and submit to them' (v. 17) indicates the presence of 'a dissident group' in the congregation.[11] Behind the command to maintain brotherly love in 13:1 there lies 'a major disruption',[12] and the author has been asked by the leaders to deal with 'the crisis'. Since he cannot come in person he has written, and his letter is 'the last resort'.[13]

This interpretation goes far beyond the evidence. It was customary for authors to add a note in their own hand at the close of a letter, and there is no reason to suppose that this one betrays our author's agitation; the injunctions he gives to the congregation in this final chapter are what we would expect. To be sure, he mentions the possibility that the leaders may have to report 'sadly' concerning the community's progress (13:17) – but at the same time he indicates that they may well do so 'with joy'! The author would be failing in his duty if he did not warn the congregation of the dangers surrounding them and urge them to be faithful, but this does not mean that he is writing to deal with a major crisis.

2. Warnings

There are, nevertheless, passages in the epistle which do spell out the possible dangers confronting the recipients, and we shall get a more balanced view of the situation if we concentrate on these. The author's concern is first mentioned in 2:1, where he writes that we (not 'you'!) must pay greater heed to what we have heard, lest we drift away from it: clearly the danger he has in mind confronts *all* Christians, not just those whom he addresses. It soon becomes clear that 'what we have heard' refers to the message of salvation brought by 'the Lord'. This note of warning is sounded four more times in

---

[8] Lindars, *Theology*, 11.
[9] Lindars, *Theology*, 6.
[10] Lindars, *Theology*, 7.
[11] Lindars, *Theology*, 7.
[12] Lindars, *Theology*, 8.
[13] Lindars, *Theology*, 8.

the course of the epistle, and becomes more specific and urgent. The first of these four warnings – against having evil, unbelieving hearts that turn away from God, so repeating the error of Israel in the wilderness – begins in 3:7–4:1, and continues in 4:11–13. In view of Israel's past failures, it is hardly surprising if the author felt it necessary to warn his congregation, as well as to encourage them. Although the warning is addressed to his 'brothers', it should be noted that he again includes himself in his warning: 'Let us take care. ... Let us make every effort' (4:1, 11).

This section in 3:7–4:13 introduces the theme of the pilgrimage of God's people, and their hope of entering into God's rest, a theme which is picked up again at the end of the epistle, in chs. 11–12. Here we find another warning, in 12:25–29, but this one is far more urgent: instead of a simple warning not to repeat the sin of the wilderness generation, who had – like us – received 'the good news' (4:2), we have a reminder that we have received something far greater than they did. You have come, our author tells his readers in 12:18–24, not to Mount Sinai, but to Mount Zion and the heavenly Jerusalem, where are gathered a great company, and Jesus himself, the mediator of a new covenant: if the wilderness generation, who ignored a warning heard from earth, did not escape destruction, how much less shall we (he again includes himself), if we ignore a warning heard from heaven! This final reminder of danger assumes the argument of the previous chapters, where the author has explained how Jesus is the mediator of a new covenant, and spelt out the significance of his 'sprinkled blood' and his entry into heaven. How, then, can they refuse the one who now speaks to them?

Although these two passages issue clear warnings about the danger of judgement awaiting those who are disobedient, there is no suggestion that those whom he addresses have actually fallen away.

In two other passages, however, the warnings become much more specific and urgent. The first of these is found in 5:11–6:12, and opens with a direct attack on the readers. They have become 'dull in understanding' (5:11). By now, they should have been able to teach others, but they are still in need of someone to teach them 'the basic elements (τὰ στοιχεῖα) of the first principles (τῆς ἀρχῆς) of the oracles of God' (5:12). Like infants, they still need milk, and are not ready for solid food, which can be digested only by the mature, who can distinguish good from evil.

A similar image is used by Paul in 1 Cor of immature believers who want to eat meat but can digest only milk (1 Cor 3:2). There is no reason to suppose, however, that our author borrowed the metaphor from Paul: it was used by others – e.g. Philo[14] – and a similar image is found in Isa 7:15.[15] We need

---

[14] Philo, *Agr.* § 2.
[15] This may well be Hebrews' source, since Isa 7:15 describes the child who is old enough to digest curds and honey as being able to distinguish between good and evil; cf. Heb 5:14.

to note, however, the implications of the image: the burden of our author's complaint is that his readers are immature, since they have failed to advance in comprehension of the meaning of 'the oracles of God' as they should. He therefore urges the community (once again, he includes himself!) to go on to maturity or perfection, leaving behind the elementary teaching about the Christ. There should be no need, he says, for him to repeat basic teaching about repentance from dead works, faith towards God, teaching about ablutions, the laying on of hands, resurrection of the dead and eternal judgement. It has often been pointed out that there is nothing specifically Christian about this list: these basic beliefs were Jewish in origin, though they were now shared by the Christian community. It was only the conviction that Jesus was the Christ that separated the two communities.

In Heb 6:4–8, the tone changes. Instead of offering his readers encouragement to progress, we have condemnation for 'those who have once been enlightened, who have tasted the heavenly gift and shared in the Holy Spirit, who have tasted the goodness of the word of God and the powers of the age to come, and then have fallen away'. These people had clearly once believed that with Christ the End had in some sense come, and that they were experiencing life in the Age to Come. But if they have now abandoned these things, they cannot again be restored to repentance. In what way, then, have they fallen away? They are, we are told, crucifying the Son of God again to their own loss, and holding him up to contempt.[16] What does this mean? Were they denying that the crucified Jesus was the Son of God? Or was it perhaps that by continuing to stress the importance of the cult, they were in effect denying that through Christ's death and resurrection they had experienced the benefits of the New Age? Once again, we have a parallel in Paul, who accused the Galatians of failing to grasp the significance of his message of Christ crucified, and so of attempting to 'nullify the grace of God'. If righteousness came through the Law, he declared, it meant that Christ died in vain. For the author of Hebrews, too, the Law was unable to make men and women perfect (7:19; 9:9), and failure to recognize this would mean that Christ had died in vain: those who insist that the sacrifices are still necessary are therefore holding the crucified Christ up to contempt.

---

[16] The verb ἀνασταυρόω, used only here in the New Testament, normally means simply 'to crucify', the ἀνα- being added for emphasis. The translation 'to crucify again' does, however, rest on the interpretation of Fathers and versions; see Westcott, *Hebrews, in loc.* Marie E. Isaacs, *Sacred Space: An Approach to the Theology of the Epistle to the Hebrews*, JSNTSup 73 (Sheffield: JSOT Press, 1992), 93, suggests that the meaning 'crucify again' is nonsense. In view of the fact that the author will go on to insist that Christ's death took place once for all, and did not need to be repeated (9:25–26), however, his point may well be that those who do not recognize this are, in effect, behaving – absurdly – as though it were necessary for Christ 'to suffer again and again' (9:26).

This admonitory section concludes with a parable emphasizing the importance of our response (vv. 7–8), and an expression of confidence in the readers (vv. 9–12). Our author is *not* condemning his readers for holding the Son of God up to contempt, but warning them against the possibility of doing so. Nevertheless, the fact that he does so shows that he fears that if they remain dull in understanding, and fail to grasp the true significance of the scriptures, they are in danger of sinning.

The other major admonitory section (10:19–32) begins by reminding the readers of what has been done for them, and once again the author uses the first-person plural, so including himself along with those whom he addresses. He urges them to have the 'full assurance' of their faith, and to hold fast to the 'confession' of their hope 'without wavering'. The source of their confidence is 'the blood of Jesus', and they are able to approach the presence of God because they know that their hearts are 'sprinkled clean'. They must not waver, but must encourage one another, not neglecting – as do some – to meet together; whether or not the 'some' were formerly members of the congregation is not clear.

Then comes the warning (vv. 26–31). For those who wilfully persist in sin after receiving knowledge of the truth, 'there no longer remains a sacrifice for sins', only judgement. This judgement is inevitable, since what these people are doing is to 'spurn the Son of God, profane the blood of the covenant by which they were sanctified, and outrage the Spirit of grace'. As in 6:6, the crucial mistake concerns their attitude to 'the Son of God', and once again it relates specifically to his death. What they have profaned is the blood of the covenant, and if we turn back to 7:22–9:22, we find that the dominant theme there was the way in which Christ's death sealed 'the better covenant' (7:22) which had been foreshadowed by the first. This was the covenant to which the Holy Spirit testified (10:15–16). No wonder, then, that to profane this blood is to outrage the Spirit of grace.

Nevertheless, the readers of the letter are encouraged to remember their former enthusiasm, and not to abandon confidence, for 'we are not among those who shrink back and so are lost, but among those who have faith and so are saved' (v. 39).

As we have seen, both these severe warnings concern the death of the Son of God, and it can hardly be accidental that they introduce and conclude the central section of the epistle, which expounds Jesus' work as high priest. At the heart of Hebrews, then, we have a chiastic structure. On either side of the central section we have these two severe warnings; before the first, we have a passage introducing the idea of Jesus as high priest, and following the second we have a passage emphasizing the importance of faith. The two 'bookends' are formed by two sections (3:1–4:13 and 11:1–12:29) which use the imagery of pilgrimage, and urge the readers to enter into what God has promised – something which their ancestors failed to do (4:5–6). The fact that they have now reached, not Sinai but Mount Zion (12:22), is due to 'Jesus, the mediator of a new covenant' and to his 'sprinkled blood' (12:24).

3:1–4:13   Imagery of pilgrimage, including *first warning*
   4:14–5:10   Introduction of idea of Jesus as high priest
      5:11–6:12   *First severe warning*
         6:13–10:18   Jesus our high priest
      10:19–32   *Second severe warning*
   10:32–11:40   The importance of faith
12:1–29   Imagery of pilgrimage, including *final warning.*

This arrangement suggests that the author's purpose is not simply to comfort his readers over the loss of the temple and to reassure them that the temple sacrifices are unnecessary. Nor, in the light of 5:11–6:3, does it seem probable that he is warning them against lapsing into Judaism. It would appear that the author's message to his readers was not 'Do not *fall back* into Judaism,' but rather, 'It is time to *move on,* and to *leave behind* your former understanding of Judaism'.[17] They must not cling to the past, but grasp what is new, for the old was meant to point forward to what has now taken place. That means that they must both acknowledge the superiority of Jesus as Son of God to previous revelation, and trust in what he has achieved by his death. The author's argument in 6:13–10:18 has set out that significance by showing that Christ has 'offered for all time a single sacrifice for sins' (10:12). At the same time, he has demonstrated that the Jewish sacrifices were ineffective and have been rendered redundant. If his readers persist in continuing to set store by the sacrifices prescribed in the Law, therefore, they will, in effect, be rejecting what Christ has now achieved. In other words, they will be spurning the Son of God, and holding him up to contempt. If Jewish Christians assume that it is necessary to go on repeating sacrifices, what are they implying about the sacrifice of Christ? By failing to comprehend that his death was effective for all time, they are in danger of behaving as though it were necessary to crucify him again. What they need to grasp is that 'where there is forgiveness of sins, there is no longer any offering' (10:18). The only sacrifices required now are those of praise to God and of mutual concern in the community (13:15–16). The community must recognize that although they truly belong to God's people, they will no longer be welcome in the Jewish synagogue. They must therefore go to Jesus 'outside the camp', even though that means that they must 'bear the abuse he endured'. For here, they are told, they 'have no lasting city', since they 'are looking for the city that is to come' (13:13–14).

---

[17] Cf. William Manson, *The Epistle to the Hebrews* (London: Hodder & Stoughton, 1951), 15–16: 'it is possible that the danger to their faith lay not in a return to Judaism as such, but in a retardation of their Christian progress by factors having their causes in the Jewish element in their Christianity, in other words, by an undue assertion of their Jewish-Christian inheritance'.

3. The Argument

It is time to turn to the rest of the book, and see how these various warnings fit into the author's argument as a whole.

The epistle begins (1:1–4) with a brief prologue. From vv. 1–2 we learn that there are both continuity and contrast with what God spoke in the past through the prophets and what he has spoken 'in these last days' through a Son. The close relationship between God and his Son is explained in vv. 2–3, and the latter's superiority to angels stated in v. 4, following a brief summary of the epistle's main theme: 'When he had made purification for sins, he sat down at the right hand of the Majesty on high'.

The rest of ch. 1 spells out the Son's superiority to the angels. This forms the basis for the warning in 2:1–4: 'If God's word, spoken through angels, was valid, and meant that every violation was punished, how can we escape if we neglect such a great salvation – the salvation announced through a Son?' A new point is introduced in 2:5. It now becomes clear that the 'Son' who is so much superior to the angels is none other than Jesus, who – paradoxically – was (in the words of Ps 8) for a time made lower than the angels, but is now crowned with glory and honour (Heb 2:9). Significantly, however, this glory and honour are obtained *through* '*the suffering of death*'. Jesus' death, therefore, is *the necessary prelude* to the glory and honour promised in Ps 8. This glory and honour were in fact promised to mankind in general, not to one individual, and it is clear that we 'do not yet' enjoy it. Now, however, we discover that Jesus is our representative, since we are told that by God's grace, he experienced this death 'for all' (Heb 2:9). The fact that he is crowned with glory and honour, therefore, is a sign that the promise of Ps 2 will one day be fulfilled for the rest of humanity. But how can he be their representative, and 'the pioneer of their salvation' (v. 10)? He shared human flesh and blood and became like his brothers in all respects (vv. 14, 17), *in order that,* through his own death, 'he might destroy the one who has the power of death, that is, the devil' (vv. 14–15). He is thus able to save those who are enslaved to the fear of death, and bring many children to God. He came to help the descendants of Abraham (v. 16) – a reminder that before he came, the Jewish nation was 'enslaved' through the work of the devil.

The author's interpretation of 'man' and 'son of man' in Ps 8 is remarkable, although many modern translators do their best to ensure that readers of the English versions miss its significance by using politically correct terms such as 'human beings' and 'mortals'! To be sure, 'son of man' is *not* used here as a title. Nevertheless, the *role of* the son of man is said to have been fulfilled by Jesus, who acts as mankind's representative. As such, the meaning of the term is close to what some have suggested is the way in which Jesus himself used the term.[18] Moreover, although the Psalmist points to future glory, the author of Hebrews insists that this glory is achieved only through death. Jesus fulfilled the role of 'man' and 'son of man' by being 'made for a while lower than the angels', and then being 'crowned with glory and honour'. This combination of 'the suffering of death' and eschatological glory, which will be shared by others, picks up the dominant themes of the 'Son of man' sayings in all four Gospels, and suggests that our author's exegesis of the Psalm is influenced by knowledge of the tradition of Jesus' sayings.

In these verses, moreover, we have a fascinating parallel to a central theme in Paul which some of us have termed 'interchange',[19] a theme which was later summed up in the famous words of Irenaeus, 'He became what we are, *in order that* we might become what he is'.[20] It was because he was 'made for a while lower than the angels' that he was 'crowned with glory'; by sharing our humanity, even to the point of death, the Son was able, through his exaltation, to fulfil on our behalf the words of Ps 8 – words which describe God's ultimate goal for humanity – and to 'bring many sons to glory' (Heb 2:10).[21] By destroying the power of death on our behalf he brings us freedom. Those who have become 'partners of Christ' (3:14) will share his glory.

Now Paul's understanding of 'interchange' is linked very closely to the idea of human solidarity, which he spells out in terms of our participation in Adam and in Christ. There are hints of this idea in Hebrews. In 2:11, for example, our author speaks of the one who sanctifies and those who are sanctified being ἐξ ἑνός. Many translators assume that this is a reference to God, but the *context* suggests that the 'one' may well signify Adam. The verses from Ps 8 which introduce this discussion speak of the place of 'man' and the 'son of man' within creation, but it is Jesus who fulfils human destiny, and he does so by sharing human flesh and blood (v. 14). Both Paul and the author of Hebrews link this idea of Christ sharing our humanity with our salvation, but whereas Paul uses the notion of solidarity to spell out how Christ's obedience, righteousness, and resurrection were able to reverse Adam's disobedience, condemnation, and death, the writer to the Hebrews links it to the theme of Jesus as our priest, a theme that is introduced at the end of ch. 2: 'Therefore

---

[18] Cf. Morna D. Hooker, *The Son of Man in Mark* (London: SPCK, 1967); 'Is the Son of Man Problem Really Insoluble?', in *Text and Interpretation: Studies in the New Testament Presented to Matthew Black*, eds. Ernest Best and R.McL. Wilson (Cambridge: Cambridge University Press, 1979), 155–168 = above, essay 6 (pp. 90–102).

[19] Cf. Morna D. Hooker, *From Adam to Christ: Essays on Paul* (Cambridge: Cambridge University Press, 1990), 1–100.

[20] Irenaeus, *Adv. Haer.* 5 *praef.*

[21] In using the word 'sons', the author was emphasizing the link between Christ and ourselves, and the privileges of status now enjoyed by all Christians, male and female alike. Modern translators who substitute the word 'children' for 'sons' obscure this link, though they are correct in understanding the author's meaning to be inclusive.

he had to become like his brothers in all things, *in order that* he might become a merciful and faithful high priest in the service of God, to make atonement for the sins of the people'. For both Paul and the author of Hebrews, it was essential that the one who brings our salvation should be fully human, just as it was essential that he should be Son of God. Christ shares our humanity in order that we may share his sonship and glory (Gal 4:4–6; Phil 2:6–7; 3:21; Heb 2:10). For Paul, this is achieved by Christ 'being made sin', so enabling us to share his righteousness (2 Cor 5:21); Christ dies our death, and sets us free from the consequences of sin by his resurrection. For the author of Hebrews, too, Jesus deals with our sins, but it is by acting as high priest, and leading us into the presence of God; because Jesus is obedient and perfect, he is the source of salvation for others who obey him and who will be perfected (Heb 5:8–9; 6:1). Whereas Paul believes that Christians will share Christ's resurrection (Rom 6:5), this author thinks of them entering the inner shrine, where Jesus, their forerunner, has already entered (Heb 6:19–20): to do this is to enter into God's rest, promised to the people of God (3:7–4:13). The two authors offer us two models of what is essentially an incarnational soteriology.

A comparison in ch. 3 between Jesus, the Son, and Moses, the servant – a reminder of the superiority of the message that has come through Christ to that brought by the prophets (1:1–2) – leads naturally into the warning given in Ps 95, where Israel is urged not to repeat the mistakes made by their ancestors in the wilderness. The author now explores the theme of pilgrimage: God's people failed to enter his sabbath rest because of their disobedience, and this is symbolized by the failure of the wilderness generation to enter the promised land. But 'today', as Ps 95 says, the possibility of entering that rest is open to those who are 'partners of Christ' (Heb 3:14). We must not repeat the failure of an earlier generation.

In 4:14, the author changes his image. Picking up the idea of Christ as high priest from 2:17, he moves from the idea of entering into the sabbath rest to that of entering into the holy of holies. The theme is introduced with a bold claim: we have a great high priest, who has passed through the heavens – none other than Jesus, the Son of God. He begins by reminding us of Jesus' qualifications to be a high priest, building on the argument of chs. 1–3. Every high priest is chosen from men, and is called by God, as was Aaron: so, too, Jesus. Because he shares our humanity, he can sympathize with our weakness, having been tested as we are (4:15); but though subject to weakness (5:2), he is nevertheless without sin (4:15), and through suffering he has learned obedience and been perfected (5:8–9). He has been appointed high priest by God, who not only designated him as his Son, but made him a priest according to the order of Melchizedek (5:5–6). In his earthly life, he offered up prayers and supplications with cries and tears; now he is the source of salvation to those who obey him.

It is at this point that we have the first clear criticism of the readers for their failure to progress in understanding (5:11–14): they need 'someone to teach them again the basic elements of the oracles of God'. The author is about to do this himself! He warns them to do better (6:1–3), condemns those who have 'fallen away' (6:4–8), and expresses his confidence in the readers themselves (6:9–12). It would seem that their failure to comprehend 'the oracles of God' concerns the meaning of the passages quoted in 5:5–6, addressing Jesus as 'Son' and 'priest'.

There follows a long section (6:13–10:18) whose theme is the high priesthood of Christ and the efficacy of his death. This central section is the core of the author's argument. He begins with God's promise of blessing to Abraham, which picks up the reference to 'promises' in 6:12. For the 'heirs of the promise', the fulfilment still lies in the future, and is nothing less than entering into the presence of God, where Jesus, their forerunner, has already gone. Chapter 7 spells out the superiority of Melchizedek to the Aaronic priesthood.[22] Since the Law could not achieve perfection, it follows that the levitical priesthood was flawed, and another order of priesthood was necessary. Jesus could not be a priest according to the order of Aaron but, as a descendant of Judah, he could be a priest according to the order of Melchizedek, and is established as 'a priest for ever' through his resurrection (7:16):[23] unlike the levitical priests, 'he holds his priesthood permanently', and unlike them, he has no need to offer sacrifices for himself, since he has been made perfect for ever (7:28; cf. 5:9).

The finality of Christ's work as high priest is demonstrated by the fact that he is seated at the right hand of God in heaven (8:1). Earthly priests offer worship in a sanctuary that is but a copy of the heavenly one, as God's words to Moses in Exod 25:40 show (Heb 8:5). Jesus is the mediator of a 'better covenant', his ministry 'more excellent'. Through Jeremiah, God declared the first covenant to be faulty; it is therefore obsolete, and has been replaced by a new one (8:13).

After describing the layout of the tabernacle, the author reminds us that only the high priest could enter the holy of holies. Even his offerings 'cannot perfect the conscience of the worshipper', but deal only with food and drink and lustrations (9:9–10). In contrast, Christ entered the 'perfect', heavenly

---

[22] Although Hebrews is the only New Testament book to refer to the work of Melchizedek, he appears to have been the subject of speculation in pre-Christian Judaism. He is the central figure in 11QMelchizedek, though he is not portrayed there as a priest. Ps 110:4 is echoed in various Jewish writings, but not in passages where Melchizedek himself is mentioned. See the discussion in David M. Hay, *Glory at the Right Hand: Psalm 110 in Early Christianity* (Nashville: Abingdon Press, 1973), 19–33.

[23] The author's phrase 'by the power of an indestructible life' neatly reminds us that Christ's priesthood was established through his resurrection from the dead.

tent, not with animal blood but with his own. He is the mediator of a new covenant, and his death redeems those whose sins could not be dealt with under the first covenant. A play on the meaning of διαθήκη, meaning 'will' or 'covenant', shows that it was necessary for the one making the covenant to die (vv. 15–18). The first covenant was inaugurated with blood, and according to the Law, everything must be purified with blood: without the shedding of blood, there is no forgiveness of sins (v. 22).

But the sanctuary was only a copy of the heavenly one, and that has been sanctified by a better sacrifice – namely Christ's own, once-for-all offering of himself. And 'having been offered once to bear the sin of many', he has no further need to deal with sin (9:28). So we see that 'the Law has only a shadow of good things to come, and not the true form of these realities' (10:1). The language is that of apocalyptic: the heavenly realities represent the true world, which already exists, since it is eternal, even though it will remain hidden until Christ appears a second time (9:28).[24]

In ch. 10, the author points out that the continual repetition of the sacrifices demonstrates that they are ineffective. But Christ has offered a much better offering, by doing the will of God, and so has abolished the sacrifices, offerings, and burnt offerings. Having 'offered for all time a single sacrifice for sins, he sat down at the right hand of God' (v. 12), a sign that his task was complete. Quoting again from Jeremiah, our author reminds us that this is the promised new covenant.

We can have confidence, therefore, to enter the sanctuary by the blood of Jesus, since he has opened up a new and living way through the curtain into the presence of God. We can have the full assurance of faith, since our hearts have been sprinkled clean from an evil conscience and our bodies have been washed with pure water (10:19–23). As we have seen, the admonitory verses that follow point to the danger of spurning the Son of God, and of profaning the blood of the covenant. The author appeals to his readers to hold fast to the hope that they have without wavering, warns them (and himself!) about the dangers of persisting in sin and spurning the remedy that has been offered (10:26–31), and appeals to them again not to abandon their former confidence in the gospel (10:32–39).

Chapter 11 spells out the meaning of faith by listing Old Testament heroes who were faithful but did not receive what they had been promised. We have returned once more to the theme of pilgrimage, and the fact that God's people have never obtained what God promised them. These heroes were all prepared to take risks; Abraham and Moses, in particular, both set out into

---

[24] See C.K. Barrett, 'The Eschatology of the Epistle to the Hebrews', in *The Background of the New Testament and Its Eschatology: Studies in Honour of C.H. Dodd,* eds. W.D. Davies and D. Daube (Cambridge: Cambridge University Press, 1964), 363–393.

the unknown. This is what the author is now urging his congregation to do. For them, however, the end of the journey is in sight, since Christ has taken his seat at God's right hand (12:2).

The last two chapters urge the readers to follow Christ's example, enduring suffering and accepting trials. Encouragement is mixed with warnings – in particular, that in 12:25–29 which, as we have seen, is based on the significance of Jesus' death and the new covenant (v. 24). It also picks up the point made in 2:1–4, which made a similar contrast between the punishments appropriate to those who neglected the message given by angels, and that given through the Lord.

Chapter 13 continues the injunctions, with a reprise of the main theme in vv. 10–13: 'We have an altar from which those who officiate in the tent have no right to eat'. The point is surely not that this altar is one from which Christians *can* eat, but that Christ's sacrifice *was not that sort of sacrifice:* the sacrifice *he* offered was a 'sin-offering' and so could not be eaten.[25] He suffered 'outside the camp', a sign that his death was 'a sacrifice for sin', in which the priests did not partake. We, therefore, must be prepared to 'go to him outside the camp' and share his suffering. Through him, we can offer a continual 'sacrifice of praise to God' (vv. 13, 15).

4. Parallels with Paul

It was at an early stage in its history that Hebrews was attributed to Paul. Although the style and vocabulary are very different from his, this attribution was not entirely absurd, since there are interesting parallels to his thought, some of which we have already noted. It is worth examining these more closely.

The parallels between the so-called 'Wisdom Christology' of Heb 1 and Col 1:15–20 (together with John 1:1–18) have often been noted. Since Colossians may be post-Pauline, however, we should note the parallels with what Paul says about the Son in passages such as 1 Cor 8:6 and 2 Cor 4:4. Both authors begin from a conviction that Jesus is the Son of God, who reveals God's character, or glory. Each of them, moreover, uses the language of Ps 110:1 in speaking of Christ's exaltation (Rom 8:34; 1 Cor 15:25; Heb 1:3, 13). Both believe that the Son is obedient to his Father (Rom 5:19; Heb 5:8). The conviction that God spoke through the prophets but now has spoken through

---

[25] Cf. Lev 6:30. The statement in Heb 13:10 is prompted by the comment that 'rules about food' are unimportant (v. 9); it emphasizes the superiority of Christ's sacrifice to those sacrifices which *could* be eaten. It cannot be intended as a reference to the eucharist, even though many commentators have argued for this interpretation – as, e. g., does James Swetnam, 'Christology and the Eucharist in the Epistle to the Hebrews', *Biblica* 70 (1989): 90.

his Son is an underlying theme in Paul (e.g. Rom 1:2–3), and both authors describe past revelation as having been given through angels, and so as inferior to the gospel (Gal 3:19; Heb 1:2–3). Both stress the superiority of Christ to Moses (2 Cor 3:7–18; Heb 3:3–6), and contrast two covenants (2 Cor 3:4–14; Gal 4:21–26; Heb 8:6–9:22). For each writer, the inadequacy of the Law was that it was unable to achieve what it promised: for Paul, that means that it was powerless to deal with sin and to make men and women righteous (Rom 8:3), while in Hebrews, the sacrifices stipulated in the Law are described as unable to take away sins and so to make perfect (Heb 10:4; 7:19). Both understand Christ as the fulfilment of what the Law commanded: for Paul, this means that Christ is the τέλος of the Law, since the purpose of the Law has been fulfilled in him (Rom 10:4), while the author of Hebrews, by spelling out Christ's work as high priest, shows how he has not only fulfilled the purpose of the cult, but has at one and the same time done away with the whole system.[26]

For both authors, the death of Christ is essential in dealing with sin. But as we have noted already, his humanity is also of vital importance to both, since it is impossible for Christ to deal with sin without sharing human flesh (Rom 8:3; Heb 2:14). For Paul, Christ deals with sin by his obedience and death, so reversing the effects of Adam's disobedience (Rom 5:19; 6:10; Phil. 2:8), while in Hebrews, he learned obedience through his suffering, and dealt with sin by offering up himself as a sacrifice (Heb 5:8; 9:12). For Paul, Christ's resurrection meant salvation and life for those who trust in him (1 Thess 5:9–10), while Hebrews describes Christ as 'the source of eternal salvation for all who obey him' (Heb 5:9), and as opening up 'the new and living way into God's presence' (10:20). For both, what Christ offers is in some sense experienced already (Rom 6:4; Heb 4:16), and is in some sense still future (Rom 6:5; Heb 6:19–20; 9:24, 28): to live the Christian life is to live in the present in the light of the future. Both speak of Christians becoming 'sons of God', and stress the fact that this status depends on their close relationship to the one who is uniquely 'Son of God' (Rom 8:1–4,14–17; Gal 4:1–7; Heb 2:10–13). That means that they are his 'brothers', and will share his glory (Rom 8:29–30; Phil 3:21; Heb 2:10–13). For both authors, Christians are wholly dependent on Christ, but whereas Paul works out his understanding of 'interchange' in terms of being 'in Christ', the author of Hebrews speaks rather of Christ as 'our pioneer', and though he describes Christians as 'partners with Christ' (3:14), he uses the same term of our relationship with one another (3:1): in other words, he thinks of Christians as members of the same company, with Christ at their head on their journey.

---

[26] Since delivering this lecture, I have discovered that a similar point was made by Manson, *Hebrews,* 167.

512 Section Six: Adam, Law, and Cult

The central theme of Hebrews – Christ's work as high priest – is, of course, unique. Yet even this reminds us of aspects of Paul's thought. It seems highly probable, for example, that in Rom 3:25 Paul has in mind the ritual of the Day of Atonement:[27] if so, then he identifies Jesus not only with the sin-offering whose blood is taken into the holy of holies, but with the ἱλαστήριον, the 'mercy seat' where reconciliation between God and his people takes place. For Hebrews, Jesus is not the *place* of sacrifice, but the one who offers the sacrifice: and since what he offers is himself, he is both priest and victim. Whereas in Rom 3, therefore, Christ is a sacrifice offered by God, in Hebrews the offering is made by Christ himself. Yet this is only to put into sacrificial language[28] an idea which Paul expresses in more traditional language by speaking of Christ 'giving himself'.[29] Both authors speak of Christ as now at God's right hand, where he makes intercession for us (Rom 8:34; Heb 7:25 and 8:1).

Like the author of Hebrews, Paul also uses the language of sacrifice for the Christian life, urging those who have been brought into a right relationship with God to present themselves 'a living, holy sacrifice, acceptable to God' (Rom 12:1; cf. Heb 13:15).

Finally, we should note that both writers share a similar eschatological framework of thought; with Christ, the old has given way to the new, which makes the regulations governing the old obsolete. Both, moreover, use apocalyptic language to express this. We have noted already that the author of Hebrews uses apocalyptic language in describing Christ's entry into the heavenly sanctuary (e.g. Heb 9:23–28); he uses it, too, in comparing Mount Sinai with Mount Zion and the heavenly Jerusalem (Heb 12:18–24). Similar imagery is used by Paul in Gal 4:21–31, where Mount Sinai is compared with 'the Jerusalem above'.[30]

What are we to conclude from these parallels? Did the author of Hebrews know Paul's letters?[31] Although this is possible, there are no obvious quotations, and dependence would be impossible to prove.[32] It is just as likely that

---

[27] This was suggested by T.W. Manson, 'ΙΛΑΣΤΗΡΙΟΝ', *JTS* 46 (1945): 1–10. On the meaning of ἱλαστήριον, see Daniel P. Bailey, 'Jesus as the Mercy Seat: The Semantics and Theology of Paul's Use of *Hilasterion* in Romans 3:25', *Tyndale Bulletin* 51 (2000): 155–158. The article summarizes the argument of Bailey's unpublished PhD dissertation.

[28] The verbs used in Hebrews are ἀναφέρω (e.g. Heb 7:27) and προσφέρω (e.g. Heb 9:14).

[29] He uses both δίδωμι (Gal 1:4) and παραδίδωμι (Gal 2:20).

[30] See Morna D. Hooker, '"Heirs of Abraham": The Gentiles' Role in Israel's Story', in *Narrative Dynamics in Paul*, ed. Bruce W. Longenecker (Louisville; London: Westminster John Knox, 2002), 85–96.

[31] Similar questions relate to Hebrews' relationship with other New Testament books – e.g. the Fourth Gospel.

[32] Our purpose is not to 'harmonize' Hebrews' teaching with Paul's, as though Paul's teaching set a standard, but to note what they have in common. See Andrew Chester's criticism of Robert J. Daly ('Hebrews: The Final Sacrifice', in *Sacrifice and Redemption: Durham Essays in Theology*, ed. S.W. Sykes [Cambridge: Cambridge University Press, 1991], 57. Cf.

the similarities are due to our author using ideas which were part of early Christian tradition. Among the 'core beliefs' which they shared, we may note the following:

1. Christ is the Son of God and obedient to his will, and the 'image' of God, who reveals God to us.

2. This 'Christ' is Jesus, who is fully human, having been totally identified with the human condition, and so able to act as our representative.

3. He 'died for our sins, according to the scriptures'.

4. With his death and resurrection, the new age has dawned, rendering the legislation intended for the old age obsolete.

5. What happened through his death and resurrection was the fulfilment of God's purpose, set out in the Old Testament, which bears witness to what has now been realized in Christ.

6. The result is that Christians are now 'sons' of God,[33] and so destined to share the glory of Christ.

5. The Author's Purpose

'Hebrews', we have assumed, is a homily addressed to a particular group of Christians. Are we now in a better position to understand their situation and problems? It would seem that they were devout Jewish Christians who had not yet, in our author's view, understood the implications of their confession of the crucified and risen Jesus as the Son of God. In what ways did this new conviction affect their former beliefs and way of life? We have suggested that at first it would have been natural for Jewish Christians to continue worshipping in the temple and synagogues. As time passed, this would have become increasingly difficult, because of the hostility of other Jews. If our author was writing after 70 CE, then the catastrophic events in Jerusalem could have provided the spark which led our author to think of Christ as replacing the cult. Moreover, there was another important force at work: theological reflection on the significance of the Christ event demonstrated that there must be some discontinuity, as well as continuity, with the past. Inevitably, this realization occurred earlier in a Gentile context: Paul quickly insisted that to compel Gentiles to become Jews was to reject the grace of God. If Christ's death and resurrection had introduced the New Age, how could one expect Gentiles to adopt the rules and symbols that belonged to the old? For Gentiles to adopt circumcision and obedience to the Law would mean that nothing

---

Robert J. Daly, *Christian Sacrifice: The Judaeo-Christian Background before Origen* [Washington, DC: Catholic University of America Press, 1978], 261–285, and *The Origins of the Christian Doctrine of Sacrifice* [Philadelphia: Fortress Press, 1978], 69–75.).

[33] See above, n. 21.

significant had taken place. Writing in a Jewish context, our author faced a similar problem, though one that in the early years was less acute. What did it mean for Jews to confess Jesus as Messiah and Son of God? What practical difference did it make to their lives? Had anything really changed? Was faith in Jesus as the Messiah simply to be 'added on' to their former beliefs, or did it necessitate significant changes?

Let us put the question in another way. Why *should* anything have changed? The answer of our New Testament authors – with the exception of James – is unanimous: it is because Christ has died and been raised. Christ's death and resurrection lay at the heart of the early Christian kerygma. But the death of Christ was not only central theologically; it was, as Paul reminds us, a scandal, and therefore demanded explanation. Early attempts to do so are found in the earliest summary of belief, in 1 Cor 15:3. The conviction that 'Christ died for our sins in accordance with the scriptures' was, Paul tells us, part of the tradition that was given to him and which he, in turn, passed on. Commentators have, to be sure, suggested that Paul himself may be responsible for the phrases 'for our sins' and 'according to the scriptures', but the former is not a normal Pauline expression,[34] and both ideas are widespread in the New Testament. Indeed, it is impossible to believe that the first Christians, faced by the dilemma of the cross, would *not* have turned to the scriptures in attempting to explain it. In one way or another, we find each of our New Testament authors trying to do so.

Those Christians who refused to face up to the scandal of the cross inevitably failed to grasp the implications of the kerygma. Some clearly fell into the temptation to ignore it, as we see from the Corinthian correspondence. The Galatians failed to recognize its significance as marking the end of the old era. It is hardly surprising if Christians found it difficult to comprehend a shameful death as part of the 'good news'.

The question 'Why did Christ die?' must have been a pressing one in the formative years. The formula quoted by Paul in 1 Cor 15:3 offers two answers. First, to the question 'Why?' in the sense 'Why did it happen?' the answer is that it was part of God's purpose, set out in scripture. Second, to the question 'Why?' in the sense 'What did it achieve?' the answer is that it was 'for our sins'. But *which* scriptures? There is no hint in 1 Cor 15:3 as to which scriptures Paul might have in mind. And *how* does Christ's death deal with our sins? Again, this is not spelt out in 1 Cor 15, though we know from the rest of Paul's writings that there were various possible answers.

'Christ died for our sins according to the scriptures'. Was this formula part of the tradition that was handed on to the author of Hebrews, as it had been to Paul? Certainly it could stand as the 'text' of his epistle. For what he

---

[34] The only parallel is in Gal 1:4. Normally Paul speaks of 'sin' rather than 'sins'.

attempts to do here is to show precisely how Christ's death could be understood to be 'for our sins', and precisely which scriptures were relevant. Clearly it was not immediately obvious how Christ's death could have been 'according to the scriptures'; even the passage that seemed to later theologians to be the obvious one – Isa 53 – was not appealed to as we would expect. Nor was it obvious how his death could deal with sins. It is not surprising, then, that our author thought it necessary to spell out precisely how Jesus' death could deal with sin, and how this was 'according to the scriptures'. The scriptures he appeals to in dealing with Christ's status and exaltation overlap with those found elsewhere in the New Testament – e.g. Pss 2 and 110 – but in dealing with Christ's death, he breaks new ground, by appealing to the tradition about Melchizedek, which is not used elsewhere in the New Testament, arguing that the one who is addressed as 'Son' is also termed 'a priest'. He explains how Christ's death dealt with sins, by drawing on the rules about sacrificial offerings set out in the Pentateuch. Here, incidentally, is the explanation as to why our author speaks about the 'tent' rather than the 'temple'. It is because his concern is not with what is (or is no longer) going on in Jerusalem, but with showing that Christ's death is *according to the scriptures,* and with spelling out the implications of that 'fulfilment'. The explanation that his death was a 'sacrifice' had been used before, but by combining this with the idea of Christ as high priest, he was able to explain how Christ could offer himself, and could himself enter into God's presence, so opening up the way to others. The problem with which he is dealing is not some new crisis of faith in the community to which he writes, but the far more basic one of trying to come to terms with the 'absurd and embarrassing fact' of Christ's death,[35] and explaining how it affects us.

Like Paul, he does so by discovering that Christ's death and resurrection were not only 'according to the scriptures', but that they were the means by which the new age had been inaugurated. Just as Paul had to rethink what it meant to be 'righteous', so our author had to rethink what it meant to be 'perfect'. Working in a Gentile context, Paul was led to see that what distinguished God's people from outsiders was not 'the works of the Law', but being 'in Christ': this being so, those Gentile Christians who accepted circumcision and thought it necessary to obey food regulations were failing to grasp the significance of the cross. The author of Hebrews believed that God's people were not made perfect by the sacrifices offered in the temple, but by Christ's self-offering and entry into heaven. Just as Paul insisted that for Gentiles to accept circumcision and obedience to the Law would be to make Christ's death of no effect (Gal 2:21–3:5), so our author, writing in a Jewish context, urges his congregation to recognize that those who continue to offer

---

[35] Chester, 'Sacrifice', 68.

sacrifices in order to deal with sin are treating Christ's death with contempt and rejecting the covenant established through his death (6:6; 10:29).

Like Paul, our author began from the presumption that Christ's life, death, and resurrection/exaltation had effected a radical change which had rendered the old system obsolete. Each of them understood that the fulfilment of God's promises meant that the regulations that had hitherto governed their lives belonged to an era that was past. Yet each was convinced that God remained faithful to his promises, and had not abandoned his people. The fact that the closest parallels between the two writers concern arguments about the relationship of faith in Jesus as Christ and Son of God to the promises and regulations set out in the Law suggests that their basic concern may have been the same, even though their situations were very different. And just as Paul's insights brought about an explosion of Christianity in the Gentile world, which eventually led to a separation from Judaism, so the author of Hebrews, by demonstrating how Christ's death had fulfilled the purpose of the cult, made his own contribution, in the Jewish-Christian community, to the 'Parting of the Ways'.

6. Postscript

Preachers should begin where their congregations are. But how are we to interpret Hebrews today, when we are so clearly not where its author was? We certainly do not begin, as his Jewish readers would have done, from an assumption that 'without the shedding of blood there is no forgiveness of sin' (9:22). Nor, indeed, do we normally interpret the regulations for the Jewish cult as a 'copy' of heavenly realities. Does our author nevertheless have any insights for us today?

Hebrews is based on the assumption that 'God spoke to our ancestors ... by the prophets'. Although what Christ has achieved through his death and resurrection undoubtedly supersedes the cult, our author by no means discards past revelation, but shows how it witnesses to the realization of God's purpose in Christ. He rejects the literalist interpretation of the text without abandoning the text itself.[36] It is a strange anomaly that so many Christians today cling to a literalist interpretation of their scriptures, something which our New Testament authors did not do.

Although our author's world is shaped by the Jewish scriptures, his starting point is in fact his conviction that God has now spoken to his people *through a Son*. That Son is Jesus, who endured death, and whom God 'has brought

---

[36] Once again, we have a parallel in Paul, who sets out his position clearly in 2 Cor 3:6–11 where he contrasts 'letter' and 'spirit'.

back from the dead' (13:20). This means that though it may appear as though Christ is being interpreted in the light of scripture, in reality it is the other way round: scripture is being reinterpreted in the light of the death and resurrection of Christ. The past has to be explained in terms of present experience.

The bulk of the epistle is given over to a description of Christ's role as priest – an idea which enables our author to explain how his death was both 'for our sins' and 'according to the scriptures'. The central chapters spell out the meaning of the phrase 'when he had made purification for sins' (1:3) in a way that was particularly relevant to the community for whom he was writing. Here, too, the author picks up the statement that, the purification accomplished, 'he sat down at the right hand of the majesty on high' (1:3; 8:1; 10:12). As a result – using the high-priestly analogy – Christians are able to approach God's throne (4:16; 7:25; 10:19–22; cf. 12:18, 22–24).

Before expounding this theme, however, the author has already explained what Christ's enthronement means for us in somewhat different language: *because* Jesus was made for a while lower than the angels, and tasted death for everyone, he has now been crowned with glory and honour, so becoming the pioneer of our salvation and bringing many sons and daughters to glory (2:5–10).

This pattern of suffering/exaltation is familiar to us from other New Testament writings, e.g. Luke 9:22; Acts 2:29–36; Phil 2:6–11. In the Gospels, it is expressed in terms of death/resurrection in the so-called 'passion predictions'. All emphasize that Christ's suffering and death were 'necessary': in other words, they were 'according to the scriptures'. The author of Hebrews, however, like Paul, works out this 'necessity' in what is essentially an incarnational soteriology: in order to restore men and women to a relationship with God, and bring them to glory, Christ was made for a while lower than the angels and tasted death on behalf of (ὑπὲρ) everyone. It was because he became like men and women in every respect that he was able to act as their high priest (2:5–18).

What our author has done, therefore, is to take the basic kerygma message and interpret it in a particular context, using the imagery of the Day of Atonement to explain how Christ's death dealt with our sins, and what his exaltation to God's right hand achieved. If we are to be true to his method, we too need to reinterpret that basic summary of the gospel in the language and culture of today.

Section Seven

Living in the New Age

35. 1 Thessalonians 1:9–10:
A Nutshell – But What Kind of Nut?

It was Adolf von Harnack who said of 1 Thess 1:9b–10 'Here we have the mission-preaching to pagans in a nutshell'.[1] His judgement has since become one of the axioms of New Testament scholarship,[2] and has rarely been challenged. Commentators on 1 Thessalonians universally describe the passage in these terms; the only debate seems to be as to whether Paul is recalling the gospel as he himself preached it to the Christians in Thessalonica, or whether he is quoting a summary which was used by other early Christian missionaries – a question that Harnack himself did not raise. The popularity of his suggestion may owe something to its attractiveness, for if it is correct, and if 1 Thessalonians is the earliest of Paul's letters, then we have here the earliest summary of the gospel in the whole New Testament – earlier, even, than 1 Cor 15:3 ff.

An important challenge to the theory was, however, made more than thirty years ago, when Johannes Munck published an article in *New Testament Studies*[3] in which he suggested that the one and a half verses in question were to be seen, not as a summary of what Paul had originally preached in Thessalonica, but as an indication of the issues which Paul is going to discuss later in the letter. I remember being very excited by this article when I first read it, and thinking that I would like to investigate the matter further: I was excited, because I myself, in lecturing on 1 Thessalonians all those years ago, had already been using these one and a half verses as a kind of peg on which to hang the substance of Paul's teaching in 1 Thessalonians 4–5 – though I had been treating the correspondence between 1:9–10 and chapters 4–5 as mere accident, not the result of careful planning on Paul's part: I had apparently

---

[1] Adolf von Harnack, *Die Mission und Ausbreitung des Christentums in den ersten drei Jahrhunderten* (Leipzig: J.C. Hinrich, 1924); ET: *Mission and Expansion of Christianity in the First Three Centuries*, trans. James Moffatt (London: Williams and Norgate, 1908), 89. Harnack was perhaps seeing the passage as a credal summary. He continues: 'The "living and true God" is the first and final thing; the second is Jesus, the Son of God, the judge, who secures us against the wrath to come, and who is therefore "Jesus the Lord"'.

[2] So, e.g., Ferdinand Hahn, *Das Verständnis der Mission im Neuen Testament*, WMANT 13 (Neukirchen-Vluyn: Neukirchener Verlag, 1963); ET: *Mission in the New Testament*, trans. F. Clarke, (London: SCM Press, 1965) who refers to the passage as a 'missionary sermon': 76, 135.

[3] Johannes Munck, '1 Thess i.9–10 and the Missionary Preaching of Paul: Textual Exegesis and Hermeneutic Reflexions', *NTS* 9 (1963): 95–110.

stumbled by accident on something whose significance I had not realized. My resolution to investigate the matter further, however, took nearly thirty years to come to fruition.

But was Munck's challenge as important as I have suggested? Perhaps I am misjudging it, for in fact it has been virtually ignored by subsequent commentators. Those who mention it apparently think it unimportant.[4] Ernest Best, whose commentary is now widely used in the English-speaking world, dismisses the argument in a sentence, largely on the basis that the vocabulary in these verses is not Pauline.[5] Yet Munck's theory is very much in accord with recent work on the literary form of epistles, for we now know that it was very common to give an indication of the content of the letter in the opening paragraph.[6] If Paul is following the contemporary pattern, and if he is doing here what he does in many of his later letters, then we would expect Johannes Munck's theory to be correct.[7]

So is Paul here looking back to what he preached, or is he looking forward to what he is going to say later in the letter? It is, of course, immediately obvious that whether or not he is doing the latter, he is certainly, to some extent at least, doing the former: he is explicitly reminding the Thessalonians of what happened when he arrived in Thessalonica and preached the gospel to them. So let us begin by considering Harnack's view and ask whether in fact 1 Thess 1:9–10 reproduces what Paul preached to them, so that it can aptly be

---

[4] Cf. Raymond F. Collins, *Studies on the First Letter to the Thessalonians*, BETL 66 (Leuven: Leuven University Press, 1984), who mentions Munck's suggestion (pp. 21–23), but then refers to him repeatedly throughout the book as though he supported the view that Paul made use of a traditional Jewish Hellenistic missionary sermon.

[5] Ernest Best, *A Commentary on the First and Second Epistles to the Thessalonians*, BNTC (London: A&C Black, 1972), 87.

[6] This accords with Aristotle's analysis of discourse in general. The opening paragraph serves as a proem or exordium. Cf. Aristotle, *Rhetoric* 3.14.1.

[7] Cf. George A. Kennedy, *New Testament Interpretation through Rhetorical Criticism* (London; Chapel Hill: University of North Carolina Press, 1984), 141 ff. who sees the proem of 1 Thess 1:2–10 as raising issues discussed in the later chapters. The question of the structure of the Pauline letters has been the subject of much recent discussion. Among the many studies on this topic we may mention the following, which deal with 1 Thessalonians in particular: Robert Jewett, *The Thessalonian Correspondence: Pauline Rhetoric and Millenarian Piety* (Philadelphia: Fortress Press, 1986), 63–78; Bruce C. Johanson, *To All the Brethren: A Text-Linguistic and Rhetorical Approach to 1 Thessalonians*, ConBNT 16 (Stockholm: Almqvist & Wiksell International, 1987); Frank W. Hughes, 'The Rhetoric of 1 Thessalonians' in *The Thessalonian Correspondence*, ed. Raymond F. Collins, BETL 87 (Leuven: Leuven University Press/Uitgeverij Peeters, 1990), 94–116 (cf. also *Early Christian Rhetoric and 2 Thessalonians*, JSNTSup 30 [Sheffield: JSOT, 1989], 19–50): Wilhelm Wuellner, 'The Argumentative Structure of 1 Thessalonians as Paradoxical Encomium', in *The Thessalonian Correspondence*, ed. Raymond F. Collins, 117–136. The significance of the thanksgiving is not affected by the debate as to whether the structure of the letters should be understood in 'rhetorical' or 'epistolary' categories; see Albert Vanhoye, 'La Composition de 1 Thessaloniciens', in *The Thessalonian Correspondence*, ed. Raymond F. Collins, 73–86.

described as 'the mission-preaching to pagans in a nutshell'; and whether, if it does, this summary is Paul's own or represents some kind of traditional credal formula which Paul took over.

Let us work backwards, and look at the second of these questions first. As we have seen, the chief reason for disputing Munck's suggestion is that he has failed to discuss what Best describes as 'the unique character of the vocabulary'. If the vocabulary and phraseology are non-Pauline then the view that Paul is quoting a ready-made formula seems inevitable, and Munck's suggestion is ruled out.[8] Since Best gives details of the evidence I shall use his comments as a basis for our discussion.

Paul reminds the Thessalonians of how they *turned to God*. The Greek verb used here is ἐπιστρέφω. Best notes that Paul tends to use the aorist of πιστεύω of entry into Christian belief.[9] Nevertheless he does use ἐπιστρέφω twice, in 2 Cor 3:16 and Gal 4:9, in both cases to describe a wholesale turning about; the former passage speaks of someone turning to the Lord, the latter of Gentiles turning back to other gods. Galatians 4 is particularly relevant, since it is describing the reverse of what is happening here. The verb seems to be precisely what is required in the present context, and far more appropriate than πιστεύω.

They turned *from idols* (there is no disputing that this is a Pauline term!) *to serve a living and true God*. Best notes that elsewhere in Paul δουλεύω is used of serving Christ, not God. This is true, though the injunction to serve the Lord in Rom 12:11 is ambiguous. But if we look once more at Gal 4:8 and 9, we find the verb used of the Galatians' former bondage to pagan deities, to whom they are in danger of turning back: once again, the verb seems entirely appropriate in the present context, where Paul is talking about serving God in contrast to idols. The terms living (ζῶντι) and true (ἀληθινῷ) are both used of God in the LXX. Best points out that ἀληθινός is used by Paul only here: but he uses ἀληθής elsewhere, e.g. of God in Rom 3:4. The adjectives seem the obvious ones to use in contrasting God with pagan deities, especially in view of their LXX background.

The Thessalonians now *wait*. The verb ἀναμένω occurs only here in the New Testament. Best notes that Paul normally uses compounds of δέχομαι: in eschatological contexts that means ἀπεκδέχομαι (Rom 8:19, 23, 25; 1 Cor 1:7; Gal 5:5: Phil 3:20). Here at last we must agree that Paul has used an unusual and unexpected word: ἀναμένω is not Pauline. But since it is not used

---

[8] Typical of the many scholars who have argued that the language is pre-Pauline are Béda Rigaux, 'Vocabulaire chrétien antérieur à la première épître aux Thessaloniciens' in *Sacra Pagina*, eds. J. Coppens, A. Descamps, and É. Massaux, *BETL* 12–13 (Gembloux: J. Duculot, 1959), 380–389, and Paul-Emile Langevin, *Jésus Seigneur et l'eschatologie: Exégèse de textes prépauliniens*, Studia 21 (Bruges ; Paris: Desclée, De Brouwer, 1967), 48–58.

[9] He notes five examples: Rom 13:11; 1 Cor 3:5; 15:2, 11; Gal 2:16.

elsewhere in the New Testament, there is nothing either to suggest that it is part of a traditional formula. We have no evidence either way.

What they wait for is the appearance of *God's Son from heaven*. The title 'Son' is used frequently by Paul, though nowhere else, as Best points out, in relation to the parousia. Also unusual, he argues, is the plural form used in the phrase ἐκ τῶν οὐρανῶν. Paul certainly uses the plural οὐρανοί elsewhere, but not with the preposition ἐκ: his normal expression is ἐξ οὐρανοῦ. Could the use of the plural here be a relic of a pre-Pauline Jewish formula? Perhaps. But the use of the plural here is odd, not so much because it is unusual for Paul – there are in fact only three occasions where he uses the phrase in the singular[10] – but because it is not found anywhere else in the New Testament: apart from this passage, the singular phrase ἐξ οὐρανοῦ is the norm. There is thus no evidence that a formula containing the expression ἐκ τῶν οὐρανῶν ever existed. Once again, we have nothing on which to base an argument, either that it is Pauline, or that it is traditional.

The one whom they await was *raised from the dead*. The verb ἐγείρω is Paul's usual one, and the only oddity here is the use of the article in the phrase ἐκ τῶν νεκρῶν, found elsewhere in the Pauline corpus only in Col 1:18 and Eph 5:14. Once again there is no evidence elsewhere that the unusual phrase is traditional, since in the rest of the New Testament the form used is always ἐκ νεκρῶν. The matter here is complicated by a textual variant, since the article is omitted by A C K and some minuscules.[11] This is not very strong evidence for its omission, but there is sufficient doubt for [27]Nestle-Aland to put the article in square brackets. The article could easily have been added by a scribe whose eye wandered for a moment from the ἐκ before νεκρῶν to the words ἐκ τῶν οὐρανῶν.

The identification of the one who is awaited from heaven with the one who was raised from the dead is sufficient explanation for the use of the title 'the Son' in this context. Incidentally, we have here a theme which is found elsewhere in Paul: confidence for the future is based on God's action in the past; it is Jesus, who has been raised from the dead, who is now awaited from heaven, and who will save us from wrath. We may compare Rom 8:34, where Paul appeals to the fact that Christ Jesus died – and still more to the fact that he was raised – as the basis for his confidence that Christ intercedes for us and that nothing can destroy us. Similarly, in Rom 5:9 ff., he argues from the fact that we have been reconciled to God through the death of his Son to the fact that we shall be saved by him – and specifically by his life – from the wrath to come.

---

[10] 1 Cor 15:47; 2 Cor 5:2; Gal 1:8.
[11] 323, 629, 945, 2464, 2495 al.

The final clause tells us that the one who is awaited is *Jesus, who will save us from the wrath to come*. The identification of the Son as 'Jesus' may well have been made here because the name means 'Saviour' and is therefore particularly appropriate in this context. The notion of the coming wrath is familiar enough in Paul, and need not delay us. His normal terms for future salvation, however, are cognates of σῴζω. The verb which he uses here, ῥύομαι, is more commonly used of deliverance from physical peril, but though Best denies that it is used by Paul elsewhere in an eschatological context[12] it is in fact used in Rom 7:24, in the appeal for deliverance from 'this body of death', and in an Old Testament quotation in Rom 11:26, where it refers to the Redeemer who will save Israel at the End: in this latter passage the verbs σῴζω and ῥύομαι appear to be synonymous.

Different scholars will assess this evidence differently. For myself, I find it insufficient to justify labelling the passage as non-Pauline. There are one or two unusual phrases, one unique verb – but any passage in Paul could easily provide as many oddities. The Pauline material we have available is too scanty for us to be able to conclude that certain words and phrases are non-Pauline. It is perhaps worth comparing these 1½ vv. with the first part of v. 9, which so far we have not considered. The verb ἀπαγγέλλω, report, is used only once more by Paul, in 1 Cor 14:25; so, too, the noun εἴσοδος occurs only once more – in 2:1, the verse immediately following this passage. But no one is going to suggest on this basis that 1:9 and 2:1 are also non-Pauline: the fact that Paul does not use this particular term elsewhere is assumed to be accidental, and it is assumed to be accidental because v. 9a is not under suspicion.

There is, moreover, a great deal in this passage which sounds very Pauline indeed. If Paul *has* taken over a traditional formula, then either he has adapted it, or his own theological position is not so far removed from what he is quoting. But there is one significant difference from other Pauline summaries of the gospel, and that is the omission of any specific reference to the death of Jesus, and therefore of any interpretative comment on that death as being 'for us'. If this passage is in fact a summary of the gospel that Paul preached to the Thessalonians, we would certainly consider this failure to refer directly to the death of Jesus very odd indeed, and we might perhaps be tempted to consider it as evidence supporting the theory that he is quoting from a traditional formula. But would it not be equally strange to find a *pre*-Pauline formulation of the gospel without any reference to the death of Jesus?[13] Can the omission in fact be explained on that basis? Is there any evidence for the suggestion that there was ever a pre-Pauline statement of the gospel which did not refer

---

[12] Best, *Thessalonians*, 85.
[13] See 1 Cor 15:3 ff.; cf. Rom 4:25, 8:32; Gal 1:4; Eph 5:2, 25; Titus 2:14, which have all been suggested as possible quotations of pre-Pauline formulae.

directly to the death of Jesus?[14] And would Paul have been happy to use it? The only possible summary passage is Rom 1:3 ff., which most commentators assume to be a pre-Pauline formula on the basis of arguments similar to those used in looking at 1 Thess 1:9–10.[15] I doubt very much whether they are correct in their assessment of that text (for reasons very similar to those being spelt out here), but it is impossible to discuss the passage here. I hope to return to it in a later paper.

We turn now from the evidence that has been held to support this theory that Paul is quoting someone else's summary to the problems involved in holding it.

The suggestion is that in writing to the Thessalonians and reminding them of the gospel which he preached to them, Paul is using the words of a traditional Christian formula which had been used by Jewish Christians before him in preaching to Gentiles. Who *were* these Jewish Christian missionaries? *Were* there any before Paul? And who were the Gentiles to whom they had been preaching? According to Luke's account in Acts, the first major evangelization of Gentiles took place in Antioch,[16] and though Paul was certainly not the initiator in this move, he was involved in the work almost from the beginning.[17] Until this point, even the members of the group associated with Stephen had confined their preaching to Jews.[18] To be sure, Luke tells us of exceptions to this rule: Philip had preached to Samaritans, and his work had been confirmed by Peter and John.[19] Philip, again, had expounded the gospel to the Ethiopian eunuch and baptized him:[20] since the Ethiopian was reading the scroll of Isaiah, he was presumably already a godfearer. Then Peter was persuaded to take the gospel to Cornelius, another godfearer, and to baptize him.[21] But these are all unusual events, and regarded

---

[14] Those who argue that the 'Q' tradition represents a 'gospel' which made no reference to the death of Jesus would no doubt maintain that this in itself was a statement of such belief. Even granted that 'Q' was a 'gospel' (which we doubt), it is difficult to believe that Paul would have considered it to be an adequate statement of Christian faith. Cf. Martin Hengel, 'Christologie und neutestamentliche Chronologie', in *Neues Testament und Geschichte: Historisches Geschehen und Deutung im Neuen Testament: Oscar Cullmann zum 70. Geburtstag,* eds. Heinrich Baltensweiler and Bo Reicke (Zürich: Theologischer Verlag, 1972), 53; ET: 'Christology and New Testament Chronology', in *Between Jesus and Paul,* trans. John Bowden (London: SCM Press, 1983), 37.

[15] The statements of the kerygma which C.H. Dodd considered so important (*The Apostolic Preaching and Its Developments* [London: Hodder & Stoughton, 1936]) all refer to the death of Jesus, but cannot be relied on as early formulations of the faith.

[16] Acts 11:20.
[17] Acts 11:25.
[18] Acts 11:19.
[19] Acts 8:4–25.
[20] Acts 8:25–40.
[21] Acts 10.

as exceptions to the norm,[22] as is seen, most clearly, in the church's opposition to Peter's actions.[23] It is only when the Christians expelled from Jerusalem after Stephen's death come to Antioch that the real breakthrough takes place.[24]

It is, of course, possible that Luke has minimized the work of other early Christian preachers because he wishes to emphasize the role of Paul – but even if we allow that evangelization among Gentiles had in fact been taking place earlier, had there been time for these missionaries to develop a summary of the gospel which had become a recognizable formula that could have been adopted by others? It has, to be sure, been suggested that the formula may have been based on Jewish (not Christian) preaching to pagans, but this would account for only part of the summary. And if there *were* any such formula, would Paul have been happy to take it over and use it, even if, as Best suggests, it was not 'wholly in agreement with his own theology'? Why *should* he have adopted a statement of the church's faith with which he did not wholly agree? Would Paul, who elsewhere denied so vehemently that his gospel had been received from men,[25] have been likely in any case to have adopted someone else's formulation of that gospel – least of all in preaching to Gentiles? It is true that he insists also that his gospel agrees with that of the other apostles,[26] and it is true that in 1 Corinthians 15 he quotes the tradition he had received from others, but that tradition concerns the death, burial and resurrection of Jesus and his appearance to the disciples, events of which he had not been an eyewitness. The *meaning* of the gospel for Gentiles had come to him by revelation (Gal 1:11 ff.). He had been entrusted by the Lord with the gospel to the uncircumcised, just as Peter had been entrusted with the gospel to the circumcised: if he received it from the Lord, he did not need to quote others' formulation of it. If what we are being asked to believe about 1 Thess 1:9–10 is true, then Paul had changed his mind radically between the writing of 1 Thessalonians and Galatians, *whichever* of them was written first.

The notion that in preaching to the Thessalonians Paul found it necessary to quote some pre-existing formula is surely extremely odd. It is difficult to imagine Paul consulting a manual on 'How to convert pagans'; difficult to suppose that he adopted and repeated versions of the Christian message for pagans worked out by others. But there is a second version of this theory that may be less difficult, and that is the suggestion that Paul is indeed quoting the

---

[22] Hengel is surely right in interpreting Ἑλληνισταί in Acts 6:1 as meaning Greek-speaking Jews, not Gentiles: 'Zwischen Jesus und Paulus', *ZTK* 72 (1975): 157–171; ET: 'Between Jesus and Paul', in *Between Jesus and Paul*, 4–11.

[23] Acts 11:1–18.

[24] Martin Hengel, *Zur urchristlichen Geschichtsschreibung* (Stuttgart: Calwer Verlag, 1984), 63–105, especially 85; ET: *Earliest Christianity*, trans. John Bowden (London: SCM Press, 1986), 71–126, especially 99 ff.

[25] Gal 1:11 ff.

[26] Gal 1:7–9; 2:1 ff.

gospel as he delivered it to the Thessalonians, but that the formulation of the gospel was his own.

Now there is one piece of evidence which might support the view that Paul is here quoting a summary of his own preaching, and that is the fact that in the two passages in Acts where Luke reports what Paul said to a Gentile audience there are fascinating echoes of 1 Thess 1:9–10. The first is in Acts 14, where Luke describes how in Lystra, Paul and Barnabas are taken to be gods come to earth in human form. In v. 15 Paul protests: 'We also are men like yourselves, and bring you good news, that you should turn from these vain things to a living God who made the heaven and the earth and the sea and everything that is in them'. Here we have an echo of 1 Thess 1:9b. The second comes in Acts 17, where Paul is brought to the Areopagus, and ends his address by saying that God has 'fixed a day on which he will judge the world in righteousness, by a man whom he has appointed, having given assurance of this to everyone by raising him from the dead'. This time we have a parallel with 1 Thess 1:10. Now unless we take the unlikely view that, in composing Paul's speeches, Luke has used non-Pauline traditional summaries, these passages can hardly be thought to support the suggestion that 1 Thess 1:9–10 is also a pre-Pauline formula. Either Luke has put into Paul's mouth words which he thought appropriate for the occasion, or he has some genuine reminiscence of the kind of thing that Paul used to say. The passages are certainly compatible with the view that Paul himself composed 1 Thess 1:9–10.

But are these verses a summary of the gospel? If so, then Acts 14:15 gives us half the gospel, and Acts 17:31 the other half! But we can hardly believe that Paul's gospel did not have more to say about the death of Christ. What Acts does is to show Paul preaching in a way appropriate to the situation. Luke is not attempting to summarize the whole gospel in either of these passages. Why should we assume that Paul is attempting to do so in 1 Thessalonians? For what no one who advocates this theory seems to notice is that vv. 9b–10 are not a summary of the Christian gospel at all – and I am not referring now to the fact that there is no reference to the death of Christ, only to his resurrection. Paul did not stand up in the marketplace in Thessalonica and deliver a message which ran: 'Turn from your pagan gods to serve a living and true God, and wait for his Son to appear from the heavens – his Son whom he raised from the dead and who will save us from wrath'. What he did was to preach the gospel, and *as a result of that proclamation,* the Thessalonians abandoned their pagan deities in order to serve the one true God, and lived in expectation of the return of his Son. Paul is not here summarizing his preaching, but describing the *effect* which his preaching had on the Thessalonians. Notice how the verses come as the climax of a passage in which he is thanking God for the way in which the Thessalonians received the gospel and for their faith, which is an example to others. Everyone has heard how he came to their city and how they responded. In other words, he is reminding the Thessalonians of the way they responded to his preaching – of their *conversion,* not of that preaching itself.

Best argues that the 'fragment' in 1 Thess 1:9–10 can be set out in two three-line stanzas as follows:[27]

> You turned to God from idols.
> to serve the living and real God.
> (and) to wait for his Son out of heaven.
>
> Whom he raised from the dead.
> Jesus who delivers us.
> from the approaching anger.

But what kind of summary is this? It is not a creed or a proclamation of the gospel, but a reminder of what their conversion meant.[28] Of course there are reminiscences of Paul's original message: but that does not mean that it sums up his entire message in a nutshell.

I find myself giving negative answers, therefore, to both the questions which I raised at the beginning. I do not think that these 1½ verses represent 'the mission-preaching to pagans in a nutshell', and I find the notion that this mission-preaching was formulated by pre-Pauline Jewish Christian missionaries even more incredible.

Let us turn, then, to the alternative suggestion made by Munck, that these verses are a summary, not of what Paul said when he first came to Thessalonica, but of what he is going to say later in the letter.

As long ago as 1939, Paul Schubert pointed out that the Pauline thanksgivings served the same function as those in the epistolary papyri, namely 'to focus the epistolary situation, i.e. to introduce the vital theme of the letter'.[29] Since then, it has become accepted that this is Paul's customary pattern. If it is the norm in his other letters, we expect it to be true of 1 Thessalonians also.[30] But where does the thanksgiving in 1 Thessalonians end and the body of the epistle begin? Most commentators take 1:1–10 as the thanksgiving, but Schubert himself came to a somewhat different conclusion.[31]

---

[27] Best, *Thessalonians*, 86. See the analysis by Gerhard Friedrich, 'Ein Tauflied hellenistischer Judenchristen: 1 Thess. 1,9f'., *Theologische Zeitschrift* 21 (1965): 508–510.

[28] Friedrich, 'Ein Tauflied', regards the passage as pre-Pauline, but thinks of it as a baptismal hymn from the Hellenistic Jewish Christian mission, reminding pagan converts of the significance of their baptism.

[29] Paul Schubert, *Form and Function of the Pauline Thanksgivings*, BZNW 20 (Berlin: A. Töpelmann, 1939), 180, see also 162.

[30] An exception is to be found in Galatians – for the reason that it has no thanksgiving! A recent short study by David Cook, however ('The Prescript as Programme in Galatians', *JTS* NS 43 [1992]: 511–519), argues that the 'programme' of the epistle is found in the expansions to the prescript in Gal 1:1–5.

[31] His discussion of 1 Thessalonians is on pp. 17–27.

In his structural analysis of Pauline thanksgivings, Schubert suggested that these took two forms.³² The first form opened with the words εὐχαριστῶ τῷ Θεῷ, followed by one, two, or three modifying participle constructions. These in turn were followed by a final clause subordinate to them. The second form began with the same opening words, followed by a causal clause introduced by ὅτι. This was then followed by a consecutive clause subordinate to it and introduced by ὥστε. In terms of content (though Schubert did not put it this way), the first form thanks God while praying that something else may happen, while the second form simply thanks him for what he has done.

Now 1 Thessalonians does not fit into either category. It begins in the first way:

Εὐχαριστοῦμεν τῷ Θεῷ πάντοτε περὶ πάντων ὑμῶν,
μνείαν ποιούμενοι ...
μνημομεύοντες ...
εἰδότες ὅ ...

but the final clause is missing, and does not appear until 3:11 ff. Before we reach that point, however, we find two more thanksgiving formulae, the first in 2:13 (which begins in the second way – Εὐχαριστοῦμεν ... ὅτι – but which again is not complete) the other in 3:9 ff., which belongs to the first type, though the opening wording is more elaborate than elsewhere:

Τίνα γὰρ εὐχαριστίαν δυνάμεθα τῷ Θεῷ ἀνταποδοῦναι περὶ ὑμῶν.

Schubert therefore argued that the thanksgiving was an extended one, finishing only at the end of chapter 3. We suspect, however, that he was misled by the repetitions of the formula into trying to force 1 Thessalonians into his theory.³³ For three reasons it seems more likely that the thanksgiving ends, as most commentators assume, at 1:10.³⁴

1. Schubert himself notes that the thanksgivings in 1 Corinthians, Philippians and 2 Thessalonians end in an 'eschatological climax'.³⁵ If this is one of the

---

³² Schubert, *Pauline Thanksgivings*, 35.

³³ Cf. Jan Lambrecht. 'Thanksgivings in 1 Thessalonians 1–3', in *The Thessalonian Correspondence*, ed. Raymond F. Collins, 192: Paul is 'anything but a slave of a schematic pattern. He freely varies words as well as constructions. He can omit elements; he breaks off, interrupts, and repeats; he sometimes changes the order. There is no need at all to distinguish with Schubert two major types of Pauline thanksgiving'.

³⁴ Other scholars, however, have followed Schubert in arguing that the thanksgiving ends only at 3:13. Cf. Peter Thomas O'Brien, *Introductory Thanksgivings in the Letters of Paul*, NTSup 49 (Leiden: Brill, 1977), 141–166; Helmut Koester, 'I Thessalonians – Experiment in Christian Writing', in *Continuity and Discontinuity in Church History: Essays Presented to George Huntston Williams on the Occasion of His 65ᵗʰ Birthday*, eds. F. Forrester Church and Timothy George (Leiden: Brill, 1979), 33–44; Johanson, *To All the Brethren*.

³⁵ Schubert, *Pauline Thanksgivings*, 4.

characteristics of a thanksgiving, then we have a splendid example of just such an eschatological climax in 1 Thess 1:10.

2. If the thanksgiving ends in 1:10, then 2:1 marks the transition to the rest of the letter. This verse corresponds with another formula discovered in Paul – this time the formula with which he opens the main part of his letters or introduces a new subject. These opening sentences were analysed by Jack T. Sanders in an article published in 1962.[36] The norm is for Paul to address his readers as ἀδελφοί, and either urge them to a particular course of action or else remind them of something, which is what happens here.

3. Schubert's analysis ignores the fact that Paul could easily break into thanksgiving outside the introductory section. This would be particularly appropriate in 1 Thessalonians. Moreover, if Schubert's own suggestion that the thanksgiving contains the theme of the epistle is correct, then perhaps this is the explanation: for Paul's sense of gratitude in 1 Thessalonians is so overwhelming that the cause of his gratitude is itself one of the themes of the letter.

It is time to look briefly at the content of the letter. Paul begins with an outpouring of thanks for the Thessalonians: in the second of the explanatory phrases following the opening Εὐχαριστοῦμεν τῷ Θεῷ he says that he remembers their work of faith, labour of love and obedience of hope in our Lord Jesus Christ. Already in this familiar triad we have indications of future concerns, for Paul will return in the body of the letter to the themes of the Thessalonians' faith (3:2–10), love (3:6, 12; 5:13) and hope (4:13–18; 5:9–11). The terms ἔργον and κόπος are also particularly appropriate in a letter which, as we shall see, will take up the theme of 'serving God' (1:10). The triad of faith, love and hope will be picked up in 5:8. Paul's thanksgiving reminds his readers of the effect the gospel had had on them, of his own manner of life among them, and of the fact that they became imitators of the apostles and the Lord (vv. 5–6). Once again we have hints here of themes that Paul is going to elaborate in chapters 2 and 3. The Thessalonians themselves became in turn an example to other Christians (vv. 7–8), who report

1. concerning the apostles, the kind of entry which they had,
2. how the Thessalonians turned to God from idols in order to serve a living and true God, and 3. how they began to wait for God's Son from heaven, the Son who was raised from the dead – namely Jesus, who will save us from the wrath to come.

Munck took the last two items of this report and argued that they pointed forward to the substance of the letter in chapters 4 and 5. In this I think he is

---

[36] Jack T. Sanders, 'The Transition from Opening Epistolary Thanksgiving to Body in the Letters of the Pauline Corpus', *JBL* 81 (1962): 348–362.

correct. In chapter 4, Paul reminds the Thessalonians of what he had taught them about how they should live and please God (vv. 1–2). Tactfully he commends them for what they are doing, but suggests that they should do so even more. In vv. 3–12 he spells out what this means – teaching which would undoubtedly be necessary in explaining to former pagans what 'serving a true and living God' involved. These first twelve verses correspond exactly to 1 Thess 1:9b.

In v. 13 a new theme is introduced: the problem of those members of the Christian community who have died. Paul reminds his readers that they believe that Jesus has died and risen; they may therefore be sure that God will bring with Jesus those who have fallen asleep: the Lord will descend from heaven, the dead will rise and the living be caught up to be with him (4:13–18). Chapter 5 continues this eschatological teaching: it describes *how* the Thessalonians are to 'wait': they are to be prepared for the Lord's coming, because God has not destined us for wrath, but to obtain salvation through our Lord Jesus Christ, who died for us, so that whether we wake or sleep we might live with him. Once again, these verses spell out what is meant by waiting for the coming of God's Son from heaven – Jesus, who was raised from the dead and who will save us from the wrath to come. Here, as in 1:10, Paul reminds his readers of the essential link between Christ's death and resurrection and their own salvation.

The final paragraph (vv. 12–22) reminds the community and its leaders of their mutual responsibilities; this, too, is very much on the theme of how they are to serve God and how they are to wait.

Munck seems to me to be on the right track. But he failed to look at chapters 2–3 – perhaps because Schubert had included them in the thanksgiving. Moreover, Ernest Best rightly criticizes him for ignoring the reference to Paul's 'entrance' (εἴσοδος) in 1:9a. Put these two details together, and I think we shall find the solution.

The first thing that 'everyone' is reporting about the Thessalonians concerns the manner of the apostle's 'entrance' among them – the visit which led to their conversion. The word εἴσοδος has two meanings – 'act of entering' and 'place of entering', and in 1 Thess 1:9 and 2:1 it clearly has the former meaning. Why does Paul describe how everyone is reporting regarding the Thessalonians how *he* came among them? The RSV and NRSV translate the word by 'welcome', suggesting that he means the response given him by the Thessalonians, but strictly it does not mean that,[37] and the *response* is in any

---

[37] James Everett Frame, *A Critical and Exegetical Commentary on the Epistles of St. Paul to the Thessalonians,* ICC (Edinburgh: T&T Clark, 1912), *in loc.* The Latin inscription. P.Oxy. 32.14, often quoted to justify this translation, does not necessarily support it. See Adolf Deissmann, *Light from the Ancient East,* trans. Lionel R.M. Strachan (London: Hodder & Stoughton, 1910), 184.

case described in the next clause, 'how you turned to God from idols'. Is there some special reason why Paul should refer here to his 'entrance', rather than simply the welcome given to him by the Thessalonians?

Turn now to 2:1. Paul begins: 'For you yourselves know, brothers and sisters, that our εἴσοδος to you was not in vain'. The response did in fact take place. But in the next few verses Paul spells out his own experience: 'You know how we suffered and were abused in Philippi; yet we had courage to speak to you in the face of great opposition; our appeal did not spring from error or impurity …' and so on. For the first twelve verses of this chapter, Paul reminds them of the manner of his preaching and his life. In vv. 13–16, which opens with the second of Paul's thanksgiving formulae, he thanks God for the response the Thessalonians gave to his preaching, and touches again on the idea that they have become 'imitators', this time of the churches in Judaea, by suffering for the gospel. But in v. 17 he returns to the theme of his own activity, and this time he deals with events which took place *after* that visit. He explains why he was unable to return to the Thessalonian community after his departure, his concern for them, and how he came to send Timothy to visit them (2:17–3:5). This section moves beyond the scope of v. 9a, which referred only to Paul's original visit, but is a natural development of the discussion; moreover, it picks up themes from 1:2–8 about the Thessalonians' faithfulness to the gospel. The good report which Timothy has brought (3:6–10) leads Paul into the third of the thanksgiving sections (3:11–13). No doubt Timothy also suggested to Paul that the Thessalonians needed encouragement in how 'to serve a living and true God', and that they were concerned about those of their number who had died.

We see, then, that in chapter 2 Paul is concerned to remind the Thessalonians of the manner of his visit to them – the theme set out in 1:9a, and that in chapter 3 he deals with the theme of what has happened since.

It would seem, then, that Munck's neglected hypothesis is even more apposite than he supposed, provided that we extend it to include the whole of what is reported in vv. 9–10, and remember that while these verses serve as a particular focus of the topics which Paul intends to discuss, the whole of this introductory chapter contains indications of the letter's theme. Vv. 9–10 of chapter 1 provide not only an 'eschatological conclusion' to the introductory thanksgiving, but a summary of the subjects with which Paul is going to deal. The nut in the nutshell is not the gospel preached to pagans, but the epistle addressed to Christian converts.

36. Called to be God's Holy People*

1. Introduction

In his book *Paul: The Man and the Myth*, published in 1998, Calvin Roetzel described sanctification as a 'neglected feature of Paul's theological grammar'.¹ He had good reason to do so. When I began to explore this topic, I was astonished to find that the idea of holiness is frequently ignored by scholars. The words 'holiness' and 'sanctification' are, e.g., both missing from Jimmy Dunn's large tome on Paul's theology.² In recent years, however, there has been a growing recognition of the importance of Paul's insistence on sanctification, a recognition reflected in books edited by Stephen Barton and by Kent Brower and Andy Johnson.³ I suspect that the reason for scholarly neglect of the topic in the past may be largely due to the fact that, ever since the time of Luther, the emphasis in Protestantism has been on justification. Paul's gospel was summed up as 'justification by faith', even though that is only one aspect of his message. Sanctification came to be seen as simply the working out of justification in an individual's life.

So what does Paul understand by 'sanctification'? And what, in particular, did he mean by addressing the members of his churches as 'saints'? Writing to his churches, Paul sometimes addresses them simply as οἱ ἅγιοι – 'the saints', or 'holy ones'.⁴ At other times he reminds them that they are *'called* to be saints',⁵ and he frequently *refers* to them as οἱ ἅγιοι.⁶ He always uses the term in the plural, with the exception of Phil 4:21, which is the exception that proves the rule, since he speaks there of πάντα ἅγιον. To be 'a saint', then, is to belong to a community.

In the Old Testament, 'to be holy' means, simply, to be separated, and the origin of the term lies in the fact that Yahweh calls Israel to be his people; they have been set aside for his purposes, separated from other nations to belong to

---

* Seminar paper given in Cambridge and Aberdeen.
¹ Calvin Roetzel, *Paul: The Man and the Myth* (Minneapolis: Fortress Press, 1999), 36.
² James D.G. Dunn, ed., *The Theology of Paul the Apostle* (Grand Rapids: Eerdmans,1998).
³ See, e.g., Stephen C. Barton, ed., *Holiness: Past and Present* (London: T&T Clark, 2003); Kent E. Brower and Andy Johnson, eds., *Holiness and Ecclesiology in the New Testament* (Grand Rapids; Cambridge: Eerdmans, 2007).
⁴ 2 Cor 1:1; Phil 1:1; cf. Col 1:2 and Eph 1:1.
⁵ Rom 1:7; 1 Cor 1:2.
⁶ Rom 8:27; 12:13; 16:2, 15; 1 Cor 6:1, 2; 14:33; 16:15; 2 Cor 13:12; Phil 4:22; Col 1:4, 12, 26; 1 Thess 3:13; 2 Thess 1:10, Phlm 5, 7.

him alone. Sometimes they are reminded that the reason they belong to him is that he brought them out of Egypt. Thus Exod 19:4–6 reads:

You have seen what I did to the Egyptians.... You shall be my treasured possession out of all the peoples. Indeed, the whole earth is mine, but you shall be for me a priestly kingdom and a holy nation.

What does it mean to be a holy nation? Holiness is what differentiates God from men and women – but those who belong to him must share in this 'otherness'. So being holy means *being like God*. In Lev 19:2, e.g., we read: 'You shall be holy, for I the Lord your God am holy'. Lev 11:44 ff. brings these two ideas – of the Exodus, and the call to be like God – together:

I am the Lord your God; consecrate yourselves, therefore, and be holy, for I am holy. You shall not defile yourselves with any swarming creature that moves on the earth. For I am the Lord who brought you up from the land of Egypt, to be your God; you shall be holy, for I am holy.

Four reasons are given for the demand that the Israelites consecrate themselves, each introduced by the Hebrew כִּי: first, 'I am the Lord your God'; second, 'I am holy'; third, 'I am the Lord who brought you up from the land of Egypt'; fourth – once again – 'I am holy'. The people are to be holy – to consecrate themselves – because God is holy, and because of what he has done for them in rescuing them from Egypt. Israel is holy, therefore, because God has graciously chosen her as his special people, and her holiness depends upon her relationship with him. 'Holiness' is essentially something that belongs to the *community*, and it entails living according to the revealed character of God.

In Leviticus, 'being holy' is defined mainly in cultic terms. Israel is separated from other nations by rules about cleanliness. This understanding of holiness is continued in Ezra-Nehemiah, at Qumran, and by the Pharisees: to be holy is to be separated from the nations. There is more to holiness in Leviticus than cultic purity and legislation about food, however. Those verses in chapter 19 introduce commands which are primarily to do with behaviour towards one's neighbours and to strangers in the land, and is punctuated by constant reminders that the one who is issuing the commands is 'the Lord your God', who (v. 36) 'brought you up out of the land of Egypt'. The prophets, also, interpreted holiness in what we would call ethical terms. God is 'the Holy One of Israel', and to speak of his holiness is to speak, in effect, of what he is. Since he himself is compassionate and just, what he requires of his people is, above all, justice and compassion for others. Those who are his people acknowledge Yahweh alone as God, and reflect his character as a righteous and loving God. For some of the prophets, this is seen as involving a *mission* to the nations. Israel has called Israel to be his holy people, and witnesses of *his* holiness.

2. Paul's Usage

When we turn to Paul, we have a problem, as we so often do, in knowing how to translate the Greek terms into English: are we to speak of 'holy ones' or of 'saints'? And what of the verb ἁγιάζω? Do we translate this as 'make holy', 'sanctify', 'dedicate', or 'consecrate'? The nouns, ἁγιασμός, ἁγιότης, and ἁγιωσύνη, can similarly be translated by 'holiness', 'sanctification', or 'consecration'. 'Consecration' reminds us that believers are made members of God's people, devoted to his service; those who *are* consecrated are expected to *be* holy; the term 'sanctification' suggests a process, the work of the Holy Spirit in their lives. We have no one English word to cover all these aspects.

Interestingly, Paul does not use the word ἅγιοι at all in Galatians. In the remaining three *Hauptbriefen*, there are three passages which refer to a particular group of Christians as οἱ ἅγιοι. These are the Christians in Jerusalem, and the passages all concern the money that Paul was collecting for their benefit.[7] Since the members of the Jewish Christian community were presumably Jewish by birth, they would, of course, have been seen as members of God's holy people, so that Paul's use of the term ἅγιοι is hardly surprising. Indeed, Paul may well have used it deliberately, in order to remind his Gentile congregations that – even though, in Christ there was neither Jew nor Greek – Jewish Christians were undoubtedly members of God's holy people, and Gentile Christians certainly had an obligation to assist them. What is more remarkable, however, is that elsewhere Paul appears to use the term of *all* Christians.[8] He *assumes* that they are all, Gentiles as well as Jews, members of God's people – the very thing about which, so it would seem, there was considerable dispute.

Perhaps the clearest statement of the fact that Gentile Christians have been incorporated into 'the saints' is found in Col 1:12. Here, the Colossians are reminded that they have been 'enabled to share in the inheritance of the saints in light'. Two problems immediately occur. First: did Paul write Colossians? On the whole, I incline to the belief that he did – you may disagree – but it is interesting to note how often the author of this epistle, whoever he was, manages to express Pauline theology in a Pauline way. Certainly this passage indicates that Paul believed – or was understood to have believed – that Gentiles now shared the inheritance given by God in the past to his 'holy ones'.

But – second problem – who *were* these holy ones? Were they God's people – i.e. Israel – or were they angels? Many commentators have argued for the latter meaning, but elsewhere in Colossians[9] ἅγιοι refers to human beings,

---

[7] Rom 15:25, 26, 31; 1 Cor 16:1; 2 Cor 8:4; 9:1, 12.
[8] See above, notes 4, 5, and 6.
[9] Col 1:2, 4, 12, 26; 3:12.

and the context suggests that it refers here to the people of God. Certainly it is human beings – the Gentiles – who now share in the inheritance, which suggests that they are now numbered among the holy ones: it makes more sense, then, to suppose that 'the holy ones' refers to the members of God's people Israel. Moreover, the 'light' in v. 12 stands in contrast to the 'darkness' of v. 13, where in a parallel statement (though now including 'us' as well as 'you') we are told that we have been 'rescued from the power of darkness' and transferred into the kingdom of 'God's beloved Son'. It is by being transferred into this kingdom of Christ that Gentiles have been made partakers of the inheritance.

When Paul – outrageously – describes *Gentiles* as 'saints', therefore, it is first and foremost a declaration of their *status*, and only then a reminder of what their calling *entails*. Writing to the Roman and Corinthian churches he addresses them as ἅγιοι, and by doing so he reminds them of this status – a status which should not be challenged. In addressing his Gentile converts as ἅγιοι, he is reminding them that they have been incorporated into the people of God. The Romans, for example, are addressed as 'those who are *called* to be his ἅγιοι, his holy people' (1:7). That letter goes on to show *how* it is that Gentiles as well as Jews have this status, in Christ. 1 Corinthians is also written to those who are called to be God's ἅγιοι, but first they are addressed as those who are already ἡγιασμένους ἐν Χριστῷ Ἰησοῦ, '*made* holy' or 'consecrated' in Christ Jesus. Here they are reminded that it is by virtue of the fact that they are 'in Christ' that they are ἅγιοι, 'members of God's holy people' – an idea expressed in a different way in 1:30, where Paul declares that 'Christ is our sanctification' – our ἁγιασμός. 2 Corinthians is addressed not only to the ἐκκλησία in Corinth, but 'to God's ἅγιοι, his holy people throughout the whole of Achaia' (2 Cor 1:1). Their call to be God's holy people will be picked up in 6:4–7:1. The term is thus (like δικαιοσύνη) primarily a soteriological one, and it is a reminder of a central tenet of Paul's theology: *Gentiles belong to the people of God because they are in Christ.*

By addressing his converts as ἅγιοι, therefore, Paul reminds them of their status within the community of God's people. How is it, then, that he fails to use it when writing to the Galatians? Would it not have been a convincing rejoinder to those who were trying to persuade them that they were *not* yet members of God's people, if he had addressed them as ἅγιοι? Surprisingly, Paul not only fails to use the term ἅγιοι, but makes no use of any of the cognate terms. Instead, he addresses the ἐκκλησίαι of Galatia – but that word is, of course, like ἅγιοι, a term that is used in the Old Testament of Israel. Gentiles are now addressed as those whom God has called out – in other words, as those who belong to the people of God. Once again, modern translations disguise the significance of the word, and it is difficult to convey its meaning, except by resorting to paraphrase. In the body of the letter, Paul argues his case by appealing to Abraham: Gentile Christians (women and slaves as well as men) are 'sons of Abraham', and so 'sons of God'; in Christ they address God as 'Abba', and so have the same status as Jews.

Now Galatians may well have been Paul's earliest letter. Or was it perhaps 1 Thessalonians? Opinion is divided, but it is interesting to note that 1 Thessalonians is addressed to 'the church in Thessalonica', and not to 'the saints'. Was it perhaps that when Paul wrote his earliest letters, the idea of addressing his converts as ἅγιοι had not yet occurred to him – even though the term ἡ ἐκκλησία, which he *does* use, conveys the same idea of belonging to God's people? In his later letters, however, the term ἅγιοι was to prove more useful in reminding his converts that they have become inheritors not only of the status of God's people but of their calling – which is to *be* 'holy'.

Secondly, then, the term ἅγιοι is a reminder to Gentile converts of what they are *meant* to be. God's holy people are expected to *be* holy – a theme found in all Paul's letters. It is important to remember that this derives from the fact that they are *already* God's holy people. As Victor Furnish expressed it: 'From the gift arises the demand'.[10] It is worth looking at how Paul deals with this, and I want to begin – somewhat perversely – with 1 Thessalonians, for even though Paul does not *address* the Thessalonians as ἅγιοι, he is certainly concerned to remind them that this is their calling.

3. 1 Thessalonians

As we have seen, Paul does not in fact use the term ἅγιοι in addressing the Thessalonians, but refers to them instead as ἡ ἐκκλησία, i.e. the called-out community – 'in God the Father and the Lord Jesus Christ'. Their new status depends on what God has done, and on their relationship to Christ. In his opening greeting, Paul reminds the Thessalonians of what their conversion meant. They had 'turned to God from idols, to serve a living and true God' (1:9). In accepting the Christian gospel, the Thessalonians had abandoned their worship of idols, and put their trust in the God of Israel, and Paul had urged them to 'lead a life worthy of God' (2:12). The link between the acknowledgement of the one true God and the manner of life expected of his people is clear. This is nothing less than the old call to Israel to 'be holy because I am holy'. In the last two chapters of the letter, he spells out something of what it means to serve a living and true God.[11]

---

[10] Victor Paul Furnish, *Theology and Ethics in Paul* (Nashville; New York: Abingdon, 1968), 156.

[11] On the links between 1 Thess 1:9 ff. and chapters 4–5, see Morna D. Hooker, '1 Thessalonians 1:9–10: A Nutshell – but What Kind of Nut?', in *Geschichte – Tradition – Reflexion*:

Paul begins by urging the Thessalonians to 'live and please God' in the manner that they learned from him – tactfully adding that they are, of course, doing just this, but should do so more and more (4:1). 'For this,' he reminds them, 'is the will of God: your sanctification' – ὁ ἁγιασμός ὑμῶν (4:3). Sanctification, he explains, means abstaining from fornication; they are to control their bodies 'in holiness', ἐν ἁγιασμῷ, and not give way to lustful passion, 'like the Gentiles who do not know God' (vv. 4–5). Paul is, of course, *writing* to Gentiles, but to Gentiles who *do* know God, having abandoned their idols to serve a living and true God. They were now members of God's people, since God had called them for holiness, ἐν ἁγιασμῷ, not impurity. In other words, they had been called to be 'saints'. To resist this call to holiness is to resist the God who has bestowed on them his Holy Spirit (v. 8). Sanctification, we now discover, is the work of the Holy Spirit.

Paul uses the term ἁγιασμός three times in this paragraph, and it is clear that the holiness required of God's people is not cultic but ethical; this is why the Thessalonian converts must abstain from fornication.[12] What is expected of them is the behaviour appropriate to the people of God. Here we find the link between idolatry and illicit sex, familiar to us from the Old Testament, in particular from the book of Hosea,[13] where adultery is a symbol for idolatry. But it is not *just* a symbol: fornication itself is forbidden to God's people. Nor is it simply a sin against God. Paul has an additional reason for his command: they should not exploit their brothers (4:6) – i.e. by sleeping with their wives. Modern readers of this passage are inclined to be indignant with what seems to them a sexist stance – surely it is the *women* who are being exploited?! The NRSV even adds the words 'or sister' to the text, in an attempt to make Paul's words more acceptable. But in Paul's world, wives were regarded as the property of their husbands, and when adultery took place the offence was against the husband. For Paul, adultery was not just a matter of individual purity, but was an offence against others, and contrary to love for one's neighbour. It is no accident that in 4:9, Paul reminds the Thessalonians of the need to love one another – once again, tactfully adding that they are of course doing so, but should do so more and more.

The Thessalonians, then – Gentiles though they are – have been chosen by the one true God (1:4), called by him to be his *ecclesia* (1:1), summoned to be members of his people, and are expected to be holy. Paul concludes his lengthy opening paragraphs with a prayer that God will strengthen their hearts so that they may be *blameless* in *holiness* before him when the Lord Jesus

---

Festschrift für Martin Hengel zum 70, Geburtstag, vol. 3: *Frühes Christentum,* ed. H. Lichtenberger (Tübingen: Mohr Siebeck, 1996), 435–448 = above, essay 35 (pp. 521–533).

[12] Paul uses the term πορνεία, which includes unlawful sexual intercourse of every kind, though v. 6 suggests that he is thinking particularly of adultery.

[13] E.g. Hos 1:2; 4:10–12; 5:3–4; 9:1; cf. Mic 1:7.

comes 'with all the saints' (3:13). The Greek term used this time is ἁγιωσύνη. At the end of the letter, he repeats this prayer:

May the God of peace *sanctify* (ἁγιάζω) you entirely, and may your whole spirit and soul and body be kept *blameless* at the coming of our Lord Jesus Christ (5:23).

The emphasis in these two prayers on being 'blameless' suggests a negative emphasis, which echoes what Paul says in 4:7 about being called in holiness, and *not* for impurity. But here, too, there is a positive emphasis. His prayer for the Thessalonians in 3:12 ff. begins with the request that the Lord will make them abound in love for one another and for all. It is this love that will lead to them being strengthened and made blameless in holiness. The prayer in 5:23 follows a passage which appeals to the Thessalonians to show love and concern for one another. Love features again in 5:8, where we have the familiar triad of faith, love, and hope. The Thessalonians are urged to put on 'the breastplate of faith and love, and for a helmet, the hope of salvation'. Why? Because 'God has destined us, not for wrath, but for obtaining salvation through our Lord Jesus Christ, who died for us ... so that we might live with him' (vv. 9 ff.). This is the behaviour that is required of those who have 'turned to God from idols, to serve a living and true God, and to wait for his Son from heaven' (1:9 ff.). It is clear, then, that holiness is not just about personal sinlessness, but about love for others. Holiness, as we have already emphasized, is expected of those who belong to God, and is thus characteristic of the *community*. The notion that arose later, which led hermits to *withdraw* from the world, was due to the fact that holiness came to be interpreted in a very individualistic way, but this is quite contrary to the biblical understanding. Remembering that God's basic command to his people was to 'Be holy as I am holy – to 'Be what I am' – we realize that this command to love arises from the fact that Paul believed that God had revealed himself to be a loving God – a theme that is once again familiar to us from the book of Hosea. No wonder he expects his converts to love one another.

Now Paul does not specifically refer to God's love for us in this letter. Nevertheless, the God in whom the Thessalonians have come to trust is, as Paul reminds them in 1:9, the living and true God – i.e. the only God, the God of Israel. He is also the Father (1:1), who raised his Son, Jesus, from the dead (1:10), and this Jesus will save us from the coming wrath. By his actions, then, he demonstrates that he is a loving God. Moreover, his love for us is reflected in Paul's own behaviour, since he was gentle with the Thessalonians, caring for them like a nurse tending infants (2:7), or a father dealing with his children (2:11). They are dear to Paul, so that he is eager to share with them not the gospel alone, but his very self (2:8). The apostle, then, is an embodiment of the gospel, precisely because he has been entrusted with the gospel.

The Thessalonians' response is acknowledged by Paul in his opening thanksgiving, where he declares that the Thessalonians 'became imitators of us and of the Lord', and became, in turn, an example to believers in Macedonia and Achaia (1:6 ff.). To be a Christian is to be like the Lord and like his apostles, and to be in turn a pattern to others. He returns to this idea in 2:14 ff., where he thanks God for the fact that the Thessalonians 'became imitators of the churches of God in Christ Jesus that are in Judaea' by suffering persecution: Gentile believers, members now of God's people, are sharing the experience of Jewish Christians.

In 1 Thessalonians, then, we can trace the story of Gentiles who turned from the worship of idols to put their trust in the one true God. God's purpose for them was their sanctification (4:3), so that they might be blameless when his Son returned. This sanctification is the work of God (3:12 ff.; 5:23), in particular the work of his Holy Spirit. In 4:8, Paul declares that anyone who rejects his teaching that God calls for holiness rejects God himself, the God who gives them his Holy Spirit, and the unusual word order – τὸ Πνεῦμα αὐτοῦ τὸ Ἅγιον – stresses the fact that God's Spirit is holy. The Thessalonians themselves are nevertheless expected to cooperate, by striving to live in a way that is worthy of God (2:12). The *motive* is their joy at receiving the gospel (1:6). Although Paul does not specifically link this manner of life with the fact that they are 'in Christ', it is noticeable that in what is probably Paul's first letter, he is already assuming that believers are 'in Christ',[14] and that, because of his death and resurrection, they live 'with him', in this life as well as the next.[15] Indeed, it is precisely this relationship to Christ – the Messiah, or God's anointed one – that makes them members of God's ἐκκλησία, and so of God's people, called to be his holy nation.

4. Romans

As we've noted already, Romans is addressed to those who are beloved, called to be saints (1:7) – language reminiscent of that which is used of Israel in the Old Testament. Yet it is clear from vv. 5–6 that the majority of the members of the Roman church were Gentiles. Christians – or, to use Paul's own expression, those who are 'in Christ' – are now members of God's people, whatever their racial origin. The gospel to which they responded told of how God had raised Christ from the dead and proclaimed him Son of God according to the Spirit of holiness – the πνεῦμα ἁγιωσύνης (1:4). This unusual phrase is undoubtedly used for a reason, and we are not surprised when, at the conclusion

---

[14] 1:1; 2:14; 3:8; 4:1, 16; 5:12.
[15] 4:14; 5:10.

of the letter, we find Paul reminding his readers of the sanctifying work of the Holy Spirit. In 15:16, he tells them that his mission as a minister of Christ Jesus to the Gentiles was to ensure that the offering of the Gentiles was acceptable to God, *sanctified* (ἁγιάζω) by the *Holy* (ἅγιος) Spirit. The Greek is ambiguous, since it is possible that Paul means 'the offering made *by* the Gentiles', but the context seems to demand that Paul is the one who makes the offering, and that the offering he makes to God is nothing less than the Gentiles whom he has won for the gospel, consecrated, or made holy to God, through the work of the Holy Spirit. These are the 'saints' who have been incorporated into the people of God.

Earlier, in chapter 6, he uses yet another term with the same root – one that we have met already in 1 Thessalonians 4: ἁγιασμός, meaning 'sanctification' (6:18 ff.). Explaining the significance of sharing Christ's death and resurrection, he declares that Christians have ceased to be slaves of sin and become slaves of righteousness. Once, he reminds them, they had presented themselves as slaves to impurity (ἀκαθαρσία) and to ever-increasing iniquity. The language echoes his words in Romans 1, where men had been handed over by God to impurity (ἀκαθαρσία), and where the whole picture is one of ever-increasing iniquity. Now, he declares, they must present themselves to righteousness for sanctification.

In this section Paul uses the notion of slavery to contrast the two ways of life – the old and the new – even though he recognizes, in v. 19, that this is only a human analogy, and not wholly satisfactory. Being under sin is indeed a form of slavery, but those who are set free from sin are able, willingly, to serve righteousness (v. 13), and they offer themselves to God as instruments of righteousness. Twice Paul speaks of men and women 'presenting' themselves – either to sin or to God, to impurity or to righteousness (vv. 15, 19). They can be instruments of wickedness or of righteousness. The verb 'to present or offer' (παρίστημι) suggests making oneself available for service. Those who do so are obedient to their masters, and in vv. 15 ff. Paul picks up this idea. Those who present themselves to someone are his obedient slaves. Having been slaves of sin, the Romans are now slaves of righteousness. This is why they must present themselves to righteousness – for sanctification – and not to impurity. This idea is clearly important for Paul, since he repeats it in vv. 20–23. Being a slave of sin leads to death, but being enslaved to God means sanctification, and leads to life. Twice, then, Paul insists that being a 'slave' of righteousness or of God means sanctification. Sanctification means being set apart for God's service.

Just as the Thessalonians had turned from their old way of life 'to serve a living and true God', so those whom Paul addresses in Romans had abandoned their old way of life in order to be slaves of God. The verb used in 1 Thess 1:9 (δουλόω) is related to the terms Paul uses in Romans 6 – δοῦλος, 'slave', and δουλωθέντες, 'enslaved'. In both letters, being God's people means serving God. Both Romans and Thessalonians had formerly owed allegiance to evil powers; now they are obedient to God – and this God had called them, not for impurity, but in holiness (1 Thess 4:7). The fact that in Romans, as in 1 Thessalonians, Paul contrasts impurity and holiness (6:19), demonstrates that for him, holiness is not *just* about status but also about one's manner of life. The question posed in Rom 6:1 – 'Shall we continue in sin?' – has been firmly answered. Sin belongs to the old way of life, righteousness to the new, and the path from old to new is found in being crucified with Christ. 'Holiness' belongs to those who are 'in Christ'.

In chapter 8, Paul expresses these two ways of life in terms of living in accordance with what he calls 'the flesh' on the one hand and 'spirit' on the other. He contrasts those who live in accordance with flesh, which has been invaded by sin, with those who live in accordance with the Spirit – the Spirit of him who raised Christ from the dead. This echo of Rom 1:4 reminds us that it is the Spirit of *holiness* who enables Christians to put to death sinful deeds and live as God's children, recreated in his image (8:14–17, 28–30).

In chapters 9–11 Paul deals with the problem of the failure of Israel – and at the same time marvels at the inclusion of the Gentiles in God's people. Attempting to explain this, he uses the image of the olive tree, introducing it in 11:16 with a double metaphor: if the firstfruits are holy, so is the whole lump of dough; if the root is holy, so are the branches. The most likely interpretation of these much-discussed images is that he is thinking of Christ. It is Christ who elsewhere is said to have been raised as the firstfruits from the dead;[16] Jews are represented as branches in the tree, not as the stock, which suggests that it is Christ who is the root on whom the branches depend. It is because *he* is holy that the branches are holy. Or, to put it more succinctly, they are holy because they are 'in Christ'.

In the first eleven chapters of Romans, Paul has explained how it comes about that Gentiles, as well as Jews, are included in the people of God, and has wrestled with the problem of Israel's failure to fulfil her calling. In the concluding chapters (12–15), he spells out the implications of being 'called to be saints'. This section deals with Christians' relations to one another and to others, and its governing principle is love. It is introduced, in 12:1, with the words 'I implore you, therefore', showing the close dependence of Paul's ethical appeal on his previous arguments. The links are made clear by the echoes in his vocabulary. He appeals to the Romans to *present* their bodies (i.e. themselves) to God (echoing chapter 6) as 'a living sacrifice, holy and acceptable to God'. In chapter 1 he described how men and women had failed to worship God; now their whole lives are offered to him in sacrifice; the bodies

---

[16] 1 Cor 15:20, 23.

that were once handed over to dishonour (1:24) are now holy. Their minds, which once failed to discern God (1:28) are to be renewed and transformed, so that they may discern God's will.

Being holy in Romans clearly refers, as in the Old Testament, to the status of those who are called to be God's people. But it is also clear that those who are so-called are required to 'be what they are' – or rather, to be what they were called to be – and that true holiness – being like God – is the goal of their calling. The process by which this happens is attributed to the sanctifying work of the Holy Spirit.

5. 1–2 Corinthians

It is in 1 Corinthians, however, that we see most clearly the tension involved in Paul's conviction that Christians are God's holy people. He begins by reminding the Corinthians of their calling. The letter is addressed to 'the church of God that is in Corinth, to those who have been sanctified in Christ Jesus, who are called to be saints' (1:2), and at the end of this first chapter he reminds them that they are 'in Christ Jesus', who is for them 'wisdom from God' – a wisdom very different from that which they have been prizing. This wisdom – the message of Christ crucified – means that Christ is for them righteousness, sanctification,[17] and redemption. Three times in this opening chapter, then, Paul reminds the Corinthians of their status as those who have been sanctified in Christ. The fact that he feels it necessary to do so, however, is suspicious, and we find the explanation later in the epistle, where we realize that the behaviour of the Corinthians is anything but holy, and demonstrates their failure to perceive the link between their status as God's people and the holiness of life that is expected of them.

A blatant example of this failure occurs in 1 Corinthians 5, where Paul complains about the sexual immorality that is taking place among them – immorality 'of a kind that is not found even among Gentiles'. Paul's words reflect his horror at finding this behaviour in the community that had been called by God to demonstrate by their lifestyle their separation from the Gentiles. The sinner must be excluded from the community. It is significant that Paul appeals to the community to remove the old leaven, and reminds them that Christ, our paschal lamb, has been sacrificed. The Christian community is the people of God: as Israel was called at the Exodus, and made God's people, so Christians have been made members of that people through the sacrifice of Christ. Paul then reminds them of his earlier letter, in which he urged them not to associate with sexually immoral persons, explaining

---

[17] The term used here is ἁγιασμός, as in 1 Thess 4:3 and Rom 6:18, 22.

them that he was not referring to 'the immoral of this world, to extortioners, to robbers, and to idolaters', but to any immoral people *within the Christian community*. Such people must be driven out. In other words, the church is holy, and must be kept so – but this does *not* mean that it should become a ghetto.

A further reminder of the holiness that is expected of those who belong to God's people comes in 6:11 where, after protesting that their behaviour is not appropriate for Christians, Paul reminds the Corinthians that, though they had once been fornicators, idolaters, adulterers, thieves, drunkards, and swindlers, they have been washed, sanctified,[18] justified, in the name of the Lord Jesus and through the Spirit of our God. As in 1:30, sanctification and righteousness – being sanctified and justified – are put side by side, expressing past, present, and future. Here also we find the familiar combination of idolatry and immorality, and it is no surprise, in 6:18, to find Paul urging the Corinthians to flee from fornication, and then later, in 10:14, to flee from idolatry. To indulge in behaviour of this kind is inappropriate for those who belong to God's people and is, in effect, to abandon worship of the one true God. The warnings were clearly very necessary, since the list of vices in 6:9 ff., some of which were sexual, some simply selfish, bears a remarkable similarity to what was apparently still going on in the Corinthian community, which had not yet wholly abandoned its pagan mentality.[19] The Corinthians might have been 'sanctified' – i.e. consecrated to God's service – but they clearly had not grasped what that entailed. In 6:19 Paul explains *why* they must flee fornication: 'don't you know', he asks, 'that your bodies are temples of the Holy Spirit?' Once again we have a reference to the sanctifying work of the Spirit.

But what are we to make of ἡγίασται in 7:14? Having just argued that a Christian must have nothing to do with a prostitute, and that to do so would be to pollute one's body – the temple of the Holy Spirit – Paul now suggests that an unbelieving husband or wife can be 'made holy' through his or her spouse, and that their children also may be 'made holy'. The context in chapter 6 was fornication, however, and here it is marriage. There, fornication was incompatible with holiness, but here, holiness is stronger than the unbeliever's 'uncleanness'. Irenaeus points us to Rom 11:16: Christ as firstfruits and root sanctifies the whole.[20] We can also refer to 1 Cor 1:30: Christ is our sanctification. If Christians are sanctified through Christ, then perhaps unbelievers can be sanctified through members of his body. Influenced by their wives, husbands, or parents, they too are perhaps being made holy.

---

[18] Paul uses the verb ἁγιάζω, as in 1:2; cf. 1 Thess 5:23.
[19] See Anthony C. Thiselton, *The First Epistle to the Corinthians*, NIGTC (Grand Rapids; Cambridge: Eerdmans, 2000), 451, referring to an analysis by Kenneth Bailey.
[20] Irenaeus, *Adv. Haer* 4.20.11.

The reference to the Corinthians' bodies as temples of the Holy Spirit in 6:19 has a parallel in 3:16 ff. This time, what the Corinthians should know is that they themselves – the Christian community – are the temple of God, that his Spirit dwells in them, and that his temple is holy. Here we have another image for those who make up the people of God – and one that reminds us of the demand in Exod 19:6 that Israel should be not only a holy nation, but a kingdom of priests. In this chapter, Paul is protesting against the divisions in the Corinthian church which threaten to destroy it – divisions that arise from their failure to comprehend the gospel of Christ crucified, and to recognize that they are the ἐκκλησία of God and owe allegiance only to him, not to human leaders such as Paul, Apollos, or Cephas. They elevate human achievement, and show by their quarrelling that they fail to recognize the work of the Holy Spirit. It is not surprising that at the end of the letter Paul elaborates the theme of the Christian community as the body of Christ, and stresses the theme of mutual dependence and support. The Spirit builds up the body through various gifts, and the greatest gift of all is that of love. Holiness is not just about an individual's standing before God, but about one's relationship to other members of the community, since as 'holy ones' they belong to God's people.

1 Corinthians demonstrates the tension between what Christians already are – God's holy people, dedicated to him – and what they are meant to be – holy in their manner of life. 'Sanctified' they may be (1 Cor 1:2; 6:11), but they still need to be 'sanctified entirely', as 1 Thess 5:23 puts it. Sanctification means not only an initial dedication to God, but a life lived in his service. Negatively, it demands abstinence from vice; positively, it requires love and concern for others. Once again, the way in which those called to be holy actually *become* holy is through the work of the Holy Spirit.

This being so, it is hardly surprising to find Paul 'boasting' in 2 Cor 1:12 that he has behaved towards the Corinthians ἐν ἁγιότητι καὶ εἰλικρινίᾳ – with 'the holiness and sincerity of God'. There is of course a variant reading here, since a few mss read ἁπλότητι (virtually a synonym for εἰλικρινία) instead of ἁγιότητι.[21] Most translators and commentators prefer ἁγιότητι, however, and if they are right, then Paul is claiming that his behaviour corresponds with the holiness and sincerity of God himself. He goes on to defend himself against charges that he had changed his mind regarding his plans to visit the Corinthians. His plans were not made κατὰ σάρκα, but in accordance with the faithfulness of God, who had established him and anointed him – together with the Corinthians. Through Christ, Paul declares, he has been able to say 'Amen' to the fact that all God's promises have been fulfilled in Christ, who did not waver, but said 'Yes' to God. Similarly, Paul himself has not wavered,

---

[21] DG *pl* lat sy ς.

but has stood firm.[22] Paul's argument presupposes the fact that God's holy people – those who are in Christ – are expected to be like God – an idea that is expressed vividly in these early chapters of 2 Corinthians, where Paul explains that he is 'always carrying in the body the death of Jesus' (2 Cor 4:10).

Embedded in the argument of 2 Corinthians we have a remarkable passage, 6:14–7:1, which is often described as an erratic boulder, since it appears at first sight to interrupt the argument. Many scholars therefore excise it – thereby creating an even greater problem, since we are left wondering (a) where it came from, and (b) how it came to be where it is. Why should an editor have inserted the passage where it apparently does not fit? It seems more likely that we have simply failed to understand Paul's train of thought. Whatever the explanation, the passage is interesting for our purposes since it is about holiness – about the need for God's people to be separate from those who are *not* 'sanctified'. Christians are not to be yoked together with unbelievers, says Paul, since there is no partnership between righteousness and lawlessness. Like Israel of old, they are required to be separate, to worship the one true God and to serve only him. There can be no agreement between the temple of God and idols, declares Paul – and *we*, he reminds them, are the temple of God, since God lives among us.

To back that up, Paul quotes the Old Testament promise: 'I will dwell among them and be their God, and they shall be my people'.[23] But he also quotes the demand: 'therefore come out from among them, and be separate', says the Lord, 'and touch nothing unclean'.[24] What *Paul* understands by 'unclean' has nothing to do with the cult, however, but concerns *moral* impurity. He urges the Corinthians to cleanse themselves from every defilement of flesh and spirit, completing their sanctification, their ἁγιωσύνη, in the fear of God (7:1).

In this passage we see how Paul assumes that Christian Gentiles have been incorporated into the history of Israel. Words of scripture once addressed to Israel are now applied to the Corinthian community. They have been called to be God's people, and commanded to be separate from others. This means that they must have nothing to do with idolatry or with anything that is unclean. Their calling is to total sanctification: their consecration is to be made complete.

---

[22] See Morna D. Hooker, 'From God's Faithfulness to Ours: Another Look at 2 Corinthians 1:17–24', in *Paul and the Corinthians: Studies on a Community in Conflict: Essays in Honour of Margaret Thrall*, eds. Trevor J. Burke and J. Keith Elliott, NTSup 109 (Leiden: Brill, 2003), 233–239 = below, essay 41 (pp. 610–615).
[23] Cf. Lev 26:12; Ezek 37:27.
[24] Isa 52:11.

6. Conclusions

1) Sanctification is often assumed to be simply about ethics – about what takes place in the Christian life *after* justification. It seems clear from the evidence that we have examined, however, that it is concerned with what E. P. Sanders famously described as 'getting in' as well as with 'staying in': in other words, the term is a soteriological one. In Christ, Gentiles as well as Jews have been consecrated as members of God's holy people. The fact that Paul addresses his Gentile converts as 'saints' is far more significant than is generally recognized.

2) Paul the Pharisee saw holiness primarily in terms of separation *from* the nations; Paul the Christian sees it as embracing them, since God has called those who once were not his people 'my people'.[25]

3) It is also often assumed that sanctification is about what happens to the *individual*. Clearly, however, the term refers primarily to the community, and part of its meaning concerns relationships within the community. It is no accident that 'saint' is only once used in the singular, in Phil 4:21 where it refers to *every* saint. It is clear, too, that the status of being 'saints' depends on the fact that believers are 'in Christ'; it is he who is their sanctification.

4) But though 'saints' have been consecrated, and are reminded that holiness is their calling, it is clear that the process of sanctification is not yet complete. It refers – like justification – to something that has taken place, that *is* taking place, and that will be completed in the future. Paul reminds those in Christ that they have been sanctified by God by their incorporation into Christ, challenges them to be what they are called to be, and assures them that they will finally *be* holy, through the ongoing work of the Holy Spirit.

---

[25] Rom 9:24, quoting Hos 2:25.

37. Christ Died for Our Sins, and Was Raised for Our Acquittal: Paul's Understanding of the Death of Christ*

In a field where there are so many uncertainties and disputes, it is comforting to be able to say one thing without fear of contradiction. No one, I imagine, would query the statement that at the heart of Paul's gospel lay the death and resurrection of Christ. 'I preached Christ crucified', he reminded the Corinthians (1 Cor 1:23) – nothing else. Except, of course, that without the resurrection, their faith was vain. These two events lay at the centre of his gospel.

But how did he understand them? Paul's doctrine of the atonement has been interpreted in many different ways down the centuries. Some commentators insist that he saw Christ's death as substitutionary; others protest that he did not. Some have pointed to his use of sacrificial language, others to the idea of our participation in Christ's death. Luther understood the idea of 'justification by faith' to be central to its meaning, while some recent exegetes have argued that this is less important than Luther supposed. At the level of *interpretation*, there seems little agreement.

The centrality of Christ's death and resurrection in Paul's message is not surprising. These were the two new events that demanded recognition. The death of the Messiah on a cross was, in Paul's own words, 'a scandal to Jews, and folly to Greeks' (1 Cor 1:23). It had to be explained. The resurrection was the world-shattering event that had changed Paul's life. Without it, there would be no Christian gospel to proclaim. Those who accuse Paul of changing the 'simple, ethical message' of Jesus into a religion centred on the cross and resurrection fail to recognize that Christ's death and resurrection were the beginning of a new era: they could not be ignored.

What explanation, then, did Paul offer for Christ's death? From time to time, in the course of his letters, Paul 'reminds' his readers of the basis of their faith in pithy, memorable summaries of the gospel. Among these are many of the summaries that scholars tend to assume are 'pre-Pauline'. It seems more likely to me that they are summaries of Paul's own teaching, but whatever their origin, they are important indications of Paul's core beliefs.

---

* This paper was originally given at the 'Exegetical Day' in Uppsala on 28 Sep 2002. It also formed the basis of a presentation at a Colloquium at Fuller Theological Seminary on 13 Feb 2003.

Perhaps the earliest of these summaries is found in 1 Thess 5:10. Paul here reminds the Thessalonians that they are destined for salvation, and not for wrath. The grounds for this belief have already been touched on in 1 Thess 1:10, where Paul has reminded them of their initial response to his preaching. They had, he says, 'turned to God from idols, to serve a living and true God and to wait for his Son from heaven – Jesus, whom he raised from the dead, and who rescues us from the coming wrath'.

Paul refers here to the resurrection and to Christians' future salvation from wrath, but says nothing about the manner of Christ's death or what that meant. That is because the Thessalonians' chief concern was whether or not they would come under divine wrath. Hence Paul reminds them of the implications of their faith; since God has raised Jesus from the dead, they can be sure of their own future salvation. In 5:10, he assures them again that they will be saved from wrath

> through our Lord Jesus Christ,
> who died for us
> in order that (whether we are awake or asleep) we may live with him.

The reference to being awake or asleep has been included by Paul because the Thessalonians have been disturbed by the death of some of their number, and he is anxious to assure them that they will nevertheless be included in the coming salvation from wrath. Without it, we have a simple two-line couplet:

> who died for us
> in order that we may live with him.

Paul's stark comment that Christ died 'for us' is balanced by an assurance that we will share his resurrection. Remarkably, however, though Paul does here refer to Christ's death, he does not this time mention his resurrection. Nevertheless, this is clearly implied in the purpose clause, introduced by the Greek word ἵνα, meaning 'in order that': he 'died for us, in order that we may live with him'. We shall discover that Paul is fond of this particular construction.

'Christ died *for us*'. What does Paul mean by this 'for us'? Some commentators assume that Paul is thinking of Christ's death as substitutionary: they assume, that is, that Christ dies *in our place*.[1] This does not seem to be an appropriate description of his teaching, however, for Christ's death does not mean that Christians do not face physical death.[2] It is possible, indeed, that the Thessalonians had assumed that this was the case, and that this is why they were disturbed by the fact that some of their number had already died (1 Thess 4:13). If so, they had misunderstood Paul's gospel: Christ's death does not put a stop to physical death *in this age*. Christians may be 'awake or

---

[1] E.g. Leon Morris, *The Cross in the New Testament* (Exeter: Paternoster, 1976), 225.
[2] 'Death to sin', also, as we shall see, is something which Christians have to *share* with Christ.

asleep' – alive or dead – when, as Paul expected would happen soon, the day of judgement came.

Had Paul been thinking of Christ's death as substitutionary, he would have written simply 'Christ died for us, in order that we might live'. In physical terms, such substitutions are possible. A famous, fictional, example occurs at the end of Dickens' novel, *A Tale of Two Cities*, when Sydney Carton takes Charles Darnay's place at the guillotine. But such events are not always fictions. A friend of mine dived under a Calcutta tram in order to save a child who had fallen beneath it, and died as a result. Her death could truly be described as substitutionary, since she died in order that the child might live. Paul, however, is using a different concept: 'Christ died', he wrote, 'in order that we might live *with him*'. He sees Christians as *sharing* the risen life of Christ.

1. Christ Our Representative

Living with Christ, however, implies also *dying* with him. That idea is expressed in another of Paul's early letters – this time in very personal terms. In Gal 2:19–21, Paul describes how he has 'died to law, *in order that* [he] might live to God'. How has this death taken place? It was by being 'crucified with Christ', so that it is now *Christ* who lives in Paul. Once again, Christ's resurrection is here implied, not spelt out. This new life derives, says Paul, from the fact that the Son of God 'loved me and gave himself *for me*'. Reverse the order of the sentences, and we see the parallel with 1 Thess 5:10:

> The Son of God loved me and gave himself for me,
> in order that I might live to God;
> and it is no longer I who live,
> but Christ who lives in me.

Twice here Paul emphasizes that the Christian must die *with* Christ: 'I have died to the law', he says, and 'I have been crucified with Christ'.

Galatians 2 fills out what is said in 1 Thess 5:10, reminding us that Christ's death on behalf of others has to be appropriated: it is those who share his death to life in the old age who will share his resurrection life. 'Christ died for us' does not mean that we escape death, but that he dies as our representative – the representative of humanity; those who in turn share his death (to sin) – an idea that he spells out in Romans 6 – will also share his resurrection.

The same ideas reappear in 2 Cor 5:14–15, where Paul writes 'One has died for all'. Once again, this sounds at first like substitution, Christ dying *instead of* all, but as we read on, we find that he explains that what he means is that Christ died *as our representative*. He immediately spells out the significance of this 'death for all':

> One has died *for all*,
> therefore *all have died*.
> And he died *for all*
> *in order that* the living might no longer live to themselves,
> but to the one who died and was raised for them.

This time, therefore, Paul has explained what he means when he says that Christ died 'for all'. It means that they, too, *have already died* – not, of course, a physical death, but a spiritual one, to sin. As usual, the consequence is life – described here, not, as in 1 Thessalonians, as life *with* Christ, but life that is centred on him, instead of on themselves. This is parallel to what he says in Gal 2:20, where he speaks of his new life as a life centred on the Son of God.

It is hardly surprising that Paul goes on, in 2 Cor 5:17, to explain that when someone is 'in Christ', there is in effect 'a new creation'. The old world (life lived as Adam lived it, dominated by sin and condemnation) has gone, and the new world (life in Christ, and the righteousness that is found in him) has arrived.

Christ died for us, Christ died for me, Christ died for all. Yet another variation on this formula appears in 1 Corinthians 15, where Paul writes: 'Christ died for our sins' (1 Cor 15:3). The link is hardly surprising. Jewish tradition saw death as the punishment for sin. Not only were criminals put to death, but the fact that all living creatures are condemned to die was explained as the result of Adam's sin. According to the story in Genesis 3, Adam and Eve were expelled from the Garden of Eden lest they take and eat the fruit of the tree of life (Gen 3:22). Death was understood to be the universal punishment for human sin, but it was universal not simply as the result of Adam's action, but because his descendants *shared* his sin.[3]

Paul notes that Christ died 'according to the scriptures', but fails to tell us *which* scriptures! Nor is it clear whether he is linking the phrase with the fact of Christ's death or with what is here said to be its purpose, to deal with sin. One possibility is that he was thinking of Isaiah 53, a passage that came to be interpreted of Christ. It is unclear whether or not that passage was understood in this way in Paul's day, though it certainly was by the time that 1 Pet 2:21–25 was written. Perhaps, like the phrase 'witnessed to by the Law and the Prophets' in Rom 3:21, the phrase 'according to the scriptures' is meant to refer to the scriptures in general.[4]

---

[3] 4 Ezra 3:21–22, 25–26; 7:48 (118).

[4] There is nothing in 1 Cor 15:3 (apart from the one word 'sins') to link Paul's statement specifically with Isaiah 53. Rom 4:25, however, may well have been influenced by this passage. See Morna D. Hooker, 'Did the Use of Isaiah 53 to Interpret His Mission Begin with Jesus?', in *Jesus and the Suffering Servant: Isaiah 53 and Christian Origins,* eds. William H. Bellinger Jr. and William R. Farmer (Harrisburg, PA: Trinity Press International, 1998), 101–103 = above, essay 8 (pp. 115–127).

In other summaries, too, Christ's death is linked specifically with sins. In Gal 1:4, the Galatians are reminded that

> Christ gave himself *for our sins*,
> so that he might set us free from this present evil age.

Another passage which links Christ's death with sins – or rather with trespasses – is Rom 4:25, which refers to those who believe in Jesus our Lord,

> who was handed over to death because of *our trespasses*,
> and was raised because of *our acquittal*
> (or 'so that we might be declared righteous').

This time, we have two parallel statements about Christ's death and resurrection: his death was the result of our trespasses, and his resurrection led to our acquittal. If we try to unpack their meaning, however, we realize that this is based on an understanding of Christ's resurrection similar to that which we find in 1 Thess 5:10:

> He was handed over to death (because of our trespasses)
> in order that we might share his acquittal (pronounced at his resurrection).

In *Christ's* death, *our* sins have been dealt with; by being raised, *he* was pronounced innocent – and *we* share his acquittal.[5]

2. Sharing in Christ's Righteousness

If Christians share Christ's resurrection, therefore, it is because, in him, they have been declared righteous. We turn back again to 2 Corinthians 5, and find that Paul explains what God has done in similar terms there:

> The one who knew no sin
> He made to be sin *for us*,
> in order that we might become the righteousness of God *in him*.

Once again, we have the familiar 'for us' and 'in order that', but the idea itself is new and shocking. Instead of Christ *dying* for us, we have him being *made sin*. What does Paul mean? We should note that he does *not* say that Christ was made a *sinner*: indeed, he specifically notes that he 'knew no sin'. The idea that he was 'made sin' is similar to one expressed in Rom 8:3, where he speaks of Christ being sent in the likeness of sinful flesh. As man, Christ was identified with the human predicament and shared the consequences of sin – estrangement from God. That he was 'made sin' was demonstrated in

---

[5] See Morna D. Hooker, 'Raised for Our Acquittal (Rom 4:25)', in *Resurrection in the New Testament: Festschrift J. Lambrecht*, eds. R. Bieringer, V. Koperski, and B. Lataire, BETL 165 (Leuven: University Press/Peeters, 2002), 323–341 = below, essay 38 (pp. 562–578).

his death, just as his resurrection demonstrated his righteousness. In 2 Cor 5:21, Paul makes no specific reference to either his death or his resurrection. Instead, he points to the *cause* of his death – human sin – and the *result* of his resurrection – our righteousness. If Christ was 'made sin', Christians 'become righteousness', and just as being made sin signified alienation from God, so being made righteousness signifies reconciliation. Once again, however, it depends on that significant phrase 'in him'. Christians share in *Christ's* righteousness. For all Paul's startling language, we recognize the similarities with what he says in Rom 4:25:

> He was handed over to death because of our trespasses,
> And was raised that we might be declared righteous.

His death was a judgement on *our* sin – a judgement whose consequences he shared. His resurrection was a vindication of his own righteousness – a vindication in whose consequences *we* share.

From 2 Corinthians we turn back to 1 Corinthians, where we find an 'echo' of 2 Cor 5:21. In chapter 1, Paul reminds the Corinthians of the absurdity of his message to them; the cross appeared to be a symbol of weakness and folly. He goes on to describe Christ Jesus as the source of wisdom and righteousness, sanctification and redemption (v. 30). Those who are in Christ share *his* righteousness.

In Gal 3:13 we find Paul using language quite as shocking as that which he uses in 2 Cor 5:21. This time he describes Christ as 'a curse'. In this passage, he links the curse pronounced by the Law on those who fail to obey it (Deut 27:26) with its declaration that a criminal whose body was hung on a tree was under a curse (Deut 21:23). Such a person himself became a curse – a source of contamination to others. Christ's death was the proclamation that, under the Law, he was a curse; in fact, however, he had become a source of blessing, and had 'redeemed' (set free) those who were under the curse pronounced by the Law. Once again, Paul links what happened to Christ and what happens to believers with the Greek word ἵνα, meaning 'in order that':

> Christ redeemed us from the curse of the Law,
> having become a curse *for us* ...
> *in order that* the blessing of Abraham might be extended, *in Christ*, to the Gentiles,
> (and) *in order that* we might receive the promised Spirit through faith.

Paul's argument here is specifically related to the role of the Law, and to his fear lest the Galatian Christians should see it as necessary to salvation. Instead of speaking of sin and righteousness, as in 2 Corinthians 5, therefore, he focuses on the more specific issues relating to the Law, which had pronounced a curse on sinners, but had not led to the blessing promised to Abraham. As a Jew, crucified by Rome, Christ had come under this curse, but the curse had been overturned; Jews had been set free from the curse which rested on those who disobeyed the Law, and its removal meant that Gentiles were no longer excluded from the blessing promised to Abraham. Jews and Gentiles alike had now received blessing, and proof of this was to be seen in the gift of the Holy Spirit. Once again, as in 1 Thess 5:10 and Gal 2:19–20, there is no specific reference to Christ's resurrection, but it is the underlying assumption of his argument: there could be no blessing without it. Just as what appeared to human eyes (which see things from the point of view of the 'flesh') to be folly and weakness proved to be wisdom and strength (1 Cor 1:25), so what seemed in the eyes of the Law (which operated in the sphere of the 'flesh') to be a curse has now been demonstrated to be the true source of blessing. In his death, Christ shared the alienation of sinners from God. By his resurrection, they share his status before God.

I have suggested that Paul's understanding of Christ as having become a curse, set out in Galatians 3, is linked with the fact that Jesus was a Jew. In the following chapter, Paul spells this out: God's Son, he writes, was 'born of a woman, born under the Law'. If we read on, we discover that what Paul says here has the familiar structure, using the Greek word ἵνα, meaning 'in order that', that we have seen in statements about Christ's death:

> God sent his Son,
> > born of a woman,
> > born under the Law,
> > *in order that* he might redeem those under the Law,
> > *in order that* we might receive adoption.

The structure is similar to that in Gal 3:13–14, but so, too, are the ideas. What Christ did in being identified with the human (and specifically Jewish) situation was done *in order that* human beings might enjoy certain blessings. In 3:13–14, as a result of being redeemed from the curse of the Law, Christians have received the promised blessing of the Spirit, and Gentiles have been included in the blessing promised to Abraham (namely, righteousness). In 4:4–5, too, Paul speaks of the redemption of those who are under the Law, and of the gift of sonship – a gift that he has already said is given to those who are 'in' Christ (3:26), and which is guaranteed by the gift of the Spirit (4:6).

If Galatians 3 and 4 offer parallel ideas, so do Galatians 4 and Romans 8. In Rom 8:3, as in Gal 4:4, we read once more that God sent his Son – this time in the likeness of sinful flesh. Once again, we find Paul insisting that Christ shared fully in our humanity. Moreover, God condemned sin in the flesh (a condemnation that, as he has already explained, led to Christ's death). The purpose this time (introduced once again by ἵνα) is said to be that the Law's requirement of righteousness should be fulfilled in us, who live according to the Spirit (Rom 8:4) – the Spirit of holiness who raised Christ (and us) from the dead (Rom 1:4); when that takes place, we receive the 'Spirit of adoption' (8:15), and so address God as 'Father', as in Gal 4:6.

In both Romans and Galatians, then, we have statements that God sent his Son to share our humanity, in order that those who are 'in him' might share his status as God's children. Paul uses the same idea elsewhere. A notable example is in Philippians, where Paul describes Jesus as being 'in the form of God', and yet taking 'the form of a slave' by sharing human likeness. There could be no greater contrast than this – especially since his action led to death on a cross (Phil 2:6–11). This passage spells out more clearly than any other what sharing the status of men and women really involved. But Paul does not explain that what Christ did was 'for us', and neither is there a ἵνα clause to explain what his self-humiliation achieved – only a triumphant 'Therefore' in v. 9, which introduces an account of how God has exalted him. This time Paul describes how Christ became man, and speaks of his death and exaltation,[6] *without* telling us what these achieve for others. But when we turn the page and read the end of chapter 3, we find that Paul here describes how believers confidently hope to *share Christ's status.* Because he experienced human humiliation and death, he will enable believers to share his glory: once again, then, the fact that Christ shared our status means that we shall share his. And sandwiched in-between these two passages in chapters 2 and 3 we have Paul's statement at the beginning of chapter 3, of how he had followed Christ's example by emptying himself of the privileges that belonged to him by birth – his status as a Jew – in order to share Christ's sufferings and death, in hope of sharing his resurrection.

If the emphasis in this letter is rather different from that in Romans and Galatians, being concerned with future hope rather than present experience, that is hardly surprising, since when Paul wrote Philippians, he was writing from prison, facing the prospect of an imminent death sentence. What he had in mind here was the end of the process, as described in Romans 8, when those who are already acknowledged as God's children would be conformed to the image of his Son, and share his glory. In Philippians, too, he uses Christ's self-humiliation in sharing our status as the basis for an appeal to the Philippians to consider others and do all things out of love for others, as did Christ.

We find a similar idea, expressed in very different language, but used once again as the basis of an ethical appeal, in 2 Cor 8:9. Here, thrown into a discussion of what we might have supposed was a very mundane subject (the need for the Corinthians to contribute to the collection that Paul is making for the benefit of poor Christians in Jerusalem!), Paul tosses a reminder of what Christ has done for *them*:

---

[6] The reference to exaltation rather than resurrection is appropriate here, since he has been stressing Christ's great humiliation.

You know the grace of our Lord Jesus Christ:
that, though he was rich, yet on your account he became poor,
in order that you, by his poverty, might become rich.

The implication is obvious: if Christ did so much for you, you certainly should help those who are poorer than yourselves. Here we see Paul adapting a central theme of his understanding of what Christ has done 'for us', and expressing it in language which will be appropriate to a particular application of its implications. Instead of speaking of Christ being born of a woman, under Law, coming in the likeness of sinful flesh, or coming in the form of a slave, he describes him as accepting 'poverty' instead of riches. Here again, however, we find the idea that Christians share *his* status. Because he became poor, they become rich. The language is, of course, metaphorical. However, it nevertheless provides a theological basis for Paul's appeal.

3. 'Interchange in Christ'

With the exception of Philippians 2–3, these statements about Christ 'being sent' or 'becoming' are parallel in structure with other statements that we looked at earlier which spell out the purpose of what Christ did in the form of clear contrasts. These were
- 1 Thess 5:10, where the result of Christ's death for us was that we live with him;
- Gal 3:13–14, where Christ became a curse for us, and the result was blessing (sonship and Spirit) for Gentiles as well as for Jews; and
- 2 Cor 5:21, where Christ became sin, with the result that we became righteousness in him.

We see, then, that whether Paul is talking about what theologians later came to speak of as the doctrine of 'incarnation',[7] or about what they termed the doctrine of 'atonement',[8] he uses similar formulae. Because he was fully human, Christ *shared the status* of men and women, and shared in what it meant to be human; this involved suffering the consequences of sin, including death. In raising him from the dead, God has declared him to be righteous, given him life, and initiated a new creation, and those who are in Christ *share his status*. It is this idea of sharing in Christ's status which an early father of the church, Irenaeus, memorably summed up when he wrote: 'Christ became what we are, in order that we might become what he himself is'.[9] He

---

[7] Rom 8:3, 29; 2 Cor 8:9; Gal 4:4–5; Phil 2:7; 3:21.
[8] Rom 4:25; 2 Cor 5:14–15; Gal 2:19–21; 3:13–14; 1 Thess 5:10.
[9] Irenaeus, *Adv. Haer.* 5 *praef.*

became what we are – and shared in all that this means – so that we might share in what *he* is.

This idea of mutual sharing seems to lie at the heart of Paul's understanding of how the human race has been reconciled to God. In trying to describe it, I have often used the term 'interchange' – a word that is intended to convey the mutuality of experience involved.[10] It should be noted that this is *not* an 'exchange' between Christ and the believer. An exchange would imply substitution. What Paul is describing is God's Son sharing fully in our humanity, and suffering the consequences of so doing, so that he shares our human death. Yet he refused to succumb to sin (2 Cor 5:21) and was obedient to God (Rom 5:19). Therefore God raised him from death, and vindicated him. Because he shared our humanity, he is able to act as our representative. He died to sin on our behalf, and has been raised to a life in which we, too, may share. Nevertheless, in order to share this new life, Paul insists that believers have to be baptized into Christ – and so, symbolically, into his death – acknowledging God's judgement on sin. Thus Christ *shares* our physical death and we *share* his death to sin and his life. This is no simple exchange! But for believers, there is certainly an exchange of experience: instead of sin, they have righteousness, instead of slavery, freedom, instead of death, life – and all because they now share the status of the Son of God, and acknowledge God himself as 'Father'.

From time to time, Paul uses various images to convey what Christ's death achieves. In Gal 3:13 and 4:15, as we have seen, he uses a word which means 'to redeem' or 'to buy back' – the word used in 'redeeming' a slave. In 1 Cor 6:20 and 7:23 he uses the simple verb 'to buy' in order to remind the Corinthians that they belong to God (cf. the similar argument in Rom 6:15–23). Earlier, in 1 Corinthians, he refers to Christ as the Passover lamb, sacrificed for us, a reminder that the blood of the Passover lamb played a crucial part in God's rescue of Israel from Egypt, and became a symbol for God's redemption of his people. And in Romans, Paul made use of two other Old Testament images, with what appears to be an allusion to the mercy seat in 3:23, and a possible reference to the sin-offering in Rom 8:3.

4. God's Righteousness

It is worth looking a little more closely at Romans 3, for here, in particular, scholars have suggested that Paul has taken over a view of Christ's death

---

[10] Cf. Morna D. Hooker, *From Adam to Christ: Essays on Paul* (Cambridge: Cambridge University Press, 1990), chs. 1–4; *Not Ashamed of the Gospel* (Carlisle: Paternoster, 1994), 20–46. The phrase 'interchange' was first used in this connection by R.P.C. Hanson, with reference to what he termed the 'interchange' between opposites experienced by Christians in 2 Cor 1:1–7; see his *II Corinthians,* Torch Commentary (London: SCM Press, 1954), 32–35.

which is really not his own. Yet it fits admirably into the argument of Romans. In chapters 1–3, Paul has demonstrated that sin is universal. He is going to go on to show how Christ, sharing the universal alienation from God, shared the universal punishment, and inaugurated a new life. What happened to all the sins that God had 'passed over' (v. 25)? Paul explains in Rom 3:21–26. What has happened, he says, is that God has revealed his righteousness, as the Jewish scriptures, both Law and Prophets, witnessed that he would (Rom 3:21). However, it has been revealed *apart from* the Law, and not on the basis of whether or not one has kept the Law (v. 21), and it is therefore effective for all who have faith (v. 22). Things have been put right as a sheer gift by the grace of God, 'through the redemption which is in Christ Jesus' (v. 24). God set him forth as a *hilasterion*, explains Paul, by means of his death. Unfortunately, there is considerable dispute as to the meaning of the noun *hilasterion*, as the various translations and paraphrases offered in modern versions demonstrate. Among these are 'a sacrifice of atonement' (NRSV and *NIB*), 'the means of expiating sin' (REB), and 'so as to win reconciliation' (JB). In the Septuagint, the word means none of these things, but refers to something which had a permanent place in the holy of holies in the temple. This seems to have been positioned above the Ark of the Covenant, where the books of Torah were kept, and is generally referred to as 'the cover of the ark' or, since this is where God was thought to dwell and the place where reconciliation between God and his people took place, the 'seat of mercy'.[11] Once a year the high priest came into the holy of holies and sprinkled blood on the *hilasterion*: it was therefore the place where atonement was made. The scene is described in Heb 9:2–7.

Why, then, do our translations prefer to speak of Christ as a sacrifice, rather than as a *place* of sacrifice? There are three reasons: one is that scholars find it difficult to imagine Paul speaking of him as a piece of furniture! The second is that they object that Christ cannot be both a sacrifice (an idea implied in the phrase 'by his death') *and* the place where sacrifice is offered. They therefore understand *hilasterion* to explain the *nature* of Christ's death: by his death, he became an atoning sacrifice. Justification for this interpretation is then found in the third argument, which is that in later Jewish literature, influenced by Greek ideas, the word *hilasterion* did come to be used in the sense of 'atoning sacrifice': notably, it was used in this sense of the death of the Maccabean martyrs (4 Macc 17:22).

Notwithstanding these objections, we have to note that the idea of Christ as *the place where God and human beings are reconciled* is a highly appropriate one for the development of Paul's argument. Nor is there any real reason why he should not have thought of Christ as both the victim and the place of

---

[11] This was how William Tyndale translated the word; he was influenced at this point by Luther, who translated the word as 'Gnadenstuhl'. The traditional translation in Heb 9:5 is 'mercy seat'.

sacrifice; the author of Hebrews does something similar in describing Jesus as both the high priest *and* the sacrifice, which he himself offers (Heb 9:11–14). Finally, Paul's use of the Old Testament elsewhere suggests that his ideas are probably drawn from the Old Testament image of the mercy seat, and reflect the way in which the word *hilasterion* is used in Exodus and Leviticus.[12]

What the ritual connected with the mercy seat provided was a method of dealing with those sins which – in spite of all the other sacrifices offered throughout the year – remained as a barrier between God and his people. In Paul's thought, too, it would seem that what God deals with are the sins that, in his forbearance, he has passed over; they have created a barrier between God and human beings and need to be removed. Once a year the high priest entered the holy of holies and, far from any human gaze, sprinkled blood on the mercy seat, in order to deal with the sins that had come between God and his people. It was a very private ceremony, for the mercy seat was hidden from public gaze. Now something very public has taken place. God has 'set forth' a new 'mercy seat' – Christ – sprinkled with blood in the sight of all (cf. Gal 3:1); he is the place of reconciliation, and by his death, sins have been dealt with once and for all. Since God has now dealt with sins, he is seen to be righteous; moreover, he has 'righted' all who have faith, having brought about reconciliation between himself and *all* people, not simply (as with the high priest) between himself and the Jews. Paul's use of 'set forth' and 'blood' here alongside the word *hilasterion* suggests that he has this imagery in mind. The blood sprinkled on the old mercy seat dealt with the sins of Israel; the blood of Jesus, who is himself the true 'mercy seat', deals with the sins of the whole world, for God is the God of Gentiles as well as of Jews, and deals with both in the same way (3:27–31). I see no contradiction between the idea of Christ as the mercy seat where God and humankind meet, and the idea of Christ as the Son of God who shared the status of a man.

There is no reason, then, to suppose that Paul is using ideas that he has 'borrowed' from others, or which do not fit with his own understanding of what the death of Jesus achieved. Sin had to be dealt with, and sacrificial imagery was appropriate to explain what had been done. When the original Passover lambs were killed, the result was freedom for Israel; the sacrifice of a sin-offering had symbolized the removal of sins; the 'mercy seat' was the place where God and his people were reconciled, through the death of an animal. Now it was no animal that had been sacrificed, but the 'one man' who was able to bring God and man together. His death had finally dealt with sin, but his resurrection had inaugurated a new era. Those who shared his death and his resurrection were members of a new creation.

---

[12] On the meaning of *hilasterion,* see Daniel P. Bailey, 'Jesus as the Mercy Seat: The Semantics and Theology of Paul's Use of *Hilasterion* in Romans 3:25', *Tyndale Bulletin* 51 (2000): 155–158. The article summarizes the argument in Dr Bailey's unpublished PhD dissertation.

In looking at Paul's teaching about how Christ's death affects the human race, we have discovered, firstly, that he insists that *the initiative is with God*. Whatever happened was the work of God himself, for it is *God* who reconciles (2 Cor 5:18–20; Rom 5:10–11), *God* who sends his Son (Rom 8:3; Gal 4:4), *God* who gives him up (Rom 4:25; 8:32), *God* who 'raised him from the dead' (Rom 8:11; 1 Thess 1:10), and *God* whose grace is seen in what Christ does for us (Rom 5:15–17). Secondly, what happened took place *through* Christ, who (as Son of God) was obedient to his will, but was also *fully human*. In order to be our representative, he had to be one with us, sharing in what it meant to be human. What he achieved was as 'the one man, Jesus Christ' (Romans 5). He shared fully in our status, and as a result, he died *for us*, not as our substitute but as our representative. Thirdly, we have seen that he is our representative not only in his death but also in his resurrection: because he has shared our status, we are enabled to share his.

'Christ died for our sins, and was raised for our acquittal'. In dying for our sins, he shared our punishment; in being raised from the dead, he enables *us* to share his righteous status before God.

38. Raised for Our Acquittal (Rom 4:25)

At the end of Romans 4, Paul concludes a lengthy discussion of Abraham's faith by returning to the key text from Gen 15:5 from which his argument had begun: Abraham's trust in God *was reckoned to him as righteousness* (4:22). Paul then makes the vital link between Abraham's faith and that of Christians, 'who trust in the one who raised Jesus our Lord from the dead' (4:24). Finally, we have a brief credal statement concerning this Jesus in 4:25:

ὃς παρεδόθη διὰ τὰ παραπτώματα ἡμῶν
καὶ ἠγέρθη διὰ τὴν δικαίωσιν ἡμῶν.

The antithesis in this couplet is described by almost all commentators as 'rhetorical'. It is obvious that the phrases have indeed been carefully balanced, but does that mean that the distinction between Christ's death and resurrection is 'purely rhetorical'?[1] Was this formula 'constructed to be verbally memorable rather than theologically precise',[2] or was the language in fact chosen with an eye to theology rather than rhetoric?

Now there are various unusual features in this brief credal summary that may point to an answer. For some, of course, these lend support to the suggestion that it is a pre-Pauline formula, but it is worth considering them in relation to what Paul says elsewhere. First, we note the double use of διά with the accusative, meaning 'because of'. The first clause is syntactically straightforward: 'he was given up [to death] because of our trespasses'. The second, however, is difficult, and the διά + accusative has to be understood as expressing the reason proleptically:[3] 'he was raised *with a view to* our acquittal'. There is, in fact, an *imbalance* in the two phrases, for though it was our trespasses that led to Christ's death, it was not our acquittal that led to his resurrection, but his resurrection that led to our acquittal. *Why* our trespasses should entail his death or *how* his resurrection could achieve our acquittal are not yet explained.

If, then, the antithesis is indeed 'purely rhetorical', it is certainly not 'pure' rhetoric. It is worth asking, therefore, whether the clumsy construction is simply the result of attempting to create a brief formula that would be 'verbally memorable', or whether the antithesis reflects Paul's deliberate

---

[1] James D.G. Dunn, *Romans 1–8,* WBC 38A (Dallas: Word Books, 1988), 241.
[2] Kenneth Grayston, *Dying, We Live* (London: Darton, Longman, and Todd, 1990), 92.
[3] C.F.D. Moule, *An Idiom Book of New Testament Greek,* 2nd ed. (Cambridge: Cambridge University Press, 1959), 54, 194.

attempt to express a *theological* point in a formula that was necessarily unbalanced. The 'handing over' was the *result* of human sin; the 'raising' led to a totally new human situation. We need to see how the statement relates to the argument of the epistle as a whole. First, however, we should take note of the immediate context, and observe that the faith shown by Abraham, which was reckoned to him for righteousness, was specifically defined in 4:17 as his trust in the God who gives life to the dead (4:17); his faith is thus the prototype of ours, since we believe in the one who raised our Lord Jesus from the dead (4:24). Both in 4:17 and in 4:22–24, faith in the one who gives life to the dead is linked with righteousness (δικαιοσύνη).

1. Romans 5:12–21

Another unusual feature of the summary in 4:25 is the use of the word δικαίωσις. It cannot be dismissed as 'pre-Pauline', since it is used again in 5:18. That passage provides an interesting commentary on 4:25, for there also we have two balancing clauses: these purport to compare Adam and Christ, though in fact contrasting them:

ἄρα οὖν ὡς δι' ἑνὸς παραπτώματος
εἰς πάντας ἀνθρώπους εἰς κατάκριμα,
οὕτως καὶ δι' ἑνὸς δικαιώματος
εἰς πάντας ἀνθρώπους εἰς δικαίωσιν ζωῆς

Although this verse, also, is not without its difficulties – the lack of a verb, the ambiguity of ἑνός, the uncertainty of the meaning of the noun δικαίωμα – the contrast is clear, since it follows on those already made between Adam and Christ in 5:12–17. In 5:18 itself, we note that we have not only the noun δικαίωσις, but a further echo of 4:25 in the word παράπτωμα. Moreover, in 5:18a the παράπτωμα of Adam is the *cause* of what came next (κατάκριμα for all), while the δικαίωσις ζωῆς for all *follows* the δικαίωμα. In other words, the cause/result pattern is similar to what we have in 4:25, even though here διά with the genitive has been used in two exactly parallel phrases, to denote the two causes of what happens to humanity:

δι' ἑνὸς παραπτώματος
δι' ἑνὸς δικαιώματος

Now at first sight, the verbal links between 4:25 and 5:18 might appear to be accidental, since the subject matter is quite different. In 4:25, the contrast is between Christ's death and resurrection, while in 5:18, it is between what happens through the actions of Adam and Christ. But 4:25 is a brief summary of the gospel – Christ died and was raised – and 5:12–21 spells out in more detail what that gospel means for humankind. The starting point of that passage is the human condition of universal sin brought about by Adam's sin, which results in turn in universal death (5:12); the remedy is then set over against the problem in a series of contrasts (5:15–19, 21). Analysis of the passage suggests that it has been carefully crafted. This is the more remarkable, since what was clearly intended to be a comparison between Adam and Christ (5:12) was broken off after telling us only about the effects of Adam's sin.

15 Ἀλλ' οὐχ ὡς τὸ παράπτωμα, οὕτως καὶ τὸ χάρισμα·
    εἰ γὰρ τῷ τοῦ ἑνὸς παραπτώματι οἱ πολλοὶ ἀπέθανον,
    πολλῷ μᾶλλον ἡ χάρις τοῦ θεοῦ καὶ ἡ δωρεὰ ἐν χάριτι
        τῇ τοῦ ἑνὸς ἀνθρώπου Ἰησοῦ Χριστοῦ
    εἰς τοὺς πολλοὺς ἐπερίσσευσεν.

16 καὶ οὐχ ὡς δι' ἑνὸς ἁμαρτήσαντος τὸ δώρημα·
    τὸ μὲν γὰρ κρίμα ἐξ ἑνὸς εἰς κατάκριμα,
    τὸ δὲ χάρισμα ἐκ πολλῶν παραπτωμάτων εἰς δικαίωμα.

17 εἰ γὰρ τῷ τοῦ ἑνὸς παραπτώματι
    ὁ θάνατος ἐβασίλευσεν διὰ τοῦ ἑνός,
    πολλῷ μᾶλλον οἱ τὴν περισσείαν τῆς χάριτος καὶ τῆς δωρεᾶς
        τῆς δικαιοσύνης λαμβάνοντες
    ἐν ζωῇ βασιλεύσουσιν διὰ τοῦ ἑνὸς Ἰησοῦ Χριστοῦ.

18 ἄρα οὖν ὡς δι' ἑνὸς παραπτώματος
    εἰς πάντας ἀνθρώπους εἰς κατάκριμα,
    οὕτως καὶ δι' ἑνὸς δικαιώματος
    εἰς πάντας ἀνθρώπους εἰς δικαίωσιν ζωῆς.

19 ὥσπερ γὰρ διὰ τῆς παρακοῆς τοῦ ἑνὸς ἀνθρώπου
    ἁμαρτωλοὶ κατεστάθησαν οἱ πολλοί,
    οὕτως καὶ διὰ τῆς ὑπακοῆς τοῦ ἑνὸς
    δίκαιοι κατασταθήσονται οἱ πολλοί ...

20 οὗ δὲ ἐπλεόνασεν ἡ ἁμαρτία, ὑπερεπερίσσευσεν ἡ χάρις,
21 ἵνα ὥσπερ ἐβασίλευσεν ἡ ἁμαρτία ἐν τῷ θανάτῳ,
    οὕτως καὶ ἡ χάρις βασιλεύσῃ διὰ δικαιοσύνης εἰς ζωὴν αἰώνιον
    διὰ Ἰησοῦ Χριστοῦ τοῦ κυρίου ἡμῶν.

Paul's first 'comparison' (5:15a) is negative: the χάρισμα and the παράπτωμα are *not* alike – a point brought out in the opening words: ἀλλ' οὐχ ὡς. They cannot be, of course, since God's gracious act is so much more powerful than human transgression. But we are not really comparing like with like: it is the *result* of Adam's transgression (death) that cannot compare with divine grace. This is spelt out in the next two lines: if, because of one man's trespass, many died, *how much more* will God's grace and gift abound in the grace of the one man, Jesus Christ. The negative side of the comparison echoes what was said in 5:12, where we were told that the sin of one led to the death of all, though the terms used there were ἁμαρτία and ἁμαρτάνω.

Another comparison (5:16a) is parallel in form to the first, and is once again introduced by οὐχ ὡς: the result of the one man's sinning and the δώρημα are *not* alike. The awkward Greek construction reflects the imbalance: as in 5:15a, what is 'compared' with the divine initiative is the *result* of one man's sin, rather than the sin itself. The contrast this time is thus between κρίμα and χάρισμα, but once again the difference is overwhelming, and this is spelt out in the next two lines: the result of the *one* transgression is judgement (κρίμα), leading to condemnation (κατάκριμα), but the gracious gift of God (χάρισμα) follows after *many* transgressions and leads to acquittal (δικαίωμα). But *whose* δικαίωμα? Commentators assume that Paul is talking about *our* 'justification', and that is probably correct, since the κατάκριμα rested on all Adam's descendants; but we are presumably sharing the verdict pronounced on *Christ,* just as we share the verdict pronounced on Adam.

5:17–18 repeat and elaborate the same theme. First, 5:17 picks up the ideas and vocabulary of 5:12 and 5:15: if, because of the παράπτωμα of one man, death reigned through the one, *how much more* will those who receive the abundance of grace and the gift of righteousness reign through the one man Jesus Christ. Once again, the contrast is not a true one, as we see in the fact that the subject of βασιλεύω is 'death' in the first half of the verse and 'those who receive the abundance of grace and the gift of righteousness' in the other. The result of Adam's sin was that *death* reigned, while the result of God's gracious act was that those who were its beneficiaries reign in *life.* Although 'death' is balanced by 'life', the comparison is inevitably skewed – this time because the second half of the verse refers to the result of God's gracious action: no wonder Paul uses the phrase πολλῷ μᾶλλον!

If 5:17 repeats and elaborates 5:15, then it seems likely that 5:18 does the same for 5:16. Certainly it uses some of the same vocabulary. Once again we are told that the παράπτωμα of one led to κατάκριμα, and this time we are specifically told that this condemnation applies to 'all'. Balancing this we are told that the δικαίωμα of one man leads to δικαίωσιν ζωῆς for all. How are these terms to be understood? To answer this question it is necessary to consider the structure of 5:18 and its relationship to what precedes and follows it. The great majority of commentators assume that in 5:18 we at last have a true contrast between Adam and Christ, introduced by ὡς ... οὕτως, and that this verse is therefore parallel to 5:19, where the disobedience of Adam is contrasted with the obedience of Christ.

In order for 5:18 to consist of a true contrast, and so be parallel to 5:19, however, it is necessary to understand δικαίωμα in 5:18 as meaning 'a righteous act', in opposition to the term παράπτωμα. The problem is that, though a few analogies are found elsewhere,[4] the word is not used in that sense in any

---

[4] The word is used in the sense of 'righteous act' in Bar 2:19; Rev 19:8; Aristotle, *Rhetoric* 1359a 25.

other Pauline writing.[5] Moreover, Paul has just used the word with the sense of 'acquittal' in 5:16, and one would expect it to have the same sense here as there. And if 5:18 does indeed, as we have argued, build on 5:16, in the same way that 5:17 does on 5:15, this increases the probability that δικαίωμα has the same sense here as it does in 5:16, and means 'acquittal' or 'vindication'.[6] In that case, even though the μὲν ... δέ of 5:16 has been replaced with ὡς ... οὕτως, suggesting a straightforward comparison, we have the same kind of skewed 'contrast' in 5:18 that we have in 5:15–17 – a contrast, that is, between the παράπτωμα of Adam, and the grace of God at work through Christ to set things right, rather than between actions of Adam and Christ:

> As through the trespass of one [came] condemnation to all
> So through the vindication of one [came] acquittal – resulting in life – for all.

If we are right, this would mean that the δικαίωμα of the one is parallel to the words in 5:15–17 that refer to God's gracious activity in Christ – χάρισμα, χάρις, δωρεά, δώρημα – defined in 5:17 specifically as ἡ δωρεὰ τῆς δικαιοσύνης, the status that follows acquittal. The logic of 5:12 is implied and completed in 5:18: just as Adam's sin led to death for all, *since all sinned,* so Christ's acquittal leads to life for all, *since all share his acquittal and his righteousness.* If Paul uses two words – δικαίωμα and δικαίωσις – with virtually the same meaning, that is necessary for reasons of euphony. The link between them is, however, necessary, for it is the acquittal of the one that leads to the acquittal of all, and the *result* of their acquittal is life.[7] 5:19 then spells out what we have suggested is implied in 5:18. If it was 'through one man' that condemnation came to all, and 'through one man' also that acquittal – leading to life – came to all, that means that it was through Adam's *disobedience* that many were made sinners, and through Christ's *obedience* that they were made righteous. Here we have what is apparently a true antithesis, which picks up and completes the contrast begun in 5:12 – though, like 5:12, it leads immediately to a parenthesis about the Law (5:20a, cf. 5:13–14). But even though the statement is a

---

[5] The term occurs only in Romans. Apart from 5:16 (where it has the sense of acquittal) and 5:18, it is used in 1:32; 2:26 and 8:4, with the sense of the divine decree or requirement. William Sanday and Arthur C. Headlam, *A Critical and Exegetical Commentary on the Epistle to the Romans,* ICC (Edinburgh: T&T Clark, 1905), 31, offered the following explanation for these different usages: δικαίωμα means 'a declaration that a thing is δίκαιον, or that a person is δίκαιος.

[6] Among the few commentators to interpret the verse in this way were H.A.W. Meyer, *Critical and Exegetical Handbook to the Epistle to the Romans,* Critical and Exegetical Commentary on the New Testament 4), ed. W.P. Dickson, trans. W.P. Dickson and John C. Moore (Edinburgh: T&T Clark, 1873), 270–273; and E.H. Gifford, *The Epistle of St. Paul to the Romans,* reprinted from The Speaker's Commentary (London: John Murray, 1886), 120.

[7] Ζωῆς is a genitive of result: F. Blass and A. Debrunner, *A Greek Grammar of the New Testament and Other Early Christian Literature,* trans. and rev. R.W. Funk (Cambridge: Cambridge University Press, 1961), §166.

straightforward antithesis, with no οὐχ and no πολλῷ μᾶλλον, the subject matter does not lend itself easily to this format, as the contrast between ἐπλεόνασεν and ὑπερεπερίσσευσεν in 5:20 makes plain. Even though the argument concludes with another antithesis (ὥσπερ ... οὕτως) in 5:21, the contrast is once again unbalanced in its theme: as sin reigned in death, so grace will reign through righteousness to life through Jesus Christ our Lord.

If the above exegesis of 5:18 is correct, then Christ's acquittal or vindication (presumably at the resurrection) is said to be the cause of ours. *Whatever* interpretation we give to δικαίωμα here, however, the link between *our* acquittal and life is clear, expressed in the phrase εἰς δικαίωσιν ζωῆς: those who receive the gift of righteousness will rule in life through the one man Jesus Christ; his δικαίωμα (whether this is understood to refer to his righteous action or to his vindication) leads to acquittal and life for all. The change from a pattern of trespass leading to condemnation and so to death, to a pattern of acquittal leading to life, takes place through the one man Jesus Christ, because of the grace of God at work in him.

If we now turn back to 4:25, we realize that the imbalance we found there is exactly parallel to the skewed parallelism we have detected in 5:15–19, 21. There, our trespasses led to Christ's death; his resurrection led to our acquittal. In chapter 5, this is explained in terms of Adam and Christ: the trespass of the one man Adam led to the condemnation and death of many (since, as 5:12 explained, all have sinned); the gracious act of God, through the one man Jesus Christ, has brought acquittal and life to many. The difference is that 4:25 focuses on the death and resurrection of Jesus and what they achieve, while 5:12–21 deal with the death and life of many, and what has caused them. But both passages link 'death' with 'trespasses' and 'life' with 'acquittal', and both concern what God has done through Christ.

Remarkably, there is no reference in 5:12–21 to Christ's death or to his resurrection. The only oblique reference to his death is in the word 'obedience'[8], contrasted in 5:19 with Adam's disobedience. What we have in Romans 5, on the other hand, is precisely what was missing in 4:25, namely an attempt to explain the *link* between trespasses and death and between acquittal and life. If we put the two passages together, we understand *why* 'our' sins led to Christ's death, and *why* his resurrection (or vindication) brought us acquittal and life (4:25): it is because not only sin and death but grace and life can work through 'one man' (5:15–21). We also understand *how* the grace of God has replaced condemnation with acquittal, and death with life (5:15–21): it is through the death and resurrection of Christ himself (4:25).

The 'skewed' pattern that we have uncovered can be represented diagramatically as follows:

---

[8] Assuming that this refers specifically to his 'obedience to death', as in Phil 2:8.

Rom 4:25	our sins →	Christ's death
		Christ's resurrection → our acquittal
Rom 5:12–21	our sins →	our death
		God's grace → our acquittal and life

Now of course the various terms used in 5:15–21 – χάρισμα, χάρις, δωρεά, δώρημα – refer to far more than Christ's resurrection[9], lending some support to the view that the contrast in 4:25 is 'purely rhetorical', and reminding us that we should be wary of separating Christ's death from his resurrection. The two of course belong together, and it would be foolish to suggest that emphasis on one is meant to minimize the importance of the other. It is, after all, in 1 Corinthians, where Paul declares that his only message to the Corinthians had been 'Christ crucified' (2:2), that he later reminds them that without belief in the resurrection, their faith is vain (15:17)! The theme of 'Christ crucified' clearly *implies* the resurrection, without which the message of the cross would indeed remain 'foolishness' and 'weakness' (1:23–25). Nevertheless, the fact that in writing to the Corinthians Paul focuses first on the theme of the cross, later on the theme of the resurrection, demonstrates that Christ's death has certain implications for Christian living (in 1 Corinthians, the absurdity of human pride [chs. 2–4], the inappropriateness of certain behaviour [chs. 5–6], which should be 'cleaned out', like old leaven [5:7]), just as his resurrection has another, related – but nevertheless different – set of implications (in 1 Corinthians 15, the certainty of our future resurrection). It may well be more than mere rhetoric that in Rom 4:25 associates Christ's death with human sin and its consequences, his resurrection with vindication and righteousness.

2. Romans 1–8

To discover whether or not this is so, we need to look at the rest of the argument in Romans 1–8. The theme of the whole letter is set out in 1:16–17: the gospel 'is the power of God for salvation to everyone who has faith – the Jew first, and also the Greek. For in it the righteousness of God is revealed from faith to faith' – an affirmation that is backed up by a quotation from Hab 2:4. Clearly related to this theme is the declaration in 1:18, parallel to that in 1:17, that the wrath of God is also being revealed against all human wickedness. The revealing of God's righteousness – the setting of things right – also inevitably involves the exercise of his wrath against evil.

---

[9] God's gracious gift in Christ presumably embraces what *we* would term 'incarnation'. Cf. 2 Cor 8:9, which speaks of Christ's grace in becoming poor; also Rom 8:3; Gal 4:4; Phil 2:6–8.

The topic of human sin and its consequences (present wrath for some; future judgement for all) is dealt with in the first three chapters of Romans. Then, in 3:21–31, we are told *how* God's righteousness has been revealed in relation to this sin. Through the *death* of Christ, sins have been dealt with, since God himself put forward Christ as a 'mercy seat',[10] the place where reconciliation between God and his people takes place. In this passage, Christ's resurrection is not mentioned: the issue is the sins that God had 'passed over' but now has dealt with. The demonstration of his righteousness 'at this present time' (3:26) reminds us not only that, in the past, sins have apparently not been punished, but that, in the future, on the day of judgement, sins which have not been dealt with will be punished. The principle on which God's righteousness operates is that of πίστις (3:22, 25, 26, 27, 28, 30, 31): his righteousness is 'revealed from faith to faith, as it is written' in Hab 2:4: ὁ δὲ δίκαιος ἐκ πίστεως ζήσεται.[11]

The relation between πίστις and δίκαιος is picked up in chapter 4, in relation to Abraham, the father of Israel. Paul's argument now centres on the theme of *resurrection*. Abraham is said to have believed in the God 'who gives life to the dead and calls things that do not exist into existence' (4:17). His faith in the promise of God to give him innumerable descendants is thus a model of the faith of his true descendants, who believe in the God 'who raised Jesus our Lord from the dead' (4:24). Since faith is often assumed by commentators to be in the *death* of Christ, it is important to recognize this emphasis on faith in the resurrection, an emphasis which will be reiterated in 10:8–9, where 'the word of faith' in one's heart is defined as belief 'that God raised Christ from the dead' and so made him Lord. It is *this* faith that leads to righteousness (10:6).

Having established that righteousness is linked to faith not only in relation to Christ's death (3:21–28, which explained how his being 'handed over' dealt with our trespasses), but in relation also to his resurrection (4:22–23, where faith in the one who gives life leads to the 'reckoning' of righteousness), Paul reminds us of these two essential elements of the gospel in 4:25:

Jesus our Lord was handed over to death for our trespasses
   and was raised for our δικαίωσις.

---

[10] For a recent defence of this interpretation of the word ἱλαστήριον here, see Daniel P. Bailey, 'Jesus as the Mercy Seat: The Semantics and Theology of Paul's Use of *Hilasterion* in Romans 3:25,' PhD thesis, University of Cambridge, 1999.

[11] The debate concerning the meaning of πίστις Χριστοῦ continues. If the genitive is subjective, this would suggest that God's righteousness is revealed from Christ's faithfulness to the faith of believers. For my own contribution to this topic, see Morna D. Hooker, 'ΠΙΣΤΙΣ ΧΡΙΣΤΟΥ', *NTS* 35 (1989): 321–342. Whatever interpretation we give to the phrase, faith and righteousness are firmly linked.

Is the 'rhetoric' of 4:25 simply dictated, then, by the fact that chapters 1–3 led up to the statement regarding the significance of Christ's death, and that chapter 4 related Abraham's faith to the resurrection? Does not Paul link the theme of 'justification' specifically with Christ's death in 3:21–31, as well as to Abraham's faith in 4:22? Why, then, should we suppose its link with Christ's resurrection in 4:25 to be significant?

The word used in 4:25 is, however, as we have already noted, δικαίωσις. Most translations render the term here as 'justification', a word which, though convenient shorthand, has little meaning in modern English, and we have therefore preferred the translation 'acquittal'. It is worth asking why Paul uses this particular word here, rather than δικαιοσύνη, the term that he has used eight times already in chapter 4. The noun δικαίωσις, like the verb δικαιόω, refers to the *action* of putting things to right. The imagery is taken from the law-court, and refers to the pronouncement of the verdict. Outside the New Testament it can refer to condemnation, leading to punishment, as well as to vindication and acquittal; here, it clearly has a positive meaning. This is what happens to those to whom faith is 'reckoned as righteousness' (4:22–24): their faith is in the God who raised Jesus from the dead, and his resurrection therefore signifies their acquittal. Moreover, as is spelt out in 5:18, acquittal on a capital charge means life. The fulfilment of Hab 2:4 is now complete: ὁ δὲ δίκαιος ἐκ πίστεως ζήσεται.

For Paul, the δικαιο- words have an eschatological meaning, and can be used both of what *has* already taken place and of what *will* take place. Insofar as sin has already been dealt with (through the death of Christ), God has brought men and women into a right relationship with himself (δικαιόω) and reconciled them to himself (καταλλάσσω). But final judgement – and so final acquittal – lies in the future. Romans demonstrates well the ambiguity of the δικαιο- words. All who believe have already been 'justified' or 'acquitted' through the death of Christ (3:24; 5:9), and by dying with Christ we have been 'acquitted from sin' (6:7). Yet Paul talks in 2:13 and 3:20 of being 'justified' or 'acquitted' in the future, something that will take place on the day of wrath, when God's righteous judgement will be revealed (2:5–16). The fact that God's righteousness and wrath have already been revealed (1:17–18; 3:21) does not annul this future judgement, which Paul still expects (5:9–10; 8:31–34; 14:10–12), a judgement that will bring both wrath (12:19–20) and salvation (13:11). But there is a clear link between what *has* taken place and what *will* take place – a link that is clearly set out in 5:8–10:

While we were still sinners, Christ died for us.
  How much more, *being justified by his death*
  Shall we be saved through him from wrath.
For if, while we were enemies, we were reconciled to God *through the death of his son*,
  How much more, *being reconciled*,
  Shall we be saved by his life.

This passage not only shows the relationship between what *has* happened and what *will* happen, but relates what *has* happened to Christ's death, what *will* to his life. The logic that links these ideas is underlined by the use in each verse of the phrase πολλῷ μᾶλλον since, as in 5:15 and 5:17, life is more powerful than death. It is through Christ's *death* that we have been set right with God (δικαιόω) and reconciled to him; it is 'through him' – and more specifically 'by his life' – that we shall be saved, i.e., saved from wrath. The distinction between what is achieved through Christ's death and through his resurrection is again understood by the majority of commentators[12] to be rhetorical, but it is parallel to the one we have in 4:25. Moreover, the use not only of πολλῷ μᾶλλον, but of the verb σῴζω shows that the emphasis is on what *will* happen.

The passage that follows, 5:12–21, which we have looked at already, sums up the argument of 1:16–5:11 in terms of Adam and Christ. We have noted already the imbalance of the comparison. Now we observe that inbuilt into the comparison there is another 'lopsided' contrast, namely between what has already taken place and what *will* happen – for though God has *already* acted in Christ, the *effects* stretch into the future: the reign of sin and death is spoken of in past tenses, but the reign of grace and of those who receive grace lies in the present and future (5:17, 21). The comparison is once again an unbalanced one, since sin and death have been defeated, and righteousness and life have triumphed. The reign of the former cannot last; the reign of the latter has begun.

The tension expressed in 5:8–10 between what God has already done and what he will do is reflected in Romans 6–8, where we find the same argument that what *will* happen is guaranteed by what *has* happened. In Romans 6, Paul deals with the suggestion that Christians should 'continue in sin, in order that grace may abound' (6:1). The idea is absurd, since Christians have been baptized into Christ's death, and have died to sin (6:2–4). But Christ has also been raised from the dead (6:4), something that has not yet happened to Christians, although we can be sure that (6:5)

> if we have been united [to him] in the likeness of his death
> we shall also [be united with] his resurrection.

So we have already 'died to sin', in order that we may 'walk in newness of life' (6:2, 4). As Professor Lambrecht has pointed out,[13] Paul here 'switches from the past tense … to a purpose clause, and … instead of speaking of our resurrection he points to a new type of behaviour.… Our resurrection lies in the future, and the quality of this future depends on the moral life that we

---

[12] An exception is Ernst Käsemann, *An die Römer,* 4th ed., HNT 8a (Tübingen: Mohr Siebeck, 1980), 130–131; ET: *Commentary on Romans,* trans. Geoffrey W. Bromiley (London: SCM Press, 1980), 139.

[13] Jan Lambrecht, *The Wretched 'I' and Its Liberation: Paul in Romans 7 and 8* (Leuven: Peeters, 1992), 18.

as baptized people must live'. Once again, we have an echo of the so-called 'rhetorical' antithesis between Christ's death and resurrection in 4:25. But this time the imbalance between death and resurrection is due to the fact that the death and resurrection *of Christ* can be spoken of as past events, while the same is not true of Christians. For them, resurrection lies in the future (6:8):

> if we have died with Christ,
> we believe that we shall also live with him.

Even though resurrection remains a future hope, however, the resurrection of Christ can be experienced in the present, where the 'indicative' of what God has done forms the basis of the 'imperative' of appropriate living. The rest of Romans 6 spells out what it means to have 'died to sin' and to 'walk in newness of life'. Christians must 'consider' themselves to be dead to sin and alive to God in Christ Jesus. Those who were 'slaves to sin' are now (paradoxically) 'slaves to righteousness' (6:16–19). Sin led to death, but righteousness leads to eternal life (6:20–23). Christians are experiencing what it means to be living 'in Christ' rather than 'in Adam'.

Rom 7:1–6 traces a similar argument in relation to the Law. Christians 'have died to the Law through the body of Christ', and therefore belong to him, who has been raised from the dead (7:4). Once again, we notice the distinction: Christians have died (with Christ), but it is Christ alone who has been raised. Yet they belong to him, and so are expected to 'bear fruit for God' and to serve him 'in the new [life] of the Spirit' (7:6). But why was it necessary to be set free from the Law? In 7:7–23 Paul picks up what he said in the asides of 5:13–14, 20, and describes at length the negative effect of the Law: through the Law, sin had brought death to those under the Law.[14] But God had rescued them 'from this body of death' through Jesus Christ (7:24–25). The Law belongs to the era dominated by sin and death (5:13–14, 20), but Christians have been discharged from the Law, having died to what held them in captivity (7:4).

If Romans 7 largely centres on the past, and on the theme of death,[15] Romans 8 turns to the present experience of Christians, and to their future hope: the Spirit of life in Christ Jesus has set those who are in Christ free from sin and death (8:1). The contrast in chapter 5 between what happens 'in Adam' and what happens 'in Christ' is now expressed in terms of 'walking according

---

[14] Although the meaning of the much-discussed 'I' in these verses remains problematic, it certainly applies to someone – or to some group of people – who had been given the Law and attempted to live by it.

[15] Whatever decision we come to regarding the identity of the 'I', Paul is certainly *not* describing the Christian life here! Such an understanding undermines the whole logic of his argument. See, e.g. Lambrecht, *The Wretched 'I'*, 73–91. For the opposite belief – that is, that Paul is here referring to a struggle within the Christian life – see the recent discussion by James D.G. Dunn, *The Theology of Paul the Apostle* (Grand Rapids: Eerdmans, 1998), 472–477.

to the flesh' and 'according to the Spirit'. The flesh leads to death, the Spirit to life, for this is 'the Spirit of him who raised Christ from the dead', who 'will give life to your mortal bodies' (8:11). But though our resurrection is future, Christ's resurrection is again experienced in the present: we live 'according to the Spirit' (8:5), and though the body is dead because of sin (8:10, cf. 6:6; 7:24), the Spirit is life *because of righteousness*. What is meant by this last phrase? Once again, we have an interesting parallel structure in 8:10:

τὸ μὲν σῶμα νεκρὸν διὰ ἁμαρτίαν
τὸ δὲ πνεῦμα ζωὴ διὰ δικαιοσύνην.

Almost all commentators take διὰ δικαιοσύνην to be exactly parallel to διὰ ἁμαρτίαν. But there is an intriguing similarity with 4:25, not only in the structure but in the theme, with sin the cause of death, and a δικαιο- word linked with life. Does the second διά perhaps have a *prospective* sense, as in 4:25? Certainly there is another irregularity in the parallelism, for πνεῦμα here refers to God's Spirit, not the human spirit.[16]

Is Paul therefore saying, not that the gift of the Spirit *follows* righteousness, but that the life-giving Spirit *leads to* righteousness? This would pick up what he has already argued in 8:4, where we are told that the δικαίωμα τοῦ νόμου is fulfilled in us through the Spirit. There too we have the twin ideas of dealing with past sin and setting things right, and once again sin is the situation that has to be dealt with, while a δικαιο- word is used of what results:

ὁ θεὸς ... κατέκρινεν τὴν ἁμαρτίαν ἐν τῇ σαρκί,
ἵνα τὸ δικαίωμα τοῦ νόμου πληρωθῇ ἐν ἡμῖν ...

Through the sending of the Son (8:3), the Law's demand for righteousness is fulfilled in believers, so it is hardly surprising if the theme of the chapter is life – the life which the Law promised[17] but was unable to give.[18]

However we interpret 8:10, the emphasis in this chapter is on present life in the Spirit – though this is in fact only what Paul calls the ἀπαρχή of what is to come (8:23).[19] 'If the Spirit of him who raised Jesus from the dead dwells in you, he who raised Christ from the dead will give life to your mortal bodies also through his Spirit that dwells in you' (8:11). Those who have received the Spirit of God's Son, and are therefore God's children, call God 'Father' (8:14–16); yet this is only the beginning of the process. We wait, says Paul – with the whole of creation – for our final adoption (8:23), when we will finally

---

[16] Cf. C.K. Barrett, *A Commentary on the Epistle to the Romans*, 2nd ed. (London: A&C Black, 1991), 149–150, who points out that the latter would require 'the spirit is alive' not 'the spirit is life'.

[17] Lev 18:5 quoted in Rom 10:5; Gal 3:12.

[18] Cf. Brendan Byrne, *'Sons of God' – 'Seed of Abraham'*, AnBib 83 (Rome: Biblical Institute Press, 1979), 91–96.

[19] Cf. his use of ἀρραβών in 2 Cor 1:22 and 5:5.

be conformed to the image of God's Son (8:29). This chapter expresses more clearly than any other passage the reality of the now/not yet existence of Christians. The tension is seen in v. 30:

> οὓς δὲ προώρισεν, τούτους καὶ ἐκάλεσεν·
> καὶ οὓς ἐκάλεσεν, τούτους καὶ ἐδικαίωσεν·
> οὓς δὲ ἐδικαίωσεν, τούτους καὶ ἐδόξασεν.

Predestination and calling are clearly past events, but glorification, though referred to with an aorist verb, is certainly not yet completed. It has been referred to in 5:2 and 8:17–25 as a future hope; to be glorified is to be conformed to the image of God's Son (8:29), and is thus the realization of God's purpose. Yet there is a sense in which glorification has already begun.[20] So, too, 'justification' – the restoration of a right relationship with God – is something that has in a sense already taken place (3:23–26; 5:1). Yet the final judgement scene – and acquittal – lie in the future. The imagery of this final judgement scene is suggested at the end of Romans 8:

> If God is for us, who is against us?
> He who did not withhold his own Son,
> but gave him up for us all,
> how will he not, with him, give us all things?

The use of παραδίδωμι echoes 4:25, and the logic is the same as that in 5:8–10: if God did this in the death of his Son, we can rely on him for the future. The same logic underlies the questions that follow:[21]

> Who will bring a charge against God's elect?
>   Will God, who justifies?
> Who will condemn?
>   Will Christ, who died?
>   rather, who was raised,
>   who is at God's right hand,
>   who also intercedes for us?

The God who has already 'justified' us will not bring a charge against us. Christ, who has died, will not condemn us. We can be confident of future vindication, since Christ, who has been raised, intercedes for us at God's right hand. The one who was handed over because of our sins was raised for our acquittal.

---

[20] 2 Cor 3:18.
[21] The whole passage is reminiscent of Isa 50:7–9.

3. The Rest of Paul

A quick survey of the rest of the Pauline literature suggests that the pattern we have found in Romans is largely repeated there. The resurrection of Christians is almost invariably referred to as a *future* event.[22] The exceptions occur – perhaps significantly – in Colossians and Ephesians, where the verb συνεγείρω is used. In Col 2:12–13 the reference is clearly to baptism, and in 3:1 the context is moral exhortation – both typical Pauline themes. In Eph 2:4–6, Christians are said not only to have been raised with Christ but to have been exalted with him to the heavenly places! The author is clearly using this imagery to describe an eschatological hope, in order to remind his readers of the ethical implications in the present. The danger of taking this language literally is seen in 2 Tim 2:18, where belief that 'the resurrection has already taken place' is specifically denied.

The gift of the Spirit, however, means that Christ's resurrection is also a present experience for believers. Galatians begins (1:1) with the declaration that God the Father raised Jesus Christ from the dead (cf. Rom 1:4), and goes on to explain that the Lord Jesus Christ 'gave himself for our sins to set us free from the present evil age' (1:4): Christ's death deals with our sins.[23] At the end of chapter 2, Paul explains that he has been 'crucified with Christ' (2:19). He does *not* say, however, that he has been *raised* with Christ. Rather, he says that he lives no longer, but Christ lives in him (2:20). Nevertheless, he continues to live 'in the flesh' – though this life is lived ἐν πίστει ... τῇ τοῦ υἱοῦ τοῦ θεοῦ. Through this faith, believers are 'justified' – that is, put into a right relationship with God.

The idea that we are enabled to live for Christ is found again in 2 Cor 5, where we once again have the idea that we share Christ's death: 'One has died for all, therefore all have died' (5:14). The purpose is that those who live might live no longer for themselves but for the one who died and was raised for them (5:15). The power of sin over us has been destroyed (5:21). Already, then, as in Rom 6, we are able to experience the resurrection life of Christ in our present lives. Something of what that present experience of Christ's resurrection means has been spelt out in the previous two chapters, but it is clear there that *our* resurrection lies in the future: 'we know that he who raised the Lord Jesus will raise us also with Jesus' (2 Cor 4:14). What we experience now is the work of the Spirit, who makes alive (3:6) and is the ἀρραβών of what is to come (5:5).

---

[22] E. g. 1 Cor 6:14 (ἐξεγείρω); 2 Cor 4:14 (ἐγείρω); 1 Cor 15:12–13, 21, 42 (ἀνάστασις); 1 Cor 15:22 (ζῳοποιέω).

[23] How it deals with them is not explained but, in 3:13, Christ's death is said to remove 'the curse of the Law'.

This tension between now/not yet is summed up in Phil 3:10–11, where Paul declares that he longs to know Christ and the power of his resurrection and the fellowship of his sufferings, being conformed to the likeness of his death, if somehow he may attain the resurrection from the dead. The somewhat surprising order – resurrection, sufferings, death, resurrection – is explained when we realize that 'the power of his resurrection' refers to Paul's *present* experience, and is what gives meaning to 'the fellowship of his sufferings' (also part of his present experience), while the hope of future resurrection is what will give meaning to his coming death – provided that it is conformed to Christ's. Compressed into one tight statement we have two ideas: the power of Christ's resurrection already transforms present experiences, and is thus the guarantee of our resurrection at the end of time.

Christ's resurrection, therefore, while experienced in the present, is the basis of our future hope. Christ's death has dealt with our sins. We can be confident that his resurrection guarantees our own. This argument is set out at length in 1 Cor 15. The statement that 'Christ died for our sins' (15:3) needs no further elaboration in this context (though the implications have been dealt with earlier in the epistle).[24] The conviction 'that he was raised on the third day' is the basis of believers' confidence that they, too, will be raised. The logic is set out in 15:20–22 and 15:42–49, and is similar to that in Rom 5:12–21: Christians are one with Christ in the same way that they are one with Adam, and they therefore share in what Christ is and does.

The argument based on Christ's resurrection is found already in 1 Thess. In 1:10, Paul reminds the Thessalonians that it is Jesus, who was raised from the dead, who will rescue them from the wrath to come. Later in the epistle he explains that, since 'Jesus died and rose again', they need have no anxiety for those who have died; the Lord will bring them with him at his coming, and then 'the dead in Christ' will rise (4:14, 16). Once again, our future resurrection is guaranteed by the fact that Christ has been raised from the dead. In 5:9–10 Paul then picks up the theme of wrath from 1:10:

God has not destined us for wrath, but to obtain salvation through our Lord Jesus Christ,
 who died for us,
 so that (whether we wake or sleep)
 we may live with him.

At first sight, Paul seems here to be using a very different argument – from Christ's *death* to our resurrection – and, by implication, a doctrine of substitution: Christ died so that we might live! A more careful reading shows that the very opposite is true, for though Christ's resurrection is not mentioned

---

[24] 'Christ died for our sins', but without the resurrection there is no release from the power of sin and death. So, if Christ was *not* raised, the Corinthians are still in their sins (15:17).

here it is clearly implied, since believers (whether at present dead or alive) will live *with him*. In other words, they will share his risen life. It is because God raised his Son from the dead (1:10) that Jesus is able to rescue us from coming wrath. The argument is similar to that in Rom 5:9–10: if Christ died 'for us', we can be sure that we will be 'saved from wrath' – 'saved by his life'.

4. Participation in Christ

It is precisely this 'with him', in this very early summary of faith, that provides the key to understanding Paul's theology. Christ's death was 'for us' – at one and the same time his own gracious self-giving and the gracious act of God himself. But if we ask 'how' his death and resurrection bring release from sin and death and lead to acquittal and life for believers, the answer is through union with Christ. The fact that Christ died *for our sins* was possible because he shared our humanity: he came 'in the likeness of sinful flesh' (Rom 8:3), was 'born of a woman' (Gal 4), was 'made sin' (2 Cor 5:21), 'became a curse' (Gal 3:13), took 'the form of a servant, being born in human likeness, and was found in the fashion of a man' (Phil 2:7). In other words, Christ has shared our life 'in Adam', the consequences of which were set out in Rom 5:12–21. But the statement that 'he was raised for our acquittal' requires *us* to share in what *he* is. Those who are baptized *into Christ* are baptized into his death (Rom 6:3), accepting God's judgement on sin; but that means they share Christ's resurrection and vindication, and though resurrection for them remains a future hope, they are able – in Christ – to share his present life and status. *In him*, they are 'righteousness' (2 Cor 5:21), and receive the blessing of the Spirit (Gal 3:14), who assures them that they are 'sons' of God (Gal 4:6–7; Rom 8:14–17) because, in Christ, they share his status, a status made plain by the resurrection (Rom 1:4). The righteousness that comes διὰ πίστεως Χριστοῦ is given to those who are 'in Christ' (Phil 3:9). His resurrection therefore involves *our* acquittal (Rom 4:25). If our interpretation of Rom 5:16 and 18 above is correct, then Paul spells out this idea there: just as the verdict pronounced on Adam is shared by those who are 'in Adam', so the verdict pronounced on Christ at the resurrection is shared by those who are 'in him'. It is because Christ is acknowledged as righteous that those who are 'in him' are also reckoned to be righteous – and *will* be reckoned to be such on the last day.

Rom 4:25 is often said to reflect the language of Isa 53, and this is certainly possible.[25] If so, it is interesting to compare another summary of faith which

---

[25] I discussed this briefly in Morna D. Hooker, 'Did the Use of Isaiah 53 to Interpret His Mission Begin with Jesus?', in *Jesus and the Suffering Servant: Isaiah 53 and Christian Origins,* eds.

is certainly influenced by that passage – 1 Pet 2:24. In many ways, this summary is closer to 1 Thess 5:14 than to Rom 4:25, for though Christ's death is linked with sins (very differently from Rom 4:25!), the *purpose* (introduced by a ἵνα clause) is said to be so that we might live. Here, however, it is a *present* living that is in mind, and the purpose is 'that we might live for righteousness'. 1 Peter reflects Pauline ideas – Christ dies for us, we live for righteousness – but without the crucial Pauline emphasis on participation. What is interesting about this passage is that the emphasis here also is on the fact that the life that follows Christ's death is characterized by δικαιοσύνη.

If commentators continue to describe the antithesis in Rom 4:25 as 'rhetorical', it is probably because they are anxious not to fall into the trap of separating Christ's resurrection from his death. Of course the two belong to one another, and it would be absurd to emphasize one over the other as 'salvific'. Ironically, however, that is precisely what has frequently been done in the course of Christian history; in much interpretation of the doctrine of the atonement, the cross has been central, the resurrection virtually ignored. Some writers have attempted to rectify this, reminding us of the importance of the resurrection for Paul's thought.[26] To uncover the logic in Paul's summary that links Christ's death with our sins and his resurrection with our acquittal is not to prise the two apart: rather it is to recognize that Rom 4:25 is a neat summary which fits in with Paul's understanding of Christ as the one who became what we are in order that – in him – we might become what he is. Perhaps this notion of 'interchange' explains *why* Paul there links our sins with Christ's death, his resurrection with our acquittal. By sharing our humanity, Christ came under the condemnation that led to death; now, by baptism into his death and resurrection, we are able to share his status of righteousness before God. Because he shared in the judgement on our sins, his death dealt with what we were in Adam; because he was raised from death, those who are in him share in his acquittal. For those who are in Christ, the reign of sin has been brought to an end with his death, and his resurrection has inaugurated the new life of righteousness.[27]

William H. Bellinger Jr. and William R. Farmer (Harrisburg, PA: Trinity Press International, 1998), 88–103 = above, essay 8 (pp. 115–127).

[26] E.g. S. Lyonnet, 'La valeur sotériologique de la résurrection du Christ selon saint Paul', *Gregorianum* 39 (1958): 295–318; D.M. Stanley, *Christ's Resurrection in Pauline Soteriology,* AnBib 13 (Rome: Biblical Institute Press, 1961). Brian McNeil, 'Raised for Our Justification', *ITQ* 42 (1975): 97–105, while emphasizing the importance of the resurrection, rightly insists that to see 'cross or resurrection' as alternatives is 'a false antithesis' (104).

[27] This essay explores further an idea that was set out in Morna D. Hooker, 'Interchange in Christ', *JTS* NS 22 (1971): 349–361. The term 'interchange' is also discussed there.

39. A Partner in the Gospel: Paul's Understanding of His Ministry

My original intention was to use as the title for this essay a phrase from 1 Cor 9:22 which is familiar to us all in the translation immortalized by the King James Version – 'All things to all men'. The phrase occurs in the passage in which St. Paul is discussing his ministry, and it is highly relevant to my theme, but clearly the sexist language of that version would not do. And it is in fact the translation which is at fault, not Paul, for in Greek his phrase is terse and impartial: τοῖς πᾶσιν γέγονα πάντα. The word 'man' simply does not occur! So I toyed with the possibility of using the non-sexist, but flabby translation in the NRSV – 'All things to all people' – but then I realized that there were other problems with the traditional rendering, in addition to the feminists' very proper objection to its masculine language. First, the phrase is meant to sum up the list of different categories of people whom Paul has been listing in the previous verses: Paul has put himself out, in different ways, for each individual group in turn, and this is simply not conveyed by the traditional translation, which suggests rather that Paul has become everything at once to everyone on earth. The REB attempts to catch the original meaning, but needs twice as many words as did Paul: 'To them all I have become everything in turn'. But none of these translations avoids the danger that the verse might be understood to be suggesting something almost dishonest in Paul's dealings with men and women, as though he were a kind of prototype of the Vicar of Bray, willing to adapt his principles according to circumstance: and whatever Paul is meaning in this passage, he is surely not suggesting, as Henry Chadwick once neatly put it, that he is 'a mere weathercock'.[1]

So what *is* the argument that Paul is attempting to sum up in this phrase? We need to begin at v. 19. The context is Paul's discussion of his rights and privileges as an apostle – rights and privileges which he has gladly foregone for the sake of winning men and women for the gospel. This chapter has sometimes been seen as a digression from the main argument in 1 Corinthians 8 and 10, which concerns the question of whether or not it is permissible to eat meat that has been offered to idols. But, of course, the argument is highly relevant to that topic, for in chapter 8 Paul has urged the Corinthians, too, to give up freedom for the sake of their fellow Christians. In support of his insistence that concern for one another is far more important than their

---
[1] Henry Chadwick, 'All Things to All Men', *NTS* 1 (1955): 261.

freedom to do what they believe to be permissible as Christians, he points to the way in which he has denied himself the reward due to an apostle. The behaviour he urges on them may prevent the downfall of a fellow Christian; the behaviour he himself has adopted has helped to *win* men and women for the gospel.

In 9:19 ff. he explains what this has meant. He has, he says, though free, enslaved himself in order to win others; to Jews, he became as a Jew, in order to win Jews; though he himself was not under the Law, he became as one who was under the Law for the sake of those who were under the Law, in order to win those who were under the Law, while to those outside the Law he became as though he were outside the Law, even though he was not himself outside the Law, in order to win those who were outside the Law; finally, to those who were weak he became weak, in order that he might win the weak. Five times over, then, Paul spells out the same theme: he became what others were, in order to win them for the gospel. Five times over, he uses the verb κερδαίνω [gain/win], introduced each time by the word ἵνα [in order that]. The first of his five points – that though he was in fact free, he made himself a slave to all – picks up the theme of the previous chapter, and may well have made his readers uncomfortable: some, at least, of the Corinthians have been glorying in their freedom; Paul gladly gives his freedom up for the sake of the gospel. The last point also – his willingness to share the weakness of the weak – echoes the theme of that section; it is the 'weak' in Corinth – that is to say, those who are hesitant about how to act in particular circumstances – who are afraid to eat idol meat, and who could be made to fall if those of their fellow Christians who are more confident and whose consciences are therefore more robust are not prepared to limit their freedom – to 'share', as it were, in the weakness of others. The second, third, and fourth statements are the most problematic, and therefore the most interesting. To Jews, says Paul, he became 'as a Jew', in order to win Jews. This time he cannot, of course, say that he became a Jew, because he was by birth a Jew; rather, he became 'as a Jew'. Perhaps because he realizes that his readers may be puzzled, he immediately explains what he means in another way: to become 'as a Jew' means that he put himself under the Law, even though he was not under the Law. Similarly, for Gentiles – for those outside the Law – he became as one outside the Law; but once again, he immediately qualifies his statement: though he put himself outside the Law, he was not outside the Law of God, for he was under the law of Christ. But whatever qualifications Paul needs to add, the point he is making is clear: as far as possible he has deliberately identified himself with those whom he has sought to win for the gospel.

So when Paul says, in v. 22, that he has become all things to them all, he is summing up his missionary endeavours. He has done it all in order – once again he uses the word ἵνα – to save some of them. The form of the statement is parallel to the previous five, except that the verb σώζω [save] replaces κερδαίνω [gain]. Then, in v. 23, he repeats this statement and defines it: 'I do it all', he says, 'for the sake of the gospel, in order that I may be a participant in it' – ἵνα συγκοινωνὸς αὐτοῦ γένωμαι. What does Paul mean by describing himself as a συγκοινωνός in the gospel? The literal meaning of the word is 'participant' or 'partner'.[2] Almost all the commentators believe that it means one who participates in the *benefits* of the gospel, and the majority of the translators agree.[3] They understand Paul to be saying: 'I do it all for the sake of the gospel, so that I may share in its blessings'. But is this the most likely interpretation? Has Paul undertaken all his missionary endeavours merely so that he himself may share in the benefits of the gospel? Is it not strange that the climax of the argument should prove to be a statement that what seemed like selfless activity undertaken to win men and women for the gospel should have as its ultimate aim his own personal salvation?

No doubt there were some evangelists, then as now, who preached a message which concentrated on the personal benefits which come to those who accept the gospel, but Paul himself has scathing things to say about this perversion of the gospel – not least in 1 Corinthians! If we understand συγκοινωνός in this way, as one who participates in the benefits of the gospel, then we must certainly stress the force of the συν-. Paul does not say simply that his aim is to be a κοινωνὸς τοῦ εὐαγγελίου [participant in the gospel] but a συγκοινωνὸς τοῦ εὐαγγελίου [fellow participant in the gospel], which suggests that his purpose is that others should join him in these benefits.[4] In this case, we should understand Paul to be saying, not 'I do all this for the sake of the gospel, so that I may share its benefits', but 'I do all this for the sake of the gospel, so that *others* may share in its benefits *with me*'. This emphasis is not normally brought out in either the translations or the commentaries however: rather, Paul is assumed to be referring primarily to his own salvation.[5]

The word συγκοινωνός can be understood in a passive sense, therefore, provided that the phrase is emphasized in this way. But are the commentators right in understanding the word to mean a passive participant? I have suggested already that Paul's accounts of his mission in vv. 22b and 23 belong together. Is it not far more logical to suggest that coming as it does at the climax of the argument of vv. 19–23, this twin statement of Paul's intentions

---

[2] For the adjective, LSJ gives the meaning 'partaking jointly of'; for the noun, 'partner'.

[3] But see R.St. John Parry, *The First Epistle of Paul the Apostle to the Corinthians* (Cambridge: Cambridge University Press, 1916), 143; NEB: 'All this I do for the sake of the gospel, to bear my part in proclaiming it'.

[4] Cf. the other occurrences of συγκοινωνός in the New Testament: Rom 11:17; Phil 1:7; Rev 1:9.

[5] Thus C.K. Barrett, *A Commentary on the First Epistle to the Corinthians,* BNTC (London: A&C Black, 1968), 216 translates: 'that I too may have my share in it'.

means that in becoming 'all things to all people', he is sharing in the gospel, not simply passively but actively also? The fact that the structure of vv. 22 and 23 is parallel to the structure of the previous five statements suggests that the meaning, also, is parallel: Paul has become all things to all people *in order to* save some; he has done it all for the sake of the gospel, *in order to* be a sharer in the gospel – and logic suggests that this means sharing in its work of salvation. Why is it, then, that neither the commentators nor the translators agree with me on this point? Why is it that they understand Paul to be introducing a new idea here, describing himself as receiving a share in the *benefits* of the gospel?

First, it has to be acknowledged that the overall theme of 1 Corinthians 9 is that of reward. In pointing to himself as an example of one who has deliberately limited his freedom and refused to demand his 'rights' for the sake of the gospel, Paul stresses the rewards that are his due as an apostle. Might we not expect him to continue this theme in v. 23? But the whole point of Paul's argument is that he has *refused* to accept any reward – save that of preaching the gospel without charge (vv. 12, 15–18). The last thing we expect to be told, therefore, is that the reward he is aiming for is his own salvation. Rather, we would expect him to insist once again that his only 'reward' is to preach the word, and to win men and women for the gospel.

Secondly, immediately after this verse, in vv. 24–27, Paul goes on to speak of the reward that comes to those who compete in the games, and says that he disciplines his own body lest, after preaching to others, he is himself rejected. Here we certainly have the idea of Paul himself hoping to share in the benefits of the gospel. Does v. 23b, then, look forward to this idea? We suggest not: firstly, because the idea that Paul's *aim* in preaching was to secure his own salvation is far removed from the *hope* he expresses in v. 27; secondly, because vv. 24–27 introduce a new argument, backed up by a new metaphor, as to why the Corinthians should discipline themselves. The reference to Paul having preached to others is incidental to the main argument, though understandable in view of the theme of the chapter.

Thirdly, there is the question of the precise meaning of the phrase ἵνα συγκοινωνὸς αὐτοῦ γένωμαι. The word συγκοινωνός, as we have seen, means 'partner', a term which implies both giving and receiving: a partner in a firm is obliged to contribute something in terms of finance and labour, but can expect to share in the firm's profits.[6] The word here could thus refer either to participation in the *benefits* of the gospel, or to sharing in the *work* of the gospel, which seems highly appropriate in the present context. This second interpretation is generally ruled out as impossible.[7] Nevertheless, the active

---

[6] The word κοινωνός is used in that sense in Luke 5:10.

[7] C.K. Barrett, *First Corinthians,* 216, who comments simply that this is not what Paul means. Cf. W.G. Kümmel, who states that 'Die Übersetzung, "Mitarbeiter am Evangelium" ist unmöglich; συγκοινωνός heisst niemals "aktiver Teilnehmer" [the translation, "co-worker

sense is a possible one for συγκοινωνός, and it makes good sense to understand it here as 'one who participates in the work of the gospel'.[8] The word αὐτοῦ [in/of it] refers to εὐαγγέλιον, a term which normally refers to the *content* of the gospel; but although it is frequently used with a verb to denote the preaching of the gospel, it is sometimes used *without* a verb to refer to the proclamation of the gospel.[9] In the present passage, Paul is very much concerned with his own proclamation of the gospel. He says that he is anxious that no obstacle should obstruct [the spread of] the gospel of Christ (v. 12); he reminds the Corinthians of the Lord's instruction that those who preach the gospel should live by the gospel [i.e., be paid for preaching it] (v. 14); and he says that his aim is that in preaching the gospel he should do so without charge, in order not to make full use of his authority in the gospel [i.e., as a preacher of it] (v. 18). The meaning that we are suggesting for v. 23 understands εὐαγγέλιον in the same sense. The phrase could thus signify that Paul sees himself as a partner with others in the work of preaching the gospel – in which case he is presumably referring to the group alluded to in v. 1 of this chapter of those people who also claim to be apostles and to have seen the Lord. As so often, Paul is on the defensive about his apostleship throughout this section, and it would not be surprising if he here claims that his labours for the salvation of the Gentiles are the proof that he is a 'partner in the gospel' in the sense that he, too, shares in the work of proclaiming it.

Yet Paul's understanding of what apostleship involves clearly differs from that of some of these other apostles: is he here perhaps going beyond the mere claim that, like them, he shares in the proclamation of the gospel? If he has refused to claim his 'rights', this is because he is determined to put no obstacle in the way of the gospel (v. 12): in other words, his behaviour is governed by the gospel itself. There is, in fact, yet a third possible way of understanding the phrase συγκοινωνὸς τοῦ εὐαγγελίου which underlines this point, and this is to take it as meaning that Paul is a partner of the gospel in the sense that he and the gospel are 'partners' in a common enterprise.[10] In other words, he is a συγκοινωνός

---

in the gospel" is impossible; συγκοινωνός never means "active participant"]' (Hans Lietzmann, *An die Korinther I–II*, 5th ed., rev. W.G. Kümmel, HNT 9 [Tübingen: Mohr, 1969], 180). For the active sense, however, we need only turn to Rev 1:9, where John describes himself as the συγκοινωνός of his readers in tribulation and sovereignty and endurance.

[8] Cf. the reference to Titus as κοινωνός ἐμὸς in 2 Cor 8:23; also to the κοινωνία of the Philippians εἰς τὸ εὐαγγέλιον in Phil 1:5.

[9] Cf. Rom 1:1, 9; 2 Cor 2:12; 10:14; Gal 2:7; Phil 2:22; 4:15. I am grateful to Mr. G.M. Styler for pointing out the relevance of this in relation to 1 Cor 9:23.

[10] The idea is not entirely without parallel in Paul, though elsewhere he speaks of his cooperation with God. Cf. 1 Cor 3:9, where θεοῦ γάρ ἐσμεν συνεργοί may mean 'we are fellow workers with God', and 1 Thess 3:2, where Timothy is described as τὸν ἀδελφὸν ἡμῶν καὶ συνεργὸν τοῦ θεοῦ, a phrase which is normally interpreted as meaning 'our brother and God's fellow worker'. C.K. Barrett, *First Corinthians*, 216, argues that in 1 Cor 9:23 this sense would require a dative, but if the word is treated as a noun rather than a participle, a genitive is the

with the gospel itself (which is in effect personified), working with a common purpose.¹¹ Paul does more than proclaim the gospel: his involvement with it is such that he is in a sense identified with it. This idea comes out clearly in many of his letters: he has been crucified with Christ,¹² and carries round in his body the death that Jesus died.¹³ If this is what he means here, then he is saying that his task as a partner in this enterprise is to share in the work of the gospel by bringing men and women to salvation. This would in effect sum up all that he has been saying in the previous verses; if this is correct, then Paul is claiming that by his manner of life in identifying with others he in fact proclaims the gospel, and thus wins men and women for Christ.

If the idea that Paul may be a 'partner *with* the gospel' is a startling one, this is perhaps because it is at odds with the Lutheran insistence that Paul saw himself simply as the passive recipient of God's grace, doing nothing: how can Paul *share* in the work of salvation? In fact, however, Paul has already described himself, in v. 22b, as saving others. It is not this that makes this particular interpretation difficult, but rather the need to personify the gospel, which has no parallel in Paul. Yet he comes close to doing so elsewhere: he describes it in Rom 1:16 as 'the power of God which brings salvation',¹⁴ and like the word of God in the Old Testament, the gospel brings life and death.¹⁵ Paul can speak of 'preaching the gospel' or of 'preaching Christ crucified',¹⁶ and the latter, like the former, is 'the power of God'.¹⁷ He tells the Corinthians that he begat them διὰ τοῦ εὐαγγελίου [through the gospel],¹⁸ and describes himself as a διάκονος [servant] of the gospel¹⁹ and as being engaged in the priestly service of the gospel.²⁰ It is possible, then, that in describing himself as a συγκοινωνός τοῦ εὐαγγελίου, Paul is claiming to be a partner *with* the gospel, sharing in the work of the gospel itself.

Whichever of these interpretations of the phrase may be the correct one, it seems highly likely that when Paul applies the word συγκοινωνός to himself,

---

only case possible. In two of the three other occurrences of συγκοινωνός in the New Testament the genitive is used of the person with whom one is a partner or fellow participant. See Phil 1:7 and Rev 1:9. Cf. 2 Cor 8:23. In 1 Corinthians 10 the phrase κοινωνοὶ τοῦ θυσιαστηρίου used in v. 18 with the sense 'partners *in* the altar', followed in v. 20 by the phrase κοινωνοὺς τῶν δαιμονίων with the sense 'partners *with* demons'.

¹¹ So Einar Molland, *Das Paulinische Euangelion: Das Wort und die Sache* (Oslo: Jacob Dybwad, 1934), 53 ff.
¹² Gal 2:20.
¹³ 2 Cor 4:10.
¹⁴ Cf. 1 Cor 15:1 ff.
¹⁵ 1 Cor 1:23 ff.; 2 Cor 2:15 ff.
¹⁶ 1 Cor 1:17, 23; Gal 1:6–9 and 3:1 ff.
¹⁷ 1 Cor 1:24.
¹⁸ 1 Cor 4:15.
¹⁹ Col 1:23; cf. Eph 3:7.
²⁰ Rom 15:16.

he does so because he sees his role not simply as that of a passive participant in the gospel, but as an active partner. The gospel of course brings benefits, which Paul expects to receive, but it must also be shared with others, and the receiving and the sharing cannot be separated; the term συγκοινωνός having an active as well as a passive meaning, describes both aspects admirably. Far from being a selfish statement that the ultimate motive he has for working as an evangelist is in order to have his share in the benefits of the gospel, he is surely saying here that the only way to receive those benefits is to share in *ministry* — to be a *partner* in the gospel in every sense of the term.

There is, I suggest, interesting support for this interpretation in the remarkable parallel between the statements concerning Paul's ministry which we have just been analysing and those summaries of the gospel which Paul uses from time to time which are sometimes described as expressing a notion of interchange. Now the term 'interchange' is not an ideal one, though I confess to having used it myself, for want of a better word, more than most: 'interchange' suggests a total reversal of roles, a substitution of the kind that takes place in *A Tale of Two Cities,* when Sydney Carton takes Charles Darnay's place on the scaffold. In fact, what Paul describes is the self-identification of Christ with men and women which, in turn, results in their sharing in what he is. In becoming what men and women are, Christ does not cease to be what he eternally is. Irenaeus expressed this idea tersely and admirably when he said that Christ became what we are, in order that we might become what he is.[21] The passages in Paul where this idea is most clearly spelt out are as follows:

2 Cor 5:21: God made Christ sin for our sake, though he knew no sin, in order that we might become the righteousness of God in him.
2 Cor 8:9: Christ became poor for our sake, though he was rich, in order that we might become rich through his poverty.
Gal 3:13: Christ redeemed us from the curse of the Law, having become a curse for us, in order that the blessing of Abraham might come upon the Gentiles, in order that we might receive the Spirit.
Gal 4:4–5: God sent his Son, born of a woman, born under the Law, in order that he might redeem those who were under the Law, in order that we might receive adoption as sons.

Similar ideas are expressed elsewhere:

Rom 8:3–4: God sent his own Son in the likeness of sinful flesh and ... condemned sin in the flesh, in order that the righteous command of the Law might be fulfilled in us.
Phil 2:6–8: Christ, being in the form of God, emptied himself, taking the form of a slave; and humbling himself, he became obedient to a slave's death on a cross. (The result is spelt out at the end of chapter 3, where Christians are transformed into the likeness of Christ's glorious body.)

---

[21] Irenaeus, *Adv. Haer.* 5 *praef.*

The common structure of these passages is as follows:

First, Christ became something (or God made him to be something); in other words, Christ accepted a state of existence which was not normal to him. He became poor, became sin, was born as a man, under the Law, came under a curse; he came in the likeness of sinful flesh, took the form of a slave. The fact that he was accepting a condition that was foreign to him is reflected in the way in which Paul often hedges his statements around with apologetic explanations. He became poor – though of course he was rich; he became sin – though of course he knew no sin; he came *in the likeness of* sinful flesh; he took the *form* of a slave: we should not misunderstand μορφή in this last statement as though it referred to something unreal; the phrase may perhaps be best interpreted as indicating status: in other words, Christ accepted the status of a slave. Only in Galatians, where Paul tends to be blunt in everything he says, does he fail to put things delicately: Christ was born of a woman (nothing docetic about that!), he was born under the Law, and he became a curse – and what endless problems that last, stark statement has caused for commentators who wanted to escape from its blunt reality! In all these statements, whether the idea is expressed bluntly or more carefully, Christ is identified with the condition of men and women.

Secondly, the purpose of this identification, introduced in every case (except in Philippians) by the word ἵνα [so that], is that men and women might share in what Christ is: might share, not in what he became in being identified with us, but in what he essentially was and is. Through the redemptive kenosis of Christ they share what he was willing to abandon; he was rich, and they too become rich; he knew no sin, and they become the righteousness of God in him; the Son of God abandoned the privileges of sonship when he came under the curse of the Law, but those who are redeemed from the curse of the Law receive a blessing instead of a curse, and have become the children of God. When he came in the likeness of sinful flesh, Christ destroyed sin in the flesh, and so allowed the righteous command of God to be fulfilled in men and women, just as it was in himself. And because the one who was in the form of God took the form of men and women, their bodies of humiliation will be conformed to his body of glory.

We begin to understand now how this 'interchange' works: it is not that Christ changes place with men and women. Though he identifies with them, he remains what he is – without sin, Son of God, in the form of God. And when they become what he is, it is because they are now identified with him – or, to use the crucial Pauline expression, because they are 'in Christ'.

Let us return to those seven parallel statements about Paul's ministry in 1 Corinthians 9. Straight away, we see that there is an obvious parallel between them and our 'interchange' formulae. Christ became what we are, he was made what we are, he was sent into our condition, *in order that* we might become what he is. Paul, in turn, became what the men and women to whom he was proclaiming the gospel were, in order that he might gain them for the gospel. And just as some of the statements about what Christ became needed modification – he became sin, *though he knew no sin,* and he came *in the likeness of* sinful flesh, where the word 'likeness' prevents us thinking of him as sinful – so, too, in the case of Paul. He came under the Law, *even though he was not under the Law*; he became as one without Law, *even though he was not without God's Law.* Only the last part of the statements is different: in those about Christ, Paul spells out the interchange: we become rich, we become children of God, and so on. But in the statements in 1 Corinthians about his own ministry, his aim – in six of the seven – is said to be that he may gain – or save – the men and women to whom he preaches. And in the seventh, it is that he may be a partner in the gospel.

Commentators are often puzzled by the paradoxical nature of these statements: how can Paul be under the Law, even though he was not under the Law, and be as one without Law, even though he was not without God's Law? Perhaps the realization that he sees himself, in Christ, as sharing in some sense in the paradox of the incarnation may provide us with the clue. What I am suggesting is that the summary of events which lies at the heart of Paul's kerygma is seen by him as the pattern for his own ministry. The apostle, sent by his Lord, acts as his representative. He proclaims the gospel, not simply in word, but in action. He is conformed to the pattern of Christ's own kenosis. Far from being a simple recipient of the benefits of the gospel, he is a partner in it. We should not be surprised to find Paul seeing his ministry in this light, for after all, there is a sense in which he sees the whole of Christian existence in these terms. In earlier studies, I have sought to show how, paradoxically, the Christian shares the kenosis of Christ in order to share the benefits which that kenosis brought about.[22] Christ shared our condition in order that we might share his, yet we need, in turn, to share his humiliation and suffering. He shared our death, in order that we might share his life, yet in order to share his life, we need to share his death. The Christian is summoned to die with Christ, to suffer with Christ, to become like him in his obedience and self-emptying. Christian atonement is never a simple matter of substitution, and neither is Christian living. It is hardly surprising, then, if Christian ministry is seen as a sharing in the pattern provided by Christ.

But if Christ is a pattern, then there is a sense in which Christians are called to imitate him. Now it is my conviction that the notion of imitation is much more significant in Pauline thought than has often been allowed. Commentators have sometimes tended to shy away from it, partly perhaps

---

[22] See Morna D. Hooker, *From Adam to Christ: Essays on Paul* (Cambridge: Cambridge University Press, 1990), 1–69, 88–100.

because, like Luther, they have felt that the idea of imitating Christ suggests human endeavour, and so conflicts with the belief that the Christian depends for salvation on the grace of God alone and can do nothing on his or her own; and partly perhaps because they have thought that in 2 Cor 5:16 Paul denies any earthly knowledge of the earthly Jesus.[23] But the theme of imitation is found relatively frequently in Paul.[24] More often than not, of course, Paul points to *himself* as the pattern for others to follow. When he urges his converts to imitate him, as he does in 1 Cor 4:16 and Phil 4:9,[25] we may well conclude that he is being immodest, but at least it does not offend Protestant theological principles. But why does he set himself up as a pattern for other believers to imitate? The answer is set out most clearly in 1 Cor 11:1, where Paul urges the Corinthians to become imitators of him, *even as he is an imitator of Christ*. This is a particularly interesting passage, and we shall come back to it in a moment. Meanwhile, we note that in Phil 3:17, Paul urges the Philippians to become fellow imitators, but this time his meaning is ambiguous, for the word he uses is συμμιμηταί, and if, as is most natural, the μου which follows is a subjective genitive, then he must mean that they are to become fellow imitators *with* him; he is suggesting, that is, that they should imitate Christ together.[26] Once again, however, I find that I am out of step with the commentators and the translators in taking the passage this way, since they almost all understand Paul to mean here that it is the Philippians who are to join together in imitating *him*: in other words, they are to be fellow imitators with one another. And I have to admit that Paul *does* appeal to himself as an example in the last four words of the verse, where he says 'even as you have

---

[23] The article contributed by W. Michaelis to *TWNT* has been extremely influential, especially in Germany. Cf. *TDNT* 4/672 ff.: 'When Paul calls himself a μιμητὴς Χριστοῦ, or when he tells the Thessalonians they must show themselves to be μιμηταὶ τοῦ κυρίου, the point is that both he and they are followers of their heavenly Lord. There is thus no thought of an imitation, whether outward or inward, of the earthly life of Jesus in either individual features or total impress. The call for an *imitatio Christi* finds no support in the statements of Paul.... Paul does not speak of true imitation of Christ or God. His reference is simply to obedient following as an expression of fellowship of life and will'. Cf. Hans Dieter Betz, *Nachfolge und Nachahmung Jesu Christi im Neuen Testament*, BHT 37 (Tübingen: Mohr Siebeck, 1967), 137–189; Eduard Lohse, *RGG* 4, 3rd ed. (1960) col. 1287 ff.

[24] See the discussions in E.J. Tinsley, *The Imitation of God in Christ* (London: SCM Press, 1960), 134–165; Edvin Larsson, *Christus als Vorbild* (Uppsala: Almquist & Wiksells, 1962), 232–270; Victor Paul Furnish, *Theology and Ethics in Paul* (Nashville; New York: Abingdon, 1968), 218–224; D.M. Stanley, '"Become Imitators of Me": The Pauline Conception of Apostolic Tradition', *Biblica* 40 (1959): 859–877, and 'Imitation in Paul's Letters: Its Significance for His Relationship to Jesus and to His Own Christian Foundations', in *From Jesus to Paul: Studies in Honour of Francis Wright Beare,* eds. Peter Richardson and John C. Hurd (Waterloo, ON: Wilfrid Laurier University Press, 1984), 127–141; Larry W. Hurtado, 'Jesus as Lordly Example in Philippians 2:5–11', in *From Jesus to Paul*, 113–126.

[25] Cf. also 2 Thess 3:7, 9.

[26] See the references in my *From Adam to Christ*, 177.

us as a model'. But perhaps Paul was not merely repeating himself here: he was a model for the Philippians; but the context makes clear that *his* model was Christ; is it not logical, then, that he should appeal to them to be fellow imitators of Christ with him?

Even if I am wrong about this passage, however, we find when we turn to 1 Thess 1:6–7 that Paul says quite clearly that the Thessalonians have become imitators both of himself *and of the Lord,* and that in so doing they have, in turn, become the pattern for other believers to imitate. The context makes clear that this 'imitation' involved suffering, which suggests that in this respect, at least, it is not something which is undertaken deliberately. A somewhat similar statement is made in 1 Thess 2:14, where Paul comments that the Thessalonians 'became imitators of the churches of God in Judaea which are in Christ Jesus' – not, to be sure, deliberately – but because they suffered the same things from their countrymen as did the Jews from theirs, who also killed the Lord Jesus and the prophets. Here again, Paul reminds the Thessalonians that they are sharing the same fate as the Lord himself. And that, of course, is a theme which Paul elaborates in terms of his own ministry in 2 Corinthians, where he speaks of carrying about in his body the dying of the Lord Jesus. But though in 1 Thessalonians he uses the language of 'imitation', the idea that Christians suffer in the same way that their Lord suffered is similar to that which Paul elsewhere expresses in terms of 'being conformed' to Christ's sufferings.

These passages in 1 Thessalonians describe an imitation of Christ which has been forced on believers by circumstance. Elsewhere, it is something to be deliberately pursued. Meanwhile, we note that there are several other passages where Paul recalls the saving activity of Christ, and urges his readers to take it as a pattern to be copied. In Rom 15:1–3, he argues that 'we who are strong ought to bear with the failings of the weak, and not to please ourselves; let each of us please our neighbour, in order to build up the community ... even as Christ did not please himself'. The advice is repeated in v. 7: 'Accept one another, as Christ accepted us'. Again, in 2 Corinthians 8, where Paul is appealing to the Corinthians to contribute to his collection for the saints in Jerusalem, he reminds them of the grace of the Lord Jesus: 'though he was rich, yet he became poor for your sake, in order that you, through his poverty, might become rich'. This is a passage we have looked at already; but notice how it continues. They, in their turn, must show the same kind of generosity – in other words, they are to follow Christ's example. In chapter 10, at the very point where Paul suddenly becomes very cross with the Corinthians, he appeals to them 'by the gentleness and magnanimity of Christ' – and goes on to argue that it is this same gentleness and magnanimity which have governed his own behaviour in dealing with them: he has followed the example of Christ.

The best-known example, however, is to be found in the introduction to the so-called 'hymn' in Philippians 2, where Paul's readers are urged to 'have the mind of Christ Jesus'. Now in fact, ever since Käsemann's influential study of this passage, the relevance of this exhortation to our theme is often denied. Käsemann argued that Paul's appeal was not to the example of the earthly Jesus, but to the events of the saving kerygma,[27] and many commentators have followed him.[28] Käsemann is certainly right to insist that the Pauline ethic does not consist *simply* in an exhortation to be like Jesus; rather it depends on the saving events of the gospel, and on the fact that the believer now lives in Christ. But the antithesis he draws between these two ideas is unnecessarily sharp: it is not a case of either/or but of both/and. This passage is one of the most difficult in the Pauline epistles, but certainly we may say that Paul sees *some* connection between Christ's self-emptying and self-humiliation and the behaviour which he thinks proper in the Christian community: the behaviour of those who are in Christ must conform to his.[29] And it is not just the self-emptying of the heavenly Christ which is to be our pattern, but the obedience of the earthly Jesus, which led him to death on a cross.

It is perhaps worth mentioning that appeals to emulate the love of Christ are found in Eph 5:2, 25, and that the first of these is linked with an appeal to imitate God himself (5:1). And before we dismiss these passages as simply post-Pauline, we should note the same idea in Rom 14:1–3, which introduces the argument about the necessity for the strong in the congregation to care for the weak: if the strong are to accept the weak, that is because God himself has already received them.

It is surely no accident that when we examine the context of all these passages, we find that this is concerned with the behaviour which is expected among Christians, and in particular with the way in which they deal with one another. It is in their lifestyle that Christians are to be imitators of Christ; moreover, in imitating him they benefit one another. Just as Christ's actions brought benefit to Christians, so the actions of his followers bring help to their fellow Christians.

We should not be surprised, then, to find that Paul applies this idea of *imitatio Christi* to his own ministry – or to discover that it is the pattern of kenosis which he sees as the model to which he should be conformed. But does he in fact link those statements in 1 Corinthians 9 (about becoming what

---

[27] Ernst Käsemann, 'Kritische Analyse von Phil 2:5–11', *ZTK* 47 (1950): 313–360; ET: 'A Critical Analysis of Philippians 2:5–11', trans. A. F. Carse, *JTC* 5 (1968): 45–88.

[28] Among these are Francis Wright Beare, *A Commentary on the Epistle to the Philippians*, BNTC (London: A&C Black, 1959), 73–78; Ralph P. Martin, *Carmen Christi: Philippians ii.5–11 in Recent Interpretation and in the Setting of Early Christian Worship* (Cambridge: Cambridge University Press, 1967) and *Philippians*, NCB (London: Oliphants, 1976).

[29] See, Hooker, *From Adam to Christ*, 88–100.

others are in order to win them for the gospel) with the example of Christ? He does.

If we turn to the end of chapter 10 we find the idea repeated, in v. 33, in language which echoes 1 Cor 9:22; this time, Paul says that he tries to please everyone in every matter (πάντα πᾶσι), seeking their advantage rather than his own, and that he does it in order to *save* them. The interesting thing about this passage is that it is followed immediately, in 1 Cor 11:1, by the appeal we noted earlier – an appeal to the Corinthians to imitate him, *as he imitates Christ*. The language, moreover, about 'pleasing others', echoes what he says about Christ in a similar context in Romans 15. Here is clear evidence that Paul modelled his own ministry on that of Christ; in becoming 'all things to all people', he was consciously conforming to the example of Christ. And indeed the link is made once again in Romans 15, for there Paul uses this appeal to Christ's example to back up a statement that those who are strong ought to bear with the failings of the weak, and not to please themselves (Rom 15:1); in the context, the meaning of this is clear. Those who are strong in faith (and Paul associates himself with them) must be prepared to identify with the weakness of those whose faith is weak. The strong must be as though weak, for the sake of the weak. Why? The reason is spelt out in the preceding chapter: 'don't let what you eat destroy the fellow Christian for whom Christ died ... it is not right to eat meat or drink wine or to do anything that makes a fellow Christian stumble' (Rom 14:15, 21). Notice that the motive expressed positively in 1 Corinthians 9 – the desire to save others – is here expressed in negative terms. Notice, too, that this ministry of self-identification with others is not something which stops at Paul, but is extended to the members of his congregation: they, too, are to become as others are, in other that others may be saved. And when we turn back to 1 Corinthians, we find that in chapter 8, Paul urges the Corinthians, in effect, to share the weakness of the weak. Why should they do so? Because if they do not, their behaviour may destroy their fellow Christians, for whom Christ died: once again, it is something Paul himself is prepared to do: 'if food causes my brother's downfall, I will abstain from meat for evermore, lest I cause him to stumble' (8:13).

Now both 1 Corinthians 8–10 and Romans 14–15 are about the problems of what may be eaten and drunk. But this is not the only context in which Paul uses this idea that he, like Christ, identifies himself with those whom he hopes to save for the gospel. The fact that in 1 Corinthians 9 he spoke of coming 'under the Law' or being 'outside the Law' for the sake of others might perhaps reflect the fact that questions about clean and unclean food were at stake, but it could suggest that wider issues are involved. So let us turn to Galatians, where Paul grapples with the problem of the Law. In 4:12, we find him appealing to the Galatians to become as he is, because he has become *as they are*: here is a fascinating echo of the interchange formulae. Its meaning is that Paul has become 'without the Law' for the sake of his Gentile converts, and it follows very quickly after the statement that Christ himself came *under the Law* in order to set free those under the Law. At first sight, Paul seems to be doing something diametrically opposite: Christ came under the Law for the sake of others; moreover, he came under the curse of the Law. But Paul puts himself *outside* the Law! That means, of course, that he too comes under its curse. What is important, however, is that in preaching the gospel, *Paul shares the condition of those to whom he ministers,* and so is conformed to the pattern of his Lord.

There are other passages, too, in which Paul appears to be claiming that his ministry is modelled on that of Christ. Let us look again at Philippians, where Paul spells out in chapter 2 the self-emptying of Christ, and then describes in the following chapter how he himself has abandoned everything he prized for the sake of Christ. Here he spells out the benefits of the gospel which he enjoys – the surpassing worth of knowing Jesus Christ his Lord, and the hope of resurrection. But it is not his own salvation alone that is his concern, for in the service of that gospel, he has learned (as did Christ), how to be abased and how to abound (4:12): we are perhaps not surprised to find that Paul's somewhat extravagant language here echoes the verb used of Christ's self-humiliation in 2:8.[30] The gospel is not merely something to which he has responded and whose benefits he enjoys; it has stamped its pattern on his whole life: he shares in the self-emptying of Christ.

Or take 2 Cor 6:10, where he describes himself as poor, yet making many rich. Here is a clear 'echo' of what he will go on to say about Christ himself in 8:9. This verse is part of the many in 2 Corinthians where Paul speaks of his ministry in terms of sharing in the sufferings of Christ for the sake of others. He carries around in the body the dying of the Lord Jesus, and he is always being given up to death for Jesus' sake; but what is the end result? 'Death is at work in us, but life in you' (2 Cor 4:10–11). The theme is spelt out in the opening chapter of the epistle: Paul shares abundantly, he says, in the sufferings of Christ, and through Christ shares abundantly in comfort too; but, he goes on, 'if we are afflicted, it is for your comfort and salvation, and if we are comforted, it is for your comfort'. Like Christ himself, Paul knows both suffering and comfort; and his experience is used by God for the comfort and salvation of others. As Victor Furnish admirably expressed it: 'Paul's suffering and serving as an apostle are to be regarded as a sort of "parable" of Christ's own saving death and resurrection'.[31]

But the most remarkable passage of all is Col 1:24, where Paul (if it is Paul) speaks of his sufferings on behalf of the Colossians (ὑπὲρ ὑμῶν), and says that

---

[30] ἐταπείνωσεν – ταπεινοῦθαι
[31] Furnish, *Theology and Ethics in Paul,* 222 ff.

these sufferings fill up what is lacking of the afflictions of Christ in his flesh. We can be sure that Paul does not mean that the sufferings of Christ himself were in any sense inadequate. Yet he understands himself to be called to share the sufferings of Christ – and it is for the sake of his body, the church. *Because they are Christ's sufferings,* they can bring benefit to others.[32]

Now one of the reasons why expositors have often been so wary of the notion of imitation is clearly the suspicion that it could be thought to undermine the uniqueness of God's saving action in Christ. If grace stands over against human endeavour, how can we 'imitate' the work of Christ? If salvation is through Christ alone, how can the sufferings of others be in any sense redemptive? The answer, of course, is that if imitation is attempted at an external level, like the imitation of the latest fashion in hairstyles or pop music, one cannot: this is indeed a version of the belief that one can save oneself by works. But the imitation Paul is describing depends on the fact that the believer is in Christ. He is thinking, that is, not of counterfeit copies, pirated without permission, but of authentic replicas which bear the stamp of the original. Perhaps, rather than talking about imitation, we should speak of Christians being conformed to the pattern of Christ – language with which Paul is certainly equally at home. To suppose that what we term 'imitation' is impossible is to ignore Paul's fundamental belief in the believer's participation in Christ. For the imitation of Christ depends on union with him, and takes place within that union: it is thus a question of believers being conformed to his image, not of copying an external pattern: what Paul desires for his converts above all else is that 'Christ be formed in them' (Gal 4:19). But if Christ is truly formed in the Christian community, does this not mean that its members will share in *his* redeeming work?

Whatever we may wish to say about Christ's death as a unique saving act is not diminished by the recognition that what he does *for* us has to be worked out *in* us. Christ's uniqueness as the one on whom salvation depends is in no sense affected, for whatever men and women are enabled to do derives from him. It is an old heresy – and one with which Paul was all too familiar – to imagine that the doctrine of salvation by grace meant that one was now free to live as one liked; to suppose that because Christ had reconciled men and women to God through his death, the Christian life meant living like

---

[32] Cf. W. F. Flemington, 'On the Interpretation of Colossians 1:24', in *Suffering and Martyrdom in the New Testament: Studies presented to G. M. Styler by the Cambridge New Testament Seminar,* eds. William Horbury and Brian McNeil (Cambridge: Cambridge University Press, 1981), 84–90. See p. 89: '... the Cross is representative and capable of being reflected and mirrored in the life of Christians. The love of God in Christ that there embraced sacrificial suffering is the pattern for the Christian. By incorporation "in Christ" he must continually seek more and more completely to reproduce it in his own life, and St. Paul believes that this can bring benefit to the Body of Christ'. Cf. also those passages where Paul describes himself or others as suffering ὑπὲρ Χριστοῦ [for the sake of Christ]: 2 Cor 12:10; Phil 1:29.

kings; that particular version of the heresy can unfortunately still be heard on certain American television stations. In contrast, Paul insists that Christians were set free (from sin and the flesh) to live 'in Christ', which certainly involves being like him; he insists, too, that being a follower of Christ means sharing in his sufferings; and dares to suggest that, precisely because they are Christ's sufferings, they can bring life and comfort to others. But whatever men and women are enabled to do as channels of salvation derives from him. The 'interchange' works only for those who are in Christ, as we can see in a remarkable passage where Paul expresses a wish to be identified with others, but cannot be. The passage in question is Rom 9:3, where Paul declares that he could wish to be *anathema,* cut off from Christ, for the sake of his fellow Jews. Commentators recognize an echo of Moses' prayer in Exod 32:32. But notice also an echo of the interchange formulae: Paul is willing to become anathema for the Jews – ὑπὲρ [τουτῶν], 'for their sake' – just as Christ became a curse for our sake. But this particular longing necessarily remains unfulfilled, for at this point he cannot imitate his Lord. By becoming a curse, Christ was able to bring blessing to others; by being made sin, he was able to become the source of righteousness. But *it is only those who are in Christ* who are able to share in what he is and who are able to be channels through whom this life can be passed on to others. However much Paul may identify with his fellow Jews, therefore, he cannot help them *by being cut off from Christ,* for were he to be cut off, he could not be the means of bringing them blessing. The paradox is that it is his union with Christ which causes him to long to save his countrymen, even were it to be at the cost of losing his own salvation.

Perhaps the key to Paul's understanding of what it means to be a minister, a partner in the gospel, is to be found in Gal 1:16, where Paul refers briefly to what we tend to describe as his conversion, but which he clearly thinks of as his call to be an apostle. He refers here to what he terms 'the time when it pleased God to reveal his son in me, in order that I might proclaim him among the Gentiles'. Once again, I find myself at odds with many of the commentators and translators, who tend to ignore the fact that Paul speaks of God revealing his son *in* him: this is surely deliberate. The revelation of Christ which is given to Paul is stamped on him, so that he himself, by his life as well as by his words, becomes the means by whom Christ is revealed to the Gentiles.

Paul's summons to his converts to imitate him was not the result of immodesty; rather it sprang from his conviction that the whole Christian community should reflect the love and compassion of Christ: there was no distinction here between apostle and community, except that the role of the apostle was to be a subsidiary model. The gospel was to be proclaimed both by Paul and by the community, not simply through the preaching of the word, but in every believer's life.

Paul's teaching on ministry has often been misunderstood – not least, perhaps, because in the final chapters of 2 Corinthians he is led to lay down the Law and exert his own authority because of the problems facing him in Corinth. People tend to remember those passages, and ignore the teaching we have been examining here. But there is another reason why little attention has been paid to what I believe to be his real understanding of ministry. The inhibition about recognizing Christ as an example has led many to ignore Paul's emphasis on Christ as a pattern to which they should be conformed. Is it not paradoxical that in shying away from this idea, Christians have looked for other models for ministry – and those models have tended to be about status and authority, instead of about kenosis? Paul, I think, would claim that when that happens, men and women have misunderstood, not simply Christian ministry, but the gospel itself.

40. Paul the Pastor: The Relevance of the Gospel*

Many years ago, as I cycled from my home in Oxford into work, I found myself confronted by a poster which announced in bold letters: 'Jesus said: "I am the Christ"'. How I was supposed to respond to this message I do not know, but in fact I nearly fell off my bicycle with surprise. My first reaction was to remonstrate with what the poster said, as though it were a statement in an undergraduate essay: 'But he didn't!' I began to explain, 'It's clear from the Gospels that Jesus did *not* go round Galilee making such open claims about himself.' But then I found myself wondering: 'What are the inhabitants of North Oxford expected to understand by this statement? What would the word "Christ" mean to them – unless, of course, they were already Christians?' Outside the context of Jewish and Christian faith, the word 'Christ' has no significance. The message might as well have been written in Chinese. So I composed myself, abandoned my dialogue with the poster, and continued to pedal my way into Oxford.

Whoever put up that poster was clearly out of touch with the world outside the church; it had not occurred to them that it would convey virtually nothing to the very people whom they were targeting. And as every preacher is taught, it is essential to begin where your congregation is, and to speak in language and idioms that they will comprehend. If you are to communicate effectively, you need to know your audience.

We tend to think of Paul as an apostle, or a theologian, but rarely stop to think that the reason why most of his letters were written was that he was also a pastor. As though to encourage us in neglecting this aspect of his work, the term 'Pastoral Epistles' is universally used of three letters which many of us consider to be post-Pauline! But were not *all* Paul's genuine letters 'pastoral' in their intent? Apart from the epistle to the Romans, of which more anon, his letters are addressed to churches which he founded,[1] and are written out of pastoral concern for his addressees. The Galatians were in danger of succumbing to what Paul regarded as a false gospel; the Thessalonians were wavering in their faith because some of their number had died; the Corinthian church was in disarray; the Philippians were apparently doing well, but they were concerned about Paul himself, who was in prison facing trial, so Paul writes to reassure them.

---

* A lecture delivered to the Irish Biblical Association in April 2008.
[1] Even Colossians, if it is a genuine letter, was written to a congregation that was an offshoot of the Pauline mission, having been founded by Paul's co-worker Epaphras.

Much scholarly analysis of his letters has created an image of St Paul as an erudite theologian writing pamphlets that would have been to a large extent incomprehensible to his readers. As we struggle with his complex exegesis of scripture, we find ourselves wondering: what would his Gentile converts have made of this? Would they have understood his arguments?[2] Did Paul make the mistake that was made centuries later by those who displayed that Oxford poster, the mistake of assuming knowledge that those whom he addressed did not possess? No one can deny that Paul was a profound thinker – one of the most formative, and many of us would say *the* most formative, theologian that the church has ever had. His letters are indeed written by a scholar. But my contention is that they were also written by a pastor; they were practical letters, intended to deal with particular problems. In other words, Paul was a practical theologian, who was in touch with his congregations.

Although some of the problems Paul had to sort out were clearly matters of doctrine, he also had to deal with moral problems. It was all very well for Paul to rush through a city, preaching the gospel, making conversions, and then moving on – but what were these young Christians meant to do next? What did their new faith signify? How should they behave? Was there, indeed, any connection between belief and behaviour? Or was moral conduct a matter of indifference to the God in whom they now trusted? Whether Paul was dealing with problems of doctrine or of behaviour, however, his method was to go back to first principles; in other words, he started from the gospel. And when he wanted to clinch an argument, he used an appropriate credal summary. In this paper, I want to examine some of these credal summaries, and consider how they relate to their context.

1. Introductions

Now one of the interesting things about these credal summaries is their great variety: Paul seems to use different language every time, and he does so, I suggest, not because he wants to ring the changes, but because he wants to express the basic core of the gospel in such a way as to demonstrate its relevance to the particular problem facing his readers.

We begin with the opening verses of Romans. In one way, Romans would seem to be a very odd place to begin if we are thinking of Paul's pastoral concerns, since this is the only one of the 'core' Pauline letters to have been written to a congregation that Paul had not himself founded: in what sense, then, could he be writing to them as their pastor? His purpose in writing the

---

[2] These questions are aptly raised by Christopher D. Stanley, in *Arguing with Scripture: The Rhetoric of Quotations in the Letters of Paul* (New York; London: T&T Clark, 2004).

letter is still debated, but clearly he wishes to ensure that the Roman congregation is aware of the gospel which he preaches; his pastoral concern arises not out of a situation that already exists in Rome, but the situation that he himself may cause by travelling there. In other words, he wishes to ensure that Christians in Rome recognize the validity of his work and that relationships between them are smooth.

But his pastoral concern surely extends to the Roman congregation itself: he is anxious that they should understand what he terms 'the depth of the riches and wisdom and knowledge of God' (Rom 11:33) – his conviction that the gospel is addressed to Jews and Gentiles alike, and that the conversion of the Gentiles will in fact herald the salvation of Israel (Rom 11:25 ff.). Not surprisingly, then, he introduces himself in his opening words by establishing his authority to write to them: he is a servant – or slave – of Christ, called to be an apostle, set apart for the gospel. Not surprisingly, too, he then summarizes 'his' gospel. And not surprisingly he hastens to point out that he is writing to the Romans because his commission is 'to bring about the obedience of faith among all the Gentiles ... including yourselves' (1:5–6).

The gospel with which he has been entrusted, Paul tells his readers, concerns God's Son, who was descended from David according to the flesh. Reference to Jesus' Davidic descent is surprisingly rare in Paul, but it is important for his argument in Romans, since it provides evidence to support his claim that Jesus is the Christ.[3] Jesus the Christ was declared Son of God with power according to the spirit of holiness by resurrection from the dead. Here are more themes that occur later in the letter: in several places Paul stresses that Jesus was the Son of God (and so obedient to the will of God);[4] the theme of God's power is picked up as early as 1:17, where we are told that the gospel is the power of God, leading to salvation to all who trust in him, while Paul's strange use of the plural in the phrase 'resurrection from the dead' – lit. 'resurrection of corpses' – hints at what we will be told later – that his resurrection brings new life to believers. The odd phrases 'according to the flesh' and 'according to the spirit' are both picked up later; and as for that strange expansion 'the spirit of holiness', that might well prepare us for what Paul is going to spell out in chapter 8, in terms of the necessity for believers to be sanctified and to live holy lives, in the power of the Spirit. Finally, we have the familiar words of the confession of faith, 'Jesus Christ our Lord'. And it is through Jesus Christ our Lord, Paul declares, that he has received grace

---

[3] Jesus' physical ancestry is picked up in Rom 9:5. Although it is often assumed that 'Christ' was already being used as a name, it would certainly have been impossible for Paul to have used the word without an awareness of its significance, which was indeed crucial for his understanding of the relationship between Christ and believers.

[4] Rom 5:10; 8:3, 29, 32.

and apostleship to bring about the obedience of faith among all the Gentiles, including the Romans themselves.

This opening credal summary, then, neatly sums up the gospel in language appropriate to the argument of the letter, establishes Paul's own authority to write to the congregation in Rome, and underlines the significant emphasis of his understanding of the gospel – that it is for Gentiles as well as for Jews. It seems clear that Paul has chosen his language very deliberately.

And that, of course, is precisely what we would expect, since it was usual in Paul's time for the opening words of a letter to sum up the theme that is going to be discussed later.[5] In other words, an introduction is not simply a way of getting started, but a kind of contents page, indicating what is going to be discussed. Romans is unusual because Paul is about to spell out what the gospel is: to explain why it was necessary for God to act in Christ, to indicate the significance of Christ's death and resurrection, and to show the place of Jews and Gentiles in God's plan.

In most of his letters, Paul's purpose is much more focused, so the opening words home in on one particular aspect of the gospel that he feels needs to be stressed. In 1 Thess 1:10, for example, after thanking God for the Thessalonians' response to the gospel, he reminds them of the assurance they had been given that Christ, having been raised from the dead, would save believers from the coming wrath:[6] later in the letter, we find that the Thessalonians are distressed by the fear that Christians who die before the return of the Lord will perish, and so not be saved from wrath. In 1 Corinthians (1:4–9), Paul thanks God for the spiritual gifts with which the Corinthians have been blessed – gifts of speech and knowledge, of which (as subsequent chapters demonstrate) the Corinthians are clearly proud – thus reminding them that these things are gifts, and so no cause for pride; at the same time, he expresses his confidence that God will make them blameless on the last day, so reminding them that their calling to be 'saints', or 'holy ones' (1:2) demands appropriate moral behaviour: these themes will occupy much of the letter. In 2 Corinthians, Paul's thanksgiving is for the consolation that has come to him through suffering, which he understands to be a sharing in the sufferings of Christ, and thus a means of bringing comfort to the Corinthians: this is to be the theme of the following chapters. In all these letters, Paul indicates in the opening thanksgivings both his pastoral concerns and the topics he plans to discuss.

---

[5] Paul Schubert, *Form and Function of the Pauline Thanksgivings*, BZNW 20 (Berlin: A. Töpelmann, 1939).

[6] On the significance of 1 Thess 1:10, see Morna D. Hooker, '1 Thessalonians 1:9–10: A Nutshell – but What Kind of Nut?', in *Geschichte – Tradition – Reflexion: Festschrift für Martin Hengel zum 70. Geburtstag,* vol. 3: *Frühes Christentum,* ed. H. Lichtenberger (Tübingen: Mohr Siebeck, 1996), 435–448 = above, essay 35 (pp. 521–533).

There is, of course, one exception to this pattern, and that is Galatians, which has no opening thanksgiving – presumably because Paul is so distraught in writing to the congregations in Galatia that he is unable to think of anything in their situation for which to thank God! Nevertheless, he is still able to *praise* God, and the longer than usual opening greeting does end in a brief doxology (1:5). Moreover, the greeting itself contains an indication of the theme of the letter – and this, as we might expect, is a brief summary of the gospel, the gospel that Paul fears the Galatians are abandoning.[7] He begins, however, as in Romans, by reminding his readers that he is an apostle – a necessary reminder if his authority is being challenged. The opening verse thus serves both to establish his own authority and to remind the Galatians of the gospel, since his commission has come 'through Jesus Christ and God the Father, who raised him from the dead' (1:1). Paul then sends grace and peace to the churches of Galatia 'from God our Father and the Lord Jesus Christ, *who gave himself for our sins to set us free from the present age*' (1:3–4). As we read the rest of the letter we realize that the problem with the Galatian Christians is that they have failed to appreciate the fact that they have been set free from the present age – the age in which the Law operated – and failed to understand that the death and resurrection of Christ have dealt with their sins. Once again, Paul seems to have chosen his vocabulary deliberately.

2. Credal Summaries

In various letters, then, we find references in the opening thanksgivings to particular aspects of the gospel that correspond to the pastoral needs of the readers, while in the opening verses of Galatians and Romans we have summaries of the gospel itself – summaries that are worded in language that is relevant to the particular ways in which Paul is going to spell out that gospel in what follows. What I find interesting, however, is that in credal summaries *elsewhere*, Paul also seems to choose language that is appropriate to the theme. His answer to any theological problem is to state the gospel, and to state it in a way that makes its relevance obvious. As a pastor, Paul is sensitive to the need to relate the gospel to the situation.

Take, for example, 1 Thess 4:14, where the particular pastoral problem has been caused by the death of some believers; it would seem that expectation of an imminent Parousia had led to a conviction that Christians would not die before the Lord returned. Paul attempts to persuade his readers that those who have died have not been lost. 'Since we believe that Jesus died and rose again,' he writes, 'even so, God will bring with him those who have died'. In

---

[7] Cf. David Cook, 'The Prescript as Programme in Galatians', *JTS* NS 43 (1992): 511–519.

other words, the gospel of Jesus' death and resurrection means life for those who have died. How can the Thessalonians be confident that this is so? In the next chapter, he spells out the answer. 'Our Lord Jesus Christ died for us,' he writes, 'so that, whether we are awake or asleep – i.e. dead or alive – we may live with him' (5:10). There is a great deal of theology packed into that statement, but we see immediately the clear relationship between creed and conviction: Jesus died and rose: *therefore we live with him*.

Now you may well tell me that 'Jesus died and rose' is a very basic form of the gospel – and so it is. Indeed, in 5:10, Paul says only 'Our Lord Jesus Christ died for us', and there is no direct reference to the resurrection! Nevertheless, the resurrection is clearly essential to the argument, since believers are to 'live *with* him'. Paul is here spelling out the implication of his words in the previous chapter, where he appealed to the fact that 'we believe that Jesus died and rose again'. Moreover, in the opening thanksgiving, as we have already seen, he singled out the resurrection of Christ as the basis of his confident hope for future salvation, reminding the Thessalonians that when they accepted the gospel, they trusted that Jesus, whom God had raised from the dead, would save them from the coming wrath (1:10). Now they are worried about the death of some of their congregation, but they have no need to be; they need simply to recall the gospel, and realize what it implies. 'God has not destined us for wrath, but for salvation through our Lord Jesus Christ, who died for us, so that whether we are awake or asleep we may live with him' (5:9–10). If God raised Jesus from the dead, then those who believe in him will share his risen life. This example demonstrates very clearly the way in which Paul appealed to the gospel when reassuring his readers. Moreover, he appeals to it in language which shows the gospel's relevance to the particular situation with which he is dealing.

For Paul, however, living with Christ – sharing his resurrection – implies also *dying* with him. That idea is not stressed in Thessalonians, but it does come to the fore in another of Paul's early letters, Galatians, where Paul wishes to stress what Christ's *death* has achieved. If 'Christ gave himself for our sins to set us free from the present evil age' (1:4), what does this mean for believers? Someone has been trying to persuade the Galatian Christians that they need to obey the Law; for Paul, that would be to abandon the freedom given them by Christ, and to return to living in the present evil age. In Gal 2:19–21, Paul expresses what Christ's death and resurrection mean in very personal terms. He describes how he himself has 'died to Law, *in order that* [he] might live to God'. How has this death taken place? It was, he says, by being 'crucified with Christ', so that it is now *Christ* who lives in Paul. The life Paul now lives is lived by trusting in the Son of God, who loved him and gave himself for him. His language echoes that introductory summary of the gospel: this is what the fact that 'Christ gave himself for our sins to set us free from the present evil age' (Gal 1:4) means for Paul: dying to the Law and living to God.

Once again, therefore, as in 1 Thessalonians, Paul appeals to the gospel, but the summary he gives at the end of chapter 2 is a very short one: simply 'the Son of God loved me and gave himself for me', and – as in 1 Thess 5:10 – Christ's resurrection is implied, not spelt out. Indeed, if we reverse the order of the sentences in Gal 2:19–20, we see the close parallel with 1 Thess 5:10. There we read:

> Our Lord Jesus Christ died for us,
> so that we might live with him.

Here we find:

> The Son of God loved me and gave himself for me,
> in order that I might live to God;
> and it is no longer I who live,
> but Christ who lives in me.

The difference between the two passages is, of course, that twice here Paul emphasizes that in order to live to God – or to allow Christ to live in him – the Christian must *die* with Christ: 'I have died to the Law', he says, and 'I have been crucified with Christ'. Galatians 2 fills out what is said in 1 Thess 5:10, reminding us that Christ's death on behalf of others has to be appropriated: it is those who *share his death to life in the old age* who will share his resurrection life. 'Christ died for us' does not mean that we escape death, but that he dies as our representative – the representative of humanity – and so dies to what Paul describes as life lived 'according to the flesh'. Those who in turn share his death to this way of living will also share his resurrection – and that means that Christ already lives in them, and that God's Spirit is at work in them.

Why the differences between the two summaries? Clearly it is because the pastoral problem Paul is dealing with in Galatians is a very different one from the one that confronts him in the Thessalonian community. The Galatians need to comprehend the fact that Christ's death frees them from the present age – and so releases them from the necessity to live under the Law; the Law was intended to deal with sin, but Christ gave himself up for our sins, and has released us once and for all from the power of sin. If the Galatians are to be set free from the present age and share Christ's resurrection life, they must first die with him.

Similar ideas reappear in another brief summary of the gospel in 2 Cor 5:14–15, where Paul writes 'One has died for all'. At first that sounds like substitution, Christ dying *instead* of all, but he goes on to explain that what he means is that Christ died *as our representative*. The reason that he feels it necessary to spell out the significance of Christ's 'death for all' is, I suggest, precisely because the Corinthians are interpreting Christ's death as a crude exchange: he dies, we live, he suffers, we do not. No, insists Paul,

> One has died *for all*,
> therefore *all have died*.
> And he died *for all*
> *in order that* those who live might no longer live to themselves,
> but to the one who died and was raised for them.

Once again, we note the parallel with 1 Thess 5:10:

> Our Lord Jesus Christ died for us,
> so that we might live with him.

Because the situation is different, however, the conclusion that is drawn is also different: in 1 Thessalonians, he is assuring his readers that they will share Christ's resurrection, whereas here, he is concerned to remind the Corinthians that they should live their lives in conformity to the gospel.

In 1 Thessalonians, Paul did not spell out either what Christ's death 'for us' might mean, or what our living 'for him' might involve, since the problem he was dealing with was simply the Thessalonians' fear that those Christians who had died would not share future salvation. He needed only to stress that all Christians would live *with* Christ. In writing to the Corinthians, he is concerned to stress that – paradoxically – Christian life involves conformity to Christ's death. This is an idea that the Corinthians have clearly failed to grasp, for they are scandalized by Paul's own understanding of ministry as a sharing in the sufferings of Christ, and reluctant to see the implications for their own manner of life. In the chapters preceding this summary of the gospel, Paul has been discussing his ministry, and his call to preach the gospel. Then, in 5:14, he appeals to the gospel that constrains him to preach:

> The love of Christ constrains us, because we are convinced that one has died for all; therefore all have died. And he died for all, so that those who live might live no longer for themselves, but for him who died and was raised for them.

For Paul, living for the one who died and was raised for him meant that he was compelled to preach this gospel, and to embody it in his manner of life.

If Christ died 'for all', Paul reminds the Corinthians, this means that Christians, too, have also died – not, of course, a physical death, but a spiritual one, to sin. The consequence is life – described here, not, as in 1 Thessalonians, as life *with* Christ, but – as in Gal 2:20 – life that is centred *on* him, instead of on themselves. The wording reflects the particular problems in Corinth. It is hardly surprising that Paul goes on, in 2 Cor 5:17, to explain that when someone is 'in Christ', there is in effect 'a new creation'. Christ's death and resurrection bring an end to one way of living and introduce something quite new. The old world has gone, and the new world has arrived.

These three short summaries all emphasize the fact that Christ died on behalf of others: he 'died for us' (1 Thessalonians), he 'died for me' (Galatians), he 'died for all' (2 Corinthians). In three different ways, Paul stresses the fact that Christ acts on our behalf and as our representative, in order that we might share his risen life: and in three different ways, he explains what that new life means. The core message is the same, the wording different, in order to deal with the particular pastoral problem.

A longer summary of the gospel is used in 1 Cor 15:3 ff. This time the pastoral problem that confronts Paul arises from the doubts expressed by some members of the Corinthian congregation concerning the future resurrection of the dead. Not surprisingly, Paul spells out not only the fact that Christ died for our sins, but that he was raised on the third day. Both his death and his resurrection, he insists, were 'in accordance with scripture', though he does not bother to quote the scriptures he has in mind. But there are two unusual elements in this credal summary. First, we are told that Christ was buried; is the reference to burial included simply to confirm the reality of Christ's death? Or is it perhaps because Paul is going to explain our future resurrection by using the analogy of seeds that are sown in the earth? Our present bodies, he says, are made of dust, and we are mortal and perishable. If Christians share Christ's resurrection, it is because he shared our death: he, too, was 'sown in dishonour, raised in glory' (v. 43). Maybe, then, Paul includes the reference to Christ's burial precisely because he is anxious to allay the Corinthians' doubts about their own resurrection.

Secondly, Paul backs up the statement that Christ was raised from the dead by giving a list of witnesses to the resurrection, in which his own name figures last. In what follows, Paul's argument that Christians are to be raised depends wholly on the fact that Christ *has* been raised: deny that, and there is no basis for belief in *our* future resurrection; affirm it, and the resurrection of believers follows. Belief in Christ's resurrection and ours belong together (v. 13). Since the Corinthians' doubts about their own resurrection are the hub of the problem, it is not surprising if Paul has on this occasion added the list of witnesses to Christ's resurrection appearances to the credal summary.

But why, we may wonder, does he say that 'Christ died for our sins' rather than simply that he died 'for us'? Is *this* significant? Or was the phrase already part of an accepted formula? That is certainly possible: the link with sins is hardly surprising. Jewish tradition saw death as the punishment for sin. Not only were criminals put to death, but the fact that all living creatures are condemned to die was explained as the result of Adam's sin. According to the story in Genesis 3, Adam and Eve were expelled from the Garden of Eden lest they take and eat the fruit of the tree of life (Gen 3:22). Death was understood to be the universal punishment for human sin, but it was universal, not simply as the result of Adam's action, but because his descendants *shared* his sin.[8]

---

[8] 4 Ezra 3:21–22, 25–26; 7:48 (118).

When we read on through 1 Corinthians 15, however, we realize that Paul is going to pick up the reference to sins. If Christ has not been raised, he insists, then the Corinthians' faith is futile, *and they are still in their sins* (v. 17). This statement leads into a discussion of the contrast between Adam and Christ: death came to men and women through Adam, and life has come through Christ (vv. 20–22, 35–57). Paul needed the particular wording of the formula that he uses in vv. 3 ff., therefore, in order to draw out the implications of the gospel for the resurrection hope. Other chapters in the epistle indicate how necessary it was for the Corinthians to make the break with their past, sinful, life. The phrase 'for our sins' was certainly an appropriate one in this context, and may well have been a Pauline addition to an earlier credal summary.

A summary of the gospel in Rom 4:25 also makes the link between Christ's death and human sin: 'He was handed over for our trespasses and raised for our δικαίωσις' – our 'rightwising'. It is difficult to know how to translate the final word, δικαίωσις, into English, which is why many translations simply render it 'righteousness', or 'justification', as though it were δικαιωσύνη. Perhaps we should translate it by 'acquittal', since its meaning seems to be that we are established as righteous – hence my use of 'rightwise'. The wording of this summary is often dismissed as a rhetorical flourish. I suggest that it is in fact carefully chosen, in order to sum up Paul's argument in Romans. In dying, Christ dealt with sin, and in being raised, he becomes the source of righteousness – right standing – before God, since we share his acquittal. There, in a nutshell, we have Paul's understanding of atonement.

In many of these summaries, Paul may be using traditional language. Elsewhere, his choice of words is unusual. In Gal 3:13, for example, we are told that 'Christ was made a curse'. Now we can hardly call this a 'mini-creed', but it is certainly a reminder of the gospel – and a very powerful one. What Paul did when he preached the gospel to the Galatians was, he says, to 'placard' Christ crucified before their eyes (Gal 3:1); and now, in writing to them, he does so again. 'Remember the gospel!' he pleads – 'the gospel of Christ crucified! What did his death do for you? Paradoxically, it was the means of bringing you blessing, and making you children of Abraham!' The Galatians are in danger of turning their backs on the gospel, but it is precisely the scandal of the cross that is the source of the blessing they seek. Paul grasps the nettle: yes, Christ was made a curse – and yet, paradoxically, he became the source of blessing.

In the next chapter, Paul gives us a very different summary of the gospel; this one is notable for concentrating on what *we* would term the 'incarnation', with only a hint at Christ's death and resurrection. God sent his Son, born of a woman, born under the Law, so that he might redeem those under the Law (here is the reference to his death), and so that we might be made sons of God. God's Son became man, in order to make both men *and* women sons; he was born under the bondage of the Law, in order to set free those who were enslaved. The language is relevant to Paul's argument in this section, which is concerned to show how all who believe in Christ are children of God by being in Christ, and have been freed from any obligation to the Law. Even what seems to us to be 'sexist' language is deliberately chosen: in becoming sons of God, those with no rights (Gentiles, slaves, women, Gal 3:28) share in what Christ is, and enjoy the privileges of sonship. They must not turn their backs on freedom by embracing the Law. Once again, the summary of the gospel is carefully worded, in order to show its implications for the Galatians.

3. Ethics

It is hardly surprising, I suppose, that when Paul wants to correct a theological misunderstanding, he goes back to the gospel, and stresses the connection by expressing it in a particular way. What is perhaps more interesting is that he does exactly the same thing when he is instructing his readers about how they should behave. But since in Jewish tradition ethics are based on theology, we should not be surprised. In Paul's understanding, the Christian life is shaped by the gospel.

1 Corinthians is a good place to begin this investigation, since the Corinthian church was clearly beset by many moral problems, some of them caused by sexual immorality. What should they do about a notorious sinner in their midst? They should remove him from the community, says Paul, in the way that one removes leaven from the house, lest it contaminate the new dough (5:7). Note how Paul assumes familiarity with Jewish customs, even to the extent of moving swiftly from the feast of unleavened bread to Passover, which was celebrated immediately after, for his instruction depends on the fact that 'Christ our Passover lamb has been sacrificed for us'. This is hardly what we expect, in a letter written to Gentiles! Would his readers have seen the point? The image of the Passover lamb was probably already known to them: the Gospels all place Jesus' death at Passover, and the link may well have featured in the Corinthians' celebration of the eucharist (1 Cor 10:16–18; 11:13–34). Moreover, words commonly used by Paul, such as 'salvation' (2 Cor 1:6; 6:2), 'righteousness', and 'redemption', suggest that he saw what happened in Christ as a new exodus, which incorporated Gentiles, as well as Jews, into the people of God. The Corinthians, then, would have understood very well why, earlier in the letter (1:30), Paul described Christ as righteousness, sanctification, and redemption. Just as Israel was saved from slavery at the exodus, when the Passover lamb was sacrificed, and was called to be God's holy people, so now those for whom Christ, our Passover lamb, has been sacrificed, have been freed from sin, and have been washed, sanctified, and

made righteous in him (6:11). Once again, therefore, Paul deals with a pastoral problem – in this case an ethical one – by appealing to the gospel, and once again his summary of the gospel is framed in language appropriate to the problem.

Some problems facing the Corinthian congregation were more complicated – notably the question as to whether or not Christians should eat meat that had been sacrificed to idols. Some of the Corinthians had argued that there was nothing wrong with it, since idols did not exist. Paul apparently agreed with them. We do indeed know that 'there is one God, the Father,' he says, 'and one Lord, Jesus Christ'. This might seem to clinch the argument, but then Paul warns the Corinthians against relying on what they know, and suggests that concern for others may be more important than knowledge. And once again he reminds them of the gospel. If they lead others, weaker than themselves, into sin, then by their knowledge they are destroying those for whom Christ died. In a discussion about what these 'clever' Corinthians knew, this stark reminder of what the gospel was about must have taken his readers aback. Interestingly, Paul seems to oppose two summaries of faith in this argument. There is one God and one Lord – yes indeed! And since the so-called 'gods and lords' are nothing, the Corinthians are right, and they can eat the meat with impunity – *provided* that they do not persuade their fellow Christians to do what they believe to be wrong, and so destroy them, for that is to sin against Christ, who died for them. At the end of the day, love for others is more important than knowledge – a principle that Paul spells out in 1 Corinthians 13, where he declares that possessing knowledge is of no value, if one does not have love.

This discussion in 1 Corinthians is the more fascinating, because it shows how Paul went about advising his congregation to deal with a problem when the proper course of action was by no means clear. If the strong Corinthian Christian eats meat, that is surely a demonstration of his faith; true – but does that action accord with the principle of self-sacrificing love seen in the death of Christ? Christ loved us and gave himself up for us; it is clear, then, that it is love that should shape the lives of Christians. This is the principle that Paul brings to bear when answering moral problems.

Problems of immorality and inappropriate behaviour within the Christian community are discussed again, in 2 Cor 6:14–18. Righteousness and lawlessness do not go together, says Paul. These verses are part of a passage (6:14–7:4) that is often described as an 'erratic boulder', which interrupts the train of thought. It has even been suggested that it is a scrap belonging to another letter, which has mysteriously made its way into 2 Corinthians.[9] If we turn

---

[9] For a full discussion of the issues, see Margaret E. Thrall, *A Critical and Exegetical Commentary on the Second Epistle to the Corinthians,* vol. 1, ICC (Edinburgh: T&T Clark, 1994), 25–36.

back to chapter 5, however, I think we will see why it is placed here. In 5:21, we find Paul reminding the Corinthians how they have 'become righteousness'. It is, of course, because they are 'in Christ'. 'If anyone is in Christ,' he writes in 5:17, 'there is a new creation. The old has passed away, and everything is new'. And then, in 5:21, 'For our sake God made the one who knew no sin to be sin, so that we might become the righteousness of God in him.' No wonder he goes on to say, in effect, 'be what you are'. But notice the way in which he chooses to remind the Corinthians of the gospel. Once again, he uses unusual language: Christ was identified with our sin, in order that we might be identified with his righteousness. Now, in chapter 6, he urges the Corinthians to think about what that means for their everyday lives.

In 8:9 we have another summary of the gospel: 'You remember the generosity of our Lord Jesus Christ – how, though he was rich, he became poor for your sake, so that we, through his poverty, might become rich'. This summary concentrates on what we would call the 'incarnation' rather than on Christ's death and resurrection, and the language is clearly chosen carefully. And the point? Why, to persuade the Corinthians to be like Christ! In other words, they should put their hands into their pockets and contribute generously to the collection for the church in Jerusalem. To refuse to do so is in effect to reject the gospel itself.

The relevance of the gospel to one's manner of life is a central theme in the letter to the Philippians. Most of Paul's letters deal with pastoral problems, and that means that their contents are largely dictated by the matters that need to be dealt with. The language Paul uses reflects those problems. Philippians is unusual because there does not seem to be any particular problem – apart, that is, from a minor disagreement between two ladies hinted at in 4:2. Although commentators have sometimes imagined huge problems within the Philippian community, the 'opponents' who are mentioned do not seem to have belonged to the church.[10] Paul's concern for the community appears to arise from his own position – in prison, facing a possible death sentence. Will he ever see his beloved Philippian church again? He writes to comfort them – and to make sure that they will carry on his work. He reminds them of the gospel – the gospel about one who was in the form of God, but was content to take the form of a slave. Whether or not Paul composed the famous passage in Philippians 2, its language is just what he needs. It speaks of Christ becoming what we are – taking human form – being obedient to death, and being exalted and proclaimed Lord.

---

[10] See Morna D. Hooker, 'Philippians: Phantom Opponents and the Real Source of Conflict', in *Fair Play: Diversity and Conflicts in Early Christianity: Essays in Honour of Heikki Räisänen*, eds. Ismo Dunderberg, Christopher Tuckett, and Kari Syreeni (Leiden: Brill, 2002), 377–395 = below, essay 42 (pp. 616–631).

This so-called 'hymn' is introduced by an appeal to the community to be like Christ — something that is possible only because they are in him: they are to be governed by the mind which was in Christ Jesus — the mind which is now theirs because they are in him. They are to follow the example of Christ — or rather, to allow him to live in them, and to live in a manner that is worthy of the gospel (1:27). Theology and ethics are welded together. The gospel is, then, a model for Christian living; and it is the model for Paul's own ministry. In the next chapter, he reminds the Philippians that he, too, had abandoned what he had — his status within Judaism; the language he uses echoes that of the hymn; his goal is to be found in Christ. Sharing his sufferings, his hope is that he will share his resurrection (3:10). For Paul, 'being in Christ' means 'being conformed to Christ', and since he models his life on the gospel, he urges the Philippians to imitate him (3:17). The hope they share is that their mortal bodies will be conformed to Christ's body of glory. Once again, Paul's language echoes the 'hymn' in chapter 2.[11]

It would seem, then, that Paul's pastoral approach is rooted in his understanding of the gospel. He starts from the conviction that the Christian life is a matter of conformity to the gospel — of living *in Christ*.[12] In dealing with problems, he is a very practical theologian. His language is chosen to fit the context, and he is prepared to express the gospel in unusual and sometimes shocking ways, in order to show its relevance. In demonstrating the relevance of the gospel to the problems confronting his congregations he shows himself to be a good pastor, as well as a profound theologian.

---

[11] See Morna D. Hooker, 'Philippians 2.6–11', in *Jesus und Paulus: Festschrift für W. G. Kümmel*, eds. E. Earle Ellis and E. Grasser (Göttingen: Vandenhoeck & Ruprecht, 1975), 151–164.

[12] It is intriguing that many of these appeals are based on statements of the gospel that have been described by some of us as statements about 'interchange'. The basic form of these is 'Christ became what we are, in order that we might become what he is', or share in what he is. See Morna D. Hooker, *From Adam to Christ: Essays on Paul*. So Philippians 2–3; Christ took the form of a slave, and came in the likeness of man, so that we might be conformed to his body of glory; Galatians 3–4: Christ became a curse, so that we might receive blessing; he came under the Law, so that those under the Law might be redeemed from it, and was born of a woman, so that we might become, as he is, sons of God; 2 Corinthians 8: he became poor, so that we might become rich; and 5: he became sin, so that we might become the righteousness of God in him. And that 'in him' is vital. It is necessary to be 'in Christ', part of the messianic community. We have to be *in* him, to share his death and resurrection, and to be conformed to the gospel.

41. From God's Faithfulness to Ours: Another Look at 2 Corinthians 1:17–24

In an earlier article, I suggested that 2 Cor 1:17–22 lent some support to the view that the phrase πίστις Χριστοῦ referred primarily to the faithfulness of Christ.[1] I argued that Paul's defence in this passage against the charge of vacillation is based on an appeal to the faithfulness of God himself (v. 18), a faithfulness that is embodied in the person of Christ, who is the 'Yes' to all God's promises (v. 19). Since Christians have been 'made firm' (v. 21), and this verb is qualified by the phrase εἰς Χριστὸν, Paul is clearly claiming that he shares in this faithfulness through his incorporation into Christ. The logic of his argument is that he is reliable because God himself is reliable. '[H]e is not guilty of vacillating – of faithlessness – because he shares in the faithfulness of God himself; and he shares in that faithfulness by his incorporation into Christ, who is the embodiment of God's faithfulness'.[2] Since some, at least, of those involved in the ongoing debate about the meaning of πίστις Χριστοῦ have failed to understand my point,[3] it seems worth exploring this suggestion in greater depth.

The situation which Paul addresses in this passage is some kind of misunderstanding between the Corinthians and himself. He has changed his original plans about revisiting them (vv. 15–16), and they have accused him of fickleness. He has behaved, they suggest, 'in a worldly fashion'[4] (v. 17), and so clearly cannot be relied on. We might perhaps have expected Paul to respond immediately to these accusations with the explanation he gives for his actions in v. 23: it had been to spare them that he had decided not to visit them again. The truth of what he says there is affirmed by the introductory oath: 'I call

---

[1] Morna D. Hooker, 'ΠΙΣΤΙΣ ΧΡΙΣΤΟΥ', Presidential Address to SNTS, 1988, NTS 35 (1989): 321–342, reprinted in Morna D. Hooker, From Adam to Christ (Cambridge: Cambridge University Press, 1990), 165–186.

[2] Hooker, 'ΠΙΣΤΙΣ ΧΡΙΣΤΟΥ', 334–35/178.

[3] E.g. James D.G. Dunn, in 'Once More, ΠΙΣΤΙΣ ΧΡΙΣΤΟΥ', in Pauline Theology, vol. 4, eds. E. Elizabeth Johnson and David M. Hay (Atlanta: Scholars Press, 1997), 61–81, reprinted as Appendix 1 in Richard B. Hays, The Faith of Jesus Christ, 2nd ed. (Grand Rapids; Cambridge: Eerdmans, 2002), 231–248. Dunn's comment, 77/267, n. 69, is puzzling. He writes: 'The same is true of 2 Cor 1:17–22 – a reference to God's faithfulness, not Christ's (pace Hooker, "πίστις Χρίστου," 177–178), though we might speak of God's faithfulness incarnated in Christ'. This, of course, is precisely what I myself had said!

[4] Thrall's translation. See Margaret E. Thrall, A Critical and Exegetical Commentary on the Second Epistle to the Corinthians, vol. 1, ICC (Edinburgh: T&T Clark, 1994), in loc.

on God as witness against me'. Although this explanation is enigmatic – since Paul thought it unnecessary to tell the Corinthians what they were being spared by his absence – it does at least offer some kind of reason for his change of plan. Vv. 18–22 offer no such explanation. Rather they maintain that the charge of fickleness is clearly inappropriate, since what Paul is and does is determined by the faithfulness of God himself.

Paul's argument begins with an appeal to the faithfulness of God: πιστὸς δὲ ὁ Θεὸς. Some commentators suggest that this should be understood as an oath-formula.[5] Others point out that the various forms of Paul's oath-formulae are quite different from this.[6] One of these formulae is, of course, used a few verses later, to introduce the argument in v. 23. Those who argue that the clause is not an oath-formula suggest, instead, that it should be interpreted as a statement from which the rest of the argument will be developed.[7] The two interpretations are not, however, mutually exclusive. Thus Furnish, who concludes that '[i]t should be interpreted … as an oath formula', nevertheless argues that Paul 'is saying, in effect, "Trust God! His promises have been fulfilled in Christ, and our own faithfulness in dealing with you has been assured by our preaching of Christ to you."'[8]

If this is indeed an 'oath-formula', then the question we should be asking is why Paul has chosen to use *this* particular formula, rather than make his usual appeal to God as his witness (as he does a few verses later, in 2 Cor 1:23), or employ, as he does elsewhere, the phrase 'God knows' (2 Cor 11:11, 31) or 'before God' (Rom 1:9; Gal 1:20). The relevance of the theme of God's own faithfulness to the argument that follows is sufficient explanation of its occurrence here. In other words, whether or not the clause is in fact an oath-formula, its significance lies in the integral relationship between God's faithfulness and Paul's own trustworthiness.

A comparison with other occurrences of the statement that 'God is faithful' reveals that they, too, link God's faithfulness with the implications for believers' own steadfastness. In 1 Cor 1:9, Paul reminds the Corinthians that 'God is faithful; by him you were called into the fellowship of his Son, Jesus Christ our Lord'. And because it is God who called them, he will, as Paul has already explained in v. 8, 'strengthen you to the end, so that you may be blameless on the day of our Lord Jesus Christ'. Similarly, in 1 Cor 10:13, he assures them that 'God is faithful, and he will not let you be tested beyond your strength, but with the testing he will also provide the way out so that you may be able to

---

[5] Among them, '[w]ith some hesitation', Thrall, *2 Corinthians*, 144.

[6] E.g. Alfred Plummer, *A Critical and Exegetical Commentary on the Second Epistle of St. Paul to the Corinthians,* ICC (Edinburgh: T&T Clark, 1915), 34–35. See Rom 1:9; 2 Cor 11:11, 31; Gal 1:20 for examples.

[7] E.g. Plummer, *2 Corinthians,* 34–35, quoting Chrysostom in support.

[8] Victor Paul Furnish, *II Corinthians,* AB (Garden City, NY: Doubleday, 1984), 135 and 145.

endure it'. A similar link is seen in 1 Thess 5:23–24. Because God is faithful, he can be relied on to keep the Thessalonians whole and blameless. It is found again in 2 Thess 3:3: those who have faith (unlike those who have none) rely upon God (v. 2), for 'the Lord is faithful; he will strengthen you and guard you from evil'. It is hardly surprising, then, that the same statement is the basis here for an argument about the character of Paul's behaviour: if God is faithful, he can be relied upon to make Paul himself firm.[9]

The accusation brought against Paul is that his word cannot be relied upon: he says both 'yes' and 'no', and the Corinthians do not know what to believe.[10] Paul insists that the accusation is unfounded: his word cannot be inconsistent, since God himself is faithful. But how does he argue from what *God* is to what *he himself* is and to his own actions? The answer, as always for Paul, is *through his relationship to Christ*. Here, the link is provided by the word λόγος, which appears to have a double meaning, since 'our word to you' is not just his own proposal to visit the Corinthians, but the 'word' which 'we' – i.e. 'Silvanus and Timothy and I' – proclaimed among them, and that word was 'the Son of God, Jesus Christ' (v. 19). The reliability of *this* word – the word of the gospel – is supported by the number of witnesses: it was proclaimed by Silvanus and Timothy, as well as by Paul. Its true guarantee, however, lies in its content, for what was proclaimed among the Corinthians was Christ.

Christ himself is clearly reliable, for he is *the Son of God,* and so shares God's faithfulness. There can be no suspicion of ambiguity here, no suggestion that *this* word is both 'yes' and 'no'; on the contrary, in him there is only a 'Yes'. That means that in him there is a 'Yes' to all the promises of God.

But what has that 'Yes' to do with Paul and his co-workers? What is the logical link between his statement concerning Christ – οὐκ ἐγένετο ναὶ καὶ οὔ – and himself – οὐκ ἔστιν ναὶ καὶ οὔ? Paul's words about Christ in v. 19 deliberately echo the charge laid against himself in v. 18. Moreover, the gospel of the Son of God was preached through Paul and his companions – δι' ἡμῶν ... δι' ἐμοῦ (v. 19) – and their preaching was thus the 'Amen' to God's 'Yes' (v. 20). Commentators interpret this 'Amen' in various ways, but the repetition of δι' ἡμῶν links it with v. 19. The 'Amen' is pronounced by those who preach the gospel – δι' ἡμῶν – but they are enabled to do so through the agency of Christ – δι' αὐτοῦ. The argument assumes, as Thrall points out, that Paul is 'Christ's ambassador through whom God himself speaks (5.20) and Christ speaks (13.3)'.[11]

---

[9] God's faithfulness – together with his righteousness and his truth – are seen as the guarantee that his purpose will be accomplished in Rom 3:3–7. See also Rom 1:17a, where ἐκ πίστεως may refer to God's faithfulness, now revealed in the gospel.

[10] The most likely meaning of v. 17b is that Paul is charged with inconsistency. For a discussion of the possibilities, see Thrall, *2 Corinthians, in loc.*

[11] Thrall, *2 Corinthians,* 147–148.

The reliability of Paul's word, then, is guaranteed because it is the 'Amen' to God's 'Yes'. This link is clearly set out in v. 20:

ἐν αὐτῷ τὸ ναί.
διὸ καὶ δι' αὐτοῦ
τὸ ἀμὴν τῷ Θεῷ πρὸς δόξαν
δι' ἡμῶν.

The proclamation and acceptance of the gospel are the 'Amen' to what God has done, in Christ, and redound to God's glory. But this Amen, too, is pronounced δι' αὐτοῦ.

'The proclamation *and acceptance* of the gospel'. Although the 'through us' refers to what God is doing through the missionaries, the 'Amen' is clearly *echoed* by those who accept their message. Not surprisingly, then, Paul includes them in his next words: 'For God confirms us, with you, into Christ' (v. 21). Though the word was proclaimed *among* the Corinthians *by* Paul (v. 19), those who accepted it are also 'in Christ', as he himself is. The significance of the participles used in vv. 21–22 has been much debated. Is the language baptismal? Are βεβαιῶν, σφραγισάμενος and δοὺς τὸν ἀρραβῶνα all legal terms?[12] The language may well be taken from the world of legal transactions, since that provided appropriate metaphors, and it may well have been used in connection with baptism, since that signified the relationship of the believer to Christ, but it is with this relationship itself that Paul is primarily concerned here, not with baptism. The unexpected use of the phrase εἰς Χριστὸν with βεβαιῶν reminds us that *it is only by being transferred 'into' Christ that believers are 'confirmed' or 'guaranteed'*. The use of the present tense suggests that God *continues* to keep Christians firm,[13] and so takes us back to the accusation made against Paul.

The remaining participles in vv. 21–22 are aorists. They refer to something that has been done and cannot be undone. Most interesting is the first, χρίσας. Following closely on the phrase εἰς Χριστὸν, it is clearly intended as a play on words. Those who have been put 'into Christ' share what he is, and have therefore been 'anointed', as he was. Paul, ever conscious of the true meaning of the term 'Christ', is probably thinking here of Christians being made members of the messianic community. As Messiah, Jesus embodies the qualities that should belong to the whole community. The fact that Christians have been sealed and given the Holy Spirit as a 'deposit', guaranteeing more to come, is yet further proof of the faithfulness of God, for it is he who has done and is doing all these things.

---

[12] See the discussion in Thrall, *2 Corinthians, in loc.*, and in C.K. Barrett, *A Commentary on the Second Epistle to the Corinthians*, BNTC (London: A&C Black, 1973), *in loc*.

[13] So Thrall, *2 Corinthians*, 159.

The accusation brought against Paul was that he had changed his travel plans. His use of the word λόγος has enabled him to argue that his word is reliable, since the word he proclaimed to them was Christ himself. If the Corinthians were still feeling contentious, they might well have accused Paul at this point of using a verbal form of sleight of hand! How, they may have wondered, can he equate the word of the gospel with his message about his movements – especially when his plans were in fact changed? The answer is found in his conviction that he, like the Corinthians, is continually 'confirmed into Christ'. Paul's 'Amen' to the gospel is spoken διὰ Χριστοῦ. But *everything* he does or says is now experienced in and through Christ. Even if his plans were changed, he himself is faithful.

Paul's conviction that his whole life is lived 'in Christ', and that his mission is part of God's purpose for the spread of the gospel, dominates the early chapters of 2 Corinthians. Paul has already used this argument that all he does is experienced through Christ in the opening verses of 2 Corinthians, where he has explained that, because he has shared in the sufferings of Christ, he has also experienced consolation διὰ τοῦ Χριστοῦ (v. 5) – sufferings and consolation which are, in turn, experienced by the Corinthians (v. 7). He will use it again in spelling out how he understands his ministry (2 Cor 3:1–6:13). It is set out most clearly in 5:16–21, where he speaks of the new creation that takes place in Christ, through whom God has reconciled the world to himself, and has entrusted Paul with the λόγος of reconciliation. Just as Paul shares in the consolation of God through Christ in 1:3–7, the life of God through Christ in 1:8–11, the glory of God through Christ in 3:1–4:6, and the righteousness of God through Christ in 5:16–21, so in 1:17–24, Paul shares in the *faithfulness* of God through Christ.

It is because Paul understands Christian life to be lived in and through Christ, that he commonly appeals to statements of the gospel and to theological principles when offering advice about Christian behaviour;[14] here he does the same in justifying his own behaviour. His first, and theological, defence against the accusation of vacillating is to appeal to the faithfulness of God himself – a faithfulness which was manifested in Christ, and which is now shared by those who are in him. In vv. 23–24, however, he deals with the accusation in a much more down-to-earth manner.

He begins, nevertheless, by calling God to be his witness – the God already declared to be faithful – so affirming the truth of his own testimony. He changed his plans, he tells the Corinthians, in order to spare them: whether he wished to spare them further discipline or sorrow (the two would presumably have been linked) he does not explain: perhaps sorrow (or pain) is primarily in his mind, since that contrasts with 'joy' in v. 24, and λύπη is in fact the subject

---

[14] See, e.g., Rom 14:9; 15:3; 1 Cor 8:11–12; 2 Cor 8:9.

of 2:1. His intention, he says, is not to control their faith (a comment probably occasioned by another Corinthian accusation!), for his concern is their joy.[15] 'For you', he says, 'stand firm in faith'. The two references to πίστις in this verse echo the theme of the previous section. Is this final πίστει in v. 24 instrumental?[16] But why, it is asked, should the Corinthians be reminded that the basis of the Christian existence is faith? Is it local?[17] But why, others ask, should the Corinthians be told here that they are standing firm in their faith? The answer to both these questions points us in the right direction. What Paul is affirming is that it is faith – or faithfulness – that makes the Corinthians stand firm, just as he himself does.

In the previous section, vv. 17–22, Paul has argued that God himself is faithful, and that he has demonstrated his faithfulness by saying 'Yes' to all his promises in Christ. The apostle and his fellow preachers said 'Amen' to that by proclaiming Christ, and God 'confirmed' the Corinthians, with them, into Christ. If they stand firm 'in faith' it is because they are in Christ. Paul is not dominating the Corinthians, but enabling them to say the same 'Amen' as he himself has given to the gospel. Christian faith is the response to God's faithfulness, but it is also a sharing in Christ's faithfulness. Believers share in Christ's faithfulness because, like him, they trust in God, and because they trust in God, who is faithfulness, they themselves stand firm.

Paul's defence against the accusation that he is fickle is that he cannot be, since God himself is not fickle. If he shares in God's faithfulness it is because he, like all Christians, has been transferred 'into Christ' and now lives in him. It is *through Christ* that he shares the faithfulness of God, and it is *in Christ* that he 'stands firm in faith', trusting in God to confirm him. 2 Cor 1:17–24 spells out one aspect of what Paul means when he says that God acts ἐκ πίστεως εἰς πίστιν (Rom 1:17).[18] It supports the view that the phrase πίστις Χριστοῦ refers primarily to the faithfulness of Christ – the embodiment of God's own faithfulness – and *consequently*, to the faith or faithfulness of those who are 'in Christ' as well.

---

[15] The phrase συνεργοί ἐσμεν τῆς χαρᾶς ὑμῶν is ambiguous. Does it mean 'fellow workers with you for your joy' or 'fellow workers with Silvanus and Timothy for your joy'? The fact that the words follow the plural κυριεύομεν supports this second interpretation. Whichever we choose, Paul's own concern is clear.

[16] So Barrett, *Corinthians, in loc.*

[17] So Furnish, *II Corinthians, in loc.*

[18] The phrase ἐκ πίστεως in Rom 1:17a has been variously interpreted as referring to 1. God's faithfulness 2. Christ's faithfulness and 3. the faith of believers. Since Paul is speaking of the way in which God's righteousness is revealed in the gospel, however, 3. is excluded. On the meaning of this phrase, see the discussion in Douglas A. Campbell, 'Romans 1:17 – A *Crux Interpretum* for the Πίστις Χριστοῦ Debate', *JBL* 113 (1994): 265–285, and literature cited there.

42. Philippians: Phantom Opponents and the Real Source of Conflict

1. Introduction: The Nature of the Opposition

Who were Paul's 'opponents' in Philippi? This much-debated question[1] should perhaps give way to the more fundamental question: *were* there any opponents within the Philippian community? That there were opponents *to* the Christian community in Philippi is plain, for they are clearly referred to in 1:28. Since very little is said about them, except that they are heading for destruction and are causing the Philippians suffering, and since there is no hint that they are preaching the 'wrong' gospel, this group must almost certainly have consisted of outsiders,[2] who were opposed to the gospel and were persecuting the Christians in Philippi, much as Paul himself had suffered at their hands.[3] What, then, is the evidence for opposition to Paul's gospel *within* the Christian community? In 3:2 Paul issues a peremptory warning against 'the dogs', who were clearly Judaizers of some kind, but the warning serves mainly to introduce a discussion of his own renunciation of Jewish privilege, which reflects Christ's own self-emptying. There is no evidence of any significant Jewish presence in Philippi, and no hint that these people were already at work in that city; the warning here seems to be a general one – be careful if you come across such people! – rather than referring to a specific, known danger. In 3:18–19 Paul refers to those who 'live as enemies of the cross of Christ', but, remarkably, says that he has often told the Philippians about them – suggesting, again, that this was a danger that had not yet invaded the community.[4] Finally, we have in 4:2–3 Paul's plea to Euodia and Syntyche 'to be of the same mind in the Lord'. Here we are clearly dealing, not with

---

[1] For a recent summary of some of the main suggestions, see Peter Thomas O'Brien, *The Epistle to the Philippians,* NIGTC (Grand Rapids: Eerdmans, 1991), 26–35. For later discussion, see Günter Klein, 'Antipaulinismus in Philippi: Eine Problemskizze', in *Jesu Rede von Gott und ihre Nachgeschichte im frühen Christentum: Beiträge zur Verkündigung Jesu und zum Kerygma der Kirche: Festschrift für Willi Marxsen,* eds. Dietrich-Alex Koch et al. (Gütersloh: Mohn, 1989), 297–313; Christoph Kähler, 'Konflikt, Kompromiss und Bekenntnis: Paulus und seine Gegner im Philipperbrief', *Kerygma und Dogma* 40 (1994): 47–64.

[2] In Philippi, the opposition was almost certainly pagan.

[3] Phil 1:30; Acts 16:19–24.

[4] It would seem that this is a different group from the 'dogs' in 3:2. For a brief summary of the issues, see Morna D. Hooker, 'Philippians', in *The New Interpreter's Bible,* eds. Leander E. Keck et al. (Nashville: Abingdon, 2000), 11/534b–535a.

false teaching or opposition to Paul (since both have wrestled side by side with Paul 'in the gospel', together with others who are all Paul's co-workers), but rather with some personal dispute. It is not surprising, then, that some recent commentators have concluded that the notion that the Philippian community had been invaded by opponents to Paul's gospel is the product of scholars' faulty 'mirror-reading' of the text.[5] There is, indeed, *no* evidence that there were *any* 'false teachers' in the Philippian community.

Our concern in this paper, however, centres on a somewhat different problem, which arises from personal rivalry rather than doctrinal opposition, and involves not the Philippians, but Paul himself. In 1:12–26, Paul explains his own situation to the Philippians, declaring that his imprisonment has in fact helped to advance the gospel, both because news of the reason for his imprisonment has spread but also because many members of the Christian community in the city where he is imprisoned[6] have been inspired by his courage and confidence in the Lord to preach the gospel.[7] Some of them, however, do so for the wrong reasons – out of strife and rivalry, and because of their own selfish ambition. Strangely, Paul does not directly condemn these people, but concludes that, whatever their motives, Christ is nevertheless being proclaimed, and that this is all that matters.

Although commentators have sometimes identified these people as 'Judaizers', it is difficult to see how this could be the case. How could he describe Judaizers as 'proclaiming Christ', when in Gal 1:6–7 he refers to their teaching as 'another gospel', and indeed quickly denies that it is a gospel at all? Suggestions that he has 'mellowed' in his opposition to the Judaizers since writing Galatians founder when we turn to Phil 3:2.[8] Moreover, there is no criticism here of the content of this group's preaching. Paul clearly recognizes these people as fellow Christians: they are included among those whom he describes as 'brothers in the Lord' (1:14), and they are said to 'speak the word' (1:14), to 'preach Christ' (1:15) and to 'proclaim Christ' (1:17). Though he

---

[5] Gordon D. Fee, *Paul's Letter to the Philippians*, NICNT (Grand Rapids: Eerdmans, 1995), 7–10; Markus Bockmuehl, *The Epistle to the Philippians*, BNTC (London: A&C Black, 1997), 18–19.

[6] Rome, Caesarea, and Ephesus have all been suggested as the place of Paul's imprisonment, but Rome is by far the most likely, and the difficulties with this solution have been exaggerated. See the major commentaries for summaries of the arguments. In this essay we shall assume that the letter was written from Rome.

[7] Paul in fact expresses this more modestly: it is others who have been made confident in the Lord by his bonds. Here we see the same paradoxical sharing of strength and consolation 'in Christ' by those who are weak and afflicted, that we find in passages such as 2 Cor 12:8–9; 1:3–7.

[8] I have argued elsewhere for the unity of Philippians, on the basis that chapter 3 reflects and continues the argument of chapter 2. See Morna D. Hooker, 'Philippians 2:6–11', in *Jesus und Paulus: Festschrift für W. G. Kümmel,* eds. E. Earle Ellis and E. Grasser (Göttingen: Vandenhoeck & Ruprecht, 1975), 151–164.

thinks they are doing the right thing for the wrong motive, they can hardly be described as 'opponents'. He refuses to regard them as rivals, even though he obviously believes that they see *themselves* as his rivals. The problem (as in 4:2–3) concerns personal conflicts rather than doctrinal disputes.

Yet this distinction between 'doctrine' and personal rivalry immediately raises a further problem. Were not the gospel and personal attitudes inextricably linked? Did not the message of Christ's own self-emptying, death, and exaltation imply the necessity for Christians to be conformed to the same pattern in their everyday lives? Certainly this seems to be Paul's basic argument throughout Phil 1:27–3:21! Did he not argue that the image of Christ must be stamped on the Christian?[9] Is it not perfectly clear that conformity to that image excludes such things as φθόνος, ἔρις and ἐριθεία?[10] Did Paul not consider personal rivalry and bickering to be a danger to the church?'[11] Is it not essential that those who preach the gospel must preach Christ, not themselves,[12] and that this must be demonstrated in the preachers' own lives?[13] Describing his call in Gal 1:16, Paul speaks of God choosing ἀποκαλύψαι τὸν Υἱὸν αὐτοῦ ἐν ἐμοί, and if we take that ἐν seriously, then Paul is placing the emphasis on Christ being revealed through what he, Paul, becomes – i.e. his manner of life – rather than through what he proclaims. This is hardly surprising, since he goes on to declare: 'It is no longer I who live, but it is Christ who lives in me' (Gal 2:20). This is why he dares to urge his converts to imitate his example.[14]

In accusing these people of preaching Christ because of envy and strife (v. 15), and as the result of selfish ambition (v. 17), it would seem that Paul is making the kind of criticism that was brought against himself in Corinth (2 Cor 4:5). We might expect him to say that their selfish ambition emptied the cross of its power, as he does in 1 Cor 1:17, when attacking the rivalry that was endemic in Corinth. In Paul's view, concern for one's self contradicts the underlying principle of the gospel, which must be reflected in concern for others. Yet here he insists that in spite of their mixed motives these preachers *are* 'proclaiming Christ'.

---

[9] Rom 6:1–11; 2 Cor 3:18.

[10] All three terms are included in the list of 'the works of the flesh' in Gal 5:19–21. Cf. also 2 Cor 12:20, where we find ἔρις and ἐριθεία in the list of what Paul regards as possible dangers to the community.

[11] Cf. 1 Cor 1–3, where those who encourage such attitudes are said to be in danger of destroying the temple of the Holy Spirit, 1 Cor 3:16–17.

[12] 2 Cor 4:5. Cf. 1 Cor 3:5–9.

[13] See, e.g., 2 Cor 4:5: 'ourselves as your slaves, for Jesus' sake'. Cf. 1 Cor 9:19–23: I have discussed this passage elsewhere; see Morna D. Hooker, 'A Partner in the Gospel: Paul's Understanding of His Ministry', in *Theology and Ethics in Paul and His Interpreters: Essays in Honor of Victor Paul Furnish,* eds. Eugene H. Lovering, Jr. and Jerry L. Sumney (Nashville: Abingdon, 1996), 83–100 = above, essay 39 (pp. 579–595).

[14] 1 Cor 4:16; Phil 3:17.

Paul's unhappiness regarding the motives of his fellow Christians in Rome surfaces again in Phil 2:20–21, when he complains that of those whom he might send to Philippi he can trust only Timothy to have the interests of the Philippians at heart, since the rest are all concerned about their own interests. The people whom Paul has in mind here are presumably a smaller group than those he refers to in 1:15, 17, and do not necessarily overlap with them, but their general attitude is similar: they are concerned with their own welfare, rather than that of others. It seems that Paul is determined that his envoy to Philippi should be the ideal role model.

Finally, we notice that there are hints that Paul believes that the same infection may be creeping into the Philippian congregation. The clearest indication of this comes in 4:2–3, where he refers to a disagreement between two leading members of the Christian community. We are not told the cause of the disagreement, and Paul does not accuse Euodia and Syntyche of rivalry and ambition, but the fact that he urges them to be of the same mind in the Lord suggests that he believes that each of them is more concerned about having her own way than with the truth of the gospel. It sounds very much as though Paul suspects that the strife and rivalry which he has encountered in Rome may be present in Philippi. If so, then the way in which he spells out the gospel in terms of Christ's self-emptying and stresses its implications for Christian living is clearly relevant to the Philippian community.[15] This perhaps explains why he is so anxious to send the right envoy to Philippi, someone who will provide the right example to the community. Yet Paul speaks warmly of these two women as having struggled alongside him in the work of the gospel; and having urged them to 'agree in the Lord', and requested his 'loyal companion' to assist them, he drops the matter: the danger appears to be minimal, and certainly does not affect Paul's overwhelming joy regarding the Philippians' genuine faith and their 'partnership in the gospel'.[16] The characteristic note of the epistle is joy, and he refers to the Philippian Christians as his 'joy and crown'[17] Whatever the dispute between the two women, it appears not to have been a major problem.[18]

We need, then, to examine further two related issues:

First, why does Paul refuse to regard the group referred to in 1:15, 17 as opponents, and insist that these people *are* preaching Christ, in spite of attitudes which might be thought to negate the gospel?

---

[15] Phil 1:27–2:18.
[16] Phil 1:5–11; 4:15–20.
[17] Phil 4:1.
[18] The recent study by Davorin Peterlin, *Paul's Letter to the Philippians in the Light of Disunity in the Church,* NTSup 79 (Leiden; New York: Brill, 1995) greatly exaggerates the problems by excessive 'mirror-reading'.

Second, what were the problems and concerns that led Paul to write the letter to the Philippians? Did it perhaps arise out of and reflect his own situation and problems as much as those of the Philippians?

2. Paul's 'Rivals' in Philippians 1:15–17

Paul's reference to those who are preaching Christ as a result of his imprisonment is set out in chiastic form, drawing a clear contrast between honest and false motives:

τινὲς μὲν καὶ διὰ φθόνον καὶ ἔριν,
τινὲς δὲ καὶ δι' εὐδοκίαν
   τὸν Χριστὸν κηρύσσουσιν·

οἱ μὲν ἐξ ἀγάπης,
εἰδότες ὅτι εἰς ἀπολογίαν τοῦ εὐαγγελίου κεῖμαι,
οἱ δὲ ἐξ ἐριθείας
   τὸν Χριστὸν καταγγέλλουσιν,
οὐχ ἁγνῶς οἰόμενοι θλῖψιν ἐγείρειν τοῖς δεσμοῖς μου.

Τί γάρ; πλὴν ὅτι παντὶ τρόπῳ
εἴτε προφάσει
εἴτε ἀληθείᾳ,
   Χριστὸς καταγγέλλεται
καὶ ἐν τούτῳ χαίρω.

On the one hand we have φθόνος, ἔρις and ἐριθεία. In Rom 1:29, φθόνος and ἔρις are both said to characterize fallen humanity, while in the following chapter (2:8), those who are doomed to wrath are those who live ἐξ ἐριθείας and who disobey the truth (ἀλήθεια). But this does not mean that these attitudes are no longer found in the Christian community! In 13:12–13, the Romans are urged to lay aside the works of darkness, which include ἔρις (here linked with ζῆλος). In 1 Cor 1:11 we learn that there are ἔριδες in Corinth and in 1 Cor 3:3, ἔρις and ζῆλος are seen as a sign that the Corinthians are not πνευματικός but σαρκικός. In 2 Cor 12:20 Paul expresses his fear that he will not find the community to be what he would like them to be: the catalogue of what he fears he *will* find includes both ἔρις and ἐριθεία. Gal 5:20–21 refers to all three terms in a list of the works of the flesh which are opposed to the Spirit, but the warning against them indicates that there is a real danger that the Galatians may succumb to them. Finally, we note that the Philippians themselves are urged to do nothing from ἐριθεία in 2:3.

It is worth noting that φθόνος and ἔρις appear together in secular Greek as attitudes which were considered to endanger the common good. Thus Dio Chrysostom (writing a little later than Paul) condemns them as opposing concord in the community, and regards them as inappropriate behaviour for the manly and high-minded.[19] In an earlier discourse,[20] he contrasts those who are motivated by concern for the good of others and those who are seeking personal glory. This is remarkably similar to Paul's antipathy to these attitudes. Yet Paul's concern goes beyond this, for he regards these things as belonging to the sphere of the flesh, not the Spirit, and it is clear in 1 Corinthians 1 that he sees them as endangering the unity of the body of Christ.

In opposition to φθόνος and ἔρις, Paul sets εὐδοκία, whose meaning is far from straightforward. Whose good will is in mind? The word's normal meaning in the LXX and New Testament is 'God's will or purpose',[21] though in Rom 10:1 Paul uses it of his own resolve.[22] But this is hardly what we understood by 'goodwill', which is the meaning normally given to the term here. The word is used again in Phil 2:13, and though some commentators interpret it there also as meaning 'goodwill', it is more naturally understood as referring to God's good pleasure or purpose: it is God who is at work in the Christian community in Philippi, bringing about the fulfilment of his will. Some have argued, therefore, that the word has the same meaning in 1:15:[23] if this is correct, what Paul is contrasting to φθόνος and ἔρις is not simply goodwill towards himself, but a willingness to be used by God for the sake of his purposes.

However we interpret this word, the issue focuses on attitudes towards Paul in the next contrast, which is between ἀγαπή and ἐριθεία. There is little need to explore the appropriateness of ἀγαπή in this context, for it sums up, as does no other term, the quality which should characterize life in the Spirit. In 1 Corinthians 13 it is the supreme gift which holds the body together – in contrast to the ἔριδες of 1:11 that are in danger of tearing it apart. Love is the very opposite of selfish ambition.

In Phil 1:16–17 the contrast between ἀγαπή and ἐριθεία is filled out and made specific by two defining clauses. On the one hand, those motivated by love know that Paul has been put in prison for the defence of the gospel. On the other, those motivated by selfish ambition are not sincere but imagine that they can increase his sufferings. It looks, then, as though the particular problem being described here has something to do with the way in which Paul's fellow Christians view his imprisonment. If the first group know that Paul has been imprisoned for the defence of the gospel, this is presumably something that the members of the second group have failed to grasp.

---

[19] Dio Chrysostom, *Or.* 77/78.37–39.
[20] Dio Chrysostom, *Or.* 38.8–9.
[21] In the Pauline literature, see Eph 1:5, 9.
[22] Cf. also 2 Thess 1:11, where the meaning is ambiguous.
[23] Bockmuehl, *Philippians, in loc.*

What exactly is Paul claiming here? The word κεῖμαι in v. 16 suggests that he thinks of himself as being 'placed' in prison or 'appointed' to be there. The purpose of this is conveyed by the word ἀπολογία, a term which was linked in v. 7 with βεβαίωσις, confirmation, and it is already clear from vv. 12–14 that his defence of the gospel has helped to spread it; his expectation of a positive outcome from this 'defence' (whatever the verdict at the trial!) will be affirmed in v. 20.

This very positive attitude towards Paul's imprisonment – that it has, in effect, been part of God's εὐδοκία – is set in contrast to a very negative view, held by the other group. Paul obviously believes that the members of this group see themselves as his rivals; if, as he says, they imagine that he will be hurt to learn of their successful preaching, then they must see *him* as a failure. Do they perhaps think that he is in danger of bringing the Christian community into disrepute, and thus *damaging* the cause? Do they think that Paul has come into unnecessary conflict with the political authorities? Do they therefore consider him an embarrassment, and rejoice that he is out of the way? Do they perhaps even believe that his imprisonment is a sign of divine punishment?

What we have in Phil 1:15, 17 is, of course, Paul's own assessment of this group's motives, and we cannot be sure that he has understood them correctly! He accuses these people of supposing (wrongly!) that they are adding to his affliction, but perhaps it is he who is wrong in his supposition that this is their motive. Certainly he seems to believe that they have misunderstood the significance of his imprisonment. He insists, therefore, that he has been set in prison in order to defend the gospel, and that his very imprisonment has served to forward it. His 'eager expectation and hope' are that he will not be put to shame and that, whatever happens to him, Christ will be exalted through him, whether by his life or his death (v. 20). Like the Corinthians, the members of this group have perhaps failed to understand the implications of the gospel, and so cannot see his sufferings as part of the paradox of the cross. Whether or not Paul is correct in thinking that they wish to cause him pain, we can be sure that their understanding of the apostolic role would have been very different from the one he sums up in 1 Cor 4:8–21[24] Paul may well be right, then, in thinking that they are to some extent motivated by ἐριθεία. Were they perhaps boasting, in effect, that if Paul had converted thousands, they would convert ten thousands?[25]

---

[24] There is no need to imagine, as do some (e.g. Robert Jewett, 'Conflicting Movements in the Early Church as Reflected in Philippians', *NT* 12 [1970]: 362–390), that 'divine-men' missionaries are the cause of the problem.

[25] 1 Sam 18:7.

Since vv. 16–17 focus on Paul, it is probable that we should understand the envy and strife of v. 15 as being directed chiefly towards him, in which case we may suppose that the εὐδοκία in that verse also concerns him. But this does not necessarily mean that we should understand the term as meaning simply 'human goodwill', for this second group's attitude towards Paul will presumably be grounded in the divine purpose. Moreover, as we have seen, these people (like Paul himself) understand Paul's chains to be themselves part of the divine purpose. They are certainly not preaching Christ because they wish to be nice to Paul! Rather, their response to Paul's imprisonment is to carry on his work of proclaiming the gospel. Human goodwill, then, seems an inadequate understanding of the term: their preaching, like his imprisonment, has its part in God's plan.

The contrast between the two groups is summed up in 1:18: Christ is being proclaimed, we are told, whether as the result of pretext (πρόφασις) or of truth (ἀλήθεια). Paul uses the term πρόφασις in 1 Thess 2:5, where he denies that his mission to the Thessalonians had been motivated ἐν προφάσει πλεονεξίας. In a similar – but much more passionate – context in 2 Corinthians 4, he insists that he has preached the word of God in an open declaration of the truth. We see, then, that these words are terms that Paul has used in defending his *own* ministry: he himself has been accused of πρόφασις, and he has claimed that, on the contrary, he is motivated by ἀλήθεια.

Remarkably, however, Paul affirms that *both* groups are proclaiming Christ; those whom he criticizes are not preaching 'another Jesus'[26] or 'a different gospel',[27] but are preaching the right gospel for the wrong reasons. If we are puzzled by his failure to condemn them, then it is perhaps partly explained by the fact that the second group's failing appears to be primarily animosity towards Paul himself. At the heart of the disagreement seems to be their unwillingness to recognize that his imprisonment is furthering the gospel. But just as the Corinthians, though 'infants in Christ', are nevertheless *in Christ*,[28] so these preachers are in Christ and are 'preaching Christ'. Their misunderstanding does not invalidate their gospel.

We need to remember also that Paul was under no illusions about the continuing existence of inappropriate attitudes and behaviour within the Christian community, as his continual warnings against them make clear. His constant appeal to his converts is: 'You are in Christ: live as those who are in Christ *should* live!' His scathing comments to the Corinthians in 1 Cor 4:8–13 are addressed to those whom in v. 14 he terms his 'beloved children'. Paul himself, as he will remind the Philippians in 3:12, does not consider himself

---

[26] As in 2 Cor 11:4.
[27] 2 Cor 11:4; Gal 1:6.
[28] 1 Cor 3:1.

to be perfect. 2 Corinthians 10–13 demonstrate that he was painfully aware of the dangers of boasting in his achievements as an apostle – a danger which besets all preachers and to which many succumb. Though the message of the cross *should* be reflected in the life of the preacher, as in the lives of all Christians, the reflection in this life is only partial, and the process of transformation incomplete.[29] It would seem, however, that the power of the gospel is sufficient to negate human failure. If the message of the cross is being effectively proclaimed, though from the wrong motives, we find that even here, the 'weakness of God', displayed in the cross, is stronger than the 'human strength' of those who proclaim it.

We turn now to our second question, and ask how this matter relates to the rest of the letter. Are the issues that concern Paul in prison reflected in the teaching directed towards the Philippians?

3. Paul's *Apologia*

The letter to the Philippians is unusual among Paul's epistles in that much of the section that follows immediately after the thanksgiving in 1:3–11 is devoted to telling the readers about his own situation. It would seem that the Philippians are concerned about him[30] and are eager to know how he fares, but Paul introduces the subject of his imprisonment in a triumphant way: 'I want you to know that what has happened to me has actually helped to advance the gospel'. He is clearly anxious that the Philippians should have no doubts about why he is in prison: it is for the defence of the gospel (v. 16). He does not wish to risk any misunderstanding of the kind that he has encountered in Rome. He seems anxious, too, to set his own view of the coming trial down on paper. Whatever happens, he is confident that he will not be put to shame, but that through their prayers and the help of the Spirit of Jesus Christ he will be vindicated before God and enabled to speak boldly, so that Christ will be 'magnified' through him. For Paul, the whole process – imprisonment, trial, verdict and possible punishment – serves to spread the gospel. The Philippians need to be reassured that what is happening to him will further God's plan, but Paul perhaps has another reason for explaining how he views his situation: Phil 1:12–26 is not only a defence against those who misunderstand his plight (vv. 15, 17) and a reassurance to the Philippians that the outcome will serve the gospel (vv. 12–20), but a 'final testimony' (in case of an unfavourable verdict at the trial) explaining the underlying principle of his ministry: 'to me, to live is Christ and to die is gain' (v. 21).

---

[29] 2 Cor 3:18.
[30] Phil 2:25–30.

One tends to assume that from 1:27 onwards, when Paul turns his attention back to the Philippians, we have a letter whose primary concern is to encourage the Philippians to 'live in a manner that is worthy of the gospel'. Yet there are frequent references to his own situation and ministry, suggesting that the manner of life he is anxious to foster in his converts is inextricably linked with this explanation of his own manner of life and ministry. This is hardly surprising, for the Philippians are 'his joy and his crown' (4:1) and his partners in the gospel (1:5). The pattern which he urges on them (of conformity to Christ's own attitudes) is the one that has governed his own ministry. His appeal to them is to join in 'imitating' him (3:17), just as he has clearly 'imitated' Christ (3:7–11).[31] There are others among them who live according to the model – τύπος – which they have in Paul. Side by side with his encouragement to the Philippians to follow this way of life (1:27–2:18) he shows how he has followed it himself (3:4–16). His argument seems to be: 'the principle that to live is Christ and to die is gain has governed my life; may it govern yours also'.

The teaching in 1:27–2:18 is clearly related to matters which affect Paul in prison, and may be prompted as much by his own experience as by what is going on in Philippi. What echoes of his own situation, then, are to be found there?

We note first that Paul begins his teaching by urging the Philippians to stand firm against opposition from outside. They must not be intimidated by their opponents, for what is taking place is 'from God' (v. 28), who has 'granted' them the privilege, not simply of believing in Christ but of suffering for his sake – an idea which is emphasized by being expressed twice (ὑπὲρ Χριστοῦ ... ὑπὲρ αὐτοῦ, v. 29), echoing the phrase used elsewhere when speaking of Christ's suffering and death 'for us'. The Philippians are thus 'having the same struggle' that they had once seen Paul engaged in (while he was among them) and now hear him to be having (in Rome). Just as Paul believes that God is at work in his own circumstances, and that he has been 'placed' in prison for the defence of the gospel (v. 16), so he believes that the opportunity to suffer for Christ has been 'granted' to the Philippians. He is confident that the outcome of his own sufferings will be σωτηρία (v. 19), and assures the Philippians that their own firmness in the face of opposition is proof of *their* σωτηρία (v. 28).

If Paul, in prison, is finding himself lacking in support from many of his fellow Christians, it is hardly surprising if he urges the Philippians to 'stand firm in one Spirit,[32] striving side by side as one person for the faith of the

---

[31] The command Συμμιμηταί μου γίνεσθε should perhaps be understood to mean 'Be imitators *with* me' – i.e. *of* Christ. For the literature on this point, see Hooker, 'ΠΙΣΤΙΣ ΧΡΙΣΤΟΥ', *NTS* 35 (1989): 332–333. But however we translate the phrase, the twin ideas that Paul and Christ are to be seen as 'models' of Christian living are both present.

[32] It is likely that πνεῦμα here, as in 2:1, refers to the Holy Spirit. For discussion of the point see the commentaries.

gospel' (v. 27). Nor is it surprising if he continues, in Philippians 2, by appealing to the 'encouragement found in Christ', the 'consolation of love', and the 'fellowship of the Spirit', and urging the Philippians to complete *his* joy by 'thinking the same thing, having the same love, being of one accord and thinking the one thing' (vv. 1–2). As in 1:15–18, we have a contrast between two attitudes: the one they should pursue has been set out in 2:1–2, where one of the key terms used in 1:16, ἀγάπη, has been picked up; now, in v. 3, where Paul sets out what they should avoid, we find the second, ἐριθεία: 'do nothing from selfish ambition or conceit'. Paul is anxious that the Philippians should get it right, and be motivated by ἀγάπη, not ἐριθεία: so far, however, the only cause of his anxiety for which we have evidence is his experience in Rome.

After repeating the contrast in v. 4, Paul sets out the basis of his appeal: the *reason* why they should be governed by love, not by selfish ambition, is that this is what the gospel itself is about. In 2:6–11 we see how Christ himself was governed by concern for others, not himself. The function of the so-called 'hymn' is both kerygmatic *and* ethical. The gospel demands that Christians have 'the same mind' that is seen in Christ and that belongs to them *in* Christ: to live in any other way is a denial of the gospel itself. Therefore the Philippians – who have 'always obeyed' Paul – must 'continue to work out' their own σωτηρία, for God is at work in them (vv. 12–13). The goal is expressed in the phrase ὑπὲρ τῆς εὐδοκίας: all is 'for the sake of his will'. The purpose of God – which in 1:15 motivated one of the groups of Christians in Rome – is worked out also in the Philippians, as they respond to the gospel and allow it to govern their lives.

Another – implied – contrast lies behind 2:14–15, where the Philippians are urged to do everything 'without complaining or arguing'. Perhaps Paul again has the ἔρις of 1:15 in mind; certainly he is thinking of the people of Israel, for the phrase is a clear echo of Deut 32:5. But the Philippians are not, like them, the 'crooked and perverse generation'; on the contrary, they shine among them like lights. So Paul returns to the thought of the opposition that confronts the Philippians, and urges them to 'hold fast[33] the word of life'. Then he will be able to boast on the day of Christ that he has not run in vain or toiled in vain.[34] In other words, the Philippians will provide the proof of the authenticity of his work. Once again, Paul may have those who criticize him in mind, and in v. 17 he appears to return to the matter that is uppermost in his mind – the possible verdict of death that looms over him. To be sure, his reference to being poured out as a libation does not necessarily

---

[33] It is possible to understand the verb ἐπέχω here as meaning 'to hold out/proffer'. So, e.g., Fee, *Philippians, in loc*. The idea of Paul's 'boasting' in them, however, suggests that he has in mind their steadfastness.

[34] The second phrase echoes Isa 49:4.

relate specifically to his death, since it can be understood of his whole ministry, but the two are closely linked, since it is the manner of that ministry that is leading him into the danger of death – just as it was Christ's self-emptying and manner of living that led to *his* death. Again, the Philippians' 'offering' could be understood to refer to the gift the Philippians have sent him – except that the offering is defined as being τῆς πίστεως. Moreover, there is a logical link (already established in v. 16) between Paul's death and the Philippians' steadfastness, and it is therefore more likely that Paul is seeing his death as a libation that accompanies the Philippians' 'sacrifice' and 'offering', which consist of lives lived in accordance with the faith of the gospel. Once again, Paul links his own situation with that of the Philippians, who are maintaining the faith.

We have noted already that in the passage immediately following this section of teaching, Paul refers again to the motives of his fellow Christians in Rome (2:21). Here the contrast is between Timothy, who will genuinely care for the Philippians' well-being, and the rest, who 'seek their own interests, not those of Christ Jesus'. Timothy's value is already known to the Philippians, since he has served (δουλεύω) with Paul in the cause of the gospel (v. 22). Paul described himself and Timothy as δοῦλοι Χριστοῦ Ἰησοῦ in 1:1,[35] and though the appellation is an honorific one,[36] it nevertheless echoes the language of 2:5–11. Paul and Timothy are the δοῦλοι of the one who is now κύριος, and proud to be so: but Christ was made κύριος because he was content to become a δοῦλος, and the manner of their service will therefore be modelled on his. Timothy will, in turn, be a model to the Philippians, whom Paul has urged to be concerned for one another's interests, not their own (μὴ τὰ ἑαυτῶν, 2:4) – unlike those referred to in 2:21, who seek τὰ ἑαυτῶν. Paul hopes to send Timothy soon (vv. 19, 23), but he is still 'confident in the Lord' that he himself will be able to come soon (v. 24). Paul's confidence surprises us, but it echoes what he said in 1:25, where his conviction that he was needed by his churches persuaded him that, in spite of his personal desire to be 'with Christ', he would 'remain' with them. Nevertheless, this has to be seen in the context of his awareness that the outcome of the trial is far from certain (1:20–23). His own convictions about what would be good for the churches are challenged throughout the epistle by the reality of his situation, and lead him to seize the opportunity to write what is in effect a 'farewell letter'.

Paul then turns from Timothy to Epaphroditus, whose return to Philippi has probably triggered the writing of the letter (2:25–30). Epaphroditus has been the Philippians' messenger and a minister to Paul in his need in captivity:

---

[35] The use of δοῦλος in a prescript is rare: see only Rom 1:1.
[36] Cf. the descriptions of Moses and David as 'my servant' in e.g. Num 12:7; Ps 89:20 (LXX 88:21).

he has endeavoured to minister to Paul on the Philippians' behalf, and has risked his life in the process. The whole passage resonates with concern for others: the Philippians for Paul and for Epaphroditus, Epaphroditus for Paul and for the Philippians, Paul for Epaphroditus and for the Philippians. Though the language is not this time picked up, the theme is again that of 2:4, since each is concerned for the interests of others.

But why, when Paul turns back to teaching, does he issue the stern warning against Judaizers in 3:2–3? There is no reason to believe that these people are already troubling the Philippians, and it may simply be that Paul is warning them against all possible dangers – understandable, if he thinks it possible that he won't have the opportunity to visit them, or even to write to them, again. The interesting fact from our viewpoint, however, is that the warning immediately triggers Paul's account of what he has done in response to the gospel – in effect, 'emptying' himself of his Jewish privileges[37] and regarding them as worthless for the sake of knowing Christ, gaining Christ, and being found in him. For Paul, as for Christ, this process lasts even to death. Once again, Paul's mind has turned to what he may soon have to face; he wants to know 'the power of Christ's resurrection', which is experienced through the 'sharing of his sufferings' and by 'being conformed to his death' (3:10). For Paul, response to the gospel means becoming like Christ and sharing his attitudes: this is what has led to his imprisonment, and to the prospect of becoming like him in death, trusting that 'to die is gain' (1:21). The process of conformity to Christ is not yet complete, and the prize is not yet won (3:12–14). Paul again links the Philippians with himself with the words Τοῦτο φρονῶμεν, echoing the command of 2:6 and showing that he and they are taking part in a common endeavour. And if any of them thinks differently, then God will reveal this to them (v. 15)! This brief reference to possible dissent is dropped as soon as it is introduced, and does not suggest that Paul suspects any serious disagreement. If anyone *does* think differently, then he is confident that he or she will be corrected.

For Paul the end is in sight, and the prize will soon be gained (v. 14). It is because he himself has given up everything for the sake of Christ and longs to share his resurrection by being conformed to his death that he dares to urge the Philippians to 'observe those who live according to the example that you have in us' (v. 17). They are to join in imitating him (or perhaps to be joint imitators *with* him),[38] but the ultimate model is, of course, Christ himself. Once again, Paul contrasts two ways of life: over against the example (τύπος) that the Philippians have in Christ, stand those who 'live as enemies of the cross' (v. 18). Why does Paul mention these 'negative models'? Clearly

---

[37] The verb, ἥγημαι and ἡγοῦμαι (*bis*), echoes ἡγήσατο in 2:6.
[38] See above, n. 31.

they have caused him much pain and distress, since he has 'often' told the Philippians about them – which suggests that they are not present in Philippi. There is nothing to indicate that these people are the 'dogs' of 3:2;[39] it is possible that they do not even claim to be Christians, though both Paul's distress at their lifestyle and the reference to 'the cross of Christ' suggest that they do. The accusation that 'their god is their belly' and that 'their minds are set on earthly things' (v. 19) makes it probable that they were living a licentious, antinomian life, believing that the gospel brings freedom from all constraint. The context suggests that the shame in which these people glory may well be sexual licence,[40] but whatever it is, it is the antithesis of true glory. Presumably Paul's words are intended as a warning against their way of life: they do not have to be physically present in Philippi for their philosophy to represent a danger. Their manner of life is precisely the opposite of the one that Paul has been advocating, for it is based on self-indulgence, and their minds are set on earthly things instead of heavenly. The way of life that Paul has been commending (πολιτεύεσθε, 1:27) is now seen to relate to a heavenly 'commonwealth' (πολίτευμα, 3:20),[41] from which Christians expect a saviour – the Lord Jesus Christ, whose exaltation was described in 2:9–11. The one who in 2:7–8 was said to have been found in fashion (σχῆμα) as a man and who humbled himself (ἐταπείνωσεν ἑαυτὸν) will now transform (μετασχηματίσει) the body of our humiliation (τὸ σῶμα τῆς ταπεινώσεως ἡμῶν); he who took the form of a slave (μορφὴ δούλου) will conform (σύμμορφον) that body to his body of glory (δόξα, in contrast to the false δόξα of v. 19), by the power that enables him to make all things subject to himself (echoing 2:9–11).

Paul's eye is clearly still on the heavenly prize. But the imagery has reverted from running a race to 'standing firm'. He urges the Philippians to stand firm 'thus' – i.e., in accordance with his teaching from 1:27 onwards. They are his joy and crown (4:1, cf. 2:16) – the symbol of victory that will be given him at the end of the race.

In 4:2–3 we finally come to a clear indication of some sort of trouble in the Philippian church. But after all that he has said, Paul apparently feels that there is little more that *needs* to be said, beyond urging them to 'think the same thing in the Lord' (4:2, echoing 2:2). He simply asks other members of the congregation to help the two women to agree, and so offer the kind of mutual support that we expect among those who share the mind of Christ.

After a few general admonitions (4:4–8) and encouragement to continue to follow Paul's teaching and example (v. 9), Paul turns again to his own

---

[39] See above, n. 4.
[40] See the commentaries for discussion of the various suggestions.
[41] The use of the term in this context suggests that Paul is not primarily concerned with civic responsibility in 1:27 pace Bruce Winter, Seek the Welfare of the City: Christians as Benefactors and Citizens (Grand Rapids: Eerdmans, 1994), 81–104.

situation in prison, and to the help that the Philippians have given him there (4:10–19); this help is 'a fragrant offering, an acceptable sacrifice, well pleasing to God' (v. 18), since these gifts, like the earlier ones they made for his work (vv. 15–16), are a 'sharing in the gospel' (1:5), modelled on Christ's self-giving.

4. Conclusion

The letter to the Philippians is not simply a pastoral letter to one of Paul's congregations. Pastoral concern is certainly part of its purpose, for in spite of Paul's expressions of confidence that he will be spared, it would seem that he is anxious to set out his understanding of the manner of life that is appropriate to Christians. In that sense, it is part of his final testimony. But it is also testimony to the underlying policy of his mission which, like his understanding of the Christian life, is modelled on the gospel story itself. If the gospel is about Christ's self-emptying and exaltation, then the Christian must be prepared to abandon concern for self, to share his sufferings and death, and so share his glory. The paradox of the cross, seen in Christian humility and final glory, is reflected in Paul's ministry: in particular, it is seen in his imprisonment – which has served to spread the gospel – and will continue to be seen in whatever happens to him, whether through his life or his death, since for him 'to live is Christ, and to die is gain'. Insofar as others are blind to this principle, and regard his imprisonment as a sign of failure, Paul's letter is a defence of his understanding of his apostolic mission.

The real source of conflict, then, is found in Rome (if that is where Paul is imprisoned), not in Philippi, and centres on Paul himself.[42] The epistle's explanation is to be found in Paul's own situation, quite as much as that of the congregation to whom he writes. In this respect, Philippians is perhaps analogous to Romans, which many have argued is addressed to Paul's own

---

[42] It is worth nothing that in 1 Clement, the deaths of Peter and Paul are attributed to ζῆλος and φθόνος (5:2), and that of Paul to ζῆλος and ἔρις (5:5) – a combination used by Paul himself in Rom 13:13 and 1 Cor 3:3. There are other interesting echoes of Philippians, such as the use of πολιτεία etc. in 2:8 and 3:4, the reference to Paul showing the way to a crown (βραβεῖον, 5:5, cf. Phil 3:14), the reference to Clement and the Corinthians being engaged in the same strife (ὁ αὐτὸς ... ἀγών, 7:1, cf. Phil 1:30) as those who preceded them, the appeal to be imitators of the prophets (μιμηταὶ γενώμεθα, 17:1), and the frequent references in the early chapters to humility (2:1; 3:1; 16:1; 19:1). The source of the jealousy, envy, and strife experienced by Peter and Paul is not specified, but the theme is introduced because it is relevant to Clement's purpose. His letter is addressed to the church in Corinth, where there are strifes and factions (ἔρεις καὶ θυμοί, 46:5), and Clement links these present controversies with the divisions which existed there in Paul's day. The parallel Clement draws between the problems that assailed the Corinthian church and those that confronted Paul himself in Rome supports our suggestion that for Paul, also, the opposition he encountered from Christians in Rome would have had obvious links with the strife within the Corinthian community.

concerns rather than those of the Romans. If so, however, it is for a very different reason: not because he was writing to a church he did not know, and whom he wishes to inform of his position, but because he is writing to a church he knows intimately. The epistle is a presentation of his gospel and of his pastoral theology. Writing to those who were his 'joy and crown', Paul ensured that his understanding of *how the gospel should be lived* was preserved. The Philippians were surely encouraged and inspired by his letter to them, not rebuked.

The irony is that once his pastoral warnings about those who might lead his converts astray became detached from their original situation, they helped to contribute to later conflict: in particular, his comments about 'Judaizers' in 3:2–3 became a source of anti-Jewish sentiment.

If this essay 'swims against the tide', and finds less conflict in the Philippian situation than Professor Räisänen himself would perhaps argue for, it is hoped that this will nevertheless make it an appropriate offering for a scholar who has never been afraid to rebel against commonly-accepted views.

43. 'Submit to One Another': The Transformation of Relationships in Christ (Eph 5:21–6:9)*

Ephesians 5:21–6:9 is one of those passages in the Pauline corpus which many Christians in the modern world find not only difficult but distasteful. It is out of harmony with the 'politically correct' beliefs of the western world, and is therefore quietly ignored by many. In Christian communities which believe that the Bible has final authority over their lives today, and must be literally obeyed, it causes pain and division.

Modern dislike of a first-century writer's cultural presuppositions are insufficient grounds for questioning whether or not he intended what he appears to have said. But what *was* his intention in writing these verses? Have later exegetes interpreted him correctly? The passage is by no means straightforward. There are three questions in particular that we need to consider.

The first concerns the place of v. 21 in the writer's argument. Does it belong to what precedes or what follows? If the latter, does it modify in some way the significance of what is demanded? In this paper I shall argue that v. 21 is indeed a crucial verse, since it invites us to read the verses that follow in a particular light.

Secondly, what is the author's primary concern in vv. 22–33? Is it with paraenesis or with ecclesiology? Did he use the *Haustafel* in his letter because he considered these rules to be important, or because they were present at this point in his source[1] and he took the opportunity to use the sections concerning wives and husbands as a 'peg' on which to hang his teaching concerning the church? To deal with this question we shall need to consider the possible origin of the code, its relevance to the issues dealt with in the rest of the letter, and the way in which the author handles the various commands.[2]

Thirdly, what is the significance of the μυστήριον of v. 32?

---

* Paper delivered at the Pauline Ecumenical Colloquium in Rome, 2004.

[1] There are clear parallels between Col 3:16–17 and Eph 5:19–20, as well as between Col 3:18–4:1 and Eph 5:22–6:9. If the author of Ephesians is not using Colossians, then they are both drawing on a common source.

[2] Similar questions were discussed in relation to the *Haustafel* in Colossians by Marlis Gielen in a paper given at the previous colloquium; see *'Le Christ Tout et en Tous' (Col 3, 11): L'épître aux Colossiens*, ed. Benoît Standaert, OSB, Série Monographique de Benedictina, Section Biblique–Oecuménique 16 (Rome: Benedictina, 2003), 89–119.

1. Eph 5:21: To what does it relate?

The ambiguity surrounding v. 21 is demonstrated by critical editions of the text, as well as by translations and commentaries. Westcott and Hort treated 5:15–6:20 as one long paragraph, but left a gap between 5:21 and 5:22; v. 21 was separated from v. 20 by a comma only. They were followed by earlier editions of Nestle-Aland and by the editors of the BFBS critical edition of 1954 and the UBS critical edition of 1966, who all began a new paragraph with v. 22. In the 26th and 27th editions of Nestle-Aland, however, the paragraph break comes *before* v. 21.

These differences are reflected by the translators. Older translations (Luther, AV and RV) indicate by their punctuation that v. 21 is to be read with what precedes, while RSV and JB both treat v. 21 as the introduction to what follows. Many modern translations appear to sit on the fence, printing v. 21 as a separate paragraph (NEB and NRSV), though some make their understanding clear by including this paragraph in the previous section (NIB) or the one that follows (REB).[3]

Does the modern preference for linking v. 21 with what follows merely reflect a distaste for the assumption of male superiority reflected in vv. 22–23, and a desire to soften it? Or is it justified by exegesis? The change in understanding indicated in the translations appears, in fact, to rest on the work of commentators. In Great Britain, older commentaries tended to follow the lead of Westcott and Hort,[4] but others began to treat v. 21 as the introduction to the *Haustafel*, or household code, rather than as the conclusion of the previous paragraph.[5] Most recent commentators now make the division before v. 21.[6]

The reasons for linking v. 21 with what precedes it are clear. Firstly, the only verb in the clause is a participle, ὑποτασσόμενοι, which appears to be dependent, like the participles in vv. 19 and 20, on the imperative πληροῦσθε in v. 18. To see mutual submission as a result of being filled with the Spirit accords

---

[3] In each case, the section headings make these divisions plain.
[4] E.g. J. Armitage Robinson, *St. Paul's Epistle to the Ephesians* (London: Macmillan, 1903); Brooke Foss Westcott, *St. Paul's Epistle to the Ephesians* (London: Macmillan, 1906).
[5] In English, as early as Thomas Kingsmill Abbott, *A Critical and Exegetical Commentary on the Epistles to the Ephesians and to the Colossians,* ICC (Edinburgh: T&T Clark, 1897), even though he followed the traditional division of the text; cf. Ernest Findlay Scott, *The Epistles of Paul to the Colossians, to Philemon and to the Ephesians* (London: Hodder & Stoughton, 1930); G.B. Caird, *Paul's Letters from Prison* (Oxford: Oxford University Press, 1976). In Germany, cf. Heinrich Schlier, *Der Brief an die Epheser* (Düsseldorf: Patmos, 1957); Joachim Gnilka, *Der Epheserbrief* (Freiburg: Herder, 1971).
[6] Ernest Best, *A Critical and Exegetical Commentary on Ephesians,* ICC (Edinburgh: T&T Clark, 1998), is an exception.

with Paul's teaching elsewhere.[7] Secondly, the command to Christians to be subject to one another forms an *inclusio* with the appeal to the community in 4:2 to treat one another with humility and love. Thirdly, it is argued that v. 21 is an inappropriate introduction to what follows, since the author's instructions to wives and husbands, children and fathers, slaves and masters, can hardly be said to demonstrate a principle of mutual subjection: it is wives who are commanded to be subject to their husbands, children and slaves who are to show obedience, and though instructions are given to husbands, fathers and masters, they are certainly not commanded to be subject to their wives, children, and slaves, but rather to show them love and tolerance. The mutuality demanded in v. 21 appears to be at odds with the teaching given in 5:22–6:9.

Forceful as this last argument may seem, it does not stand up to scrutiny, however, for though grammatically the participle ὑποτασσόμενοι may depend on the verb in v. 18, its meaning clearly links it to the section that follows. Moreover, wherever we decide to insert paragraph breaks, the paradox remains. Side by side we have, first, a demand that Christians submit to one another, and second, a code of rules where one partner in each relationship is clearly dominant. We cannot solve the apparent contradiction simply by assigning v. 21 and v. 22 to different paragraphs.

The other arguments for refusing to link v. 21 with the *Haustafel* are equally weak. Although v. 21 has no finite verb, v. 22 lacks a verb altogether,[8] and the command to wives must therefore depend on the participle in v. 21. There is no problem with this, however, if ὑποτασσόμενοι is being used as an imperative.[9] As for the suggested *inclusio* between 4:2 and 5:21, one can point to alternative patterns: e.g. 4:2 is echoed by 5:2, and 5:21 by 5:33. Moreover, the repetition of language does not necessarily mean that a section is being brought to a conclusion: on the contrary, it may simply indicate that an author is exploring different ways in which an idea is applied. In Ephesians 4–6, our author is clearly concerned to spell out what it means to live a life worthy of the gospel (4:1), and he uses the verb περιπατεῖν repeatedly (4:1, 17; 5:2, 8, 15). This way of life certainly involves mutual respect and concern, a theme which pervades the whole section, but which is stressed in 4:2, 32; 5:21.

Are there, then, any *positive* reasons for regarding v. 21 as the introduction to what follows? First, as we have already noted, v. 22 (according to the reading

---

[7] See Phil 2:1–4.

[8] It is, to be sure, only P[46] and B, supported by Cl and Hier[mss], which read a text without a verb. The vast majority of mss add some form of the verb ὑποτάσσω. Nevertheless, the shorter text is more likely to have been the original, since a verb would have been a necessary addition when 5:22–33 came to be used as a lectionary reading.

[9] See F. Blass and A. Debrunner, *A Greek Grammar of the New Testament*, trans. Robert W. Funk (Cambridge: Cambridge University Press, 1961), § 468(2). Cf. Rom 12:9–13; 1 Pet 2:18; 3:1, 7, 9.

of P[46] and B) lacks a verb, and so depends on the verb in v. 21. The command in v. 21 is, then, a *necessary* introduction to what follows. Secondly, the theme of v. 21 – mutual subordination – is relevant to the *Haustafel*, even though the subordination advocated there is definitely *not* mutual. 5:21 is therefore *relevant* as an introduction to what follows. Thirdly, v. 20 is in effect a doxology, and a fitting ending to the previous section. The instruction to the readers to be careful how they live in v. 15 has been spelt out with three negatives and three positives (μὴ ... ἀλλά): 'do not behave as though you were fools, but as those who are wise', 'do not be foolish but understanding', 'do not be drunk with wine but be filled with the Spirit'. Although v. 21 returns to a theme which has pervaded the whole letter, it is hardly an appropriate conclusion to this particular paragraph. If we detach it from vv. 22 ff., it has no real reason for being where it is.

There would seem, then, to be no compelling reasons for linking v. 21 with what precedes, and very good reasons for seeing it as the introduction to what follows. This, however, by no means solves the problem of this verse, for we still have to decide whether our author intended his readers to read the *Haustafel* in the light of 5:21, and was aware of the tension between the mutuality of this verse and the hierarchical commands that follow, or whether it is merely 'a verse constructed to permit the transition from what preceded to the section of tradition' that follows.[10]

2. The Household Code: Origin and Use

Eph 5:22–6:9 contains problems of its own. First, what is the relationship between this passage and similar codes (Col 3:18–4:1; 1 Pet 2:18–3:7)? Is Ephesians 5:22–6:9 based on Col 3:18–4:1, or are they both, together with 1 Pet 2:18–3:7 and other more fragmentary codes,[11] based on pre-Christian teaching? If so, were the Christian household codes influenced primarily by similar teaching found in secular Greek literature,[12] or by that used in the world of Hellenistic Judaism?[13]

---

[10] Ernest Best, *Essays on Ephesians* (Edinburgh: T&T Clark, 1997), 195.
[11] E.g. 1 Tim 2:8–15; 6:1–2; Titus 2:1–10.
[12] The importance of the Greek literature was stressed by Martin Dibelius, *An Die Kolosser, Epheser, an Philemon*, 3rd ed., HNT, ed. H. Greeven (Tübingen: Mohr Siebeck, 1953), 48–50, and by Karl Weidinger, *Die Haustafeln, ein Stück urchristlicher Paraenese*, UNT 14 (Leipzig: J. C. Hinrichs, 1928). See also David Balch, *Let Wives be Submissive: The Domestic Code in 1 Peter*, SBL monograph series 26 (Atlanta: Scholars Press, 1981).
[13] Cf. Ernst Lohmeyer, *Die Briefe an die Kolosser und an Philemon* (Göttingen: Vandenhoeck & Ruprecht, 1930), Kolosser 152–156; James E. Crouch, *The Origin and Intention of the Colossian Haustafel*, FRLANT 109, (Göttingen: Vandenhoeck & Ruprecht, 1972).

The parallels suggest that the Christian versions of the code owe something to their predecessors, and the influence is likely to have been via the synagogue – i.e. through Hellenistic Judaism.[14] In fact, however, the *origin* of the material does not much affect our understanding of the author's *use* of the household code. He has clearly taken over traditional teaching used by Christians before him, and adapted it. Like the author of Colossians, he offers us a thoroughly Christianized version of the code, since the motive underlying every command makes reference to Christ/the Lord; all these relationships are to be seen in the light of the fact that both parties are 'in Christ'. Like the author of Colossians, also, he expands one section of the code, though he chooses to concentrate on the commands to wives and husbands, rather than on that to slaves.

The existence of similar codes in the ancient world may, however, be relevant to our understanding of the inclusion of this particular code here. The author is writing to Gentiles (2:11; 3:1), and he considers it necessary to remind them that as Christians they must live like Gentiles no longer (4:17). He describes the Gentile way of life as 'alienated from the life of God', and contrasts it with the new way of life they are called to live in Christ (4:18). It seems unlikely, then, that he would spell out the new life by 'recycling' a code used in the Gentile world. On the other hand, if such codes were familiar to his Gentile Christian readers, they would present a challenge to the Christian community. In what sense had their lives been transformed by their new faith? Gentile by birth, these Christians were living in a hostile, pagan world. It is possible that this teaching was intended to remind them that their behaviour should now *excel* that of their pagan neighbours. Even what was good in their old way of life had been transformed by the fact that they were now 'in Christ'. What had hitherto simply been regarded as social obligation was now the necessary result of being 'members of his body'. But *in what way* had the old social code been excelled? And how were its demands to be reconciled with what Paul had written in Gal 3:28, where he insisted that 'there is no such thing as Jew or Greek, slave or free, male and female', since all are one in Christ Jesus.[15] Did these social codes perhaps seem irrelevant to Gentile Christians claiming freedom in Christ?

Yet our author has also stressed the fact that these former Gentiles were now included in the people of God, and had been made fellow heirs *with the Jews* of his promises to his people (3:6). It would be entirely natural and logical to apply to the Christian community – a new body, created out of

---

[14] See, e.g., Eduard Lohse, *Die Briefe an die Kolosser und an Philemon* (Göttingen: Vandenhoeck & Ruprecht, 1968), 222 (ET: *Colossians and Philemon,* Hermeneia, ed. Helmut Koester, trans. William R. Poehlmann and Robert J. Karris [Philadelphia: Fortress Press, 1971], 156).

[15] Cf. 1 Cor 12:13.

two – a Christianized version of the Jewish teaching being used in the synagogues. If these household codes were familiar to Hellenistic Jews, it would seem appropriate to adapt and apply them to those who now claimed to be members of God's people.

3. 5:21 in the Context of the Letter

If we are to understand the significance of Eph 5:21–6:9, we need to see it in the context of the whole epistle. This, of course, raises problems. Unless we dismiss not only the evidence of Acts but of 1 Corinthians as well,[16] this letter was clearly *not* written by Paul to the Ephesians. Pauline authorship being unlikely,[17] the link with Ephesus is possible, but with both author and destination uncertain, any information regarding the situations in which and to which it was written must be derived from the letter itself.

The theme of the letter, as is usual in the Pauline epistles, is set out in the opening thanksgiving.[18] It is 'the mystery of [God's] will', made known to us by being set forth in Christ (1:9). His will was active at the very beginning of time, when God chose us in Christ (1:4), and has been demonstrated in the inheritance which we have obtained in Christ (1:11). This inheritance – which means the redemption of God's people – will be enjoyed only in the future, when God's will is fully worked out. The themes of past predestination, present redemption, and future fulfilment are all held together in the opening paragraph.

This opening thanksgiving is noted for its christocentric emphasis and rhythmic structure. Notable, too, is its emphasis on the θέλημα of God (vv. 5, 9, 11). The μυστήριον of God's will is said to be his purpose 'to gather up all things in Christ, whether in heaven or on earth' (1:10). This theme is elaborated in the following paragraphs. The author prays that his readers may be given the insight to understand what is the hope to which God has called them and what are the riches of their inheritance – an inheritance guaranteed by Christ's resurrection and exaltation. All things have been put under his feet, and he has been set over all things for the sake of the church, which is his body (1:15–23).

The next two chapters explore the significance of Christ for those who are members of his body. Believers have been raised with Christ and have

---

[16] Contrast 1 Cor 15:32; 16:8 with Eph 3:2.
[17] It is impossible to discuss the arguments for and against Pauline authorship here, but difficulties with language, style, developments in theology and situation, together with the overlap with Colossians, all suggest that it was not written by Paul himself.
[18] Paul Schubert, *Form and Function of the Pauline Thanksgivings*, BZNW 20 (Berlin: A. Töpelmann, 1939).

been seated with him in the heavenly places (2:6); in him, Gentiles by birth have been made one with Jews, since he has broken down the dividing wall between them, and through his death they have both been reconciled to God in one body (2:11–16). He has proclaimed peace to all, and through him both Jew and Gentile – and in particular the readers of this epistle – have access in one Spirit to the Father (2:17–18): those who were once strangers and aliens are now members of God's household, part of a structure which grows into a holy temple in the Lord, Christ himself being the keystone (2:19–22).

The author then reminds his readers of Paul's insight into 'the mystery of Christ', formerly hidden but now revealed; this 'mystery' is the fact that Gentiles have been made fellow heirs with Jews, 'members of the same body and sharers of the promise in Christ Jesus through the gospel' (3:4–6). Paul's own role has been to take this gospel to the Gentiles, and to bring to light the divine plan concerning this mystery; this meant that, through the church, God's wisdom was being made known to the rulers and authorities in the heavenly places, so fulfilling God's eternal purpose (3:7–11; cf. 1:11). This section of the letter concludes with a prayer which, like the opening thanksgiving, is trinitarian in structure, followed by a doxology (3:14–21).

With this emphasis in the first part of Ephesians on God's plan to gather up all things in Christ, a plan that is now embodied in the church, it is not surprising that the paraenesis of chapters 4–6 centres on the life of the Christian community and its dependence upon Christ. In their life together, Christians must show humility, gentleness, patience and love (4:2), and demonstrate the unity of the Spirit in the bond of peace – a peace established by Christ himself (2:14–17). There is one body, one Spirit, one hope, one Lord, one faith, one baptism, and there is one God and Father, who is the basis of this unity (4:4–6). The gifts poured out by Christ are poured out on *the church*, not on individuals, in order to build up the body of Christ and bring all into unity and maturity in Christ (4:7–13). Once again, the members of the community are described as growing – not, this time, into a holy temple, but into Christ himself, from whom the whole body is being itself built up (4:15–16).

So the readers must live no longer as their fellow Gentiles do, for they have been taught to abandon their old way of life – 'the old man' – and to clothe themselves with the new. The use of the term ἄνθρωπος suggests that the author is thinking of Adam and Christ.[19] Lust and impurity result from being in Adam, but those who are in Christ share his righteousness and holiness (4:17–24). Their behaviour must be governed by the fact that they are 'members of one another' (4:25). Because their new way of life is grounded

---

[19] Although the author uses plural verbs and pronouns, he applies singular terms to both pagans and Christians – νοῦς, διάνοια, καρδία, πνεῦμα (vv. 17, 18, 23) – indicating that he is thinking of corporate life.

in what God has done, the author appeals (in a typically Pauline way) to the gospel: God in Christ has forgiven you – so you must be imitators of him and forgive one another; Christ loved us and gave himself up for us – so you must live in love (4:32–5:2).[20] The gospel is to be reflected in the behaviour of the community. Its members must have nothing to do with any behaviour that is inappropriate for those who are 'saints' and citizens of the kingdom of God (5:3–7). And since they have been brought out of darkness into light, they must behave as children of light (5:8–14). Their new way of life is expressed in worship, speaking together and joining together in singing psalms and hymns and spiritual songs (5:15–20).

The debate as to whether v. 21 belongs to what precedes or to what follows it reminds us that 5:22–6:9 itself is closely linked with the preceding verses, and is an integral part of the paraenetical section. That means that the behaviour expected of the various groups addressed in these verses is understood by the author to be yet another way in which Christians are expected to respond to the summons to lead a life worthy of their calling (4:1).

The language of that summons is reminiscent of Phil 1:27, and the instructions in 4:2–3 echo the opening verses of Philippians 2. As we have already noted, the verb περιπατεῖν is repeated throughout these chapters (4:17; 5:2, 8, 15). The author's concern is to remind his readers of the way of life appropriate to them – a way of life which, as he has already explained in 2:10, has been prepared for them, and which depends on what God has done for them in Christ (2:8–9).[21]

Nor is it surprising if the author sums this up in terms of mutual submission, for throughout his epistle he has emphasized the supremacy of Christ. In developing the Pauline images of the church as Christ's body[22] and as a temple,[23] he has referred to Christ as the head of the body[24] and as the cornerstone or keystone of the temple.[25] But if there is to be harmony in the body, and if the temple is to be joined together securely, there needs to be mutual recognition of the place of each individual in the community ἐν φόβῳ Χριστοῦ. The respect of each member of the community for the others is an expression of their allegiance to Christ.

---

[20] Similar appeals to the gospel are made by Paul in Rom 15:1–3, 7–8; 1 Cor 5:7; 7:23; 2 Cor 8:8–9; Phil 2:3–11.
[21] This way of life stands in contrast to the manner in which they previously lived (2:2).
[22] 1 Cor 12:4–31; Rom 12:3–8.
[23] 1 Cor 3:10–17; 2 Cor 6:16.
[24] Eph 1:22–23; 4:15–16; 5:23. Cf. Col 1:18; 2:19.
[25] Eph 2:20–22.

4. Christology and Paraenesis

It is clear from the repeated use of phrases such as ὡς τῷ κυρίῳ (5:22; 6:7), ὡς τῷ Χριστῷ (5:24; 6:5) and καθὼς ὁ Χριστός, (5:25, 29), that the instructions in 5:21–6:9 are intended to remind the readers of what it means to live in Christ. Their theme, therefore, is very much that of the preceding one and a half chapters. In spelling out how husbands should behave, the author appeals to the gospel itself (5:25, 29); in urging wives to be subject to their husbands, and slaves to obey their masters, he instructs them to behave 'as though to Christ/the Lord' (5:22; 6:5, 7), and so appeals to their common life in Christ. Commentators have often noted that these instructions are addressed only to Christians and that they ignore the problems faced by husbands and wives in a 'mixed' marriage, or by slaves serving non-Christian masters. The teaching has even been described as 'pastorally defective', and been said to indicate 'a serious lack of imagination as to the real world'.[26] This criticism is unfair: rather than blaming the author for failing to do what we expect, we should ask *why* he has chosen to address these particular groups.

The author's purpose is clearly *not* to attempt to offer comprehensive advice to all possible situations. Like Colossians, Ephesians presents a picture of life as it should be lived *in the Christian community*, and is concerned with relationships *within* that community, consisting as it does of 'blameless children of God in the midst of a crooked and perverse generation' (Phil 2:15), rather than with offering advice to individuals confronted with particular questions regarding relationships with outsiders. In this respect, the use of the code in Ephesians may be compared with similar teaching used in the synagogue, where those addressed could be assumed to be members of God's people. We may contrast the way in which 1 Peter, dealing with the problems of relations between Christians and outsiders, adapts the material to deal with the particular problems of slaves serving non-Christian masters and of mixed marriages (1 Pet 2:18–3:2).[27] Perhaps it is because Colossians and Ephesians are concerned with describing 'life in Christ' that they alone contain what we tend to regard as complete codes, while the Pastoral Epistles, which are primarily concerned with practical problems relating to particular groups, use fragments of the code.[28]

When we remember the place of the *Haustafel* in the argument of the letter as a whole, it no longer seems strange that one section of it – the verses addressed to husbands – has been expanded to the extent that 'it would almost

---

[26] Best, *Commentary on Ephesians*, 526.
[27] The question of mixed marriages is dealt with by Paul in 1 Cor 7:12–16, though without use of material from the code.
[28] 1 Tim 2:8–15; 6:1–2; Titus 2:1–10.

seem that this concern [for the relationship between Christ and the church] has nearly eclipsed the *Haustafel* itself'.[29] But the use of the *Haustafel* in Ephesians is not simply an excuse to expound the author's teaching about the relationship between Christ and the church, any more than his primary purpose is to introduce teaching about marriage. His main concern in this section is to demonstrate how the various possible relationships between Christians should reflect the mutual love which ought to permeate the whole body of Christ. It may be an exaggeration to say that 'marriage and the family are of interest to him only because they illustrate the call to Christian obedience in the church',[30] but certainly his main aim is to explain how this call to Christian obedience should be implemented. The relationship between husbands and wives offers him a golden opportunity to remind his readers of the link between the gospel and Christian living, between God's plan to unite all things in Christ and the mutual respect which should be demonstrated by all members of Christ's body.

In 5:23–33, the author compares the relationship between husband and wife with that between Christ and the church; he urges husbands to love their wives, quoting a traditional formula concerning Christ's death (5:25), a formula that he has already used in 5:2: Χριστὸς ἠγάπησεν τὴν ἐκκλησίαν καὶ ἑαυτὸν παρέδωκεν ὑπὲρ αὐτῆς. This time, however, 'the church' has replaced the more Pauline 'me' and 'us'.[31] In a very similar way, the author of 1 Peter expands one section of the household code in 2:18–25 – that addressed to slaves – by appealing to the example of Christ, who suffered for the sins of others, and is thus seen as a model for those slaves who are being unjustly punished. Colossians and Ephesians, too, both expand that section of the code, but not by appealing to the example of Christ: instead, slaves are simply urged to obey their earthly masters as though they were serving the Lord, remembering that the Lord will both reward and punish them (Col 3:22–25; Eph 6:5–8).

The fact that in 5:25 the author uses the formula that he has already employed in 5:2 may perhaps throw some light on the thorny problem of how to reconcile 5:21 and 5:22–6:8. The justification for dividing the text *after* v. 21 lay in the fact that its message was seen as compatible with the preceding chapters but *not* with the *Haustafel*. Eph 4:1–5:20 do, indeed, describe the life of the Christian community in a way that might well be summed up in the words: 'Be subject to one another, out of reverence for Christ'. When the author turns to the particular relationships discussed in 5:22–6:8, however,

---

[29] J. Paul Sampley, *'And the Two Shall Become One Flesh'*, SNTSMS 16 (Cambridge: Cambridge University Press, 1971).

[30] John Muddiman, *A Commentary on the Epistle to the Ephesians*, BNTC (London: Continuum, 2001), 254.

[31] In 5:2 he uses ἡμᾶς (or ὑμᾶς in some mss).

the same rule should apply, and the fact that the discussion is introduced by v. 21 indicates that he understood it to apply here also. As we have seen, his discussion refers only to *Christians* – i.e. to relationships *within* the Christian community. What is demanded of those within these relationships must be consistent with the manner of life which characterizes those who are 'in Christ' – a manner of life that derives from and reflects the self-sacrificial love of Christ himself. These various relationships, then, should be characterized by the same mutual respect for others which pervades the entire community.

At this point, however, our author might appear to be confronted by a major problem, for he now refers to three relationships in which there is a clear imbalance: in first-century culture, whether Greek, Roman, or Jewish, husbands exercised authority over their wives, fathers over their children, and masters over their slaves. It is clear that he has no desire to challenge the structures of society, and he probably saw neither the need to make changes nor the possibility of doing so. Indeed, he may well have been unaware of any inconsistency between 5:21 and the *Haustafel*. His task was to show how the mutual love and respect which he had been advocating in the rest of his letter should permeate these specific relationships.

The verb ὑποτάσσω signifies submission to another. In 5:21, the passive participle used with ἀλλήλοις indicates a 'voluntary yielding in love'.[32] Looking back over the paraenetical section, we notice that it began by showing how the unity of the church was built up by Christ's gifts to the church – apostles, prophets, evangelists, pastors and teachers. These gifts mean that certain men and women are expected to exercise this authority over others, and that the rest of the community accepts this. The humility and mutual forbearance in love demanded in 4:2 do not simply mean that every member of the community must give way to everyone else and say 'after you'! Rather, they mean that all the members of the community must recognize the authority given to certain members and be subject to them *in their various fields of responsibility*. Similarly, when in 5:21 the author demands that the members of the community are subject to one another, this does not mean that no one has the authority to command others. Rather, it suggests that all should be concerned for the well-being of others. By stressing the *mutuality* of the subordination, the readers are reminded that they are *all* 'in Christ', and that this means that *both* sides in each relationship must be prepared to respect the other. The conventions governing the relationships discussed in the *Haustafel* were integral to life in the first century, and could not be challenged, but for those 'in Christ' these relationships could be radically changed.

---

[32] William F. Arndt and F. Wilbur Gingrich, *A Greek-English Lexicon of the New Testament*, 2nd ed. (Chicago; London: University of Chicago Press, 1979).

It is clearly significant, then, that in 5:25 the author repeats the appeal to Christ's self-giving love first made in 5:2. There, the appeal was addressed to *all* the members of the community: they were to be kind and tender-hearted to one another; they were to forgive one another and to love one another – 'just as Christ loved us and gave himself up for us'. The argument employed in this passage is similar to one that is used by Paul himself in his appeals to his congregations: Christ became poor for your sakes, so you must share your riches with others (2 Cor 8:9); Christ did not please himself – so we must please our neighbours rather than ourselves (Rom 15:1–3); Christ humbled himself, and was obedient even to the extent of dying on the cross – so you, too, must show humility and obedience (Phil 2:8, 3, 12). The appeal is to the example of Christ, but it is also to the gospel events which have brought about the readers' redemption and made them members of the body of Christ. They cannot *refuse* to love as Christ loved them without denying the basis of their inheritance.

But now in 5:25 the same command is given to one particular group: husbands must love their wives, just as Christ loved the church and gave himself up for her. If the command to love others could be understood as an appropriate expression of 'mutual submission' when used in 5:2, there is no reason to deny that it is equally appropriate when addressed to one particular group in 5:25. Our problem arises from the fact that very different things are being required from husbands on the one hand and wives on the other. Although there is no verb in 5:22, the attitude which wives should show to their husbands is clearly assumed to be a demonstration of the one demanded in the ὑποτασσόμενοι of v. 21. Indeed, this is spelt out in v. 24: wives must be subject to their husbands, while husbands must love their wives (v. 25). Yet it is obvious that the command in 5:2 is *also* addressed to a community in which some exercise authority over others, which means that some will command and others obey. There, too, different things are demanded of different members of the community. Loving others with a Christ-like love does not mean anarchy, but an acceptance of the authority given by God to certain people.

For the author of Ephesians, the authority of husband over wife is certainly God-given. He begins from the assumption that 'the husband is the head of the wife' (5:23). No explanation for this statement is given – presumably because it was accepted Christian teaching (cf. 1 Cor 11:3) – and we are left to deduce whether 'head' is used in the sense of 'ruler' or 'source'.[33] Since the author is certainly advocating that wives must be subject to their husbands,

---

[33] For a recent discussion of this issue, and an indication of recent relevant literature, see Anthony C. Thiselton, *The First Epistle to the Corinthians,* NIGTC (Grand Rapids: Eerdmans, 2000), 812–822.

it is clear that the metaphor implies rule, an idea that is stressed in relation to Christ's rule over creation in Eph 1:22. But the notion of the church as the body of Christ, introduced in 1:23, is used again in 4:15–16, where Christians grow up into Christ, the head, on whom the body's growth depends. Christ's headship implies here that he is both the goal and the source of the body's existence. The notion of 'source' is implicit in the reference to Gen 2:21–23 in 1 Cor 11:8: the first woman was made from the first man, and he is therefore her head. The same verse seems to be in mind in Ephesians 5, since in v. 31 we have a quotation of Gen 2:24: 'for this reason a man shall leave his mother and father and be joined to his wife, and the two shall become one flesh'.

The author's primary interest, however, is in the analogy between the relationships that exist between husband and wife on the one hand, and Christ and the church on the other. A husband's attitude to his wife should mirror the love of Christ for the church. The 'imitation' of God and Christ demanded of all Christians in 5:1 is to be demonstrated in the love of a husband for his wife – which includes, of course, a willingness to sacrifice himself for her sake. Similarly, the attitude of a wife to her husband should mirror that of the church to Christ. Both attitudes fall under the general rubric in v. 21: 'Be subject to one another out of reverence for Christ'.

All this, however, could have been expressed far more briefly than it is, as can be seen by comparing Eph 5:22–33 with Col 3:18–19: Eph 5:23–24 and 25b–33 are expansions of the original commands. The author of Colossians chose to elaborate only one of the commands – that to slaves. The author of Ephesians, however, has taken the opportunity to expand the command to husbands, and in particular to spell out the significance of two key ideas in his analogy – ideas which have already been referred to earlier in the epistle. The first is the sacrifice made by Christ in giving himself up for the church (5:2), the second the relationship between Christ and the church as head and body (1:22–23; 4:15–16).

Our author may, of course, simply have taken the opportunity to explore these ideas here. On the other hand, he may have developed this analogy because he wished to demonstrate how personal relations are changed by being 'in Christ'.

A comparison with Colossians suggests that the reciprocal nature of the relationships between those who are in Christ is being deliberately stressed. This, of course, is what we should expect, following on from Eph 5:21. In *Colossians*, wives are urged to be subject to their husbands, and children to obey their parents 'in the Lord', while the behaviour of slaves to their masters is linked four times to their allegiance to the Lord. Nothing similar, however, is said to the men: husbands are merely urged to love their wives, and fathers told not to provoke their children; only masters (κύριοι) are reminded that they have a Master (κύριος) in heaven (Col 3:18–4:1). In *Ephesians*, this same injunction to masters is repeated, and fathers are instructed to bring up their children 'in the discipline and instruction of the Lord', while husbands are urged to love their wives, 'just as Christ loved the church'. Both wives and slaves are instructed to behave ὡς τῷ κυρίῳ/Χριστῷ (5:22; 6:5, 7), and children are again told to obey their parents ἐν κυρίῳ – unless, that is, we accept the alternative reading which omits these words:[34] even without them, however, the instruction is backed up by an appeal to God's commandment to children to honour their parents. There is thus *some* reference to the Lord in the commands addressed to all six groups.

5. Transformed Relationships

At this stage in our argument we need to turn back once more to the early chapters of the epistle and remind ourselves of the author's key argument. In chapters 1–3 he reminded his readers of God's plan to gather up all things in Christ (1:10), and of the way in which this plan has been inaugurated in the reconciliation of Jews and Gentiles to God in one body through Christ's death (2:16). Paul's insistence that in Christ there is neither Jew nor Greek (Gal 3:28) has been demonstrated in the life of the church, where circumcision and uncircumcision are no longer important.[35] But what of those other distinctions that Paul claimed had no place in Christ – slave and free, male and female? Although all Christians – Gentiles as well as Jews – could claim to be descendants of Abraham and sons of God, and so enjoy equal status before God in Christ, it was plain that some were men and some were women, some slave and some free. If the reconciliation of Jew and Gentile in Christ meant that the barrier between them had been broken down (1:11–22), what was to be said about men and women, slaves and free?

It is possible that Paul's teaching in Gal 3:28 had led to unrest among women and slaves. There, of course, he was arguing that being 'justified' – brought into a right relationship with God and made a full member of his people – does not depend upon race, sex, or status: such distinctions are unimportant, as far as *salvation* is concerned. But just as Paul's insistence on freedom from law was misunderstood by those who interpreted it as a justification for antinomianism, so his insistence that all Christians were one in Christ may have encouraged demands from women for recognition of equality in society, and from slaves for emancipation. There are signs in Paul's

---

[34] The words are thought by many to be an addition to the text, possibly on the analogy of Col 3:20. They are, however, widely attested, e.g. by P[46] A D vg. sy. co.

[35] The author is writing to a predominantly *Gentile* community (2:11), but is anxious to remind his readers that the body of Christ – the church – is made up of both Jews and Gentiles. *Outside* the church, these distinctions continued.

own letters that such demands were being made, and that he was anxious lest they brought the church into disrepute.[36] For Paul, being in Christ *transformed* human circumstances: circumcision and uncircumcision were unimportant, since neither could affect one's relationship with God; being a slave was also unimportant, since the Christian slave was a freedman in the Lord's service – just as the freedman was the Lord's slave.[37] As for the distinction between male and female, there is an important difference between this contrast and the other two referred to in Gal 3:28. Whereas it was possible for the distinction between Jew and Gentile to be removed (whether by conversion or apostasy, circumcision or the surgical disguise of circumcision), and it was possible for a slave to buy his freedom or for someone to lose his liberty, it was *not* possible in the ancient world for a male to become female or *vice versa*.[38] The possibility of change here lay in the *relationship* between the sexes, namely marriage, and it is this topic that Paul considers alongside those of circumcision/uncircumcision and slavery/freedom in 1 Cor 7:25–40. Marriage brought male and female into a specific relationship, and it is this specific relationship with which our author is concerned in Eph 5:22–33.

The matter discussed here is thus a very different one from that with which Paul was concerned in Gal 3:28. There, the question at issue was the inclusion of all categories of person *in Christ*. Here, our author is dealing with the question of how those who *are* in Christ relate *to one another*. As far as being in Christ is concerned, Paul had made it clear that there is no distinction: it makes no difference to one's relationship with Christ whether one is circumcised or uncircumcised, male or female, slave or free. But those who are in Christ are involved in 'horizontal' relationships as well as 'vertical'. The slave has a particular relationship with his master, as does the husband with his wife, and the child with its father. Our author clearly believes that in the Christian community these relationships were transformed: wives are still expected to submit to their husbands, but now it is 'as to the Lord' (5:22); children are still commanded to obey their fathers – but it is 'in the Lord' (6:1); slaves are required to serve their earthly masters, but now it is 'as slaves of Christ', and 'as to the Lord' (6:6–7). The author's elaboration of the first relationship spells out what this means: the attitude which wives are expected to show towards their husbands is the same attitude that the church is required to show towards Christ, since the church is the body, Christ its head. And since the husband

---

[36] For possible agitation among the women, see 1 Cor 11:2–16; 14:34–36. Cf. Crouch, *Colossian Haustafel*, 121–145.

[37] 1 Cor 7:17–24. Many slaves must have aspired to win their freedom, and teaching such as Gal 3:28 may have encouraged them in their hopes.

[38] It is significant that Paul distinguishes between the pairs, using οὐδέ in the first two – 'Jew or Greek', 'slave or free' – but καί in the last – 'male and female'.

is seen as the head of the wife, the relationship between them should mirror the relationship between Christ and the church.

That means, on the other side, that husbands must love their wives as Christ loved the church (5:25). This time, the author's elaboration of his basic material is more complex. He repeats what he said in 5:2 – that Christ gave himself up for the church – but now he spells out the purpose of his self-sacrifice in language which is appropriate not only to the image of sacrifice, but to that of marriage as well. The sacrificial language is in fact applied to the *church*: through Christ's self-sacrifice, *she* becomes ἁγία καὶ ἄμωμος (v. 27).[39] This idea is mingled with that of the preparation of the bride in the bridal bath, and her presentation to the bridegroom (by the bridegroom himself!), in all her glory. Yet the analogy is incomplete, for in spite of the οὕτως in v. 28, there is no reason to believe that our author regarded the husband as in any sense the *saviour* of his wife. Rather, the husband is being called on to follow the example of Christ by loving and cherishing his wife – just as Christ loves and cherishes the church, his body.

These two ecclesiological expansions (Eph 5:23–24 and 25b–33) appear at first to be intrusions into the main argument, providing the author with the opportunity to explore the relationship between Christ and the church. Nevertheless, they do perform an important function in relation to the theme of this section, since the author points us back once again to the central tenets of the gospel message by insisting that Christ is the Saviour of the church (5:23), that he gave himself up for her and sanctified her (5:25–27), and that he is responsible for her life and well-being (5:29). The church exists because of what Christ has done, and he is the source of her life, the head upon which the body depends (cf. 4:16). These comments are thus by no means an aside; on the contrary, they link the particular commands directed to husbands and wives with the main theme of the paraenetic section: Christ has brought all things into a unity (4:3–6), and the church, which is his body, must therefore demonstrate this unity and harmony in its life, its members joined to one another in mutual love (4:2, 15, 16; 5:2).

Intermingled with the imagery of 'head' and 'body' in Eph 5:22–33, then, we have the idea of the church as the bride of Christ. In fact this idea is not specifically spelt out, and is merely implied by analogy, by the vocabulary, and by the application of Gen 2:24. The image is more clearly used by Paul himself in 2 Cor 11:2, and its background is the Old Testament image of Israel as the bride of Yahweh.[40] In 1 Cor 6:15–19 he applies the idea to *individual* Chris-

---

[39] Here is an echo of the Pauline understanding of 'interchange': by his self-giving, Christ has made his people what he himself is – 'holy and without blemish'. Cf. Morna D. Hooker, *From Adam to Christ: Essays on Paul*, (Cambridge: Cambridge University Press, 1990), 11–69.

[40] Hos 1–3; Isa 50:1; 54:1–8; Ezek 16.

tians – in a passage where he also refers to individuals as members of Christ's body and as temples of the Holy Spirit. Appalled by Corinthian immorality, Paul warns his readers that they must not sleep with prostitutes, since to be joined with a prostitute is to be made 'one flesh' with her – to make members of Christ members of a prostitute.

The author of Ephesians uses the quotation from Genesis more positively, though his purpose in quoting it is far from clear. In 5:28–29 he has urged husbands to love their wives as they do their own bodies, and appealed to the example of Christ's love for the church. The rationale is apparently given in v. 30 – 'because we are members of his body', but this is hardly what we expect.[41] Logically, the explanation should have been 'because the church is his body'. By stressing that we are all members of that body, however, the author reminds us of the link between Christ's love for the church and the love of husbands for their wives. Those who are members of his body must mirror the behaviour of Christ. In contrast to union with a prostitute, which is *inappropriate* for a member of Christ's body, the union of a man with his wife is a participation in the love shown by Christ for his body.

This close link between the two relationships surely provides the answer to the much-debated question as to whether the quotation from Gen 2:24 in v. 31 is applied to the union between a man and his wife, or to that between Christ and the church. The answer must be both. The verse is clearly related to the former – indeed, that is its original significance. Its literal meaning continues the theme of Eph 5:25a and 28, and is picked up again in v. 33. But it is clear, too, that our author understands it to refer to Christ, since he says so plainly in v. 32, and it would seem, as we shall see, that for him this is its primary meaning. Once again, however, the analogy goes only so far: the verse is not meant to be understood as an allegory. The 'punch-line' is found at the end: 'The two will become one flesh'.

6. The Meaning of μυστήριον

The author terms this coming together a μυστήριον, and gives his explanation: although the literal meaning is clearly to the union of husband and wife, he believes that it refers also to the relationship between Christ and the church. The term μυστήριον obviously means more here than simply 'a secret'. It has been argued[42] that it refers to the mysterious meaning hidden within an Old

---

[41] Commentators are by no means agreed as to the correct reading in v. 30, though most conclude that the shorter text (which is better attested) is more likely to be original, and that the quotation from Gen 2:23 is an addition. An exception is Muddiman, *Ephesians*.

[42] E.g. by F.F. Bruce, *The Epistles to the Colossians, to Philemon and to the Ephesians,* NICNT

Testament text, and is the equivalent of the Hebrew רז; used at Qumran.[43] Since the term is used here to refer to an interpretation of scripture that is far from literal, this would seem to be correct. Nevertheless, in view of the fact that it has been used several times previously in the epistle, it is worth asking whether the term may have a more precise significance.[44] Does μυστήριον simply refer to the 'hidden meaning' that is to be found in this particular text,[45] or is it *a hidden meaning which has been spoken of previously in the epistle*? This latter possibility has been advocated by several exegetes,[46] and in view of the significance given to the term elsewhere in the epistle, it is worth summarizing the evidence for this interpretation.

The term μυστήριον is first used in 1:9, where God is said to have revealed to us 'the mystery of his will', in accordance with the purpose set out in Christ. This is then explained as being a plan for the fullness of time; this plan is 'to unite all things in him – things in heaven and on earth'. As we read on to the end of this chapter, we learn how this plan is being brought to fulfilment in the realization of the inheritance planned for us (vv. 11, 18): God has placed Christ at his right hand in the heavenlies, far above every ruler and authority and power and dominion, and has put all things under his feet and given him as head over all things to the church, which is his body (1:20–23).

In chapter 3, the term is used three times: we are reminded first of all that the μυστήριον was made known by revelation to Paul (v. 3), who possesses insight into what is now more narrowly defined as 'the μυστήριον of Christ' (v. 4). In v. 6 we are told the content of this μυστήριον: it is that Gentiles have been made fellow heirs (with the Jews), members of the same body and co-partakers of the promise in Christ Jesus through the gospel. Paul's task has been to preach this gospel to the Gentiles, and to make known the plan of the mystery which has been hidden in God from eternity (vv. 8–9). This is so that, through the church, the manifold wisdom of God might be made known to the rulers and authorities in the heavenlies, according to the eternal purpose which has been realized in Christ Jesus (vv. 10–11). Although the

---

(Grand Rapids: Eerdmans, 1984), 394 ff. Cf. Markus Barth, *Ephesians: Translation and Commentary on Chapters 4–6,* AB (Garden City, NY: Doubleday, 1974), 641–647.

[43] Cf. 1QpHab 7:1–5.

[44] Cf. Günther Bornkamm, μυστήριον (C3b) *TWNT/TDNT* 4. Cf. Thorsten Moritz, *A Profound Mystery: The Use of the Old Testament in Ephesians,* NTSup 85 (Leiden; New York: Brill, 1996), 117–152, at 142–146.

[45] Chrys C. Caragounis, *The Ephesian Mysterion: Meaning and Content,* ConBNT 8 (Lund: LiberLäromedel/Gleerup, 1977), 59, assumes that '5:32 is a special use of the term', and omits it from his discussion of the meaning of the word elsewhere in the epistle. Raymond E. Brown, 'The Semitic Background of the New Testament Mysterion (II)', *Biblica* 40 (1959): 82–84, also believed that the use of the term μυστήριον was unlike every other occurrence in Ephesians – and, indeed, in the rest of the New Testament.

[46] E.g. by Paul Sampley in his important study of this passage, *One Flesh,* 86–96. See also Andrew T. Lincoln, 'The Use of the Old Testament in Ephesians', *JSNT* 14 (1982): 30–36.

μυστήριον here is said to concern the inclusion of Gentiles into the community of God's people, the overall theme is the same as in chapter 1: 'to unite all things in Christ'. Key-terms are picked up from the earlier passage: σοφία (1:8; 3:10); γνωρίζω (1:9; 3:3, 10); οἰκονομία (1:10; 3:9); ἐν τοῖς ἐπουρανίοις (1:20; 3:10); ἀρχὴ καὶ ἐξουσία (1:21; 3:10); πρόθεσις (1:11; 3:11).

Apart from 5:32, the only other occurrence of the term μυστήριον is in 6:19, which speaks of Paul proclaiming 'the mystery of the gospel': for our author, the phrase would seem to refer to the message of this epistle – the apostle's insight into the divine plan.

In the rest of the epistle, then, the μυστήριον is the divine plan, formerly hidden (3:5) but now revealed (1:9–10; 3:9–10). This plan was in accord with God's eternal purpose (1:4–10; 3:11). This plan was to sum up all things in Christ (1:10), which meant incorporating Gentiles into God's holy people (1:14; 3:6), so making them members of Christ's body (1:23; 3:6). In this plan the church has a special place (1:21–23; 3:10).

The use of μυστήριον in 5:32 appears different because it refers to something hidden – and revealed – *in scripture*. If we were to have asked the author of Ephesians how and where the μυστήριον of chapters 1 and 3 was hidden, however, he would undoubtedly – being a disciple of Paul – have answered 'in scripture'! Like the μυστήριον in chapters 1 and 3, this μυστήριον in chapter 5 refers to the significance of Christ, which means that it was previously hidden, but has now been revealed. That this μυστήριον is in accord with God's purpose goes without saying, for it refers to what God is said to have decreed in Genesis. Moreover, it refers to another aspect of the bringing together of all things referred to in 1:10, and once again the special role of the church in God's plan is to the fore. This time, instead of referring to the bringing together of Jew and Gentile *within* the church, as in 3:3–6, the μυστήριον concerns the union of Christ with the church itself. Gen 2:24 is not, however, just a proof-text with a hidden message – the church is Christ's bride – but a text which relates the unity of Christ with his church to the unity that should exist within that church between husband and wife. It is because of (ἀντὶ τούτου) the fundamental unity of Christ with his church (Eph 5:29b–30), that a husband must love his wife as his own body (vv. 28–29a).[47] The author is well aware of the important shift in meaning that he finds in the Genesis text, and draws attention to this by prefacing his interpretation with the words ἐγὼ δὲ λέγω. The bond between husband and wife

---

[47] See J. Coppens, '"Mystery" in the Theology of Saint Paul and its Parallels at Qumran' reprinted in *Paul and Qumran: Studies in New Testament Exegesis,* ed. Jerome Murphy-O'Connor (London: G. Chapman, 1968), 132–158. Markus Barth, *Ephesians,* 639, suggests that the phrase refers to the argument in vv. 25–30. Coppens' suggestion that it refers only to vv. 29b–30 makes better sense, however.

no longer depends on Eve's creation from Adam's side, as in Gen 2:23–24, but on Christ's love for the church.[48]

If we were correct in seeing the *Haustafel* as an integral part of the paraenetic section of the epistle, and if that section is in turn closely related to the theological affirmations of chapters 1–3 and is intended to demonstrate how the unity brought by Christ is to be lived out in the church, then it is not surprising if our author finds the μυστήριον Χριστοῦ embedded in Gen 2:24, which at the literal level refers to husband and wife. The μυστήριον concerns the bringing together of all things in Christ (1:10). It includes the union of Christ with the church and of Jew with Gentile *within* that church. It includes also the very special union of husband and wife, which mirrors that of Christ with his body. It is hardly accidental that what is said about husbands loving their wives as themselves echoes the command in Lev 19:18 to love one's neighbour as oneself, for Paul himself had linked that summary with the command to the whole community to 'serve one another in love'.[49]

What, however, of the other relationships? Here, the author has less to say. Nevertheless they, too, are 'in the Lord'. In these relationships there is need on the one hand for obedience – from children and slaves – and for considerate behaviour on the other. The most problematic element in 6:1–4 is the reference to the 'first commandment with a promise', accompanied by the quotation of Exod 20:12. In what sense is this commandment 'first'? Does the word have a temporal meaning – i.e. the first to be given – or does it mean 'foremost'? If the former, then we might assume that the author is indicating that this is the first commandment in the decalogue to be linked to a promise. The problem is that the second of the Ten Commandments, which prohibits the making of idols (Exod 20:6) is also linked with a promise, though this is in fact far less specific than the one in v. 12.[50] In Exod 20:6, the reward is mentioned incidentally, whereas in 20:12, it is spelt out clearly. If the term means 'foremost' then this could mean that the commandment is either the most important, or the most difficult. Since it can hardly be described as the most important, some commentators suggest that it is to be understood as 'foremost in difficulty'.[51] The Midrash on Deuteronomy describes the commandment as the 'heaviest' – the most difficult to obey – whereas the commandment in Deut 22:6–7 concerning birds' nests is the 'lightest'. Even if this

---

[48] Coppens, 'Mystery', 147, suggests that it is to emphasize this shift that the author has used ἀντὶ τούτου, instead of the Septuagintal phrase, ἕνεκεν τούτου. Since there is no reference to Gen 2:23 in Ephesians, the phrase can hardly refer to the creation of Eve. Ernest Best, *Commentary on Ephesians*, 552, argues that τούτου has no referent, and is used here simply because it is part of the quotation; this does not explain the use of ἀντί in a quotation which otherwise agrees with the LXX.

[49] Gal 5:13–14; Cf. Rom 13:8.

[50] Cf. Andrew T. Lincoln, *Ephesians*, WBC (Dallas: Word Books, 1990), 404.

[51] Cf. Schlier, *Der Brief an die Epheser*, 281. See Rab. Deut. 6.

tradition was known in the first century, however, it could hardly have been familiar to the readers of this epistle! This question regarding the meaning of the phrase has puzzled commentators since the time of the Fathers, and there is no obvious answer. Since the command to honour one's parents is the only one of the Ten Commandments which is specifically linked with a promise ('do this ... so that ...'), it is possible that the author meant simply that it was 'foremost' – i.e. 'a commandment of the greatest importance' – and that it also had a promise attached to it.[52]

More important for our purpose is the fact that our author is pointing to the promise attached to the command. Surprisingly, this concerns reward in this life, and there is no attempt to reinterpret the promise in terms of reward in the future age. Slaves, by contrast, being without promise in this world, are promised reward from the Lord hereafter (6:8). Indeed, they are promised that they and their masters will be judged on equal terms by their common Lord. As for the present, their lives are transformed by the fact that the service they render to their masters is carried out 'as slaves of Christ'.

7. Conclusion

These verses in Ephesians are in many ways alien to the modern world.

Not surprisingly, our author has been blamed for imposing patriarchal and repressive rules on society, and for encouraging the oppression of women and the institution of slavery. Even his authoritarian attitude regarding children and the propriety of disciplining them is out of sympathy with what is regarded as appropriate today. But of course he was not imposing new rules, but reinterpreting the rules which were common in the ancient world. We cannot blame him for what the modern world regards as politically incorrect views, since these attitudes were part of ancient society. Relationships in the ancient world *were* asymmetrical. What is remarkable is the way in which our author endeavoured to view them through the lens of living in Christ. The question he addressed was this: *how* did the fact that Christians of whatever sex or status were all 'in Christ' affect their relationships with one another?

Our author attempted to deal with this question in relation to the society in which he lived. The tragedy was that Christians of a later generation regarded his words as 'law', and so took his underlying assumptions regarding the structures of society as part of the 'given'. His analogy between Christ and the church on the one hand, husband and wife on the other, was now understood to give theological justification for women's continuing subordination.[53] In the

---

[52] See comment in Arndt and Gingrich, *A Greek-English Lexicon of the New Testament*, on πρῶτος, 1ca.

[53] Cf. the words of Elisabeth Schüssler Fiorenza, *In Memory of Her* (London: SCM Press,

same way, for centuries, it was assumed that our author's teaching regarding slaves and masters was equivalent to a ratification of the institution of slavery. If we are to be faithful to our author's method, however, we need to seek answers to the questions he raised in terms that are appropriate for our own time, not to take over the answers he gave in his. We need to go back to first principles and ask the basic question as to what light the gospel sheds on our dealings with our fellow Christians. What does it mean for us, in the twenty-first century, to live as members of the body of Christ? In what ways would relationships between Christians be transformed if *all* the partners involved in them were prepared to 'submit to one another in the fear of Christ'?

1983), 270: 'It must be recognized that this christological modification of the husband's patriarchal position and duties does not have the power, theologically, to transform the patriarchal pattern of the household code, even though this might have been the intention of the author. Instead, Ephesians christologically cements the inferior position of the wife in the marriage relationship'.

44. 'The Sanctuary of His Body': Body and Sanctuary in Paul and John[*]

May 2017 marks the centenary of the birth of Kingsley Barrett, possibly the greatest British New Testament scholar of the twentieth century, and his work continues to guide today's scholars and to suggest new avenues for exploration. This article is written as an appreciation not only of his scholarship, but of his friendship over many years. The core of his outstanding contribution to New Testament studies is to be found in his work as a commentator, and this study concentrates on four of the books on which he wrote commentaries – the Gospel of John, and Paul's letters to the Romans and the Corinthians – and though the title comes from John, it is concerned primarily with the theology of Paul.

My title comes from John, however, because I was intrigued by John's reference to 'the sanctuary of his body' in John 2:19, a phrase which brings together two words used by Paul in describing the church. Was there, I wondered, any overlap between Paul and John?

Commenting on Jesus' saying about the destruction of the sanctuary in John 2:19, Kingsley noted that the two verbs used there, λύσατε and ἐγερῶ, 'destroy' and 'raise', have the same object, and concluded that the *body* that is to be raised up in v. 21, where John speaks of 'the sanctuary of his body', must therefore be Christ's own, and cannot be the church, 'understood in terms of the familiar Pauline image'.[1] Kingsley nevertheless thought it reasonable 'to suppose that John was aware of this image', and that 'there may be a secondary reference to it'.[2] Was he right? My purpose is to approach this question from the other end, as it were, and to examine the link between the sanctuary and the body, the ναός and the σῶμα, in the letters of Paul – a link that may conceivably have led John to coin this phrase.

---

[*] This paper was originally written for a seminar in honour of Kingsley Barrett (4 May 1917–26 August 2011), soon after his death, and it seems appropriate to review it again, in the centenary year of his birth.

[1] C.K. Barrett, *The Gospel According to St. John: An Introduction with Commentary and Notes on the Greek Text,* 2nd ed. (London: SPCK, 1978), 201.

[2] Barrett, *The Gospel According to St. John,* 201.

1. 'Sanctuary' in 1 Corinthians

In 1 Corinthians, Paul uses the term ναός, sanctuary, twice. On the first occasion, in 3:16, he asks the Corinthian church: 'Do you not know that you are the sanctuary of God, and the Spirit of God dwells in you?' On the second, in 6:19, his question is: 'Do you not know that your body is a sanctuary of the Holy Spirit in you?' The close similarity between these two sayings is obvious:

οὐκ οἴδατε ὅτι ναὸς Θεοῦ ἐστε καὶ τὸ πνεῦμα τοῦ Θεοῦ οἰκεῖ ἐν ὑμῖν;

οὐκ οἴδατε ὅτι τὸ σῶμα ὑμῶν ναὸς τοῦ ἐν ὑμῖν ἁγίου πνεύματός ἐστιν οὗ ἔχετε ἀπὸ Θεοῦ;

Both questions are addressed to the same people, and both describe them as a sanctuary – that is, as the place where the Spirit of God is found. The contexts of the two passages are, however, very different, and it will help our discussion if we examine these.

The first passage is found in that section of the epistle, 1 Cor 3:5–4:21, where Paul is discussing the place and work of apostles and teachers in the church, a section which in turn forms part of the discussion in chs. 1–4 of the divisions in the Corinthian church. Paul begins in 3:5 by speaking of himself and Apollos as gardeners in the service of God, then changes the metaphor to that of building: Paul laid the foundation of the Corinthian church, and others have built upon it. Here a distinction is made between the good workmen who build well and who will receive a reward, and those who are shoddy workmen and who add rubbishy material to the building; the latter will have their work destroyed by fire, although they themselves will be saved. It is at this point that Paul reminds his readers that the building that is being constructed is no ordinary one, but the sanctuary of God. In 3:17 we meet a third group of people who are concerned with this building; they, however, are not helping to build the sanctuary but are destroying it, and these men will neither receive a reward nor be saved, but will be destroyed. Since it is the Corinthian church which is addressed here as the ναὸς Θεοῦ, the men who are destroying the sanctuary are presumably those who are destroying the unity of the Corinthian church by splitting it into cliques; by teaching the Corinthians to say 'I am of Paul' or 'I am of Apollos' (3:1–4), these men are destroying the sanctuary where τὸ πνεῦμα τοῦ Θεοῦ dwells. The verses which follow (3:18–23) take up again the themes of wisdom and party strife found in chs. 1–2; the destroyers are those who have taught the Corinthians to glory in human wisdom (vv. 18–20) and in men, 'whether Paul or Apollos or Cephas'.

The second question occurs in 1 Cor 6:12–20, a section which takes up again the subject of fornication, already dealt with in the previous chapter. Paul now explains why fornication is incompatible with Christian faith, and shows the inadequacy of what appear to be slogans used by some of the

Corinthians who, presumably under the influence of Greek ideas, place the body on a level with the belly and think that both can be given over to the satisfaction of appetites (vv. 12–13). On the contrary, insists Paul, the body belongs to the Lord, and the Lord to the body. Paul's argument is based upon his own Hebraic concept of the σῶμα as a totality of personality; as such it can be joined either to a harlot, through σάρξ, or to the Lord, through πνεῦμα (vv. 16–17). Because both of these relationships involve the body, they can, although so different, be described in similar terms. 'Do you not know that your bodies are limbs of Christ?' asks Paul (v. 15); but the μέλη Χριστοῦ can be taken away and made πόρνης μέλη, and the man who is κολλώμενος τῷ Κυρίῳ becomes instead κολλώμενος τῇ πόρνῃ. Anyone who commits fornication, therefore, sins against his own body (v. 18) – and yet his body is not his own, since it is the temple of the Holy Spirit (v. 19). The Corinthians are not their own because they have been bought with a price, and they should therefore glorify God in their body (v. 20).

2. Resurrection and Morality

In this summary of Paul's discussion in 1 Cor 6, I have so far omitted to mention v. 14, which seems at first sight to be an aside, leading Udo Schnelle to argue that it is a post-Pauline gloss.[3] It is, I maintain, on the contrary, the basis of Paul's argument. 'By his power, God has both raised the Lord, and has raised/is raising/will raise us up'. The manuscripts are in confusion regarding the tense of the second verb, being uncertain as to whether it is an aorist, present or future. P[46] and its correctors support all three readings! All the translations and commentaries I have consulted plump for the future. Kingsley, for example, pointing to the parallel in 2 Cor 4:14, argues that 'It is because *the body* will not simply pass away but will be raised up that men must avoid using it for fornication'.[4] When this paper was first delivered I agreed with him, noting that the link between Christ's resurrection and our own future resurrection is affirmed in ch. 15 of this epistle. But recently I have changed my mind, for the context of 2 Cor 4:14 is very different from the argument here, being concerned with the contrast between present weakness and future glory, whereas the reason for Paul's statement in 1 Cor 6:14 is spelt out in the next verse, and concerns the relationship between Christ and believers. It is, of course, possible that Paul has simply dropped a credal summary – 'God raised

---

[3] Udo Schnelle, '1 Kor 6:14 – Eine nachpaulinische Glosse', *NT* 25 (1983): 217–219.

[4] C.K. Barrett, *A Commentary on the First Epistle to the Corinthians,* BNTC (London: A&C Black, 1968), 148. Barrett refers here to Günther Zuntz, *The Text of the Epistles: A Disquisition upon the Corpus Paulinum. The Schweich Lectures of the British Academy, 1946* (London: Oxford University Press, 1953), 256–257.

the Lord and will also raise us by his power' – into the argument. But that argument depends on the fact that Christians are *already* members of Christ's risen body: it is precisely because they are raised with Christ that believers are limbs and organs of his body.

Bruce Metzger also opts for the future, citing not only 2 Cor 4:14 but 1 Cor 6:13, where Paul uses the future καταργήσει, which Metzger describes as 'correlative'.[5] He argues that the context makes it 'necessary' to take 'raise up' in 1 Cor 6:14 as future. But the future fate of 'the belly' can scarcely be 'correlative' with the resurrection of the body. Far more significant is Paul's declaration in v. 11 that 'you were washed, you were sanctified' (i.e. made members of God's holy nation), 'you were justified' (i.e. brought into a relationship with God).[6] How did all this happen? Why, because God raised the Lord and raised us up also (v. 14). This being so, we are members of his body and bound to behave in a certain way. The context demands that our resurrection must in some sense have happened or be happening already. It may be objected that elsewhere Paul always speaks of the resurrection of believers as a future event. True, but he frequently speaks of believers' present experience of life in/with Christ (e.g., Rom 6:4, 11; 2 Cor 5:14–15; Gal 2:19–20; Phil 3:10). Although the resurrection of believers is a future event, there is for Paul a sense in which it can be said to have taken place already. In other words, whichever of the three readings in v. 14 is correct, Paul's argument is that Christ's resurrection involves our own, and that this dictates our present manner of life.

The fact that we share Christ's resurrection should be well-known to the Corinthians, as is indicated by his next words: οὐκ οἴδατε ὅτι, 'Don't you know?' In both 1 Cor 3:16 and 6:19, Paul begins his question with this phrase, which he often uses to introduce ideas which are known – or at least *should* be known – to his readers. In 5:6, for example, he asks whether they do not know that a little leaven is enough to make a lump of dough rise, a matter of common knowledge; in 6:2 he asks, 'Do you not know that the saints will judge the world?', a doctrinal point with which he thinks they ought to be familiar. In these cases, the phrase serves as a gentle reminder of something which Paul's readers had apparently forgotten or overlooked. The probability is, therefore, that here in 6:15, as well as in 3:16 and 6:19, he is dealing with ideas which he has already touched upon in the instruction he gave to his Corinthian converts.

οὐκ οἴδατε ὅτι τὰ σώματα ὑμῶν μέλη Χριστοῦ ἐστιν;

Do you not know that your bodies are limbs of Christ?

---

[5] Bruce M. Metzger, *A Textual Commentary on the Greek New Testament*, 2nd ed. (London: United Bible Societies, 1994), 486.
[6] Cf. Rom 8:30.

It is for this reason that they will be raised up. But it is for this reason, also, that they must shun fornication. Those who are limbs of Christ have been 'washed, sanctified, justified in the name of the Lord Jesus Christ and in the Spirit of our God' (1 Cor 6:11). The question in v. 16 has a close connection with the one which follows it in v. 19: 'Do you not know that your body is a temple of the Holy Spirit?' Indeed, it is precisely because the σώματα of the Corinthian Christians are μέλη Χριστοῦ that Paul can go on to describe them as sanctuaries of the Holy Spirit; the term which was applied to the Christian community as a whole in 3:16 is clearly appropriate for the bodies of the individual members of that community. Unlike the Greek idea of man as God's temple, which is essentially individualistic, Paul's primary understanding is that of the *community* as a temple; in this, of course, his ideas are close to those found at Qumran, where the Council of the Community is described as 'a House of Holiness for Israel',[7] in which true worship was offered. Hence here, when Paul thinks of the individual as a sanctuary, it is only because individual believers are μέλη Χριστοῦ.

3. The 'Body' in 1 Corinthians

The term μέλη Χριστοῦ is a strange one, whose peculiarity is disguised for us, both by its familiarity and by the usual translation 'members of Christ'. This translation fails to convey the down-to-earth character of the Greek word μέλη, which means literally 'limbs' or 'organs'. In modern usage, the word 'member' has lost its metaphorical origins, but neither Paul nor his readers could have used the word without thinking of the σῶμα of which each individual μέλος was a part. One cannot have limbs or organs without a body, and if the σώματα referred to in 1 Cor 6:15 are in fact only limbs, they are limbs of the body which is discussed in 1 Cor 12. In that chapter, Paul explores the image of the σῶμα Χριστοῦ and its limbs or organs, and sets out the link between the two. His argument can be summed up in his words in 12:27:

ὑμεῖς δὲ ἐστε σῶμα Χριστοῦ καὶ μέλη ἐκ μέρους.

Significantly, he introduces the image in this passage because he is speaking of the work of the one Holy Spirit within the Christian community, and the spiritual gifts given to individuals for the sake of the whole community. In 1 Cor 6:15, also, the reference to the μέλη Χριστοῦ inevitably links the σῶμα of a believer, which is a ναός of the Holy Spirit, with the σῶμα of Christ, within which the Holy Spirit is at work. There is an essential link between the body and the Holy Spirit.

---

[7] 1QS 8:5–9. Strict rules about the purity of Council members follow.

'Do you not know?' asks Paul. So why had the Corinthians failed to see the relevance of his teaching to their way of life? It is possible that his own argument, that the present σῶμα ψυχικόν will be raised as a σῶμα πνευματικόν (1 Cor 15:44), was already familiar to the Corinthians; if so, this might well have led his opponents to argue that there is no link between the two, and that what one does while in the former is irrelevant to the latter. There is obvious logic in this position. For Paul, however, there is an essential link between the two modes of existence, for it is the σῶμα that is 'sown' that is raised. There is continuity between the two, because Christ – himself man, 'Adam' – has died to the former and been raised to the latter (1 Cor 15:22). The resurrection of the dead comes through a human being (15:21), and those who are in Christ die and rise with him and will bear his image (15:49). It is only an extreme futuristic eschatology that severs the link between 'now' and 'then'. As Paul argues in 2 Corinthians, we are *already* being transformed into the image of the Lord (3:18). What we *shall* be should be seen in what we are now. But all depends on the fact that Christians have died with Christ to the old life – and *that,* as he explains in Rom 6, means dying to sin. Christ was raised, he tells us, οὕτως καὶ ἡμεῖς ἐν καινότητι ζωῆς περιπατήσωμεν (Rom 6:4). A neat translation is impossible, but basically he means 'so that we might conduct ourselves as those who have set out on a new life'.

1 Corinthians 6:14, then, is not a digression, but a summary of Paul's gospel, which reminds us of the implications that he draws elsewhere. Here his point is that our bodies belong to the Lord, who has been raised by God from the dead; by that same power we too will be raised – how, then, can those who are *already* joined to Christ as his limbs or organs be joined to a prostitute?

4. Parallels – Significant or Accidental?

Let us return to the two questions that Paul poses about the sanctuary of God. The context of 1 Cor 6:19 is, as we have seen, very different from that of 3:16, but the two passages share the idea that the sanctuary is in danger. In 3:16 the sanctuary – the Christian church – faces destruction by being torn apart through the tendency to disunity. In 6:19, the sanctuary is the σῶμα of the believer, and its threatened destruction lies in being torn away from the Lord through fornication.

If we now put together the various sayings which we have quoted, we find that Paul has instructed the Corinthians as follows:

3:16: *You* are the sanctuary of God, indwelt by the Holy Spirit.
6:19: *Your body* is the sanctuary of the Holy Spirit from God within you.
6:15: *Your bodies* are limbs of Christ.
12:17: *You* are the body of Christ, and as individuals you are limbs of that body.

In these statements, the subject is either 'you' (the Christian community) or 'your body/bodies' (i.e. individuals). More interesting is the variation on the right-hand side, where we find that the church is both the body of Christ and the sanctuary of God, and that the individual Christian also is both a limb of Christ and a sanctuary of the Holy Spirit. Chapters 3 and 6 both use the image of a sanctuary, and both stress the concept of holiness, while chs. 3 and 12 are both concerned with unity. Chapters 6 and 12 both use the noun σῶμα and speak of Christians as μέλη Χριστοῦ, which seems to imply the idea of the church as the σῶμα Χριστοῦ, though it is only in ch. 12 that the term is actually used. All three passages speak of the work of the Holy Spirit.

The question that intrigues me is this: are the images of the ναὸς Θεοῦ or ναὸς ἁγίου πνεύματός and of the σῶμα Χριστοῦ simply parallel images that just happen to overlap in 1 Cor 6, or is there an underlying relationship between them? It would be false logic to assume that because two images refer to the same ideas, they are to be identified. The closest we have come to such an identification so far is in 1 Cor 6:15, where Christians' bodies are identified as 'limbs/organs' of Christ, and each body is then said to be a ναός of the Holy Spirit (v. 19). It is the Fourth Evangelist who brings the words together, and he is speaking – primarily at least – of the crucified and resurrected body of Jesus, not the church. To deal with these questions we need to look at other passages where Paul uses these two images. But first we must consider what he meant by describing the church as the ναὸς Θεοῦ.

5. The Church as the Sanctuary of God

In the LXX, ναός is used of the sanctuary, the holy place which contained the holy of holies, the dwelling-place of God. In pre-exilic days, the sanctuary was considered to be God's dwelling-place in a very real sense, to the extent that the Jews came to think that its destruction was impossible. When it *was* destroyed, the idea of the new temple became part of the eschatological hope: the restored sanctuary would be a symbol that God was once again in the midst of his people. This hope is expressed in Isa 28:16, which reads, in the LXX, 'Behold I lay in Zion for a foundation a stone, a tried stone, a precious stone of sure foundation, and he who believes shall not be ashamed'. This stone would be the foundation of the rebuilt sanctuary, and with the building's restoration the people would know that God was again dwelling in his holy mountain Zion (Joel 3:17). With God once more in the midst of Israel, his Spirit would be poured out on his people (2:27–29).

It was perhaps Paul's own words about laying a foundation in 1 Cor 3:10–11 (though it is he himself who lays it there, not God!) which led him to use the image of the sanctuary in vv. 16–17. We may compare his reference here to Jesus Christ as the only foundation with his argument in Rom 9:33, where he combines Isa 28:16 with words taken from Isa 8:14, which (in the Hebrew) refers to God himself as a sanctuary and a rock of offence – a trap and a snare to the Jews, causing many of them to stumble and fall. The combined reference reads:

See, I am laying in Zion a stone that will cause people to stumble, and a rock that will make them fall (πέτραν σκανδάλου); and whoever believes in him will not be put to shame.

Paul's argument is based on the assumption that the eschatological hope is fulfilled, and that God is again found in the midst of his people. In 1 Cor 1:23 he has already used the idea that Christ crucified is a σκάνδαλον, a stumblingblock to the Jews, and foolishness to Greeks, but to Christians, strength and wisdom. Now Christ is the foundation of the ναός (3:11), and human power and wisdom have no place there (3:18–23).

The same idea is found in 2 Cor 6:16–18, where Paul declares, 'we are the sanctuary of the living God' (ναὸς Θεοῦ), and follows this statement with another collection of quotations, drawn chiefly from Lev 26, Ezek 37, Isa 52, Ezek 20 and 2 Sam 7. Together, these quotations remind us of the covenant God made with his people; he promises to be their God, and their response must be to be a holy people, separate from their neighbours. The quotation from 2 Sam 7:14 takes God's promise to David regarding his son, but applies it to those who – *through* David's son – are now God's sons and daughters.

In this paragraph, Paul is addressing the Christian community as though it were Israel, because, as he reminds them in 2 Cor 1:1, Christians are 'saints' – i.e. holy ones. Since this is so, they must cleanse themselves 'from every defilement of flesh and spirit, making holiness perfect' (7:1). The fact that the *community* is God's sanctuary has consequences for individual Christians.

2 Corinthians 6:14–7:1 is regarded by many commentators as an intrusion into the text of 2 Corinthians. Kingsley himself believed that it was integral to the epistle, and in a paper given to celebrate his ninetieth birthday, I, too, argued that the passage should be regarded as part of the letter, since it followed on logically from what precedes it.[8] In 1 Cor 1:30, Paul writes that Christ is 'our righteousness and sanctification'; those who now live in him must therefore be righteous and holy – a theme which recurs repeatedly in both 1 and 2 Corinthians. In 2 Cor 5:21 he declared that Christ, who knew no sin, was made sin, so that we might become the righteousness of God. In 6:1–10 he spells out how he himself has wielded 'the weapons of righteousness', and how the life and resurrection of Christ have been seen in his ministry. Now he turns to the Corinthians and reminds them that God's righteousness

---

[8] Morna D. Hooker, 'On Becoming the Righteousness of God: Another Look at 2 Cor 5:21', *NT* 50 (2008): 373–374 = above, essay 28 (pp. 401–415).

and sanctification must be seen in their lives also: they are 'to make holiness perfect'.

2 Corinthians 6:14–7:1 is therefore the climax of – not an intrusion into – the argument of the passage beginning in 2 Cor 3:2, which is primarily a defence of Paul's ministry and his gospel. True, he now speaks about what *the Corinthians* must do, but that is the logical outcome of Paul's own work. I am always suspicious of artificial chiastic structures, unearthed by commentators in biblical texts, but I suggest that the shape of Paul's argument falls into a natural chiasm, which is 'bookended' by the accounts in 1:15–3:1 and 7:2–8:24 of the misunderstanding between himself and the Corinthians, his original plans to visit the Corinthians via Macedonia, and his concern for Titus. Throughout these sections, Paul is dealing with the accusation of someone in Corinth to the effect that he is always commending himself. Not surprisingly, then, most of what lies in between concerns Paul's ministry, and he begins with a passage which might well seem to confirm the accusation brought against him, since he compares himself with Moses and declares that his own ministry is greater than that of Moses! If Moses was the minister of a covenant that brought condemnation, Paul is minister of a covenant that brings righteousness (3:4–18). That ministry is, of course, directed towards the Corinthians, for what he does is undertaken in order that life may be at work in them (4:12); everything is for their sake (v. 15). So how should they respond? It is not until 6:14–7:1 that Paul spells this out, and it is surely significant that this is done in language that reminds them that *they* are now God's people and the temple of the living God. The old has been done away with, since in Christ there is a new creation (5:17), brought into existence when God said, 'Let there be light' and revealed his glory in the face of Jesus Christ (4:6). If ch. 3 recalls God's covenant with Israel on Sinai, it is appropriate that 2 Cor 6:14–7:1 should recall that same covenant, together with the one made with David, and remind God's people of what he offers and requires of them.

But what of the material that comes in between these two significant passages? After declaring that God 'has shone in our hearts to give the light of the knowledge of the glory of God in the face of Jesus' face' (2 Cor 4:6), Paul spells out what this means; paradoxically, it means persecution and affliction of all kinds, even death itself, in order that the Corinthians may experience life. 'Reflecting the image of Christ' means conformity to the way of the cross.

In 2 Cor 5:11–13 we have a reminder of the underlying dispute, as Paul once again denies that he is commending himself. Then he restates the gospel: it is that Christ 'died for all, in order that the living might live no longer for themselves, but for the one who died and was raised for them' (v. 15). Then he once again spells out what this means in terms of his ministry. He has indeed commended himself, he admits, in afflictions, hardships, calamities, distress, the list goes on; but he has commended himself also by purity, patience, holiness, and love. Once again, Paul accepts that to be a minister of the gospel is to be conformed to its pattern; and so he is in a position to appeal to the Corinthians to accept his authority, to follow his teaching, and to see the implications of the gospel for their lives.

Exploring 2 Cor 6:14–7:1 has again taken me on something of a digression, but it has, I hoped, helped to show the logic of Paul's reasoning throughout this section. Just as Moses was commissioned to call Israel to be God's holy people, so now Paul's task is to summon believers to be 'the temple of the living God'. This underlying logic is important when we come to the final passage in which we may have an allusion to the idea of the body as a sanctuary, 2 Cor 5:1–10. Reference to digressions reminds me that I recently found myself disagreeing with Kingsley, because he describes these verses in his commentary as 'a digression'.[9] So, was he right in describing their purpose here as simply that of 'illustrating further the relative unimportance of the earthenware container',[10] or does Paul's argument here develop further what he says in the previous chapter?

Paul has been arguing, as we have already seen, that the glory of God is revealed in his ministry in a paradoxical way. The 'treasure' is contained in 'clay jars' (2 Cor 4:7), a metaphor that conveys well the vulnerability of human life; but though he is continually being given up to death for Jesus' sake, the life of Jesus is made visible in his mortal flesh (4:11). Paul describes his flesh here as θνητός, mortal, a term he uses in 1 Cor 15:53–54 when describing the change that takes place at the End. His faith is founded on the fact that God 'raised the Lord Jesus', and he is confident that God will therefore 'raise us also with Jesus' (2 Cor 4:14). This statement, as we noted earlier, is parallel to 2 Cor 6:14 and fulfils a similar function: there, it was the basis for Paul's teaching about the proper use of the body, which, as a 'limb' of Christ's body, was a sanctuary of the Holy Spirit; here, it is the basis for Paul's belief that, though our outer nature is decaying, our inner nature is being renewed, and that present affliction will be replaced by eternal glory (vv. 16–18).

In 2 Cor 5:1 he uses a new metaphor: instead of clay pots we have earthly tents – equally fragile. When his is destroyed, he will have 'a building from God, a house not made with hands, eternal in the heavens'. Discussion of 2 Cor 5:1–10 usually concentrates on the question 'Has Paul changed his mind?' Has he abandoned the notion of future resurrection for a hope of being straight away 'at home with the Lord' (v. 8)? The answer is that Paul combines both these ideas in other texts! He cheerfully uses them side by side

---

[9] C.K. Barrett, *A Commentary on the Second Epistle to the Corinthians*, BNTC (London: A&C Black, 1973), 149.

[10] Barrett, *Second Epistle to the Corinthians*, 149.

and apparently sees no conflict between them.[11] But the question that concerns so many commentators is in fact irrelevant, for Paul's purpose here is not to discuss this particular question, but to hammer home the point he has been making in ch. 4. At present, he is being put to death and yet is alive – alive not simply metaphorically but physically. But even if the point comes when physical death overwhelms him, the experience of 'the life of Jesus in our body' (4:10) will continue; indeed, Kingsley, commenting on this verse, insists that 'the primary reference here is to future resurrection'.[12] Now, in 5:1, Paul expresses this hope in a new way: 'we have a building from God, a house not made with hands, eternal in the heavens'.

This phrase is remarkable because it echoes the saying in Mark 14:58, where Jesus is accused of claiming that he would destroy the present sanctuary and build another, 'not made with hands' – the Marcan equivalent of the Johannine saying with which we began.[13] Its occurrence in both gospels suggests that a genuine saying may underlie Mark 14:58.[14] Both evangelists use the word ναός, though both do so in passages referring to Jesus' activity in the temple, ἱερόν (Mark 14:49; John 2:14–15). Does Paul have temple imagery in mind here? Certainly, he describes the 'earthly dwelling', which he expects to be destroyed, as a tent, reminding us of the original desert sanctuary. Whether or not Paul is familiar with a tradition going back to Jesus, the hope that God himself would replace the temple was part of the Jewish eschatological hope, and the idea of a heavenly temple – the pattern for what will be set up in the Age to Come – is widespread in biblical and pseudepigraphical writings.[15] It is possible, then, that Paul was influenced by this hope, rather than by a dominical saying. Some commentators argue that Paul has in mind the church, which came into being through the death and resurrection of Christ, and that he is thinking here of the community rather than the individual.[16]

---

[11] 1 Thess 4:14–17; Phil 1:23 and 3:20–21.

[12] Barrett, *Second Epistle to the Corinthians*, 140.

[13] Among those who see this echo as significant are André Feuillet, 'La demeure céleste et la destinée des chrétiens: Exégèse de 2 Cor. 5,1–10 et contribution à l'étude des fondements de l'eschatologie paulinienne', *RSR* 44 (1956): 161–192, 360–402; for Feuillet, the heavenly dwelling is the resurrection body of Christ (377–378). Similarly, Jean-François Collange, *Énigmes de la deuxième épître de Paul aux Corinthiens: Étude exégétique de 2 Cor. 2,14–7,4*, SNTSMS 18 (Cambridge: Cambridge University Press, 1972), 179–198. On the significance of the temple saying, see also R.F. Hettlinger, '2 Corinthians 5.1–10', *SJT* 10 (1957): 174–194; E. Earle Ellis, 'II Corinthians V. 1–10 in Pauline Eschatology', *NTS* 6 (1960): 211–224.

[14] See also Mark 13:2.

[15] See, e.g. 2 Bar. 4:2–6; 4 Ezra 10. In Exod 25:9, 40; 26:30; 27:8, we find the idea that the earthly sanctuary is a copy of the heavenly pattern. See also Wis 9:8; T. Levi 3:4–6; Enoch 90:29; 4Q174; and Heb 8:2. For a discussion of this hope, see R.J. McKelvey, *The New Temple: The Church in the New Testament*, Oxford Theological Monographs 3 (Oxford: Oxford University Press, 1969), 1–41.

[16] John A.T. Robinson, *The Body: A Study in Pauline Theology* (London: SCM Press, 1952), 73–80; Ellis, 'II Corinthians'.

He may well have this corporate aspect in mind, but if this verse *is* the climax of 2 Cor 4:7–18, we can expect it to affirm his belief that his own 'tent' will not be 'crushed ... forsaken ... [or] destroyed'. As long as he continues 'in this tent' he groans, even though he is sure of the final outcome, of which God's Spirit is the guarantee (5:2–5). Here Paul picks up the words he used about the Spirit in 2 Cor 1:22: present experience is a pointer to what is to come. But what is the basis of Paul's confidence? Once again, it was expressed in 4:14: 'we know that the one who raised the Lord Jesus will raise us also *with Jesus*'.

The constant reminders in 2 Cor 4:7–15 that Paul is *already* experiencing, and is confident that he *will* experience, the risen life *of Jesus,* support the suggestion that there may be an echo here of the tradition about the sanctuary recorded in Mark 14:58. It is worth noting that in these verses the name 'Jesus' occurs six times – an unusual concentration, to say the least – so focusing our attention on the earthly Jesus who was himself 'afflicted ... persecuted ... struck down'. The saying about the sanctuary was understood by John to refer to Jesus' own body. If Paul did know that saying, then he might well have spoken of his own body as a tent that is destroyed and replaced by a heavenly building. 2 Corinthians 5:1–10 is the culmination of what he has described as 'carrying in the body the dying of Jesus' (4:10), and 'being given up to death for Jesus' sake' (4:11) in order that the life of Jesus might be made visible in his mortal flesh, for now the mortal is swallowed up by life (5:4).

As we have already noted, Paul speaks of the mortal (θνητός) giving way to immortality in 1 Cor 15:53–54; there, also, he uses the image of being swallowed up (κατεπόθη), and both words reappear here; in 1 Corinthians, death is swallowed up in victory, while here it is the mortal that is swallowed up by life. The physical body, which bore the image of 'the man of dust', is raised a spiritual body, bearing the image of 'the man of heaven' (vv. 44, 49). A similar idea is expressed in Phil 3:21, where Paul triumphantly declares that Christ 'will transform the body of our humiliation that it may be conformed to the body of his glory'. In 2 Corinthians, transformation into the image of Christ is understood to be a gradual process, already taking place in our present bodies, where the paradoxical glory of the cross is already visible, but culminating in the stage when the mortal is swallowed up by life, a process described in language that appears to recall the tradition of a heavenly temple.

6. The Church as Christ's Body

Finally, we must look very briefly at Paul's use of the image of the body of Christ. We have already noted his use of the idea that believers' σώματα are 'limbs' or 'organs' of Christ in 1 Cor 6:15. We have seen, too, how he picks up this image and explores it in 1 Cor 12:12–31. It is noteworthy that it is introduced there in the context of a discussion about the gifts of the Spirit (12:4–11; 12:27–14:40). All Christians are baptized into the one body in the one Spirit (12:13). The Spirit unites all Christians, and gives them a diversity of gifts, in order to build up the body. The same ideas reappear in Rom 12:3–8, though this time they are introduced by Paul's appeal to his readers 'to offer [their] bodies to God, a living sacrifice, holy and acceptable to him; this is the spiritual service you owe' (v. 1). Paul uses cultic language here, but this time he describes the believer as a *sacrifice,* rather than as a sanctuary. Significantly, it seems that it is the reference to believers' σώματα in v. 1 that leads Paul to remind the Romans that they are μέλη of another σῶμα, and that they are 'one body in Christ'. This passage does not refer directly to the Holy Spirit, but does speak about 'spiritual service', and to 'gifts' (v. 6), presumably of the Spirit.

It is significant that, in all these passages, what Paul says about individual Christians is dependent on the fact that they belong to the community of those who are in Christ. 1 Corinthians 3:16–17 is about the unity of the church, which must not be destroyed by individualistic factions. 1 Corinthians 6:19 speaks of an individual's body as a sanctuary – but *only* because he is a 'limb of Christ', and belongs to him. In 1 Cor 12 Paul addresses the Corinthians as 'the body of Christ'; spiritual gifts given to individuals are intended for the good of the whole community. In 2 Cor 6:16 he declares that Christians are 'the sanctuary of the living God' – though that has implications for individual believers. 2 Corinthians 5:1, I have argued, is primarily about Paul's own body rather than the church, and might therefore seem to be the exception to the rule, but what he affirms about it is true because 'the one who raised the Lord Jesus will raise us also with Jesus' and 'will bring us with you into his presence' (2 Cor 4:14); certainly the relationship with Christ – and so with others who belong to him – is essential. In Rom 12, reference to believers' σώματα soon turns to a discussion of the σῶμα of which they are part.

The role of the Holy Spirit is another unifying element in all of these passages. The ναός is by definition the place where the Spirit dwells,[17] while the σῶμα Χριστοῦ is the body that is built up by the spiritual gifts given to its various limbs and organs.[18] As for the possible reference to Paul's own body as a sanctuary in 2 Cor 5:1, and the clear reference to the Christian community as God's sanctuary in 2 Cor 6:16, these follow the fundamental statement in 3:17–18 that those who turn to the Lord, who is the Spirit, are changed into his image and reflect his glory. If Paul's body is changed, it is because he reflects the dying and rising of Christ in his body; by sharing his death,

---

[17] 1 Cor 3:16; 6:19.
[18] See especially the references to the Spirit in 1 Cor 12:4, 7, 8, 9 (*bis*), 11 (*bis*), 13 (*bis*).

he is transformed into his glory;[19] if believers are God's holy people and his sanctuary, it is because they have turned to the Lord who is the Spirit. The work of the Spirit, uniting and sanctifying, is fundamental throughout.

Was it perhaps Paul's experience of the dying and rising of Christ in his own body (2 Cor 4:10), together with the conviction that this experience brought resurrection life to others (v. 12), which led Paul to describe *the church as the body of Christ*? What had happened to Christ's own body – suffering, death, resurrection, and glory – is reflected in the bodies of his followers because they are 'in Christ', and so part of *his* body. But the reason why all the 'limbs of Christ' belong to one body is because they were baptized into that body by the one Spirit (1 Cor 12:13) – the Spirit that dwells in all Christians – which is why, together, they are the sanctuary of the Holy Spirit. Was Paul himself aware of the traditions underlying John, which linked Christ's body with the sanctuary? And what is our judgement regarding the question about John 2:21, with which we began? The answers to all these questions must inevitably be tentative, but regarding this last one, the evidence we have examined is, I suggest, sufficient to allow us to conclude that Paul himself linked the ideas of body and sanctuary, and that there is therefore good reason to believe that Kingsley was right to suggest that John may well have been aware of Paul's description of the church as the body of Christ and that this idea may therefore be hinted at when he spoke of 'the sanctuary of his body'.

---

[19] Cf. Phil 3:10–11.

45. 'Sola Fide': The Wrong Slogan?*

In the evening I went very unwillingly to a society in Aldersgate Street, where one was reading Luther's preface to the *Epistle to the Romans*. About a quarter before nine, while he was describing the change which God works in the heart through faith in Christ, I felt my heart strangely warmed. I felt I did trust in Christ, Christ alone for salvation; and an assurance was given *me* that He had taken away *my* sins, even *mine*, and saved me from the law of sin and death.[1]

The importance of Martin Luther's teaching on Romans for John Wesley's so-called 'conversion' and theology was typical of much of Protestantism for centuries. 'The change which God works in the heart through faith in Christ' is nothing less than 'justification by grace through faith', which was so important for Luther – and, before him, for Paul himself. The centrality of faith (or trust), the emphasis on the individual's experience, and the reference to law, are all part of this tradition. But was Luther's own understanding properly represented by the way in which the Lutheran doctrine of *sola fide* had come to be interpreted, or was his teaching distorted by his followers? And – an even more fundamental question – did Luther himself distort Paul?

For Wesley, as for so many Protestants, Luther was the great interpreter of Paul. It was Luther's understanding of Galatians and Romans – whose message he describes in his Preface to Romans as 'purest Gospel' – that formed the basis of the 'Theology of Paul' that I myself was taught as an undergraduate. But in the late twentieth-century his reliability as a Pauline exegete was challenged – initially by Krister Stendahl, who pointed out 'a fact' that was at one and the same time obvious and yet ignored: 'that sayings which originally mean one thing later on were interpreted to mean something else, something which was felt to be more relevant to human conditions of later times'.[2] Examples of this are to be seen in the New Testament itself: the sayings of Second Isaiah, for example, already a reinterpretation of the events of the exodus, are now read as prophecies of the salvation experienced in Jesus,[3]

---

* I am grateful to Professor Donald Hagner for his encouragement in completing this essay.

[1] John Wesley, *Journal*, 24 May 1738. If I begin this essay with a quotation from John Wesley, it is not simply because of my own Methodist heritage, but in recognition of the contribution made by Diarmaid MacCulloch to the training of Methodist ministers in his first academic position, as Lecturer at Wesley College Bristol – a humble prelude to a dazzling career, but one that brought lasting benefit to those he taught.

[2] Krister Stendahl, *Paul among Jews and Gentiles: And Other Essays* (Minneapolis: Fortress, 1976), 94.

[3] For a discussion of one aspect of this issue – the many different Jewish and Christian

and by the time that the Gospels are written down, Jesus' parables are being reinterpreted in the light of the experience of the early Christian communities, and adapted to the problems that confronted them.[4] Moving to more recent times, the biblical texts that were once seen as endorsing the patriarchal and hierarchical economic structures of society as part of the divine will are now interpreted by feminist and liberation theologians as containing a message of liberation and equality for all humanity.[5]

It was this reinterpretation of Romans and Galatians in a different context, Stendahl argued, that warped scholars' understanding of Paul's original message. Whereas the problem that had chiefly concerned Paul had been the role of the Gentiles in God's plan – and what Israel's rejection of the gospel meant for her own fate[6] – Luther read his own battle with sixteenth-century Roman Catholicism into Paul's arguments about 'works' and the Law, and so understood his words as an attempt to wrestle with the problem of how a sinner found a gracious God. For Stendahl, the notion that Paul was describing his guilt as he struggled with sin until finding liberation in Christ was due to the way that first Augustine, then Luther, had read Romans. Subsequent commentators had followed their lead and had supposed that the heart of Paul's message was to be found in Rom 3:21–8:39, with chapters 9–11 being treated as a mere appendix to his argument.

Paul believed that he had been called to evangelize the Gentiles, and he spelled this out in his letters to Galatia and to Rome, the two letters in which he justified his understanding both of his calling and of the gospel he proclaimed.[7] Having acknowledged Jesus as Christ and Son of God, his basic problem was to reconcile his presuppositions as a loyal Jew with this new conviction that his mission was to preach to Gentiles: how could they, by definition outsiders, become included in the people of God? Paul's discussions of justification (or righteousness) take place in the context of this problem. It would seem, then, that Paul's primary purpose had *not* been to protest against human efforts to earn righteousness, but rather to argue for the inclusion of Gentiles in God's people without their first becoming Jewish. But once this particular issue ceased to be a problem for the church, and Paul's letters

---

interpretations of the 'servant' referred to in Isa 52:13–53:12 – see Murray Rae, 'Texts in Context: Scripture and the Divine Economy', *JTI* 1 (2007): 23–45.

[4] See, e.g., the classic discussion by Joachim Jeremias, *The Parables of Jesus*, trans. S.H. Hooke (London: SCM Press, 1963).

[5] Contrast the traditional interpretation of biblical references to slavery, held for centuries, which assumed that slavery had been established by divine decree, with the 91-page pamphlet *A Condensed Anti-Slavery Bible Argument, by a Citizen of Virginia,* written in America by George Bourne in 1845, when emancipation had become a possibility, in which he argued that commonly accepted understandings of biblical texts were 'perversions'.

[6] Stendahl, *Paul*, 85: 'Rom. 9–11 is not an appendix to chs. 1–8, but the climax of the letter'.

[7] Rom 1:5, 13; 11:13; 16:26; Gal 1:16; 2:2, 7–9.

were being read as part of the canon of scripture addressed to the faithful, they were inevitably interpreted in a different way. The problem that was in danger of tearing the church apart in its earliest years was no longer an issue for Christians of later generations; it did not concern Luther, any more than it concerns Christians today. Paul's letters had been addressed to 'outsiders' and were concerned with the changes in their lives which becoming 'insiders' entailed; but now they were being read by and to those who had long belonged to the Christian community. How were his arguments relevant to individual believers? Luther did what every good pastor should do, interpreting what he understood to be the message of scripture to the needs of his congregation. 'Justification by – or *through* – faith' was assumed to be the heart of Paul's gospel; and that included the rejection of the 'works' of the Law as a means to righteousness.

One of the major shifts which had taken place, well before the time of Luther, had been the final break of Christianity with Judaism. The opposition of Jews to the gospel drove Jews and Christians apart, and as early as in the Fourth Gospel, 'the Jews' were being portrayed as Jesus' opponents. In the second century, Marcion attempted to cut the ties of Christianity to Judaism by rejecting the Old Testament – which inevitably meant that his understanding of Paul was totally distorted. At some stage, though when and how is disputed, Christianity ceased to be a Jewish sect, but the years of in-fighting had left their mark and contributed to the growth of 'anti-Semitism'. It is hardly surprising if this attitude influenced biblical interpreters, and if Paul came to be understood as rejecting everything Jewish, condemning both 'the Jews' and 'the Law'. This anti-Semitism was part of Luther's world, and explains his vitriolic language about Jews, but he transferred Paul's arguments to his own situation. Paul's words about works and faith, law and grace, seemed highly appropriate to his own battle with the mediaeval church's claims about merit and indulgences.

Sadly, biblical interpreters – with a few notable exceptions – continued to interpret Paul as the opponent of Judaism and the Law. The emphasis on faith, not works (of the Law) stressed by Luther meant that Paul's gospel was regarded as the antithesis of Judaism. This view was challenged by the work of one or two twentieth-century scholars, in particular E.P. Sanders, who, building on the work of others, argued that not only Paul but Judaism had been misunderstood, since it was not a religion of legalistic works-righteousness.[8] Keeping the Law was not seen by Jews as the way of *entering* the covenant between God and his people, but the way of *maintaining* it. For Paul, what was wrong with the Law was simply the fact that 'following the law does

---

[8] E.P. Sanders, *Paul and Palestinian Judaism* (London: SCM Press, 1977).

not result in being found in Christ'.[9] How could it? In the post-Holocaust world Sanders' insights found a ready audience, and his work, together with that of Stendahl, initiated the so-called 'new perspective' on Paul.

One of the results of these developments has been the fact that Pauline scholars have blamed Luther for leading Protestant exegetes astray by distorting the message of Paul. 'Justification by faith' is no longer seen as the heart of Paul's gospel; after all, it is only Romans and Galatians that discuss it – because of the particular issues with which they deal. But just as subsequent interpretation may have distorted our understanding of Paul, did later Lutheran theology perhaps lose sight of some of Luther's own insights? Did the emphasis on faith, the hallmark of Protestant orthodoxy, obscure equally important aspects of the gospel? Some recent explorations of his writings suggest that this may be so.

One distortion, highlighted by Richard Hays, is the way in which emphasis has been placed on the Reformation catch-phrase *sola fide* to such an extent that faith itself, it is claimed, has sometimes been seen as a 'work', and that Paul is therefore seen as replacing one 'anthropocentric' view (works) with another. But while it may be true that some of Luther's followers turned *pistis* into 'a bizarre sort of work',[10] this was definitely not Luther's own view. On the contrary, as he states in the Preface to Romans, 'Faith is a divine work in us. It changes us and makes us to be born anew of God. It kills the old Adam and makes altogether different people'.[11] In his *Disputation on Justification*, he criticises the view that faith is a work; rather faith has been 'poured into us', by the Holy Spirit.[12]

This misinterpretation of Luther's understanding of faith as 'anthropocentric' rather than 'Christo-centric' has been entwined in recent discussion with arguments about the meaning of *pistis Christou* in Paul's letters, a phrase which occurs particularly in passages where he is discussing 'righteousness' (or 'justification').[13] Does he mean 'faith in Christ', as has been assumed by the vast majority of exegetes, or 'the faith/faithfulness *of* Christ himself'? Or

---

[9] Sanders, *Paul*, 550.
[10] Richard B. Hays, 'ΠΙΣΤΙΣ and Pauline Christology: What Is at Stake?', in *Pauline Theology*, vol. 4: *Looking Back, Pressing On*, eds. E. Elizabeth Johnson and David M. Hay (Atlanta: Scholars Press, 1977), 35–60. Reprinted in Richard B. Hays, *The Faith of Jesus Christ: The Narrative Substructure of Galatians 3:1–4:11*, 2nd ed. (Grand Rapids; Cambridge, UK; Eerdmans, 2002), 272–297, at 56/293. Hays is careful to stress that this is not Luther's own view.
[11] Luther, *Preface to the Epistle of St Paul to the Romans*, 1522, *LW* 35:370 = *WA* 7:11.
[12] Luther, *LW* 34:153.
[13] In German, *die Rechtfertigung*. Discussion is made more complicated in English by the use of different terms (based on 'right' and 'just' to translate Greek words deriving from the stem *dikaio-*. We have 'righteousness', 'justice', and 'justification' for the noun, 'righteous' and 'just' for the adjective, but when we come to the verb, tend to use 'to justify', since 'to right' is used only of boats or wrongs. Some scholars use the Anglo-Saxon 'to rightwise' or 'to set things right').

is his meaning perhaps more fluid than grammarians suggest? This topic has been widely discussed, which means that we cannot explore it here,[14] but must simply note that, however we interpret Paul's use of this phrase, faith was for Luther the gift of God, as it was for Paul, even though Luther clearly understood *pistis Christou* to refer to the believer's faith *in* Christ. In a recent article, Jonathan Linebaugh has defended the view that for Luther himself *sola fide* is thoroughly *Christo*-centric – it is, after all, faith *in Christ* – and reminded us of the words of Karl Barth: 'What is the *sola fide* other than a faint echo of the *solus Christus*?'.[15] Linebaugh writes: 'Whatever Luther thought faith in Jesus Christ was, he certainly did not regard it as the human contribution to salvation'.[16]

In this article Linebaugh is defending the traditional understanding of *pistis Christou* as meaning 'faith *in* Christ', and he is of course correct in maintaining that we do not have to translate the phrase as 'Christ's faith/faithfulness' in order to avoid an 'anthropocentric' view of faith. What (*contra* Linebaugh) I suggest the translation 'faith/faithfulness of Christ' *adds* to our understanding of Paul is to *emphasize* what Christ has achieved, through his *pistis*, his faithfulness to God. Paul's gospel centred on the death and resurrection of Christ; it is only through their relationship to him that believers share in what he is and does – and they are able to share in that *because* of what he is and does: Christians put their faith (or trust) in the one who trusted in God and was himself trustworthy, and so share in his righteousness. Interestingly, Luther comes close to expressing this idea when, in his *Commentary on Galatians*, he writes that faith 'takes hold of Christ in such a way that Christ is the object of faith, *or rather not so much the object but, so to speak, the One who is present in faith itself*'.[17] This stress on Christ as 'present in faith' rather than the 'object of faith' not only answers those who suggest that faith came to be seen as a human 'work', but hints at the ambiguity in the Greek phrase *pistis Christou*. Luther continues:

It is Christ who forms and trains faith or who is the form of faith. Therefore the Christ who is grasped by faith and who lives in the heart is the true Christian righteousness, on account of which God counts us righteous and grants us eternal life.[18]

---

[14] There is a vast amount of literature on this topic. For my own views on the issue, see Morna D. Hooker, 'ΠΙΣΤΙΣ ΧΡΙΣΤΟΥ' *NTS* 35 (1989): 321–342; Morna D. Hooker, 'Another look at πίστις Χριστοῦ', *SJT* 69 (2016): 46–62 = above, essay 29 (pp. 416–431).

[15] Jonathan Linebaugh, 'The Christo-Centrism of Faith in Christ: Martin Luther's Reading of Galatians 2.16, 19–20', *NTS* 59 (2013): 535–544; Karl Barth, *Church Dogmatics,* vol. 4, part 1: *The Doctrine of Reconciliation,* eds. G.W. Bromiley and Thomas F. Torrance, trans. G.W. Bromiley (Edinburgh: T&T Clark, 1956), 632.

[16] Linebaugh, 'Christo-Centrism', 540.

[17] *Sic ut Christus sit objectum fidei, imo non obiectum, sed, ut ita dicam, in ipsa fide Christus adest.* Luther, *Commentary on Galatians, LW* 26:129; *WA*: 40/1:228, 34–229, 15, emphasis mine.

[18] Luther, *LW* 26:130; *WA*: 40/1:229, 9.

Similarly, a little later in the commentary he writes 'This is the true faith *of Christ and in Christ*, through which we become members of his body'[19] – a statement that underlines the role of Christ.

Christ is not so much the object of faith as 'the one who is present *in* the faith'; 'the true faith of Christ and in Christ'; both these statements, together with the slogan *Christus forma fidei* – 'Christ the form of faith' – underline the fact that for Luther, faith is thoroughly Christo-centric. Moreover, whatever he understands by the words 'of Christ', faith is linked to 'membership' of Christ.

1. Union with Christ

This brings us to the idea of union with Christ or 'participation', to use the word which is commonly used in contemporary explorations of Paul's theology. In another article written in reaction to Richard Hays' criticisms of post-Reformation understanding of Paul, Stephen Chester explored the relationship between participation and justification.[20] Hays had described the lack of any 'coherent account of the relation between the doctrine of justification and *christology*' as 'the greatest weakness of the traditional post-Reformation understanding of "faith" and "justification" in Paul'.[21] Once again, however, we should note that Hays' criticism is brought against post-Reformation understanding rather than against Luther himself. But here, too, his criticism is linked with the argument about the meaning of the phrase *pistis Christou*, and so traced back to Luther's emphasis on *sola fide*: the translation 'faith *in* Christ' places the emphasis on the individual's own faith, while 'faith/faithfulness *of* Christ' stresses the idea of the believer's participation in Christ.

Chester argues that although 'the Reformation tradition of interpreting Paul's soteriology primarily in terms of justification by faith' is founded on the views of Luther, and although he understood *pistis Christou* to mean 'faith in Christ', Luther himself 'displays a profoundly participatory understanding of justification'.[22] Noting the way in which Luther's views appear to vary, according to the situation, and as his ideas developed,[23] Chester comments that

---

[19] Luther, *Commentary on Galatians, LW* 26:357, emphasis mine: *Ea est vera fides Christi et in Christum, per quam membra fimus corporis eius. WA* 40/1:546, 21 ff.

[20] Stephen Chester, 'It is No Longer I Who Live: Justification by Faith and Participation in Christ in Martin Luther's Exegesis of Galatians', *NTS* 55 (2009): 315–337. See also Olli-Pekka Vainio, *Justification and Participation in Christ: The Development of the Lutheran Doctrine of Justification from Luther to the Formula of Concord (1580)* (Leiden; Boston: Brill, 2008).

[21] Hays, *Faith*, xxix (his emphasis).

[22] Chester, 'No Longer', 317.

[23] The same can be said of Paul himself!

his views on justification are 'particularly difficult to pin down'.[24] Although Luther sometimes uses forensic language, and interprets Paul's words in terms of God's judgement of sin, he interprets the verdict of acquittal to be just because the believer is 'cloaked in Christ's righteousness'.[25] Righteousness is imputed to those who in fact are sinners, and this 'is accomplished by imputation on account of the faith by which I begin to take hold of Christ'.[26] This 'faith takes hold of Christ and has him present, enclosing him as the ring encloses the gem. And whoever is found having this faith in the Christ who is grasped in the heart, him God accounts as righteous'.[27] The imputation of righteousness to the believer clearly involves participation in Christ.

It is intriguing to notice a possible hint of this idea of participation in the work of Paul's earliest interpreter, Luke. The fullest account of Paul's theology offered us by Luke in the Acts of the Apostles is found in the speech on the Areopagus in chapter 17, and hardly encourages us to think that he has fully understood Paul's gospel. Christ's resurrection is simply said to give assurance that God 'would judge the world in righteousness by a man whom he has appointed' (v. 31). Yet earlier, in chapter 13, the resurrection of Jesus, is declared to be 'good news', since 'through this man forgiveness of sins is proclaimed to you' (v. 38). The next verse spells out what this means, namely that 'in this man everyone who believes is justified' (v. 39). As so often, the Greek is ambiguous! Does 'in him' go with 'everyone' or with 'believes'? The weight of tradition supports the latter, but the word order suggests the former.

These two passages in Acts demonstrate two different emphases that have been given to the word 'righteousness'. In chapter 17, the emphasis is on judgement – and punishment: God is portrayed as the just judge. In chapter 13, however, Paul proclaims the 'good news' of God's forgiveness through Jesus, in whom everyone is 'right-wised'. Luther himself moved from the former understanding to the latter, as he demonstrates in his comments on Rom 1:17 towards the end of his life, where he recounts how he had been taught to think of righteousness as referring to God's punishment and wrath, but had come to realize that 'the righteousness of God is that by which the righteous lives by a gift of God, namely by faith'.[28]

For Luther, the participation of the believer in Christ's righteousness is explained in terms of what Lutheran scholars often refer to as a 'happy exchange', whereby Christ takes human sins upon himself, and gives the believer his own righteousness. By 'exchange' he is referring to the idea that Paul describes most clearly in Gal 3:13, where he writes of Christ redeeming

---

[24] Chester, 'No Longer', 318.
[25] Chester, 'No Longer', 320.
[26] Luther, *LW* 26:232 = *WA* 40:367.
[27] Luther, *LW* 26:32 = *WA* 40:233.
[28] Luther, *Preface to Latin Writings*, *LW* 34:336–337; *WA* 54:185–186.

us from the curse of the Law by himself becoming a curse – for us – in order that we might receive blessing, and in 2 Cor 5:21, where he declares that Christ was made sin for us in order that we might become the righteousness of God – *in him*. Luther uses the term 'exchange' when commenting on Psalm 22:2 in *An Offering to the Church of God in the Last Days*. He writes:

> That is the mystery which is rich in divine grace to sinners: wherein by a wonderful exchange our sins are no longer ours but Christ's and the righteousness of Christ not Christ's but ours. He has emptied Himself of His righteousness that He might clothe us with it, and fill us with it. And He has taken our evils upon Himself that He might deliver us from them … in the same manner as He grieved and suffered in our sins, and was confounded, in the same manner we rejoice and glory in His righteousness.[29]

Although this sounds like an exchange, there is in fact an imbalance; sinners lose their sins, but even though Christ is said to 'empty' himself of righteousness, the righteousness with which he clothes sinners remains his. To be 'clothed with' or to 'put on' Christ, as he explains in his commentary on Galatians, is to put on 'the forgiveness of sins, righteousness, peace, comfort, joy in the Holy Spirit, salvation, life, and Christ himself'.[30]

The idea itself is expressed as early as 1516 in a letter written to George Spenlein:

> Lord Jesus, you are my righteousness, just as I am your sin. You have taken upon yourself what is mine and have given to me what is yours. You have taken upon yourself what you were not and have given to me what I was not.[31]

Once again, although the sin is 'taken' by Christ and the righteousness is freely given to the sinner, this is not what the commercial world would term a true 'exchange', since the righteousness remains Christ's. It is rather a matter of a mutual *sharing* in what the other is.

In his *Commentary on Galatians*, Luther describes how Christ:

> became the greatest thief, murderer, adulterer, robber, desecrator, blasphemer, etc., there has ever been anywhere in the world.… He is a sinner, who has and bears…. all the sins of all men in his body.… Christ was not only found among sinners, but of His own free will and by the will of the Father He wanted to be the associate of sinners, having assumed the flesh and blood of those who were sinners and thieves and who were immersed in all sorts of sin. Therefore when the Law found Him among thieves, it condemned and executed Him as a thief.[32]

For Luther, the key is found in the words 'for us'. A little further on he writes:

> With gratitude and with a sure confidence, therefore, let us accept this doctrine, so sweet and so filled with comfort, which teaches that Christ became a curse for us, that is, a sinner

---

[29] Luther, *WA* 5:608.
[30] Luther, *LW* 26:353; *WA* 40/1, 541.
[31] Luther, *LW* 48:12.
[32] Luther, *LW* 26:277, *WA* 40:433, 27–28.

worthy of the wrath of God; that He clothed Himself in our person, laid our sins upon His own shoulders, and said: 'I have committed the sins that all men have committed'. Therefore He truly became accursed according to the Law, not for Himself but, as Paul says, ὑπὲρ ἡμῶν.... By this fortunate exchange with us He took upon Himself our sinful person and granted us His innocent and victorious Person. Clothed and dressed in this, we are freed from the curse of the Law, because Christ Himself voluntarily became a curse for us, saying: 'For My own Person of humanity and divinity I am blessed, and I am in need of nothing whatever. But I shall empty Myself (Phil 2:7); I shall assume your clothing and mask; and in this I shall walk about and suffer death, in order to set you free from death'.[33]

Luther vigorously rejects the normal interpretation of Gal 3:13 by commentators who side-stepped the idea that Christ could have been made a curse, complaining that 'Jerome and his present-day followers rack their miserable brains over this comforting passage in an effort to save Christ from the fancied insult of being called a curse';[34] the best that Luther can say of this exegesis is that it is 'a zealous attempt to defend the honor and glory of Christ'.

The example of Luther's 'happy exchange' most frequently referred to is found in his 1520 publication *The Freedom of the Christian*, with reference to Ephesians 5. Luther links this chapter with Hosea 1–2, suggesting that in Paul's analogy what belongs to the bridegroom (i.e. righteousness) is exchanged with what belongs to the bride (i.e. sin). Faith:

unites the soul with Christ as a bride is united with her bridegroom. By this mystery, as the Apostle teaches, Christ and the soul become one flesh [Eph 5:31–32]. And if they are one flesh and there is between them a true marriage – indeed the most perfect of all marriages, since human marriages are but poor examples of this one true marriage – it follows that everything they have they hold in common, the good as well as the evil. Accordingly the believing soul can boast of and glory in whatever Christ has as though it were its own, and whatever the soul has Christ claims as his own.... Christ is full of grace, life, and salvation. The soul is full of sins, death, and damnation. Now let faith come between them and sins, death, and damnation will be Christ's, while grace, life, and salvation will be the soul's; for if Christ is a bridegroom, he must take upon himself the things which are his bride's and bestow upon her the things that are his. If he gives her his body and very self, how shall he not give her all that is his? And if he takes the body of the bride, how shall he not take all that is hers?[35]

This is certainly an exchange – grace for sins, death for life, salvation for damnation – but I wonder whether that term is adequate for what Luther is trying to describe.[36] In a true exchange, *A* can exchange places with *B*, as

---

[33] Luther, *LW* 26:283 ff.; *WA* 40/1:442–443.

[34] Later commentators would also have fallen under Luther's condemnation! See Ernest De Witt Burton, *A Critical and Exegetical Commentary on The Epistle to the Galatians*, ICC (Edinburgh: T&T Clark, 1921), 171; James D.G. Dunn, *A Commentary on the Epistle to the Galatians*, BNTC (London: A&C Black, 1993), 177.

[35] Luther, *LW* 31:351–352, *WA* 7:25, 34.

[36] He himself does not use the term here.

Sydney Carton did with Charles Darnay in *A Tale of Two Cities*, but what Paul is attempting to describe involves a sharing in what the other is and experiences. It is for this reason that I myself have preferred to use the term 'interchange' for passages such as Gal 3:13 and 2 Cor 5:21, where Paul is clearly thinking of something which involves participation in what the other is.[37] Admittedly, this term also – reminiscent as it is of Spaghetti Junction – is not ideal, though the image of a recovery truck *joining itself* to a broken-down car on a motorway and then successfully towing it in the opposite direction may convey something of what is involved! The truck does not change places with the car, but by joining itself to the car's predicament (the analogy is clearly inadequate!), enables the car to become mobile. This idea of 'interchange' lies at the heart of Pauline teaching – the idea that Christ becomes what we are in order that, *in him*, we might become what he is, which is basically an *incarnational* model:[38] i.e., because Christ, by becoming man, *shares* our humanity and state of sinfulness, together with what that brings, we are able to share his righteousness and what *that* brings.

Luther refers again to the image of marriage found in Ephesians 5 in his *Commentary on Galatians*:

But faith must be taught correctly, namely, that by it you are so cemented to Christ that He and you are as one person, which cannot be separated but remains attached to Him forever and declares: 'I am as Christ'. And Christ, in turn, says: 'I am that sinner who is attached to Me, and I to him. For by faith we are joined together into one flesh and one bone'. Thus Eph 5:30 says: 'We are members of the body of Christ, of His flesh and of His bones', in such a way that this faith couples Christ and me more intimately than a husband is coupled to his wife. Therefore this faith is no idle quality; but it is a thing of such magnitude that it obscures and completely removes those foolish dreams of the sophists' doctrine – the fiction of a 'formed faith' and of love, of merits, our worthiness, our quality, etc.[39]

Significantly, Luther notes that the Christian is 'joined' to Christ 'more intimately than a husband is coupled to his wife', just as earlier he had acknowledged that 'human marriages are but poor examples of this one true marriage'. It would seem that he recognizes that the marital image is insufficient to convey an attachment which he describes as being 'cemented to Christ'. What he is describing is once again 'participation', or 'interchange', which comes about through Christ becoming what we are.

Judging by passages in his writings such as those quoted above, it would seem that this idea was of central importance for Luther as well as for Paul, since they suggest that by the term 'exchange' Luther was thinking primarily of something which takes place because the believer is *in Christ*. By faith,

---

[37] See among other articles, those gathered in Hooker, *From Adam to Christ*.
[38] Cf. Rom 8:3; Gal 4:4–5; Phil 2:7.
[39] Luther, *LW* 26:168–169; *WA* 40/1:285, 24–286, 20.

the believer participates in the attributes of Christ, because he is 'clothed in Christ'. It is an idea which seems to permeate both men's writings. In 1 Cor 1:30, for example, Paul reminds the Corinthians that they are 'in Christ Jesus, who has become our wisdom, and righteousness, and holiness, and redemption', and this idea is echoed by Luther in his *Sermo de duplici iustitiae* (1518):

> Through faith in Christ, therefore, Christ's righteousness becomes our righteousness ... and all that he has becomes ours; rather, he himself becomes ours.... He who trusts in Christ exists in Christ; he is one with Christ, having the same righteousness as he.[40]

The same passage from 1 Corinthians – linked with Johannine vocabulary – is echoed in another sermon, preached as early as 1514:

> Just as the word of God became flesh, so it is certainly also necessary that the flesh may become word. In other words: God becomes man so that man may become God. Thus power becomes powerless so that weakness may become powerful. The Logos puts on our form and pattern, our image and likeness, so that it may clothe us with its image, its pattern, and its likeness. Thus wisdom becomes foolish so that foolishness may become wisdom, and so it is in all other things that are in God and in us, to the extent that in all these things he takes what is ours to himself in order to impart what is his to us.[41]

What Luther is expressing here is better described as 'interchange', rather than as 'exchange', since, as he goes on to say, God does not stop being God, and man does not stop being man. Luther's words in this passage echo the idea expressed by Irenaeus, which so brilliantly sums up Paul's theology: 'Christ was made what we are, in order that he might make us what he is'.[42] It is not a matter of Christ and humanity *exchanging* places; rather, because Christ becomes man, men and women are enabled, *through union with him*, to become what Christ is. We might well use of Christ himself the famous slogan *simul justus et peccator*! As Luther himself expresses it:

> He became Law to the Law, sin to sin, and death to death, in order that He might redeem me from the curse of the Law, justify me, and make me alive. And so Christ is both: while he is the Law, he is liberty; while he is sin, he is righteousness, and while he is death, he is life. For by the very fact that he permitted the Law to accuse him, sin to damn him, and death to devour him he abrogated the Law, damned sin, destroyed death, and justified and saved me.[43]

In the teaching of Paul, the idea of 'interchange' brings together the doctrines of 'incarnation' and 'atonement'. It is because Christ was born as a man that he was able to overcome sin. Luther took seriously Paul's statements in

---

[40] *Two Kinds of Righteousness*. See Martin Luther, *Martin Luther: Selections from His Writings*, ed. John Dillenberger (Garden City, NY: Anchor Books, 1961), 87 ff.
[41] Luther, *In Natali Christi*, WA 1:28, 25–32.
[42] Irenaeus, *Adv. Haer.* 5 praef.
[43] Luther, *LW* 26:163; *WA* 40/1:278, 22–28.

Gal 3:13[44] that Christ was 'made a curse' and in 2 Cor 5:21 that 'Christ became sin', maintaining – in words as shocking as Paul's – that Christ was 'the greatest sinner'.[45]

Another suggestion regarding an alternative to the term 'exchange' has been offered by a Finnish scholar, Tuomo Mannermaa, who is a leading member of a group of Finnish scholars who have joined in the criticism of the traditional 'Lutheran' understanding of Luther's theology, which emphasized the forensic understanding of Christ's death. Mannermaa suggests that a more accurate expression of Luther's meaning is found in another phrase which he uses, 'communication of attributes' (*communicatio idiomatum*):[46] the believer becomes a participant in what Christ is. He has even argued that this implies *theosis*, or divinization, bringing him close to Greek Orthodox interpretation of Paul. Although we may hesitate to describe this as 'deification',[47] we do find Luther writing of Christians becoming 'participants in the divine nature'.[48] The idea that, in Christ, we share his righteousness and become *like* him is Pauline to the core, and was clearly central to Luther who, like Paul, saw incarnation and atonement as inseparably joined.[49] The contribution of Mannermaa and his colleagues in rediscovering neglected parts of Luther's teaching supports our belief that the idea that Christians are made righteous through sharing in Christ's righteousness, and that in him they *continue* to live and to grow, is of central importance to both Paul and Luther.[50]

2. Sola Fide

It seems clear that the idea of union with Christ and what that involves – whether we call it 'participation', 'interchange', or 'communication of attributes' – was at least as important for Luther as the interpretation of justification

---

[44] See above, n. 34.

[45] Luther, *Commentary* on Psalm 22:1.

[46] Tuomo Mannermaa, *Christ Present in Faith: Luther's View of Justification*, ed. Kirsi Stjerna (Minneapolis: Fortress Press, 2005), 21. Mannermaa has stressed the importance of union with Christ for Luther; on this, see also Marcus Johnson, 'Luther and Calvin on Union with Christ', *Fides et Historia* 39 (2007): 59–77.

[47] The terms 'deification' and 'theosis' have been used of Paul's own teaching by Michael J. Gorman, e.g. in his *Inhabiting the Cruciform God: Kenosis, Justification, and Theosis in Paul's Narrative Soteriology* (Grand Rapids: Eerdmans, 2009).

[48] Cf. Luther's sermon on the letter to the Ephesians, *Predigt* (1525), where (referring to 2 Peter 1) he declares 'that we are to become participants in the divine nature and ... have Him, the Lord Himself, dwelling in us in His fullness', *WA* 17/1:438, 14–28.

[49] See Mannermaa, *Christ Present in Faith* throughout.

[50] I have discussed some of the issues raised in this article, including the contribution of the Finnish school, in an expanded version of a presentation at a seminar on Luther held in Cambridge in 2017: Morna D. Hooker, 'Luther – Faithful Exegete of Paul', in *Luther and Philosophies of the Reformation*, ed. Boris Gunjević (London: Bloomsbury, 2023), 23–38.

as a forensic transaction which has dominated Protestant interpretation of Paul ever since the Reformation. But what of this latter concept? Clearly it had some role in Paul's thought, and this is hardly surprising, for although the 'new perspective' on Paul has attacked the traditional emphasis on justification as a legal judgement, this understanding was part of Paul's own teaching. The problem has centred on the meaning of the Greek verb *dikaioō*. The idea that it means 'to impute righteousness' (to consider x to be righteous) rather than 'to impart righteousness' is based on the fact that its basic meaning is 'to set things right', and hence to 'acquit' or to 'vindicate' those who are recognized as righteous. The idea that those who are vindicated or acquitted are those who are 'in Christ' is consistent with this. For Paul, to be 'justified' is to be declared righteous in the sight of God, but this depends on being joined to Christ, and so sharing in *his* righteousness – something that becomes possible for those who share in his death and resurrection. Paul sums up this idea in Gal 2:19–20:

> Through the Law I died to the Law, so that I might live to God. I have been crucified with Christ, and it is no longer I who live, but Christ who lives in me. And the life I now live in the flesh I live by faith in (*or* by the faithfulness of) the Son of God, who loved me and gave himself up for me.

Luther comments:

> It is unprecedented and insolent to say: 'I live, I do not live; I am dead, I am not dead; I am a sinner, I am not a sinner; I have the Law, I do not have the Law'. But this phraseology is true of Christ and through Christ. When it comes to justification, therefore, if you divide Christ's Person from your own, you are in the Law; you remain in it and live in yourself, which means that you are dead in the sight of God and damned by the Law....[51]

For him, as for Paul, sharing in Christ's righteousness came about through sharing in his death and resurrection.

By a strange irony, the writings of Paul, who protested against imposing the Law on Gentile converts and who insisted that what was written by the Spirit on human hearts was far greater than what was written on stone, were themselves treated for centuries as though written on stone for all time – or rather, what he was *thought* to have written, since his words have so frequently been misunderstood. The same fate, it would seem, has befallen Luther, since what he meant by 'justification' and by 'faith' have similarly been misinterpreted, and what he was thought to have said was turned into a doctrine which was accepted by later generations. 'Justification by faith' became the slogan of Protestant orthodoxy. Whatever Luther and other Reformers believed, and whatever official church pronouncements said, the slogan was frequently interpreted primarily as a reference to a forensic transaction, and the important emphasis on union with Christ was forgotten.

---

[51] Luther, *LW* 26:168; *WA* 40/1:285, 12–17.

Was this perhaps because Luther's fight with Rome meant that the emphasis was laid on faith in opposition to works, and the idea of union with Christ received far less attention? Or was it perhaps the slogan *sola fide* which was to blame? Certainly that *sola* seems to lay all the stress on faith, and unless what is meant by 'faith' is spelt out, it is as easy to distort this as any other slogan. Barth was right when he said that the *sola fide* was 'a faint echo of the *solus Christus*'[52] – but perhaps it was *too* faint! When the emphasis shifts from the grace of God at work in Christ to the response of the believer, Paul's insights and Luther's own teaching are distorted and turned into a doctrine which loses sight of what both men had seen as essential. When later generations emphasize particular aspects of past teaching which are relevant to their situation, this is a legitimate interpretation of the text; but when their understanding is codified into a creed which believers are told they must accept, the result can be stultifying.

Since we began with the words of John Wesley, honesty demands that we admit, sadly, that it seems that he was one of those who missed one important aspect of Luther's interpretation of Paul, for though he admired Luther's writings, his sermon on 'Justification by faith'[53] fails to pick up Luther's emphasis on union with Christ. Perhaps it was because, for Wesley, the important concept of having 'the mind of Christ' was associated with the idea of a subsequent sanctification.

And so we return to the question we raised at the beginning of this essay: was Luther himself guilty of distorting Paul's teaching, as some Pauline scholars have argued? Did the inevitable reinterpretation resulting from the very different situations in which Luther lived and worked and the very different problems which confronted him – the reinterpretation which was highlighted by Stendahl – destroy Paul's insights or preserve them? Some things he undoubtedly got wrong: Luther's attitude to Jews, for example, which today seems so reprehensible, but which reflects the attitudes of his own day, is a long way from that of Paul, who expressed himself willing to be cut off from Christ for the sake of his fellow countrymen.[54] The chief problem faced by Luther was not 'how to *get into* the people of God' but 'how to *stay in*' (to use Sanders' terms) – in other words 'how to *behave* as members of his people' (issues discussed by Paul in the so-called 'ethical' sections of his letters. When Luther read Galatians and Romans he was applying their teaching to a very different situation, and his interpretation of those letters to the teaching of the church of his day was both appropriate and necessary.

---

[52] See above, n. 15.
[53] John Wesley, *Sermons on Several Occasions* (London: Epworth Press, 1944), 49–61.
[54] Rom 9:3.

Regarding Paul's teaching on righteousness (or justification) however, it would seem that the emphasis on 'forensic justice' and on 'faith, not works' which has characterized so much later teaching is precisely that — an emphasis on one part of Luther's teaching at the expense of other aspects of his thought. The criticism that the doctrine of justification was not integrated into Christology in much post-Lutheran Protestant theology is understandable. But in spite of reading Paul in a very different situation, the 'real' Luther is much closer to Paul than we might have supposed, and his teaching was faithful to the heart of the Pauline gospel, which proclaimed the crucifixion and resurrection of Christ, and saw union with Christ as the way to salvation. The idea that, in Christ, believers share his righteousness is Pauline to the core, and was clearly central to Luther, who, like Paul, saw incarnation and atonement as inseparably joined: 'justification' is indeed through faith, but it takes place *in Christ*, who — sharing *our* human nature — shares *his* righteousness with believers and transforms them into his own likeness.

Details of First Publication

The following journals and publishers have granted permission to reproduce the articles, papers, and chapters included in this volume:

1. *New Wine in Old Bottles: A Discussion of Continuity and Discontinuity in Relation to Judaism and the Gospel*
London: University of London, 1984.

2. 'Christology and Methodology'
New Testament Studies 17 (1970): 480–487.

3. 'On Using the Wrong Tool'
Theology 75 (1972): 570–581.

4. 'In His Own Image?'
Pages 28–44 in *What about the New Testament? Essays in Honour of Christopher Evans*. Edited by Morna D. Hooker and Colin Hickling. London: SCM Press, 1975.

5. 'T.W. Manson and the Twentieth-Century Search for Jesus'
Bulletin of the John Rylands Library, 86 (2004): 77–98.

6. 'Is the Son of Man Problem Really Insoluble?'
Pages 155–168 in *Text and Interpretation: Studies in the New Testament presented to Matthew Black*. Edited by Ernest Best and R.McL. Wilson. Cambridge: Cambridge University Press, 1979.

7. 'The Son of Man and the Synoptic Problem'
Pages 189–201 in vol. 1 of *The Four Gospels 1992: Festschrift Frans Neirynck*. Edited by Frans Van Segbroeck, C.M. Tuckett, G. Van Belle, and J. Verheyden. Leuven: Leuven University Press/Peeters, 1992.

8. 'Did the Use of Isaiah 53 to Interpret His Mission Begin with Jesus?'
Pages 88–103 in *Jesus and the Suffering Servant: Isaiah 53 and Christian Origins*. Edited by William H. Bellinger Jr. and William R. Farmer. Harrisburg, PA: Trinity Press International, 1998.

9. 'Good News about Jesus Christ, the Son of God'
Pages 165–180 in *Mark as Story: Retrospect and Prospect*. Edited by Kelly R. Iverson and Christopher W. Skinner. Atlanta: Society of Biblical Literature, 2011.

10. 'The Nature of New Testament Theology'
Pages 75–92 in *The Nature of New Testament Theology: Essays in Honour of Robert Morgan*. Edited by Christopher Rowland and Christopher Tuckett. Oxford: Blackwell, 2006.

11: 'Chalcedon and the New Testament'

Pages 73–93 in *The Making and Remaking of Christian Doctrine: Essays in Honour of Maurice Wiles*. Edited by Sarah Coakley and David Pailin. Oxford: Clarendon Press, 1993.

12. '"What Doest Thou Here, Elijah?": A Look at St. Mark's Account of the Transfiguration'

Pages 59–70 in *The Glory of Christ in the New Testament: Studies in Christology in Memory of George Bradford Caird*. Edited by L.D. Hurst and N.T. Wright. Oxford: Clarendon Press, 1987.

13. 'Mark's Use of Scripture'

Originally entitled 'Mark'. Pages 220–230 in *It is Written: Scripture Citing Scripture: Essays in Honour of Barnabas Lindars, SSF*. Edited by D.A. Carson and H.G.M. Williamson. Cambridge: Cambridge University Press, 1988.

14. 'Isaiah in Mark's Gospel'

Pages 35–49 in *Isaiah in the New Testament: The New Testament and the Scriptures of Israel*. Edited by Steve Moyise and Maarten J.J. Menken. London: Continuum, 2005.

15. 'Trial and Tribulation in Mark XIII'

Bulletin of the John Rylands Library 65 (1982): 78–99.

16. 'Traditions about the Temple in the Sayings of Jesus'

Bulletin of the John Rylands Library 70 (1988): 7–19.

17: 'Creative Conflict: The Torah and Christology'

Pages 117–136 in *Christology, Controversy and Community: New Testament Essays in Honour of David R. Catchpole*. Edited by David G. Horrell and Christopher M. Tuckett. Leiden: Brill, 2000.

18. 'Uncomfortable Words: The Prohibition of Foreign Missions (Matt 10:5–6)'

Uncomfortable Words X, *The Expository Times* 82 (1971): 361–365.

19. 'The Beginning of the Gospel'

Pages 18–28 in *The Future of Christology: Essays in Honor of Leander E. Keck*. Edited by Abraham J. Malherbe and Wayne A. Meeks. Minneapolis: Fortress Press, 1993.

20. 'Beginning from Moses and from All the Prophets'

Pages 216–230 in *From Jesus to John: Essays on Jesus and New Testament Christology in Honour of Marinus de Jonge*. Edited by Martinus C. de Boer. Sheffield: JSOT Press, 1993.

21. 'John's Baptism: A Prophetic Sign'

Pages 22–40 in *The Holy Spirit and Christian Origins: Essays in Honor of James D.G. Dunn*. Edited by Graham N. Stanton, Bruce W. Longenecker and Stephen C. Barton. Grand Rapids: Eerdmans, 2004.

22. 'John the Baptist and the Johannine Prologue'

New Testament Studies 16 (1970): 354–358.

23. 'The Johannine Prologue and the Messianic Secret'

New Testament Studies 21 (1974): 40–58.

24. '"There's Glory for You!": Death and Glory in John's Gospel'
Unpublished lecture delivered in Cambridge.

25. 'Paul: Apostle to the Gentiles'
The 28th St Paul's Lecture, under the auspices of the London Diocesan Council for Christian-Jewish Understanding, given at St Botolph's Church, Aldgate on November 16th, 1989. *Epworth Review* 18 (1991): 79–89.

26. 'Adam *Redivivus*: Philippians 2 Once More'
Pages 220–234 in *The Old Testament in the New Testament: Essays in Honour of J. L. North*. Edited by Steve Moyise. JSNTSup 189. Sheffield: Sheffield Academic Press, 2000.

27. 'Christ: The "End" of the Law'
Pages 126–146 in *Neotestamentica et Philonica: Studies in Honor of Peder Borgen*. Edited by David E. Aune, Torrey Seland, and Jarl Henning Ulrichsen. NTSup 106. Leiden: Brill, 2003.

28. 'On Becoming the Righteousness of God: Another Look at 2 Cor 5:21'
Novum Testamentum 50 (2008): 358–375.

29. 'Another Look at πίστις Χριστοῦ'
Scottish Journal of Theology 69 (2016): 46–62.

30. '2 Corinthians 5:1–10 in Context'
Pages 165–195 in *2 Thessalonians and Pauline Eschatology: For Petr Pokorný on His 80th Birthday*. Proceedings of the 42nd Meeting of the Colloquium Oecumenicum Paulinum, 2012. Edited by Christopher Tuckett. Leuven: Peeters, 2013.

31. 'Artemis of Ephesus'
Journal of Theological Studies 64 (2013): 37–46.

32. 'The Authority of the Bible: A New Testament Perspective'
Ex Auditu 19 (2003): 45–64.

33. 'Where is Wisdom to Be Found? Colossians 1:15–20'
Pages 116–128 in *Reading Texts, Seeking Wisdom: Scripture and Theology*. Edited by David F. Ford and Graham Stanton. London: SCM Press, 2003.

34. 'Christ, the "End" of the Cult'
Pages 189–212 in *The Epistle to the Hebrews and Christian Theology*. Edited by Richard Bauckham, Daniel R. Driver, Trevor A. Hart, and Nathan MacDonald. Grand Rapids: Eerdmans, 2009.

35. '1 Thessalonians 1:9–10: A Nutshell – But What Kind of Nut?'
Pages 435–448 in vol. 3: *Frühes Christentum* of *Geschichte – Tradition – Reflexion: Festschrift für Martin Hengel zum 70. Geburtstag*. Edited by Hermann Lichtenberger. Tübingen: Mohr Siebeck, 1996.

36. 'Called to Be God's Holy People'
Unpublished seminar paper presented in Cambridge and Aberdeen.

37. 'Christ Died for Our Sins, and Was Raised for Our Acquittal: Paul's Understanding of the Death of Christ'

Originally entitled '"Who Died for Our Sins, and Was Raised for Our Acquittal": Paul's Understanding of the Death of Christ'. *Svensk Exegetisk Årsbok* 68 (2003): 59–71.

38. 'Raised for Our Acquittal (Rom 4:25)'

Pages 323–341 in *Resurrection in the New Testament: Festschrift J. Lambrecht*. Edited by R. Bieringer, V. Koperski and B. Lataire. *BETL* 165. Leuven: University Press/Peeters, 2002.

39. 'A Partner in the Gospel: Paul's Understanding of His Ministry'

Pages 83–100 in *Theology and Ethics in Paul and His Interpreters: Essays in Honor of Victor Paul Furnish*. Edited by Eugene H. Lovering, Jr. and Jerry L. Sumney. Nashville: Abingdon, 1996.

40. 'Paul the Pastor: The Relevance of the Gospel'

Proceedings of the Irish Biblical Association 31 (2009): 17–31.

41. 'From God's Faithfulness to Ours: Another Look at 2 Corinthians 1:17–24'

Pages 233–239 in *Paul and the Corinthians: Studies on a Community in Conflict: Essays in Honour of Margaret Thrall*. Edited by Trevor J. Burke and J. Keith Elliott. NTSup 109. Leiden: Brill, 2003.

42. 'Philippians: Phantom Opponents and the Real Source of Conflict'

Pages 377–395 in *Fair Play: Diversity and Conflicts in Early Christianity: Essays in Honour of Heikki Räisänen*. Edited by Ismo Dunderberg, Christopher Tuckett, and Kari Syreeni. Leiden: Brill, 2002.

43. '"Submit to One Another": The Transformation of Relationships in Christ (Eph 5:21–6:9)'

Pages 163–188 in *Ethik als Angewandte Ekklesiologie: Der Brief and die Epheser*. Edited by Michael Wolter. Leuven: Peeters, 2005.

44. '"The Sanctuary of His Body": Body and Sanctuary in Paul and John'

Journal for the Study of the New Testament 39 (2017): 347–361.

45. '"Sola Fide": The Wrong Slogan?'

Pages 25–39 in *Contesting Orthodoxies in the History of Christianity: Essays in Honour of Diarmaid MacCulloch*. Edited by Ellie Gebarowski-Shafer, Ashley Null and Alec Ryrie. Woodbridge, Suffolk: Boydell Press, 2021.

List of Illustrations

Page 68: *Fig. 1*. Thomas Walter Manson (1893–1958), Rylands Professor 1936–1958 Copyright of the University of Manchester.

Page 466: *Fig. 2*. Second-century statue of Artemis of Ephesus, National Archaeological Museum in Naples. Photo: author.

Bibliography

Abbott, Thomas Kingsmill. *A Critical and Exegetical Commentary on the Epistles to the Ephesians and to the Colossians.* ICC. Edinburgh: T&T Clark, 1897.
Ackerman, James S. 'The Rabbinic Interpretation of Psalm 82 and the Gospel of John: John 10:34'. *HTR* 59 (1966): 186–191.
Aletti, Jean-Noël. *Colossiens 1,15–20.* AnBib 91. Rome: Biblical Institute Press, 1981.
Allen, Willoughby C. *A Critical and Exegetical Commentary on the Gospel According to St. Matthew.* 3rd ed. ICC. Edinburgh: T&T Clark, 1912.
Anderson, Hugh. 'The Old Testament in Mark's Gospel'. Pages 280–306 in *The Use of the Old Testament in the New and Other Essays: Studies in Honor of William Franklin Stinespring.* Edited by James M. Efird. Durham, NC: Duke University Press, 1972.
–. *The Gospel of Mark.* London: Oliphants, 1976.
Arndt, William F. and F. Wilbur Gingrich. *A Greek-English Lexicon of the New Testament.* 2nd ed. Chicago; London: University of Chicago Press, 1979.
Arnold, Clinton E. *The Colossian Syncretism: The Interface between Christianity and Folk Belief at Colossae.* WUNT 2/77. Tübingen: Mohr Siebeck, 1995.
Ashton, John. *Understanding the Fourth Gospel.* Oxford: Clarendon Press, 1991.
Augustine. *St Augustine: On the Spirit and the Letter.* Translated by W.J. Sparrow Simpson. London: SPCK, 1925.
Bacon, Benjamin W. *Studies in Matthew.* London: Constable, 1930.
Badenas, Robert. *Christ the End of the Law: Romans 10.4 in Pauline Perspective.* JSNTSup 10. Sheffield: JSOT Press, 1985.
Bailey, Daniel P. 'Concepts of *Stellvertretung* in the Interpretation of Isaiah 53'. Pages 223–250 in *Jesus and the Suffering Servant: Isaiah 53 and Christian Origins.* Edited by William H. Bellinger Jr. and William R. Farmer. Harrisburg, PA: Trinity Press International, 1998.
–. 'Jesus as the Mercy Seat: The Semantics and Theology of Paul's Use of *Hilasterion* in Romans 3:25'. PhD thesis, University of Cambridge, 1999.
–. 'Jesus as the Mercy Seat: The Semantics and Theology of Paul's Use of *Hilasterion* in Romans 3:25'. *Tyndale Bulletin* 51 (2000): 155–158.
Balch, David. *Let Wives be Submissive: The Domestic Code in 1 Peter.* SBL monograph series 26. Atlanta: Scholars Press, 1981.
Barbour, R.S. *Traditio-Historical Criticism of the Gospels: Some Comments on Current Methods.* London: SPCK, 1972.
Barclay, John M.G. 'Death and Early Christian Identity'. Pages 131–153 in *Not in the Word Alone: The First Epistle to the Thessalonians.* Edited by Morna D. Hooker. Monographic Series of *Benedictina* 15. Rome: Abbey of St Paul Outside the Walls, 2003.
Barr, James. *The Semantics of Biblical Language.* Oxford: Oxford University Press, 1961.
Barrett, C.K. 'Q: A Re-examination'. *ExpTim* 54 (1943): 320–323.
–. *The Gospel According to St John: An Introduction with Commentary and Notes on the Greek Text.* London: SPCK, 1955; repr., 1958; 2nd ed., 1978.
–. *A Commentary on the Epistle to the Romans.* BNTC. London: A&C Black, 1957; 2nd ed., 1991.

–. *The Holy Spirit and the Gospel Tradition*. London: SPCK, 1958.
–. 'The Background of Mark 10.45'. Pages 1–18 in *New Testament Essays: Studies in Memory of Thomas Walter Manson, 1893–1958*. Edited by A.J.B. Higgins. Manchester: Manchester University Press, 1959.
–. 'The Eschatology of the Epistle to the Hebrews'. Pages 363–393 in *The Background of the New Testament and Its Eschatology: Studies in Honour of C.H. Dodd*. Edited by W.D. Davies and David Daube. Cambridge: Cambridge University Press, 1964.
–. *Jesus and the Gospel Tradition*. London: SPCK, 1967.
–. *A Commentary on the First Epistle to the Corinthians*. BNTC. London: A&C Black, 1968 = New York: Harper & Row, 1968.
–. *A Commentary on the Second Epistle to the Corinthians*. BNTC. London: A&C Black, 1973.
–. 'Romans 9.30–10.21: Fall and Responsibility of Israel'. Pages 99–130 in *Die Israelfrage nach Röm 9–11*. Edited by Lorenzo De Lorenzi. Rome: Abbey of St Paul Outside the Walls, 1977.
–. 'Luke'. Pages 231–244 in *It is Written: Scripture Citing Scripture: Essays in Honour of Barnabas Lindars*. Edited by D.A. Carson and H.G.M. Williamson. Cambridge: Cambridge University Press, 1988.
–. *A Critical and Exegetical Commentary on the Acts of the Apostles*. vol. 2. ICC. Edinburgh: T&T Clark, 1998.
Barth, Karl. *The Epistle to the Romans*. Translated by E.C. Hoskyns. Oxford: Oxford University Press, 1933.
–. *Church Dogmatics*. vol. 4, part 1: *The Doctrine of Reconciliation*. Edited by G.W. Bromiley and Thomas F. Torrance. Translated by G.W. Bromiley. Edinburgh: T&T Clark, 1956.
Barth, Markus. *Ephesians: Translation and Commentary on Chapters 4–6*. Anchor Bible. Garden City, NY: Doubleday, 1974.
Barton, Stephen C., ed. *Holiness: Past and Present*. London: T&T Clark, 2003.
Bash, Anthony. *Ambassadors for Christ*. WUNT 2/92. Tübingen: Mohr, 1997.
Beare, Francis Wright. *A Commentary on the Epistle to the Philippians*. BNTC. London: A&C Black, 1959.
–. 'Sayings of the Risen Jesus in the Synoptic Tradition'. Pages 161–181 in *Christian History and Interpretation: Studies Presented to John Knox*. Edited by William R. Farmer, C.F.D. Moule and R.R. Niebuhr. Cambridge: Cambridge University Press, 1967.
–. 'The Mission of the Disciples and the Mission Charge: Matthew 10 and Parallels'. *JBL* 89 (1970): 1–13.
Beasley-Murray, George R. *Jesus and the Future*. London: Macmillan, 1956.
–. *A Commentary on Mark Thirteen*. London: Macmillan, 1957.
Beavis, Mary Ann. *Mark's Audience: The Literary and Social Setting of Mark 4:11–12*. Sheffield: JSOT, 1989.
Belleville, Linda L. *Reflections of Glory: Paul's Polemical Use of the Moses-Doxa Tradition in 2 Corinthians 3.1–18*. JSNTSup 52. Sheffield: JSOT Press, 1991.
Best, Ernest. 'Spirit-Baptism'. *NT* 4 (1960): 236–243.
–. *The Temptation and the Passion: The Markan Soteriology*. SNTSMS 2. Cambridge: Cambridge University Press, 1965; 2nd ed., 1990.
–. *A Commentary on the First and Second Epistles to the Thessalonians*. BNTC. London: A&C Black, 1972.
–. *Essays on Ephesians*. Edinburgh: T&T Clark, 1997.
–. *A Critical and Exegetical Commentary on Ephesians*. ICC. Edinburgh: T&T Clark, 1998.

Betz, Hans Dieter. *Nachfolge und Nachahmung Jesu Christi im Neuen Testament*. BHT 37. Tübingen: Mohr Siebeck, 1967.
—. *Galatians*. Hermeneia. Philadelphia: Fortress, 1979.
Bieringer, R. 'Sünde und Gerechtigkeit Gottes in 2 Korinther 5,21'. Pages 461–513 in *Studies on 2 Corinthians*. Edited by R. Bieringer and Jan Lambrecht. Leuven: Peeters, 1994.
Bilezikian, Gilbert G. *The Liberated Gospel: A Comparison of the Gospel of Mark and Greek Tragedy*. Grand Rapids: Baker, 1977.
Black, Matthew. 'The Son of Man Problem in Recent Research and Debate'. *BJRL* 45 (1963): 305–318.
—. *An Aramaic Approach to the Gospels and Acts*. Oxford: Clarendon Press, 1967.
—. 'The Christological Use of the Old Testament in the New Testament'. *NTS* 18 (1971): 1–14.
—. *Romans*. 2nd ed. NCB. London: Marshall, Morgan and Scott, 1989.
Blass, F. and A. Debrunner. *A Greek Grammar of the New Testament and Other Early Christian Literature*. Translated and revised by Robert W. Funk. Cambridge: Cambridge University Press, 1961 = Chicago: University of Chicago Press, 1961.
Bockmuehl, Markus. *The Epistle to the Philippians*. BNTC. London: A&C Black, 1997.
—. '"The Form of God" (Phil. 2:6): Variations on a Theme of Jewish Mysticism'. *JTS* NS 48 (1997): 1–23.
—. ed. *The Cambridge Companion to Jesus*. Cambridge: Cambridge University Press, 2001.
Boismard, M.E. *St John's Prologue*. Translated by Carisbrooke Dominicans. London: Blackfriars, 1957.
Boobyer, G.H. *St Mark and the Transfiguration Story*. Edinburgh: T&T Clark, 1942.
Booth, Roger P. *Jesus and the Laws of Purity*. Sheffield: JSOT, 1986.
Borgen, Peder. *Bread from Heaven*. NTSup 10. Leiden: Brill, 1965.
—. 'God's Agent in the Fourth Gospel'. Pages 137–148 in *Religions in Antiquity: Essays in Memory of Erwin Ramsdell Goodenough*. Edited by Jacob Neusner. Leiden: Brill, 1968; repr. in *The Interpretation of John*. Edited by John Ashton. London: SPCK, 1986, 67–78.
—. 'Observations on the Targumic Character of the Prologue of John'. *NTS* 16 (1970): 288–295.
—. 'Logos was the True Light'. *NT* 14 (1972): 115–130; repr. in *Logos Was the True Light*, by Peder Borgen. Relieff 9. Trondheim: Tapir, 1983, 95–110.
—. *Logos Was the True Light*. Trondheim: Tapir, 1983.
—. 'Jesus Christ, the Reception of the Spirit and a Cross-National Community'. Pages 220–236 in *Jesus of Nazareth: Lord and Christ*. Edited by Joel B. Green and Max Turner. Grand Rapids: Eerdmans, 1994; repr. in *Early Christianity and Hellenistic Judaism*, by Peder Borgen. Edinburgh: T&T Clark, 1996, 253–272.
Bornkamm, Günther. *Jesus of Nazareth*. Translated by Irene and Fraser McLuskey with James M. Robinson. London: Hodder & Stoughton, 1960.
Bourne, George. *A Condensed Anti-Slavery Bible Argument, by a Citizen of Virginia*. New York: S.W. Benedict, 1845.
Bowen, Clayton R. 'The Fourth Gospel as Dramatic Material'. *JBL* 49 (1930): 292–305.
Bowman, John W. *The Intention of Jesus*. London: SCM Press, 1945.
Brandon, S.G.F. *Jesus and the Zealots: A Study of the Political Factor in Primitive Christianity*. Manchester: Manchester University Press, 1967.
Brooke, George J., ed. *The Significance of Sinai Traditions About Sinai and Divine Revelation in Judaism and Christianity*. Leiden: Brill, 2008.

Brower, Kent E. and Andy Johnson, eds. *Holiness and Ecclesiology in the New Testament*. Grand Rapids; Cambridge: Eerdmans, 2007.

Brown, Raymond E. 'The Semitic Background of the New Testament Mysterion (II)'. *Biblica* 40 (1959): 70–87.

—. *The Gospel According to John, I–XII*. New York: Doubleday, 1966.

—. *The Birth of the Messiah: A Commentary on the Infancy Narratives in Matthew and Luke*. London: Chapman, 1977.

Bruce, F. F. 'Hebrews'. Pages 1008–1019 in *Peake's Commentary on the Bible*. Edited by Matthew Black. London: Thomas Nelson, 1962.

—. *The Epistles to the Colossians, to Philemon and to the Ephesians*. NICNT. Grand Rapids: Eerdmans, 1984.

—. *Romans*. 2nd ed. NCB. Grand Rapids: Eerdmans, 1989 = London: Marshall, Morgan and Scott, 1989.

Bühner, Jan-Adolf. *Der Gesandte und sein Weg im vierten Evangelium*. WUNT 2/2. Tübingen: Mohr, 1977.

Bultmann, Rudolf. *Die Geschichte der synoptischen Tradition*. Göttingen: Vandenhoeck & Ruprecht, 1921.

—. *Jesus and the Word*. Translated by Louise Pettibone Smith and Erminie Huntress. New York: Scribner, 1934.

—. *Theology of the New Testament*. Vol 1. Translated by Kendrick Grobel. London: SCM Press, 1952.

—. *Das Evangelium des Johannes*. 17th ed. Göttingen: Vandenhoeck & Ruprecht, 1962.

—. *The History of the Synoptic Tradition*. Translated by John Marsh. Oxford: Blackwell, 1963.

—. 'ΔΙΚΑΙΟΣΥΝΗ ΘΕΟΥ'. *JBL* 83 (1964): 12–16; repr. in *Exegetica*. Edited by E. Dinkler. Tübingen: Mohr Siebeck, 1967, 470–475.

—. 'Jesus und Paulus'. Pages 210–229 in *Exegetica*. Edited by E. Dinkler. Tübingen: Mohr Siebeck, 1967.

Burch, Ernest W. 'Tragic Action in the Second Gospel: A Study in the Narrative of Mark'. *The Journal of Religion* 11 (1931): 346–358.

Burkert, Walter. *Greek Religion: Archaic and Classical*. Translated by John Raffan. Oxford: Blackwell, 1985.

Burkitt, F. C. 'W and Θ: Studies in the Western Text of St Mark (continued)'. *JTS* 17 (1916): 139–152.

Burney, C. F. 'Christ as the ΑΡΧΗ of Creation'. *JTS* 27 (1926): 160–177.

Burton, Ernest De Witt. *A Critical and Exegetical Commentary on The Epistle to the Galatians*. ICC. Edinburgh: T&T Clark, 1921.

Bussche, Henri van den. *Jean: Commentaire de l'Evangile Spirituel*. Paris: Desclée de Brouwer, 1967.

Byers, Andrew J. *Ecclesiology and Theosis in the Gospel of John*. SNTSMS 166. Cambridge: Cambridge University Press, 2017.

Byrne, Brendan. *'Sons of God' – 'Seed of Abraham'*. AnBib 83. Rome: Biblical Institute Press, 1979.

Cadman, William H. *The Open Heaven: The Revelation of God in the Johannine Sayings of Jesus*. Edited by G. B. Caird. Oxford: Blackwell, 1969.

Caird, G. B. 'Expository Problems: The Transfiguration'. *ExpTim* 67 (1956): 291–294.

—. 'The Development of the Doctrine of Christ in the New Testament'. Pages 66–80 in *Christ for Us Today*. Edited by Norman Pittenger. London: SCM Press, 1968.

—. 'The Glory of God in the Fourth Gospel: An Exercise in Biblical Semantics'. *NTS* 15 (1969): 265–277.
—. *Paul's Letters from Prison*. Oxford: Oxford University Press, 1976.
—. *New Testament Theology*. Edited by L.D. Hurst. Oxford: Clarendon, 1994.
Calvert, D.G.A. 'An Examination of the Criteria for Distinguishing the Authentic Words of Jesus'. *NTS* 18 (1972): 209–219.
Campbell, Douglas A. 'Romans 1:17 – A *Crux Interpretum* for the ΠΙΣΤΙΣ ΧΡΙΣΤΟΥ Debate'. *JBL* 113 (1994): 265–285.
—. 'An Echo of Scripture in Paul and its Implications'. Pages 367–391 in *The Word Leaps the Gap: Essays on Scripture and Theology in Honor of Richard B. Hays*. Edited by J. Ross Wagner, C. Kavin Rowe and A. Katherine Grieb. Grand Rapids; Cambridge: William B. Eerdmans, 2008.
Caragounis, Chrys C. *The Ephesian Mysterion: Meaning and Content*. ConBNT 8. Lund: LiberLäromedel/Gleerup, 1977.
Casey, P. Maurice. 'The Corporate Interpretation of "One like a Son of Man" (Dan. VII 13) at the Time of Jesus'. *NT* 18 (1976): 167–180.
—. 'The Son of Man Problem'. *ZNW* 67 (1976): 147–154.
—. 'The Use of the Term "Son of Man" in the Similitudes of Enoch'. *Journal for the Study of Judaism in the Persian, Hellenistic and Roman Period* 7 (1976): 11–29.
—. *Son of Man: The Interpretation and Influence of Daniel 7*. London: SPCK, 1979.
Catchpole, David R. 'The Synoptic Divorce Material as a Traditio-Historical Problem'. *BJRL* 57 (1974): 92–127.
—. 'The Law and the Prophets in Q'. Pages 95–109 in *Tradition and Interpretation in the New Testament: Essays in Honor of E. Earle Ellis for His 60th Birthday*. Edited by Gerald F. Hawthorne with Otto Betz. Grand Rapids: Eerdmans, 1987 = Tübingen: Mohr, 1987.
—. *The Quest for Q*. Edinburgh: T&T Clark, 1993.
Chadwick, Henry. 'All Things to All Men'. *NTS* 1 (1955): 261–275.
Chester, Andrew. 'Hebrews: The Final Sacrifice'. Pages 57–72 in *Sacrifice and Redemption: Durham Essays in Theology*. Edited by S.W. Sykes. Cambridge: Cambridge University Press, 1991.
Chester, Stephen. 'It is No Longer I Who Live: Justification by Faith and Participation in Christ in Martin Luther's Exegesis of Galatians'. *NTS* 55 (2009): 315–337.
Chilton, Bruce and Craig A. Evans, eds. *Studying the Historical Jesus: Evaluations of the State of Current Research*. New Testament Tools and Studies 19. Leiden: Brill, 1994.
Colani, Timothée. *Jésus-Christ Et Les Croyances Messianiques De Son Temps*. 2nd ed. Strasbourg: Truettel et Wurtz, 1864.
Collange, Jean-François. *Énigmes de la deuxième épître aux Corinthiens: Étude exégétique de 2 Cor. 2:14–7:4*. SNTSMS 18. Cambridge: Cambridge University Press, 1972.
Collins, Raymond F. *Studies on the First Letter to the Thessalonians*. BETL 66. Leuven: Leuven University Press, 1984.
Conzelmann, Hans. *Die Mitte der Zeit: Studien zur Theologie des Lukas*. Tübingen: Mohr, 1954; ET: *The Theology of St Luke*. Translated by Geoffrey Buswell. London: Faber and Faber, 1960.
—. 'Gegenwart und Zukunft in der synoptischen Tradition'. *ZTK* 54 (1957): 277–296.
—. 'Jesus Christus'. Columns 619–653 in *Die Religion in Geschichte und Gegenwart*. vol. 3. Edited by Hans von Campenhausen et. al. Tübingen: Mohr, 1959.
—. *An Outline of the Theology of the New Testament*. Translated by John Bowden. London: SCM Press, 1969.

Cook, David. 'The Prescript as Programme in Galatians'. *JTS* NS 43 (1992): 511–519.
Coppens, J. 'Le « mystère » dans la théologie paulinienne et ses parallèles qumrâniens'. Pages 142–165 in *Littérature et théologie Pauliniennes*. Edited by A. Descamps et al. Recherches Bibliques 5. Bruges: Desclée de Brouwer, 1960 ; ET: '"Mystery" in the Theology of Saint Paul and its Parallels at Qumran'. Pages 132–158 in *Paul and Qumran: Studies in New Testament Exegesis*. Edited by Jerome Murphy-O'Connor. London: G. Chapman, 1968.
Cranfield, C. E. B. *A Critical and Exegetical Commentary on the Epistle to the Romans*. vol. 1: *Introduction and Commentary on Romans I–VIII*. ICC. Edinburgh: T&T Clark, 1975.
—. *On Romans and Other New Testament Essays*. Edinburgh: T&T Clark, 1998.
Crossan, John Dominic. *The Historical Jesus: The Life of a Mediterranean Jewish Peasant*. Edinburgh: T&T Clark, 1991.
Crouch, James E. *The Origin and Intention of the Colossian Haustafel*. FRLANT 109. Göttingen: Vandenhoeck & Ruprecht, 1972.
Cullmann, Oscar. 'Le caractère eschatologique du devoir missionaire et de la conscience apostolique de S. Paul: Étude sur le κατέχον (-ων) de 2. Thess. 2:6–7'. *RHPR* 16 (1936): 210–245.
Dabeck, P. 'Siehe, es erschienen Moses und Elias' (Mt. 17.3)'. *Biblica* 23 (1942): 175–189.
Daly, Robert J. *The Origins of the Christian Doctrine of Sacrifice*. Philadelphia: Fortress Press, 1977 = London: Darton, Longman & Todd, 1978.
—. *Christian Sacrifice: The Judaeo-Christian Background before Origen*. Washington, DC: Catholic University of America Press, 1978.
Daube, David. *The New Testament and Rabbinic Judaism*. London: Athlone Press, 1956.
Davies, W. D. *Paul and Rabbinic Judaism*. 2nd ed. London: SPCK, 1955.
Davies, W. D. and Dale C. Allison. *A Critical and Exegetical Commentary on the Gospel According to Saint Matthew*. Vols. 1–3. ICC. Edinburgh: T&T Clark, 1988, 1991, 1997.
Davies, W. D. and E. P. Sanders. 'Jesus: From the Jewish Point of View'. Pages 618–677 in *Cambridge History of Judaism*. vol. 3. Edited by William Horbury, W. D. Davies, and John Sturdy. Cambridge: Cambridge University Press, 1999.
Deissmann, Adolf. *Licht vom Osten*. Tübingen: Mohr, 1909; ET: *Light from the Ancient East*. Translated by Lionel R. M. Strachan. London: Hodder & Stoughton, 1910.
—. *St. Paul: A Study in Social and Religious History*. Translated by William E. Wilson. London: Hodder & Stoughton, 1926.
Delobel, J. 'The Fate of the Dead According to 1 Thes 4 and 1 Cor 15'. Pages 340–347 in *The Thessalonian Correspondence*. Edited by Raymond F. Collins. Leuven: Leuven University Press, 1990.
Dibelius, Martin. *Die Formgeschichte des Evangeliums*. Tübingen: Mohr, 1919.
—. 'Zur Formgeschichte der Evangelien'. *Theologische Rundschau* 1 (1929): 185–216.
—. *An Die Kolosser, Epheser, an Philemon*. 3rd ed. HNT. Edited by Heinrich Greeven. Tübingen: Mohr Siebeck, 1953.
Dobschütz, Ernst von. *Die Thessalonicher-Briefe*. KEK 10. Göttingen: Vandenhoeck & Ruprecht, 1909.
Dodd, C. H. *The Epistle of Paul to the Romans*. London: Hodder & Stoughton, 1932.
—. 'The Framework of the Gospel Narrative'. *ExpTim* 43 (1932): 396–400; repr. in *New Testament Studies*, by C. H. Dodd. Manchester: Manchester University Press, 1953, 1–11.
—. 'The Mind of Paul: Change and Development'. *BJRL* 18 (1934): 69–110; repr. as 'The Mind of Paul: II' in *New Testament Studies*, by C. H. Dodd. Manchester: Manchester University Press, 1953, 83–128.
—. *The Apostolic Preaching and Its Developments*. London: Hodder & Stoughton, 1936.

—. *The Parables of the Kingdom,* 3rd ed. London: Nisbet, 1936.
—. *The Interpretation of the Fourth Gospel.* Cambridge: Cambridge University Press, 1953.
—. *The Founder of Christianity.* New York: Macmillan, 1970 = London: Collins, 1971.
Downing, F. Gerald. *The Church and Jesus: A Study in History, Philosophy and Theology.* London: SCM Press, 1968.
—. *Jesus and the Threat of Freedom.* London: SCM Press, 1987.
—. *Christ and the Cynics.* Sheffield: JSOT Press, 1988.
Drury, John. *Luke.* J.B. Philips' Commentary. London: Collins, 1973.
—. *Tradition and Design in Luke's Gospel.* London: Darton, Longman & Todd, 1976.
Dunn, James D.G. *Baptism in the Holy Spirit.* SBT 2/15. London: SCM Press, 1970.
—. 'Spirit-and-Fire Baptism'. *NT* 14 (1972): 81–92.
—. *Christology in the Making: A New Testament Inquiry into the Origins of the Doctrine of the Incarnation.* London: SCM Press, 1980.
—. *Romans 1–8.* WBC 38A. Dallas: Word Books, 1988.
—. *Romans 9–16.* WBC 38B. Dallas: Word Books, 1988.
—. *A Commentary on the Epistle to the Galatians.* BNTC. London: A&C Black, 1993 = Peabody, MA: Hendrickson, 1995.
—. *The Epistles to the Colossians and to Philemon: A Commentary on the Greek Text.* Grand Rapids: Eerdmans, 1996 = Carlisle: Paternoster, 1996.
—. 'Once More, ΠΙΣΤΙΣ ΧΡΙΣΤΟΥ'. Pages 61–81 in *Pauline Theology.* vol. 4. Edited by E. Elizabeth Johnson and David M. Hay. Atlanta: Scholars Press, 1997; repr. as Appendix 1 in *The Faith of Jesus Christ,* by Richard B. Hays. 2nd ed. Grand Rapids; Cambridge: Eerdmans, 2002, 231–248.
—. *The Theology of Paul the Apostle.* Grand Rapids: Eerdmans, 1998 = Edinburgh: T&T Clark, 1998.
Earl, Donald. 'Prologue-Form in Ancient Historiography'. *ANRW* 1/2 (1972): 842–856.
Edwards, Richard A. *The Sign of Jonah in the Theology of the Evangelists and Q.* SBT 2/18. London: SCM Press, 1971.
Elliott, Mark W. 'Πίστις Χριστοῦ in the Church Fathers and Beyond'. Pages 277–289 in *The Faith of Jesus Christ: Exegetical, Biblical, and Theological Studies.* Edited by Michael F. Bird and Preston M. Sprinkle. Milton Keynes: Paternoster, 2009 = Peabody, MA: Hendrickson, 2009.
Ellis, E. Earle. 'II Corinthians V. 1–10 in Pauline Eschatology'. *NTS* 6 (1960): 211–224.
Emerton, J.A. 'The Interpretation of Psalm 82 in John 10'. *JTS* NS 11 (1960): 329–332.
Evans, C.F. 'The Central Section of St Luke's Gospel'. Pages 37–53 in *Studies in the Gospels: Essays in Memory of R.H. Lightfoot.* Edited by D.E. Nineham. Oxford: Blackwell, 1957.
Evans, Craig A. *Life of Jesus Research: An Annotated Bibliography.* Rev. ed. New Testament Tools and Studies 24. Leiden: Brill, 1996.
Farmer, William R. *The Gospel of Jesus: The Pastoral Relevance of the Synoptic Problem.* Louisville: Westminster/John Knox, 1994.
Farrer, Austin M. *A Study in St Mark.* London: Dacre Press, 1951.
—. *St Matthew and St Mark.* London: Dacre Press, 1954, 2nd ed. 1966.
—. 'On Dispensing with Q'. Pages 55–88 in *Studies in the Gospels: Essays in Memory of R.H. Lightfoot.* Edited by D.E. Nineham. Oxford: Blackwell, 1955.
Farris, Stephen. *The Hymns of Luke's Infancy Narratives.* JSNTSup 9. Sheffield: JSOT Press, 1985.
Fee, Gordon D. *Paul's Letter to the Philippians.* NICNT. Grand Rapids: Eerdmans, 1995.

—. 'Wisdom Christology in Paul: A Dissenting View'. Pages 251–279 in *The Way of Wisdom: Essays in Honor of Bruce K. Waltke*. Edited by J.I. Packer and Sven Soderlund. Grand Rapids: Zondervan, 2000; repr. in Gordon D. Fee, *To What End Exegesis?* Grand Rapids: Eerdmans, 2001 = Vancouver: Regent College Publishing, 2001, 351–378.

Feuillet, André 'La Demeure Céleste et la destinée des chrétiens : Exégèse de 2 Cor. 5,1–10 et contribution à l'étude des fondements de l'eschatologie paulinienne'. *RSR* 44 (1956): 161–192, 360–402.

Fitzmyer, Joseph A. Review of *An Aramaic Approach to the Gospels and Acts*, by Matthew Black. *CBQ* 30 (1968): 417–428.

—. 'The Matthean Divorce Texts and Some New Palestinian Evidence'. *Theological Studies* 37 (1976): 197–226.

—. *The Gospel According to Luke I–IX*. AB. New York: Doubleday, 1981.

—. *The Gospel According to Luke X–XXIV*. AB. New York: Doubleday, 1985.

Fleischer, Robert. 'Neues zu Kleinasiastischen Kultstatuen'. *Archaeologischer Anzeiger* 98 (1983): 81–93.

Flemington, W.F. 'On the Interpretation of Colossians 1:24'. Pages 84–90 in *Suffering and Martyrdom in the New Testament: Studies presented to G.M. Styler by the Cambridge New Testament Seminar*. Edited by William Horbury and Brian McNeil. Cambridge: Cambridge University Press, 1981.

Fossum, Jarl E. *The Image of the Invisible God*. Göttingen: Vandenhoeck & Ruprecht, 1995.

Frame, James Everett. *A Critical and Exegetical Commentary on the Epistles of St. Paul to the Thessalonians*. ICC. Edinburgh: T&T Clark, 1912.

Friedrich, Gerhard. 'Ein Tauflied hellenistischer Judenchristen: 1 Thess. 1,9f'. *Theologische Zeitschrift* 21 (1965): 502–516.

Friesen, Steven J. *Twice Neokoros*. Religions in the Graeco-Roman World 116. Leiden: Brill, 1993.

Fuchs, Ernst. *Studies of the Historical Jesus*. Translated by Andrew Scobie. SBT 42. London: SCM Press, 1964.

Fuller, Reginald H. *The New Testament in Current Study: Some Trends in the Years 1941–1962*. London: SCM Press, 1963.

—. *The Foundations of New Testament Christology*. London: Collins, 1965.

Furnish, Victor Paul. *Theology and Ethics in Paul*. Nashville; New York: Abingdon, 1968.

—. *II Corinthians*. AB 32A. Garden City, NY: Doubleday, 1984.

Gerhardsson, Birger. *Memory and Manuscript: Oral Tradition and Written Transmission in Rabbinic Judaism and Early Christianity*. Lund: Gleerup, 1961.

Gibbs, J.M. 'Mark 1,1–15, Matthew 1,1–4,16, Luke 1,1–4,30, John 1,1–51: The Gospel Prologues and Their Function'. Pages 154–188 in *Studia Evangélica*. vol. 6. Edited by E.A. Livingstone. Berlin: Akademie Verlag, 1973.

Gielen, Marlis. 'Die Haustafel des Kolosserbriefes (3,18–4,1). Herkunft, Intention und Integration in die briefliche Schlussparänese 3,17.18–4,6'. Pages 89–119 in *'Le Christ Tout et en Tous' (Col 3,11): L'épître aux Colossiens*. Edited by Benoît Standaert. Série Monographique de Benedictina. Section Biblique Oecuménique 16. Rome: Benedictina, 2003.

Gifford, E.H. *The Epistle of St. Paul to the Romans*. Reprinted from The Speaker's Commentary. London: John Murray, 1886.

Glasson, T. Francis *The Second Advent: The Origin of the New Testament Doctrine*. London: Epworth Press, 1945; 3rd ed., 1963.

—. *Moses in the Fourth Gospel*. London: SCM Press, 1963.

Gnilka, Joachim. *Der Epheserbrief.* Freiburg: Herder, 1971.

Goguel, Maurice. 'Jésus et les origines de l'universalisme chrétien'. *RHPR* 12 (1932): 193–211.

Gorman, Michael J. '"Although/Because He Was in the Form of God": The Theological Significance of Paul's Master Story (Phil 2:6–11)'. *JTI* 1, no. 2 (2007): 147–169.

—. *Inhabiting the Cruciform God: Kenosis, Justification, and Theosis in Paul's Narrative Soteriology.* Grand Rapids: Eerdmans, 2009.

Goulder, M.D. 'Characteristics of the Parables in the Several Gospels'. *JTS* NS 19 (1968): 51–69.

Grayston, Kenneth. 'The Study of Mark XIII'. *BJRL* 56 (1974): 371–387.

—. *Dying, We Live: A New Enquiry into the Death of Christ in the New Testament.* London: Darton, Longman, and Todd, 1990 = New York: Oxford University Press, 1990.

Grimm, Werner. *Weil ich dich liebe: Die Verkündigung Jesu und Deuterojesaja.* Bern: Herbert Lang, 1976.

Guilding, Aileen. *The Fourth Gospel and Jewish Worship: A Study of the Relation of St. John's Gospel to the Ancient Jewish Lectionary System.* Oxford: Clarendon Press, 1960.

Haenchen, Ernst. *The Acts of the Apostles.* Translated by Bernard Noble et al. Oxford: Blackwell, 1971.

Hahn, Ferdinand. *Christologische Hoheitstitel. Ihre Geschichte im frühen Christentum.* Göttingen, 1963; ET: *The Titles of Jesus in Christology.* Translated by Harold Knight and George Ogg. London: Lutterworth Press, 1969.

—. *Das Verständnis der Mission im Neuen Testament.* WMANT 13. Neukirchen-Vluyn: Neukirchener Verlag, 1963; ET: *Mission in the New Testament.* Translated by Frank Clarke. London: SCM Press, 1965.

Hanson, Anthony Tyrrell. *Jesus Christ in the Old Testament.* London: SPCK, 1965.

—. *Studies in Paul's Technique and Theology.* London: SPCK, 1974.

Hanson, R.P.C. *II Corinthians.* London: SCM Press, 1954.

Harman, A.M. 'Missions in the Thought of Jesus', *The Evangelical Quarterly* 41 (1969): 131–142.

Harnack, Adolf von. 'Über das Verhältnis des Prologs des vierten Evangeliums zum ganzen Werk'. *ZTK* 2 (1892): 189–231.

—. *Die Mission und Ausbreitung des Christentums in den ersten drei Jahrhunderten.* Leipzig: J.C. Hinrich, 1906; ET: *Mission and Expansion of Christianity in the First Three Centuries.* Translated by James Moffatt. London: Williams and Norgate, 1908.

Harrisville, Roy A., III. 'ΠΙΣΤΙΣ ΧΡΙΣΤΟΥ: Witness of the Fathers'. *NT* 36 (1994): 233–241.

Hartman, Lars. *Prophecy Interpreted: The Formation of Some Jewish Apocalyptic Texts and of the Eschatological Discourse Mark 13 Par.* ConBNT. Lund: Gleerup, 1966.

Harvey, A.E. *Jesus and the Constraints of History.* London: Duckworth, 1982.

Haussleiter, Johannes. *Der Glaube Jesu Christi und der christliche Glaube: Ein Beitrag zur Erklärung des Römerbriefes.* Erlangen: Deichert, 1891.

Hay, David M. *Glory at the Right Hand: Psalm 110 in Early Christianity.* Nashville: Abingdon Press, 1973.

Hays, Richard B. 'ΠΙΣΤΙΣ and Pauline Christology: What Is at Stake?'. Pages 35–60 in *Pauline Theology.* vol. 4: *Looking Back, Pressing On.* Edited by E. Elizabeth Johnson and David M. Hay. Atlanta: Scholars Press, 1977; repr. in *The Faith of Jesus Christ: The Narrative Substructure of Galatians 3:1–4:11*, by Richard B. Hays. 2nd ed. Grand Rapids; Cambridge, UK; Eerdmans, 2002, 272–297.

—. *The Faith of Jesus Christ: An Investigation of the Narrative Substructure of Galatians 3.1–4.11*. SBL Dissertation Series 56. Chico, CA: Scholars Press, 1983; 2nd ed., Grand Rapids; Cambridge: Eerdmans, 2001; repr., 2002.

Hengel, Martin. 'Christologie und neutestamentliche Chronologie'. Pages 43–67 in *Neues Testament und Geschichte: historisches Geschehen und Deutung im Neuen Testament: Oscar Cullmann zum 70. Geburtstag*. Edited By H. Baltensweiler and B. Reicke. Zurich: Theologischer Verlag, 1972 = Tübingen: Mohr Siebeck, 1972; ET: 'Christology and New Testament Chronology'. Pages 30–47 in *Between Jesus and Paul,* by Martin Hengel. Translated by John Bowden. London: SCM Press, 1983.

—. 'Zwischen Jesus und Paulus'. *ZTK* 72 (1975): 151–206; ET: 'Between Jesus and Paul'. Pages 1–29 in *Between Jesus and Paul,* by Martin Hengel. Translated by John Bowden. London: SCM Press, 1983.

—. *Zur urchristlichen Geschichtsschreibung*. Stuttgart: Calwer Verlag, 1979; ET: *Acts and the History of Earliest Christianity*. Translated by John Bowden. London: SCM Press, 1979; repr. in *Earliest Christianity*. Translated by John Bowden. London: SCM Press, 1986.

Herbert, A. G. '"Faithfulness" and "Faith"'. *Theology* 58 (1955): 373–379.

Héring, Jean. *The Second to the Corinthians*. Translated by A. W. Heathcote and P. J. Allcock. London: Epworth, 1967.

Hettlinger, R. F. '2 Corinthians 5.1–10'. *SJT* 10 (1957): 174–194.

Higgins, A. J. B. *Jesus and the Son of Man*. London: Lutterworth, 1964.

—. 'Is the Son of Man Problem Insoluble?'. Pages 70–87 in *Neotestamentica et Semitica: Studies in Honour of Matthew Black*. Edited by E. Earle Ellis and Max Wilcox. Edinburgh: T&T Clark, 1969.

Hill, David. *The Gospel of Matthew*. NCB. London: Oliphants, 1972.

Hindley, J. C. 'Towards a Date for the Similitudes of Enoch. An Historical Approach'. *NTS* 14 (1968): 551–565.

Hofius, Otfried. 'Das vierte Gottesknechtslied in den Briefen des Neuen Testamentes'. *NTS* 39 (1993): 414–437.

Holmén, Tom. 'Doubts about Double Dissimilarity: Restructuring the Main Criterion of Jesus-of-history Research'. Pages 47–80 in *Authenticating the Words of Jesus*. Edited by Bruce Chilton and Craig A. Evans. New Testament Tools and Studies 28/1. Leiden: Brill, 1999.

Holtz, Traugott. *Untersuchungen über die alttestamentlichen Zitate bei Lukas*. Berlin: Akademie Verlag, 1968.

Hooker, Morna D. *Jesus and the Servant: The Influence of the Servant Concept of Deutero-Isaiah in the New Testament*. London: SPCK, 1959.

—. 'Adam in Romans I'. *NTS* 6 (1960): 297–306; repr. in *From Adam to Christ,* by Morna D. Hooker. Cambridge: Cambridge University Press, 1990, 73–84.

—. 'A Further Note on Romans I', *NTS* 13 (1967): 181–183; repr. in *From Adam to Christ,* by Morna D. Hooker. Cambridge: Cambridge University Press, 1990, 85–87.

—. *The Son of Man in Mark*. London: SPCK, 1967 = Montreal: McGill University Press, 1967.

—. 'John the Baptist and the Johannine Prologue'. *NTS* 16 (1970): 354–358 = essay 22 (pp. 316–320).

—. 'Christology and Methodology'. *NTS* 17 (1971): 480–487 = essay 2 (pp. 29–37).

—. 'Interchange in Christ'. *JTS* NS 22 (1971): 349–361; repr. in *From Adam to Christ,* by Morna D. Hooker. Cambridge: Cambridge University Press, 1990, 13–25.

—. 'The Prohibition of Foreign Missions (Matt 10:5–6)'. Uncomfortable Words X. *The ExpTim* 82 (1971): 361–365 = essay 18 (pp. 265–272).

—. 'On Using the Wrong Tool'. *Theology* 75 (1972): 570–581 = essay 3 (pp. 38–49).

—. 'Were There False Teachers in Colossae?' Pages 315–331 in *Christ and Spirit in the New Testament: Studies in Honour of Charles Francis Digby Moule*. Edited by Barnabas Lindars and Stephen S. Smalley. Cambridge: Cambridge University Press, 1973; repr. in *From Adam to Christ: Essays on Paul,* by Morna D. Hooker. Cambridge: Cambridge University Press, 1990, 121–136.

—. 'The Johannine Prologue and the Messianic Secret'. *NTS* 21 (1974): 40–58 = essay 23 (pp. 321–340).

—. 'In His Own Image?' Pages 28–44 in *What about the New Testament? Essays in Honour of Christopher Evans*. Edited by Morna D. Hooker and Colin Hickling. London: SCM Press, 1975 = essay 4 (pp. 50–63).

—. 'Philippians 2:6–11'. Pages 151–164 in *Jesus und Paulus: Festschrift für W. G. Kümmel*. Edited by E. Earle Ellis and Erich Grässer. Göttingen: Vandenhoeck & Ruprecht, 1975; repr. in *From Adam to Christ,* by Morna D. Hooker. Cambridge: Cambridge University Press, 1990, 88–100.

—. 'Interchange and Atonement'. *BJRL* 60, no. 2 (1978): 462–481; repr. in *From Adam to Christ: Essays on Paul,* by Morna D. Hooker. Cambridge: Cambridge University Press, 1990, 26–41.

—. 'Is the Son of Man Problem Really Insoluble?' Pages 155–168 in *Text and Interpretation: Studies in the New Testament presented to Matthew Black*. Edited by Ernest Best and R. McL. Wilson. Cambridge: Cambridge University Press, 1979 = essay 6 (pp. 90–102).

—. *Pauline Pieces*. London: Epworth Press, 1979 = *A Preface to Paul*. New York: Oxford University Press, 1979.

—. 'Beyond the Things That Are Written?: St Paul's Use of Scripture'. *NTS* 27 (1981): 295–309; repr. in *From Adam to Christ: Essays on Paul,* by Morna D. Hooker. Cambridge: Cambridge University Press, 1990, 139–154.

—. 'Trial and Tribulation in Mark XIII'. *BJRL* 65 (1982): 78–99 = essay 15 (pp. 216–234).

—. *New Wine in Old Bottles: A Discussion of Continuity and Discontinuity in Relation to Judaism and the Gospel*. The Ethel M. Wood Lecture delivered at the Senate House, University of London on 14 February 1984. London: University of London, 1984 = essay 1 (pp. 11–26).

—. *Continuity and Discontinuity*. London: Epworth, 1986.

—. '"What Doest Thou Here, Elijah?": A Look at St. Mark's Account of the Transfiguration'. Pages 59–70 in *The Glory of Christ in the New Testament: Studies in Christology in Memory of George Bradford Caird*. Edited by L. D. Hurst and N. T. Wright. Oxford: Clarendon Press, 1987 = essay 12 (pp. 179–189).

—. 'Mark'. Pages 220–230 in *It is Written: Scripture Citing Scripture: Essays in Honour of Barnabas Lindars, SSF*. Edited by D. A. Carson and H. G. M. Williamson. Cambridge: Cambridge University Press, 1988 = 'Mark's Use of Scripture', essay 13 (pp. 190–199).

—. 'Traditions about the Temple in the Sayings of Jesus'. *BJRL* 70 (1988): 7–19 = essay 16 (pp. 235–247).

—. 'ΠΙΣΤΙΣ ΧΡΙΣΤΟΥ'. Presidential Address to SNTS, 1988. *NTS* 35 (1989): 321–342; repr. in *From Adam to Christ,* by Morna D. Hooker. Cambridge: Cambridge University Press, 1990, 165–186.

—. *From Adam to Christ: Essays on Paul*. Cambridge: Cambridge University Press, 1990; repr., Eugene, OR: Wipf and Stock, 2008.

–. *A Commentary on the Gospel According to St. Mark*. BNTC. London: A&C Black, 1991; repr., Peabody, MA: Hendrickson, 1993.
–. 'Paul: Apostle to the Gentiles'. The 28th St Paul's Lecture, under the auspices of the London Diocesan Council for Christian-Jewish Understanding, given at St Botolph's Church, Aldgate on November 16th, 1989. *Epworth Review* 18 (1991): 79–89 = essay 25 (pp. 359–370).
–. 'The Son of Man and the Synoptic Problem'. Pages 189–201 in vol. 1 of *The Four Gospels 1992: Festschrift Frans Neirynck*. Edited by Frans Van Segbroeck, C.M. Tuckett, G. Van Belle, and J. Verheyden. Leuven: Leuven University Press/Peeters, 1992 = essay 7 (pp. 103–114).
–. 'Beginning from Moses and from All the Prophets'. Pages 216–230 in *From Jesus to John: Essays on Jesus and New Testament Christology in Honour of Marinus de Jonge*. Edited by Martinus C. de Boer. Sheffield: JSOT Press, 1993 = essay 20 (pp. 285–297).
–. 'The Beginning of the Gospel'. Pages 18–28 in *The Future of Christology: Essays in Honor of Leander E. Keck*. Edited by Abraham J. Malherbe and Wayne A. Meeks. Minneapolis: Fortress Press, 1993 = essay 19 (pp. 275–284).
–. 'Chalcedon and the New Testament'. Pages 73–93 in *The Making and Remaking of Christian Doctrine: Essays in Honour of Maurice Wiles*. Edited by Sarah Coakley and David Pailin. Oxford: Clarendon Press, 1993 = essay 11 (pp. 160–176).
–. *Not Ashamed of the Gospel: New Testament Interpretations of the Death of Christ*. Carlisle: The Paternoster Press, 1994 = Grand Rapids: Eerdmans, 1995.
–. '1 Thessalonians 1:9–10: A Nutshell – But What Kind of Nut?' Pages 435–448 in vol. 3, *Frühes Christentum* of *Geschichte – Tradition – Reflexion: Festschrift für Martin Hengel zum 70. Geburtstag*. Edited by Hermann Lichtenberger. Tübingen: Mohr Siebeck, 1996 = essay 35 (pp. 521–533).
–. 'A Partner in the Gospel: Paul's Understanding of His Ministry'. Pages 83–100 in *Theology and Ethics in Paul and His Interpreters: Essays in Honor of Victor Paul Furnish*. Edited by Eugene H. Lovering, Jr. and Jerry L. Sumney. Nashville: Abingdon, 1996 = essay 39 (pp. 579–595).
–. *Beginnings: Keys That Open the Gospels*. London: SCM Press, 1997.
–. *The Signs of a Prophet*. London: SCM Press, 1997 = Harrisburg, PA: Trinity Press International, 1997.
–. 'Did the Use of Isaiah 53 to Interpret His Mission Begin with Jesus?' Pages 88–103 in *Jesus and the Suffering Servant: Isaiah 53 and Christian Origins*. Edited by William H. Bellinger Jr. and William R. Farmer. Harrisburg, PA: Trinity Press International, 1998 = essay 8 (pp. 115–127).
–. 'Adam *Redivivus*: Philippians 2 Once More'. Pages 220–234 in *The Old Testament in the New Testament: Essays in Honour of J.L. North*. Edited by Steve Moyise. JSNTSup 189. Sheffield: Sheffield Academic Press, 2000 = essay 26 (pp. 371–383).
–. 'Creative Conflict: The Torah and Christology'. Pages 117–136 in *Christology, Controversy and Community: New Testament Essays in Honour of David R. Catchpole*. Edited by David G. Horrell and Christopher M. Tuckett. Leiden: Brill, 2000 = essay 17 (pp. 248–264).
–. 'Philippians'. Pages 534b–535a in *The New Interpreter's Bible*. vol. 11. Edited by Leander E. Keck et al. Nashville: Abingdon, 2000.
–. '"Heirs of Abraham": The Gentiles' Role in Israel's Story'. Pages 85–96 in *Narrative Dynamics in Paul: A Critical Assessment*. Edited by Bruce W. Longenecker. Louisville: Westminster John Knox Press, 2002.

—. 'Philippians: Phantom Opponents and the Real Source of Conflict'. Pages 377–395 in *Fair Play: Diversity and Conflicts in Early Christianity: Essays in Honour of Heikki Räisänen*. Edited by Ismo Dunderberg, Christopher Tuckett, and Kari Syreeni. Leiden: Brill, 2002 = essay 42 (pp. 616–631).

—. 'Raised for Our Acquittal (Rom 4:25)'. Pages 323–341 in *Resurrection in the New Testament: Festschrift J. Lambrecht*. Edited by R. Bieringer, V. Koperski, and B. Lataire. *BETL* 165. Leuven: University Press/Peeters, 2002 = essay 38 (pp. 562–578).

—. 'The Authority of the Bible: A New Testament Perspective'. *Ex Auditu* 19 (2003): 45–64 = essay 32 (pp. 468–487).

—. 'Christ: The "End" of the Law'. Pages 126–146 in *Neotestamentica et Philonica: Studies in Honor of Peder Borgen*. Edited by David E. Aune, Torrey Seland, and Jarl Henning Ulrichsen. NTSup 106. Leiden: Brill, 2003 = essay 27 (pp. 384–400).

—. 'From God's Faithfulness to Ours: Another Look at 2 Corinthians 1:17–24'. Pages 233–239 in *Paul and the Corinthians: Studies on a Community in Conflict: Essays in Honour of Margaret Thrall*. Edited by Trevor J. Burke and J. Keith Elliott. NTSup 109. Leiden: Brill, 2003 = essay 41 (pp. 610–615).

—. *Paul: A Short Introduction*. Oxford: One World, 2003; repr. as *Paul: A Beginner's Guide*, Oxford: One World, 2008.

—. 'Where is Wisdom to Be Found? Colossians 1:15–20'. Pages 116–128 in *Reading Texts, Seeking Wisdom: Scripture and Theology*. Edited by David F. Ford and Graham Stanton. London: SCM Press, 2003 = essay 33 (pp. 488–496).

—. '"Who Died for Our Sins, and Was Raised for Our Acquittal": Paul's Understanding of the Death of Christ'. *Svensk Exegetisk Årsbok* 68 (2003): 59–71 = 'Christ Died for Our Sins, and Was Raised for Our Acquittal: Paul's Understanding of the Death of Christ', essay 37 (pp. 549–561).

—. 'John's Baptism: A Prophetic Sign'. Pages 22–40 in *The Holy Spirit and Christian Origins: Essays in Honor of James D. G. Dunn*. Edited by Graham N. Stanton, Bruce W. Longenecker and Stephen C. Barton. Grand Rapids: Eerdmans, 2004 = essay 21 (pp. 298–315).

—. 'T. W. Manson and the Twentieth-Century Search for Jesus'. *BJRL* 86 (2004): 77–98 = essay 5 (pp. 67–89).

—. 'Isaiah in Mark's Gospel'. Pages 35–49 in *Isaiah in the New Testament: The New Testament and the Scriptures of Israel*. Edited by Steve Moyise and Maarten J.J. Menken. London: Continuum, 2005 = essay 14 (pp. 200–215).

—. '"Submit to One Another": The Transformation of Relationships in Christ (Eph 5:21–6:9)'. Pages 163–188 in *Ethik als Angewandte Ekklesiologie: Der Brief und die Epheser*. Edited by Michael Wolter. Leuven: Peeters, 2005 = essay 43 (pp. 632–653).

—. 'The Nature of New Testament Theology'. Pages 75–92 in *The Nature of New Testament Theology: Essays in Honour of Robert Morgan*. Edited by Christopher Rowland and Christopher Tuckett. Oxford: Blackwell, 2006 = essay 10 (pp. 143–159).

—. 'On Becoming the Righteousness of God: Another Look at 2 Cor 5:21'. *NT* 50 (2008): 358–375 = essay 28 (pp. 401–415).

—. 'Christ, the "End" of the Cult'. Pages 189–212 in *The Epistle to the Hebrews and Christian Theology*. Edited by Richard Bauckham, Daniel R. Driver, Trevor A. Hart, and Nathan MacDonald. Grand Rapids: Eerdmans, 2009 = essay 34 (pp. 497–517).

—. 'Paul the Pastor: The Relevance of the Gospel'. *Proceedings of the Irish Biblical Association* 31 (2009): 17–31 = essay 40 (pp. 596–609).

–. 'Good News about Jesus Christ, the Son of God'. Pages 165–180 in *Mark as Story: Retrospect and Prospect*. Edited by Kelly R. Iverson and Christopher W. Skinner. Atlanta: Society of Biblical Literature, 2011 = essay 9 (pp. 128–142).
–. '2 Corinthians 5:1–10 in Context'. Pages 165–195 in *2 Thessalonians and Pauline Eschatology: For Petr Pokorný on His 80*th *Birthday*. Edited by Christopher Tuckett. Leuven: Peeters, 2013 = essay 30 (pp. 432–459).
–. 'Artemis of Ephesus'. *JTS* 64 (2013): 37–46 = essay 31 (pp. 460–467).
–. 'Another Look at πίστις Χριστοῦ'. *SJT* 69 (2016): 46–62 = essay 29 (pp. 416–431).
–. '"The Sanctuary of His Body": Body and Sanctuary in Paul and John'. *JSNT* 39 (2017): 347–361 = essay 44 (pp. 654–667).
–. '"Sola Fide": The Wrong Slogan?'. Pages 25–39 in *Contesting Orthodoxies in the History of Christianity: Essays in Honour of Diarmaid MacCulloch*. Edited by Ellie Gebarowski-Shafer, Ashley Null and Alec Ryrie. Woodbridge, Suffolk: Boydell Press, 2021 = essay 45 (pp. 668–682).
–. 'Luther – Faithful Exegete of Paul'. Pages 24–38 in *Luther and Philosophies of the Reformation*. Edited by Boris Gunjević. London: Bloomsbury, 2023.
Horbury, William. *Jewish Messianism and the Cult of Christ*. London: SCM Press, 1998.
Howard, George F. 'On the "Faith of Christ"'. *HTR* 60 (1967): 459–465.
–. 'The "Faith of Christ"'. *ExpTim* 85 (1974): 212–215.
–. 'Faith of Christ'. Pages 758–760 in *The Anchor Bible Dictionary*. vol. 2. Edited by David N. Freedman. New Haven: Yale University Press, 2008.
Howard, Wilbert F. *The Fourth Gospel in Recent Criticism and Interpretation*. Revised by C.K. Barrett. London: Epworth Press, 1955.
Hübner, Hans. *Das Gesetz in der synoptischen Tradition*. Witten: Luther-Verlag, 1973.
Hughes, Frank W. *Early Christian Rhetoric and 2 Thessalonians*. JSNTSup 30. Sheffield: JSOT, 1989.
–. 'The Rhetoric of 1 Thessalonians'. Pages 94–116 in *The Thessalonian Correspondence*. Edited by Raymond F. Collins. BETL 87. Leuven: Leuven University Press/Uitgeverij Peeters, 1990.
Hunn, Debbie. 'Debating the Faithfulness of Jesus Christ in Twentieth-Century Scholarship'. Pages 15–32 in *The Faith of Jesus Christ: Exegetical, Biblical, and Theological Studies*. Edited by Michael F. Bird and Preston M. Sprinkle. Milton Keynes: Paternoster, 2009 = Peabody, MA: Hendrickson, 2009.
Hurtado, Larry W. 'Jesus as Lordly Example in Philippians 2:5–11'. Pages 113–126 in *From Jesus to Paul. Studies in Honour of Francis Wright Beare*. Edited by Peter Richardson and John C. Hurd. Waterloo, ON: Wilfrid Laurier University Press, 1984.
–. *Lord Jesus Christ: Devotion to Jesus in Earliest Christianity*. Grand Rapids: Eerdmans, 2003.
Isaacs, Marie E. *Sacred Space: An Approach to the Theology of the Epistle to the Hebrews*. JSNTSup 73. Sheffield: JSOT Press, 1992.
–. *Reading Hebrews & James: A Literary and Theological Commentary*. Macon, GA: Smyth & Helwys, 2002.
Janzen, J. Gerald. 'Coleridge and *Pistis Christou*'. *ExpTim* 107 (1996): 265–268.
Jeremias, Joachim. *Jesus' Promise to the Nations*. Translated by S.H. Hooke. London: SCM Press, 1958.
–. *The Parables of Jesus*. Rev. ed. Translated by S.H. Hooke. London: SCM Press, 1963.
–. 'Die älteste Schicht der Menschensohn-Logien'. *ZNW* 58 (1967): 159–172.
–. *New Testament Theology, Part 1: The Proclamation of Jesus*. Translated by John Bowden. London: SCM Press, 1971.

Jewett, Robert. 'Conflicting Movements in the Early Church as Reflected in Philippians'. *NT* 12 (1970): 362–390.
–. *The Thessalonian Correspondence: Pauline Rhetoric and Millenarian Piety*. Philadelphia: Fortress Press, 1986.
Johanson, Bruce C. *To All the Brethren: A Text-Linguistic and Rhetorical Approach to 1 Thessalonians*. ConBNT 16. Stockholm: Almqvist & Wiksell International, 1987.
Johnson, Luke Timothy. 'Romans 3:21–26 and the Faith of Jesus'. *CBQ* 44 (1982): 77–90.
Johnson, Marcus. 'Luther and Calvin on Union with Christ'. *Fides et Historia* 39 (2007): 59–77.
Johnson, Marshall D. *The Purpose of the Biblical Genealogies*. 2nd ed. Cambridge: Cambridge University Press, 1988.
Jonge, Marinus de and A.S. van der Woude. '11Q Melchizedek and the New Testament'. *NTS* 12 (1966): 301–326.
Kähler, Christoph. 'Konflikt, Kompromiss und Bekenntnis: Paulus und seine Gegner im Philipperbrief'. *Kerygma und Dogma* 40 (1994): 47–64.
Käsemann, Ernst. 'Kritische Analyse von Phil 2:5–11'. *ZTK* 47 (1950): 313–360; ET: 'A Critical Analysis of Philippians 2:5–11'. Translated by A.F. Carse. *JTC* 5 (1968): 45–88.
–. 'Das Problem des historischen Jesus'. *ZTK* 51 (1954): 125–153; ET: 'The Problem of the Historical Jesus'. Pages 15–47 in *Essays on New Testament Themes*. Translated by W.J. Montague. SBT 41. London: SCM Press, 1964.
–. 'Gottesgerechtigkeit bei Paulus'. *ZTK* 58, no. 3 (1961): 367–378; ET: '"The Righteousness of God" in Paul'. Pages 168–182 in *New Testament Questions of Today*. Translated by W.J. Montague and Wilfred F. Bunge. London: SCM Press, 1969.
–. *Exegetische Versuche und Besinnungen*. vol. 1. 2nd ed. Göttingen: Vandenhoeck & Ruprecht, 1960; ET: *Essays on New Testament Themes*. Translated by W.J. Montague. SBT 41. London: SCM Press, 1964.
–. *Exegetische Versuche und Besinnungen*. vol. 2. 2nd ed. Göttingen: Vandenhoeck & Ruprecht, 1965; ET: *New Testament Questions of Today*. Translated by W.J. Montague and Wilfred F. Bunge. London: SCM Press, 1969.
–. *An die Römer*. 4th ed. HNT 8a. Tübingen: Mohr, 1980; ET: *Commentary on Romans*. Translated by Geoffrey W. Bromiley. London: SCM Press, 1980.
Keck, Leander E. 'The Introduction to Mark's Gospel'. *NTS* 12 (1966): 352–370.
Kee, H.C. 'The Function of Scriptural Quotations and Allusions in Mark 11–16'. Pages 165–188 in *Jesus und Paulus*. Edited by E. Earle Ellis and Erich Grässer. Göttingen: Vandenhoeck & Ruprecht, 1975.
Kennedy, George A. *New Testament Interpretation through Rhetorical Criticism*. Chapel Hill; London: University of North Carolina Press, 1984.
Kertelge, Karl. '*Rechtfertigung*' *bei Paulus*. Münster: Aschendorff, 1967.
Kiddle, M. 'The Death of Jesus and the Admission of the Gentiles in St. Mark'. *JTS* 35 (1934): 45–50.
Kilpatrick, G.D. *The Origins of the Gospel According to St. Matthew*. Oxford: Clarendon Press, 1946.
–. 'The Gentile Mission in Mark and Mark 13:9–11'. Pages 145–158 in *Studies in the Gospels*. Edited by D.E. Nineham. Oxford: Blackwell, 1957.
Kingsbury, Jack Dean. *Matthew: Structure, Christology, Kingdom*. Philadelphia: Fortress, 1975.
Kittel, Gerhard. 'Πίστις Ἰησοῦ Χριστοῦ bei Paulus'. *TSK* 79 (1906): 419–436.
Klein, Günter. 'Antipaulinismus in Philippi: Eine Problemskizze'. Pages 297–313 in *Jesu Rede von Gott und ihre Nachgeschichte im frühen Christentum: Beiträge zur Verkündigung Jesu*

und zum Kerygma der Kirche: Festschrift für Willi Marxsen. Edited by Dietrich-Alex Koch et al. Gütersloh: Mohn, 1989.

Klijn, A. F. J. 'I Thessalonians 4,13–18 and its Background'. Pages 67–73 in *Paul and Paulinism: Essays in Honour of C. K. Barrett*. Edited by Morna D. Hooker and S. G. Wilson. London: SPCK, 1982.

Knibb, Michael A. *The Ethiopic Book of Enoch: A New Edition in the Light of the Aramaic Dead Sea Fragments*. In consultation with Edward Ullendorff. Oxford: Clarendon Press, 1978.

Knox, John. *The Death of Christ: The Cross in New Testament History and Faith*. London: Collins, 1959.

Knox, Wilfred L. *The Sources of the Synoptic Gospels*. vol. 2. Edited by Henry Chadwick. Cambridge: Cambridge University Press, 1957.

–. *St Paul and the Church of the Gentiles*. Cambridge: Cambridge University Press, 1961.

Koester, Helmut. 'I Thessalonians – Experiment in Christian Writing'. Pages 33–44 in *Continuity and Discontinuity in Church History: Essays Presented to George Huntston Williams on the Occasion of His 65th Birthday*. Edited by F. Forrester Church and Timothy George. Leiden: Brill, 1979.

Koet, B. J. *Five Studies on Interpretation of Scripture in Luke-Acts*. Leuven: Leuven University Press/Uitgeverij Peeters, 1989.

Kümmel, W. G. *Promise and Fulfilment: The Eschatological Message of Jesus*. Translated by Dorothea M. Barton. London: SCM Press, 1957.

Lagrange, Marie-Joseph. *Évangile selon Saint Matthieu*. 3rd ed. Paris: J. Gabalda, 1927.

Lambrecht, Jan. *Die Redaktion der Markus-Apokalypse: literarische Analyse und Strukturuntersuchung*. Rome: Päpstliches Bibelinstitut, 1967.

–. 'Thanksgivings in 1 Thessalonians 1–3'. Pages 183–205 in *The Thessalonian Correspondence*. Edited by Raymond F. Collins. BETL 87. Leuven: Leuven University Press/Uitgeverij Peeters, 1990.

–. *The Wretched 'I' and Its Liberation: Paul in Romans 7 and 8*. Leuven: Peeters, 1992.

–. *Understanding What One Reads II: Essays on the Gospels and Paul*. Leuven: Peeters, 2011.

Lambrecht, Jan and Richard W. Thompson. *Justification by Faith: The Implications of Romans 3:27–31*. Wilmington, DE: Michael Glazier, 1989.

Lane, William L. *Hebrews 1–8*. WBC. Dallas: Word Books, 1991.

Lang, Friedrich Gustav. *2. Korinther 5,1–10 in der neueren Forschung*. BGBE 16. Tübingen: Mohr, 1973.

–. 'Kompositionsanalyse des Markusevangeliums'. ZTK 74 (1977): 1–24.

Langevin, Paul-Emile. *Jésus Seigneur et l'eschatologie: Exégèse de textes prépauliniens*. Studia 21. Bruges; Paris: Desclée, De Brouwer, 1967.

Larsson, Edvin. *Christus als Vorbild*. Uppsala: Almsquist & Wiksells, 1962.

Leenhardt, Franz J. *The Epistle to the Romans: A Commentary*. Translated by H. Knight. London: Lutterworth, 1961.

Leivestad, Ragnar. 'Der apokalyptische Menschensohn ein theologisches Phantom'. *Annual of the Swedish Theological Institute*, 6 (1968): 49–105.

–. 'Exit the Apocalyptic Son of Man'. NTS 18 (1972): 243–267.

Lietzmann, Hans. *An die Korinther I–II*. 5th ed. Revised by W. G. Kümmel. HNT 9. Tübingen: Mohr, 1969.

Lightfoot, J. B. *Saint Paul's Epistle to the Galatians*. 10th ed. London; New York: Macmillan, 1890.

Lightfoot, R. H. *The Gospel Message of St. Mark*. Oxford: Clarendon Press, 1950.

Lincoln, Andrew T. *Paradise Now and Not Yet*. Cambridge: Cambridge University Press, 1981.
—. 'The Use of the Old Testament in Ephesians'. *JSNT* 14 (1982): 16–57.
—. *Ephesians*. WBC. Dallas: Word Books, 1990.
Lindars, Barnabas. *The Gospel of John*. NCB. London: Marshall, Morgan and Scott, 1972 = Grand Rapids: Eerdmans, 1972.
—. *Jesus Son of Man: A Fresh Examination of the Son of Man Sayings in the Gospels in the Light of Recent Research*. London: SPCK, 1983.
—. *The Theology of the Letter to the Hebrews*. New Testament Theology. Cambridge: Cambridge University Press, 1991.
Lindgård, Fredrik. *Paul's Line of Thought in 2 Corinthians 4:16–5:10*. WUNT 2/189. Tübingen: Mohr Siebeck, 2005.
Linebaugh, Jonathan. 'The Christo-Centrism of Faith in Christ: Martin Luther's Reading of Galatians 2.16, 19–20'. *NTS* 59 (2013): 535–544.
Lohmeyer, Ernst. 'Die Verklärung Jesu nach dem Markus-Evangelium'. *ZNW* 21 (1922): 185–215.
—. *Die Briefe an die Kolosser und an Philemon*. Göttingen: Vandenhoeck & Ruprecht, 1930.
—. *Das Evangelium des Markus*. 17th ed. Göttingen: Vandenhoeck & Ruprecht, 1967.
Lohse, Eduard. *Die Briefe an die Kolosser und an Philemon*. KEK. Göttingen: Vandenhoeck & Ruprecht, 1968; ET: *Colossians and Philemon*. Edited by Helmut Koester. Translated by William R. Poehlmann and Robert J. Karris. Hermeneia. Philadelphia: Fortress Press, 1971.
Lowe, John. 'An Examination of Attempts to Detect Developments in St Paul's Theology'. *JTS* 42 (1941): 129–142.
Luther, Martin. *Martin Luther: Selections from His Writings*. Edited by John Dillenberger. New York: Anchor Books, 1962.
Luz, Ulrich. *Matthew 1–7: A Commentary*. Translated by Wilhelm C. Linss. Edinburgh: T&T Clark, 1990.
Lyonnet, S. 'La valeur sotériologique de la résurrection du Christ selon saint Paul'. *Gregorianum* 39 (1958): 295–318.
—. 'Pauline Soteriology'. Pages 820–865 in *Introduction to the New Testament*. Edited by A. Robert and André Feuillet. New York: Desclée, 1965.
Mack, Burton L. *A Myth of Innocence: Mark and Christian Origins*. Philadelphia: Fortress Press, 1988.
Malherbe, Abraham J. 'The Beasts at Ephesus'. *JBL* 87 (1968): 71–80.
Mannermaa, Tuomo. *Christ Present in Faith: Luther's View of Justification*. Edited by Kirsi Stjerna. Minneapolis: Fortress Press, 2005.
Manson, T.W. *The Teaching of Jesus: Studies of Its Form and Content*. Cambridge: Cambridge University Press, 1931; 2nd ed., 1935.
—. 'Is It Possible to Write a Life of Christ?' *ExpTim* 53 (1942): 248–251.
—. 'The Life of Jesus: A Study of the Available Materials'. *BJRL* 27, no. 2 (1943): 323–337.
—. 'The Foundation of the Synoptic Tradition: The Gospel of Mark'. *BJRL* 28, no. 1 (1944): 119–136.
—. 'ΙΛΑCΤΗΡΙΟΝ'. *JTS* 46 (1945): 1–10.
—. *The Sayings of Jesus: As Recorded in the Gospels According to St Matthew and St Luke*. London: SCM Press, 1949; originally published in Part II of *The Mission and Message of Jesus*, by H.D.A. Major, T.W. Manson, and C.J. Wright. London: Nicholson and Watson, 1937.
—. 'The Son of Man in Daniel, Enoch and the Gospels'. *BJRL* 32 (1950): 171–193.

–. 'The Cleansing of the Temple'. *BJRL* 33, no. 2 (1951): 271–282.
–. '2 Cor. 2[14–17]: Suggestions Towards an Exegesis'. Pages 155–162 in *Studia Paulina: In Honorem Johannis de Zwaan Septuagenarii*. Edited by Jan N. Sevenster and W.C. van Unnik. Haarlem: Erven F. Bohn, 1953.
–. *The Servant-Messiah: A Study of the Public Ministry of Jesus*. Cambridge: Cambridge University Press, 1953.
–. *Jesus and the Non-Jews*. London: Athlone Press, 1955.
–. 'The Life of Jesus: Some Tendencies in Present-day Research'. Pages 211–221 in *The Background of the New Testament and Its Eschatology*. Edited by W.D. Davies and D. Daube. Cambridge: Cambridge University Press, 1956.
–. 'Realized Eschatology and the Messianic Secret'. Pages 209–222 in *Studies in the Gospels: Essays in Memory of R.H. Lightfoot*. Edited by D.E. Nineham. Oxford: Blackwell, 1957.
–. *Studies in the Gospels and Epistles*. Edited by Matthew Black. Manchester: Manchester University Press, 1962.
–. *On Paul and John: Some Selected Theological Themes*. Edited by Matthew Black. London: SCM Press, 1963.
Manson, William. *Jesus the Messiah: The Synoptic Tradition of the Revelation of God in Christ*. London: Hodder & Stoughton, 1943.
–. 'The ΕΓΩ ΕΙΜΙ of the Messianic Presence in the New Testament'. *JTS* 48 (1947): 137–145.
–. *The Epistle to the Hebrews*. London: Hodder & Stoughton, 1951.
Marcus, Joel. *The Way of the Lord: Christological Exegesis of the Old Testament in the Gospel of Mark*. Louisville: Westminster/John Knox, 1992.
–. *Mark 1–8*. AB. New York: Doubleday, 1999; repr., 2000.
Marsh, Clive. 'Quests of the Historical Jesus in New Historicist Perspective'. *Biblical Interpretation* 5 (1997): 403–437.
Marshall, I. Howard. *The Gospel of Luke*. NIGTC. Exeter: Paternoster Press, 1978.
Martin, Ralph P. *Carmen Christi: Philippians ii.5–11 in Recent Interpretation and in the Setting of Early Christian Worship*. Cambridge: Cambridge University Press, 1967.
–. *Philippians*. NCB. London: Oliphants, 1976.
Martyn, J. Louis. *Galatians*. AB. New York: Doubleday, 1997.
Marxsen, Willi. *Der Evangelist Markus: Studien zur Redaktionsgeschichte des Evangeliums*. Göttingen: Vandenhoeck & Ruprecht, 1959.
Masson, Charles. *Les deux épîtres de Saint Paul aux Thessaloniciens*. CNT 11a. Neuchâtel/Paris: Delachaux & Niestlé, 1957.
Matlock, R. Barry. 'Saving Faith: The Rhetoric and Semantics of πίστις in Paul'. Pages 73–90 in *The Faith of Jesus Christ: Exegetical, Biblical, and Theological Studies*. Edited by Michael F. Bird and Preston M. Sprinkle. Milton Keynes: Paternoster, 2009 = Peabody, MA: Hendrickson, 2009.
Mauser, Ulrich. *Christ in the Wilderness*. London: SCM Press, 1963.
McKelvey, R.J. *The New Temple: The Church in the New Testament*. Oxford Theological Monographs 3. Oxford: Oxford University Press, 1969.
McNeil, Brian. 'Raised for Our Justification'. *ITQ* 42 (1975): 97–105.
Meeks, Wayne A. *The Prophet-King: Moses Traditions and the Johannine Christology*. NTSup 14. Leiden: Brill, 1967.
Meier, John P. *A Marginal Jew*. 3 vols. AB. New York: Doubleday, 1991, 1994, 2001.
Metzger, Bruce M. *A Textual Commentary on the Greek New Testament*. 2nd ed. London: United Bible Societies, 1994.

Meyer, Ben F. *The Aims of Jesus*. London: SCM Press, 1979.
Meyer, Eduard. *Ursprung und Anfänge des Christentums*. 3 vols. Stuttgart: J.G. Cotta, 1921–1923.
Meyer, H.A.W. *Critical and Exegetical Handbook to the Epistle to the Romans*. Critical and Exegetical Commentary on the New Testament 4. Edited by W.P. Dickson. Translated by W.P. Dickson and John C. Moore. Edinburgh: T&T Clark, 1873.
Meyer, Paul W. 'Romans 10:4 and the End of the Law'. Pages 59–78 in *The Divine Helmsman: Studies on God's Control of Human Events*. Edited by James L. Crenshaw and Samuel Sandmel. New York: Ktav, 1980.
Milik, J.T., ed. *The Books of Enoch: Aramaic Fragments of Qumrân Cave 4*. With the collaboration of Matthew Black. Oxford: Clarendon Press, 1976.
Minear, Paul S. 'A Note on Luke XXII 36'. *NT* 7 (1964): 128–134.
–. 'Luke's Use of the Birth Stories'. Pages 111–130 in *Studies in Luke-Acts*. Edited by Leander E. Keck and J. Louis Martyn. Nashville: Abingdon Press, 1966 = 'Luke's Use of the Birth Narratives' in London: SPCK, 1968 version.
Molland, Einar. *Das Paulinische Euangelion: Das Wort und die Sache*. Oslo: Jacob Dybwad, 1934.
Moo, Douglas J. *The Old Testament in the Gospel Passion Narratives*. Sheffield: The Almond Press, 1983.
Moritz, Thorsten. *A Profound Mystery: The Use of the Old Testament in Ephesians*. NTSup 85. Leiden; New York: Brill, 1996.
Morris, Leon. *The New Testament and the Jewish Lectionaries*. London: Tyndale Press, 1964.
–. *The Cross in the New Testament*. Grand Rapids: Eerdmans, 1965; repr., Exeter: Paternoster, 1976.
Moule, C.F.D. 'The Biblical Conception of "Faith"'. *ExpTim* 68 (1957): 157.
–. *An Idiom Book of New Testament Greek*. 2nd ed. Cambridge: Cambridge University Press, 1959.
–. Review of *Jesus and the Servant*, by Morna D. Hooker. *Theology* 62, no. 472 (1959): 429–430.
–. 'The Influence of Circumstances on the Use of Eschatological Terms'. *JTS* NS 15 (1964): 1–15.
–. 'St Paul and Dualism: The Pauline Conception of Resurrection'. *NTS* 12 (1966): 106–123.
–. 'Mark 4:1–20 Yet Once More'. Pages 95–113 in *Neotestamentica et Semitica*, Edited by E. Earle Ellis and Max Wilcox. Edinburgh: T&T Clark, 1969.
–. 'The Manhood of Jesus in the New Testament'. Pages 95–110 in *Christ, Faith and History: Cambridge Studies in Christology*. Edited by S.W. Sykes and J.P. Clayton. Cambridge: Cambridge University Press, 1972.
–. 'Neglected Features in the Problem of "the Son of Man"'. Pages 413–428 in *Neues Testament and Kirche, Festschrift für Rudolf Schnackenburg*. Edited by Joachim Gnilka. Freiburg: Herder, 1974.
–. *The Origin of Christology*. Cambridge: Cambridge University Press, 1977.
Moulton, James Hope. *A Grammar of New Testament Greek*. vol. 1: *Prolegomena*. Edinburgh: T&T Clark, 1908.
Muddiman, John. *A Commentary on the Epistle to the Ephesians*. BNTC. London: Continuum, 2001.
Munck, Johannes. *Paul and the Salvation of Mankind*. Translated by Frank Clarke. London: SCM Press, 1959.

—. '1 Thess i.9–10 and the Missionary Preaching of Paul: Textual Exegesis and Hermeneutic Reflexions'. *NTS* 9 (1963): 95–110.
Murphy-O'Connor, Jerome. *The Theology of the Second Letter to the Corinthians*. Cambridge: Cambridge University Press, 1991.
Myers, Benjamin. 'From Faithfulness to Faith in the Theology of Karl Barth'. Pages 291–308 in *The Faith of Jesus Christ: Exegetical, Biblical, and Theological Studies*. Edited by Michael F. Bird and Preston M. Sprinkle. Milton Keynes: Paternoster 2009 = Peabody, MA: Hendrickson, 2009.
Neirynck, Frans. 'ΑΠΟ ΤΟΤΕ ΗΡΞΑΤΟ and the Structure of Matthew'. *ETL* 64 (1988): 21–59; repr. in *Evangelica II 1982–1991: Collected Essays*. Edited by Frans van Segbroeck. *BETL* 99. Leuven: Leuven University Press/Uitgeverij Peeters, 1991, 141–182.
Nineham, D.E. 'The Order of Events in St. Mark's Gospel – an examination of Dr. Dodd's Hypothesis'. Pages 223–239 in *Studies in the Gospels: Essays in Memory of R.H. Lightfoot*. Edited by D.E. Nineham. Oxford: Blackwell, 1955.
—. *The Gospel of St Mark*. Pelican New Testament Commentaries. Harmondsworth: Penguin, 1963.
—. '... et hoc genus omne'. Pages 199–222 in *Christian History and Interpretation: Studies Presented to John Knox*. Edited by William R. Farmer, C.F.D. Moule, and R.R. Niebuhr. Cambridge: Cambridge University Press, 1967.
—. 'Jesus in the Gospels'. Pages 45–65 in *Christ for Us Today*. Edited by Norman Pittenger. London: SCM Press, 1968.
O'Brien, Peter Thomas. *Introductory Thanksgivings in the Letters of Paul*. NTSup 49. Leiden: Brill, 1977.
—. *The Epistle to the Philippians*. NIGTC. Grand Rapids: Eerdmans, 1991.
Orlinsky, Harry M. and Norman H. Snaith. *Studies on the Second Part of the Book of Isaiah*. VTSup 14. Leiden: Brill, 1967.
Osborne, Robert E. 'Paul and the Wild Beasts'. *JBL* 85 (1966): 225–230.
Oster, Richard. 'The Ephesian Artemis as an Opponent of Early Christianity'. *Jahrbuch für Antike und Christentum* 19 (1976): 24–44.
—. 'Numismatic Windows into the Social World of Early Christianity: A Methodological Inquiry'. *JBL* 101 (1982): 195–223.
—. 'Ephesus as a Religious Center under the Principate, I: Paganism before Constantine'. Pages 1661–1728 in *Aufsteig und Niedergang der römischen Welt* II/18/3. Edited by H. Temporini and W. Haasa. New York: DeGruyter, 1990.
Palmer, Humphrey. *The Logic of Gospel Criticism*. London; New York: St. Martin's Press, 1968.
Parry, R.St. John. *The First Epistle of Paul the Apostle to the Corinthians*. Cambridge: Cambridge University Press, 1916.
Perrin, Norman. *Rediscovering the Teaching of Jesus*. London: SCM Press, 1967.
—. 'The Literary *Gattung* "Gospel" – Some Observations'. *ExpTim* 82 (1970): 4–7.
—. *What is Redaction Criticism?* London: SPCK, 1970.
Pesch, Rudolf. *Naherwartungen: Tradition und Redaktion in Mark 13*. Düsseldorf: Patmos-Verlag, 1968.
Peterlin, Davorin. *Paul's Letter to the Philippians in the Light of Disunity in the Church*. NTSup 79. Leiden; New York: Brill, 1995.
Plevnik, Joseph. *Paul and the Parousia: An Exegetical and Theological Investigation*. Peabody, MA: Hendrickson, 1997.

Plummer, Alfred. *An Exegetical Commentary on the Gospel According to St. Matthew.* London: Elliot Stock, 1909.
—. *A Critical and Exegetical Commentary on the Second Epistle of St. Paul to the Corinthians.* ICC. Edinburgh: T&T Clark, 1915.
Portefaix, L. 'The Image of Artemis Ephesia – a Symbolic Configuration Related to Her Mysteries?' Pages 611–617 in *100 Jahre österreichische Forschungen in Ephesos.* Edited by H. Friesinger and F. Krinzinger. Vienna: Verlag der Österreichischen Akademie der Wissenschaften, 1999.
Quesnell, Quentin. *The Mind of Mark: Interpretation and Method through the Exegesis of Mark 6,52.* Rome: Pontifical Biblical Institute, 1969.
Rae, Murray. 'Texts in Context: Scripture and the Divine Economy'. *JTI* 1 (2007): 23–45.
Räisänen, Heikki. 'Paul's Theological Difficulties with the Law'. Pages 301–320 in *Studia Biblica 1978.* Edited by Elizabeth A. Livingstone. JSNTSup 3. Sheffield: JSOT Press, 1980.
—. *Paul and the Law.* WUNT 29. Tübingen: Mohr, 1983.
Rawlinson, A.E.J. *The Gospel According to St Mark.* Westminster Commentaries. London: Methuen, 1925.
Rese, Martin. *Alttestamentliche Motive in der Christologie des Lukas.* Gütersloh: Mohn, 1969.
Reumann, John. 'Philippians 3.20–21 – a Hymnic Fragment?'. *NTS* 30 (1984): 593–609.
Rhoads, David, and Donald Michie. *Mark as Story: An Introduction to the Narrative of a Gospel.* Philadelphia: Fortress, 1982; 2nd ed. Edited by David Rhoads, Joanna Dewey, and Donald Michie. Minneapolis: Fortress, 1999.
Riesenfeld, Harald. *Jésus Transfiguré.* Copenhagen: E. Munksgaard, 1947.
Rigaux, Béda. *Saint Paul: Les épîtres aux Thessaloniciens.* EBib. Paris: Gabalda, 1956.
—. 'Vocabulaire chrétien antérieur à la première épître aux Thessaloniciens'. Pages 380–389 in *Sacra Pagina.* Edited by J. Coppens, A. Descamps, and É. Massaux. *BETL* 12–13. Gembloux: J. Duculot, 1959.
Robinson, J. Armitage. *St. Paul's Epistle to the Ephesians.* London: Macmillan, 1903.
Robinson, John A.T. *The Body: A Study in Pauline Theology.* London: SCM Press, 1952.
—. *Jesus and His Coming: The Emergence of a Doctrine.* London: SCM Press, 1957.
—. 'The Relation of the Prologue to the Gospel of St John'. *NTS* 9 (1963): 120–129.
—. *The Priority of John.* London: SCM Press, 1985.
Roetzel, Calvin. *Paul: The Man and the Myth.* Minneapolis: Fortress Press, 1999.
Rowland, Christopher. *The Open Heaven: A Study of Apocalyptic in Judaism and Early Christianity.* London: SPCK, 1982.
—. *Christian Origins: An Account of the Setting and Character of the Most Important Messianic Sect of Judaism.* 2nd ed. London: SPCK, 2002.
Sampley, J. Paul. *'And the Two Shall Become One Flesh'.* SNTSMS 16. Cambridge: Cambridge University Press, 1971.
Sanday, William and Arthur C. Headlam. *A Critical and Exegetical Commentary on the Epistle to the Romans.* ICC. Edinburgh: T&T Clark, 1905.
Sanders, E.P. *The Tendencies of the Synoptic Tradition.* Cambridge: Cambridge University Press, 1969.
—. *Paul and Palestinian Judaism.* London: SCM Press, 1977.
—. *Jesus and Judaism.* London: SCM Press, 1985.
—. *Paul.* Oxford; New York: Oxford University Press, 1991.
Sanders, Jack T. 'The Transition from Opening Epistolary Thanksgiving to Body in the Letters of the Pauline Corpus'. *JBL* 81 (1962): 348–362.
Schlier, Heinrich. *Der Brief an die Epheser.* Düsseldorf: Patmos, 1957.

Schmidt, Karl L. *Der Rahmen der Geschichte Jesu*. Berlin: Trowitzsch, 1919.
Schmiedel, Paul Wilhelm. 'Gospels'. Columns 1761–1898 in *Encyclopaedia Biblica*. vol. 2. Edited by Thomas Kelly Cheyne and John Sutherland Black. London: A&C Black, 1901.
Schnackenburg, Rudolf. *The Gospel According to St. John*. vol. 1. London: Burns & Oates, 1968.
Schnelle, Udo. '1 Kor 6:14 – Eine nachpaulinische Glosse'. *NT* 25 (1983): 217–219.
Schubert, Paul. *Form and Function of the Pauline Thanksgivings*. BZNW 20. Berlin: A. Töpelmann, 1939.
–. 'The Structure and Significance of Luke 24'. Pages 165–186 in *Neutestamentliche Studien für Rudolf Bultmann*. Edited by Walther Eltester. BZNW 21. Berlin: Töpelmann, 1954.
Schulz, David. 'Recensionen'. Review of *Einleitung in Das Neue Testament*, by Johann Gottfried Eichhorn, and *Lehrbuch der historisch-kritischen Einleitung in die kanonischen Bücher des Neuen Testaments*, by Wilhelm Martin Leberecht de Wette. *Theologische Studien und Kritken* 2 (1829): 563–636.
Schulz, Siegfried. 'Markus und das Alte Testament'. *ZTK* 58 (1961): 184–197.
Schürer, Emil. *The History of the Jewish People in the Age of Jesus Christ (175 BC–AD 135)*. A new English version revised and edited by Geza Vermes and Fergus Millar. 3 vols. Edinburgh: T&T Clark, 1973–1987.
Schüssler Fiorenza, Elisabeth. *In Memory of Her*. London: SCM Press, 1983.
Schweitzer, Albert. *The Quest of the Historical Jesus*. Translated by W. Montgomery. London: A&C Black, 1910.
Schweizer, Eduard. *Erniedrigung und Erhöhung bei Jesus und seinen Nachfolgern*. Zürich: Zwingli-Verlag, 1955; ET: *Lordship and Discipleship*. London: SCM Press, 1960.
–. 'Der Menschensohn'. *ZNW* 50 (1959): 185–209.
–. 'The Son of Man'. *JBL* 79 (1960): 119–129.
–. 'The Son of Man Again'. *NTS* 9 (1963): 256–261.
–. *Das Evangelium nach Markus*. Das Neue Testament Deutsch. Göttingen: Vandenhoeck & Ruprecht, 1967; ET: *The Good News According to Mark*. Translated by Donald H. Madvig. London: SPCK 1971.
Scobie, Charlie. *John the Baptist*. London: SCM Press, 1964.
Scott, Ernest Findlay. *The Fourth Gospel: Its Purpose and Theology*. Edinburgh: T&T Clark, 1920.
–. *The Epistles of Paul to the Colossians, to Philemon and to the Ephesians*. London: Hodder & Stoughton, 1930.
Segal, Alan F. *Two Powers in Heaven: Early Rabbinic Reports about Christianity and Gnosticism*. Leiden: Brill, 1977.
Seiterle, Gérard. 'Artemis – Die Grosse Göttin von Ephesos'. *Antike Welt* 10 (1979): 3–16.
Seitz, Oscar J. F. 'Gospel Prologues: A Common Pattern?' *JBL* 83 (1964): 262–268.
Sevenster, Jan N. 'Some Remarks on the ΓΥΜΝΟΣ in II Cor. V. 3'. Pages 202–214 in *Studia Paulina: In Honorem Johannis de Zwaan Septuagenarii*. Edited by Jan N. Sevenster and W. C. van Unnik. Haarlem: Erven F. Bohn, 1953.
Snodgrass, Klyne R. 'Streams of Tradition Emerging from Isaiah 40:1–5 and Their Adaptation in the New Testament'. *JSNT* 8 (1980): 24–45.
Stacey, W. David. *Prophetic Drama in the Old Testament*. London: Epworth, 1990; repr., Eugene, OR: Wipf & Stock, 2018.
Standaert, Benoît H. M. G. M. *L'Evangile selon Marc: Composition et genre littéraire*. Brugge and Zevenkerken: Sint Andriesabdij, 1978.

Stanley, Christopher D. '"Under a Curse": a Fresh Reading of Galatians 3.10–14'. *NTS* 36 (1990): 481–511.
–. *Arguing with Scripture: The Rhetoric of Quotations in the Letters of Paul*. New York; London: T&T Clark, 2004.
Stanley, D.M. '"Become Imitators of Me": The Pauline Conception of Apostolic Tradition'. *Biblica* 40 (1959): 859–877.
–. *Christ's Resurrection in Pauline Soteriology*. AnBib 13. Rome: Biblical Institute Press, 1961.
–. 'Imitation in Paul's Letters: Its Significance for His Relationship to Jesus and to His Own Christian Foundations'. Pages 127–141 in *From Jesus to Paul: Studies in Honour of Francis Wright Beare*. Edited by Peter Richardson and John C. Hurd. Waterloo, ON: Wilfrid Laurier University Press, 1984.
Stanton, Graham. 'Incarnational Christology in the New Testament'. Pages 151–165 in *Incarnation and Myth: The Debate Continued*. Edited by Michael Goulder. London: SCM Press, 1979.
–. 'Mr Cupitt on Incarnational Christology in the New Testament'. Pages 170–173 in *Incarnation and Myth The Debate Continued*. Edited by Michael Goulder. London: SCM Press, 1979.
–. 'Stephen in Lucan Perspective'. Pages 345–360 in *Studia Biblica 1978*. Edited by Elizabeth A. Livingstone. JSNTSup 3. Sheffield: JSOT Press, 1980.
–. 'Matthew'. Pages 205–219 in *It is Written: Scripture Citing Scripture: Essays in Honour of Barnabas Lindars*. Edited by D.A. Carson and H.G.M. Williamson. Cambridge: Cambridge University Press, 1988.
–. *A Gospel for a New People: Studies in Matthew*. Edinburgh: T&T Clark, 1992.
Stauffer, Ethelbert. *Jesus and His Story*. Translated by Dorothea M. Barton. London: SCM Press, 1960.
Steenburg, Dave. 'The Case Against the Synonymity of *Morphē* and *Eikōn*'. *JSNT* 34 (1988): 77–86.
Stendahl, Krister. 'Quis et Unde?' Pages 94–105 in *Judentum, Urchristentum Kirche: Festschrift für Joachim Jeremias*. Edited by Walther Eltester. BZNW 26. Berlin: Töpelmann, 1960.
–. *Paul among Jews and Gentiles: And Other Essays*. Minneapolis: Fortress, 1976.
Stettler, Christian. *Der Kolosserhymnus*. WUNT 2/131. Tübingen: Mohr Siebeck, 2000.
Stuhlmacher, Peter. *Gerechtigkeit Gottes bei Paulus*. FRLANT 87. Göttingen: Vandenhoeck & Ruprecht, 1965.
Suhl, Alfred. *Die Funktion der alttestamentlichen Zitate und Anspielungen im Markusevangelium*. Gütersloh: Mohn, 1965.
Sundkler, Bengt. 'Jésus et les païens'. *RHPR* 16 (1936): 462–499.
Swete, Henry B. *The Gospel According to St. Mark*. London: Macmillan, 1898.
Swetnam, James. 'Christology and the Eucharist in the Epistle to the Hebrews'. *Biblica* 70 (1989): 74–95.
Taylor, Vincent. *The Gospel According to St. Mark*. London: Macmillan, 1952; repr., 1957.
Telford, William R. *The Barren Temple and the Withered Tree*. JSNTSup 1. Sheffield: JSOT Press, 1980.
Theissen, Gerd. *A Theory of Primitive Christian Religion*. London: SCM Press, 1999.
Thiselton, Anthony C. *The First Epistle to the Corinthians*. NIGTC. Grand Rapids: Eerdmans, 2000 = Carlisle: Paternoster, 2000.
Thomas, Kenneth J. 'Torah Citations in the Synoptics'. *NTS* 24 (1977): 85–96.
Thrall, Margaret E. 'Elijah and Moses in Mark's Account of the Transfiguration'. *NTS* 16 (1970): 305–317.

–. *A Critical and Exegetical Commentary on the Second Epistle to the Corinthians*. vol. 1. ICC. Edinburgh: T&T Clark, 1994.
Tinsley, E.J. *The Imitation of God in Christ*. London: SCM Press, 1960.
Tödt, H.E. *Der Menschensohn in der synoptischen Überlieferung*. Gütersloh: G. Mohn, 1959; ET: *The Son of Man in the Synoptic Tradition*. Translated by Dorothea M. Barton. London: SCM Press, 1965.
Torrance, Thomas F. 'One Aspect of the Biblical Conception of Faith'. *ExpTim* 68 (1957): 111–114.
Trebilco, Paul. *The Early Christians in Ephesus from Paul to Ignatius*. WUNT 166. Tübingen: Mohr Siebeck, 2004.
Trilling, Wolfgang. *Das Wahre Israel*. 3rd ed. München: Kösel, 1964.
Turner, C.H. 'ὁ υἱός μου ὁ ἀγαπητός'. *JTS* 27 (1926): 113–129.
Turner, Nigel, and James Hope Moulton. *A Grammar of New Testament Greek*. vol. 3: *Syntax*. Edinburgh: T&T Clark, 1963.
Upton, Bridget Gilfillian. *Hearing Mark's Endings: Listening to Ancient Popular Texts Through Speech Act Theory*. Leiden: Brill, 2006.
Vainio, Olli-Pekka. *Justification and Participation in Christ: The Development of the Lutheran Doctrine of Justification from Luther to the Formula of Concord (1580)*. Leiden; Boston: Brill, 2008.
Valloton, Pierre. *Le Christ et la foi: Etude de théologie biblique*. Geneva: Labor & Fides, 1960.
Vanhoye, Albert. 'La Composition de 1 Thessaloniciens'. Pages 73–86 in *The Thessalonian Correspondence*. Edited by Raymond F. Collins. BETL 87. Leuven: Leuven University Press/Uitgeverij Peeters, 1990.
Vermes, Geza. 'The Use of בר נש / בר נשא in Jewish Aramaic'. Pages 310–330 (Appendix E) in *An Aramaic Approach to the Gospels and Acts*, by Matthew Black. 3rd ed. Oxford: Clarendon, 1967.
–. 'He is the Bread'. Pages 256–263 in *Neotestamentica et Semitica: Studies in Honour of Matthew Black*. Edited by E. Earle Ellis and Max Wilcox. Edinburgh: T&T Clark, 1969.
–. *Jesus the Jew: A Historian's Reading of the Gospels*. London: Collins, 1973.
–. *Jesus and the World of Judaism*. London: SCM Press, 1983.
–. *The Religion of Jesus the Jew*. London: SCM Press, 1993.
Vielhauer, Philipp. 'Gottesreich und Menschensohn in der Verkündigung Jesu'. Pages 51–79 in *Festschrift für Günther Dehn*. Edited by Wilhelm Schneemelcher. Neukirchen: Kreis Moers, 1957.
–. 'Jesus und der Menschensohn'. *ZTK* 60 (1963): 133–177.
Walker, William O. 'The Origin of the Son of Man Concept as Applied to Jesus'. *JBL* 91 (1972): 482–490.
–. 'The Son of Man Question and the Synoptic Problem'. *NTS* 28 (1982): 374–388.
Wallis, Ian G. *The Faith of Jesus Christ in Early Christian Traditions*. SNTSMS 84. Cambridge: Cambridge University Press, 1995.
Wanamaker, C.A. 'Philippians 2.6–11: Son of God or Adamic Christology?' *NTS* 33 (1987): 179–193.
Watson, Francis. 'By Faith (of Christ): An Exegetical Dilemma and its Scriptural Solution'. Pages 147–163 in *The Faith of Jesus Christ: Exegetical, Biblical, and Theological Studies*. Edited by Michael F. Bird and Preston M. Sprinkle. Milton Keynes: Paternoster, 2009 = Peabody, MA: Hendrickson, 2009.
Watson, Nigel. *The Second Epistle to the Corinthians*. London: Epworth, 1993.
Watts, Rikki E. *Isaiah's New Exodus in Mark*. WUNT 2/88. Tübingen: Mohr Siebeck, 1997.
Weeden, Theodore J. *Mark – Traditions in Conflict*. Philadelphia: Fortress Press, 1971.

Weidinger, Karl. *Die Haustafeln, ein Stück urchristlicher Paraenese.* UNT 14. Leipzig: J.C. Hinrichs, 1928.
Wellhausen, Julius. *Das Evangelium Matthaei.* 2nd ed. Berlin: Georg Reimer, 1914.
Wendland, Heinz-Dietrich. *Die Briefe an der Korinther.* 7th ed. Göttingen: Vandenhoeck & Ruprecht, 1954.
Wesley, John. *Sermons on Several Occasions.* London: Epworth Press, 1944.
Westcott, Brooke Foss. *The Epistle to the Hebrews.* 2nd ed. London: Macmillan, 1892.
–. *St. Paul's Epistle to the Ephesians.* London: Macmillan, 1906.
Whybray, R. Norman. *Thanksgiving for a Liberated Prophet: An Interpretation of Isaiah Chapter 53.* JSOTSup 4. Sheffield: JSOT Press, 1978.
Wiles, Maurice F. *The Spiritual Gospel: The Interpretation of the Fourth Gospel in the Early Church.* Cambridge: Cambridge University Press, 1960.
–. *The Divine Apostle: The Interpretation of St. Paul's Epistles in the Early Church.* Cambridge: Cambridge University Press, 1967.
–. 'Does Christology Rest on a Mistake?' *Religious Studies* 6 (1970): 69–76.
–. *The Remaking of Christian Doctrine.* London: SCM Press, 1974.
Williams, Sam K. *Jesus' Death as Saving Event: The Background and Origin of a Concept.* Missoula, MT: Scholars Press, 1975.
–. 'Again Pistis Christou'. *CBQ* 49 (1987): 431–447.
Wilson, S.G. *Luke and the Law.* Cambridge: Cambridge University Press, 1983.
Wink, Walter. *John the Baptist in the Gospel Tradition.* London: Cambridge University Press, 1968.
Winter, Bruce. *Seek the Welfare of the City: Christians as Benefactors and Citizens.* Grand Rapids: Eerdmans, 1994 = Carlisle: Paternoster, 1994.
Wright, N.T. *The Epistles of Paul to the Colossians and to Philemon.* Leicester: Inter-Varsity, 1986; repr., Grand Rapids: Eerdmans, 1988.
–. 'Poetry and Theology in Colossians 1.15–20'. *NTS* 36 (1990): 444–468.
–. *Jesus and the Victory of God.* London: SPCK, 1996.
Wuellner, Wilhelm. 'The Argumentative Structure of 1Thessalonians as Paradoxical Encomium'. Pages 117–136 in *The Thessalonian Correspondence.* Edited by Raymond F. Collins. BETL 87. Leuven: Leuven University Press/Uitgeverij Peeters, 1990.
Yates, John Edmund. *The Spirit and the Kingdom.* London: SPCK, 1963.
Yates, Roy. '"The Worship of Angels": (Col 2:18)'. *ExpTim* 97 (1985): 12–15.
–. *The Epistle to the Colossians.* London: Epworth, 1993.
Young, Frances. 'A Cloud of Witnesses'. Pages 13–47 in *The Myth of God Incarnate.* Edited by John Hick. London: SCM Press, 1977.
Zahrnt, Heinz. *The Historical Jesus.* Translated by John Bowden. London: Collins, 1963.
Ziesler, J.A. 'The Transfiguration Story and the Markan Soteriology'. *ExpTim* 81 (1970): 263–268.
Zuntz, Günther. *The Text of the Epistles: A Disquisition upon the* Corpus Paulinum. *The Schweich Lectures of the British Academy, 1946.* London: Oxford University Press, 1953.

Index of Ancient Sources

Hebrew Bible

Genesis
1   23, 281, 353, 375, 376, 398, 468, 476, 491, 492
1:1–5   285, 334
1:1–3   159
1:1   283, 285, 395, 396, 489
1:2   301
1:3   375, 394, 474
1:26 ff.   344
1:26–27   371
1:26   154, 371, 397, 398
1:27   193, 251, 254, 375, 381
2   375, 376
2:4   284
2:7   376
2:18   375
2:21–23   644
2:22   375
2:23–24   651
2:23   648, 651
2:24   193, 251, 254, 289, 644, 647, 650, 651
2:25   452
3:7   452
3:8   344
3:10 ff.   452
3:22   373, 552, 604
5:1   284
6:17   299
15   386
15:5   562
15:6   402, 403, 428
22:2   195, 212
22:12   195
22:16   195
26:24   212
37:20   198
49   219
49:11   198

Exodus
1–15   277
3   252, 259
3:1–6   342
3:6   172, 193
3:12   259
3:14   259
4:22   146
7:1   173
14:21   139
14:31   212
15:1–19   491
16   139
16:1–12   382
17:1–7   382
17:6   394
19–20   259
19:3–7   256
19:3   256
19:4–6   535
19:6   546
19:16   346
20:2   172
20:6   651
20:8–11   195
20:12–16   193
20:12   191, 205, 651
21:17   191, 205
22:22   198, 252
23:20   132, 191, 200, 207
24:1   296
24:8   198
24:15 ff.   186, 197
24:15   256
24:16   180
25:9   450, 664
25:40   450, 508, 664
26:30   450, 664
27:8   450, 664
30:12   214
30:13   257
31:14   195
32   381
32:32   594
33–34   23, 335–337, 353, 492

33	334, 342, 375	*Numbers*	
33:7–11	335, 342	6:3	286
33:12–34:8	285	6:6	259
33:12–23	334	11:16	296
33:12–13	257	11:26–29	197
33:13	334, 335	12:7	627
33:14	257	14:18	336
33:16	335	20:7–13	394
33:17–23	319, 335	22:35	198
33:17	338	27:17	197
33:18–23	158, 485	28:9–10	258
33:18	334	30:2	191, 205
33:19	335, 336, 397		
33:20	335	*Deuteronomy*	
33:22 ff.	23	1–26	295
33:22	336	1:15–18	168
34	23, 181, 281, 336,	4:6	493
	398, 471, 472, 475,	4:32	198
	476	4:35	194, 210
34:4–7	158	5:16–20	193
34:4	256	6:4 ff.	194
34:5–7	335, 336	6:4	210
34:5	186, 336	6:5	210
34:6	335, 336	6:13	254
34:7	23	6:16	254
34:21	195	6:25	411
34:29 ff.	180	8:3	254
34:29–35	188	10:17	302
34:29–30	472	13:1–3	198
34:33–35	472	15:11	198
34:34	393, 473	16:18	296
40:35	185	17:6	198
		17:17	251
Leviticus		18:15–19	296
6:30	510	18:15	151, 182, 186, 197, 261,
11	251		295
11:21 ff.	195	18:21–22	294
11:44 ff.	535	19:15	198
11:45	423	21:22 ff.	198
14:2 ff.	196	21:22	399
17:16	298	21:23	403, 404, 554
18:5	389, 399, 402, 484,	22:6–7	651
	573	23:21–23	191, 205
19:2	535	23:25	195
19:18	194, 651	24	193, 252
19:36	535	24:1–4	251, 254
21:11	259	24:1	289
23:42 ff.	184	24:17–22	252
24:5–9	195	25	193
25:24–26	214	25:5–10	252
25:51	214	27:26	390, 402, 404, 554
26	256, 661	30	20
26:12	547	30:4	198

30:12 ff.	389, 484	*Esther*	
30:12–14	389, 484	2:9	335
30:15–20	256	2:17	335
31:14–15	259		
31:23	259	*Job*	
32	219	9:8	139
32:5	382, 626	23:10	301
32:10	215	28	489
32:49	297	28:1–27	490
34:1	297	28:12–19	490
34:3	297	28:12	489
34:10	183, 257	28:23–27	489
		28:28	490
Joshua			
1:1–9	259	*Psalms*	
7	404	2	505, 515
		2:7	146, 151, 195, 212
1 Samuel		8	6, 95, 105, 170, 505, 506
1–2	286	8:4 ff.	155
2:10	151	8:4–8	152
18:7	622	8:4	152
21:1–6	250	8:5	378
		8:6	378, 380
2 Samuel		8:7	154
3:18	212	18:16	299
5	239	19:7 (LXX 18:8)	257
5:8	239	22	133, 135
7	661	22:1 (21:2)	213
7:14	146, 661	22:2	675
		22:7 (21:8)	212
1 Kings		22:23 (21:24)	336
1:28–40	140	24:8	302
8:27	173	32 (31)	386
17:17–24	261	33 (32)	490
19:1–3	134	33:6	490
19:19–21	261, 295	51:2	298
		51:7	298
2 Kings		62:12 (61:13)	96, 109
1:8	202, 298	66:10	301
1:9–12	295	69:10	243
2:1–12	261	74:19	461
2:4	297	75:8	213
2:9–15	296	77:19–20	139
4:32–37	261	80:8	154
4:42–44	139	80:14	154
5:10–14	298	80:17	152, 154
		82	168
1 Chronicles		82:6	168, 327
28	219	84:5 (4)	188
		86:15	336
Nehemiah		89:8–9	139
9:17	336	89:20 (88:21)	627
		95	507

98	424	13	228
102:16	344	13:10	133, 209, 228
102:21–22	344	13:13	211
103:8	336	19:2	211
106:11	299	20	299
110	133, 515	20:3	212
110:1	105, 106, 146, 249, 258, 510	22:13	460
		25:6	366
110:4	508	26:19	308
118 (117)	133	27:13	109
118:22–23	208	28	386, 481
118:22	210, 237, 386	28:7	211
119	166	28:16	210, 386, 387, 481, 482, 660, 661
119:89	256		
119:130 (118:130)	257	29	191
145:8	336	29:13	133, 204–206, 210, 250
148	133	29:18–19	291
		30:27–28	307
Proverbs		30:28	300
1:7	490	32:15	301
8	24, 339, 489, 490	34	228
8:22–35	159	34:4	133, 209, 228
8:22–31	166	35:5–6	115, 133, 291, 308
8:22	395, 396, 489, 490	35:5	211
8:23–31	490	35:6–7	300
8:35	490	35:9	214
9:10	490	40–55	491
24:12	109	40	201, 202, 290
		40:2	121
Isaiah		40:3–5	491
1:16	298	40:3	132, 201, 202, 204, 207, 209, 254, 310
1:25	301		
2:2–4	366	40:5	342
4:3	301	40:8	256, 491
4:4	300, 301, 307, 314	40:9	201
5	237	40:12–31	491
5:1–2	133, 208	40:18	211
5:2	208	40:24	307
5:3–7	208	41:14	214
5:5	208	41:15–16	307
6	204, 208, 343, 348	41:18	300
6:9–10	133, 203, 290	42	212, 310
6:10	203, 329	42:1–9	1
7:14	115, 260	42:1–4	117, 209, 212
7:15	501	42:1	195, 210–212
8	386, 481	43:1	214
8:14	210, 386, 387, 481, 482, 661	43:2	491
		43:3 ff.	214
8:21	211	43:11–21	491
9:1–2	209	43:14	214
9:6	173	43:16	139, 210
10:2	211	43:25	211
11:2	210	44:3–4	300

44:3	301	54:1–8	647
44:13	381	54:13	477
44:22–23	214	55:10–13	491
44:24	214	56	239
45:13	214	56:7	133, 206, 209, 237, 245, 246
45:21–23	491		
45:21	133, 210	56:9	461
47:3	452	58:6	290
48:10	301	60:6	201
49:1–6	1, 212	61	150, 157, 260, 290, 291, 308, 309
49:4	626		
49:24 ff.	211	61:1–4	301
49:24	133	61:1–2	209, 290, 291
50:1	647	61:1	151, 201, 308
50:4–11	1	61:2	290
50:4–9	212	62:4	210
50:6	211, 213	62:12	214
50:7–9	574	63:9	214
51:6	133, 211	64:1 (63:19)	211
51:10	139	65:4	133, 211
51:13–16	491	66:15	307
51:17	211, 213	66:24	133
51:22	211		
52–53	118	*Jeremiah*	
52	661	4:11–12	307
52:3	214	4:11	300
52:5	478	4:14	298, 300
52:7	201	5:5	257
52:8	188	6:29–30	301
52:11	547	7:4	479
52:12	116	7:5–15	246
52:13–53:12	1, 212	7:9–10	478
52:15	117, 125	7:11	207, 236, 245
53	1, 2, 54, 84, 115–121, 123–125, 127, 213, 214, 293, 348, 515, 552, 577	7:22 ff.	251
		8:13	140
		9:7	301
		16:1–9	259
53:1	117, 125, 329	19:1–13	299
53:3	212	31:31–33	392
53:4	118, 121, 122, 125	31:33	471
53:5	118, 121, 122, 127	47:2–4	299
53:5b	122	50:6	267
53:6	118, 213		
53:7–8	292	*Ezekiel*	
53:7	117, 212, 213	1:26–28	343
53:8	117	4:9–17	299
53:9	118	16	647
53:10	120, 121, 123	16:37	452
53:10–11	214	17:5–6	300
53:11 ff.	127	20	661
53:11	213, 214	23:29	452
53:12	117, 118, 120–122, 213, 294	24:15–18	259
		29:3 ff.	461

34:5	461	2:28–29	301, 314
34:6	267	2:30 ff. (3:3 ff.)	228
34:8	461	3:17	660
34:11 ff.	267		
34:25	461	*Amos*	
34:28	461	2:16	452
36:25–28	300		
36:26–28	471	*Jonah*	
37	661	2:5–6	299
37:27	547	4:2	336
39:29	301		
47	243	*Micah*	
47:1–12	300	1:7	539
		4:1–3	366
Daniel		4:1	236
7	1, 6, 77, 78, 90, 95, 99–102, 113, 125, 170, 343, 461	7:1	140
		Habakkuk	
7:9–10	343	2:4	388, 402, 425, 426, 428, 568–570
7:9	180		
7:13	73, 74, 100, 101, 105, 140, 152, 209, 213	2:17	461
		Zephaniah	283
12:1	226		
12:7	221		
12:11	226	*Zechariah*	
12:12	223	8:23	366
		12:10	300
Hosea		12:12	188
1–3	647	13:1–2	298
1–2	676	13:1	300
1:2	539	13:4	298
2:3	452	13:7	134, 135, 213
2:12 (2:14)	461	13:9	301
2:25	548	14:4	221
4:10–12	539	14:16–19	185
5:3–4	539		
6:6	251, 254, 258	*Malachi*	
9:1	539	3	181
9:10	140	3:1–12	303
9:16	140	3:1–4	140, 304
11:1	146	3:1	132, 134, 191, 200, 207, 246
12:9 (10)	185		
12:14 (13)	183	3:2–4	207, 301
		3:5	252
Joel		4	181
2:10	209	4:4–5	297
2:13	336	4:5–6	135
2:27–29	660	4:5	134, 202

OT Apocryphal/Deuterocanonical Books

Apocalypse of Abraham
                    283

Apocalypse of Moses
20–21   344
20:1 ff.   452

Assumption of Moses
10:5   228

Baruch
2:19   565

2 Baruch
4   450
4:2–6   664

3 Baruch
4:16   452

1 Enoch
37–71 (*Similitudes of Enoch*)
                  90, 113
38–71   74
38:2   426
38:4   494
39:4   450
45   173
46:4–8   113
50:1   494
53:6   426
62:5–14   113
62:15 ff.   451
69:26–29   113
80:4 ff.   228
90:29   664

2 (4) Esdras
2:45   451
3:21–22   552, 604
3:25–26   552, 604
5:44 ff.   228
6:53–59   152
7:48   552, 604
7:95   494
7:97   494
10   664
10:25–57   450
13:10   307
13:11   300

Jubilees
1:23   300

4 Maccabees
17:22   559

Sirach
15:1   490
17:3   398
24   24, 166, 339, 489, 490
24:1–12   395
24:8   490
24:9   490
24:23–26   493
24:23   166, 490
43:31   336
45:1–5   335
51:26   257

Testaments of the Twelve Patriarchs

Testament of Levi
3:4–6   450, 664
4:1   228

Testament of Issachar
5:2   479
7:6   479

Testament of Dan
5:3   479

Testament of Job   283

Tobit   283

Wisdom of Solomon
6–10   489
6:4   490
6:18   490
7   24
7:22–10:21   166
7:22–26   159
7:22   395, 490
7:25–26   490
7:26   397
9:1–2   159, 397, 490
9:8   450, 664
9:15   449
10:15–21   491
11:1–4   394, 492

New Testament

Matthew
1:1–4:16	284	5:17–18	15, 475
1–2	156, 281, 284	5:17	16, 157, 256
1:1–17	334	5:19	16
1:1	145, 281, 284	5:20	255
1:2–17	284	5:21–48	188, 475
1:16	281	5:21–22	157
1:17	281	5:22	310
1:18	145, 281, 284	5:23	257
1:20	281	5:27–30	310
1:21	282	5:48	256
1:22–23	132, 254, 286	7:1–5	310
1:23	259	7:13–27	310, 314
2	282, 333	7:19	310
2:4	281	7:21–23	256
2:5–6	132, 254, 281, 286	7:24–27	157
2:15	132, 254, 281, 286	7:28	255
2:17–18	132, 286	8	269
2:18	254	8:11 ff.	268, 282
2:23	132, 254, 280, 286	8:11	282
3–4	281	8:17	117, 254, 286
3:1–4:17	280	8:18–34	268
3	281	8:19	151
3:1	202, 298	8:20	92
3:2	299, 310	8:21–22	258
3:3	132, 200, 254	9	269
3:5	308	9:6	299
3:6	299, 313	9:13	254
3:7–10	202, 310	9:17	11, 258
3:10	306, 309, 310	9:36	266, 267
3:11	299, 311, 313	9:37 ff.	267
3:12	306, 309, 310	10	96, 223, 224, 269
3:13–17	6	10:1	309
3:16	210	10:2–4	265
3:17	210, 211	10:5 ff.	268, 269, 270
4:4	254	10:5–16	265
4:7	254	10:5–7	231
4:10	254	10:5–6	271
4:11	280	10:5b–6	266, 268, 269
4:14–16	132, 254	10:6	268
4:14	286	10:7	269
4:15–16	209	10:8	269
4:17	150, 269, 280, 310	10:15	110, 310
4:18–22	256	10:16	266
4:23	150	10:16b	268
5–7	157, 314	10:17 ff.	266, 269
5	158, 255	10:17–23a	267
5:1	157, 255	10:17–22	265, 267
5:3–4	290	10:17–21	223
5:17–21	25	10:18 ff.	269
5:17–20	188, 254, 255, 492	10:19–20	309
		10:20	309

10:22	267	13:50	310
10:23	96, 110, 224, 231, 267, 268	13:52	258
		13:54–58	291
10:23a	267	13:57	151
10:23b	267, 268, 269	14:2	298
10:24 ff.	267, 269	14:8	298
10:24	268	14:25	210
10:32 ff.	96, 109	15:1–20	199, 254, 258, 261
10:32	96	15:7–9	254
10:37	259	15:11	255
11:2–6	254	15:12–20	255
11:5–6	290	15:16	255
11:7–15	257	15:21–28	268
11:10	132, 200, 254	15:24	266, 268
11:11–12	298	16:4 ff.	268
11:12	257	16:14	298
11:13	257	16:16	147
11:19	92, 159, 257	16:21	147
11:20–24	310	16:27	109, 110
11:25–30	159, 257	16:28	96, 97, 111, 180, 231
11:25–27	151, 492	17:2	180
11:25	257	17:13	298
11:27	169, 257, 258	17:27	257
11:28	257	18:8	310
12	125	18:9	310
12:1–8	258	18:23–35	310
12:5	258	19:3–12	199
12:7	254	19:3–9	254, 255
12:9–14	486	19:9	199
12:17–21	117, 254	19:10–12	255
12:17	286	19:11	199
12:18–21	209, 271	19:16–22	258
12:18	310	19:28	96, 111, 256
12:22–32	310	20:28	120, 125
12:24–37	309	21	239
12:28	309, 310	21:4–5	254
12:32	92	21:4	286
12:33–34	310	21:9	239, 254
12:38–42	258	21:13	254
12:39 ff.	112	21:14–16	239
12:40	96	21:16	254
13	112	21:31	240
13:13	203	21:42	210, 254
13:14 ff.	349	21:43	240, 268
13:14–15	254, 290	22	240
13:14	286	22:1–14	310
13:24–30	111, 231, 310	22:7–10	240
13:35	254, 286	22:11–14	452
13:36–43	231, 310	22:34–40	479
13:40	310	22:41–46	258
13:41	96, 110	22:44	254
13:42	310	23	220, 258
13:47–50	310	23:1–39	310

23:2	258	28:18	98
23:23	254	28:19	258, 282, 309, 314
23:35–36	240		
23:37–39	220, 240, 241	*Mark*	
24	111, 112, 224, 225, 267	1–8	61
24:2	240	1	196, 200, 212, 246
24:9	309	1:1–15	129, 275, 277
24:14	224, 269	1:1–13	129, 131, 135, 137–139, 156, 201, 211, 275, 277, 281, 304, 321, 322
24:15	254		
24:16	267		
24:20	257	1:1–3	209
24:26–28	227	1:1	131, 132, 137, 138, 143, 145, 156, 321, 334
24:27	96, 111		
24:29	254	1:2 ff.	190
24:30–31	152	1:2–13	280
24:30	96	1:2–8	135
24:30a	112	1:2–3	133–135, 200, 205, 249, 282
24:30b	109, 110, 111		
24:35	256	1:2	144, 191, 205, 207, 254, 281
24:37–44	97		
24:37	96, 112	1:3	129, 132, 200, 254
24:39	96, 112	1:4–8	137
24:42	112	1:4–6	202
24:43 ff.	112	1:4	203, 298
24:44	96, 112	1:5	308
24:45–51	97	1:6	195, 298
25	240	1:7–8	135, 281, 303
25:1–46	310	1:7	211
25:14–30	229	1:8	202, 305
25:31–46	256, 268	1:9–13	302
25:31	96, 111	1:9–11	202, 303
25:41	310	1:9	156
26	240	1:10 ff.	332
26:2	96	1:10	137, 210–212, 281
26:28 ff.	125	1:11	137, 138, 151, 186, 195, 210, 211, 281, 302, 323, 331
26:28	299		
26:31	254		
26:39	147, 211	1:12–13	211, 304
26:42	147	1:13	277, 280
26:53	240	1:14–8:21	131, 135, 137, 138
26:54	254	1:14–3:6	250
26:56	254	1:14–15	277
26:60	240	1:14	134, 135, 137, 139, 150, 187, 203, 277, 305, 322, 323
26:64	110		
26:63–65	147		
27:9	254, 286	1:15	150, 203, 304, 323
27:25	270	1:16–20	305
27:39–42	240	1:17	311
27:43	240	1:21	249
27:45–54	6	1:22	150, 195, 252
27:46	410	1:24	139, 302, 304
27:51	241	1:27	150, 196, 302, 323
28:18–20	269	1:32–34	311

1:34	131, 139, 145	4:30	156, 210, 211
1:40–2:12	304	4:33–34	204
1:40–45	252, 304	4:35–41	253, 302, 304
1:44	15, 188, 196, 249	4:38	151
2:1–3:6	52	4:41	139, 150, 186, 302, 323, 331
2:1–12	304		
2:5–7	139	5:1–15	304
2:7	210, 211	5:1–13	302
2:10	92, 134	5:3	133, 135, 210, 211
2:13–17	304	5:4	211
2:17	304	5:7	138, 139, 302, 331
2:18–20	253	5:11	211
2:21–22	253	5:15	186, 302
2:22	11	5:21–34	304
2:23–3:6	195	5:23	304
2:23–28	249	5:28	304
2:24	195	5:33	186, 302
2:25	250	5:34	304
2:26	195	5:35–43	139, 304
2:28	92, 134, 196, 250	5:42	302
3:1–6	198, 304, 486	6	331
3:1	249	6:1–6	139, 291
3:4	304	6:4	151
3:6	195	6:7 ff.	265
3:7	303	6:7	305, 309
3:11	138, 139, 302, 331	6:8	266
3:13–19	253, 265	6:13	305
3:14–15	305	6:14 ff.	182
3:20–30	282, 303, 322	6:14–29	135, 137
3:21	210, 211	6:14–16	136, 139, 140
3:22–30	197, 304, 309	6:14	298
3:22	150, 302	6:15	151, 182
3:23–30	150	6:17–29	305
3:27	133, 135, 139, 210, 211, 302	6:24	298
		6:28	298
3:29–30	303, 304	6:30–44	139, 253, 304
3:29	139, 304, 305, 322	6:34	197
4	207, 210, 216	6:37	305
4:1–20	314	6:43	139
4:1–9	203, 207	6:45–52	253
4:3	156	6:47–52	139
4:9	156	6:48	210
4:10–12	140	6:50	186
4:10–11	156	6:56	304
4:11–12	204, 206	7	193, 196, 199, 210, 250, 254, 287, 288
4:11	156		
4:12	133–135, 156, 203, 205, 208, 249, 254, 290, 349	7:1–30	304
		7:1–23	205, 250, 258, 261
4:12a	203	7:1–13	191, 192, 206
4:13–20	203	7:1–5	192, 205
4:14	156	7:1	204
4:24	232	7:2 ff.	192
4:26	156	7:5	191

7:6–13	206	9:11	135, 156, 211
7:6–8	205, 206	9:12 ff.	188, 212, 249
7:6–7	133–135, 204–206	9:12–13	135, 181, 305
7:6	249	9:12	134, 136, 147, 190, 210
7:8	191, 195, 205	9:13	134, 136, 182, 187
7:9–13	191, 204–206	9:14–13:37	131, 135, 137, 138
7:9	194, 195, 205	9:14–29	305
7:10 ff.	188	9:18	302
7:10	191, 249	9:30–37	140
7:11	191	9:31	6, 92, 120
7:13	194	9:33–34	134
7:14–16	192	9:34 ff.	54
7:14	206	9:37	150
7:15	192, 206, 251	9:38–40	197
7:17–23	192, 206, 251, 252, 289	9:41	131
7:19	192, 193, 199, 263, 289	9:43	206
7:21 ff.	192	9:45	206
7:31–37	304	9:48	133, 135, 206, 210
7:37	133, 135, 210, 211	10	192, 251, 254, 289
8	109	10:1	303
8:1–10	139, 253, 304	10:2 ff.	199
8:14–21	139	10:3	188
8:15	232	10:4	133, 135
8:18	249	10:5	195
8:22–9:13	131, 135, 137, 138	10:6–8	249, 251
8:22–26	61, 140, 304	10:6–7	133, 135
8:25	298	10:9	193, 289
8:27–9:1	189	10:10–12	199, 252
8:27–30	140, 149	10:11–12	193, 289
8:27	137	10:17–22	193, 253, 258
8:28	151, 182	10:19–20	133, 135
8:29	130, 131, 145, 179	10:19	188, 195, 249
8:31–38	6, 152	10:26	304
8:31–33	149	10:32–45	140
8:31	92, 94, 134, 179	10:32–40	74
8:33	305, 327	10:32	134
8:34–38	140, 181, 305	10:33 ff.	92
8:34	74	10:33	6, 120
8:35	223, 304	10:34	210, 211, 213
8:38	92, 96, 99, 108–111, 134, 140, 179, 180, 189	10:37	189
		10:38–39	305
9	181, 189, 212	10:38	138, 211, 213, 282
9:1–13	281	10:40	55
9:1	57, 111, 179–181, 231	10:43–45	152
9:2–13	187, 197	10:45	54, 55, 92, 120, 125, 150, 154, 210, 213, 214, 271, 304, 305
9:2–8	253		
9:2	140		
9:7–9	332	10:46–52	304
9:7	137, 138, 147, 151, 179, 189, 195, 211, 282, 322, 331	10:52	134, 304
		11–16	190
		11–12	209
9:9	133, 179	11	77, 208, 219, 220, 229, 235–237, 243, 247
9:11–12	137		

11:1–10	236	12:38	232
11:1	198	12:40	198, 210, 211
11:2	198	12:41–43	209
11:3	207	12:41	208
11:9–10	133, 135	13	97, 99, 198, 209, 210, 216–220, 224, 233, 238, 242, 265
11:11	140, 207, 235		
11:12–19	304		
11:12–14	140, 207, 305	13:1–2	221
11:15–19	140, 207	13:1	208
11:17	133, 135, 206, 210, 236–238, 249, 254	13:2	238, 244, 664
		13:4	221
11:18	235, 236	13:5–8	221, 223
11:20–24	207	13:5	223, 230
11:20–21	305	13:6–9	228
11:20	140, 235	13:6–8	222
11:23	235	13:6	221, 226, 233
11:27–33	136, 137, 140, 208, 236, 281, 304	13:7	221, 224
		13:8	210, 211, 221
11:27	208, 236	13:9–13	223, 238, 267
11:28	150, 302, 323	13:9	223, 224, 230
12	193, 207, 219, 220, 236, 237	13:10	142, 223–225, 314
		13:11–13	224
12:1–12	208, 245	13:11	198, 223, 305, 309, 322
12:1	133, 135, 210	13:12	223
12:3	238	13:13	304
12:6	138, 140, 195, 282	13:14 ff.	238
12:7	198	13:14–20	225
12:8	220, 237	13:14	220, 226, 230, 233
12:9	236, 271	13:14b	267
12:10–11	133, 135, 237, 249, 254	13:15–20	228
12:10	210, 237	13:19	198
12:12	208, 237	13:20	304
12:14	151	13:21	131, 141
12:17	237	13:21–31	208
12:18 ff.	193	13:21–23	226
12:18–27	252	13:22	198, 233
12:19	133, 151	13:23	227, 230
12:20	135	13:24 ff.	229, 230
12:26	133, 135, 188, 249	13:24–27	227, 229
12:28–34	194, 198, 209, 252	13:24–25	133, 135, 209, 249, 254
12:28–31	479	13:26–27	152, 209
12:28	195	13:26	97, 109–113, 140, 141, 189
12:29 ff.	188		
12:29–30	249	13:27	238
12:31	195, 249	13:28–31	230
12:32	133, 135, 210	13:28	209
12:33	238	13:30 ff.	229
12:35–37	140, 208, 249, 250, 331	13:31	133, 135, 210, 211
12:35	131, 281	13:32	138, 141, 229
12:36	133, 135, 254, 322	13:33 ff.	231
12:36b	105	13:33	230
12:38–44	238	13:34–37	97
12:38–40	245, 252	13:35–37	112

13:35	112, 230	15:38	141, 209, 220, 239
14	220, 238, 242, 243	15:39	137, 138, 156, 157, 282,
14:1–15:47	131, 137, 138		302, 331, 332
14:1–2	136	15:42–47	136
14:1	179, 219	15:42	198
14:3–9	141	16:1–8	129, 141
14:7	198	16:6	136
14:10–11	136	16:8	130, 141, 186
14:12–16	249		
14:18	213	Luke	
14:21	92, 134, 135, 190, 213, 249	1–2	57, 156, 279, 281, 285–287, 294, 295, 297, 333
14:24	55, 125, 198, 210, 213, 253, 305	1	281
		1:1–4	59, 60, 280, 283, 333, 334
14:26–31	74	1:15	286
14:27	134, 135, 213, 249, 254	1:32	281
14:33–39	6	1:35	281
14:33	139	1:39	15
14:35–36	150	1:69	281
14:36	147, 151, 211, 213	2	282, 289
14:49	134, 135, 150, 210, 212, 236, 249, 664	2:4	281
		2:9	345
14:50	305	2:11	145, 281
14:55–59	198	2:13	345
14:58	209, 220, 238, 244, 449, 450, 664, 665	2:22–24	260
		2:22	282, 288
14:61–63	147	2:23	282, 288
14:61–62	149	2:24	282, 288
14:61	131, 137, 138, 157, 179, 189, 210, 213	2:26	145, 281
		2:27	282, 288
14:62	97, 98, 99, 109, 110, 111, 130, 137, 140, 213, 238	2:29–32	271
		2:30–32	144
14:65	211, 213	2:32	282, 287
14:66–72	305	2:35	282
15	125, 131, 137, 220	2:39	282, 288
15:1–15	136	2:41	260
15:2	130	2:52	280
15:5	213	3–4	281
15:9	130, 157	3:1–4:13	280
15:12	130	3	281
15:16–20	130	3:2–3	202
15:18	157	3:3	298, 307, 308
15:19	213	3:4–6	132, 290
15:24	249	3:4	200
15:26	131, 157	3:6	287
15:27	210, 213	3:7–14	202
15:28	117, 213, 292	3:9	306, 307
15:29	209, 220, 239	3:10–15	313
15:30–31	157, 304	3:10–14	308, 309
15:32	130, 131, 158	3:16	307, 308, 311, 313
15:34	133, 213, 249, 410	3:17	306, 307
15:34–35	135	3:18	313
15:35–36	136, 137		

3:22	290	7:20	298
4–11	314	7:21	291
4	291, 292	7:22	157
4:1–13	288	7:27	132, 200
4:1	282, 290	7:28	308
4:4	260	7:31–35	309
4:8	260	7:33	298
4:12	260	7:34	92
4:13	280	7:36–50	309
4:14–15	290	7:39	261, 293, 309
4:14	282, 290, 308	7:41–43	309
4:16–7:23	297	8:10	203, 290, 349
4:16–30	287, 290	8:26–39	287
4:16–21	150, 157	9	109
4:16–19	260	9:1 ff.	265
4:16	260	9:1	309
4:18–19	209	9:2	266
4:18	150, 151, 157, 282	9:8	151, 261, 293
4:19	309	9:19	261, 293, 298
4:21	308	9:22	293, 517
4:23	292	9:26	109
4:24	151, 261, 292, 293	9:27	111
4:25–27	261	9:28–36	295
4:31–7:23	260	9:31 ff.	345
4:33–37	308	9:31	125, 183, 260, 295, 296
4:38–41	308	9:32	183
4:43–44	308	9:35	261, 296
5:1–11	308	9:44	206, 293
5:10	582	9:46–48	54
5:12–16	308	9:46	206
5:17–26	308	9:48	206
5:27–28	308	9:51–18:30	297
5:32	150	9:51–62	297
5:36	262	9:51	261, 295, 296
5:37–38	262	9:57–62	261
5:37	11	9:58	92
5:39	262	9:59–62	261
6:5	308	10:1–18:30	296
6:6–11	308, 486	10:1 ff.	265
6:9	288	10:1	287, 295
6:17–49	157, 262	10:3–16	266
6:20–49	308, 314	10:3	266
6:20–21	290	10:4 ff.	266
6:20	157	10:16	296
6:40	267	10:17–24	261
7:1–10	287	10:21–22	151
7:11–17	261, 296, 308	10:22	169
7:16	261, 293	10:24	296
7:18 ff.	291	10:25–28	194, 288, 296, 479
7:18–23	260, 291	10:29 ff.	288
7:18–20	308	10:30–37	287
7:19	157	10:39	296
7:20–21	291	10:42	296

11:13	309	18:18–21	296
11:15–23	309	18:31 ff.	293, 294
11:20	309	18:31	261
11:28	296	18:35	297
11:29–32	296	19:1–10	55
11:30	96, 112	19:10	150
11:37–41	206	19:12–27	229
12	96	19:41–44	241
12:8 ff.	96, 109	20:16	287
12:8	92, 96, 112	20:17	210
12:10	92	21	113, 265
12:11–20	309	21:27	109, 113
12:13	151	21:34–36	97
12:36–40	229	21:36	96, 113
12:39 ff.	112	22	125
12:40	96, 112	22:19–20	296
13	241	22:17 ff.	55
13:1–9	241	22:24–30	125
13:1–5	241	22:27	54
13:6–9	241	22:28–30	296
13:10–17	288	22:37	117, 118, 261, 292–294
13:16	291	22:48	92, 96
13:22–30	241	22:69	110
13:28–30	287	22:70–71	147
13:31–33	241	23:31	241
13:33	151, 261, 293	23:35	292
13:34–35	241	23:45	242
14	240	23:47	260
14:1–6	486	24	295, 297
14:3	288	24:1–12	293
14:15–24	287	24:7	96, 293
14:35	296	24:13–27	294
16:16–18	261	24:19	151, 261, 293
16:16	261, 262, 289	24:25	294
16:17	261	24:26	183, 345
16:18	261, 289	24:27	188, 261, 285, 294
16:29–31	261, 296	24:36–49	294
16:29	188	24:44–45	261
16:31	188	24:44	294
17	112	24:46	314
17:11–19	287	24:47	287, 294
17:20–30	231	24:49	307, 314
17:21	226		
17:22–37	308	*John*	
17:22	96, 112	1	23, 325, 333, 335, 337–339, 353, 491, 492
17:23	226		
17:24	96, 112	1:1–34	334
17:25	96, 293	1:1–18	156, 159, 263, 264, 280, 281, 321, 330, 398, 491, 510
17:26	96, 112		
17:30	96, 112		
18:8	96, 112	1:1–5	319
18:14	295	1:1	165, 167, 332, 336
18:18–27	288	1:3	319

1:5	319, 320	1:49	325
1:6–9	310	1:51	114, 263
1:6–8	281, 316–319, 325	2	243
1:7–8	318	2:1–11	157
1:9–13	319	2:11	322, 345
1:9	318	2:13–22	157
1:10	319	2:13	157
1:11–13	328	2:14–15	664
1:11	335	2:17	243, 263
1:12 ff.	330, 338	2:18	347
1:12–14	5	2:19–22	449
1:12	168, 492	2:19	654
1:14–18	189, 320, 334, 335	2:21	654, 667
1:14	5, 23, 161, 165, 264, 281, 318, 319, 335, 337, 345	2:22	347
		3	169
		3:1–21	157
1:15	189, 281, 310, 311, 316–319, 325, 337	3:1–13	325
		3:5	312
1:16–18	319	3:13–15	5
1:16	335–337, 397	3:13	114
1:17–18	158, 264	3:14 ff.	113, 349
1:17	257, 281, 335, 336, 476	3:14–21	325
1:18	145, 167, 168, 257, 279–281, 335, 336	3:14	114
		3:15	326
1:18b	336	3:16–21	314
1:19 ff.	317	3:16–19	312
1:19–51	280, 281	3:16	5, 147, 151, 158
1:19–36	322	3:17	146
1:19–28	318, 325	3:19–21	264, 326
1:19	280, 310, 311, 323, 330	3:19	322
1:20 ff.	331	3:22–24	312
1:20	318	3:22	311
1:21	189	3:25–30	322
1:23	201, 263, 310	3:26	311, 320
1:24–27	311	3:33	320, 326
1:24	310	3:36	326
1:25	331	4	243
1:26	311	4:1–30	312
1:27	311	4:1–26	157
1:29–36	325	4:1–15	264
1:29–34	318	4:1–2	311
1:29–30	311	4:14	312
1:29	264	4:19	151
1:30	311, 317, 318	4:21	347
1:31	311, 320	4:23	264, 347
1:32–34	311, 332	4:25–26	149
1:32	320	4:26	325
1:33	311	4:29	331
1:34	320	4:34	350
1:35–37	311	4:46–5:47	347
1:36	264	4:46–54	157
1:41	145, 325	4:54	347
1:45	188	5:1	157

5:2–9	157	6:60	327
5:16–47	166	6:62	114, 327
5:17 ff.	325, 326	6:63	312, 477
5:17	325	6:68–69	477
5:19 ff.	347	6:68	328
5:19–47	157	7:14–52	166
5:19	167	7:16	167
5:20–23	149	7:18	348
5:24–26	326	7:19–24	264
5:24	458	7:21–24	348
5:25	347	7:22 ff.	322
5:26	322	7:25–30	326
5:27	114	7:31	331
5:28 ff.	347	7:37–39	312
5:28	458	7:38–39	264
5:30	143, 158	7:38	243, 263, 312
5:36–47	348	7:39	312
5:36	350	7:40	151
5:37 ff.	21, 326, 329, 338	7:41 ff.	326
5:37–47	326, 328	7:41–42	281
5:37–40	476	7:41	331
5:37	322, 335	8	326
5:39–47	166, 264, 398	8:12 ff.	326
5:45–46	476	8:12–59	157, 166
5:46 ff.	328	8:12	322, 336
5:46	346	8:14 ff.	326
6	5, 348	8:23–30	326
6:1–14	157, 476	8:23	167
6:4	157	8:28	113, 325, 349
6:5–59	264	8:31	326, 328
6:14	151, 476	8:32	322
6:16–21	157	8:37	326, 328
6:25–59	157	8:38	322
6:27	114	8:39 ff.	326
6:28	477	8:39–59	398
6:29	477	8:42 ff.	328
6:32–35	476	8:42–47	326
6:32	139	8:44–46	326
6:35	336	8:46–47	143
6:37–40	477	8:47	327
6:40	458	8:51–55	327
6:41 ff.	326	8:53	330
6:41–65	166	8:58 ff.	326
6:42	330	8:58	167, 264, 311, 327
6:44–47	477	9	329, 349
6:45–46	477	9:1–12	157
6:45	263	9:5	322, 326
6:46	335	9:13–41	157
6:48–51	476, 477	9:28–29	166, 329
6:51 ff.	326	9:29	326
6:51–58	327	9:33	167
6:53	114	9:35–41	166
6:58	476	9:37	325

9:39	326	14:6	336
10	168	14:7 ff.	322
10:1–39	157	14:9	345
10:7	336	14:16–17	312
10:9	336	14:23 ff.	327
10:10	150	14:26	312
10:11	336	14:28	167
10:14	336	15	169
10:19–39	166	15:1–11	154
10:22–38	157	15:1	336
10:22	157	15:5	336
10:24 ff.	325	15:20	155
10:30–39	326	15:25	188, 263
10:30	167, 168	15:26	312
10:34–36	327	16:3	322
10:34	168, 188, 263	16:7–11	312
10:37–38	143, 167	16:7	312
11:1–53	157	16:13–15	312
11:4	322, 348	16:13	312
11:15	348	17	5, 336, 350, 458
11:24–25	149	17:1–5	147
11:25 ff.	348	17:1–4	322
11:25	264, 322, 336, 458	17:4	350
11:28	151	17:5	311, 337
11:40	348	17:6	327
11:48	348	17:8	327
11:55	157	17:12	263
12	125, 329	17:14	322, 327
12:13	263	17:17	322, 327
12:15	263	18:20 ff.	325
12:23 ff.	349	18:28	125, 264
12:23–33	157	18:34 ff.	326
12:23–28	158	18:36	326
12:23	113, 350	18:37–38	326
12:27	147	19:6 ff.	326
12:27–28	150	19:9	326
12:28	144	19:24	263
12:34	113, 188	19:28	263
12:35 ff.	322	19:30	147, 312, 350
12:37–43	348	19:33	125
12:38	117, 263	19:34	264
12:40	204, 263	19:36	263, 264
12:41	24	19:37	263
12:44–50	327	20:9	263
12:46	322	20:21–23	312, 314
13	219	20:22	312
13:16	155	20:23	312
13:18	263	20:28	158, 167, 168
13:31 ff.	113, 350	20:31	145, 149
13:31–32	158	21:19	350
14–17	330		
14–16	312	Acts	
14:2	449	1	296

1:5	307	15:8–9	307
1:6	308	16:19–24	616
1:8	309, 314	16:37	460
1:9–10	296	17	528, 674
2	305, 313	17:31	528, 674
2:1–4	307	18:8–21	463
2:2	307	18:18	464
2:16–21	314	18:21	464
2:22	309	18:22	464
2:29–36	517	19	462, 467
2:32	144	19:8–12	463
2:36	144, 145, 155	19:8	463
2:38	307	19:10	463
2:43	309	19:17	463
3:13	144	19:21	462, 463
3:14	426	19:23–41	464
3:15	144	19:26	463
3:18–21	144	19:27	465
3:22	296	19:28–41	462
3:26	144	19:35	464
4:11	237	20	219
5:42	145	20:1	462
6:1	527	20:16	463, 498
6:13 ff.	242	20:29	461
6:14	262	22	460
7	25, 242	22:3	70
7:52	426	22:14	426
7:56	95, 152	22:15	148, 361
8	125, 292	22:25–29	460
8:4–25	526	26:16–18	148
8:25–40	526	26:17 ff.	361
8:32 ff.	117	28:20	263
9	361	28:23	188
9:15	148, 361	28:26–27	204, 290
10	363, 526	28:28	290
10:34–48	399		
10:39	399	Romans	
10:43–44	307	1–8	379, 388, 483, 568
10:44	399	1–4	442
11	69	1–3	559, 570
11:1–18	399, 527	1	1, 381, 542
11:13–18	307	1:1–4	144, 424
11:15–17	363	1:1–3	147
11:16	307	1:1	583, 627
11:19	526	1:2–4	428
11:20	526	1:2–3	511
11:25	526	1:2	200, 425, 469, 472, 485
13:38	674	1:3 ff.	126, 332, 526
13:39	674	1:3–4	378, 379, 381, 388, 430
13:46	287	1:3	146, 151, 154
14	528	1:4	154, 351, 541, 543, 555, 575, 577
14:15	528		
15	69	1:5–7	431

1:5–6	541, 598	3:21–26	412, 426–428, 431, 559
1:5	148, 390, 485, 669	3:21–22	386
1:6	424	3:21	366, 388, 428, 475, 478, 483, 487, 552, 559, 570
1:7	424, 534, 537, 541		
1:9	147, 424, 583, 611	3:22	388, 418, 429, 483, 559, 569
1:13	669		
1:16–5:11	571	3:23–26	574
1:16–17	413, 424, 568	3:23	154, 354, 477, 558
1:16	287, 584	3:24	429, 559, 570
1:17–18	570	3:25–26	388
1:17	388, 412, 428, 483, 568, 598, 615	3:25	70, 388, 512, 559, 569
		3:26	569
1:17a	425, 426, 612, 615	3:27–31	560
1:17b	426	3:27	386, 388, 483, 569
1:18–32	155	3:28	386, 483, 569
1:18	568	3:30	569
1:23	154, 354, 477, 494	3:31	17, 19, 20, 359, 384, 430, 569
1:24	544		
1:28	544	4	155, 386, 391, 562, 570
1:29	620	4:3	428
1:32	566	4:17	563, 569
2	477	4:22–24	563, 570
2:1–16	434	4:22–23	569
2:5–16	570	4:22	562, 570
2:5	442	4:24–25	428
2:8	620	4:24	562, 563, 569
2:12–16	477	4:25	118, 125–127, 425, 431, 442, 525, 552–554, 557, 561–563, 567–574, 577, 578, 605
2:13	477, 570		
2:14–15	477		
2:14	478		
2:16	442, 478	5–8	442
2:17–3:20	390	5–6	427
2:17–24	478	5	126, 154, 354, 377, 380, 429, 561, 567, 572
2:25–29	477		
2:25–27	477	5:1	442, 574
2:26	566	5:2	574
2:27	478	5:6–11	428
2:29	477, 479	5:6	376
3	512, 558	5:8–11	378
3:2–3	384	5:8–10	570, 571, 574
3:2	428	5:8–9	377
3:3–7	612	5:8	144, 354, 376
3:4	523	5:9–10	442, 570, 577
3:5	388, 412	5:9 ff.	524
3:10	426, 428	5:9	376, 429, 570
3:19–4:6	386, 483	5:10–11	377, 561
3:19–22	386, 387, 482, 483	5:10	147, 376, 409, 429, 430, 598
3:19	188, 469		
3:20	386, 570	5:11	409
3:21–8:39	669	5:12–21	126, 154, 155, 371, 376, 379, 382, 428–431, 563, 567, 568, 571, 576, 577
3:21 ff.	390		
3:21–31	155, 569, 570		
3:21–28	569	5:12–19	448

5:12–18	377	6:15	542
5:12–17	563	6:16–19	572
5:12	564–567	6:16	426
5:13–14	566, 572	6:18 ff.	542
5:14	397	6:18	544
5:15–21	567, 568	6:19	542, 543
5:15–19	564, 567	6:20–23	542, 572
5:15–17	154, 376, 429, 561, 566	6:22	544
5:15–16	143	7	155, 385, 390, 479, 483, 572
5:15	127, 428, 565, 566, 571		
5:15a	564, 565	7:1–6	20, 572
5:16	127, 428, 565, 566, 577	7:4	572
5:16a	565	7:6	479, 572
5:17–18	565	7:7–23	572
5:17	127, 425, 428, 565, 566, 571	7:11	367, 368
		7:12	19, 25, 359, 385, 479, 483
5:18–19	376		
5:18	127, 425, 563, 565–567, 570, 577	7:14	385, 479, 483
		7:22	385, 448, 483
5:18a	563	7:23	385, 483
5:19	127, 158, 426, 427, 510, 511, 558, 565–567	7:24–25	572
		7:24	525, 573
5:20–21	154	7:25	385, 483
5:20	127, 567, 572	8	126, 373, 374, 375, 378, 381, 429, 543, 555, 556, 572, 574, 598
5:20a	566		
5:21	127, 425, 426, 443, 564, 567, 571		
		8:1–4	511
6–8	571	8:1	127, 428, 479, 572
6–7	410	8:2	385, 390, 483
6	126, 127, 305, 442, 542, 551, 575	8:3 ff.	126, 443
		8:3–4	379, 381, 430, 479, 485, 585
6:1–11	618		
6:1	543, 571	8:3	19, 146, 147, 154, 159, 162, 373, 374, 378, 385, 428, 483, 487, 511, 553, 555, 557, 558, 561, 568, 573, 577, 598, 677
6:2–4	571		
6:2	571		
6:3–5	443		
6:3	127, 153, 577		
6:4	127, 351, 443, 511, 657, 659	8:4	430, 555, 566, 573
		8:5	573
6:5–11	127	8:10	573
6:5	153, 154, 443, 507, 511, 571	8:11	434, 443, 561, 573
		8:14–21	374
6:6–7	127	8:14–20	126
6:6	573	8:14–17	373, 430, 511, 543, 577
6:7	570	8:14–16	573
6:8	443, 572	8:14–15	147
6:10–14	426	8:14	378
6:10	511	8:15 ff.	443
6:11	443, 657	8:15	32, 45, 555
6:12–14	127	8:17–25	574
6:13	415, 542	8:17	74, 444
6:15 ff.	542	8:18–39	155
6:15–23	558	8:18–30	371

8:18	354, 434	10:4	20, 21, 384, 385, 390, 392, 393, 412, 473, 481, 483, 484, 485, 511
8:19–25	154		
8:19–21	434		
8:19	154, 378, 414, 443, 444, 523	10:5	389, 399, 484, 573
		10:6–10	389, 484
8:21	354, 430	10:6	569
8:23	443, 523, 573	10:8–9	569
8:24 ff.	434	10:8	159
8:24	443, 444	10:9	145, 158, 365, 386, 481
8:25	523	10:11–17	386
8:27	534	10:11	386, 481
8:28–30	382, 543	10:12–13	386, 481
8:29 ff.	354	10:13	145
8:29–30	511	10:16	117, 329
8:29	147, 154, 373, 374, 378, 397, 430, 431, 443, 557, 574, 598	11	155
		11:7–10	405
		11:9	405
8:30	154, 374, 444, 447, 574, 657	11:11	367
		11:13	669
8:31–34	570	11:15	409
8:32	147, 378, 430, 525, 561, 598	11:16	543, 545
		11:17	581
8:34	146, 390, 510, 512, 524	11:25 ff.	225, 598
8:38 ff.	451, 457	11:25–36	155
8:39	371	11:26	525
9–11	204, 271, 369, 384, 480, 543, 669	11:33	598
		11:36	395
9–10	391	12–15	543
9	385, 386	12	666
9:1–5	153, 155, 387, 482	12:1	480, 512, 543, 666
9:3	594, 682	12:2	180, 480
9:4–5	271, 391	12:3–8	639, 666
9:5	146, 598	12:4–5	153
9:6	384, 388, 483	12:6	666
9:23	384, 480	12:9–13	634
9:24	548	12:11	523
9:30–10:10	480	12:13	534
9:30–33	387, 482, 483	12:19–20	570
9:30–32	385, 480	13:8–10	480
9:30–31	387, 388, 482	13:8	479, 651
9:30	385, 388, 389, 411, 478, 481–483	13:9	367
		13:11 ff.	434, 442
9:31	390	13:11	523, 570
9:31a	386	13:12–13	620
9:32	385, 389, 481, 484	13:13	630
9:33	386, 387, 388, 396, 405, 482, 661	14–15	591
		14:1–3	590
10	20, 125	14:9	614
10:1	388, 483, 621	14:10–12	570
10:2	388	14:15	591
10:3 ff.	339	14:21	591
10:3	388, 389, 411, 412, 483, 484	14:23	69
		15–16	69

15	125, 591	2:1	448
15:1	591	2:2–5	351
15:1–3	589, 639, 643	2:2	568
15:3	614	2:6–8	351
15:4	469	2:7	339
15:7–8	639	3	660
15:7	589	3:1–4	408, 655
15:8	270	3:1	623
15:16	542, 584	3:2	501
15:18	390, 424, 485	3:3	620, 630
15:21	117	3:5–4:21	655
15:25	536	3:5–9	618
15:26	536	3:5	523, 655
15:31	536	3:9	583
15:33	69	3:10–17	639
16	69	3:10–11	660
16:2	534	3:11–17	153
16:15	534	3:11	661
16:20	69	3:16 ff.	449, 546
16:24	69	3:16–17	244, 618, 660, 666
16:25 ff.	339	3:16	450, 493, 655, 658, 659, 666
16:25	389, 484		
16:26	148, 390, 424, 485, 669	3:17	655
16:27	69	3:18–23	655, 661
		3:18–20	655
1 Corinthians		4:5	493
1–4	655	4:8–21	622
1–3	618	4:8–13	623
1–2	655	4:14	623
1	395, 396, 621	4:15	407, 584
1:2	534, 544, 546, 599	4:16	409, 588, 618
1:4–9	599	5–6	568
1:7	523	5	544
1:8	611	5:6	657
1:9	611	5:7	568, 606, 639
1:10	437	5:13	367
1:11	620	6	545, 660
1:17	584, 618	6:1	534
1:18–25	351, 448	6:2	534, 657
1:23 ff.	584	6:9 ff.	545
1:23–25	413, 568	6:11	314, 545, 546, 657, 658
1:23	396, 405, 549, 584, 661	6:12–20	655
1:24	382, 395, 396, 411, 493, 496, 584	6:12–13	656
		6:13	657
1:25	555	6:14	575, 656, 657, 659
1:29	411	6:15–19	647
1:30	339, 382, 389, 395, 396, 411–414, 426, 483, 493, 496, 537, 545, 554, 661, 678	6:15	656–660, 665
		6:16–17	656
		6:16	658, 666
		6:18	545, 656
1:31	411	6:19	244, 449, 545, 546, 655–660, 666
2–4	568		
2	339	6:20	558, 656

7:11	409	12:8	666
7:12–16	640	12:9	666
7:14	545	12:11	666
7:17–24	646	12:12–31	666
7:23	558, 639	12:12–27	153
7:25–40	646	12:13	636, 666, 667
8–10	591	12:17	659
8	396, 579, 591	12:27–14:40	666
8:5	145	12:27	658
8:6	146, 163, 382, 395, 396, 492, 510	13	607, 621
		14:21	188
8:11–12	614	14:25	525
8:13	591	14:33	534
9	582, 586, 590, 591	14:34–36	646
9:1	583	15	375, 377, 379, 432–434, 435, 439, 444, 448, 449, 451, 457, 459, 527, 568, 605, 656
9:12	582, 583		
9:14	583		
9:15–18	582		
9:18	583	15:1 ff.	584
9:19 ff.	580	15:2	523
9:19–23	581, 618	15:3 ff.	521, 525, 604, 605
9:22	579, 580, 582, 591	15:3	514, 552, 576
9:22b	581, 584	15:11	523
9:23	581–583	15:12–19	440
9:23b	582	15:12–13	575
9:24–27	582	15:13	604
9:25–27	461	15:17	442, 568, 576, 605
9:27	582	15:20–28	155
10	396, 579	15:20–27a	154
10:1–5	314, 395, 492	15:20–23	433, 440
10:4	394, 396	15:20–22	442, 576, 605
10:13	611	15:20	435, 543
10:14	545	15:21–22	371, 376, 378
10:16–18	606	15:21	448, 575, 659
10:18	584	15:22	440, 575, 659
10:20	584	15:23	378, 433, 543
10:33	591	15:24–28	147, 376, 381
11	376, 383	15:24	378
11:1	407, 409, 588, 591	15:25	146, 510
11:2–16	646	15:26	451
11:3	375, 381, 643	15:27–28	380
11:7	375	15:27	154
11:8	644	15:28	378
11:10	376	15:30–33	440
11:13–34	606	15:30–32	433
11:25	400	15:30	460
11:29	314	15:31	460
12	658, 660	15:32	460–464, 637
12:3	145	15:35–58	440
12:4–31	639	15:35–57	371, 605
12:4–11	666	15:35–49	380
12:4	666	15:36	457
12:7	666	15:37	440, 452

15:42–54	441	1:19	610, 612, 613
15:42–50	371	1:20	612, 613
15:42–49	154, 382, 440, 442, 448, 576	1:21–22	613
		1:21	610, 613
15:42	575	1:22	573, 665
15:43	351, 604	1:23–24	614
15:44	659, 665	1:23	610, 611
15:45–49	440	1:24	614, 615
15:45	376	1:30	606
15:46	397	2:1	615
15:47–49	376	2:12	583
15:47	376, 380	2:14–17	70
15:49	377, 397, 433, 449, 659, 665	2:15 ff.	584
		2:16	70
15:50	440	3–4	339, 475, 476, 477, 492
15:51–57	451	3	22, 23, 70, 188, 338, 364, 375, 381, 382, 391, 407, 478, 662
15:51–55	456		
15:51	433, 434, 440		
15:52 ff.	445	3:1–6:13	614
15:52	432, 433, 440	3:1–4:6	338, 382, 470, 476, 614
15:53 ff.	432, 441, 450, 451, 456	3:1–6	145
15:53–54	440, 452, 663, 665	3:1–3	474, 495
15:54	451, 453, 457	3:1–2	471
15:56	442	3:1	446
16:1	536	3:2	414, 662
16:8	460, 461, 498, 637	3:3	407, 471
16:9	463, 467	3:4–18	662
16:15	534	3:4–14	511
16:22	145	3:4–11	447
		3:4–5	471
2 Corinthians		3:6–11	516
1–2	446	3:6	392, 400, 471, 472, 473, 575
1:1–7	558		
1:1–2	423	3:7–18	353, 382, 511
1:1	534, 537, 661	3:7	392, 472, 473
1:3–7	353, 407, 614, 617	3:8–9	392
1:5	74, 614	3:8	472
1:6	606	3:9	392, 472
1:7	409, 614	3:10	392, 472
1:8 ff.	433	3:11	392, 472, 473
1:8–11	614	3:12–4:6	371
1:8–10	462	3:12–18	392, 393, 447, 472
1:11	409	3:12	472
1:12	546	3:13	392, 446, 473
1:15–3:1	662	3:14	472–474
1:15–22	423	3:15	473
1:15–16	610	3:16	393, 473, 523
1:17–24	614, 615	3:17–18	666
1:17–22	610, 615	3:17	393
1:17	610	3:18	154, 180, 338, 374, 393, 394, 397, 407, 444, 449, 453, 454, 474, 492, 574, 618, 624, 659
1:17b	612		
1:18–22	611		
1:18	610, 612		

4	354, 398, 623	5:6–9	433
4:1–6	189, 447	5:6–8	451, 454
4:1	392, 474	5:6	454, 456
4:2 ff.	393	5:8 ff.	437
4:2	474	5:8	445, 456, 457, 663
4:3	474	5:9	435, 454, 457
4:4–6	353	5:10	407, 452, 454
4:4	22, 338, 374, 382, 394, 397, 423, 446, 447, 474, 492, 510	5:11–13	662
		5:11	407, 454
		5:12	454
4:5	394, 454, 618	5:13	407
4:5–6	474	5:14–21	415
4:6 ff.	189	5:14–15	401, 408, 412, 551, 557, 602, 657
4:6	22, 338, 375, 382, 394, 474, 475, 492, 662		
		5:14	407, 454, 575, 603
4:7–18	450, 456, 665	5:15	441, 454, 455, 575, 662
4:7–15	665	5:16–21	614
4:7	447, 449, 663	5:16	408, 588
4:8 ff.	447	5:17	154, 408, 447, 455, 552, 603, 608, 662
4:8–12	407		
4:10 ff.	447	5:18 ff.	413
4:10–12	447	5:18–20	409, 561
4:10–11	592	5:18–19	401, 412
4:10	453, 547, 584, 664, 665, 667	5:18	408, 409
		5:18a	409
4:11–12	407	5:18b	409
4:11	663, 665	5:19	143, 408, 409, 429
4:12	412, 447, 662, 667	5:19b	409
4:13 ff.	448	5:20	413, 612
4:13–15	447	5:20a	409
4:14	438, 451, 454, 456, 575, 656, 657, 663, 666	5:21	6, 126, 154, 162, 165, 374, 401, 403, 406, 410, 412, 413, 426, 455, 507, 554, 557, 558, 575, 577, 585, 608, 661, 675, 677, 679
4:15	407, 448, 662		
4:16–18	456		
4:16	448, 453		
4:17 ff.	449		
4:17	456	5:21b	415
5	374, 401, 406, 433–435, 453, 457, 459, 554, 575, 609	6:1–10	661
		6:1	413
		6:2	413, 606
5:1–10	433, 436, 446, 456, 663, 665	6:3	413
		6:4–7:1	537
5:1–5	433, 451, 456	6:4 ff.	455
5:1	446, 449, 450, 453, 663, 664, 666	6:6 ff.	455
		6:6	154
5:2–5	450, 665	6:7	413
5:2–4	451	6:8–10	455
5:2	450, 451, 453	6:9	413
5:3	451–453, 553	6:10	413, 592
5:4	450, 451, 453, 456, 665	6:11	607
5:5 ff.	454	6:14–7:4	607
5:5	454, 457, 573, 575	6:14–7:1	244, 414, 455, 547, 661–663
5:6–10	445		

6:14–18	607	1:20	611
6:14	663	2–3	428
6:16–18	661, 663	2	69, 551
6:16	414, 450, 639, 666	2:1 ff.	527
7:1	414, 547, 661	2:2	669
7:2–8:24	662	2:7–9	669
8–9	414	2:7	361, 583
8	589, 609	2:15	401
8:4	414, 536	2:16	148, 367, 421, 431, 523
8:8–9	639	2:19 ff.	441
8:9	154, 161, 162, 165, 373, 374, 407, 413, 415, 455, 556, 557, 568, 585, 589, 592, 608, 614, 643	2:19–21 2:19–20 2:19 2:20	551, 557, 601 403, 555, 602, 657, 680 455, 457, 575 147, 153, 402, 420, 425, 431, 445, 512, 552, 575, 584, 603, 618
8:23	583, 584		
9:1	536	2:21–3:5	515
9:8–10	415	3–4	609
9:10–15	407	3	366, 374, 410, 555
9:12	536	3:1–4:11	422, 423
10–13	624	3:1 ff.	584
10	589	3:1–5	399, 402, 442, 471
10:14	583	3:1	560, 605
11:2	647	3:2	390
11:4	623	3:3	391
11:11	611	3:6–18	431
11:23–29	433	3:6–9	402
11:23–27	461, 467	3:6	403
11:31	144, 611	3:7	403
12:8–9	617	3:8	405
12:10	593	3:10–14	391
12:20	618, 620	3:10	390, 402, 404
13:3–4	407, 413	3:11–12	391
13:3	612	3:12	391, 399, 573
13:12	534	3:13 ff.	126, 406
		3:13–14	555, 557
Galatians		3:13	162, 374, 401, 403, 411, 554, 558, 575, 577, 585, 605, 674, 676, 677, 679
1	361		
1:1–5	529		
1:1	403, 474, 575, 600		
1:3–4	600	3:14	165, 577
1:4	441, 512, 514, 525, 553, 575, 601	3:15–29 3:15–20	400 391
1:5	600	3:16	153
1:6–9	584	3:19	390, 394, 474, 511
1:6–7	617	3:21	17, 20, 391, 402, 405
1:6	623	3:22	391, 405
1:7–9	527	3:23	402, 405
1:8	524	3:24	20, 390
1:11 ff.	527	3:25	405
1:12	474	3:26–4:7	374
1:13 ff.	360	3:26–29	153
1:15–16	474	3:26	147, 403, 441, 555
1:16	441, 447, 594, 618, 669	3:27	153, 441, 453

3:28	147, 165, 375, 606, 636, 645, 646	1:11–22	645
3:29	403	1:11	637, 638, 649, 650
4	373, 381, 391, 523, 555, 577	1:14	650
		1:15–23	637
		1:18	649
4:1–7	378, 441, 511	1:20–23	649
4:1	391	1:20	650
4:3	378	1:21–23	650
4:4 ff.	126, 441	1:21	650
4:4–6	147, 403, 507	1:22–23	639, 644
4:4–5	374, 431, 555, 557, 585, 677	1:22	644
		1:23	337, 644, 650
4:4	146, 147, 154, 161, 162, 374, 381, 405, 498, 555, 561, 568	2:2	639
		2:4–6	575
		2:6	638
4:5	165	2:8–9	639
4:6–7	577	2:10	639
4:6	32, 45, 442, 555	2:11–16	638
4:8	523	2:11	636, 645
4:9	523	2:14–17	638
4:12	591	2:16	645
4:15	558	2:17–18	638
4:19	148, 593	2:18–22	244
4:21–31	400, 450, 512	2:19–22	638
4:21–26	511	2:20–22	639
4:28–30	442	3	650
5:2–6	480	3:1	636
5:5	442, 523	3:2	637
5:11	405	3:3 ff.	339
5:13–14	651	3:3–6	650
5:13	480	3:3	649, 650
5:14	367, 400, 480	3:4–6	638
5:16–26	442	3:4	649
5:16	480	3:5	650
5:19–21	618	3:6	636, 649, 650
5:20–21	620	3:7–11	638
5:21	442	3:7	584
6:1–2	480	3:8–9	649
6:2	159, 400	3:9–10	650
6:8	442	3:9	650
6:17	74	3:10–11	649
		3:10	650
Ephesians		3:11	650
1–3	645, 651	3:14–21	638
1	650	4–6	634, 638
1:1	534	4:1–5:20	641
1:4–10	650	4:1	634, 639
1:4	637	4:2–3	639
1:5	621, 637	4:2	634, 638, 642, 647
1:8	650	4:3–6	647
1:9–10	650	4:4–6	638
1:9	621, 637, 649, 650	4:7–13	638
1:10	637, 645, 650, 651	4:15–16	638, 639, 644

4:15	647	6:1–4	651
4:16	647	6:1	646
4:17–24	638	6:5–8	641
4:17	634, 636, 638, 639	6:5	640, 645
4:18	636, 638	6:6–7	646
4:23	638	6:7	640, 645
4:25	638	6:8	652
4:32–5:2	639	6:19	650
4:32	634		
5	650, 676, 677	*Philippians*	
5:1	590, 644	1–2	435, 446
5:2	525, 590, 634, 639, 641, 643, 644, 647	1	435, 445
		1:1	534, 627
5:3–7	639	1:3–11	624
5:8–14	639	1:5–11	619
5:8	634, 639	1:5	409, 583, 625, 630
5:14	524	1:6	444
5:15–6:20	633	1:7	581, 584, 622
5:15–20	633, 639	1:10	435, 444
5:15	634, 635, 639	1:12–26	445, 617, 624
5:18	633, 634	1:12–20	624
5:19–20	632	1:12–14	622
5:19	633	1:14	69, 617
5:20	633, 635	1:15–18	620, 626
5:21–6:9	632, 635, 637, 640	1:15	617–619, 621–624, 626
5:21	632–635, 639, 641–644	1:16–17	621, 623
5:22–6:9	634, 639	1:16	622, 624–626
5:22–6:8	641	1:17	617–619, 622, 624
5:22 ff.	635	1:18	623
5:22–33	632, 634, 641, 644, 647	1:19	625
5:22–23	646	1:20–26	435
5:22	633, 634, 640, 643, 645, 646	1:20–23	627
		1:20	445, 457, 622
5:23–24	644, 647	1:21	457, 624, 628
5:23	639, 643, 647	1:23	435, 437, 454, 457, 664
5:24	640, 643	1:25	627
5:25–30	650	1:27–3:21	618
5:25–27	647	1:27–2:18	619, 625
5:25	525, 590, 640, 641, 643, 647	1:27	446, 609, 625, 626, 629, 639
5:25a	648	1:28	616, 625
5:25b–33	644, 647	1:29	74, 593, 625
5:27	647	1:30	616, 630
5:28–29	648	2–3	379, 446, 557, 609
5:28–29a	650	2	95, 162, 351, 372, 373, 380, 381, 382, 435, 446, 556, 590, 592, 609, 617, 626, 639
5:28	647, 648		
5:29	640, 647		
5:29b–30	650		
5:30	648, 677	2:1–11	445
5:31–32	676	2:1–4	634
5:31	644, 648	2:1–2	626
5:32	632, 648–650	2:1	625
5:33	634, 648	2:2	629

2:3–11	639	3:10 ff.	435
2:3	620, 626, 643	3:10–11	576, 667
2:4	626, 627, 628	3:10	74, 351, 445, 609, 657
2:5–11	627	3:11	431
2:6–11	374, 379, 381–383, 427, 431, 444, 517, 556, 626	3:12–14	628
		3:12	623
2:6–8	445, 568, 585	3:14	628, 630
2:6–7	373, 507	3:15	628
2:6	352, 371, 380, 382, 383, 445, 628	3:17–18	427
		3:17	409, 588, 609, 618, 625, 628
2:7–8	162, 629		
2:7	372, 373, 378, 445, 557, 577, 676, 677	3:18–19	616
		3:18	628
2:8	158, 431, 511, 567, 592, 643	3:19	629
		3:20 ff.	435, 444, 445
2:9–11	146, 444, 629	3:20–21	162, 374, 664
2:9–10	165	3:20	145, 433, 445, 450, 454, 523, 629
2:9	435, 556		
2:11	145, 158	3:21	165, 379, 431, 444, 445, 507, 511, 557, 665
2:12–13	626		
2:12	427, 643	4:1	619, 625, 629
2:13	621	4:2–3	616, 618, 619, 629
2:14–15	626	4:2	608, 629
2:15–16	409	4:4–8	629
2:15	367, 640	4:5	444
2:16	435, 444, 627, 629	4:9	409, 588, 629
2:17	626	4:10–19	630
2:19	627	4:12	592
2:20–21	619	4:15–20	619
2:21	627	4:15–16	630
2:22	583, 627	4:15	583
2:23	627	4:18	630
2:24	627	4:21	534, 548
2:25–30	624, 627	4:22	534
3–4	435, 446		
3	371, 374, 375, 428, 435, 445, 446, 556, 585, 617	*Colossians*	
		1	337, 397, 400, 491
3:2–3	628, 631	1:2	534, 536
3:2	391, 446, 461, 616, 617, 629	1:4	534, 536
		1:9–12	493
3:3	391	1:9	493, 494
3:4–16	625	1:10	489, 493
3:4–10	391	1:12	534, 536, 537
3:4–6	368	1:13	537
3:5 ff.	361	1:15 ff.	23
3:6	388, 391, 483	1:15–20	159, 334, 337, 375, 396, 488, 489, 491, 493–495, 510
3:7–17	445		
3:7–11	625		
3:7	445	1:15–17	337, 382
3:8–10	412	1:15–16	382, 491, 493
3:8–9	374	1:15	374, 382, 397, 494
3:9	388, 389, 411, 412, 431, 445, 483, 484	1:16	495
		1:17–18a	491

1:17	493	1:9	362, 525, 532, 538, 540, 542
1:18	524, 639		
1:18a	493	1:9a	525, 532, 533
1:18b–20	491, 493	1:9b	528, 532
1:19	337	1:10	147, 436, 528, 530–532, 540, 550, 561, 576, 577, 599
1:20	396, 495, 496		
1:23	584		
1:24	74, 448, 592	2–3	532
1:25 ff.	339	2	531, 533
1:26	339, 494, 534	2:1–12	533
1:27	494	2:1	525, 531–533
1:28	493	2:5	623
2:1	494	2:7	540
2:2 ff.	339	2:8	540
2:2–3	496	2:9a	533
2:2	494	2:11	540
2:3	494	2:12	538, 541
2:6	495	2:13–16	533
2:8–15	494	2:13	530
2:8–10	489	2:14 ff.	541
2:8	495	2:14	541, 589
2:9 ff.	337, 338	2:15 ff.	244
2:12–13	575	2:17–3:5	533
2:15	489	2:17	533
2:16–23	489	3	530, 531, 533
2:19	639	3:2–10	531
2:20	495	3:2	583
2:23	494	3:6–10	533
3:1	494, 575	3:6	531
3:9	382	3:8	541
3:10	338, 374, 375, 397, 495	3:9 ff.	530
3:12–17	495	3:11 ff.	530
3:12	536	3:11–13	533
3:16–17	632	3:12 ff.	540, 541
3:18–4:1	632, 635, 644	3:12	531
3:18–19	644	3:13	530, 534, 540
3:20	645	4–5	439, 521
3:22–25	641	4	435, 448, 531, 532, 542
		4:1–2	532
1 Thessalonians		4:1	539, 541
1:1–10	529	4:2	437
1:1	539–541	4:3–12	532
1:2–10	522	4:3	539, 541, 544
1:2–8	533	4:4–5	539
1:4	539	4:6	539
1:5–6	531	4:7	540, 543
1:6 ff.	541	4:8	539, 541
1:6–7	589	4:9	539
1:6	539, 541	4:13 ff.	437
1:7–8	531	4:13–18	531, 532
1:9 ff.	540	4:13	436, 437, 439, 532, 550
1:9–10	521, 522, 526–529, 533	4:14–17	664
1:9b–10	521, 528		

4:14	436, 438–440, 541, 576, 600	*Hebrews*	
		1–3	507
4:15–17	438	1	337, 491, 505, 510
4:15	445, 454	1:1–14	493
4:16 ff.	448	1:1–4	159, 334, 337, 505
4:16	437, 438, 440, 458, 541, 576	1:1–2	257, 505, 507
		1:1	144
4:17	437–439, 448	1:2–3	505, 511
5	448, 531, 532	1:3	510, 517
5:8	439, 531, 540	1:4	505
5:9 ff.	540	1:13	510
5:9–11	531	2	5, 95, 337
5:9–10	511, 576, 601	2:1–4	505, 510
5:10	127, 435, 440, 455, 457, 458, 541, 550, 551, 553, 555, 557, 601–603	2:1	500
		2:5–18	155, 517
		2:5–10	517
		2:5	505
5:12–22	532	2:6–8	6
5:12	541	2:6–7	155
5:13	531	2:9	189, 505
5:14	578	2:10–13	511
5:23–24	612	2:10	337, 338, 493, 505–507
5:23	540, 541, 545, 546	2:11	506
		2:14–15	505
2 Thessalonians		2:14	505, 506, 511
1:10	534	2:16	505
1:11	621	2:17	505–507
2	221, 222, 224, 226, 227, 233	3	189
		3:1–4:13	503, 504
2:1	439	3:1–6	189, 257, 475, 492
2:4	233	3:1	511
2:9	233	3:2	418
3:2	612	3:3–6	511
3:3	612	3:7–4:13	501, 507
3:7	588	3:7–4:1	501
3:9	588	3:14	506, 507, 511
		4:1	501
1 Timothy		4:2	501
2:8–15	635, 640	4:5–6	504
6:1–2	635, 640	4:11–13	501
		4:11	501
2 Timothy		4:14–5:10	504
2:18	575	4:14	507
3:14–17	468	4:15	507
		4:16	511, 517
Titus		5:2	507
2:1–10	635, 640	5:5–6	507, 508
2:14	525	5:8–9	507
		5:8	510, 511
Philemon		5:9	508, 511
5	534	5:11–6:12	501, 504
7	534	5:11–6:3	504
		5:11–14	508

5:11	501	10:32–39	509
5:12	501	10:39	503
5:14	501	11–12	501
6:1–3	508	11:1–12:29	503
6:1	507	11	509
6:4–8	502, 508	11:1	419
6:6	503, 516	12:1–29	504
6:7–8	503	12:2	510
6:9–12	503, 508	12:18–24	501, 512
6:12	508	12:18	517
6:13–10:18	504, 508	12:22–24	517
6:19–20	507, 511	12:22	504
7	508	12:24	504, 510
7:16	508	12:25–29	501, 510
7:19	502, 511	13:1	500
7:22–9:22	503	13:9	510
7:22	503	13:10–13	510
7:25	512, 517	13:10	510
7:27	512	13:13–14	504
7:28	508	13:13	498, 510
8:1	508, 512, 517	13:15–16	504
8:2	450, 664	13:15	510, 512
8:5	508	13:17	500
8:6–9:22	511	13:18–19	500
8:13	508	13:20	517
9–10	159	13:22	499
9:2–7	559		
9:5	70, 559	James	
9:9–10	508	5:16	426
9:9	502		
9:11–14	560	1 Peter	
9:12	511	2	118, 125
9:14	512	2:4–8	244, 386, 481
9:15–18	509	2:6	387
9:22	509, 516	2:7	237
9:23–28	512	2:18–3:7	635
9:24	511	2:18–3:2	640
9:25–26	502	2:18–25	641
9:26	502	2:18	634
9:28	509, 511	2:21–25	552
10	509	2:22–25	118
10:1	492, 509	2:24	127, 578
10:4	511	3:1	634
10:12	504, 509, 517	3:7	634
10:15–16	503	3:9	634
10:18	504		
10:19–32	503, 504	2 Peter	
10:19–23	509	1	679
10:19–22	517		
10:20	511	1 John	
10:26–31	503, 509	2:18	227
10:29	516	4:9–10	146
10:32–11:40	504	4:14	146

Revelation
1:9   581, 583, 584
6:11   451

9:9   451
13   461
19:8   565

Dead Sea Scrolls

Damascus Document (CD)
3.20   344
4.20–5.5   251

1QH
17:15   344

1QM   283

1QpHab
7:1–5   649
12   461

Rule of the Community (1QS)
1:2–3   254
3:6–9   300

3:6   307
4:7 ff.   451
4:20–21   300, 307
8:5–9   658
10:11   411

4Q
159   257
174   664
175   17

11Q13 (11Q Melchizedek)
            168, 508

11QTemple
57:17–19   251

Greek and Roman Literature

Aristotle

Poetica
7   277
10–12   129
10–11   276
10   276
11   276
12   276, 277
14   276
16   276
18   275
23–24   277

Rhetorica
1.3.6 (1359a)   565
3.14   129, 277
3.14.1   522

Dio Chrysostom

Orationes
38.8–9   621
77/78.37–39 621

Homer

Iliad
21.470   465

Other Jewish, Rabbinic, and Related Literature

Mishnah

Nedârîm.
9:1   206

Babylonian Talmud

'Abodah Zarah
5a   168

Ketubbôt
8a   381

Rôš Hašânâh
17b   336

Šabbât
31a   479
88b   339

Sanhèdrin
38b   344, 494
91b   188

Sûkkâh
51b   188

Midrash

Rabbah Genesis
1.1   163
1.1.4   339
11.2   344, 494
12.6   344, 494
21.7   373

Rabbah Exodus
32.1   168
32.7   168

Rabbah Leviticus
4.1   168
11.3   168, 339

Rabbah Numbers
7.4   168
16.24   168

Rabbah Deuteronomy
6   651
7.12   168

Rabbah Song of Songs
1.2.5   168

Rabbah Ecclesiastes
3.16.1   168

Sipra
89b   479

Targum

Neofiti
Exodus 16:15   328

Hellenistic Jewish and Christian Literature

Ezekiel the Tragedian

The Exagoge   277
68–89   173

Josephus

Antiquities
15.11.5   220
18.5.2   298

Jewish War
5.5.4–6   220

Philo of Alexandria

De agricultura
§ 2   501

De cherubim
127   490, 491, 492

De confusione linguarum
146   337
147   397

De fuga et inventione
101   397

De migratione Abrahami
130   166

De somniis
1.62   396
1.75   396
2.189   173
2.45   397

De vita Mosis
1.158   173

Legum allegoriae
1.43   397
2.86   24, 395, 491, 492
3.96   381, 398

Quod deterius potiori insidari soleat (Det.)
115   24

Sibylline Oracles
3:798 ff.   228

Nag Hammadi/Gnostic Texts

Gospel of Thomas
31 291

Christian Authors and Works

1 Clement
2:1	630
2:8	630
3:1	630
3:4	630
5:2	630
5:5	630
7:1	630
16:1	630
17:1	630
19:1	630
46:5	630

Aquinas

Summa Theologiae
3a, q.7, a.3 419

Athanasius

De Incarnatione contra Apollinarium
54 165

Orationes contra Arianos
2.6.9 418

Augustine

De spiritu et littera
9 419

Eusebius

Historia ecclesiastica
3.39.15 128

Ignatius

To the Romans
5:1 461

Irenaeus

Adversus Haereses
3.1.2 128
4.20.11 545
5 *praefatio* 1, 162, 403, 439, 441, 444, 506, 557, 585, 678

Martyrdom of Polycarp
8.2 146

Origen

Homiliae in Lucam
24 308

Tertullian

On the Resurrection of the Flesh
48 462

Index of Modern Authors

Abbott, Thomas Kingsmill 633
Ackerman, James S. 168
Aletti, Jean-Noël. 489
Allen, Willoughby C. 270
Allison, Dale C. 255, 257, 259, 284
Anderson, Hugh 180, 200
Arndt, William F. 422, 642, 652
Arnold, Clinton E. 489
Ashton, John 167, 172, 264

Bacon, Benjamin W. 270
Badenas, Robert 384, 484
Bailey, Daniel P. 70, 123, 512, 560, 569
Balch, David 635
Barbour, R.S. 82
Barclay, John M.G. 436
Barr, James 421
Barrett, C.K. 51, 69, 99, 289, 305, 307, 316, 317, 319, 332, 335, 351, 387, 393, 401, 406, 409, 413, 432, 436, 446, 449, 452, 453, 460, 462, 478, 481, 482, 573, 581–583, 613, 615, 654, 656, 663, 664
Barth, Karl 80, 417, 421, 672, 681
Barth, Markus 649, 650
Barton, Stephen C. 136, 534
Bash, Anthony 409
Beare, Francis Wright 270, 590
Beasley-Murray, George R. 217, 222, 227
Beavis, Mary Ann 276
Belleville, Linda L. 471
Best, Ernest 58, 128, 307, 437, 522, 523–525, 527, 529, 532, 633, 635, 640, 651
Betz, Hans Dieter 404, 588
Bieringer, R. 412
Bilezikian, Gilbert G. 275, 276
Black, Matthew 90–92, 95, 100, 114, 237, 385
Blass, F. 634
Bockmuehl, Markus 88, 371–373, 381, 383, 435, 617, 621
Boismard, M.E. 334, 337
Boobyer, G.H. 180, 184
Booth, Roger P. 192
Borgen, Peder 167, 285, 334, 398, 399, 476
Bornkamm, Günther 81, 82
Bourne, George 669

Bowen, Clayton R. 332, 333
Bowman, John W. 151
Brandon, S.G.F. 84
Brooke, George J. 355
Brower, Kent E. 534
Brown, Raymond E. 282, 316, 317, 319, 649
Bruce, F.F. 481, 497, 648
Bühner, Jan-Adolf 167
Bultmann, Rudolf 13, 29, 39, 41, 44, 54, 58, 72, 74, 75, 80–82, 84, 86, 119, 149, 151, 217, 218, 270, 306, 317, 412, 413, 443
Burch, Ernest W. 275
Burkert, Walter 465
Burkitt, F.C. 246
Burney, C.F. 396, 489
Burton, Ernest De Witt 676
Bussche, Henri van den 334, 336
Byers, Andrew J. 5
Byrne, Brendan 573

Cadman, William H. 319
Caird, G.B. 144, 179, 185, 338, 633
Calvert, D.G.A. 47
Campbell, Douglas A. 424, 426, 615
Caragounis, Chrys C. 649
Casey, P. Maurice 74, 91, 92, 100, 104, 105, 108
Catchpole, David R. 248, 251, 261
Chadwick, Henry 579
Chester, Andrew 512, 515
Chester, Stephen 673, 674
Colani, Timothée 216–218
Collange, Jean-François 450
Collins, Raymond F. 522
Conzelmann, Hans 16, 29, 33, 41, 57, 59, 286, 381
Cook, David 529, 600
Coppens, J. 650, 651
Cranfield, C.E.B. 69, 416, 424, 443, 478
Crossan, John Dominic 87
Crouch, James E. 635, 646
Cullmann, Oscar 224

Dabeck, P. 296
Daly, Robert J. 512, 513

Daube, David 86, 255
Davies, W.D. 86, 252, 257, 284, 334, 450
Debrunner, A. 418, 566, 634
Deissmann, Adolf 420, 532
Delobel, J. 436
Dewey, Joanna 128, 137
Dibelius, Martin 39, 72, 75, 80, 635
Dobschütz, Ernst von 437
Dodd, C.H. 80, 83, 85, 125, 126, 271, 335, 433, 435, 447, 526
Downing, F. Gerald 30, 31, 32, 87
Drury, John 56
Dunn, James D.G. 70, 161, 298, 313, 314, 372, 382, 404, 422, 478, 494, 534, 562, 572, 610, 676

Earl, Donald 278, 279
Edwards, Richard A. 52, 54
Elliott, Mark W. 418
Ellis, E. Earle 450, 664
Emerton, J.A. 168
Evans, C.F. 50, 63, 295, 320
Evans, Craig A. 88

Farmer, William R. 84, 115
Farrer, Austin M. 56
Farris, Stephen 286
Fee, Gordon D. 617, 626
Feuillet, André 450, 664
Fitzmyer, Joseph A. 92, 102, 251, 283, 292
Fleischer, Robert 466
Flemington, W.F. 448, 593
Fossum, Jarl E. 355
Frame, James Everett 437, 532
Friedrich, Gerhard 529
Friesen, Steven J. 464
Fuchs, Ernst 84, 86
Fuller, Reginald H. 29, 30, 32, 35–37, 40, 41
Furnish, Victor Paul 393, 409, 446, 450, 452, 455, 473, 538, 588, 592, 611, 615

Gerhardsson, Birger 83
Gibbs, J.M. 283
Gielen, Marlis 632
Gifford, E.H. 566
Gingrich, F. Wilbur 422, 642, 652
Glasson, T. Francis 77, 96, 336
Gnilka, Joachim 633
Goguel, Maurice 271
Gorman, Michael J. 352, 679
Goulder, M.D. 56
Grayston, Kenneth 126, 219, 562

Grimm, Werner 214
Guilding, Aileen 56

Haenchen, Ernst 463
Hahn, Ferdinand 74, 84, 90, 96, 152, 267, 270, 521
Hanson, Anthony Tyrrell 337, 393, 426
Hanson, R.P.C. 393, 558
Harman, A.M. 270
Harnack, Adolf von 321, 521, 522
Harrisville, Roy A., III 418
Hartman, Lars 233
Harvey, A.E. 87, 207, 245, 246
Haussleiter, Johannes 420
Hay, David M. 508
Hays, Richard B. 405, 417, 421–423, 671, 673
Headlam, Arthur C. 566
Hengel, Martin 86, 526, 527
Herbert, A.G. 421
Héring, Jean 393, 473
Hettlinger, R.F. 450, 453, 664
Higgins, A.J.B. 90, 91, 96
Hill, David 280
Hindley, J.C. 90
Hofius, Otfried 123
Holmén, Tom 82
Holtz, Traugott 294, 295
Hooker, Morna D. 1–4, 13, 23, 31, 34–36, 38, 46, 50, 55, 57, 60, 67, 70, 82, 84, 86, 90, 91, 94, 108, 115, 126, 129, 136, 152, 162, 164, 165, 174, 181, 189, 197, 207, 214, 253, 262, 281, 283, 285, 288, 298, 304, 322, 325, 334, 348, 352–354, 374, 377, 392, 397, 398, 400, 403, 405, 409, 416, 423, 436, 439, 445, 448, 455, 474, 476, 484, 488, 492, 506, 512, 538, 547, 552, 553, 558, 569, 577, 578, 587, 590, 599, 608–610, 616–618, 625, 647, 661, 672, 677, 679
Horbury, William 87
Howard, George F. 405, 421
Howard, Wilbert F. 317
Hübner, Hans 190
Hughes, Frank W. 522
Hunn, Debbie 416, 422
Hurtado, Larry W. 87, 588

Isaacs, Marie E. 499, 502

Janzen, J. Gerald 420
Jeremias, Joachim 44–47, 83, 85, 267, 268, 270, 271, 669

Jewett, Robert 522, 622
Johanson, Bruce C. 522, 530
Johnson, Andy 534
Johnson, Luke Timothy 421, 429
Johnson, Marcus 679
Johnson, Marshall D. 282
Jonge, Marinus de 168

Kähler, Christoph 616
Kähler, Martin 80, 89
Käsemann, Ernst 20, 29, 41, 81, 82, 334, 411–413, 443, 571, 590
Keck, Leander E. 129, 275, 277, 284
Kee, H.C. 190
Kennedy, George A. 277, 522
Kertelge, Karl 412
Kiddle, M. 271
Kilpatrick, G.D. 223, 270
Kingsbury, Jack Dean 280
Kittel, Gerhard 420
Klein, Günter 616
Klijn, A.F.J. 436
Knibb, Michael A. 90, 91
Knox, John 35, 90
Knox, Wilfred L. 268, 436
Koester, Helmut 530
Koet, B.J. 291
Kümmel, W.G. 268, 582, 583

Lagrange, Marie-Joseph 270
Lambrecht, Jan 219, 416, 430, 449, 530, 571, 572
Lane, William L. 499
Lang, Friedrich Gustav 276, 432, 452
Langevin, Paul-Emile 523
Larsson, Edvin 538
Leenhardt, Franz J. 443
Leivestad, Ragnar 33, 36, 46, 91, 104
Lietzmann, Hans 449, 583
Lightfoot, J.B. 404
Lightfoot, R.H. 38, 49, 56, 81, 99, 184, 220, 238, 275, 321–323, 332
Lincoln, Andrew T. 449, 649, 651
Lindars, Barnabas 74, 105, 108, 113, 499, 500
Lindgård, Fredrik 432
Linebaugh, Jonathan 672
Lohmeyer, Ernst 184, 283, 299, 635
Lohse, Eduard 396, 588, 636
Lowe, John 433, 434, 457
Luther, Martin 70, 165, 419, 431, 534, 549, 559, 588, 633, 669–682
Luz, Ulrich 310
Lyonnet, S. 412, 578

MacCulloch, Diarmaid 668
Mack, Burton L. 87
Major, H.D.A. 72
Malherbe, Abraham J. 460
Mannermaa, Tuomo 679
Manson, T.W. 1, 67–89, 100, 268, 272, 306, 330, 512
Manson, William 222, 497, 504
Marcus, Joel 201, 206, 299
Marsh, Clive 88
Marshall, I. Howard 292
Martin, Ralph P. 590
Martyn, J. Louis 428
Marxsen, Willi 230
Masson, Charles 437
Matlock, R. Barry 418
Mauser, Ulrich 185
McKelvey, R.J. 664
McNeil, Brian 578
Meeks, Wayne A. 335, 336
Meier, John P. 87, 298, 299
Metzger, Bruce M. 657
Meyer, Ben F. 87
Meyer, Eduard 75
Meyer, H.A.W. 566
Meyer, Paul W. 387, 482
Michie, Donald 128, 137
Milik, J.T. 90
Minear, Paul S. 57, 286, 292, 333
Molland, Einar 584
Moo, Douglas J. 213, 292
Moritz, Thorsten 649
Morris, Leon 56, 550
Moule, C.F.D. 2, 6, 84, 102, 327, 352, 421, 422, 452, 457, 562
Moulton, James Hope 416, 418
Muddiman, John 641, 648
Munck, Johannes 224, 521–523, 529, 531–533
Murphy-O'Connor, Jerome 453
Myers, Benjamin 417

Neirynck, Frans 280
Nineham, D.E. 31, 38, 80

O'Brien, Peter Thomas 530, 616
Orlinsky, Harry M. 121, 122
Osborne, Robert E. 461
Oster, Richard 463, 465

Palmer, Humphrey 39
Parry, R.St. John 581

Perrin, Norman 13, 29–32, 34, 38, 41, 44, 45, 53, 56–60, 76, 83, 91, 105
Pesch, Rudolf 219, 232
Peterlin, Davorin 619
Plevnik, Joseph 438
Plummer, Alfred 270, 611
Portefaix, L. 466

Quesnell, Quentin 58

Rae, Murray 669
Räisänen, Heikki 19, 384, 631
Rawlinson, A.E.J. 72
Rese, Martin 292
Reumann, John 445
Rhoads, David 128, 137
Riesenfeld, Harald 184
Rigaux, Béda 437, 523
Robinson, J. Armitage 633
Robinson, John A.T. 96, 113, 316, 317, 450, 664
Roetzel, Calvin 534
Rowland, Christopher 87, 170, 173

Sampley, J. Paul 641, 649
Sanday, William 566
Sanders, E.P. 13, 40, 86, 87, 235, 245, 252, 400, 404, 424, 548, 670, 671, 681
Sanders, Jack T. 531
Schlier, Heinrich 633, 651
Schmidt, Karl L. 72, 76
Schmiedel, Paul Wilhelm 46, 385, 481
Schnackenburg, Rudolf 319
Schnelle, Udo 656
Schubert, Paul 278, 529–532, 599, 637
Schulz, David 69
Schulz, Siegfried 190
Schürer, Emil 86
Schüssler Fiorenza, Elisabeth 652
Schweitzer, Albert 80, 83
Schweizer, Eduard 33, 52, 95, 99
Scobie, Charlie 317
Scott, Ernest Findlay 330, 633
Segal, Alan F. 170
Seiterle, Gérard 466
Seitz, Oscar J.F. 280, 334
Sevenster, Jan N. 452
Snaith, Norman H. 121
Snodgrass, Klyne R. 201
Stacey, W. David 298, 299, 307, 348
Standaert, Benoît H.M.G.M. 275–277
Stanley, Christopher 390, 405, 597

Stanley, D.M. 578, 588
Stanton, Graham 26, 175, 257, 260
Stauffer, Ethelbert 81
Steenburg, Dave 371, 372
Stendahl, Krister 282, 668, 669, 671, 681
Stettler, Christian 491
Stuhlmacher, Peter 412
Suhl, Alfred 190, 200
Sundkler, Bengt 272
Swete, Henry B. 52
Swetnam, James 510

Taylor, Vincent 80, 85, 201, 271, 306
Telford, William R. 220, 229, 236
Theissen, Gerd 87
Thiselton, Anthony C. 395, 545, 643
Thomas, Kenneth J. 191
Thompson, Richard W. 430
Thrall, Margaret E. 181, 393, 407, 414, 432, 449, 452, 473, 607, 610, 611–613
Tinsley, E.J. 588
Tödt, H.E. 74, 84, 90, 96
Torrance, Thomas F. 421
Trebilco, Paul 464, 467
Trilling, Wolfgang 271
Turner, C.H. 77, 323,
Turner, Nigel 418

Upton, Bridget Gilfillian 129

Vainio, Olli-Pekka 673
Valloton, Pierre 421
Vanhoye, Albert 522
Vermes, Geza 46, 74, 86, 91, 94, 99, 102, 104, 105, 108, 152, 254, 328
Vielhauer, Philipp 33

Walker, William O. 103–108, 114
Wallis, Ian G. 418
Wanamaker, C.A. 381–383
Watson, Francis 425
Watson, Nigel 432
Watts, Rikki E. 132, 201, 202, 204
Weeden, Theodore J. 60–62, 130
Weidinger, Karl 635
Wellhausen, Julius 270
Wendland, Heinz-Dietrich 414
Wesley, John 419, 668, 681
Westcott, Brooke Foss 497, 502, 633
Whybray, R. Norman 121, 122
Wiles, Maurice F. 161, 172–175
Williams, Sam K. 124, 405

Wilson, S.G. 288
Wink, Walter 317
Winter, Bruce 629
Woude, A.S. van der 168
Wright, C.J. 72
Wright, N.T. 87, 488, 491
Wuellner, Wilhelm 522

Yates, John Edmund 303
Yates, Roy 488
Young, Frances 175

Zahrnt, Heinz 30
Ziesler, J.A. 185, 186
Zuntz, Günther 656

Index of Subjects

Abraham 15, 18, 153, 167, 172, 264, 268, 326–328, 330, 365, 386, 391, 402, 403, 405, 431, 498, 509, 538, 585
– descendants of, heirs of 18, 19, 195, 282, 328, 333, 366, 402, 403, 498, 505, 538, 605, 645
– faith of 403, 405, 562, 563, 569, 570
– God of 172, 259, 361
– lesser than 398
– promises to 20, 147, 287, 365, 367, 384, 391, 400, 402, 403, 405, 406, 480, 508, 554, 555
– *see also* Seed
Acquittal 428, 442, 549–578, 605, 674
Adam 1, 2, 6, 15, 126, 127, 152, 154, 155, 163–165, 174, 344, 352, 354, **371–383**, 397, 398, 400, 423, 426, 428, 429, 440–442, 444, 448, 452, 492, 494, 495, 506, 552, 563–567, 571, 572, 576–578, 605, 638, 651, 659, 671
– descendants of 126, 565, 604
– disobedience of, fall of, sin of 126, 154, 164, 344, 354, 373, 375, 377, 382, 383, 426, 430, 442, 506, 511, 552, 564–567, 604
– first and last 154, 376, 382, 397, 441, 444
– image of God 154, 164, 352, 354, 372–383, 397, 398, 400, 423, 440, 494
– Second Adam 165, 400
Adoption, adoptionism 126, 161, 162, 443, 555, 573, 585
Antichrist 226, 227, 232, 234
Antithesis 13, 20–22, 26, 59, 126, 252, 268, 337, 562, 566, 567, 572, 578, 590, 629, 670
Apocalypse, apocalyptic 29, 41, 46, 73, 79, 87, 99, 180, 209, 216–228, 267, 283, 344, 436, 438, 450, 509, 512
Aramaic 32, 35, 44–47, 49, 71, 83, 91, 92, 99, 101, 102, 105, 146, 152, 267
Atonement 1, 5, 67, 118, 124, 125, 127, 162, 293, 507, 549, 557, 559, 578, 587, 605, 678, 679, 682
– Day of 70, 512, 517
Authenticity 13, 24, 29–36, 38, 41–49, 51, 74, 76, 81–83, 85, 86, 91, 92, 104, 119,
125, 131, 137, 188, 216, 252, 257, 268, 270, 271, 471, 593, 626
– inauthentic 33–35, 46, 48, 94

Baptism, baptize 6, 19, 60, 126, 127, 135–138, 187, 259, 280, 282, 290, 291, 305, 453, 526, 529, 572, 575, 613, 638, 667
– into Christ, into Christ's death 153, 403, 406, 426, 427, 441, 442, 447, 558, 571, 577, 578
– of John 207, 298–315, 318, 320
– of repentance 133, 135, 187, 203, 298, 313
– with fire 301, 306–310, 313
– with the Holy Spirit 6, 135, 136, 187, 299, 301–315, 325, 366
– *see also* John the Baptist
Birth 5, 14, 16, 129, 132, 148, 154, 161, 162, 221, 260, 277, 282, 285, 286, 288, 289, 294, 312, 333, 345, 361, 362, 365, 374, 478, 496, 536, 556, 580, 636, 638
– *see also* Seed
Blessing 69, 126, 165, 189, 256, 268, 301, 363–366, 374, 391, 399, 402–406, 410, 411, 508, 554, 555, 557, 577, 581, 585, 586, 594, 605, 609, 675
Blood 5, 55, 170, 198, 301, 339, 376, 440, 442, 462, 501, 503–506, 509, 512, 516, 558–560, 675
Bread 5, 114, 139, 169, 250, 258, 299, 327, 328, 348, 363, 398, 476, 477, 606

Chalcedon 61, 160, 161, 171–176
Chiasm, chiastic 306, 319, 387, 482, 503, 620, 662
Christology 19, **29–37**, 43, 48, 60–62, 84, 115, 143, 149, 151, 153, 156, 158, 161, 165, 171–173, 175, 208, 248–250, 262–264, 279, 287, 331, 334, 381, 383, 386, 396, 397, 400, 417, 422, 481, 493, 640, 653, 673, 682
– false 60, 61, 340
– Son of man 105, 106, 155
– wisdom 24, 159, 334, 337, 395–397, 489, 493, 510

Circumcision 15, 17–19, 287, 363–366, 391, 442, 447, 448, 480, 498, 513, 515, 527, 646
- Uncircumcision 527, 645, 646

Cleanliness 157, 192, 195, 196, 199, 251, 252, 254, 287, 289, 298–301, 304, 305, 414, 503, 509, 535, 547, 568, 591, 661
- uncleanliness 138, 139, 150, 191, 192, 199, 254, 277, 287, 289, 300, 302–305, 308, 309, 323, 331, 545, 547, 591
- see also Temple

Continuity 1, 11–26, 85, 87, 116, 152, 153, 208, 248, 253, 261, 263, 310, 394, 398, 440, 505, 513, 659
- discontinuity 1, 3, 12, 13, 21, 152, 513

Covenant 55, 144, 271, 296, 363, 365, 390, 411, 469, 485, 490, 516, 661, 662, 670
- Ark of 559
- Blood of 198, 503, 509
- Covenantal nomism 400, 424
- Mediator of 501, 504, 508, 509
- Mosaic 20, 24, 365, 662
- Old and new 13, 253, 337, 338, 366, 369, 392, 393, 400, 446, 471–478, 486, 510, 511

Creation, creative 23–25, 34, 40, 43, 48, 49, 52, 105, 107, 119, 153, 163, 171, 173–175, 259, 264, 300, 301, 305, 379, 382, **394–397**, 400, 443, 444, 450, **489–492**, 506, 573, 651
- agent of 319, 337, 395, 400, 490, 492–495
- and redemption 354, 400, 491, 493
- day of 22, 468
- goal of 396, 397
- light of 22, 23, 338, 340, 398, 447, 492
- lordship over 164, 644
- new 154, 165, 284, 396, 408, 415, 447, 455, 457, 552, 557, 560, 603, 608, 614, 662
- plan for 344, 354, 376, 382
- renewal and restoration of 155, 314, 344, 373, 375, 434
- story 249, 251
- Word of God at 166, 264, 283, 319, 337, 338, 394–396, 491, 495
- work of 158, 166, 170, 171, 337, 339, 493

Credal summaries 439, 442, 448, 488, 521, 523, 562, 597, 599, 600, 604, 605, 656

Criteria 13, 29–33, 35, 41–49, 82, 83, 87, 127, 312

Criticism
- form 34, 35, 38–41, 47, 51, 53, 59, 72, 75, 78, 80, 81, 84, 85, 128
- redaction 47, 50–60, 75, 85, 95, 128, 218
- source 46, 50, 51, 58, 84, 85, 217
- traditio-historical 29, 31, 41, 43, 91

Crucifixion 77, 117, 129–131, 137, 141, 147, 209, 213, 239, 240, 270, 292, 293, 349–352, 354, 396, 399, 406, 413, 420, 434, 441, 448, 496, 502, 504, 513, 543, 544, 546, 549, 551, 554, 568, 575, 584, 601, 602, 605, 660, 661, 680, 682

Curse 126, 140, 162, 207, 235, 241, 374, 390, 391, 399, 402–406, 410, 554, 555, 557, 575, 577, 585, 586, 592, 594, 605, 609, 675, 676, 678, 679

David 15, 124, 140, 154, 196, 219, 238, 239, 248–251, 258, 263, 268, 281, 282, 286–288, 300, 333, 378, 386, 423, 430, 598, 627, 661, 662

Devil 254, 326, 328, 505
- see also Satan

Discontinuity, see Continuity

Divorce 81, 133, 192, 199, 251, 252, 254, 255, 261, 289, 475
- see also marriage

Ecclesiology 400, 539, 632, 647

Elect 96, 97, 109, 110, 112, 152, 173, 198, 209, 227–229, 231, 238, 242, 267, 344, 574

Elijah 133–137, 140, 179–189, 197, 202, 212, 253, 260, 261, 263, 286, 287, 291, 295–297, 305, 311, 331, 345

Elisha 139, 261, 287, 291, 296

Eschatology, eschatological 36, 44, 73, 83, 152, 174, 184, 201, 216–218, 221, 225, 226, 231, 243, 314, 351, 412, 433, 434, 439, 457, 506, 512, 523, 525, 530–533, 570, 659
- expectation 112, 174, 181, 233
- goal 377, 382, 443
- hope 36, 104, 439, 575, 660, 661, 664
- judge, judgement 84, 112, 238, 314
- Son of man, sayings 32, 33, 36, 45, 74, 78, 84, 90–95, 98, 99, 104–108, 110, 112–114, 267
- temper 44, 82
- tension 443, 451, 456, 457

Ethics, ethical 73, 261, 400, 417, 495, 496, 535, 539, 543, 548, 549, 556, 575, 590, 606–609, 626, 681
Eucharist 314, 327, 510, 606

Faith 12, 14, 17–20, 22, 29, 41, 58, 62, 79–82, 85–86, 115, 144, 145, 148, 150, 151, 155, 172, 176, 223, 236, 248, 268, 304, 324, 336, 338–340, 351, 359, 364, 367, 368, 399, 402, 403, 405, 414, **417–431**, 435, 439, 440, 445, 448, 456, 460, 462, 468, 469, 481–485, 493, 496–499, 502–504, 509, 514–516, 526, 528, 531, 533, 540, 549, 550, 554, 559, 560, 568–570, 575, 577, 591, 596, 598, 605, 607, 612, 615, 619, 627, 638, 655, 663
– and works 19, **385–391,** 402, 477, 480–485, 670
– confessions of 151, 239
– eyes of 324, 329
– justification by 534, 549, 575, **668–682**
– new 11, 62, 174, 361, 363–365, 489, 497, 499, 597, 636
– obedience of 148, 424, 427, 431, 485, 598, 599
– of Abraham 18, 403, 405, 562, 563, 569, 570
– of the church 11, 83, 87, 88, 527
– of the gospel 625, 627
– *see also* Pistis Christou
Faithfulness 1, 15, 16, 49, 61, 77, 110, 112, 124, 125, 140, 141, 171, 181, 222, 223, 227, 230, 231, 234, 257, 336, 342, 349, 350, 364, 366, 384, 387, 411, 417, **421–431**, 461, 475, 482, 500, 507, 509, 516, 533, 546, 569, **610–615**, 653, **670–673**, 680, 682
– of Jesus to Torah 248–253, 259, 288
– to Jewish heritage 20, 171, 340, 384
– unfaithfulness 16, 428
Flesh 5, 114, 154, 287, 300, 322, 330, 366, 402, 430, 448, 511, 555, 575, 593, 594, 618, 620, 663, 665, 677, 680
– according to 154, 326, 378, 408, 430, 443, 543, 573, 598, 602
– and blood 5, 170, 339, 440, 505, 506, 675
– heart of 145, 300, 471
– sinful, weakness of 19, 126, 162, 373, 378, 379, 385, 390, 400, 410, 430, 443, 483, 553, 555, 557, 577, 585–587,
– two become one 644, 648, 676

– versus Spirit 173, 312, 325, 363, 391, 442, 443, 479, 543, 547, 573, 621, 661
– word made, word became 5, 17, 23, 116, 165, 166, 169, 264, 319, 320, 322, 323, 329, 330, 336, 337, 339, 340, 345, 476, 486, 492, 678
– *see also* Incarnation
Forerunner 135–137, 182, 187, 188, 236, 253, 254, 282, 305, 322, 333, 346, 507, 508

Galilee 52, 141, 142, 150, 161, 230, 241, 266, 270, 277, 290, 293, 303, 308, 323, 326, 347, 596
Gamaliel 70
Gentiles 19, 146, 155, 209, 237, 239, 240, 287, 289, 396, 410, 434, 442, 462, 469, 494–496, 513, 523, 560, 580
– and righteousness 385, 388–390, 399, 401, 426, 480–483, 485
– and the Law 158, 251, 263, 363–370, 399, 477, 478, 480, 489, 498, 513, 515, 580, 646, 680
– as holy **536–548**, 646
– blessing of Abraham to 18, 153, 403–406, 411, 480, 498, 538, 554, 555, 557, 585, 645
– Elijah and Elisha helping 287, 291
– inclusion of, inheritance of 18, 141, 144, 153, 244, 282, 384, 498, 536, 537, 543, 606, 636, 638, 645, 649–651, 669
– mission to 20, 117, 146, 191, 224, 225, 263, 287, 290–292, 294, 399, 498
– Paul as apostle to 145, 146, 148, **359–370**, 398, 399, 422, 424, 474, 516, 526–528, 583, 592, 594, 597–599, 649, 669
– prohibition of mission to **265–272**
Glorification 113, 147, 157, 168, 189, 312, 332, 336, 338, 339, 346, 349, 350, 354, 434, 444, 447, 448, 472, 574, 656
Glory 95, 96, 328, 329, **341–355**, 371, 375, 376, 384, 397, 441, 444, 446, 447, 449, 452, 456, 472, 474–477, 480, 490, 494, 505–507, 517, 580, 604, 613, 621, 629, 630, 647, 655, 662, 663, 667, 675, 676
– and Adam 154, 163, 344–346, 352, 354, 371, 373, 375, 382, 397, 400, 492, 494
– at Sinai 22–24, 158, 166, 180, 181, 189, 334–336, 338, 342–346, 348–350, 353, 382, 392–395, 397, 398, 400, 446, 447, 472–476, 485, 492, 495
– at the transfiguration **179–189**, 295, 345

Index of Subjects

- bring many sons to 5, 170, 171, 493, 506, 517
- crowned with, enthroned in 6, 111, 113, 170, 173, 505, 506, 517
- enter into 294, 345, 349
- future, coming in 46, 47, 92, 108, 111, 152, 180, 231, 256, 344, 345, 354, 434, 444, 506, 656
- in the cross 144, 158, 506, 665
- power and 57, 92, 97, 98, 109, 141, 228, 353, 440
- reflected 170, 171, 180, 337, 343, 344, 352, 353, 374, 375, 382, 394, 397, 400, 423, 447, 472–475, 477, 492, 666
- revealed, seen 166, 168, 180, 319, 320, 331, 332, 334, 337–340, 342–354, 374, 381, 382, 392–395, 398, 400, 407, 434, 444, 447, 449, 454, 472, 474–476, 492, 495, 510, 662, 663, 665
- sharing, conforming 6, 55, 165, 170, 179–181, 374, 430, 431, 442, 444, 492, 494, 507, 511, 513, 556, 586, 609, 614, 629, 630, 665

Grace 21, 127, 143, 154, 161, 164, 256, 269, 335, 354, 361, 366, 376, 407, 413, 415, 426, 428–430, 442, 502, 503, 505, 513, 557, 559, 561, 564–568, 571, 584, 588, 589, 593, 598, 600, 668, 670, 675, 676, 681
- and truth 23, 166, 189, 319, 336, 339, 345, 398, 476

Haustafel 632–635, 640–642, 651
Heresy 14, 60–62, 171, 172, 340, 593, 594
Herod 135, 237, 255, 282, 331
Hilasterion, *see* Mercy seat
Holy Spirit, *see* Spirit

Image of Christ 382, 440, 441, 453, 618, 662, 665
Imitation 445, 587–589, 593, 644
Incarnation 5, 6, 116, 161, 162, 164, 165, 167–169, 171, 173–175, 311, 318–320, 330, 339, 373, 374, 376, 378, 413, 486, 495, 496, 507, 517, 557, 568, 587, 605, 608, 610, 677–679, 682
Inheritance 11, 17, 18, 147, 165, 193, 253, 286, 288, 296, 344, 402, 440, 442, 504, 536–538, 637, 643, 649
Interchange 1–5, 126, 127, 162, 165, 168, 170, 374, 403, 405, 407, 411, 439, 444, 506, 511, 557, 558, 585–587, 591, 594, 609, 647, 677–679

Jerusalem 21, 59, 183, 204, 230, 233, 236, 239, 241, 249, 282, 294, 295, 300, 301, 303, 309, 310, 318, 344, 346, 347, 361, 363, 407, 464, 497, 498, 515, 527, 536, 556, 589, 608
- destruction of 12, 209, 221, 227, 232, 233, 241, 243, 244, 299, 513
- going to 55, 77, 133, 134, 140, 198, 207–209, 219, 236, 243, 260, 261, 287, 293, 463, 464, 497, 498
- heavenly 501, 512
- lament over 220, 240, 241

Jesus of History, Quest of historical Jesus 34, 47, 48, 51–53, 58, 59, 61, 74, 76, 78–89, 119, 128, 150, 155, 169, 228, 233, 320, 322, 340
John the Baptist 6, 132, 134–138, 140, 181, 182, 185, 186, 188, 189, 200–203, 211, 236, 247, 260, 280, 281, 286, 291, 294, 298–320, 322, 324, 325, 331, 333, 337, 339, 340

Kapporeth 70
- *see also* Mercy seat
Kerygma 80, 514, 517, 587, 590, 626
Kingdom of God 6, 44, 45, 55, **72, 73,** 78, 156, 226, 255, 261, 268, 286, 289, 292, 296, 304, 308, 310, 326, 329, 367, 378, 537, 639
- coming of 57, 84, 91, 97, 111, 112, 179, 231, 270, 272, 289, 323
- entering 206, 240, 261, 282, 287, 288, 312
- exclusion from 240, 241, 270, 272
- inheriting 400, 442
- not far from 194, 209
- proclamation of 83, 111, 129, 139, 149, 150, 169, 204, 261, 270, 277, 323
Kingdom of heaven 16, 111, 268, 288

Lamb 117, 264, 311, 318, 320, 324, 544, 558, 560, 606
Law
- End of 14, 20, 24, 384–400, 482–485
- Fulfilment of 14, 20, 158, 256, 337, 390, 479, 485
- Law and gospel 13, 17, 19, 20
- Mosaic 191, 194, 198, 256, 282, 288, 294, 297
- Works of 19, 367, 386, 390, 391, 402, 403, 419, 421, 428, 483, 498, 515
Logos 161, 166, 167, 283, 319, 320, 330, 396–398, 493, 678

Lord 139, 167, 168, 202, 263, 300, 301, 342–344, 362, 389, 473, 474, 490, 644–646, 651, 652
- acknowledge as 86, 126, 365, 379
- as title 93, 102, 145, 146, 151, 156, 158, 164, 333, 386
- at home with 433, 435, 451, 454, 456, 457, 663
- coming of, return of 132, 140, 202–205, 210, 230, 231, 299, 432, 433, 442, 451, 454, 456, 532, 599, 600
- confidence in 617, 627
- day of 134, 135, 182, 209, 221, 222, 226–228, 299, 303, 439, 446, 611
- glory of 180, 185, 342, 343, 349, 351, 374, 393–395, 449, 454, 474
- imitate 541, 589, 594
- meet 437, 439, 454
- one 607, 638
- of the Sabbath 250, 258
- please 454, 457
- raised, risen 43, 269, 345, 353, 438, 442, 448, 456, 562, 563, 569, 575, 576, 656, 657, 663, 665, 666
- return of 231, 433, 454, 456
- same mind in 616, 619, 629
- serving, servant(s) of 79, 124, 231, 523, 641
- Spirit of 290, 308, 474
- temple of 246, 247, 479
- turn to 353, 355, 393, 473, 474, 523, 666, 667
- way of, way for 133–136, 182, 186, 187, 202, 203, 207, 210, 246, 286, 301, 310, 318, 400
- word(s) of 47, 49, 186, 438, 472, 490
- worthy of 247, 489, 493
Luther, Lutheranism 13, 51, 70, 165, 384, 419, 422, 431, 534, 549, 559, 584, 588, 633, 668–682

Marcan priority, *see* Source
Marriage 193, 239, 240, 251, 252, 261, 289, 545, 640, 641, 646, 647, 653, 676, 677
Mercy seat 429, 512, 558–560, 569
Messiah, messiahship 18, 62, 79, 95, 100, 115, **129–135, 140–147, 151–154, 156–158,** 172, 174, 179, 227, 236, 238–241, 258, 263, 269, 271, 304, 330–332, 354, 362, 365, 367, 398, 499, 541, 549, 613
- acknowledge, confess as 149, 324, 325, 498, 514

- as identity, title 18, 102, 120, 130, 137, 138, 149, 151–152, 156
- coming 18, 208, 238
- false, pseudo 221, 222
- rejected 12, 62, 220, 239, 241, 243, 269, 271, 272
- stone as 386, 481
- suffering 2, 115, 131, 134, 140, 157, 294
Messianic 17, 18, 46, 48, 74, 79, 90, 91, 100, 133, 179, 180, 229, 236, 249, 254, 268, 329–331, 426, 609
- age 229, 236, 360, 369
- claims 31, 33, 36, 43, 91, 222, 317, 378
- pretenders 221, 222, 227
- prophecy 17, 115, 249, 254
- secret 324, 327, 332, 338
- self-consciousness 36, 88, 151
- titles 18, 36, 46, 91, 93, 152, 426
Metaphor 145, 163, 172, 208, 228, 237, 298, 313, 332, 344, 349, 375, 387, 392, 432, 440, 450, 451, 453, 460–462, 464, 465, 467, 471, 482, 501, 543, 557, 582, 613, 644, 655, 658, 663, 664
Ministry 36, 55, 57, 71, 74–77, 79, 80, 88, 102, 115, 116, 124, 129, 136, 147, 150, 152, 203, 207, 209, 211, 254, 260, 268–271, 286, 290, 291, 303–305, 309, 314, 315, 322, 324, 331, 345, 362, 401, 447, 508, 587
- in Galilee 52, 303
- of John the Baptist 132, 281, 310
- of Moses 22, 353, 392, 393, 446, 472, 473, 475
- of Paul 117, 353, 392, 393, 401, 407–410, 412–415, 434, 446–448, 454–456, 458, 463, 470–474, 485, 579, 585–587, 589, 590–592, 595, 603, 609, 614, 623–625, 627, 630, 661–663
Miracles 117, 118, 125, 150, 253, 304, 323, 330, 331, 345, 349, 492
Mission, missionary 36, 71, 90, 101, 102, 115, 119, 127, 134, 153, 155, 233, 286, 290, 304, 314, 362, 364, 413, 526, 527, 529, 535, 580, 613, 622
- of John the Baptist 134, 135, 202, 236, 315, 320
- of Paul 219, 362, 364, 398, 410, 424, 427, 433, 441, 498, 521–523, 542, 581, 596, 614, 623, 630, 669
- to Gentiles 224, 263, 287, 291, 292, 498
- prohibition of 265–272
Moses 15, 16, **21–25,** 124, 133, 139, 151, 166, 168, 170, 171, 173, 174, **191–199,**

205, 214, 219, 249, **251–264,** 277, 282, 285, 289, **294–298,** 314, 319, 326, 328, 329, **334–338, 342–346, 348–350,** 353, 365, 375, 389, 392–395, 398, 400, 446, 447, 473, 475–477, 484–486, 490, 492, 495, 507–509, 594, 627, 663
- and Elijah 181–189, 197, 253, 260, 263, 295, 298, 345
- and the prophets 62, 140, 261, 294, 296, 297, 340, 399
- face of 22, 180, 181, 338, 342, 343, 353, 392–394, 472, 473, 475
- greater than 25, 139, 140, 157, 169, 173, 180, 188, 189, 192, 195, 196, 199, 251, 252, 255, 256, 263, 264, 348, 353, 394, 472, 508, 511, 662
- on Mount Sinai 19, 22, 24, 158, 166, 180, 181, 186, 188, 189, 339, 342, 344–346, 365, 375, 382, 392, 394, 397, 472, 475, 492, 494–496
- teaching of 12, 16, 25, 188, 192, 195, 199, 251, 252, 255, 259, 262, 263, 296
- *see also* Law (Mosaic)

Nazareth 79, 81, 150, 161, 176, 242, 290, 292, 297, 303, 330, 340

Obedience 1, 26, 73, 100, 124, 140, 148, 256, 288, 344, 364, 369, 382, 389, 390, 400, 403, 424, 427, 430–431, 442, 479, 484, 485, 513, 515, 531, 542, 543, 558, 588, 599, 634, 641, 643, 651
- disobedience 26, 154, 164, 242, 344, 352, 368, 377, 380, 382, 426, 442, 501, 506, 507, 511, 565–567
- of Christ 6, 102, 116, 126, 147, 154, 157, 158, 162–164, 171, 186, 192, 352, 354, 373, 377, 378, 382, 390, 426, 427, 429–431, 442, 506, 507, 510, 511, 513, 561, 565–567, 585, 587, 590, 598, 608, 643
- of faith 148, 390, 424, 427, 431, 485, 598, 599

Paraenesis 217, 632, 638, 639–645, 647
Parousia 57, 73, 94, 97, 102, 110, 113, 175, 224, 230, 231, 269, 432–442, 444–452, 454, 456–459, 524, 600
Participation 5, 422, 506, 549, 577, 578, 581–583, 593, 648, 673, 674, 677–679
Passion 6, 21, 35, 57, 73, 92, 94, 114, 120, 134, 136, 137, 141, 147, 157, 194, 198, 213, 214, 219, 220, 238, 249, 282, 292, 293, 294, 322, 517,
Pauline thanksgivings 278, 407, 522, 529–533, 541, 599–601, 624, 637, 638
Persecution 94, 95, 97, 110, 219, 224, 225, 232–234, 238, 265–267, 269, 270, 541, 616, 662
Pharisees 15, 16, 112, 133, 191–196, 204, 205, 220, 237, 240, 249–252, 254–255, 258, 262–264, 288, 289, 308–311, 329, 348, 349, 361, 535, 548
Peter 35, 61, 77, 128, 130, 133, 139–141, 144, 179, 182–186, 253, 307, 328, 345, 350, 361–363, 367, 399, 526, 527, 630
Pilate 130, 136, 141, 157, 241, 326
Pistis Christou 428, 671–673
Priest, priesthood 18, 130, 196, 235, 237, 244, 250, 258, 310, 311, 318, 348, 506–508, 510, 512, 515, 517, 535, 546, 584
- high priest 98, 109, 130, 131, 137, 138, 141, 147, 149, 157, 159, 171, 238, 240, 350, 503, 504, 507, 508, 511, 512, 515, 517, 559, 560
Prologue
- Greek and Latin 129–131, 276, 277
- Hebrews 505
- Johannine 5, 17, 156, 165–167, 263, 275, 281, 282, 310, 316–340, 345, 353, 476
- Josephus 278
- Lucan 156, 280, 281, 285, 295, 333
- Matthean 156, 280, 281, 333
- Marcan 129–131, 134–135, 137–139, 156, 275–283, 304, 324, 325, 333
Prophecy, prophetic 18, 36, 84, 87, 94, 95, 121, 133, 171, 186, 189, 204, 209, 216, 218–222, 225, 227, 233, 242, 245, 251, 261, 272, 283, 286, 290, 293, 294, 298, 299, 301, 303–306, 313, 314, 348, 389, 484, 668
- fulfilment of 15, 132, 98, 249, 260, 289, 307, 308, 455, 472
- messianic 17, 115, 249, 254
- of the temple's destruction 238–240, 242, 245
Prophet(s) 23, 36, 43, 140, 144, 158, 161, 166, 170, 181, 183, 186–189, 197, 198, 200, 202, 222, 227, 228, 241, 248, 262, 281, 285, 289, 291, 298–301, 342–344, 389, 469, 471, 472, 485, 505, 507, 510, 516, 535, 589, 630, 642
- false 198, 222, 227, 233, 234, 300
- Isaiah 2, 118, 129, 132, 200, 202, 206, 211, 214, 215, 343

Index of Subjects 763

- Jesus as 84, 139, 151, 156, 157, 182, 183, 186–188, 260–263, 290, 293, 294–297, 309, 331, 476
- John the Baptist as 202, 203, 298, 311, 314
- Law and 14–17, 24, 25, 181, 254, 256, 257, 261, 263, 366, 367, 369, 370, 386, 388, 390, 399, 428, 475, 477, 478, 483, 486, 487, 495, 552, 559
- Moses and 62, 140, 185, 187, 188, 254, 261, 285, 294–297, 340, 399

Q, *see* Source
Qumran 17, 31, 43, 86, 104, 124, 244, 254, 298, 344, 461, 535, 649, 658

Reconciliation 143, 377, 408–410, 413–415, 419, 455, 494, 512, 554, 559, 560, 569, 614, 645
Redemption 1, 2, 54, 147, 155, 163, 174, 175, 214, 337, 354, 373, 395, 400, 411, 415, 429, 443, 444, 491, 493, 544, 554, 555, 558, 559, 586, 593, 606, 637, 643, 678
Reformation 411, 671, 673, 680
Repentance 6, 124, 132, 133, 135, 150, 187, 203, 204, 241, 247, 269, 294, 296, 298, 299, 304, 305, 307–309, 313, 314, 344, 502
Resurrection 127, 133, 136, 155, 183, 193, 194, 237, 238, 243, 269, 270, 293, 312, 351, 354, 403, 406, 430, 438–440, 450, 451, 457, 496, 506–508, 511, 514, 527, 528, 549–551, 553–555, 562–563, 592, **598–605**, 608, 637, 657, 659–661, 667, 682
- and acquittal 553, 562, 567, 568, 570, 577, 578
- and new era 502, 513, 515, 516, 549, 560, 603
- death and 3, 14, 16, 90, 94, 95, 98, 99, 106, 107, 112, 116, 126, 130, 134, 138, 143–145, 147, 148, 154, 179, 188, 194, 213, 286, 291, 292, 294, 305, 346–348, 361, 365, 368, 369, 399, 400, 408, 413, 429, 430, 436, 438, 440, 469, 496, 498, 502, 513, 515–517, 532, 541, 542, 549, 553, 562, 563, 571, 572, 578, 664, 672
- faith and 430, 460, 549, 569, 570
- pointing to, prediction of 94, 114, 213, 179, 346–349, 517
- power of 194, 353, 435, 445, 576, 628

- present and future 126, 154, 241, 377–379, 423, 432–435, 439, 440, 442, 443, 448, 456, 458, 459, 502, 568, 571–573, 575–577, 604, 656, 657, 663, 664
- righteousness and 368, 413, 425, 542, 554, 568, 569, 577, 578, 674
- sharing in 153, 154, 429, 431, 439, 443, 507, 550, 551, 553, 555, 556, 560, 561, 571, 577, 578, 601–604, 609, 628, 657, 680
- vindication and 94, 98, 99, 102, 110, 126, 554, 567, 568, 577
Revelation 12, 13, 20, 21, 23, 25, 63, 141, 148, 156, 158, 166, 168, 171, 180, 186, 199, 256, 257, 263, 287, 311, 320, 324, 325, 334, 337–339, 345, 348, 350, 361, 382, 389, 392, 394, 398, 407, 425, 428, 434, 443, 474, 476, 477, 484, 493, 494, 496, 504, 511, 516, 527, 594, 649
- self-revelation 15, 22–25, 166, 168, 171, 173, 249, 252, 261, 336, 345, 397, 399, 470, 472, 476, 486, 487
Righteousness, righteous 6, 16, 18, 19, 22, 110, 111, 135, 147, 213, 214, 217, 255, 260, 268, 269, 308, 312, 339, 354, 361, 364, 367, 374, 401, 406, 442, 447, 450, 451, 472, 506, 528, 535, 542–545, 547, 552, 559–563, 565–573, 577, 578, 594, 605–609, 661, 662, 669–671
- and the law 368, 385–392, 399, 402, 405, 419, 430, 475, 477–485, 490, 502, 511, 515, 573, 585, 670
- of God 366, 386, 388, 401, 410–415, 417, 422, 424–431, 455, 475, 568, 569, 585, 586, 608, 609, 612, 614, 615
- share in 126, 127, 165, 507, 553–555, 557, 558, 561, 566, 638, 672–682
- suffering and 95, 101, 120, 123, 125, 213
Rightwising 126, 376, 377, 386, 401–403, 405, 406, 411, 426, 442, 444, 605, 671

Sabbath 195, 196, 249, 250, 258, 260, 288, 349, 486, 507
Sacrifice 15, 159, 171, 214, 238, 243, 245, 246, 252, 254, 257, 258, 260, 304, 346, 418, 466, 480, 497, 499, 502–504, 508–512, 515, 516, 543, 544, 549, 558–560, 593, 606, 607, 627, 630, 642, 644, 647, 666
Sadducees 193, 194, 238, 252, 310
Saints 74, 77, 79, 100, 125, 241, 359, 407, 414, 424, 431, 494, 534, 536–544, 548, 589, 599, 639, 657, 661

Salvation 16, 44, 55, 59, 129, 133, 144, 150, 164, 168, 169, 171, 201, 203, 204, 210, 231, 268, 290, 295, 299, 300, 303–305, 309, 310, 353, 389, 415, 417, 427, 436, 448, 484, 500, 506–507, 511, 532, 554, 568, 570, 576, 581, 582, 584, 588, 592–594, 598, 606, 645, 672, 675, 676
- coming, future 132, 525, 550, 601, 603
- day of 413, 434, 439, 442
- for the Gentiles 271, 272, 282, 287, 292, 367, 424, 583
- hope of 439, 540
- of individuals 175, 360, 422
- of Israel 282, 286, 314, 424, 491, 598
- pioneer of 5, 155, 170, 505, 517
- rejecting 292, 368
- revealing 143, 411, 412
- through Jesus, source of 601, 668, 682

Sanctification 155, 346, 411, 414, 415, 427, 503, 506, 509, 534, 536, 537, 539, 540–542, 544–548, 554, 598, 606, 647, 657, 658, 661, 662, 667, 681

Sanctuary 238, 244, 387, 450, 482, 508, 509, 512, 654, 655, 658–661, 663–667

Satan 35, 57, 139, 156, 211, 260, 262, 280, 282, 288, 290, 291, 302–305, 322–324, 349
- *see also* Devil

Seed 111, 267, 440, 452
- of Abraham 153, 391, 403, 431, 498, 604
- of David 154, 378

Servant 1, 2, 72, 79, 97, 115, 117, 120–125, 151, 154, 171, 189, 211, 212, 214, 229, 230, 231, 254, 257, 263, 268, 287, 291, 293, 346, 352, 411, 474, 475, 492, 507, 577, 584, 598, 627, 669

Sign(s) 12, 33, 47, 60, 109, 112, 140, 153, 159, 163, 209, 215, 221, 222, **224–234**, 243, 282, 283, 332, **346–349**, 351, 363, 403, 404, 466, 505, 509, 510, 620, 622, 630, 645
- and discourses 157, 166, 324, 338
- and wonders, miracles 150, 198, 227, 233, 309, 330, 331, 347–349, 476
- of destruction 207, 208, 226, 228, 232, 233, 243, 244
- of the covenant 365, 366
- prophetic 298, 299, 301, 306

Sin, sinful 20, 110, 120, 121, 125, 155, 214, 242, 304, 328, 359, 374, 385, 391, 426, 427, 443, 479, 483, 501, 503, 507, 509–512, 514–517, 539, 542, 543, **550–578**, 602–608, 659, 668, 669, 674–679

- and Adam 127, 154, 354, 373, 380, 382, 442, 564–567, 604
- flesh 162, 373, 430, 443, 553, 555, 557, 577, 585–587, 594
- forgiveness of, cleansed of 294, 298–300, 304, 307, 308, 312, 509, 516, 674, 675
- sinner 113, 121, 124, 126, 240, 291, 293, 304, 309, 367, 377, 544, 553–555, 566, 570, 606, 669, 674, 675, 677, 679, 680
- vicarious 115, 117, 122, 123, 126, 127, 401, 406, 410, 411, 415, 455, 507, 509, 557, 577, 585, 594, 608, 609, 661, 675, 679

Sinai 19, 20, 22, 24, 26, 158, 166, 168, 180, 181, 188, 189, 296, 334–336, 338, 339, 342, 344–346, 353, 365, 369, 375, 382, 392, 394, 396–398, 400, 471, 472, 475–477, 490, 492–496, 501, 504, 512, 662

Sitz im Leben 34, 36, 38–40, 59, 60, 78, 85

Slavery 118, 214, 359, 365, 371, 373, 382, 391, 403, 414, 426, 441, 505, 530, 538, 558, 580, 598, 606, 618, 634, 636, 640–642, 644–646, 651–653, 669
- form of 162, 383, 444, 556, 557, 585, 586, 608, 609, 629
- of sin, of righteousness 328, 380, 414, 427, 542, 543, 572

Son of God 5, 6, 128, 131, 132, 134, **137, 138,** 141, 142, **146–149,** 156, 157, 162–164, 171, 176, 188, 189, 239–242, 258, 263, 281, 282, 285, 302, 304, 311, 320, 324, 325, 327, 331, 332, 347, **377–383,** 398, 420, 423, 430, 441, 498, 502–504, 507, 509–511, 513, 514, 516, 521, 541, 551, 552, 558, 560, 561, 586, 598, 601, 602, 612, 669, 680
- as title 102, 151, 154, 333, 377, 381

Son of man 2, 5, 47, 70, 72, 73, 79, 88, 89, 90–114, 148, 169, 171, 173, 180, 187–190, 196, 210, 212, 214, 243, 263, 327, 349, 350, 355
- Coming 36, 45, 47, 57, 111–112, 141, 179, 208, 224–234, 238, 242, 256, 308, 345
- Daniel 7 1, 6, 72–74, 77–79, 90, 95, 99–102, 105, 113, 120, 125, 140, 152, 170, 187, 209, 325, 343
- Elijah 133–136, 187, 212
- Judge 114, 240, 310, 345
- Psalm 8 6, 95, 152, 154, 155, 170, 505, 506
- Sabbath 250, 258
- Sayings 33, 46, 47, 55, 57, 152–154, 506

- Suffering 46, 61, 134, 140, 293, 294
- Title 32, 33, 36, 44, 46, 84, 103–114, 120, 151–155

Source
- common source 103, 107, 632
- Griesbach hypothesis 103, 107, 108
- Marcan priority 84, 105, 108, 119, 128, 265
- Q 51, 55, 56, 96, 201, 261, 308, 313
- two-source hypothesis 103, 106, 107

Spirit (Holy) 16, 22, 25, 145, 151, 154, 169, 173, 212, 259, 280–282, 290, 296, **300–314,** 318, 320, 322, 325, 332, 333, 363, 364, 366, 368, 369, 376, 378, 391–393, 399, 402, 403, 405, 430, 434, 442, 443, 450, 454, 471–475, 479, 480, 486, 487, 495, 502, 503, 541–543, 545, 546, 554, 555, 557, 572, 573, 577, 585, 598, 613, 620, 621, 624–626, 638, 655, 665–667, 671, 675, 680
- baptize with 6, 135, 136, 187, 299, 301–303, 305–315, 325, 366
- gift(s) of 311–313, 333, 363, 403, 406, 555, 573, 575, 666
- filled with 286, 290, 294, 633, 635
- power of 139, 287, 290, 303, 308, 309, 598
- sanctuary of, temple of 244, 545, 546, 618, 648, 656, 658–660, 663, 667
- work of, activity of 12, 144, 150, 197, 202, 281, 282, 304, 312, 314, 323, 324, 471, 487, 495, 536, 539, 541, 542, 544–546, 548, 575, 602, 658, 660, 667

Stone of stumbling, stumbling-block 386–388, 481, 482, 496, 661

Submit, submission 118, 344, 388, 483, 500, 632–653

Substitution 122, 123, 127, 549–551, 558, 576, 585, 587, 602

Synoptic Problem 51, 84, 103–114

Temple 15, 19, 24–26, 76, 86, 153, 194, 206–210, 219–221, 226, 228, 229, **232–247,** 258, 264, 282, 287, 304, 346, 347, 363, 386, 414, 449, 450, 464, 478, 479, 481, 497, 498, 504, 513, 515, 547, 559, 618, 638, 639, 658, 660, 662–664
- cleansing of 77, 140, 206, 219, 245–247, 346
- curtain 137, 141, 209, 239, 241, 242
- destruction of 18, 209, 219–221, 229, 232–234, 238–247, 262, 347, 499
- heavenly 450, 664, 665
- of the Holy Spirit 545, 546, 618, 648, 656, 658

Torah 13, 20, 21, 24, 62, 70, 188, 191, 193, 194, 196, 248–257, 259, 261–264, 284, 328, 329, 333, 336, 337, 339, 359, 360, 364, 369, 386, 395, 397, 398–400, 469, 476, 477, 490–495, 498, 559

Transfiguration 138, 179–189, 197, 211, 263, 295–297, 345

Truth 21, 25, 36, 52, 62, 88, 102, 115, 130, 133, 137, 140, 141, 156, 157, 182, 186, 189, 211, 279, 285, 312, 320, 321, 324–333, 338–341, 347, 352, 367, 369, 398, 422, 425, 432, 474, 487, 492, 503, 610, 612, 614, 620, 623
- blind to 327, 329
- grace and 23, 166, 189, 319, 336, 339, 345, 398, 476
- hidden 156, 325, 331, 338
- of the gospel 408, 470, 471, 619
- whole 31, 43, 487

Unclean, *see* Cleanliness

Union (with Christ) 19, 127, 153, 154, 420, 425, 577, 593, 594, 650, 651, 673–682
- *see also* Participation

Vicarious suffering 2, 115, 120–125, 293

Wine, wineskins 11–26, 55, 243, 253, 258, 262, 340, 346, 591, 635

Wisdom 24, 84, 87, 139, 159, 166, 170, 173, 257, 296, 339, 351, 355, 369, 382, 394–397, 411, 415, 448, 470, 488–496, 544, 554, 555, 598, 638, 649, 655, 661, 678
- *see also* Christology (wisdom)

Wrath 213, 228, 244, 301, 377, 406, 429, 439, 442, 521, 524, 525, 528, 531, 532, 540, 550, 568–571, 576, 577, 599, 601, 620, 674, 676

Wissenschaftliche Untersuchungen zum Neuen Testament

Edited by Jörg Frey (Zürich)

Associate Editors:
Markus Bockmuehl (Oxford) · James A. Kelhoffer (Uppsala)
Tobias Nicklas (Regensburg) · Janet Spittler (Charlottesville, VA)
J. Ross Wagner (Durham, NC)

WUNT I is an international series dealing with the entire field of early Christianity and its Jewish and Graeco-Roman environment. Its historical-philological profile and interdisciplinary outlook, which its long-term editor Martin Hengel was instrumental in establishing, is maintained by an international team of editors representing a wide range of the traditions and themes of New Testament scholarship. The sole criteria for acceptance to the series are the scholarly quality and lasting merit of the work being submitted. Apart from the specialist monographs of experienced researchers, some of which may be habilitations, *WUNT I* features collections of essays by renowned scholars, source material collections and editions as well as conference proceedings in the form of a handbook on themes central to the discipline.

WUNT II complements the first series by offering a publishing platform in paperback for outstanding writing by up-and-coming young researchers. Dissertations and monographs are presented alongside innovative conference volumes on fundamental themes of New Testament research. Like Series I, it is marked by a historical-philological character and an international orientation that transcends exegetical schools and subject boundaries. The academic quality of Series II is overseen by the same team of editors.

WUNT I:
ISSN: 0512-1604
Suggested citation: WUNT I
All available volumes can be found at *www.mohrsiebeck.com/wunt1*

WUNT II:
ISSN: 0340-9570
Suggested citation: WUNT II
All available volumes can be found at *www.mohrsiebeck.com/wunt2*

Mohr Siebeck
www.mohrsiebeck.com